The Wainwrights in Colour

The Wainwrights in Colour

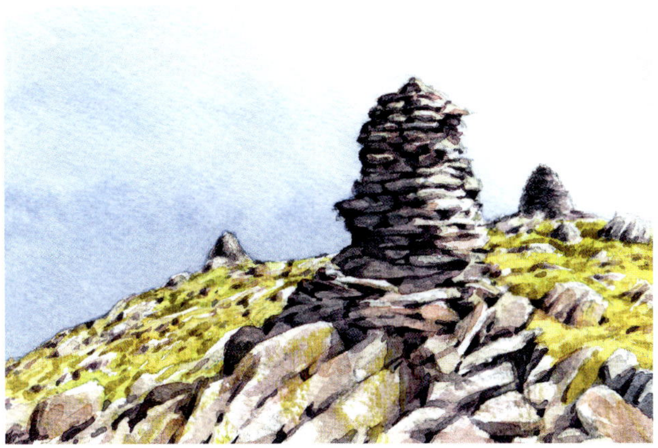

Andy Beck

This book is number 2404 of a single edition of 5000 copies.

First published in Great Britain 2017
By Double Z Publishing, Andy Beck Images Ltd.
Old West End Garage, Bowes,
Co. Durham. DL12 9LW

ISBN 978-0-9955762-0-9

Printed and bound by Elanders
North Tyneside.

The Wainwrights in Colour Book
is dedicated to
my faithful companions
who accompanied me in turn throughout the whole journey.

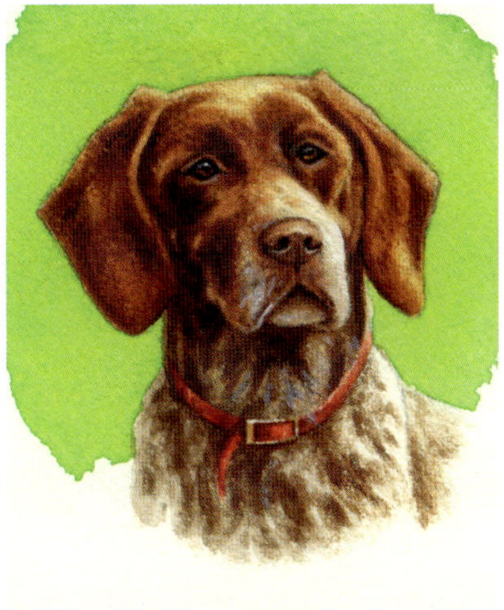

Zoe
A pointer/ springer cross.
Sturdy, steadfast and reliable who was a pleasure to be with.

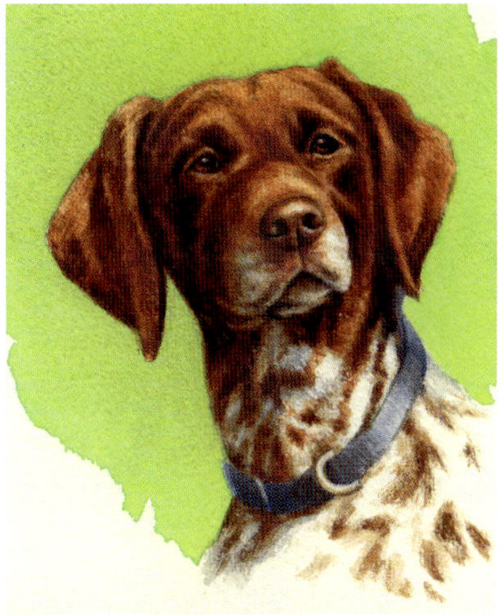

Zeta
The daughter of Zoe.
Completed her Wainwright round with me on Starling Dodd 10/9/09.

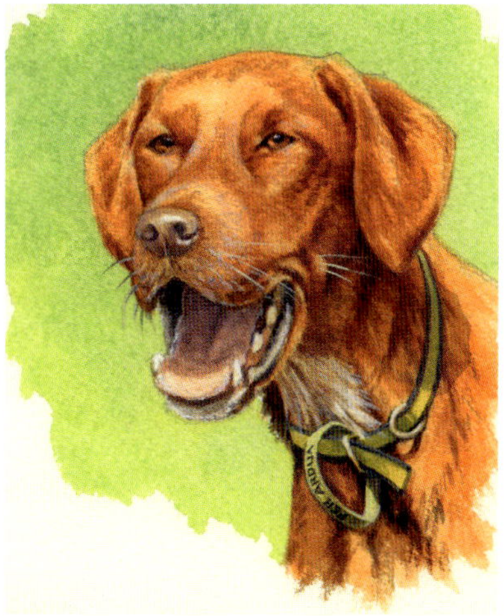

Bailey
A setter/ visla cross recruited from The Dogs Trust.
Completed his Wainwright round with me on Outerside 10/9/14.

Contents

Foreword

By Derry Brabbs, acclaimed photographer who collaborated with Wainwright in a series of later books.

To a casual observer, two hundred and fourteen may appear to be a random number of no particular significance; perhaps a mediocre total posted by the England cricket team in a Test match, or maybe the number of votes separating political candidates in a marginal seat ? However, to serious aficionados of the Lakeland fells and mountains, that figure will be instantly recognised as the total number of fells covered in his seven book series of Pictorial Guides by the iconic author and fellwalker, Alfred Wainwright. Those 214 fells, crags and summits have become collectively known as 'The Wainwrights' and although they can never compete in terms of height or stature with their Scottish counterparts, (the Munros) they have given renewed impetus to many people's visits to Cumbria.

Expeditions invariably feel more worthwhile and satisfying if a specific target has been set and subsequently achieved, whether it be the conquering of one new summit, or well over 200 ! As someone who has spent years following in Wainwright's footsteps with cameras and tripod, I can only begin to imagine what a Herculean task those seven books represented and am doubly amazed that Andy Beck has mustered the stamina and resolve to reprise them.

However, to look at it in purely physical terms is to completely overlook one vital ingredient – love. AW was completely and utterly captivated by the allure of the fells and that love radiated from every page of his books. It is impossible not to look at Andy's work without sensing that same empathy with the landscape and also a huge amount of respect for the artist whose original work he has emulated through his chosen medium of watercolour.

I may have evolved into an accomplished landscape photographer, but it has always irked me that I am totally incapable of equally artistic endeavour with brush or pencil and stand in awe of artists who have the ability to transform a blank canvas or sheet of paper into a stunning representation of a particular scene. AW's pen and ink drawings breathed more life into inanimate lumps of rock than could reasonably be imagined but I was slightly heartened to note that he was one of the worst photographers on the planet!

Andy Beck also uses a camera to record his subjects for reference but unlike Wainwright, who photographed and drew predominately in black and white, Andy's colour work has breathed new life into the all too frequently sombre rocky landscapes of the Lake District. Anyone who regularly visits the region knows only too well that it has its own 'weather-forecast immune' microclimate and I was frequently driven off the hills by bad light when the exact opposite had been predicted !

Andy's project could be perceived as having progressed well beyond a labour of love into the realms of masochism, but that is the effect the Lakeland mountains have upon those who get to know them. From an artist's perspective, it is akin to being the gambler who cannot walk away from a fruit machine, firmly believing that the next pull of the handle will be the jackpot. We all strive to portray the Lake District in its best possible light but regardless of how good the results we manage to achieve, there is always the niggling worry that the light might be even better tomorrow.

This atmospheric collection of watercolours is such an impressive body of work, I feel exhausted by simply contemplating the endeavour that went into its planning and execution and AW would have definitely approved.

Acknowledgements

Although this was basically a one-man project it couldn't have been completed without the help of others. Most importantly, my wife and best friend Esther, whose support through good times and bad enabled me to see this idea through to conclusion. Peter Ditchburn for not only his input which made the venture viable but also his prolonged patience. All of the clients who purchased the original works, too many to mention by name and many of whom waited longer than expected to obtain their fells, again, thank you for your patience. Derek Cockell and David Johnson for their additional insights into Wainwright and the Pictorial Guides. Dik Stoddart and Andrew Stainthorpe for their design skills. Others who helped me in locating some of the more obscure references and those on private land including Ian Tyler - mining expert, Ms Betty Walker of Eller's, Martin Robinson of Thrang Crag, Dr Margaret Bradshaw - botany expert, and Andrew Leaney. Like AW, I usually walked alone with only the dogs to accompany me as I sought out references, Esther was there at times but thanks must go to three other occasional companions who put up with my unusual routes and sense of humour: Lesley Ritchie, Frances Kate Alderson and Jenny Whalley.

For material used in the production of this book: Derry Brabbs for kindly writing the Foreword and for the use of the image of Wainwright on the dust jacket, Rosemary Gutteridge, the daughter of Ken Shepherd for the kind permission to use the photograph on page 11, Mr T.C.Bell of Tirrel for his information on the Romans on High Street. The staff of Kendal Museum, the staff of Kendal Archive Centre. The Westmorland Gazette. Frances Lincoln Publishing (see page 344). Thanks also to Alan Fentiman for filming and producing the short film of The Wainwrights in Colour, a copy of which is included at the back of this book.

Last but not least, thanks must go to the Wainwright Estate and family, namely the late Betty Wainwright and Wainwright's step-daughters Jane King and Annie Sellar for their approval and support in this venture which hopefully helps to keep the memory and skills of the man himself, Alfred Wainwright, in the public domain.

A. Wainwright

The life of Alfred Wainwright has been well documented but I consider it worth including some background information on the man whose most famous legacy is the series of pocket-sized books, the seven Pictorial Guides to the Lakeland Fells on which this whole project is based.

Wainwright was born on 17th January 1907 into a working class family in Blackburn, the youngest of four children. His father, Albert, was an itinerant stonemason with a drink problem and his mother Emily, who kept family and home together with little means. By studying hard at school young Alfred, a tall, lanky red-haired lad, got himself away from the cotton mills and into a better line of work, that of an office boy in the Borough Engineer's Office at the age of 13. Three years later, he was transferred to the Accountancy office and by further studies and promotion he was able to work his way up the ladder until in 1948 he became Borough Treasurer in Kendal, a position he held until retiring in January 1967.

It was only in 1930 when at the age of 23 Wainwright had his first taste of the Lake District. On holiday from work in Blackburn he and his cousin, Eric Beardsall, took the bus to Windermere and on a sunny afternoon in June they ascended to the summit of Orrest Head, where he was spellbound by the scene that confronted him, his first sighting of the Lakeland Fells that were to become such a big part of his life in future years.

In December 1931 he married a 22 year-old mill worker, Ruth Holden. It didn't take long before he realised that this was a mistake. However, they did have a son, Peter, born in February 1933. Wainwright continued to visit the Lake District on holidays until his move to Kendal in 1941.

A period from November 1952 until Christmas 1965 saw Wainwright writing the Pictorial Guides to the Lakeland Fells. Working during the week, writing and drawing up the fell descriptions in the evenings and walking at the weekends was to be his routine, a thirteen-year plan which he completed one week ahead of schedule. By now his marriage to Ruth was over, their divorce was finalised in June 1968. In 1970 Wainwright remarried, his second wife being Betty McNally some 15 years his junior with two daughters, and someone whom he had been in contact with for some time. They were happily married for 21 years until his death in January 1991.

Once the Pictorial Guides were completed, Wainwright continued to write and work on many other books under his own name including his famous A Coast to Coast Walk but also sketchbooks and large format books illustrated by photographers, such as Derry Brabbs. Other authors called on Wainwright to provide illustrations for their books, which he did.

At the time of writing the Pictorial Guides, Alf, as he was known by friends, was a tall man, at least 6'2" and about 14 stone in weight. His red hair turned white with age. Those who properly knew him described him as shy with a dry sense of humour, to some this attitude came over as being grumpy. It seems the "AW" name tag only came into use in his later life, most likely taken from his signature at the end of each guidebook. Many people fail to appreciate his generous side, especially his donations to good causes. Wainwright was a man of the first part of the 20th century, attitudes to women, work and life in general were different than they are today. Even he would admit that he wasn't perfect but then, none of us are.

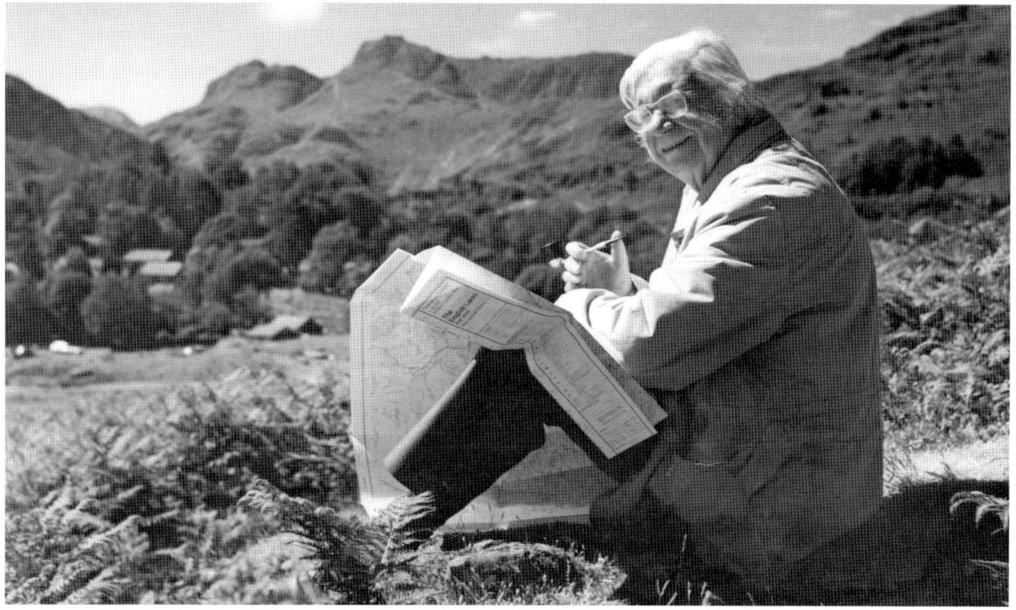

Wainwright and the Pictorial Guides

There is no definitive date as to when Wainwright first came up with the idea of producing a series of guidebooks to the Lakeland fells. Correspondence to friends as far back as 1943 hinted at producing a book on the fells but this was to be more of a book of drawings, not a guidebook. AW's move to Kendal in 1941 enabled him to more regularly explore the fells which were now on his doorstep and no doubt he used already published guidebooks such as Baddeley's Thorough Guide to the English Lakes to find routes and points of interest. In fact, guidebooks had been produced for a long time before AW came on the scene, but his were to be different.

Originally, his plan was to produce a two volume guide covering 229 fells, eastern and western. This was altered at some point to three books before eventually ending up with seven volumes and 214 fells. Wainwright divided the region up into the seven sections mostly using lakes and valleys as boundaries and each fell description follows the same basic content pattern: an illustrative drawing of the fell, natural features narrative, a map, routes of ascent, the summit, the view and ridge routes. Where space allowed Wainwright included further illustrations and notes of interest, often with his own humorous asides. He began this thirteen-year task in November 1952 with pages on Dove Crag in the eastern fells.

The task posed various challenges for AW. As he didn't drive he was at the mercy of public transport for most but not all of his trips. It was usual for him to be at the bus stop twenty minutes early so his walking days had to be planned by the clock. Weather could also be a problem, low cloud and mist would have curtailed his plans. This is particularly pertinent to his summit views, every distant fell had to be seen and annotated, a task requiring not only clear weather but also concentration.

The technique for producing the guides was unique, each page designed and planned so that the text and illustrations fitted neatly without looking cramped. Remarkably the pages were drawn to the size that they were to be reproduced in print, no reduction or cut and pasting. When the illustrations are studied closely the level of detail is remarkable, some drawn with the aid of a magnifying glass. All the work was completed with a traditional dip pen and ink using the finest nibs available. Noticed errors would usually have meant the complete re-drawing of the page but one or two did slip through the net. After an initial design review and the scrapping of the first 100 pages, all main text blocks were then justified on both sides with the words cleverly spaced to fit the line, such was the man's attention to detail.

Once complete, each guide was printed locally and at the author's own expense. Initially he had considered making this a limited edition book of only 2000 copies just to cover the printing costs but thankfully the print run continued, making it available to all. Whilst other guidebooks have come and gone, some of which try to emulate something of Wainwright's guides, these seven volumes produced fifty years ago still stand the test of time especially when used in conjunction with an up to date map and a bit of common sense.

Innominate Tarn (after A. Wainwright) A sketch that I produced to test my skills at drawing in a "Wainwright" style.

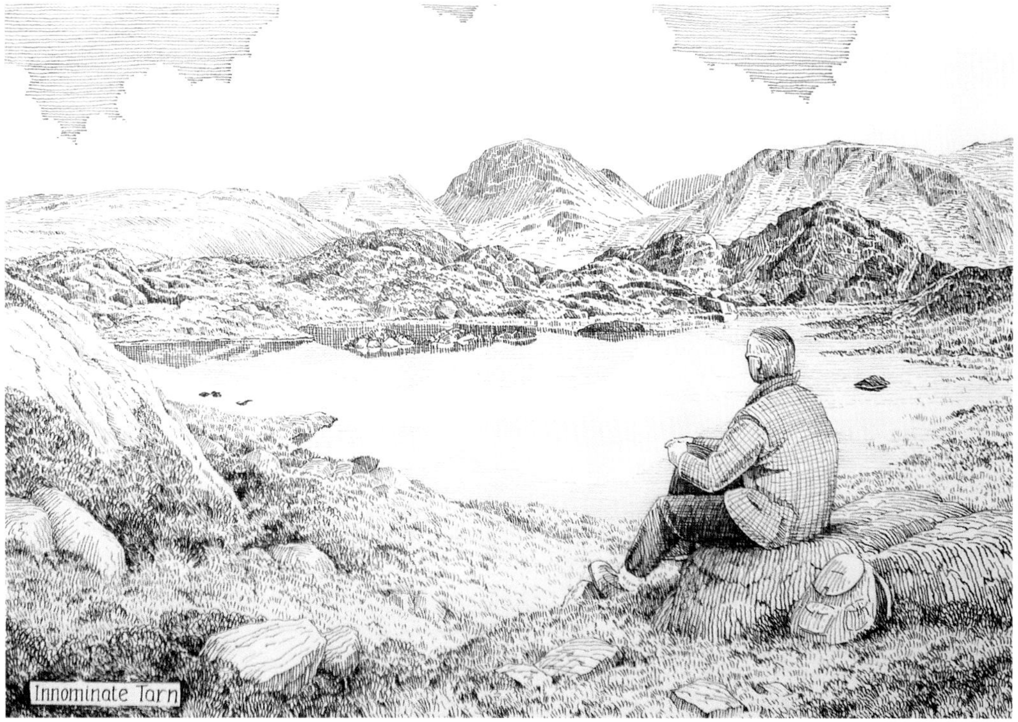

Introduction

It is hard to imagine that what started with a casual view back to Red Pike from Black Crag high above Mosedale would begin a journey for me which would take over my life for the best part of 10 years. A late afternoon walk over Yewbarrow, Red Pike and Pillar on a warm summer's day on 2nd July 2006 took me along the narrow path contouring towards Black Crag from Red Pike. A casual glance back to the distinct summit I had just crossed presented a scene which looked so familiar to me yet I hadn't been this way before. A quick rummage in my rucksack and I pulled out my relevant Wainwright Pictorial Guide, Book Seven, The Western Fells, flicking to the Red Pike (Wasdale) chapter. There it was, a small drawing of the view before me, depicted by Wainwright in his usual highly detailed pen and ink style. By chance I had stopped at almost the exact location from where he must have taken his photograph for later use all those years ago, albeit in a different season. Just for the sake of it I also took a similar photograph, just to record the event. So that was it, that's how it started, no big plan to take it further, just the happy coincidence of standing where AW stood for that brief moment. By the time Esther, the dogs and I returned to the campsite at Wasdale Head an idea had begun to form in my mind about painting that scene as a watercolour comparison sketch of AW's drawing, but more than that, how about painting a selection of the other sketches? It actually took some time to develop the idea fully, to visit every single location for all the sketches in the seven Pictorial Guides, photograph the scene and then paint it as a small watercolour. Little did I realise at that time just how many there were and how big a challenge this would be. It meant wiping my "Wainwright" tick list slate clean and starting from scratch and not only standing on every summit, but locating the off route places that AW explored as he worked on his unique guidebooks to the Lakeland Fells.

I had several concerns to address before embarking on the project. Firstly was the copyright of the images but this really was not an issue. AW's Pictorial Guides and drawings are copyrighted but not the subjects which he drew, and as I was producing sketches from my own photographs I was free to paint the scenes as I wished. Secondly, I didn't wish to upset the Wainwright family so I contacted Jane King, one of Wainwright's stepdaughters, and informed her of my plan which she then relayed to her sister and her mother Betty, who graciously all gave their approval. Thirdly, and most importantly for me was the question as to whether it would be a practical proposition, after all, painting is my sole income and to dedicate so much time to such an undertaking was a risk, and I would have to put to one side all other work. It wasn't to be all plain sailing,

Once I had decided to proceed with the project a plan developed. At this point I should add that for the purpose of this project I was using the original versions of the Pictorial Guides. These are the unadulterated versions, every word is Wainwright's, every page laid out in his well-planned design and more importantly every single sketch that he intended to illustrate the 214 fells is included. I took the relevant copies of my guides with me on every single walk, occasionally having to carry two books as every so often a sketch was drawn from one region looking into another (see the Red Screes chapter). As a consequence, my set of Pictorial Guides have had personal notes added, lost their dust-jackets and are now looking rather tatty but I am sure AW would see this as good use of his works. Regrettably, the revised guides tend to dilute the work of Wainwright with pages being removed, layout designs altered and sketches being edited, either by being deleted or importing sketches from other later Wainwright works. The narrative has been changed to record alterations to the routes which I can understand, but to take it further and add in notes, some of which have happened since AW's passing, takes the revisions too far in my opinion. To me the original versions of the Pictorial Guides are like having one man's personal journal in my pocket, a friendly guide with humour and detail that I know comes from the pen of Wainwright himself. There is no denying that some of the routes and facts may be out of date but there is pleasure to be had in finding these alterations out for oneself, a journey of discovery. No revision will be up to date, fully accurate and without error and in all my time on the fells, AW's original versions in conjunction with the up to date maps haven't failed me (I am not a user of GPS technology) and the Countryside and Rights of Way Act 2000 basically allows walkers to almost wander at will across open land and explore the hidden places away from the crowds.

There followed a close scrutiny of every single drawing in the books and each possible location was plotted on my Ordnance Survey maps complete with a directional arrow and code so that I knew which way to look when I was on site. Then it was a case of planning routes to link as many of these locations together in each walk. This made for some very interesting routes. Wherever possible I would try and replicate the season in the drawing, which was not easy to determine in his black and white illustrations. To match the snow conditions which he illustrated in some drawings meant planning walks just at the right time. Leaving home to drive over to the fells and walk to a location just to record one single scene with snow cover was not unusual for me, made more difficult if the A66 at Stainmore, not far from home, was blocked. Trees that he drew in leaf could be any season apart from mid-winter and some had grown to almost obscure the required view when in leaf, entailing a return visit in winter when the tree was bare and thus revealing the scene. The weather was to be a major factor in acquiring the photographs. The challenge was to observe what he depicted, easy enough for close quarters detail but more of an undertaking when distant horizons are 16 miles or more away. On many occasions I would arrive at a summit cairn only to find that a distant fell in his illustration was obscured from my view by low cloud; this meant a return visit on a better day. Another additional complication which I had to take into account on occasions was the direction of the sunlight, a detail which proved frustrating more than once. To arrive at the correct point only to find the bright sun was behind the subject and rendered the fell or crag as a silhouette was cause for many a return trip when the sun was in a more suitable position. Often the light was poor and made the subject flat and lacking detail so as time was limited I often had to make the best of a bad job and work with the photograph as it was, and in the studio try and add some extra life into the work. Producing all of these sketches in the field would have been totally impractical. Some locations are in what would be classed as unsafe positions on steep scree slopes or on a narrow ridge, others such as fell summits would have meant working whilst in the vicinity of other walkers, having a clear view of a summit cairn to complete a sketch would have been often impracticable. Besides, precision was the key, and it would have been impossible to sketch whilst lining up the scene with Wainwright's drawing exactly. By being as precise as possible I was often able to deduce in which position Wainwright took each photograph, sometimes sitting, whilst possibly having a smoke, kneeling or bent down, or even standing at his full 6'3" height when I then had to hold my camera above my eye level to gain the exact photographic perspective for the reference.

After three years of work, in September 2009 I decided to hold an exhibition of the project. This was at the Rheged Discovery Centre near Penrith. It allowed me to promote the work as well as enabling visitors to purchase completed fells or to order others which were still in progress. I was overwhelmed by the response. With 6000 plus visitors over a six week period nearly all of the fells were either purchased or ordered during the exhibition. It was confirmed to me that no one had undertaken such a project before, either as photographs or sketches. The uniqueness of my idea certainly drew attention. With the exhibition closed and a full order book all I had to do then was complete the whole challenge. Here I have to admit I underestimated the time element, frustrated by weather and other problems in the field was compounded by the fact that I was still running my gallery in Barnard Castle, which restricted my walking time and painting. Reluctantly in 2012 I decided to close the outlet to solely concentrate on fulfilling the order book for the Wainwrights in Colour, a decision which with hindsight I should have taken much earlier.

I continued to gather the references and produce the sketches. During the process of this project not only have I completed two full rounds of the Wainwright fells but visited most summits on several occasions. This involved 1747 miles of walking and 587,992 feet of ascent including 628 summit visits in total but with many walks not requiring a visit to any top. Throughout the book I have added the date on which I obtained the reference photograph for that painting, this gives a sense of the number of trips required to achieve my aim. Like Wainwright, nearly all of my walks were undertaken solo, with only a few walks in the company of others. This allowed me to concentrate on the task in hand especially as often I would check and re-check the precise locations which could add a great deal of time to a walk, and here I could appreciate one of the reasons that Wainwright avoided contact with people on the fells: he was on a mission, time spent in idle chat with others may have caused him to lose concentration or even worse, miss his bus home. I spent several nights wildcamping out on the fells, enjoying the experience that Wainwright himself had. I of course had the dogs as company and a comfortable tent in which to eat and sleep whereas he had no such luxuries, preferring to sit and smoke during the hours of darkness.

My method of producing the sketches in the studio is explained in the Artist's notes on page 16 and I decided that the presentation of the original work should be as individual fells with all the sketches for each fell being mounted in one single frame as a montage. This was easy enough for those fells with half a dozen or less paintings but the larger works such as Blencathra involved some intricate layout design to present the numerous sketches in a balanced and neat format.

Here in the book you will find all of the sketches. The original plan was just to include the majority of the paintings in the book but it soon became apparent to me that all the sketches should be included to portray the full story, so now the complete 1509 are featured, wherever possible in proportion and in order as they are in the guidebooks. I should make it clear that I haven't included the panoramic views shown in the Pictorial Guides. In these AW tended to exaggerate the distant fells for identification purposes, in reality and the way I would depict them would mean that the horizons would be rather flat and uninteresting. Where Wainwright included a self-portrait which he did once in every book I have placed myself in that same location and pose which I have further explained on page 190. Where space has allowed I have also written short articles relevant to Wainwright and the Lake District which I hope will be if interest to readers. In places I have identified minor mistakes or errors in AW's work, this is done purely to highlight these few cases and not to criticise his wonderful work. Like him, this book is also all my own work, from conception to completion with no editorial input, so it is to be expected that small errors may have been overlooked for which I apologise in advance.

During this undertaking I have taken time to research Wainwright, his background and life, but more importantly his methods of working in the production of the Pictorial Guides. The tingle on the back of my neck when I knew I was standing on the exact spot to take a reference photograph as he had done was a feeling that lasted throughout. More intense was the effect when it was at one of the many unfrequented places where the grass still grows strongly underfoot, away from the masses and where perhaps I would like to think that only Wainwright had previously stood to admire the same scene. These places do still exist. Many are illustrated here, away from the masses and where peace and solitude can still be found. All you have to do is seek them out.

Artist's Notes

It was in 1988 that I turned professional as an artist, following 12 years of service in the RAF Regiment. Painting, sketching has always been a passion. Growing up in Northern Ireland I spent my school holidays cycling along the North Antrim coast and stopping off to capture the dramatic cliffs and castles in pencil and watercolour purely for my own entertainment. I left school with four 'O' levels, one of which was Art, my only formal training in the subject. Professionally my normal range of work has been wildlife and landscapes from areas which I have explored throughout the UK. When the idea of The Wainwrights in Colour came into my head little did I realise how much of a difficult challenge it would be. Usually us artistic types like to convey our own interpretations of what we see and feel in the landscape but no such freedom for me here. Using Wainwright's illustration compositions as a template I had to restrict my views, almost having to use tunnel vision to edit out peripheral features and concentrate on the "Wainwright" view.

In all of the sketches I used a similar method to that used by AW, taking a photograph on site from the exact position that he used, then back in the studio using that image to draw and paint the scene. I only used the Pictorial Guides as a reference and not to copy, after all, I was producing the scenes as they are today and not just a watercolour version of his pen and ink drawings. In my work I decided to increase the dimensions of the sketches as producing such detail in watercolour to his scale would have been impractical if not impossible. So my watercolours were twice as wide and twice as high as the drawings in the guides. It was not unusual for Wainwright to occasionally add some artistic license into his illustrations. Hills were given a more pronounced profile, background details were omitted and foreground details adjusted for better composition. By comparing my sketches and notes to his drawings it will be seen where these more obvious liberties were taken. This isn't a criticism of his work, just an observation. One area where Wainwright varied the amount of work in his drawings was in the sky. The depiction of billowing clouds rarely served a purpose for him, in fact it used up valuable writing space. To me it was a space to add a feeling of sense of weather conditions or time of day.

Over such a period of time and producing over 1500 sketches I realise that my style of work has slightly changed, hopefully for the better, but as the fells were not completed in any order I hope that this change will not be too obvious to the reader of this book.

As for the materials used, throughout the project I used the same watercolour paper, Saunders Waterford 200lb Not surface which I stretched to prevent cockling even on the smallest of sketches, more of a habit than a need at this size. Using a fairly restricted palette of ten colours across the complete collection of sketches meant that no matter what the subject or season all mixed hues have a continuity of base colours. Out of interest these were: French Ultramarine, Cerulean Blue, Lemon Yellow, Cadmium Yellow, Raw Sienna, Burnt Sienna, Light Red, Cadmium Red, Alizarin Crimson and Payne's Grey. Very occasionally I applied touches of white gouache as body colour, mostly to highlight patches of snow. It could be said that my watercolour technique is fairly traditional in letting the white of the paper provide some lightness to the washes. In producing the sketches, I normally worked on one fell at a time with the prepared drawings laid out on the workbench in my studio. As a group the sketches had initial basic washes applied to skies and landforms so that they had a continuity of colour across the set for each fell. Of course this method was only applied if all of the relevant references were acquired in the same season or at about the same time of day.

Once all the sketches for the fell were complete they were scanned and then mounted and framed which in keeping with the whole project were tasks I undertook myself, my years of professionally framing artwork coming in useful especially as every framed fell was unique in size and layout.

The Eastern Fells

Most of the thirty five fells in this region are within an area which lies between Threlkeld in the north and Ambleside to the south. The western boundary is formed by Thirlmere and Dunmail Raise whilst the eastern edge is Ullswater and the Kirkstone Pass. Helvellyn is perhaps the most well known mountain in this group being one of the most popular of all the fells with its main attraction being Striding Edge. The Fairfield Horseshoe is a classic route, a circuit of eight hills which can be completed in a full single day beginning and ending in Ambleside.
Anyone new to the district and fellwalking will find that The Eastern Fells area has plenty to offer in the way of variety, from the grassy rounded tops of the Dodds to the exciting eastern ridges of the Helvellyn group.

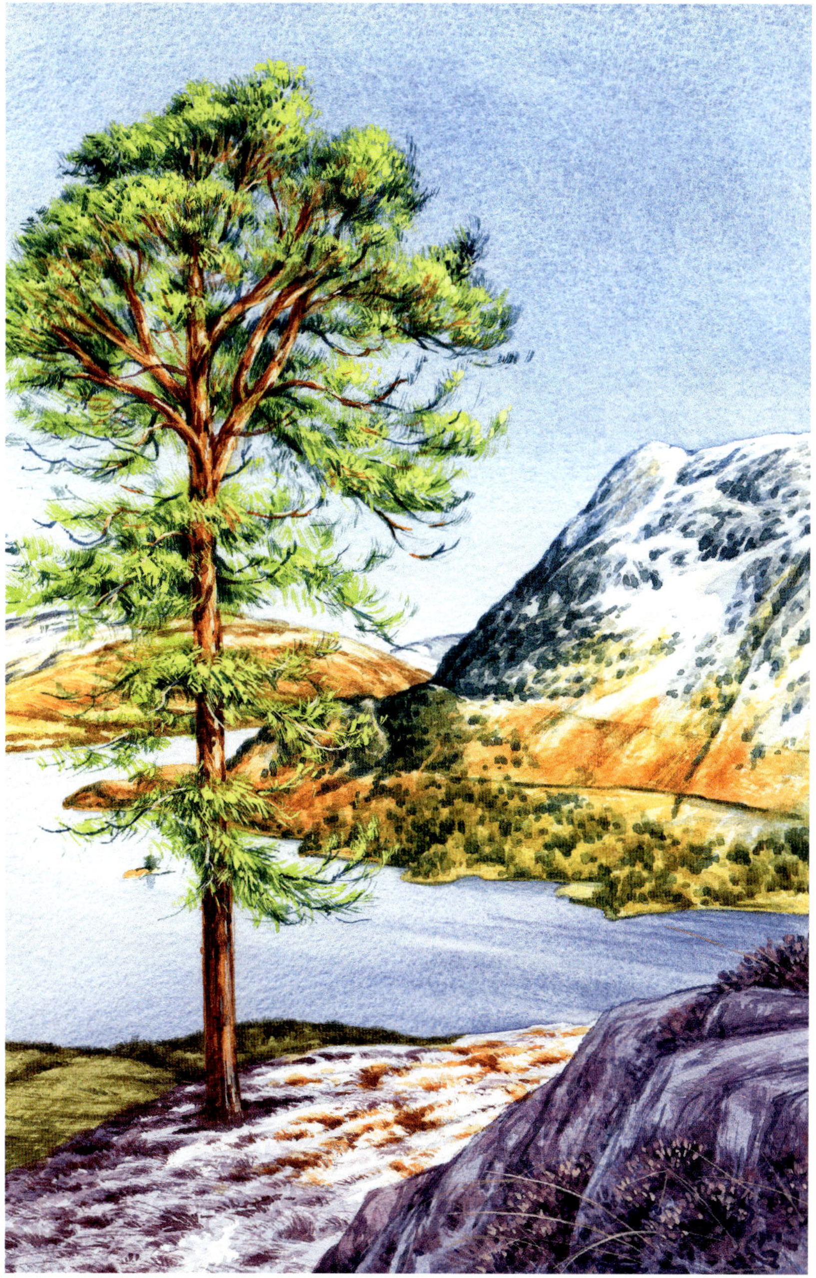

Frontispiece- Ullswater from Keldas 6/2/09

The wooded height of Keldas still provides wonderful views but being on the eastern extremity of the area covered by Book One the vistas from here are generally of Ullswater and to the east. Consequently the flank of Place Fell which lies within the Far Eastern region is the dominant feature in this sketch. Gowbarrow Fell is now obscured by the more mature pine tree. Due to the passage of time it was difficult to determine if this was the exact tree in AW's drawing but it has similarities in shape and position.

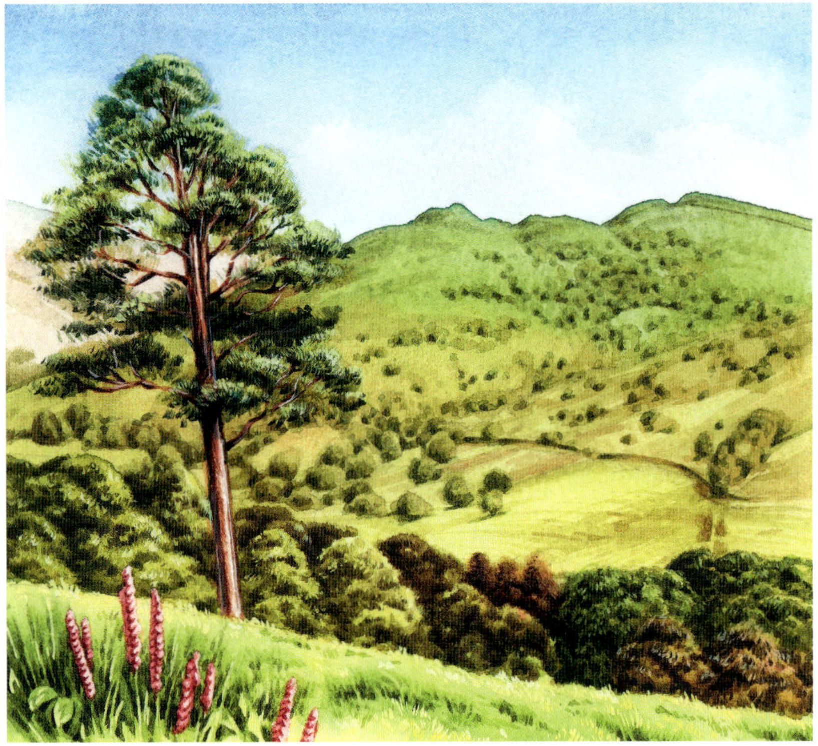

From Keldas 30/6/09
The location of this viewpoint is from about 70 yards to the south of Keldas summit. A couple of the mature pines shown in his illustration have fallen, leaving just this one specimen.

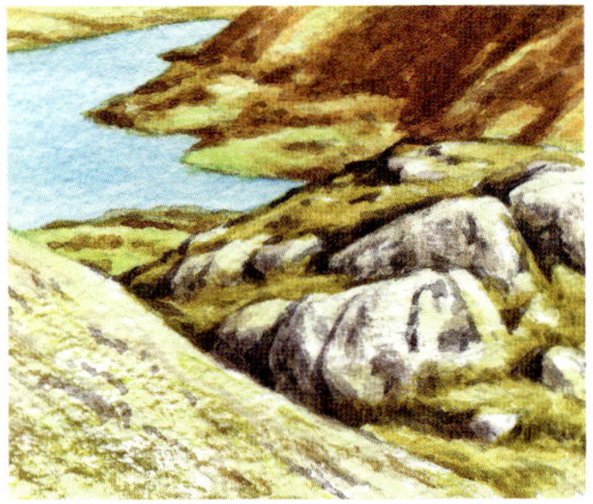

The lower cairn 18/9/07
Seen from the actual summit with Ullswater behind, the small cairn in AW's drawing has all but gone.

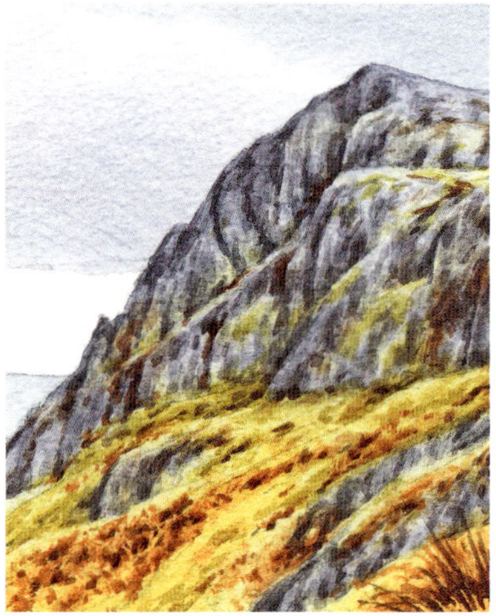

The summit from the south 18/9/07
The fine details of Wainwright's illustration with the tiny point of rock at the lower left ensured I had found the correct location for this view of the crag.

Arnison Crag

Rising up behind the village of Patterdale this fell is ideal for a simple wander. The little effort needed is rewarded with fine views of the southern reaches of Ullswater. Most often it is climbed in conjunction with a visit to Birks. This fell did not appear on Wainwright's original list for inclusion.

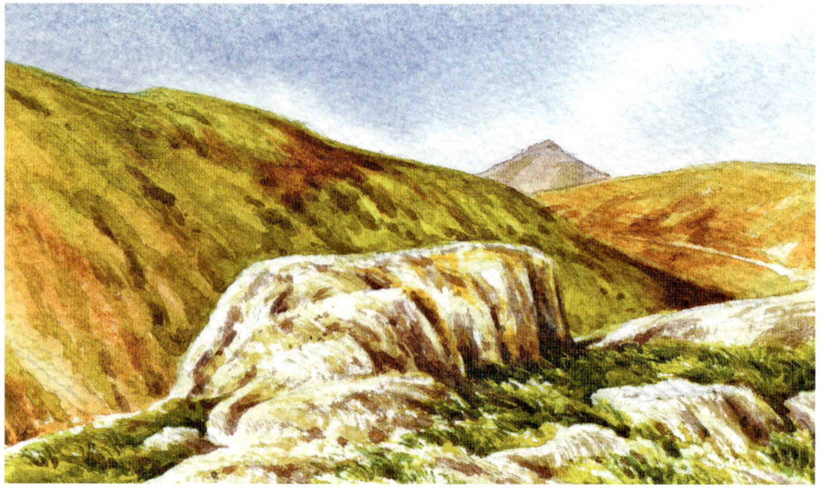

The summit 18/9/07
There is a grassy dome of a similar height 200 yards to the south, but this is the true summit of the crag. The cairn has been moved off the rock platform to a lower position on the grass just out of view on the right.

Ullswater 18/9/07
The view from the summit is not unlike the one of the lower cairn (left), in which I have included the distant Great Mell Fell which AW omitted.

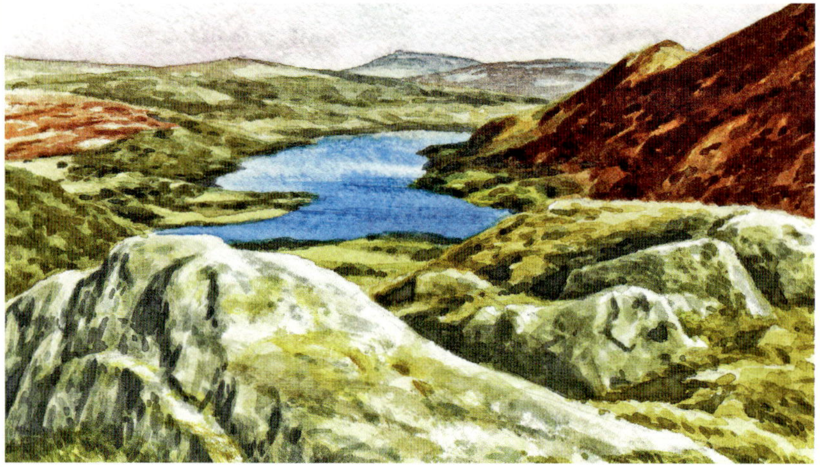

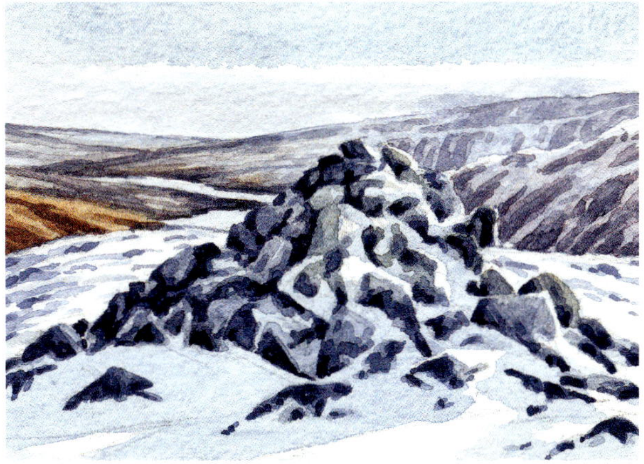

The cairn at 2318' 6/2/09
Often mistaken for the true summit (see right) this more substantial cairn has a fine view of Ullswater and was the only measured point of the fell on AW's maps.

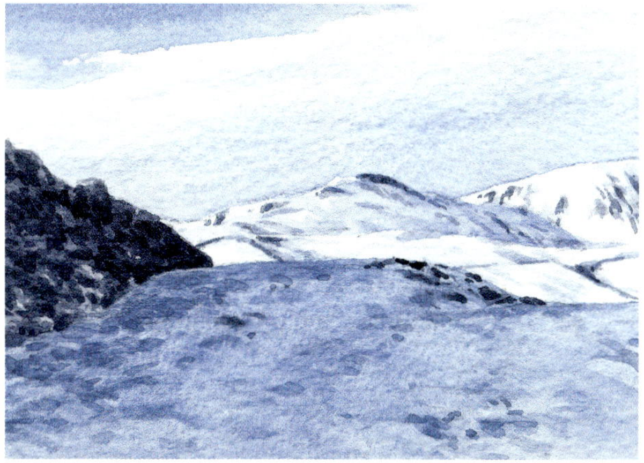

The highest point 6/2/09
Adjacent to the wall and fairly flat, the low cairn of this, the actual summit is often just ignored by walkers as they head onwards towards Striding Edge.

Birkhouse Moor

As part of the backdrop to the village of Glenridding, the fell is often ascended as a first climb towards Striding Edge and Helvellyn. The small knoll of Keldas featured in some of these sketches is worthy of a detour. It is private ground with a permissive footpath leading to the summit.

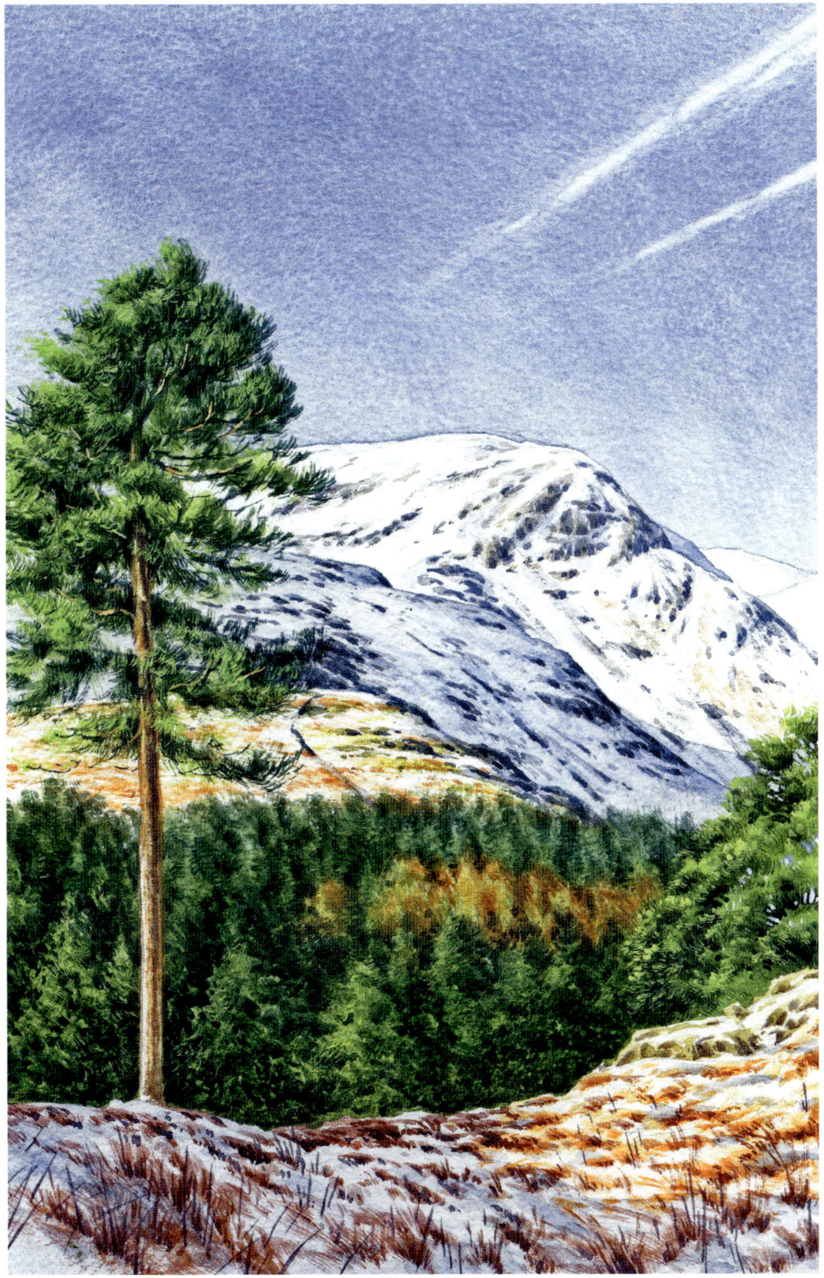

From near Lanty's Tarn 6/2/09
A mature wood now surrounds the tarn. By standing further back, a little way up the slopes of Keldas I was able to include this lone pine similar to the one in the guide.

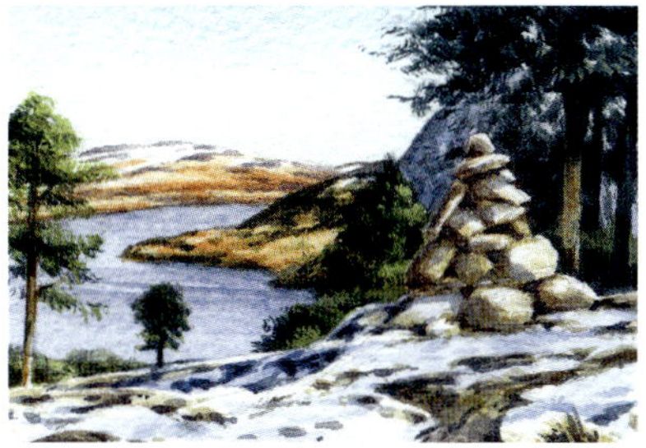

The summit of Keldas 6/2/09
The quality cairn has now gone and it has been replaced with a small heap of stones which cannot be classed as a permanent feature.

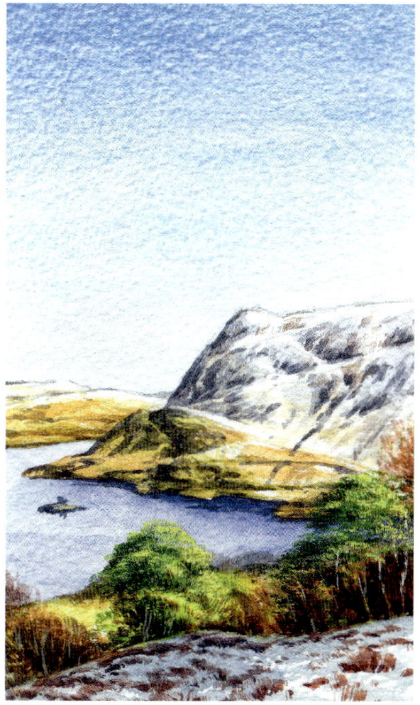

Ullswater from Keldas 6/2/09
I was unable to find a pair of trees here to match his drawing, many have been felled since AW's visit.

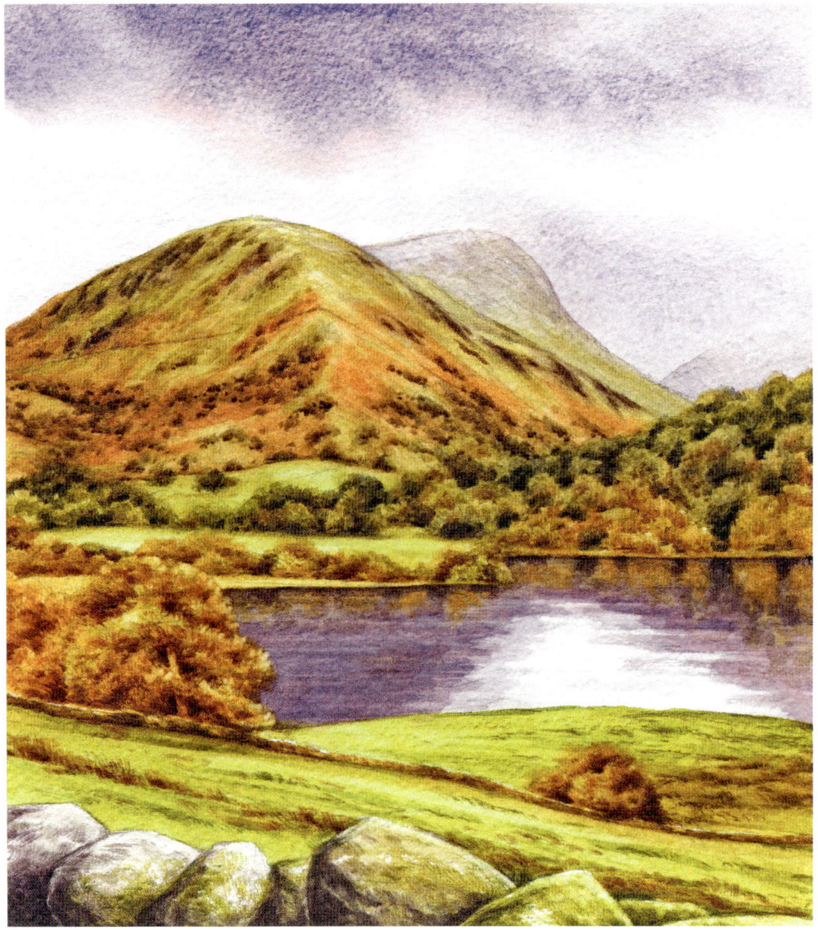

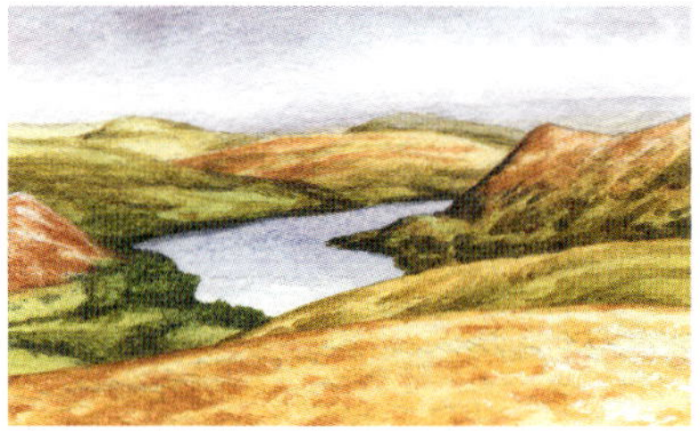

Ullswater 6/3/09
This view of the lake is from a point to the north east of the summit.

From Ullswater 14/10/08
Seen from across the upper reaches of the lake, AW totally omitted the fell of St. Sunday Crag behind, possibly to avoid confusion with his main subject or perhaps it was obscured by poor weather.

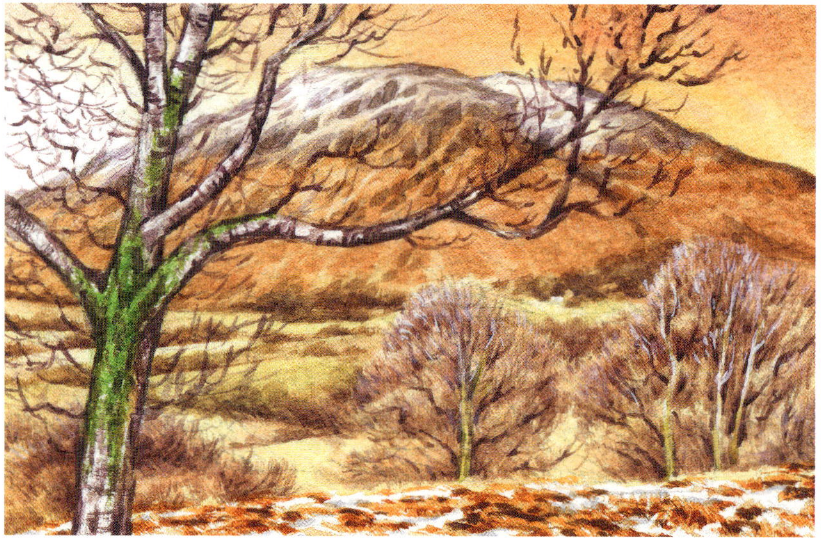

Place Fell from Glemara Park 6/3/09
It was difficult to find the exact trees in AW's drawing, they may have long since gone, but I found these to be very similar in shape and location. On maps of the day the park was either Glemarah or Glenamara (as it is today), the spelling Glemara only seems to appear in the Pictorial Guide.

The summit 18/9/07
The cairn is still small in scale but the observant will spot the Ordnance Survey ground bolt right beside it.

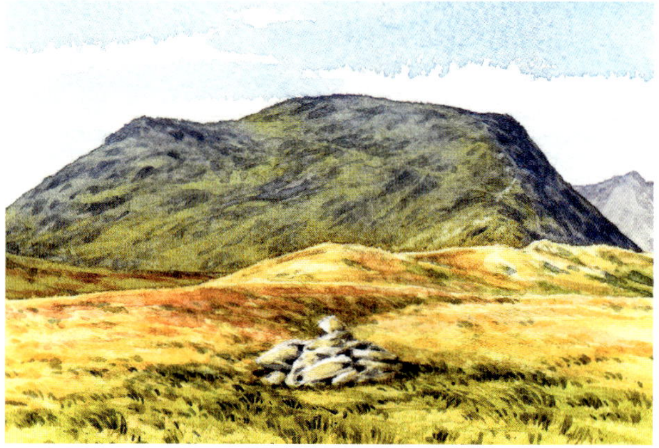

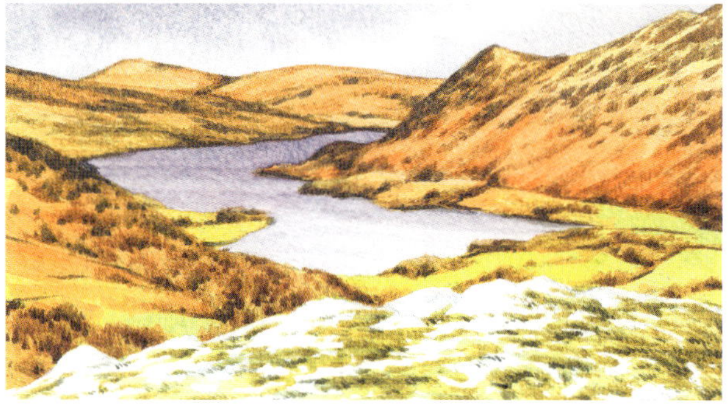

Ullswater from Thornhow End 6/3/09
This is a better aspect of the southern end of the lake than the comparative view from near the summit.

Birks

The relatively flat top of this fell means that most visitors stride out across the grassy plateau towards St. Sunday Crag. The views of Ullswater from Thornhow End are excellent as are those into Grisedale which give some of the best views of the dramatic ridges of Dollywaggon Pike and Nethermost Pike.

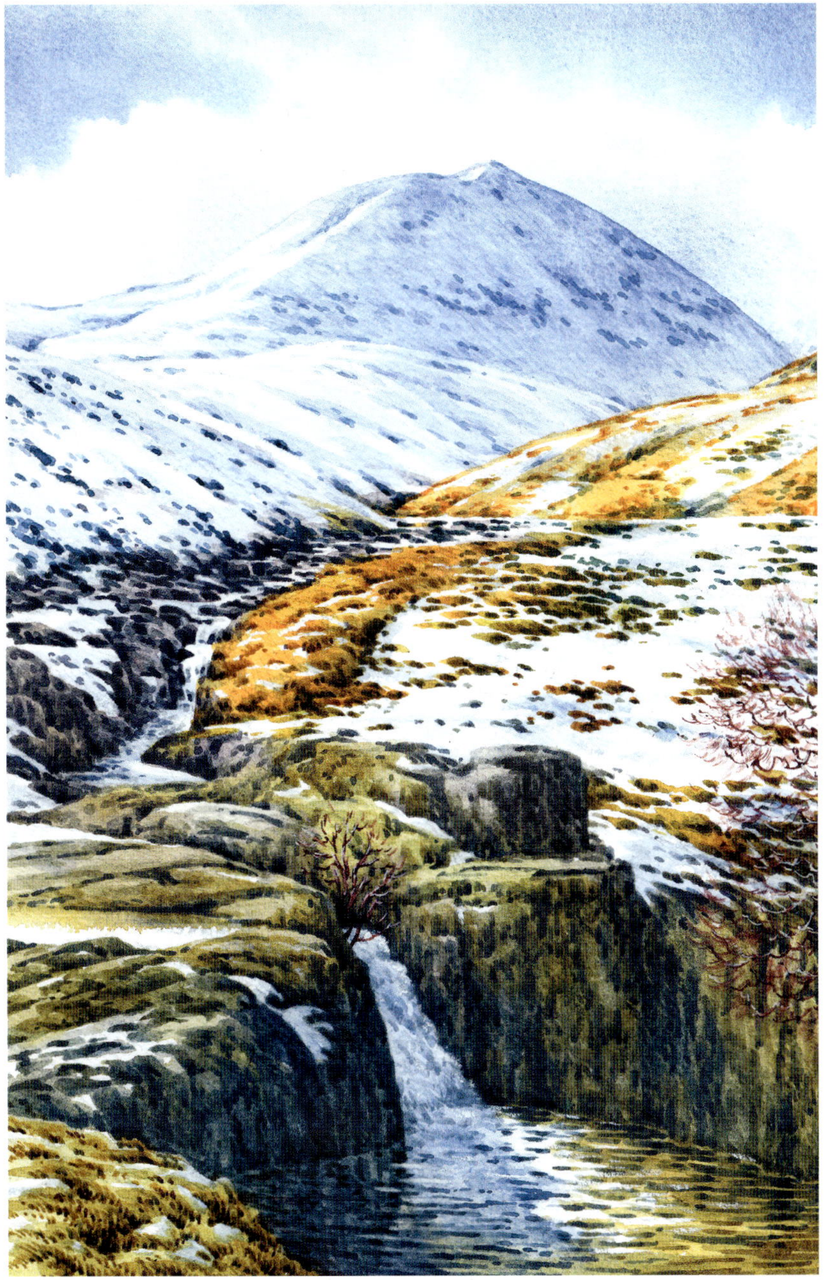

Catstycam

The name of the fell has had various derivations over the years but on today's O.S. maps Catstye Cam is used. From its summit there is a fine view of the whole of the Striding Edge ridge leading up to Helvellyn. Catstycam is often the last top on a round that has taken in that ridge.

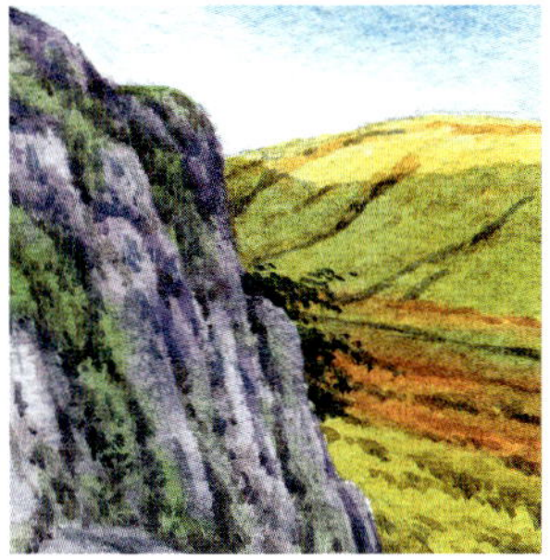

The aqueduct 11/12/09
Time has taken its toll on the wooden structure, remnants of the framework lie rotting at the foot of the crag but the stunted juniper tree clings on.

From Glenridding Beck 6/3/09
It was perfect weather to capture this scene, bright sunshine on a snow covered peak. AW gave it a little more of a dramatic point than it has in reality but Catstycam still is a most shapely of mountains.

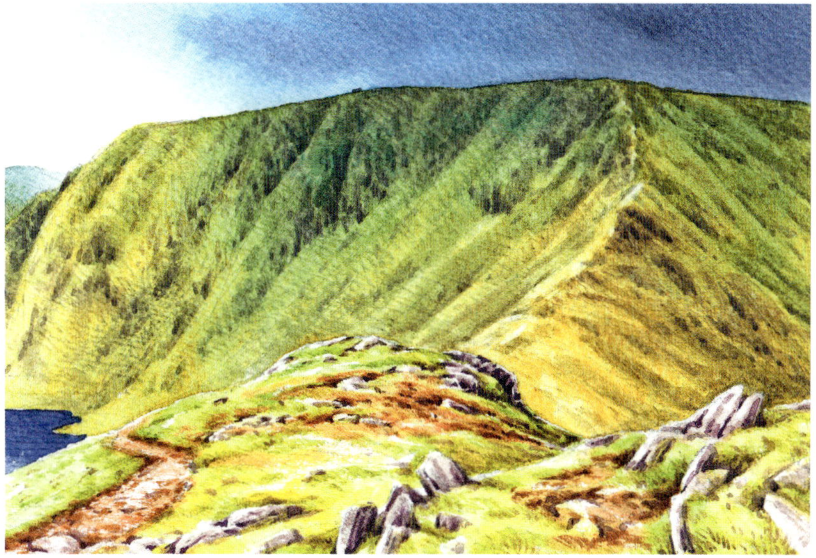

Helvellyn and Swirral Edge 25/9/09
In the intervening years, due to the popularity of the route the path has worn out the grass on the near rise. As it steeply rises up to Helvellyn the Edge has areas of loose rock and soil and needs to be crossed with care.

Keppelcove Tarn

The burst banks 11/12/09
When this terminal moraine dam failed in October 1927 it caused severe flooding in Glenridding. It has hardly changed since AW's day.

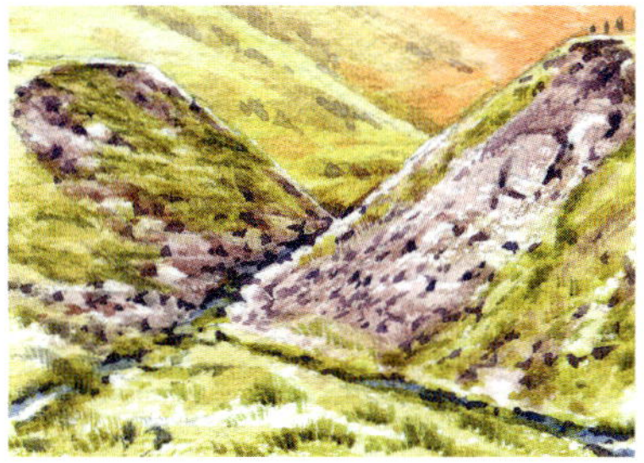

The breached dam 11/12/09
When this concrete structure also failed in 1931 it was left almost as it can be seen today with the large gaping hole at its base.

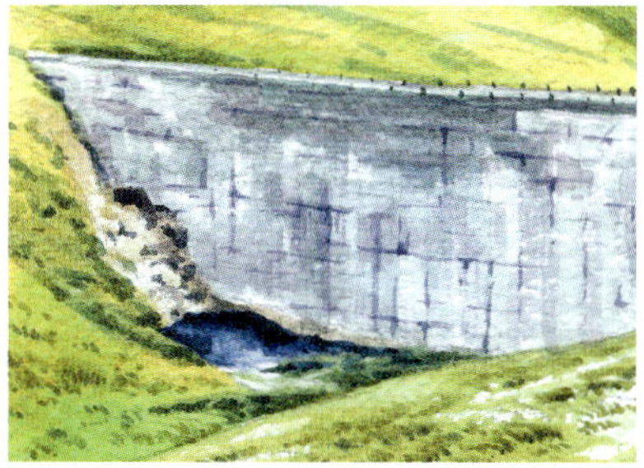

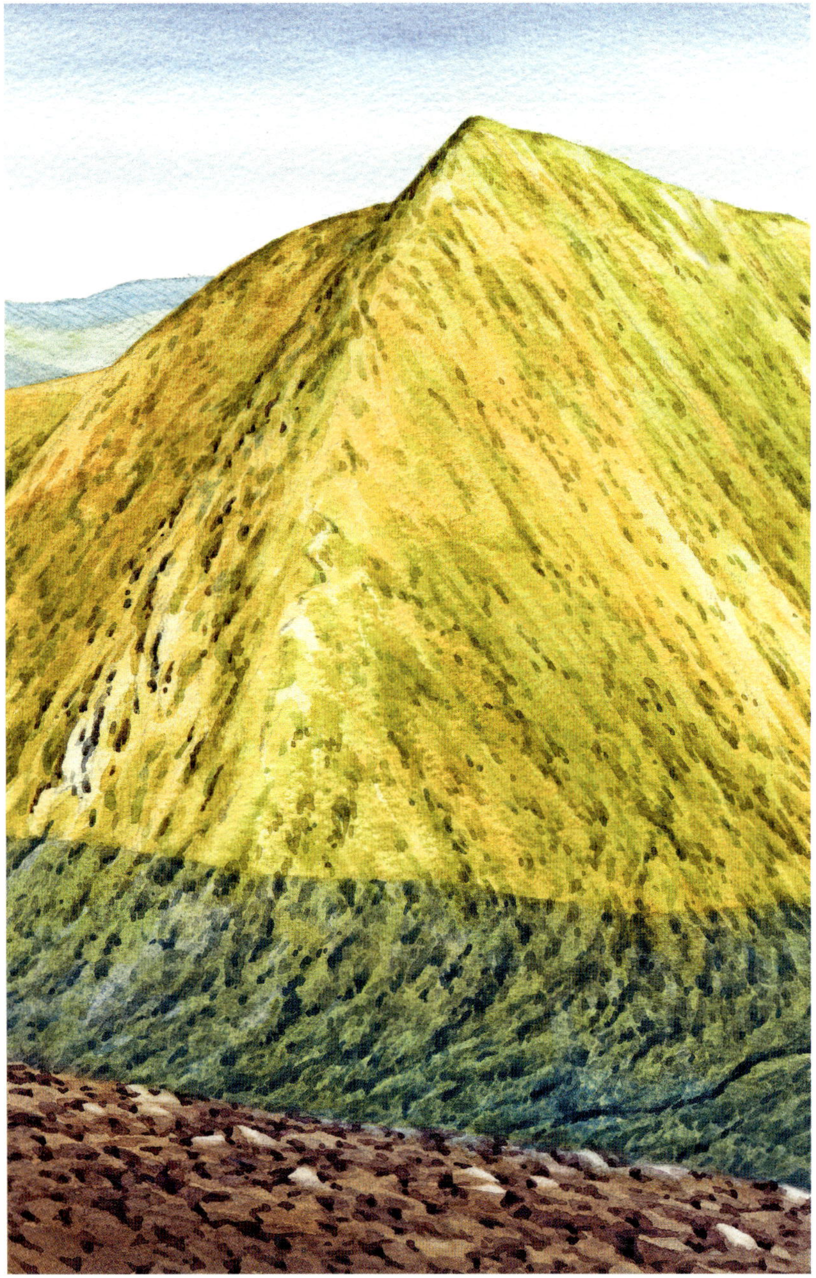

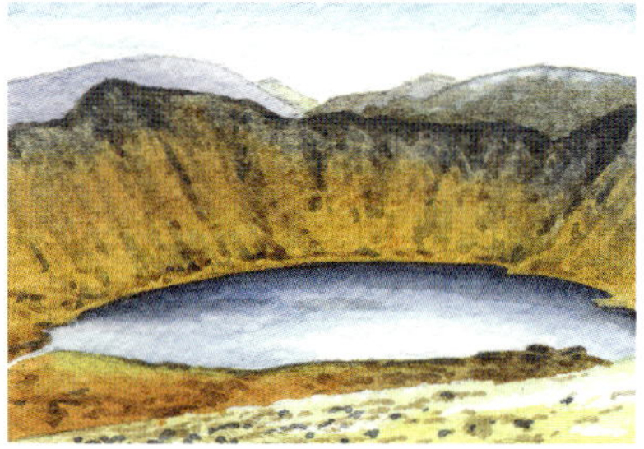

Striding Edge and Red Tarn
11/12/09
The whole of the edge in profile.

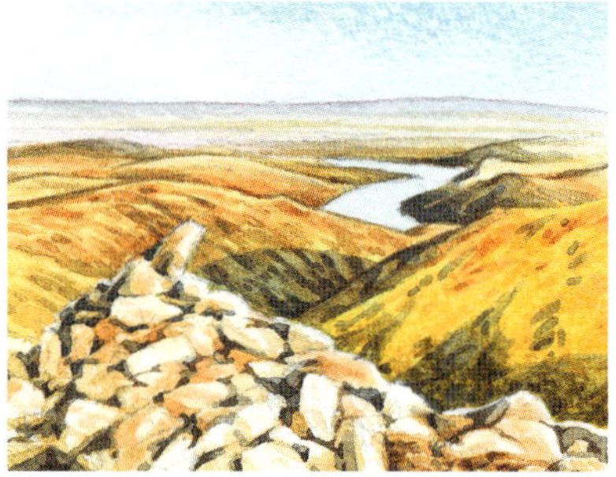

Ullswater 11/12/09
A similar sketch to the main summit drawing but from a slightly different angle.

The North-west ridge from White Side 14/6/09
From this location, almost at the top of White Side's east ridge and across Brown Cove the gradient to Catstycam's summit looks rather daunting. Either in ascent or descent the route is steep with some loose sections underfoot.

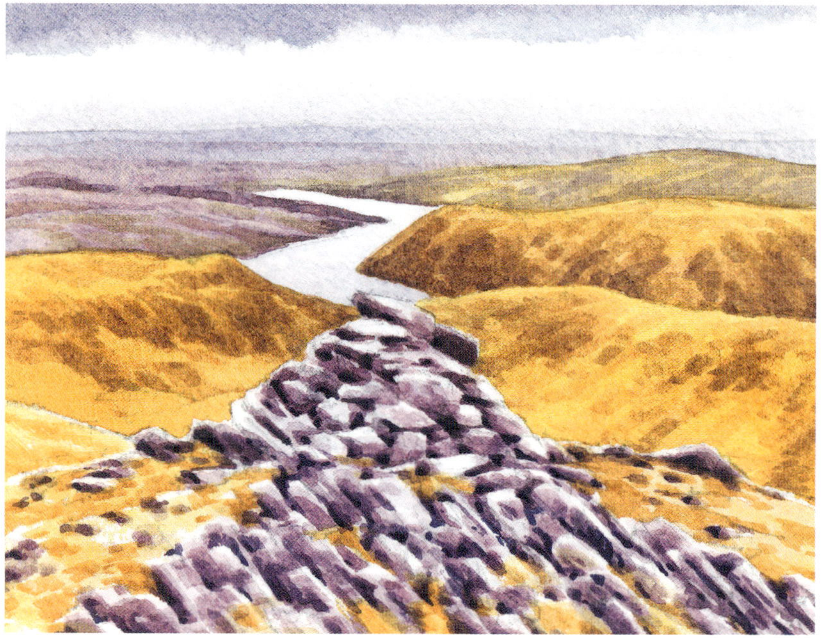

The summit 25/9/09
The cairn is perched on this small summit with a superb view of Ullswater. Whilst the neighbouring top of Helvellyn is always popular Catstycam's lofty height is much less so. The views are extensive and in the right weather this is a place to spend some time and enjoy the wide panorama.

Raise 11/12/09
Away in the distance Blencathra is framed by the tops of Raise and Great Dodd. On the flank of the fell can be seen the zigzag of the old pony track that used to take tourists to Helvellyn from Glenridding.

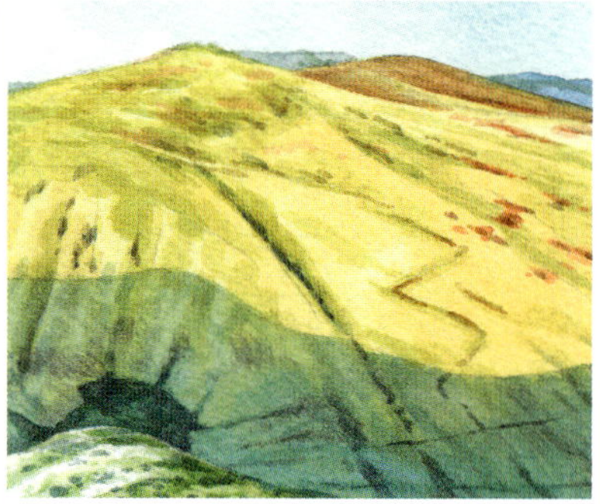

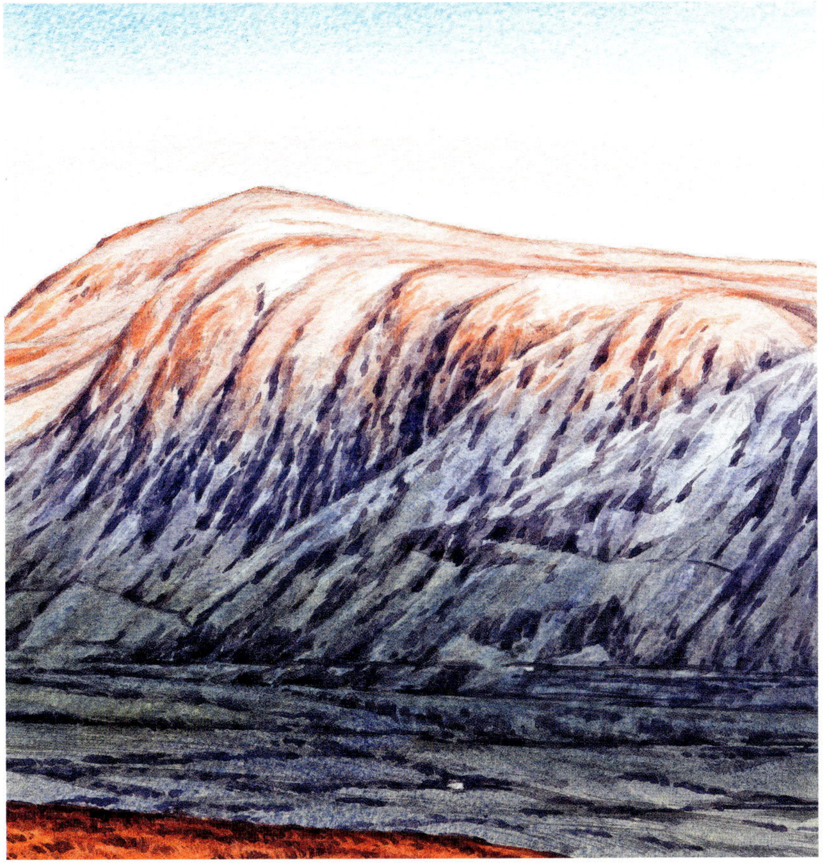

From High Rigg 10/2/09
I had visited High Rigg on several occasions but never when the winter snows coated the slopes of Clough Head as in the drawing in the Pictorial Guide. Then, late one afternoon as I was driving home from a walk on Catbells I saw the winter sun on the fell. Parking up at the St. John's church I made a mad dash to the summit before the light was gone. As I reached the top, the last rays of the sun cast a pink winter glow on the upper contours of Clough Head as the frosted valley of St John's in the Vale was cast into the darkness, fair reward for my 11 minute sprint from car to summit.

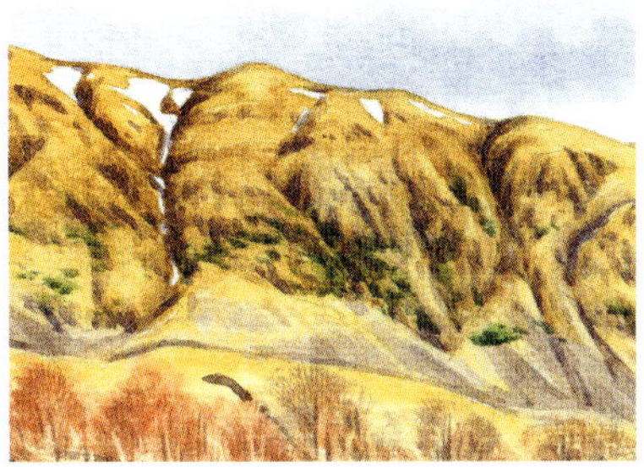

Wanthwaite Crags 16/3/10
As viewed from the main St. John's in the Vale road. The route of Fishers Wife's Rake is on the far right of this sketch.

Bramcrag Quarry 6/3/11
Now being used as a storage ground for old machinery and building materials.

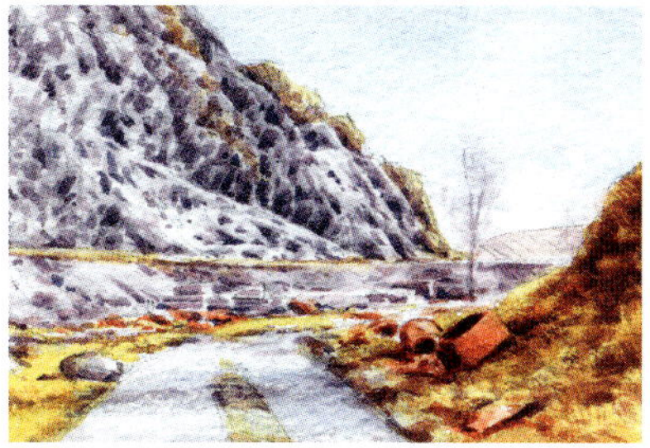

The cairn on White Pike 6/3/11
My first visit to this location was at the end of a long day, the light had gone and it was almost dark so a second visit was required just to obtain my reference photograph.

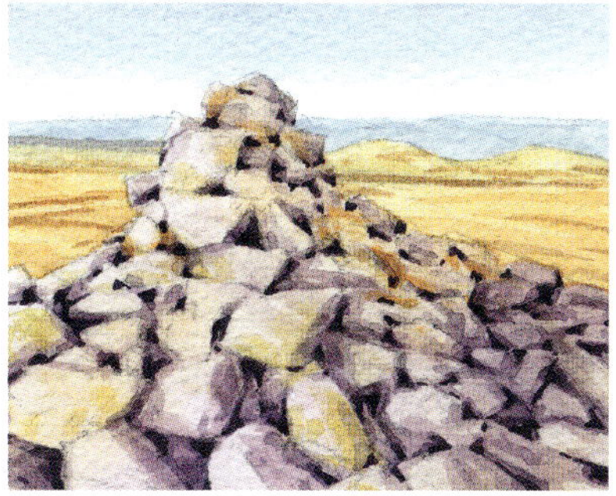

Clough Head

On the Ordnance Survey maps available to Wainwright at the time, Clough Head was the name given to the amphitheatre under Red Screes on the north face of the hill. Only on the one inch Bartholomew map is Clough Head shown as the title of the fell, next to the height of 2381'. As the northernmost of the range of fells that run like a spine through The Eastern Fells, Clough Head offers fine views of the ridges of Blencathra to the north from its summit.

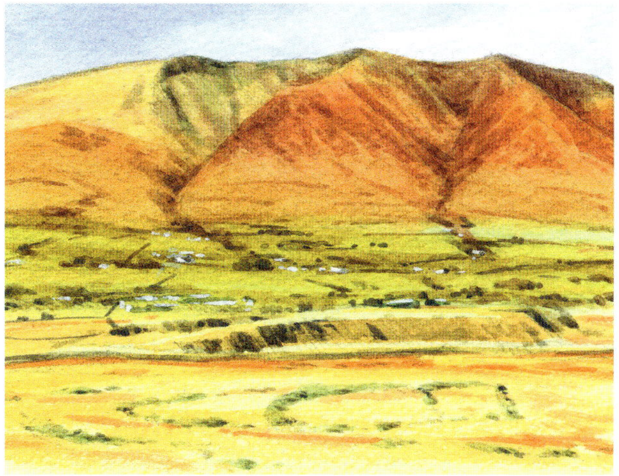

Blencathra from the British Village 26/3/09
Viewed from a rise just to the north of the Old Coach Road. The layout of the old village can still be seen.

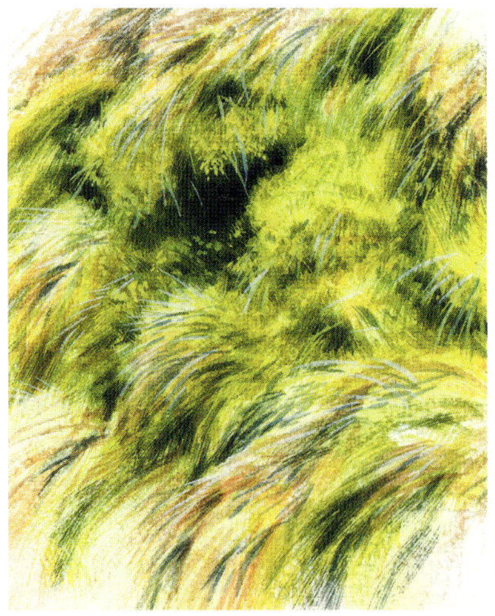

Hause Well 6/3/11

It took a couple of visits and a bit of detective work to find this spring. Now overgrown with moss and grass the clue to the well's location is the water which puddles on the coach road even on the driest of days just below the fence. I concede that it doesn't make a classic sketch but it was all part of the task of recording every single scene.

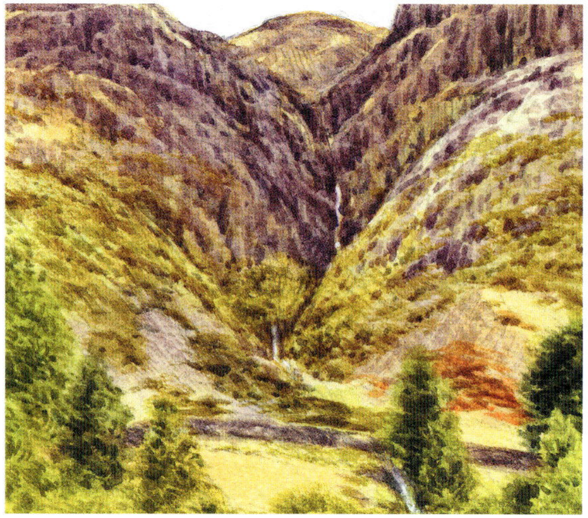

Sandbed Gill 1/9/09

As this view is actually from the valley road I pass by here quite often. I chose a day when the falls in the gorge were in full flow to obtain my reference and to give the sketch added detail.

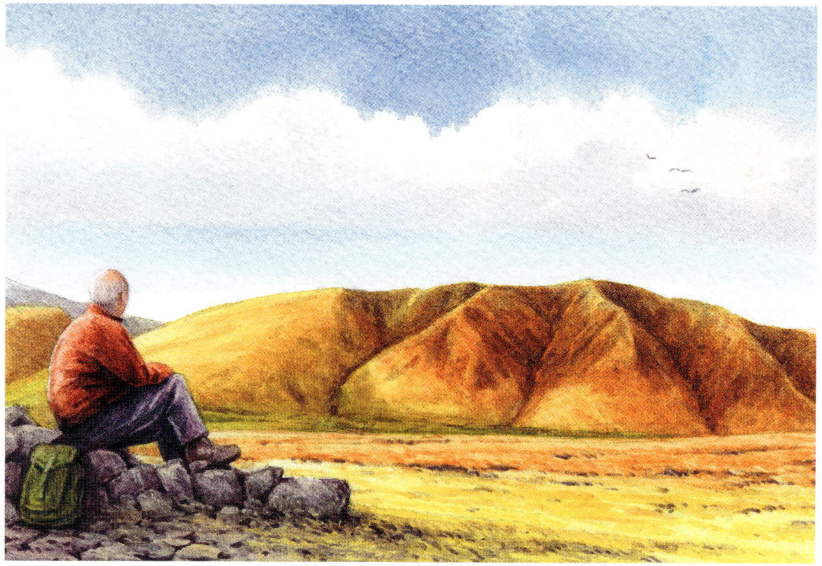

Blencathra from Clough Head 6/3/11

Wainwright's self portrait in Book One has him puffing on his pipe admiring the ridges and gullies of Blencathra. He exaggerated the mountain by some degree and unusually he left plenty of space for sky, clouds and even a couple of birds. I can only assume this was done as a page filling ploy. As with all of his self portraits, I have taken the liberty of putting myself in his place complete with rucksack but without the pipe.

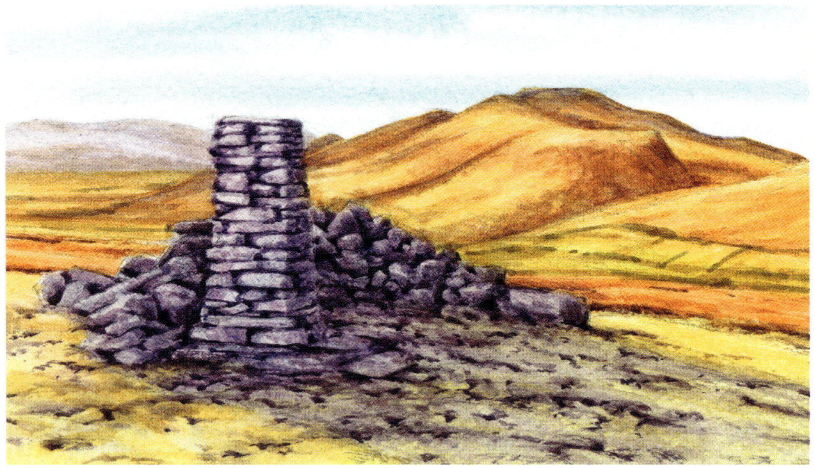

The summit 6/3/11

Hardly changed since his day with the view to Skiddaw and the north-western fells away to the left. By then moving slightly to one side AW was able to get the view of Blencathra needed for the drawing top right, but he used himself as foreground interest instead of the triangulation pillar which must have been a fairly new construction on his visit.

Calfhow Pike 26/3/09

A fortress on the flat ridge between Clough Head and Great Dodd, the rocky outcrop of Calfhow Pike is worthy of a visit. In compiling his original list of fells AW actually put Calfhow Pike down as a fell in its own right.

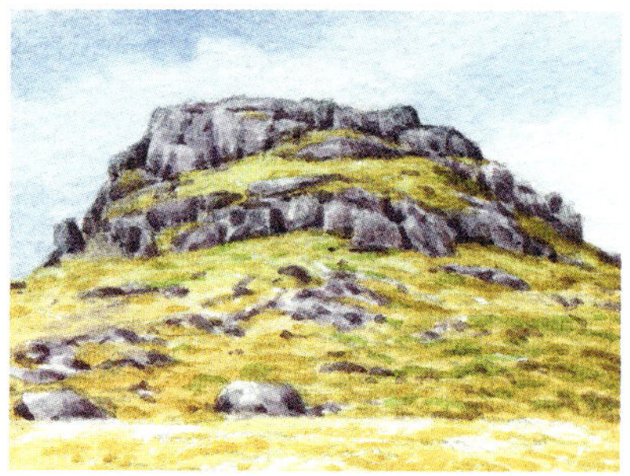

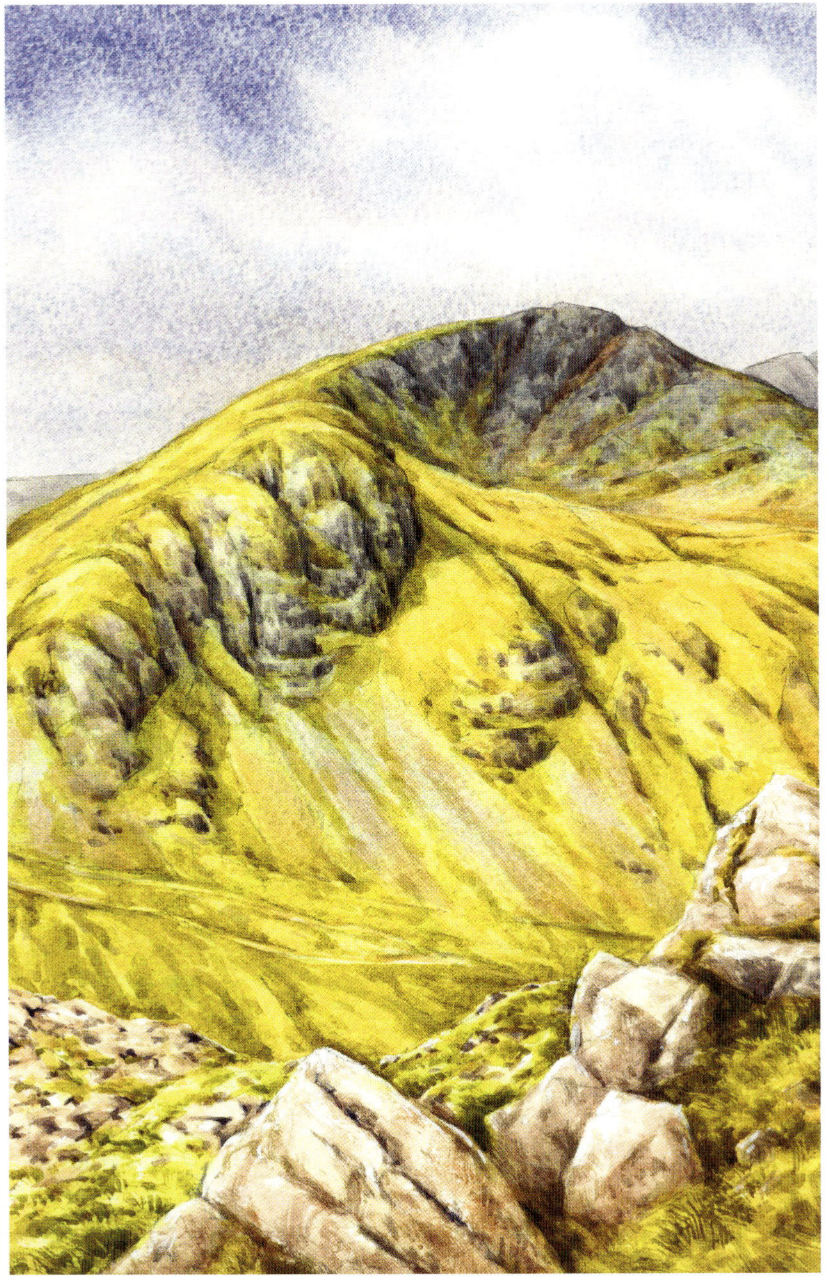

Dollywaggon Pike

When ascending the hill from Grisedale Tarn the first encounter is with the steep uniform slopes of the fell. The main pathway which has undergone some repair work zigzags up the slopes and will take you directly to Helvellyn beyond. A detour is needed from the main path to attain the actual summit from where there are exciting views over the fell's craggy eastern flanks.

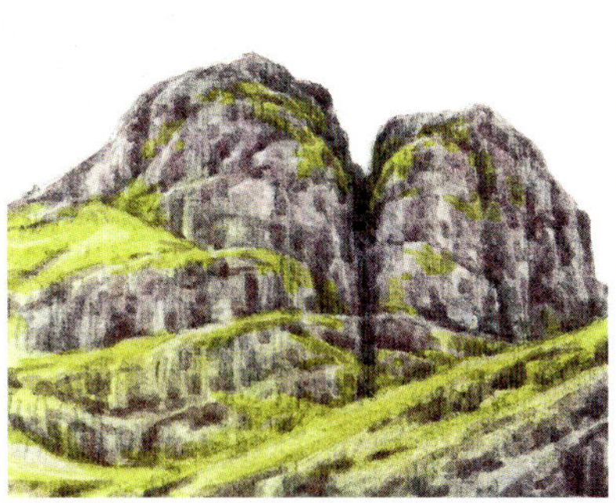

Falcon Crag 25/9/09
As seen towering above the path between Ruthwaite Lodge and Grisedale Tarn.

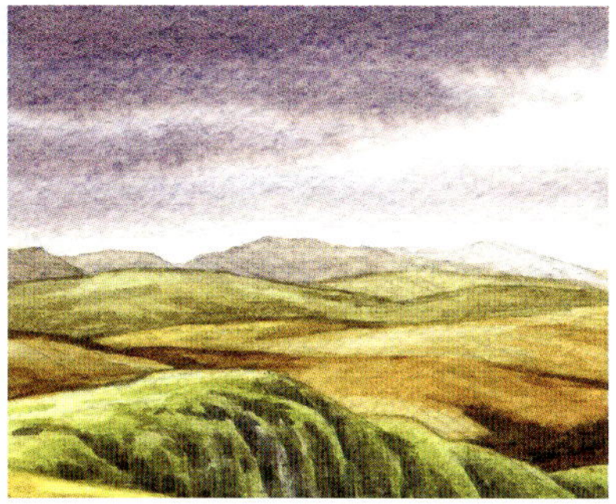

The Grasmoor Fells 25/9/09
Shown in a more realistic, flatter shape here than in AW's drawing.

The summit 25/9/09
The far cairn has diminished but the near one has grown. The fence post is no more and bare patches of grass show the popularity of the location.

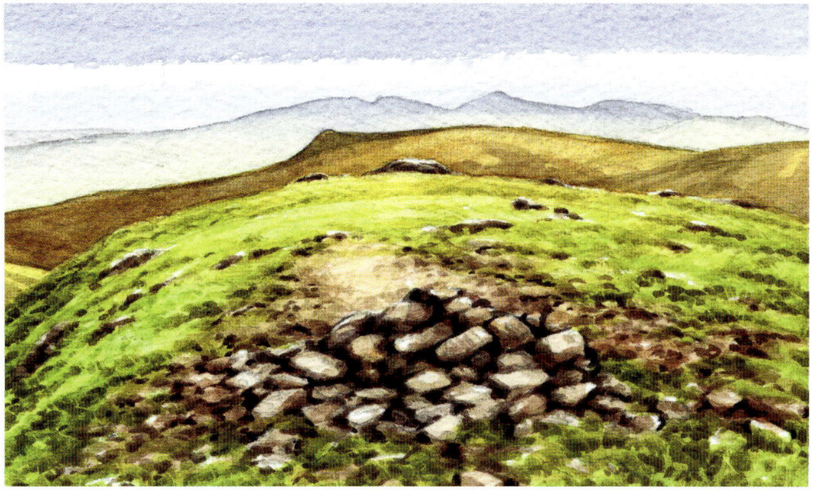

From Deepdale Hause 18/9/07
This is an excellent vantage point to assess the crags and coves of the east facing side of Dollywaggon Pike. Its profile is not quite as dramatic as depicted in his drawing or even in this sketch but it is impressive none the less.

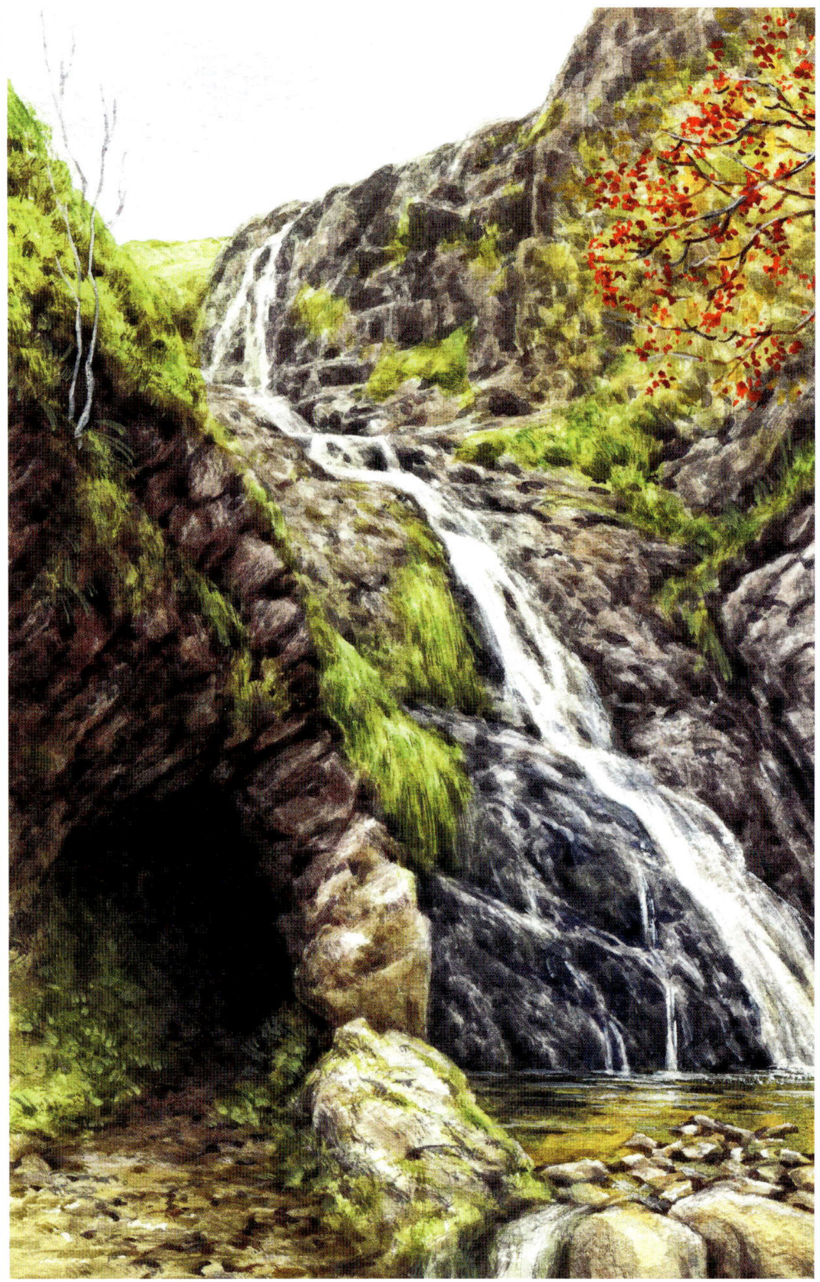

Caves and Cascades, Ruthwaite 25/9/09

A mature rowan on the right is about the only tree left from the original scene. Many of the rocks and boulders at the base of the falls have also gone leaving a shallow pool.

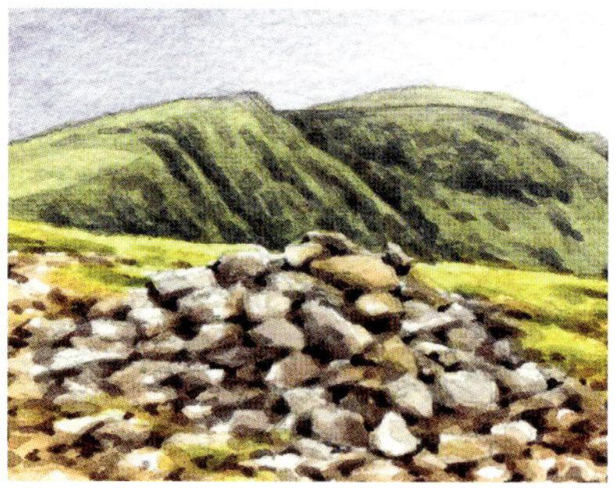

Looking north 25/9/09

High Crag and then Nethermost Pike viewed over the western cairn of the summit plateau.

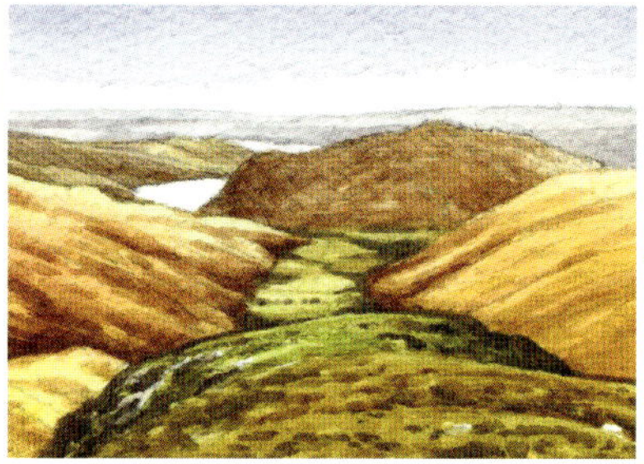

Ullswater and Place Fell 25/9/09

From the top of The Tongue which rises up from the Grisedale valley.

The Tarn Crag gullies 25/9/09

A good example of Wainwright's full exploration of the fells. These gullies are well to the east of the main path and even today there is no sign of visitors. His location for both scenes was close to precipitous drops.

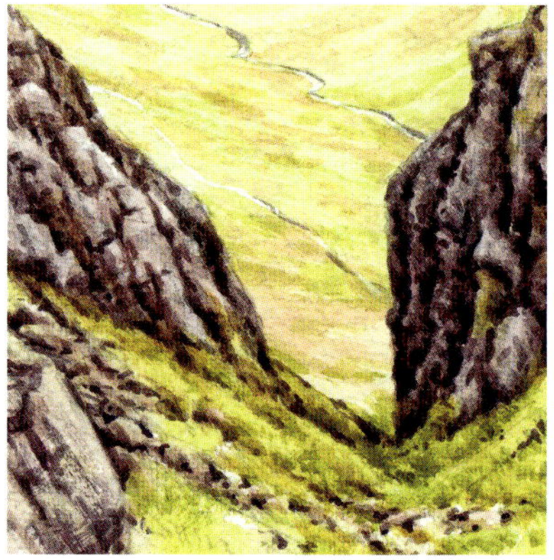

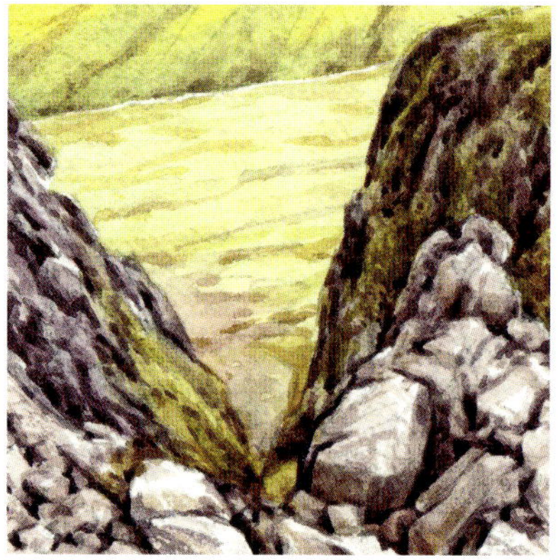

Raise Beck

Between the regular slopes of Dollywaggon Pike and Seat Sandal is a steep, narrow and almost straight valley that runs east to west. Down through this ravine over a series of cascades flows Raise Beck. Once out of the ravine the natural route of the beck was then to turn left in the direction of Grasmere. When the Thirlmere dam was constructed in the 1890s a subterranean aqueduct was constructed to take the water south via Dunmail Raise and beyond. Some years later, the water authority decided to divert the beck northwards to catch its waters in the reservoir. So now, whilst the surface water of the beck heads north in parallel to the A591, directly underneath it the aqueduct carries the supplies in the opposite direction on its 95 mile route to Manchester.

In December 2015 after a period of exceptional heavy rainfall in this locality the area was devastated by heavy flooding. Tremendous amounts of water from both Raise Beck and Birkside Gill combined to cause serious damage to the main road north of Dunmail Raise making it totally impassable for months, only re-opening in May 2016. Raise Beck isn't always the gentle stream as it often appears.

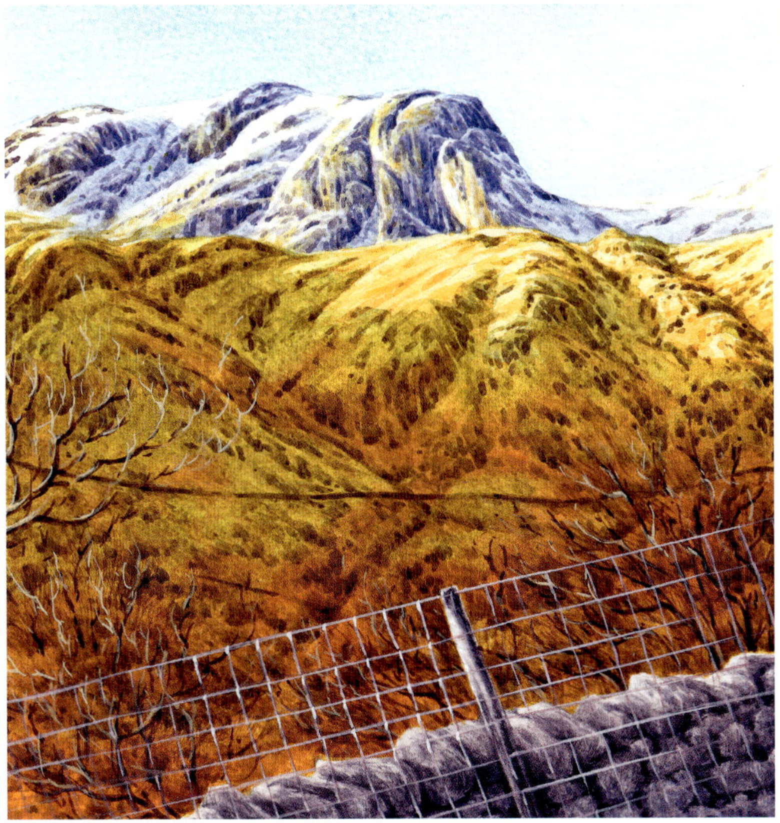

Dove Crag

Many walkers will take in this fell as part of the round of the Fairfield Horseshoe. It has areas worthy of further exploration, especially when approached from Dovedale. Today Dove Crag is well know for the shelter, The Priest's Hole which is accessible via an airy path. Even though there is no mention or detail of this cave in the guide, AW did know of it as it is listed in his notebook but not crossed off, perhaps he never visited it whilst researching the book. Dove Crag was the first fell to come under his pen at the start of the Pictorial Guides on 9th November 1952.

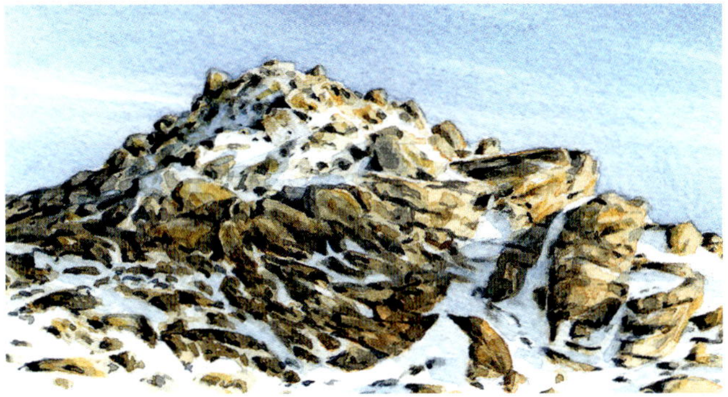

The summit 25/11/08
Now a low sprawling heap occupies the rock platform.

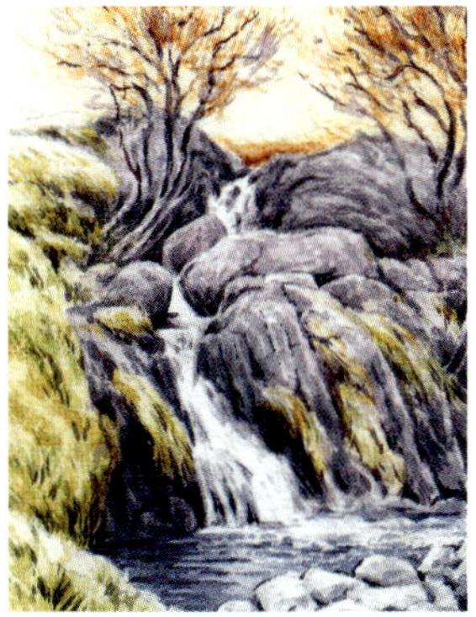

Dove Falls 25/11/08
One of a series of charming small cascades in Dovedale.

From Dovedale 25/11/08
Seen from the ascending path beyond Hartsop Hall.

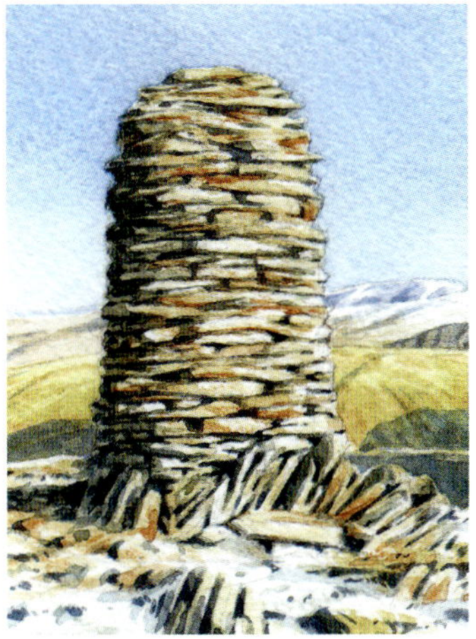

The cairn on High Bakestones 25/11/08
A fine tower of stones that's located away from a main path or summit possibly accounts for its longevity. In the recent past it has had at least three copies nearby but these have now gone, leaving the original tall cairn standing alone.

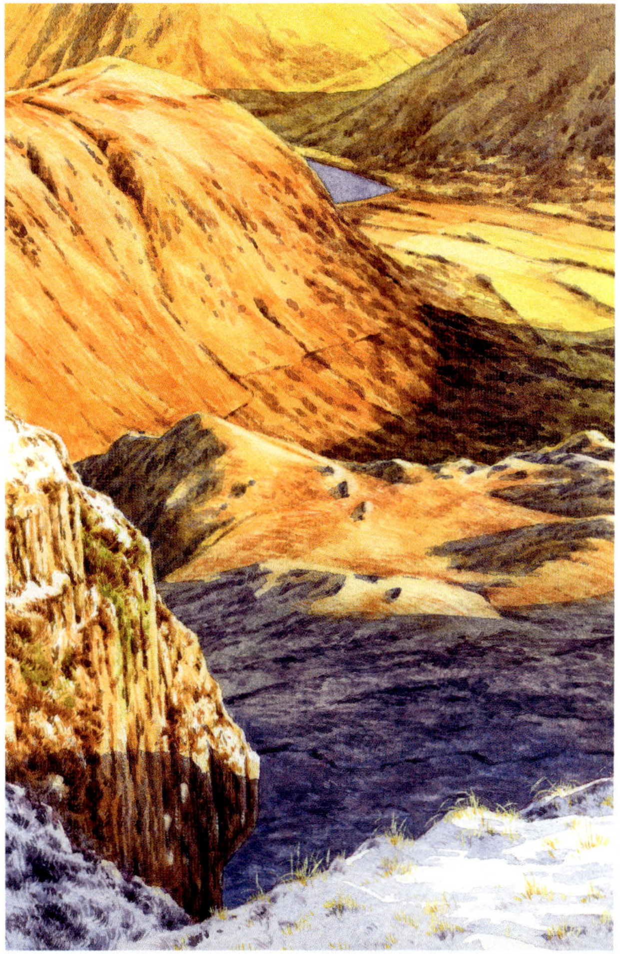

Dovedale, from the top of Easy Gully 25/11/08
A perfect winter's day to capture the scene with the shadow on the bottom left almost matching AW's original drawing. This was a precarious spot, fresh snow on grass over a sheer drop so I retreated quickly once I had obtained my reference photograph.

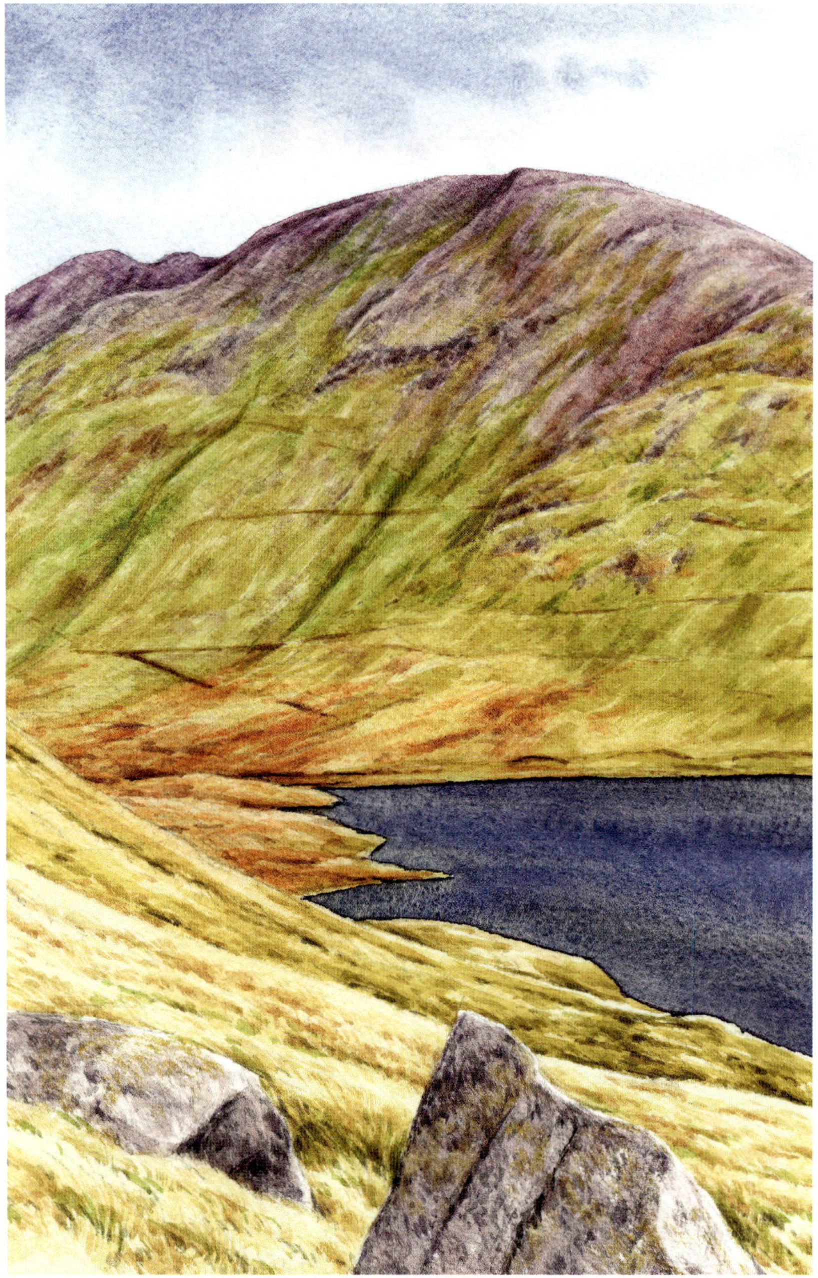

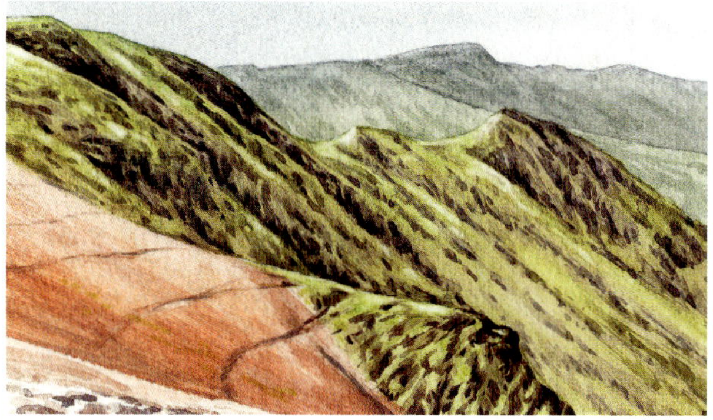

Cofa Pike and the north-east ridge 18/9/07
From the unfrequented, pathless Greenhow End spur.

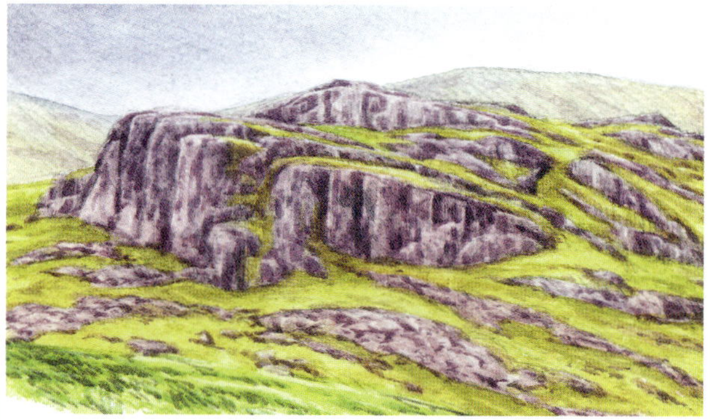

Black Crag from Rydal Head 1/9/09
Included is the Great Rigg to Fairfield ridge behind.

The Crags of Fairfield

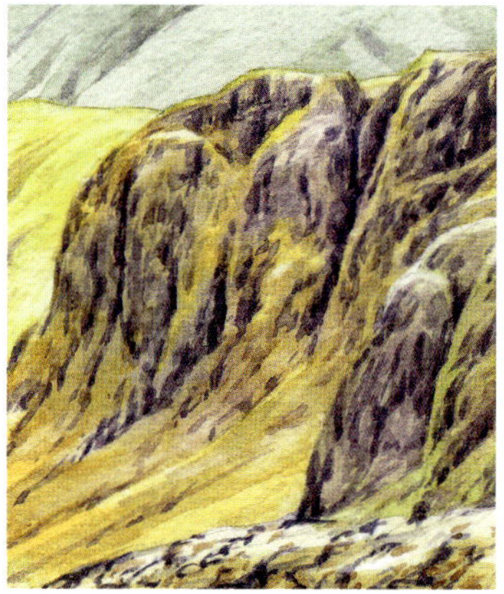

Greenhow End 18/9/07
A view similar to "The north face of Fairfield" but from nearer to Cofa Pike.

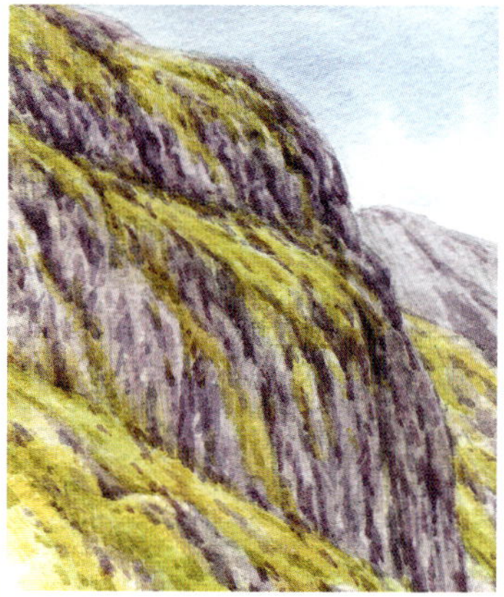

Scrubby Crag 18/9/07
A short deviation from the path at Link Hause leads to the viewpoint.

Fairfield

Giving its name to an enjoyable horseshoe walk Fairfield makes for a great focal point for a long day out from Ambleside or Rydal, providing all round grand views, weather permitting.

From Grisedale Tarn 25/9/09
The angular foreground rocks are off to one side of the main path on the north side of the tarn. The fell is more rounded in reality than it is shown in the guide.

The summit 18/9/07 With Helvellyn beyond.

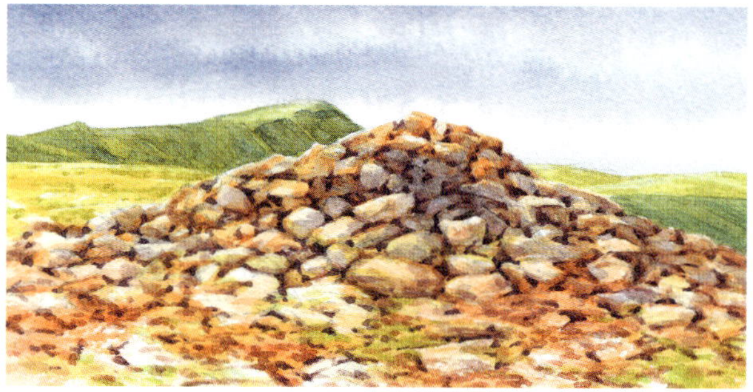

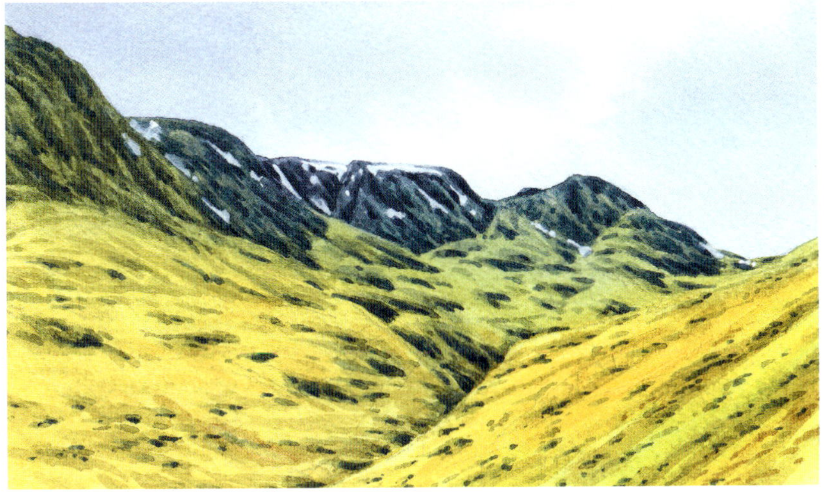

The head of Deepdale 18/9/07
AW gave the scene more drama but it is still an impressive location.

The cliffs of Fairfield, from Greenhow End 18/9/07
This view is obtained from the grassy col along Greenhow End's ridge.

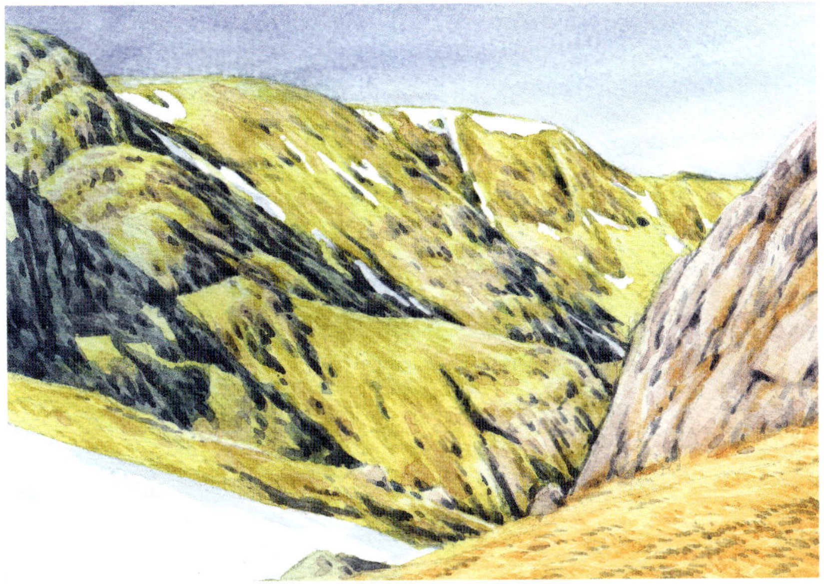

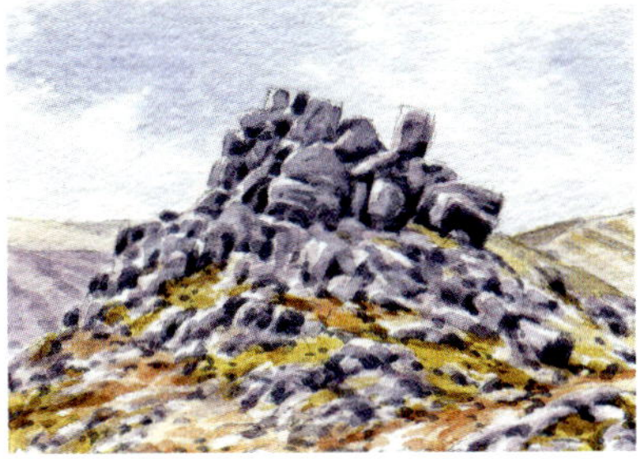

Rocks on Cofa Pike 18/9/07
As viewed when approaching on the ridge to the south.

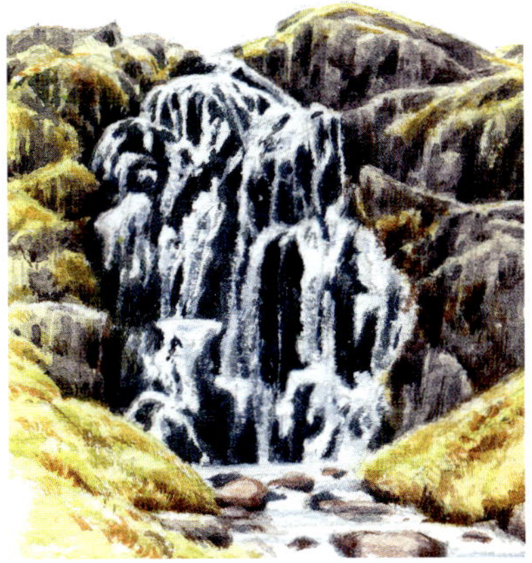

Cascade, Tongue Gill 2/1/09
Almost frozen solid during a very cold period around the new year.

The north face of Fairfield 18/9/07
Careful planning allowed me to visit the scene when the last of the snows clung on in the gullies almost as it is depicted in the guide. Far below lies Deepdale.

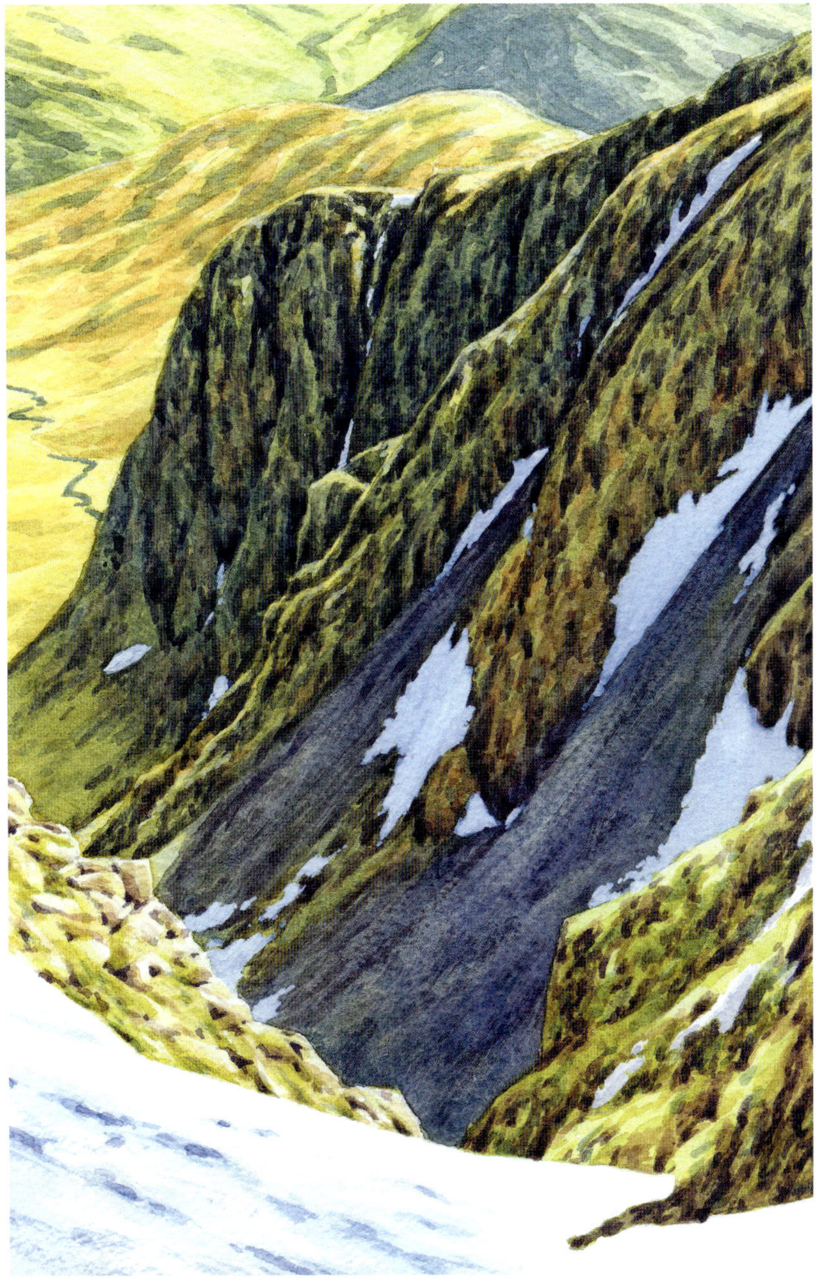

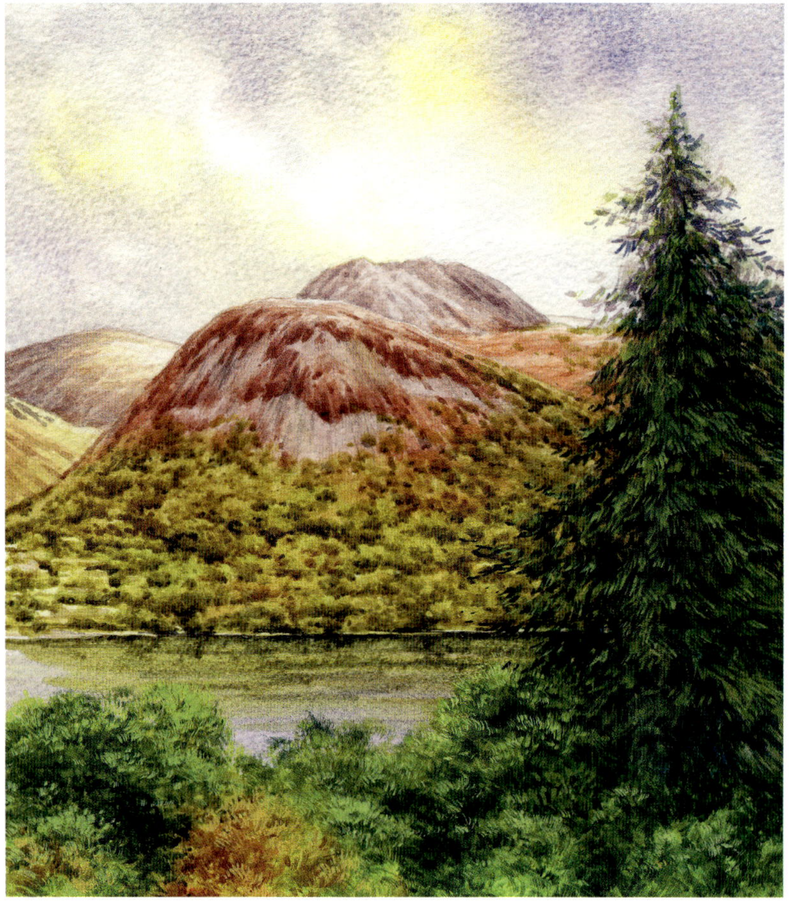

From Ullswater (Sheffield Pike behind)14/10/08
Amazingly, the trees in the foreground still bear a striking similarity in shape to the ones in Wainwright's drawing even after all this time.

Glenridding Dodd

In the Pictorial Guide Glenridding Dodd is one of the few fells without a drawing of the summit and its cairn even though AW indicated the presence of one. This fell out of all 214 qualifies as being the one to which Wainwright gave the least worded description.

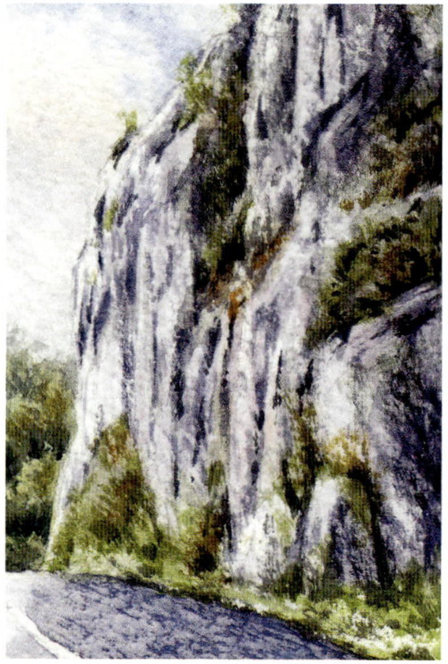

Stybarrrow Crag 14/10/08
This is no place to linger as it is right on the busy road to Glenridding.

Looking down on Glenridding 14/1/08
This shows the expansion of the village now from a point east of the summit.

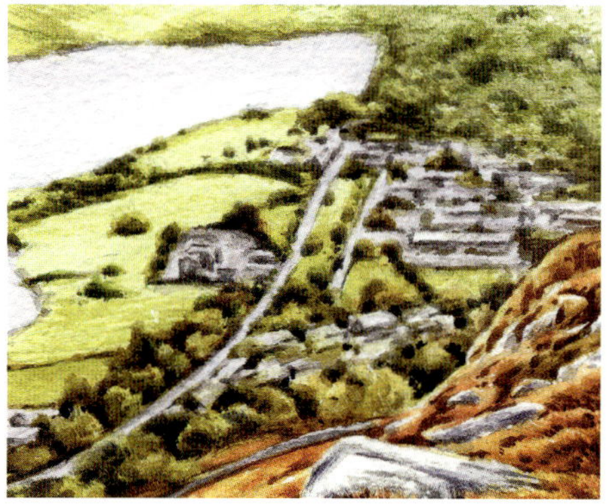

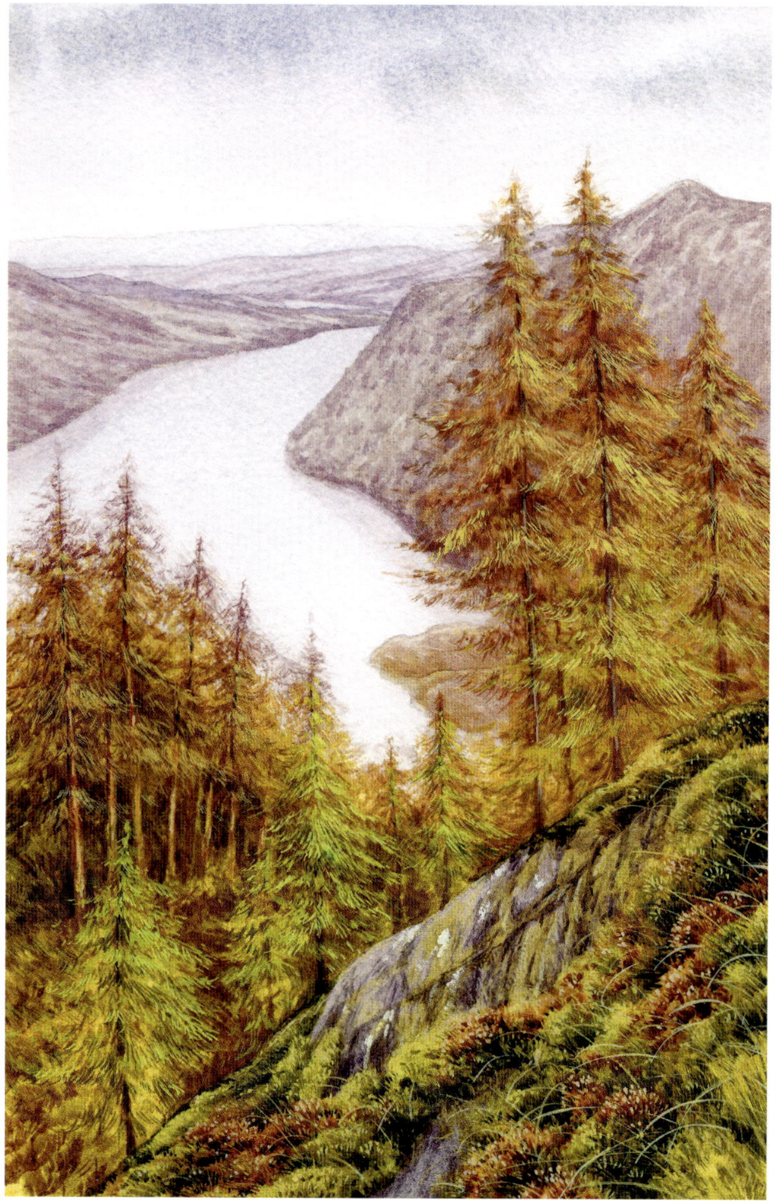

Ullswater and Birk Fell 14/10/08
As viewed from above the fell's north facing slopes on a dull, misty day.

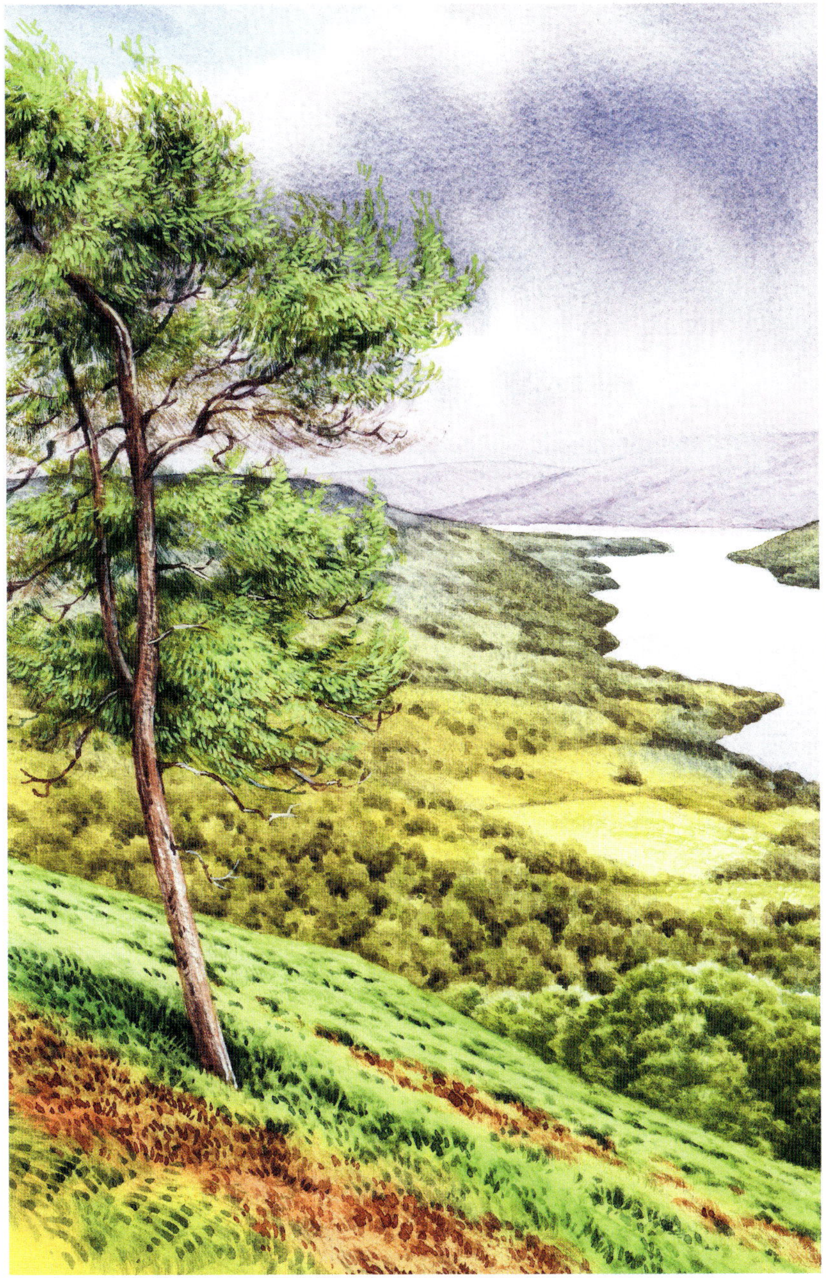

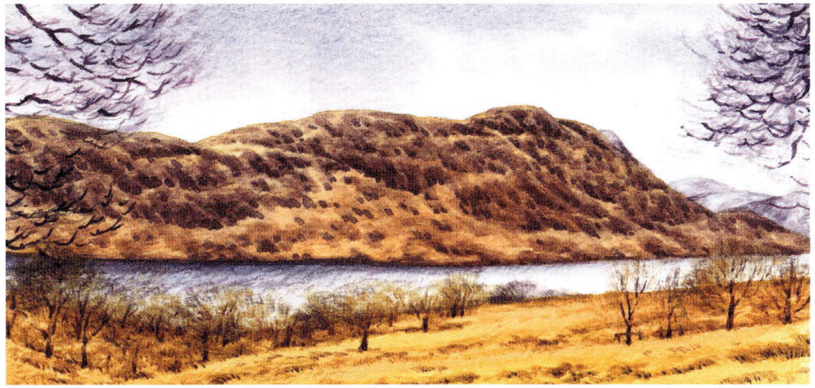

Place Fell and Ullswater from Gowbarrow Park 16/3/10
The scene from the path leading from Park Brow to Aira Force.

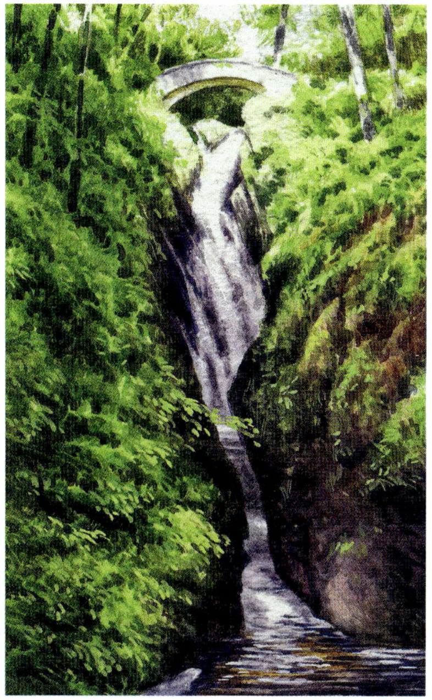

Aira Force 19/06/09
A classic view of this popular fall.

Gowbarrow Fell

This is a delightful fell for family exploration. In the main, well made paths lead to its various attractions whether it's the waterfalls, the summit or the viewpoints on Green Hill or Yew Crag. A cafe at the lower car park is the added bonus.

From Brown Hills 30/06/09
The dead pine in his drawing has since fallen and lies close by, now replaced by this youngster which I considered worth including. Its new growth almost obscures the fell but this is still a fine prospect of the lower reaches of Ullswater.

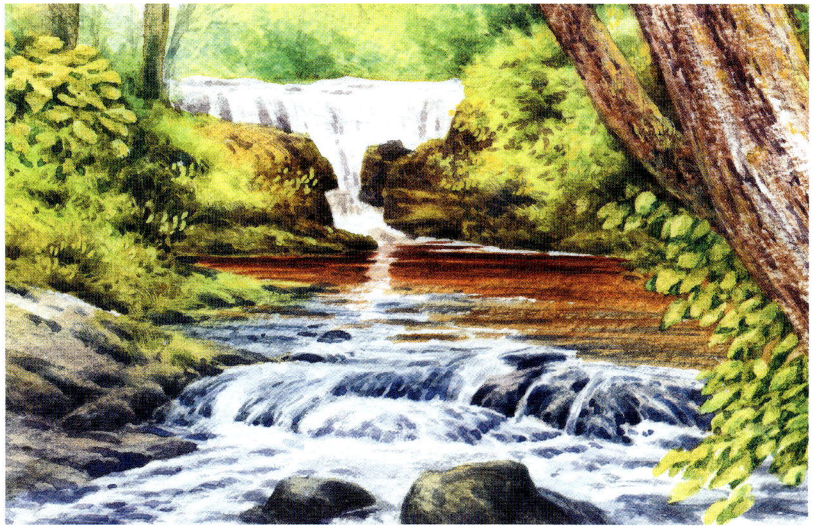

High Force 19/06/09
A few hundred yards upstream of the popular Aira Force, High Force squeezes through the rock gap.

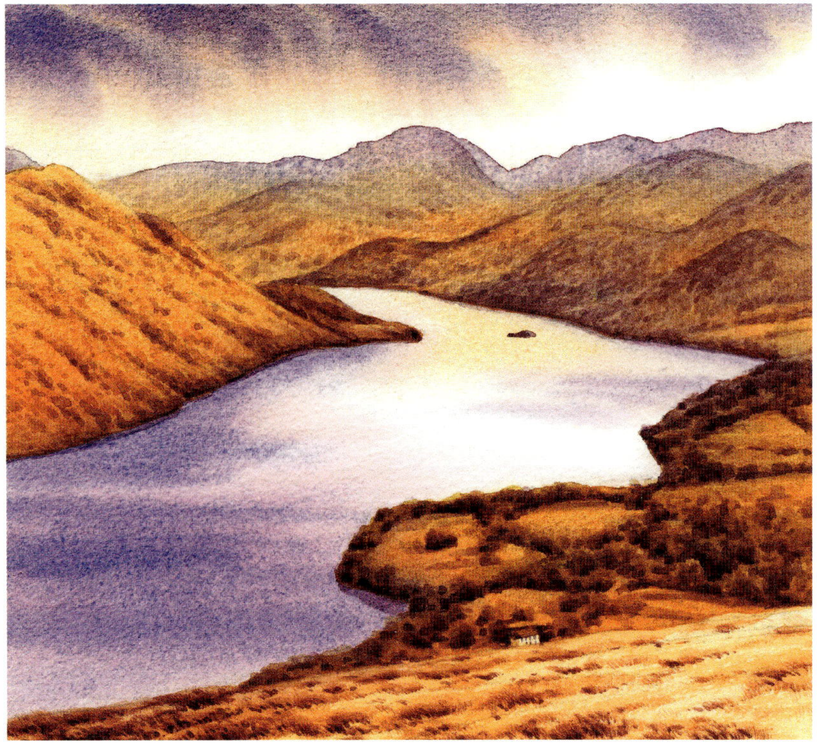

The Head of Ullswater from Green Hill 29/4/08

A fine location to watch the last light of the day fade over the head of the lake and the hills to the south.

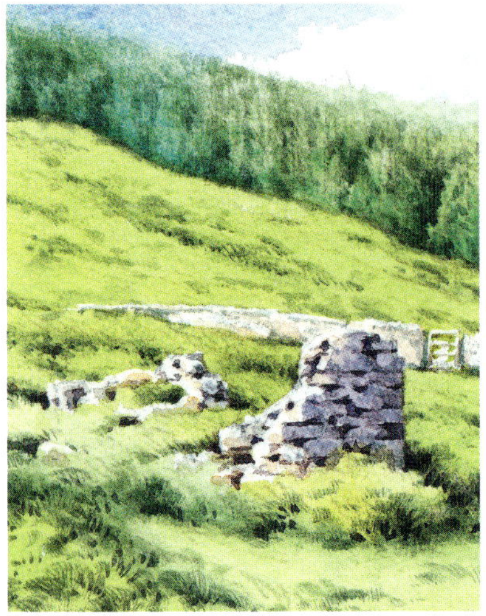

The shooting box 19/06/09

Low ruins are all that are left of this reminder of days gone by.

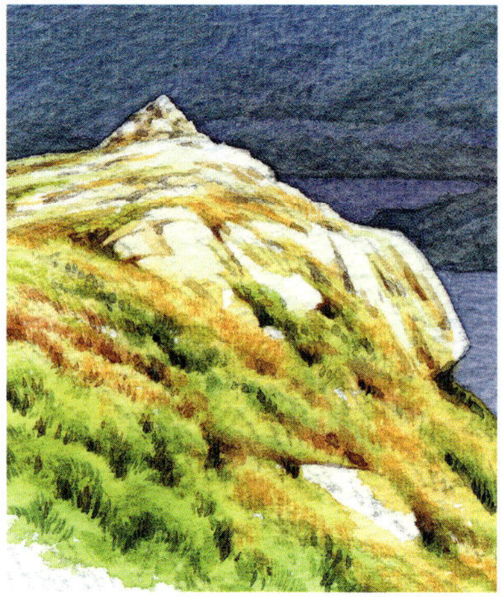

Cairn on Yew Crag 19/06/09

It is worth the detour to visit this fine cairn topped viewpoint.

Yew Crag 21/9/10

A break in the canopy of Dobbin Wood provides the required view.

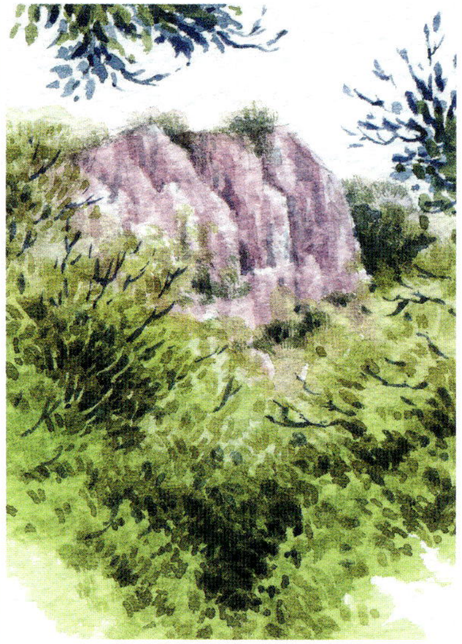

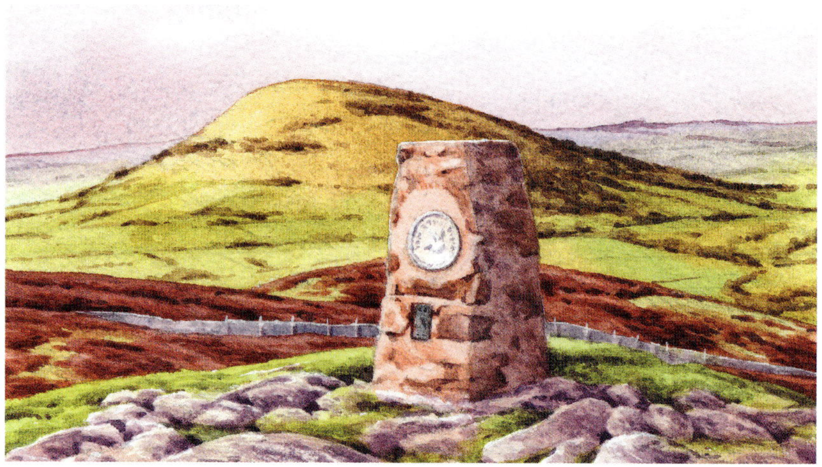

The summit 19/06/09

The building of Ordnance Survey triangulation columns was still ongoing as AW worked on the guides (see page 47). Affixed to the face of this one is the usual brass flush bracket and a National Trust plaque.

The summit ridge 29/4/08

Heather adorns the fell top and a few red grouse still reside hereabouts.

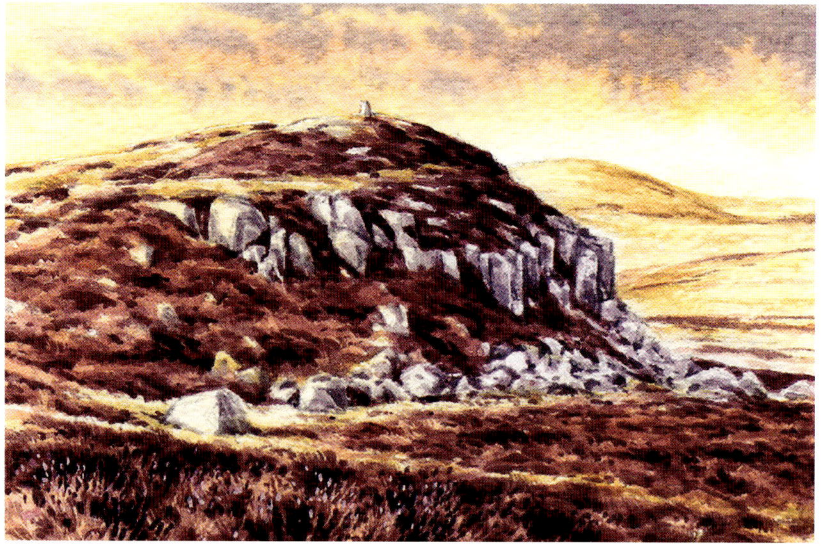

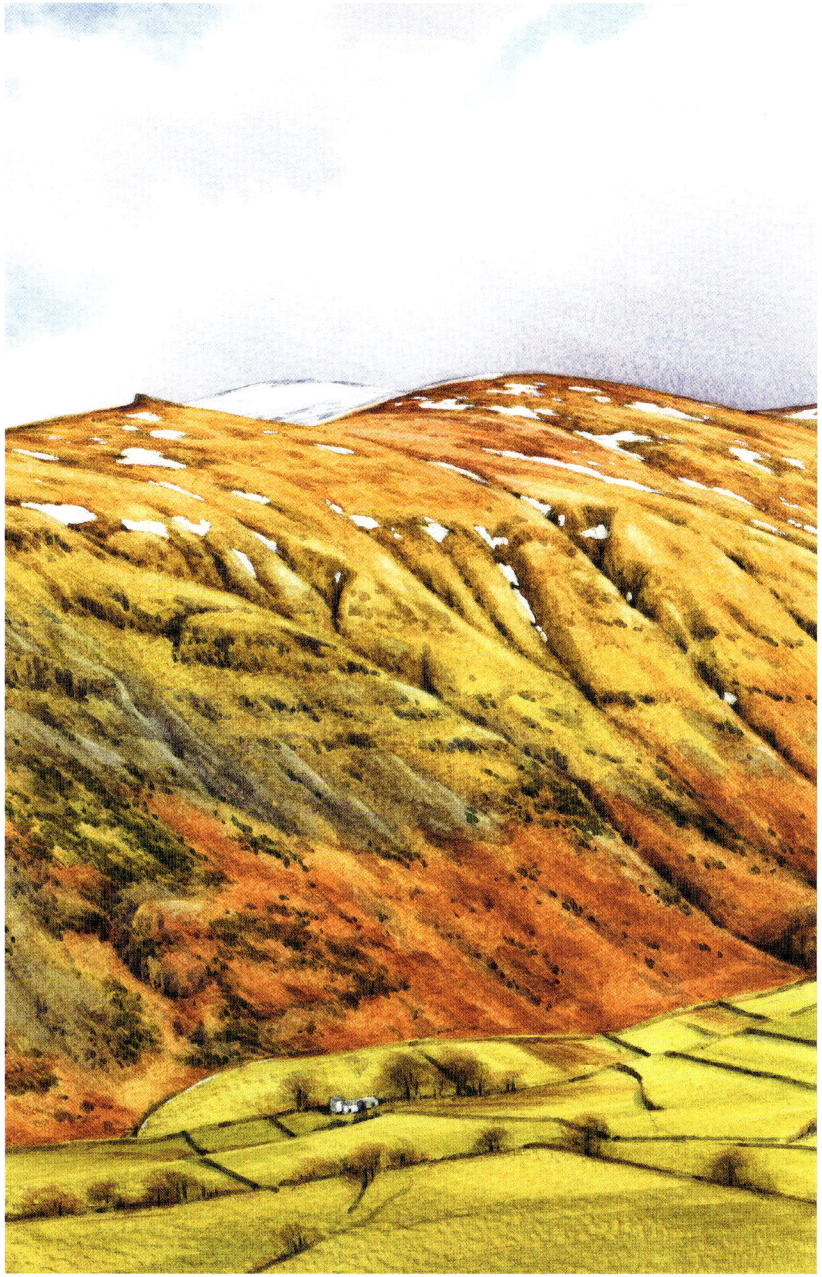

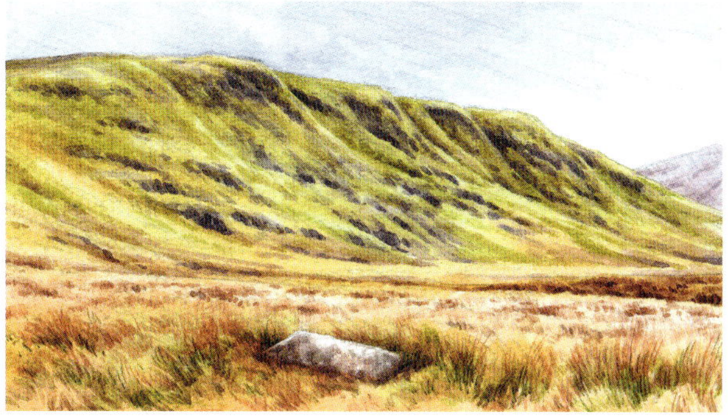

Wolf Crags 26/3/09 From the old coach road with the lone stone in the foreground acting as a marker.

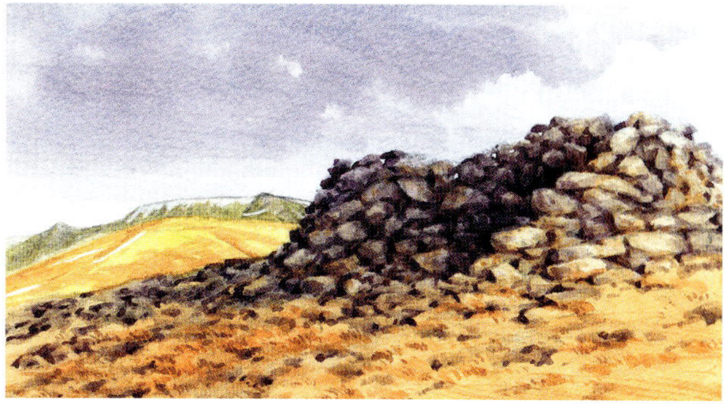

The summit 26/3/09
A cairn now adorns the top , 80 yards from this shelter.

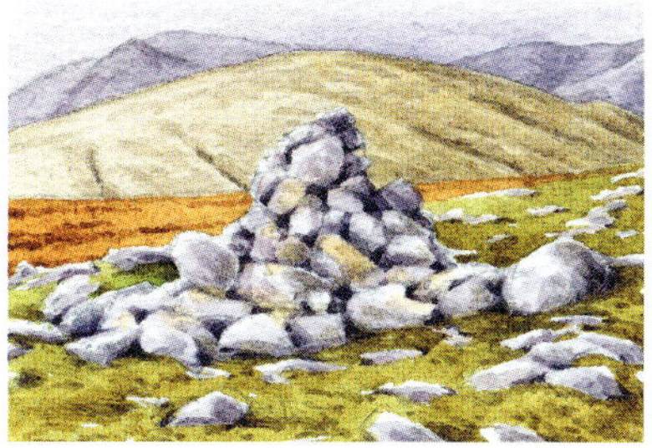

The cairn on Randerside
19/06/09 Skiddaw over on the left.

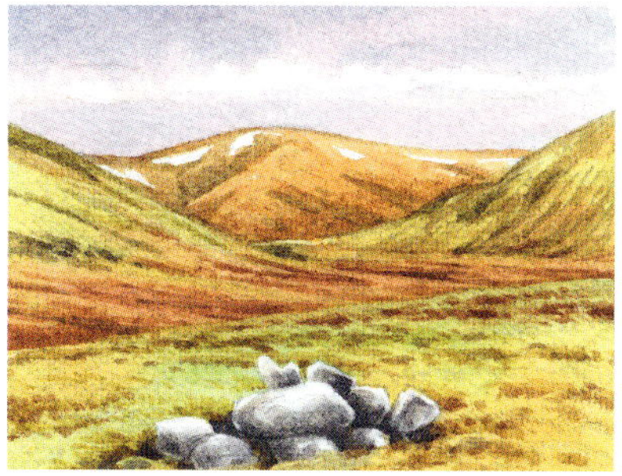

The cairn on High Brow
19/06/09 Almost totally unchanged.

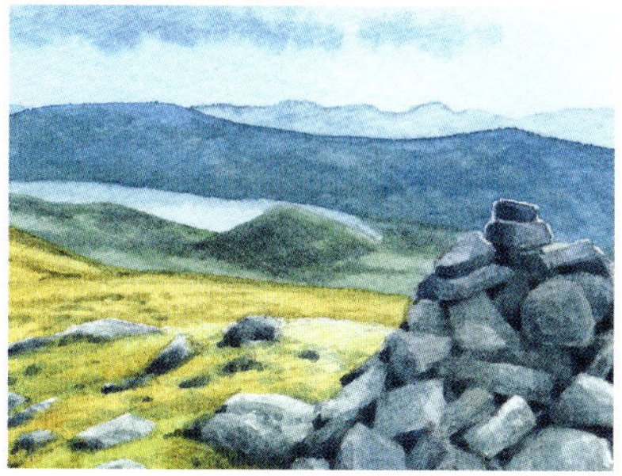

Thirlmere from Calfhow Pike
19/06/09 The cairn is now bigger.

Great Dodd

The fells to the north of Sticks Pass are all similar in terrain, fairly gentle slopes of short grass and good paths. Collectively they are sometimes known as "The Dodds" and several can be easily visited on a good walking day.

From High Rigg 16/3/10
AW exaggerated the shape of the fell in his drawing. Viewed from 100 yards east of High Rigg's top.

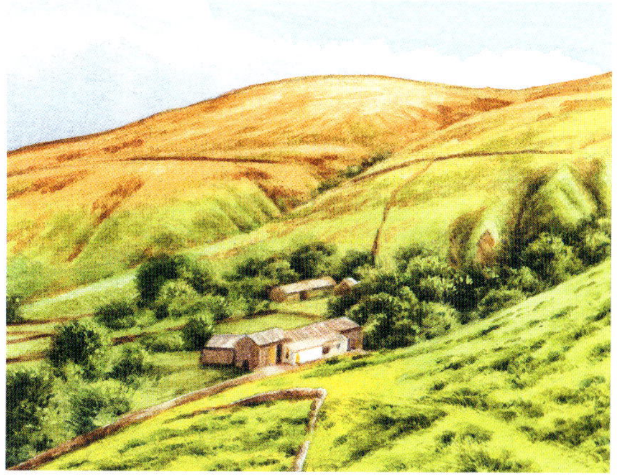

Dowthwaitehead
30/06/09
From the path under Dowthwaite Crag.

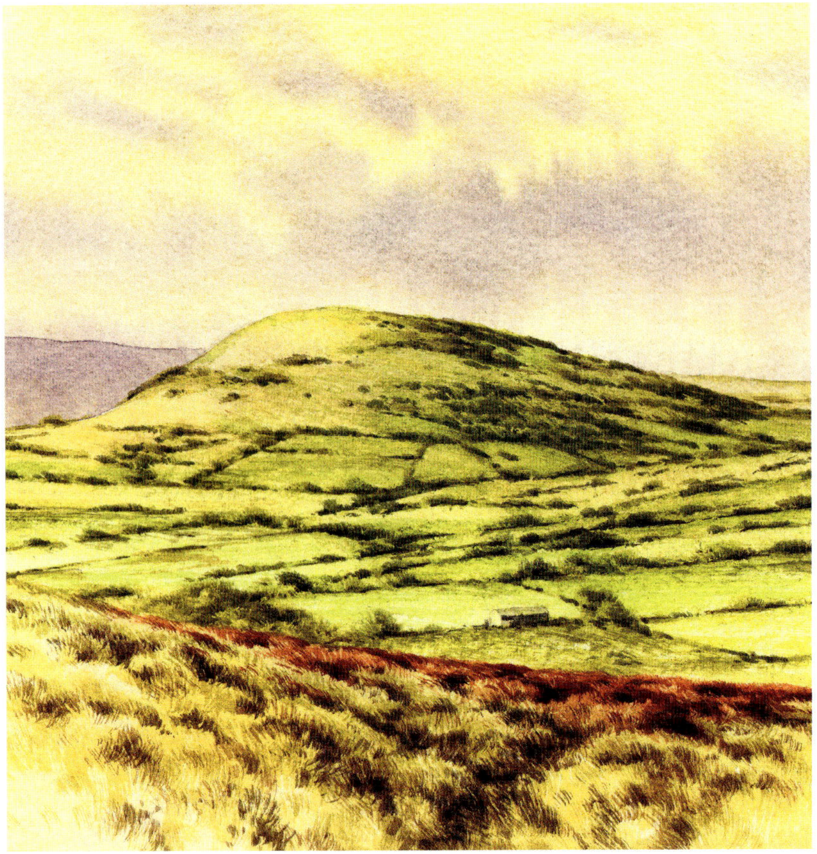

From Great Meldrum 19/06/09
This viewpoint, north east of Gowbarrow Fell is away from any recognised footpath but it does provide a pleasing view of Great Mell Fell. The farm buildings in the valley are about the only change in the intervening years.

Great Mell Fell

Rounded slopes covered in a mixture of grass and mixed woodland give Great Mell Fell a parkland feel. The rifle range which was in use in Wainwright's day can still be seen when looking at the fell from the north. The range is still private property whereas most of the rest of the fell is open access land.

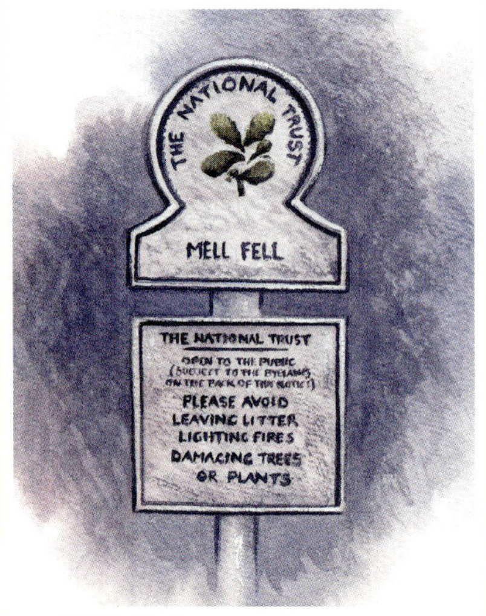

National Trust sign 5/3/08
With the rifle range now being defunct it seemed appropriate to replace the War Department sign with its modern equivalent.

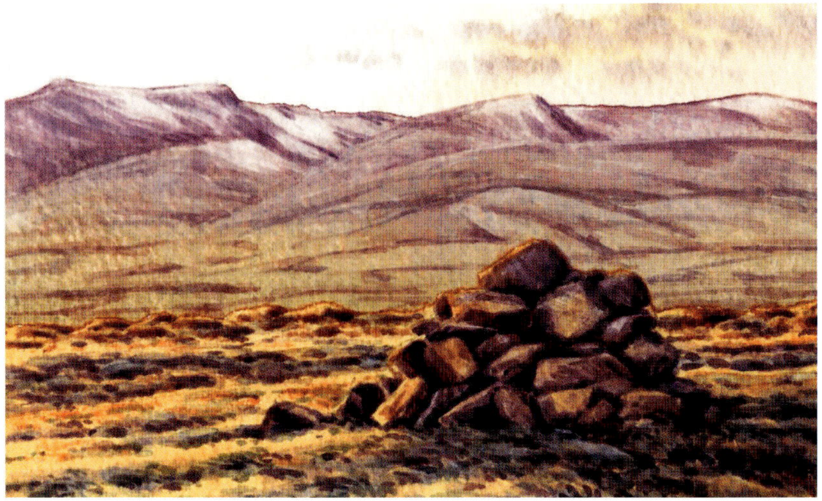

The summit 5/3/08
The small post has gone and the stones thereabouts have been gathered together to form a meagre cairn on this flat summit plateau. The winter slopes of the Blencathra group in the evening sun form the backdrop.

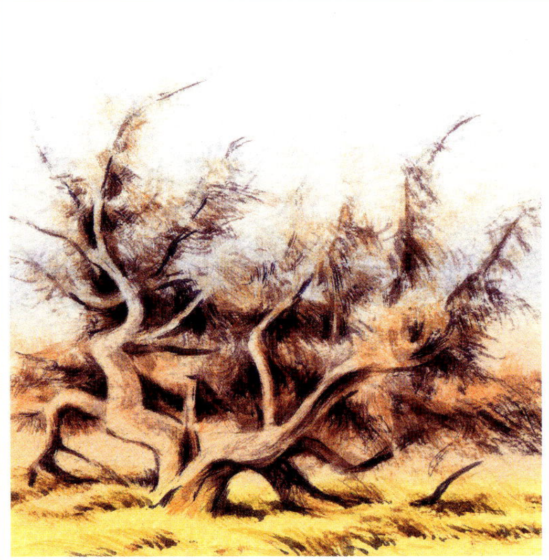

The highest tree 5/3/08
You could be forgiven for thinking that AW's description would have made the locating of this tree a fairly easy affair but there are others at a similar altitude. Given the fact that his sketch shows a windblown tree in a pretty poor state I wasn't hopeful that it would still be there. However, my diligent search paid off, now more mature but still showing the same basic form, the tree lives on.

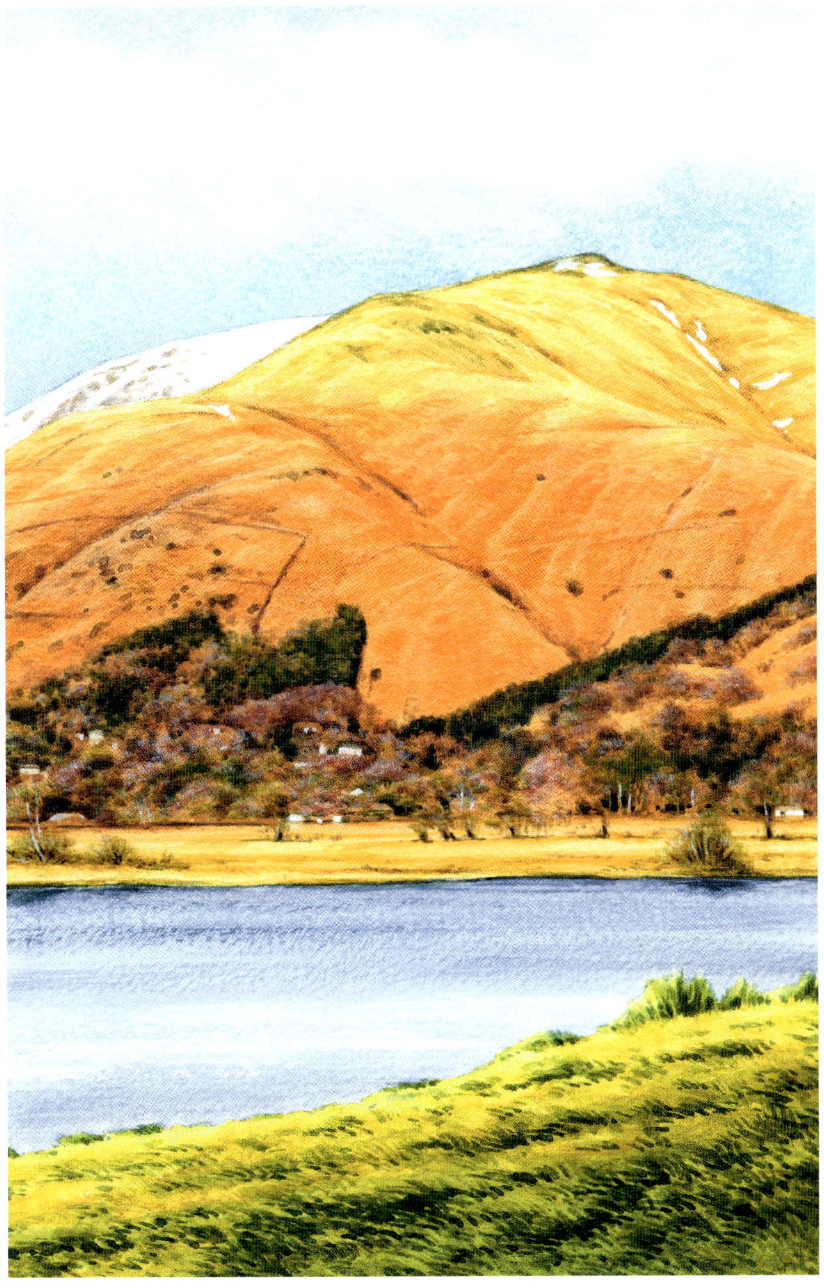

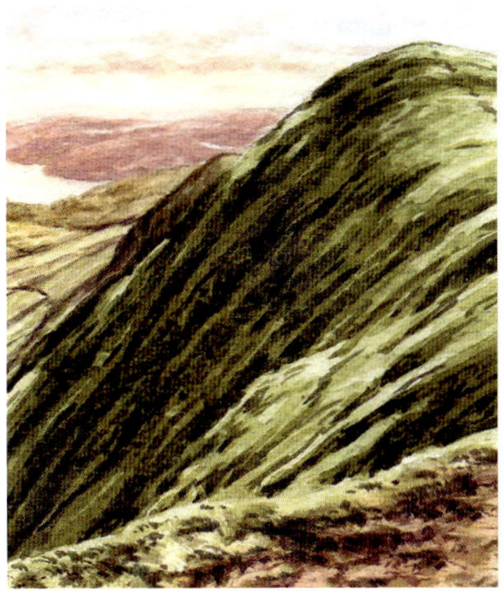

The east face 2/1/09
Windermere lies far below away in the distance in this view from the path north of the summit.

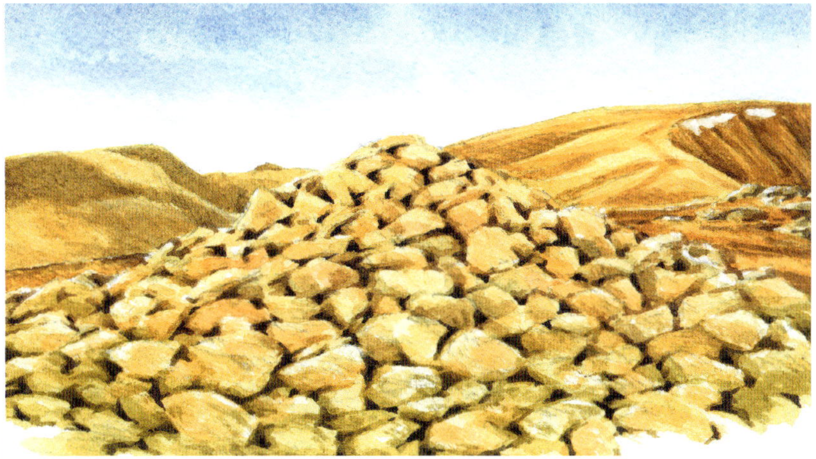

The summit 2/1/09
A cairn that was formerly known as Greatrigg Man has grown and spread over the years and is now a substantial pile.

Great Rigg

Great Rigg is hardly more than one of the undulations of the long ridge which leads south from Fairfield. This fell may lay claim to the most tarns and lakes in view from any fell summit, ten in total.

Cascades, Greenhead Gill
24/6/09
Being frozen solid on my first visit I had to return again to be able to depict these falls in full flow.

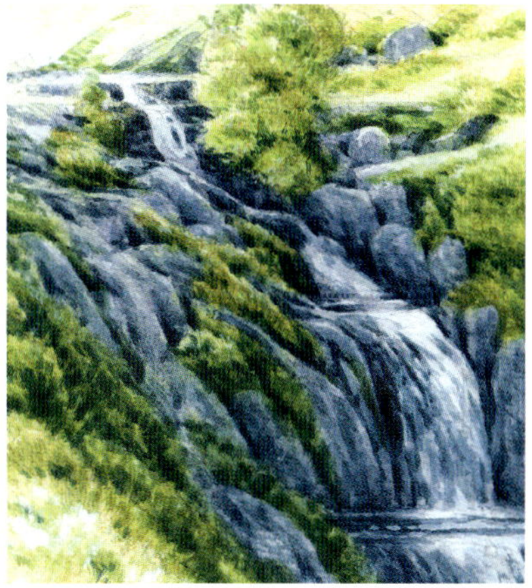

From Grasmere 16/3/10
It looks simple enough to locate this viewpoint, somewhere along the Grasmere - Red Bank road but his drawing was a little confusing. Stone Arthur is in fact connected to Great Rigg by a rising ridge and from no angle can Great Rigg take on such a peak like form as depicted in the guide. By lining up the slopes and gullies knew I was in the correct location. It was a case of Wainwright using a little more artistic license than usual for his illustration.

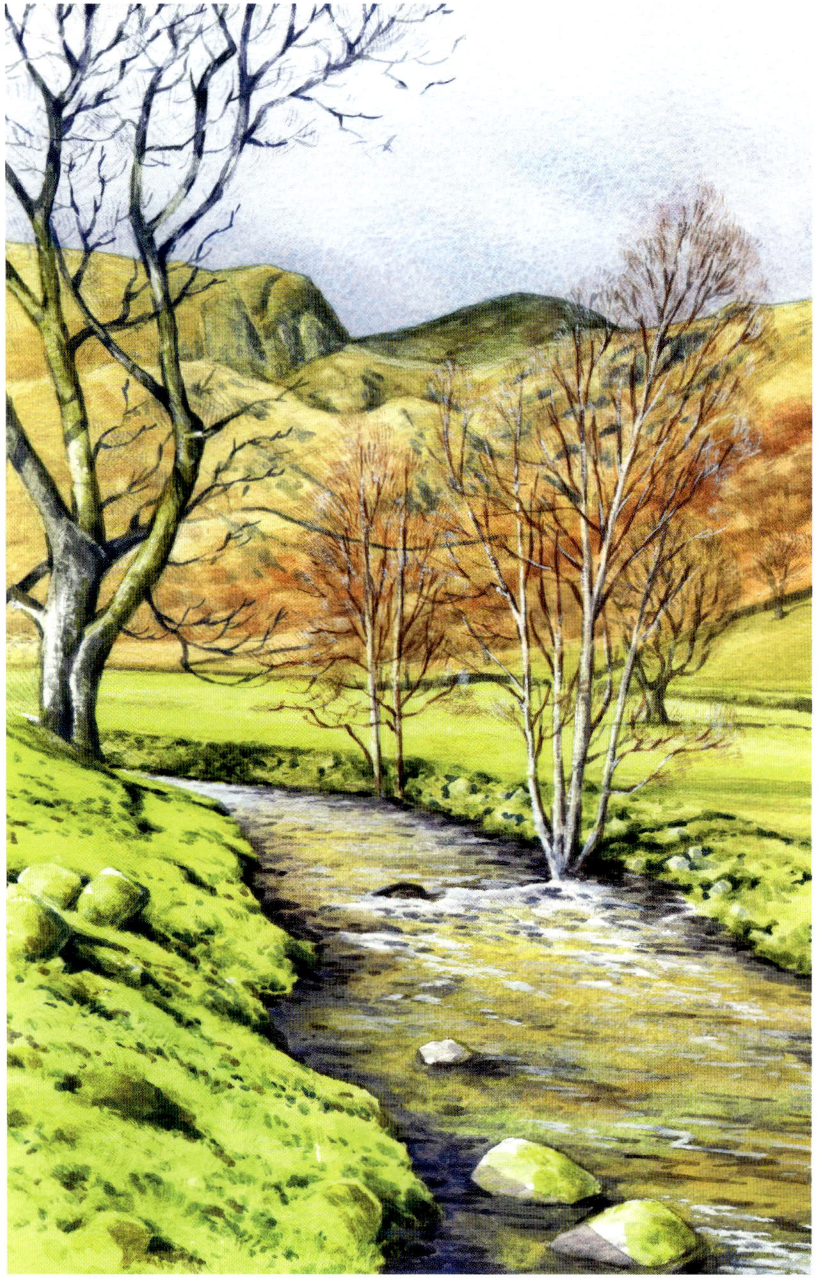

Hart Crag

Being another of the fells which feature on the Fairfield Horseshoe route and I cannot imagine that there are too many walkers who make Hart Crag the only goal for a day out. The direct ascent routes from Rydal and Patterdale are relatively quiet.

From Dovedale 6/3/11

This view is obtained by standing on the small bridge that spans Hartsop Beck. When the trees are in full leaf the fell is mostly obscured, much to my frustration on my first visit. The beck is now wider and Hart Crag is not quite the dominant feature as it is shown to be in the Pictorial Guide.

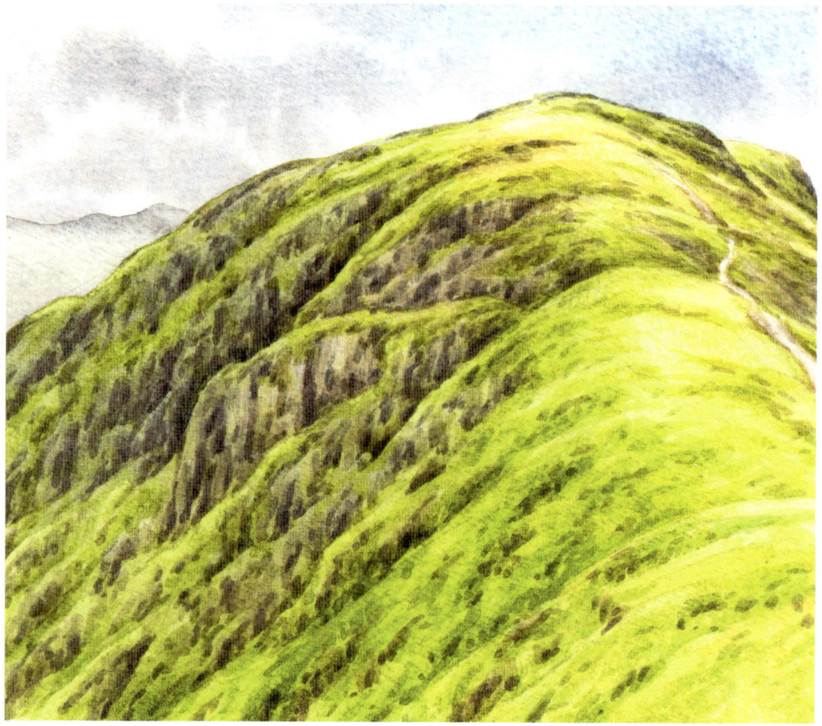

The north face 18/9/07

Descending the slopes of Fairfield near Scrubby Crag you will be faced with this profile. Sadly I didn't get there when the snow was present.

The summit 18/9/07

The far cairn in his drawing is now almost gone. The backdrop is made up of the Far Eastern Fells.

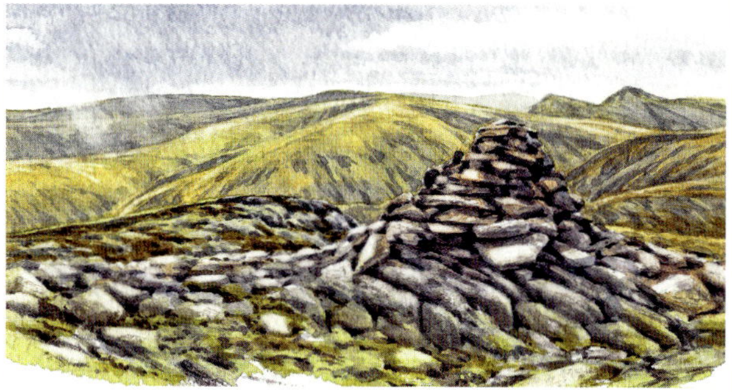

Looking west 18/9/07

Western fells form the skyline, including Great Gable.

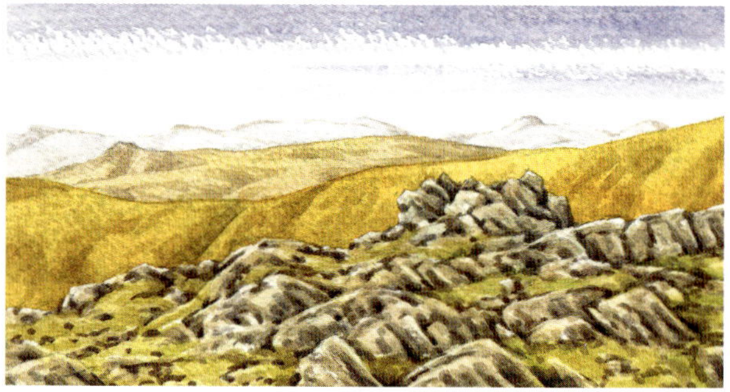

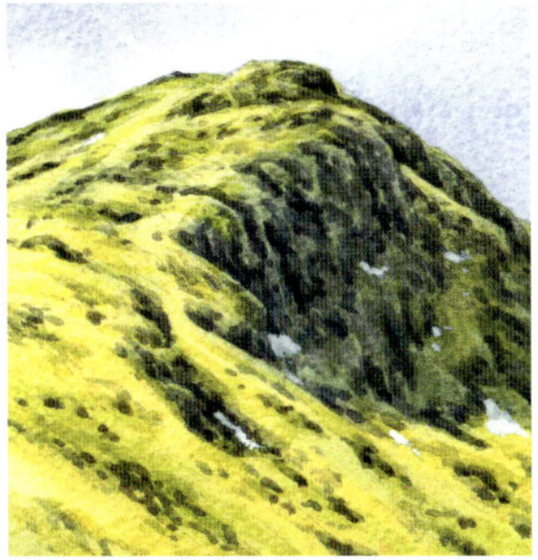

The summit from the north east 12/4/10

As you approach from the ridge above Link Cove this is the view of the fell ahead.

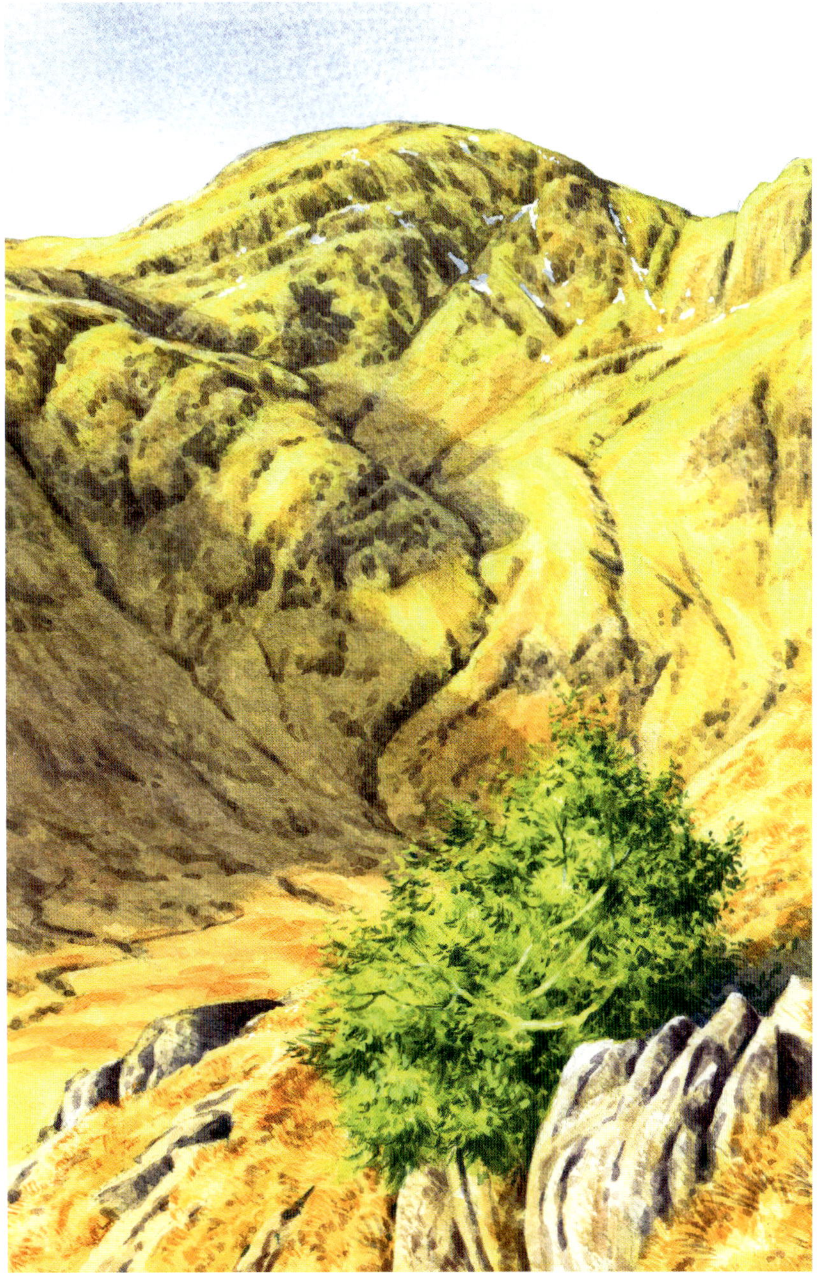

From the east ridge of St Sunday Crag 12/4/10

It was a challenge to climb this ridge whilst attempting to locate the tree in the foreground, that's if it still even existed. Persistence paid off, not much different from fifty years ago, the holly clings on. This in my opinion is a better view of the fell than shown on the main page. AW probably thought so too, by making it a full page drawing there were no distracting items such as the title or map. The Hart Crag from Dovedale scene in the main chapter illustration, as nice as it is lacks this rugged strength.

The trees that still stand firm.

When scrutinising the illustrations in the Pictorial Guides I would usually do so to ascertain the location and angle of view that AW had positioned himself in to obtain his reference photograph, but I was also looking for clues as to during what season he had been there, not only snow lying in shaded gullies but even better the foliage on the trees. Of course this scheme fell apart if the tree depicted was an evergreen. In the course of the project I came to realise that evergreen trees or shrubs that grow high on the fellsides are either holly, juniper or gorse. The latter two favour growing in dense groups whereas the holly is more of a loner and a single dark rounded low tree featured as foreground interest in AW's sketches was nearly always of this type. What was surprising to me is that in the intervening fifty years these trees were not only still surviving but had retained almost the same size and form such as the example on the left. It's as if they were in a time warp. There of course more hollies on the fells than the four depicted in the Pictorial Guides but it is clear that Wainwright was attracted to draw them as they were a strong feature to place in an illustration. Apart from the one on this page hollies also feature in Hartsop above How (page 39), Swirl How (page 196) and Mellbreak (page 322).

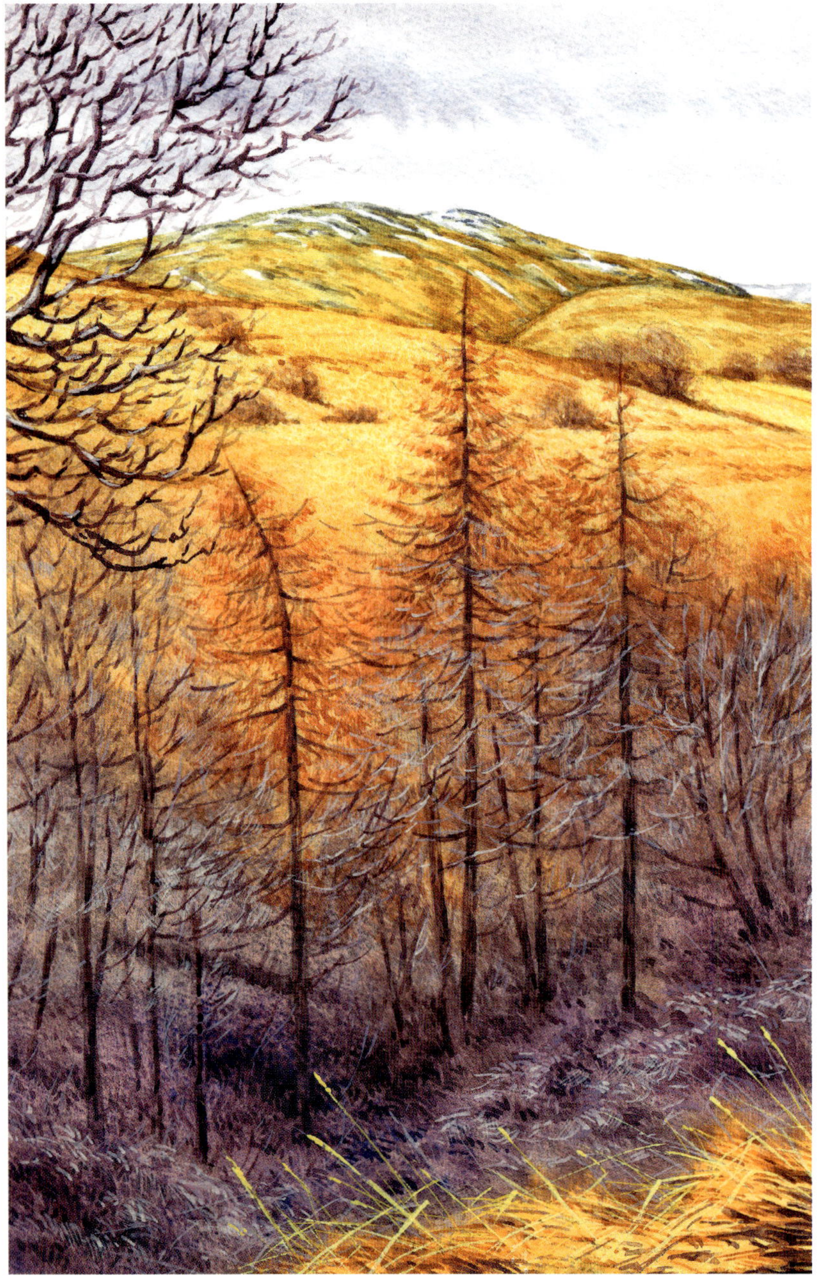

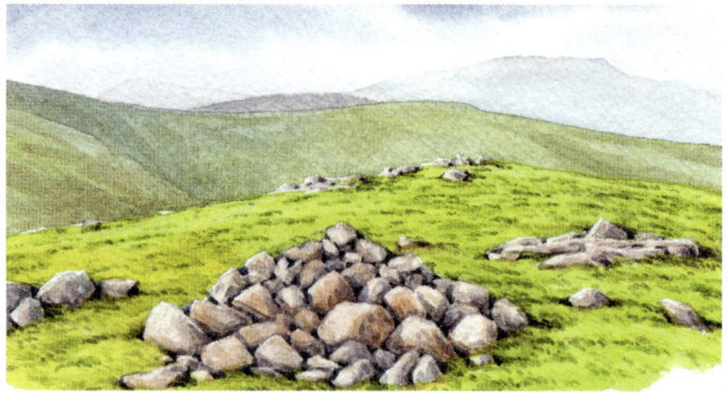

The summit 30/6/09
On the highest point the cairn is just a jumble of rocks, a better cairn is 100 yards to the north east.

Ullswater from the Brown Hills 30/6/09
I did locate this leaning stump of an old tree near the wall on Glencoyne Brow. It would be remarkable if it was the same one as in the guidebook illustration.

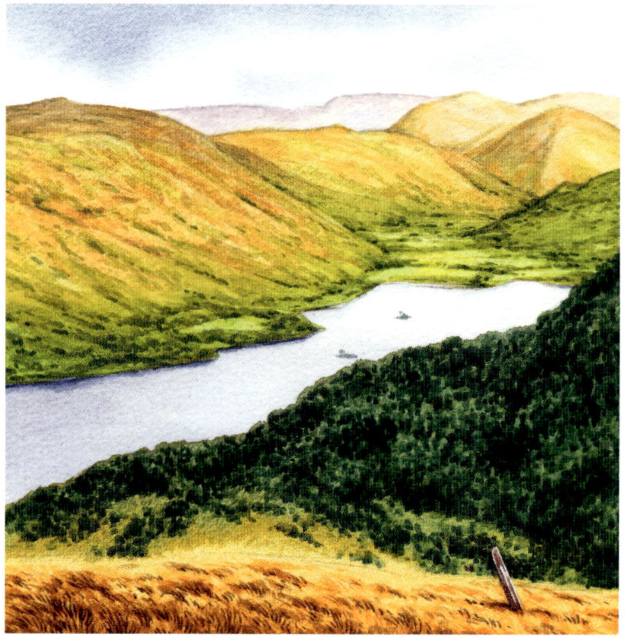

Hart Side

Being located to the east of the "Dodds", Hart Side is one of those fells out on a limb, and routes will have to be planned carefully to include this in a full hill day. The path alongside the wall under Brown Hills provides wonderful views of Ullswater.

From Dockray 16/3/10
From the road near Gill Edge this view of the fell is almost screened by the trees which on this winter's morning sat in a frost pocket.

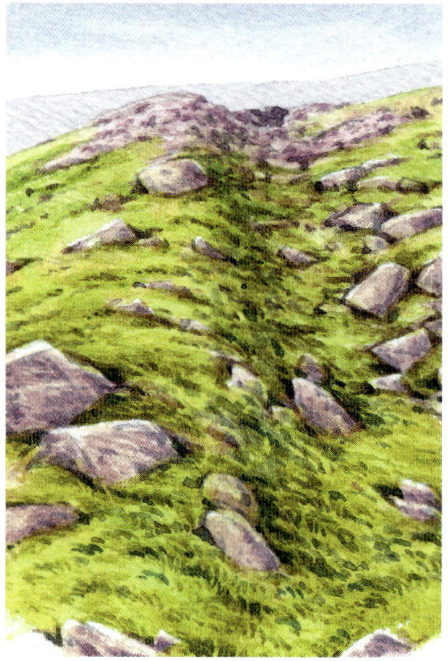

The ditch on the summit
30/6/09 A wind shelter has been built at the far end of this trench.

The cave 30/6/09
Scaffolding poles lean randomly against the opening to deter entry.

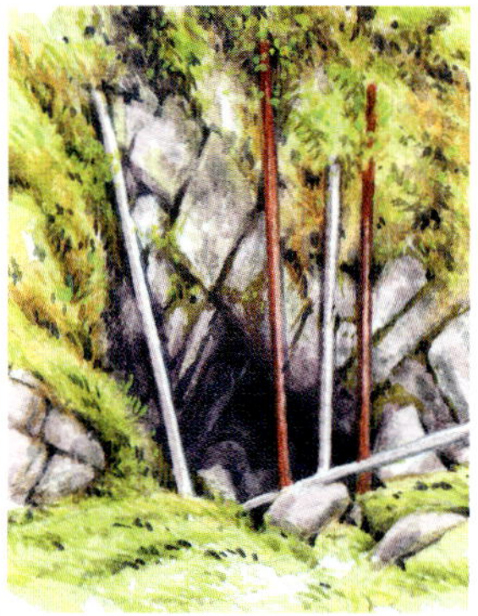

The Wainwright List

It is not clear when AW actually came up with the final total of 214 for the fells to be featured in his seven Pictorial Guides, it may only have been as he was working his way though the fells for book seven. His method of working on hills in each book at random meant that it would have been easy to dismiss or include subjects as he saw fit. It is a fact that in the course of compiling the original list of the fells he did consider quite a number of other high points which he deemed not suitable for inclusion or featured these tops as part of other fells on the 214 final list, such as Helvellyn Lower Man which became a part of the Helvellyn chapter.

There is often a debate as to why certain fells were included or excluded (see Mungrisdale Common page 233) but there is one argument that cannot be contested: the Wainwright list has always been and will always be the 214. The name "The Wainwrights" is one given over to this list, when it was first used is unclear but AW certainly knew of this tag but there is little evidence to show that he promoted it.

It is well known that AW preferred to read maps more than he did books and in his early days of fellwalking he must have pored over those available to him at that time, namely the one inch Ordnance Survey and Bartholomew maps of the day. From these he listed the measured heights and fell names which appealed to him either in actual height or location within his planned boundaries for the Pictorial Guides. The one criteria of the fells on his original lists was that they were all over the 1000′ contour. Castle Crag didn't appear on these lists but did make the final 214 proving the flexibility of Wainwright's system as he progressed through the guides. During the years of his explorations he added 28 other fells to his list which had not previously been considered. In total Wainwright's list was made up of 260 fells*, whittled down to 214.

At the publishing of the last guide the full list of "Wainwright" fells was available to the public, maybe not written in stone but certainly published on paper, never to be amended. This is one man's personal choice of fells, not defined by some mathematical equation or quality control but purely contrived by looking at maps and walking the terrain. What makes this list subject to discussion is the fact that we all could probably come up with reasons why we consider the Wainwright list to be flawed but it is immaterial, it isn't our list.

* My intention is to make this full list of 260 fells available shortly.

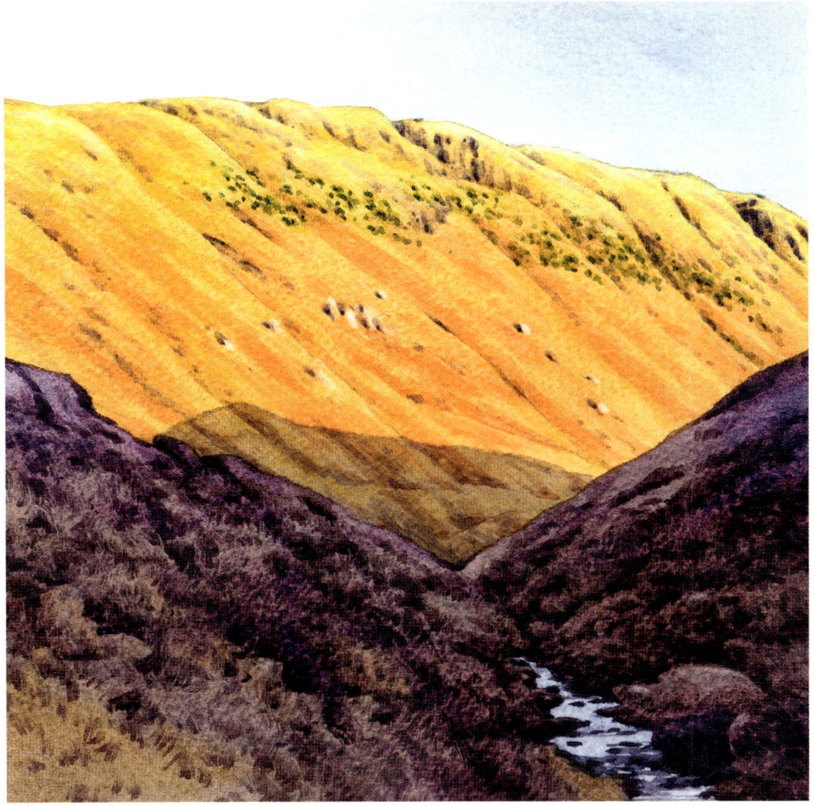

From Hunsett Cove 25/11/08

The early morning winter light on the fell side contrasts with the cold depths of the Cove. There are few signs of paths here even now so this location is rather off-track. The small tree on the left has long since gone. Gill Crag in the guidebook is shown as being more angular than the reality.

Hartsop Above How

The long rising ridge from Deepdale Bridge to Hart Crag hardly seems justified for inclusion on Wainwright's list as an individual fell but there it is, probably due to it being named on maps of the time. A slight outcrop of rock forms the summit but I have yet to find a cairn of any size there on my visits.

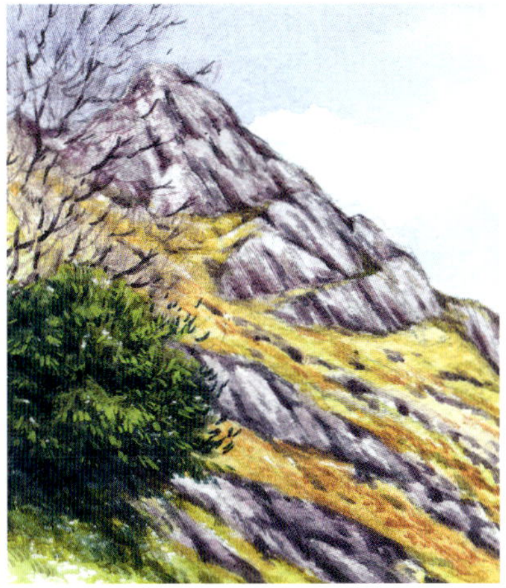

Dovedale Slabs 6/3/11

Once the correct profile of the slabs was identified I then located the holly tree. This point is roughly up on the 1300′ contour line and above the path at a point opposite The Stangs.

The summit 12/4/10

AW's drawing could not be simpler but my inclusion of the Fairfield fells beyond helps to rectify this. Any cairn here is only temporary.

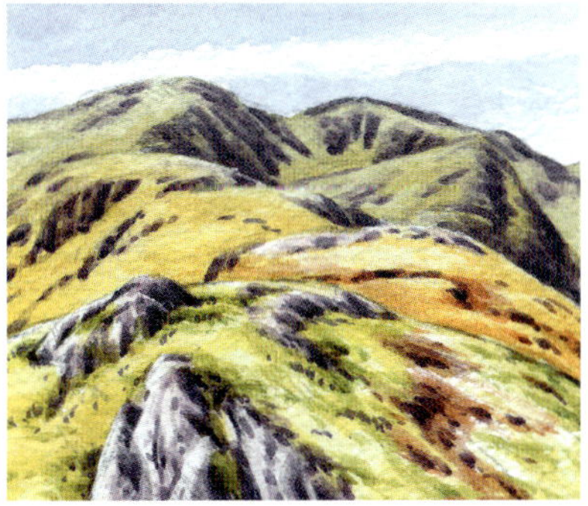

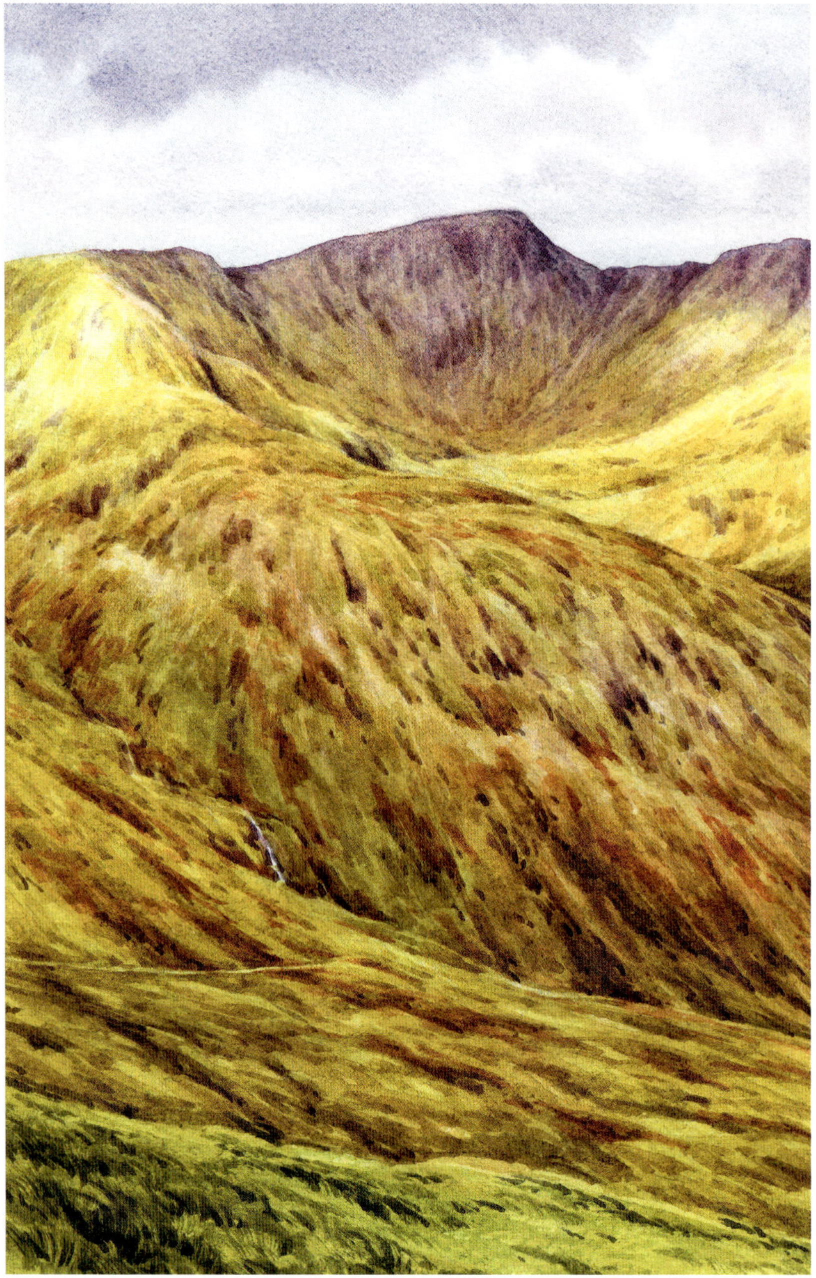

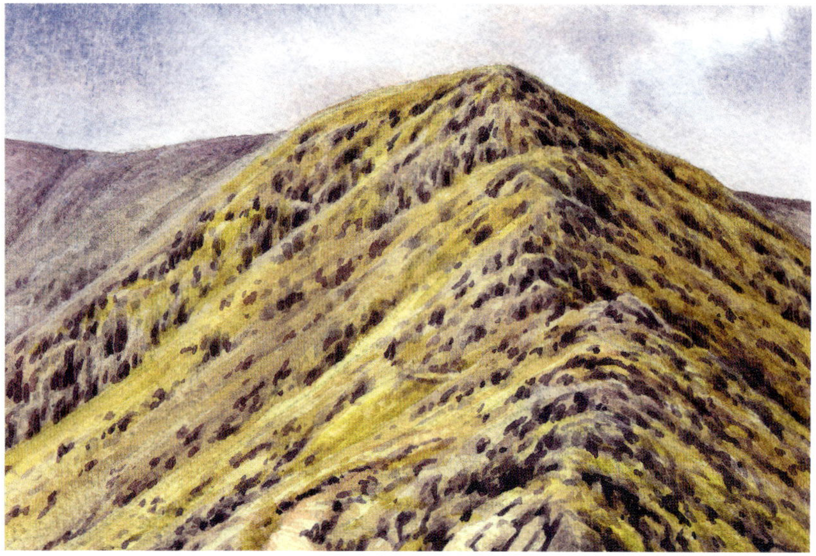

Swirral Edge 19/4/11
Not a ridge to be taken lightly.

Helvellyn

Supposedly this is the most popular of all fells with its gentle western side in strict contrast to the rugged crags and ridges which face east. In days gone by visitors to the area were able to reach the summit on pony via the more gentle slopes of the mountain.

From the south-west ridge of St Sunday Crag 18/9/07
From this angle the summit and Striding Edge are seen over the sunlit Nethermost Cove.

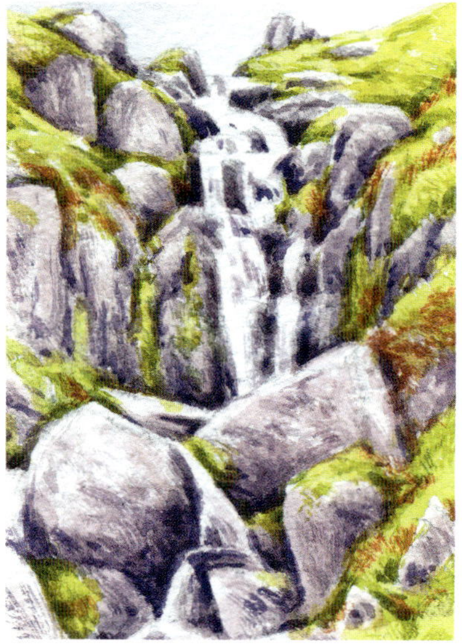

Helvellyn Gill 19/8/10
Viewed from deep in the gorge and away from the main path.

Helvellyn from Red Tarn
19/4/11 With the same boulders still in place in the foreground.

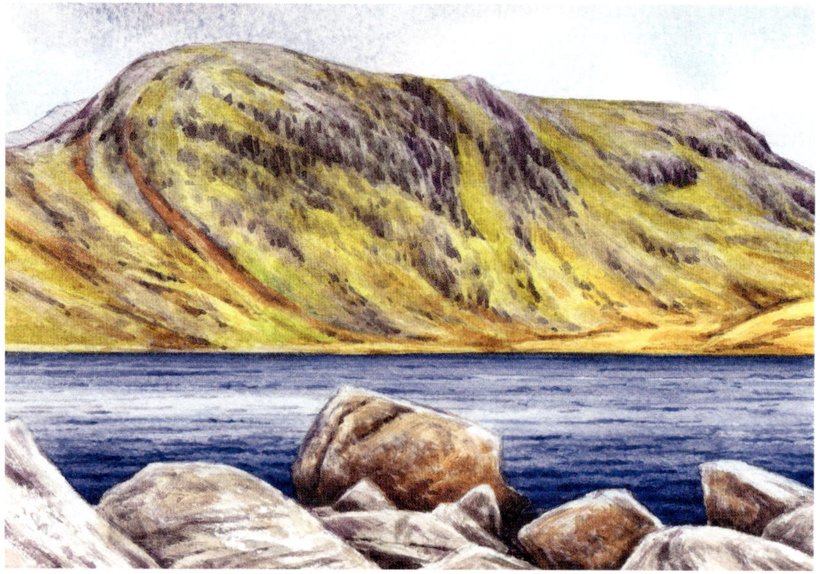

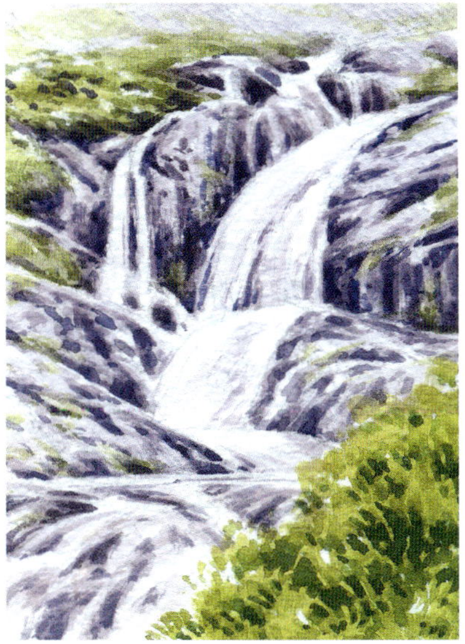

Whelpside Gill 10/8/10
A short detour off the path, this 20′ cascade is worth a visit.

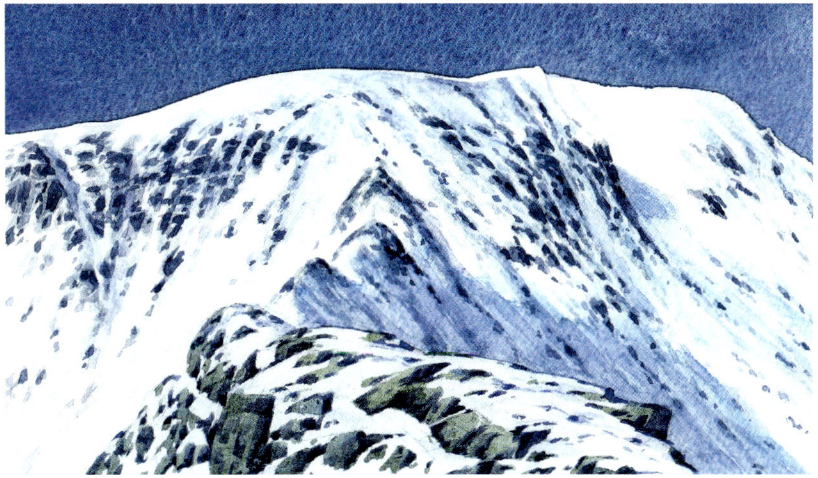

The summit from Striding Edge 6/3/09
It would be a very unwise person who attempts a traverse of this ridge without the proper equipment and experience in conditions such as depicted in this watercolour sketch. Days like these are simply stunning but can come with danger.

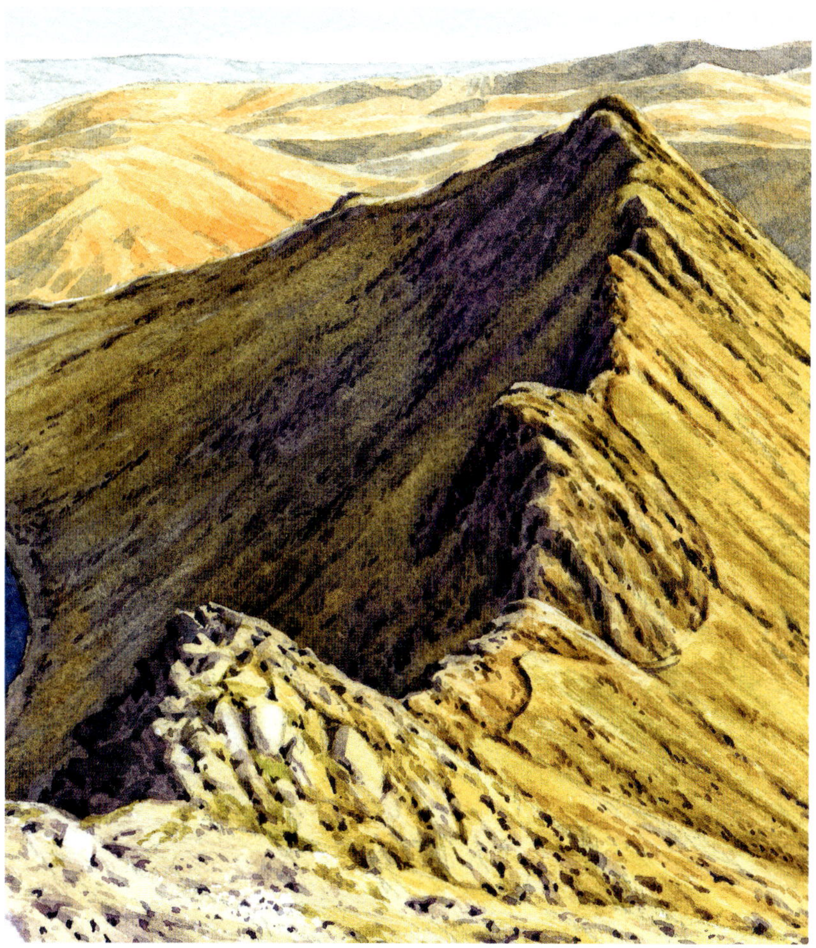

Striding Edge 11/12/09
This is the most popular ridge in the district that requires some amount of hands-on work. The adventurous will follow the edge along the very crest whereas a slightly lower, less exposed path may be taken for those without experience for most of the length. However, the easier path that once avoided the chimney which can be seen in this sketch as part of the middle peak has since been removed so this short scramble cannot be avoided. Wainwright's original guide still provides ample detail to traverse this ridge. The paths are clearly defined on the ground so are easy enough to follow. Be prepared for this ridge to be busy.

The summit 11/12/09
The small cairn that sits on the highest point is in no better shape now than it was in AW's day.

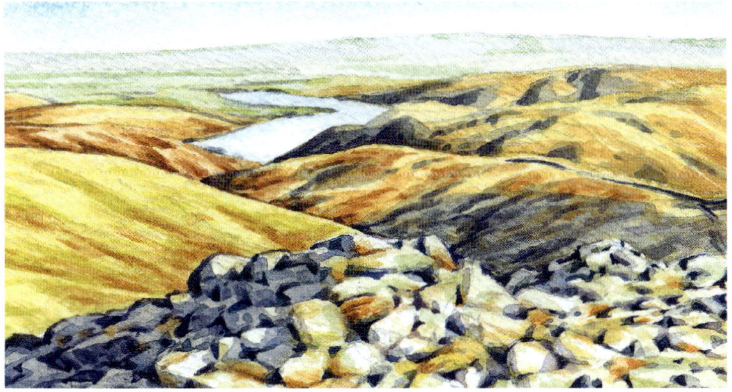

Whelpside Gill Spring 25/9/09
It is not easy to locate but the crystal clear water flows up though bright green mosses and tastes better than any bottled equivalent, maybe because it is free.

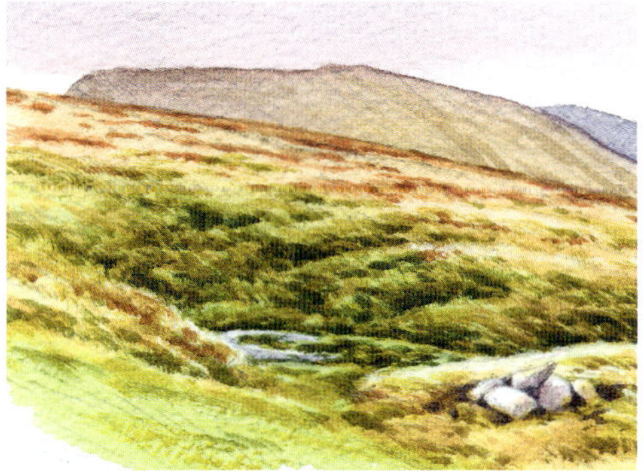

The Monuments of Helvellyn

Helvellyn Lower Man

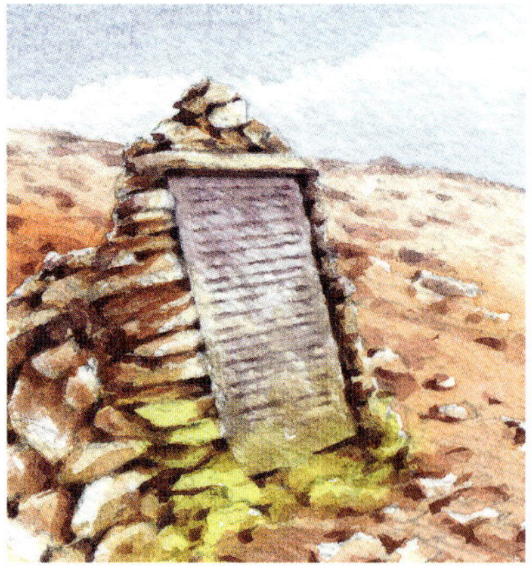

The Gough Memorial 25/9/09

A substantial engraved tablet set into stones. On my last visit in the autumn of 2015 it was in dire need of repair but I understand that it has since been repaired.

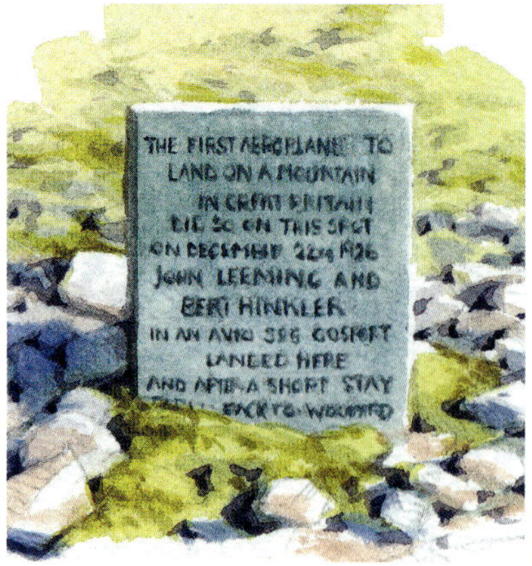

The aeroplane landing 11/12/09

At the time of my visit the slab stands proud of the nearby stones. It is adjacent to the path just south of the shelter.

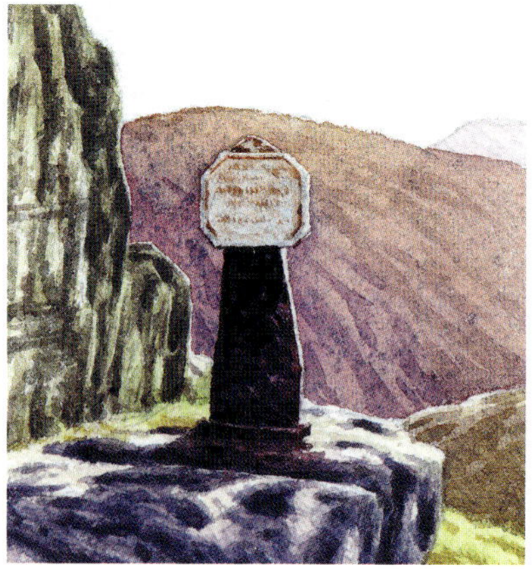

The Dixon Memorial 11/12/09

When tackling Striding Edge and heading towards Helvellyn your mind may be on the task ahead so you may be forgiven for missing this painted metal fixture on your left.

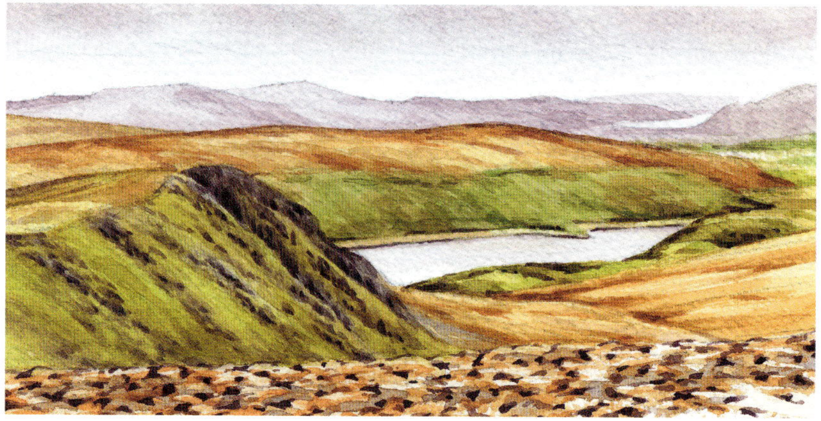

Looking north-west 11.12.09

Thirlmere and Bassenthwaite Lake can both be seen from this point just to the north-west of the Lower Man summit.

Summit of Lower Man 11/12/09

Snow clings to the eastern edges of Helvellyn from this now lesser sized cairn.

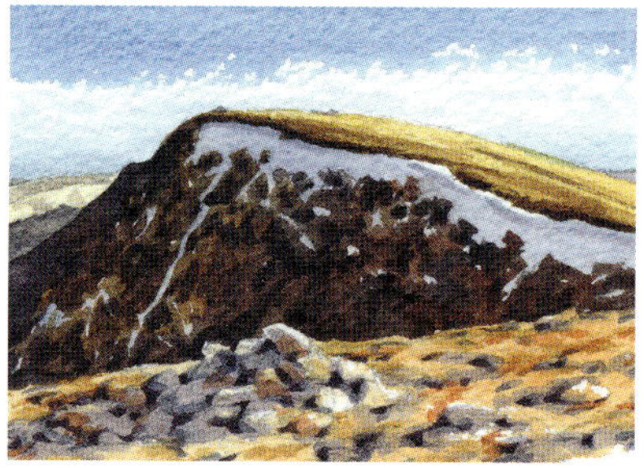

Helvellyn Observations.

In all my days out on the fells it came to my attention that Helvellyn and its near neighbours appear to have the longest winters of all the fells. As I was on Crinkle Crags on 3rd October 2008 away in the distance Helvellyn had a good covering of snow, all other fells in view were bare. This first sign of winter was seen on other early winter days in following years too. At the other end of the season the deep snow that forms the best cornice in the area, on the curving east face of the summit, remains there well into the spring when nearly all other snow has gone from other fells.

As for Helvellyn Lower Man, not many subsidiary summits of fells get a full neatly designed page to themselves as well as featuring by name in over eighty view descriptions from distant hills. This is possibly accounted for by the fact that Helvellyn Lower Man was on AW's original list of fells for the Pictorial Guides. It also has the distinction of being one of only eight named tops over 3000' on the 1:25,000 O.S. maps of the Lake District.

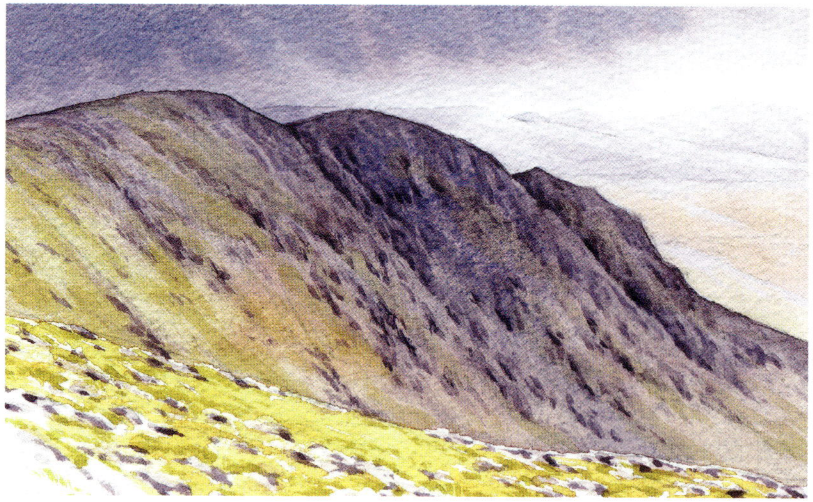

Browncove Crags 11/12/09

To obtain this correct profile you have to be some way down the north ridge towards White Side.

Seeing the wood for the trees

Apart from the occasional falling of a chunk of crag or the alterations to the terrain by man the hard landscape of the lakeland fells remains almost unaltered over the last fifty years. This means that in the main my task of finding the locations for all the illustrations resulted in me producing sketches quite similar in look to those of Wainwright but there was one feature which regularly caused me to either move to another nearby location or even return in a different season and that was trees.

Whilst AW artistically included young saplings as foreground interest such as in the fell page for Stone Arthur (page 60) it was often the case that they had since grown up to such a height or density that they obscured the required view. In these instances I took the liberty of moving to the nearest point that allowed me an unrestricted view of the main subject matter such as illustrated on this page. There were other instances where the featured trees had gone completely leaving the view unobstructed such as in the main Low Pike sketch (page 48) in another case the trees had been felled completely opening up a more extensive vista such as that of the view from Dodd summit (page 219).

However, there were occasions where I realised that by returning when the deciduous trees were bare in winter I would be able to stand at the correct position and see though the trees to depict the view with perhaps a little artistic license (for example Hart Crag page 36, High Pike page 45 and Brock Crags page 72). This added time and inconvenience to my agenda but I feel the extra effort was worth that to produce a more accurate result.

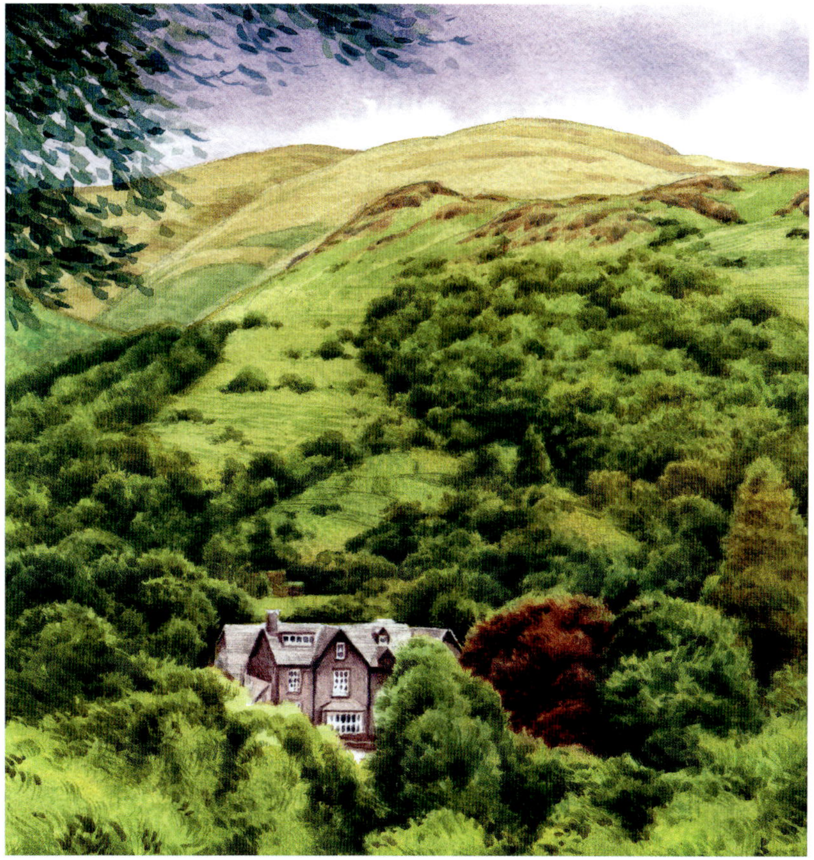

From Grasmere 30/7/09

The intervening years have turned young saplings into mature trees. Standing on the path in AW's drawing I was deep in the wood of Butharlyp Howe with the view obscured. By moving slightly south in the park the fell came into full view approximately 50 yards from his original location.

Heron Pike

The fact that this fell only warranted four pages in the Pictorial Guide speaks for itself. Its rounded grass covered top has two separate small rocky outcrops of which the southernmost is the actual summit.

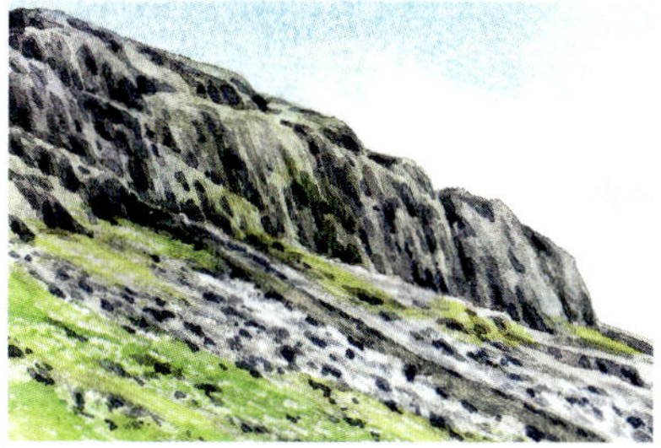

Erne Crag 1/9/09

From the ridge to Great Rigg I descended into Blind Cove to obtain this view which is off the valley path, and here a decent sized rock provides a good seat. Ideal for a smoke, take a photograph and to make notes perhaps.

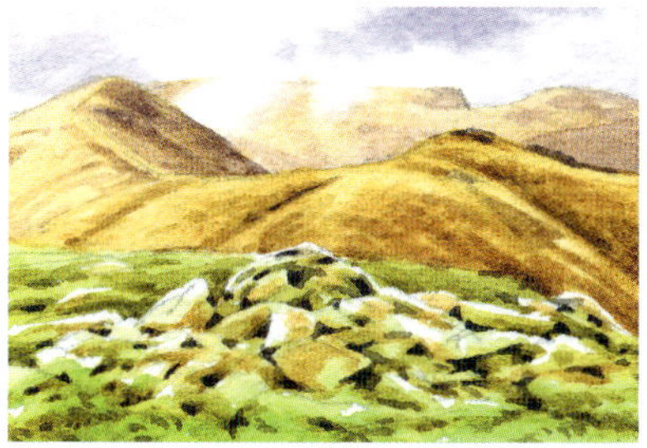

The summit 1/9/09

Just as I reached this point a break in the clouds revealed Fairfield and Hart Crag beyond, just what I required for my reference photograph. A small cairn now marks the top.

High Hartsop Dodd

Approaching the Kirkstone Pass from the direction of Patterdale your eye is drawn to the shapely peaks ahead. The one over to the right past Brotherswater is High Hartsop Dodd. It rises from the valley floor almost as a symmetrical peak which then continues as a ridge up to Little Hart Crag. Its eastern neighbour, Middle Dodd, bears a striking similarity and both afford fine views back down to Brotherswater and the valley to the north.

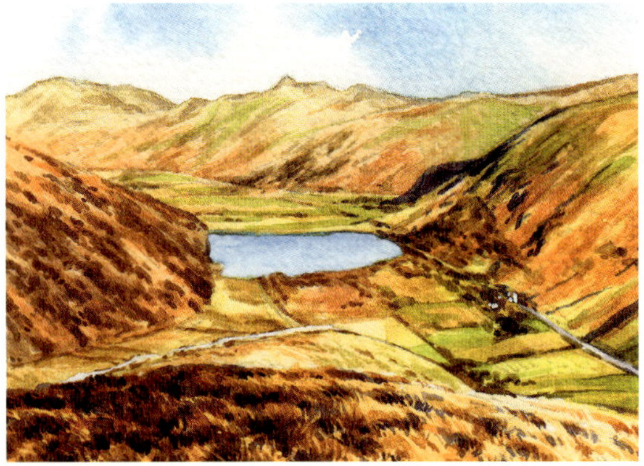

Brotherswater 25/11/07

An excellent view of the valley from north of the summit just as the ridge descends steeply.

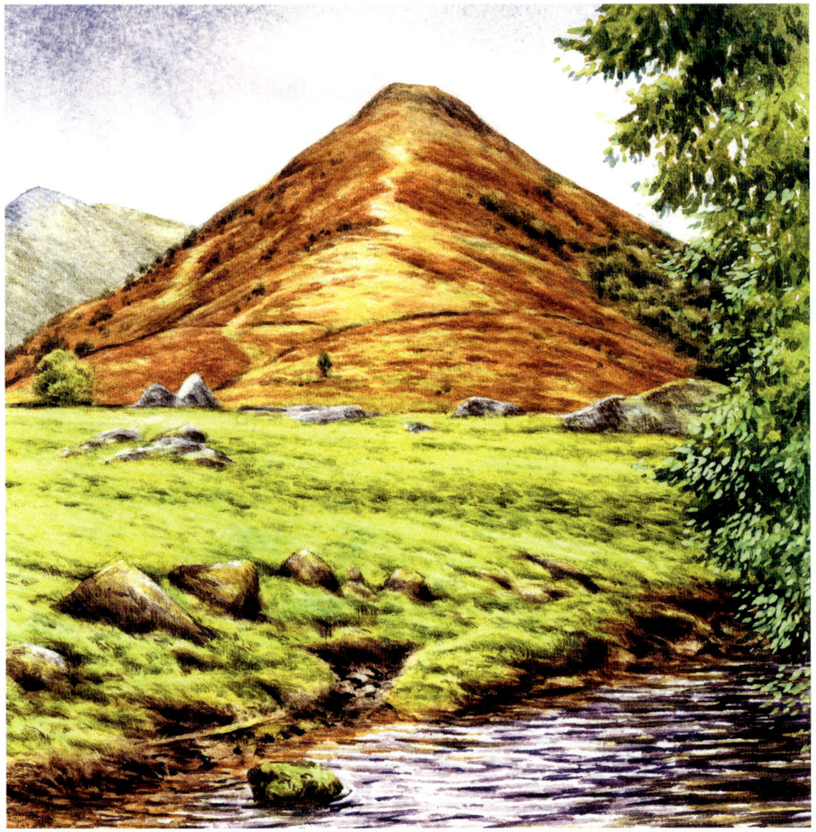

From Hartsop Beck 21/9/10

Seen from a point very close to the location for the sketch of Hart Crag, the fell is not such an angular peak as depicted in AW's illustration.

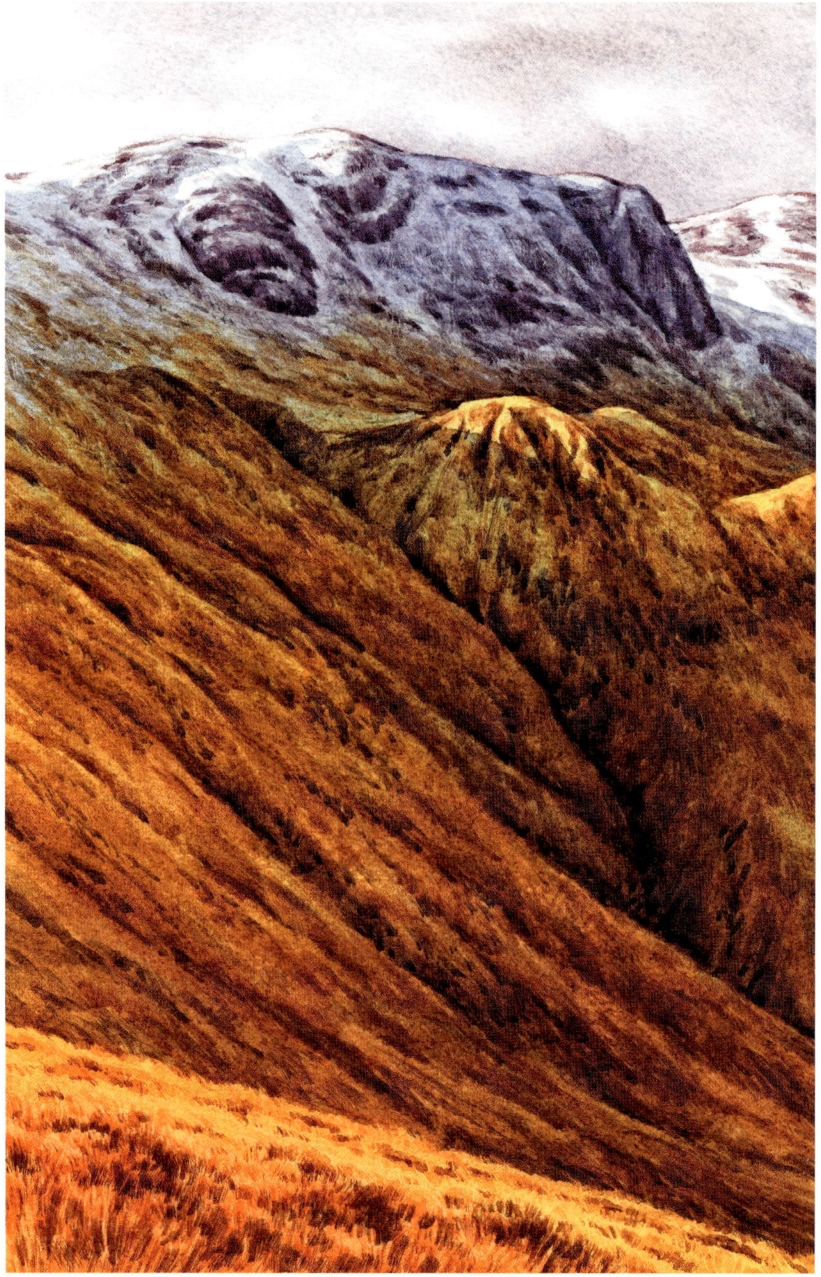

Dove Crag and Hoggett Gill, from High Hartsop Dodd 25/11/08

A fine winter's day on several fells allowed me to capture this scene in similar conditions as in AW's drawing with the late afternoon sun hitting the top of Stand Crags. This is another fell without a view of the summit as there was no cairn or feature to draw back then. Only a small mound of stones was there on my last visit.

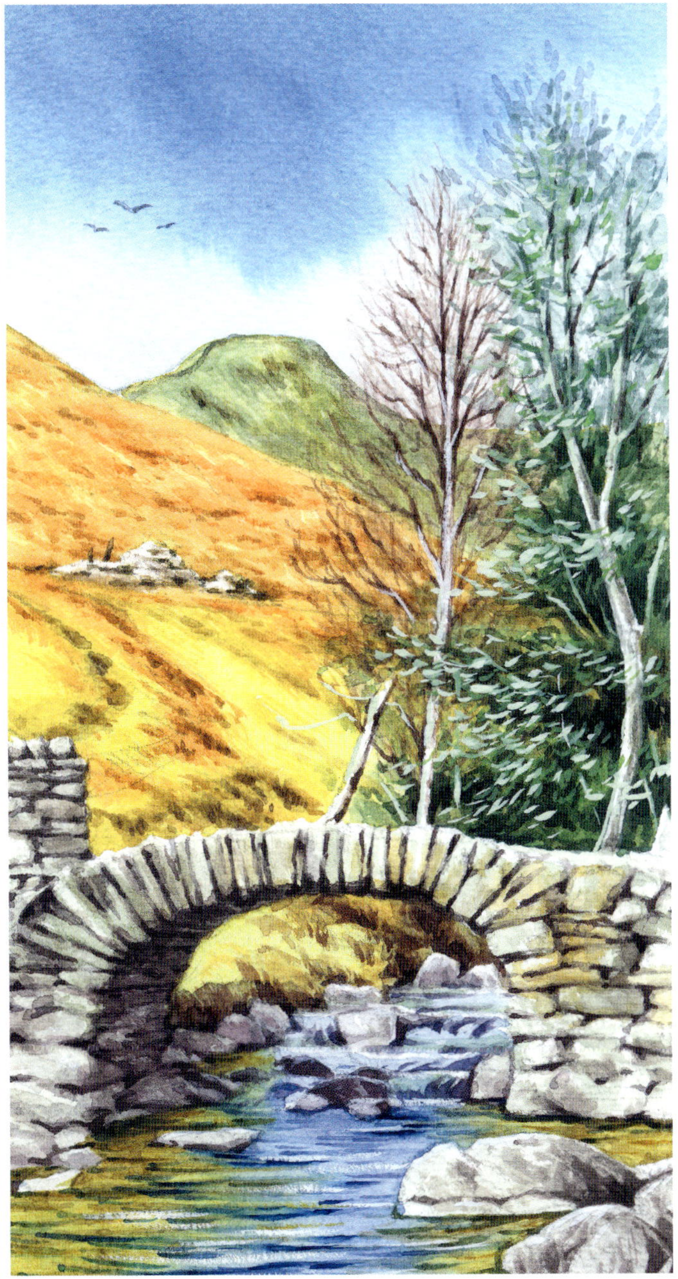

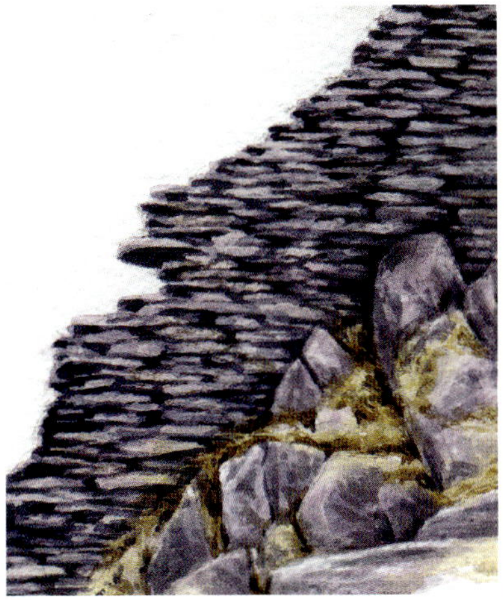

The wall 18/9/07
Locating this exact section of the wall required a slow, considered descent looking for features which may have no longer been in place. The bedrock was the clue I needed but sadly the wall requires repair.

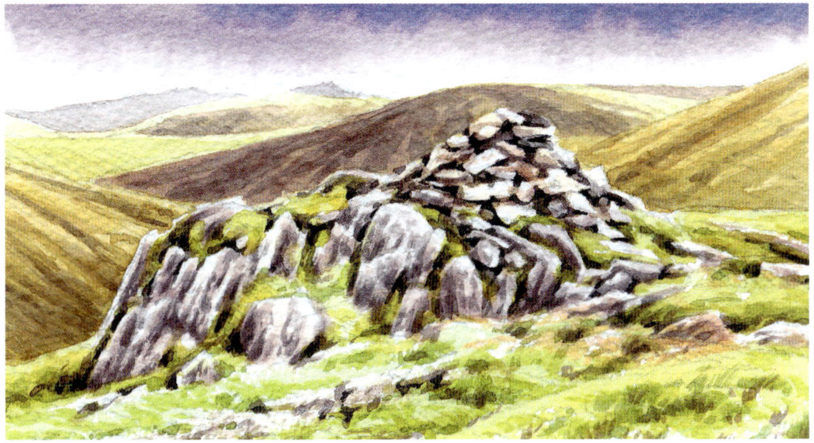

The summit 18/9/07
Gone is the neat cairn, now just a pile of rocks on an eroded rock platform.

From Scandale 16/3/10
His drawing is in mid-winter, I missed such an opportunity in the weather.

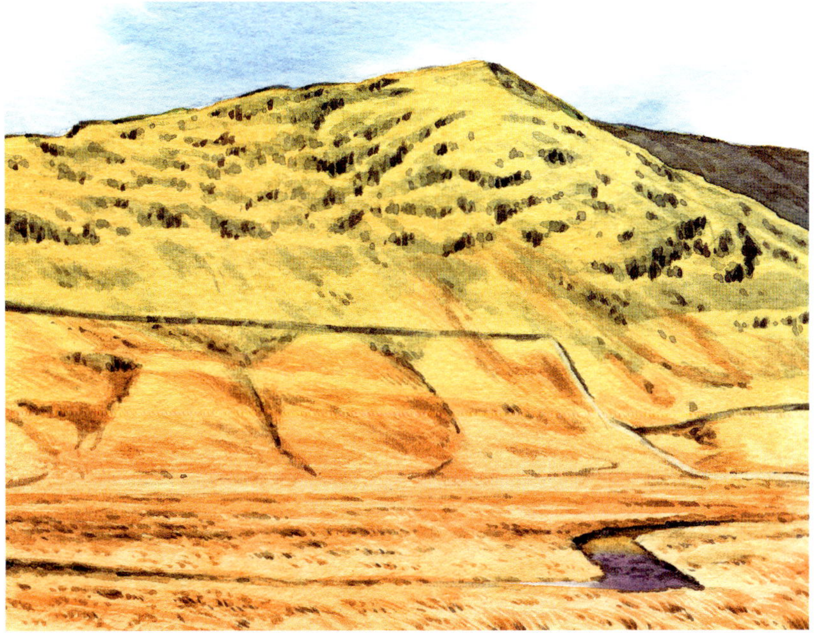

High Pike

Uniquely in the seven guides the main fell drawing fills half a page vertically. His description of High Pike with its similarities to features on Everest relates to the conquering of the world's highest mountain in May 1953, just about the time when AW was working on this book.

From High Sweden Bridge 6/3/10
My original visit to obtain this scene was in high summer, by returning in winter meant that the trees were bare, giving a less obscured view.

Little Hart Crag

At the height of the High Hartsop Dodd Ridge, the upper reaches of this fell are like a fortress raised up above the nearby landscape. Situated between both Red Screes and Dove Crag a visit to the summit is worth the short detour.

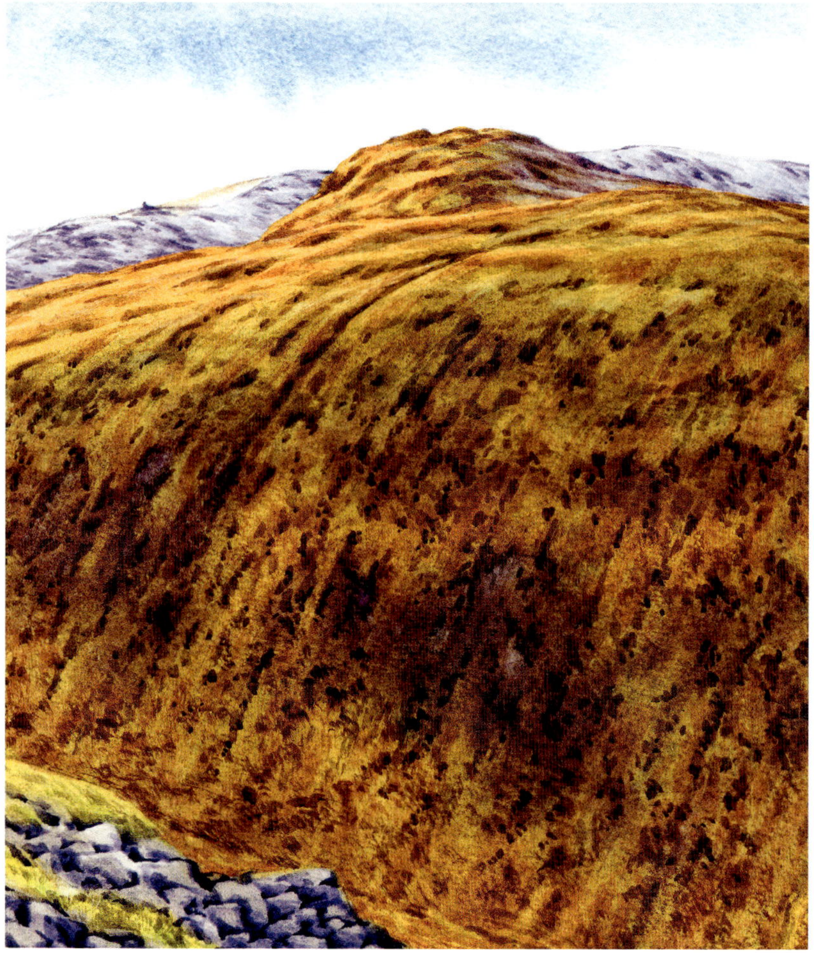

From Middle Dodd 25/11/08

Omitting the background fells meant that AW could concentrate the eye of the reader on the featured fell. My sketch shows the full scene which includes the tall cairn of High Bakestones away to the left.

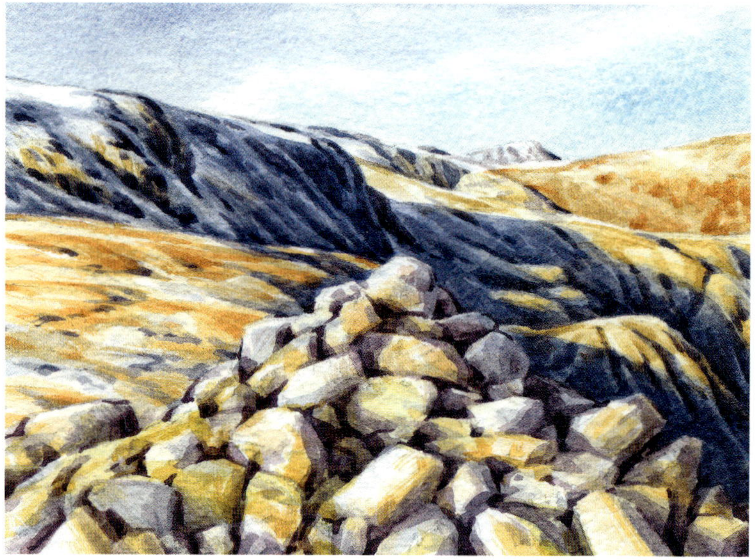

The summit 25/11/08

Now larger in volume, the main cairn identifies the higher of the two tops.

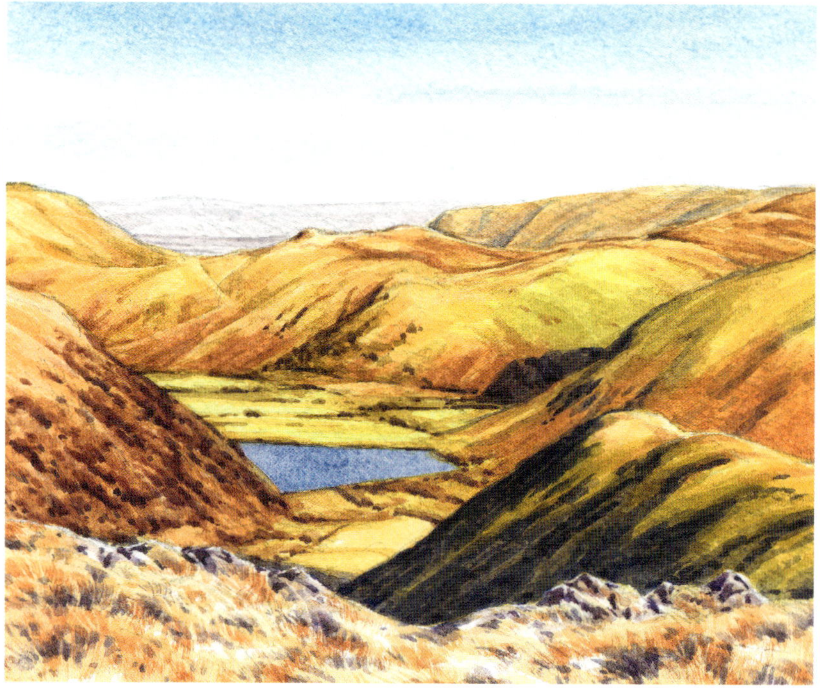

Hartsop from the summit 25/11/08

This vista must have appealed to AW, with slight variations it also appears in the High Hartsop Dodd and the Middle Dodd chapters. One may think that this was a good location to include a view of Scandale which he described as being delightful. Perhaps due to the fact it is to the south and towards the sun he was unable to photograph it with enough detail for the scene to feature in a drawing.

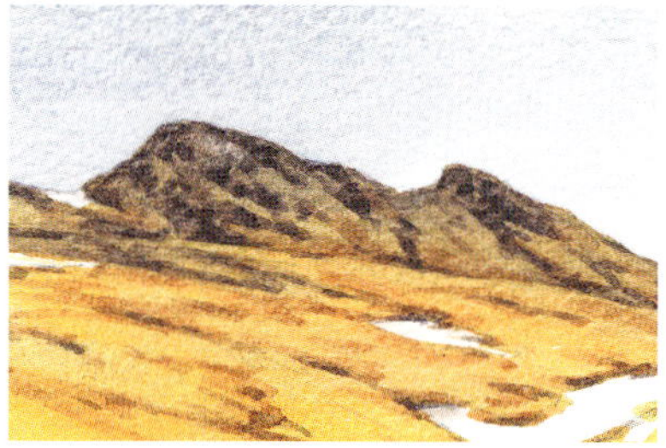

The summit from the south 25/11/08

The top section of the fell as seen from the track to Scandale Pass.

Measuring up - The Triangulation of the fells.

Something solid to lean against after struggling to the summit or a convenient pedestal on which to strike a pose, dotted across the fells these solid columns often mark the highest points of some of our favourite fells but why are they there and why not on every top?

They are of course part of a scheme to accurately measure the landscape of the country for mapping. Basically the process involved the measurement of angles between three known points to features in the landscape, these known fixed points were the triangulation stations. These measurements then allowed the accurate plotting of the features on a map. The construction of these pillars on some of the points by the Ordnance Survey began in 1936 and continued until 1962 by which time a countrywide network of 6,500 had been built. Columns found on the Lakeland Fells were built to one design and are known as Hotine Pillars, after the designer. All are 4 feet high and are built over a fixed Lower Centre Mark which is 30 inches below ground level and topped with a concrete block above which is another Centre Mark, then a vertical metal (or cardboard) tube, all encased in the tapering pillar that we are all familiar with. On the very top is a brass spider on which the surveyors theodolite was placed to take the measurements. Not all columns are on the highest point of a hill, such as Harter Fell (Southern). In most parts of the country the columns were built of concrete but in more inaccessible places such as the high lakeland fells local stone was used bound together with mortar, thus reducing the need to import all of the approximate 40 cwt (2000 kg) of materials needed to construct each pillar. Only two pillars on the Wainwright Fells are made of concrete, High Street and Skiddaw. The columns nearly always have a numbered brass flush bracket with a benchmark attached to one of the faces. Where building a pillar was impractical due to the bedrock etc. then other markers were put in place such as concrete rings (Blencathra and Branstree) or ground bolts (many various locations such as Birks and Grisedale Pike). Due to modern GPS technology the system of triangulation columns has mostly become redundant, the once measured accuracy of 20m across the whole country has now been reduced to just 3mm over the same area.
At the time of AW writing the Pictorial Guides the process of building the pillars was ongoing that is why the pillar on Gowbarrow Fell (right) didn't appear in his illustrations or chapter. Other columns or obvious triangulation markers that have been built on the fells since his visits include Loadpot Hill (column) and Branstree (concrete ring). He did miss the concrete ring on Blencathra though which was built around 1953 and on his visits was covered by a small cairn. Ground bolts are common on the fells but are often covered in the same manner by summit cairns.

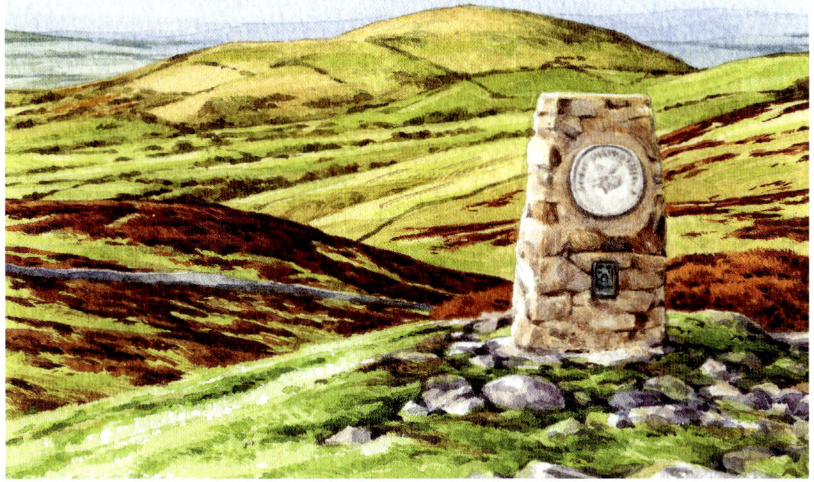

From Gowbarrow Fell 29/4/08

The second time that this triangulation column is featured, previously in the Gowbarrow Fell chapter the cairn in his illustration was most likely used to construct the column (see left). By taking a photograph looking slightly to the right AW was able to get two scenes from the one location.

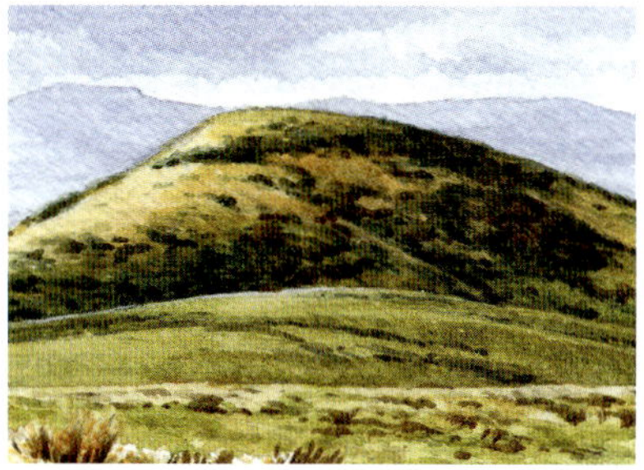

Great Mell Fell from Little Mell Fell 29/4/08

A short walk north-west from Little Mell Fell's summit will bring this scene into view.

The summit 29/4/08

Gone are the collection of stones at the summit. The column stands in a dip of the neatly cropped turf. As well as Great Mell Fell, Blencathra is also in this view, left out in the Pictorial Guide.

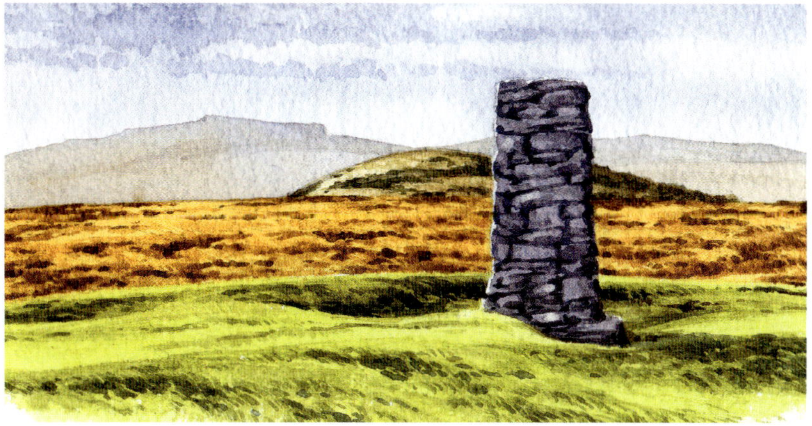

Little Mell Fell

At just over a third of a mile from the road at The Hause by my reckoning this is the shortest distance to the top of any fell from a road. Public access from other points is possible as the fell is mostly open access but be aware of the private land to the north close to Thackthwaite.

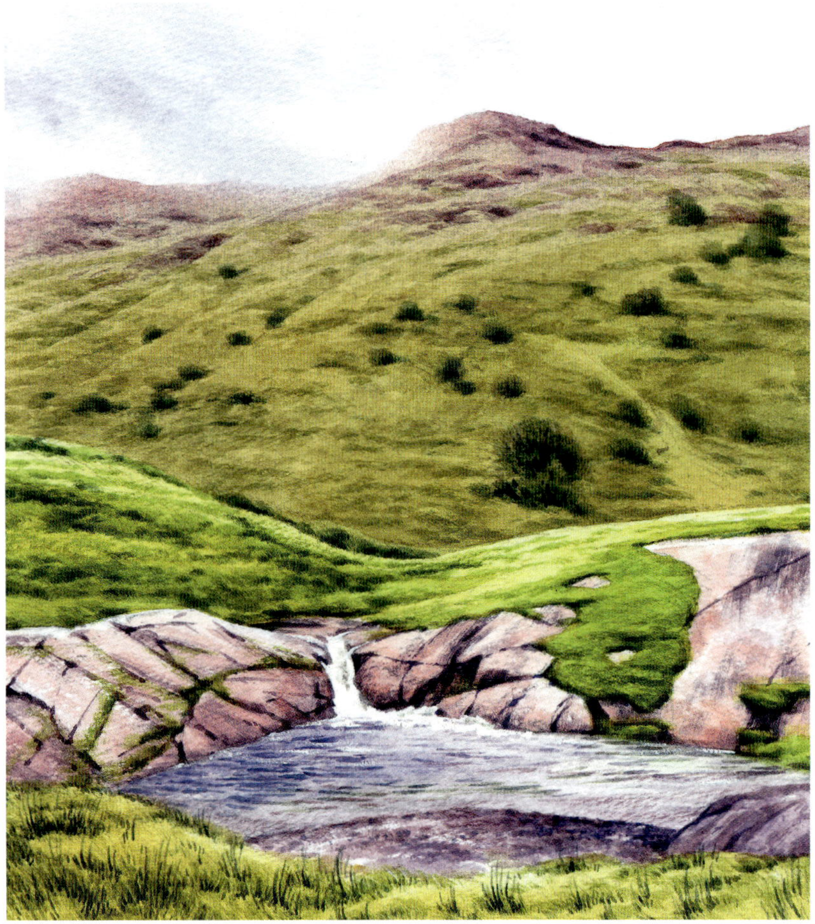

From Rydal Beck 1/9/09
The tree which was on the left of the illustration has now gone but its roots still protrude from the grass. I just managed to obtain a brief view of the peak of the fell as low cloud brushed the tops. The shallow pool of water is a popular location for paddling and swimming and is known as Buckstones Jump. An unusual feature is the pink smooth bedrock which is exposed around this location.

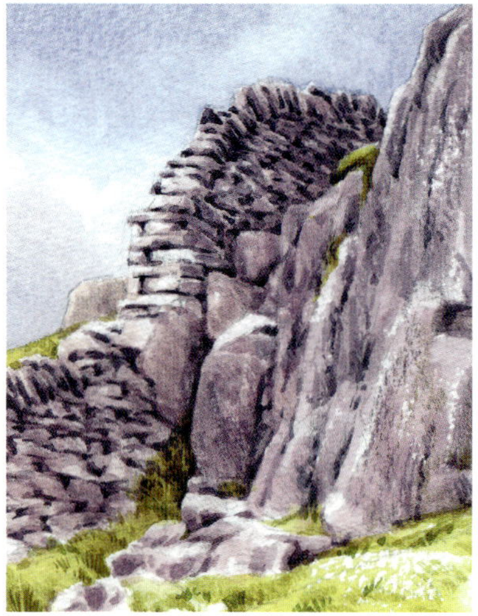

The rock-step 18/9/07
If this feature is encountered whilst undertaking the whole of the route of the Fairfield Horseshoe, then it is likely to be the only time you will have to get your hands on rock. You may be too busy negotiating the crag to take notice of the skilful bit of dry stone walling alongside.

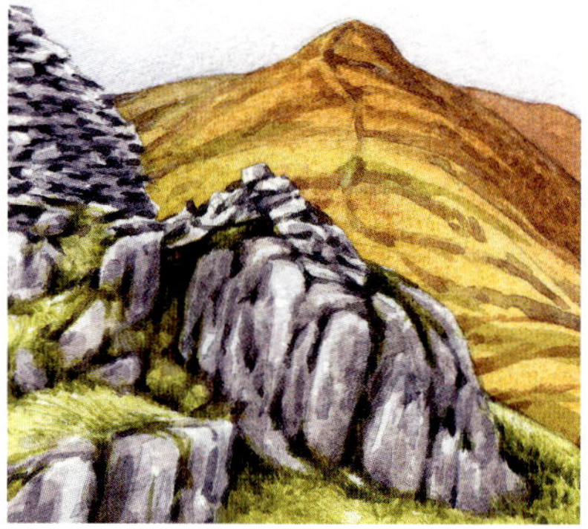

The summit 18/9/07
The highest point on a small rock platform near the wall supported a small cairn on my visit.

Low Pike

Both this and its neighbour, High Pike, form definite peaks on the ridge to the west of Scandale. A pleasant half day can be spent walking from Ambleside to this fell taking in High Sweden and Low Sweden bridges as part of the outing. Low Pike is one of the eight fells of the popular Fairfield Horseshoe.

High Sweden Bridge 18/9/07
Once again this delightful packhorse bridge is featured, this time from a slightly different angle to that shown in the High Pike chapter. The arch is lower in reality and the wall and gate are more recent than in AW's day. Sweden in the title is derived from an old Norse word for burnt or singed, most likely the moorland around here was cleared of scrub by burning.

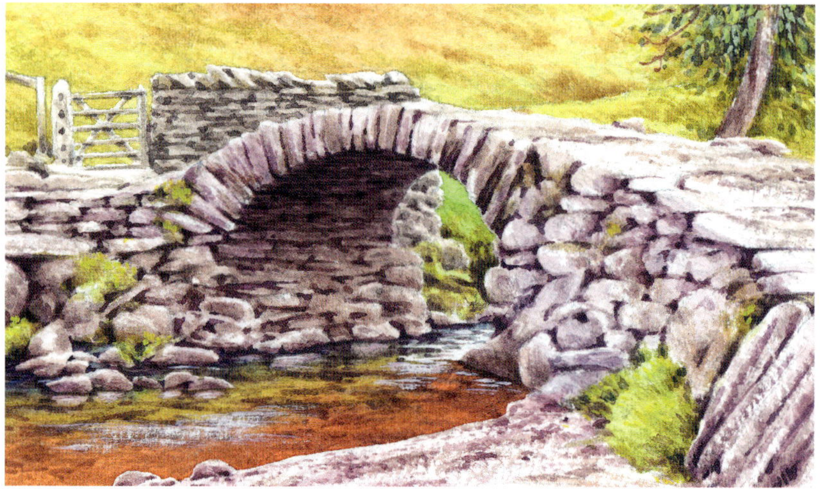

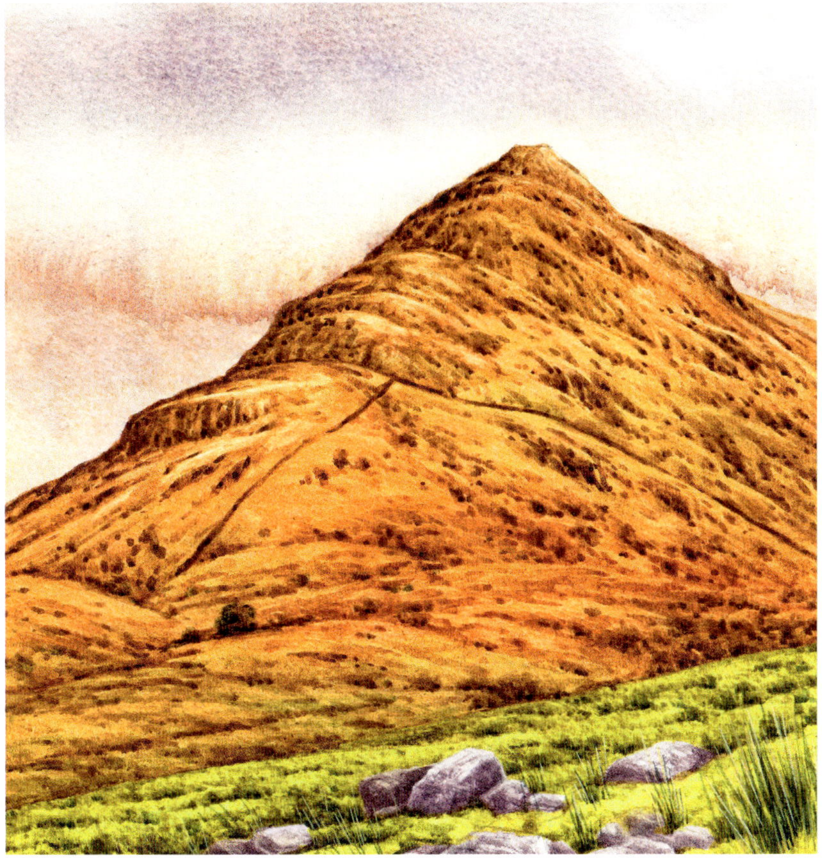

From Caiston Glen 25/11/08
Even though there was snow on the higher ground on this winter's day it did not extend down the fell side enough to allow me to portray the scene as in Wainwright's seasonal illustration. It was nearly five o'clock in the evening when I reached this point and the light was fading fast.

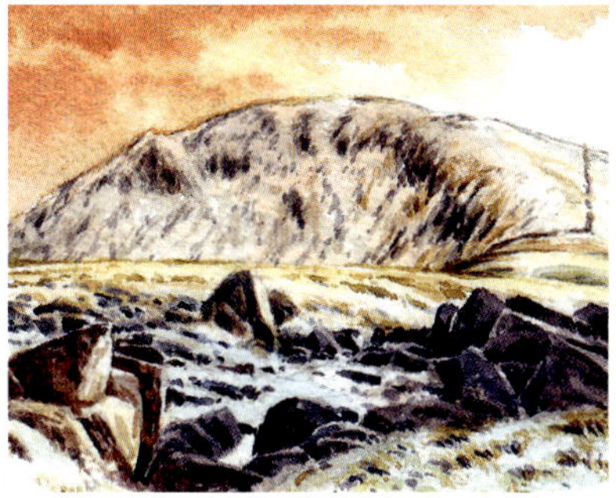

Red Screes 25/11/08
In the centre of the sketch the two pointed rocks remain in place but others have been moved to supplement the nearby cairn.

Middle Dodd

Suitably named as this lies between High Hartsop Dodd and Hartsop Dodd which all have a similarity of shape when viewed from the north. The direct route up the full length of the north ridge from the wall near Kirkstone Beck is comparable to the Wasdale Head to Kirk Fell route in straightness but not in angle of ascent or height gained. I suggest trying this one first.

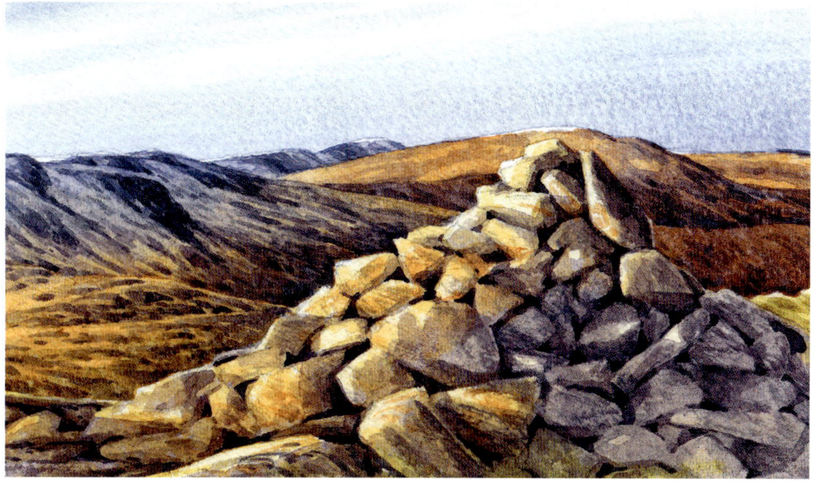

The summit 25/11/08
A more substantial cairn now sits on the highest point of the fell.

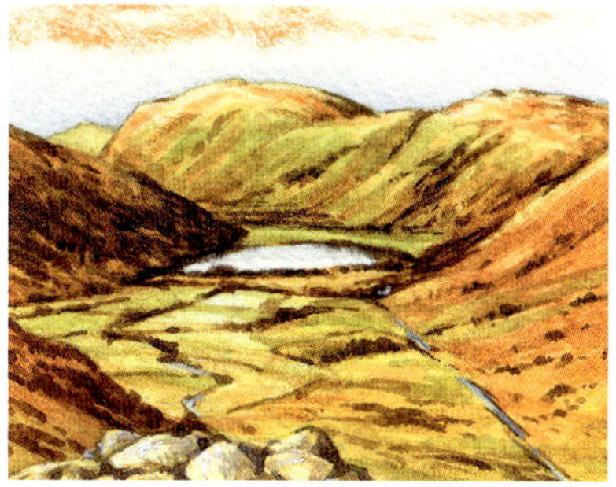

Looking north 25/11/08
The Kirkstone Pass road leads the eye down to Brotherswater and Place Fell.

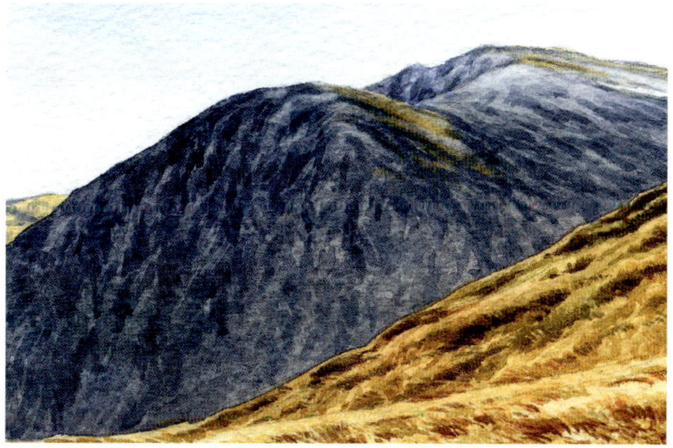

Middle Dodd with Red Screes behind from High Hartsop Dodd 25/11/08
A simple enough view from near the summit of the neighbouring fell.

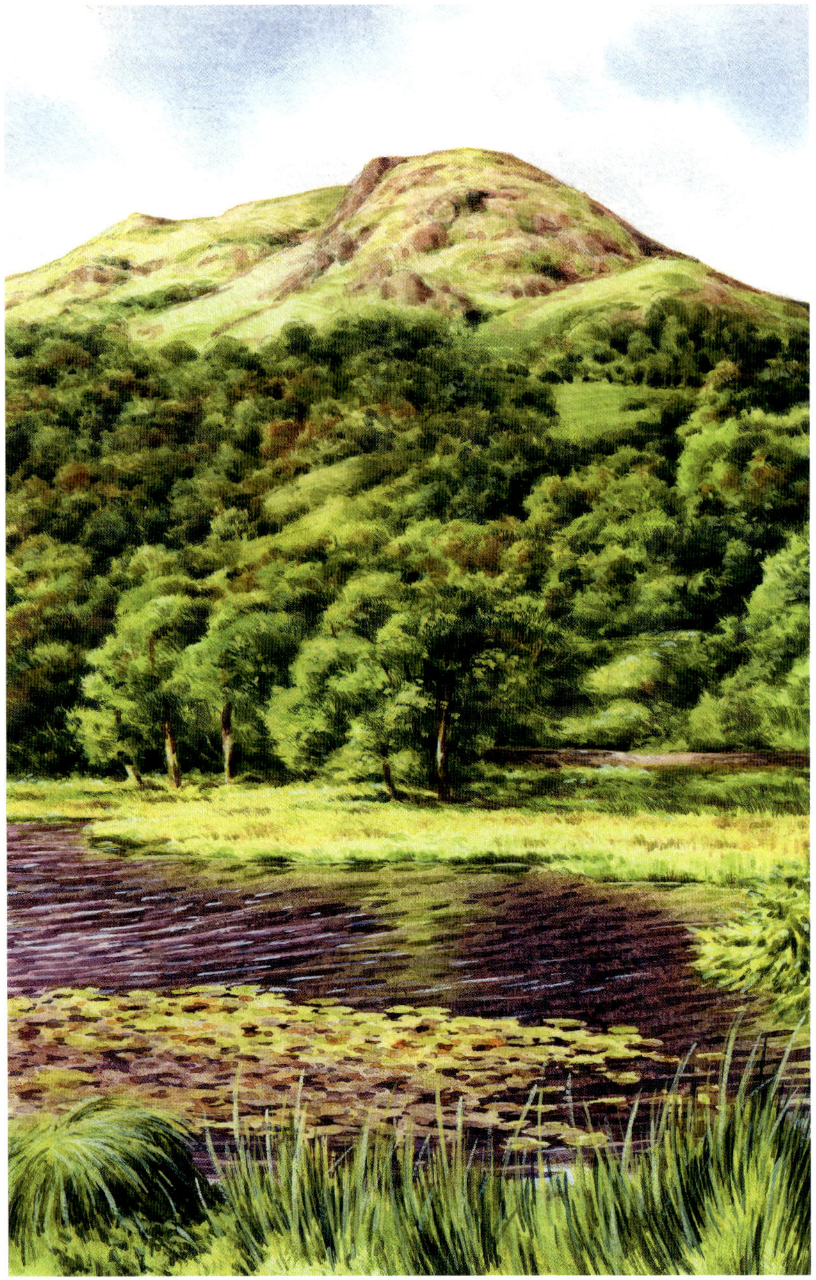

From Rydal Water 27/7/10
All evidence of the mooring and the boat in his drawing have now gone. The fell side is now more wooded but some of the trees on the far side of the water have gone to expose more of the roadside wall.

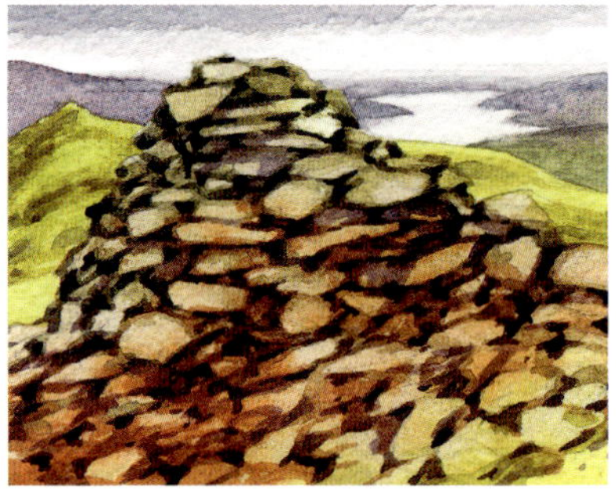

The summit 16/8/09
Sitting some 15 yards to the west of the main path a visit to the actual summit requires a slight digression in your route. Windermere is in view from this point.

The stone slab 16/8/09
Just adjacent to the path and near a small crag lies the stone cover for the Thirlmere aqueduct. It is easily overlooked in passing but hidden underneath the cover is an amazing example of engineering to transfer water through the hills.

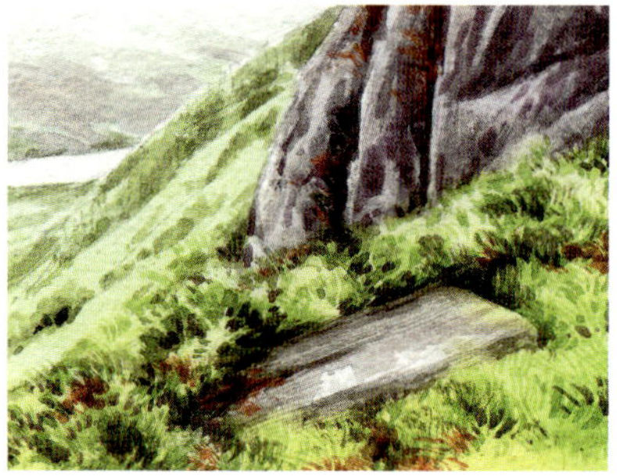

Nab Scar

If undertaking the Fairfield Horseshoe in a clockwise direction, Nab Scar will be your first summit of the day. A handy place for a breather after the ascent from Rydal, this provides good views of the Coniston Fells and the Scafells. Of course if you are travelling in the other direction your mind will possibly be on imminent refreshments in Rydal. Nab Scar did not feature on Wainwright's original list of fells for inclusion in the guides.

Wainwright's changing views

Whilst writing Book One it is clear that AW was developing the design of the Pictorial Guides as he went along. An obvious design improvement came in the format of the views, the tiny silhouette drawings of fells and the boxed corner sketches only appeared in the Catstycam, Dollywaggon Pike and Nethermost Pike chapters. Evidence shows that the small fell shapes were drawn on location in his notebook and were probably time consuming to produce accurately. Featuring them in the design limited his space for including many other lesser fells so the method was amended to allow him to give a more detailed view in later chapters. I would speculate that these three views were some of his first that he completed in the radial style, they served the purpose so he didn't re-draw or update them for the guide and thus gives us an insight to his progression of design.

Wainwright had two methods of depicting the views, either as the radial or the outline panoramas. AW listed the fells seen from each summit which required a clear 360 degree view, it is unclear why he chose one design over the other for a particular fell in the guides. Many radial views fitted into one page whereas panoramas take up two or more pages so page allocation for a chapter may have played a major part in this choice.

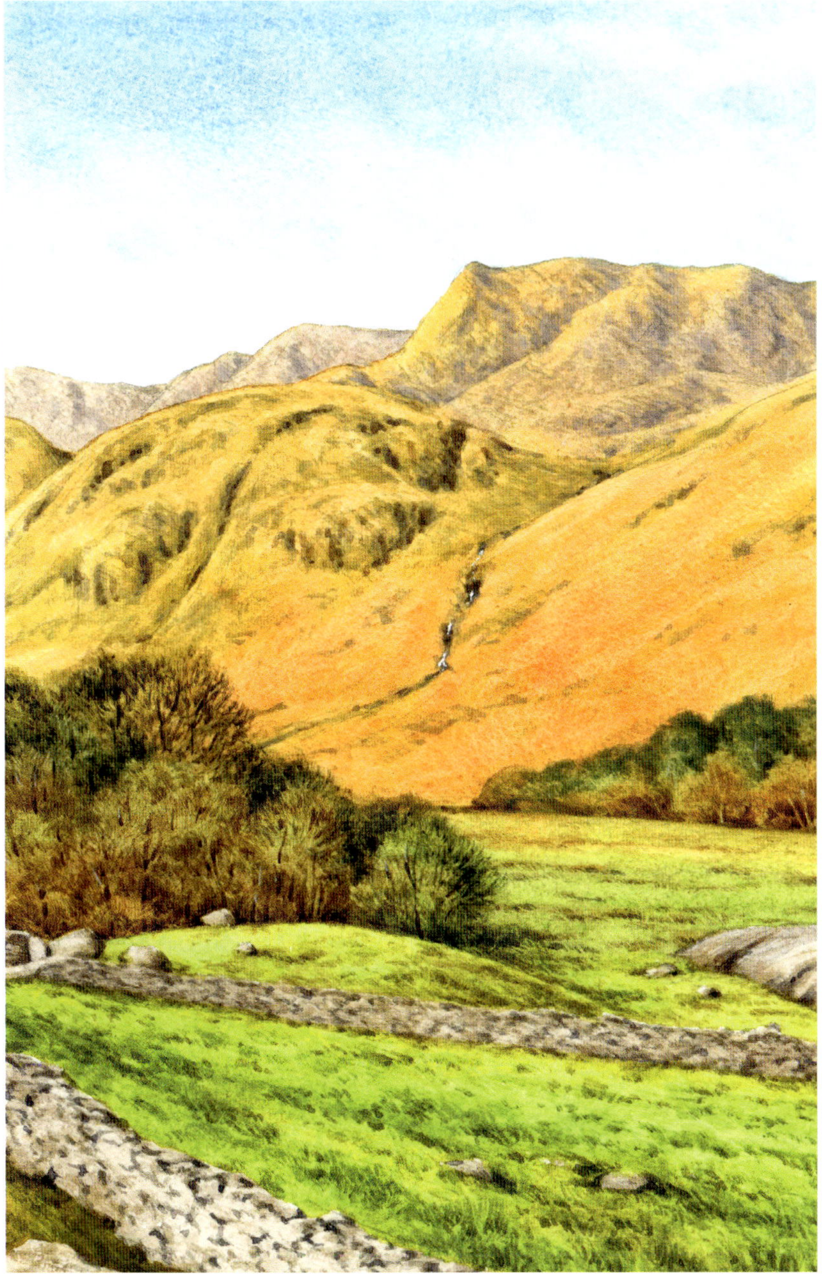

Nethermost Pike

It is overshadowed by its close next door neighbour Helvellyn in popularity but Nethermost Pike is a great alternative to that fell. An ascent up the East Ridge from Nethermost Beck is an exciting route which even today is quiet and almost pathless, but from here you can observe the queue of fellwalkers on the adjacent Striding Edge. A visit to Hard Tarn in Ruthwaite Cove is a must and you are unlikely to see another soul here.

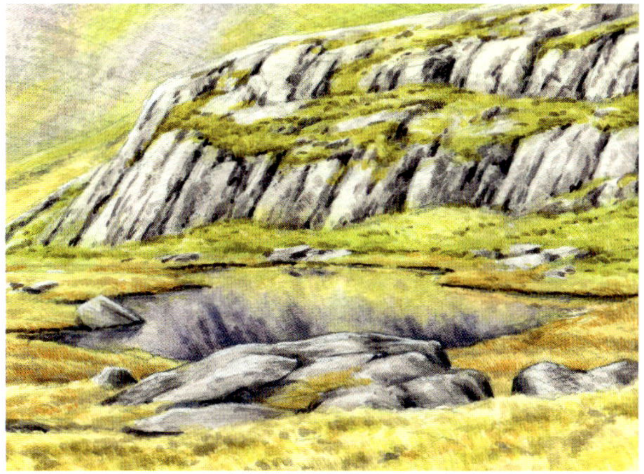

Hard Tarn 19/4/11

Possibly the least visited of all the featured tarns in the Pictorial Guides, Hard Tarn lies well away from the beaten track. A small sheet of water that sits in a slight shallow basin of rock. As AW says, it's "a gem".

From Grisedale 19/4/11

Not long after the sun rose I reached this viewpoint just west of Elmhow as the warm light touched the fells and filled the valley.

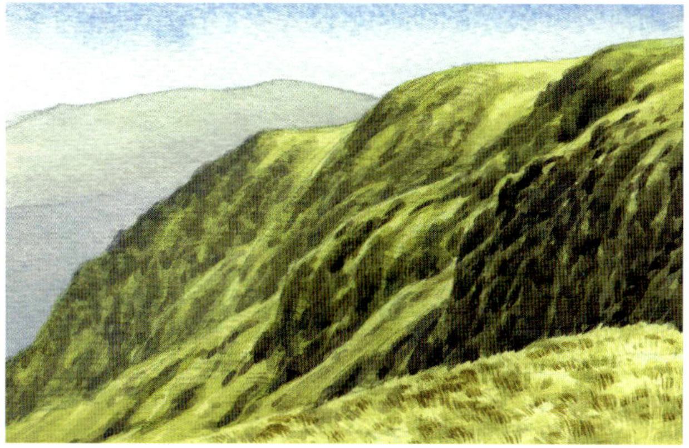

The North Face 19/4/11

Keeping close to the edge high above Nethermost Cove I was able to match this scene even though AW had left out the fell behind. As seen from near Lad Crag.

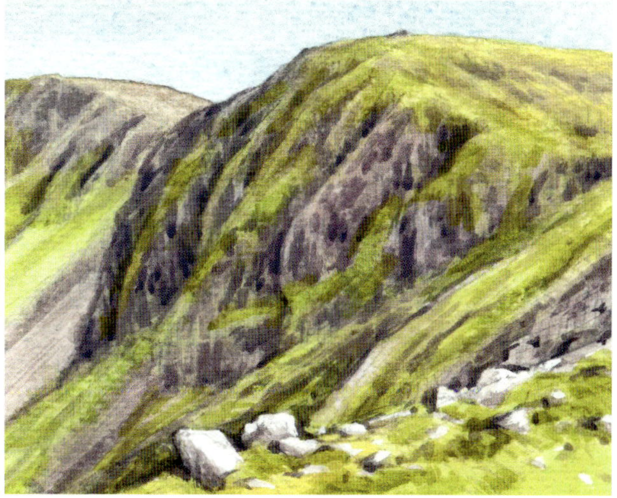

High Crag 25/9/09

From the edge above Nethermost Crag the aspect of High Crag with Dollywaggon Pike beyond.

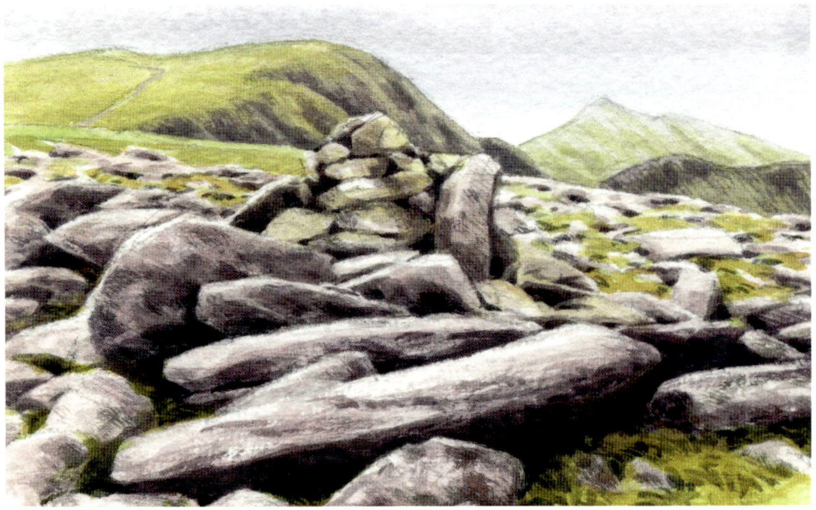

The summit 25/9/05

Large slabs of rock lie in place but considering the amount of other stones available here the summit cairn remains mostly unchanged. The possible reason for this could be that the main path passes some 100 yards or so to the west. I would guess many walkers don't actually visit this summit and go to the other cairn 100 yards to the north west.

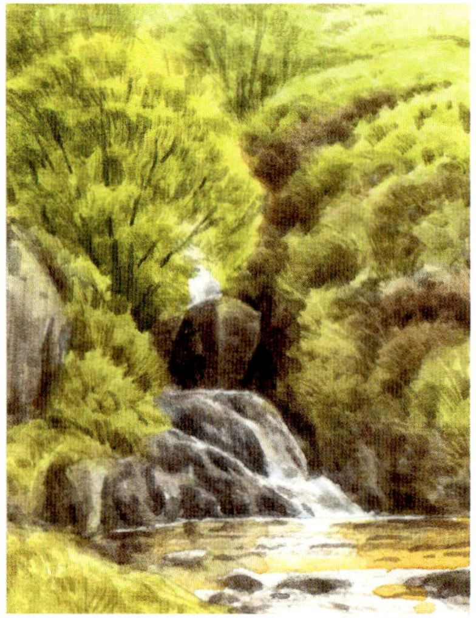

The tree on the left now obscures the main waterfall here. If time had allowed I would have returned in winter when the trees were bare to provide a clearer view.

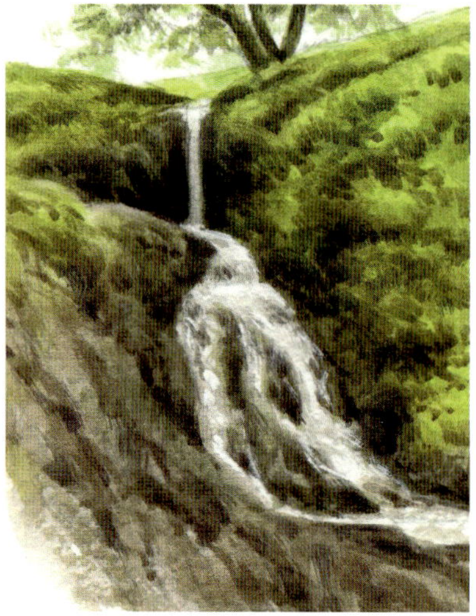

This cascade is almost as it appears in the Pictorial Guide drawing.

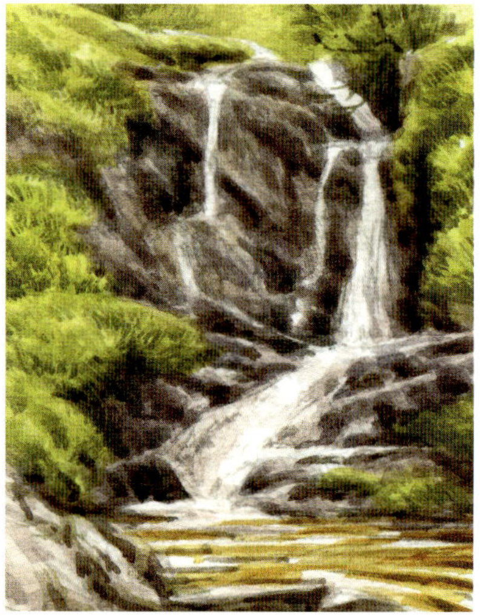

Perhaps due to an increased flow this fall has now a couple of extra runnels of water.

Cascades in Birkhouse Gill 27/6/11

Even though Birkhouse Gill is marked on the map as well as in the guide it was quite a task to locate and identify the exact falls as shown on page 8 of the fell chapter. The falls are only marked in the pages of Dollywaggon Pike. Fortunately, as the gill can clearly be seen from the main road near Dunmail Raise I observed the amount of water in the falls each time I drove past and when they looked suitable for painting I walked up to explore the gill and its many falls to obtain the required references.

Helvellyn 19/4/11

Away from the path and staying a safe distance from the edge I walked north from the summit until this view lined up to match the drawing in the Pictorial Guide.

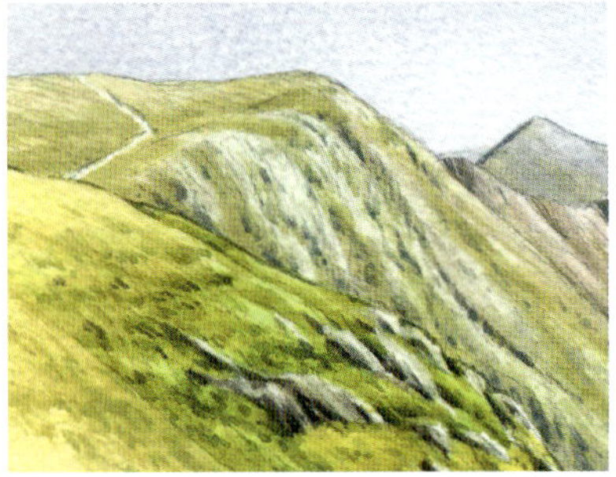

Ullswater, Place Fell and Grisedale 25/9/09

The scene from near the top of the east ridge.

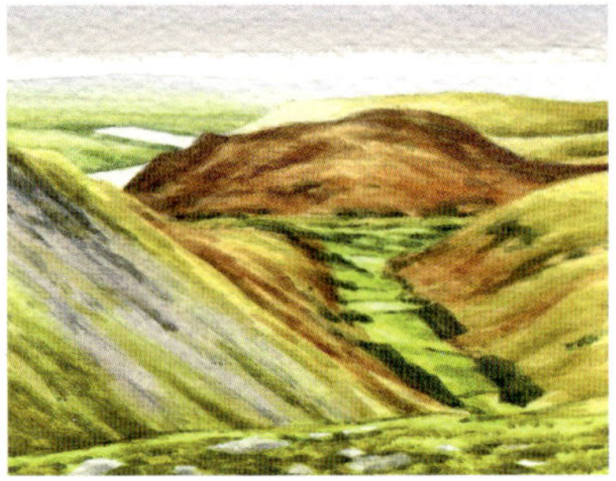

St. Sunday Crag 19/4/11

The foreground rise is actually the top of the east ridge with the rough north-west flank of St. Sunday Crag far behind.

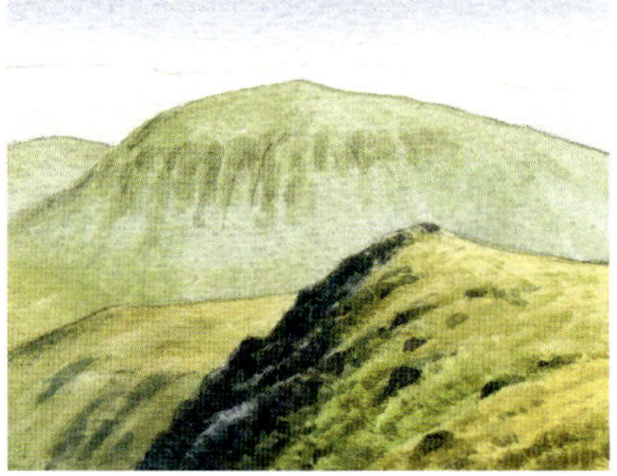

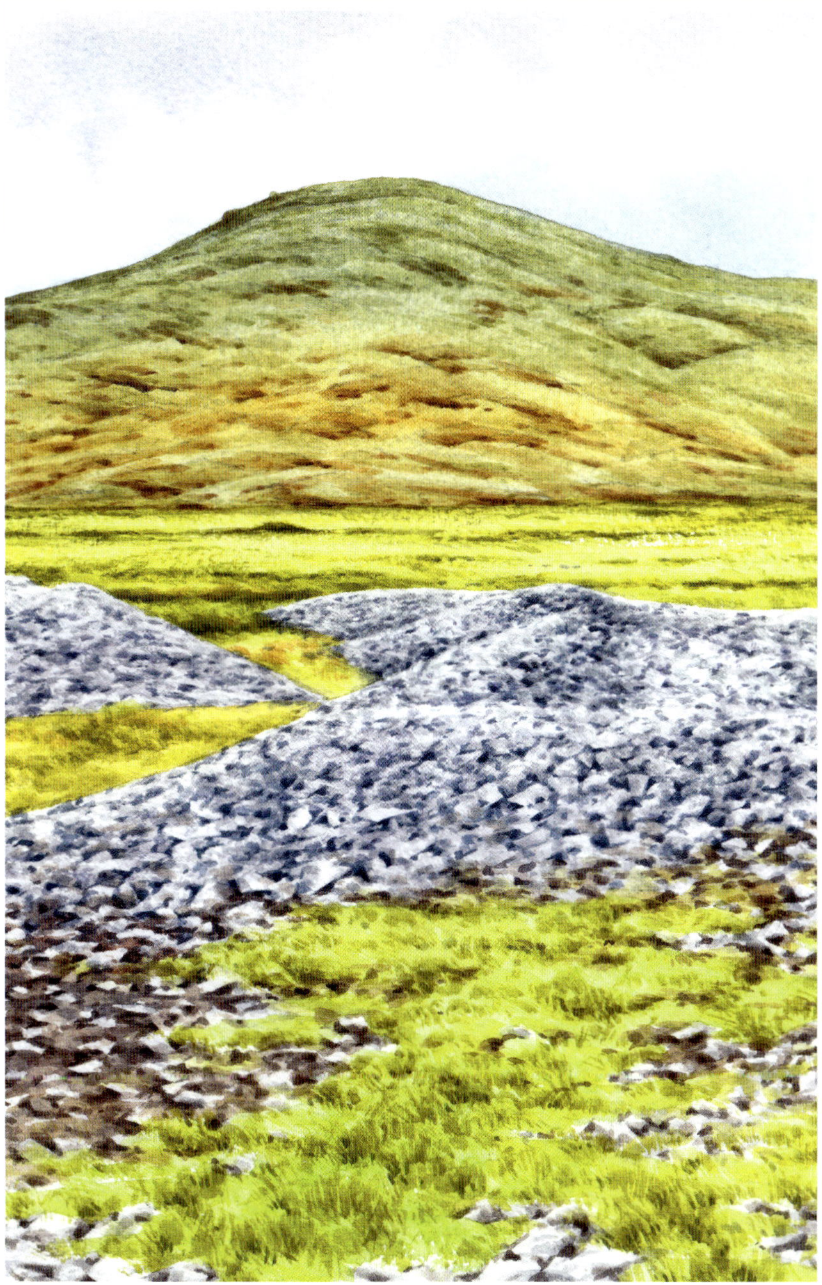

The summit of Stang 14/6/09

A slight detour from the path alongside the old flue will take you to this rocky topped rise and its good view of Birkhouse Moor.

Raise

Just one of the fells which form a long chain north from Helvellyn towards Clough Head, Raise has the unusual feature for these hills of areas of exposed patches of rough rock close to the summit. It also is home to a fully operational ski lift when the winter weather is favourable.

From Sticks Reservoir (Now gone) 12/9/10

Even though the water has long since drained away, by lining up elements in his drawing such as the small island in what was the reservoir I was able to identify the exact location for this sketch.

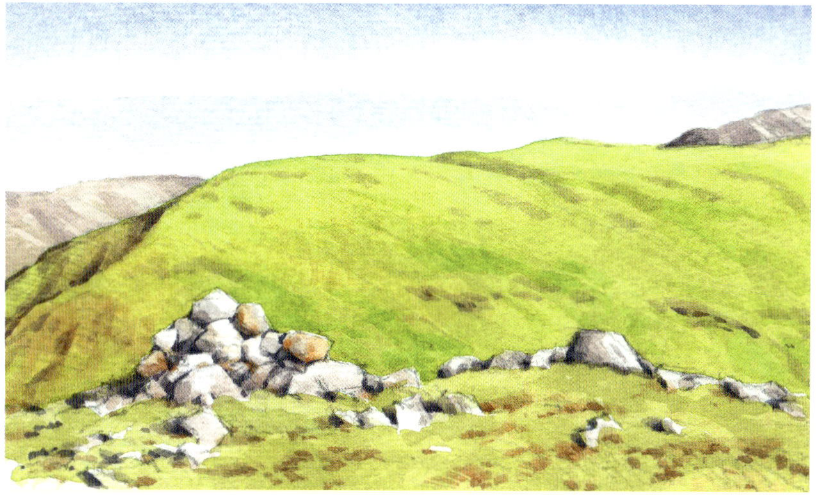

The summit 14/6/09

Now the summit cairn is a sizeable and neat construction made up of the coarse rocks which are exposed hereabouts. It took Wainwright eight visits to this summit to obtain a clear view to annotate the distant fells in his panoramic view.

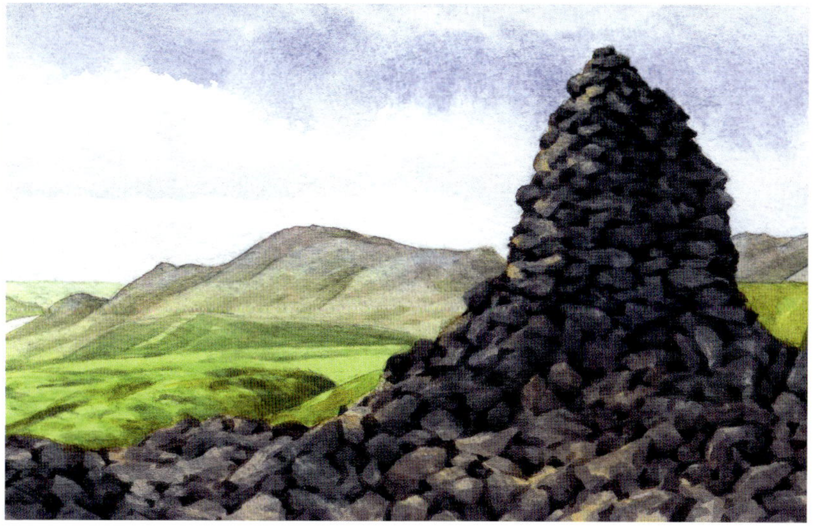

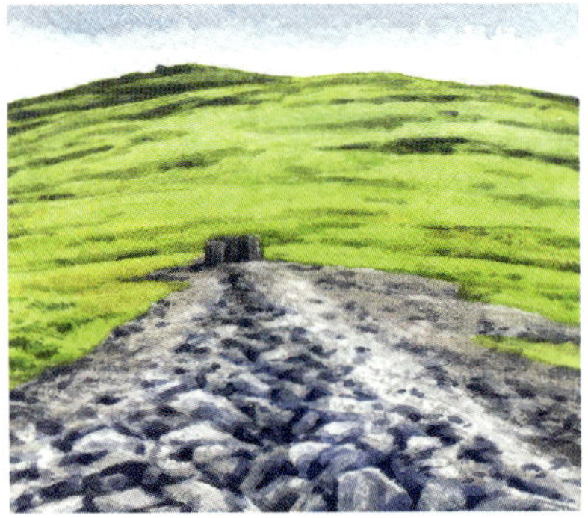

The mine chimney and flue
14/6/09
Looking up the slopes to Raise.

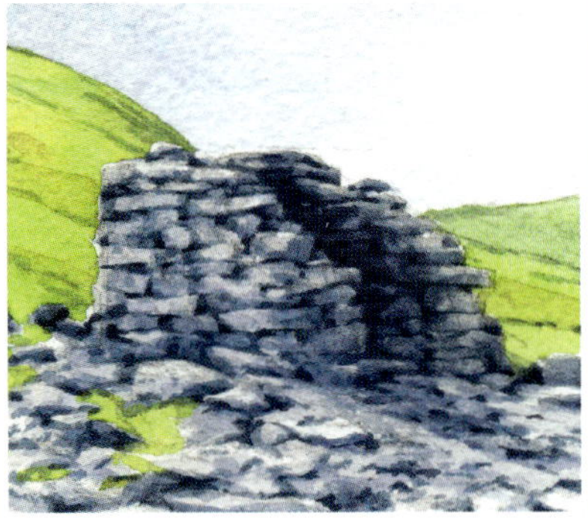

The chimney 14/6/09
Some shape still remains of this feature but it is now not as high as shown in the guide.

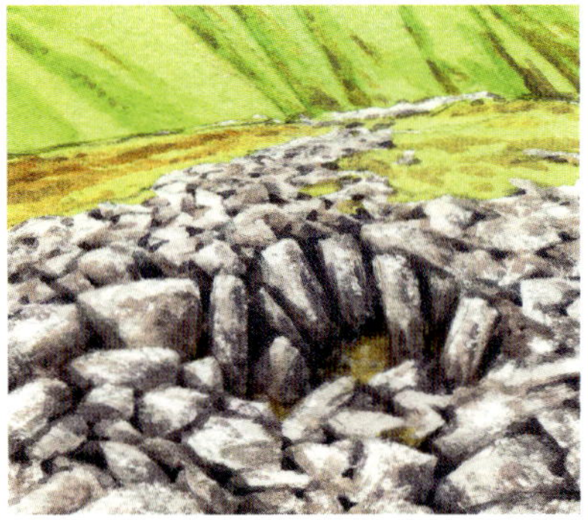

The collapsed flue 14/6/09
This section which Wainwright illustrated has now collapsed.

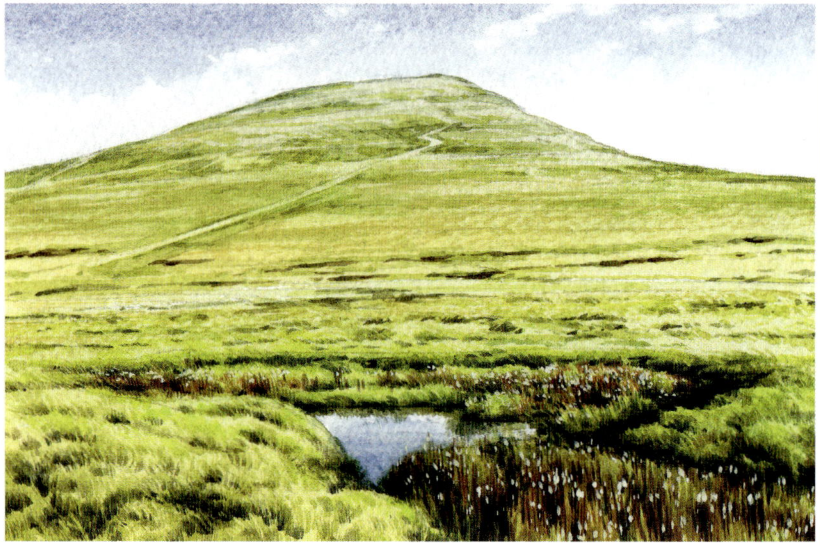

Raise from Sticks Pass 14/6/09
The small tarn has become more overgrown in the passing years and can on occasions be dry. The path which can be seen in my sketch is now a wide made trail which leads directly up the fell side towards the summit .

The Aqueduct Mystery
On studying page 4 in the chapter for Raise in the guide I was curious to AW's labelling of the "Disused Aqueduct" on the line connecting the Lead Mine to the chimney. As I have spent many a time walking around the area of the Swaledale lead mines it is obvious to me that this is in fact a flue to draw the smoke and poisonous gases away from the Smelting Mills and not a waterway.
The reason for AW's error is simple. On the 6 inch O.S. map of 1900 a very short section of aqueduct is shown, carrying the Water Cut over the flue towards the reservoir. Where they crossed the word Aqueduct was printed close to the line of the chimney, causing the confusion. This error has not been corrected in the revised guides.

Glenridding and Ullswater, from Stang End 14/6/09
This is a fine viewpoint of the valley which is accessed by a little off path walking but the reward on a good day is well worth the effort.

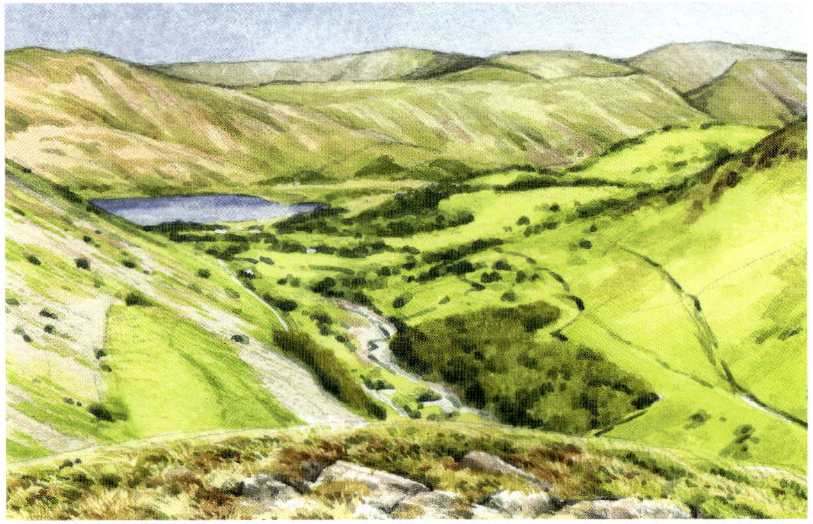

Sticks Pass
At 2420′ Sticks Pass is a high level route between Thirlmere to the east and Ullswater to the west. Its name came from a line of sticks which used to mark the route, they are no longer in place. At one time this would have been the highest pass in the whole of the area in regular use. More often than not it is now crossed by walkers heading north or south. Mickledore at 2650′ would claim the title of highest pass.

The Rock Tor 14/6/09
A short walk east of the summit will reach this outcrop which can be seen from some distance on the side of the fell.

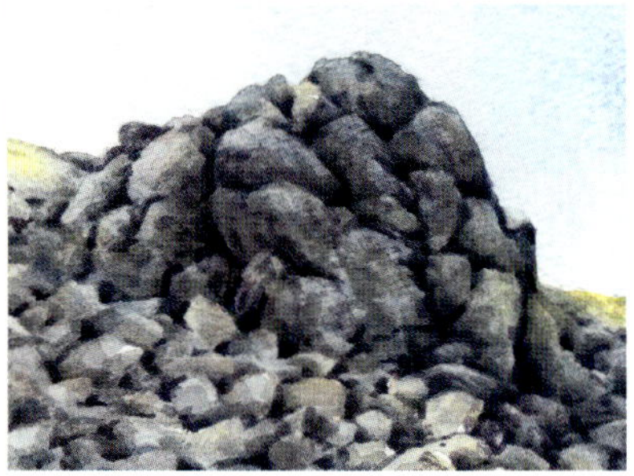

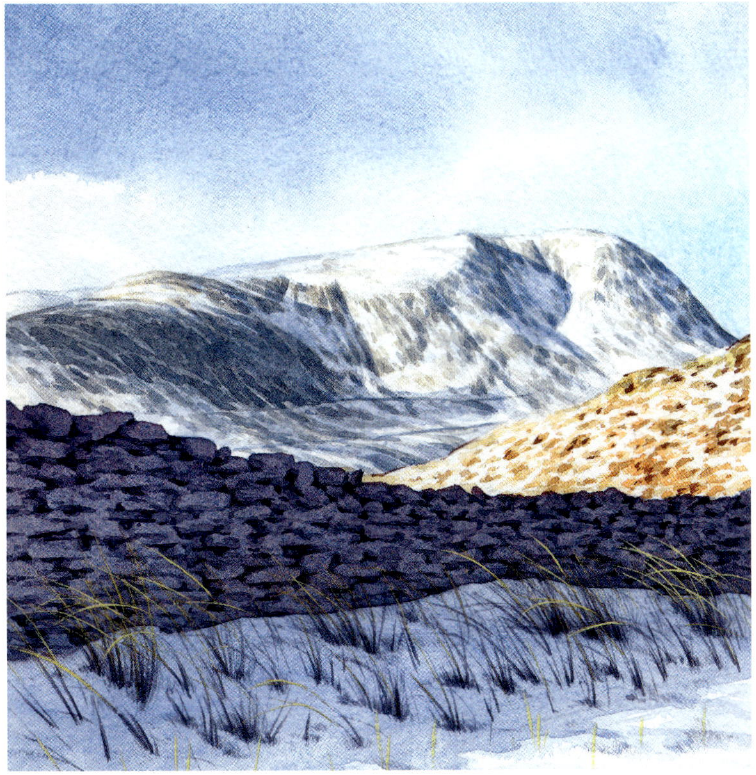

From Wansfell 6/2/09
Unusually, this drawing of Red Screes in the eastern fells was done from a location within the boundaries of the Far Eastern Fells. The wintery conditions depicted in his drawing possibly put paid to AW venturing on to higher fells on this day. The snowdrift by the wall was not quite as deep on my visit.

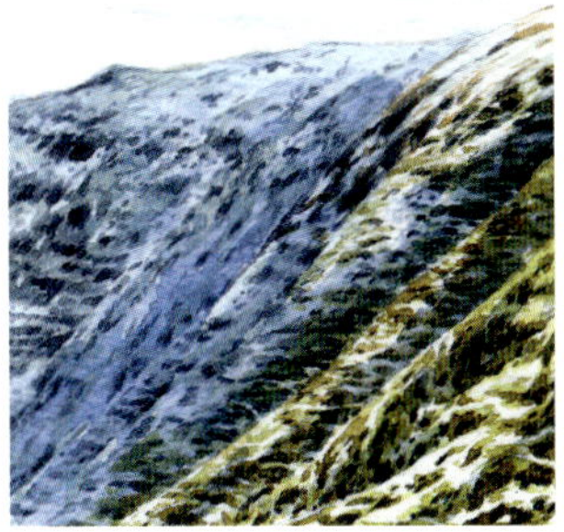

The south-east combe
25/11/08
From the east path.

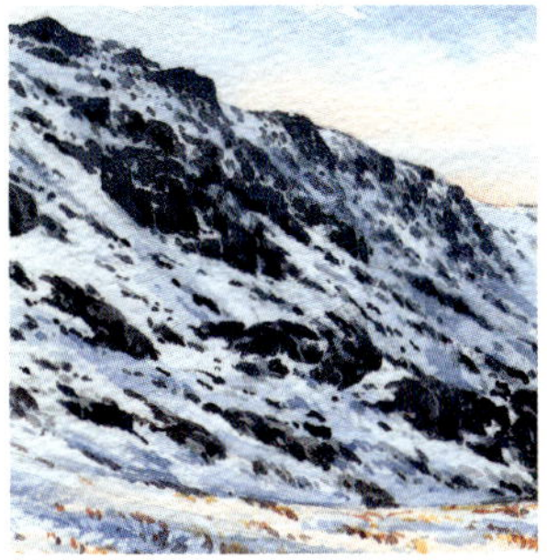

The north-east combe
25/11/08 Viewed from a rocky knoll east of the top.

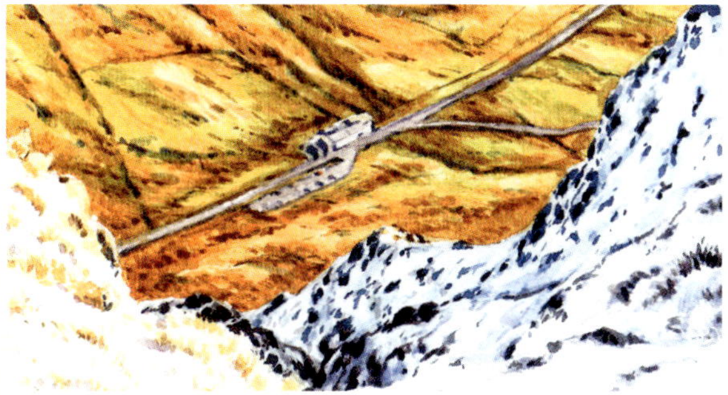

Looking down on the Kirkstone Pass Inn
25/11/08
The car park at this popular location is larger today.

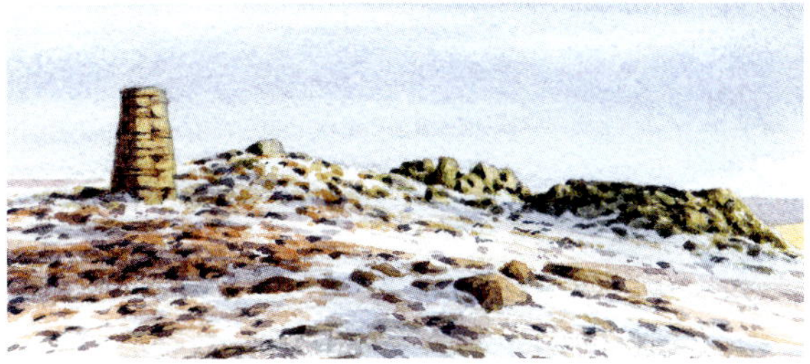

The summit 25/11/08
The huge summit cairn of Wainwright's era has been used to form rough shelters nearby.

The Kirk Stone 1/4/08
From which the pass gets its name.

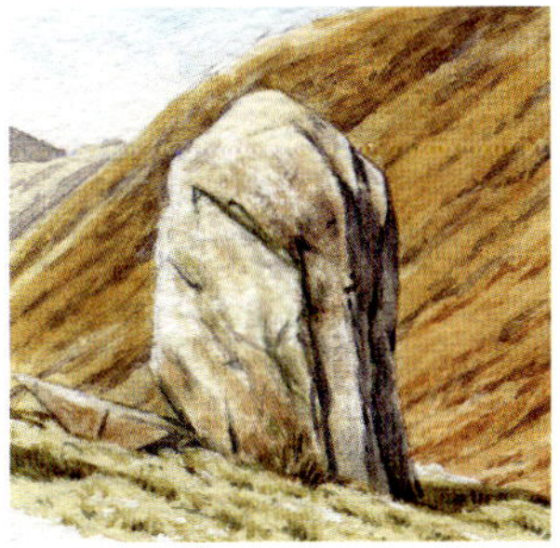

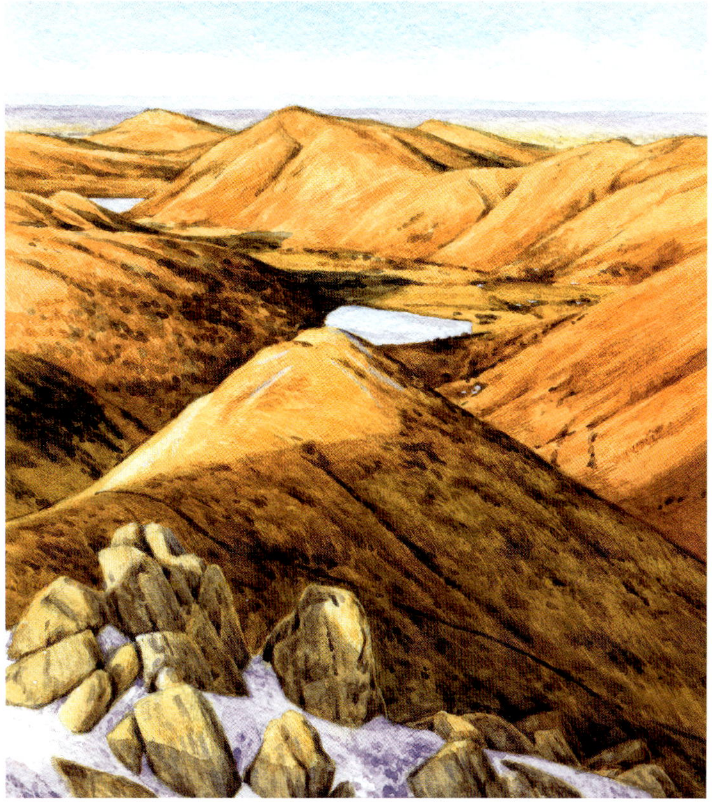

Patterdale from the summit 25/11/08
A splendid view to the north over the top of Middle Dodd.

Red Screes

The summit of the Kirkstone Pass is framed by the slopes of St. Raven's Edge to the east and the much more impressive face of Red Screes to the west. Many walkers climb this fell direct from the pass, under 1 mile in length but very steep in places, at least the Inn is there when you safely return.

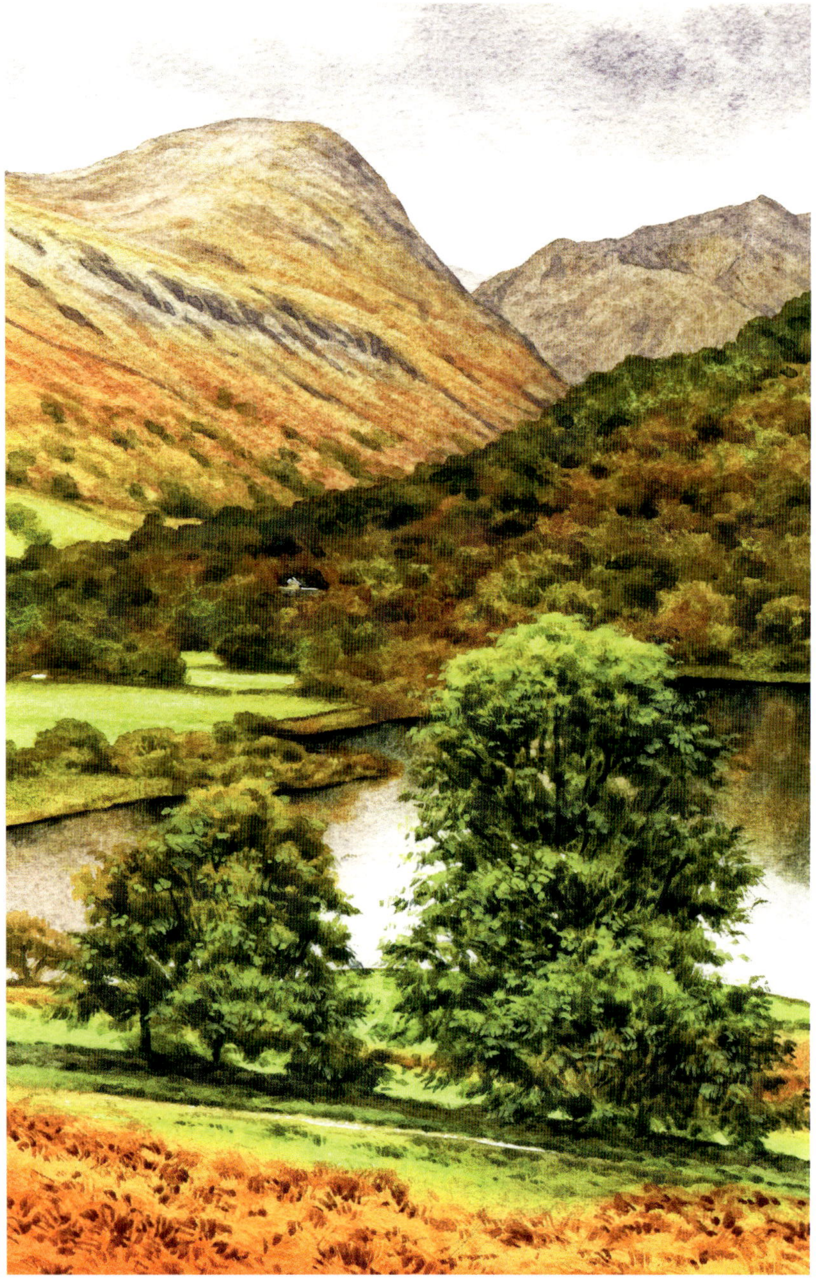

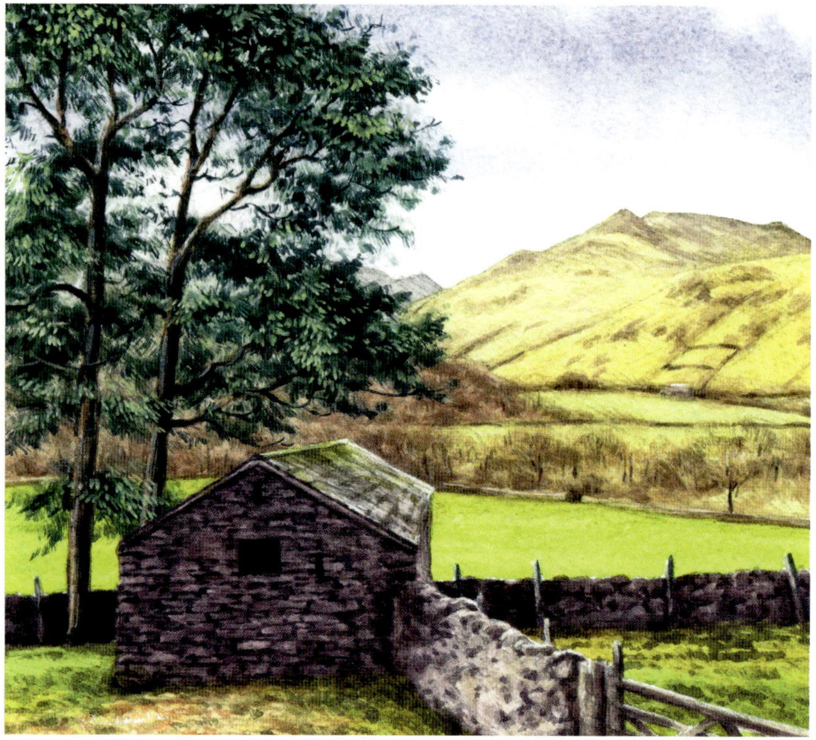

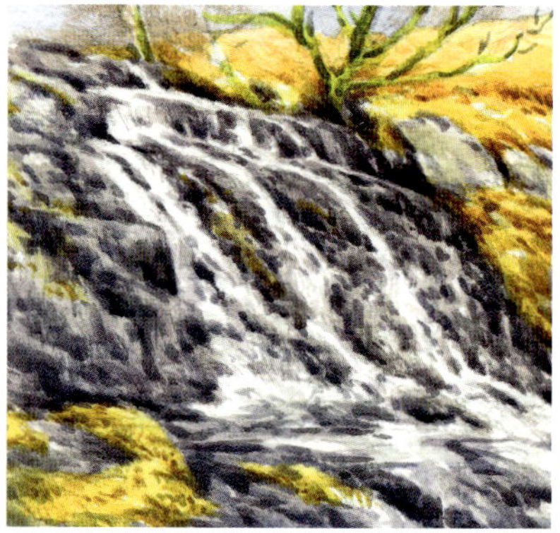

Coldcove Gill 16/3/10
Falls in a quiet setting adjacent to the path up to Latterhaw Crag.

The East Ridge, from Dubhow 6/3/11 The pines are more mature and I have drawn the fell more to a realistic scale.

St. Sunday Crag from Grisedale Tarn 21/8/10
Including Ullswater and beyond.

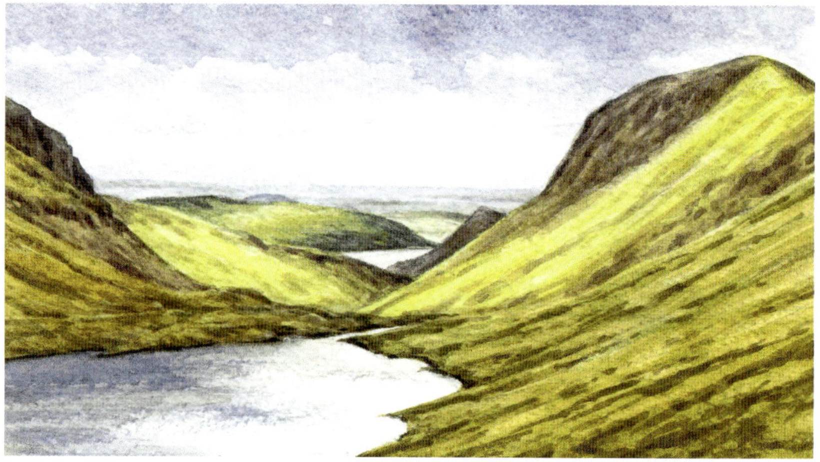

Saint Sunday Crag
A shapely fell which is often admired from Fairfield's top but the best views of the north-western craggy face can be seen from Nethermost Pike.

From Ullswater 14/10/08
The popular path under Place Fell provides some wonderful views, this being one of them. Taken from close to the point of reference for the main drawing of Birks.

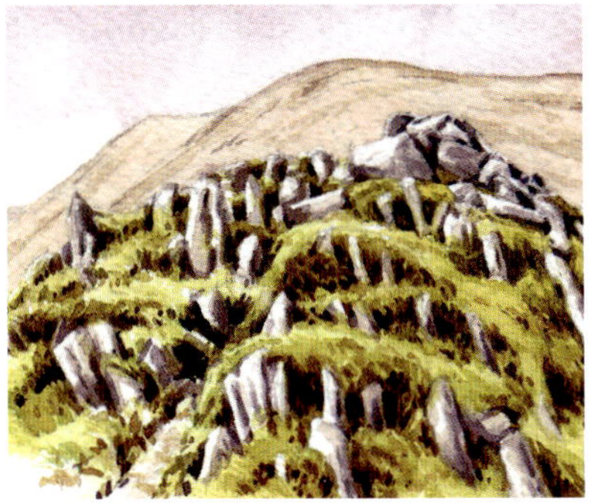

Summit of Gavel Pike 18/9/07

More rocks are now exposed through the grass but the small cairn still marks the top of this subsidiary peak. Gavel Pike was a surveyed height on old maps and consequently was on AW's first list but then was incorporated into this chapter for the guidebook.

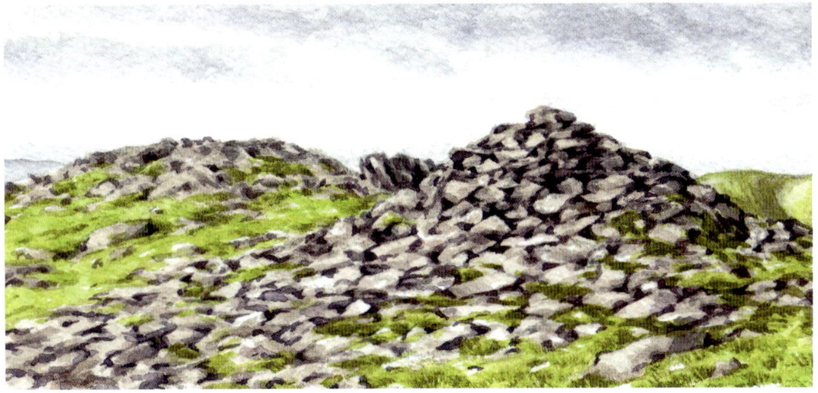

The summit 18/9/07

The far cairn has mostly gone and the nearest has lost its shapely form.

The view from the north cairn 18/9/07

What was once a fine stone pillar has now been reduced to an untidy heap. There is no disputing the grand view from this prominent location.

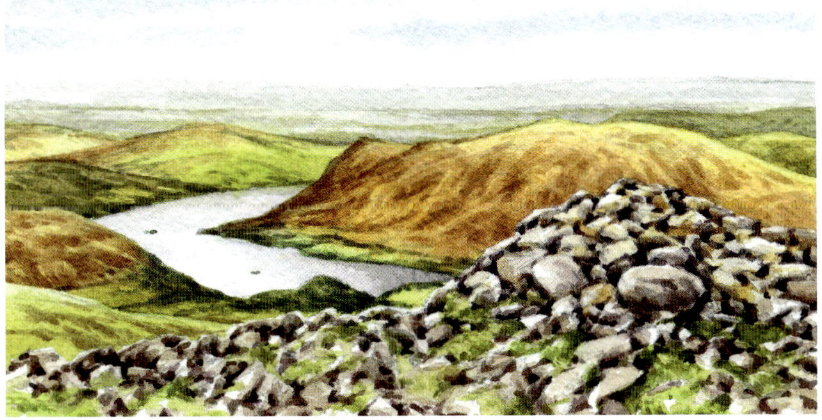

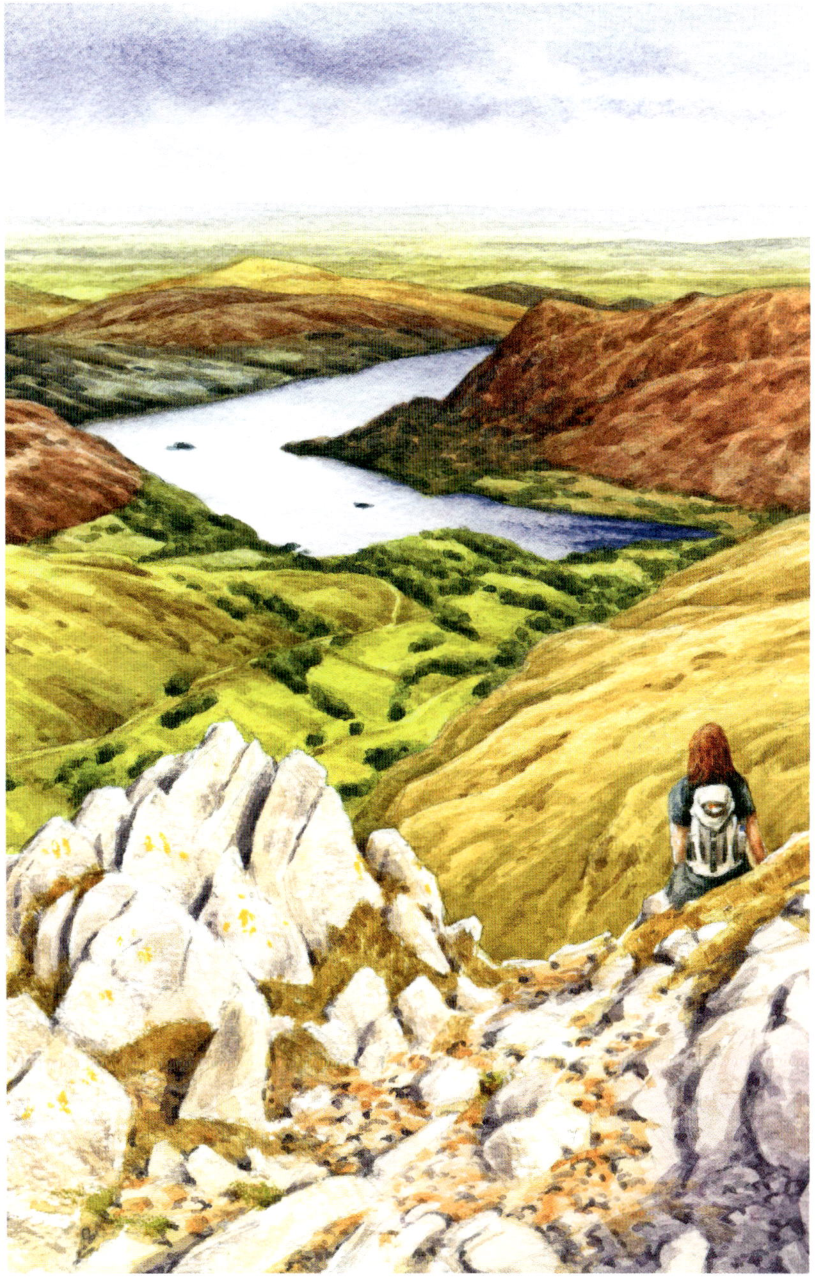

Ullswater from the north-east ridge 18/9/07

Wainwright included a lone figure sitting admiring the view as have I but my model is more appropriately attired. The ground actually drops away rather steeply at that point so both versions use elements of artistic license to achieve the pleasing result. Note how the near grass has been eroded to reveal the bare earth.

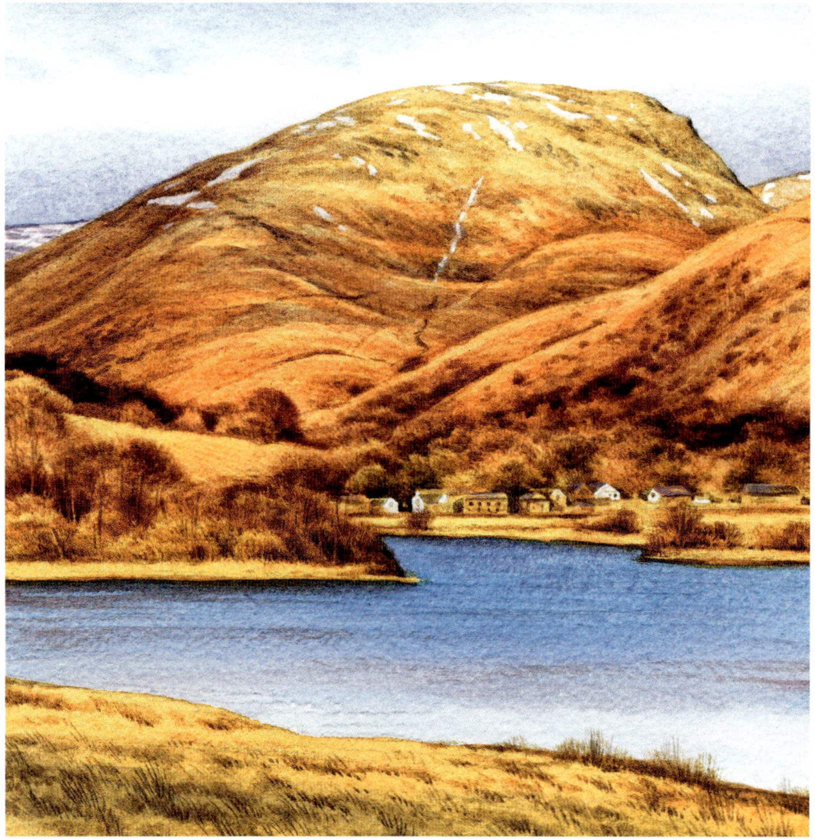

From Grasmere 16/3/10
Late winter colours on the fell side above the village.

Seat Sandal

A rounded mound of a fell when seen from Grasmere but the west side has steep rough ground. On old maps the name was used for not only the fell but also for the ground north of Raise Beck. Recent maps now show that area as Willie Wife Moor, perhaps to avoid confusion.

Ullswater from Seat Sandal (below left) 19/8/10. Seen from near the old wall on the summit.

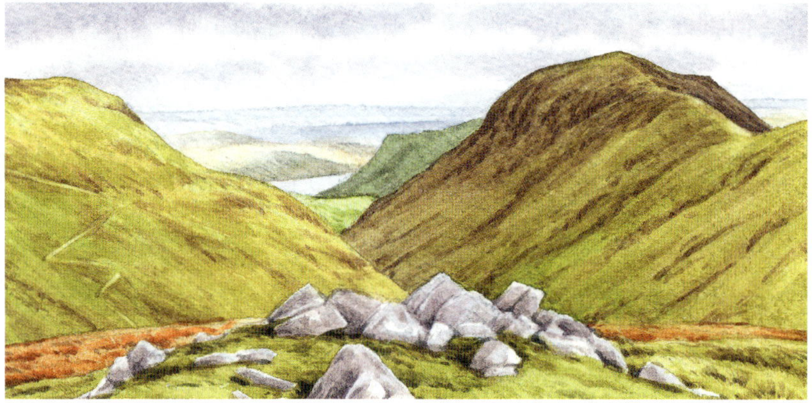

Cascade, Raise Beck 10/9/10
Part of the upper rock lip has gone, changing the shape of the falls.

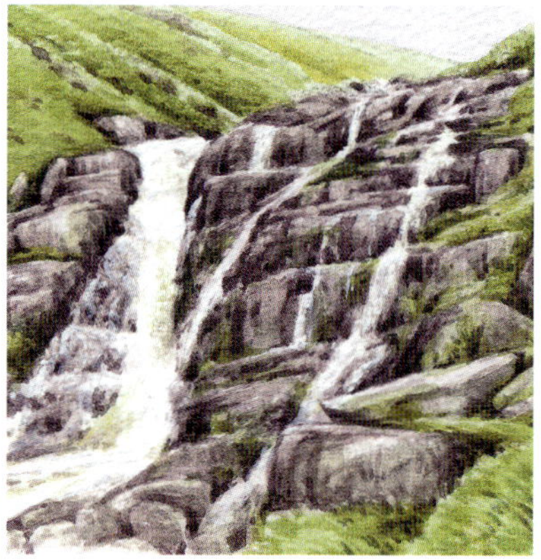

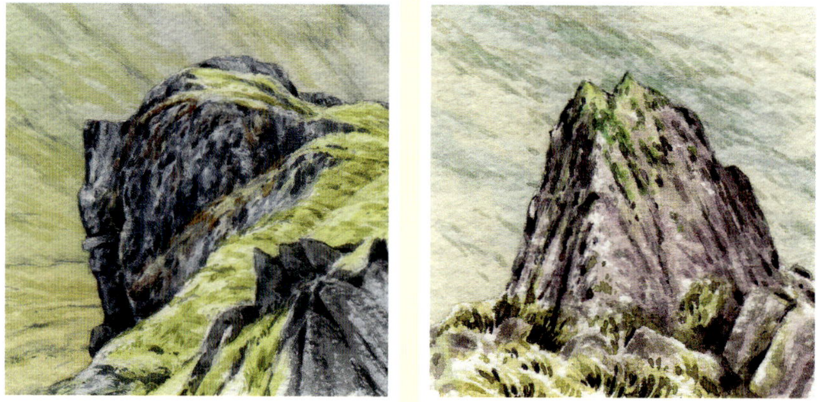

Gavel Crag 2/1/09
A large portion of the nose of the crag has fallen into the valley. By looking at the original drawing it can be seen that the crag fractured at a point just below the letter "t" of the word arête. Due to the collapse the rock in the right hand sketch is now much less pointed.

The summit 18/9/10
Neatly framed by St. Sunday Crag and Fairfield the cairn sits on the flat grass plateau of the summit. Like many others it has increased in volume.

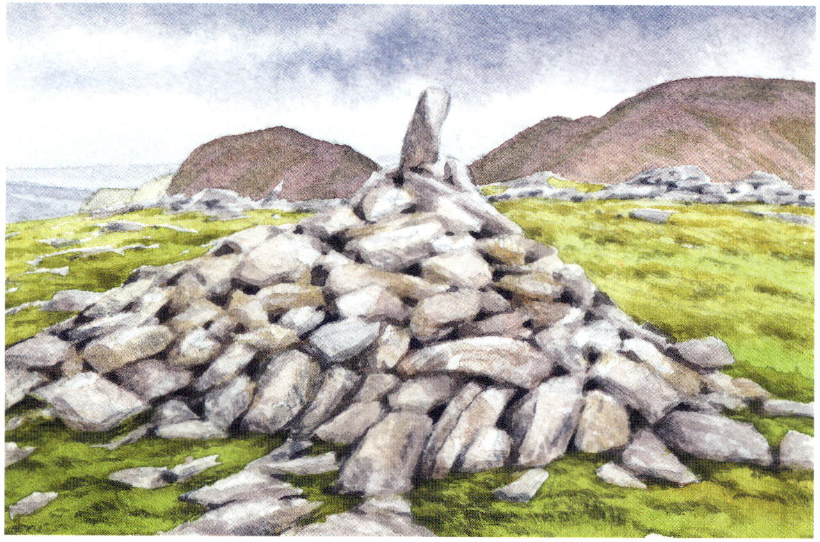

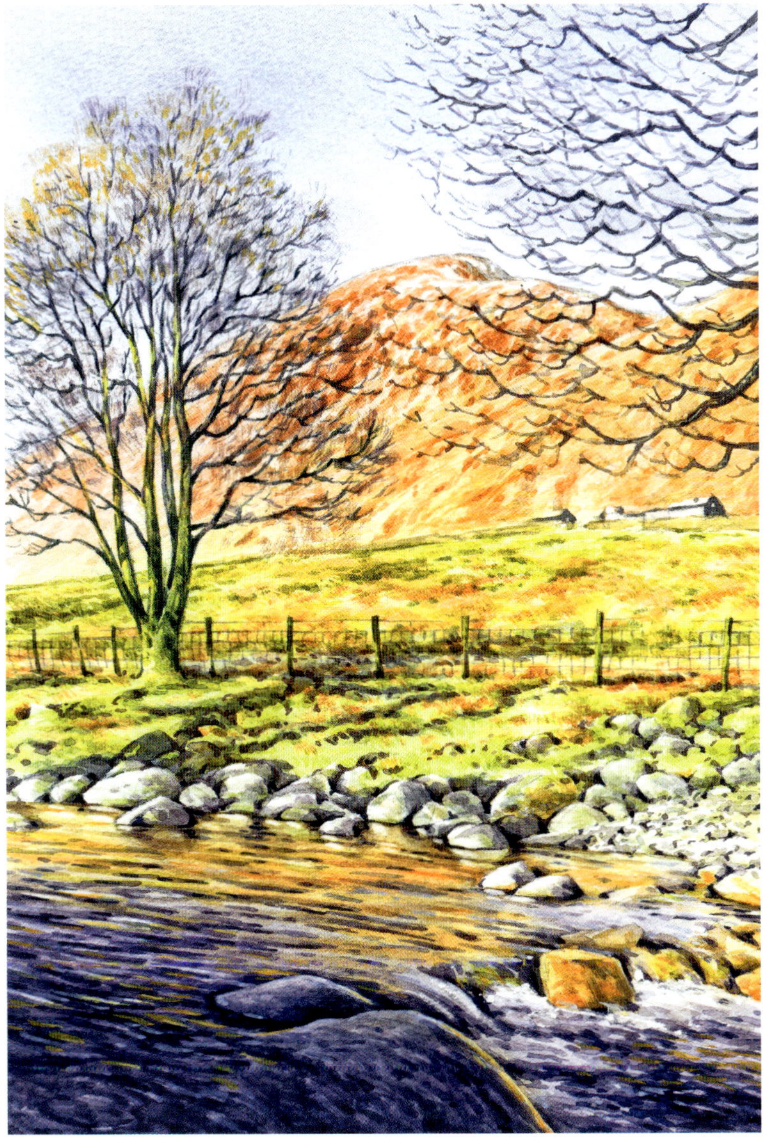

From Glenridding 6/2/09
Trees have grown up to obscure AW's illustrated view. I had to resort to walking up alongside the beck until this similar aspect reveals itself, about 100 yards from the original location.

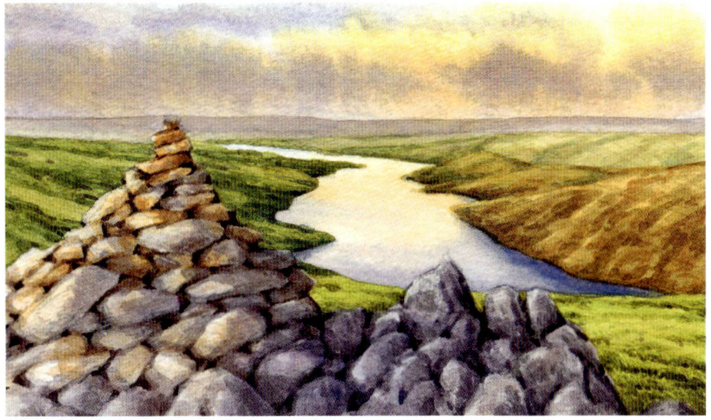

The summit 14/6/09.
It was 9.30 in the evening as I stood here on the summit to get this reference. Thank goodness for long summer days.

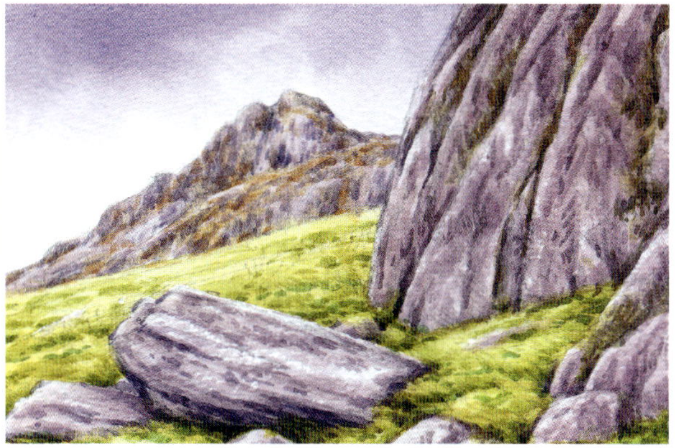

Heron Pike from the east 12/9/10
From the path by Glencoyne Wood.

Sheffield Pike

The steep southern flanks of the fell are a mixture of rock and heather which in the height of summer presents a glorious pattern of colour. A good half day walking route is from Glenridding up to the youth hostel and then back over the tops of Sheffield Pike and Glenridding Dodd.

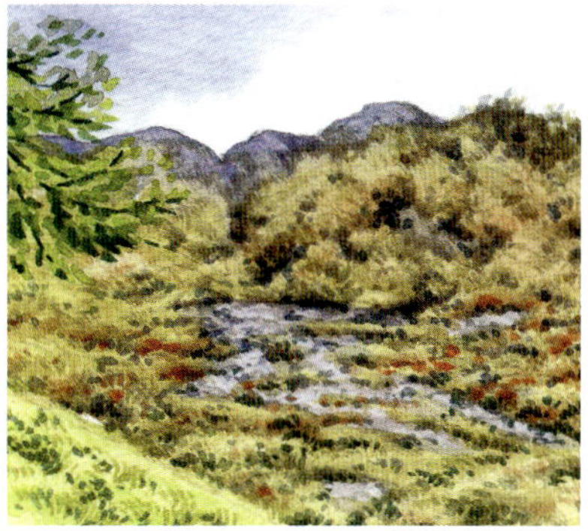

Black Crag 12/9/10
Looking up to the crag from the bottom of the overgrown scree slope.

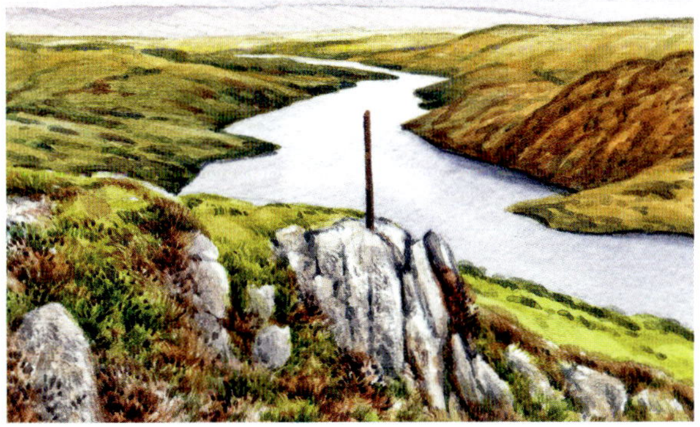

Ullswater from Heron Pike 14/6/09
The iron fence post still firmly in place on the edge of the crag.

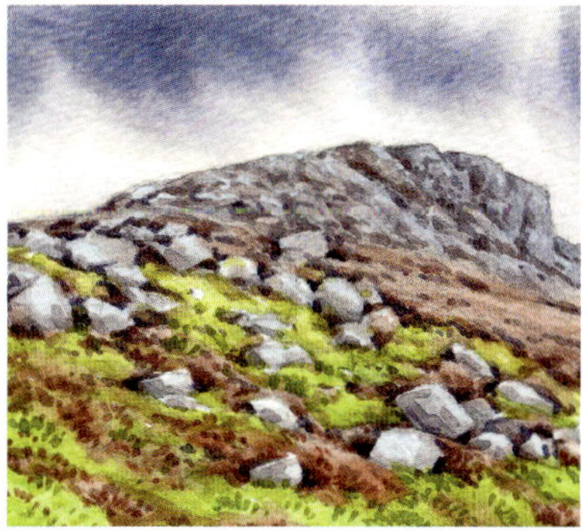

Heron Pike 12/9/10
Heather, bilberries and rocks under the crag.

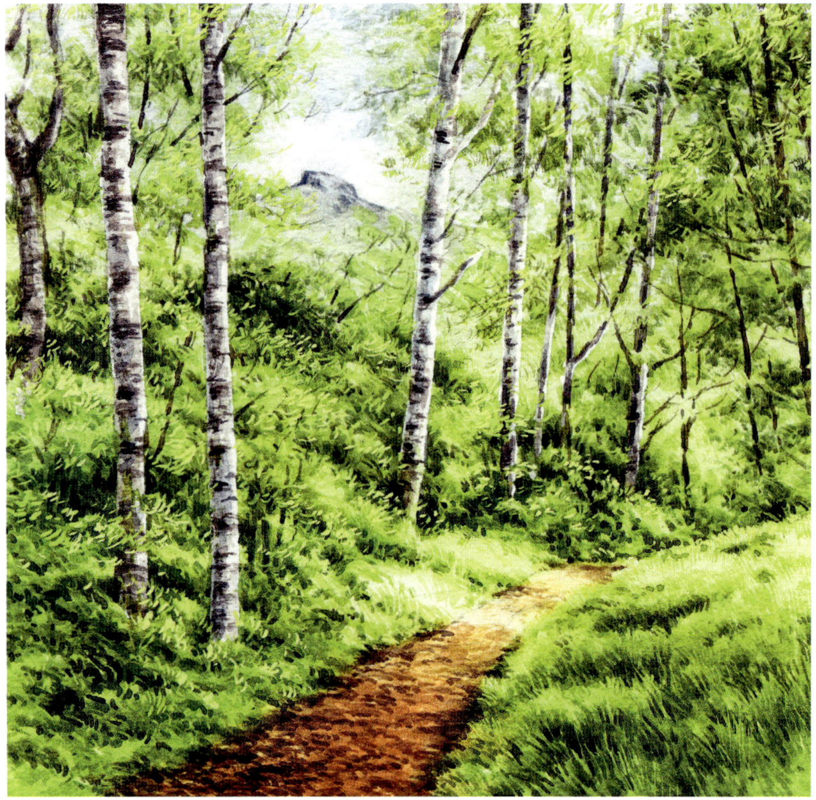

From Grasmere 24/6/08
The title does not give much of a clue as to the viewpoint location. Some detective work was required before I realised it was from Butharlyp Howe. When within the woods I was not confident of success due to the tree growth, however all was not lost for a break in the canopy revealed the fell top from just about the correct place meaning that the view could still be captured.

Stone Arthur

A rocky outcrop crowns the end of the south-west ridge of Great Rigg. Hardly a fell in its own right but it does provide an aerial view of Grasmere village and the lake. A pleasant couple of hours can be spent walking to the fell's top from Grasmere.

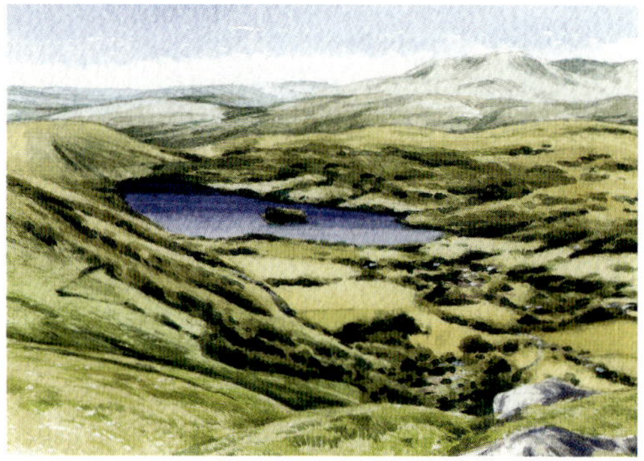

Grasmere, from the summit 24/6/09
There was no summit cairn in AW's day and on the several visits I have made only once or twice has a cairn been in situ.

The summit, from the west 2/1/09
I recall this location vividly. We had been on Fairfield late in the afternoon and I required this reference. We were contouring the fell side "off path" under Rigg Crags so that the approach to the outcrop could be made from the west. Suddenly the evening winter sun dropped below the clouds directly though Wrynose Pass and I ran the last few hundred yards to the exact location and managed to photograph the scene, just as the last rays of sun illuminated the summit rocks.

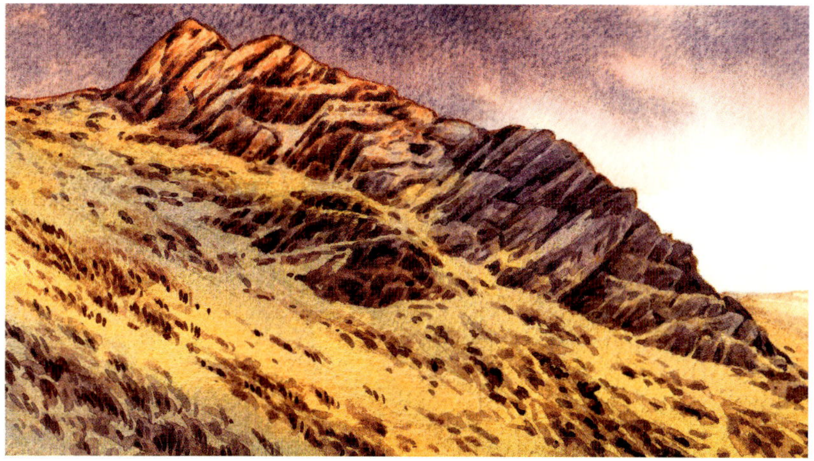

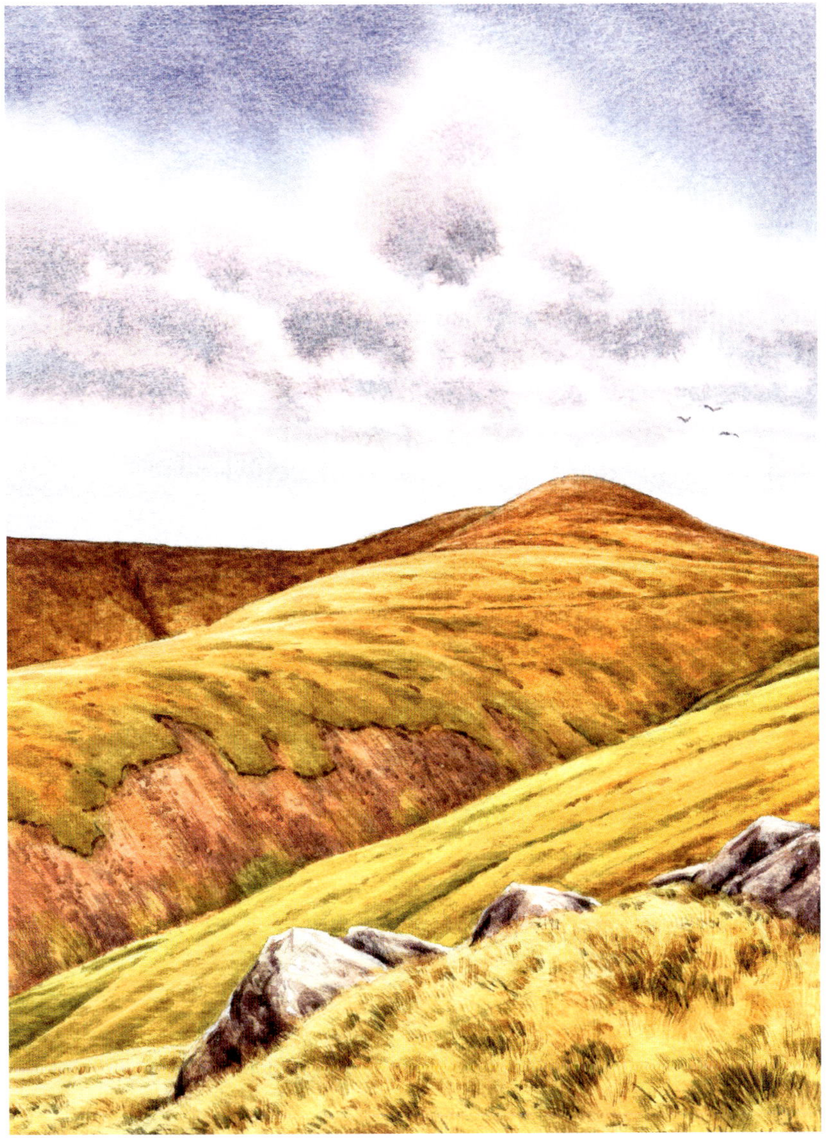

From Brown Crag 30/10/07
To make the hill fit the page, AW exaggerated the fell's shape and included some billowing clouds to fill what would have been an area of blank paper. My version is a more accurate representation.

Stybarrow Dodd

With almost unbroken rounded grassy slopes, Stybarrow Dodd is hardly a hands-on mountain, more like a hands in pockets one. Only at Deepdale Crag is the bedrock exposed. The bonus is that the views are excellent in nearly all directions.

Stannah Gill 31/10/07
There are several falls in the gill and some time was spent locating the exact one for this sketch.

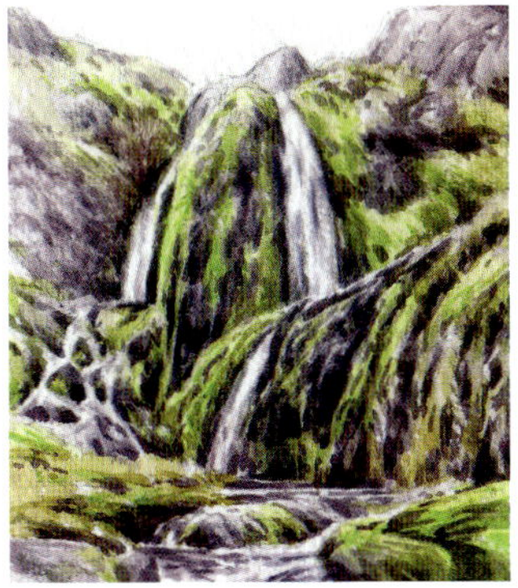

Deepdale Crag 14/6/09
Just east of the summit plateau but hardly worthy of a visit.

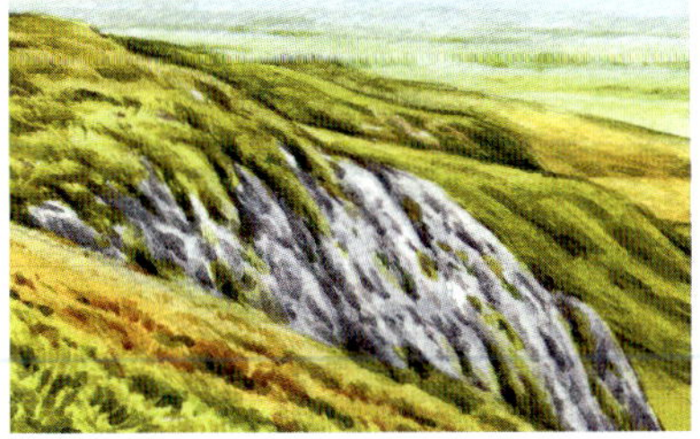

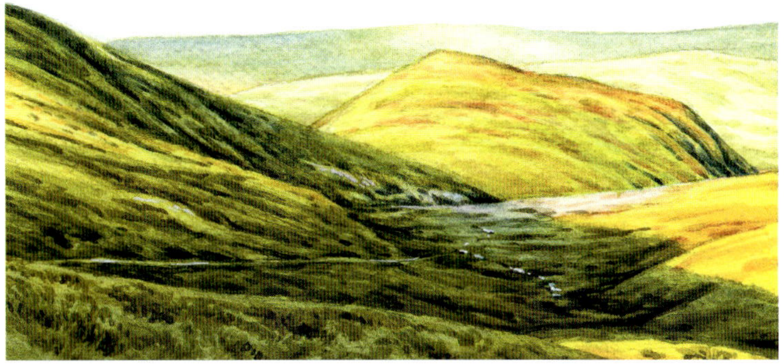

Sticks Pass looking east to Sheffield Pike 14/6/09
The reservoir has gone, leaving areas of bare gravel in the valley.

The summit 31/8/10
The slate slab that once stood on the lower summit has now been incorporated into this main cairn.

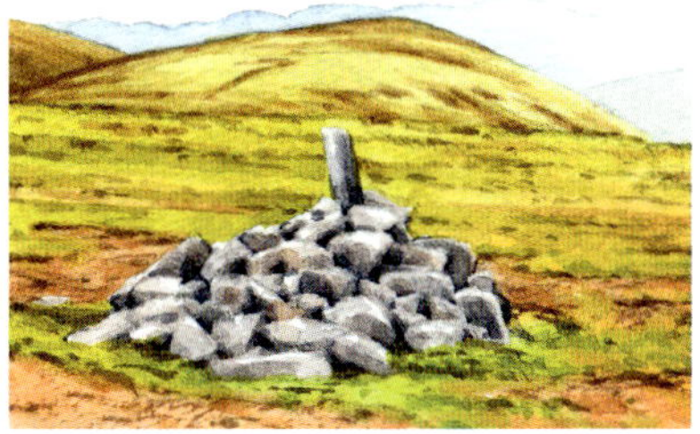

Ullswater from the east slope of Green Side 14/6/09
Glencoyne leads towards the lake.

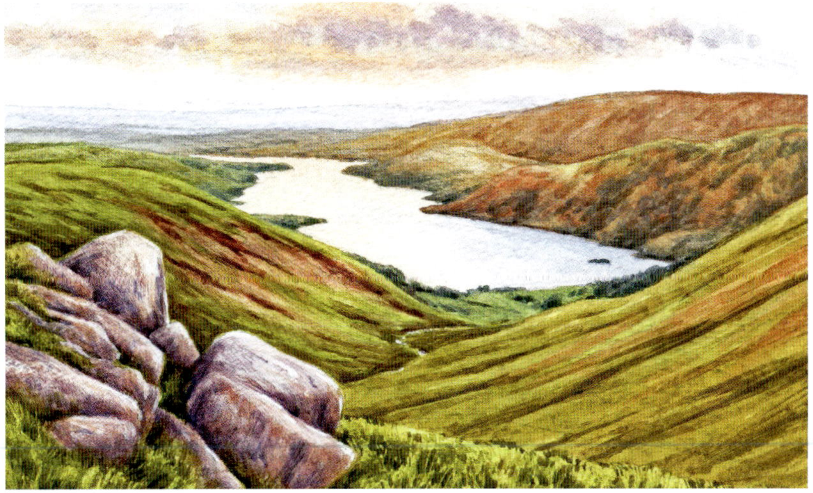

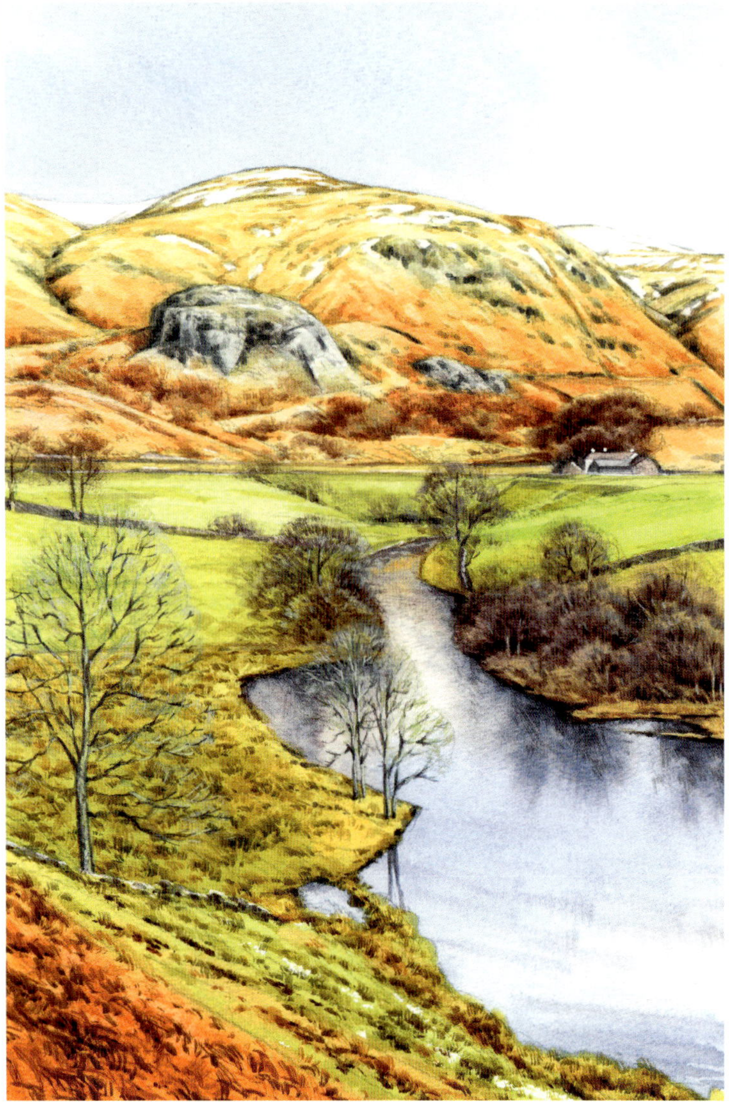

From Smathwaite 16/3/10
On a first viewing, some people may be disappointed that the fell does not actually rise to a peak as shown in AW's drawing. It is in fact more rounded as shown here, a trait of other fells in the range. Castle Rock lives up to its name on the smooth fell side.

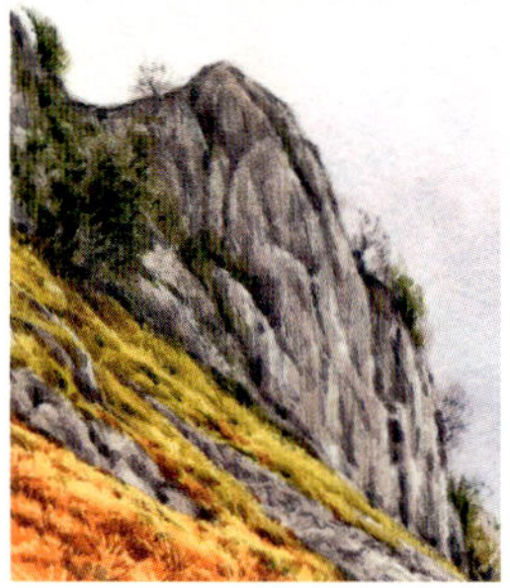

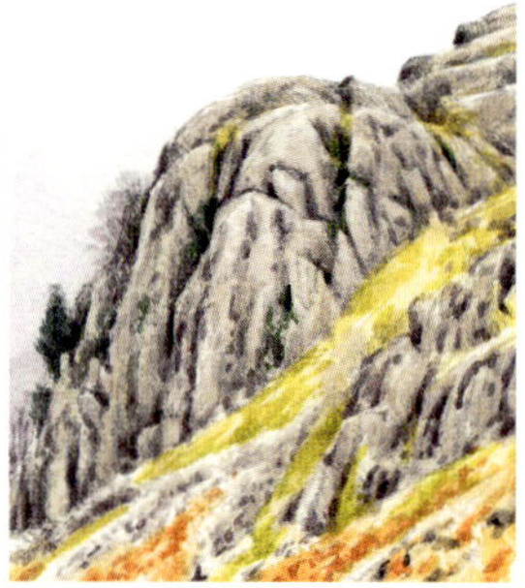

The Castle Rock of Triermain 14/3/12
From the north (left) and from the south (right) this west facing crag is well known to climbers. In 2011 a warning was issued of a potential collapse of a large portion of the north face. At the time of writing (January 2017) this had not happened.

Watson's Dodd

The name Dodd (or Dod on older maps) is given to bare rounded hills in the Lake District and other regions. Watson's Dodd is therefore an apt title although who the fell is named after is still uncertain.

The summit 26/3/09
To reach the cairn a detour of some 100 yards will have to be made from the main Dodd's ridge path.

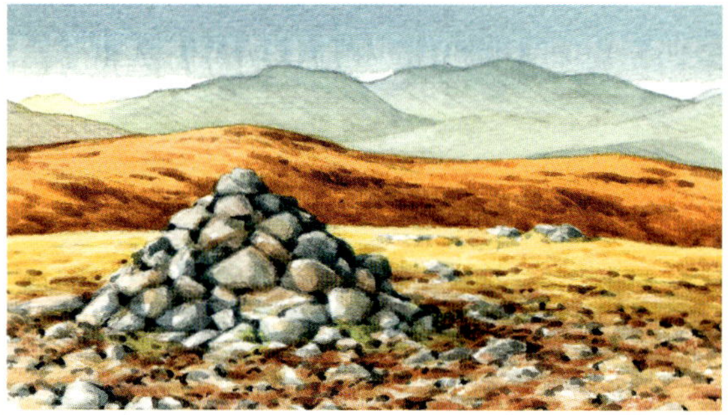

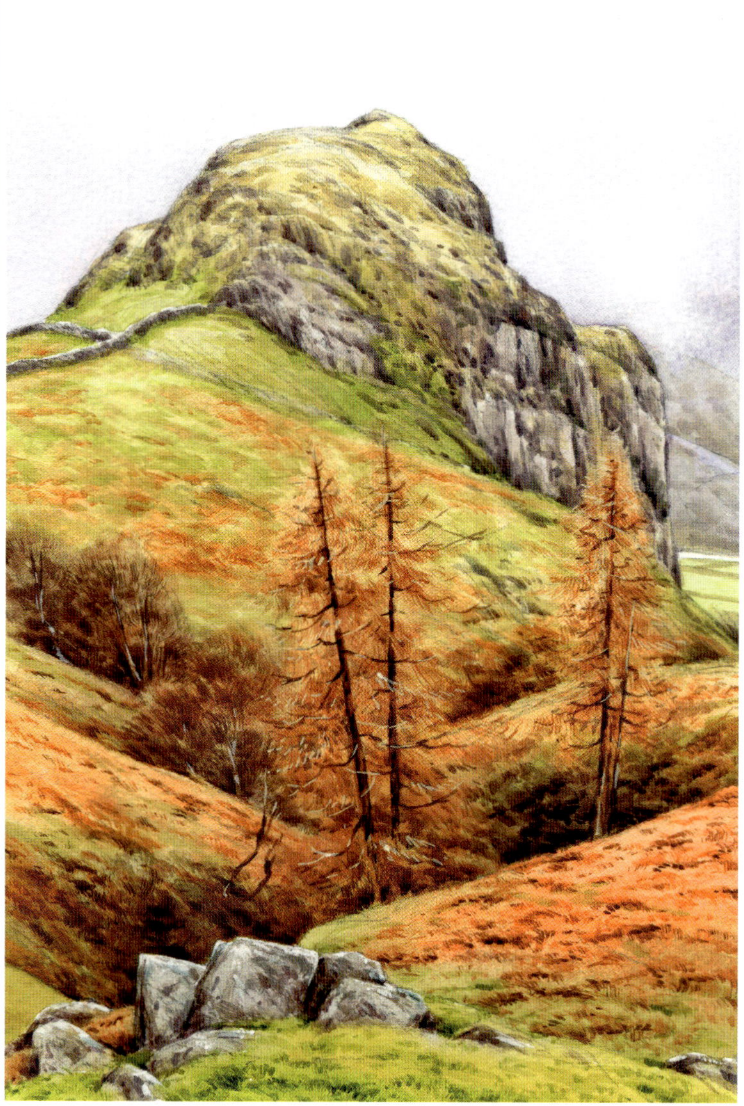

Castle Rock and Mill Gill 14/3/12
It is a fine outcrop of rock and a climber's playground, worthy of AW's full page drawing even when seen on a dull, damp but atmospheric day such as this. Some of his individual trees can still be identified in the scene today.

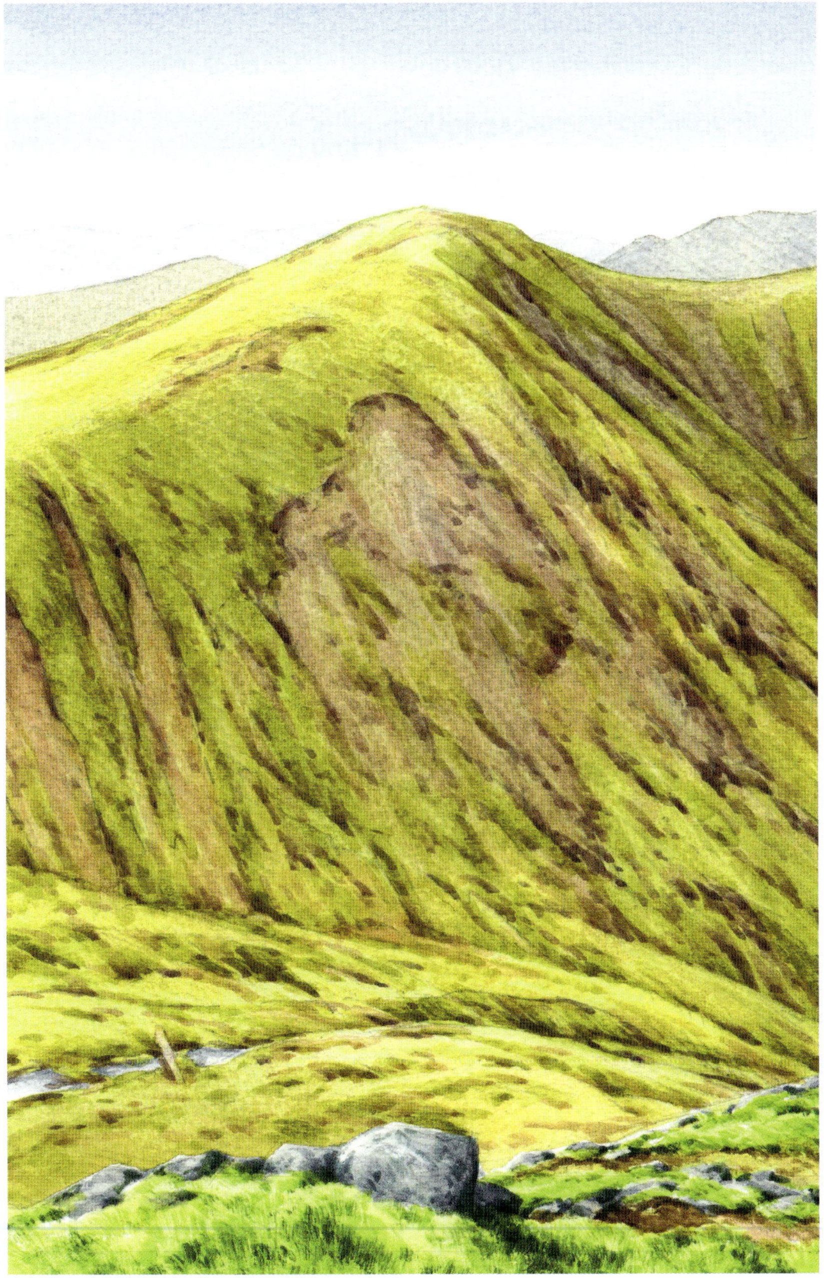

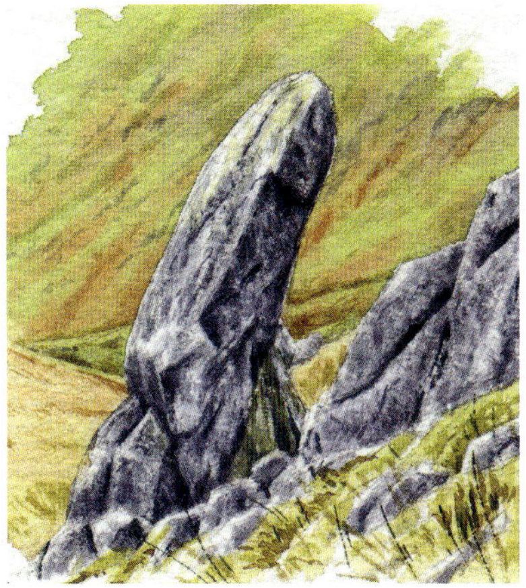

Rock pinnacle, Brown Crag 30/10/07

At only a height of four feet, this stone would not merit inclusion in chapters of more rugged fells.

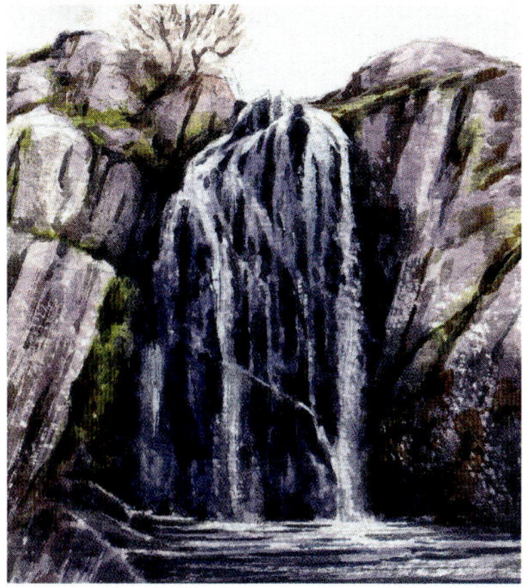

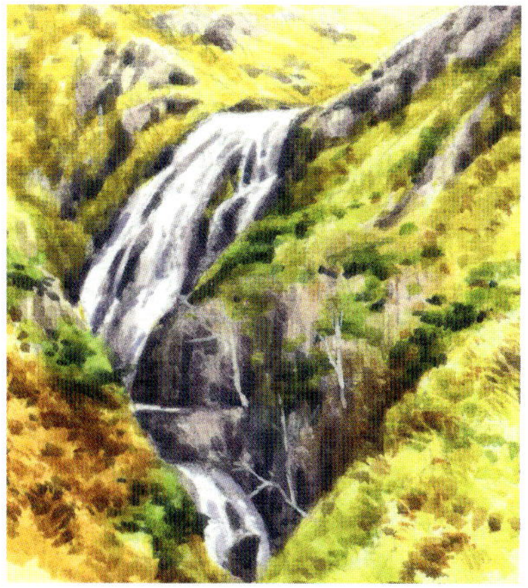

Waterfalls in Fisher Gill 30/10/07

There are several waterfalls in the gorge of Fisher Gill and to find the exact ones in these sketches required some deviation away from the path into the depths of the ravine. Since completing these sketches I have noticed that some of these gills have been fenced off and planted with trees. Soon these charming falls and others will be obscured from view.

White Side

Keppel Cove on the eastern side of the fell provides an area of bare rock and scree on what would otherwise be a large grassy fell. A good path from the village of Glenridding leads directly to the summit from where there are extensive views of many fells.

From Catstycam 25/9/09

A position on the north-west ridge of Catstycam provides this prospect of the fell and the hills beyond.

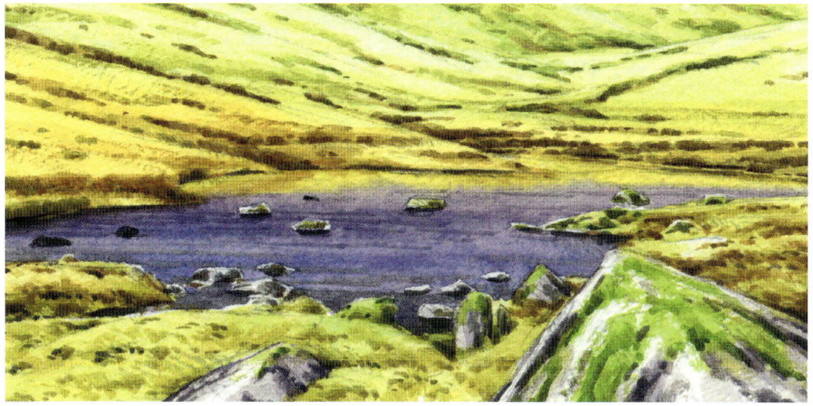

Tarn in Brown Cove 11/12/09

A curiosity here for me. Wainwright produces a fairly plain drawing of the tarn but close to this point are the interesting remains of an old stone built dam across the outlet which, artistically, would have perhaps made a better subject. He only marks a ruin at this place and not a dam.

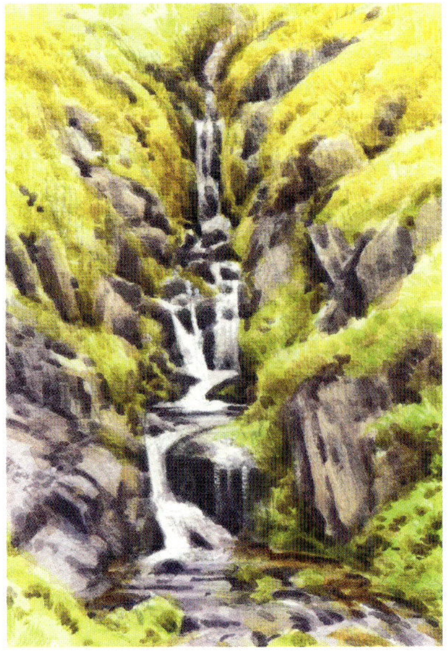

Rocky Gorge, Brund Gill
30/10/07
A narrow ravine hidden away on the hill side with a series of falls.

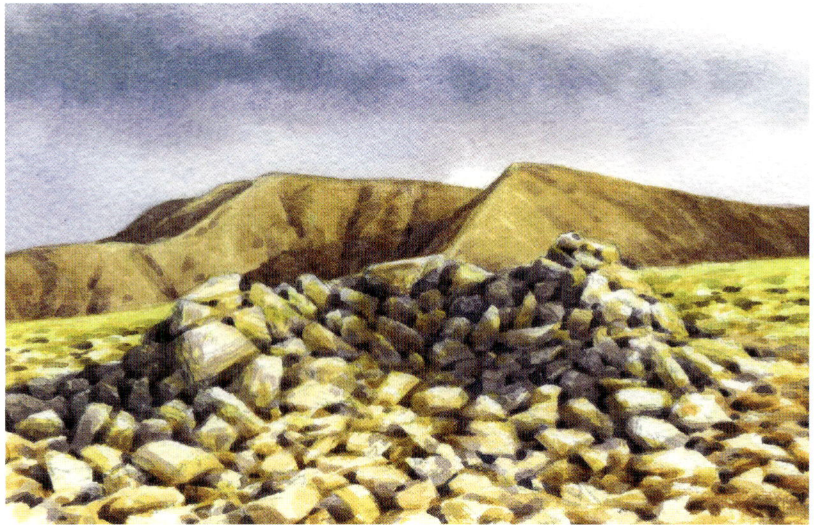

The summit 14/6/09
The cairn has been enlarged and shaped into a basic wind shelter.

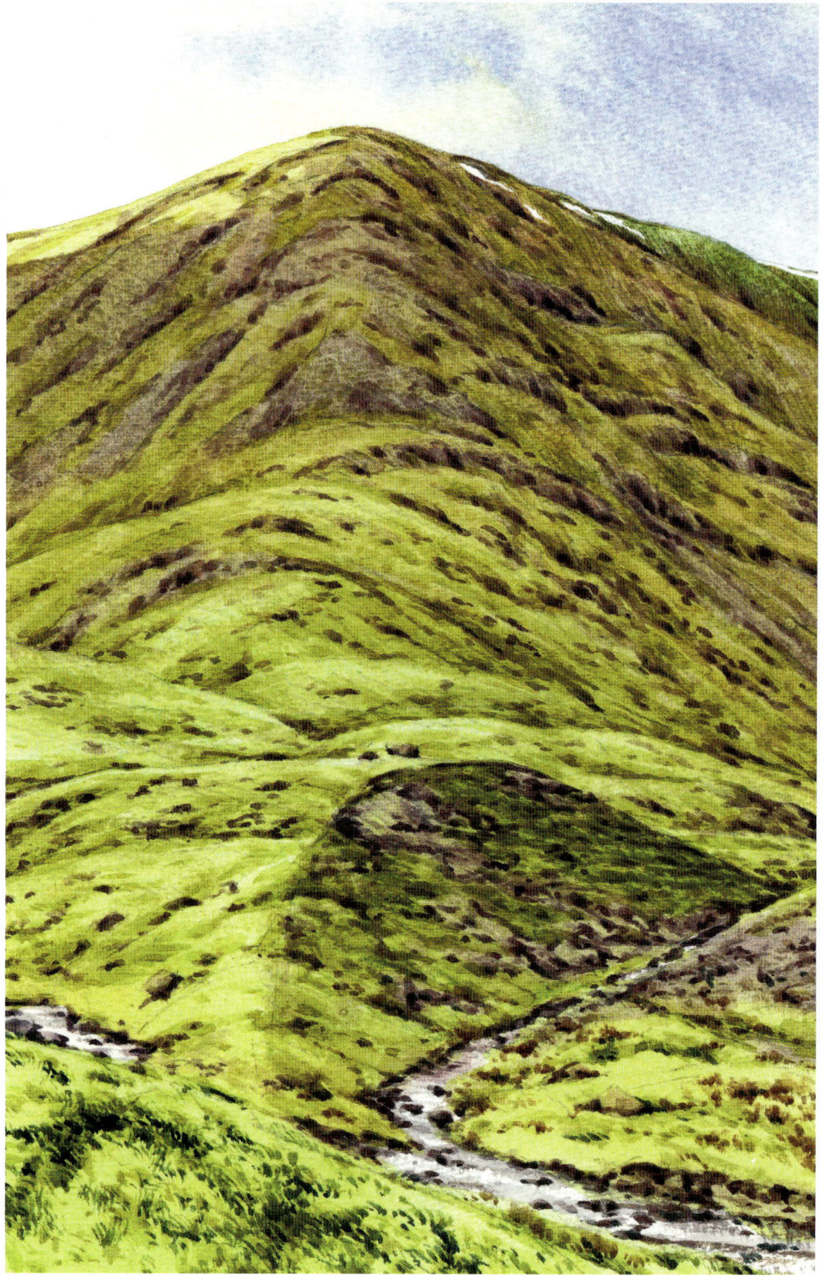

The East Ridge 11/12/09
The burst banks of Keppelcove Tarn are slowly being reclaimed by nature. The ridge itself is still not a regular route for walkers. I climbed it one winter's day, the snow and ice over the stony, loose ground made for a rather exciting ascent.

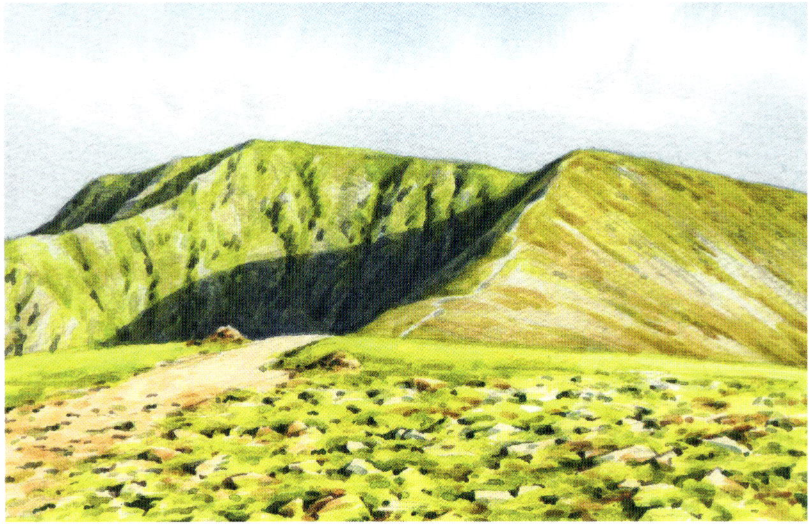

The ridge south 14/6/09
An illustration not unlike the one of the summit, but this time from a point on the broad path south of the top which gives a better view of the bulk of Helvellyn.

The Far Eastern Fells

In the second book of the series Wainwright covered the thirty six fells which are to the east of the Ullswater and Kirkstone Pass boundary. The landscape in this region is generally pleasant in nature more than dramatic, with grassy gentle ridges connecting many of the fells. On 8th June 1930, long before the work on the Pictorial Guides, Wainwright first set foot on the high Lakeland Fells which would become such a major part of his life. It was here in the Far Eastern Fells that he chose to take those initial steps of his fellwalking experiences.

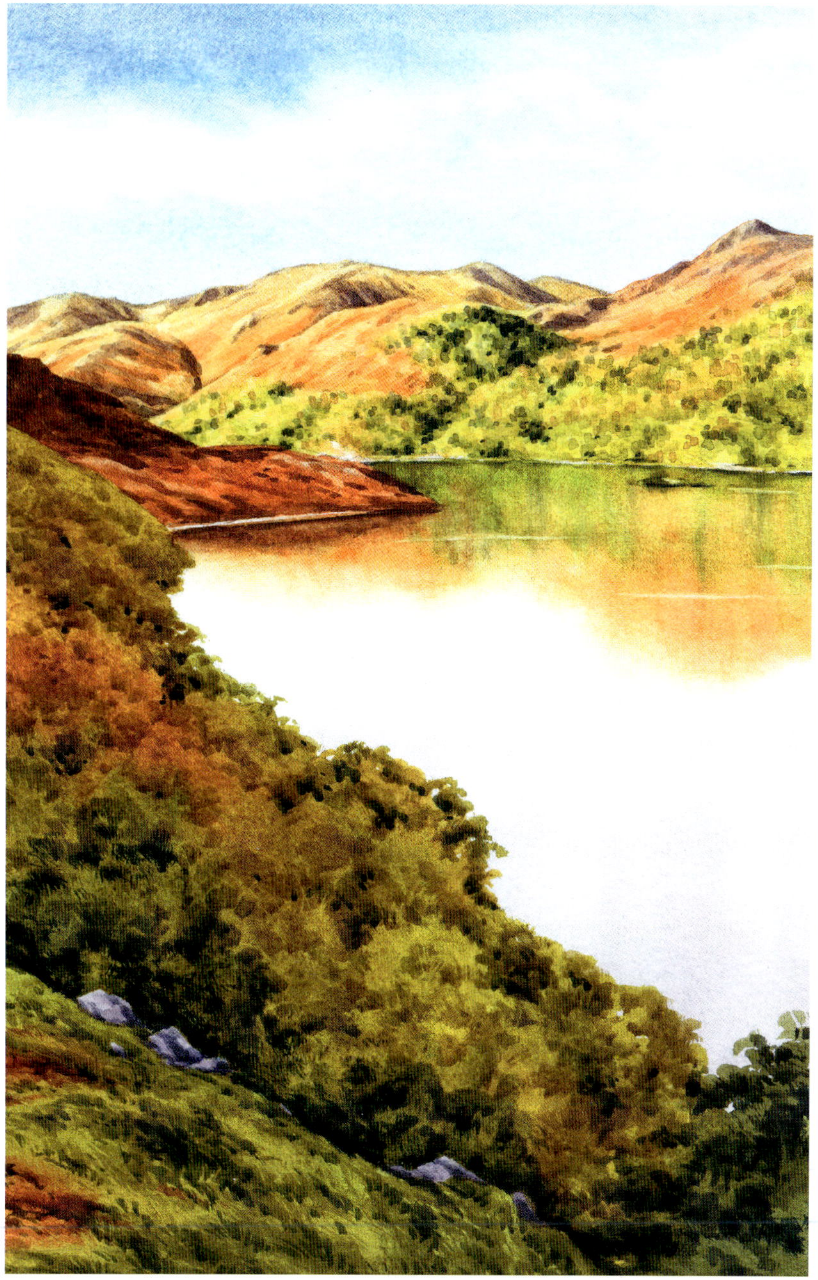

Frontispiece - Ullswater from near Silver Crag 12/10/09

The lakeside path under the slopes of Place Fell was described by AW as *"the most beautiful and rewarding walk in Lakeland"* and this page gave him the opportunity to illustrate the scene. Once again as in the frontispiece of Book One, he has chosen to fill the page with a view of fells from another region, this time looking south towards the Helvellyn range of the Eastern Fells.

Angletarn Pikes

Topped by a pair of rocky peaks the fell is perhaps best known for its delightful tarn which many walkers pass by on the way to or from High Street's summit.

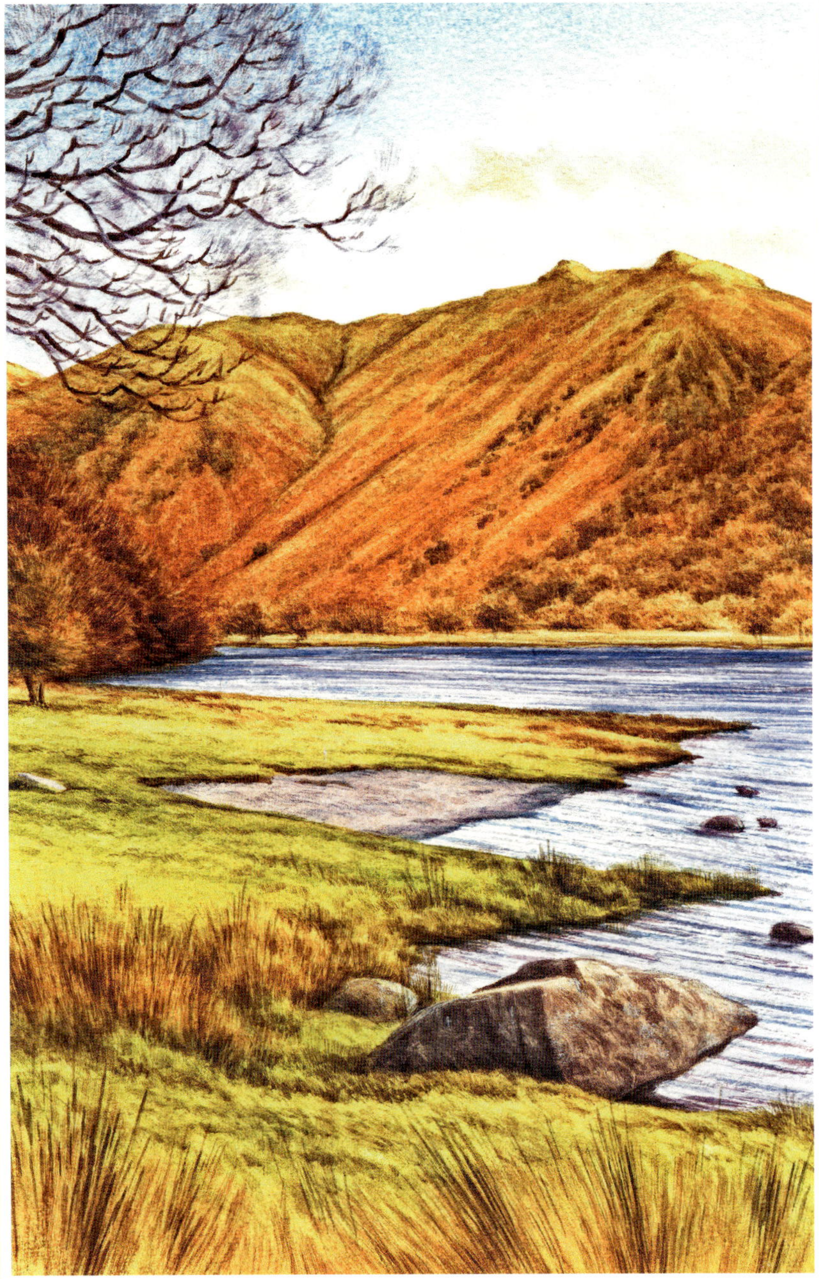

From Brotherswater 25/11/08

The shoreline has changed shape over time but the angular rock in the foreground still defines the location of AW's point of view.

Red Screes and Brotherswater from the top of Dubhow Beck 30/10/11

A fine vista from the narrow path that contours around the slopes of Stony Rigg.

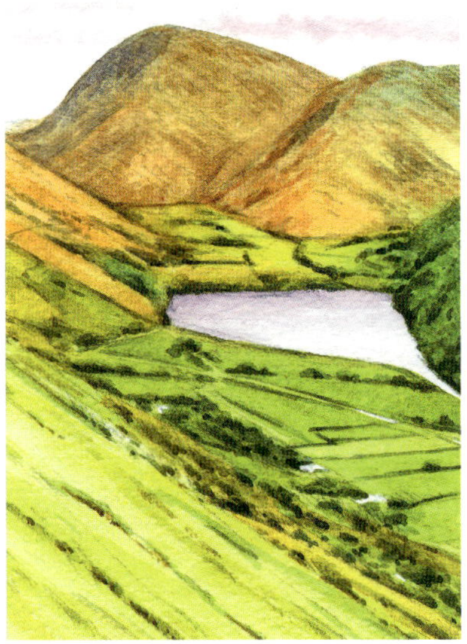

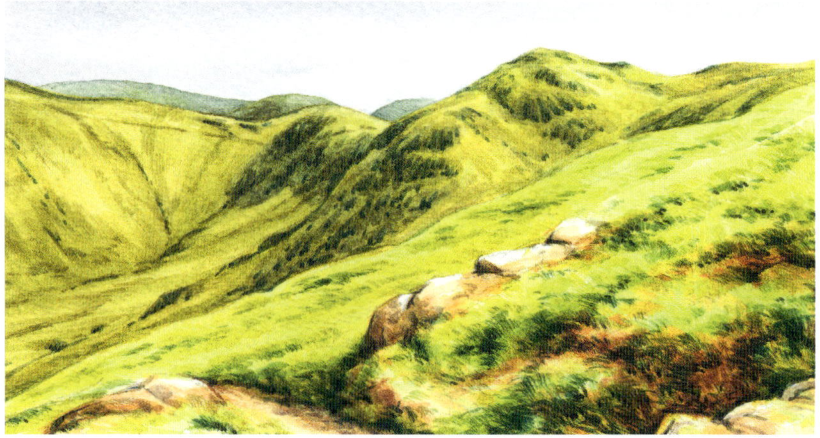

Heck Crag from the Patterdale - Martindale path 5/7/09

The head of Bannerdale from the path just as it descends from the Beda Fell ridge.

The north (main) summit 2/9/08

A heather clad outcrop indicates the highest point of the fell, it overlooks a peat bog and the other lower top.

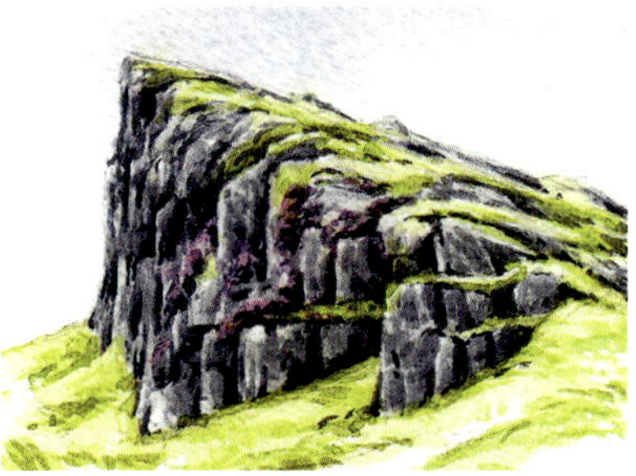

Angle Tarn from the south summit 2/9/08

An untidy small cairn with a fine commanding view of the tarn.

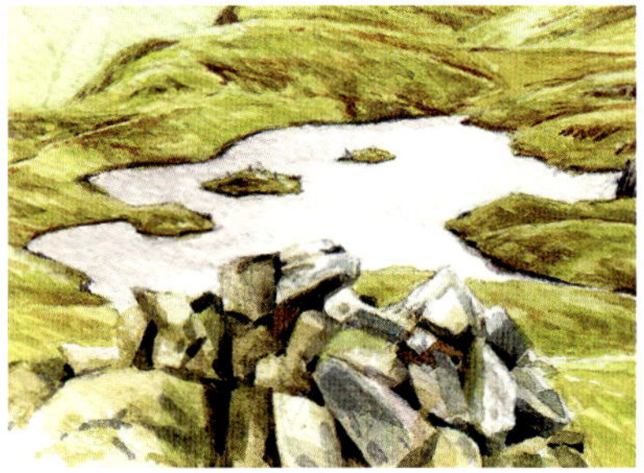

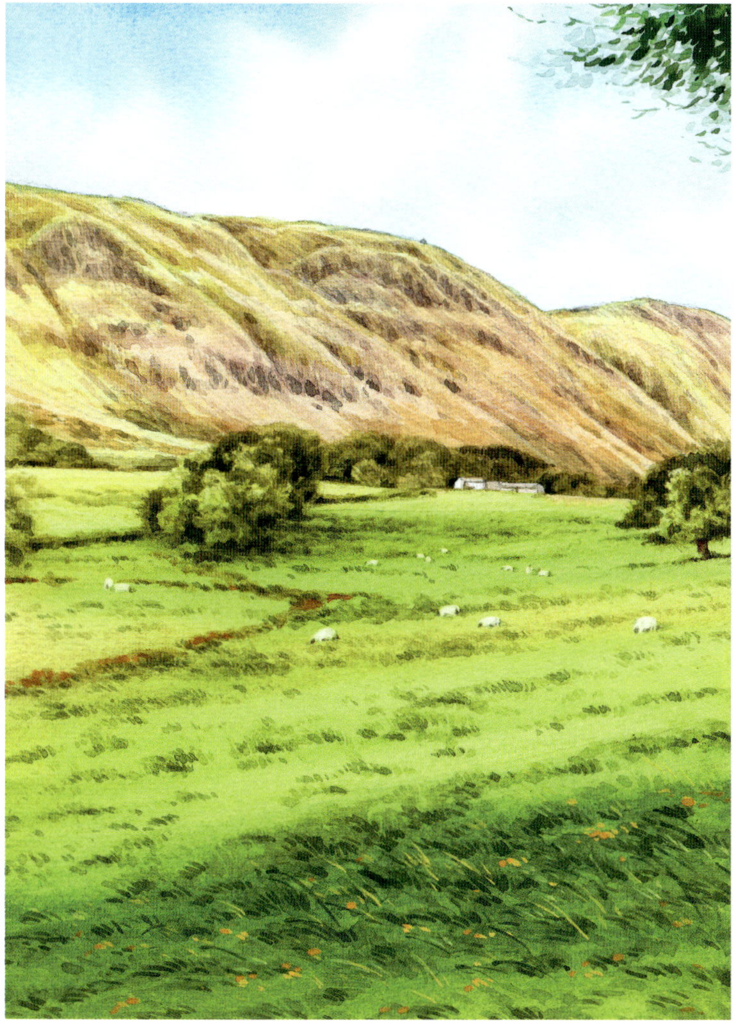

Arthur's Pike

The northernmost of the Far Eastern Fells, Arthur's Pike sits above the flat pastureland that meets Ullswater. The craggy western face of the fell is in contrast to the other sides which are mostly uniform grassy slopes.

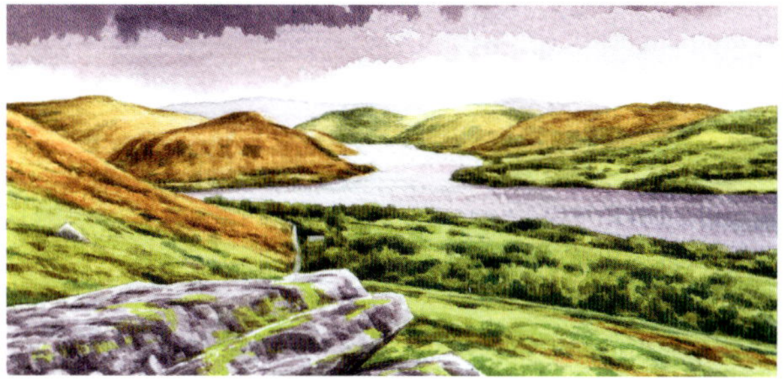

Ullswater from the Howtown path 26/5/10
The scene from under Auterstone Crag.

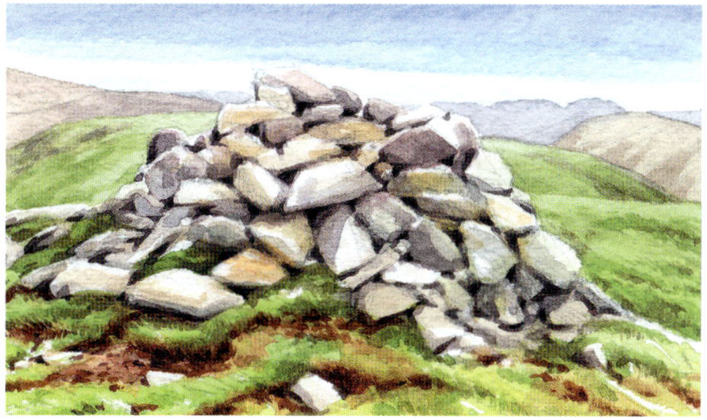

The Summit 24/6/08
This larger cairn now occupies the top of the fell.

From the Howtown road 25/9/09
Viewed from just inside the field as the hedgerow is now too high to see over.

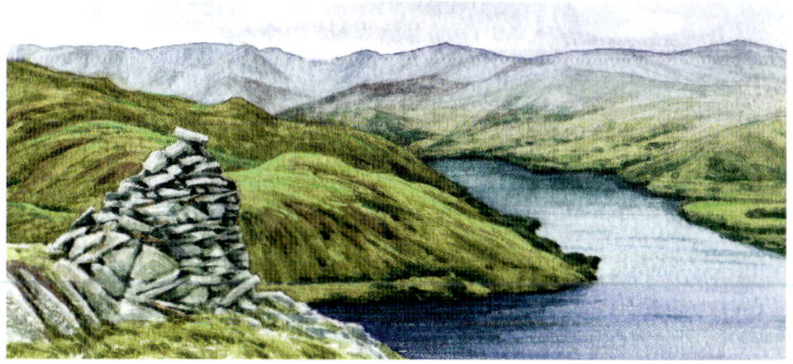

Swarthbeck Gill 26/5/10
This view of the gorse and tree lined steep ravine is from the Howtown path near Swarthbeck Farm.

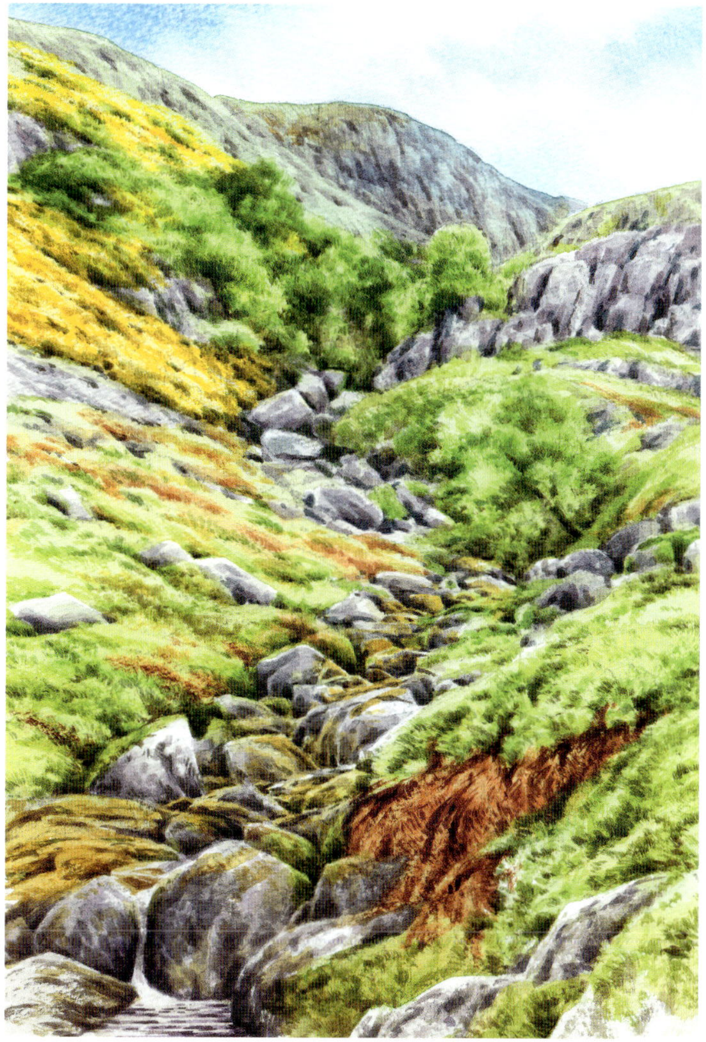

Ullswater from the beacon 24/6/08
The beacon remains almost as it was in his drawing, the view is timeless.

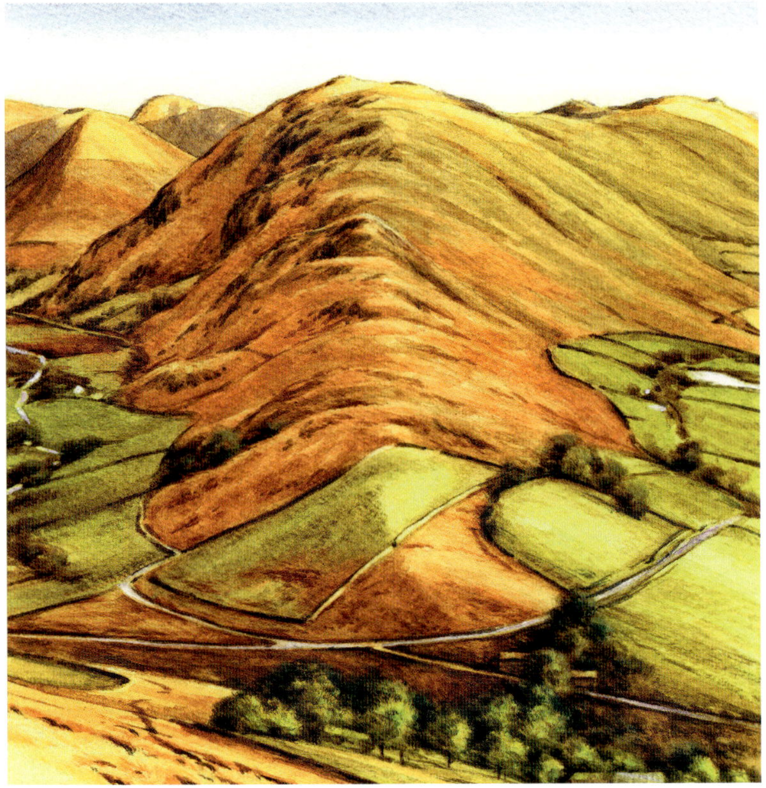

From Hallin Fell 21/4/09
About half way up the south eastern path of Hallin Fell this scene comes fully into view. Clearly showing where fell meets pasture.

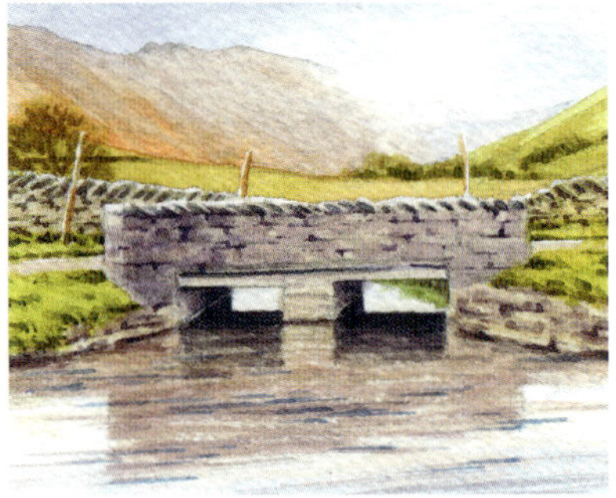

Bridge in Boardale 26/5/10
Obviously rebuilt since AW's day.

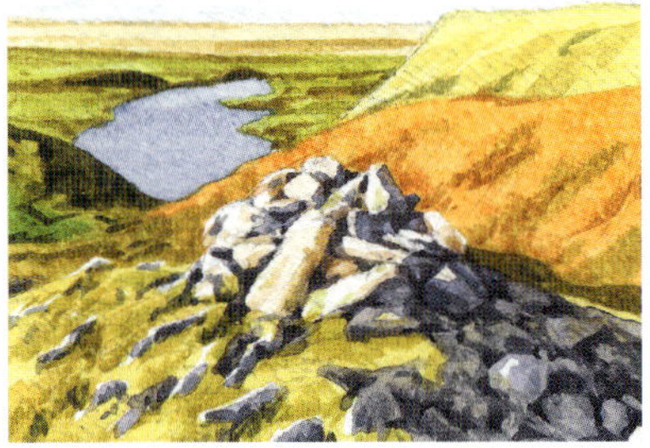

The summit 21/4/09
Looking north to Ullswater.

The ridge south 2/9/08
The cairn above Broad Crags with the path on the left which leads on to Angletarn Pikes.

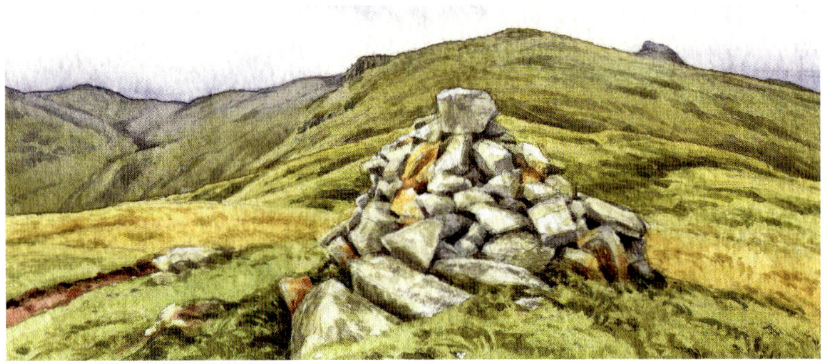

Beda Fell

Forming a defining ridge between Martindale and Boredale this fell provides wonderful views of the hidden farmland as well as the high fells which surround these quiet valleys. AW's spelling of "Boardale" only appears on the 1 inch scale maps of the time, larger scale maps used the spelling Boredale.

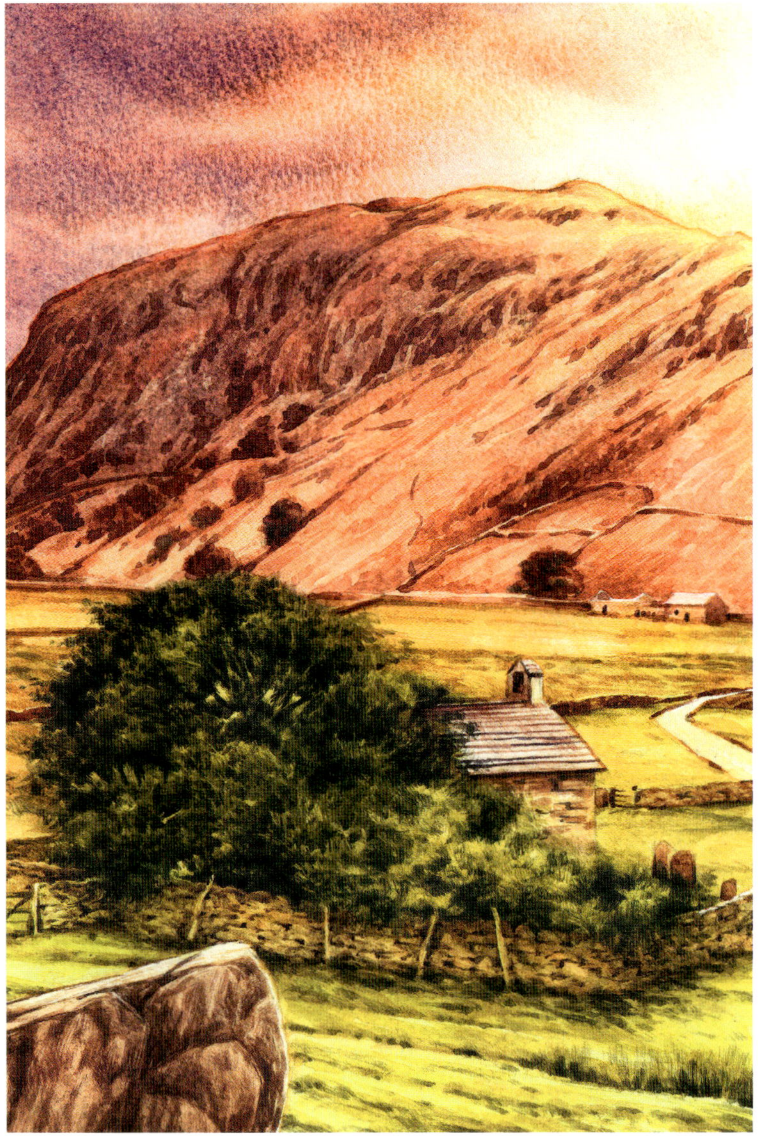

Beda Fell from Martindale Old Church 21/4/09
AW's drawing depicted a late afternoon scene with the light coming from the west. So that is how I have depicted it, with the glow of the setting sun over the ridge. He omitted the farm at Knicklethorns.

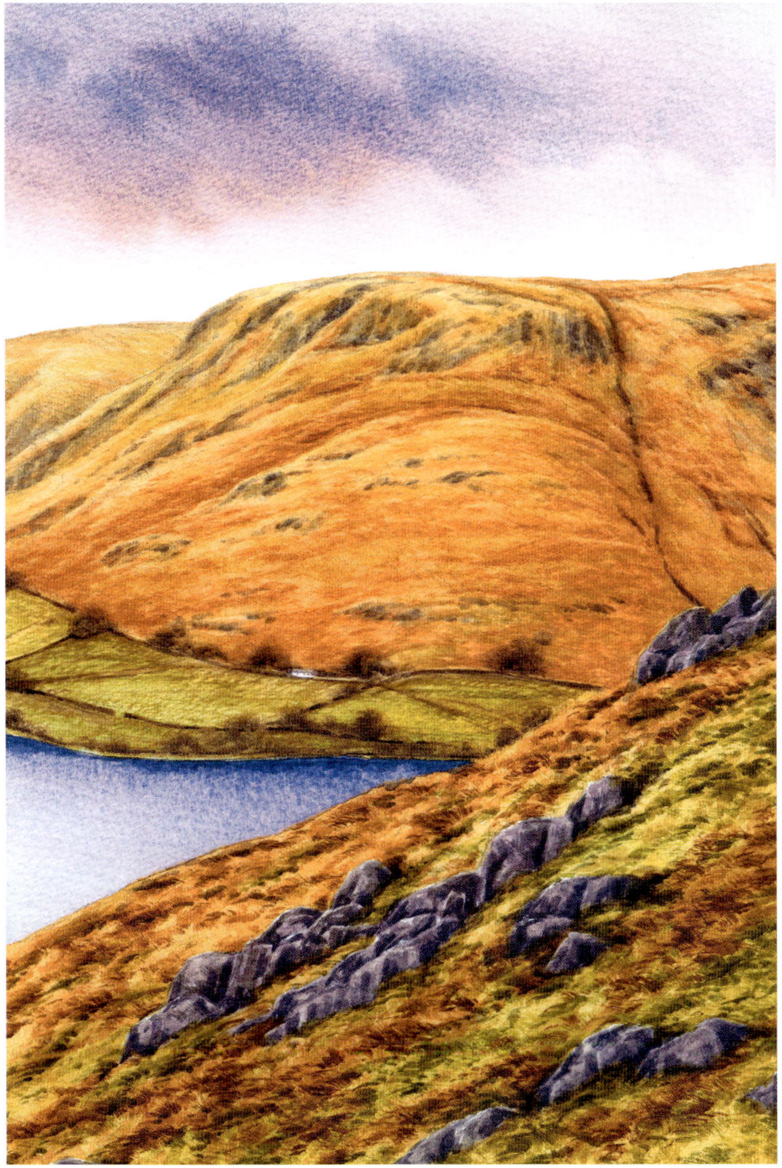

From Hallin Fell 13/3/09

This aspect of Bonscale Pike can be observed from the slopes of Hallin Fell, not far from the northern cairn and overlooking Howtown Wyke.

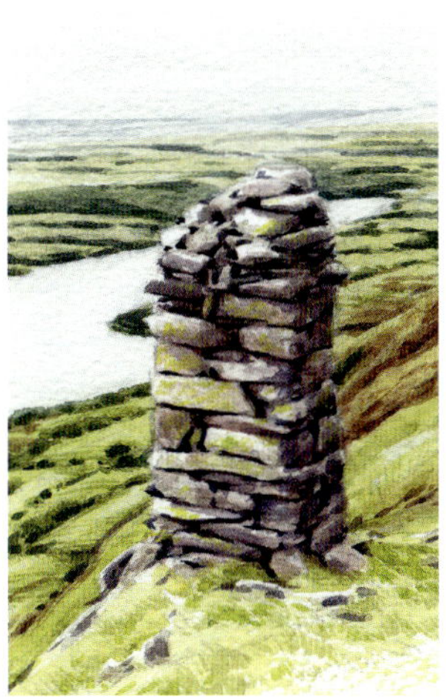

Bonscale Tower 24/6/08

This is the original column which remains virtually unchanged but now has a new companion above it.

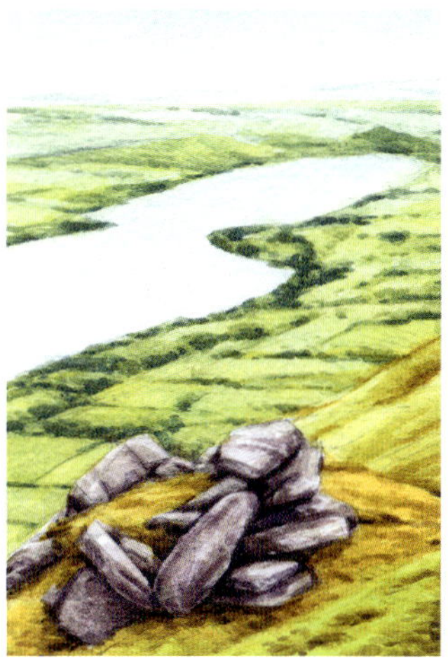

The higher pillar 29/2/12

This *"effort of amateurs"* has all but gone. A more recent tower now stands above the one shown on the left.

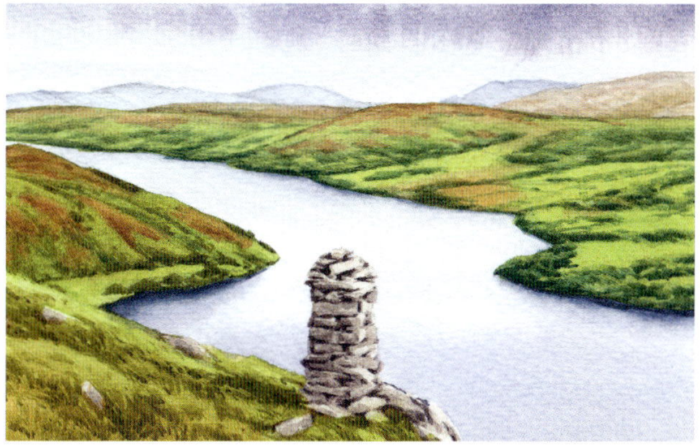

Ullswater: the middle reach 24/6/08

Wainwright opted to include the more professionally constructed tower in this view and it has stood the test of time to still be seen today.

Standing stone 24/6/08

Three of the standing stones have been re-erected but this one that AW drew now lies flat. Reference to these stones has been deleted from the revised guides.

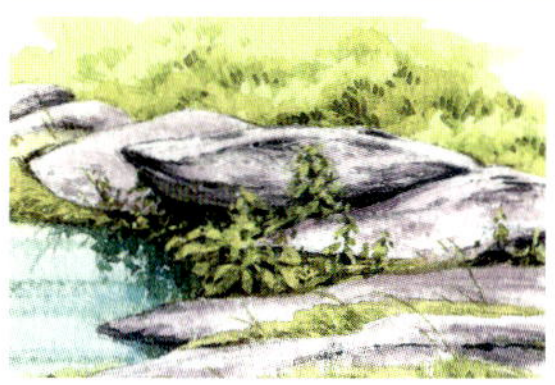

Bonscale Pike

Wainwright didn't rate this fell too highly but personally I have enjoyed my visits. The views over Ullswater are a delight and the stone towers add interest to many a photograph. A pleasant couple of hours walking can take in this fell from the ferry terminal at nearby Howtown.

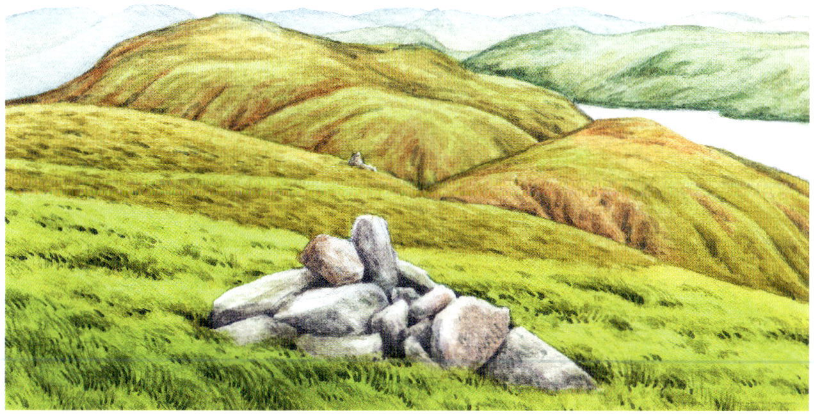

The summit 24/6/08

As Wainwright rightly states, this cairn doesn't mark the highest point, more of a good viewpoint. The site of the fallen pillar can just be seen beyond.

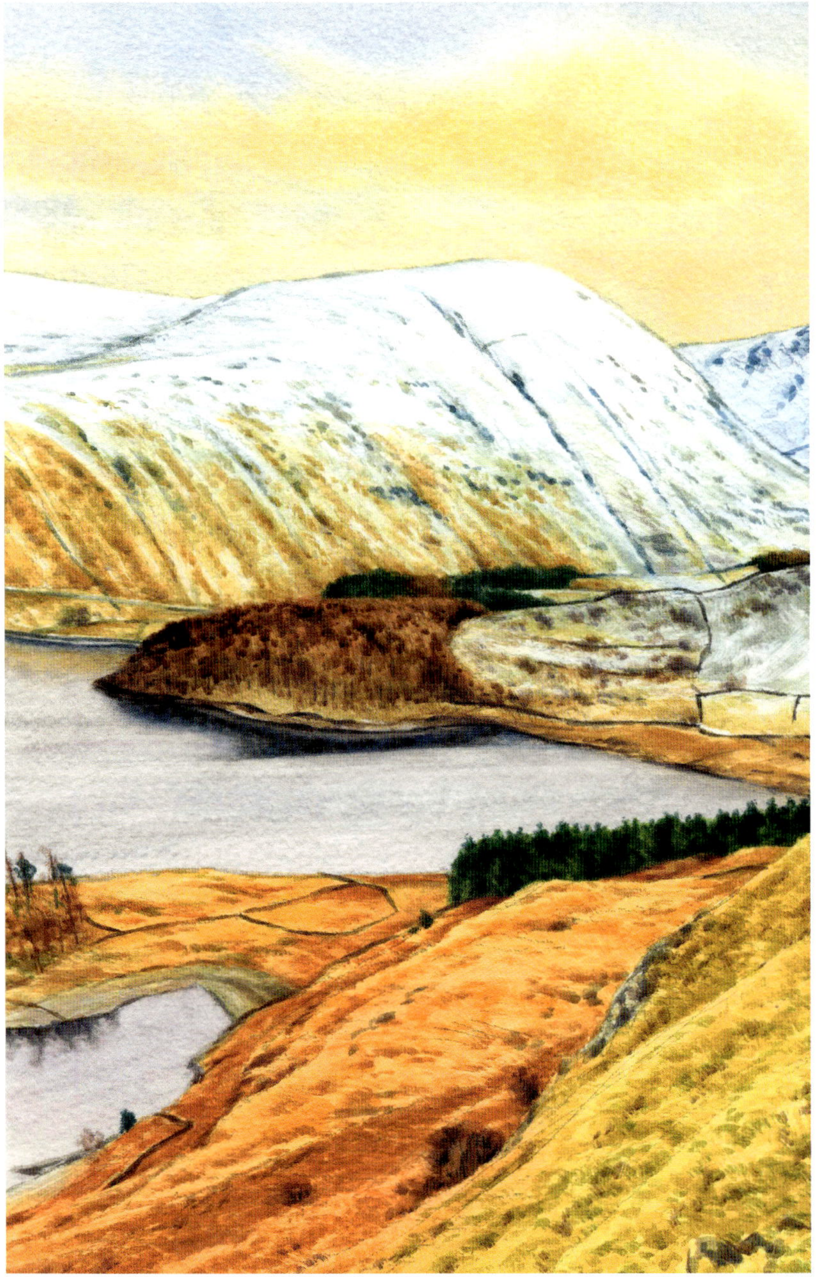

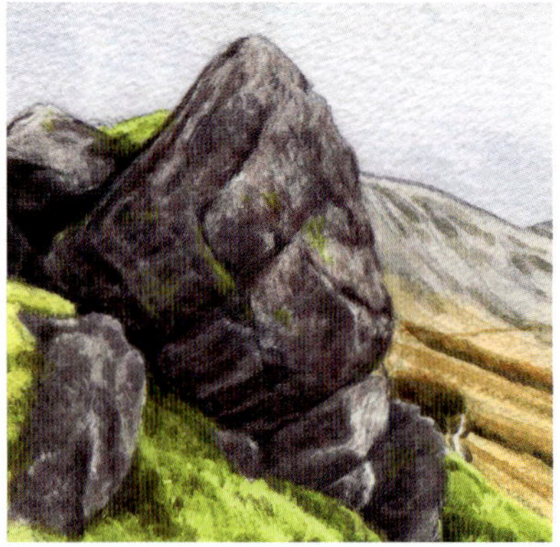

Hollow Stone 17/3/09
The shelter space is limited and its regular occupants would appear to be sheep. Its close proximity to the road perhaps offered AW some shelter from the elements as he waited for the bus.

From the south-east ridge of High Raise 2/3/10
Nearing the end of a great winter's day walk I managed to capture this scene as the muted afternoon light was fading. Apart from a new stand of conifers the scene still remains relatively unchanged.

Branstree

A rounded mound of a hill which sits near the head of Mardale. It isn't overly exciting but an ascent of the north ridge affords some fine views of the near fells of Mardale Ill Bell and High Street. Usually it is visited as part of a route around Mardale Head which may incorporate other more interesting fells.

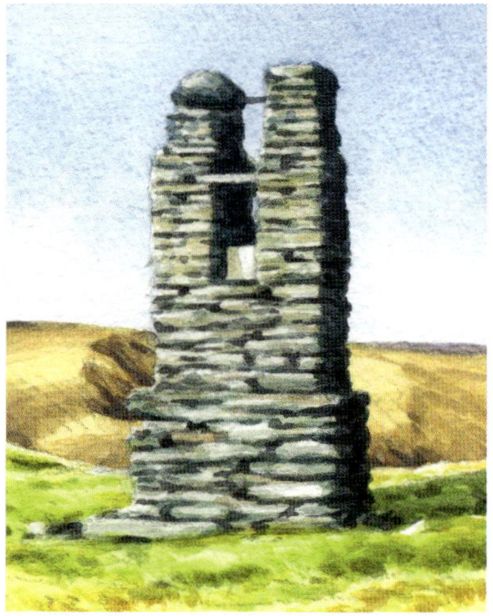

The survey post 17/3/09
One of several such features in this region. Used in the construction of the Haweswater aqueduct.

The cairn on Artlecrag Pike 17/3/09
There are now a pair of matching cairns here and without background detail in his sketch it took some deduction as to which was the correct one and the correct angle of view. The clue was the low W shaped pointed rocks to the right of the cairn's base.

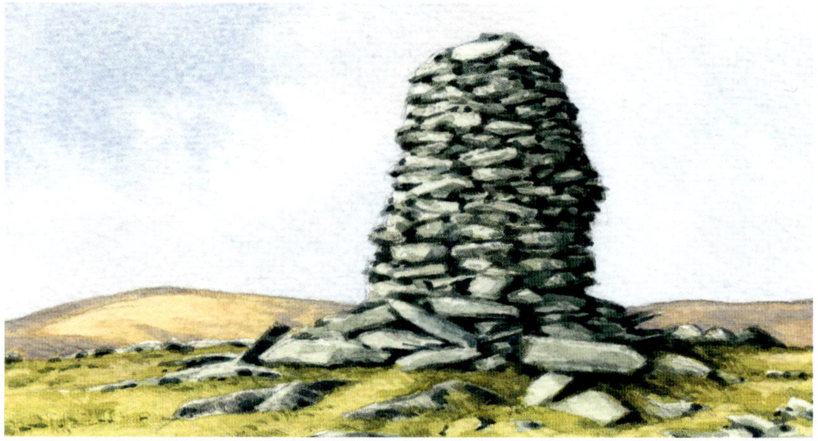

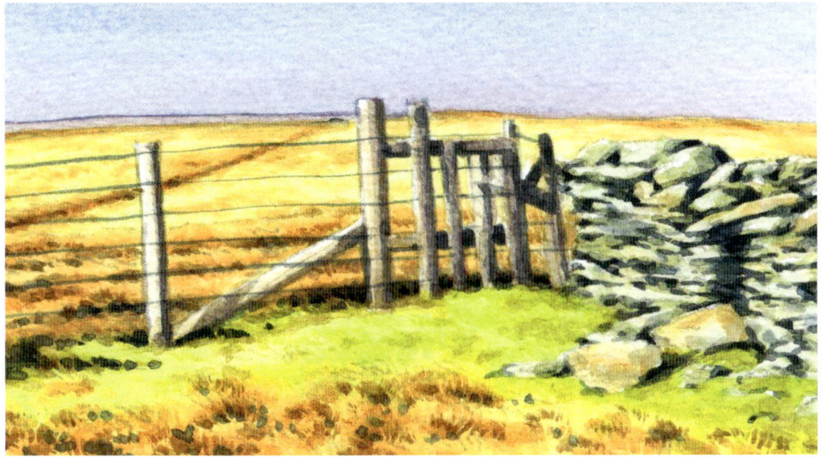

The summit 17/3/09

In AW's day there was nothing of interest to illustrate the actual highest point so he chose to draw the nearby wall end and fence. The ground level triangulation station concrete ring at the summit was built in early 1961, some years after AW completed his work on this book. The ring is one of only two on the Wainwright fells, the other being on Blencathra. A small cairn of a couple of dozen stones now sits adjacent to it.

Harter Crag from the slopes of Branstree 17/3/09

When ascending the fell from the direction of Gatesgarth Pass a pause for breath on the steep incline will provide this view.

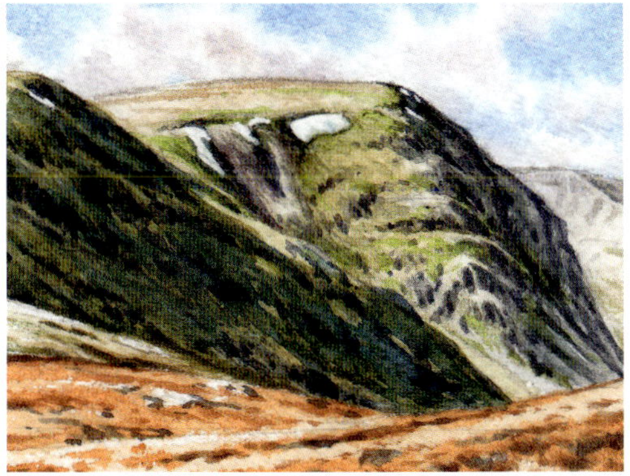

Mosedale Cottage 10/5/09

At one time used as a shepherd's hut the neat cottage is now adopted as a mountain bothy. The building has had a coat of white paint and the roof was modified in recent years. Inside it is tidy and fairly clean, please respect it if you pay a visit.

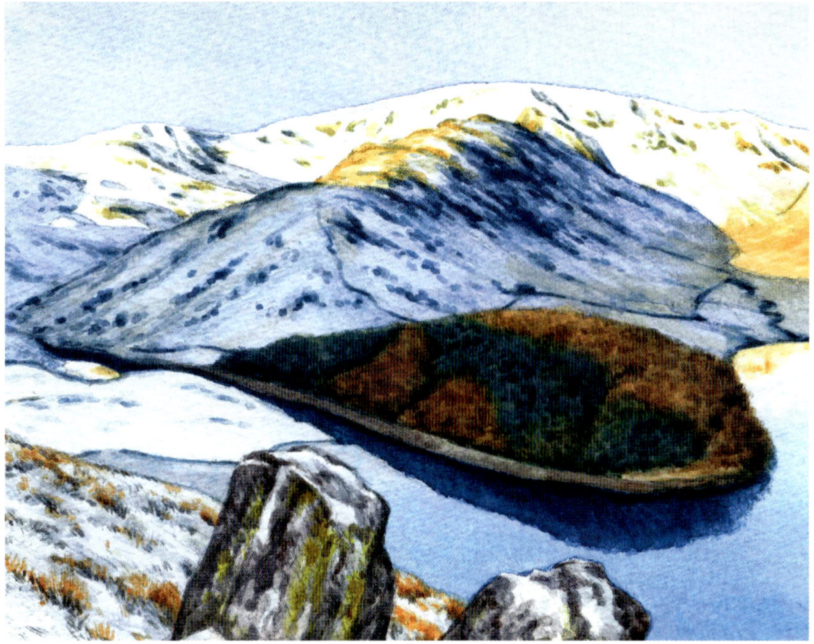

High Street from the north ridge 2/3/10

As well as this view, the ascent of the north ridge provided the references for two other sketches in the High Street and Mardale Ill Bell chapters hence the similarity in the weather conditions in all three of my sketches.

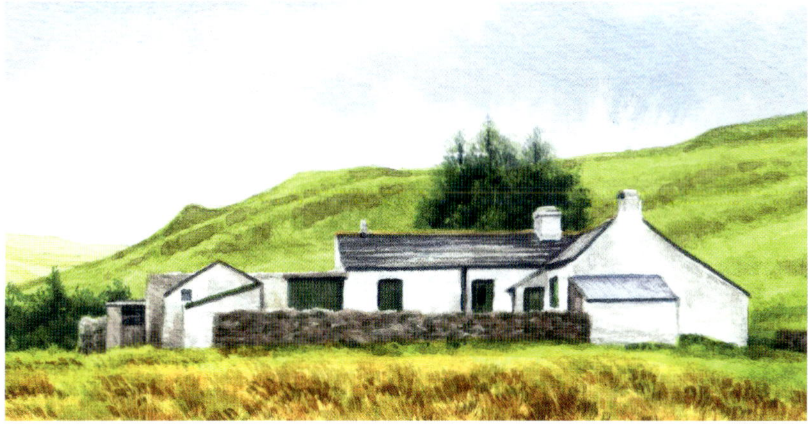

Where Eagles Soared

Throughout the district many high crags and a few fells have names taken from types of raptors which in times past must have frequented these locations and give an indication of how widespread these species were. Today, whilst wandering the fells it is possible to see some of these birds such as kestrels, buzzards, peregrine falcons and if you are lucky, merlins. Ospreys have also returned to breed in the area in recent years. Most famous of all though were the golden eagles which resided in the valley of Riggindale near Haweswater (seen in the sketch on the left). Eagles had returned to the Lake District in the 1950s and a pair first bred near Haweswater in 1969. A total of 16 chicks were fledged at this site and another four elsewhere in the region. When the last female died in 2004 a single male was left on his own in Riggindale. Sadly in April 2016, at the age of about 20 he disappeared from the scene possibly dying from old age, we may never know. A lack of quality habitat and food in the area means that it is unlikely we will witness these beautiful birds soaring over the Lakeland Fells in the foreseeable future. Perhaps one or two from southern Scotland will see the Cumbrian hills as a good place to set up home in the years ahead.

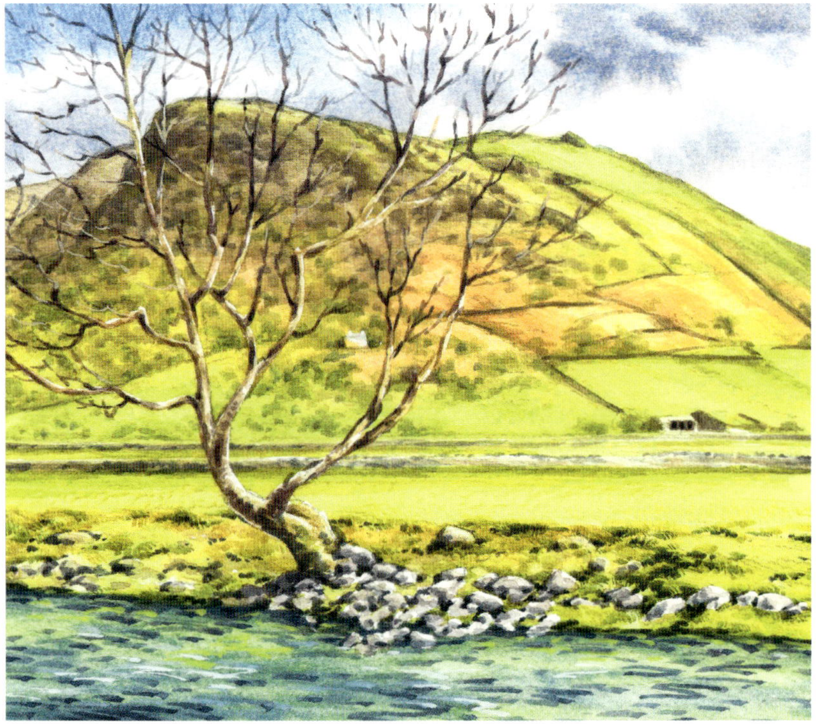

The summit looking south
5/7/09

A late walk on a fine summer's evening provided me with the opportunity to obtain these two summit views. Gray Crag and Raven Crag flank Threshwaite Glen. It was 7.20 pm and a perfect quiet time to be up on the fells.

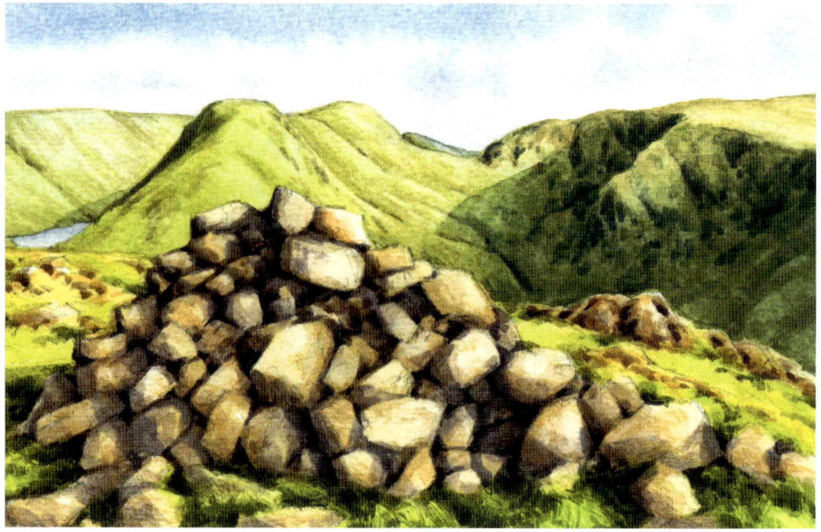

From Goldrill Beck 6/4/11

This viewpoint is from the west bank of the stream not far from the Cow Bridge car park. My first visit to obtain the photograph was thwarted by the tree being in full leaf so a return was required during early Spring. Even then, I have had to artistically "prune" the tree for a reasonably clear view of the fell, as well as other foreground branches which overhang on this side of the beck.

Brock Crags

Positioned some 400 yards to the west of the main Patterdale to High Street path, Brock Crags is often bypassed by casual walkers. From its summit almost half of the Eastern Fells are in view as well as many other tops in all directions. A place certainly worthy of a detour especially on a clear day.

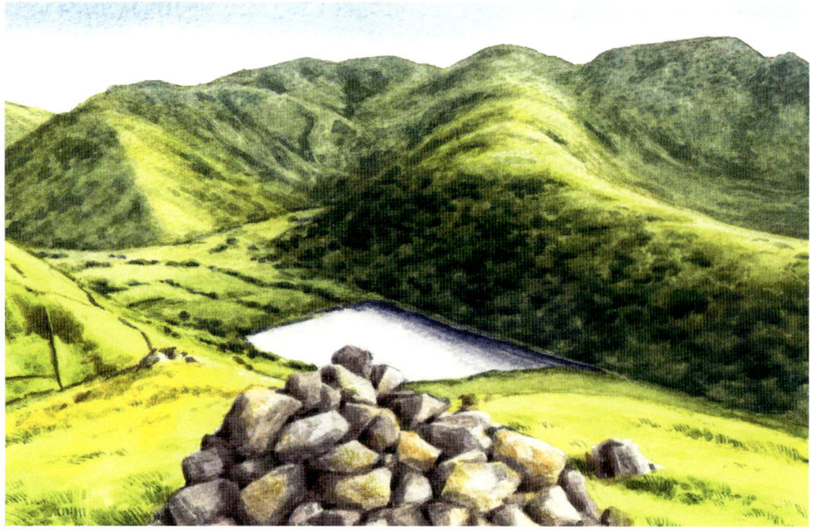

The summit looking south-west 5/7/09

By moving slightly to the left behind the cairn this aspect was easily captured with the Fairfield range as the main subject. Both views almost join into a panorama.

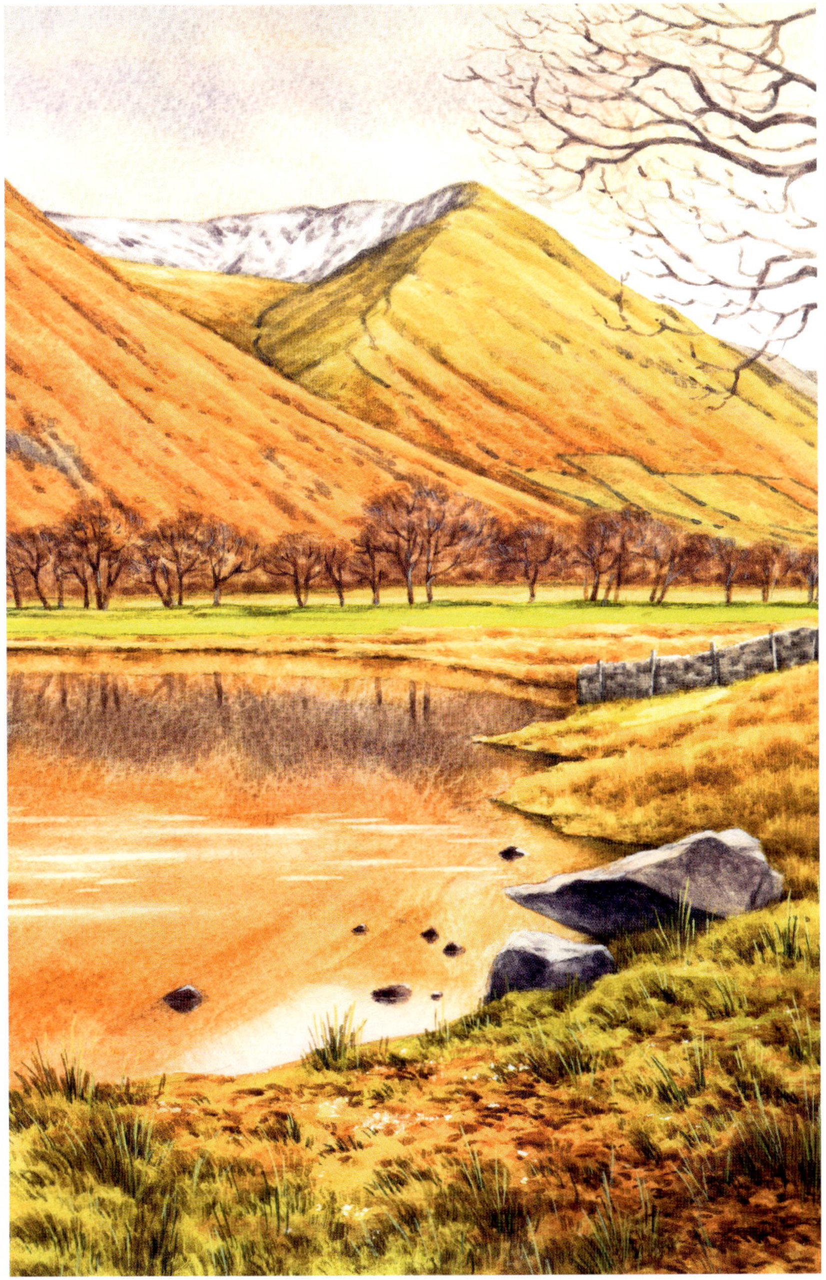

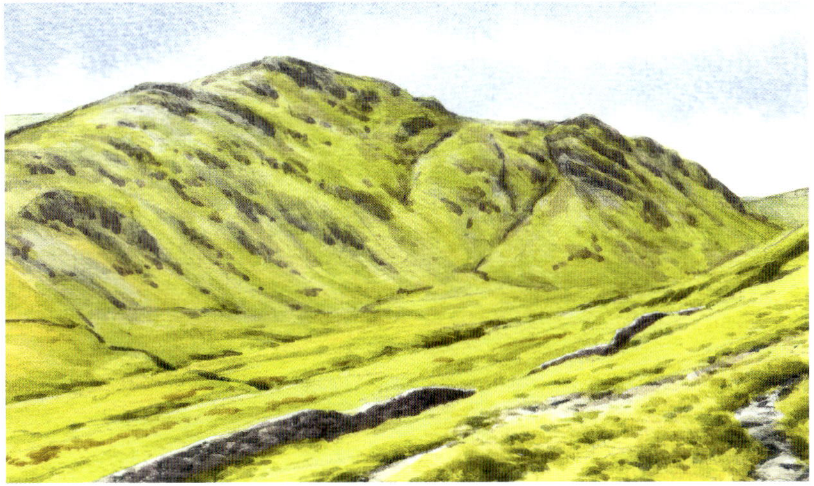

Caudale Moor from below Scot Rake 8/6/10

Once again I was out of luck in trying to obtain this reference in winter conditions. The path here leads up to Threshthwaite Mouth.

Caudale Moor

Forming the east wall of the Kirkstone Pass, the fell rises up from behind the Inn. Caudale Moor is the name given to the whole fell whereas Stony Cove Pike is really just the summit name. A choice of any of the six ridges will lead you to the top, my favourite being the north-west route past the old derelict quarry.

Threshthwaite Cove from Threshthwaite Mouth 20/9/11

My visit to the fell on 20/2/09 was timed to capture the snows filling the gullies as in AW's drawing but unfortunately the mist came down and impaired my view. The return visit had to be made in a different season.

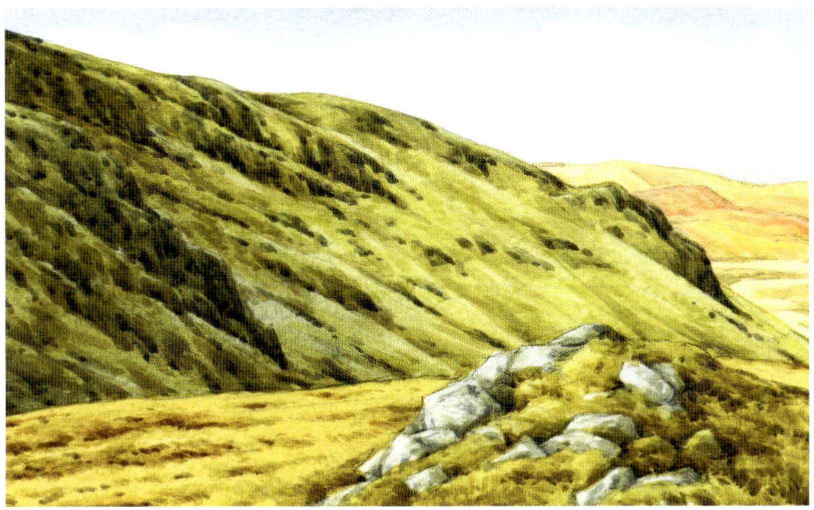

From Brotherswater 25/11/08

Snow hangs in the uppermost reaches of Caudale Moor's corrie on a winter's day, late afternoon. This is the classic view of the fell seen from the lane to Hartsop Hall.

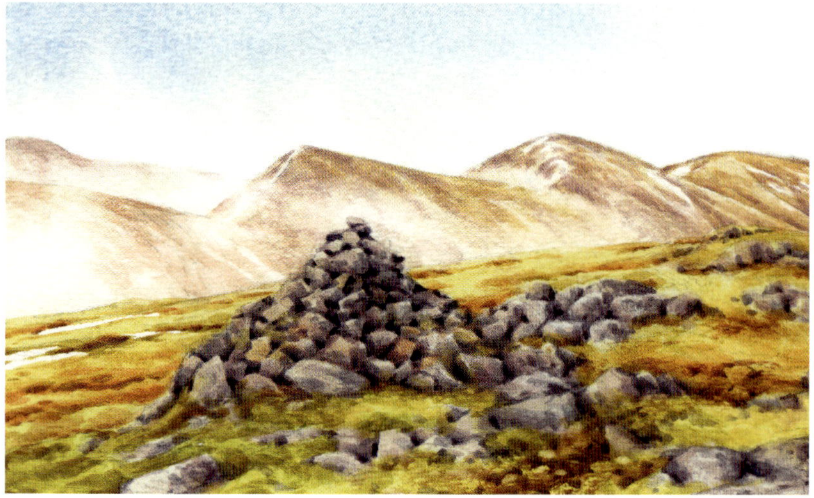

The summit 19/2/09

The low cloud in the valley nearly curtailed my mission but for a few brief moments it cleared to reveal the required vista including Ill Bell.

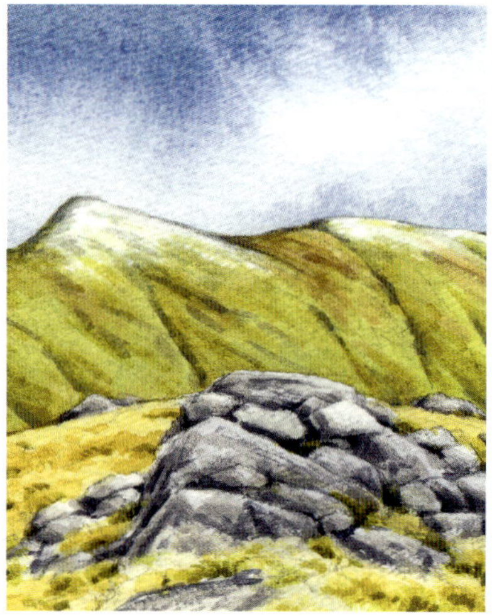

Cairn on Hart Crag above Woundale 1/12/09

There still stands a cairn on the nearby Pike How but the one featured in the guidebook on Hart Crag has collapsed. Around the platform of rock lies the evidence. The terrain behind confirmed that I was at the right location.

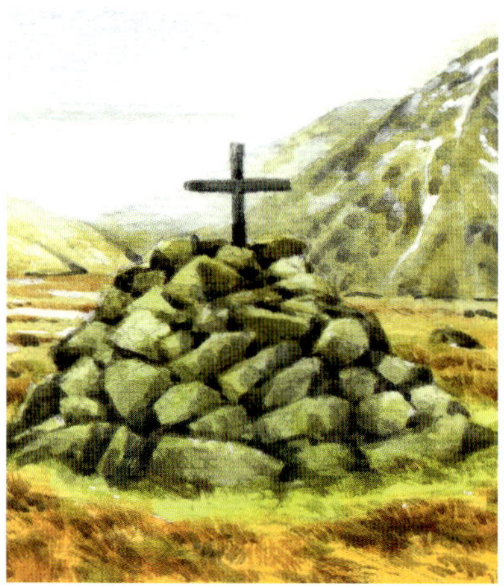

Mark Atkinson's Monument 19/2/09

The cairn which is a memorial to a former landlord of the Kirkstone Pass Inn is now larger, and I am pretty certain the wooden cross will not be the original. Still, it is a fine place for a cairn of remembrance.

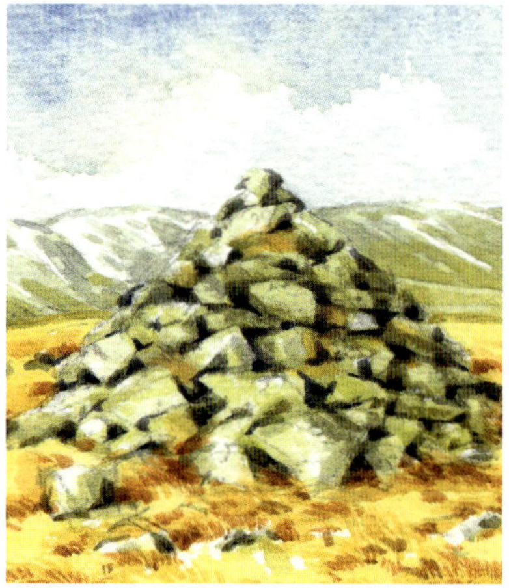

Cairn above the north west ridge 19/2/09

Only the shadow in his drawing gave me a clue as to from which direction to photograph the now enlarged cairn. It means that Dove Crag and St Sunday Crag feature as a backdrop in my sketch.

Red Screes and Middle Dodd from the north west ridge 19/2/09

A fine vista of two of the eastern fells from the far eastern area with an almost aerial aspect of the road through the Kirkstone Pass. Wansfell is seen through the gap and the Coniston Fells appear over Middle Dodd.

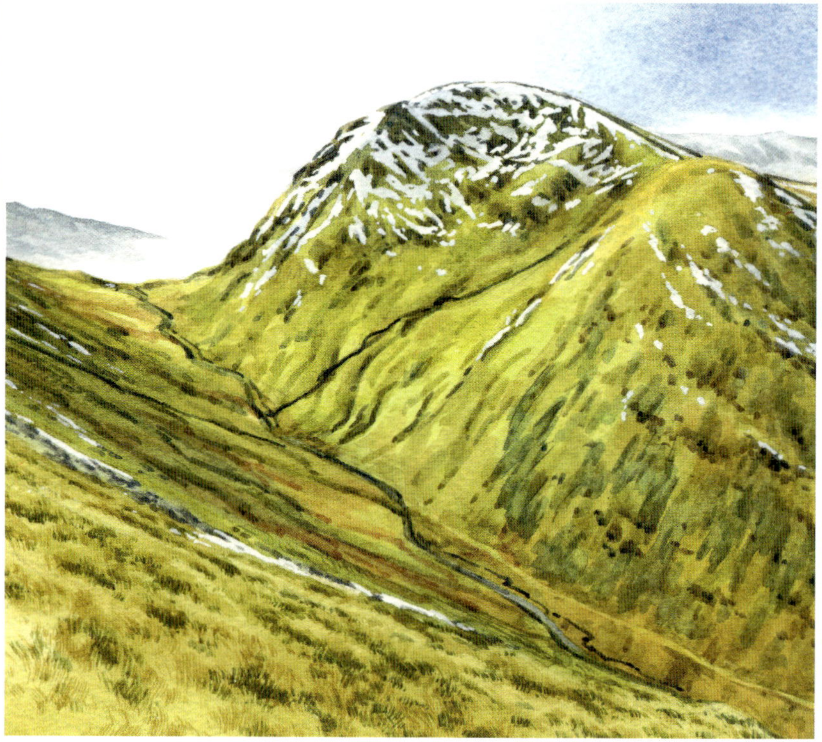

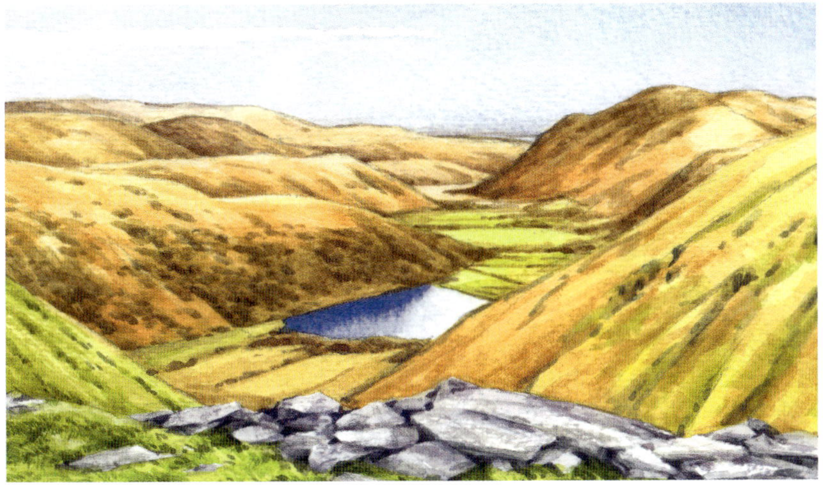

Ullswater and Brotherswater from Caudale Quarry 19/2/09
The workers in this now disused quarry probably didn't have much time for admiring the views but they really are extensive and breathtaking.

Caudale Head 19/2/09
I had timed my walk perfectly and was rewarded by capturing the scene almost as AW drew it with the snow in the dips and gullies.

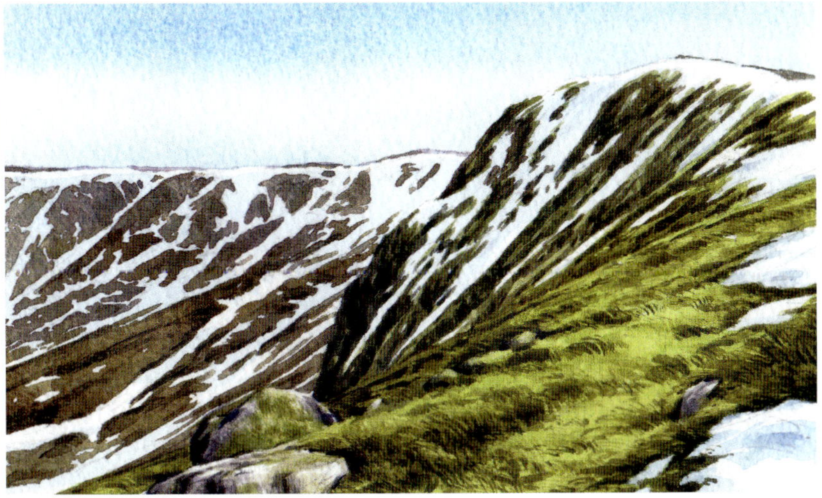

Raven Crag 19/2/09
Again an example of the similar winter conditions to Wainwright's day out. He did exaggerate the Crag in his drawing to be more vertical than the reality but it is still an impressive feature above Threshthwaite Cove.

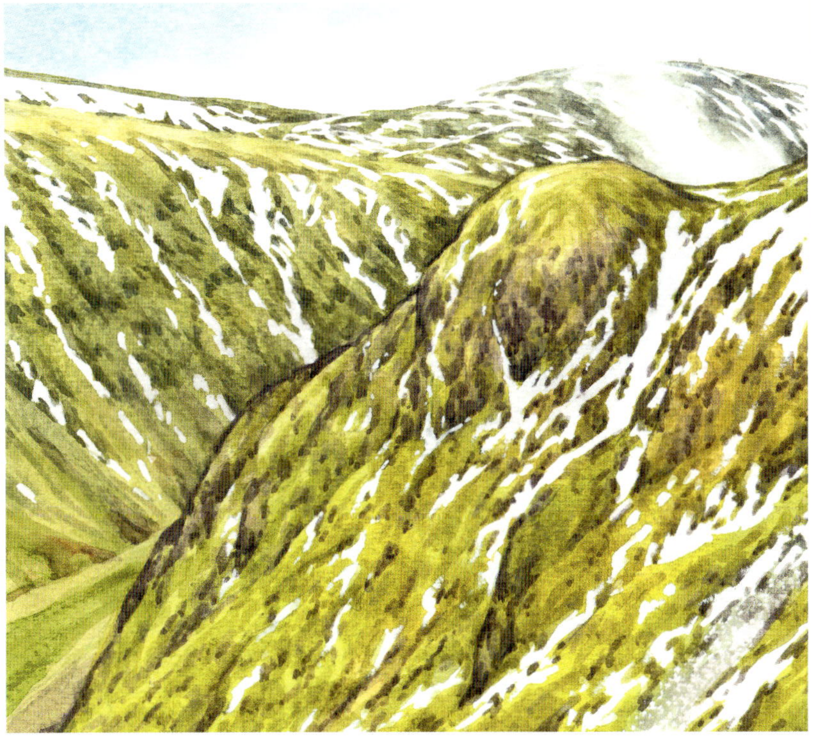

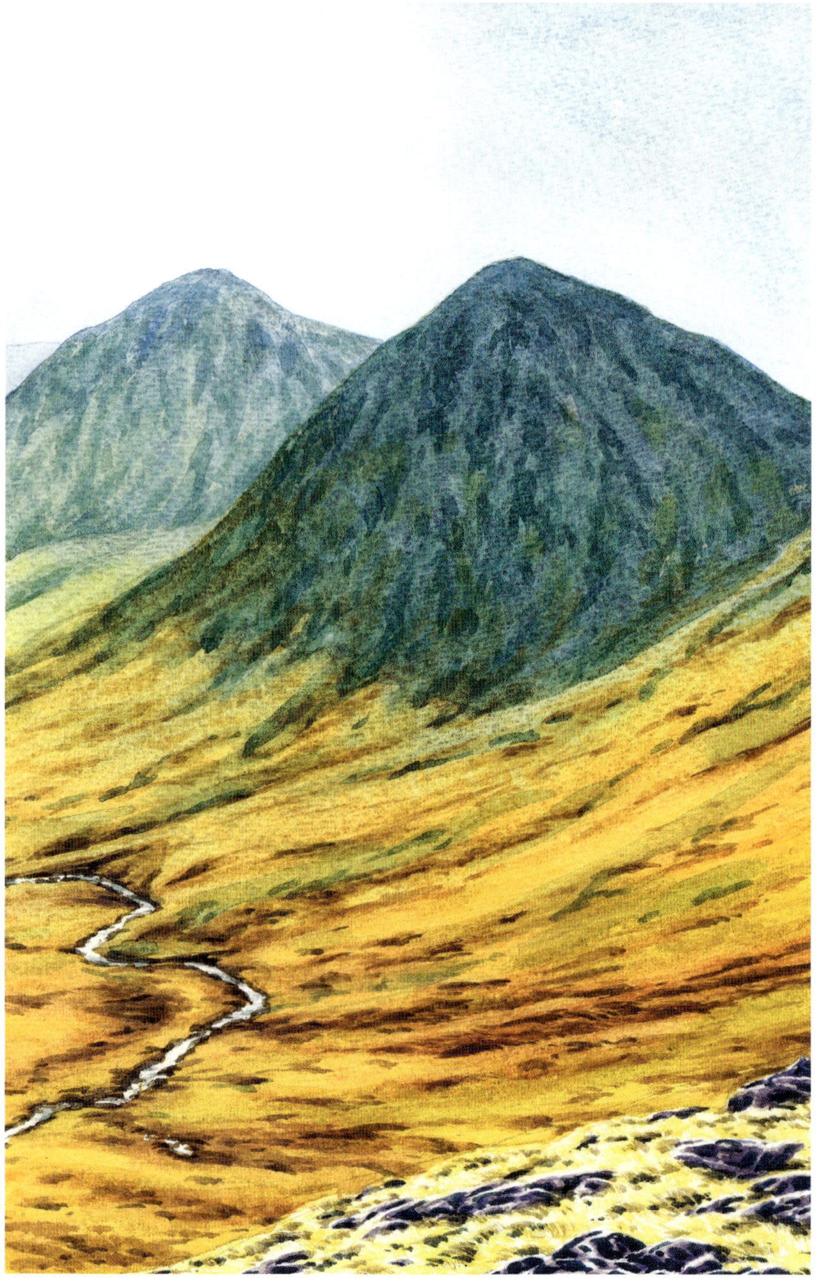

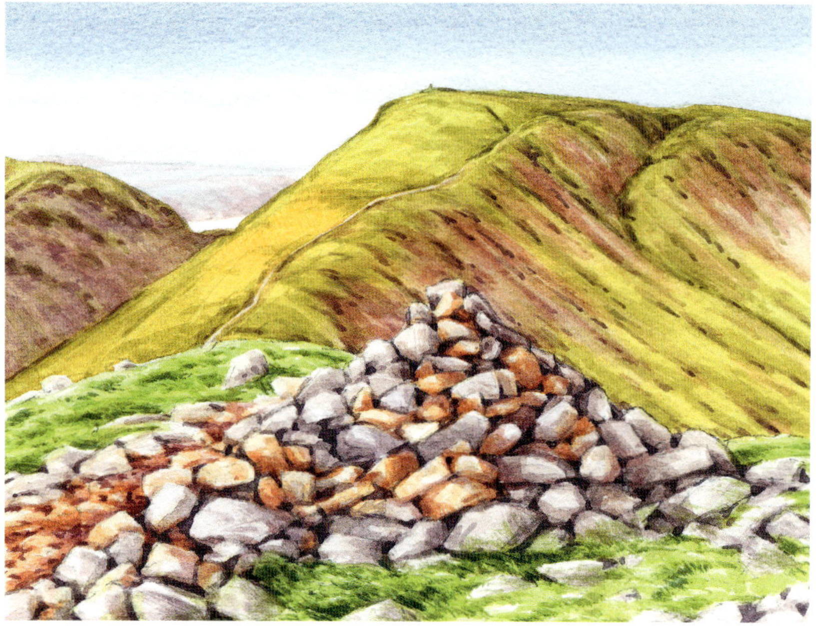

The summit 6/5/07
Nowadays the well worn path to the summit of Thornthwaite Crag is much more pronounced. It has had to undergo some recent repairs to prevent further erosion, a necessary downside of the popularity of the fells today. Ullswater can just be seen through Threshthwaite Mouth.

Froswick

In shape Froswick must be Ill Bell's twin brother and appropriately they are joined at the hip. The fine ridge walk from Garburn Pass to Thornthwaite Crag passes over this fell as well as Ill Bell and Yoke, a route which can make up part of the classic eight fell Kentmere Horseshoe round.

Ill Bell from Froswick 10/10/10
Looking across Over Cove to the crags of Ill Bell. The north east ridge seen here is an exciting steep route of ascent of that fell.

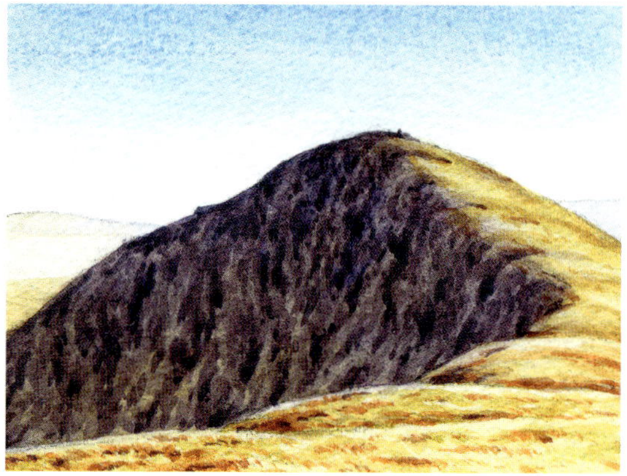

From Gavel Crag 10/10/10
This is an example of me being at the right place at the wrong time. From about halfway up the steep loose scree slope of Gavel Crag the fells and river lined up perfectly but as the view was to the south the strong sun in a cloudless sky totally flattened the scene. Time did not allow me to return on a day when conditions may have been better.

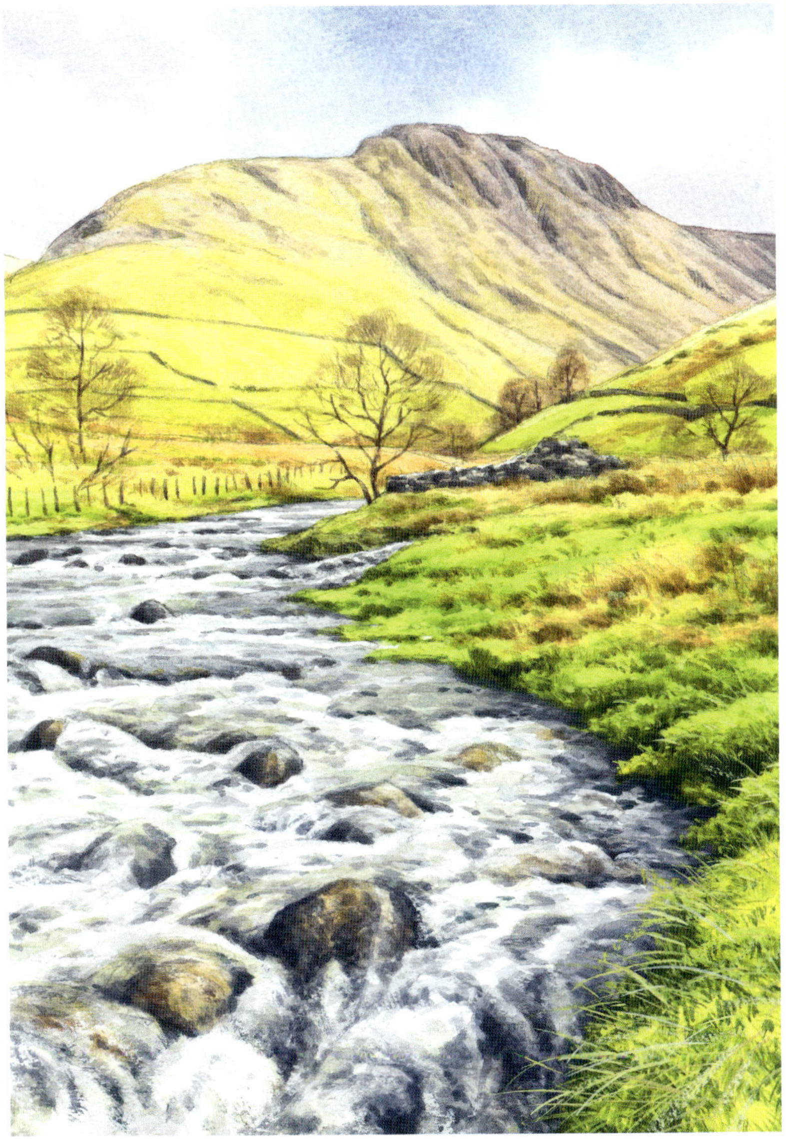

From Hartsop 6/3/11
The original scene was viewed from the bridge that crosses Pasture Beck but now trees obscure the fell from that point. This is the nearest clear view to that position, on the south bank.

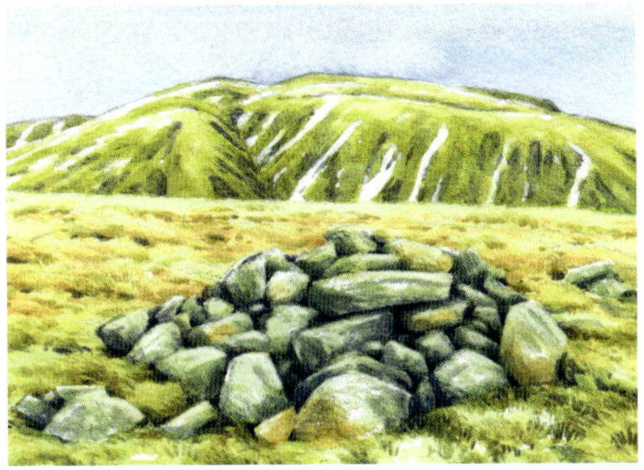

The summit 20/2/09
An untidy cairn marks the highest point.

Gray Crag

When viewed from Brock Crags this fell has almost the look of a volcano but it is in fact a long ridge coming north from Thornthwaite Crag. Its profile can best be observed from the west shore of Brotherswater.

Thornthwaite Crag from point 2331' 20/2/09
Devoid of the small cairn on my visit, just a small patch of bare earth marks where AW's cairn was.

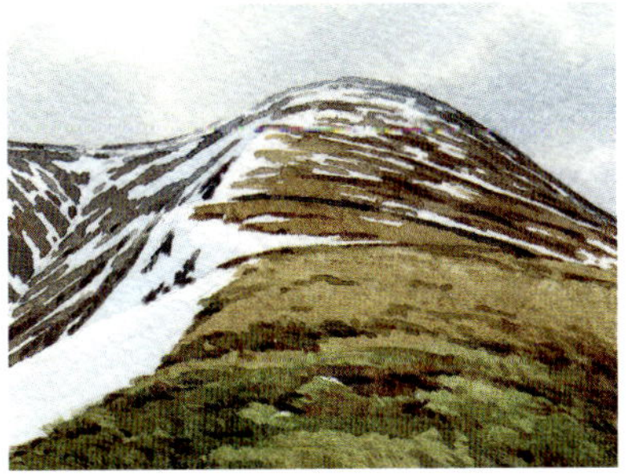

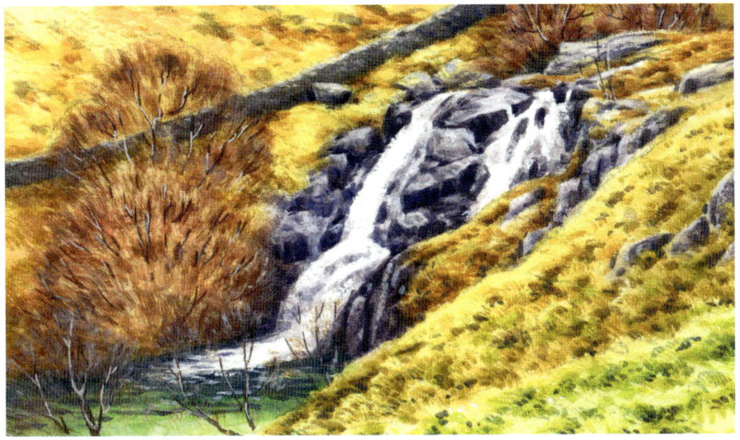

Cascades above the (former) filter house 20/2/09
As seen from the path up to the lake.

Wath Bridge 20/2/09
At first glance it would appear that the single stone slab bridge, perhaps the biggest in the area, has been replaced. Close inspection however will reveal that in fact the slab is still there but now encased within this framework of wooden rails and concrete.

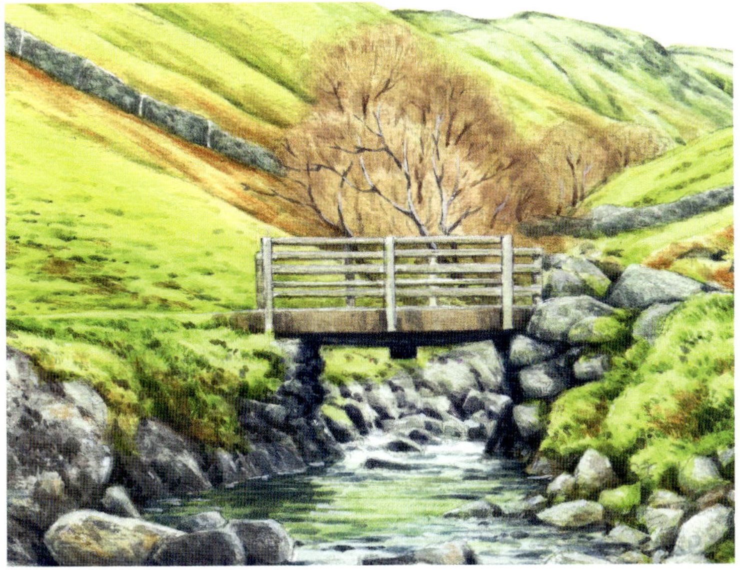

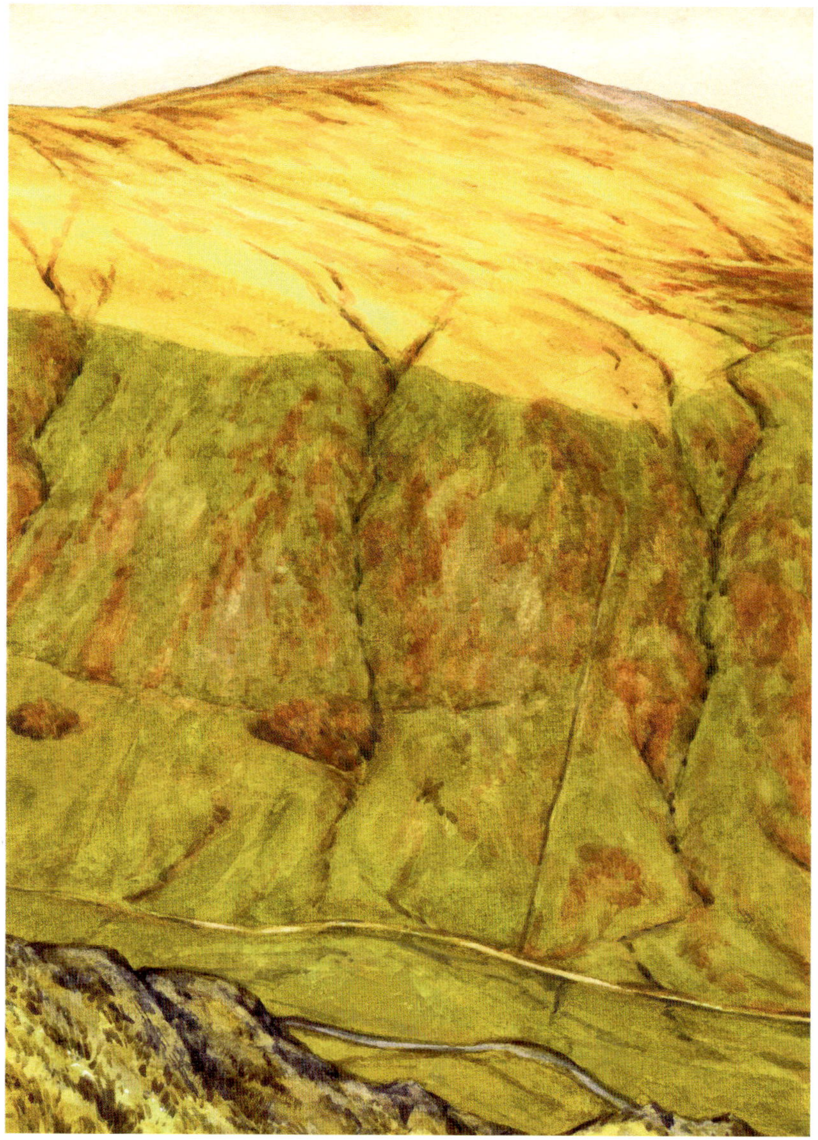

From Shipman Knotts 19/10/11
Snow in the gullies enhanced the shape of the fell in Wainwright's depiction. I was unable to re-create the scene due to this visit being in a different season. I was lucky with the late afternoon light though.

Grey Crag

Normally accessed by walkers from the quiet valley of Longsleddale, Grey Crag is the easternmost of all the Wainwright fells. Many leave this area until after they have explored the more exciting and popular regions.

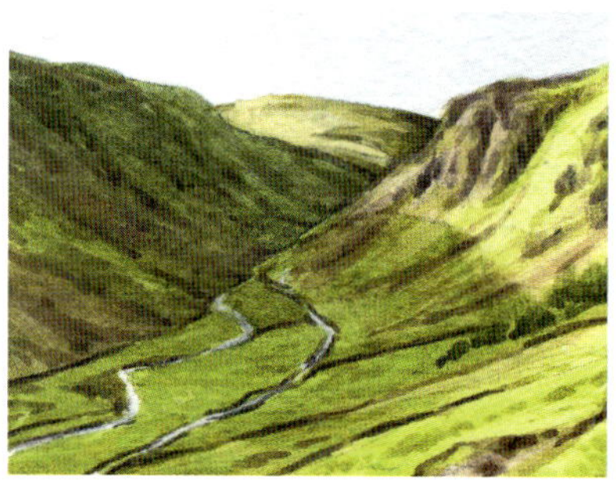

The head of Longsleddale
10/5/09
Adam Seat at the end of the valley.

The survey post on Great How 10/5/09 A concrete structure occupying a fine viewpoint.

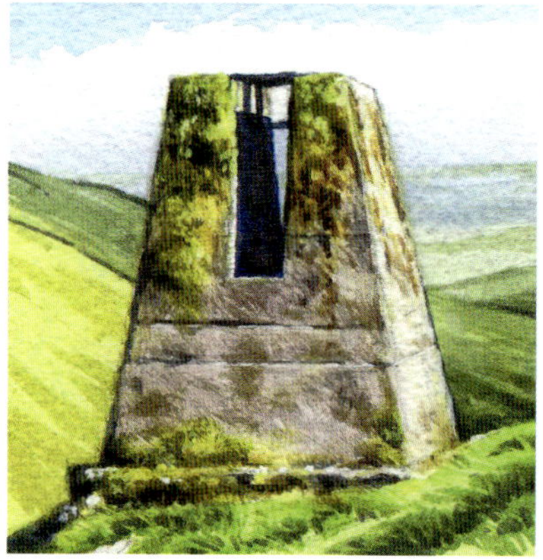

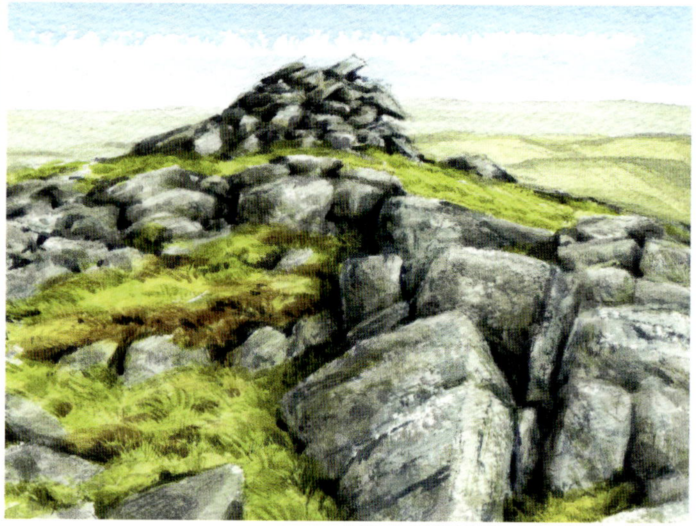

The summit 10/5/09
The large angular block in the foreground gave me the clue to the correct direction from which to view the summit cairn.

The cairn on Harrop Pike
10/5/09
In a more popular location it is unlikely that this neat old pillar would still be standing.

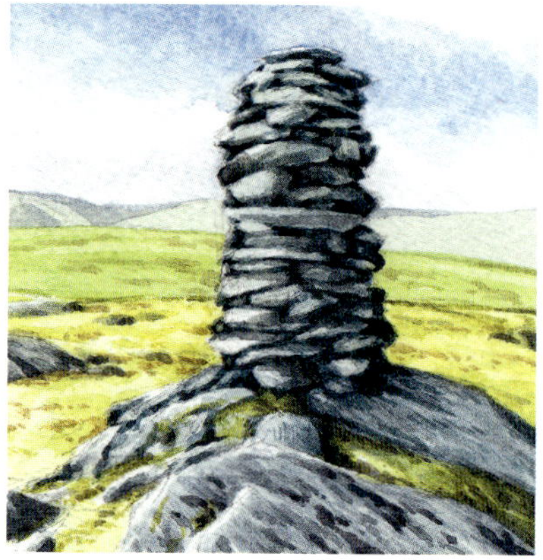

Mere Crag 10/5/09
This is one of those features which few people visit, footpaths in this area are practically nonexistent.

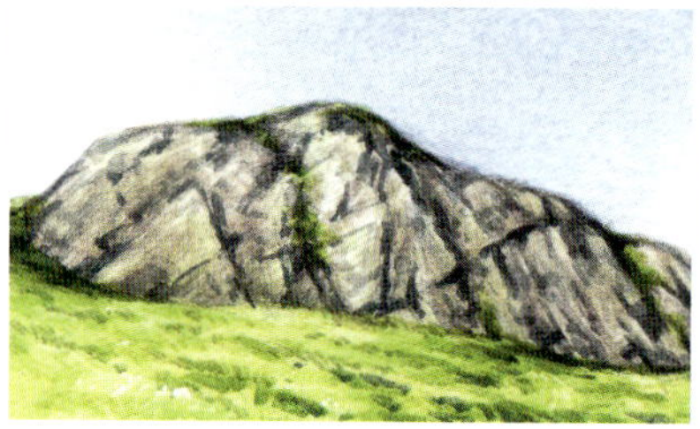

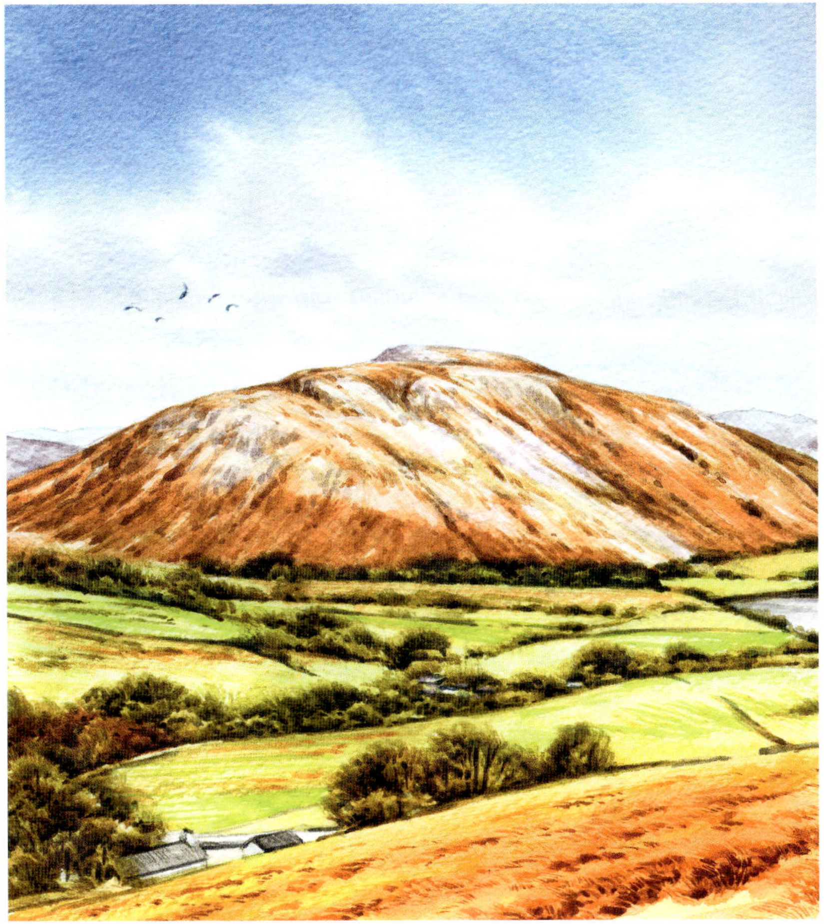

From above Mellguards 25/9/09

A vantage point on the slopes of Bonscale Pike provides this view of the fell over Howtown. The delightful couple of houses of Mellguards are just to the bottom left. The drawing in the guide exaggerated the shape of the hill, possibly just to fill the page. In reality the fell has more subtle proportions like those illustrated here.

The summit 13/3/09

The highest point is adorned by a sturdy beacon which commands a fine position overlooking the lake. However, since Wainwright drew it the beacon had lost about a quarter of its height so that is how I have painted it, as I saw it in 2009. The good news is that in the Spring of 2014 the beacon was completely rebuilt not only to the height of his drawing but slightly higher.Iit now stands about 12 feet tall and is once again restored to its former glory.

Hallin Fell

With its northwestern slopes reaching right to the edge of Ullswater, Hallin Fell sits as a guardian of Boredale and Martindale. It is a simple fell, no crags or ridges to speak of and neatly cropped turf over most of its surface. With good car parking at the top of The Hause above Howtown it is no wonder that Hallin Fell is a popular location. The views from the top are more than enough reward for the reasonably easy stroll up the clear paths.

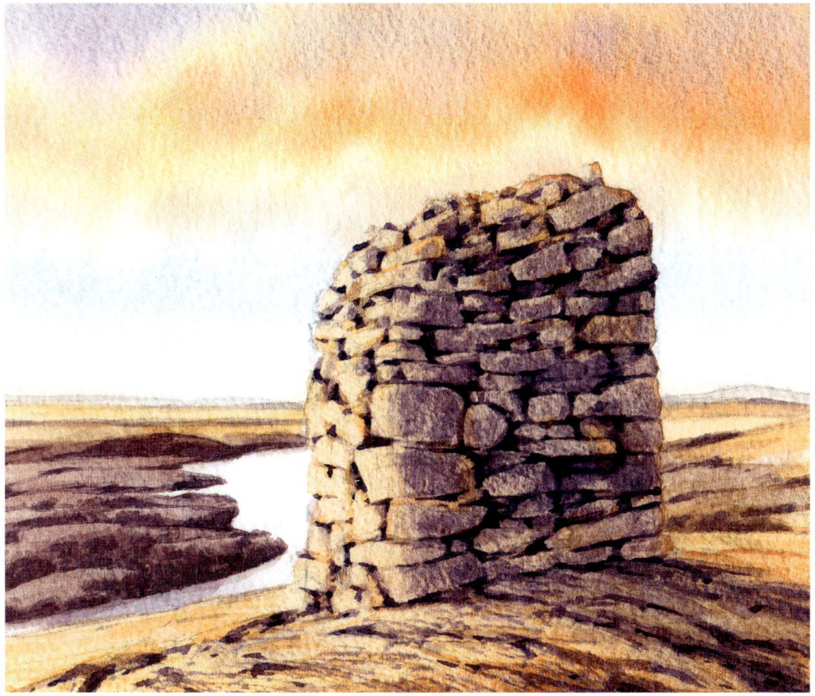

The lower reach of Ullswater from the north cairn 13/3/09

If upon reaching the main summit you find it a little busy then I recommend you have a short wander over to this area. The views north are well worth it and you will be away from the crowds.

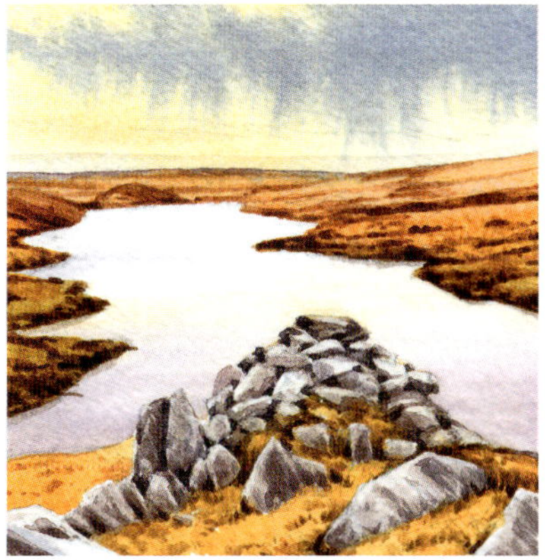

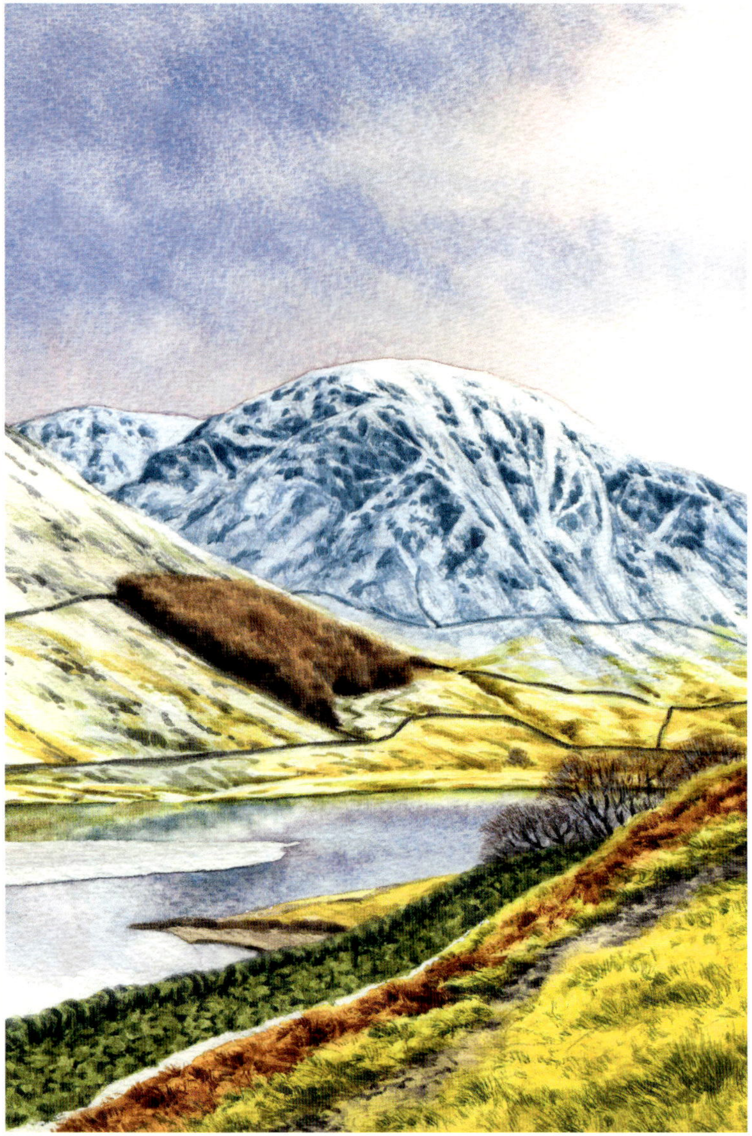

From The Rigg 2/3/10

Only a short time after getting the main reference for Branstree I was able to obtain this image. The trees have been felled here but quite a plantation has grown on the opposite side of the lake.

Harter Fell

Driving along the valley to Mardale Head one's eyes are drawn to the dominating face of Harter Fell. These rough crags are the harsher aspect of a fell which has more gentle approaches from other directions.

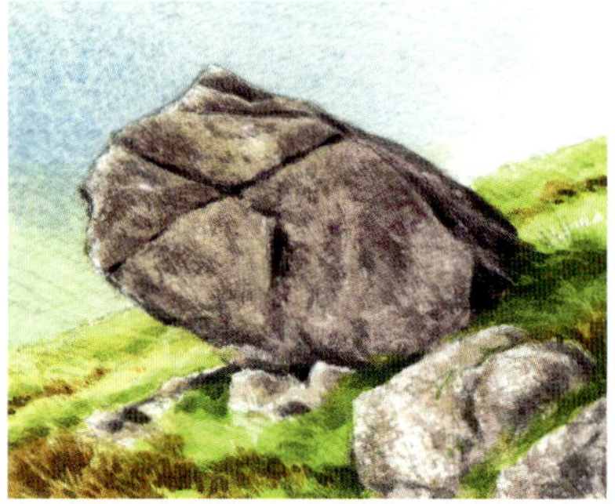

Ull Stone from the east 10/10/10

Away from any path this large boulder obviously drew AW's eye.

Ull Stone from the north 10/10/10

Marked on the map it is possibly the only boulder to give its name to a watercourse in the district.

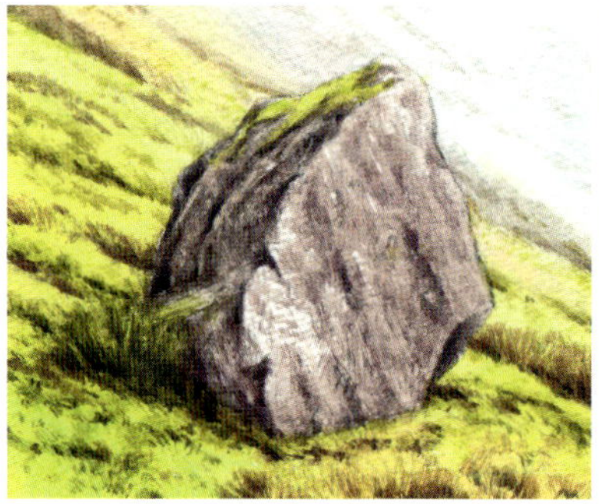

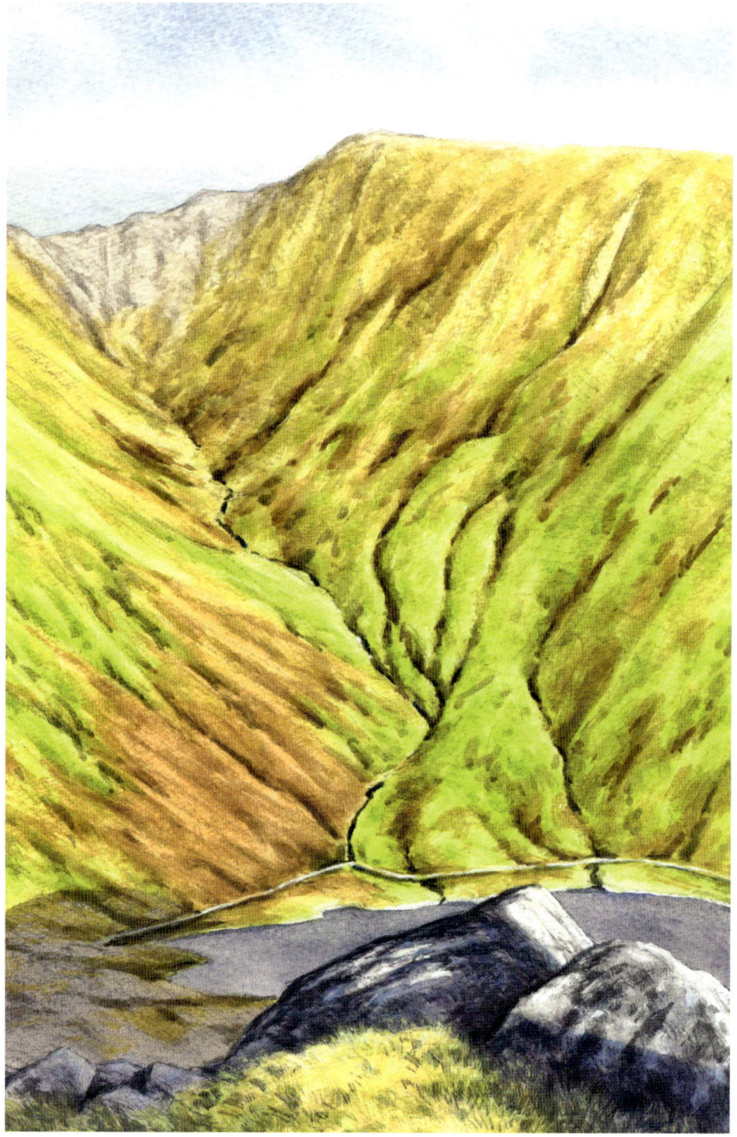

The west face of Harter Fell 10/10/10

It only required a short walk down the ridge of Ill Bell to match the view. After diligent searching I couldn't find the foreground rock to match his but AW may have invented the one in his drawing.

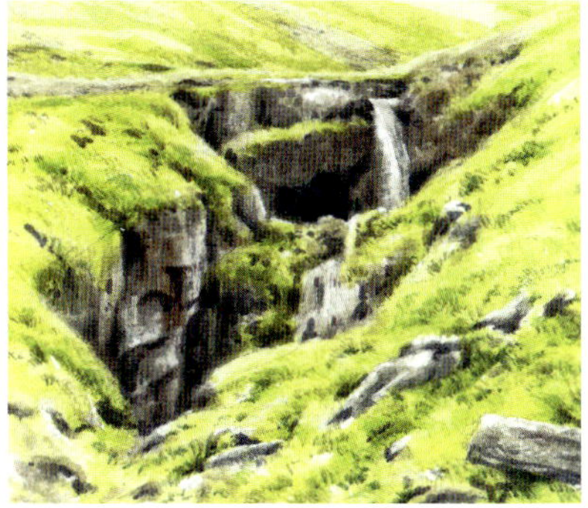

The disappearance of Wren Gill 10/5/09 The old quarry is well worth a visit but care is needed.

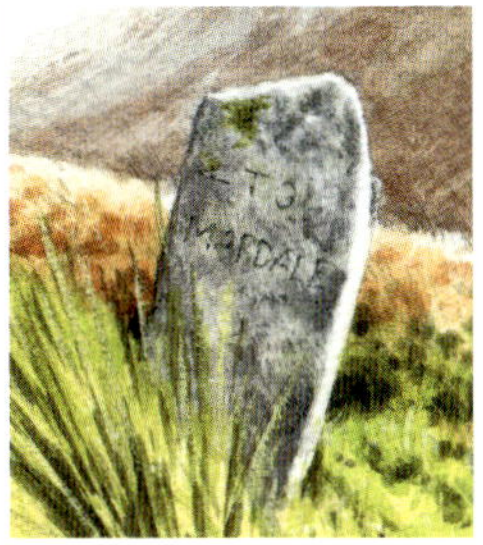

The direction sign 10/10/10 The wording is still just about legible on this old slate route marker.

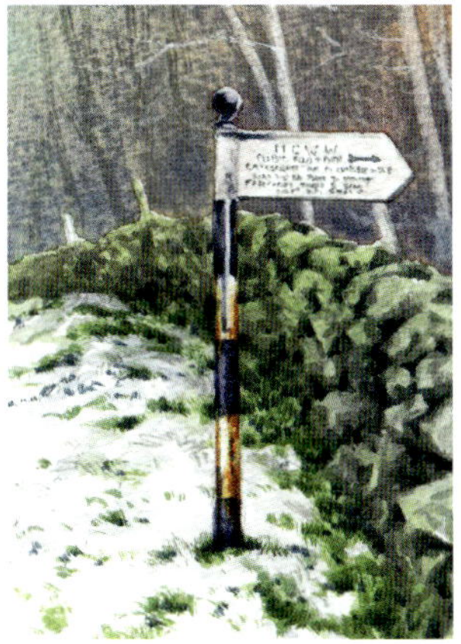

Manchester Corporation signpost 23/1/09 This signpost is the one at the Mardale Head car park. The left hand sign has gone and the one remaining is larger with extra wording, a more recent version perhaps.

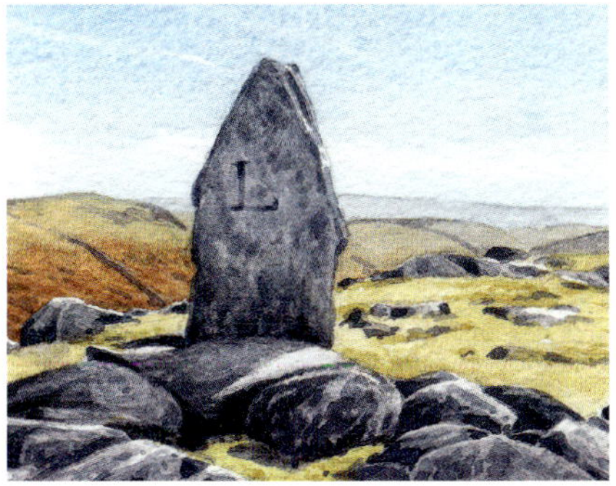

Boundary stone on Adam Seat 17/3/09 Away from the path a fence has to be crossed to visit this site. From nearby there is a grand view of Longsleddale.

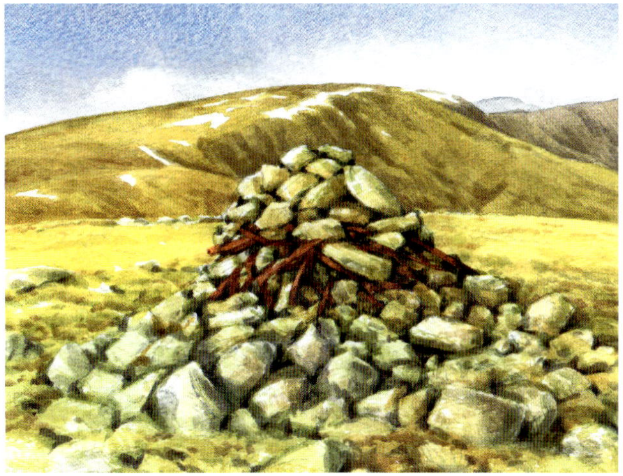

The summit 17/3/09 The summit cairn still includes some of the twisted metal of the old fence gathered from close by. A new post and wire fence now crosses the summit plateau.

Small Water 17/3/09 Nestled in the hollow below Nan Bield Pass, Small Water is a jewel of a tarn in rugged surroundings.

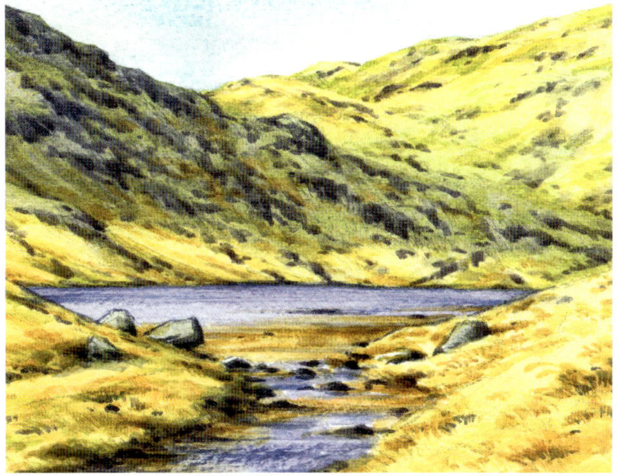

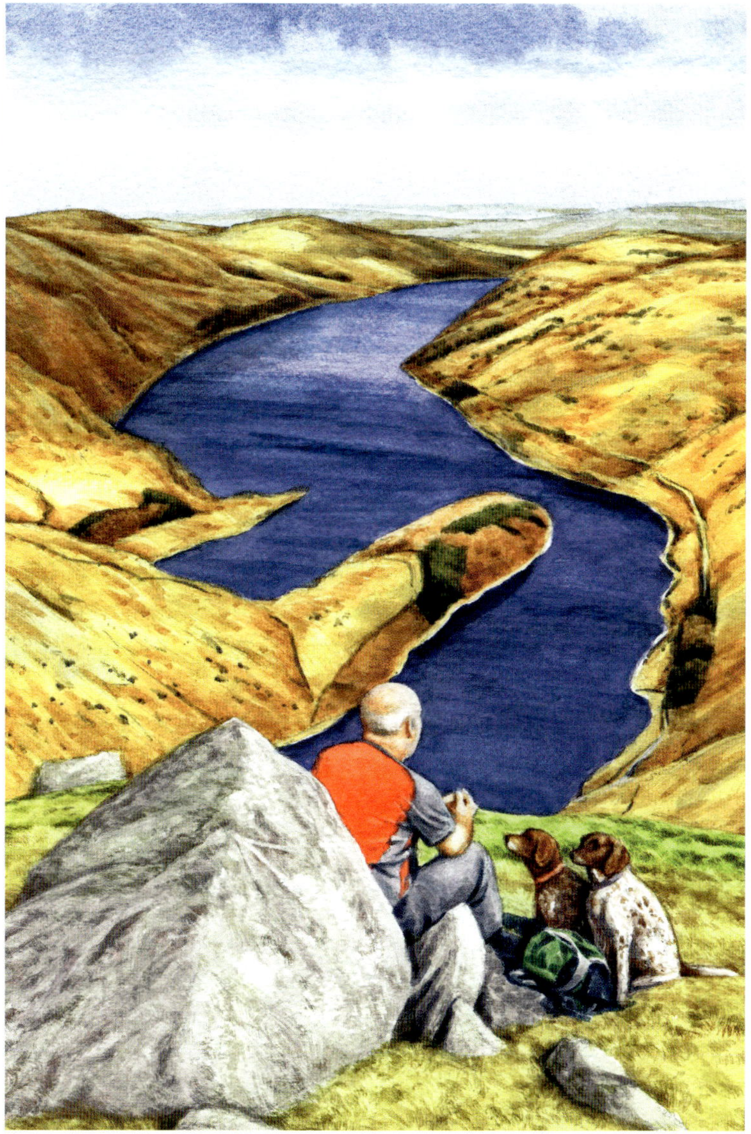

Haweswater from the third cairn 17/3/09 In the second of AW's self portraits I took the liberty of including both dogs in this sketch as sadly it was to be Zoe's last walk with us, we lost her unexpectedly the very next day. This was a special walk.

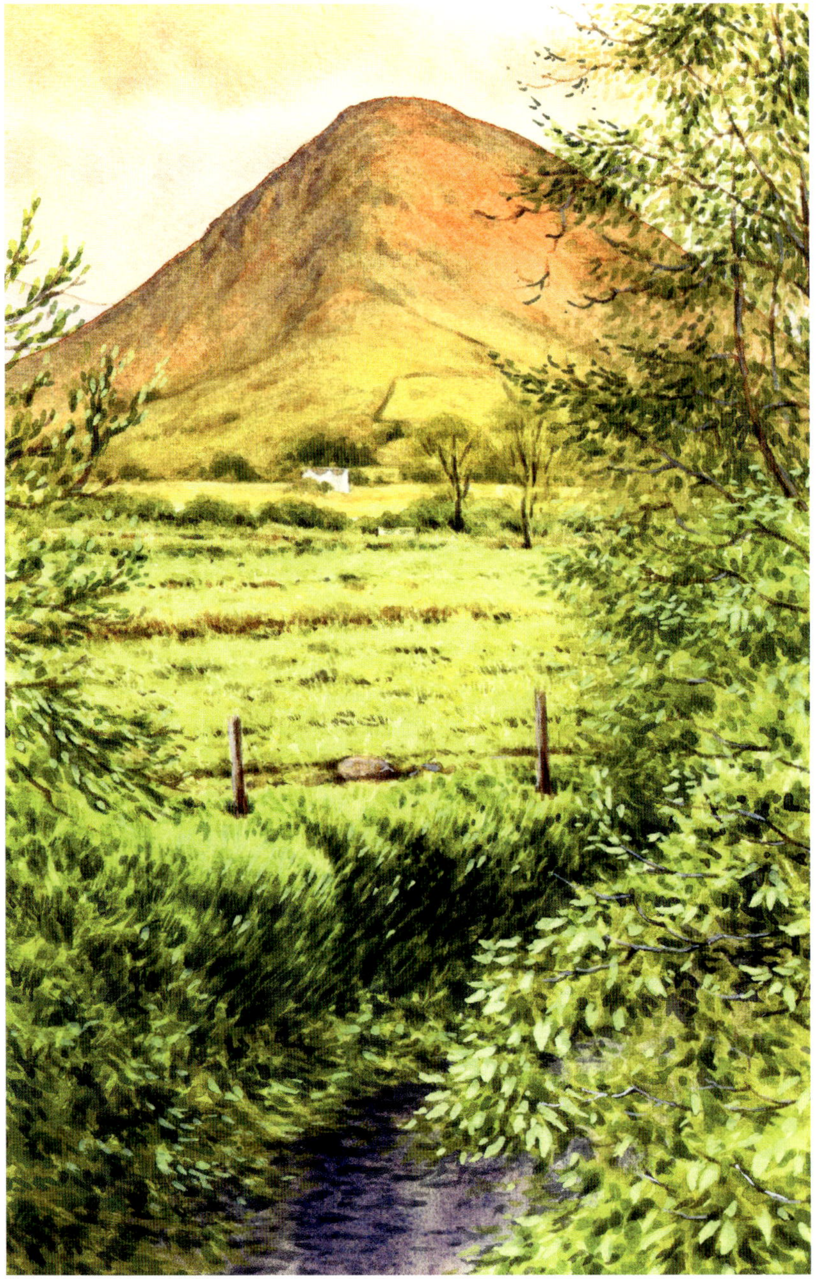

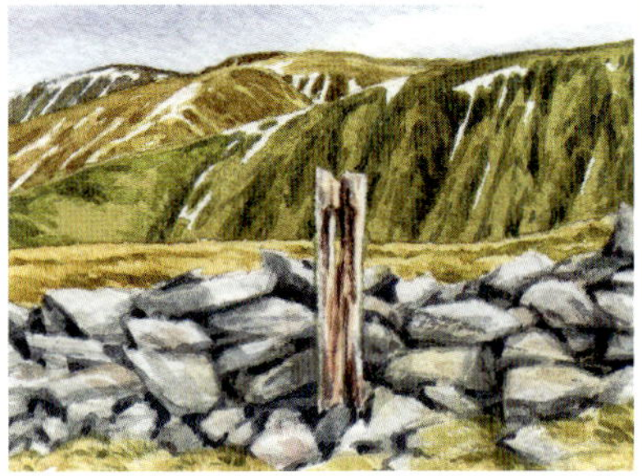

The summit 20/2/09
Amazingly the post still stands but the wall is derelict. A cairn is close by but this is the highest point.

Hartsop Dodd

Taking its name from the small hamlet at its base the fell forms one of the ridges up to Caudale Moor. From the north it has a simple evenly sloped shape which replicates its nearby neighbours just to the east.

Dovedale 20/2/09
Another route planned to capture the same seasonal conditions with snow on the fell tops. A 150 yard downhill walk east from the summit reveals this exact scene.

From Goldrill Beck 29/5/09
A position on the roadside 200 yards north of Cow Bridge car park is the location for this viewpoint.

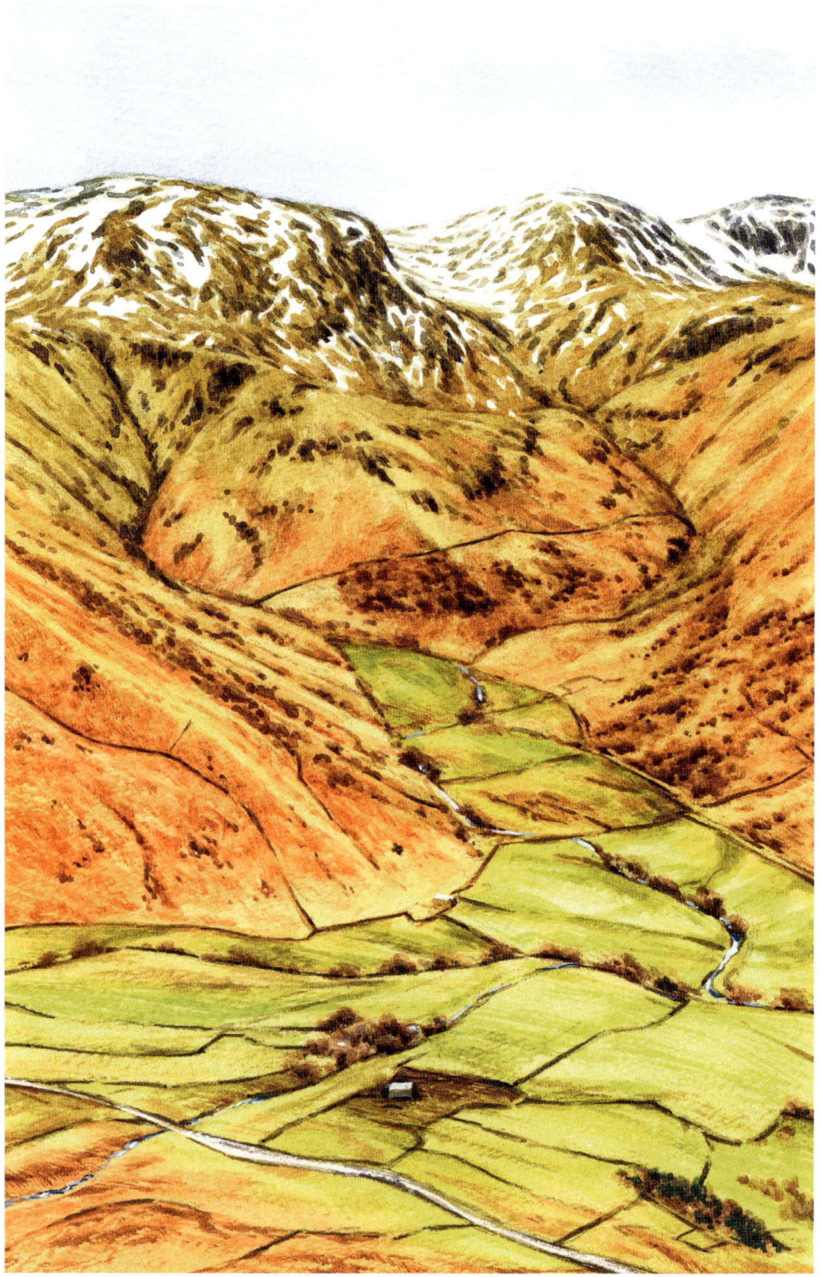

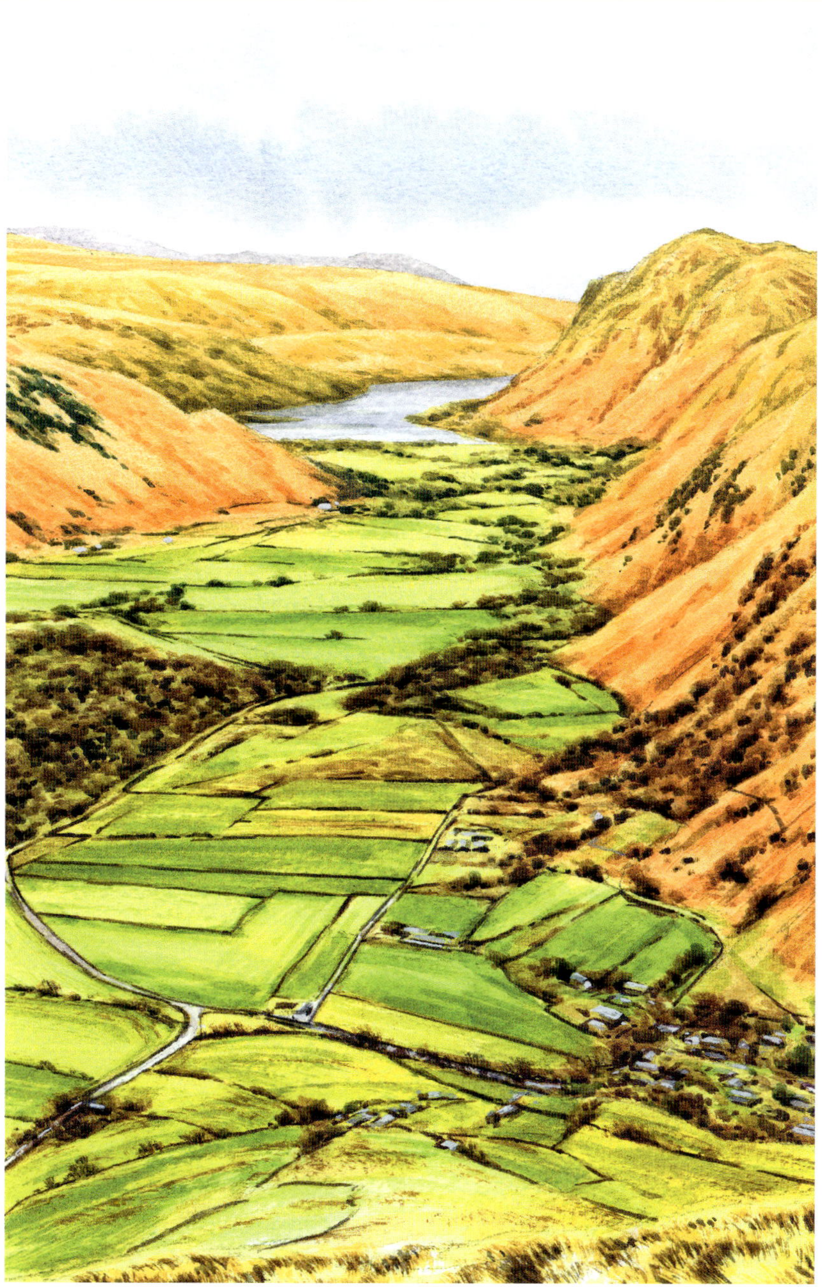

Patterdale 20/2/09

From a high point on the north ridge this fine landscape is revealed. The scene is relatively unchanged except perhaps for the large new sheds attached to farms. The field boundaries are practically identical to those of fifty years ago.

Fixing the fells

It is a sad reality that the massive increase of people walking over the fells in the last 150 years has a downside. The hard bedrock of the fells is in the main covered with a tenuous cloak of thin topsoil and turf which struggles to withstand the huge unnatural pressure of thousands of pairs of boots. Routes and footpaths that were once only used by local people, shepherds and traders are now being pounded daily but the wear and tear on such paths is not a new phenomenon. Even as far back as the early 19th century reports of deterioration of routes were being recorded but now it is on a much bigger scale. Everyone will have their own opinion as to whether Wainwright and his guidebooks are to blame for the majority of this damage (see Wainwright and Tourism p194) but there is no going back, the damage is done and can only get worse. It isn't as if this issue is just a problem in this region though, footpath erosion is now a serious concern throughout the country in the upland areas.

Path erosion just isn't down to volume of walkers. Many factors come into play both physical, such as drainage, altitude, angle of slope and type of vegetation and also human factors, level of use, popularity of route and type of activity. Basically the trampling of vegetation on paths kills it off which leads to exposure of the soil making it prone to being washed away and boots (and bike tyres) break up the soil further. Before long a channel has formed exposing rough rocks which are awkward to walk on so then people walk to either side of the channel making the path even wider and the damaging process is repeated. All fellwalkers will have witnessed this deterioration and no matter how careful we are we contribute to the problem by the very fact that we use the paths.

A survey of the whole of the National Park was carried out in the 1990s and 180 paths were shown to be in need of repair. The Upland Path Landscape Restoration Project began in 2002 setting out to tackle many of the erosion issues. Various groups now work together with a continuing programme of footpath repair such as The National Trust and Natural England, with the trust having four teams working on repairs lead by rangers who, with the help of volunteers use their expertise to carry out these works in all weathers. Various methods of repair are used depending on the severity of the damage and the environment. There is no denying that repaired paths at first can look unsightly but it must be remembered that these fixes are intended for the long term and not just for now. Nature needs help and the work done by these teams with their years of experience on the heavy scars caused by us walkers can only assist to prevent further damage and allow the fells to recover for future generations. So, whilst the zigzag path down the slopes of Sail isn't perfect I have yet to read of someone coming up with a better solution to fix what was a 20 feet wide scar on very fragile terrain. Already it is blending into the landscape and as long as people either walk on the raised path or stay well off (ideally at least 15m) to one side it can only improve. To find out more about this work or perhaps even to volunteer visit the website at: www.fixthefells.co.uk

Fix the Fells

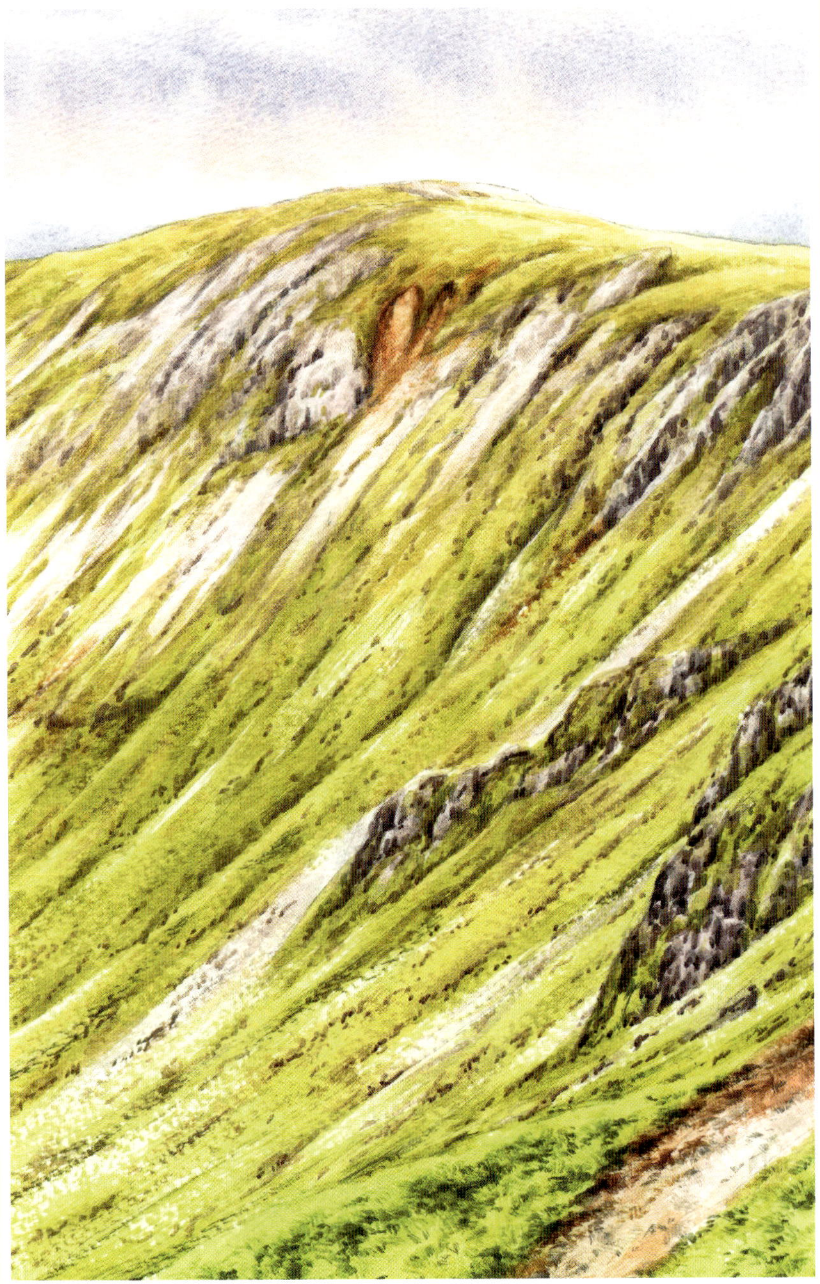

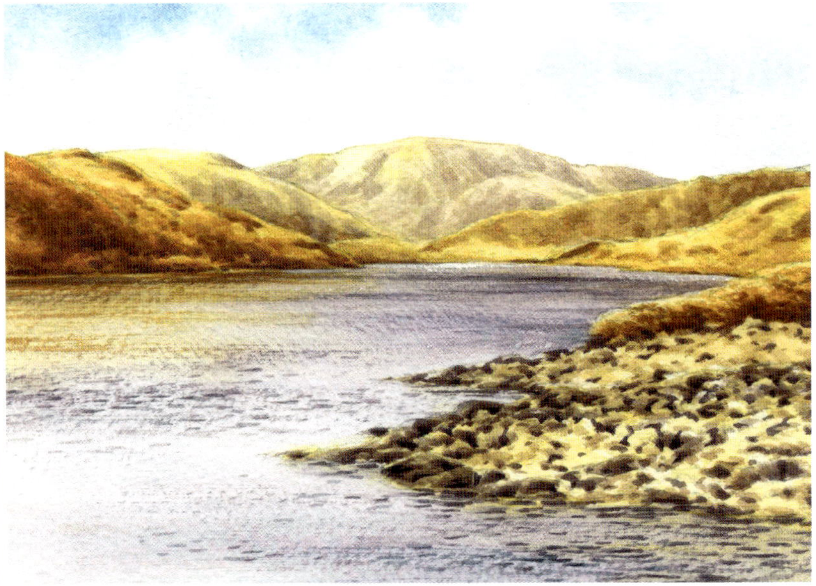

Haweswater from Measand

18/3/12

The path on the west shore of the reservoir heading south reveals fine views of the fells at the head of the water. It's a quiet route most often used by those walking the Coast to Coast long distance path.

The British Fort 2/3/10

An excellent choice of location for a stronghold, with a far reaching view down the valley to the high Pennine hills. Prior to the Haweswater dam construction in the 1930s, this would have been a wonderful viewpoint for this tranquil valley and its natural lake and the surrounding farmsteads.

High Raise

In keeping with many of the other Far Eastern Fells, High Raise is mostly covered in short cropped grass. Only Whelter Crags on its east side exposes any expanse of rock. It is one of the rolling hills which form a line heading north from High Street.

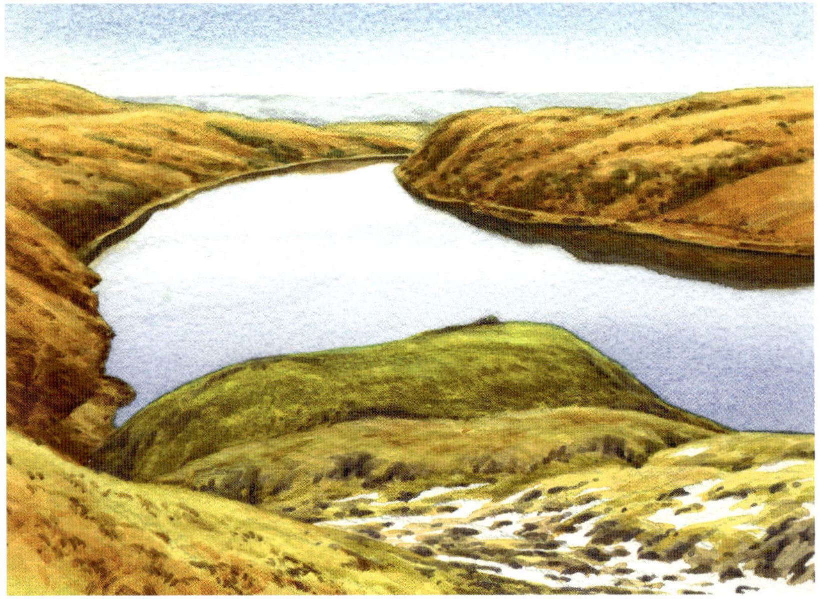

From the col below The Knott

24/6/08

Make a short detour away from the path to the lip of the col above Ramps Gill to obtain this view.

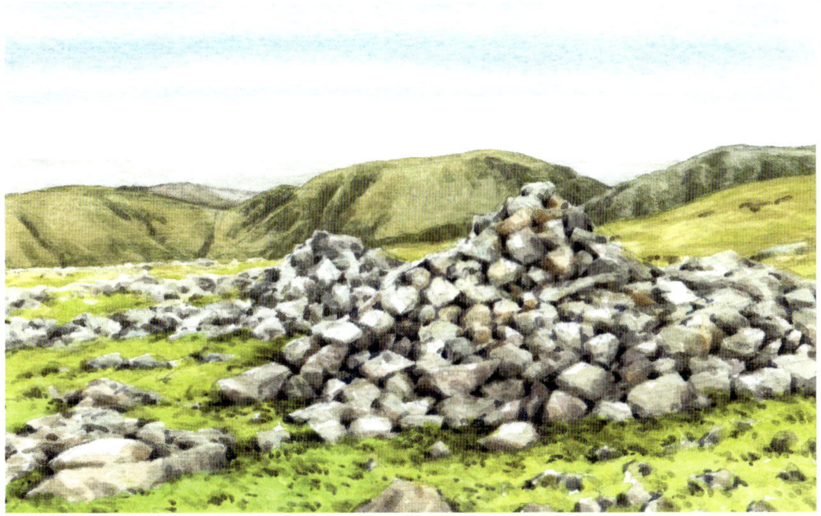

The summit 24/6/08

The cairn and its neighbouring wind shelter remain fairly unchanged over the years considering there is plenty of building material to hand in the form of rocks and stones to expand the two constructions.

The tumulus and cairn on Low Raise 18/3/12

On my first visit here the wind blown snow made the cairn look like an igloo so a second trip was required to produce a more recognisable image.

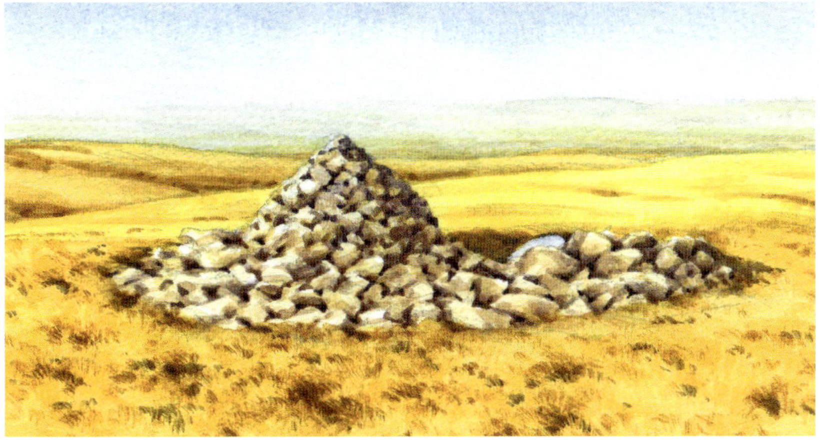

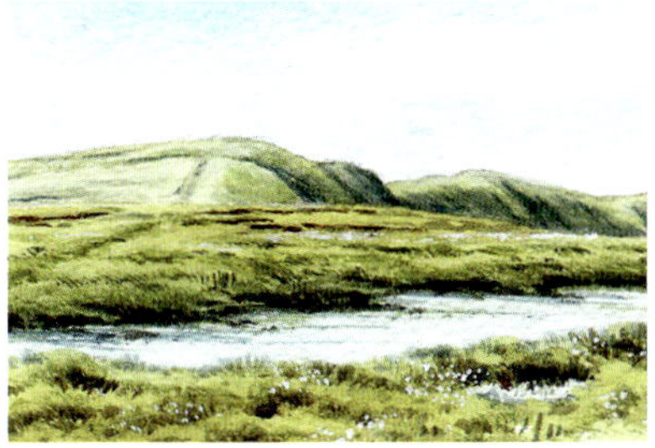

Redcrag Tarn 24/6/08

The tarn is now larger than shown in his drawing. In summer Cotton Grass covers the bog with waving heads of soft white flowers.

Whelter Beck and Whelter Crags 18/3/12

In comparing AW's drawing with the actual scene on location I was able to identify many of the rocks and details apart from the close foreground which he shows as a pool. The beck in reality drops away steeply here with another small fall. My conclusion was that he changed it slightly to make a better composition for the page.

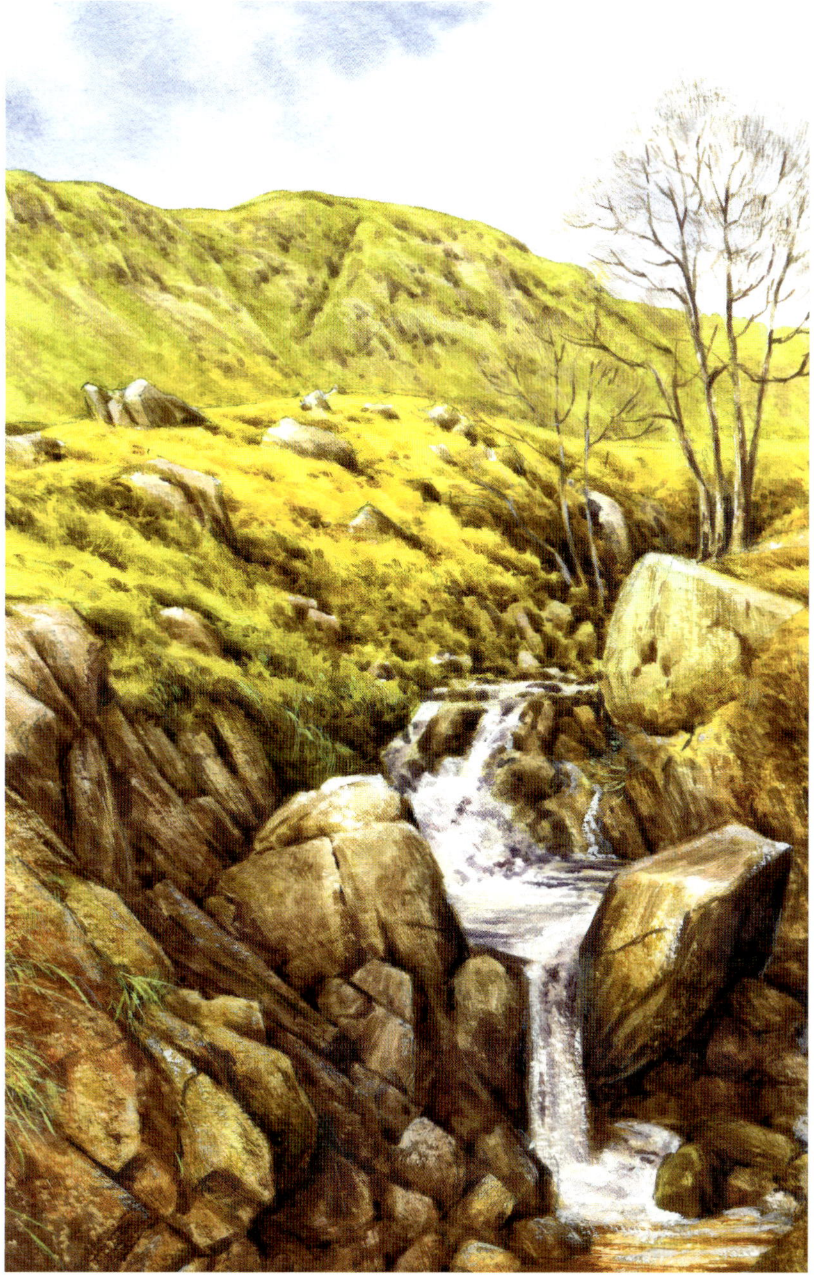

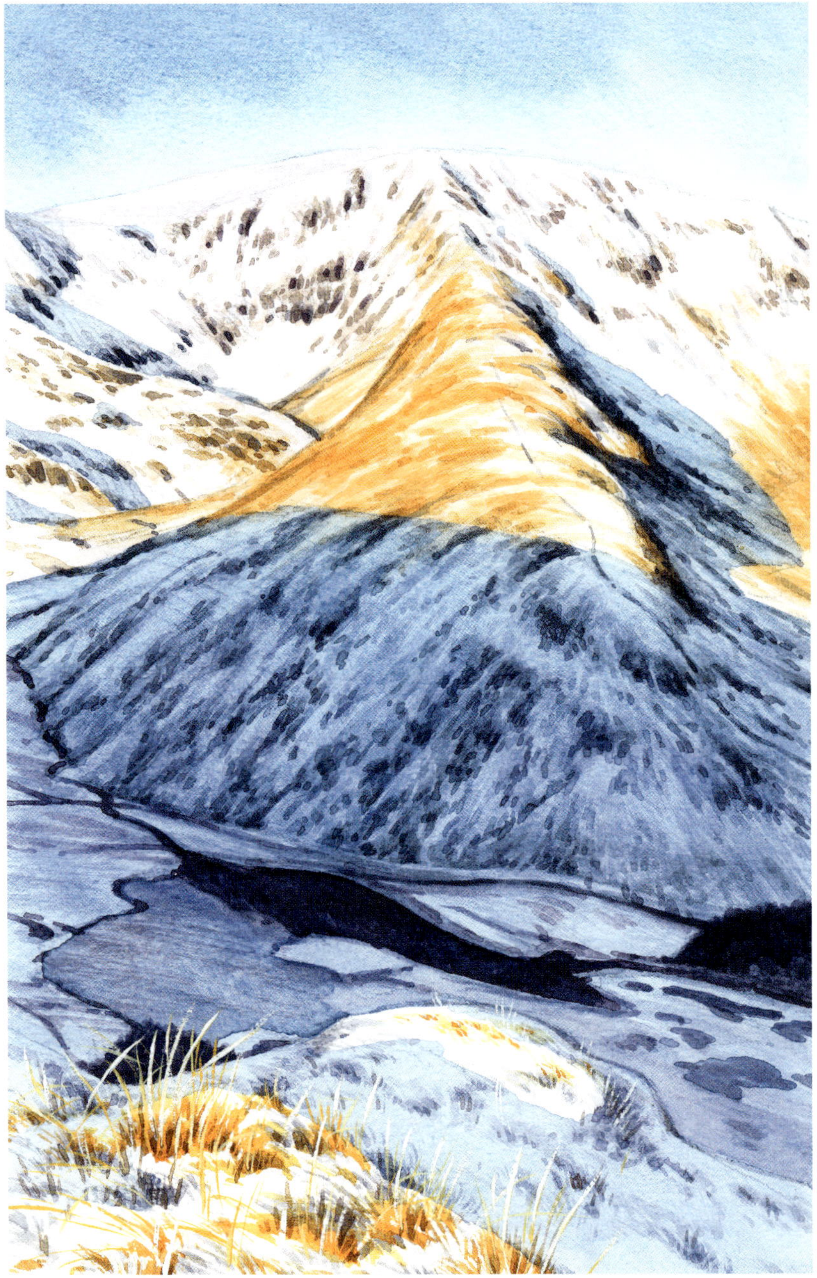

High Street

Being the loftiest of the Far Eastern Fells, High Street has drawn visitors throughout time and so it continues today. Its broad flat summit plateau has witnessed various meetings and events which is reflected in the alternative name of Racecourse Hill. Without a shadow of a doubt the best route to the summit is that from Mardale Head with almost one mile of east west walking in a near perfect straight line to the top of Long Stile along the Rough Crag ridge.

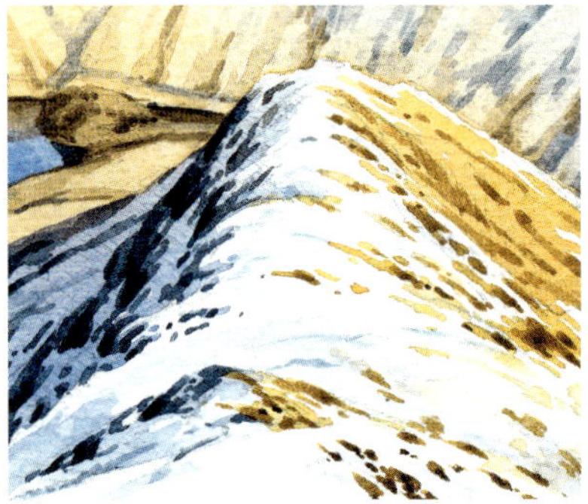

Rough Crag from Long Stile 2/3/10

Looking down the full length of this excellent walkers ridge.

From the north ridge of Branstree 2/3/10

Early morning winter sunshine on the Rough Crag ridge. Haweswater was partially iced over after a period of cold weather. This view is from slightly higher on the ridge than the one in the Branstree chapter.

Hayeswater from the Roman Road 2/3/10

Once again, I have included the distant fells which Wainwright omitted. The inclusion of birds in his drawing was out of character, my guess is that it was an attempt to disguise stray blobs of ink from his pen.

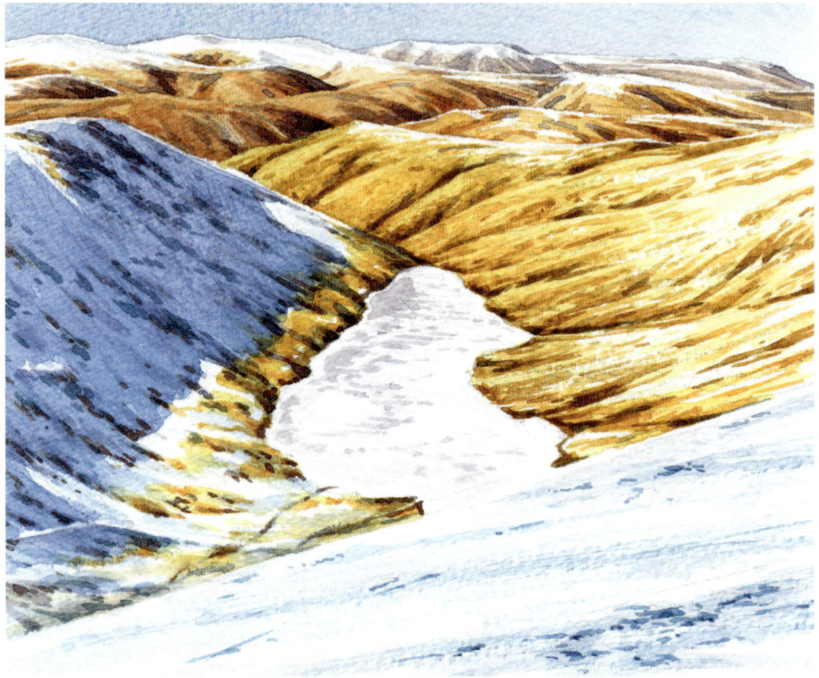

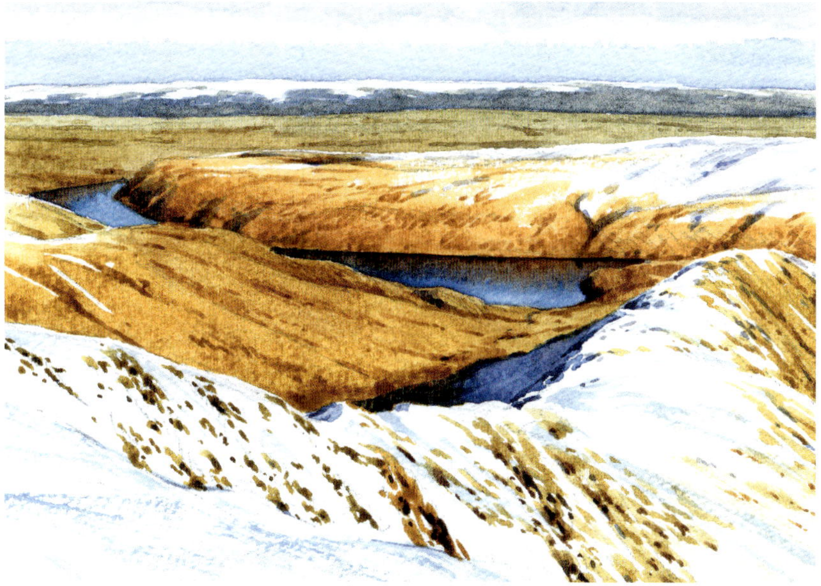

Haweswater from above Long Stile 2/3/10
The extensive visibility of this bright winter's day allowed me to include the snow capped Pennine fells as the far horizon.

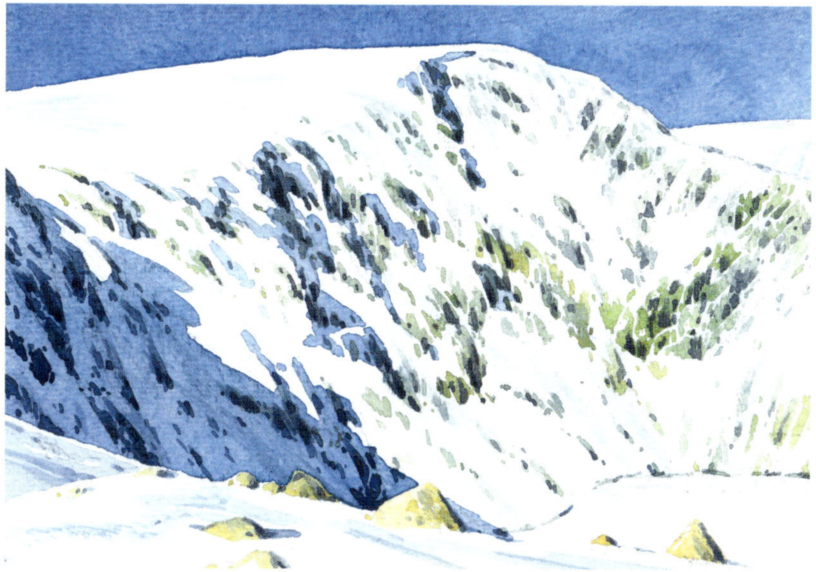

High Street from Mardale Ill Bell 2/3/10
My main reason for this day's trip was to obtain this reference in these winter conditions. Not only did I achieve this goal but many of the other scenes for High Street looked so good in their snow covered form that I have included them throughout the chapter. This point is someway down Piot Crag.

The summit 24/6/08
The ridge wall was fallen in his day and it is in an even worse state now. However it is of no consequence, the sheep around here roam at will. There are only two concrete triangulation pillars on the Wainwright fells, this being one of them, with most being constructed of local stone.

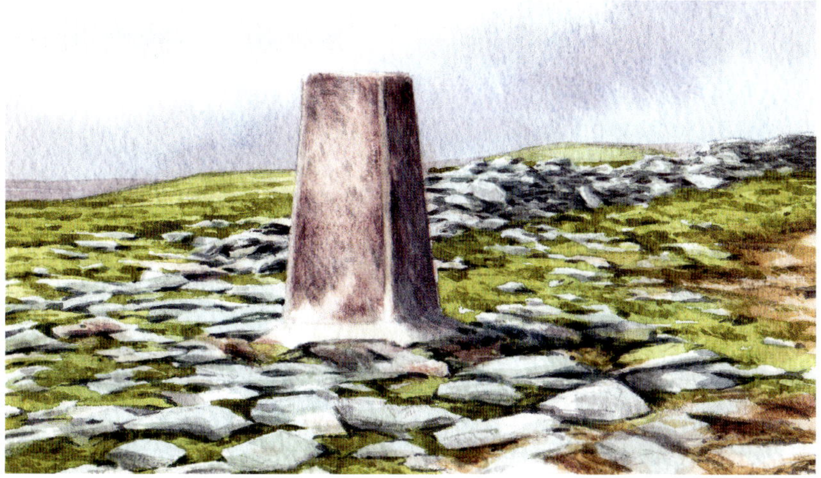

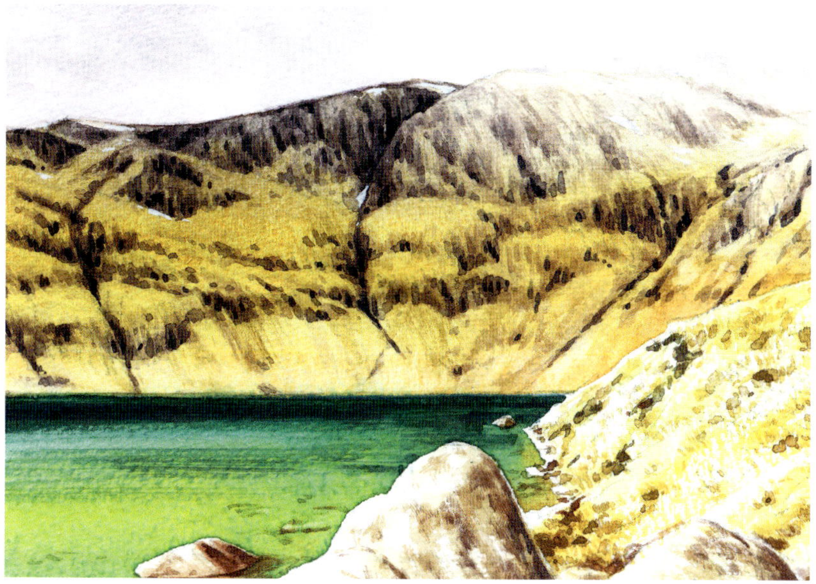

Blea Water Crag 17/3/09
A patient wait resulted in the cloud just lifting enough for me to capture the required photograph. The overcast conditions turned the water into this almost turquoise green. It may be something to do with its depth at over 200′ making it the deepest tarn in Lakeland. It is also a SSSI site partially due to its montane flora and it is regarded as one of the best examples of a Lake District corrie tarn.

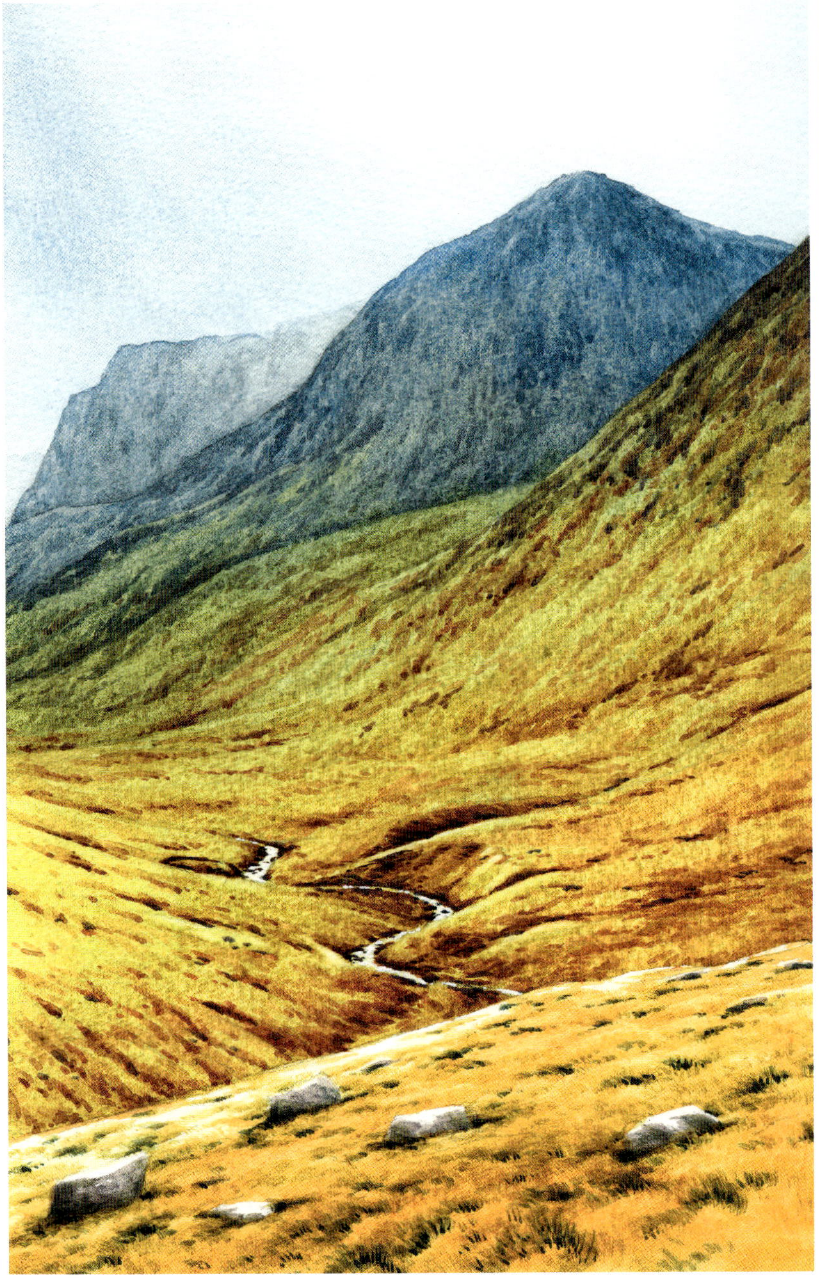

From upper Kentmere 10/10/10
As with my painting for Froswick from Gavel Crag the sun was in totally the wrong position for picking out the best detail. This area near Hall Cove is almost pathless and still unfrequented.

Ill Bell

The distinctive peak of Ill Bell is recognisable from many distant summits and the bell-like shape certainly lives up to its name. The two adjoining fells of Yoke to the south and Froswick to the north make this a fine section of mountain ridge. The north east spur which heads up from the Kentmere Valley is an exciting route of ascent. The fell was named as Hill Bell on both the 6 inch O.S. map of 1900 and the 2½ inch map of 1961 but Ill Bell is now the recognised name.

The Ill Bell ridge, from Stile End 29/5/09
These two field barns are fine examples of their type and both were fully restored in the summer of 2006. They really make a perfect foreground for a classic Lake District scene.

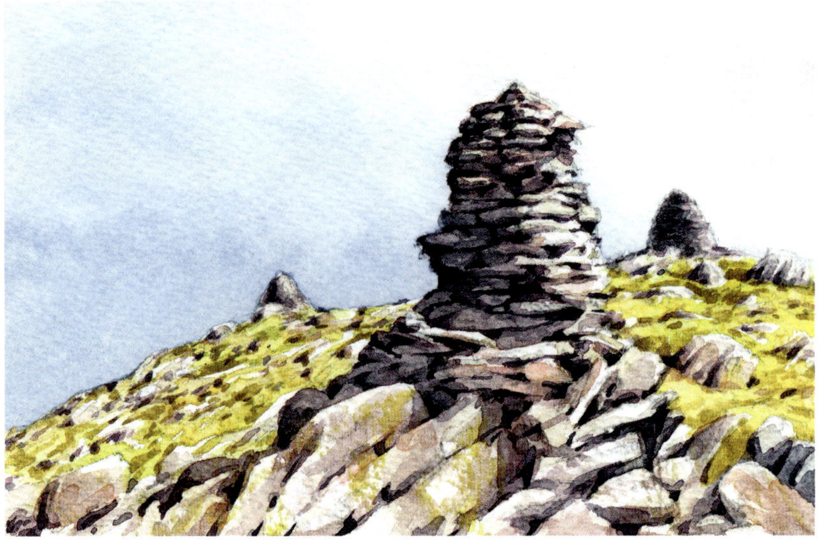

The summit 29/5/09
The group of cairns are a distinctive feature of Ill Bell's summit but now only three stand, not four as in his drawing. The missing one sat between the two on the right. On a following visit after I had produced this sketch I was dismayed to find the near cairn reduced to a mere heap so some restoration work was undertaken to put that right.

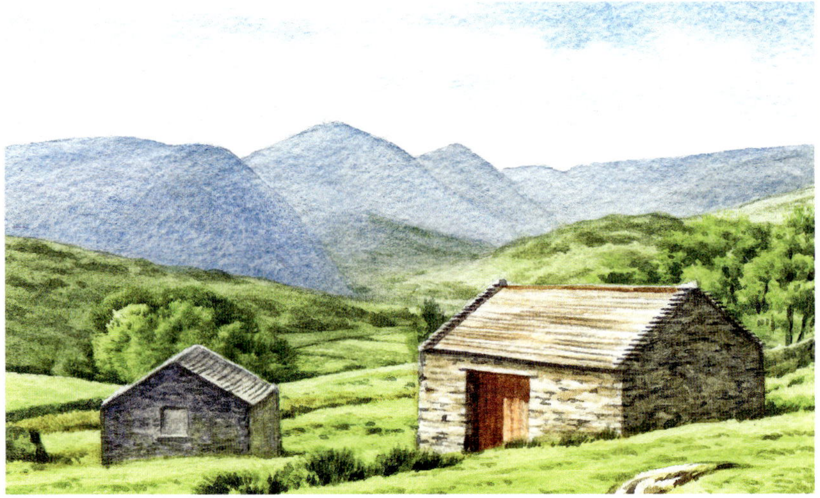

The main cairn 29/5/09

This is the largest of the three cairns and it sits on the highest point. Its shape and structure would indicate that it has had some rebuilding since AW's day.

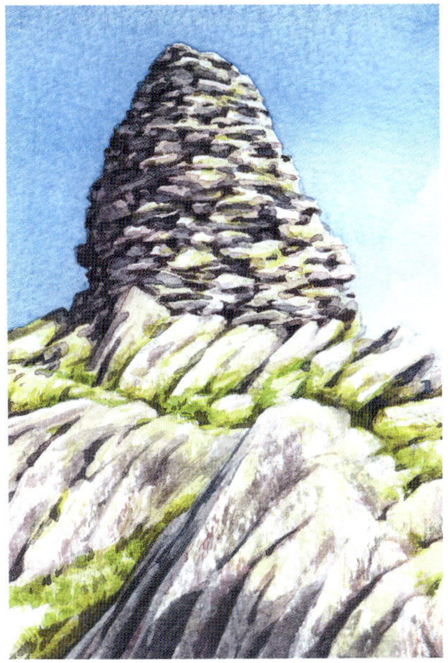

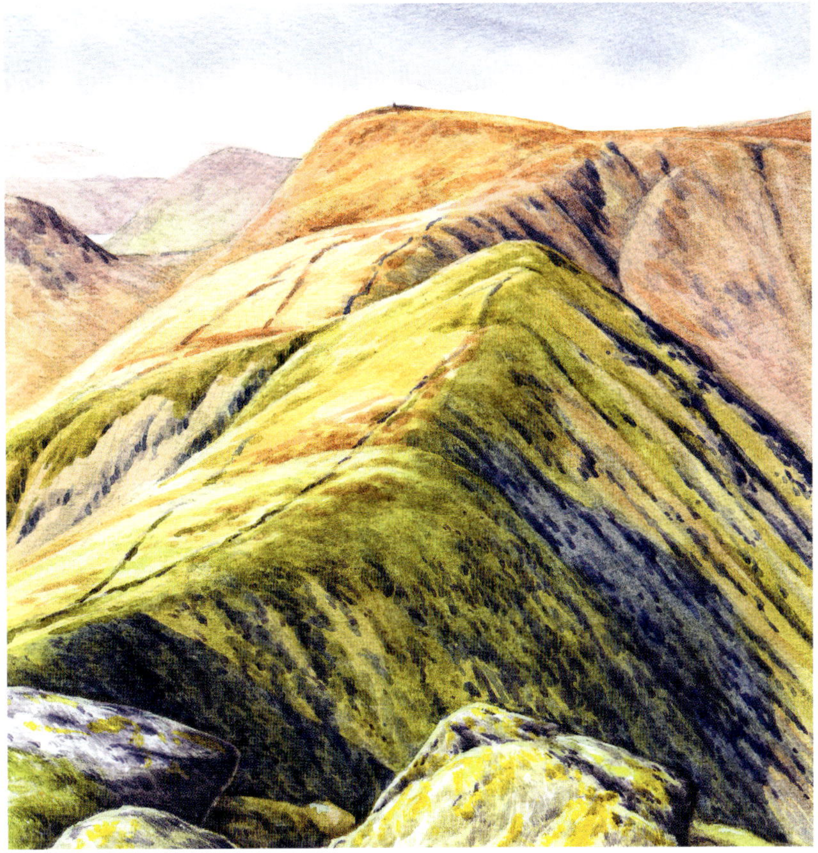

Thornthwaite Crag and Froswick 6/5/07

The ridge path to Froswick is now much more defined but it fails to spoil this dramatic scene.

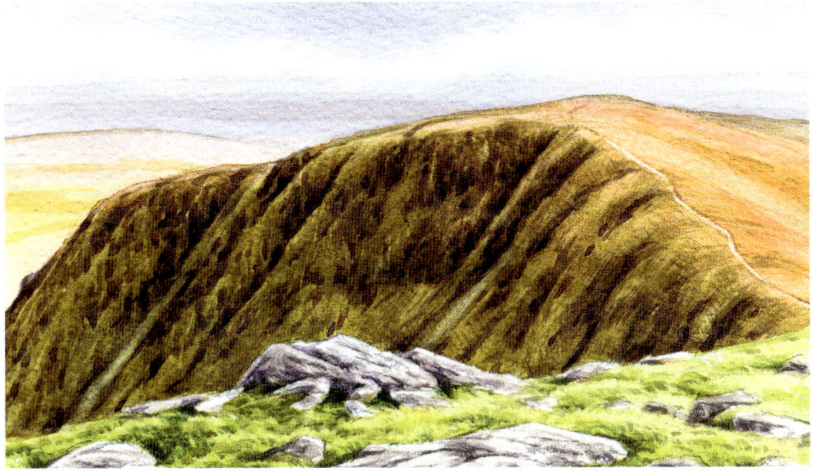

Rainsbarrow Cove and Yoke 6/5/07

The path that runs along this ridge has undergone some restoration due to the increase in footfall. None the less, the work is now blending in nicely and provides a solid pathway along the length of the route.

Ill Bell and the head of Kentmere 10/10/10

Just north of the isolated farm at Hartrigg this impressive prospect of the Upper Kentmere valley comes into view.

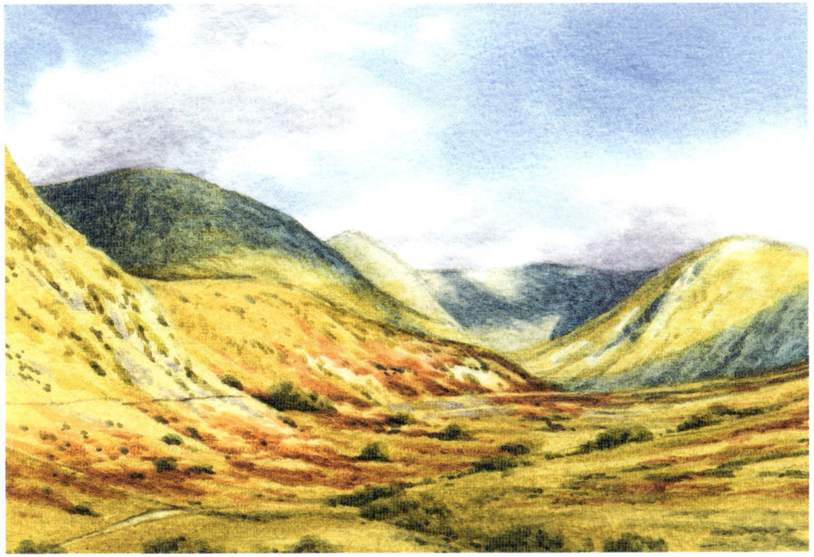

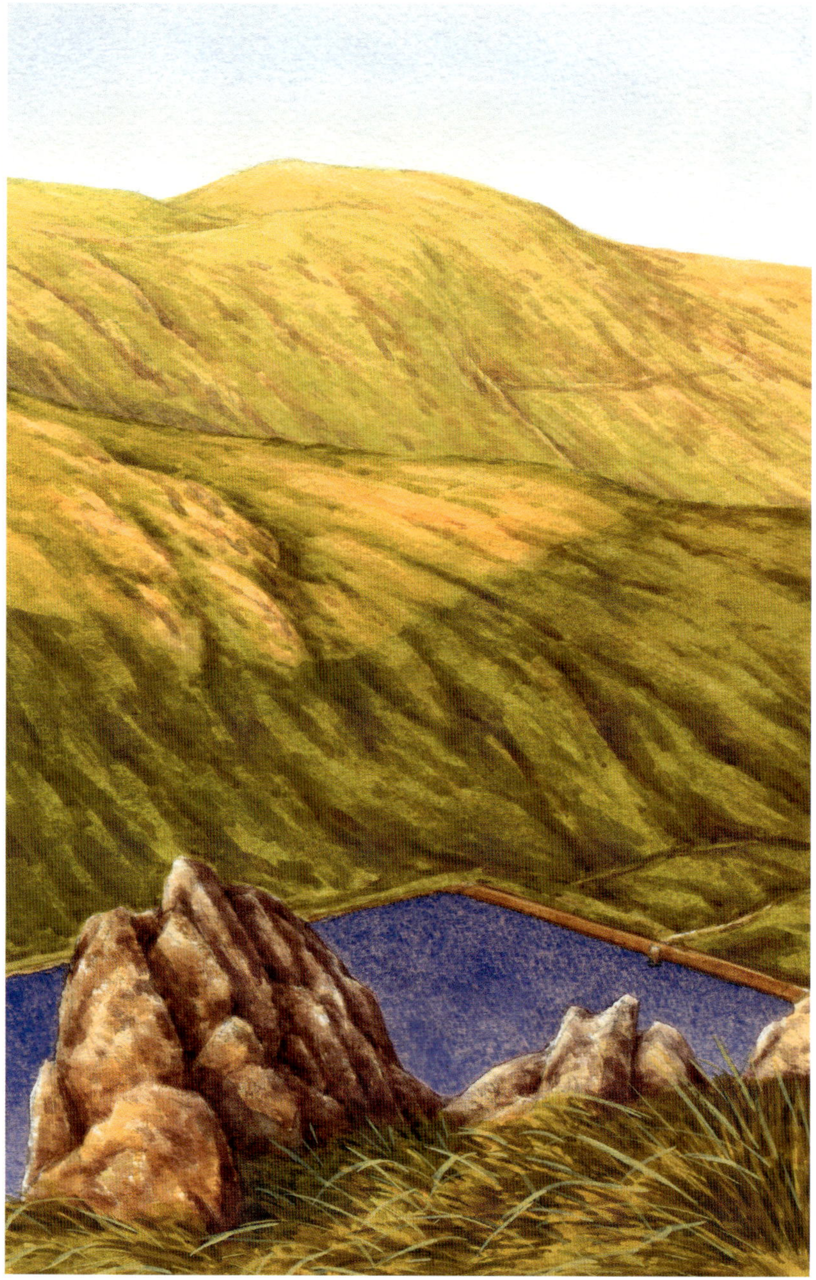

Kentmere Pike

A pike or peak in name only, rather just a rounded top on the ridge south from Harter Fell. Its western facing grassy slopes contrast with the crags and gullies of the face which drops down into the Longsleddale valley to the east. It is mostly visited as part of the Kentmere round.

From Ill Bell (north east ridge) 10/6/13

It took two attempts to achieve this location, the first time the weather was rather poor and all was shrouded in mist and drizzle. The next visit proved more fruitful although the rocks may have had some artistic interpretation by AW.

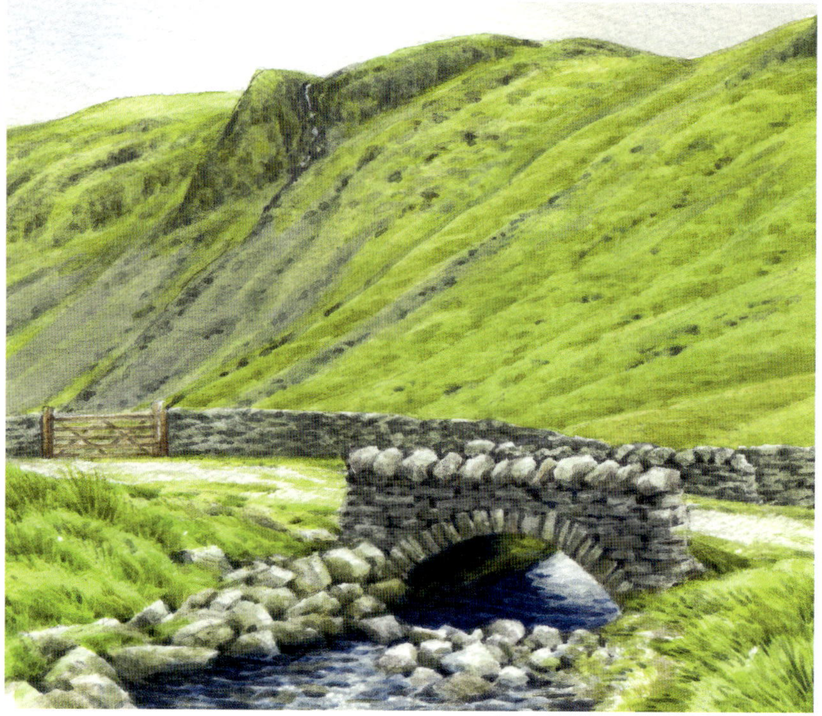

Steel Pike from the quarry road 10/5/09

The old bridge has been replaced on this lane that leads up and over the Gatesgarth Pass into Mardale.

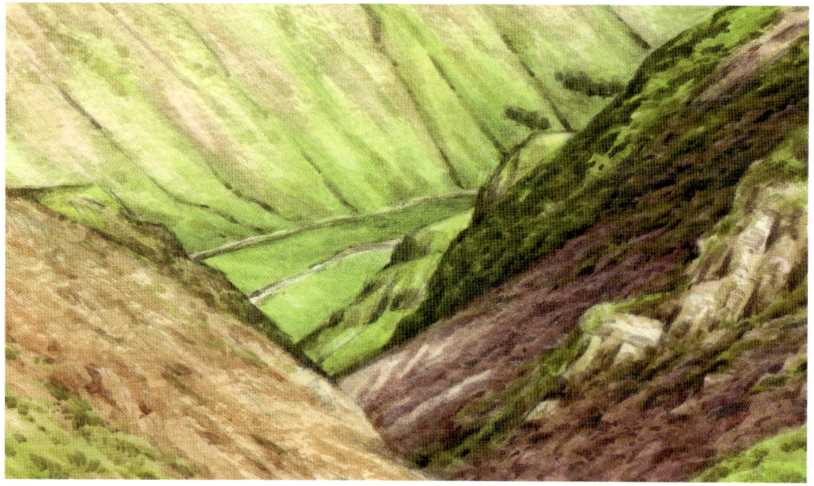

Looking down a scree gully, eastern flank 29/5/09

This dramatic cleft lies east of the recognised path. Far below is the quarry road in Longsleddale alongside the River Sprint.

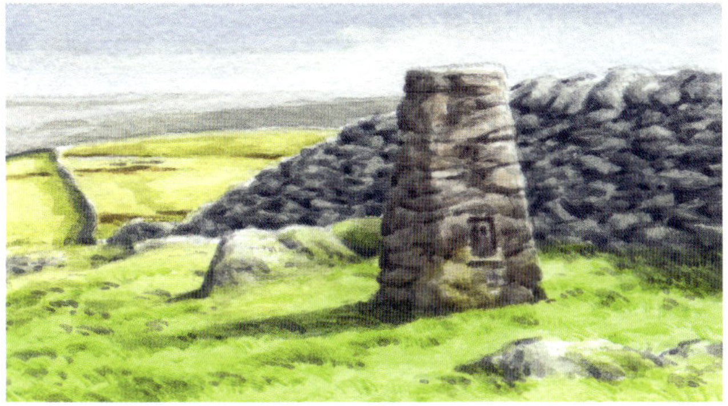

The summit 29/5/09
An unusual feature of Kentmere Pike are the summit markers. A small cairn sits atop a rock platform on the west side of the wall whereas to the east of the wall stands the O.S. pillar.

Goat Scar from Longsleddale
10/5/09
Remarkably the scene is relatively unchanged since Wainwright's day with even the trees bearing similar proportions to his drawing. The location is just along the old quarry road from Sadgill bridge.

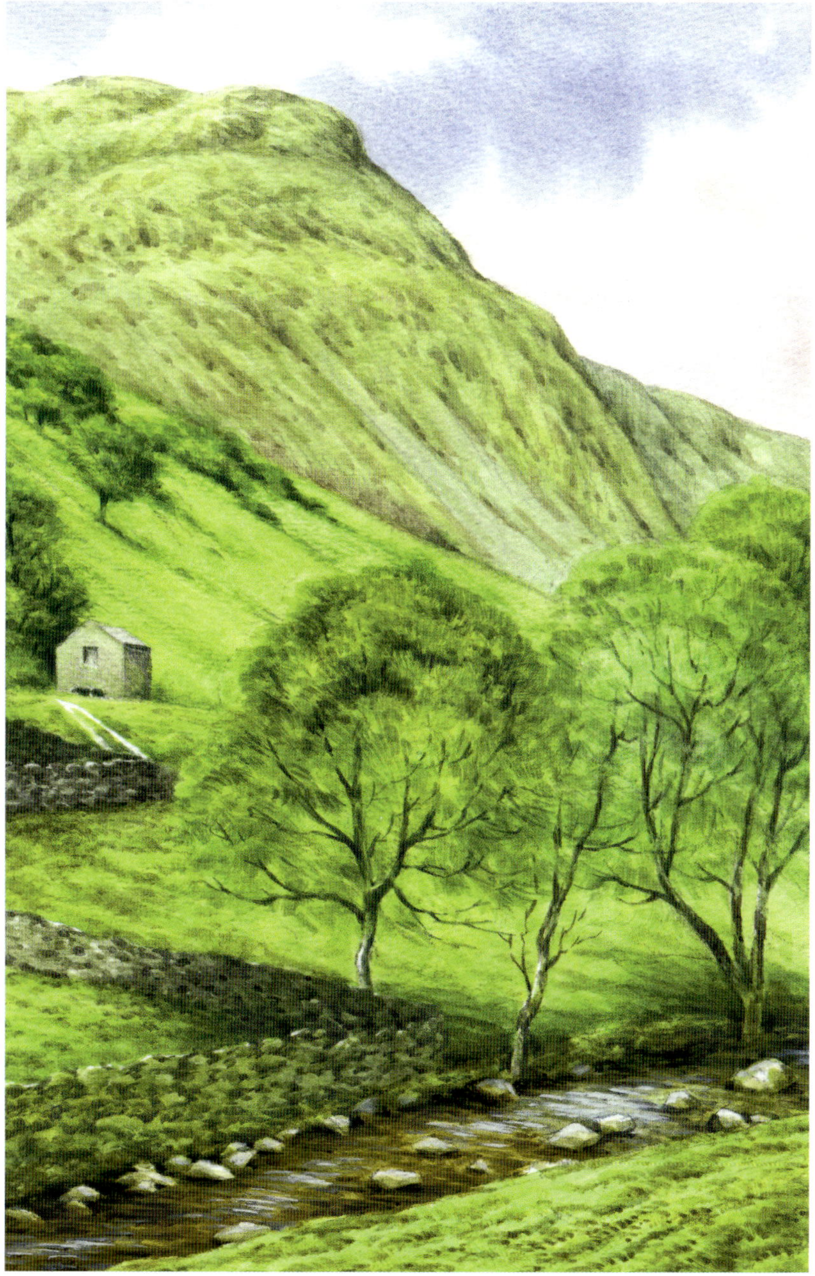

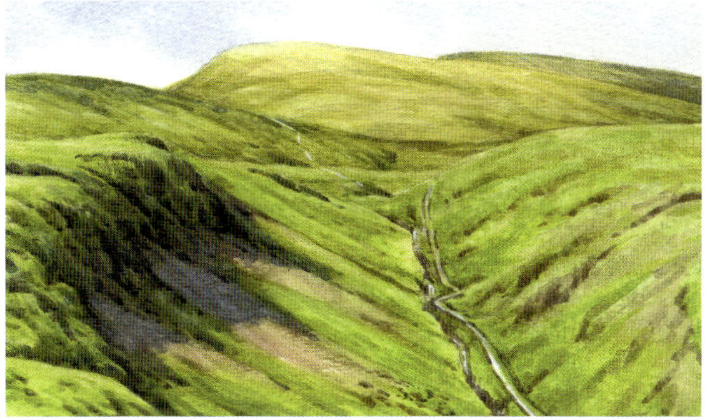

Branstree and the head of Longsleddale from Goat Scar 29/5/09
This sketch would almost stitch together with the one on the left to give a wide angle panoramic view of the valley head.

The eastern face with Harter Fell beyond from Goat Scar 29/5/09
This location is a marvellous place to view almost the whole length of Longsleddale. This sketch shows the aspect to the north.

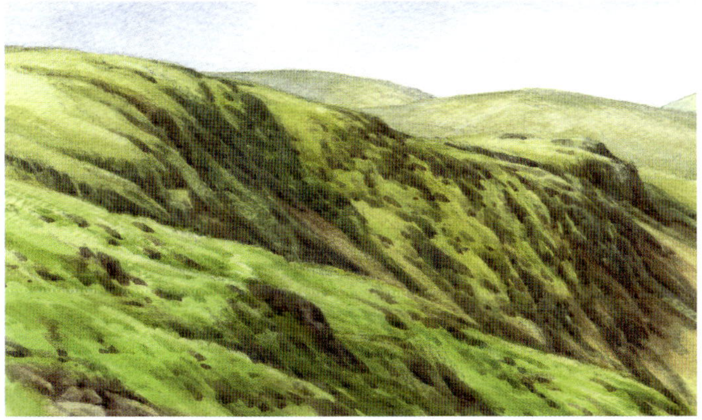

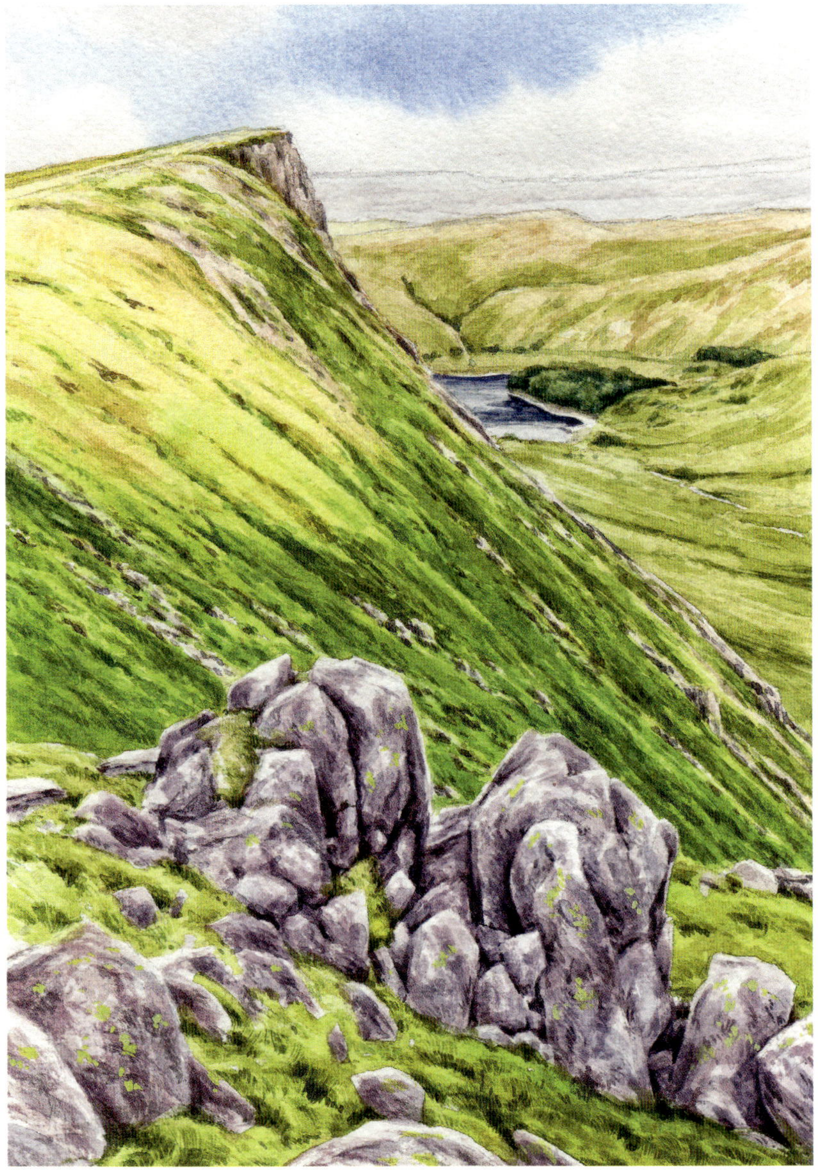

From Twopenny Crag 24/6/08
Actually this rocky outcrop, which took some finding, is 200 yards north of Twopenny Crag but it is the best location to view the fell's angular shape.

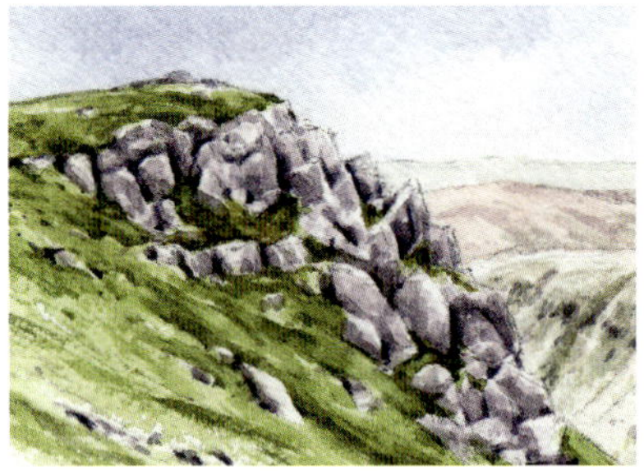

The summit crags 24/6/08
Looking eastwards from 100 yards west of the summit.

The summit 24/6/08
There now sits a larger summit cairn right on the edge of the drop.

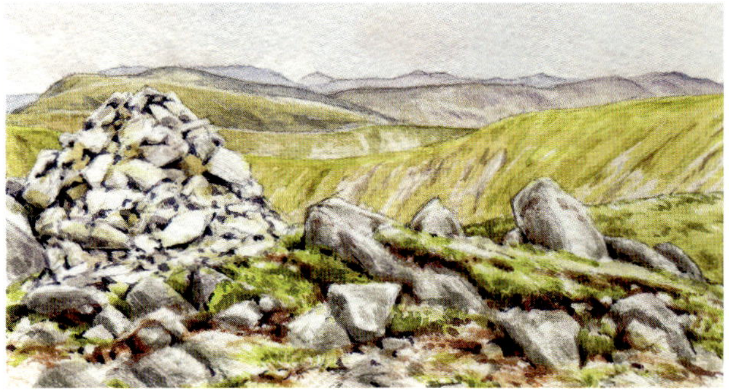

Kidsty Pike

With a wedge like shape when seen in profile Kidsty Pike is identifiable from some distance. This is one of the few fells which required only a single day to obtain all the references as they are within an area near to the summit. The popular Coast to Coast path crosses the summit.

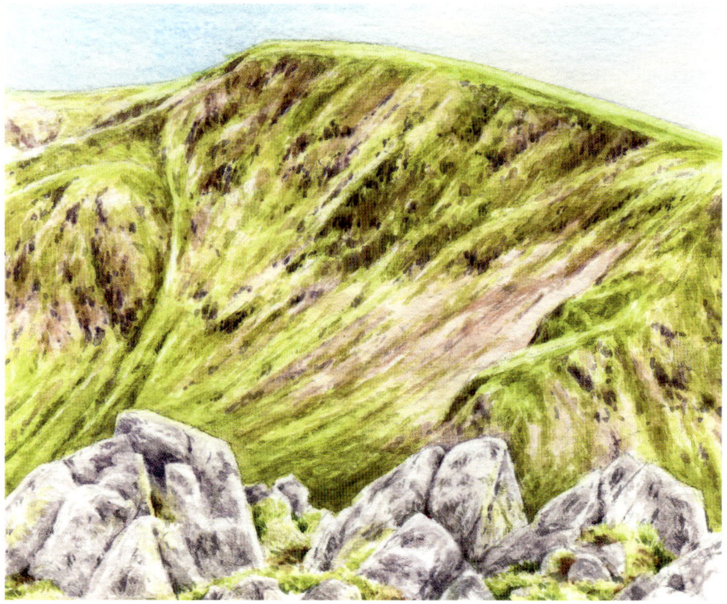

High Street 24/6/08
Near the cairn this is the view across to Hause Crag and the upper section of Long Stile.

Selside Pike and Haweswater 24/6/08
A short distance to the east of the summit this scene comes into full view.

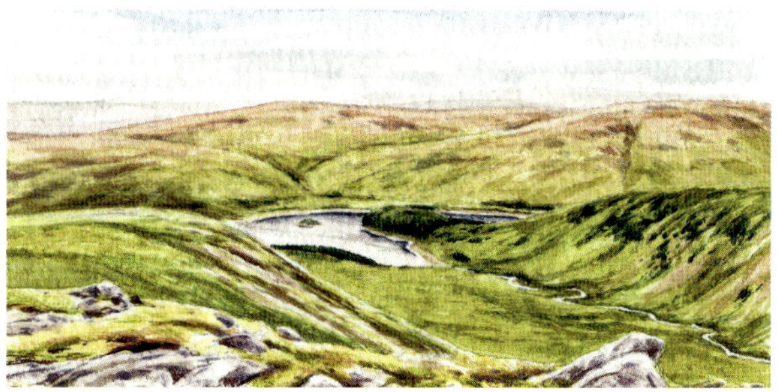

Lakes and tarns

The Lake District lives up to its name; there is hardly a square mile in the region without a body of water, large or small. Lakes are normally defined by their size being generally larger than tarns but only one in the area is actually named as a lake, Bassenthwaite Lake, the others being meres or waters. It is accepted that there are sixteen lakes in the district but not all are within the region covered by the Pictorial Guides, such as Devoke Water which lies to the south west, but it does get a mention in the Green Crag chapter. The largest lake is Windermere, in fact it is the largest body of freshwater in England. The deepest at 258 feet is Wastwater. Several of the lakes are reservoirs such as Thirlmere and Haweswater but Hayeswater (right) which at one time supplied drinking water to Penrith, has now been returned to being a tarn after the dam was removed in 2014.

Tarns are numerous, in fact so many that it would be an almost impossible task to produce a definitive list of them all, especially as some of a decent proportion are not even named. A geographical definition of a tarn is a mountain lake or pool which is sited in a cirque formed by glacial action but I have seen comprehensive lists of lakeland tarns which include pools of water on upland bog, which obviously do not fit into this category. Many tarns are in delightful settings especially when seen on a flat calm day with mountains reflected in their mirror-like surface. Some such as Angle Tarn or Sprinkling Tarn are very popular locations but it is worth exploring the more out of the way tarns which are relatively untouched. In the process of obtaining references for this project I have found some watery gems, even one or two missed by Wainwright himself. It would be easy to list them but better perhaps to let you go and find these jewels for yourself and then pick your own favourites. If you are looking for the highest tarn then you need to visit Long Top on Crinkle Crags where at 2800 feet is a pool of water ideal for dipping your toes on a hot day and should really be called Long Top Tarn: currently it is unnamed on maps. Wainwright classed Broadcrag Tarn as the highest standing water in the area. This was not a mistake on his part but he was referring to the 2 ½ inch map of the day where Broadcrag Tarn was marked in blue to indicate standing water whereas the higher Foxes Tarn on Scafell and Long Top Tarn on Crinkle Crags were not. Curiously the substantial unnamed tarn (or more accurately pool) that now lies on the "saddle" of Blencathra was not mentioned in the Pictorial Guide, and maps of the day do not indicate its presence even though they do now. It has obviously come into existence since the 1960s.

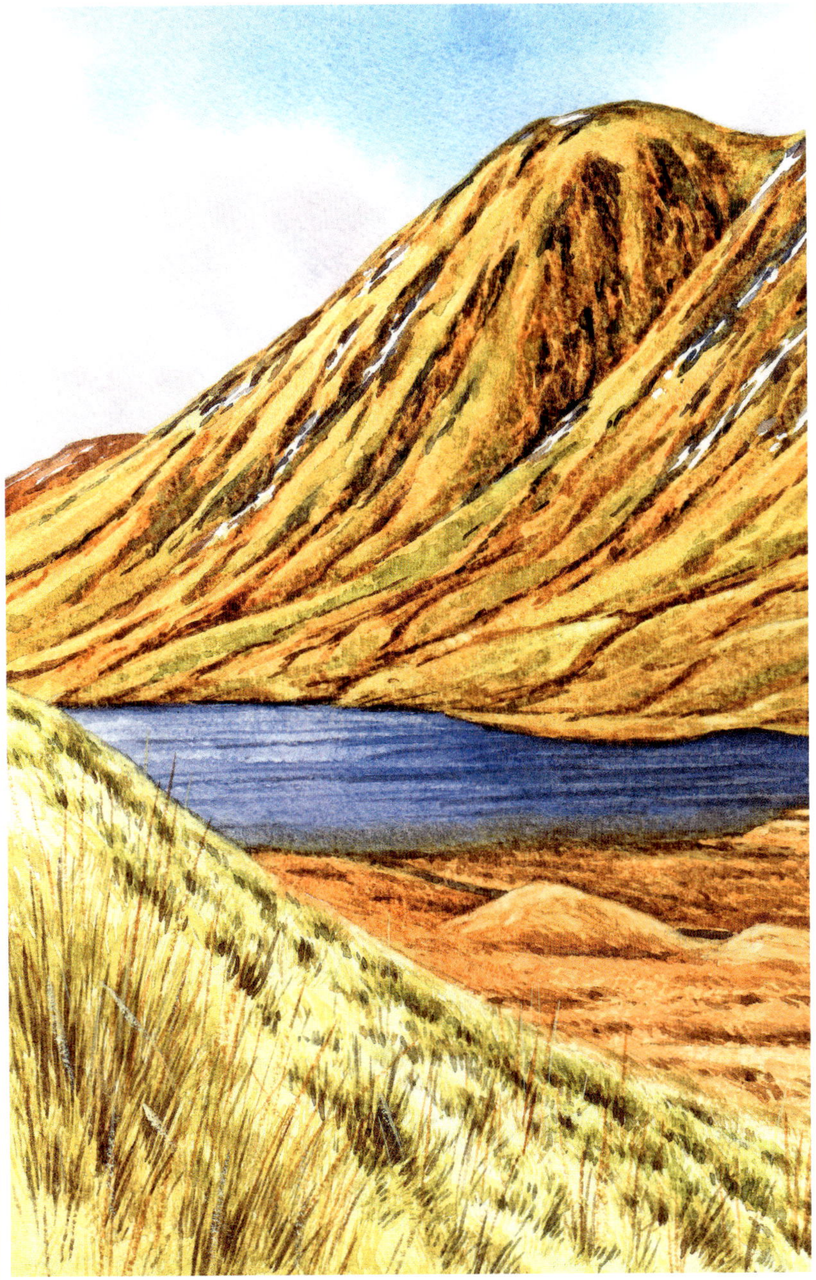

The Knott

Undoubtedly this fell is most usually visited by walkers as they are going to or from High Street from Hartsop or Patterdale. A slight diversion off the main path takes you to the unassuming top. The view west from the summit is rather impressive though.

From Hayeswater Gill 20/2/09

Since I completed this sketch the dam at the far end of the reservoir has been removed resulting in the lowering of the water level leaving an unsightly shoreline scar which will take years to recover, if ever. Surely the dam could have been replaced with a more natural embankment which could have maintained the water level and with it the natural look of the lake?

The summit 24/6/08

The summit cairn has grown at the expense of the nearby fallen wall.

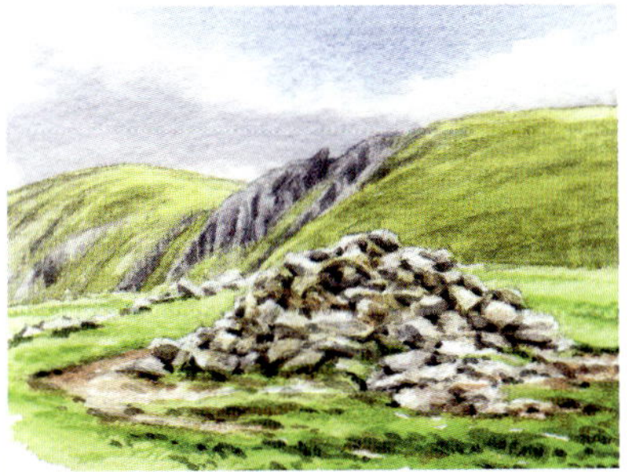

The antiquities and oddities of Moor Divock

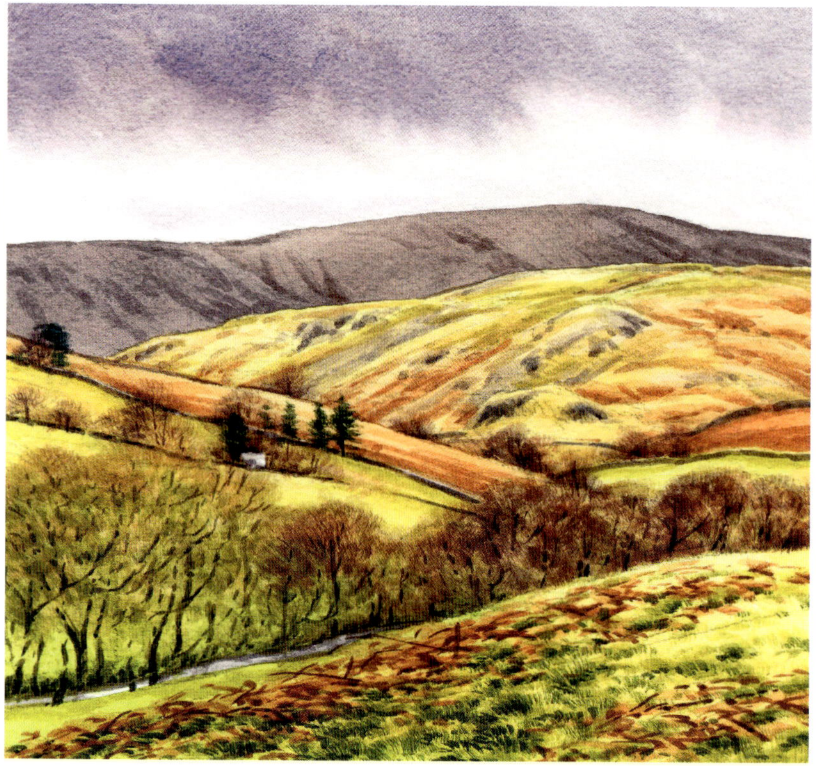

From Sandwick 13/3/09
A valley scene with Loadpot Hill only forming the distant skyline. Sandwick is a small collection of houses close to the east shore of Ullswater.

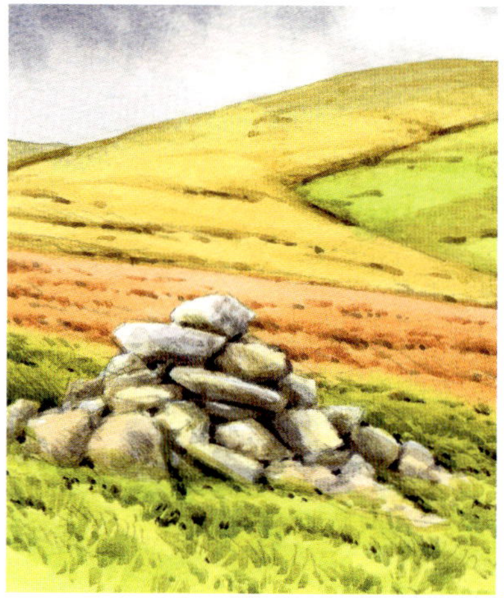

The beacon on The Pen 12/7/12
Now a heap of stones rather than the once impressive taller beacon.

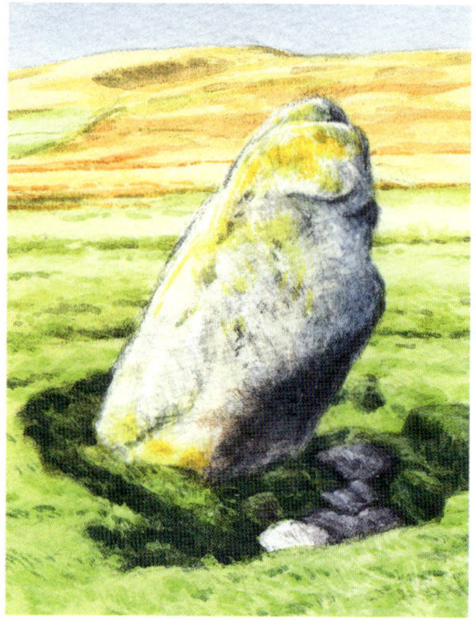

Cop Stone 16/10/09
At about 5' high this is the last one remaining of what once was an avenue of standing stones. AW's *"oddly sited signpost"* is no more.

Loadpot Hill

This is more of an area of open moorland than a fell, with very little in the way of rocky outcrops or crags. What it lacks in geographical drama it makes up for in sites of antiquity and historical interest. It is extensive in area, taking up five pages in maps alone, more than any other fell in all of the Pictorial Guides.

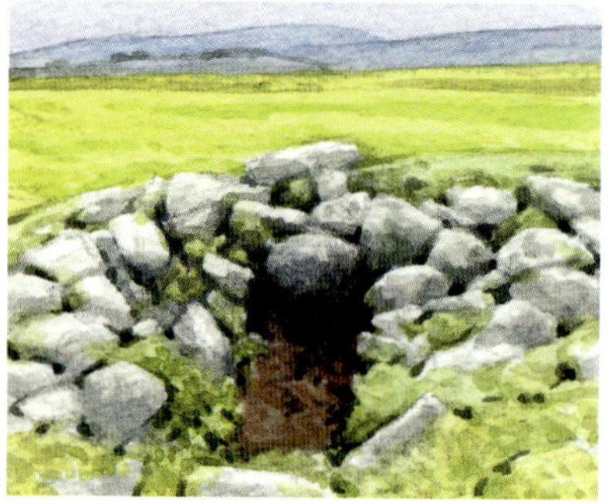

Tumuli 24/6/08
This excavated pit may not be the first of the tumuli which he drew but the skyline was similar.

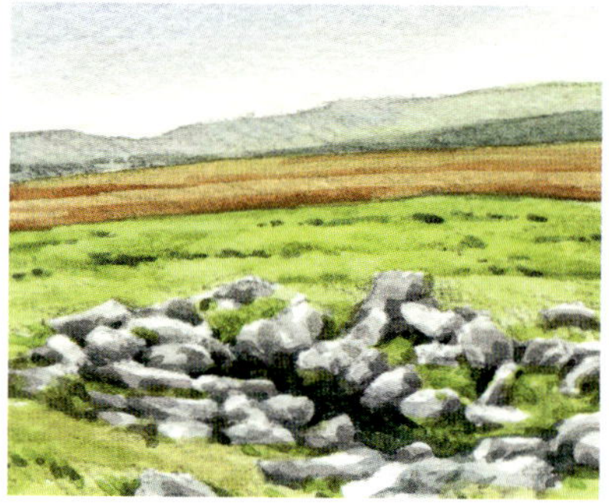

Tumuli 24/6/08
One of many in this area so to locate it required some guesswork with only the far horizon as a clue.

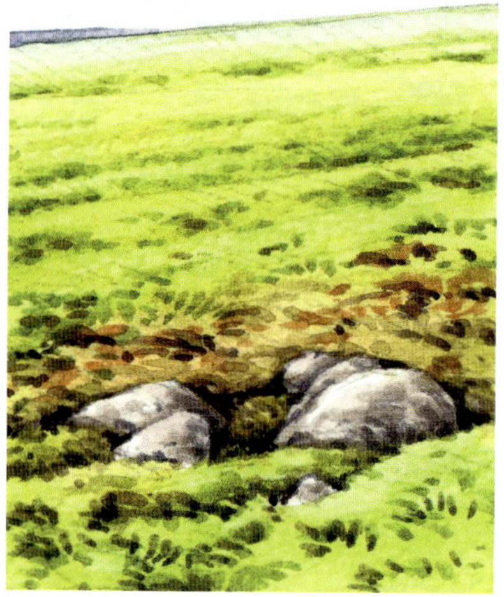

The boundary stone 24/6/08

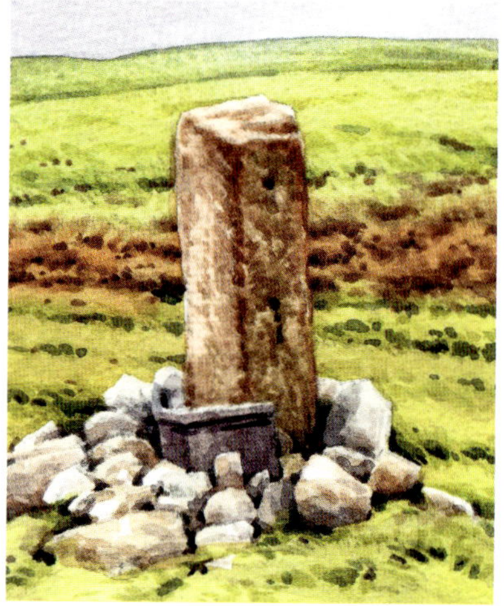

The boundary post 24/6/08

An explanation: The boundary post being wooden has decayed and gone. The boundary stone which was sited up and behind the post as shown in AW's drawing has consequently been moved down to the track side to replace the wooden post, complete with the metal angle section which stays in place. The site where the boundary stone originally stood only has the supporting rocks left in place. A case of two becoming one and hence the confusion in the titles of my two sketches above.

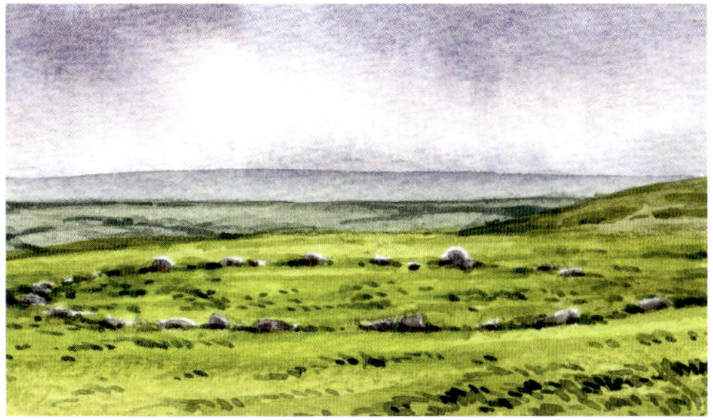

Stone Circles (a) 24/6/08

This stone circle was marked as The Cockpit on maps of the time but perhaps due to its historic "sporting" use AW decided to not to refer to this name. It is positioned just to one side of the Roman road which crosses the moor.

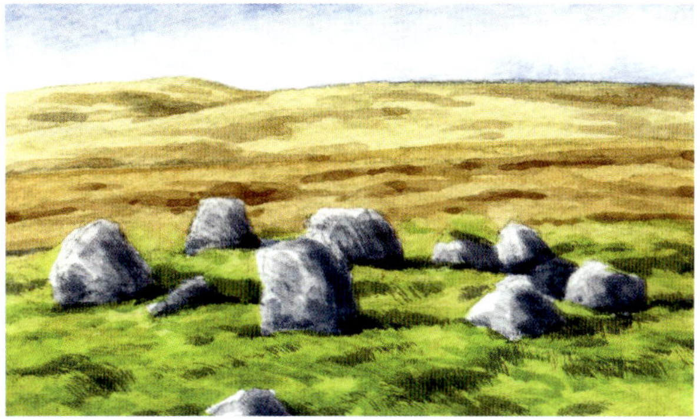

Stone Circles (b) 16/10/09

There are several such features on Moor Divock, this one is sited just to the north west of The Cop Stone.

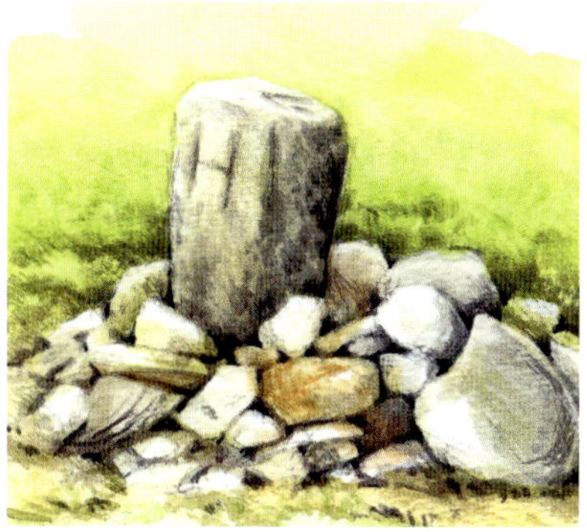

The summit 24/6/08

The boundary stone still sits amongst the pile of quartz rocks with a faded benchmark on the top. Wainwright does refer to the engraved letter L for Lowther but not the H on the other face which was for Harrison, a landowner in Longsleddale. Nearby now stands a triangulation pillar which sits on a slightly higher point than this, it was constructed several years after Wainwright's visit.

Chimney, Lowther House

24/6/08

The chimney stack of this former shooting hut which was built in the early years of the 20th century is now almost in a state of total collapse but it does provide some form of shelter from the elements. The footings of the walls can be seen as can a crumbling concrete floor nearby.

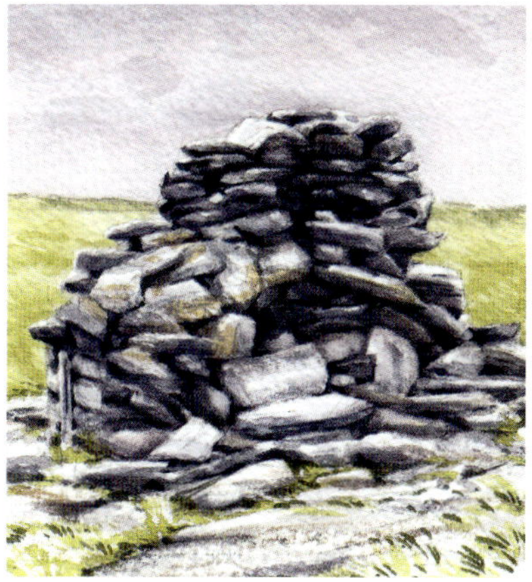

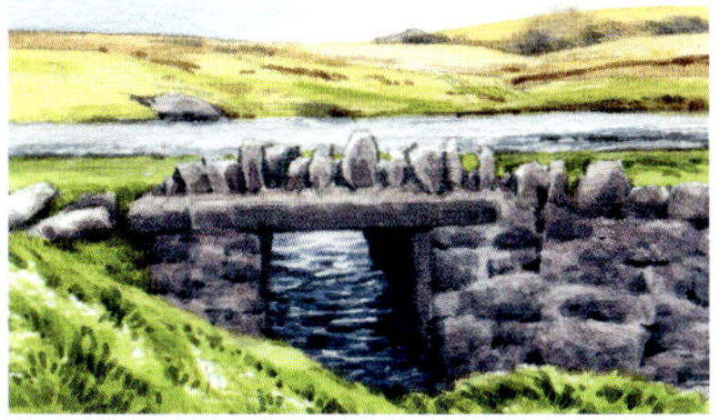

Bridge in Heltondale 16/10/09

There is nothing special about this little bridge but after six pages purely of maps and ascent drawings, AW possibly felt the need for a little sketch to break the monotony and fill a small gap so this met the requirement. Its location is only marked at the bottom right of Loadpot Hill 7.

Fusedale and Ullswater from Dodd Gill 29/10/11

The hidden valley of Fusedale from the steep descent alongside the gill.

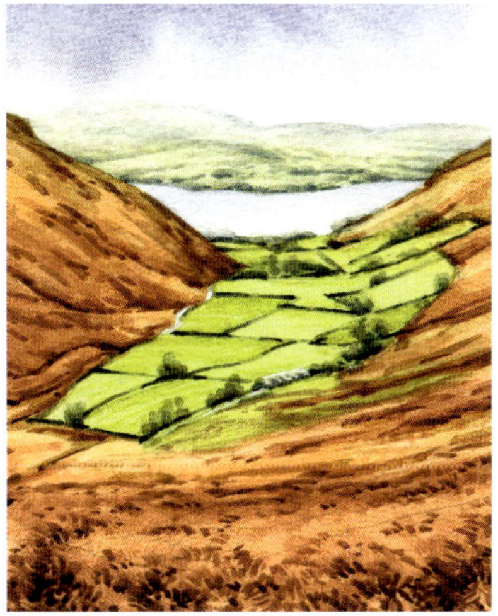

Brock Crag and Ullswater

26/5/10

A fine view reached by leaving the path near Brock Crag Tarns and heading west for 100 yards.

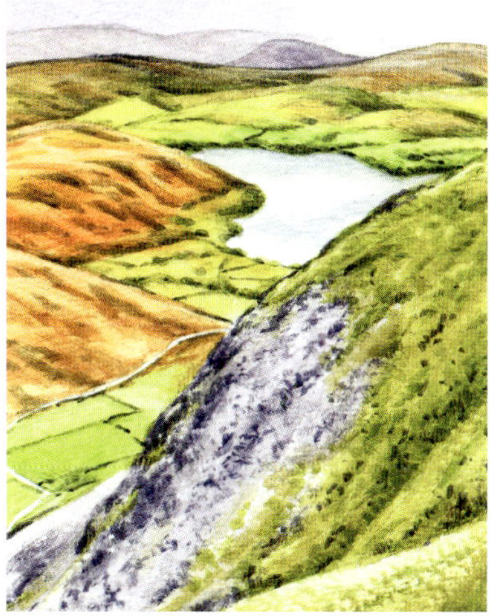

The Romans on Loadpot Hill

The history of High Street roman road is well documented but what is less well known is the part that Loadpot Hill played in the activities of the Romans, who had a large industrial city close by on the shores of Ullswater c45 A.D. The road itself passed over the summit of the fell and was a dual carriageway in the area. The name Loadpot derives from the name for the large hole north of the summit where haematite iron ore (lode) was quarried. Other stone and waste material from this quarry was used to metal the High Street road. Close to the summit of the fell is a large spring which is marked by a large glacial rock, supposedly a roman altar. The water from this spring and others supplied canals and reservoirs which serviced the ore extraction operations. These canals and aqueducts are often mistaken for sunken lanes and roads. The whole area of this fell is steeped in history in which the Romans played a major role.

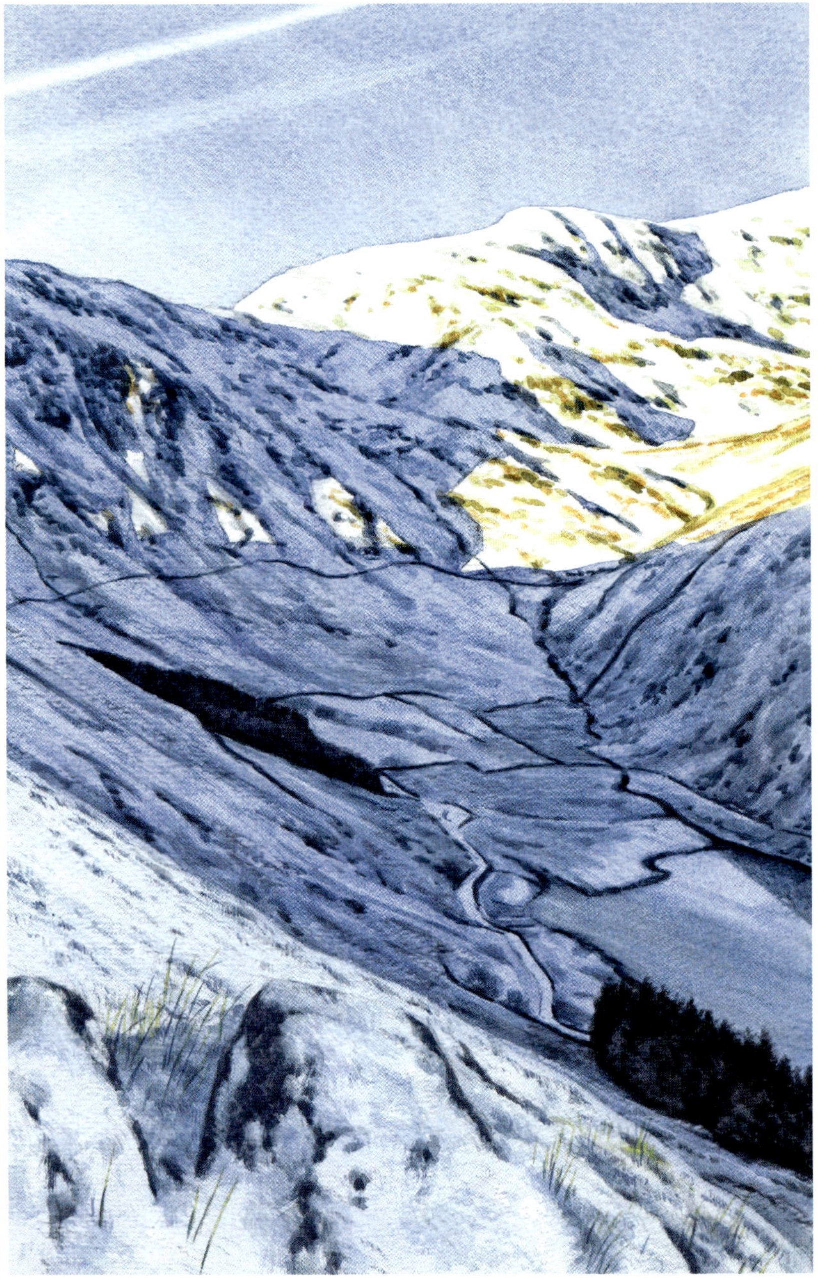

Mardale Ill Bell

Situated at the very head of the Kentmere valley this fell lacks any real character of note when approached from that southerly aspect. The north eastern quarter of the fell is a different matter. Dramatic cliffs, splendid tarns and interesting routes of ascent, this is where the best assets of Mardale Ill Bell are to be found.

From the north ridge of Branstree 2/3/10

First light of a winter's day strikes the slopes of Mardale Ill Bell. The head of the Haweswater reservoir is iced over. Seen from a location close to that of scenes from the High Street and Branstree chapters.

The north face from Blea Water 17/3/09

This is a delightful location, cliffs drop into the deep, dark water and due to the sheltered position the surface of the tarn is often flat calm. When I am past walking the high fells this is the sort of place I will continue to revisit.

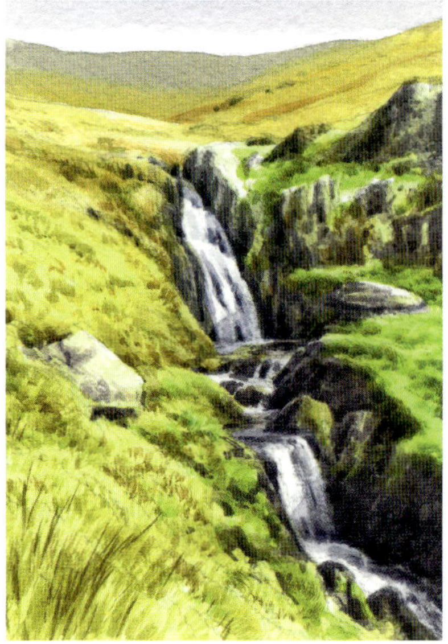

Waterfalls, River Kent below Hall Cove 10/10/10

A remote and delightful location.

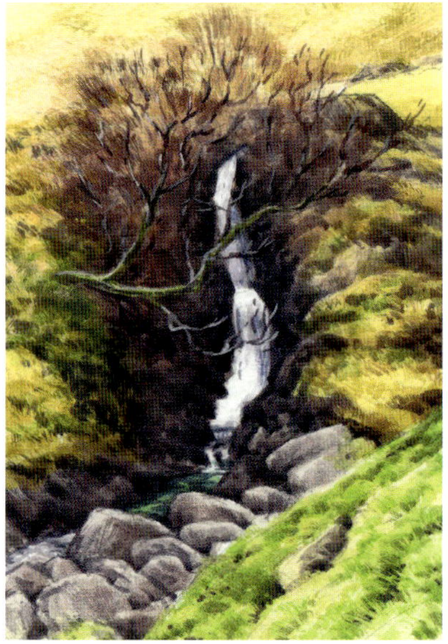

Dodderwick Force 17/3/09

Seen from near the good path that leads up towards Blea Water.

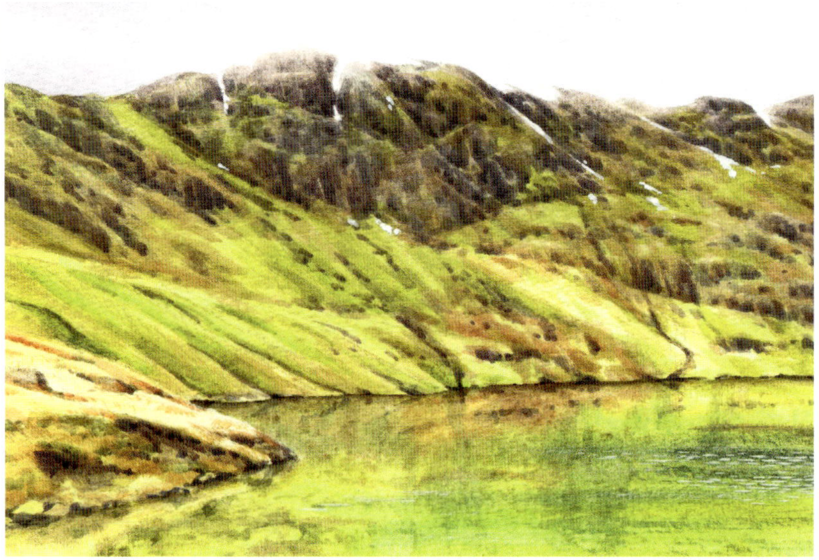

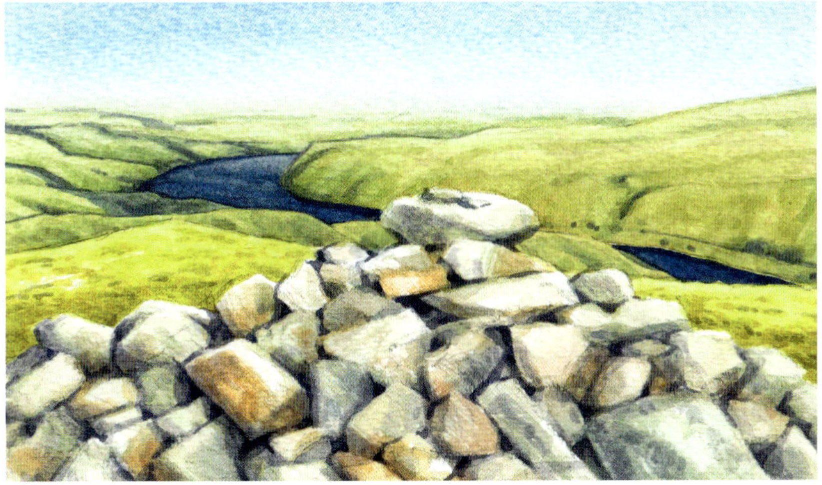

The summit 29/5/09
A sprawling mound occupies the top and it would obscure the view of Haweswater if it all was featured in this sketch. By including just the uppermost section of the cairn I was able to capture the required scene.

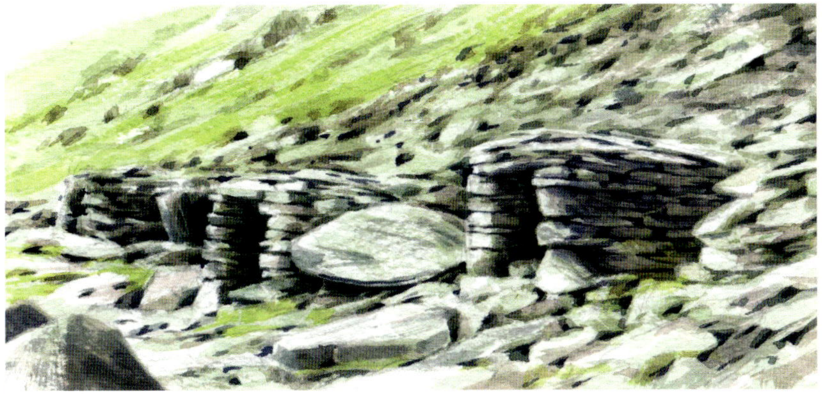

The stone shelters at Small Water 17/3/09
Still reasonably intact these diminutive and basic shelters must have served their purpose. Only really inclement weather would have caused travellers to have taken shelter here, with Mardale Green so close by.

Haweswater and Small Water from the Nan Bield ridge 29/5/09
The impressive view to the north along the length of the valley. It is a popular viewpoint between the fell's summit and Nan Bield Pass.

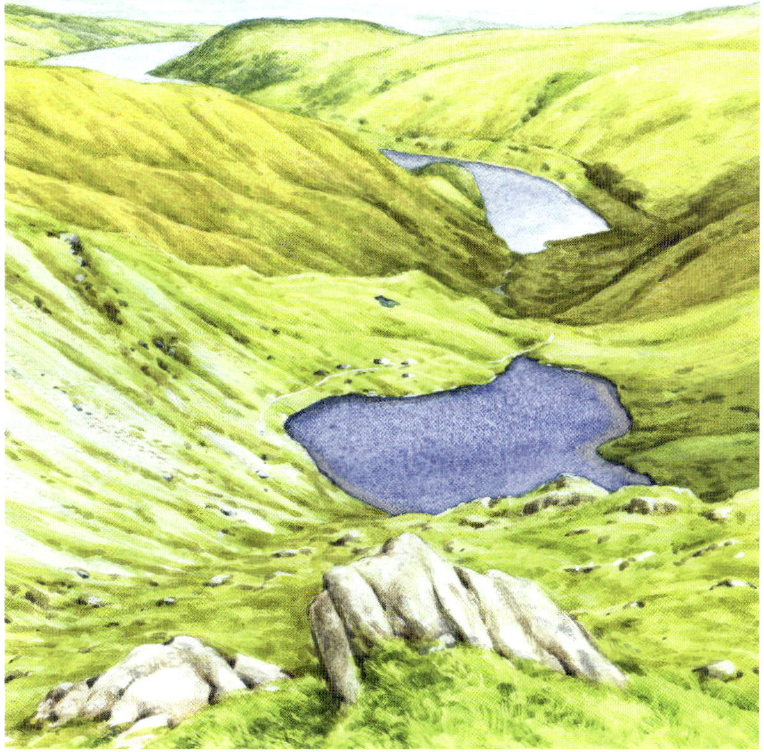

Mardale Green lost village

It is hard to imagine now just how beautiful the valley of Mardale would have been prior to the construction of the dam and the consequent flooding of the area back in the late 1930s. Then the natural lake in the valley was known as Hawes Water, comprising of High Water and Low Water. With the coming of the reservoir not only were the buildings such as the church, pub, numerous dwellings and farmsteads of Mardale Green all demolished but more importantly a whole community was dispersed against their will. At times of prolonged dry weather the low water levels of the reservoir reveal a few sad remnants of the past, old field walls and the faint outlines of farm buildings exposed as a reminder to the days gone by. Only the take off tower near the Haweswater Hotel has any permanent reminder of the past. It was constructed from the stone and windows of the village church.

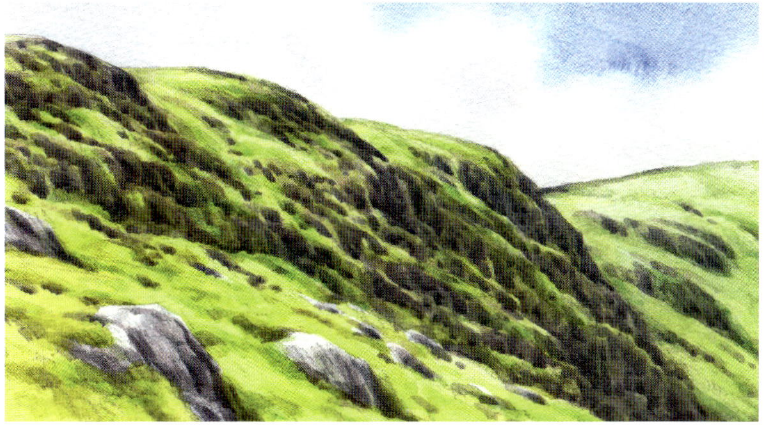

The summit crags 29/5/09
To reach this viewpoint you must either ascend or descend the north ridge. The path is indistinct but not too difficult.

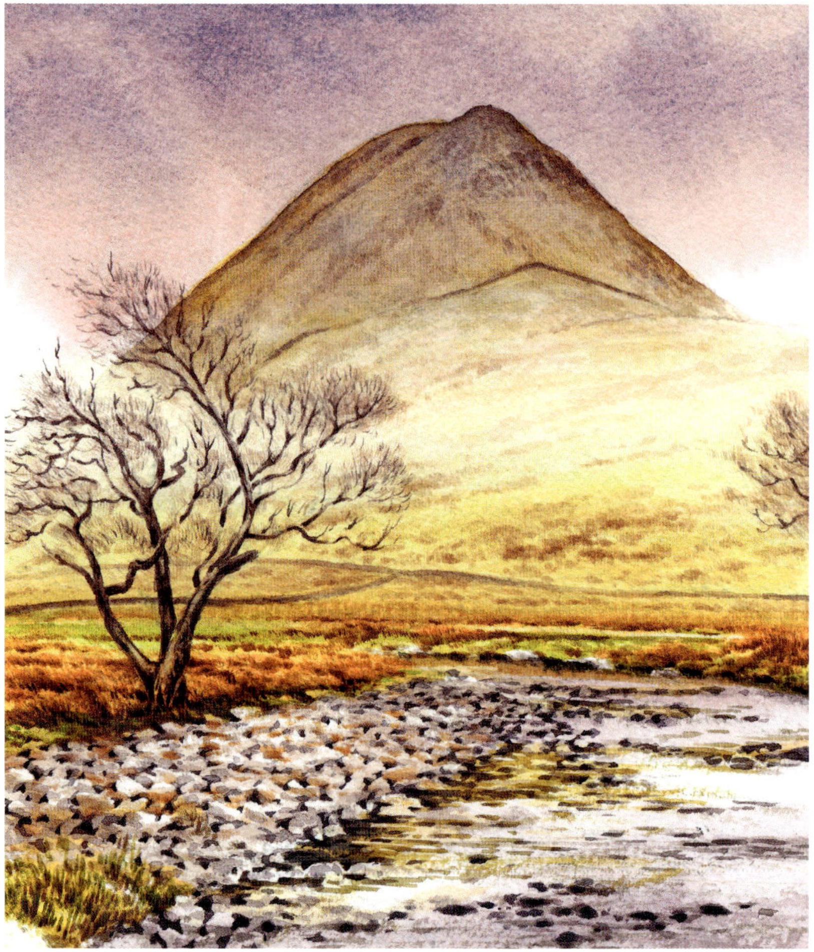

From Rampsgill Beck 21/4//09

The mist in the valley was just clearing as I arrived at the correct location. Now the riverbed is much wider but the lone tree on the bank stands firm.

Note: This location is on private ground and permission was gained for me to access this site. I have read of walkers using the lane between the dale road and The Bungalow but there is no public right of way here, please respect the landowner's rights.

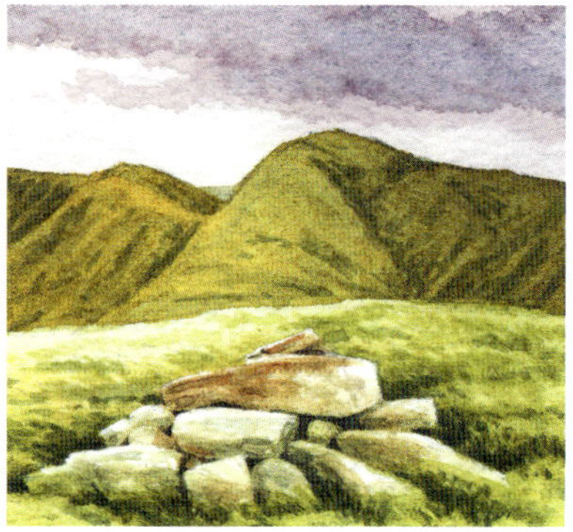

The summit 5/7/09

A small cluster of stones marks the highest point with Rest Dodd in the distance. The ground in between is a peaty bog. My advice would be to make this journey either in winter when the ground is frozen or during a very dry summer. You have been warned.

The Nab

This fell is formed by the high spur of land that protrudes from the north slope of Rest Dodd and the summit is at the most northerly high point. Even though this area is within open access land, due to the deer management walkers are requested to use the well signed preferred routes which avoids disturbance of the wild deer. I have never found this request to be an issue.

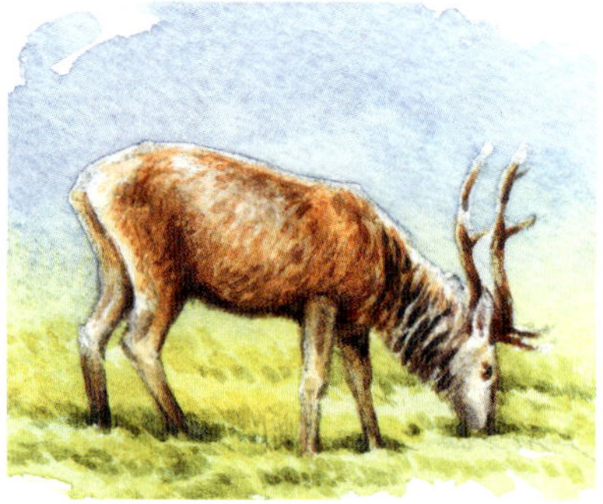

Red Deer

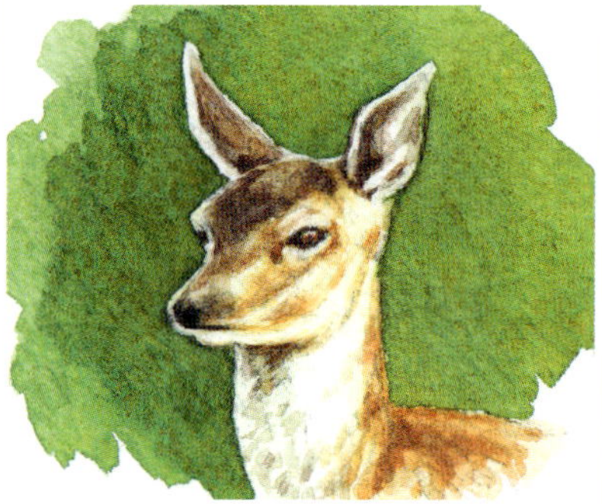

Red Deer Hind

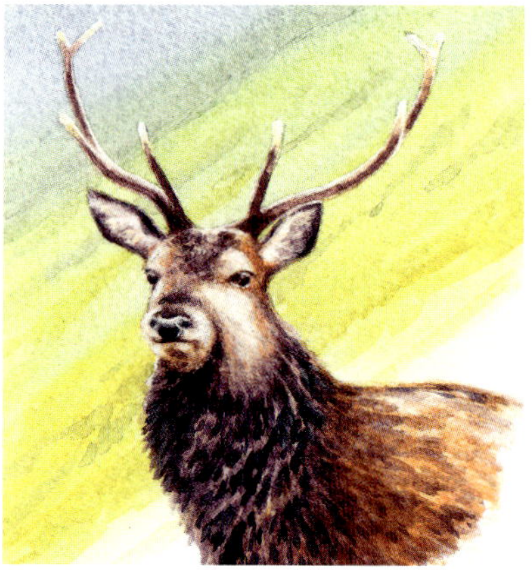

Red Deer Stag

Martindale Deer Forest

This area is home to the oldest native red deer herd in England and the deer can be seen throughout the year, but they blend in well to the fell sides so it takes a keen eye to spot them sometimes despite the fact they are about 400 in number. In autumn the stags will be in rut and their bellowing can be heard echoing throughout the area. Red deer are actually quite widespread in some of the neighbouring valleys.

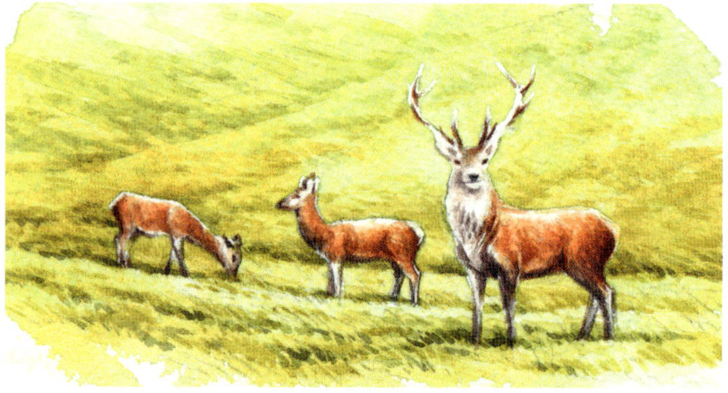

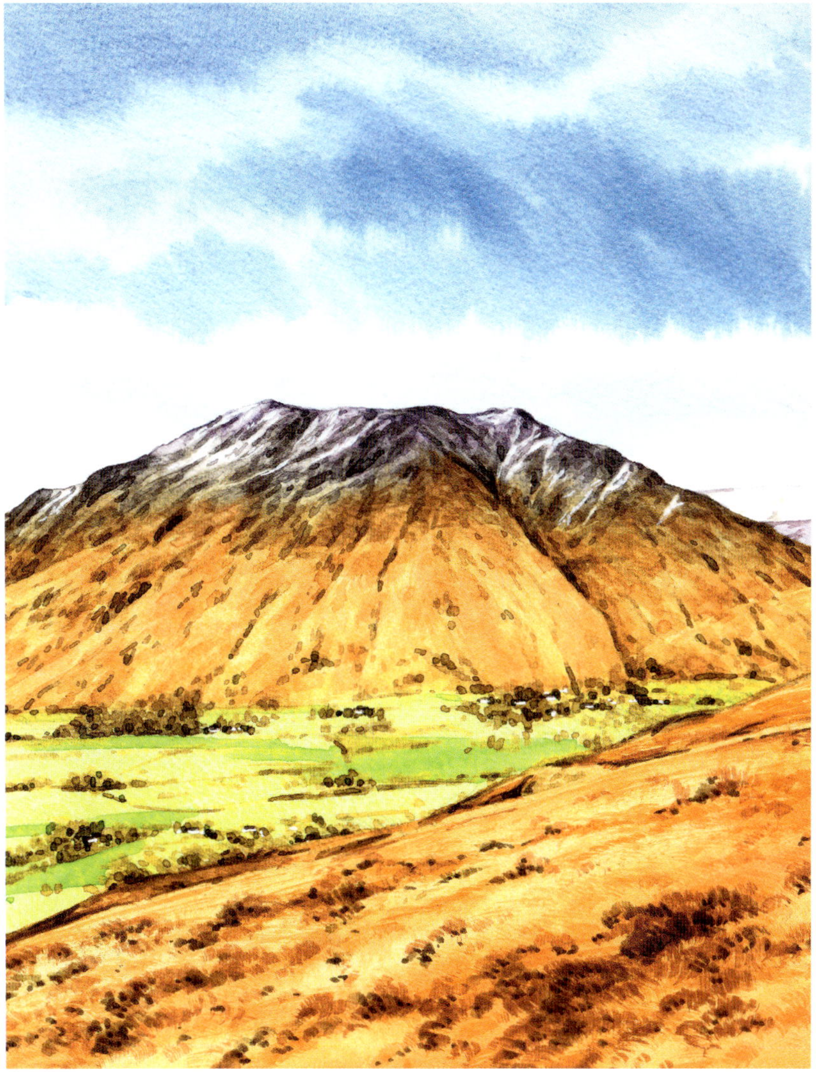

From Birks 6/3/09

It was always a trial to obtain references for this series of sketches with the fells in similar seasonal conditions to AW's drawings. In this painting I really needed the snow line to be down by a couple of hundred feet more to match his illustration, but it was not to be. There was just enough snow to help define the crags and gullies of the upper section of the fell.

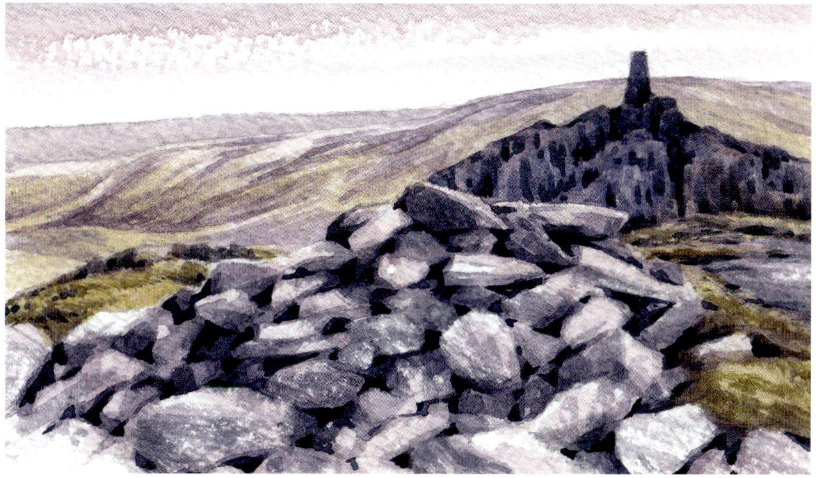

The summit 14/10/08

The design of the pages for this chapter meant that AW was only able to squeeze a small sketch of the summit cairn into the bottom right corner of one of the ten pages. Having more freedom with space I have included not only the cairn but the distant triangulation column which he mentions in the description.

Place Fell

This is a fine fell, full of interest and its higher ground provides some excellent views in all directions. This is reflected in the fact that he gives over four pages to illustrate the view, the only time he does so for any fell in Book Two. This may explain why he only found room to include two sketches in the chapter. I have visited the fell on several occasions but on each visit I have found something new of interest. I have promised myself to return one day and fully explore it in depth.

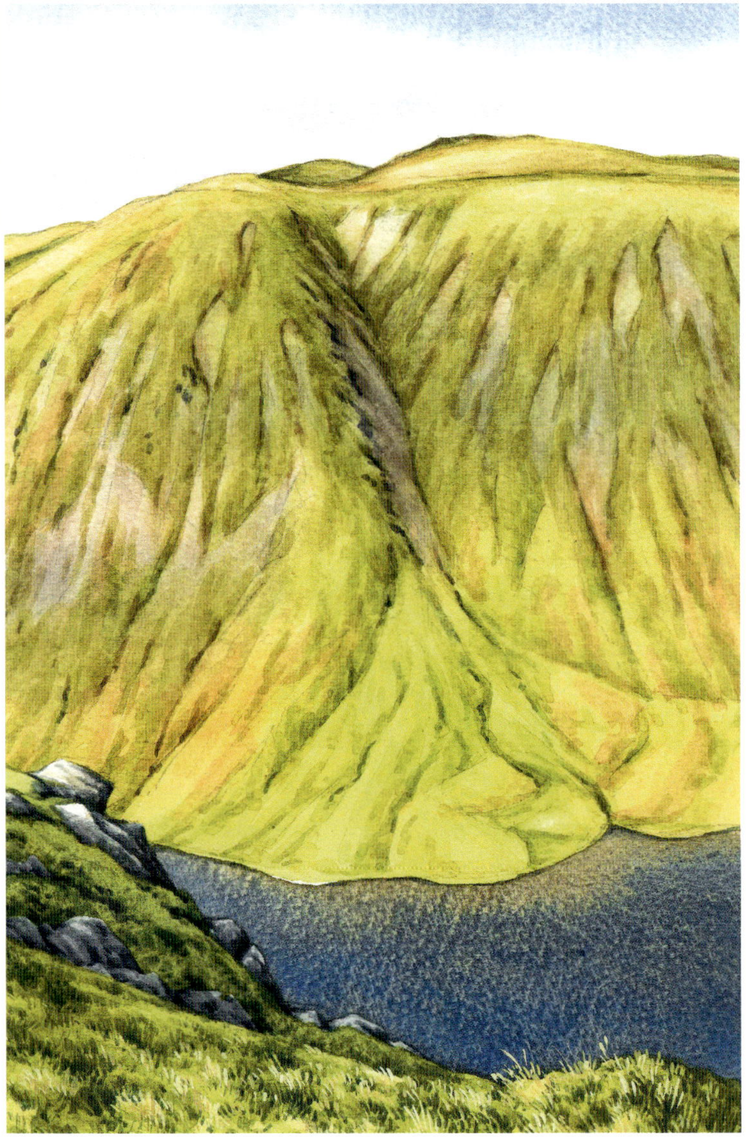

From Gray Crag 20/09/11
This is a unique drawing by AW in the Guides for he has had to include three fell summits in one main fell chapter view, The Knott on the left, Rampsgill Head on the right and High Raise in between.

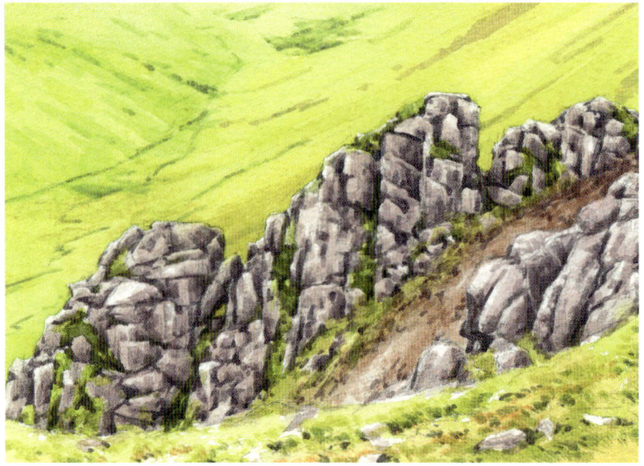

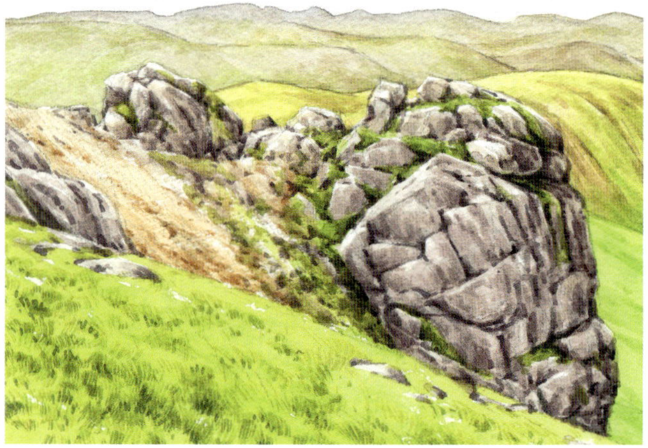

Rampsgill Head

The fine rock scenery to the north of the summit is possibly the most exciting feature of this fell. The view from there down into the valley is excellent and if you are lucky you will spot the herd of red deer.

The summit crags
24/6/08
The arête from the south (above) looking down into the valley of Ramps Gill.
The eastern aspect (top right) with the Helvellyn range in the far distance.

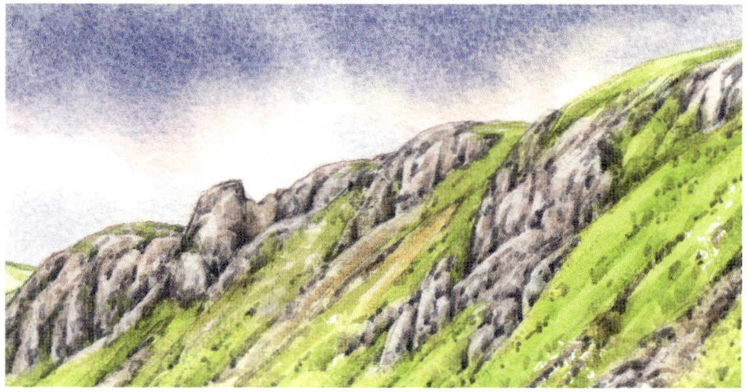

The crags above the north west face 24/6/08
Viewed from the col between Rest Dodd and The Knott.

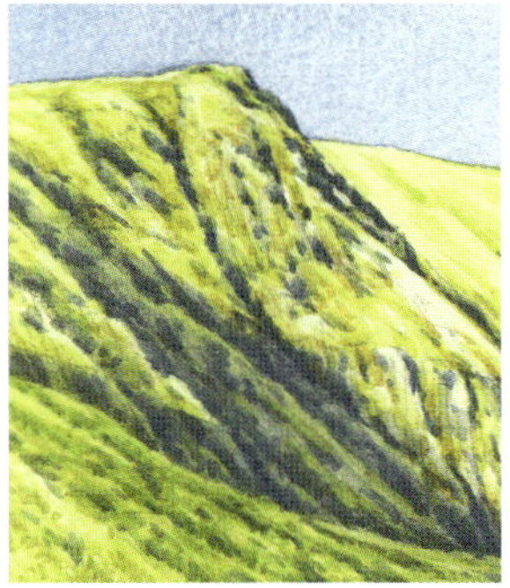

The summit 24/6/08
The untidy pile of rocks which mark the top. Looking southward in the direction of High Street. There is a better cairn just to the north west, overlooking Martindale.

Twopenny Crag 2/3/10
Seen from the path above the Straits of Riggindale.

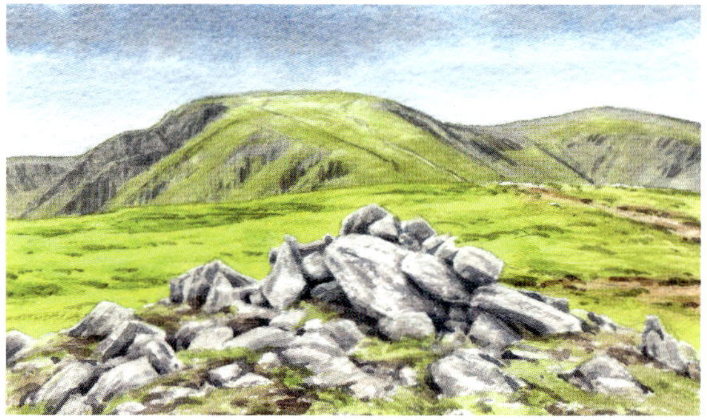

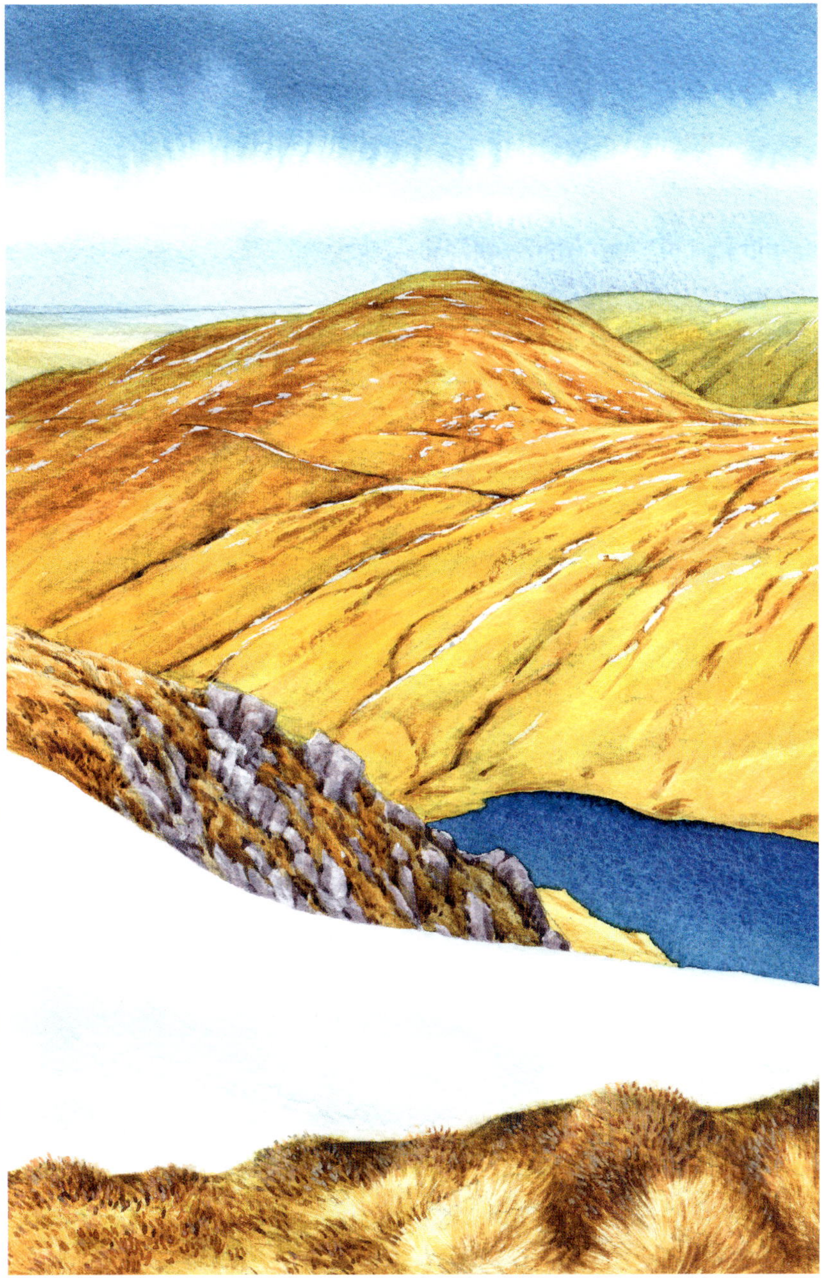

Rest Dodd

There is nothing at all remarkable about Rest Dodd, the majority of its slopes are grassy and almost uniform in shape. Only to the east does it steepen to drop down into the Ramps Gill valley. There is no doubt that many walkers will visit this top in conjunction with a plan to proceed over to the summit of The Nab.

From Gray Crag 20/2/09

This reference was obtained from nearly the same point as the one for Rampsgill Head but in a different season. Not quite the pointed hill shape as shown in AW's illustration so my sketch has a more representative shape with the distant fell of High Raise shown behind. A large snow drift fills the foreground gully.

The summit 2/9/08

The flagpole in his drawing which he also indicated on the summit map has long since gone, but that helped to confirm which cairn I was to sketch as there are three hereabouts now, but only one has this exact view. Not only is The Nab shown here but also the far distant fells beyond.

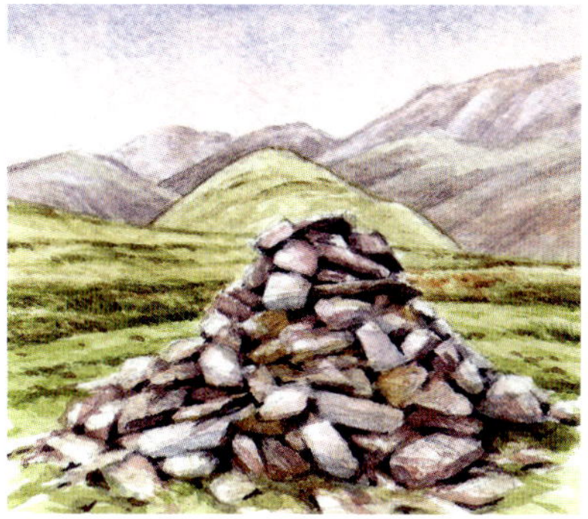

Buck Crag and Heck Crag from Satura Crag 2/9/08

Only a couple of stones now mark the top of this crag. There are one or two anomalies in AW's drawing: he greatly exaggerated the shape of Buck Crag and then past Heck Crag he completely omitted Place Fell behind. He did sometimes simplify distance possibly due to poor weather or to keep the important elements distinct, but in his sketch he drew some far detail which appears to be of his own invention.

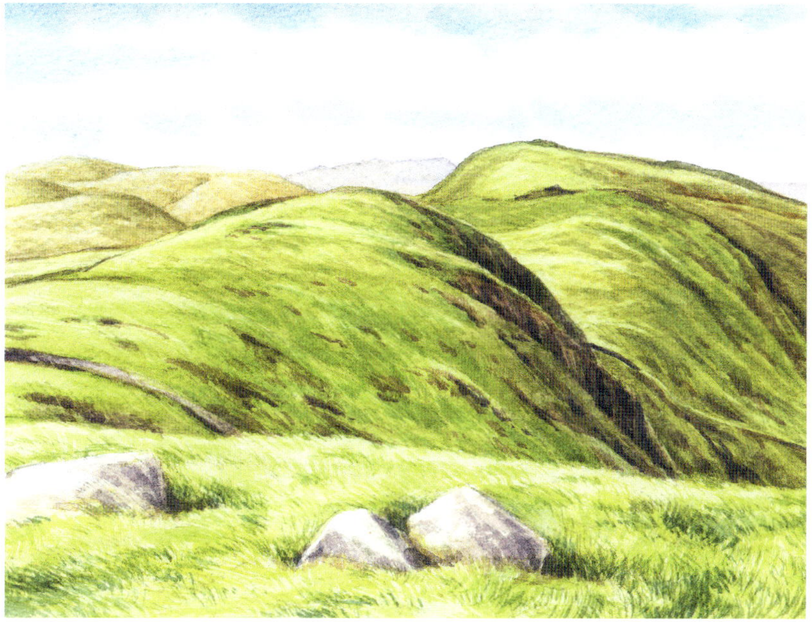

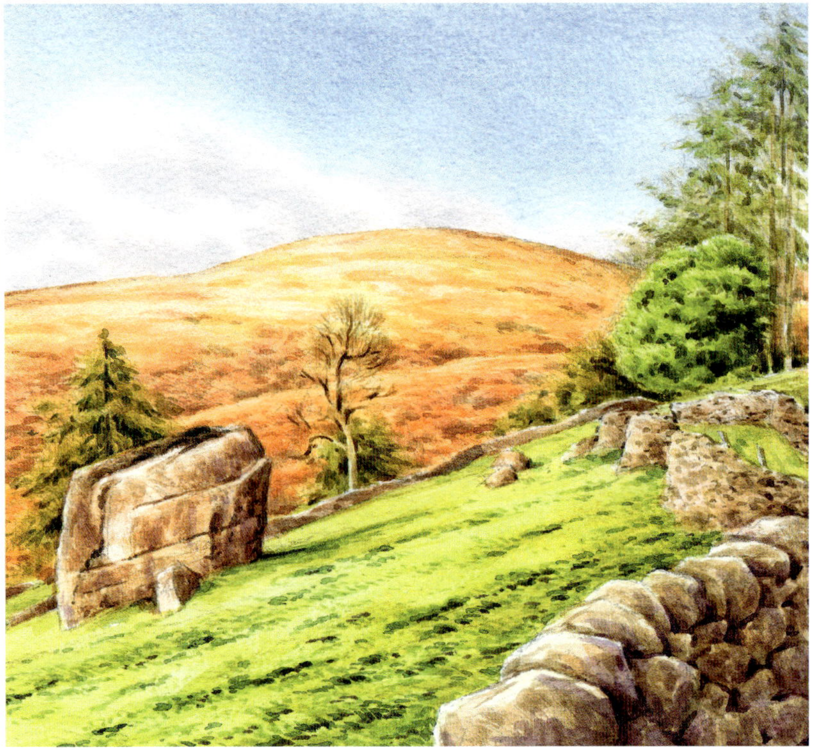

From Badger Rock 21/4/09
This large boulder sits in a field to the south of the Garburn Pass lane just west of Kentmere village.

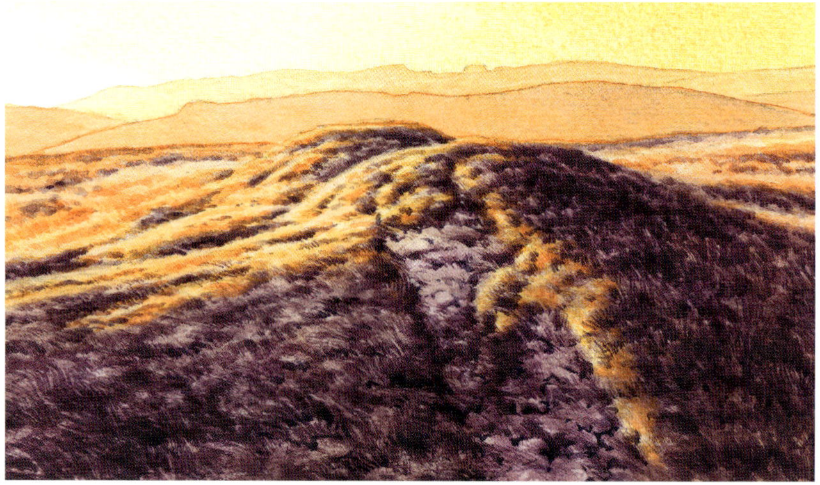

The summit mound 10/10/10
This was the scene at just after 5 pm as the late afternoon sun was setting. Wansfell is the middle ridge with Great Gable 15 miles in the distance.

Sallows

This fell and the neighbouring Sour Howes are positioned south of the Garburn Pass, and a pleasant half day can be spent walking to both summits. Troutbeck Church makes a good starting point. I recall a day in May 2009 when I included these two fells in a very long day which covered 14 hills in total, basically a clockwise round from the church at Kentmere to Kidsty Pike and back.

Sallows from Ullthwaite Bridge 21/4/09
Mature trees now hide the buildings at Croft Head but the scene is mostly unchanged from how AW saw it.

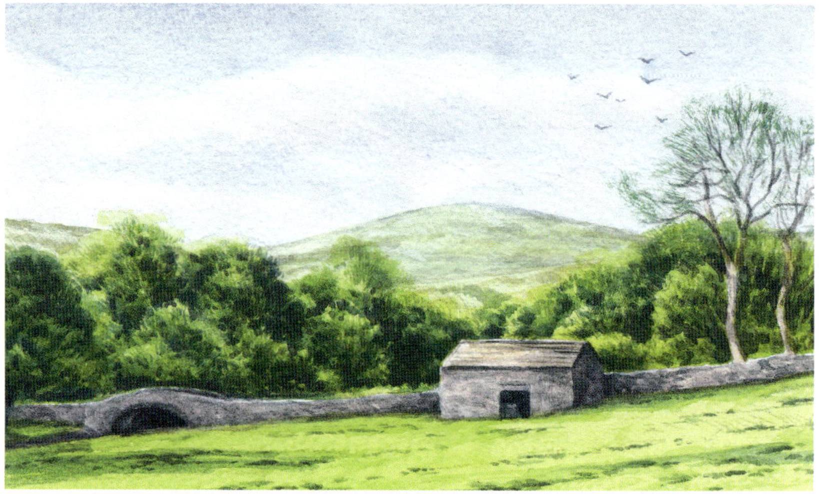

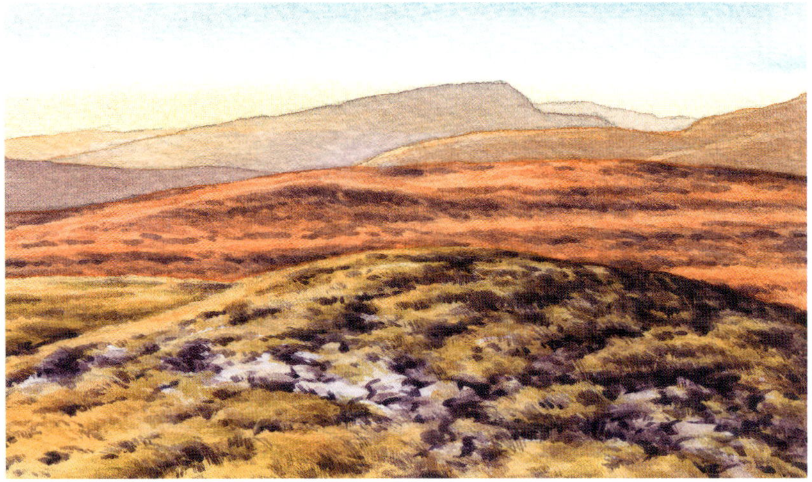

The summit 10/10/10
The long, natural bank which marks the highest point still has no cairn of note. This is looking from the very top to the north west.

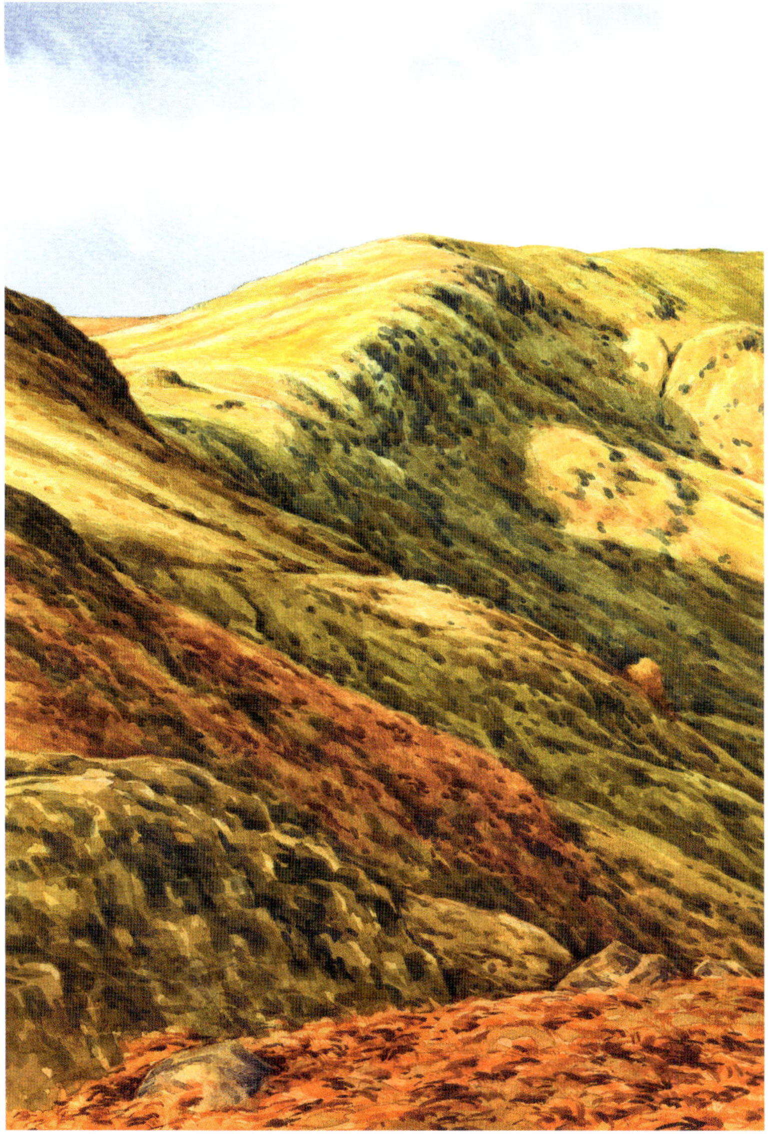

From Mosedale Beck near the waterfalls 28/10/11
This view is obtained only by leaving the recognised path near the falls. I knew I had found the correct location only when the rocky knoll in the saddle matched the positioning in AW's drawing.

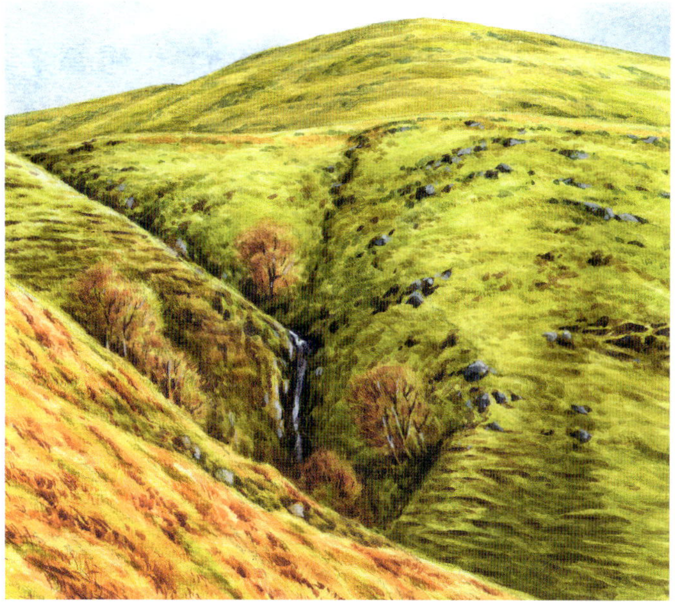

Selside Pike from the old corpse road 17/3/09
Rowantreethwaite Beck tumbles into the steep sided ravine.

Selside Pike

The easiest and possibly the most popular way to visit this fell is by walking from Mardale Head. The route has merits, including fine views from the Old Corpse Road but the delightful approach along the quiet valley of Swindale should be completed at least once.

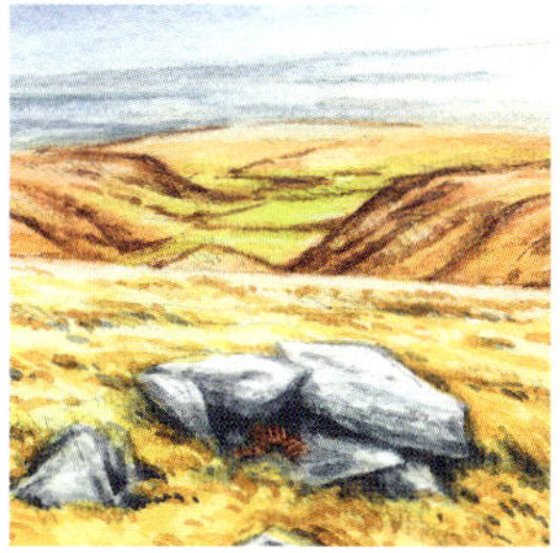

Slate Cairn 17/3/09
The upright slate has fallen but the cairn is still there although all references to it have been erased from the revised guide.

The summit 17/3/09
A shelter has been formed from the substantial sized cairn.

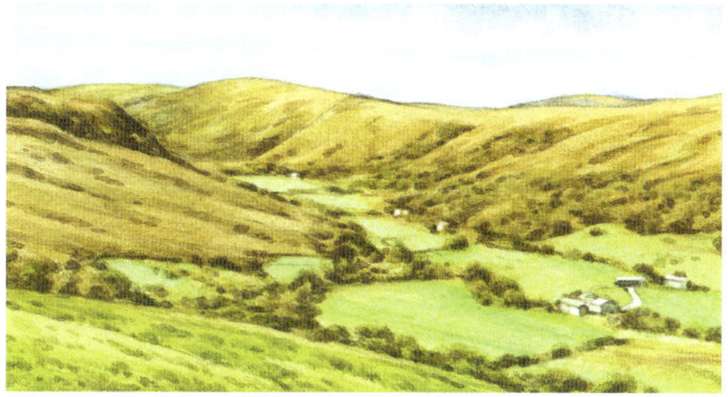

Swindale 15/8/11
Unusually this view is from a location not even covered by AW's Pictorial Guide maps. It is looking to Selside Pike from near Starling Gill, Tailbert.

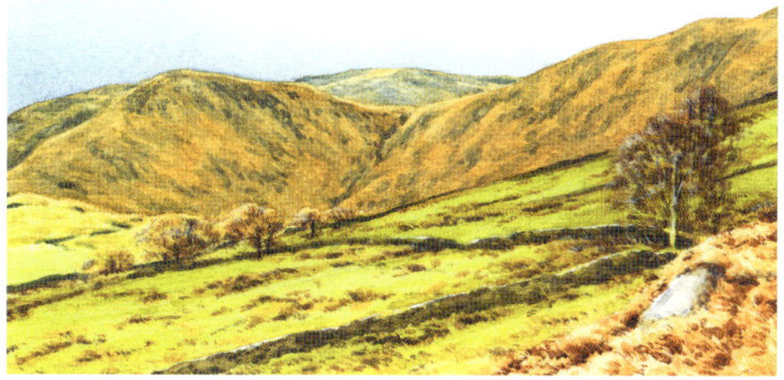

Swindale Head 28/10/11
By lining up the walls and the tree I was able to locate this position exactly near Thorny Knott.

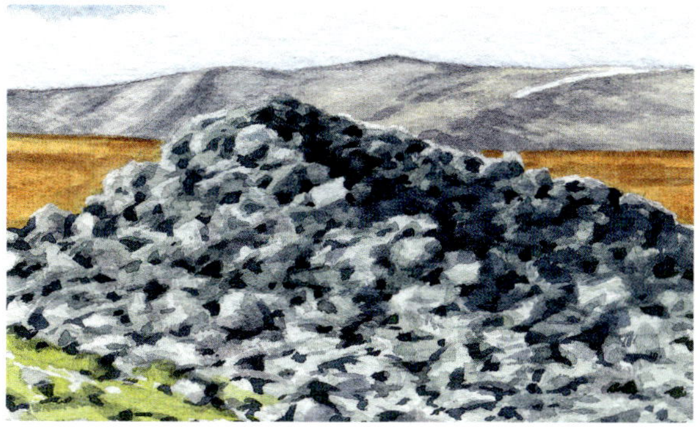

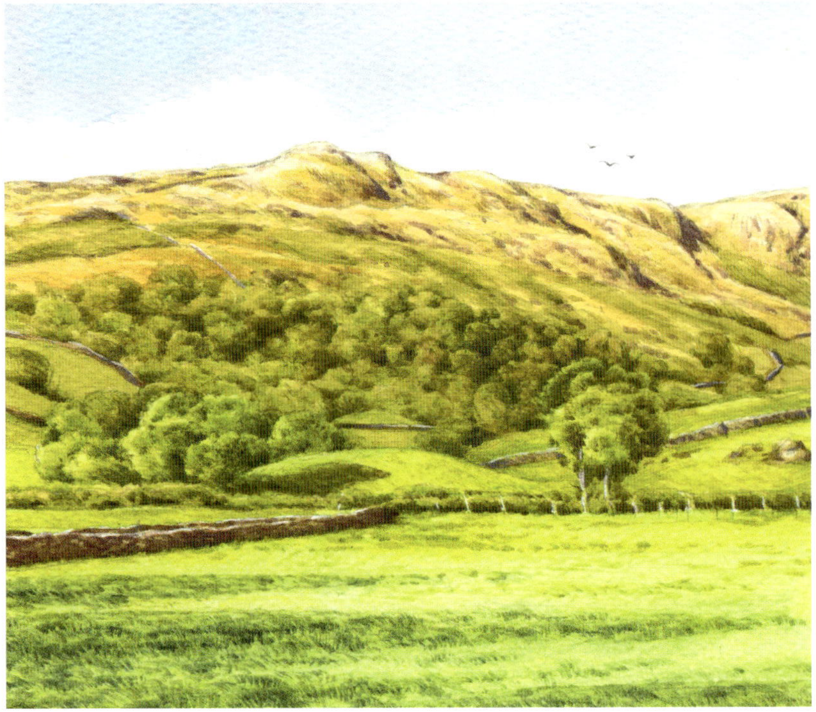

From Stockdale 28/9/13
Some fells are just not all that inspiring for a sketch. AW gave this view of Shipman Knotts some enhancement whereas I left it the way it actually looks. Even so, it took me two visits to this point at Stockdale Bridge to get something to work with, as the first day the light was flat and lifeless.

Shipman Knotts

On reading his introduction to the fell it seems that AW only featured Shipman Knotts as a separate hill in its own right due to the fact that it has more exposed rock than the rest of Kentmere Pike, its parent fell. But it was named as a surveyed height on his maps so that most likely influenced him to include it as one of the 214 fells. When walked in a clockwise direction Shipman Knotts will be the last fell of the classic Kentmere Round.

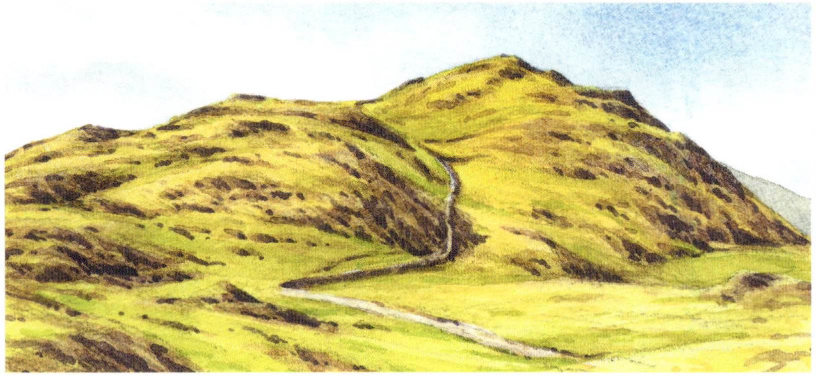

The summit from the south
29/5/09
The wall winds its way up over the fell towards the summit. The path runs alongside it on the left.

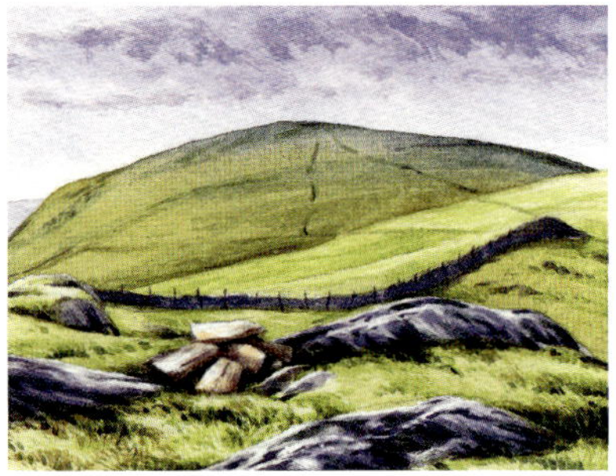

The summit 29/5/09
This is Wainwright's summit with a view towards Kentmere Pike and positioned to the east of the wall which on this day sported a small cairn. Most visitors to the fell will be happy enough to class the rocky outcrop to the west of the wall as the summit which must only be a matter of inches lower, if at all. Avoid damaging the labours of the dry stone waller by climbing the wall. Those who are adamant about visiting the Wainwright top should use the path to the east of the wall from Goat Scar.

The summit ridge from Goat Scar 29/5/09
Rough Crags drop down towards the Longsleddale valley on the left. There is a path which keeps to the left of the wall which passes through a gate and then will take you to Wainwright's summit (see left).

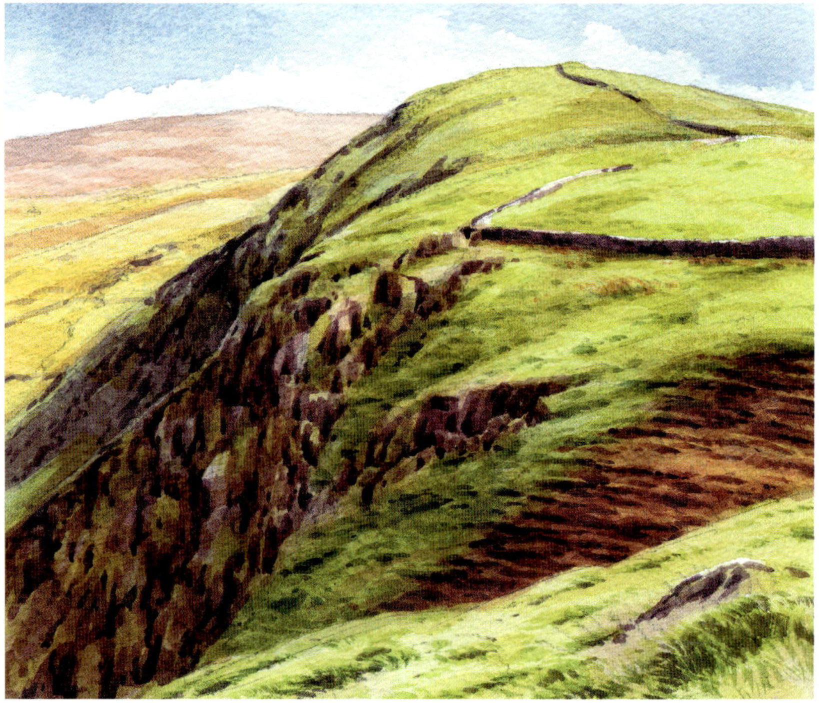

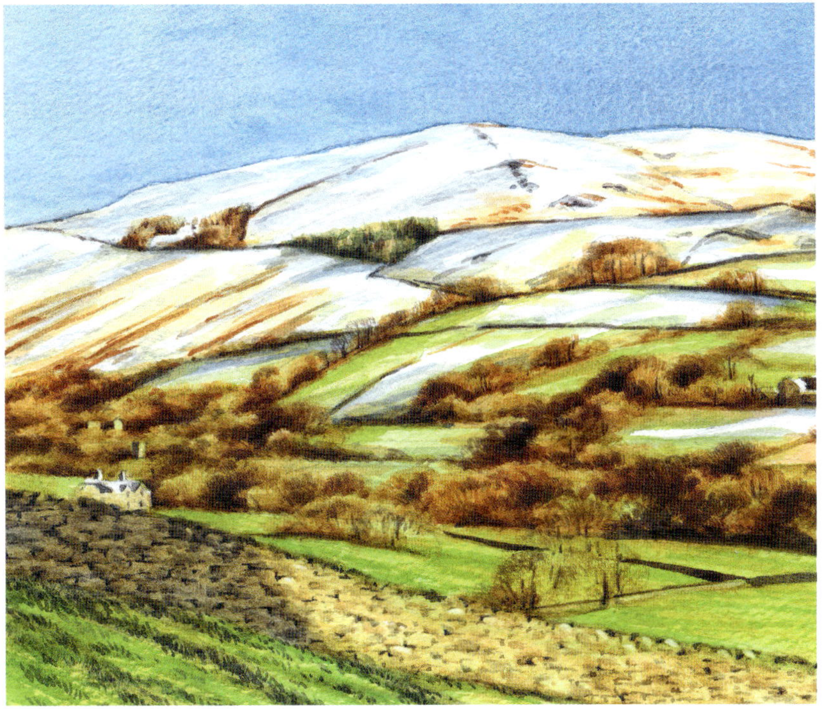

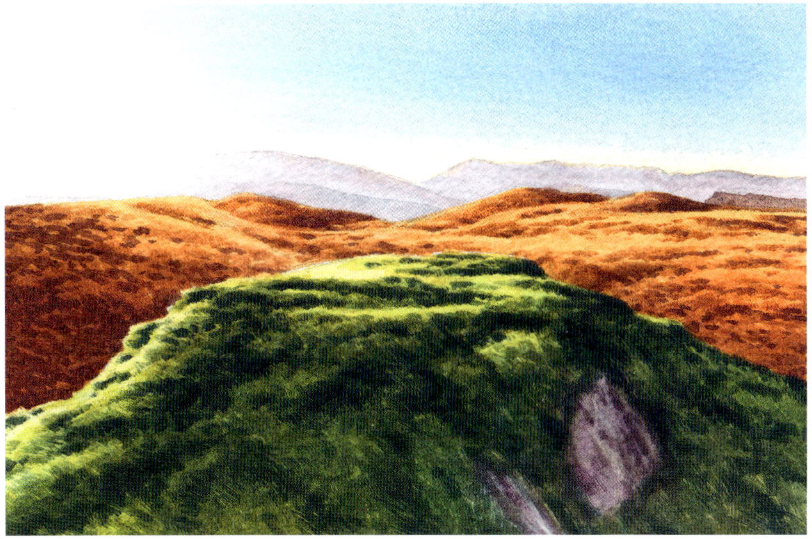

The summit 10/10/10

Finding any cairn here is not guaranteed, and identifying the true summit especially in poor conditions can be a challenge as the area has several raised hillocks of similar height. This was to be my penultimate summit of the day and the sun was low in the sky. From here it was on to Sallows where I was just in time to catch the last of the evening light.

From Troutbeck 6/2/09

It is interesting here to compare how the field boundaries, highlighted by the snow in both Wainwright's illustration and my sketch, have changed, if at all. With the trees in the foreground of AW's drawing having grown tall I had to move slightly left by fifty yards to obtain the clearest view.

Applethwaite Quarry 16/1/09

Due to the fact that the old quarry is now much more overgrown I had to spend some time in its depths searching for this view but sure enough, the spoil heap and trees matched Wainwright's scene. I even stumbled across the rusty old weighbridge that he mentions.

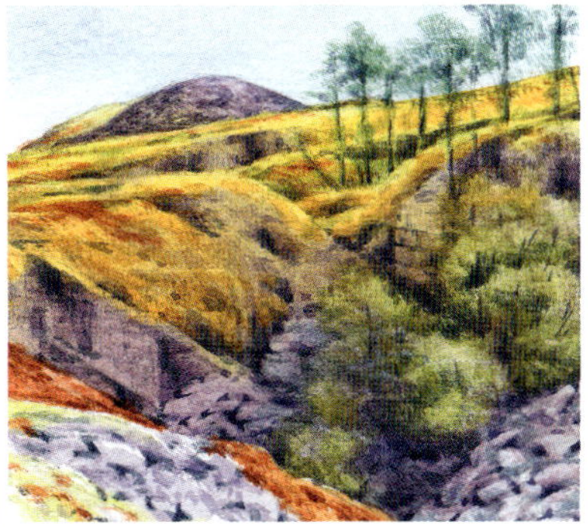

Red Screes from Sour Howes 10/10/10

AW's title as a location description for this aspect is rather vague and I spent some time wandering around trying to line up all the ridges in the view. It is actually north of the summit on the way to Moor Head.

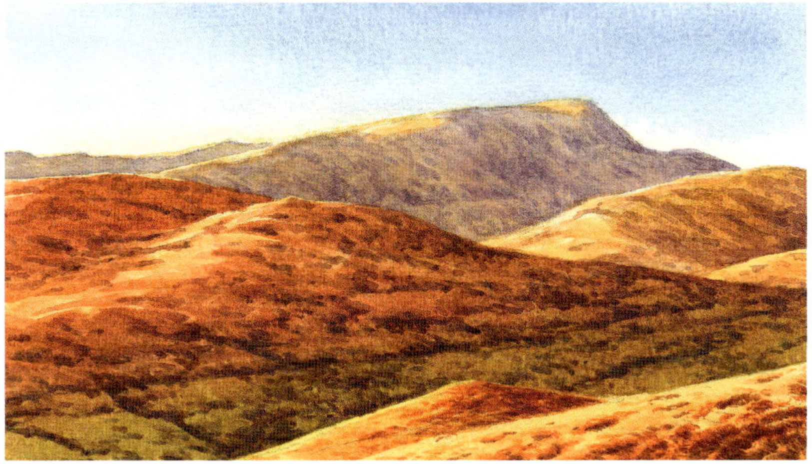

Sour Howes

On the opposite side of the valley to the village of Troutbeck the gentle slopes of this fell lead on to higher ground of the Ill Bell ridge further north. The Garburn Road skirts around its north western flanks to the Kentmere Valley beyond and this makes a fine initial route to reach the highest sections of the fell, providing excellent views towards the Kirkstone Pass.

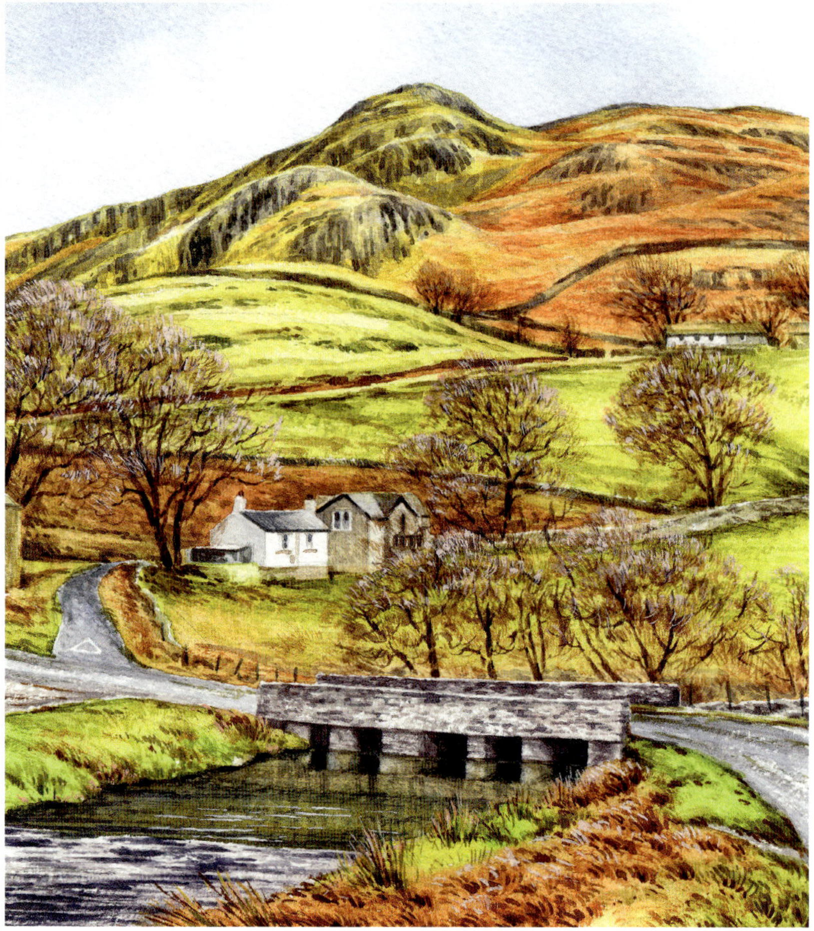

From Howe Grain Beck 13/3/09
The changes to this scene over the past fifty years are minimal, the house has gained a coat of white paint and the far wall of the bridge has been altered but that is really about all. The give way sign on the road is a bit out of place, not much traffic passes this way even today.

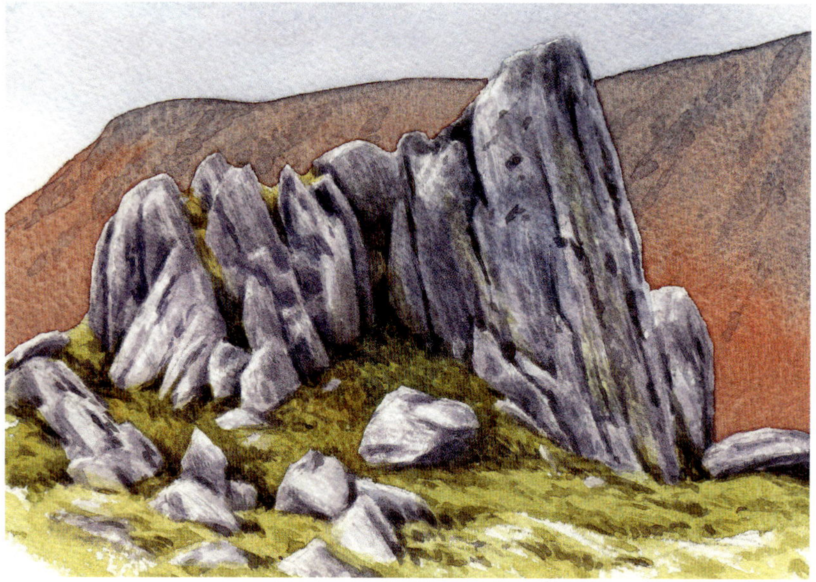

The summit 21/4/09
It may be small in height but many a higher fell cannot claim to have such a craggy summit which even has its own name, Pikeawassa. Who needs a summit cairn when nature has built one as good as this? Bonscale Pike is the fell in the background.

Steel Knotts

The height of the pass between Howtown and Martindale is flanked by two minor fells, Hallin Fell to the north and Steel Knotts to the south. Both can easily be achieved by parking at the top of the pass and making your choice. The merits of Steel Knotts are the superb views south along Martindale and the final easy scramble to the very top, a natural crown of rocks on which aspiring young mountaineers can practise.

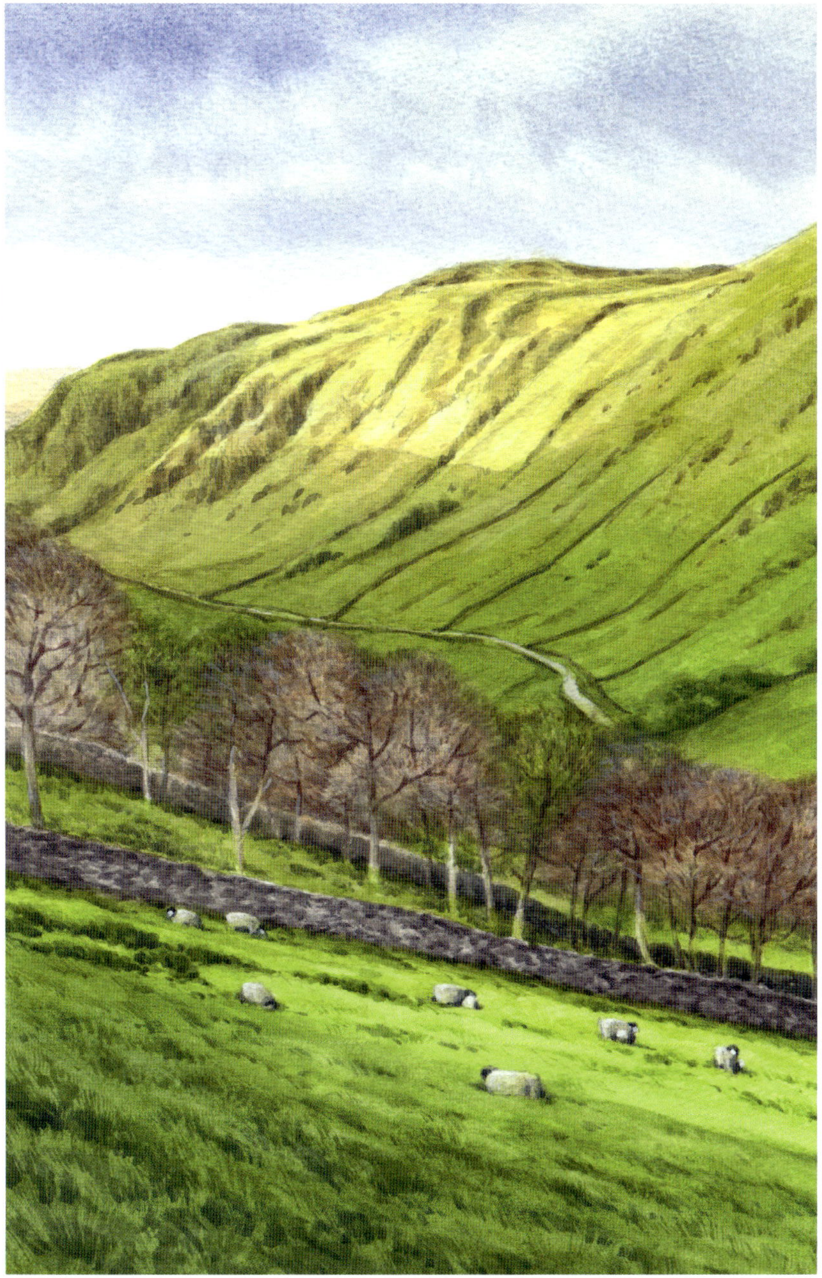

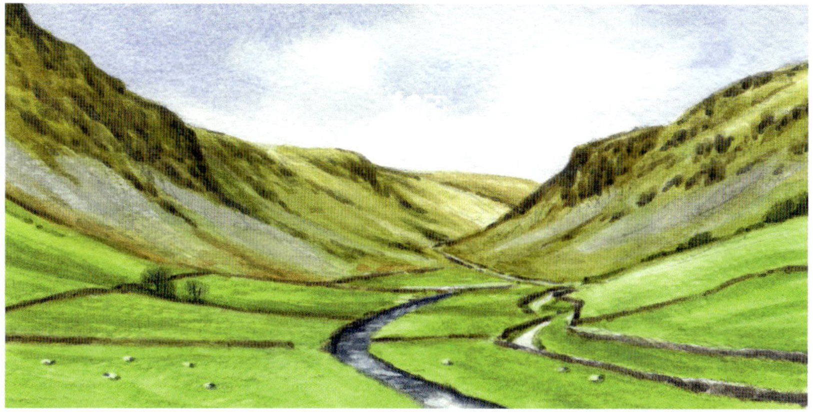

The head of Longsleddale 10/5/09
The River Sprint winds its way down the valley with the old road nearby. Goat Scar on the left and Buckbarrow Crag on the right.

Tarn Crag

Lying to the east of the rather secluded Longsleddale Valley this fell is most often included with a visit to its near neighbour, Grey Crag. The twin rock walls of Goat Scar and Buckbarrow Crag tower above the pastures in the valley bottom, and the old quarry road that heads up and over the Gatesgarth Pass at the far end of the valley.

From Sadgill Wood 10/5/09
A more recent copse of trees on the south edge of Sadgill Wood meant I had to obtain my view from slightly higher up the track which leads over to Kentmere. Even so, the bridge at Sadgill is still obscured by the trees.

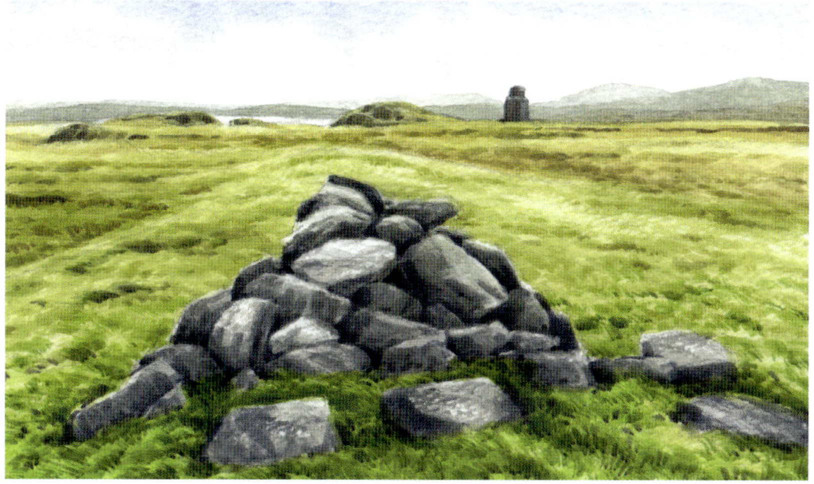

The summit 10/5/09
Even though the summit cairn has slightly increased in size, it is the survey column some 100 yards distant which dominates this high ground. This was constructed as part of the engineering of the Haweswater aqueduct, several others are to be found in this region, not all to the same design.

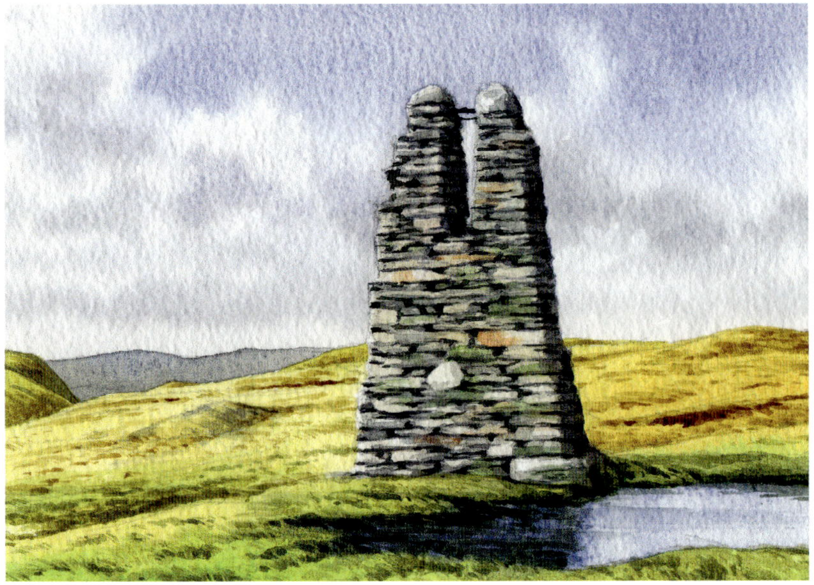

The survey column 10/5/09
With a bit of searching a few remnants of the wooden platform on which the surveying engineers stood were found partially buried in the peat on my visit.

Kentmere Pike across Longsleddale 10/5/09
Goat Scar and the craggy face of the fell from 70 yards west of the column.

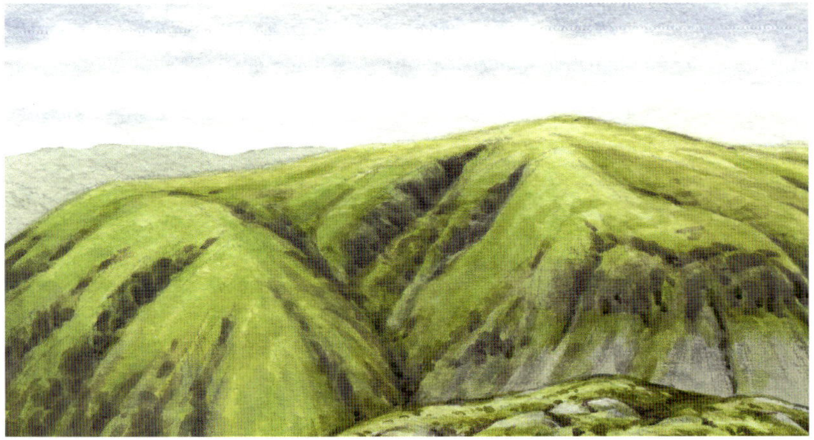

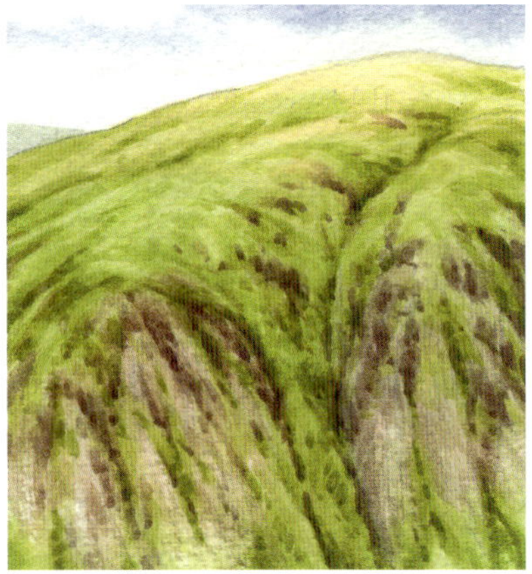

From Goat Scar 29/5/09
The view across the valley.

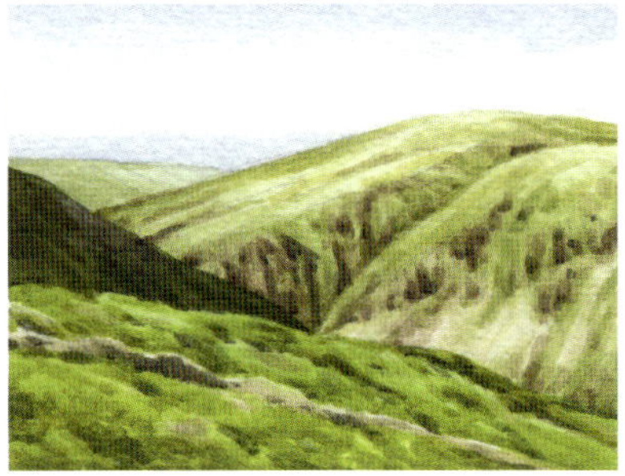

From Shipman Knotts 29/5/09
A very similar view to the one above, both in winter conditions in his drawings. Something I was not able to capture in my sketches.

Buckbarrow Crag 10/5/09
A haunt of climbers with a variety of routes on its buttressed face. It is also home to ravens that nest on the high narrow ledges.

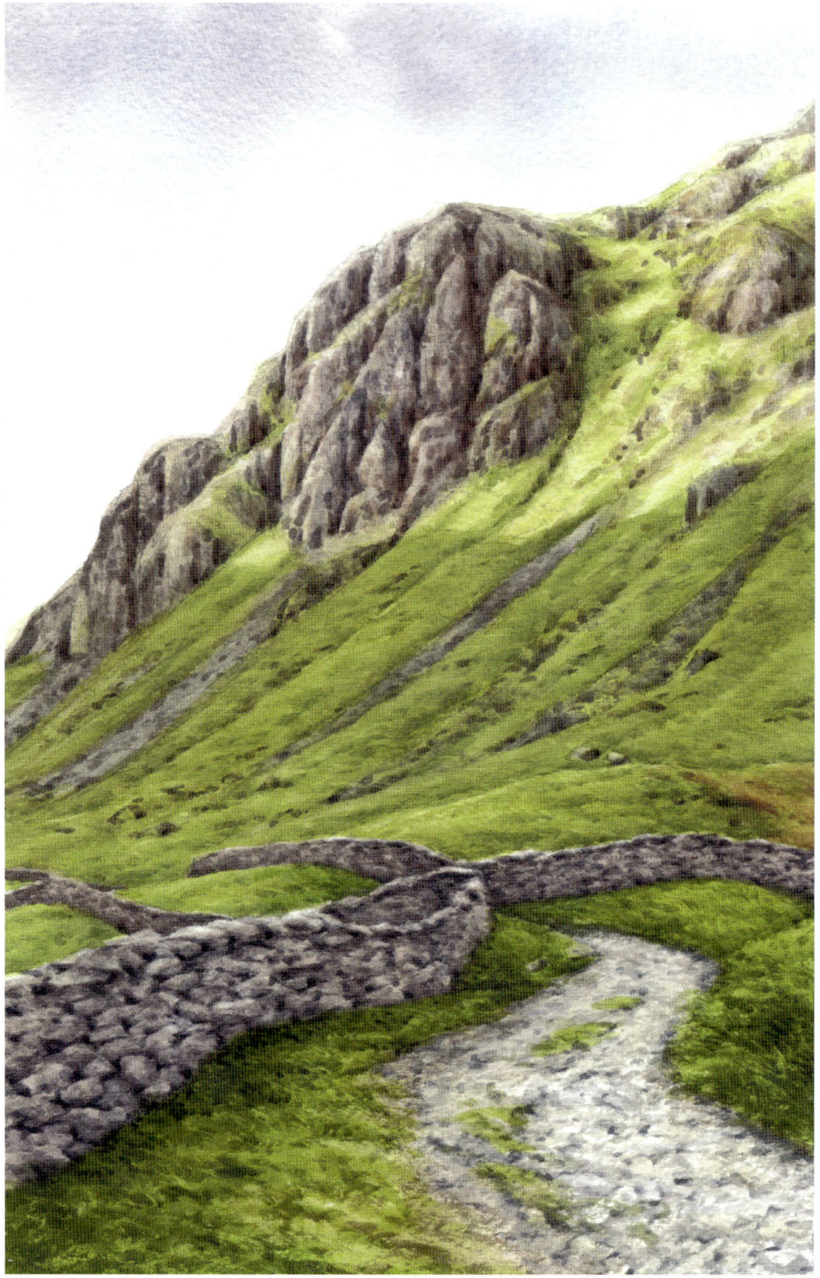

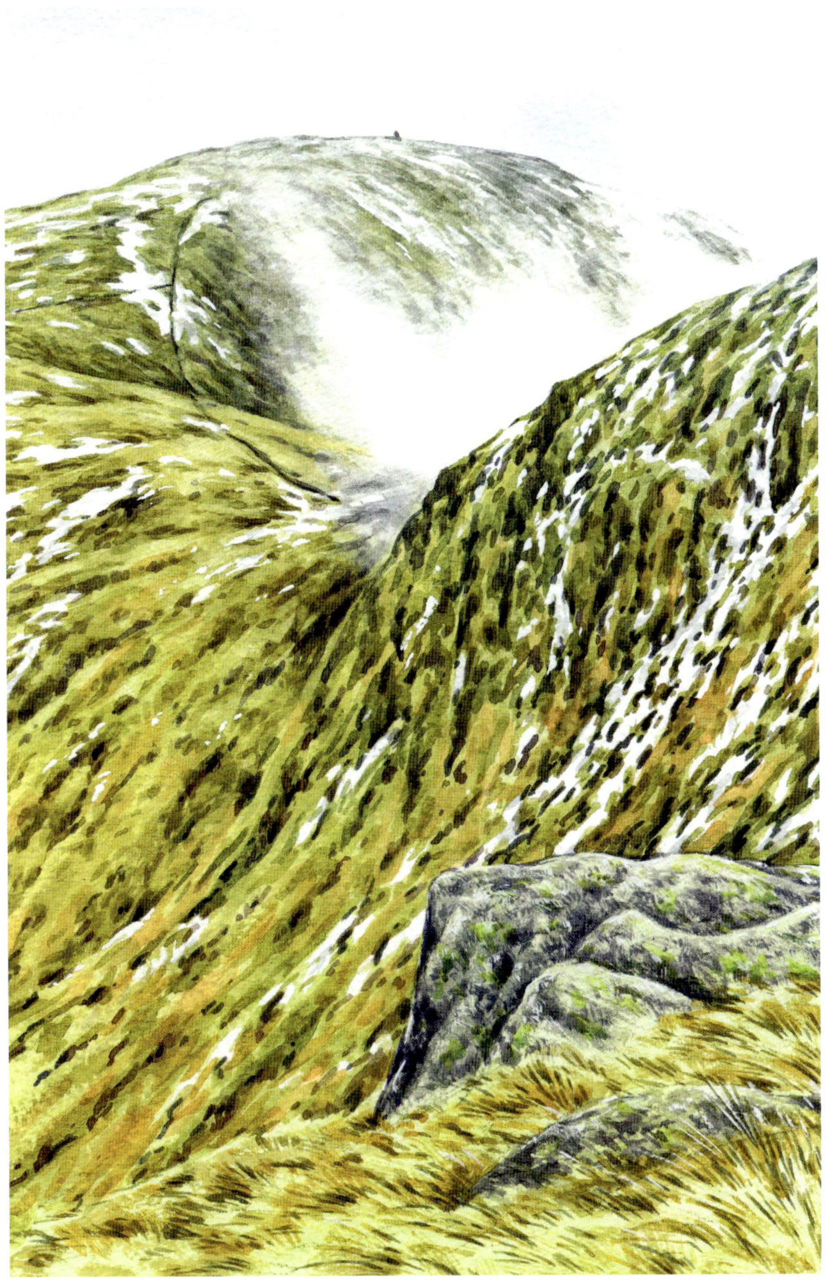

Looking north to Ullswater 20/9/11

This location is from a point on the path that drops down into the cove, about 70 yards north of the saddle of the pass itself.

Thornthwaite Crag

It is not clearly documented but it would appear that this would have been the very first major fell that AW ever climbed, the first of many, doing so on 8th June 1930 aged just 23. He was then en route to Pooley Bridge from Windermere and he approached via Scot Rake.

From Caudale Moor 20/2/09

I was lucky here, I had planned my timing for this picture as I knew the last of the lying snow would be similar to his illustration. After a period spent "off-path" looking for the foreground rock the low cloud spilled over Threshthwaite Mouth, and within minutes the scene was shrouded and hidden from view.

Looking south towards Windermere 20/9/11

Troutbeck Tongue in the middle of the valley. I have not included the sheep skull in the cairn shown in AW's drawing, it had long gone.

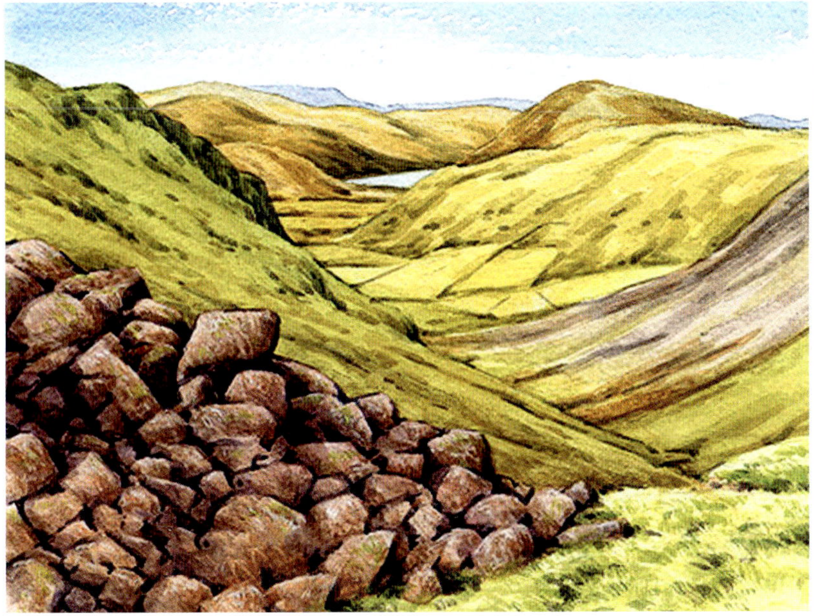

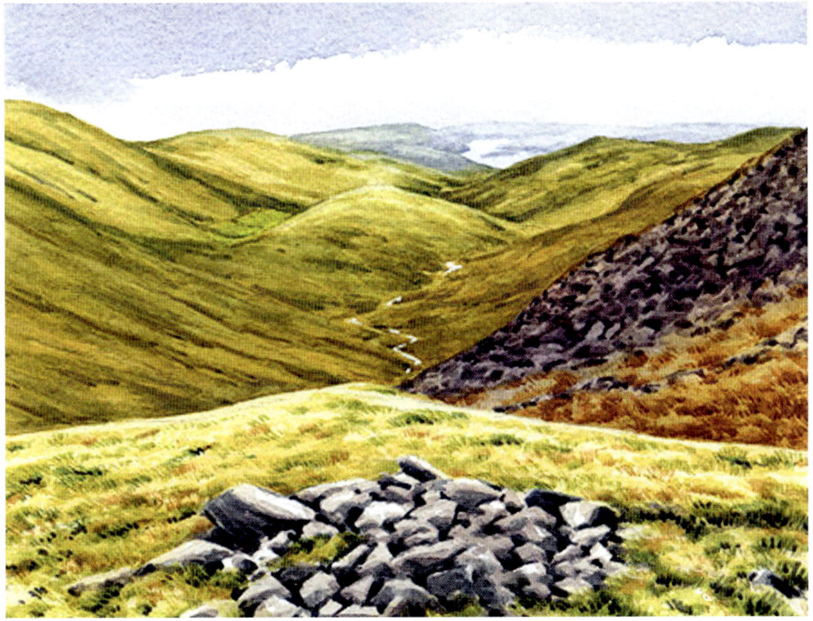

Hayeswater 20/9/11

Wainwright describes in the guide how this was once a reservoir for the Penrith area. As I mentioned in the chapter on The Knott the reservoir has now been returned to a more natural lake. Even though the water level has dropped the shape and size of the lake remains relatively the same.

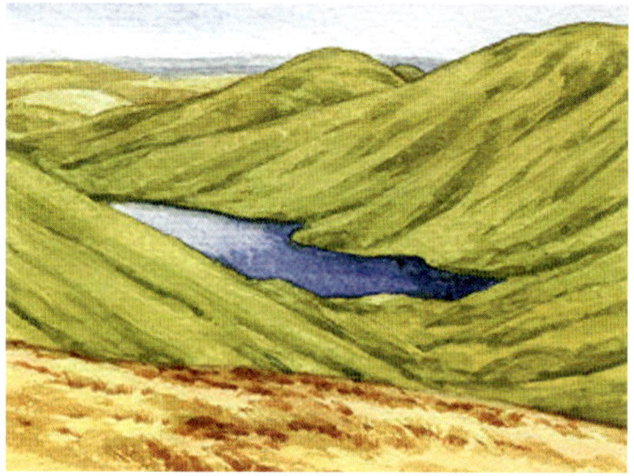

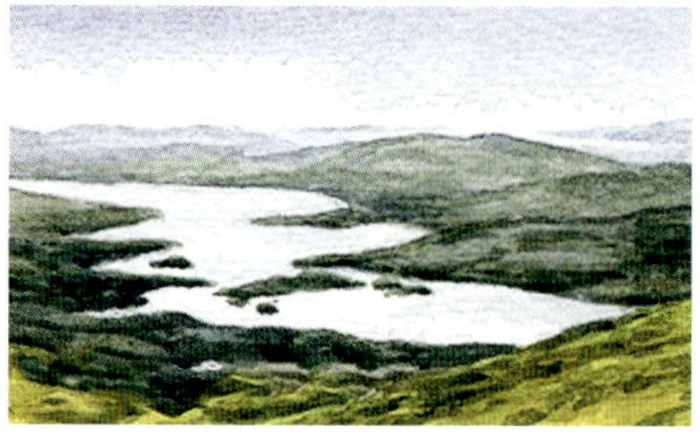

Windermere 20/9/11

The stretch of water leads off to the south. Unusually his drawing has a straight line to indicate the distant horizon.

Thornthwaite Beacon 24/6/08

The top few feet of this impressive tower have fallen since AW's day but this is still a fine tower of stone. Perhaps in the near future some restoration work will be undertaken as has been done to the beacon on Hallin Fell, scaffolding will be required though. At its base a benchmark is engraved into the rock.

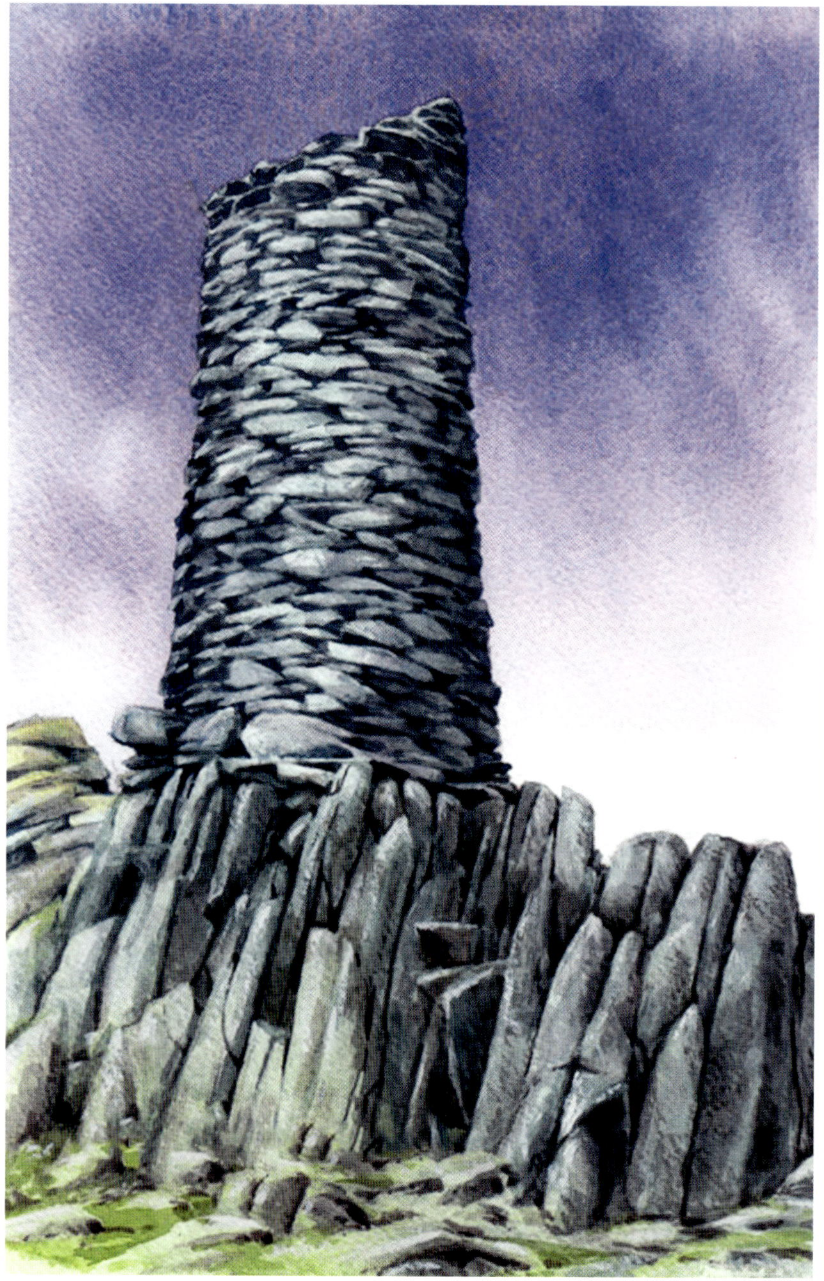

Thornthwaite Crag from the south ridge of Caudale Moor

20/9/11

My first attempt to get this awkward reference was thwarted due to poor visibility. The snowy conditions underfoot were perfect to replicate his view, but I could see only 20 yards so another visit was called for, sadly after the snow had melted away. The foreground rocks are part of the tumbled down wall.

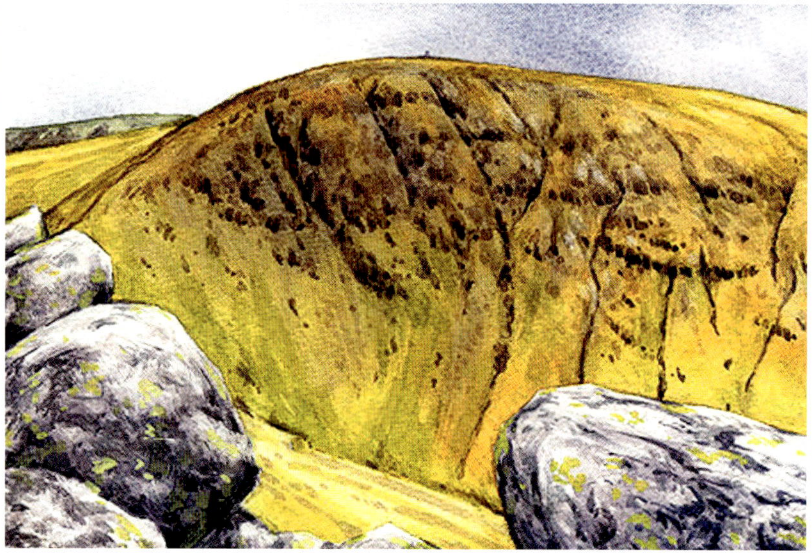

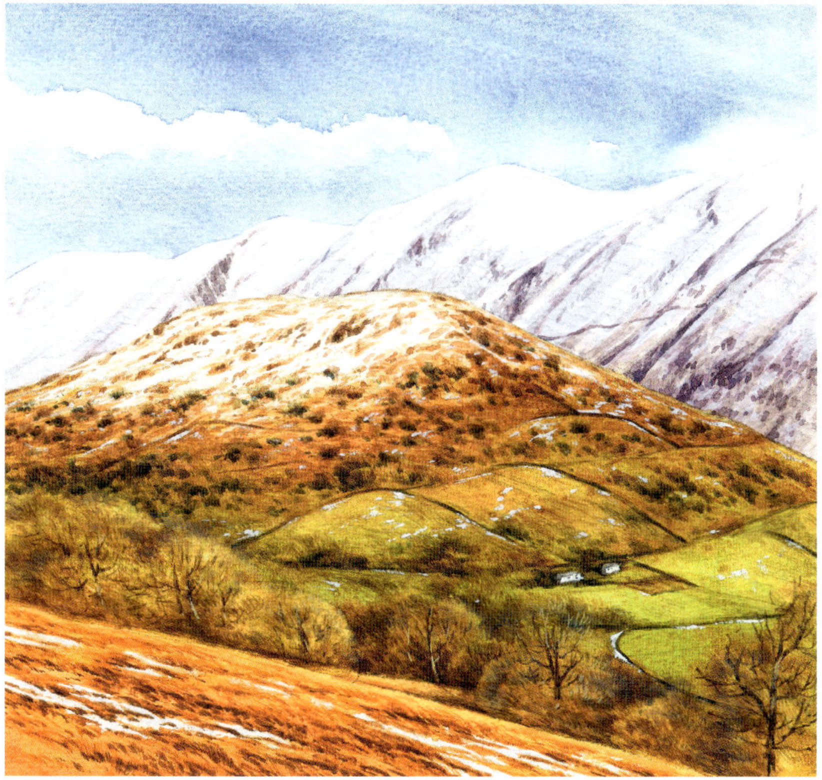

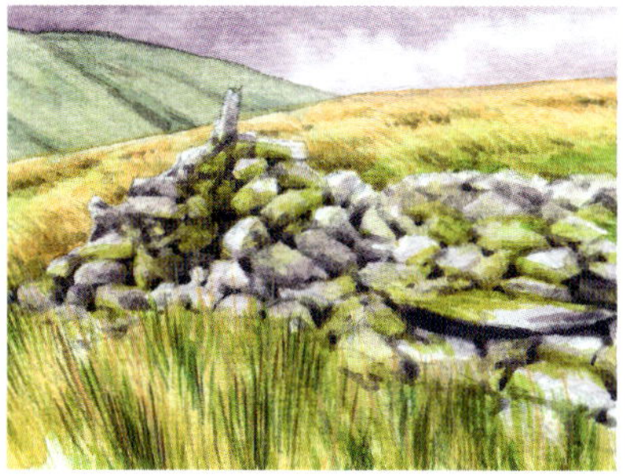

The old cairn 10/5/09

The nearby tree has gone but the old stone shelters are still here.

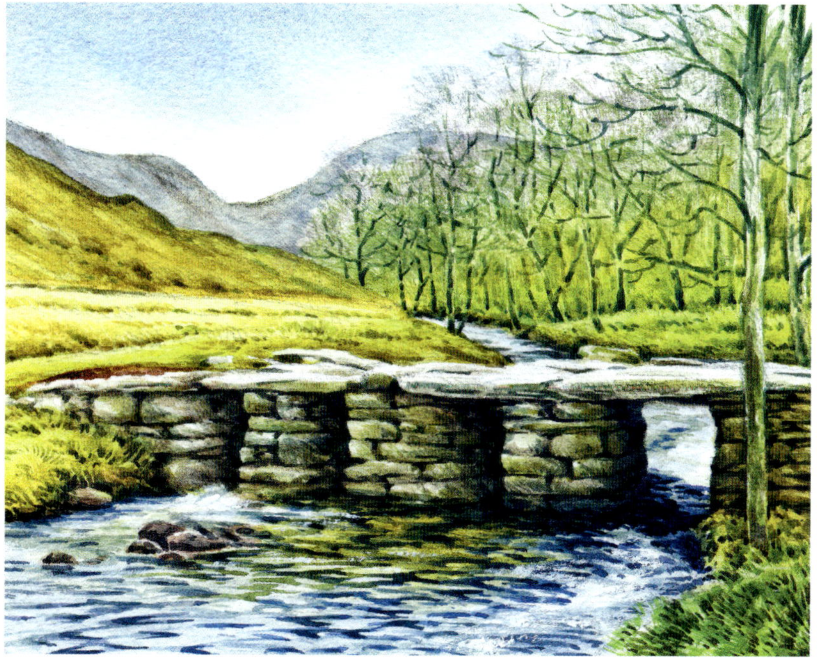

Slate Bridge, Trout Beck 10/5/09

A few months after my visit severe floods hit the lake district which resulted in this ancient bridge, one of the best examples of this "Clapper" type in the district, being badly damaged. Luckily within a short period it was fully restored to how it is depicted here.

The summit 24/6/08

A more pronounced cairn now sits on the highest point. I recall seeing a badger here as we approached before it scurried off.

Troutbeck Tongue

If it wasn't for the one mile approach along Ing Lane which has to be made on foot, then this would be a much more popular fell. Sited in the middle of the Troutbeck valley and at the base of the Ill Bell ridge, Troutbeck Tongue is a charming little fell and the pleasant route along the lane is one of its attractions.

From the Kirkstone to Windermere road 6/2/09

There is a small lay-by on the east side of the road from where you can view this scene. By then looking slightly right from the same point you will also see the view for the main page of Yoke. His sketches practically overlap.

Windermere and the Troutbeck valley 24/6/08

From the summit cairn and a fine location to spend some time.

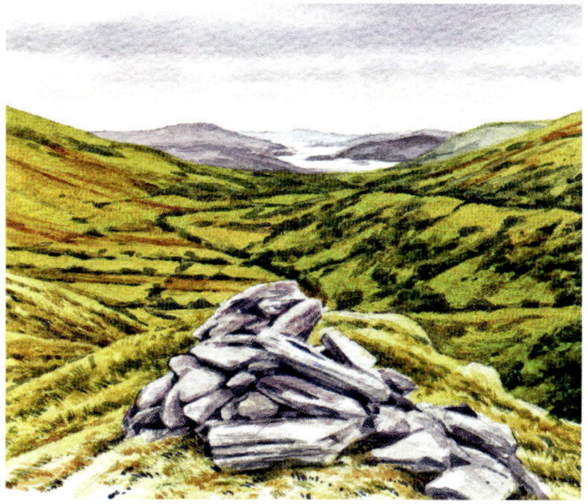

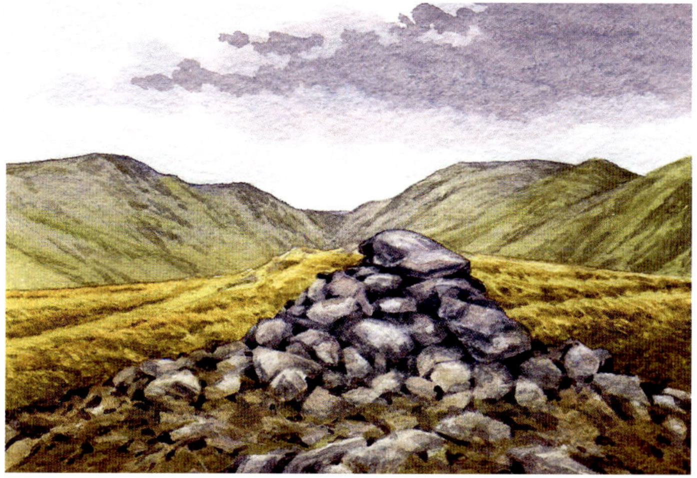

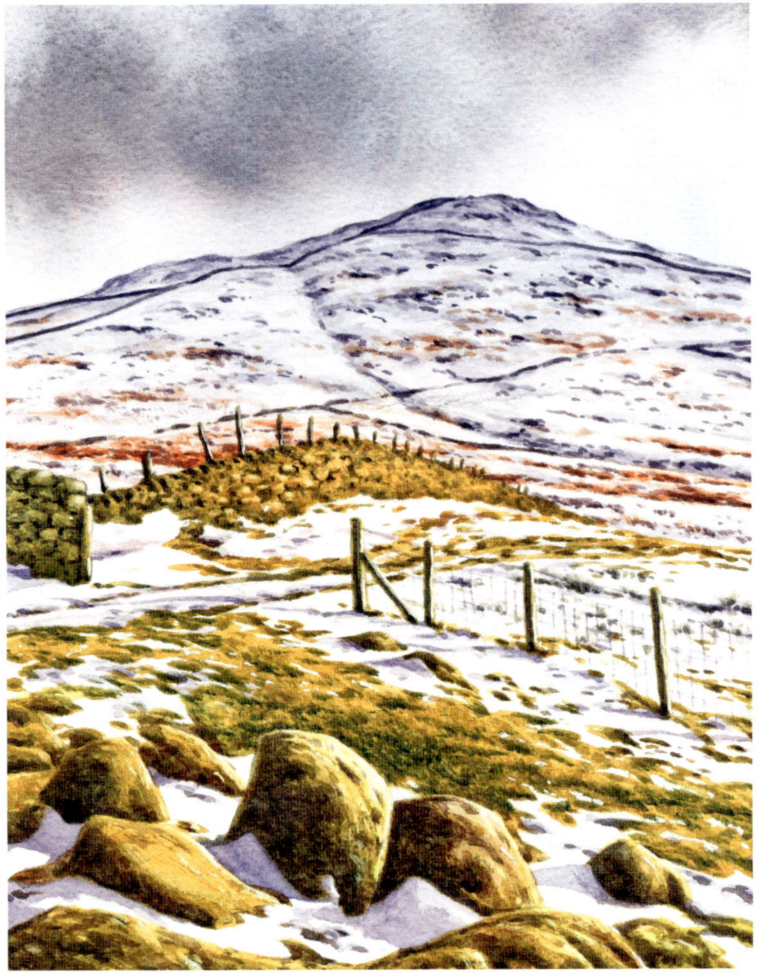

From High Grove 6/2/09
There wasn't quite as much snow on my visit as in Wainwright's drawing. The old tree has gone and there is now a more recent fence.

Wansfell
This is Ambleside's local fell, forming a ridge to the east of the town. Wansfell Pike at the southern end of the ridge has a commanding view of the town but is not the summit.

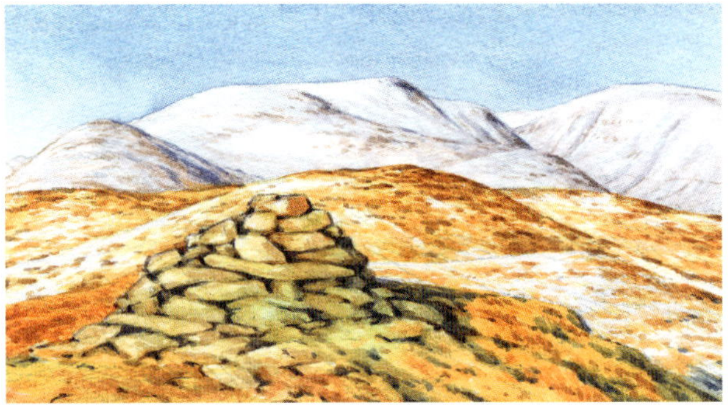

The summit 6/2/09
The view north from the cairn that marks AW's summit and the highest point of Wansfell. The rise beyond is sometimes referred to as Baystones and is slightly lower.

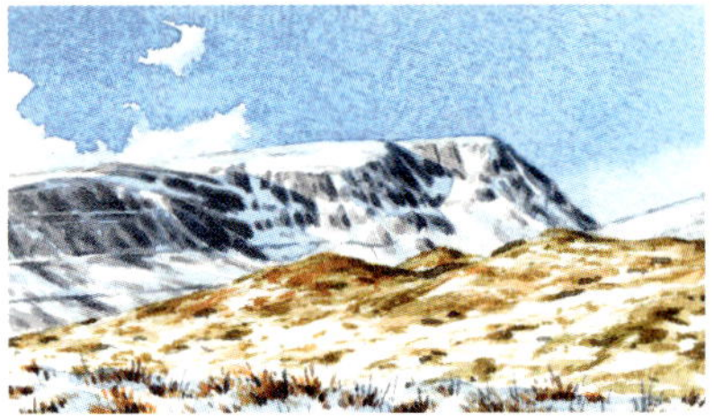

Red Screes 6/2/09
Snow covers the fell as it did on AW's visit here.

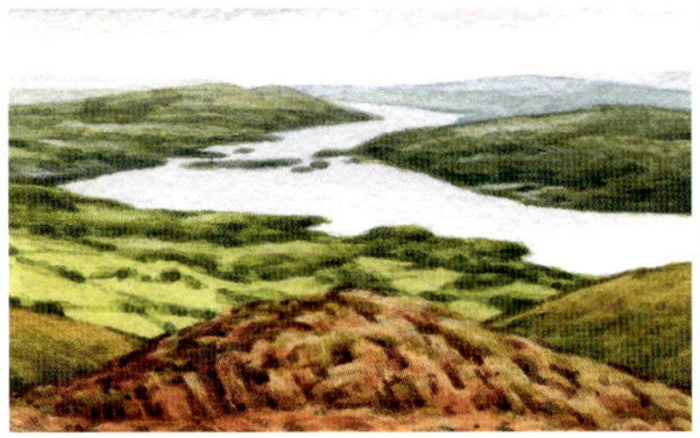

Windermere from Wansfell Pike 9/9/07
This point is often mistaken for the summit.

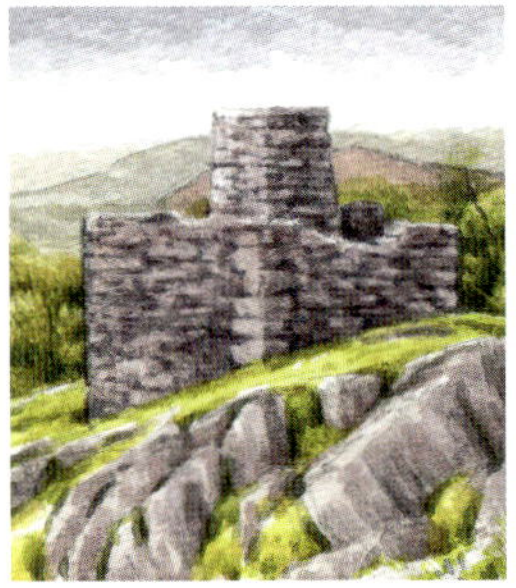

Aqueduct Observatory 9/9/07
Finding the right building, as there are three, and then lining it up for the sketch was a bit of a challenge. The clue was in the shape of the bedrock in the foreground.

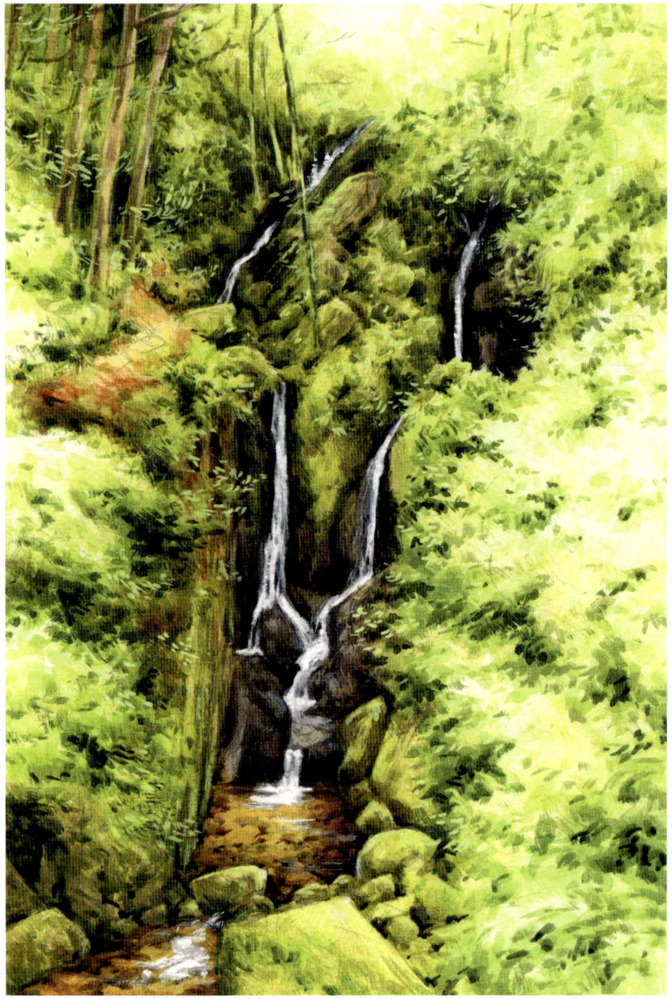

Stock Ghyll Force 9/9/07
A popular tourist attraction and only a short but pleasant walk from the centre of the busy town of Ambleside.

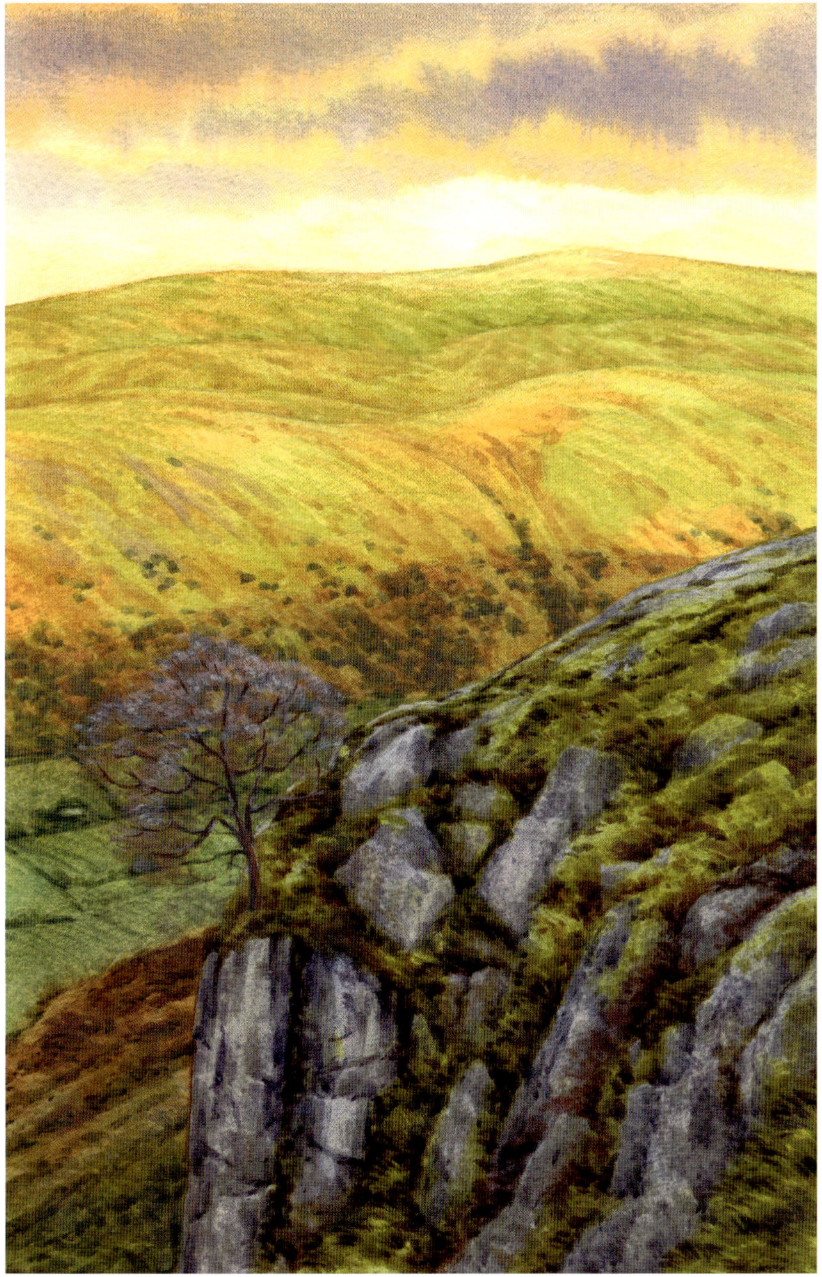

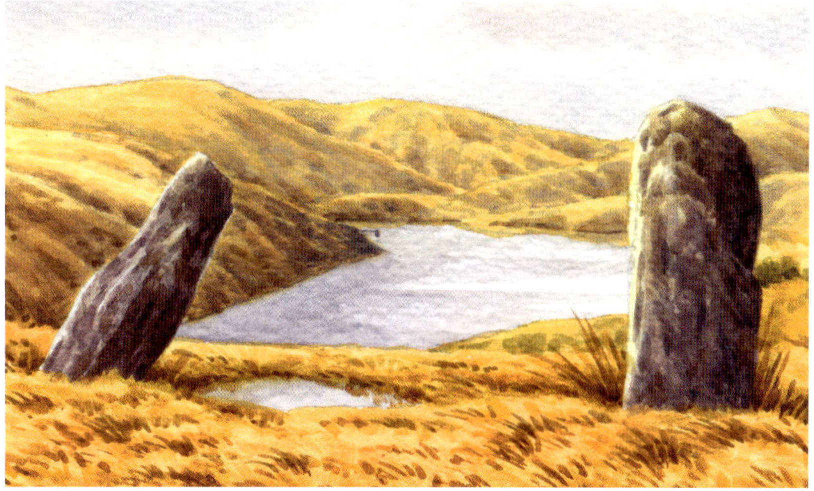

Haweswater and the Standing Stones above Burn Banks 18/3/12
The excellent view south along almost the full length of the reservoir from this location near Four Stones Hill.

Wether Hill

If it wasn't for the small group of stones marking the summit most walkers would just pass by the highest point of the fell. It is a featureless rise along the high ground between Loadpot Hill and High Raise. You have to explore the locality to find anything of real interest.

From Beda Fell 21/4/09
The late afternoon sun casting shadows on the slopes of the fell. The outcrop in the foreground is part of Allen Crag near Beda Head.

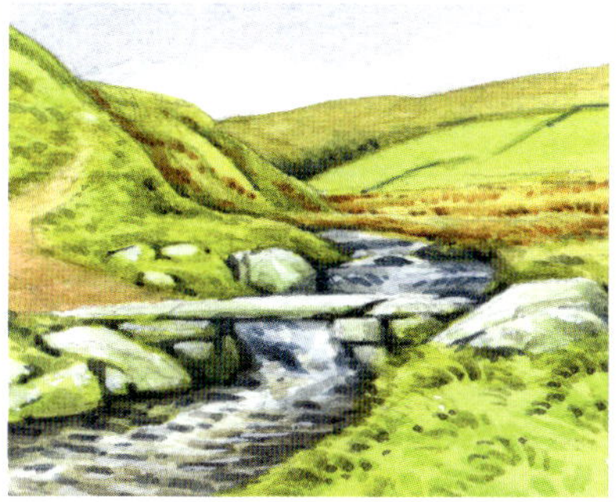

Slate bridge, Cawdale Beck
26/3/09
The ascent of Wether Hill from the east via the Hause is not a popular route, so this stone bridge will be unfamiliar to many.

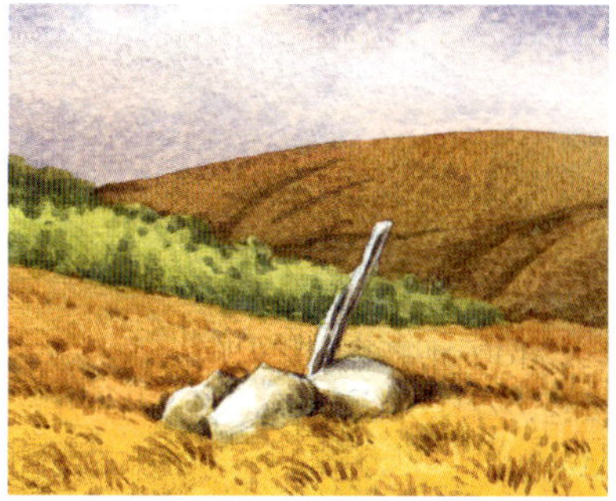

The stake on Hause End
15/8/11
It would be nice to think this short post was the remnant of the original stake. If so, it has been joined by one or two more stones.

Waterfalls, Hows Beck 13/3/09
AW indicates waterfalls near the village of Bampton but the beck has several falls. These ones can actually be seen from the bridge in the village, but permission had to be gained to get this view as they are now on private ground. The falls have changed course and are overgrown.

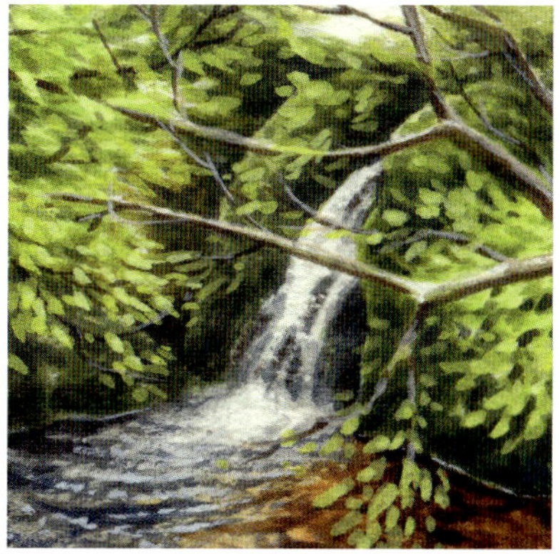

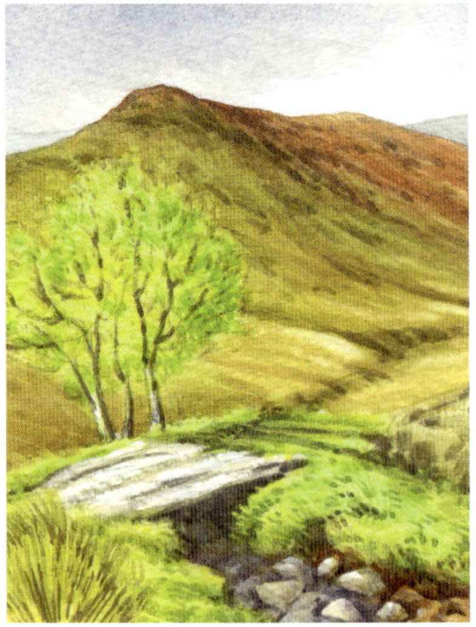

Steel Knotts from Fusedale
21/4/09
A small slate bridge carries the footpath across Groove Gill.

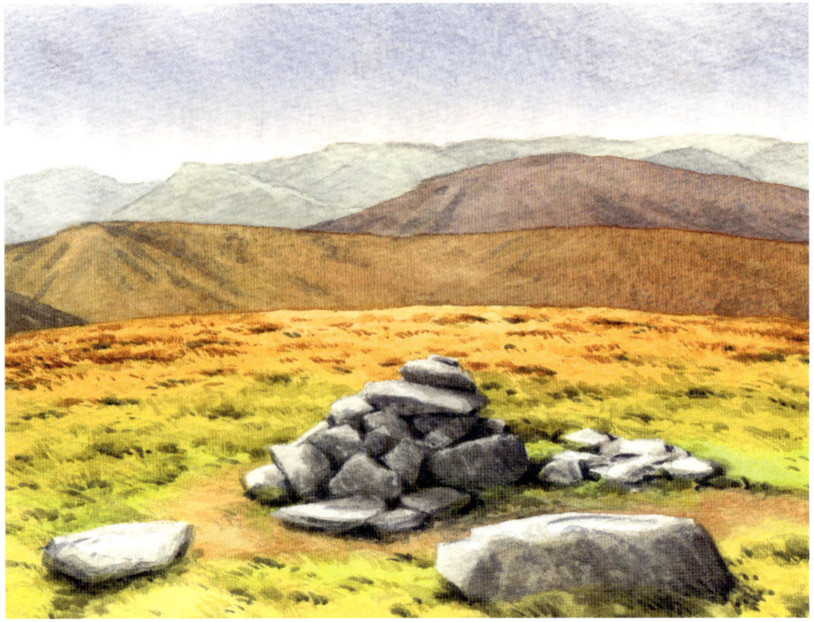

The summit 21/4/09
A few stones have been gathered locally to make the cairn slightly larger, the boundary stone is still one of them. The post has disappeared.

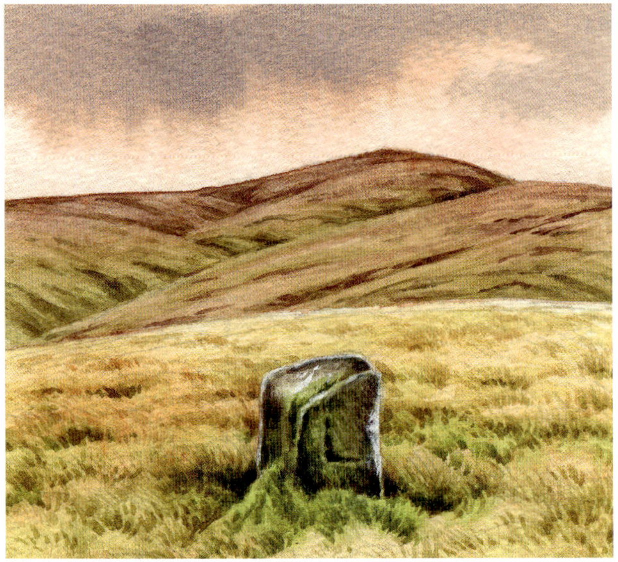

The boundary stone, High Kop
21/4/09
Some distance from the path on the eastern slopes this small engraved stone stands only about one foot tall, mosses and ageing blend it into the surroundings. It takes a bit of finding.

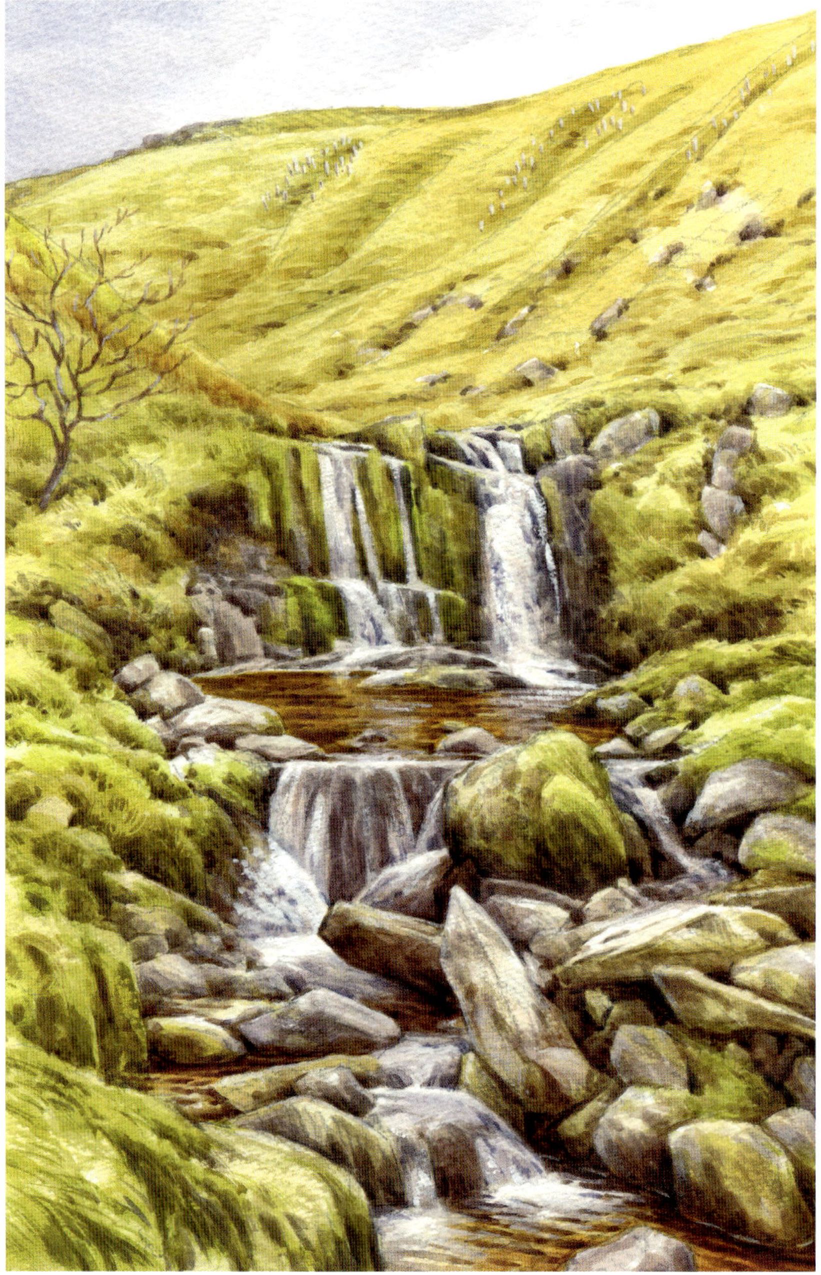

Measand Beck 18/3/12
You could not wish for a more secluded location for a picnic by a waterfall. Its remote location is possibly the only drawback.

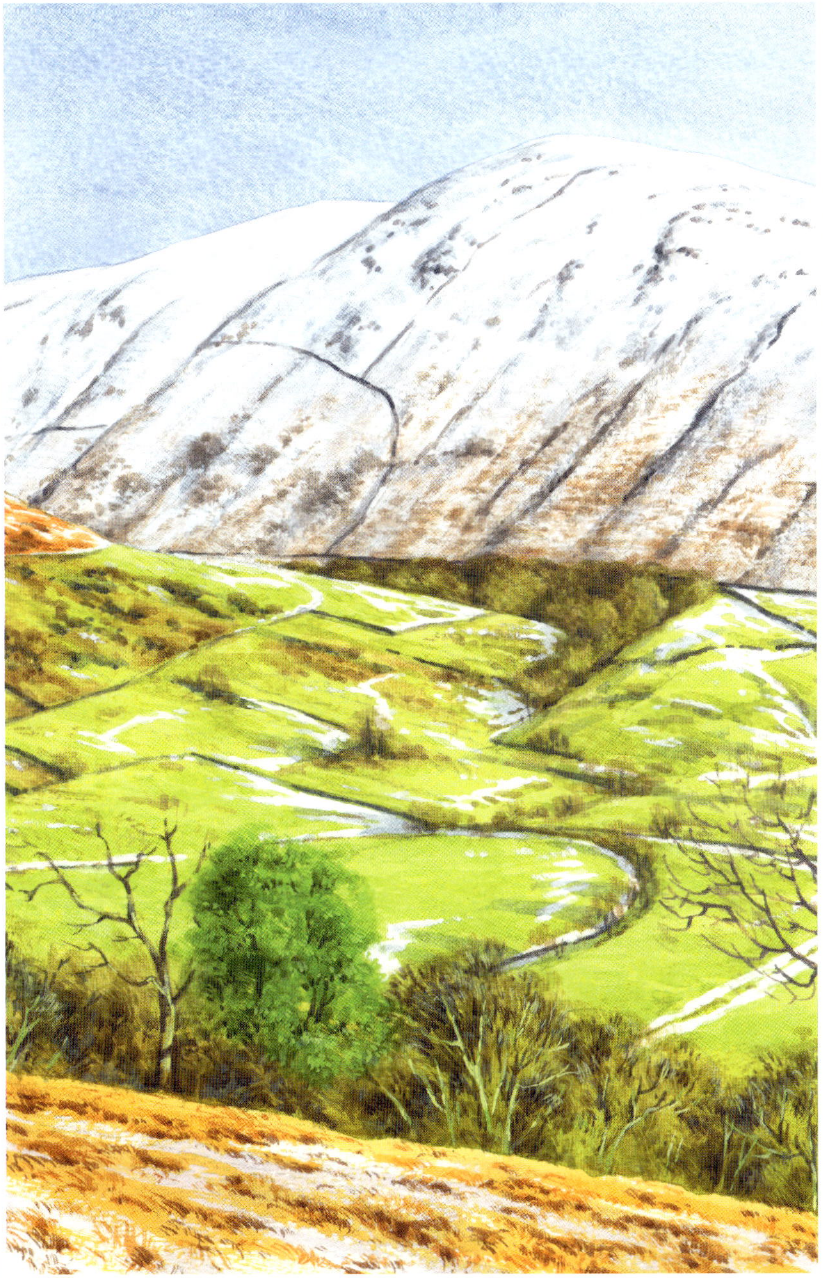

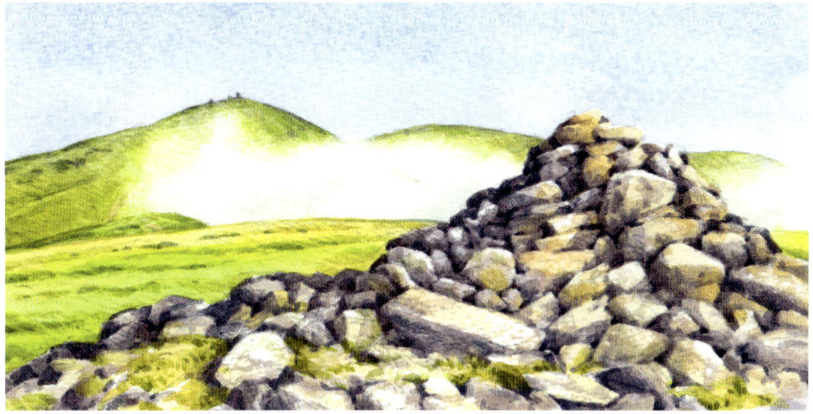

The summit 29/5/09

Since completing this sketch I have revisited the summit and found that a new post and wire fence is now in place, replacing the one from AW's day. Two unnamed tarns are also close by to the north, not marked by Wainwright in the original Pictorial Guide.

Yoke

Its neighbouring fell, Ill Bell steals all the limelight on the ridge which separates the Kentmere and Troutbeck valleys. Yoke is the first fell on a clockwise circuit of the Kentmere Horseshoe round.

From the Kirkstone to Windermere road 6/2/09

In similar winter conditions to AW's drawing, this viewpoint across the Troutbeck Valley is a good place to study the western flanks of the full Ill Bell ridge.

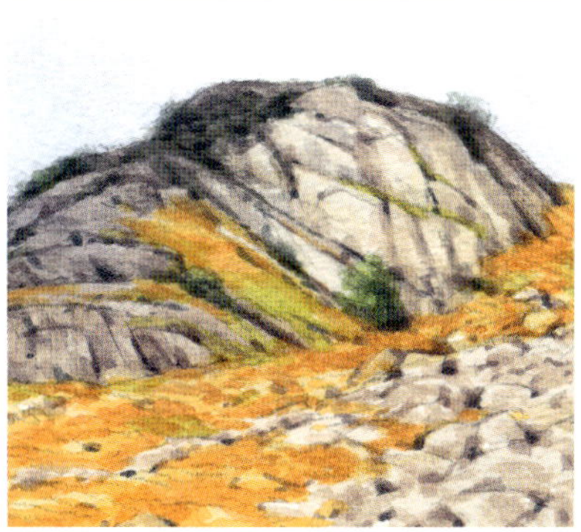

Buck Crag 10/6/13

Easy to locate on the map but harder to find the exact view on the ground. Matching the pointed rock and the background meant being on territory which even he didn't mark as a route to explain why he was there.

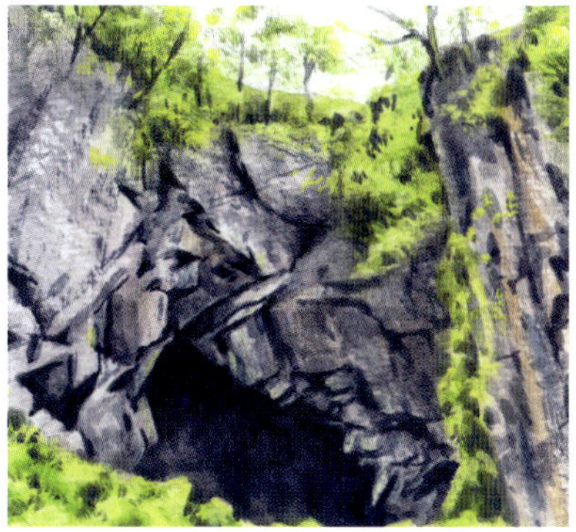

Park Quarry 10/5/09

Only the curious will have visited this site in recent years as its position is away from the main path in the valley. AW's drawing is rather odd as it only shows the very top of this huge cavern entrance. It appears as if he ran out of space in his page layout.

Raven Crag 10/10/10

A large face of rock seen from the lane which leads up to Hartrigg.

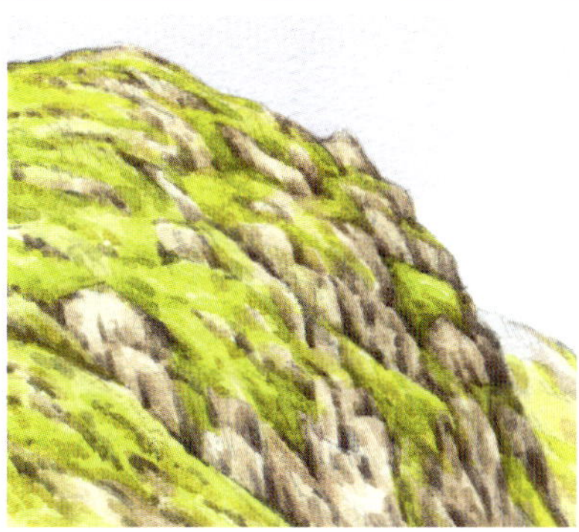

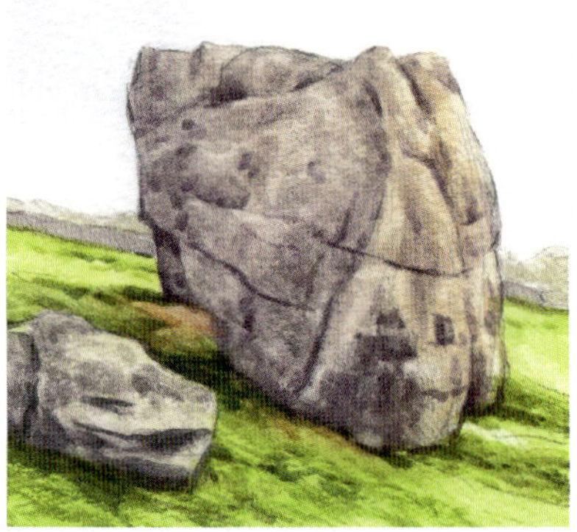

Badger Rock, West Face 21/4/09
It is worth a short detour into the field for a close inspection of this massive boulder.

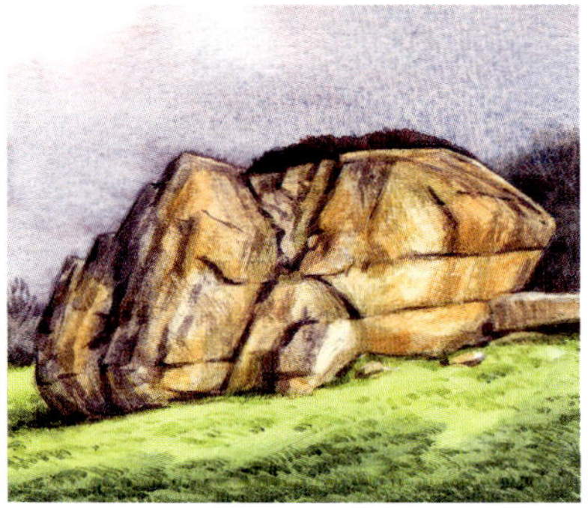

Badger Rock, East Face 21/4/09
Catching the early morning sun. A popular location for bouldering, there are over 20 recognised routes on this one rock.

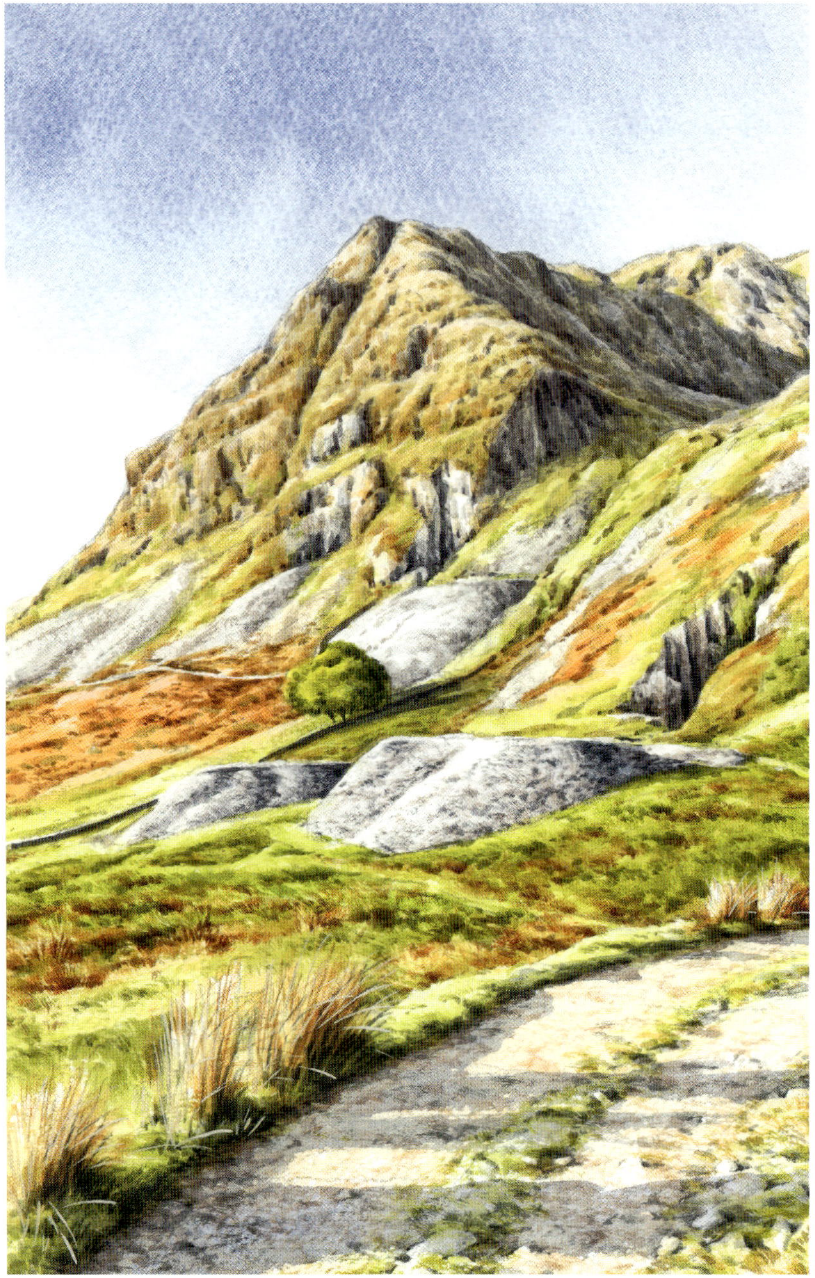

Rainsbarrow Crag 10/10/10
Of all the references that I needed to obtain for this project there are only one or two locations that I have needed to revisit to confirm that I had the correct image. This is one of them. I had already drawn the sketch and whilst in the process of adding the watercolour I knew that something wasn't quite right even though the fell shape and composition was mostly true, making allowances for AW's exaggeration. It turns out that I had been some distance short on the track when taking my photograph so I had to return to the site and confirm the detail before going on to complete the work. As it happens, it gave me a great opportunity to explore a new route for me and one not listed in the Pictorial Guides, that of the ascent of Yoke by the ridge above Rainsbarrow Crag, seen here in the sunlight. It was an exciting, adventurous and unfrequented route. All in all, a very productive return visit.

The Central Fells

With only 27 fells included in this, Wainwright's third Pictorial Guide, The Central Fells, the book certainly is the thinnest of the seven. What it lacks in volume it makes up for in variety. Ranging from the sodden terrain of Armboth Fell to the high drama of the Langdale Pikes this region has the rough boundaries of Great Langdale, Borrowdale and the Thirlmere valley. Many pleasant hours can be spent exploring the high ground of these parts.

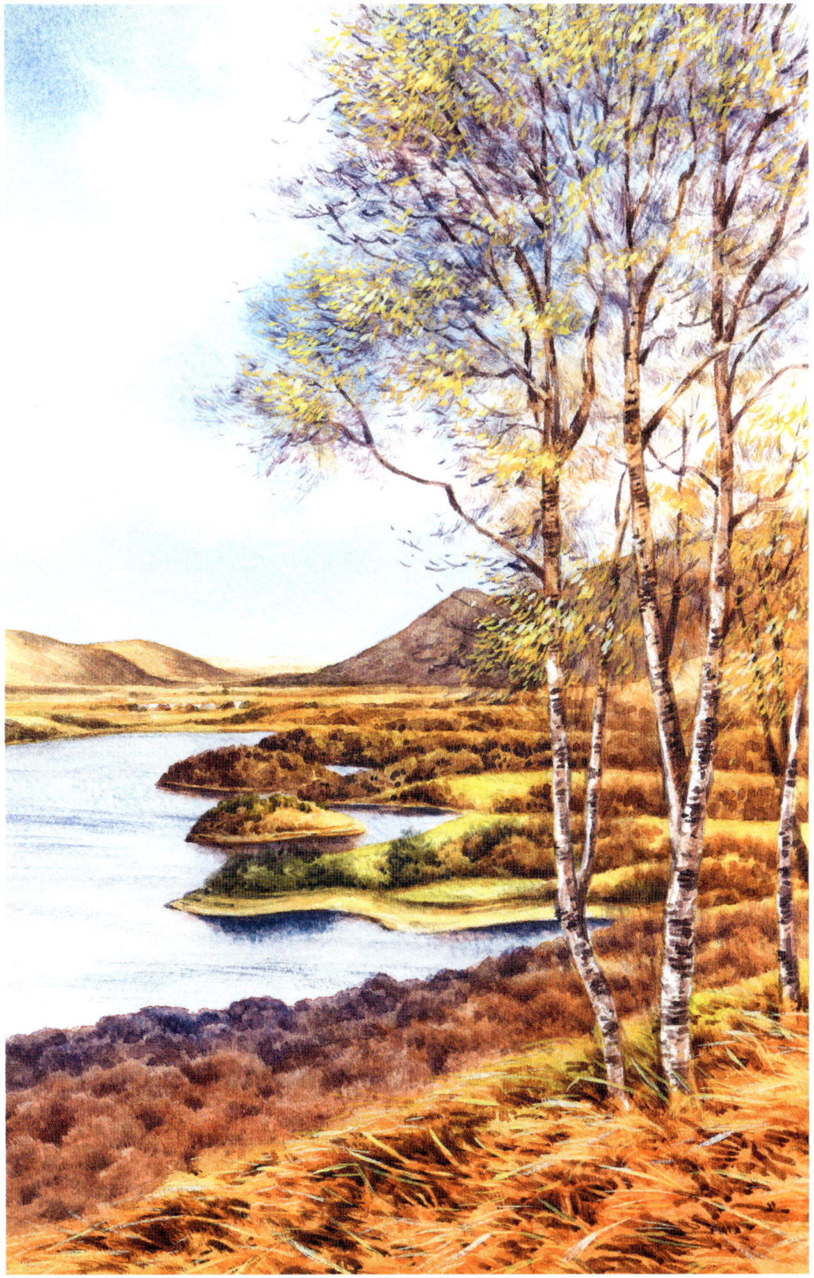

Frontispiece - Derwentwater from near Cat Gill 20/4/10

By taking the path on the south side of Cat Gill near Walla Crag it is only a short diversion to this open terrace on which grows a fine stand of birch trees, AW even indicated them on his drawing in Walla Crag 4. Revealed from here is not only this fine prospect of the northern end of Derwentwater but also stunning views across to the north-western fells. Once again, it is a frontispiece illustration which does not feature the fells contained within the volume.

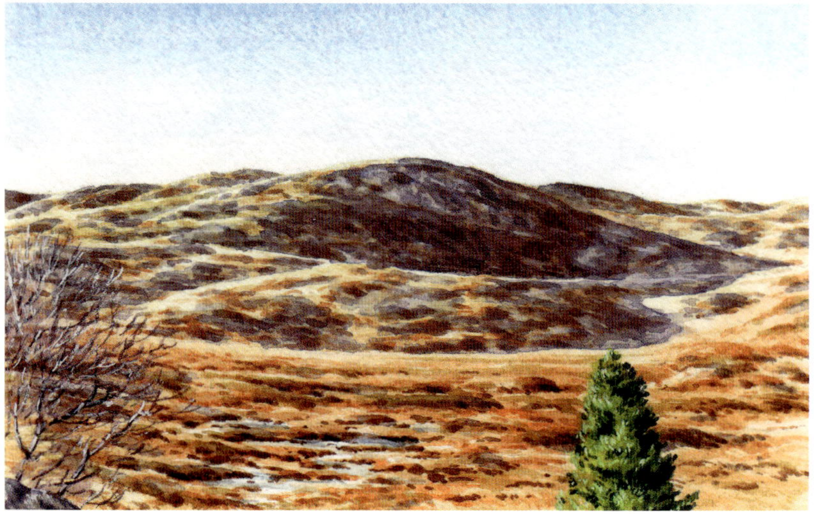

From Fisher Crag 15/11/07
Few fells have such an uninspiring profile for either the artist or photographer. This, in AW's opinion was obviously the best angle to illustrate the fell. All but one of the foreground conifers have been felled.

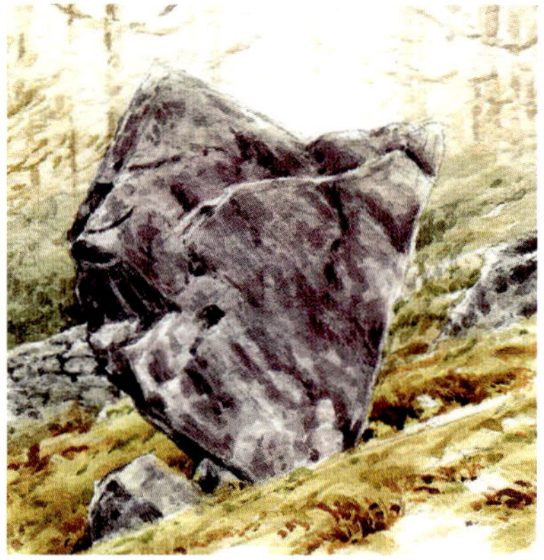

A balanced boulder 15/11/07
There are other such balanced boulders nearby such as the more famous Tottling Stone, this one being adjacent to the path up from Armboth is very accessible.

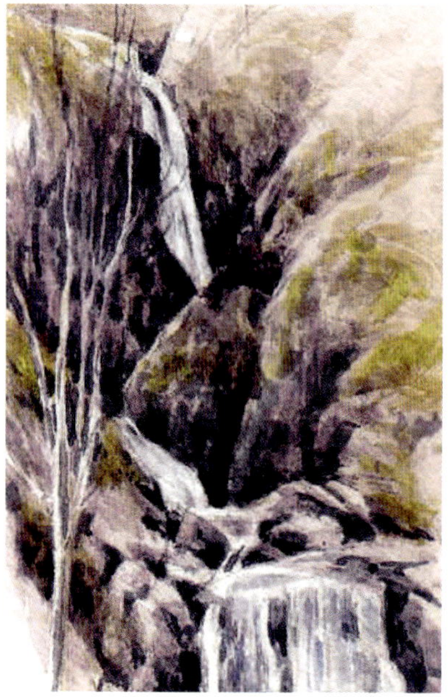

Waterfalls in Launchy Gill 1
4/3/08
The lower cascade which is now partially hidden by trees.

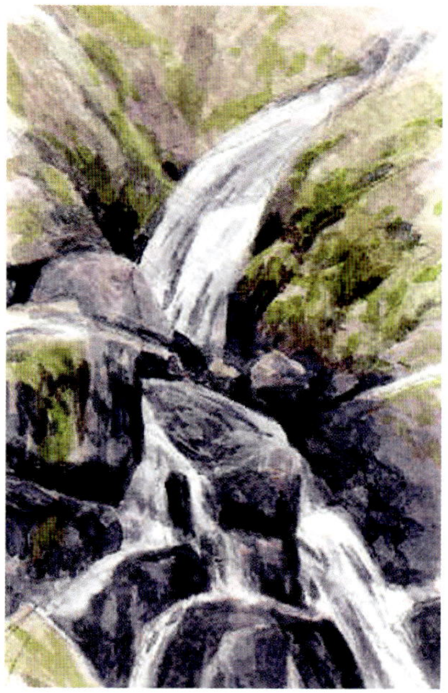

Waterfalls in Launchy Gill 2
4/3/08
The upper fall, made more impressive after heavy rain.

Armboth Fell

This is a fell with a poor reputation, even AW wrote that it wasn't really worth climbing. Yes, the panoramic view of fells from the summit is good but the surrounding ground is wet, really wet. On one of my visits I was lucky, a long period of cold winter weather had left the sponge-like terrain frozen solid, and I took a direct line from High Tove to Armboth Fell on firm ground, a rare achievement.

The shepherd's cairn 15/11/07
The wedge shaped boulder has lost its cairn off its sloping surface.

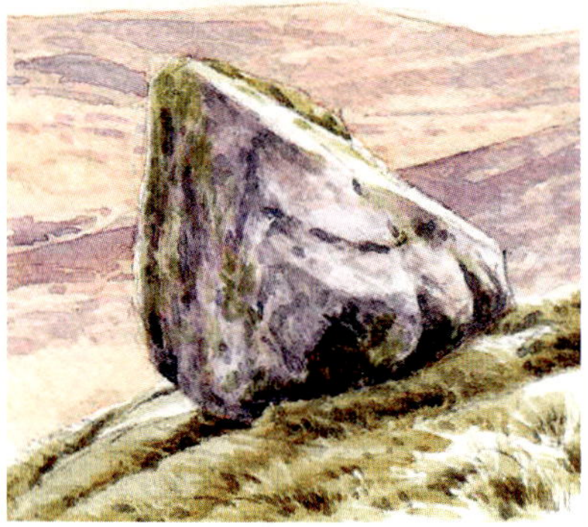

The summit 15/11/07
Surely one of the strangest "summit confusions" in all of the Pictorial Guides. The other prominence that AW mentions, 300 yards to the north east is about 20′ higher and it is now recognised as the actual summit.

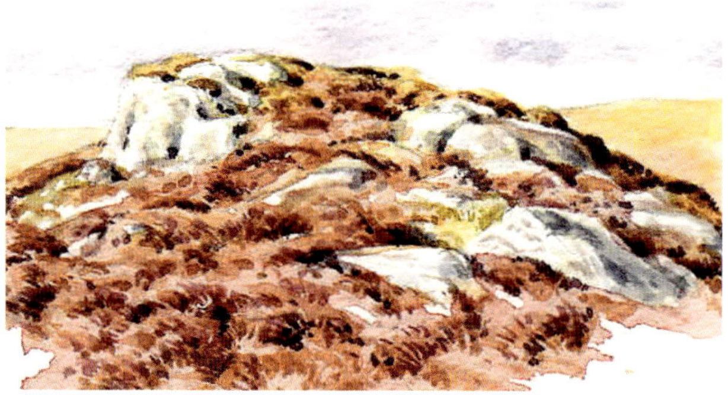

View from Fisher Crag 4/3/08
Today the clear top of this crag is just outside the open access land but I doubt if visitors will be prosecuted for venturing onto this high point.

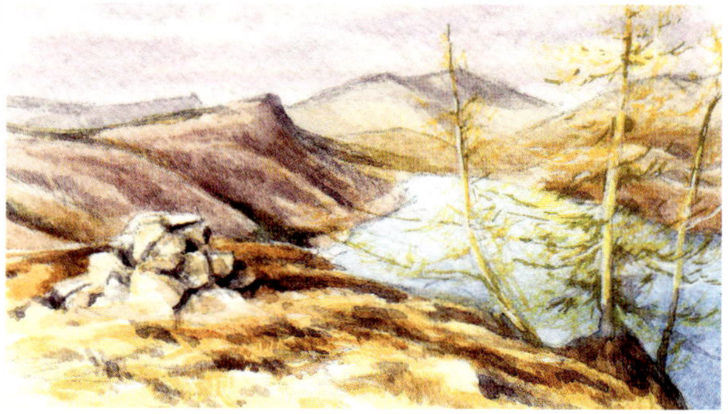

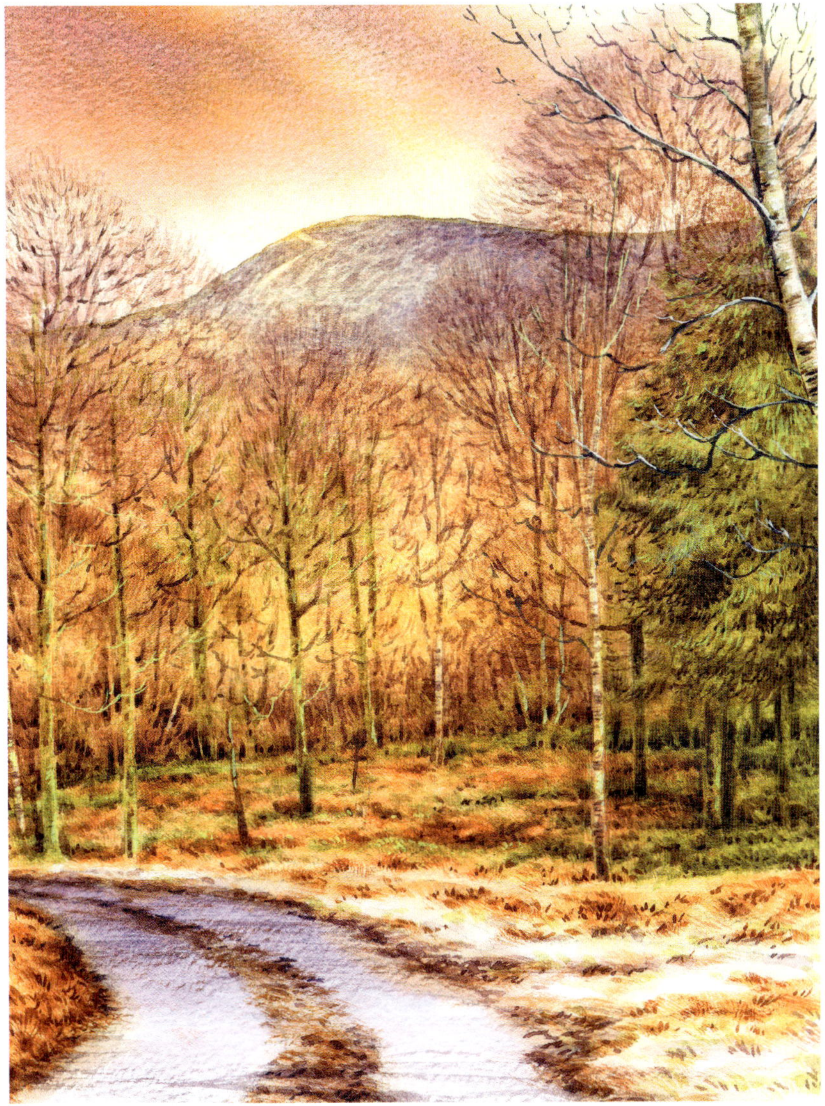

From Ashness Wood 4/1/09
This delightful mixed woodland now almost hides the fell from view. I was lucky that my visit was in winter when the bare trees provided the best opportunity to picture the top section of hill. This single track road leads down to Ashness Bridge from the hamlet of Watendlath.

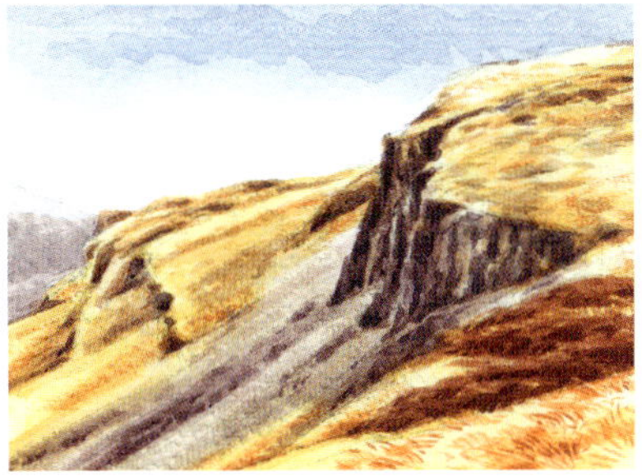

The Shoulthwaite Crags
20/4/10
The view of the crags from near Dodd Crag, not an easy viewpoint for me to locate as it is away from any hint of a footpath. Goat Crag is the nearest cliff with Iron Crag beyond.

Bleaberry Fell

I would have to fully agree with Wainwright in the fact that Bleaberry Fell affords fine views especially to the north. I do recall standing near the summit on a crisp November evening as the sun sent shafts of light across the vale of Keswick, illuminating the ridges of Blencathra and the Skiddaw massif. It made for one of those memorable fellwalking experiences.

The summit from the ruined cottage 20/4/10
The walls of the cottage are now more tumbledown but still easy to find. Some of the paths in this vicinity have undergone some recent erosion repairs.

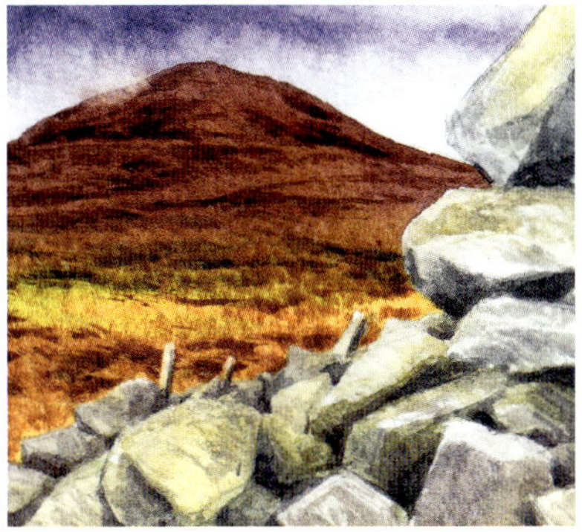

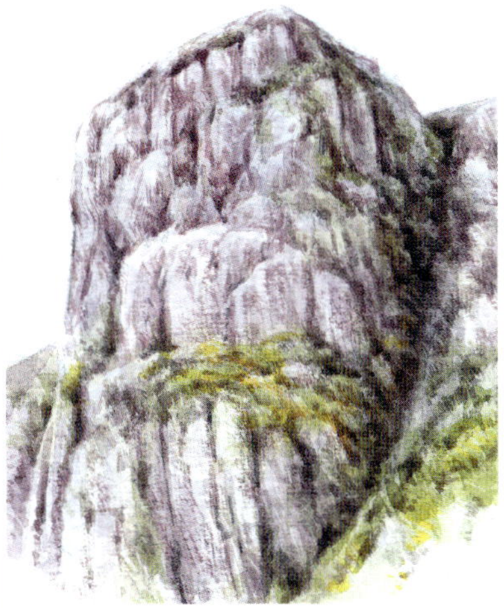

Falcon Crag 20/4/10
Access to the foot of this crag is difficult, only a few climbers seem to use this route and as a result dense gorse encroaches onto the path. The Crag is aptly named, on my visit the rock face was out of bounds to climbers due to nesting peregrines which wheeled overhead as I passed below their domain.

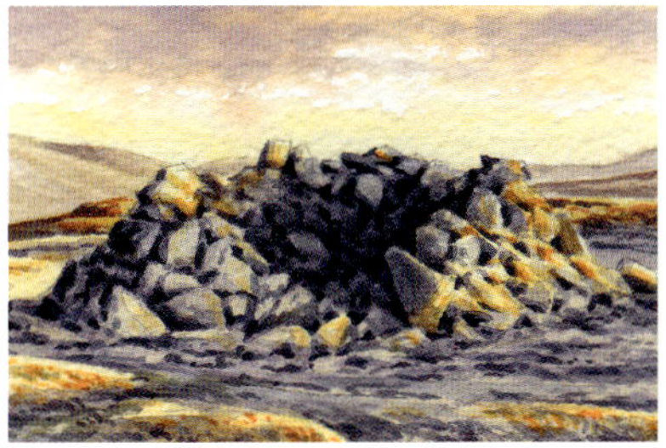

The summit 4/1/09
What once was a simple cairn has now been reworked into a decent sized wind shelter.

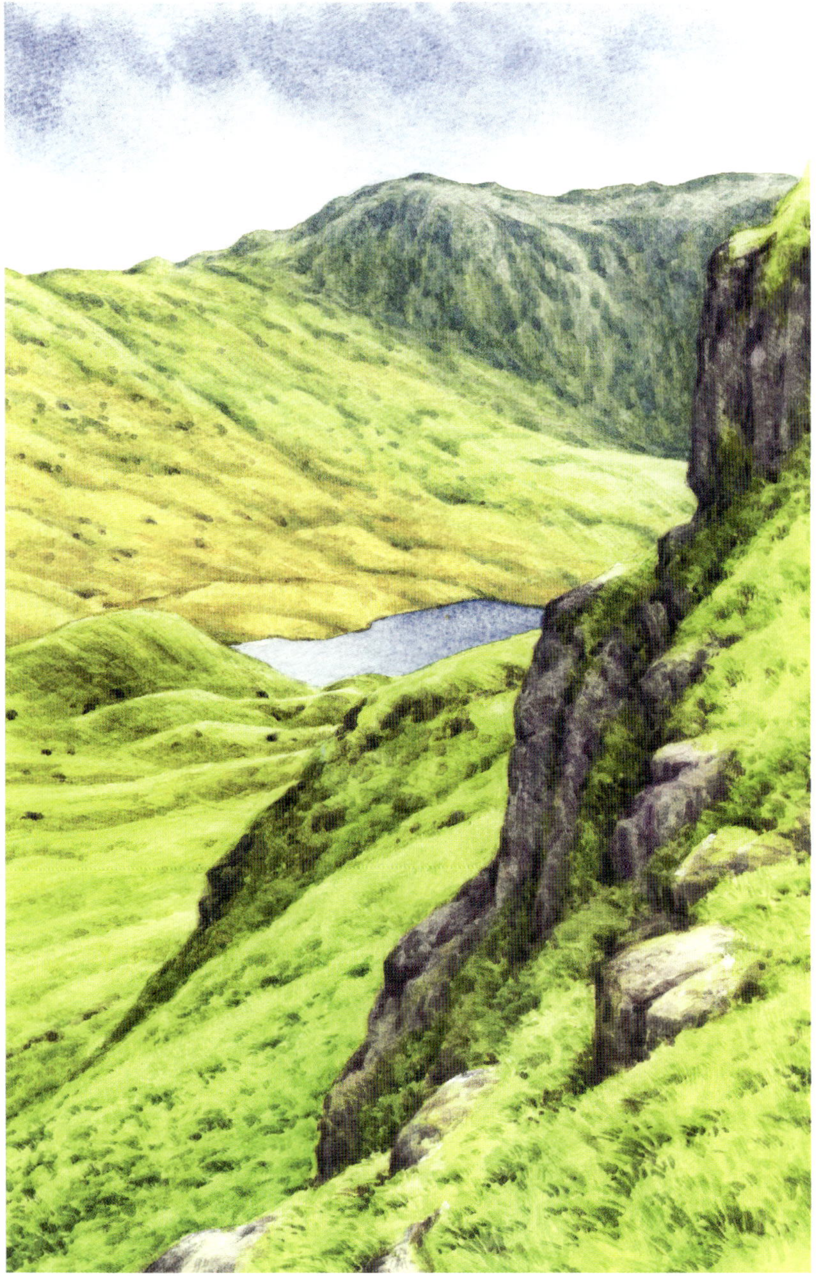

Blea Rigg

In the right conditions, the east-west route from Silver How to High Raise is a rather pleasant journey affording fine views over Langdale to the south and Easedale to the north. Blea Rigg is mid-way along this ridge. Elements of the fell such as Whitegill and Great Castle How are worth exploring but remain unknown to many walkers.

From Greathead Crag 2/6/09

Not only is this a good view of the fell but also of the area around Easedale Tarn. Greathead Crag is part of the east ridge of Tarn Crag.

The Split Boulder 12/8/09

This unusual boulder is easily visited as it is a short distance from the New Dungeon Ghyll Hotel.

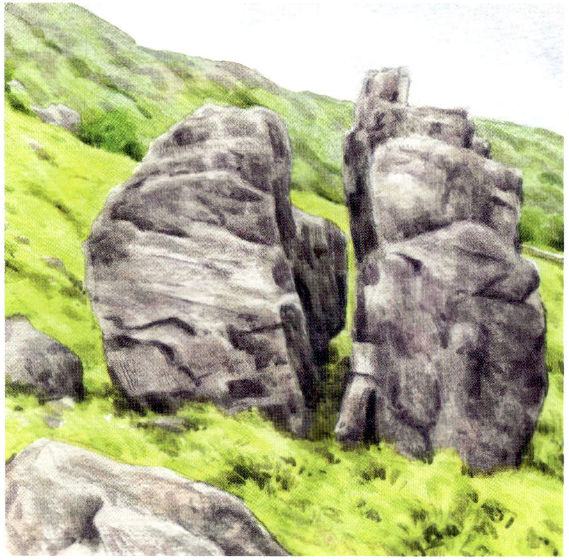

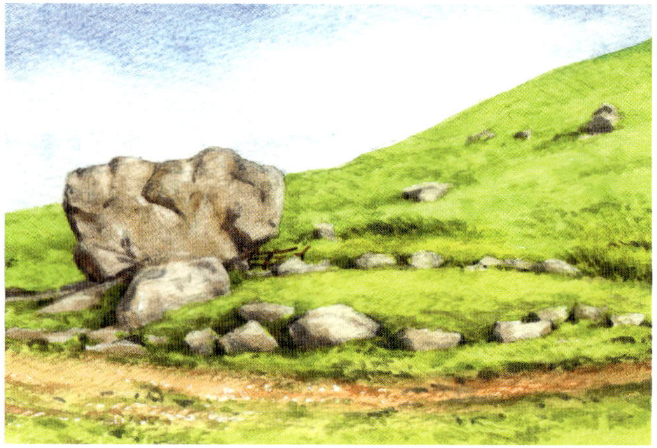

The ruins of the refreshment hut at Easedale Tarn 2/6/09

Nothing of the structure of the building remains apart from the large boulder which formed one corner of the hut. Rocks placed in a oval roughly mark out the building's footprint. An old rusty, twisted iron seat under the boulder gives a hint to days gone by.

The summit 2/6/09

There are several high points to Blea Rigg which can be confused with this summit, situated about 80 yards east of the shelter stone. One can be seen from the other.

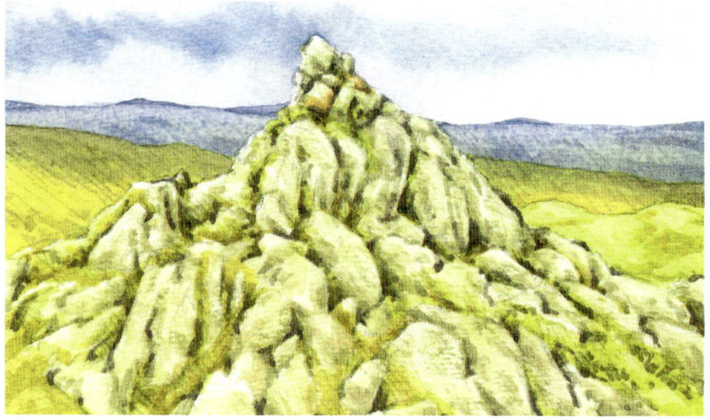

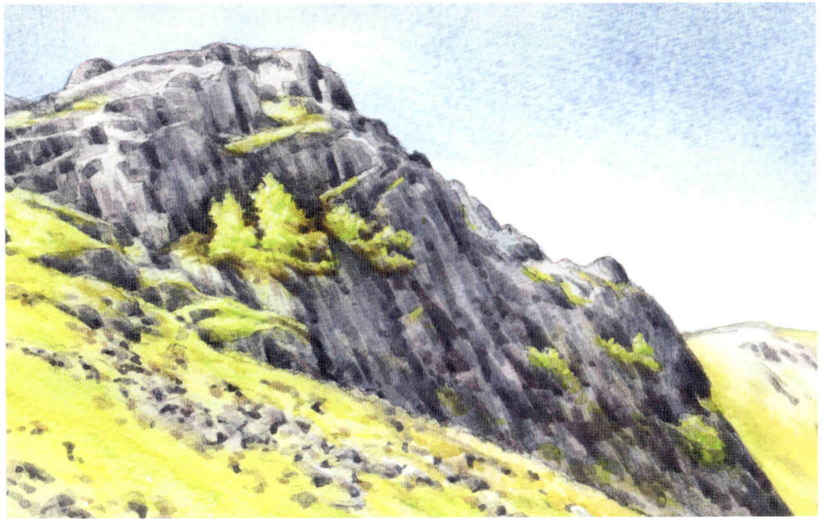

Blea Crag 2/6/09
The northern face of the fell is shaped by this crag with young birches clinging to the narrow shelves of rock. There is a very pleasant, almost secret grassy rake which passes over the top of this crag.

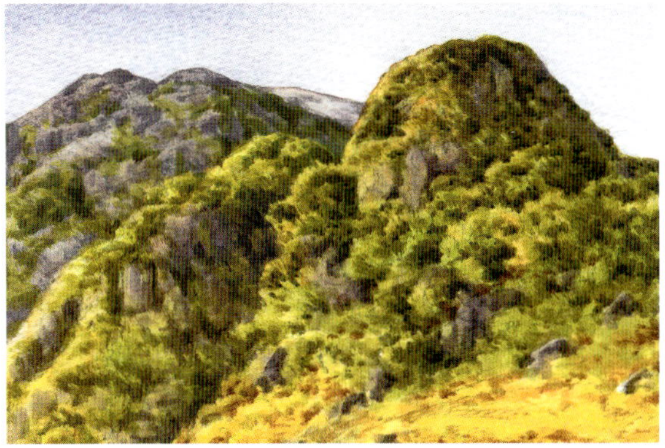

Yew Crag 1/2/12
This was one of the few days when I had a fellow walker as a companion and I recall our comments as we struggled through dense gorse thickets to get to this location. In omitting the background fell AW made the task of finding the exact place harder but when we accomplished my task there was a sigh or two of relief before we continued on up to the ridge. Yew Crag was on AW's original list of potential fells for the Pictorial Guides.

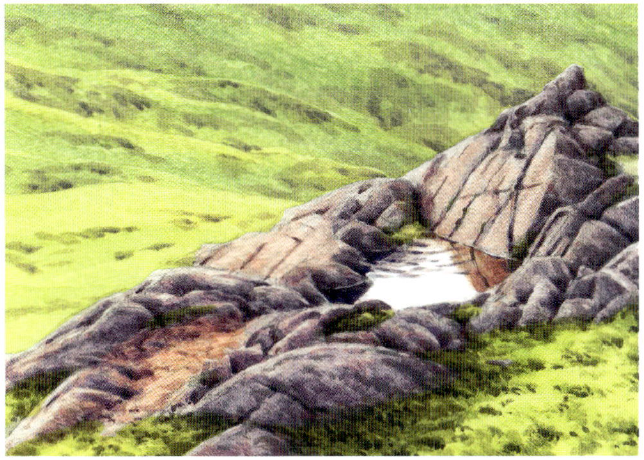

The rock pool 2/6/09
Only those who are familiar with the Pictorial Guide will make the slight detour off the path to locate this miniature pool which is one of those interesting natural curiosities which AW located on his explorations.

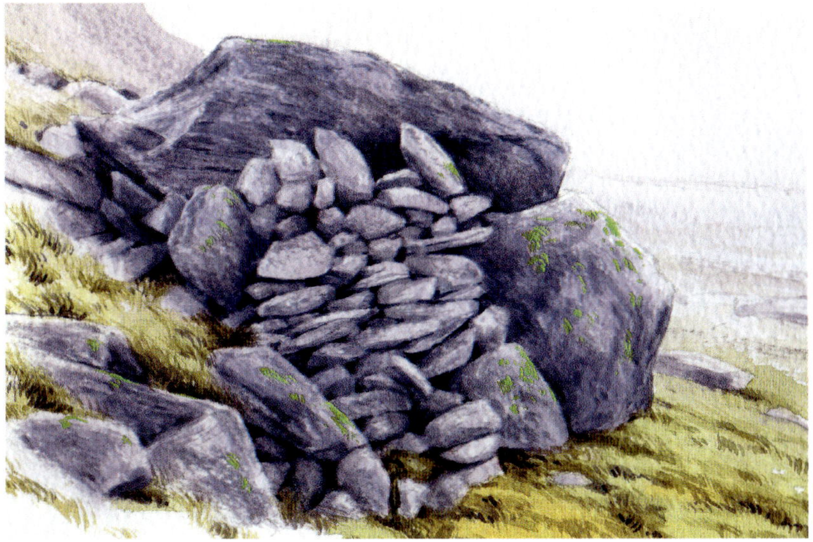

The Shelter Stone 14/9/08
Cloud had descended as I walked the ridge on this day and the only reference I was able to tick off was this one of the shelter which now has a bigger wall at this end, the other open side allows access.

Whitegill Crag 23/5/12
An ascent of this steep and rough gully takes you into the domain of serious climbers. It is one of those places not often frequented by casual walkers.

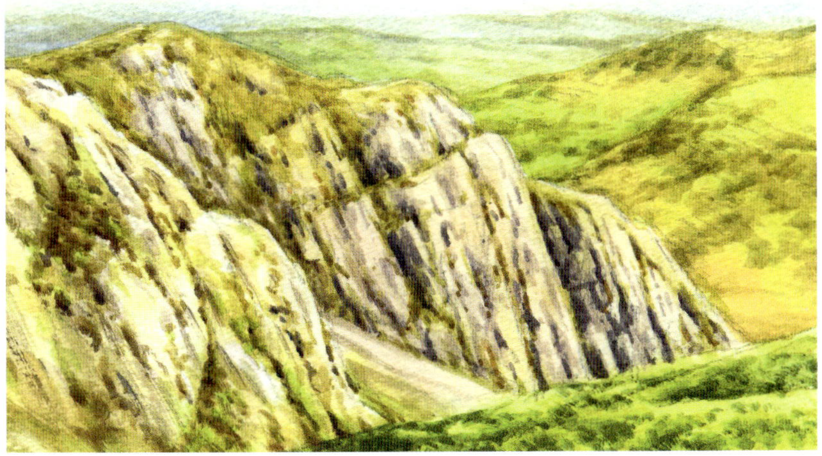

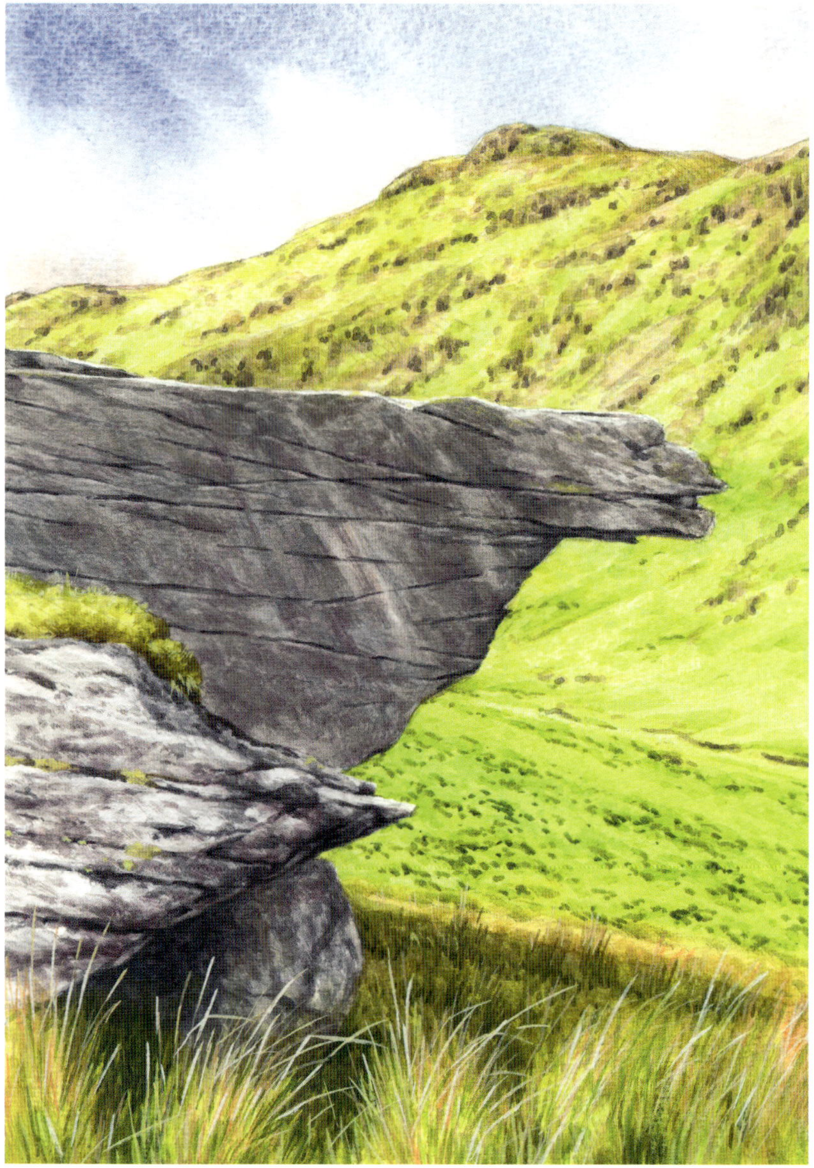

From the boulders below Deer Bield Crag 2/6/09
This huge block is easily identified due to its gargoyle like feature. The top surface is flat and a fine place to observe Far Easedale on a sunny day.

Calf Crag

Located at the western end of Far Easedale, Calf Crag sits on the ridge which also features both Helm Crag and Gibson Knott. All can be accessed in a walk from Grasmere.

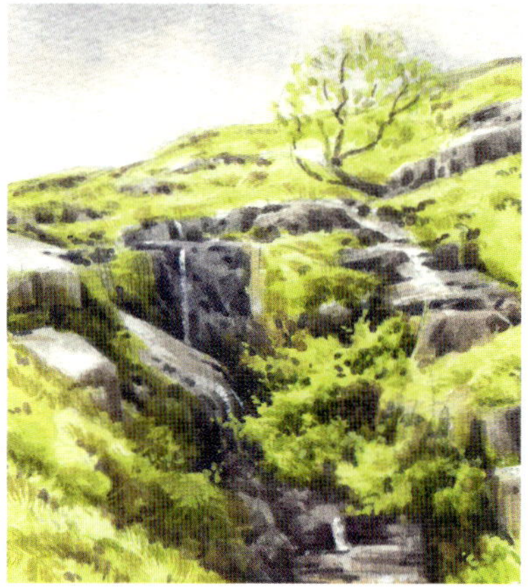

Waterfalls, Far Easedale 2/6/09
A hot period prior to my visit meant that the gill was almost dry.

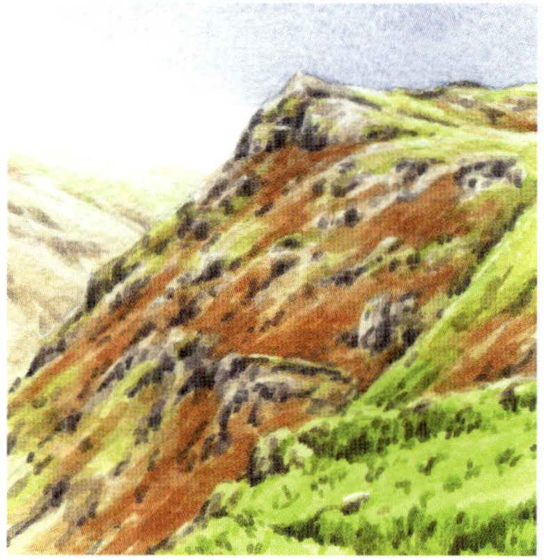

Pike of Carrs 14/9/08
Seen from the eastern approach along the ridge from Gibson Knott.

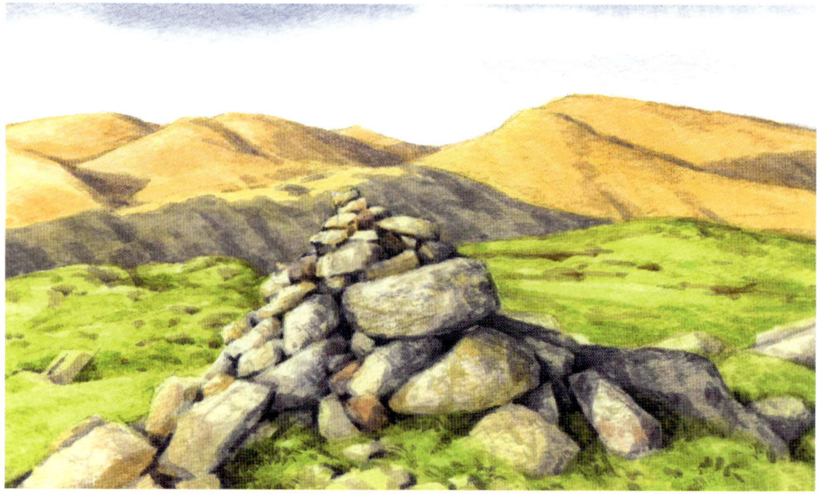

The summit 2/6/09
A small increase in the size of the cairn which marks the highest point.

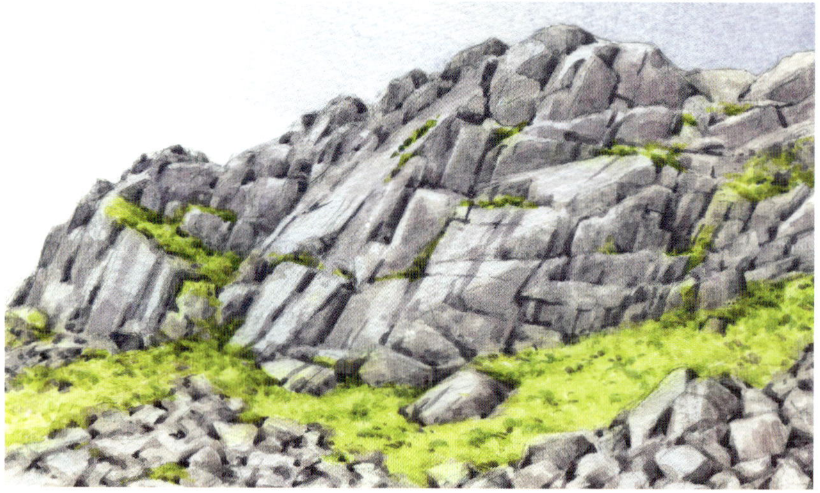

The summit crags 14/9/08
This aspect of the crags is obtained by venturing just south of the summit itself. The path here is faint and unfrequented.

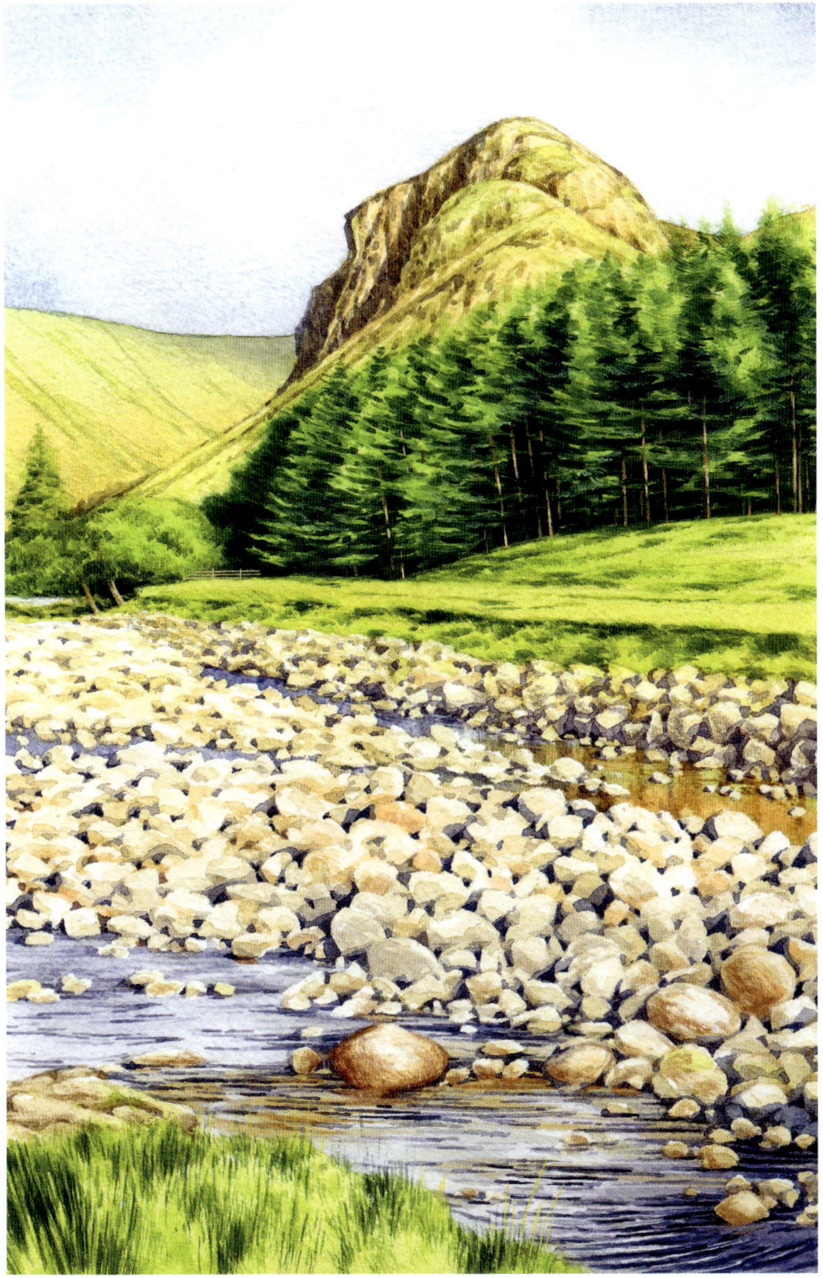

Eagle Crag

Wainwright was right in his description of Eagle Crag, it is a beautiful fell. Sitting as it does in the valley with less angular neighbours on all sides, this hill just asks to be climbed. The easy route of ascent is by coming at it from the south via the Greenup valley. A much more exciting route, and without too many difficulties is the direct ascent up the face of Heron Crag.

The summit 24/6/09

In the course of this project I had to visit this top on three occasions with the last being in April 2013. On that day the small neat cairn which had obviously stood there for some time, judging by the unweathered rock at its former position, had now been cast asunder. Why do people do this and what is achieved? Why can't they just spend their time admiring the wonderful views?

From Stonethwaite Beck

24/6/09

In principle it would seem quite easy to walk alongside the beck and find this exact location. The reality is slightly different. The river is now much wider with the left bank having been washed away, and in fact the river in the distance has changed course moving out of view to the left. A new conifer plantation has appeared on the right but the single tree in AW's drawing still stands, giving me a reference point for my correct position.

With hindsight I can see that I have drawn the top section of the fell more acute that it is in reality, something that AW himself was prone to doing in some of his fell illustrations.

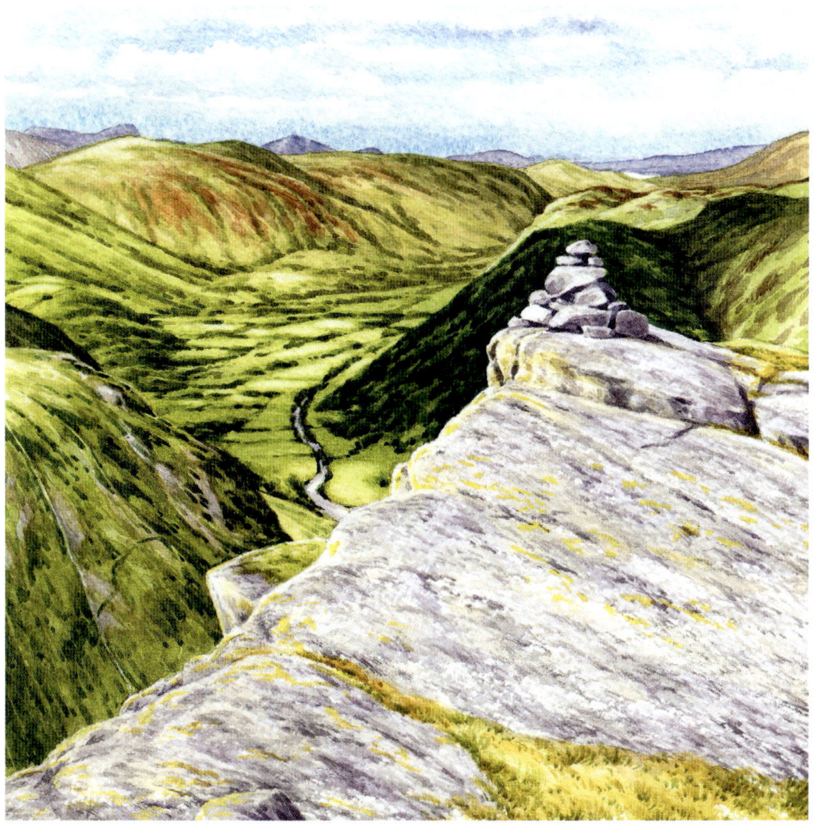

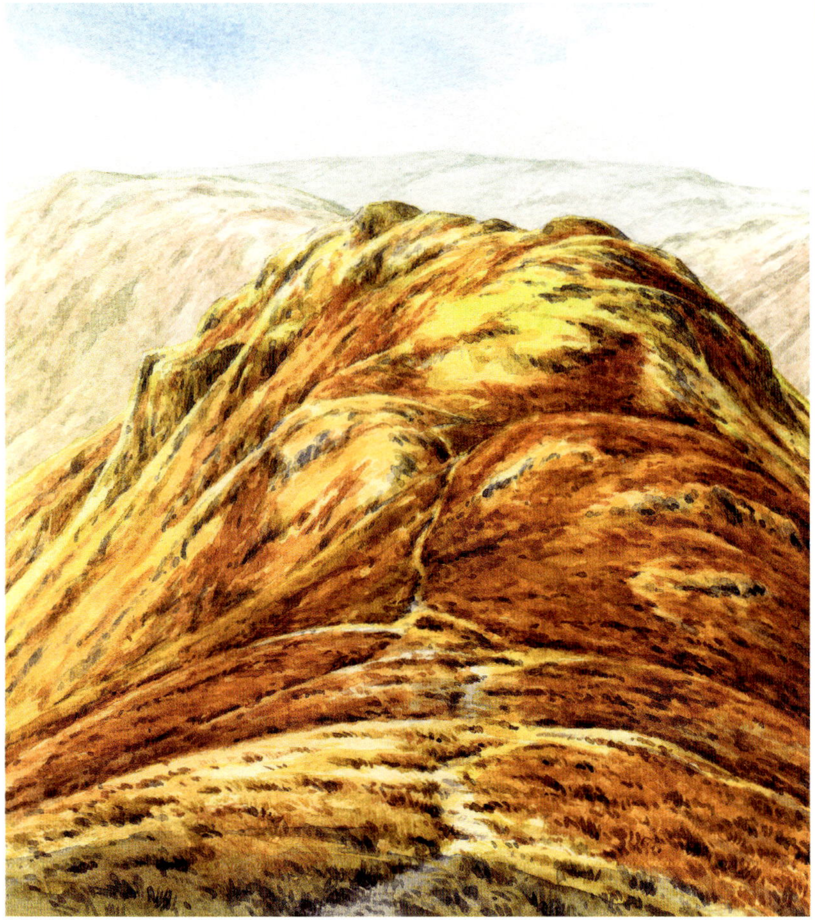

From Helm Crag 14/9/08
Unusually for one of his main chapter drawings AW hinted at the fell behind which in this case is Calf Crag. This made my job easier, all I had to do was walk west from the summit of Helm Crag on the ridge to Gibson Knott, and then when the two elements matched his drawing I knew I was in the correct place. I have not only included Calf Crag but also Ullscarf in the far distance. If only acquiring every reference had been this easy.

Gibson Knott

Few in number are the fells where a single footpath that crosses the top is about the only practical access. For that reason Gibson Knott is usually reached as part of a ridge walk which covers the north side of Far Easedale. A good round route can also take in Tarn Crag across the valley to the south.

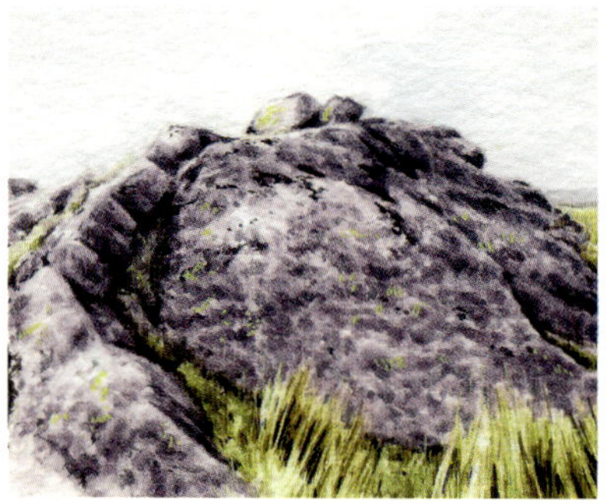

The summit 14/9/08
With several rocky knolls in the vicinity of similar height it is difficult to determine the true top without modern equipment. This is the point of AW's choice, still with just a rock or two on the top.

Horn Crag 14/9/08
The crag looks slightly different when the background of Far Easedale is included in the scene as shown here. This valley supports quite a few dense patches of Juniper (see right) of which one can be seen here.

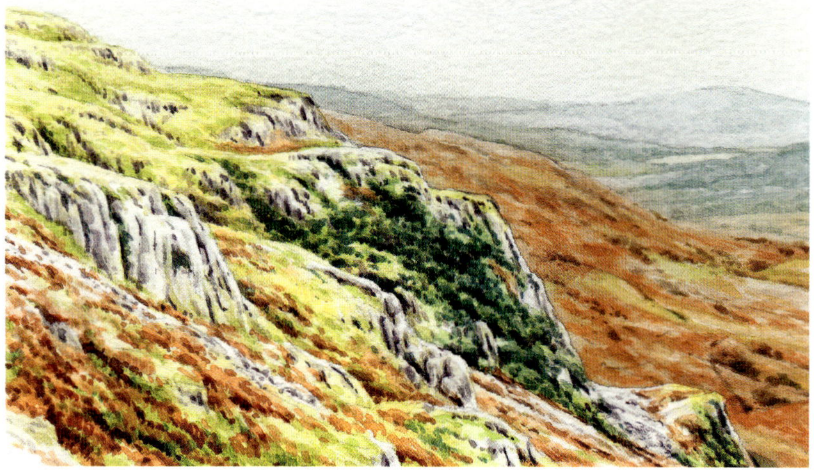

Tough times for Juniper

Areas in the central and eastern fells are home to large natural stands of juniperus communis - common juniper. This evergreen coniferous shrub is reasonably widespread across the country but the Lake District and Teesdale are its strongholds in England. As the glaciers of the last ice age retreated juniper was one of the first species of plant to colonise the harsh landscape of Cumbria, easily finding a home at altitudes of 2000′ or more. It is very slow growing but it has been used for several purposes including the flavouring of gin and in the making of gunpowder. The dense canopy provides good habitat for many species of wildlife and the now scarce Ring Ouzel feeds on the berries.

Unfortunately this hardy shrub is under threat, not only from problems with the tree self seeding, the browsing by sheep and red deer but also from a fungal disease, phytophthora austrocedrae. This causes the plant to turn orange or brown and then die back completely.

In 2011 the Uplands for Juniper project began work to survey and assess the decline of the juniper and consequently several thousand juniper saplings were planted by conservation teams to help stem the decline in this important native species.

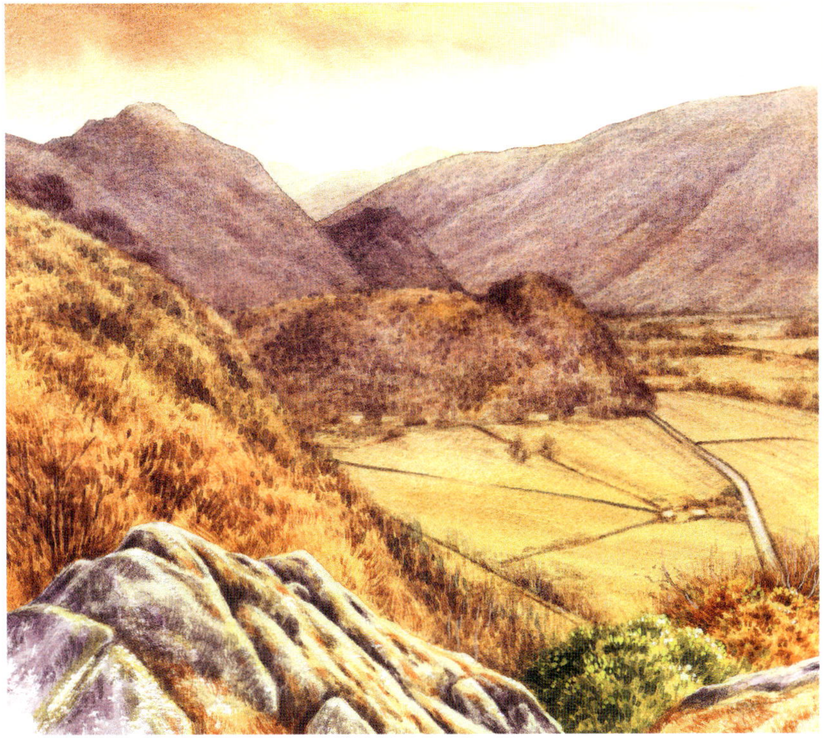

King's How, from Shepherds Crag 7/3/10
It was only due to my need to photograph this scene that I even considered how to reach Shepherds Crag and its summit, an area previously unknown to me but popular with climbers. Although the fading light was very poor, after all, it was nearly half past six on a March evening, I was impressed with this vantage point over Borrowdale and I plan to revisit.

Grange Fell

The high ground between Watendlath and Grange in Borrowdale has several interesting rocky outcrops protruding through a dense cover of heather. There are two distinctive summit peaks, Brund Fell and King's How both of which Wainwright listed as individual fells initially before finally combining them both under the name of Grange Fell.

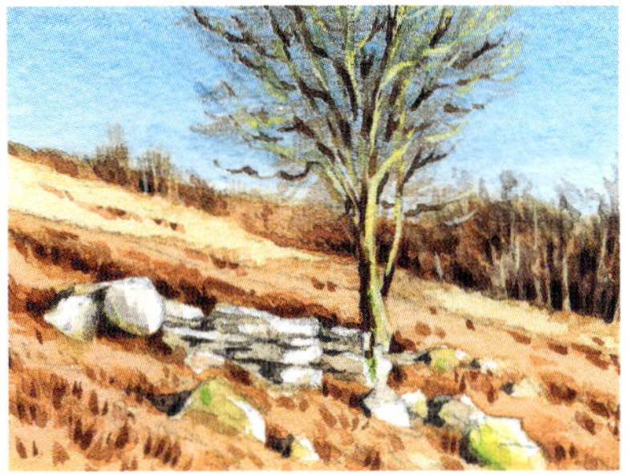

Hut (shelter) 7/3/10
One can only wonder at the purpose for constructing a small hut on the fell side as there are no signs of mining or any major through route near here. Now sadly a complete ruin, reduced almost to just the footings. The lone tree outlives the man-made structure. Wainwright's small and delicate detailed drawing has since been eradicated from the revised guide.

Jopplety How 23/7/08
This rocky tor with the quirky name is some 80 yards east of the summit of Brund Fell. Coarse rock covered with a cap of heather.

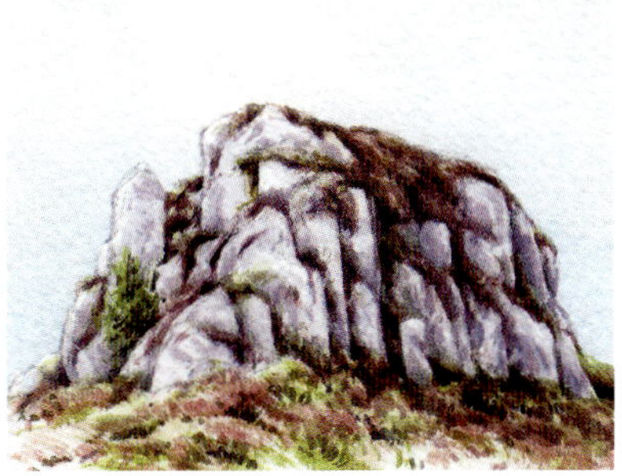

The summit 14/9/08
With several rocky platforms near the highest point of Brund Fell, determining which was the actual Wainwright top was made more interesting as the small cairn in his drawing had been dismantled. Some time was spent marrying up bedrock to his small illustration but my persistence paid off.

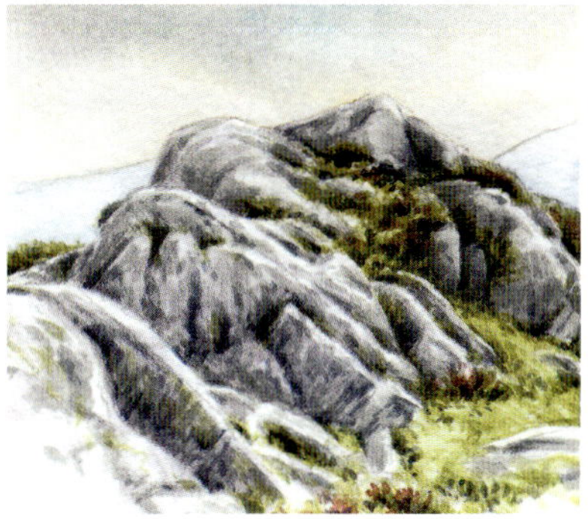

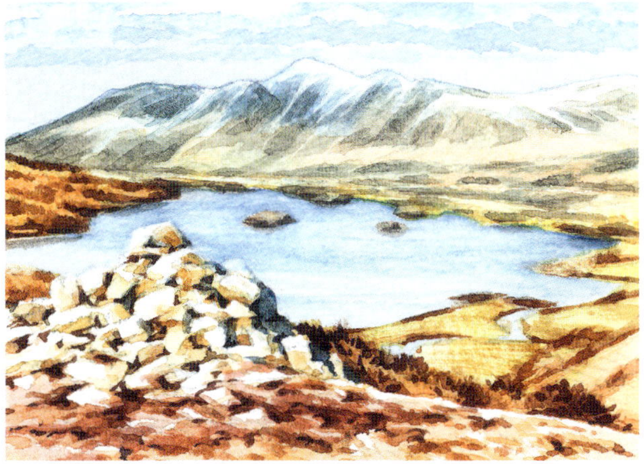

The summit of King's How 7/3/10
Even though this is the lower and most northerly of the two summit cairns, for views this one wins the competition with an almost full aspect of Derwentwater with the Skiddaw range as a distant backdrop.

The north ridge of King's How 7/3/10

The path in this area is faint and care had to be taken as vegetation covered loose boulders underfoot, but the richness of the late winter colours in the afternoon light were glorious.

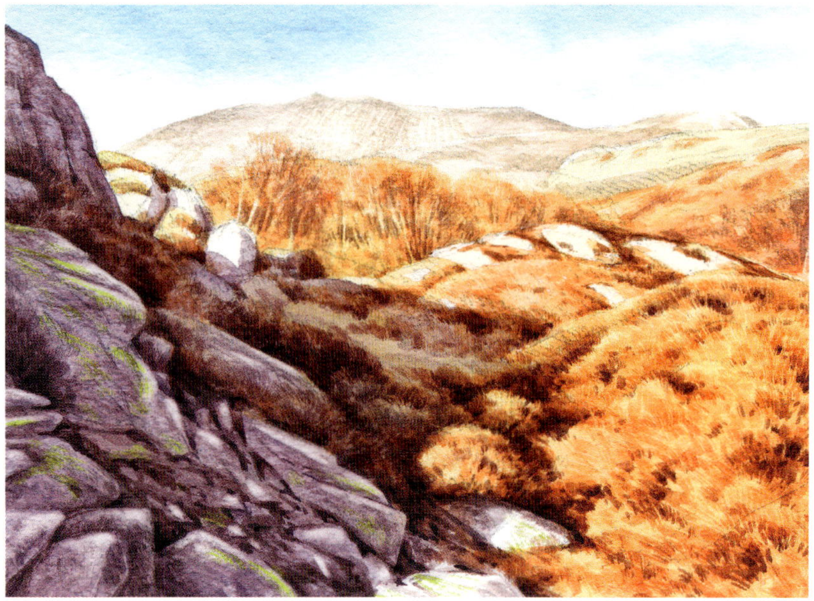

Crossing the Bridge

Wainwright liked his bridges, in fact he included over forty illustrations of bridges in one form or another in the seven Pictorial Guides. Whether is was the simple plank that he drew in Haycock 7 (which has since been upgraded, see page 310) or the more elaborate double arched stone construction of Scale Bridge (page 330) he obviously was attracted by them. Whilst many are in the form of the simple modern wooden footbridge a good number are of the old packhorse variety, dating back hundreds of years, used by traders to transport goods throughout the area on the backs of ponies and horses, but they were also used by farmers moving stock. Many of these traditional bridges are soundly constructed and are a clever feat of engineering. Low walls edge the arch so that panniers would not become snagged. Others are a simple "clapper" design where a single slab of stone supported by stone piers, the best example of this is the one in the Troutbeck valley (page 111).

The reason why so many featured in the guides is quite simple: in remote areas of the fells a man-made feature such as a bridge is not only of interest but adds variety to the illustrations and is indicated as a feature on many routes. Only two of the stone built bridges shown in the original guides have been lost and replaced with modern designs.

Looking north from the top of Brund Fell 23/7/08

Even though the view from here is not quite as good as the one from the nearby lower top of King's How it is still a fine vista. The angular large blocks of rock make a good contrast to the more rounded distant fells.

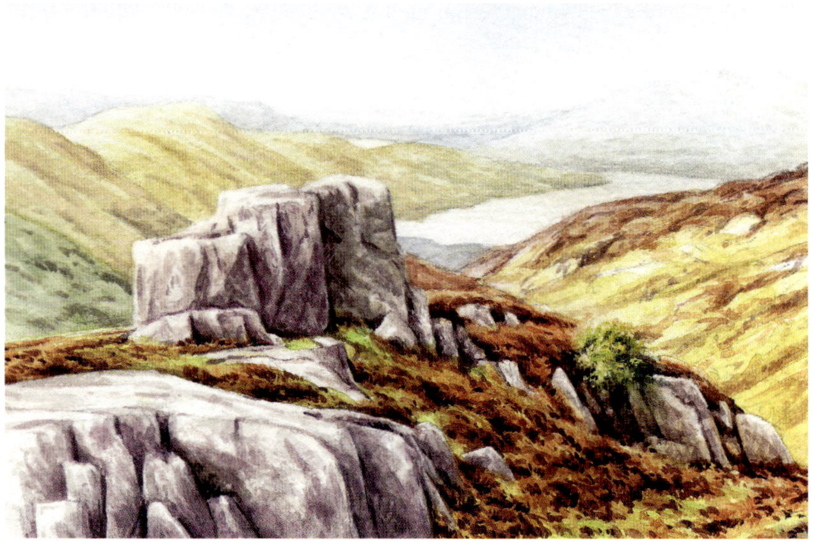

Borrowdale from the lower slopes of Brund Fell 7/3/10

AW's title gave me little in the way of clues to precisely pinpoint this view and I spent a fair amount of time seeking out possible locations. Fate was on my side though as after some time wandering across the open fell, just when the light was fading, I joined the main path between Watendlath and Rosthwaite and there it was, the actual scene in front of me, complete with the same mature conifers on the right.

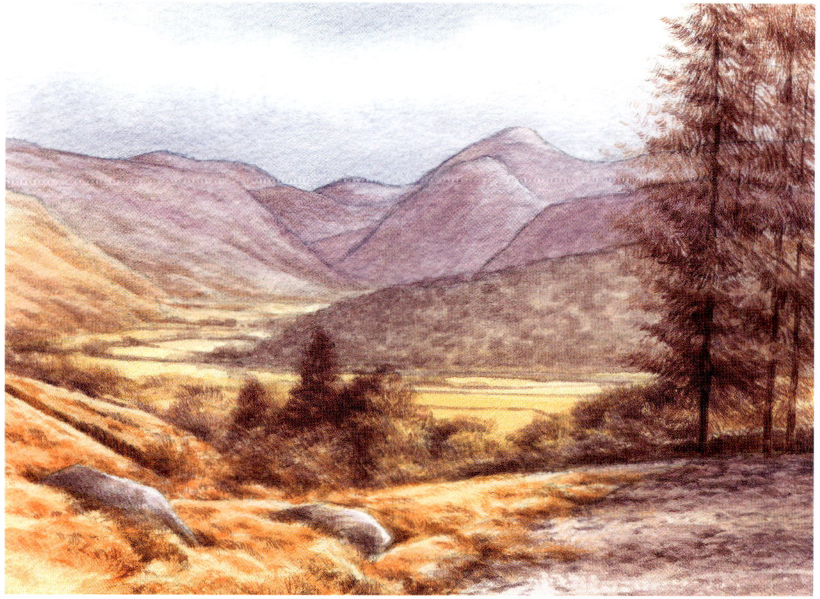

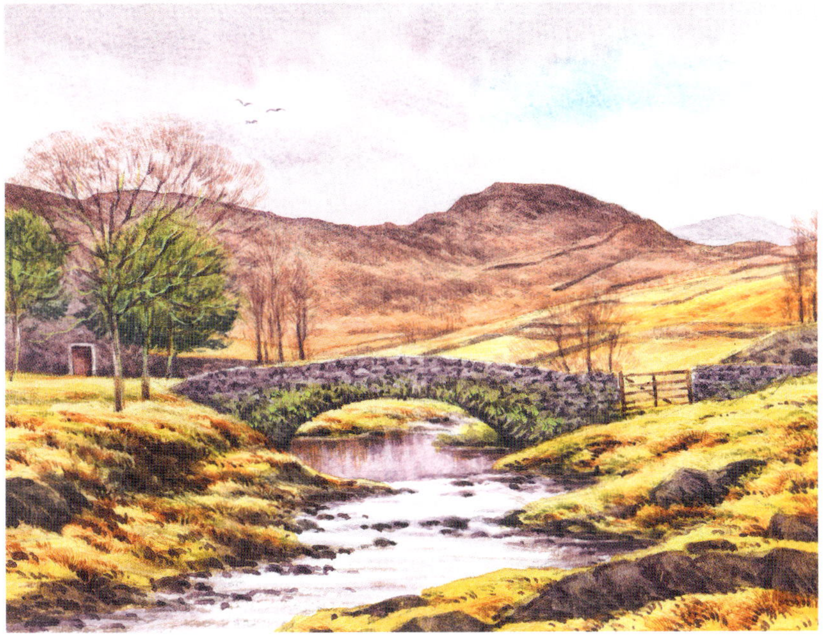

From Watendlath 7/3/10
A classic lakeland view which has been captured by many an artist and photographer. The stream is the outflow of Watendlath Tarn which from this point is obscured from view by the old packhorse bridge. The bridge underwent repairs in 2016 following the storms of the previous winter.

Great Crag

Some fells are at their best when visited in certain seasons and weather conditions. Great Crag and Grange Fell are such hills,. Pick a sunny day in late summer for then you will be walking across delightful and interesting terrain when the dense cover of heather of the upper heights will be in full bloom. Not only are these fells neighbouring geographically but also sequential in the Pictorial Guide. If you plan your walk so that you reach the idyllic hamlet of Watendlath for lunchtime you should find that refreshments are available before you continue your journey. Possibly the perfect day out on two of the lower fells.

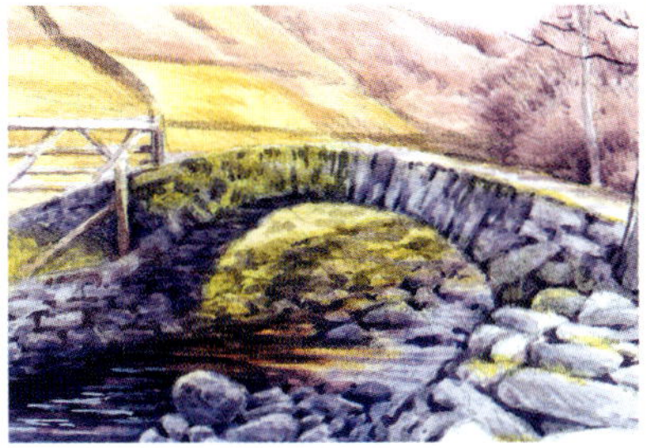

Footbridge, Bleatarn Gill 7/3/10
Contrary to what you may read in the Pictorial Guides, this bridge is located on private land so I had to obtain permission to visit the site. Surrounding undergrowth has since been cleared.

Great Crag from Watendlath Tarn 7/3/10
This view is taken from the shore path on the west side of the tarn.

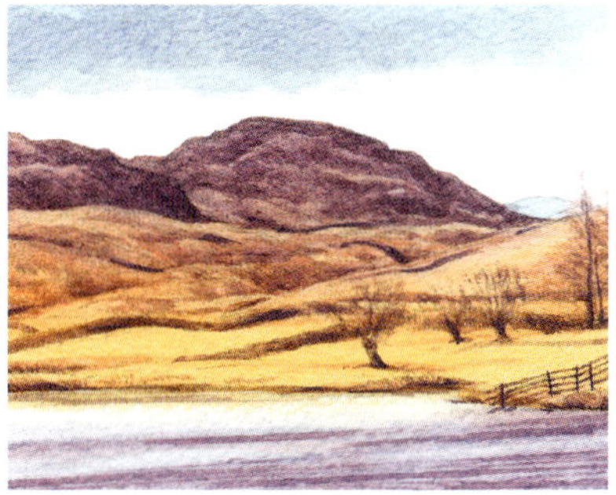

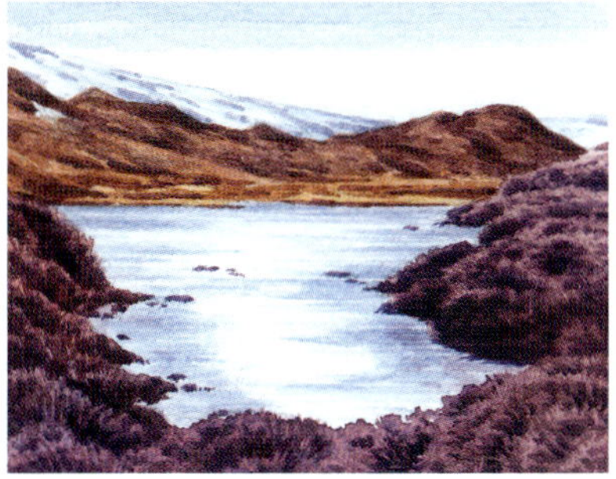

Dock Tarn 7/3/10
On this visit the waters of the tarn were completely frozen over. This is a delightful stretch of water with heather all around.

The summit 7/3/10
Wainwright chose to use this location as a viewpoint for three illustrations, this one, High Raise 1 and Ullscarf 1. By moving position slightly to take the photographs he was able to achieve varying scenes. I was able to do the same, consequently all of my sketches from here, obtained within moments of each other have a similar seasonal feel.

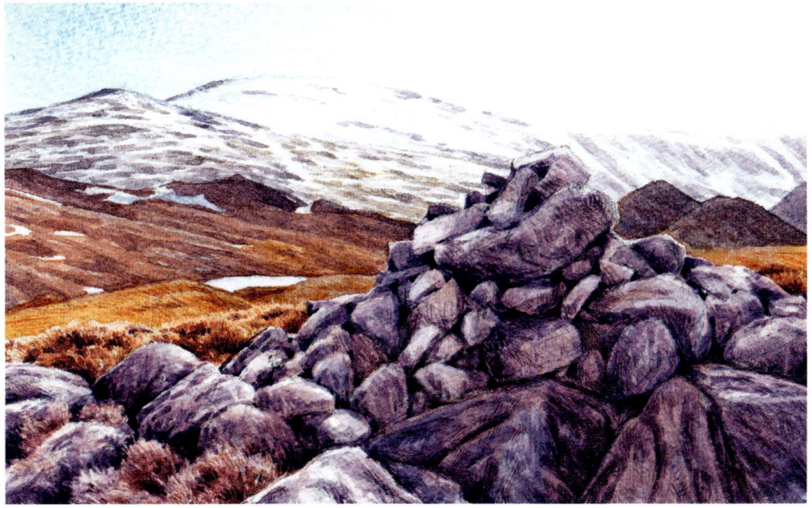

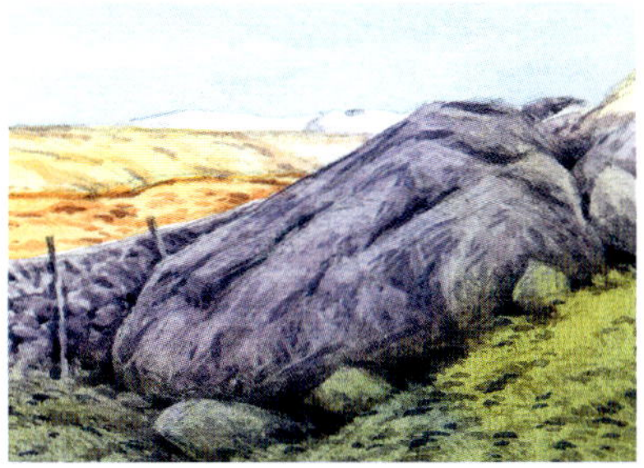

The boulder 7/3/10
The short wall that once sat on top of the boulder has now fallen and the stones fill the pool at the base of the rock. AW drew the boulder more rounded than it actually is possibly to fit the limited space on the page.

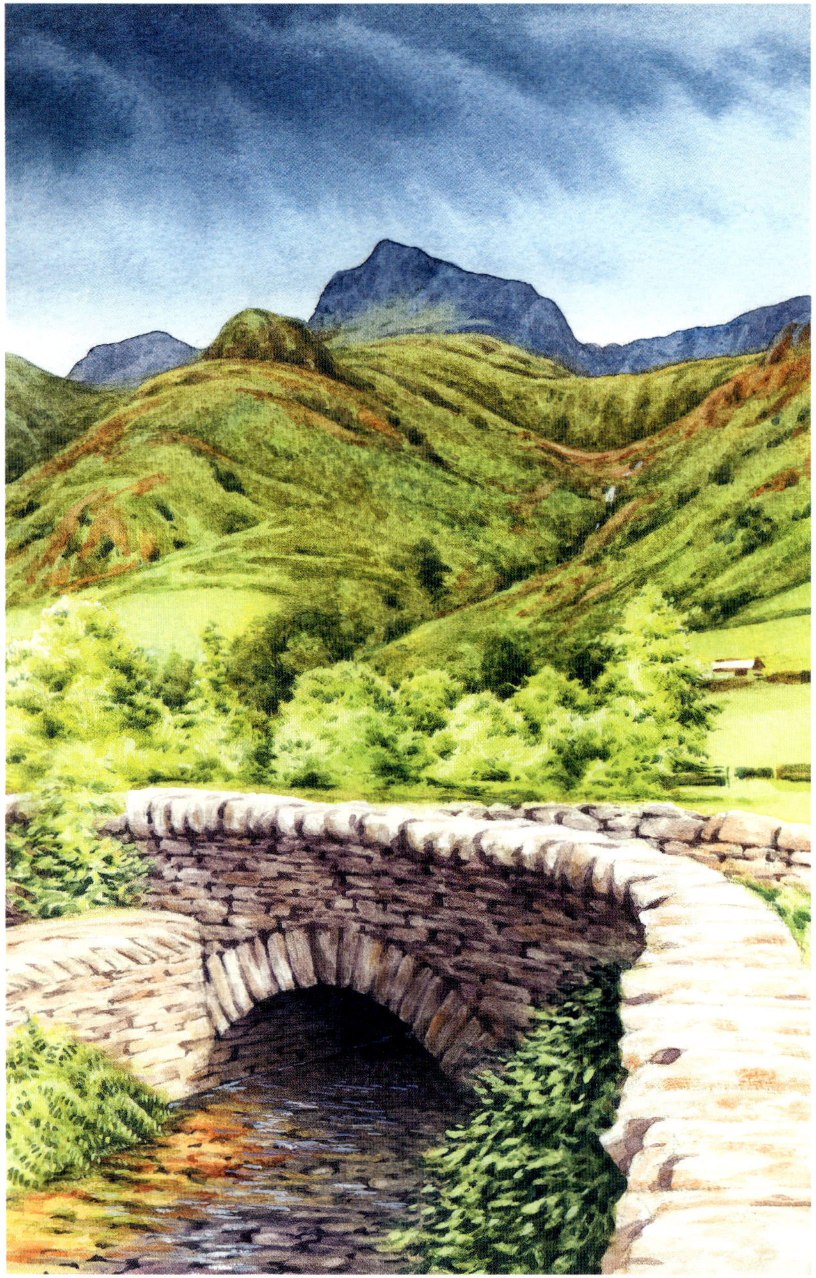

From Great Langdale Beck

12/8/09

The peak of the fell dominates this scene with Pike How being the prominent feature halfway up the fell side. Trees obscure the New Dungeon Ghyll Hotel but Stickle Ghyll is clearly seen.

Harrison Stickle

Central in the cluster of fells that make up the Langdale Pikes, Harrison Stickle is also the highest at just over 2400'. These mountains seem to just rise up from the Great Langdale valley floor which gives those who are not so fit and able the chance to get up close and personal with high lakeland fells.

The Langdale Pikes 26/7/10

This drawing in the guide book didn't need a title, one of the finest aspects of the high fells in the whole of the district. Seen from near Chapel Stile.

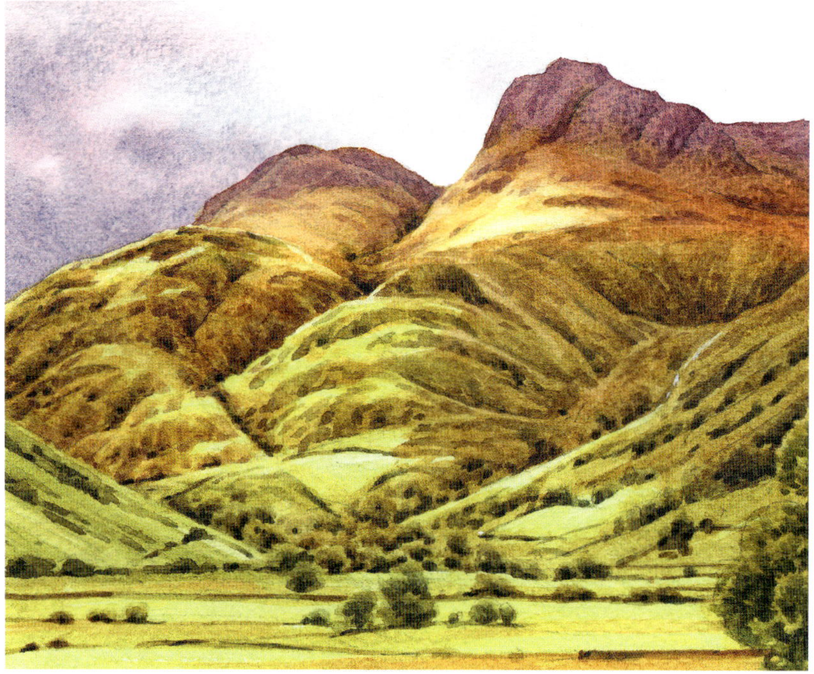

The Ravines of Dungeon Ghyll

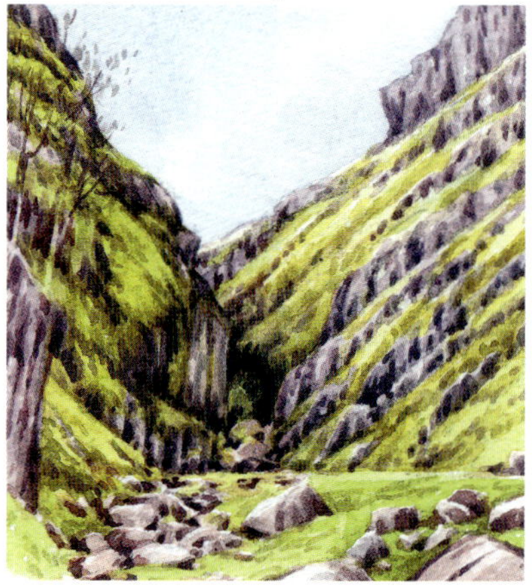

The upper ravine 12/8/09

Access to the ghyll is easy here near the 1700' contour but there is no distinct path.

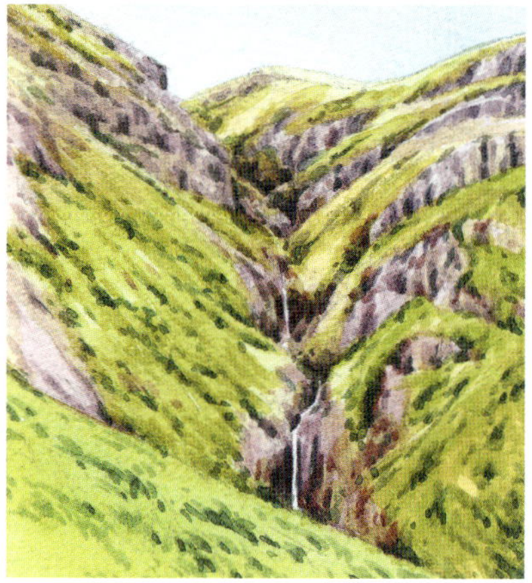

The middle ravine 12/8/09

This dramatic view is obtained from the lower section of the path which leads up to the west of Thorn Crag.

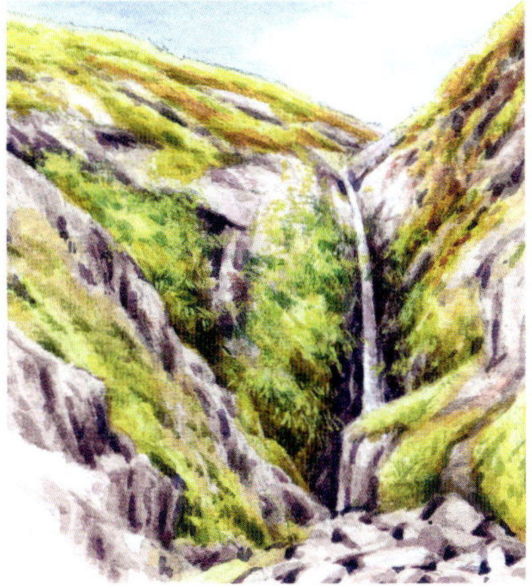

The middle ravine 12/8/09
If this waterfall was more easily accessible it would be one of the most popular in the area.

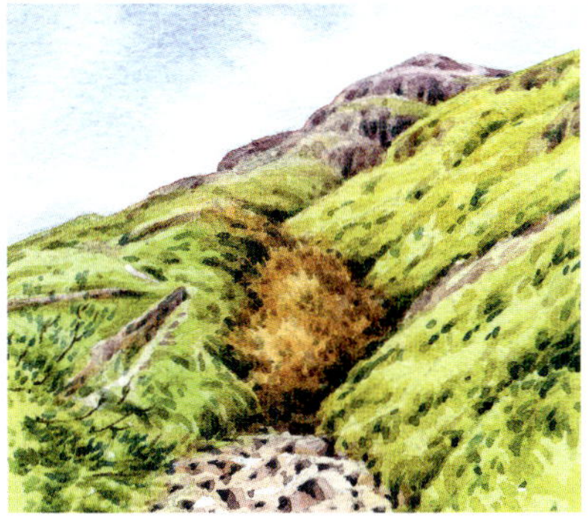

The lower ravine 12/8/09
The waterfall is hidden from view by the trees at this point where the path crosses the river bed.

The summit from Pike How 12/8/09
The sun illuminated the rock in the foreground just as I was taking my photograph, adding impact to my sketch.

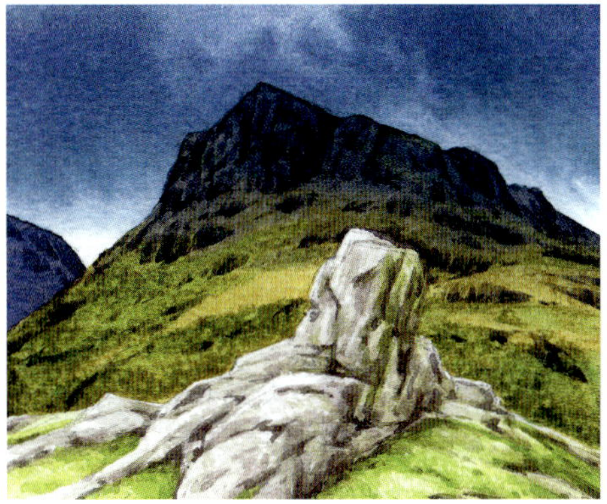

The summit from Stickle Tarn 12/8/09
A classic view across this secluded but popular tarn.

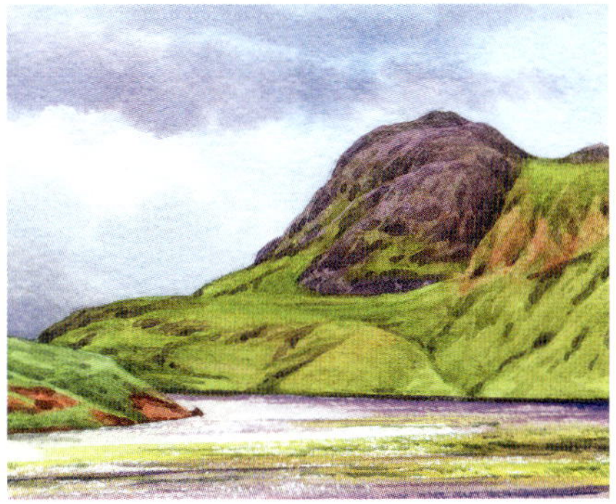

Harrison Stickle from Loft Crag 12/8/09
Steep crags form the southern face of the fell's upper section.

The summit 12/8/09
An untidy pile of rocks marks the highest point of the fell at the northern end of the summit plateau.

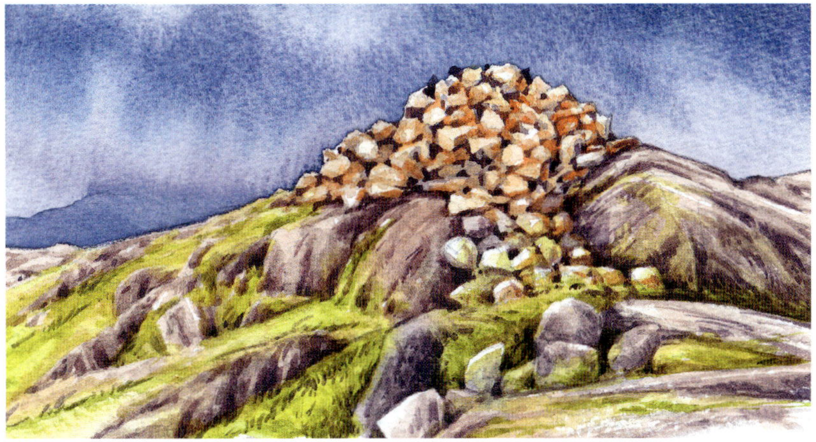

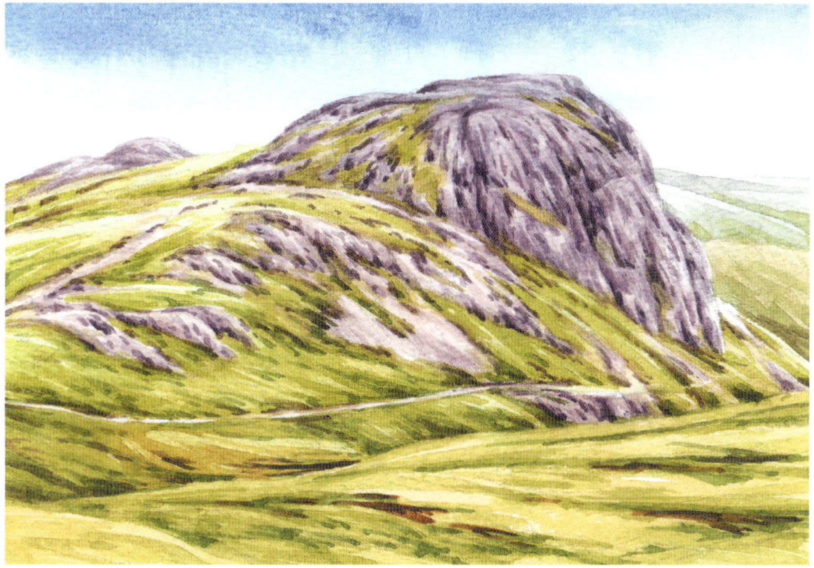

Pavey Ark from the path 12/8/09
The route to Pavey Ark is now defined by a well worn path across ground which has lost much of the turf. I have included the distant hills.

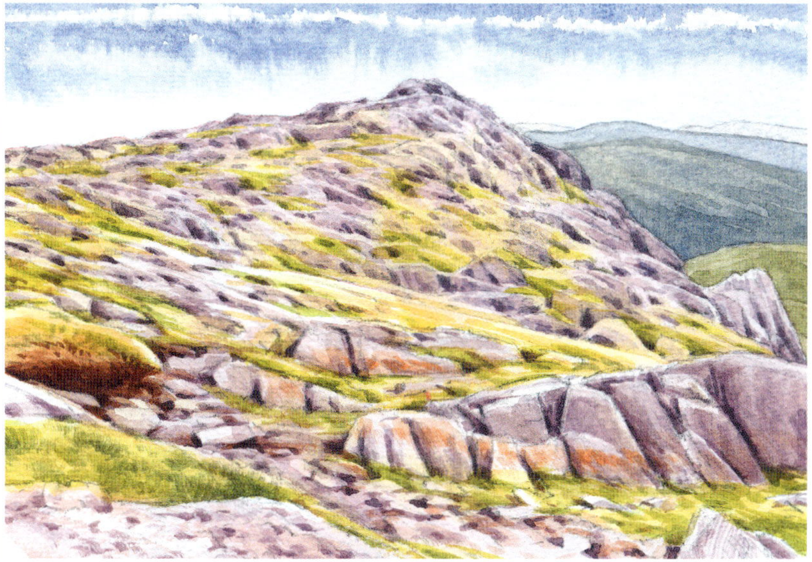

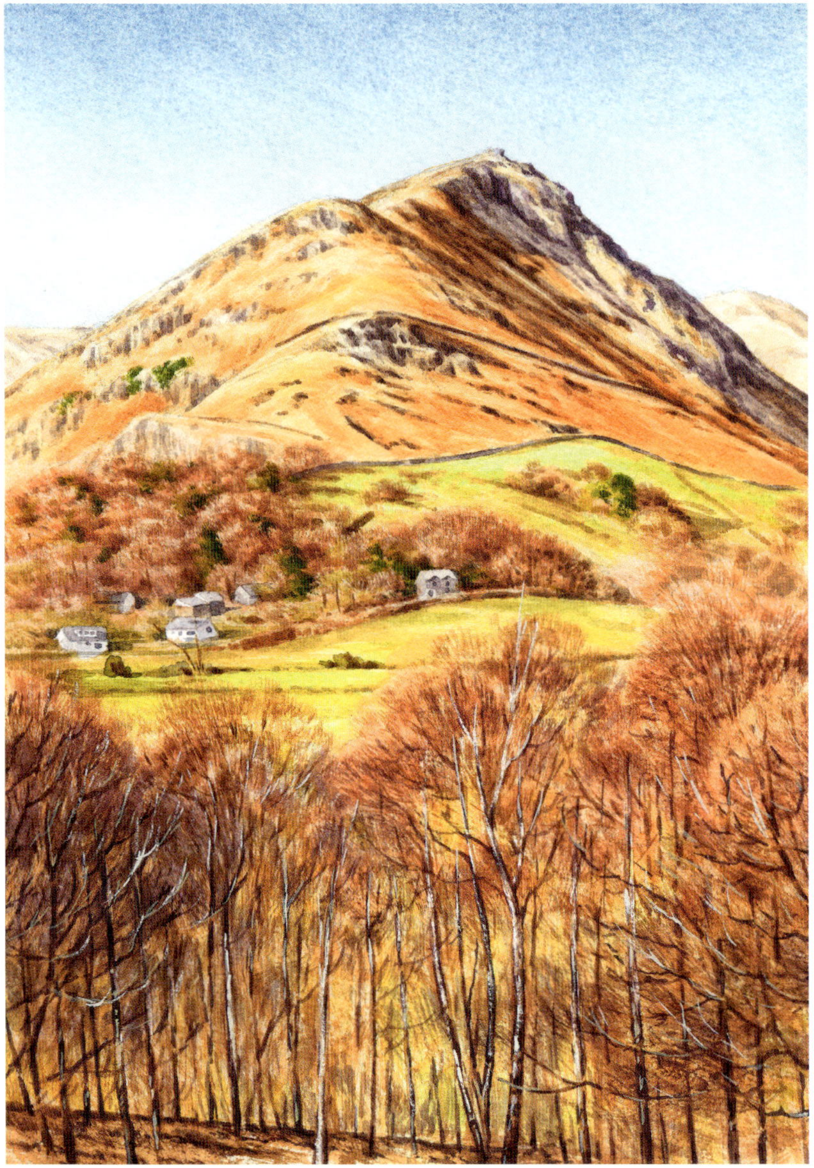

From Grasmere 4/3/08
I was forced to find a slightly higher viewpoint within the grounds of Butharlyp Wood to obtain a clear view of the fell over the birch trees.

The summit 14/9/08
Famously Wainwright was unable to muster courage to surmount this rock pinnacle and therefore it is the only fell which he failed to reach the highest point. Climbing just wasn't his thing.

Helm Crag

Being situated just to the north of the village of Grasmere probably accounts for the popularity of this fell. The paths to its summit ridge are clear and well made but as with all fells, those who venture out onto these hills should go well prepared. Helm Crag is topped by rocky features, some of which even have nicknames such as The Lion and the Lamb, and The Howitzer.

Summit Scene 2/6/09
Steel Fell forms the background to this view of the summit rocks.

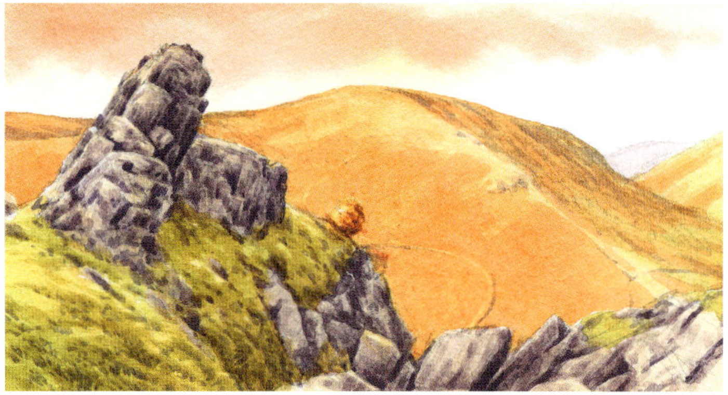

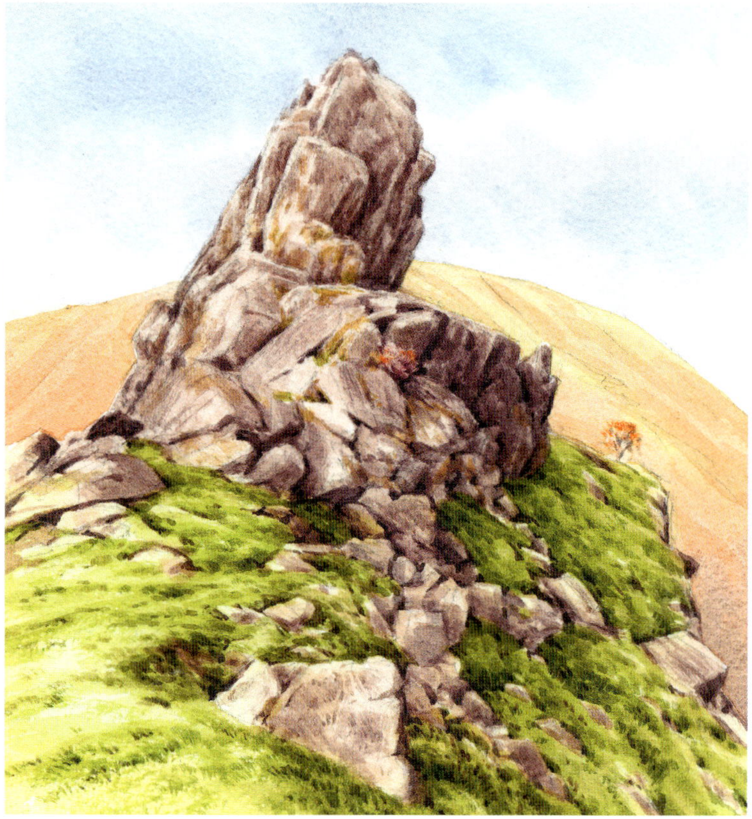

The summit rocks from the north
2/6/09 In ascending from the north-east this cleft will come into view.

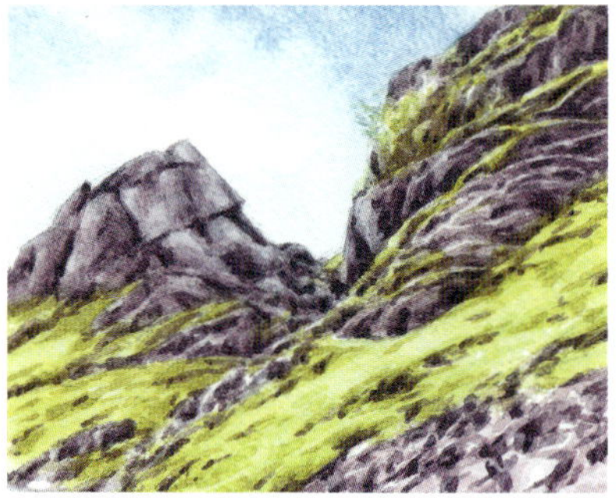

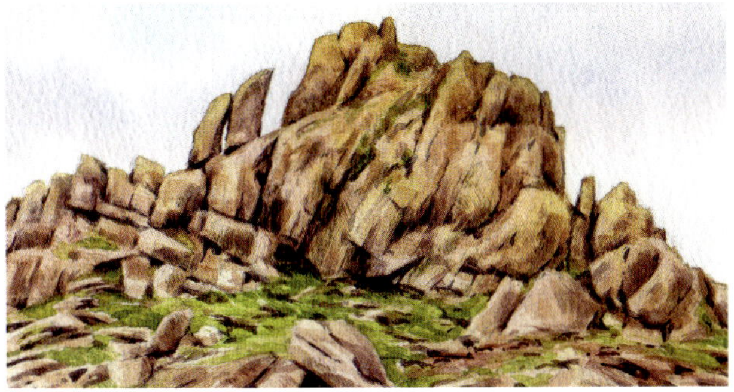

The summit 14/9/08
This is the same rocky tor as shown on the previous page but as seen from the south-west.

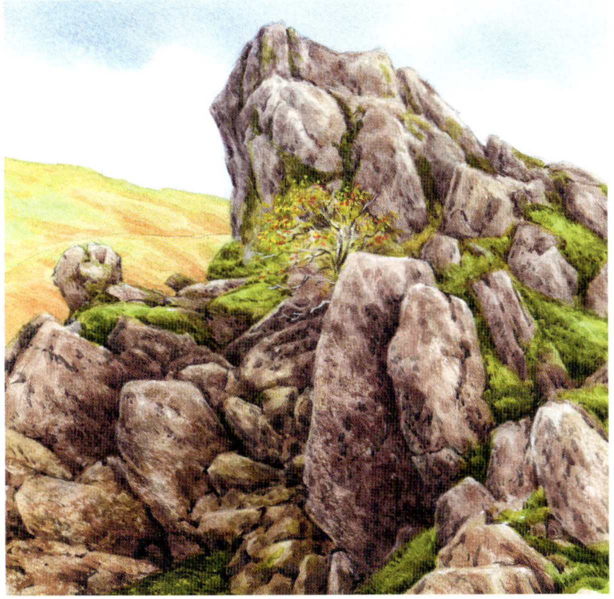

The summit 14/9/08
These rocks are those seen from Grasmere village and from that angle they have gained the name The Lion and The Lamb.

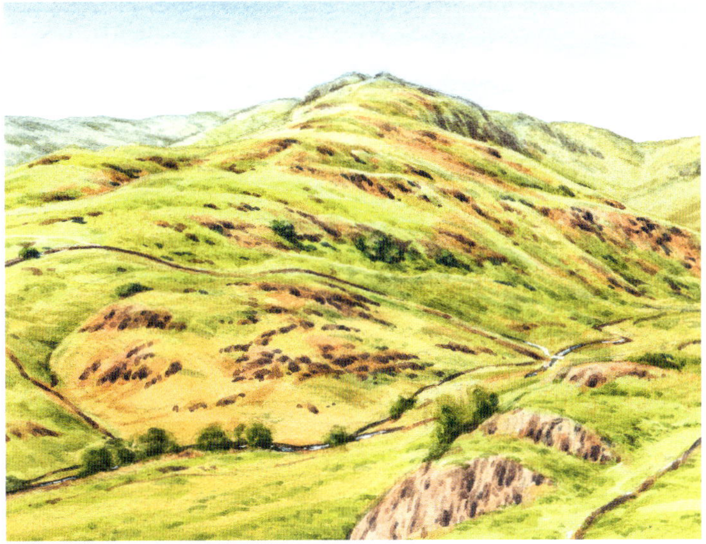

Tarn Crag 2/6/09
Unlike my depiction, AW's drawing shows the scene in winter conditions. Time restrictions meant that I was unable to capture the same conditions for this view and the sketch below.

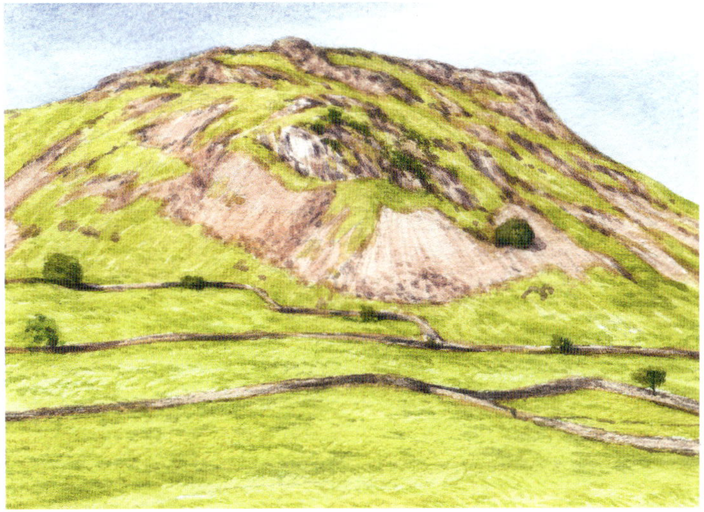

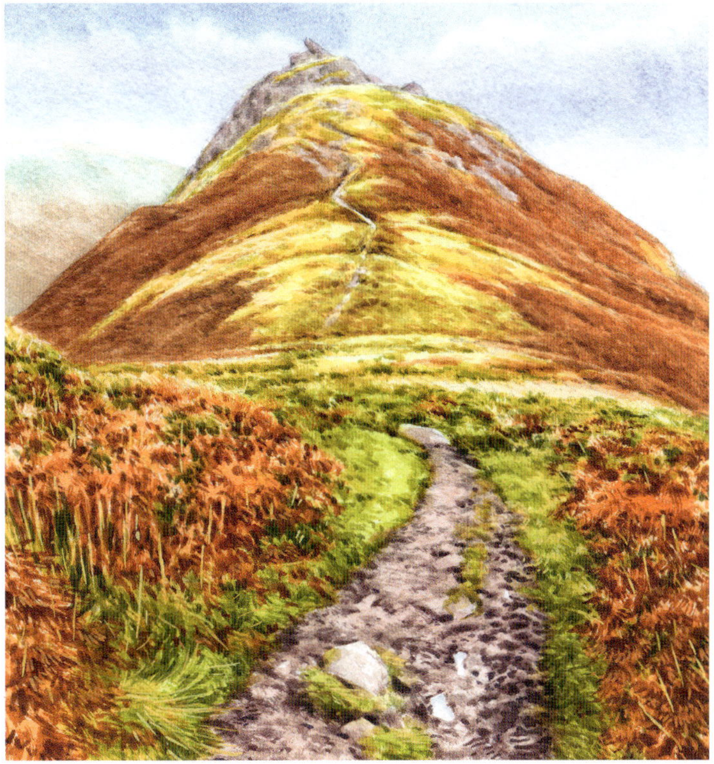

Helm Crag, from the path to Gibson Knott 14/9/08
A steep ascent of Helm Crag lies ahead with the unique summit rocks as your goal. The ridge walk from Calf Crag and over Gibson Knott has been relatively easy up until this point, here the way ahead makes a definite steep gain in height.

The north east face 2/6/09
By aligning the layout of the walls in AW's drawing with the actual scene on the ground I was able to accurately locate this exact viewpoint.

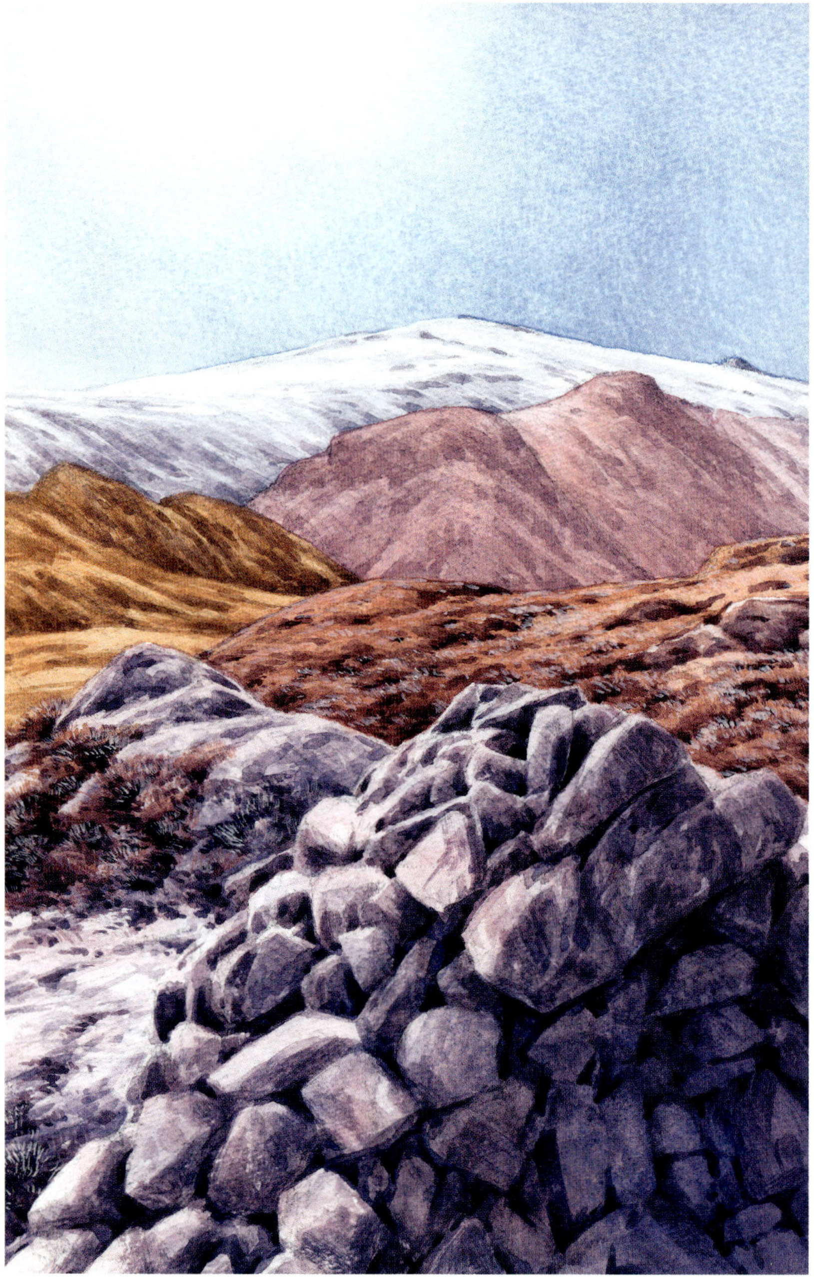

High Raise

There is no real drama with High Raise, no wild gushing waterfalls or sheer drops. It does however hold a fairly central position in all of the Wainwright fells and is the highest in this central region. Not surprising then that the panorama from the top, given the right conditions, provides extensive views of over eighty fells. Naming them all (without the aid of the guide book) will while away some time.

From Great Crag, Watendlath Fell 7/3/10
Looking towards a bright winter sun in a clear blue sky is not ideal for either a photograph or painting. High Raise is a fell of gentle character: AW's illustration over exaggerates the reality. The summit cairn in the foreground has been added to by some degree. With interest it should be noted the term Watendlath Fell as used here in the title by Wainwright is only ever mentioned twice, neither of those times in the Great Crag (Watendlath Fell) chapter.

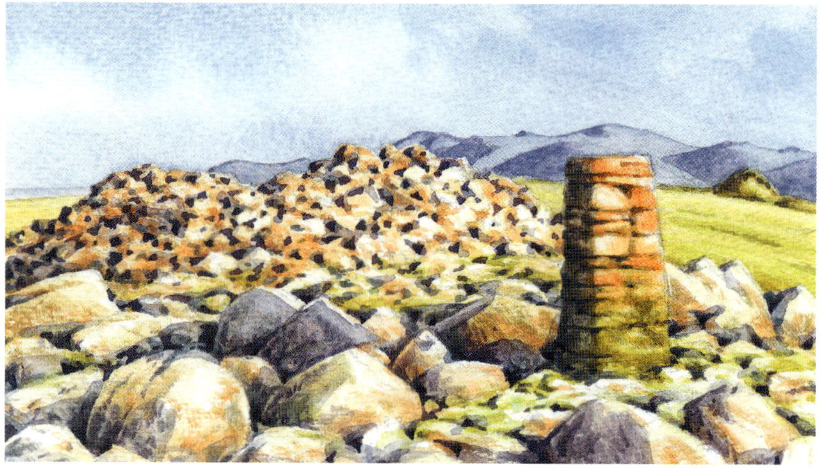

The summit 2/6/09
What once was a big cairn has now been remodelled into a substantial shelter. The Coniston Fells form the skyline behind the survey column.

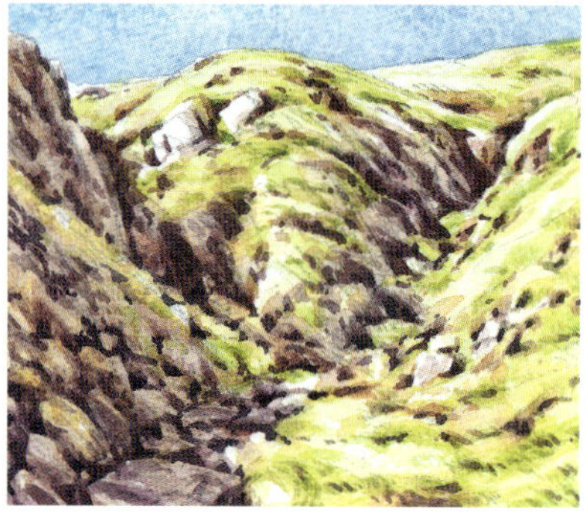

Bright Beck 28/4/11
A direct ascent of High Raise via Bright Beck will not be on everyone's to do list and the lack of a distinct path means the route is not in favour. Generally walkers like to be out in the open not deep in such shaded and damp ravines.

Long Crag 24/6/09
Taking the direct, fairly pathless route from Sergeant's Crag to High Raise will be on mostly featureless ground. A few groups of rocks will be passed including these which AW used as foreground interest in his drawing.

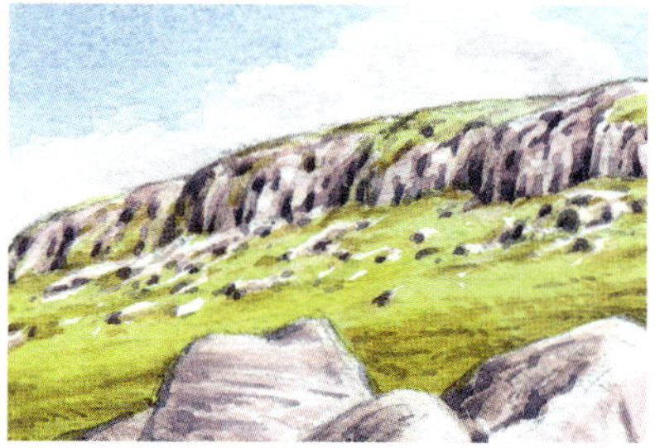

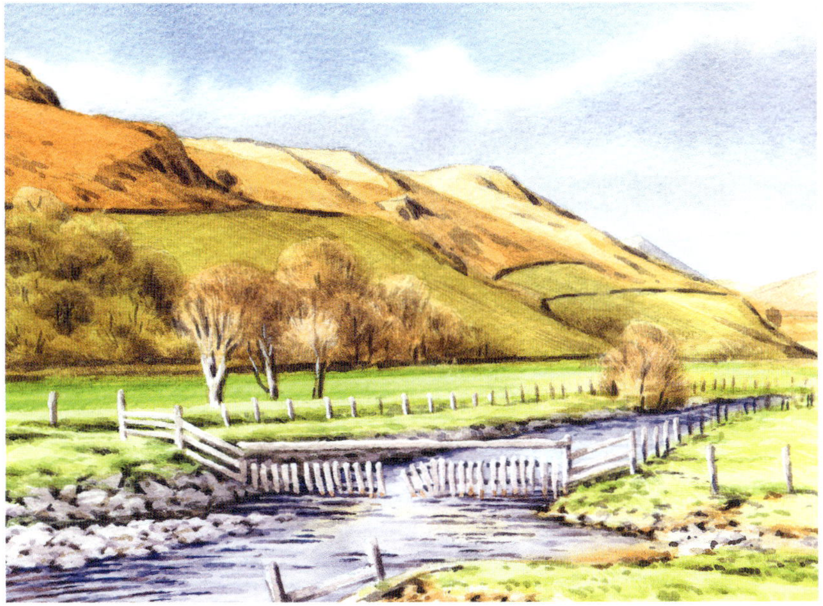

From Sosgill Bridge 5/3/08
A full covering of snow featured in AW's illustration but I was unable to capture similar conditions. New fence work has been added to the scene and the trees on the far bank have been pollarded. Lonscale Fell just peeks round the slopes of the hill. In December 2015 severe flooding affected this area badly. A bridge to the nearby Low Bridge End Farm upstream was totally washed away but remarkably the single arched Sosgill Bridge, just out of view to the left, withstood the deluge.

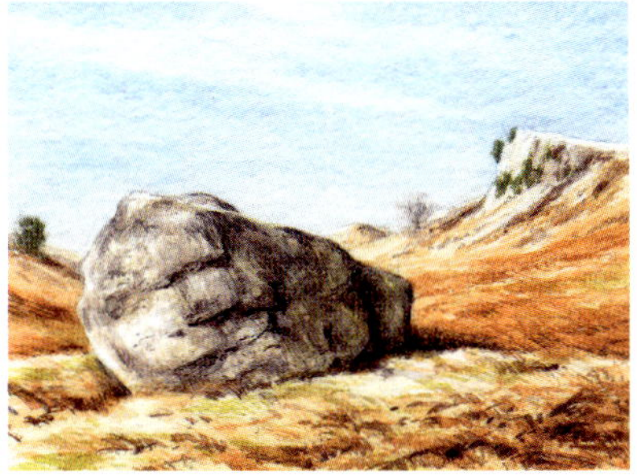

Woodcock Stone and Mart Crag 5/3/08
Located just to the east of the A591, this large boulder probably gets its name from the fact that its shape, with some imagination, is similar to that of a sitting woodcock when it is viewed from this angle.

High Rigg

I have always found High Rigg to be a convenient fell for a short walk. The easy route to the top is a short ascent from the youth centre by the church. However, High Rigg offers more than this. A really pleasant couple of hours can be spent exploring the undulating top with its numerous small tarns. Include a visit to the nearby Tewet Tarn to the north to complete the expedition.

The church of St. John's in the Vale 4/3/08
Daffodils surround the church in the spring and the ancient yews give this place of worship an air of peace and solitude. The heating system has obviously been updated as the chimney on the roof has been removed.

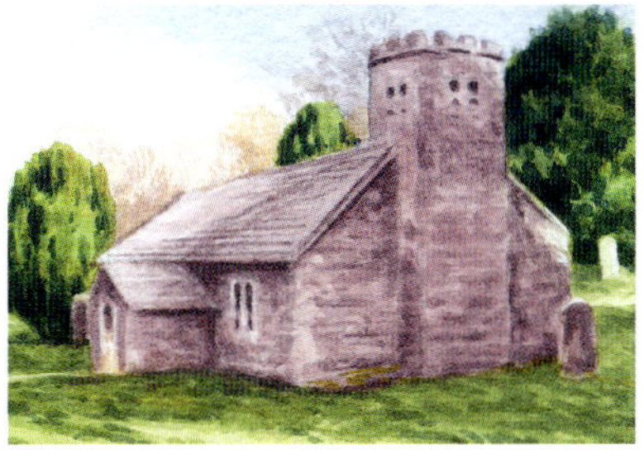

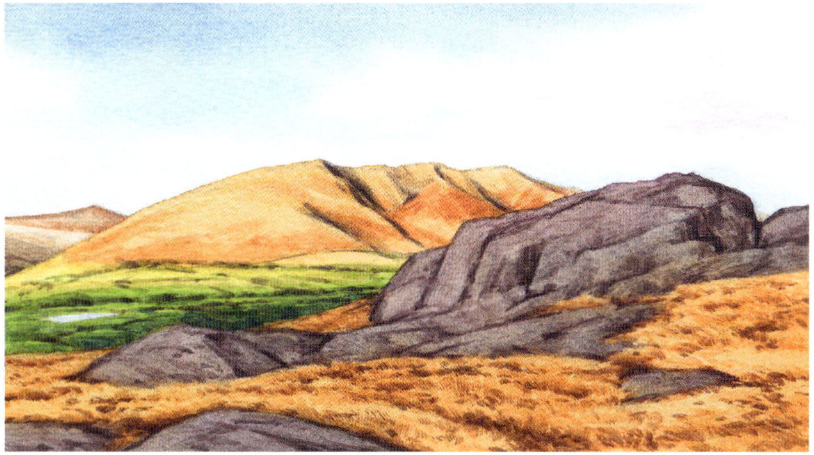

The summit 9/11/09
For some reason the cairn has at some time been moved to a lower position on the ground just to the right and out of view. Tewet Tarn is over to the left.

Looking south to Helvellyn 4/3/08
I noted in his drawing that AW must have observed this scene at the close of the day. This evening visit of mine was planned so the light was coming from the same direction with the snow adding to the atmosphere.

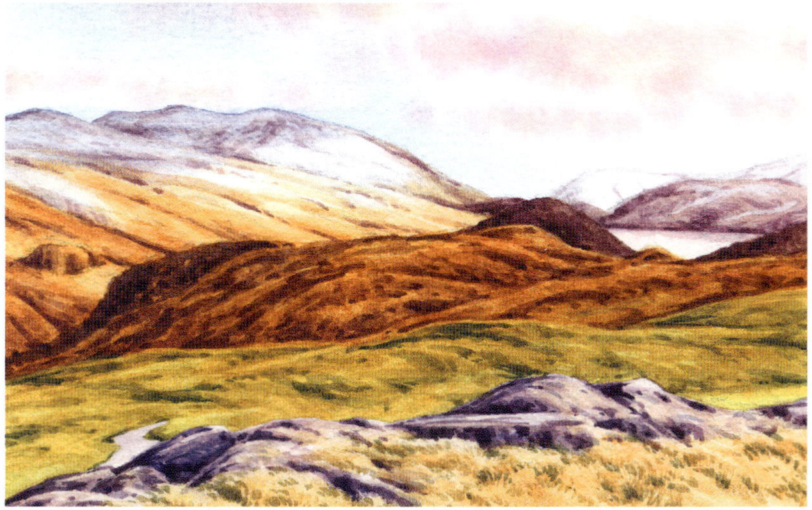

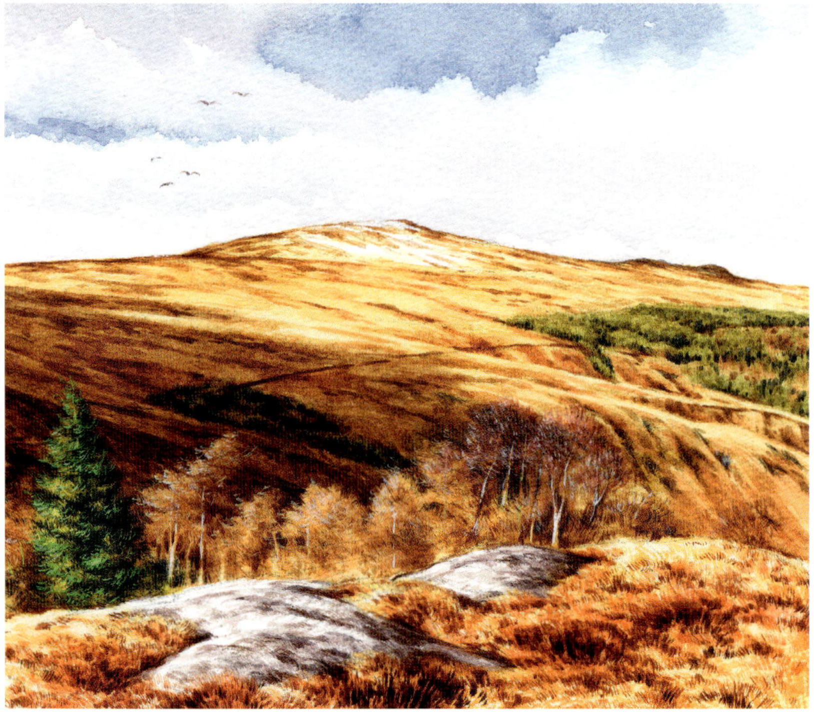

From Fisher Crag 15/11/07
Fortunately the high ground on Fisher Crag has remained free from forestation, allowing me to observe the scene as Wainwright had seen it.

High Seat

Aptly named as a fell, High Seat at just under 2000' is the highest area of ground north of Ullscarf towards Keswick. The views in all directions are extensive. There is a drawback though, the routes to adjacent fells from its summit are wet and boggy.

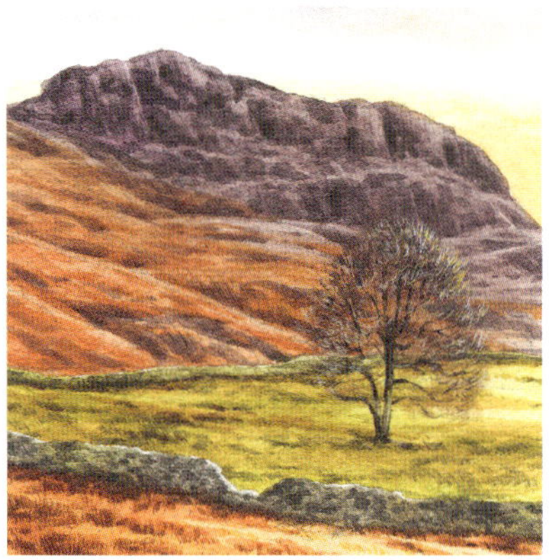

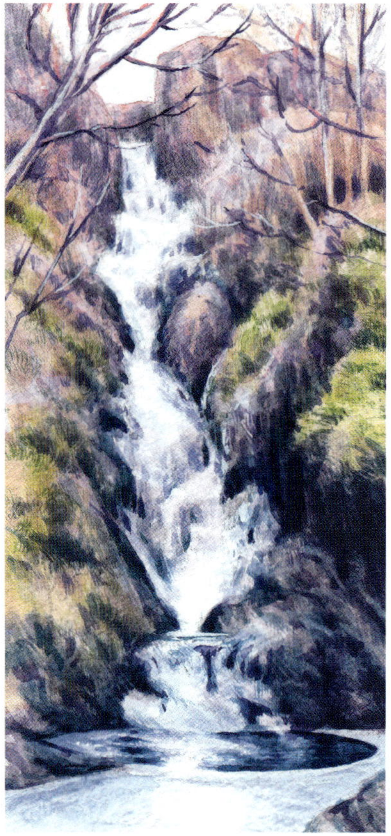

Waterfalls in Ashness Gill 4/1/09
This tall impressive cascade was nearly frozen solid on my visit.

Ashness Bridge 4/1/09
AW opted to depict this popular bridge from the downstream side.

Reecastle Crag 4/1/09
Viewed late one winter's evening from a field near Thwaite House.

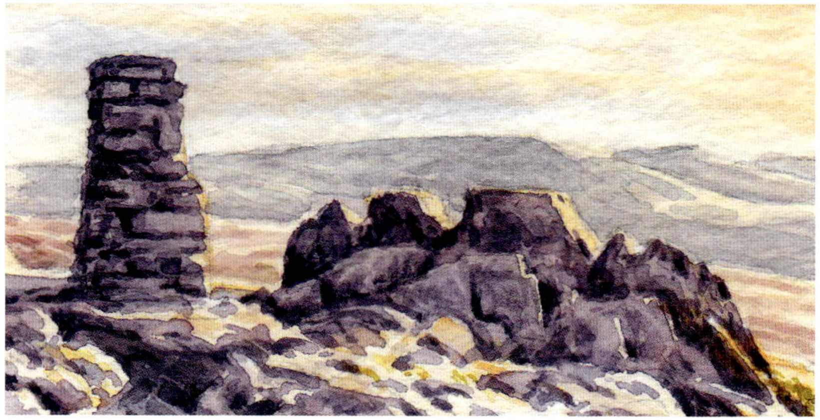

The summit 15/11/07
A late afternoon visit to this fell top and its triangulation pillar. A cairn sits close by to the west. To the east by 100 yards is the other top named Man.

Watendlath from Goat Crags 4/1/09 This location provides a fine view of the hamlet far below.

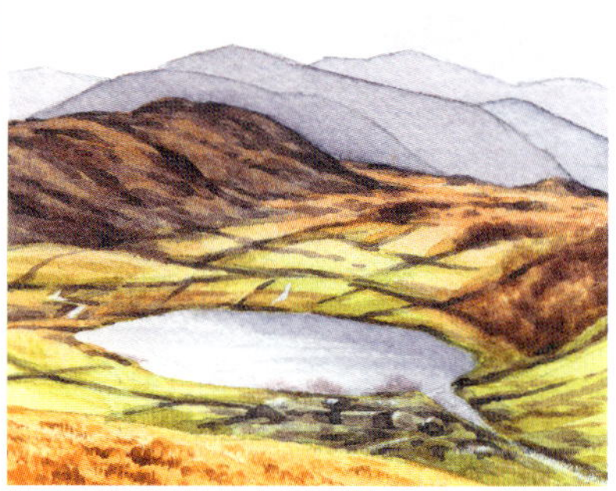

Litt's Memorial 15/11/07 (bottom right) Few walkers will stumble across this memorial of two standing stones by chance. They are dedicated to John Litt who died in March 1880. Both are about two feet high.

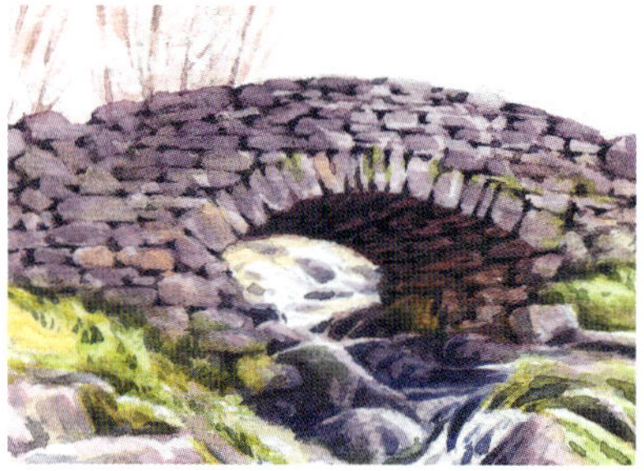

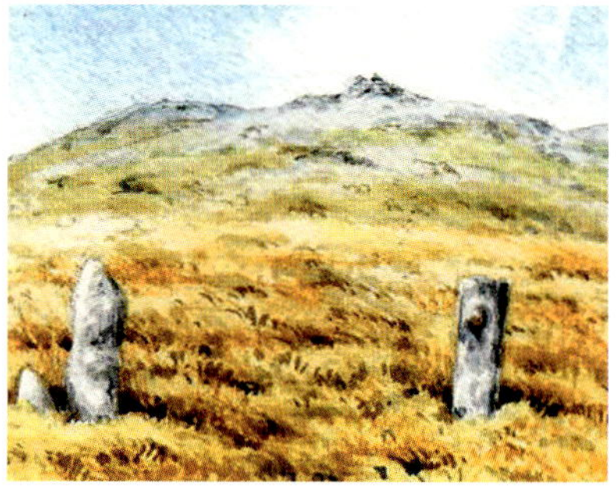

When is a summit not a summit?

Those who have studied the Wainwright Pictorial Guides in some depth may have noticed that Wainwright's definition of the summits of some fells was questionable but I have yet to read anywhere of an explanation of how these anomalies came about. In my research for this project and book I have spent many hours pondering as to how and why AW not only designed his books but also how he came up with his final list (see page 39).Much of this time was spent poring over his original maps, photographs and notebooks which I feel gave me a better insight to the man behind the Pictorial Guides. As mentioned in that previous article the maps Wainwright used in the late 1940s and early 1950s were the 1 inch Ordnance Survey and Bartholomew maps .They lacked detail but these were the ones he referred to in plotting his initial list of fells as the set of 2½ inch maps were not fully published at the time. By coincidence, at the time of his writing the process of triangulation of the country was underway and not complete (see page 47) so the only heights of any accuracy on his maps were those dating back many years, and were based on the levelling system in conjunction with the benchmarks.

When Wainwright selected a fell on the map for his list he used the marked Trigonometrical Point* on that hill as a height reference even though it was not necassarily the highest point. A good example of this is Seathwaite Fell in Book 4 where the measured point of 1970′ on the map is on the northern end of the fell at the cairn shown in the guide. Here, Wainwright acknowledges there is higher ground to the south above the 2000′ contour but he depicts the summit as this marked point. Another example of this is Thunacar Knott (see page 149). Some fells had conflicting heights when the two maps were compared but usually he opted for the O.S. height in the fell description. 24 of the other fells in the 214, even though they were distinct in their own right didn't have a trigonometrical point so for these he always used the term "approx." after his estimation of the height, such as Knott Rigg in Book 6. A few other fells have summits which AW determined and indicated the highest points but the current recognised summit is in a different location. An example of this is Maiden Moor (see page 274) where there is now a small cairn on the footpath close to the edge of the summit plateau which was not there in Wainwright's time: this is now deemed to be the summit. He estimated the highest point to be about 100 yards south east of this cairn's position but the ground is so flat here that it is hard to pinpoint the true top. Only when you stand at his "summit" does the peak of Bowfell make an appearance to the left of Blea Crag. The most glaring summit confusion occurs on Armboth Fell. There was no trigonometrical point so AW estimated the height at 1570′ on a small heather covered rock platform where, in his day was a small cairn (see right) but there can be no disputing the fact the actual summit lies 300 yards to the north east on a large rounded mound of rock that resembles the upturned hull of a boat. How he got this one so wrong we can only guess, bad weather perhaps? Another interesting summit is that of the infamous Mungrisedale Common. The spot height of 2068′ on AW's O.S. map is about 40 yards from the the small cairn that marks the supposedly highest point now meaning perhaps that very few have stood on AW's true summit of that fell.

There are many summits where questions have been asked about Wainwright's calculations regarding height but of course we now have the advantage of accurate surveying and GPS systems so we can easily find the highest point of any fell within a matter of inches (or centimetres if you prefer) back in the 1950s and 60s things were simpler.

*Trigonometrical Points predate the days of the construction of the Triangulation Columns and were usually just small cairns on the ground, the stones of these cairns may later have been used in the construction of the columns (see page 47).

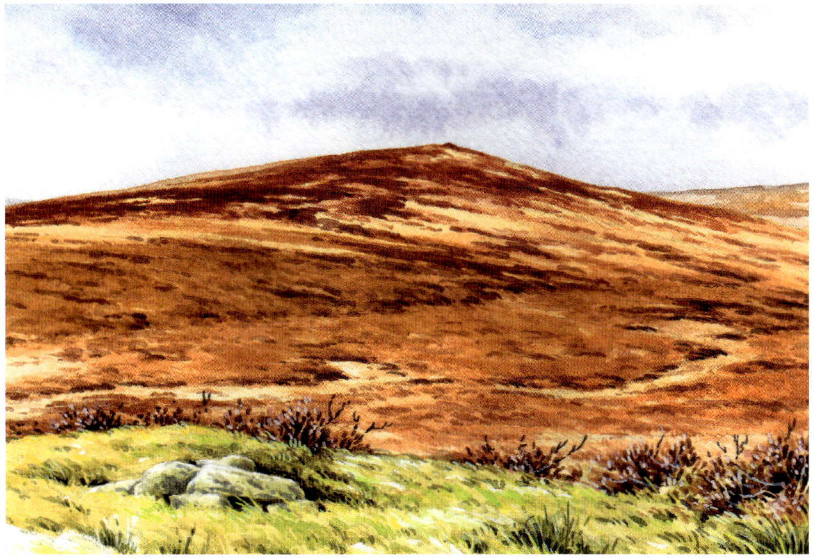

From Armboth Fell 15/11/07

The slopes of High Tove are uninspiring to artists, even the tarn in AW's drawing has practically grown over. Interestingly this viewpoint is of course from Wainwright's summit of Armboth Fell and not the true summit which is of bare rock. The foreground cairn is now almost non-existent.

High Tove

The days when folk passed over High Tove in numbers as a means to cross this ridge as described by Wainwright are long gone. My guess is that this fell is now more normally visited by those who are ticking off certain fell-walking lists and good planning sees them also "bagging" Armboth Fell on the same walking route.

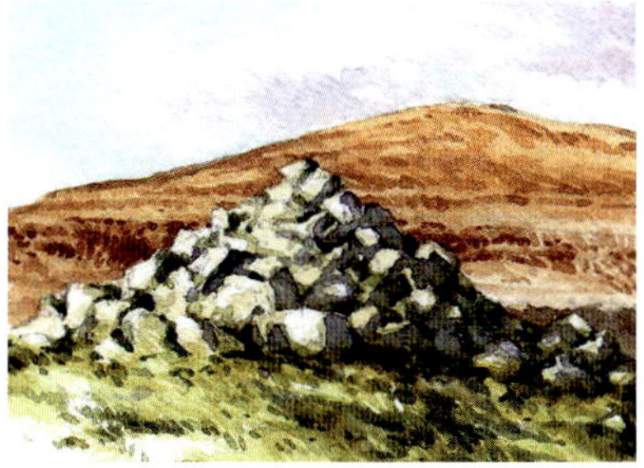

The summit 15/11/07

With High Seat beyond, the cairn has lost its wooden post and grown by a substantial amount.

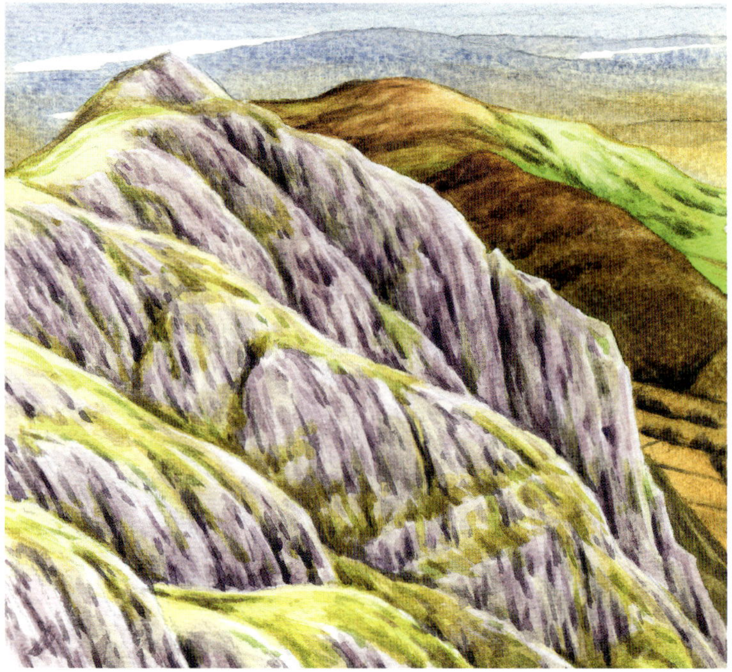

From Pike o' Stickle 12/8/09
Lingmoor Fell appears over the shoulder of Gimmer Crag.

Loft Crag

A true peak with a pointed top and a bold craggy face that almost reaches the valley floor. Loft Crag is enjoyed by walkers and climbers alike.

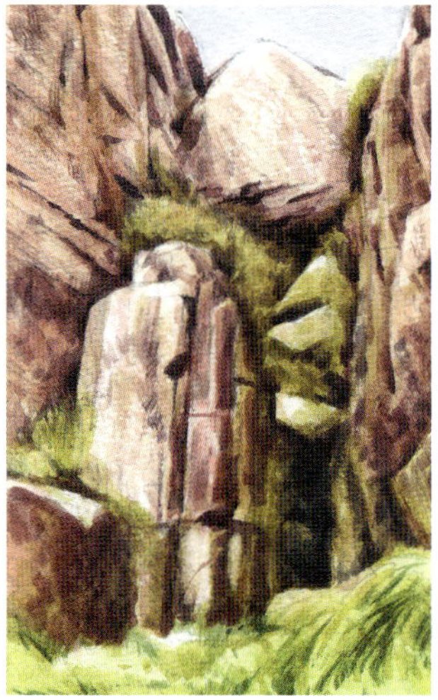

The chockstone pitch 12/8/09
A damp and mossy cleft where few venture. Care is needed in the ascent of this obstacle. Behind you the valley floor seems a long way down, and you are correct, it is.

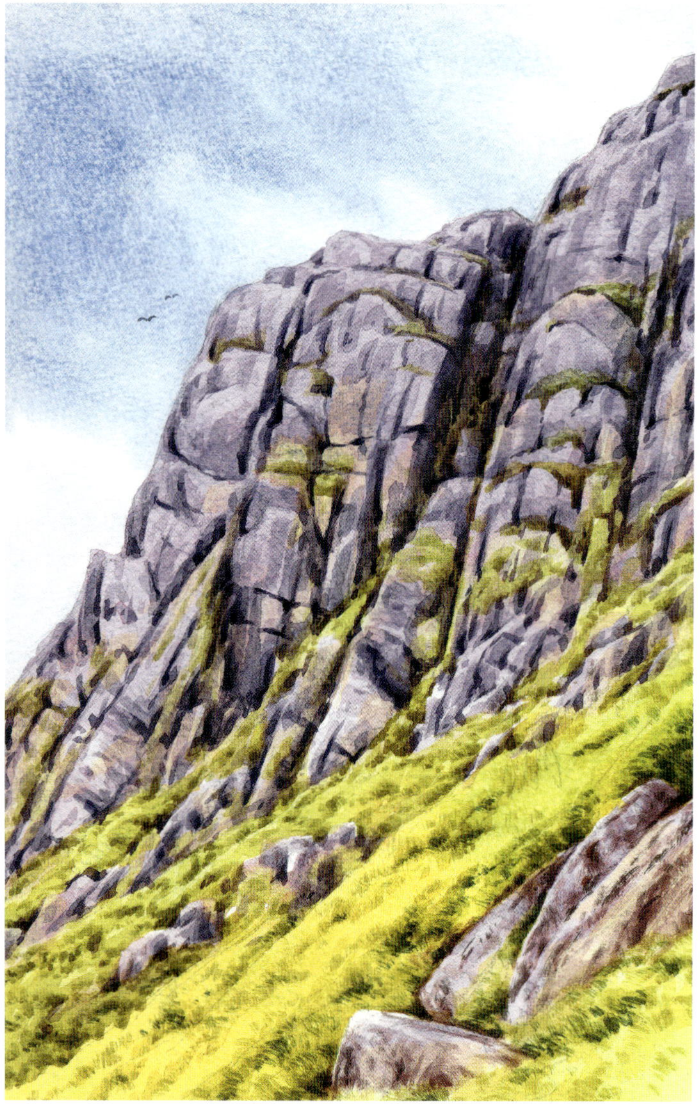

Gimmer Crag, south east face 12/8/09
By making this crag more vertical in his drawing AW made it more impressive and it also meant that it fitted his page better. This is more like the angle that it is in reality.

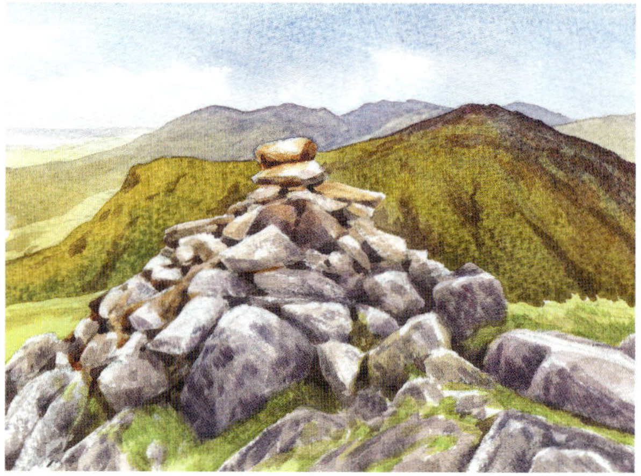

The summit 15/11/07
Comparatively unchanged in size, the cairn sits atop the crag and from here is a fine view across the valley to Pike o' Blisco and the distant Coniston Fells.

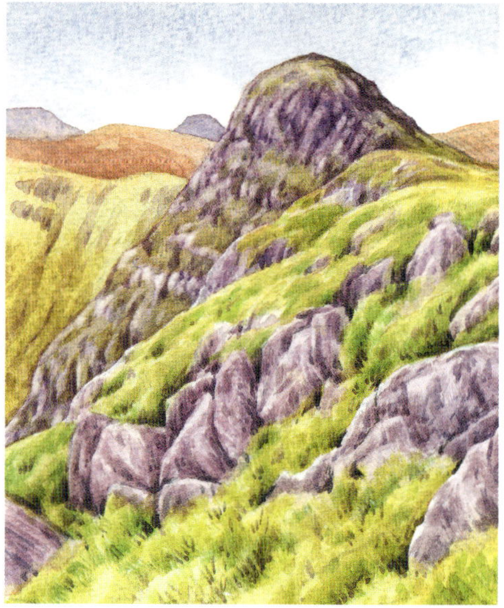

Pike o' Stickle 12/8/09
The easily recognisable top with Great Gable five miles away beyond it.

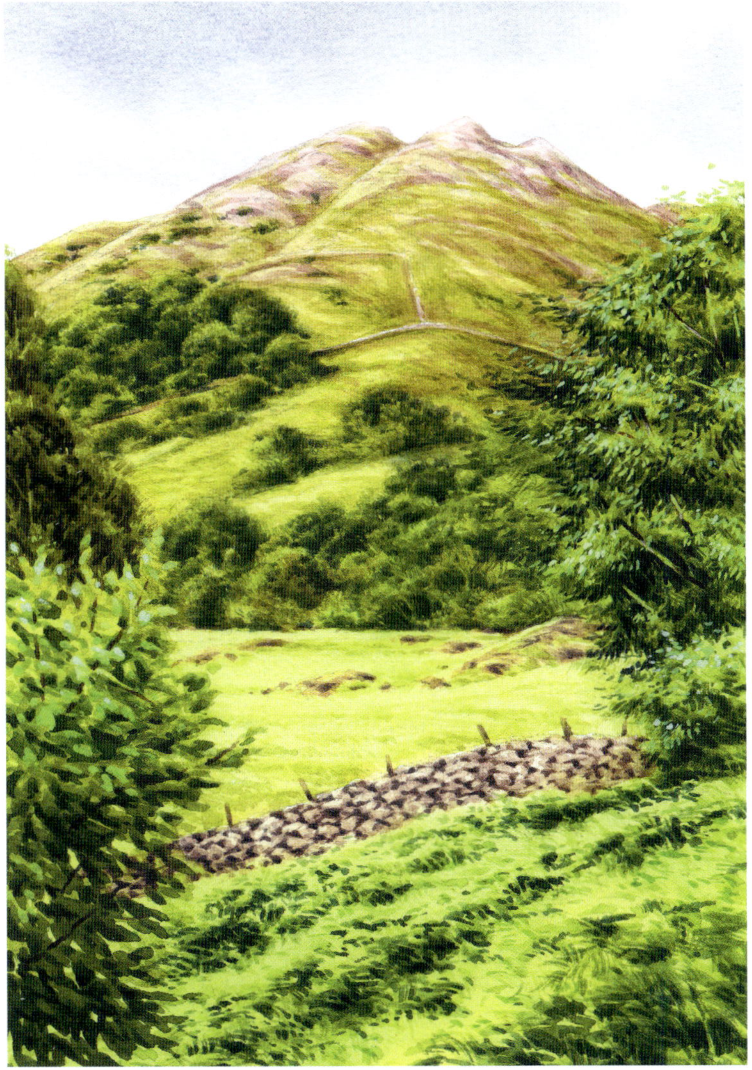

From Mandale Bridge 26/7/10
These days the bridge is completely surrounded by dense undergrowth and trees which obscure the view of the fell, no matter what the season. To obtain a clear view I had to resort to moving up the beck for 80 yards until this aspect of Loughrigg Fell was seen.

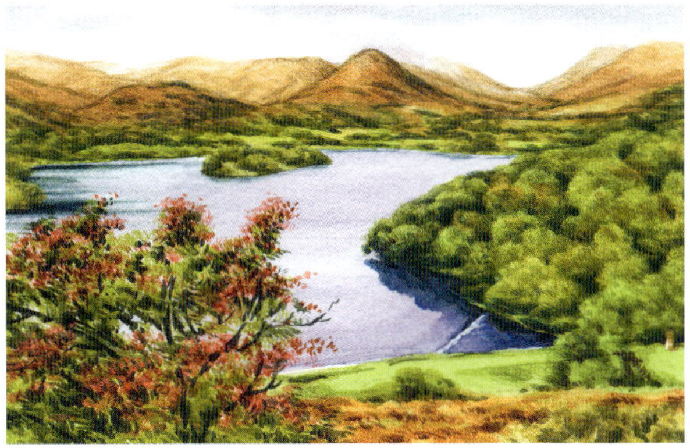

Grasmere from Loughrigg Terrace 19/9/08
A fine view over the lake from this popular fell side.

Loughrigg Fell

This is what I would class as a family fell. With easy access from Ambleside, Loughrigg has some well made paths, great views, places of interest and plenty of room to freely explore. All in all, a neat little fell worthy of a visit.

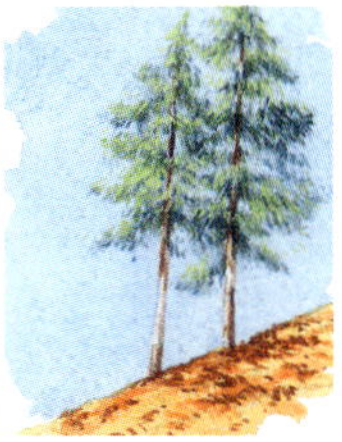

AW doodled two pines to break up a page of text.

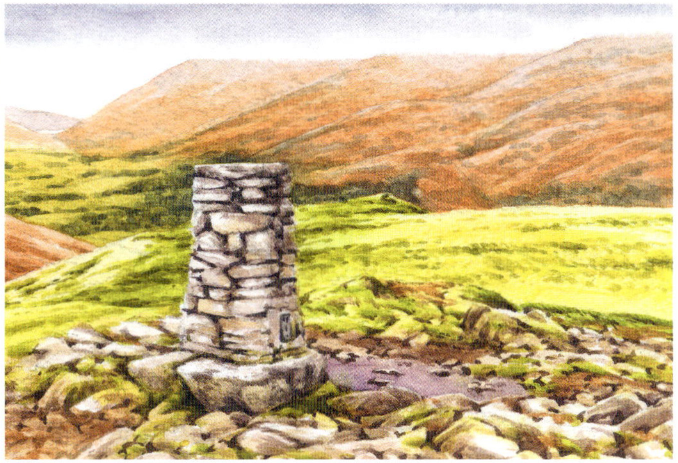

The summit 19/9/08
The big summit cairn has now been cleared away completely.

The big cave 1/10/07
The entrance to the slate quarry, now abandoned.

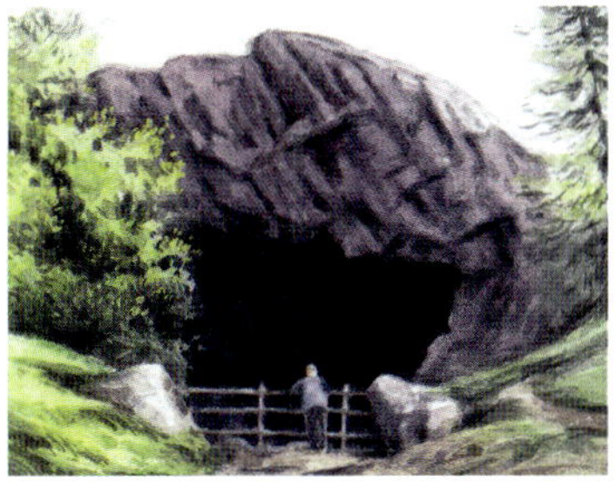

Loughrigg Tarn 19/09/08
A most pleasing pastoral scene with the tarn side cottages.

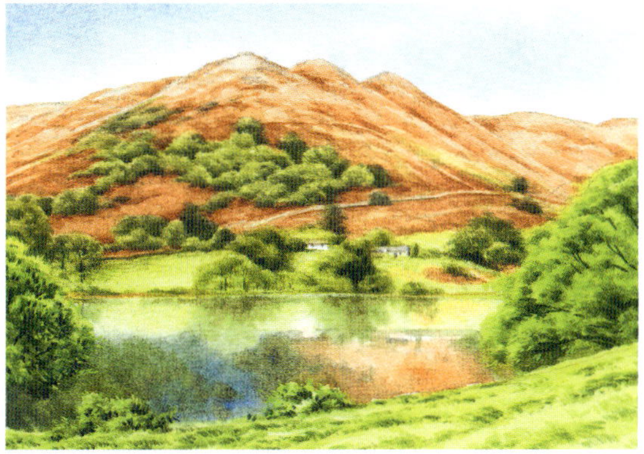

The cairn on Ivy Crag 19/9/08
A small affair but with great views down Windermere.

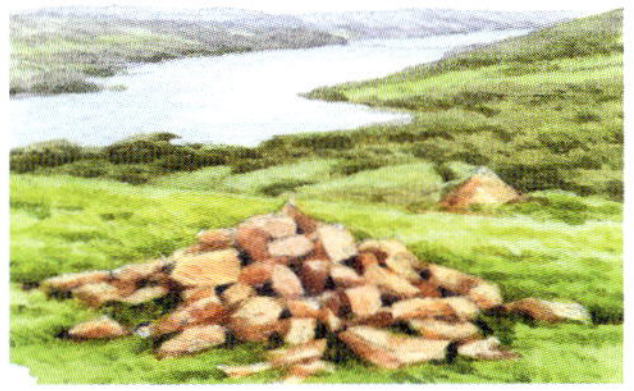

Todd Crag summit 1/9/09
A small outcrop of rock.

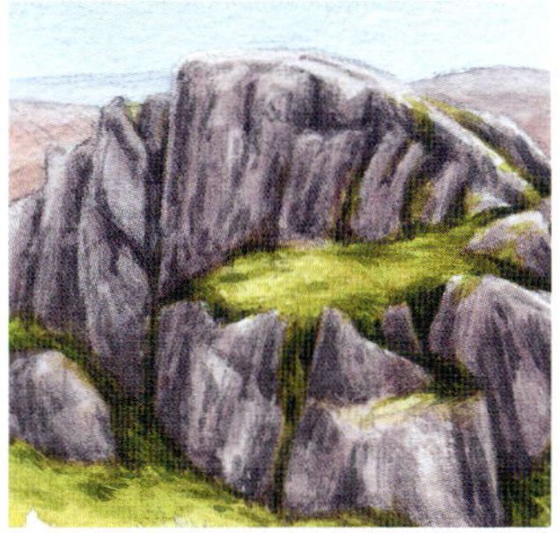

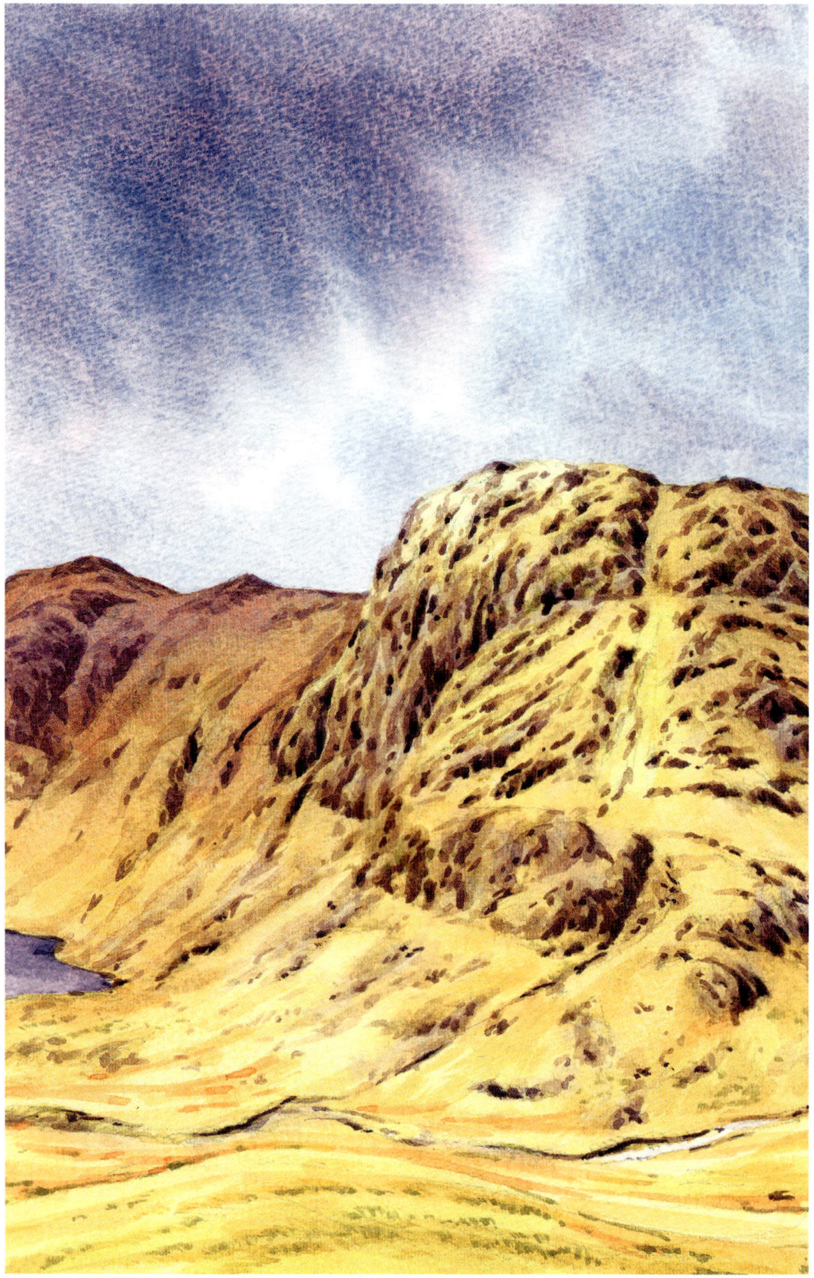

Pavey Ark

As Wainwright states in the Pictorial Guide, Pavey Ark is really the eastern boundary of Thunacar Knott but he decided to describe them as two separate fells. By doing so he was not only able to add another fell into the Central fells list and fill out the book but he could give the crag of Pavey Ark its own chapter. Sadly this was to the detriment of Thunacar Knott which instead of being the summit of a fell with fine assets became an almost featureless rise in the ground with a meagre six pages of description to its name.

From the western slopes of Blea Rigg 28/4/11

Clever use here by AW of images for the Pavey Ark chapter. Whilst the full page sketch on Pavey Ark 10 (see far right), the view across Stickle Tarn is a much more dramatic and classic view of the fell it would have had to lose some of its fine detail and composition by the placing of the title and map if used as the chapter page. By using this more unusual profile view as the main illustration he was able to use the map to obscure Harrison Stickle which detracts from the main featured fell. He also heightened the shape of Pavey Ark quite considerably to try and fill the page. Consequently by using this image he was able to give the full frontal view of the fell a full uncluttered page which it deserves.

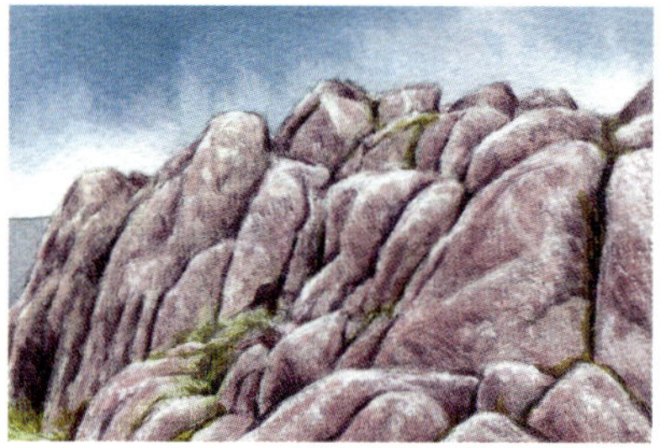

The summit 12/8/09

The top of the Ark has an area of rocky platforms some of which are very similar in height. On this visit the true top was missing its cairn but by careful study of AW's detailed drawing I was able to match the cracks and fissures of this outcrop to confirm that I had the correct summit view.

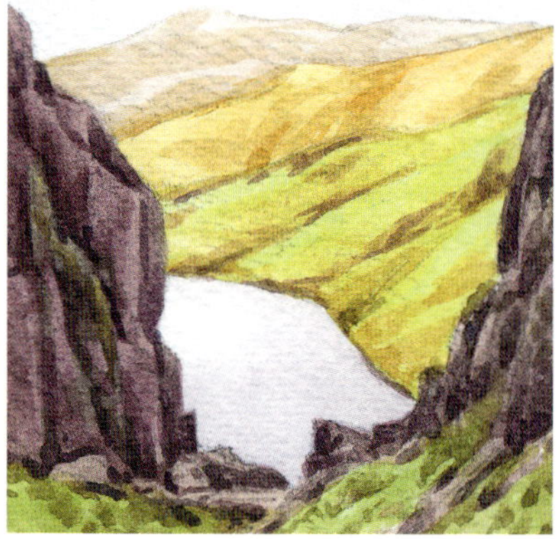

View from the top of Easy Gully 12/8/09

Stickle Tarn lies far below and in the distance are the Coniston Fells.

The North Rake 23/5/12

I completely missed this view on an earlier visit to this area so a return trip was called for but walks around the Langdale Pikes area are always a pleasure.

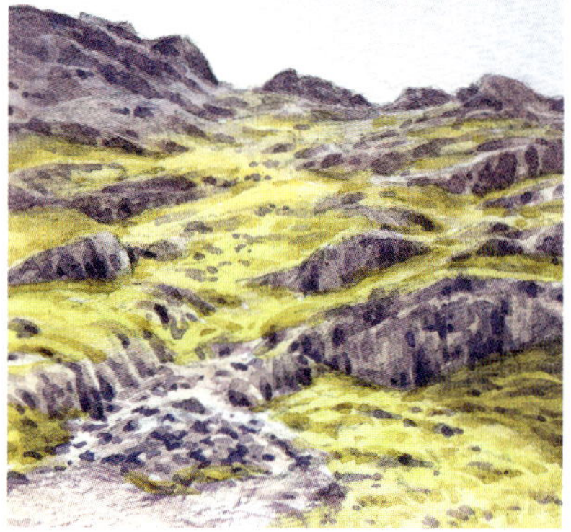

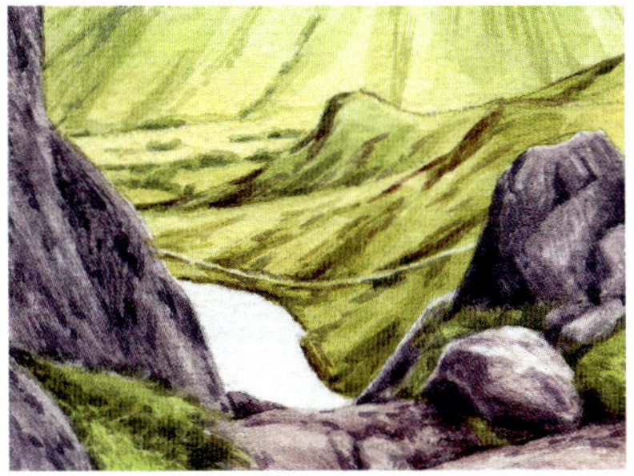

The entrance to Jack's Rake from above 12/8/09

This is the gap that walkers will pass though as they near the top of the fell after completing the Rake.

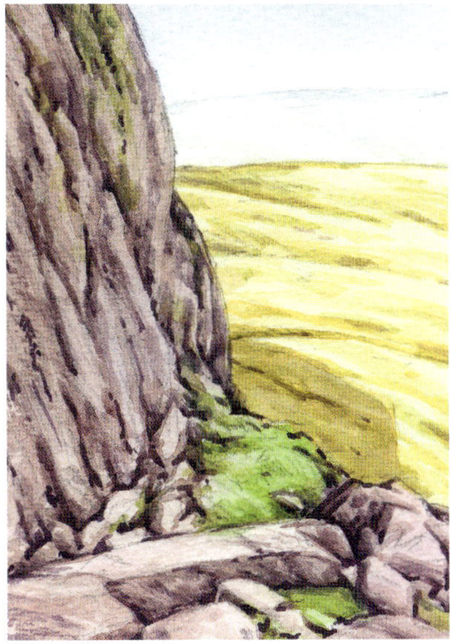

Looking back to the platform below Gwynnes Chimney 23/5/12

Both this view and the one below left were taken from the same safe location on Easy Terrace where AW felt the most comfortable. This sketch shows the route that we had just ascended with the background detail of the slopes of Blea Rigg some distance lower.

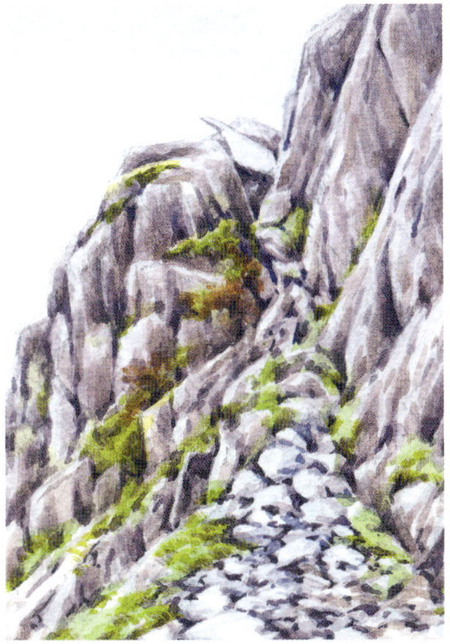

Looking up the Rake to the groove 23/5/12

Once again, seen from the Easy Terrace. At the top of the groove a large flake of rock now lies at an angle. It has fallen into place in more recent years. It has no official name but I have seen it referred to as The Gun due to its shape.

Jack's Rake

I have decided to place the sketches for this iconic Lake District route together on this page of Pavey Ark. Wainwright must have had some trepidation about venturing here as on his first visit he went with company which was very unusual for him. He did revisit the route on his own at least once after that trip. Due to the nature of the terrain his excellent description of the route in the original guide is still accurate except that is for three trees (Mountain Ash) of which now only one (the 2nd) is obvious being adjacent to the path. A new additional sapling now grows at the foot of the steep groove halfway up the route. It is a route classed as a Grade 1 scramble so it should only be undertaken by those who are confident in tackling such terrain.

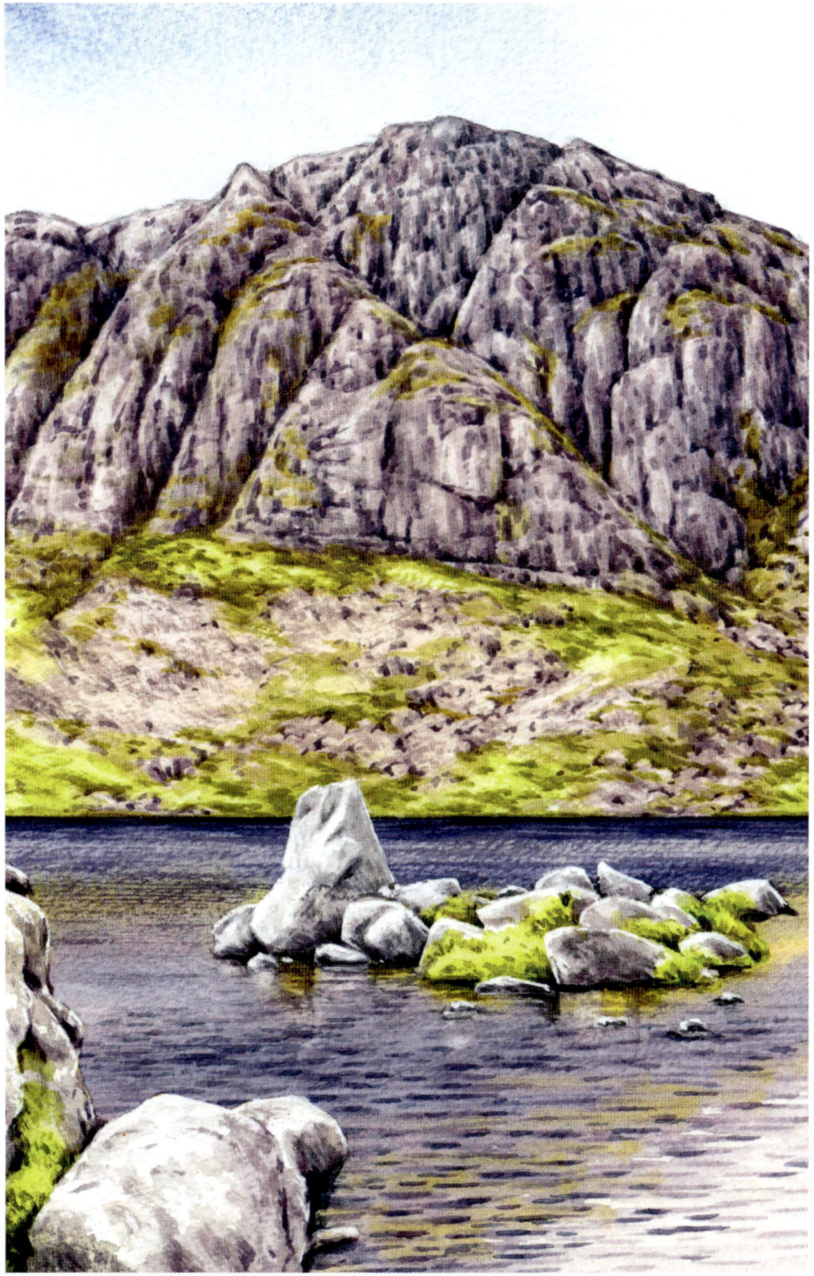

Pavey Ark 12/8/09

This view of the imposing face of the crag of Pavey Ark across Stickle Tarn was, in AW's opinion, *"superior to all others of this type in Lakeland"* and I would tend to agree with him. An interesting feature of this scene is that in the intervening fifty years the small island has suffered natural erosion and the soil has been washed away gradually and left the rocks of the island in place.

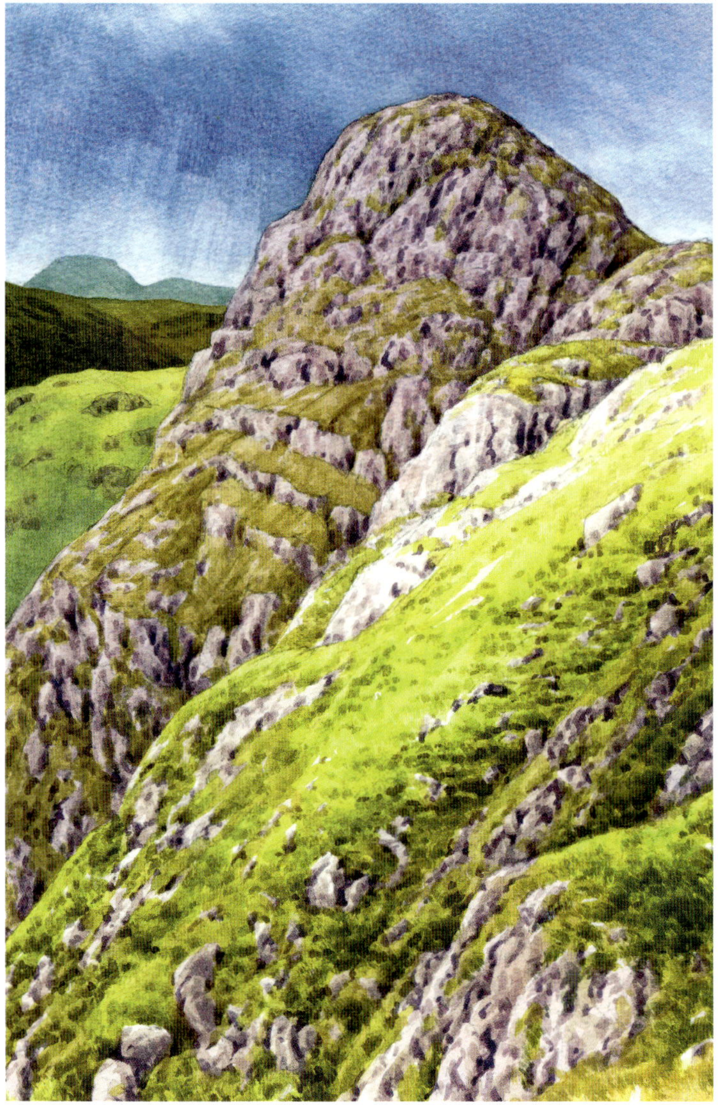

From Gimmer Crag 12/8/09
As I climbed out of the narrow cleft above the chock stone on Loft Crag this scene with the sunlight illuminating the upper slopes of Pike o' Stickle presented itself, just as in AW's drawing. Few other fells have such a distinctive profile.

Pike o' Stickle

The rounded rocky domed top of this fell is a feature which is easily identified from afar. Its very steep and craggy south eastern front is impregnable to walkers but from the northern side access to the summit is a relatively easy affair. It is usually visited as part of a route which takes in the other Langdale Pikes.

The Stone Axe Factory

There were several locations in the Langdale area where the greenstone was worked into these Neolithic tools. Pike o' Stickle is perhaps the most famous of these, with the location of a small cave near the scree slope (right) where many artefacts of axe production have been found, giving us a visual link to the past. Langdale axes have been found throughout the whole of the UK.

Stone axe found on Pike o' Stickle
The axe below is another example of a similar size and shape from the collection of Mr. R.G. Plint. As part of my research the one shown in AW's sketch could not be found in the current collection at Kendal Museum.

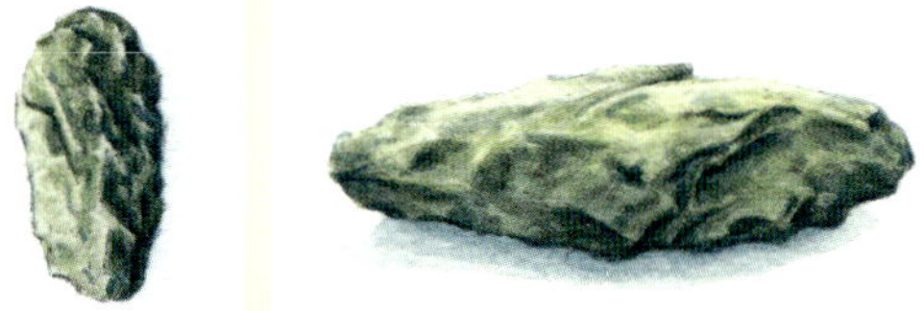

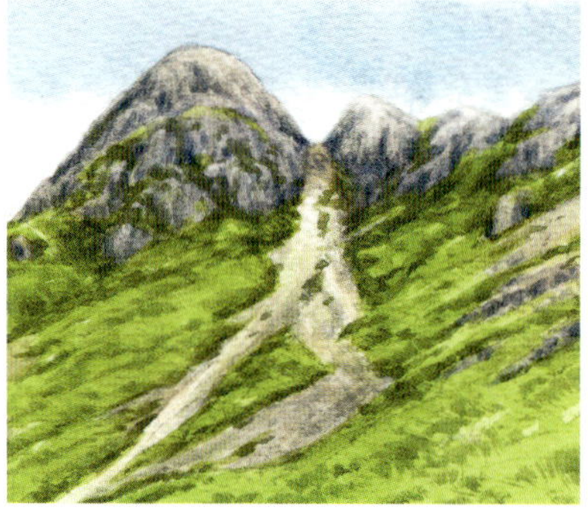

The south scree, from Mickleden 8/7/09
A very steep run of loose rocks.

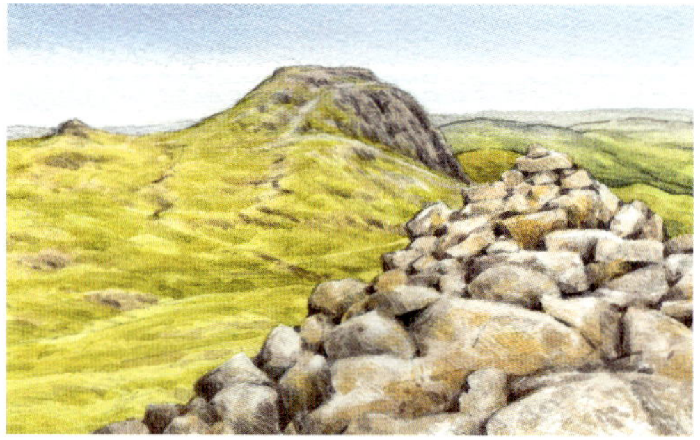

The summit 12/8/09
The path to the top of the fell leads you up a short rocky outcrop. Harrison Stickle behind.

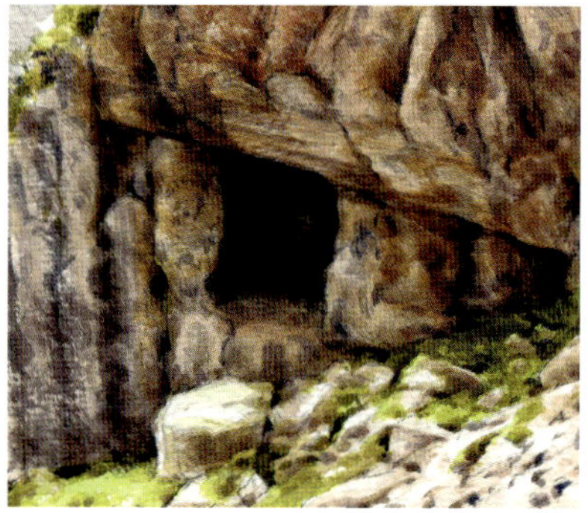

The man made cave 12/8/09
This small recess in the rock face may have provided shelter from the weather as ancient man worked the stone from the area. Stone chippings litter the floor.

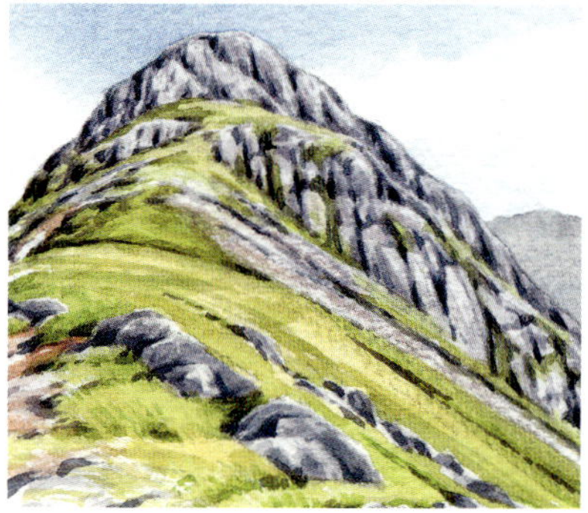

The summit of Pike o' Stickle from the north-west 12/8/09
A distinctive dome of rock.

The cairn on Martcrag Moor 12/8/09
A small cairn placed on this rock platform, well away from any regular path.

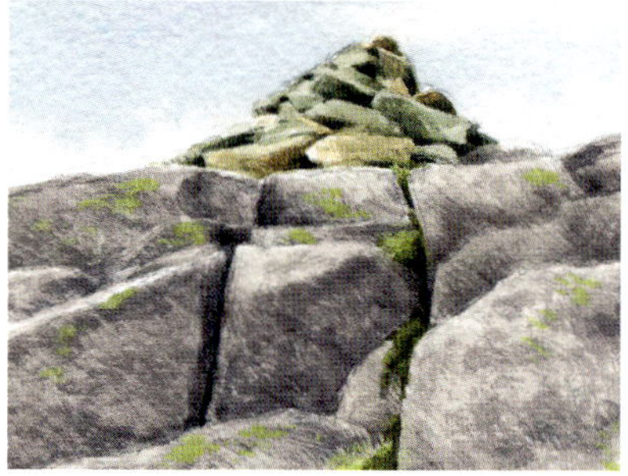

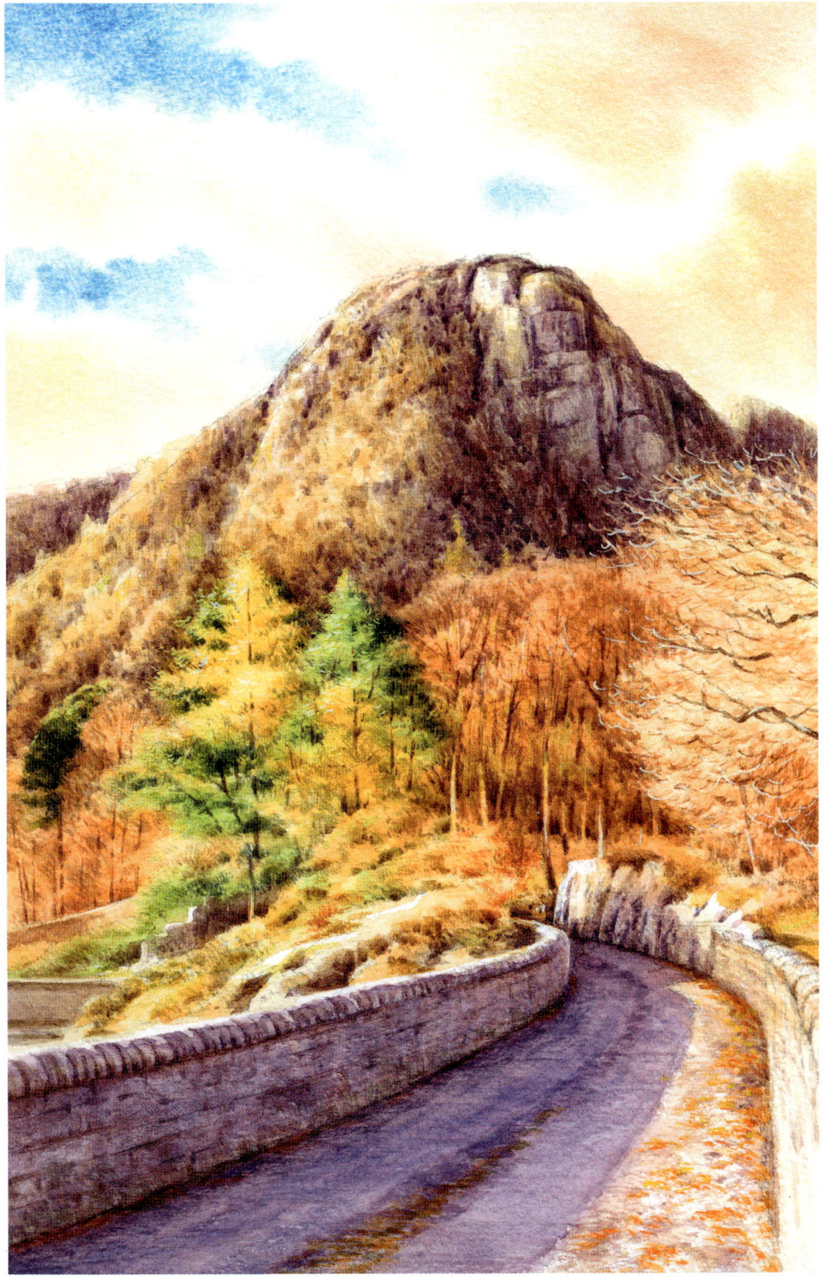

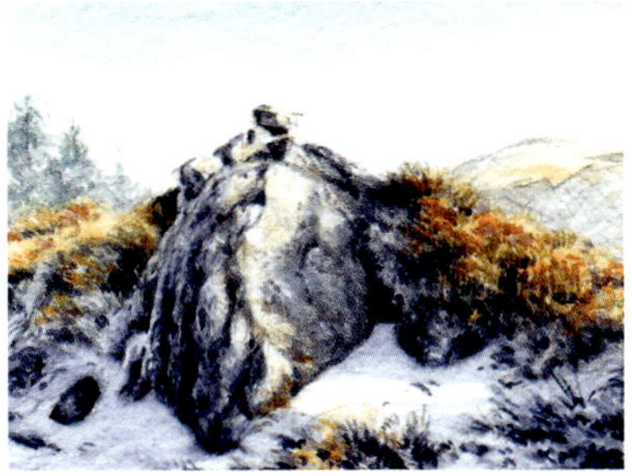

Raven Crag

Sited near the northern end of Thirlmere, this fell is easily reached from the small car park near the dam. A simple there and back route to the summit using paths through the forest will only take up an hour or so of your time. Linking Raven Crag in a walk to neighbouring fells is a bit more of a challenge.

From the Thirlmere dam 4/3/08
The Crag is still mostly covered in forest apart that is from the sheer face where trees can't take hold. Only the very observant will notice that the walls of the dam have had alterations and the drainage system has more recently been removed.

The summit 4/3/08
The screen of trees near here to which Wainwright referred have now gone from the eastern aspect, revealing a clear view of the northern end of Thirlmere. A few small stones form the basis of a cairn on the rock outcrop. More recently a wooden walkway leads up through the trees to the very summit, culminating in a viewing platform complete with handrail.

Thirlmere 26/7/10
It took more than one visit to locate the exact position for this, the view into which AW later added himself for this book's self portrait. The trees on the right are now decayed whereas the ones on the left of his image have all been felled. His distant hills are portrayed in a more dramatic fashion than in reality. This whole viewing point is more open now than in Wainwright's day.

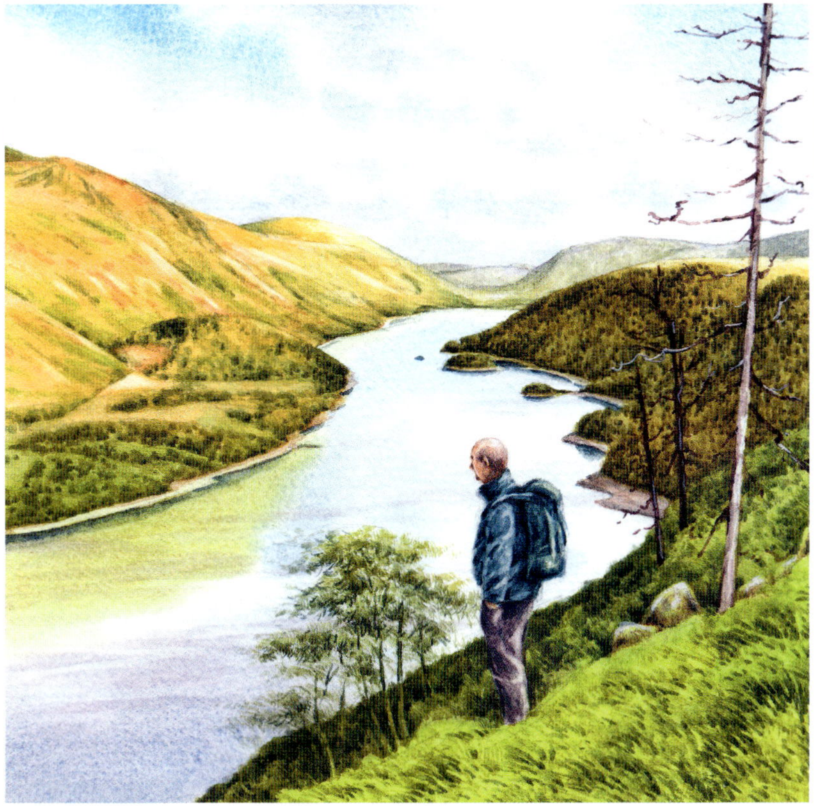

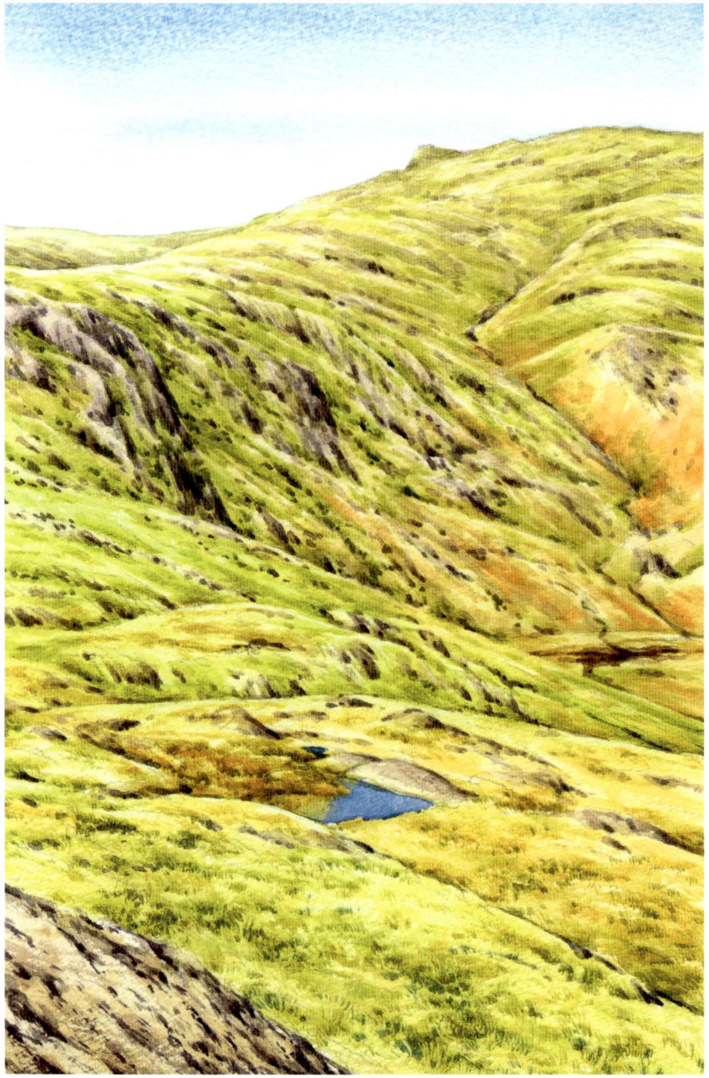

Sergeant Man

Being a named measured height and also offering a top that requires a bit of a steep climb ensured that this fell made it onto Wainwright's final list.

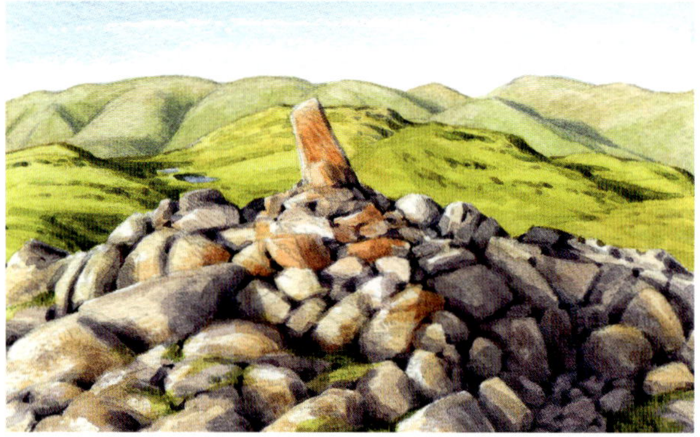

The summit 2/6/09

The stone column in AW's drawing didn't last, it was already down by 1961. Today it is just a heap of rocks.

From Great Castle How 28/4/11

Sergeant Man is really only the small peak on the skyline. AW's options for a better fell portrait were limited.

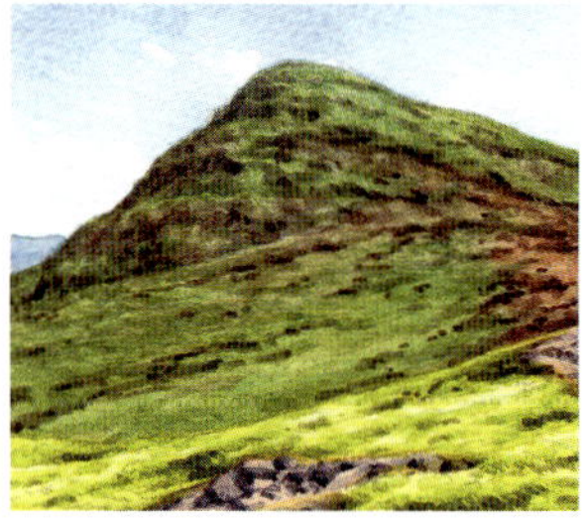

Belles Knott 2/6/09

It is not as pointed as in his drawing but this is still a definite peak shape. The stream was no more than a trickle at the time of my visit.

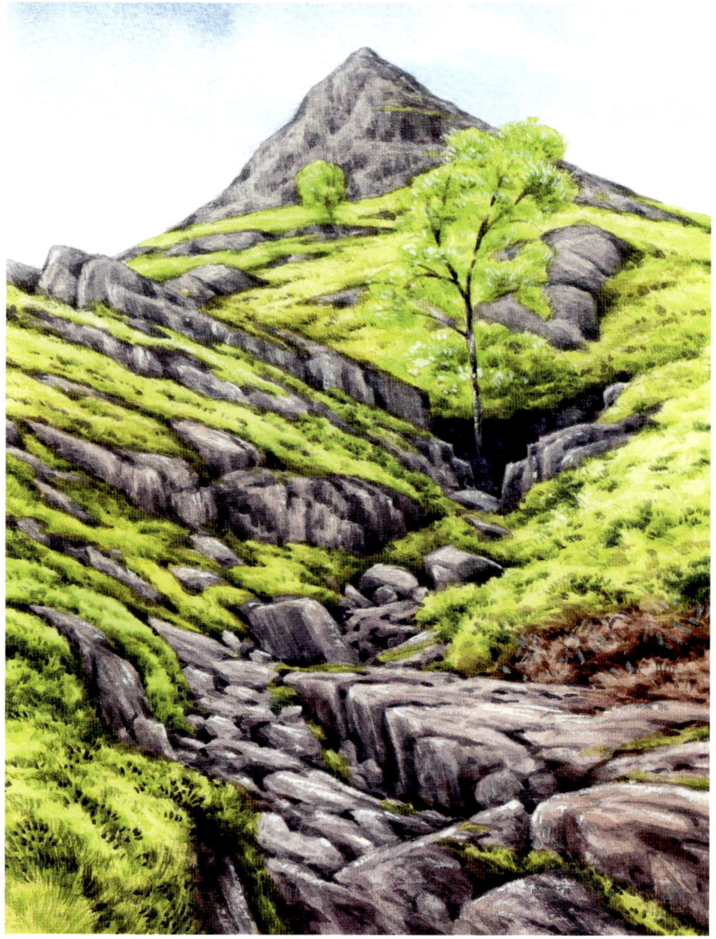

The summit from the east 2/6/09 (above)

The final approach to the summit.

The summit from the rock slab 2/6/09 (right)

The rounded top seen in profile.

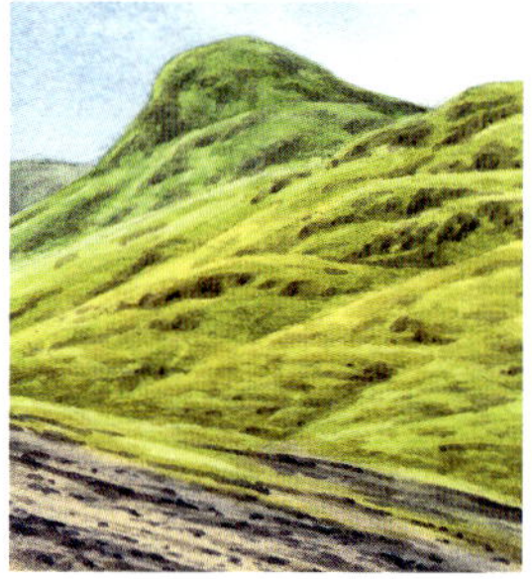

The small peak 2/6/09

The early evening sun lit this rocky outcrop. It was just after 7.30 p.m. and the light was just stunning.

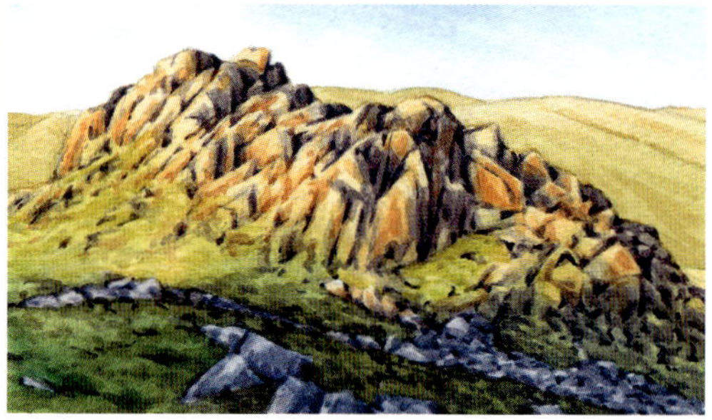

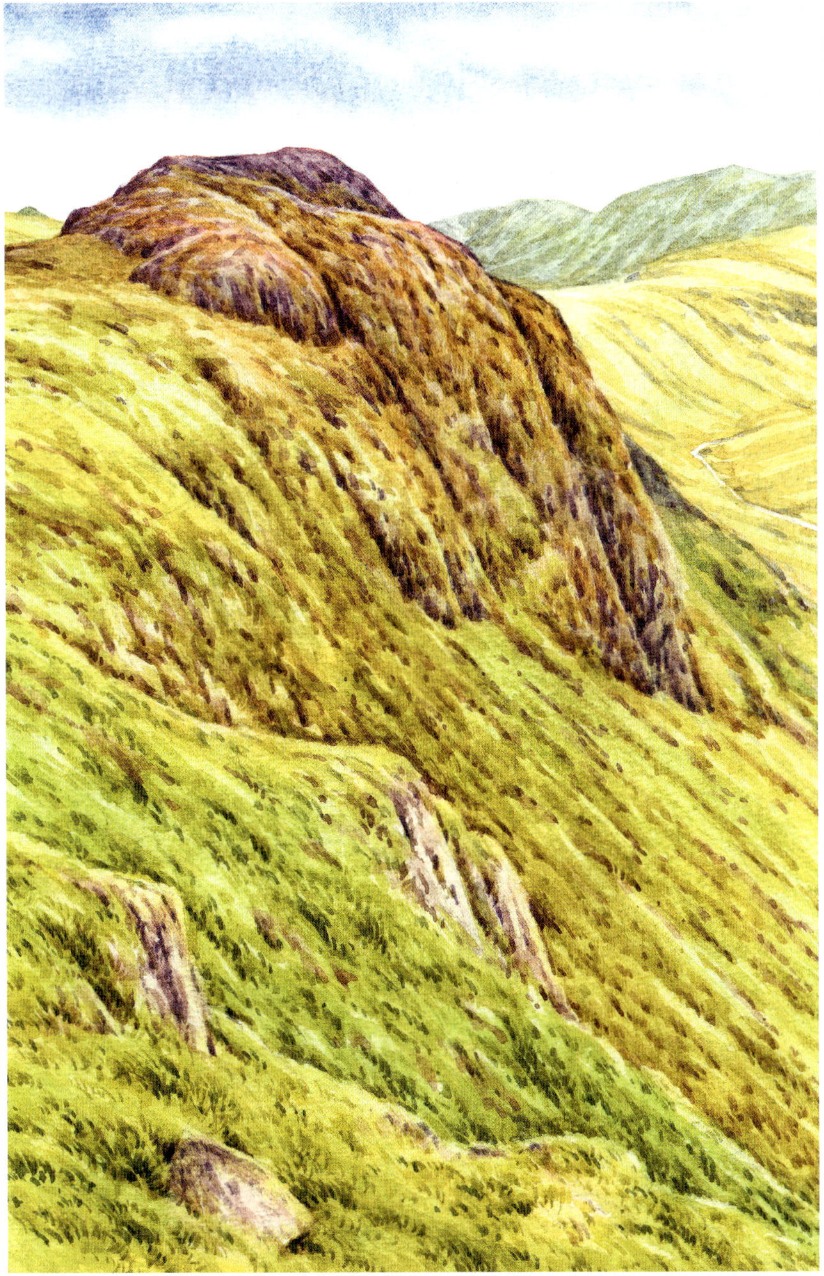

Sergeant's Crag

The tall eastern wall of the beautiful and quiet Langstrath valley is formed by the high and rough slopes of both Eagle Crag and Sergeant's Crag. It is usual for both of these close neighbours to be combined as part of one walk as they are only half a mile apart.

From Eagle Crag 24/6/09

This viewpoint is not only excellent for seeing the profile of Sergeant's Crag but also the whole length of the valley which is also seen in the sketch below.

Sergeant's Crag and Langstrath from the north 7/3/10

This vista is actually viewed from High Crag on Great Crag.

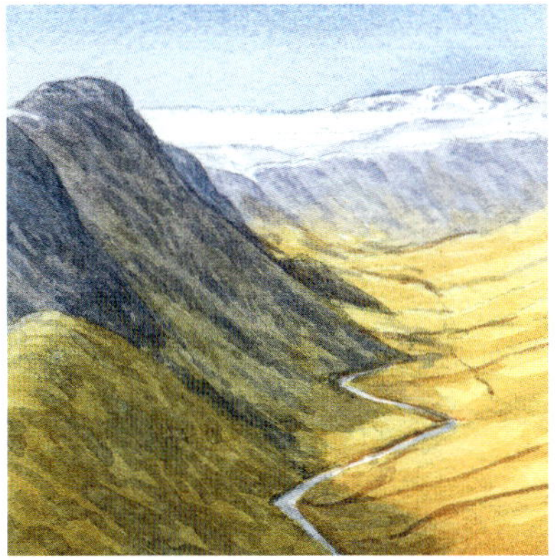

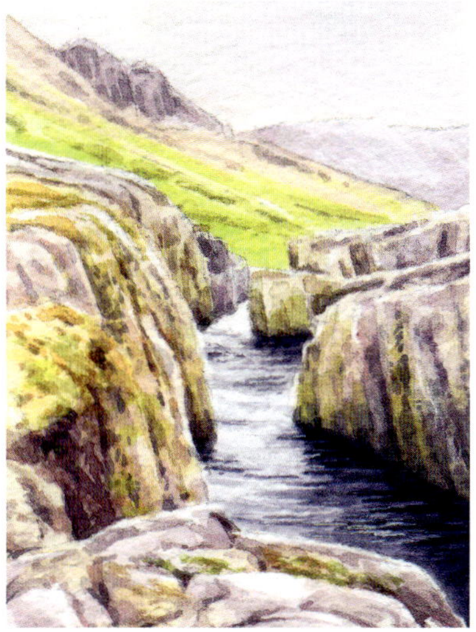

Blackmoss Pot 9/11/08

Through this narrow ravine flows Langstrath Beck. The deep pools of crystal clear water reveal the colourful rocks of the river bed.

The summit 9/1/08

An untidy cairn sits on the highest point of the fell which is formed by a platform of bare rock. The view is impressive, especially to the east.

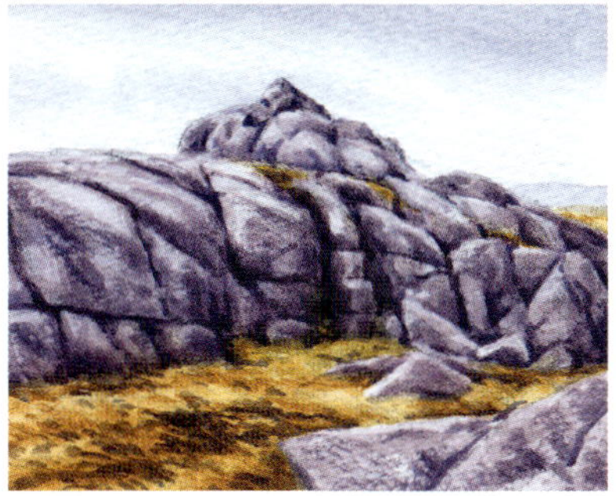

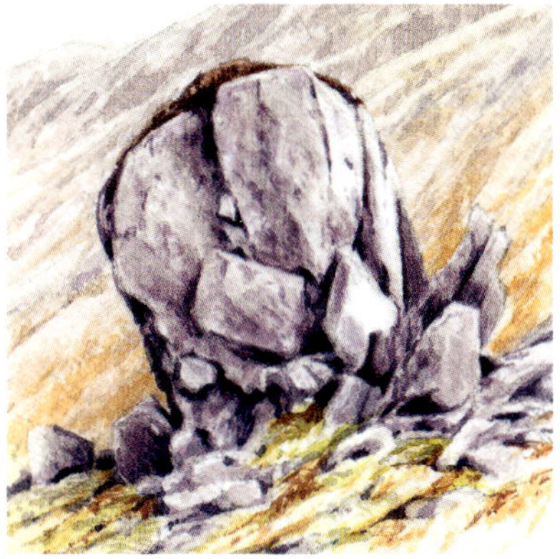

Blea Rock 9/11/08

This huge boulder with its cap of heather has come to rest at the base of the cliffs of the crag. It is named on the O.S. maps.

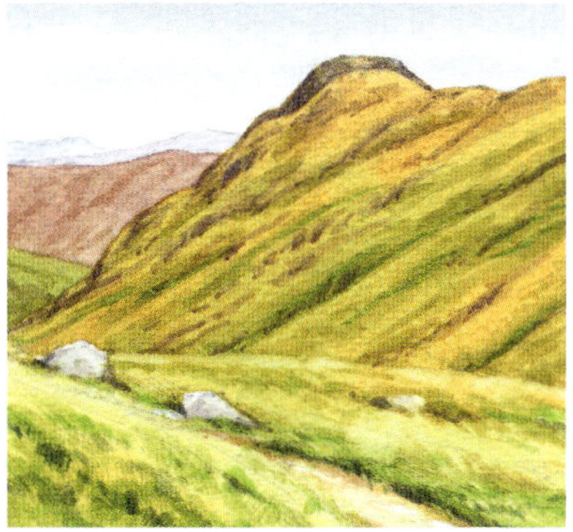

Sergeant's Crag from Stake Pass 12/8/09

As you descend into Langstrath on the recently repaired path this aspect of the fell appears.

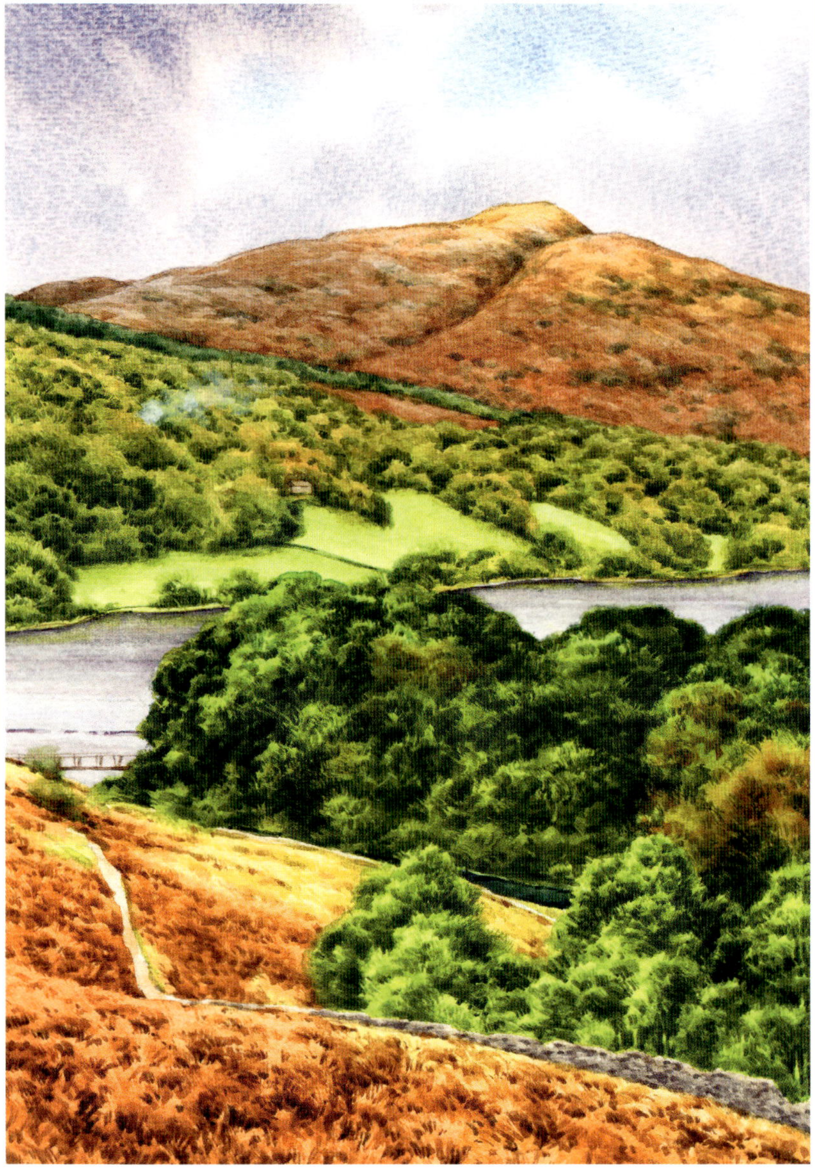

From Loughrigg Terrace 19/9/08
The view of the fell from this popular walking route shows that the wooded areas near Silver How have not altered very much over the recent years.

Langdale Pikes from the tarns below Lang How 28/4/11
AW obtained his reference in winter conditions, I was unable to achieve the similar seasonal image.

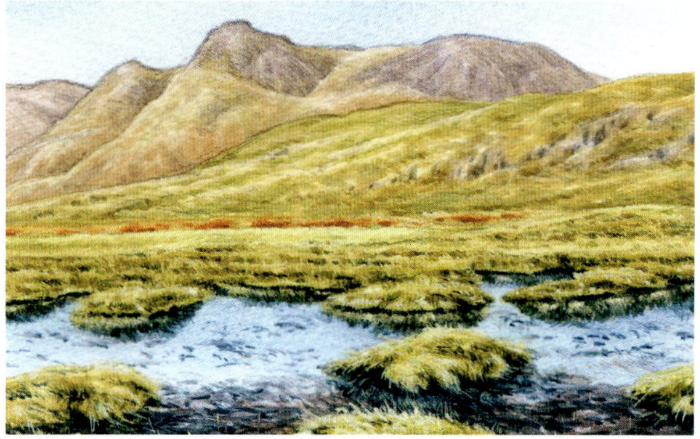

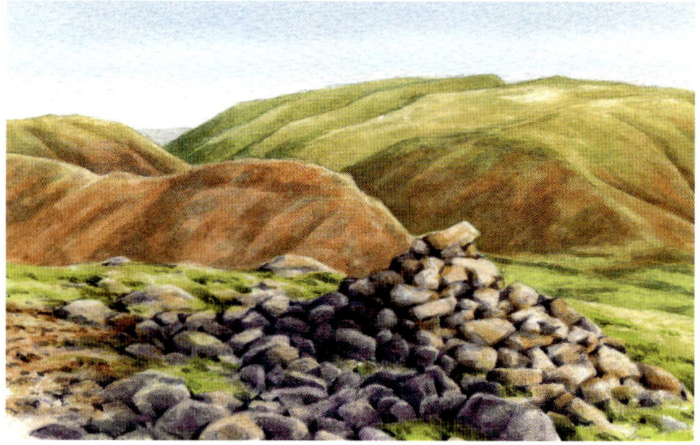

The summit 14/9/08
The bulk of the Helvellyn range beyond Helm Crag and Steel Fell can be appreciated from this point.

The stone man above Meg's Gill 14/9/08
Only by lining up the background outline of AW's drawing was I able to determine the former location of the tall column of stones which has now totally gone.

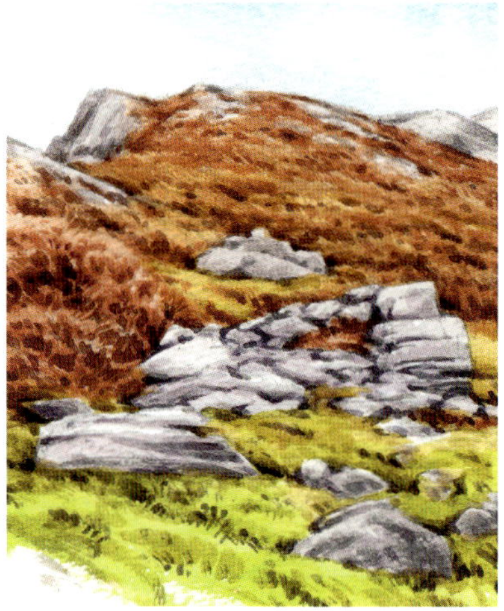

Silver How

Grasmere is a good starting point for the exploration for this rather pleasant fell. If combined with a visit to Blea Rigg the high views of Great Langdale from the route are excellent.

Meg's Gill 28/4/11
This viewpoint was easy enough for me to locate as Wainwright even marked it in Silver How 6.

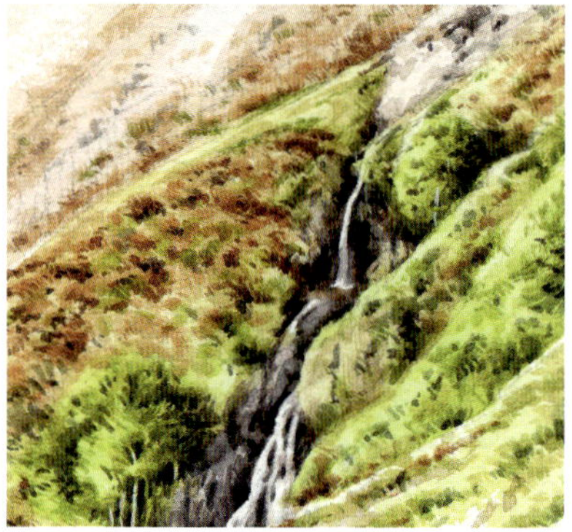

Cairn on the ridge 28/4/11
By moving some of the rocks of the rough cairn I confirmed that this was the exact required site.

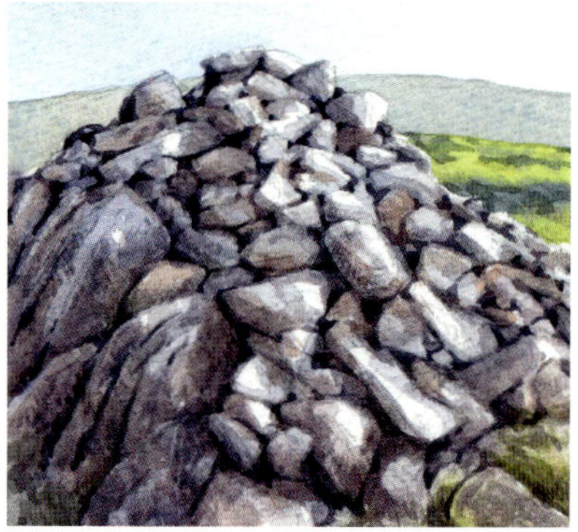

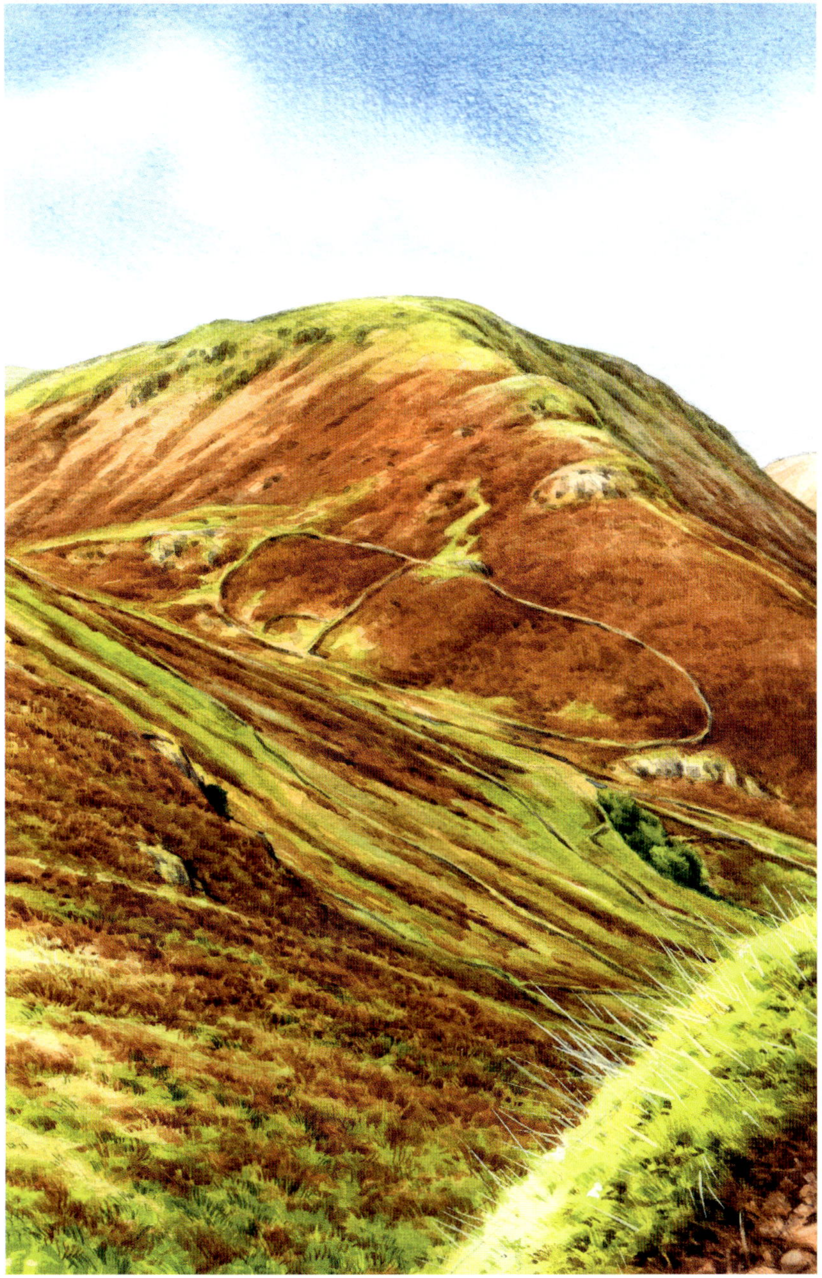

Steel Fell

The steep regular eastern slopes of Steel fell level out at the base to form the pass of Dunmail Raise which carries the main road between Keswick and Ambleside. The fell has two definite ridges basically coming from the north and south both of which are enjoyable routes of ascent to the summit. To the west the fell is linked to Calf Crag across easy but wet high ground.

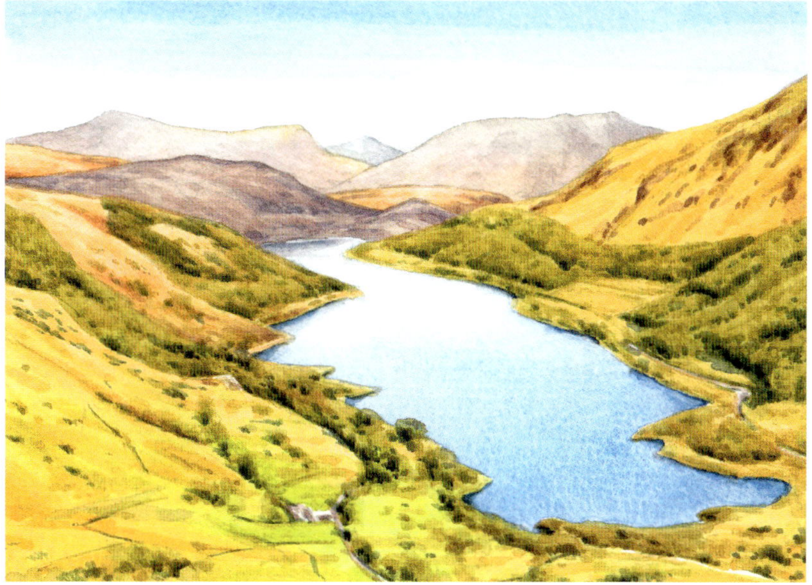

From Helm Crag 14/9/08

It was from this point, half way up the path on north west slopes of Helm Crag that Wainwright took his photograph for his drawing. The main illustration for the Gibson Knott chapter is from close to this spot, most likely taken within minutes of each other.

Thirlmere from the north ridge 27/3/12

To achieve this same view I had to make a slow descent of the ridge with guidebook in hand until all the elements of AW's drawing came into view. Note how in his illustration the water levels of Thirlmere are quite low, the southern end is shallow and the flat bed often is revealed here.

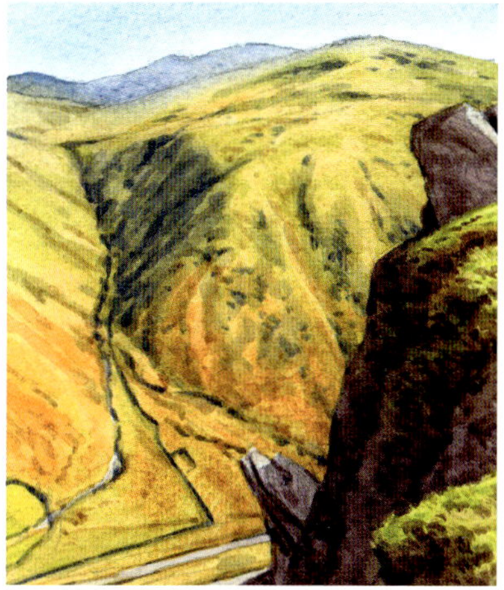

Raise Beck from the gully 27/3/12

There are no signs of the tree that once clung to the crag. Dunmail Pass lies far below.

The old cairn on Dunmail Raise 24/6/09

The word "Raise" is actually an old name for a cairn and this one that sits between the two carriageways of road is certainly old but its true original purpose for construction is still unclear. Being the reputed site of the death of King Dunmail is perhaps the more romantic story.

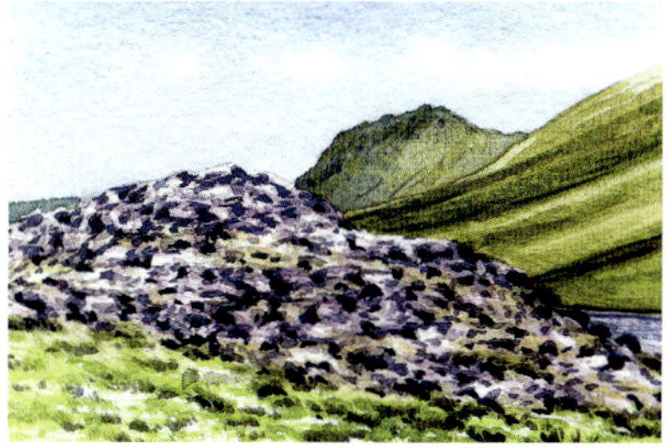

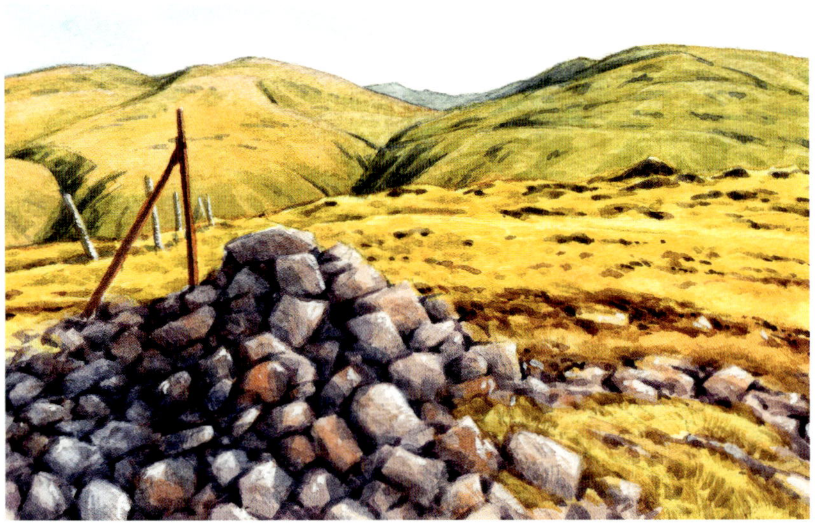

The summit 27/3/12
The cairn has now been enlarged so much so that it now partially incorporates the old iron fence post. The tangle of wires of the fence shown in Wainwright's drawing have been removed along with some of the other metal posts.

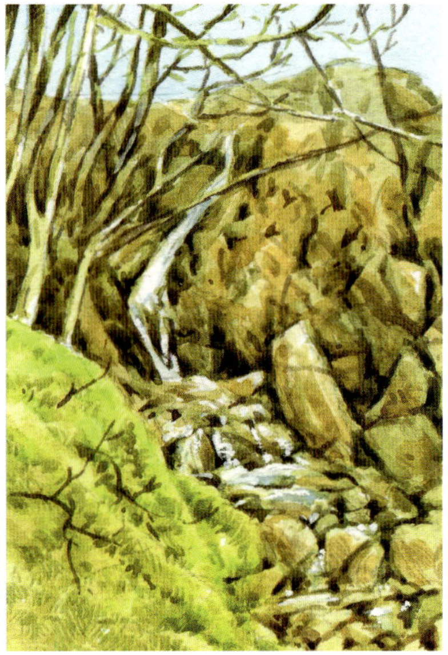

Waterfall in the Greenburn valley 26/3/12
I had visited this location on another day and the thick foliage obscured the feature so this trip was planned for earlier in the year so that the trees were bare. There are three falls marked on maps of the burn of which this is the middle one.

The upper part of the south-east ridge 27/3/12
As I took this route of ascent I passed by a couple of rocky outcrops on the ridge but only this one exactly matches his scene. This is a fine way to ascend the fell, pleasant terrain and not too steep for which I was grateful as at this time I was carrying all my wild camping equipment.

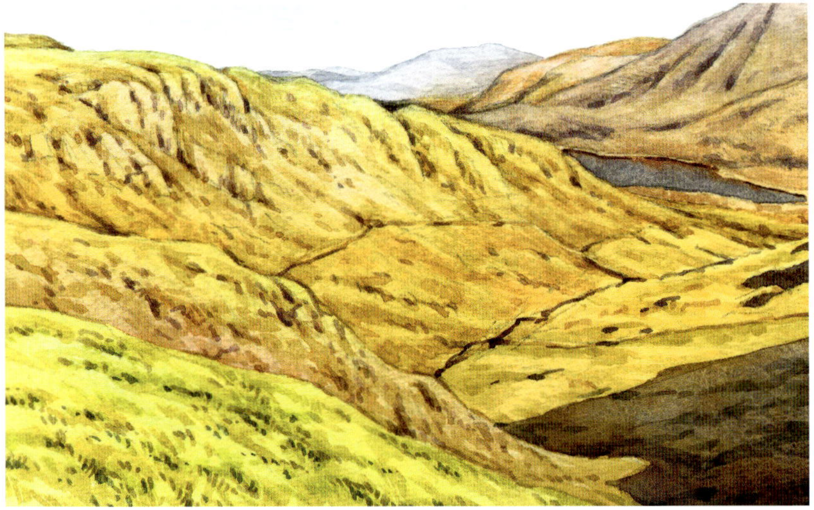

Nab Crags and the Wyth Burn valley 26/3/12
This view is obtained by taking a short detour away from the path between Steel Fell and Calf Crag. Blencathra is the fell on the horizon. Note how in this title AW has split Wythburn, in regards to the valley, into two words whereas in most other instances he has it as one word.

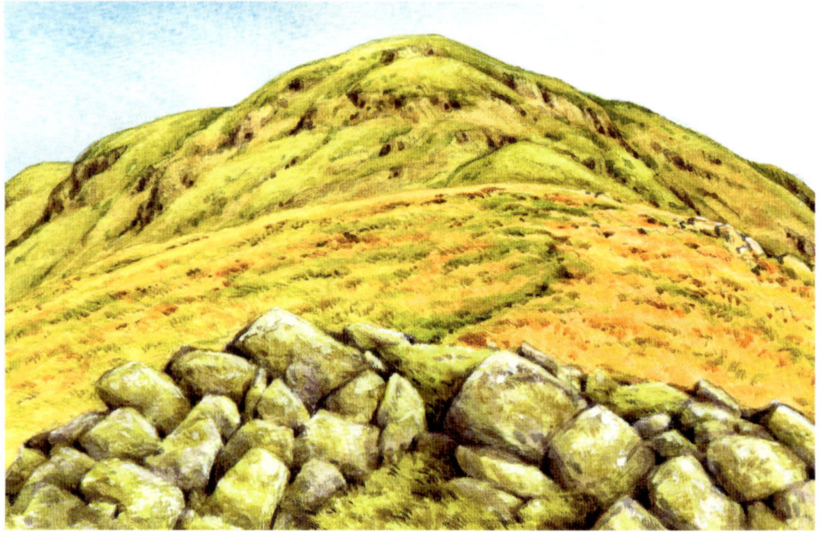

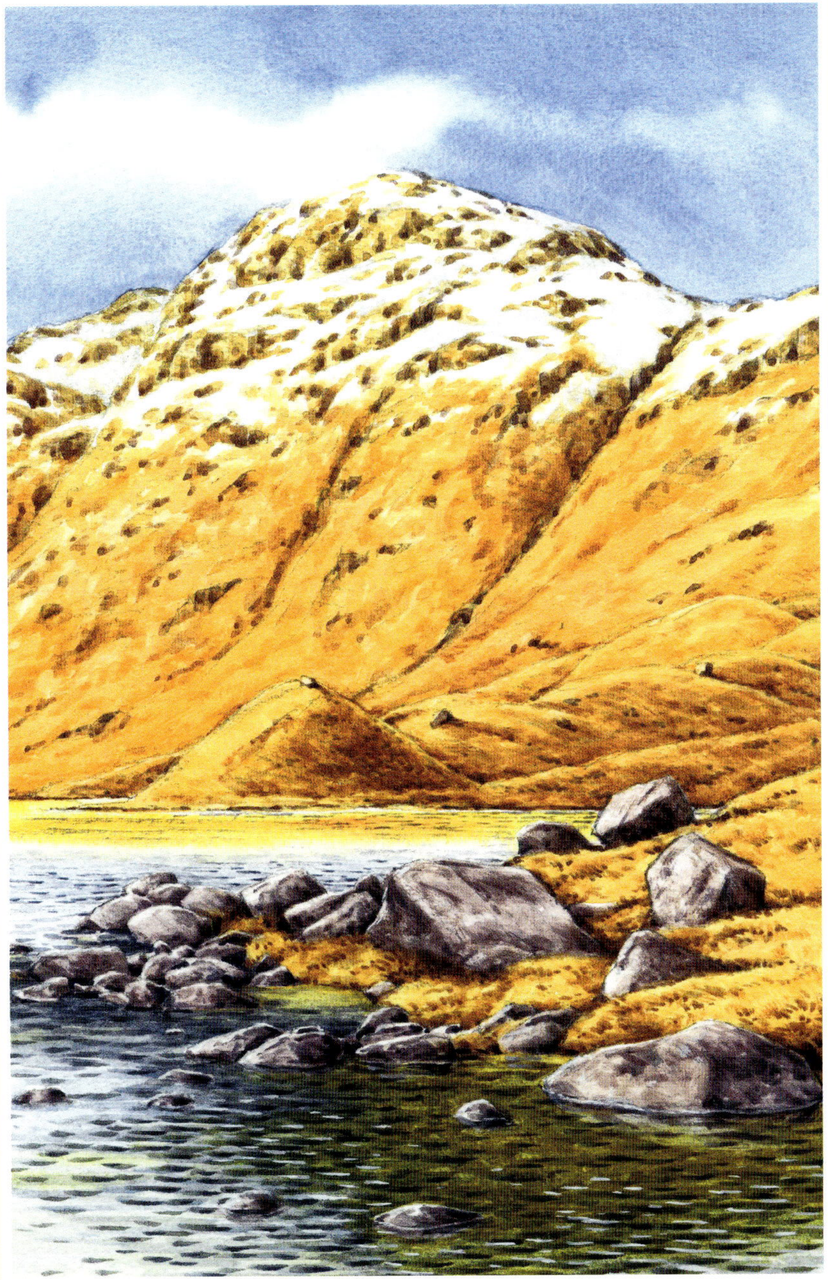

Tarn Crag

This fell along with Calf Crag to the north are unique in the fact that they both feature on all four maps in the current paper version of the Explorer range from the Ordnance Survey covering the whole of the Lake District. Tarn Crag is the dominant fell above the popular Easedale Tarn.

From Easedale Tarn 1/2/12

At this exact location, just at the outlet of the tarn I managed to capture this scene on a previous visit at the height of summer. However, on this later walk I was attracted by the winter scene with the rich colours which made for a more appealing subject to use in this sketch for the project.

Deer Bield Crag 2/6/09

This is a familiar crag to climbers with several named routes up its face. The crag has in recent years changed shape, doing so one night in the summer of 1997 when large slabs of rock fell from the face. The two pointed flakes of rock at the top right of AW's drawing are now gone but the same foreground boulders which he featured are still identifiable.

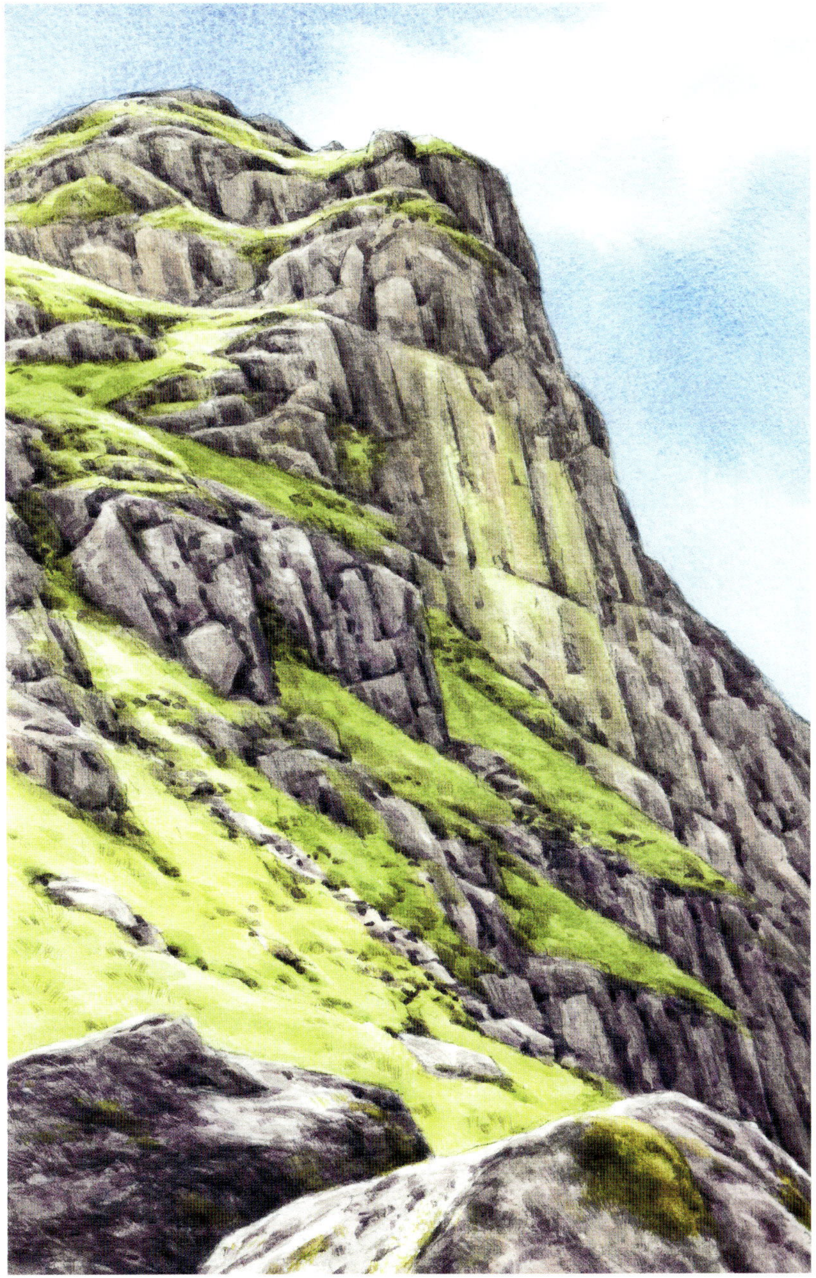

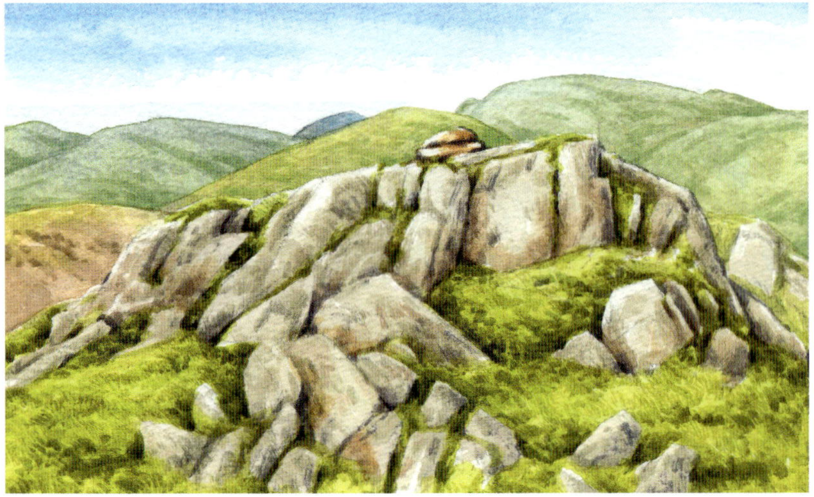

The summit 2/6/09

A couple of stones form the cairn on the small top. The more impressive lower cairn 200 yards to the south gives a dramatic view of Easedale Tarn.

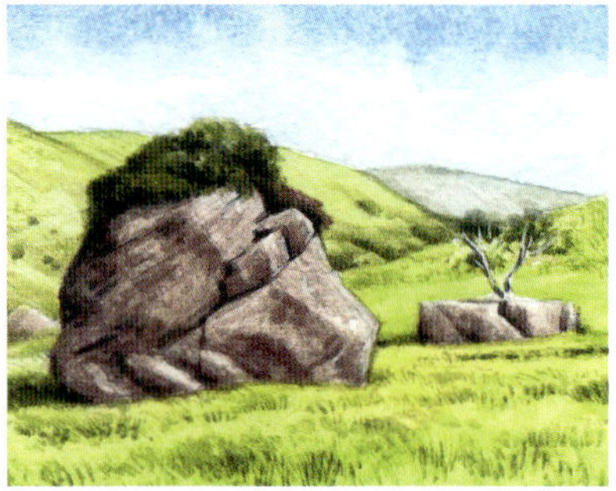

Interesting boulders 2/6/09

The larger rock has a cap of turf and daubed on one side in white paint is "Grasmere" with a directional arrow but it is faint. The smaller rock behind has a single tree growing from its crevice.

The summit crags 8/4/11

The outline of the crags are not as angular as shown in AW's drawing. The top can be reached with ease.

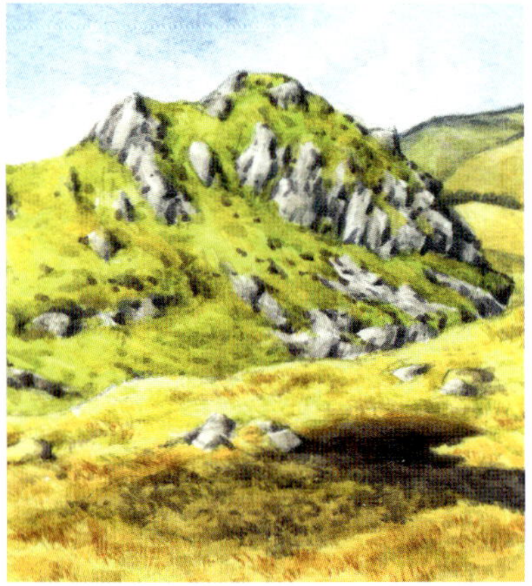

Tarn Crag and its east ridge from Easedale 28/4/11

This is a new bridge that was built in 1997 as a replacement for the old packhorse bridge and it is actually marked as New Bridge on the map.

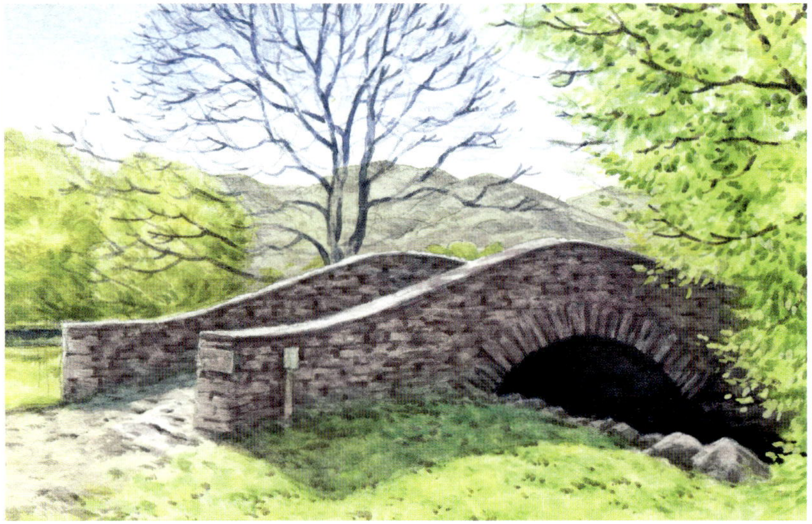

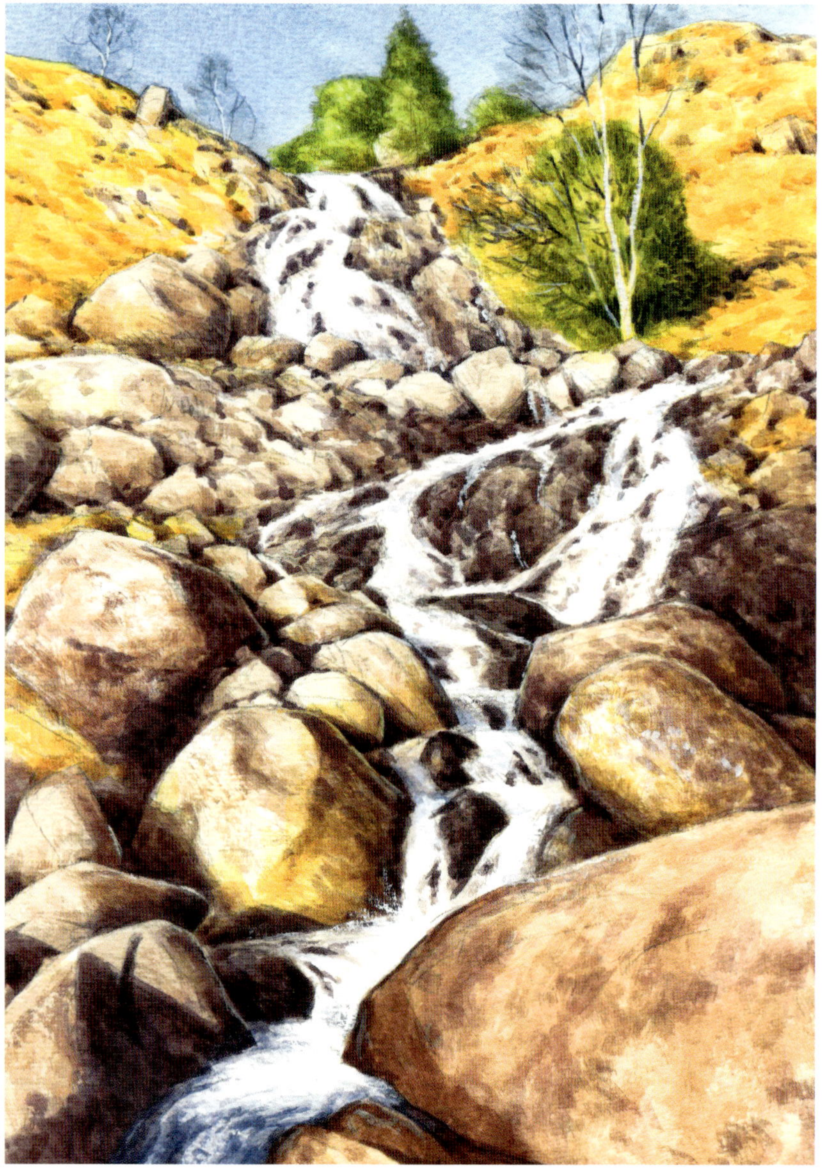

Sour Milk Gill 1/2/12

The lower waterfall may have changed course but the foreground rocks are almost identical, including the cracked one at the bottom left.

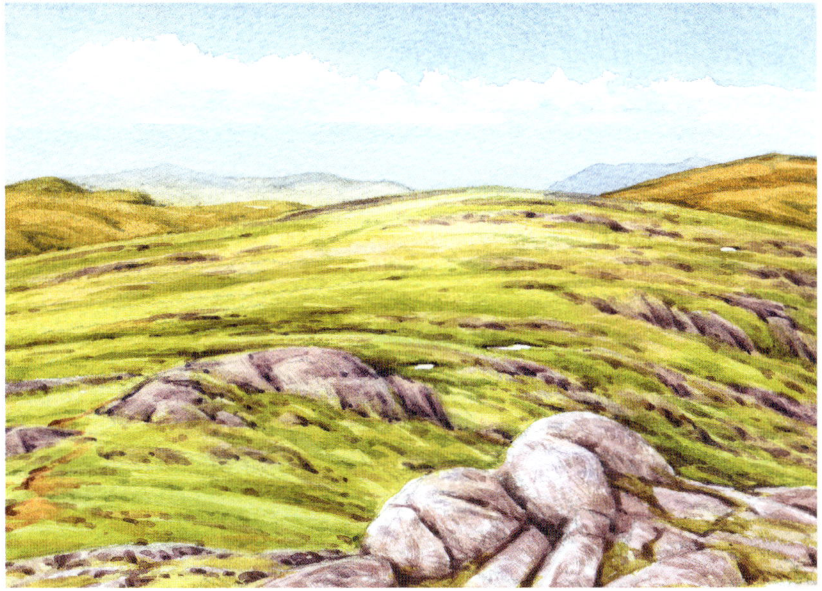

From Harrison Stickle 12/8/09

The view north from Harrison Stickle is hardly impeded by the top of Thunacar Knott. There are a couple of small pools in the middle distance but they are not marked in the guides but are on the O.S. maps.

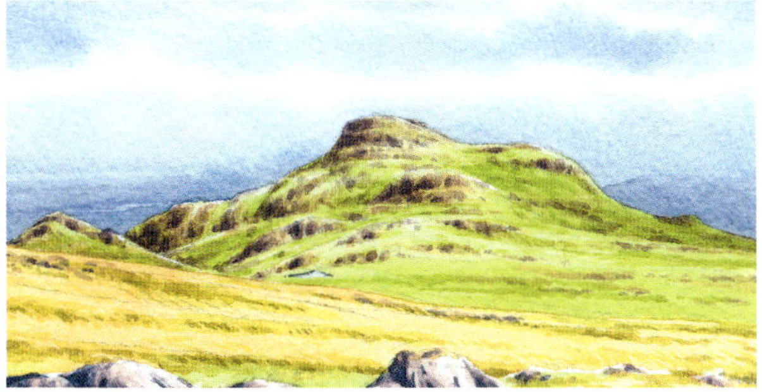

Harrison Stickle (from point 2362') 12/8/09

The rounded top of this nearby fell provides at least some interest to the sketches in this chapter. Very few fells in the Pictorial Guides have such limited possibilities for artistic work as that of Thunacar Knott.

Thunacar Knott

There is nothing exciting about this fell either visually, geographically or historically. It is a rounded rise in the landscape between Harrison Stickle and High Raise with a few rocky outcrops and one or two small tarns to break up the monotony of the short cropped turf. As its near neighbours are more interesting Thunacar Knott is often overlooked by casual walkers.

The summit confusion

Thunacar Knott is one of those fells where the true summit is not easily identified as the two high points have only a difference of approximately 10 feet. The casual reader of Wainwright's pictorial guide will assume that his illustration of the cairn just under the title "The Summit" (top right) depicts the highest point. He does however go on to explain that this is the "recognised" top and that higher ground does lie some distance to the south (bottom right). AW took his lead for the summit illustration from the 1 inch O.S. map which had this point (2351') as the only surveyed height on the fell. Those who are ticking off the "Wainwrights" should perhaps visit both summits, the true and the recognised, just for peace of mind. For more information about confusing summits see page 135.

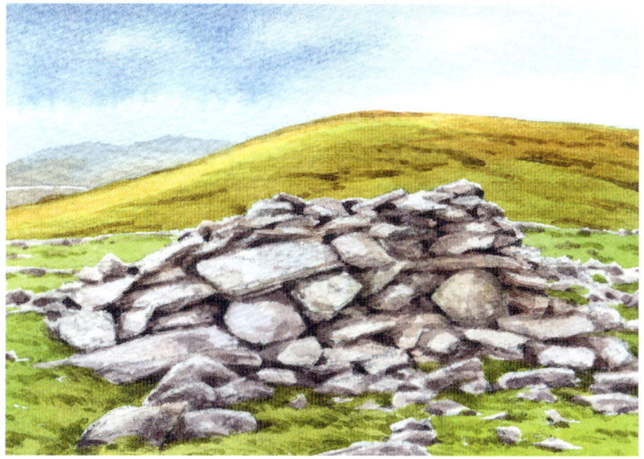

The summit 12/8/09

This cairn, shown in the guide as a neat construction is now just a jumble of rocks. There are other cairns on the high ground including one on point 2362'.

The main summit from point 2362' with High Raise beyond 12/8/09

This high ground is littered with boulders so a detailed search was required to find the angular striated block in the foreground used in AW's drawing. The elongated tarn can just be seen in the dip with the "summit" beyond. There is a cairn close to this point now, some yards to the right.

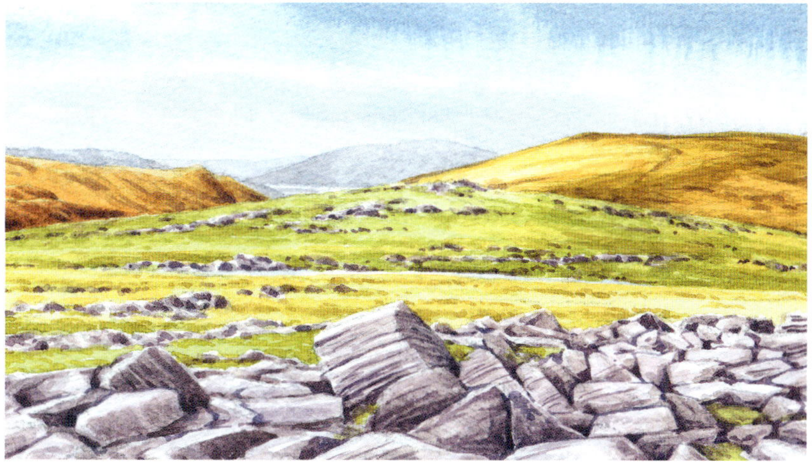

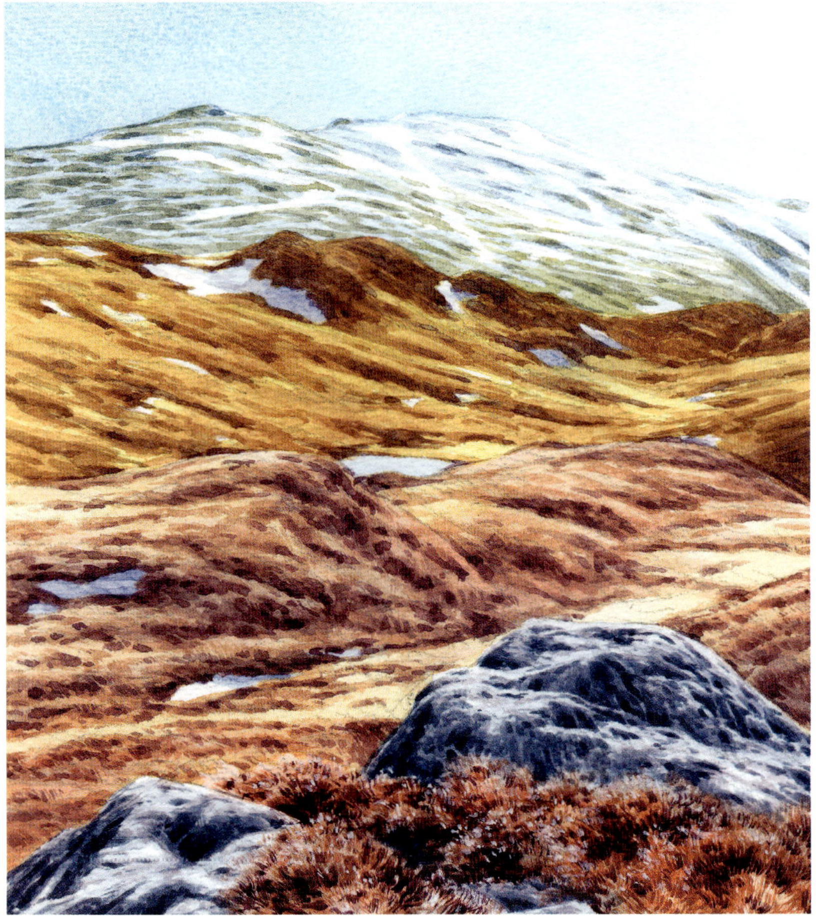

From Great Crag, Watendlath Fell 7/3/10
This sketch is very similar to that of the summit of Great Crag but by taking a pace or two to the left AW was able to omit the cairn from this scene. Patches of snow linger in the shaded depressions and in the centre of the sketch is the frozen Dock Tarn.

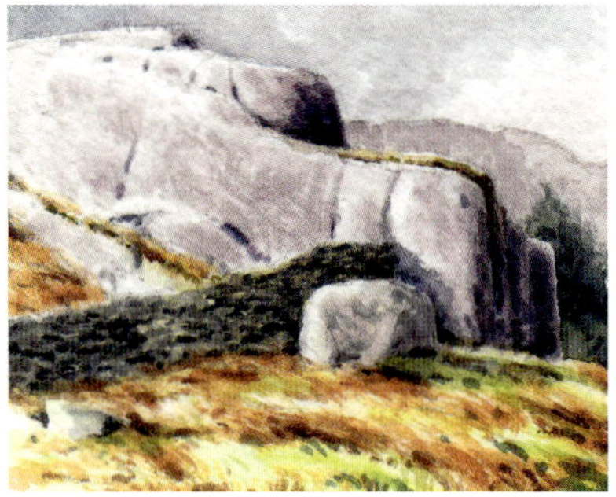

Binka Stone 5/3/08
A huge outcrop of rounded rock with a wall butting up to it. The two trees are no longer there.

Ullscarf

The area that surrounds the summit of this fell is rather bland with one main path crossing the ground in a north south direction following the line of the old fence which can now only be traced in places. In poor weather good navigation skills are required as reference points on the fell are few and far between.

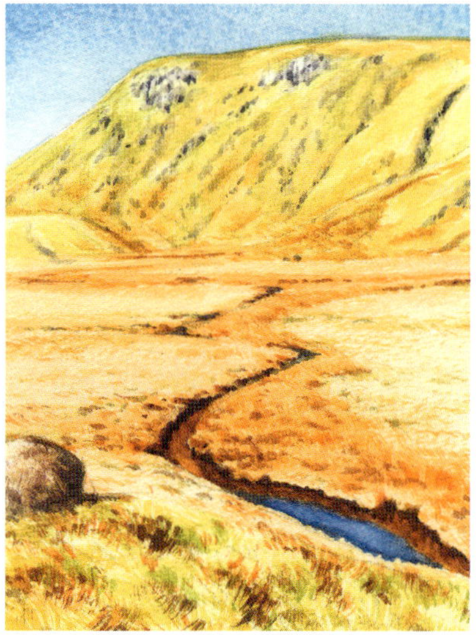

The bog 26/3/12
The upper section of the valley is generally flat and poorly drained.

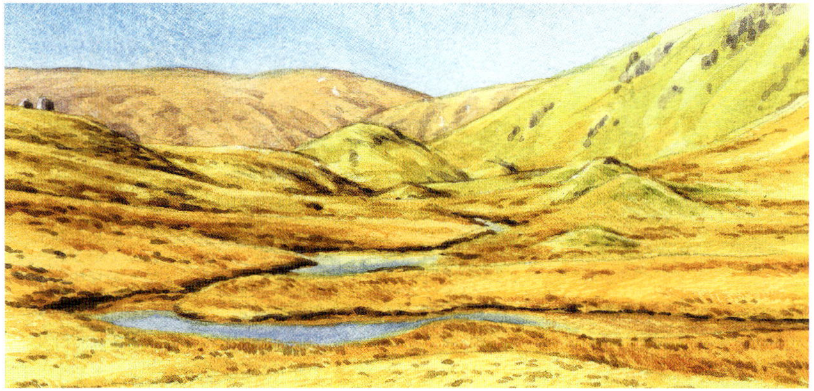

Wythburn Head Tarns 26/3/12
AW omitted the far skyline of High Raise most likely for the sake of simplicity. The two angular boulders on the left were a good reference point for my sketch.

The Wythburn Valley
a study in desolation

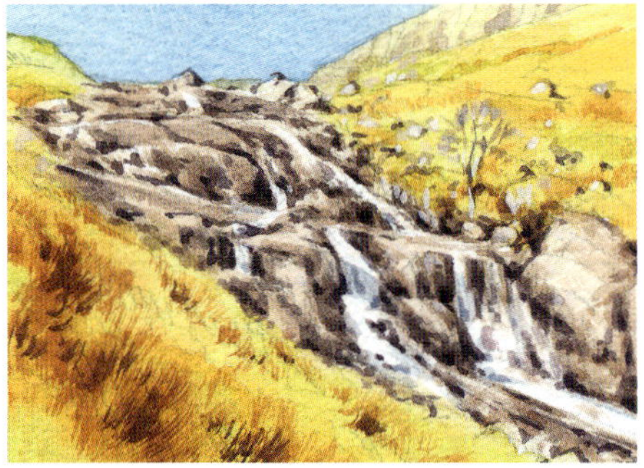

The highest waterfall
26/3/12
The falls were not in full flow on the day of my visit but were impressive none the less. They are located just below the Wythburn Head Tarns.

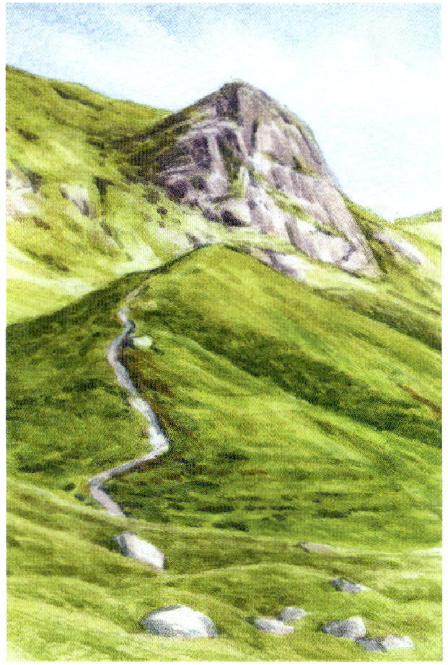

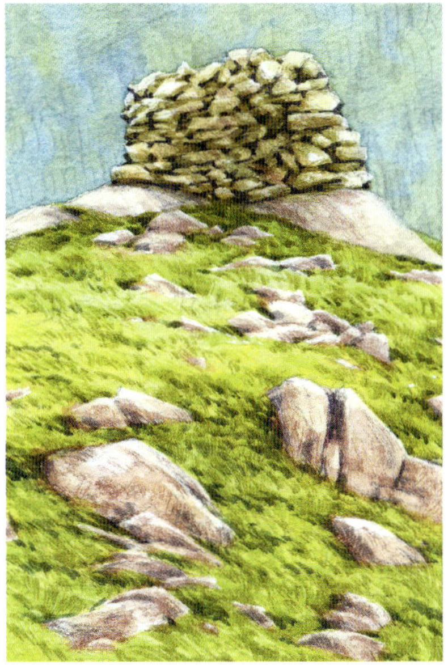

The Beacon, Nab Crags 25/7/12

It is clear from the Pictorial Guide that Wainwright had already made plans for the page layout of Ullscarf 9 and when he learnt of the destruction of The Beacon he was not only upset but it left a space where the drawing would no longer be relevant, so he vented his anger of the Beacon's demise within the frame already allocated for the illustration.

Since publication of the guide The Beacon has been rebuilt (no doubt he would be pleased) and therefore I have taken this opportunity to fill the equivalent gap with a sketch of how The Beacon looks these days. The structure is more like a short section of 6' high wall than a square cairn. By comparing it to the image of Lining Crag on the left it can be visualised as to how perhaps Wainwright's planned page would have had a neatly balanced look.

This is the only instance in the whole of the Wainwrights in Colour project where I have produced a sketch that didn't appear in the seven Pictorial Guides but I felt that this situation warranted the inclusion of The Beacon.

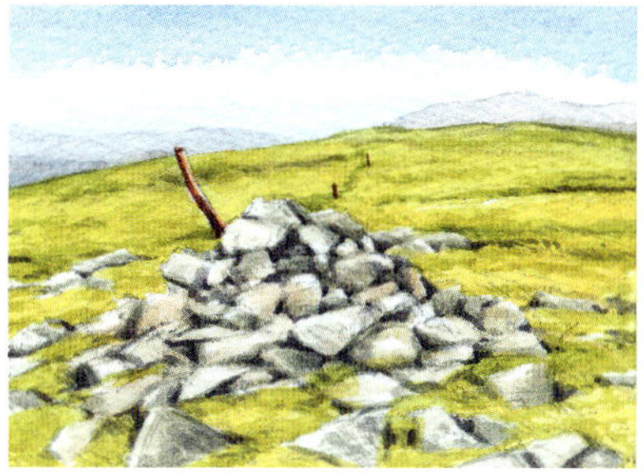

The summit 24/6/09

The drawing by Wainwright is just a simple detail of the cairn with the fence beyond, this meant that it was either looking to the north or south. Only the slight rise in the background indicated that the correct direction would be looking northwards.

Lining Crag, Greenup 24/6/09

The distinct path that rises up alongside the crag is a popular route as it is part of the Coast to Coast walk.

The tarn and point 2081' 24/6/09

A small cairn crowns this rise in the landscape, some distance from the main footpath. It is more likely to be the work of shepherds than passing walkers. This permanent tarn is marked on the map on which it is nameless but I have seen it referred to as Greenup Edge Tarn.

Standing Crag 26/3/12

This is again another sketch where I was looking directly towards the bright sun. The footpath skirts around the crag to the left. The fence stretches across the middle of this, the smallest of the three tarns here. The other two tarns are just over to the right out of view.

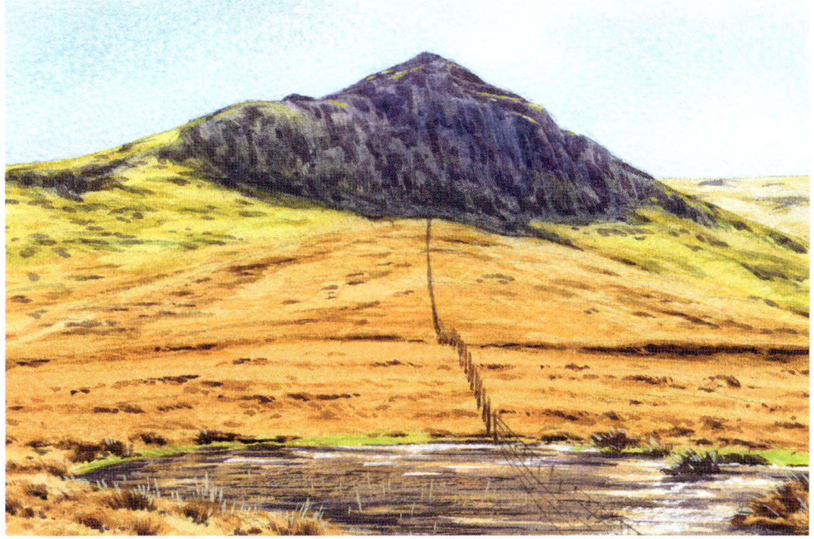

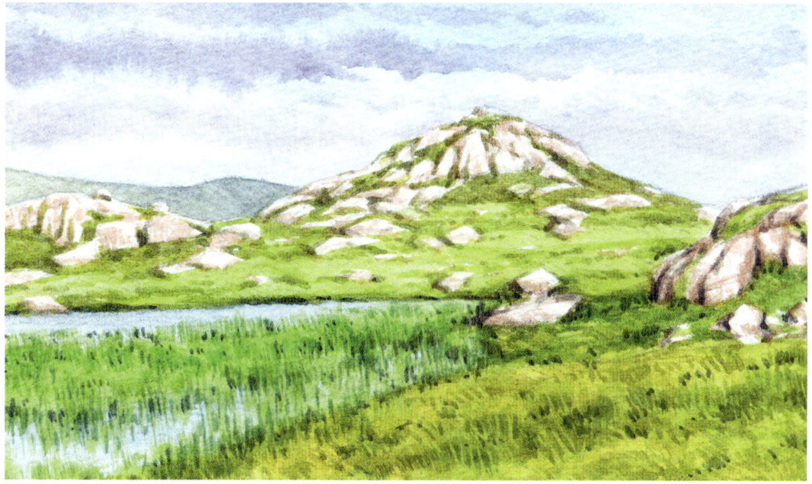

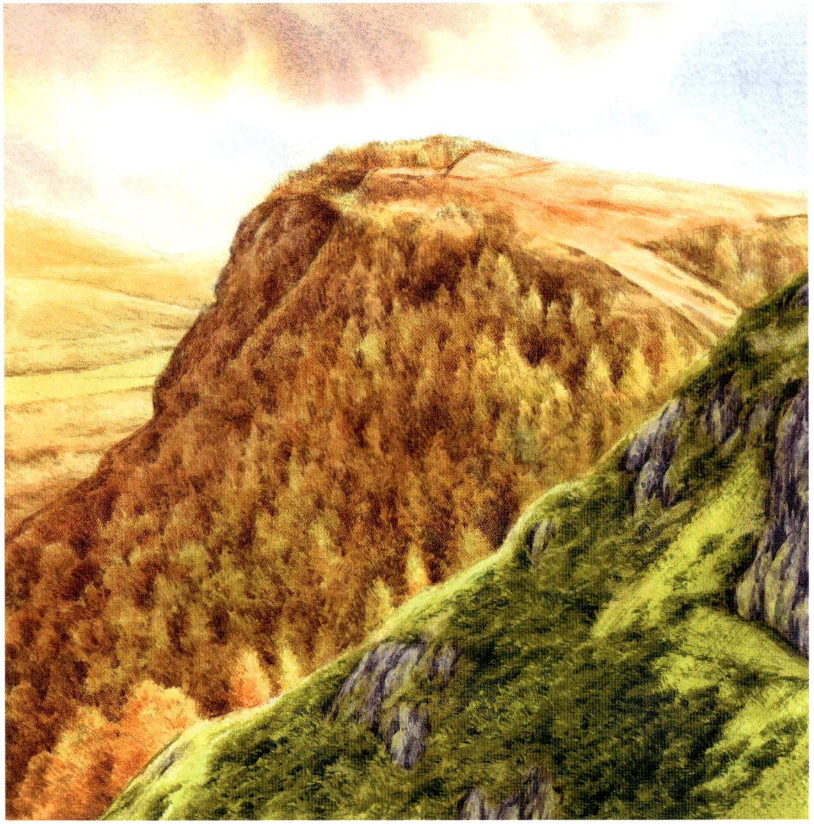

From Falcon Crag 20/4/10
An early start to my day enabled me to be at the required location on Falcon Crag as the morning sun streamed down the ravine of Cat Gill. The scene is relatively unchanged over the years.

Walla Crag
In his Bleaberry Fell chapter Wainwright explains that Walla Crag is more properly part of Bleaberry Fell but he separates them, putting this down to the popularity of the Crag in its own right for visitors to Keswick. Given the choice I would opt for a visit to nearby less frequented Falcon Crag, the views are just as good especially down towards Borrowdale and to the west.

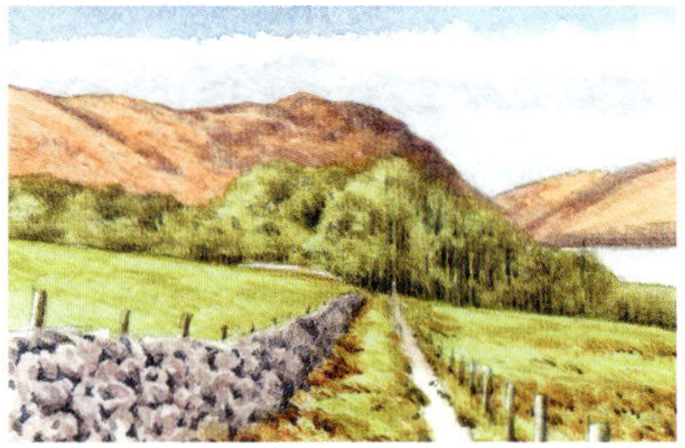

From near Rakefoot 20/4/10
The footpath leads from near the Castlerigg camp site towards Great Wood.

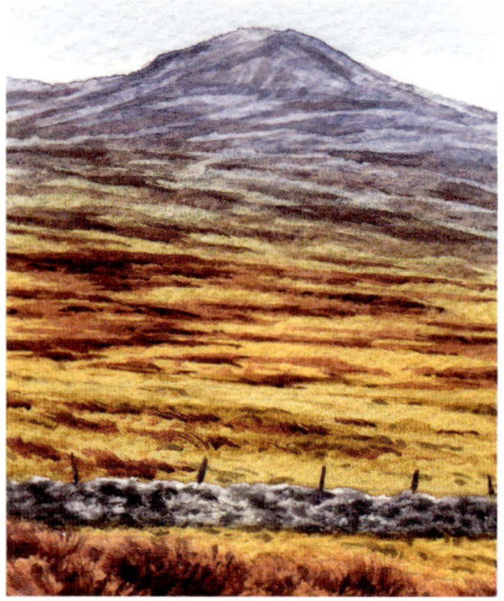

Bleaberry Fell 7/3/10
The scene looking south east from just by the new position of the summit cairn. The route between here and the top of Bleaberry crosses Low Moss which as the name suggests can be rather damp. Recently a new hard path was made, not only easier to walk on but also to prevent further damage to the Moss itself and its delicate flora and fauna.

The summit 20/4/10
The view from this flat bare rock top accounts for the fells popularity as well as the fact that a visit can be achieved in a short walk from Keswick. This aspect depicts the Coledale fells in the north western region. The summit cairn has been moved to a position behind this point.

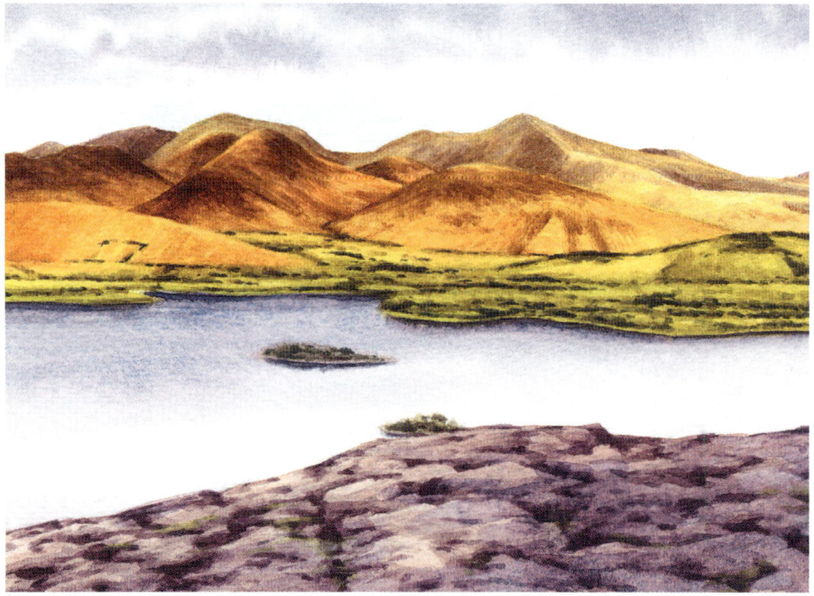

Waterfalls in Cat Gill 20/4/10
The trees in the plantation have now grown to such an extent that a clear view of these falls is almost impossible to achieve.

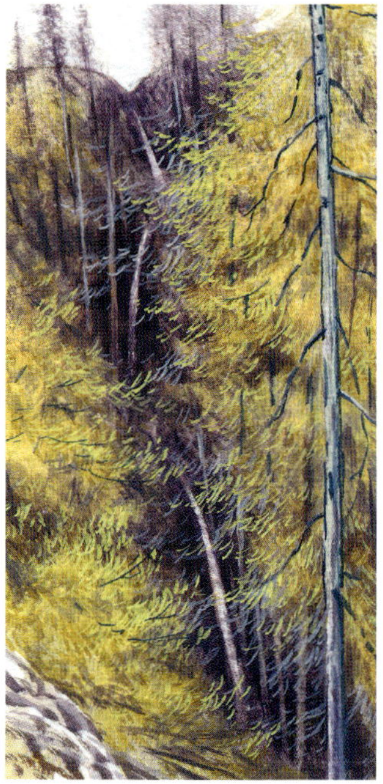

The Southern Fells

Book four in the series features 30 fells including some of the giants both in altitude and popularity. Understandably this meant that the volume was crammed full of detail and in fact space became short so that unusually, some chapters didn't get their own maps and had to share this information with other fells. No doubt that this is the most popular book of the series as within the pages are classic fells such as Scafell Pike, Crinkle Crags, Bowfell and the Coniston Fells, all described with Wainwright's usual attention to detail.

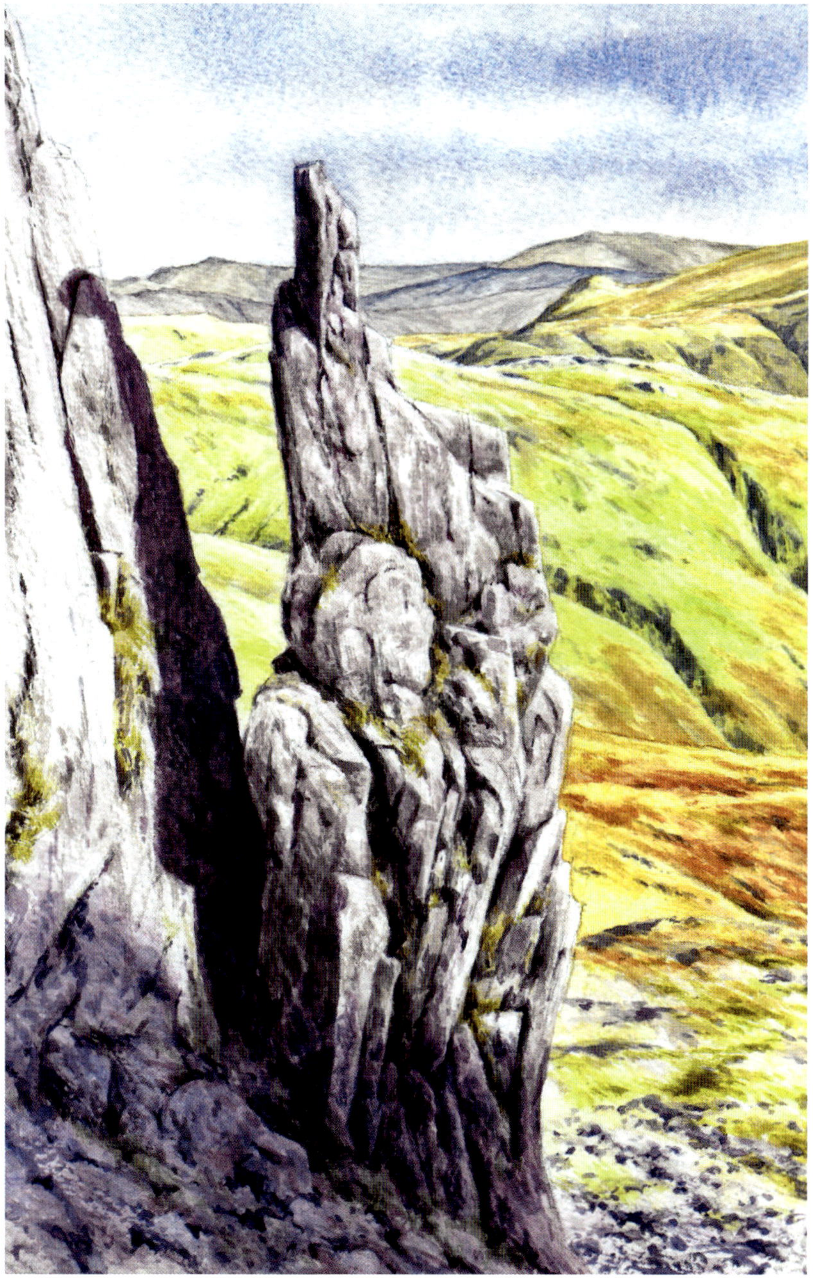

Frontispiece - Gladstone's Finger, Gladstone Knott 3/10/08

In the Victorian era this pinnacle of rock was noted as a tourist attraction but these days very few make the effort to pay it a visit. Locating it wasn't easy, with an early expedition finding me in a very risky position on the crags of Great Cove. To prevent further similar situations I reluctantly resorted to asking Derry Brabbs for information to its precise location as he had photographed it for Wainwright's book, Favourite Lakeland Mountains. I took to approaching Gladstone's Knott from Oxendale and Issac Gill so that from below I could scan the rock face to pinpoint this feature. My efforts paid off and a steep ascent of the scree gully at the Finger's base allowed me to obtain the reference without further serious risk to myself. The Finger stands at about 40' high and it is only from this angle that it appears as a separate pillar of rock. From here a steep climb up the loose scree gully brought me out to the flatter terrain near Great Knott Tarn.

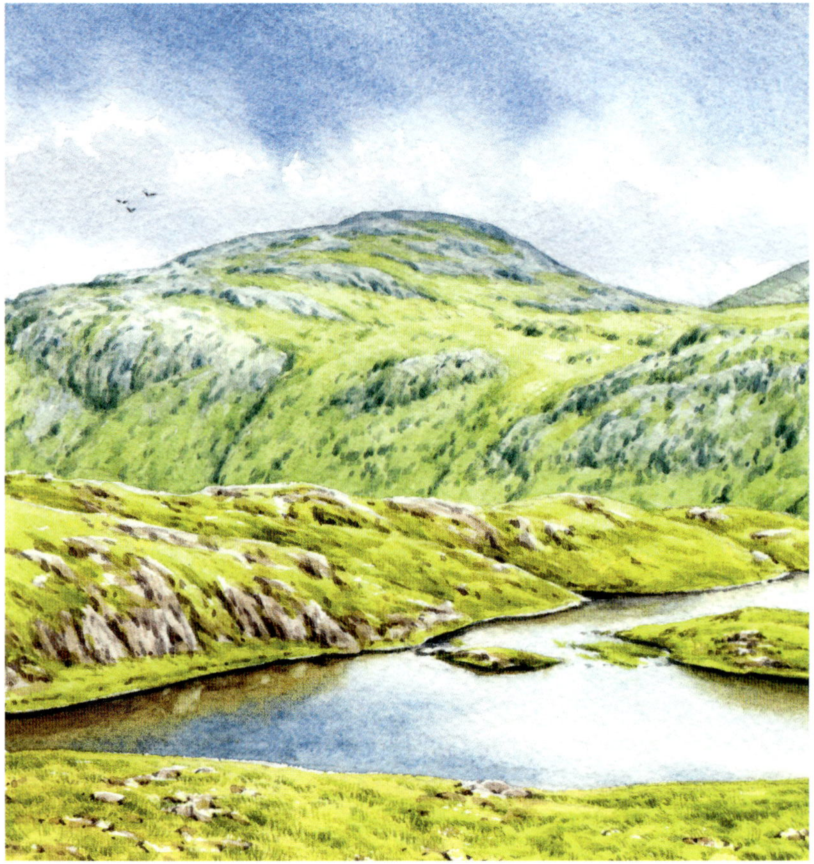

From Sprinkling Tarn 12/6/09

This tarn is located on the Seathwaite Fell ridge and is adjacent to the Langdale to Sty Head path. This view towards Allen Crags is not as impressive as that to the south, that of the near vertical face of Great End.

Allen Crags

Many walkers will have passed by this fell and not given it much attention as they head to the summit of Scafell Pike. Its position just to the south of Esk Hause means that it is not on the main thoroughfare but on a pleasant ridge which also includes Glaramara and Rosthwaite Fell.

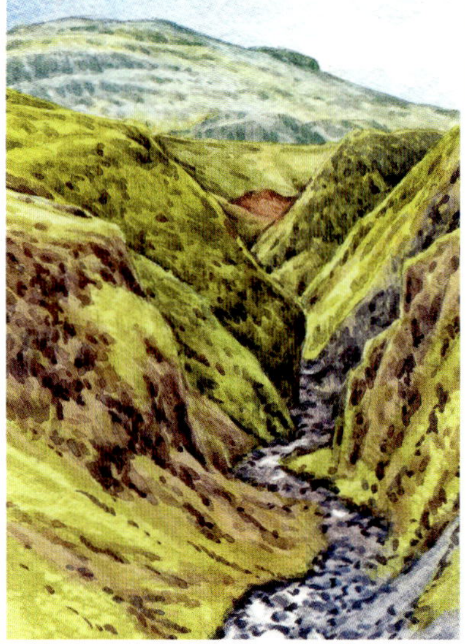

From Ruddy Gill 10/4/11

This view into the gill is obtained from the Sty Head path just at a point where the gill takes a sharp turn and the path from Seathwaite comes in from the north.

Looking northwest 3/10/08

The bulk of Great Gable and other hills in the western fells region form a backdrop over Sprinkling Tarn. As seen from a point to the west of the path from Esk Hause to Allen Crags' summit.

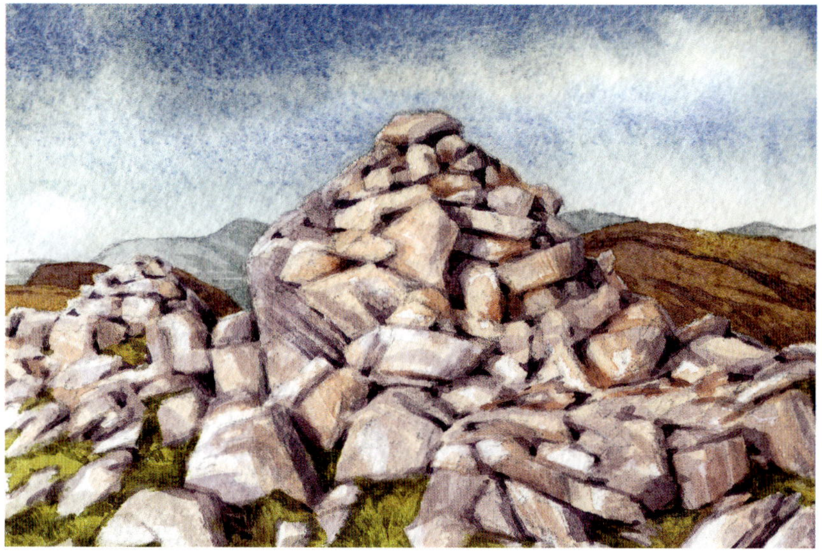

The summit 3/10/18

The very top of the fell is fairly rocky but the highest point has a large block of rock on which is the summit cairn, 10 yards to the north is a smaller cairn. Glaramara summit can be seen over to the right.

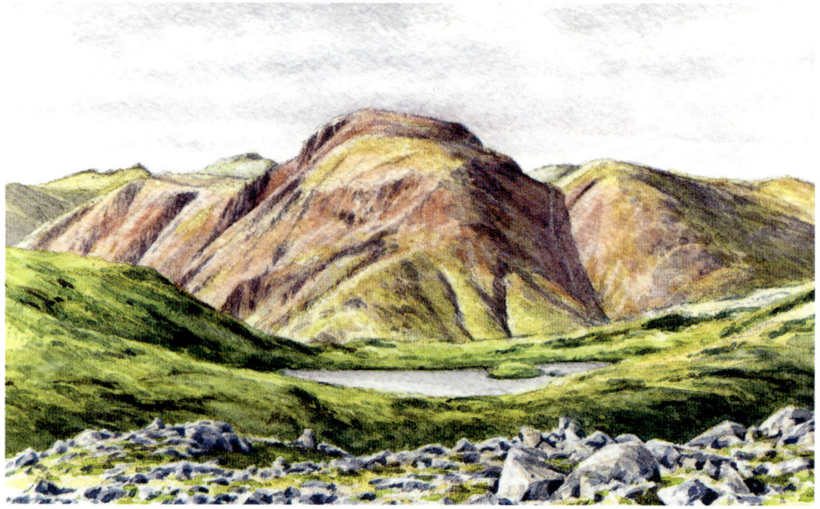

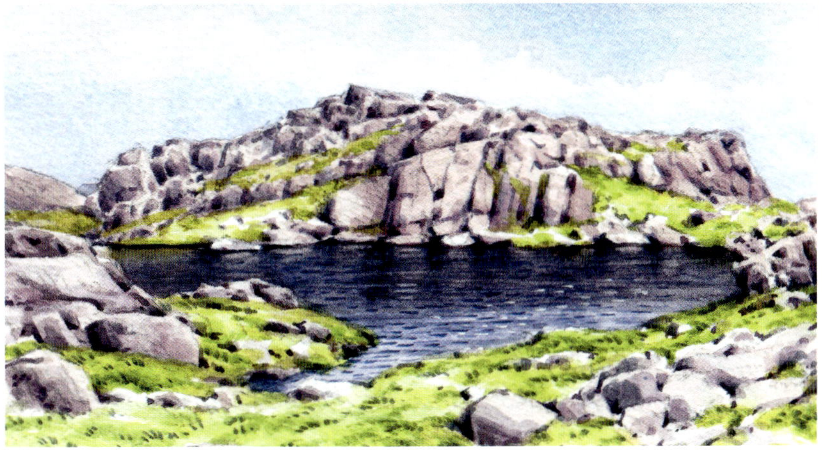

A perfect mountain tarn 12/6/09

The footpath that traverses the ridge between Allen Crags and Glaramara passes by several tarns, some of which are named such as High House Tarn. This one, which AW chose to place in the guide is nameless but he is right, it is a perfect tarn, especially as the rocky outcrop on the far side drops vertically into the water.

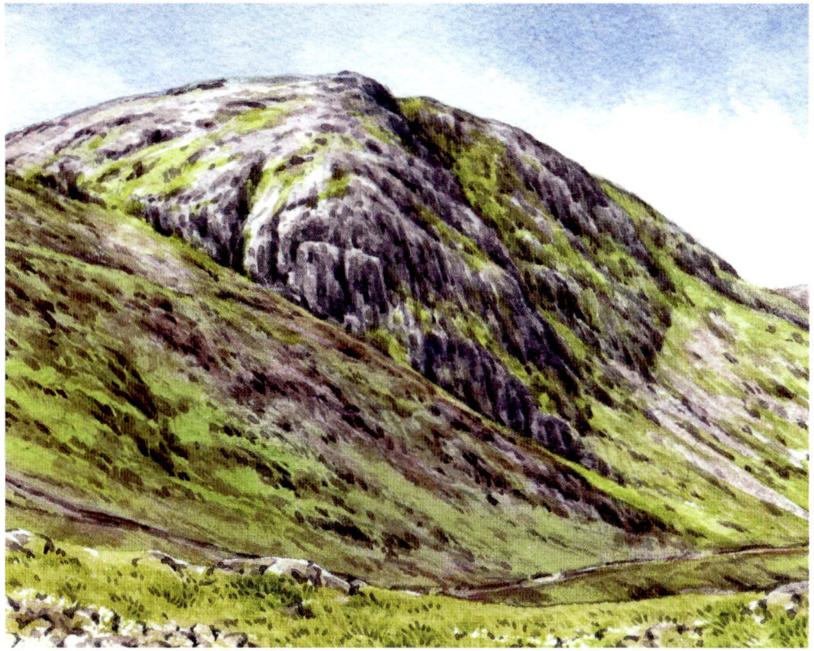

Great End from Allen Crags 12/6/09

This imposing crag towers above the Sty Head path which can be seen at the bottom right. This massive rock face is popular with climbers.

Allen Crags from Grains Gill 10/4/11

The path from Seathwaite to Esk Hause gains height in the valley of Grains Gill. This view is from the open fell after the top gate. The tree in his drawing could not be found and the stream in the foreground was now diverted.

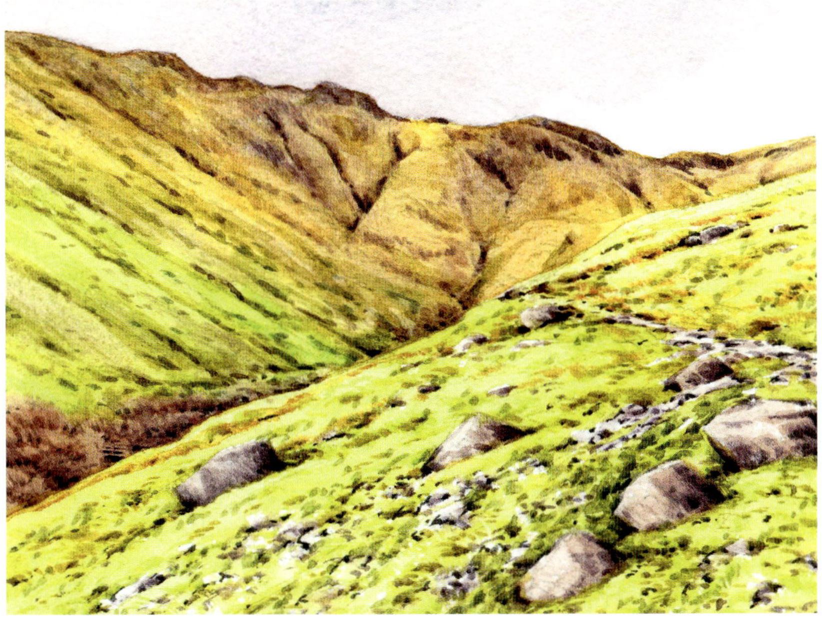

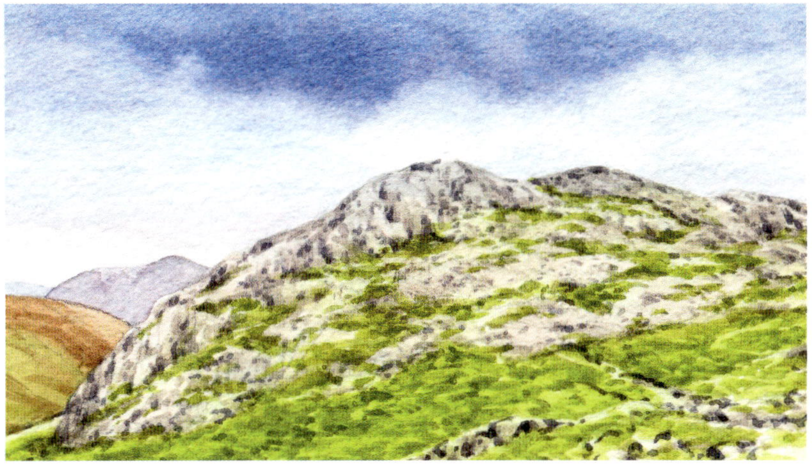

Glaramara 12/6/09

This illustration was used mainly to identify the summits of Glaramara for those using the footpath from Allen Crags. The main summit is the one on the right of the two high points even though it looks lower from here.

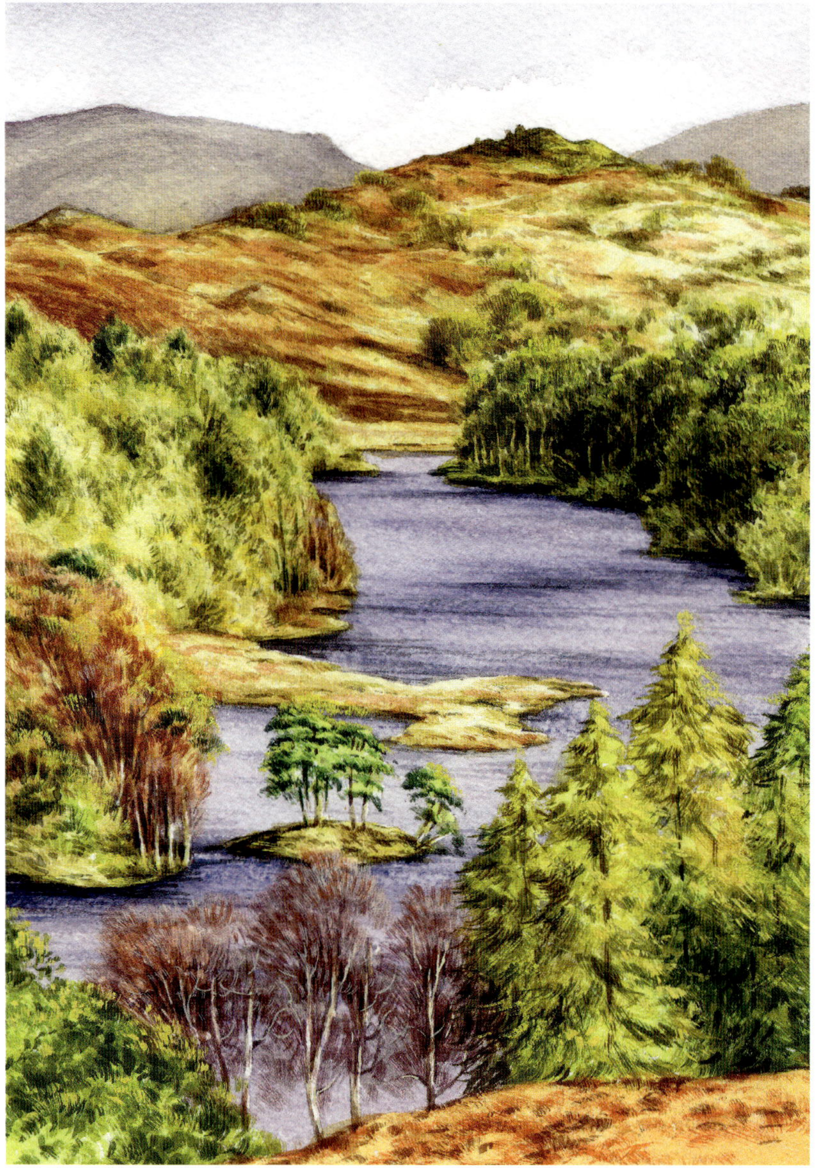

From Tarn Hows 2/9/07
Some trees have gone, some have grown up but the view over the popular tarn towards the fell and those beyond remains relatively unchanged.

Black Fell

Many visitors to the delightful location of Tarn Hows will have a pleasant stroll around the well made paths that encircle The Tarns*. With a little extra planning the route can be extended and the summit of Black Fell can be visited by taking the footpath that passes through Iron Keld Plantation. Weather permitting, the views from there of the distant fells to the north will provide good reward for the effort.

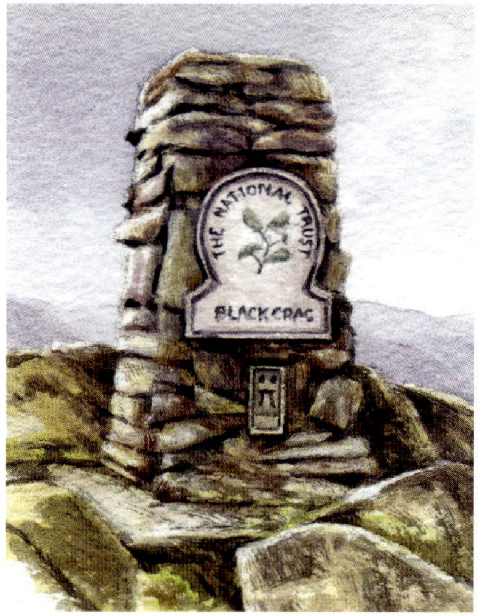

The summit 2/9/07
Fixed to the triangulation pillar is a National Trust plaque with the name Black Crag. This isn't an error, the summit is known by this name whereas the whole fell is known as Black Fell.

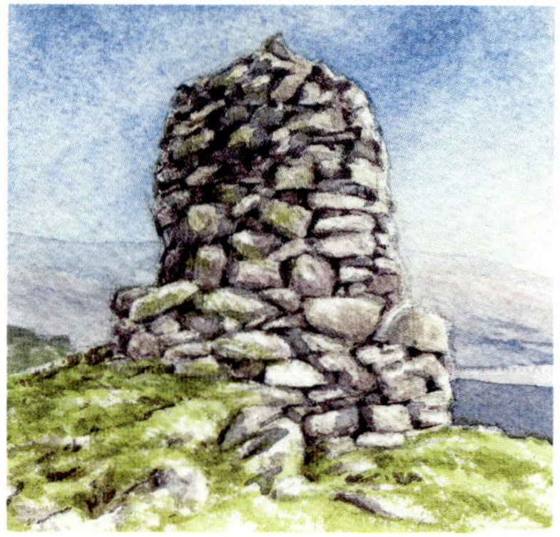

The south-east cairn 2/9/07
In AW's drawing the cairn was in a state of partial collapse. More recently it has been repaired and the lower section has a ledge which forms a seat. The view to the south from here is of Esthwaite Water and the southern reaches of Windermere.

*The Tarns

The name on the current Ordnance Survey maps "The Tarns" is confusing as there is actually just one tarn. However, originally at this site were three tarns, High Tarn , Middle Tarn and Low Tarn. In the late 1800s the landowners, the Marshall family, had some of the area landscaped which included the construction of a small dam at Low Tarn, this resulted in the raising of the water levels which consequently made three tarns into one. In 1930 the land was bought by Beatrix Heelis (Beatrix Potter) and from there it came under the ownership of The National Trust. Tarn Hows is the name given to the area of land around The Tarns.

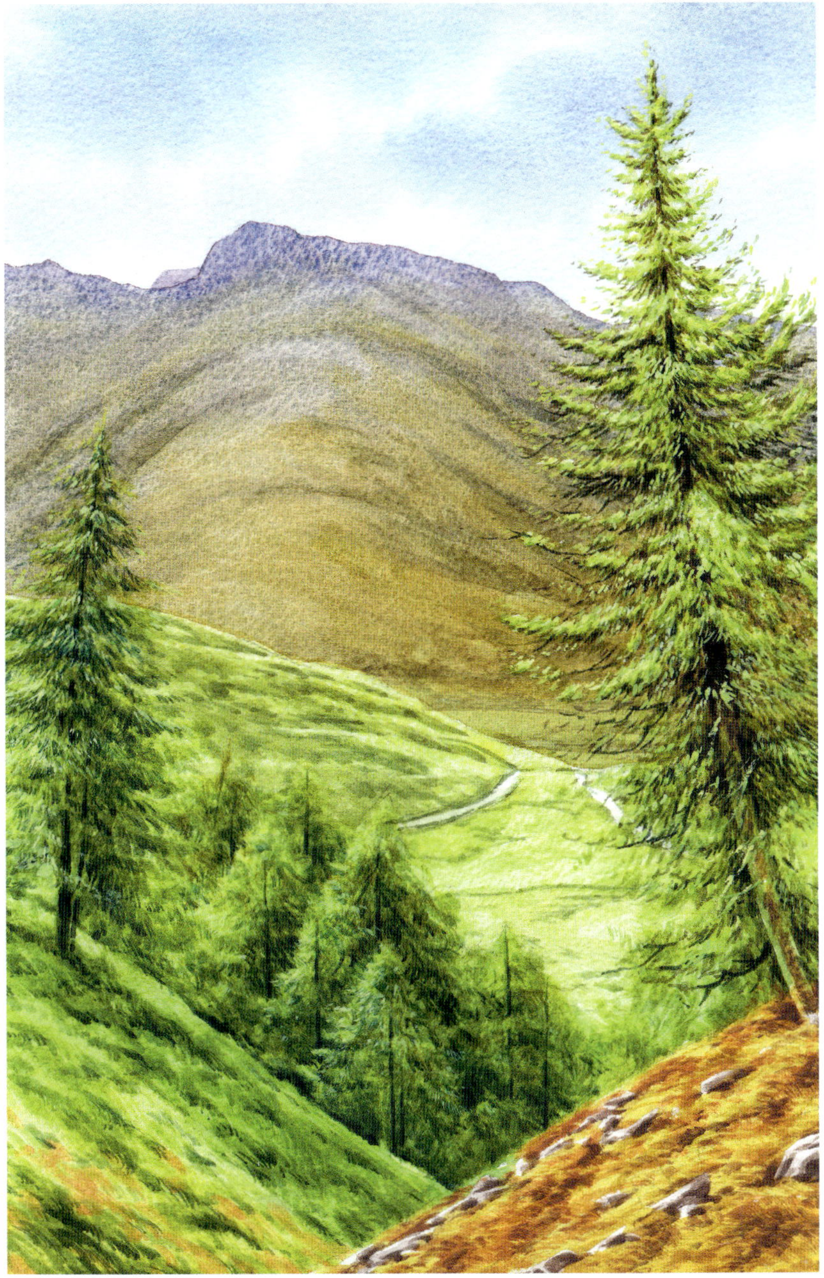

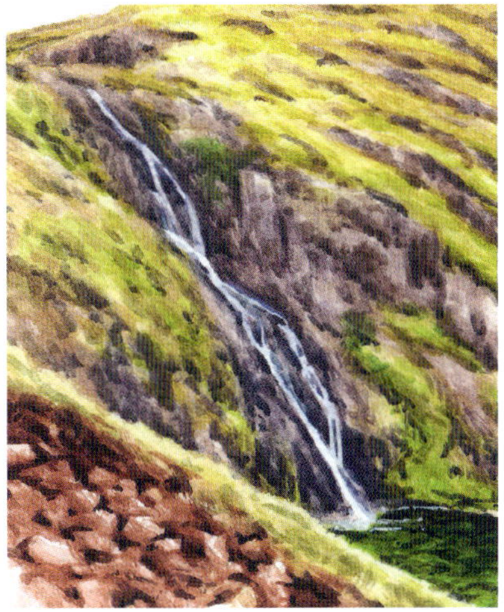

Whorneyside Force 23/9/08
A long waterslide into a clear pool. The ground where I stood had suffered recent landslides and the path in some sections was gone.

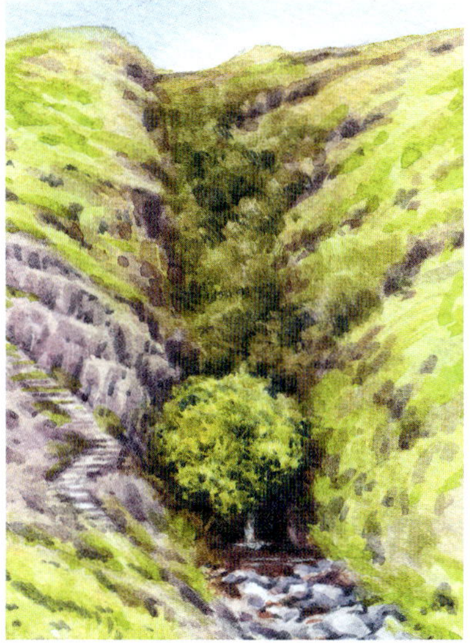

Hell Gill 24/7/11
The trees now obscure most of the falls. The footpath up to the left has been repaired and pitched.

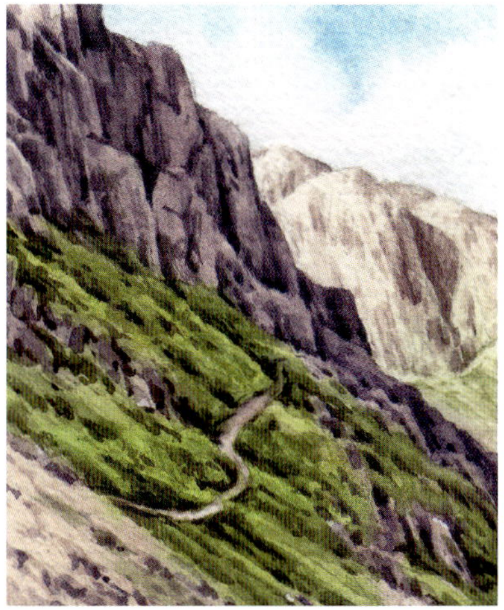

The climbers traverse 3/10/08
This narrow path passes over steep ground in places. Seen here from near The Band, the first section had been covered by a landslip.

Bowfell

The fact that Wainwright put this fell in his list of the top six is justified, it is a mountain as a mountain should be, full of character and interest. Bowfell is positioned centrally in a group of other Lakeland giants. Now named on O.S. maps as Bow Fell, the one word name Bowfell that AW used, was popular in the late 18th to mid 19th century period.

From Lingmoor Fell 29/5/11
The view that AW chose to illustrate Bowfell is taken from the gully that leads up from Bleatarn House to Lingmoor summit. Thankfully, even now the trees do not obscure the full scene.

Crinkle Crags 8/7/09
The Three Tarns in the col are still there, the one on the left is prone to change though, sometimes full and close to the original shape or sometimes, like here, almost empty.

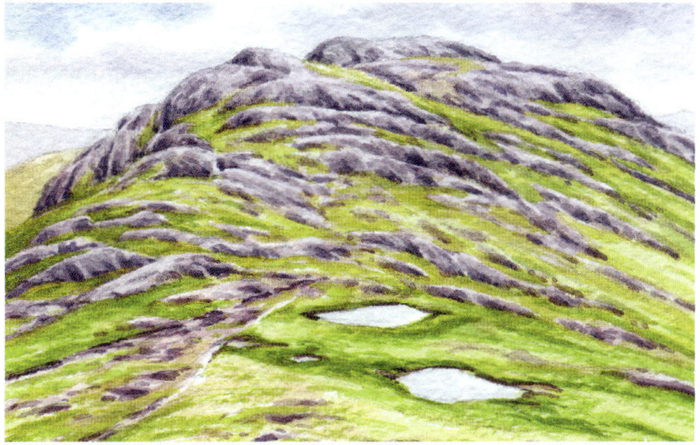

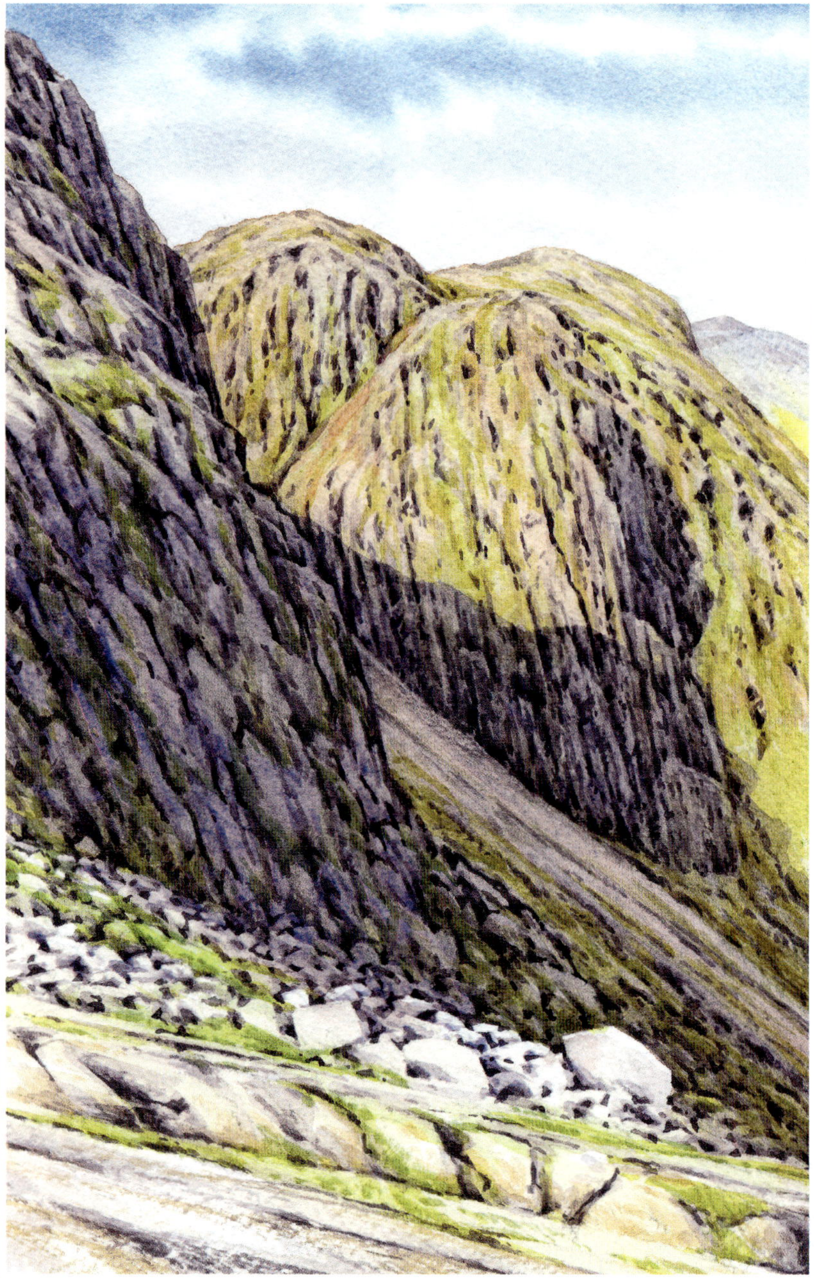

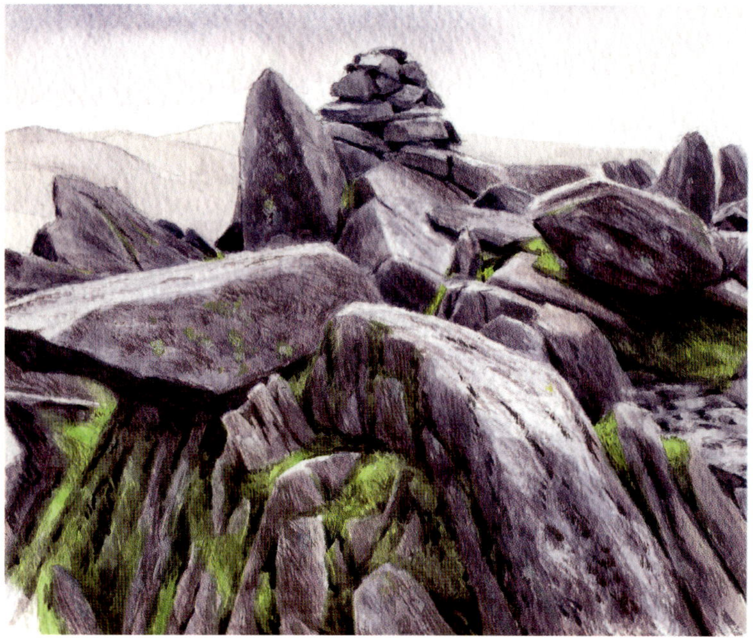

The summit 3/10/08
Even though background detail was lacking in his drawing it was fairly easy to match the required angle of view for this sketch as the majority of rocks matched AW's illustration, all that is bar one, the big chunk on the left lying flat. At about the size of a kitchen table this weighty slab just wasn't there in Wainwright's day. It did however show signs of being at some time shattered from an outcrop several feet out of the picture to the left. My only conclusion from evidence hereabouts is that a lightning strike must have hit this pointed rock and blasted it to the place where it now rests. Well, that is my theory.

Cambridge Crag and Bowfell Buttress 8/7/09
Standing on the broad, regular surface of the Great Slab this is a grand place to view the impressive crag of Bowfell Buttress. The boulder field in the mid-distance still supports the large single rock shown in the bottom right of Wainwright's drawing which made a good reference point for my sketch.

Three views from The Band

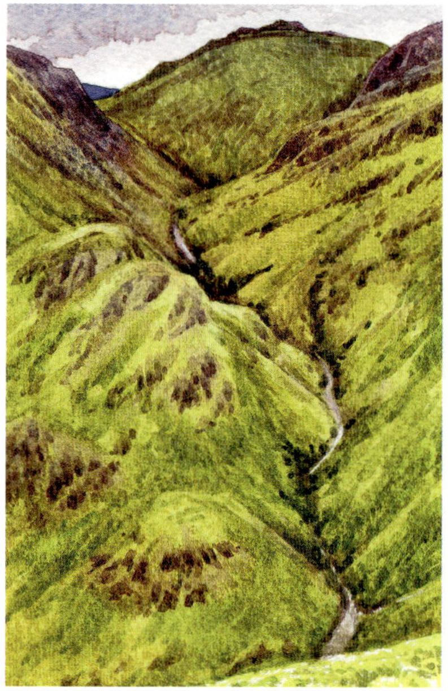

Browney Gill and Cold Pike
8/7/09
As seen from below White Stones.

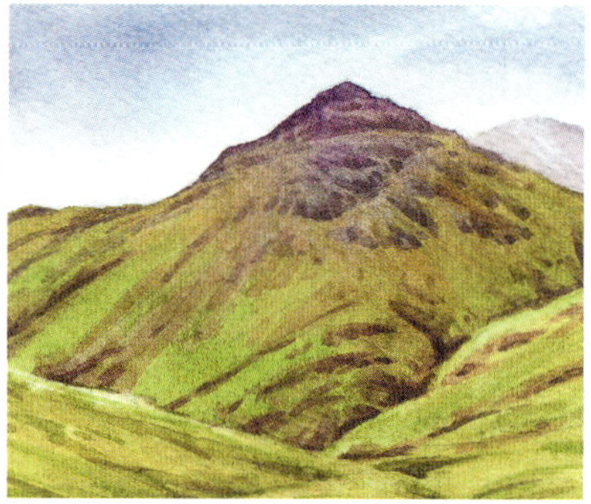

Pike o' Blisco 8/7/09
This view is from above Buscoe Sike near the top of The Band.

Pike o' Stickle 8/7/09

Wainwright squeezed this subject on to the page and thus enhanced its drama. Viewed from The Band just above the intake walls.

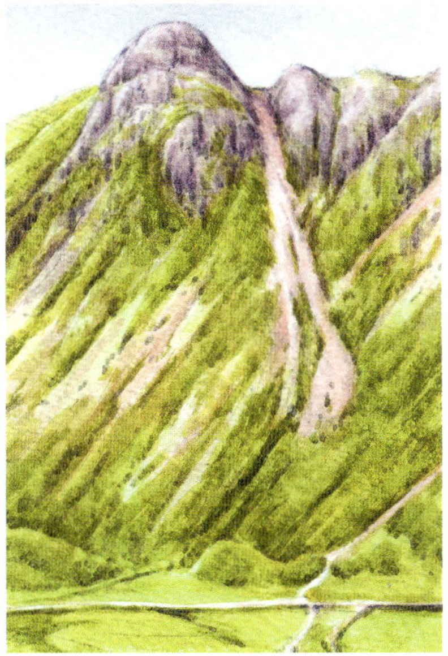

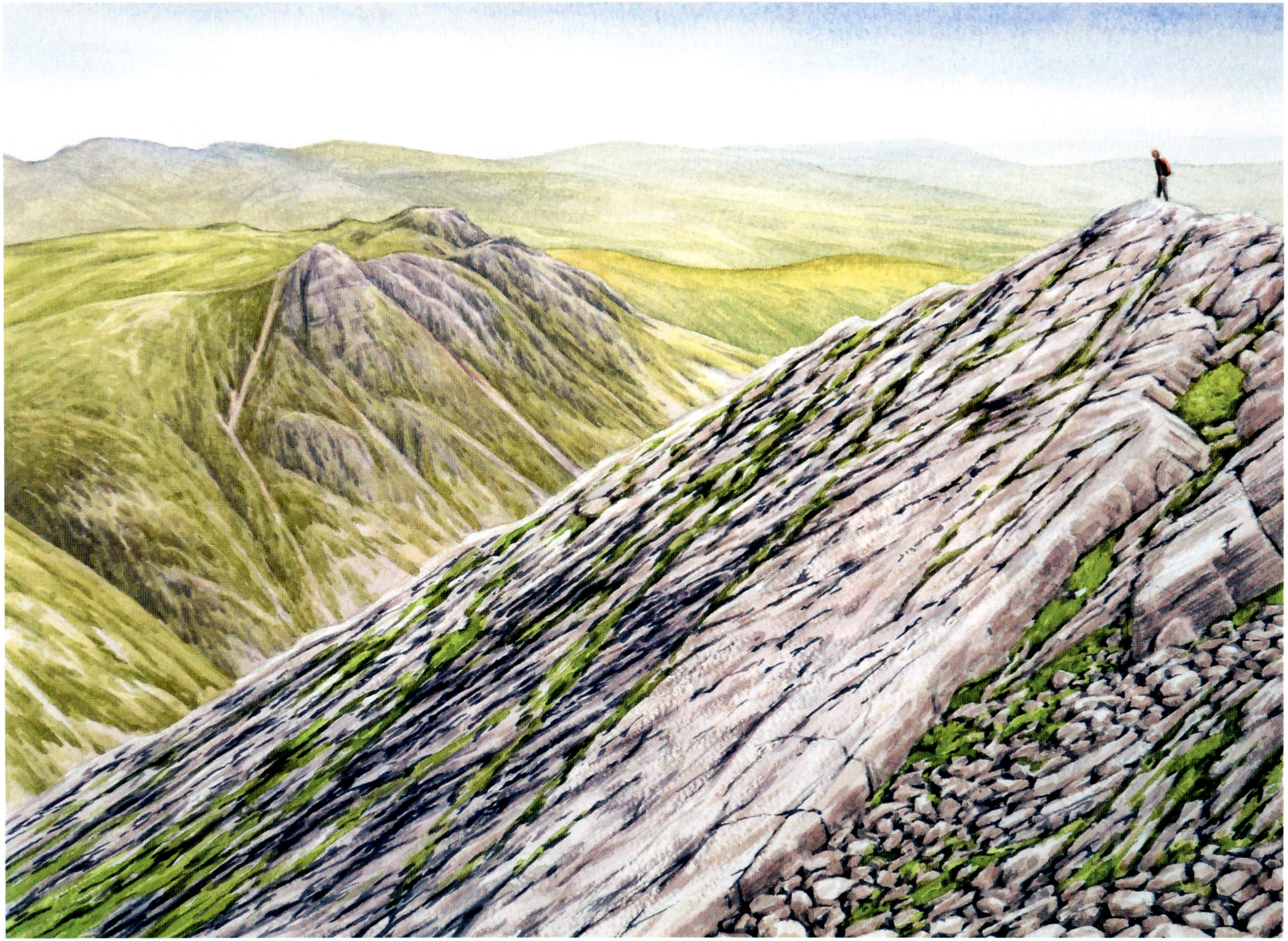

The Great Slab of Flat Crags

3/10/08

AW chose to draw this feature in all its glory in a double page spread, one of only three in all of the Pictorial Guides, complete with a walker for scale. I was able to persuade someone whom I had just met whilst ascending from the climbers traverse to go and pose in place as no doubt many others have done to emulate AW's drawing. I have included the full background of the Fairfield range in the distance.

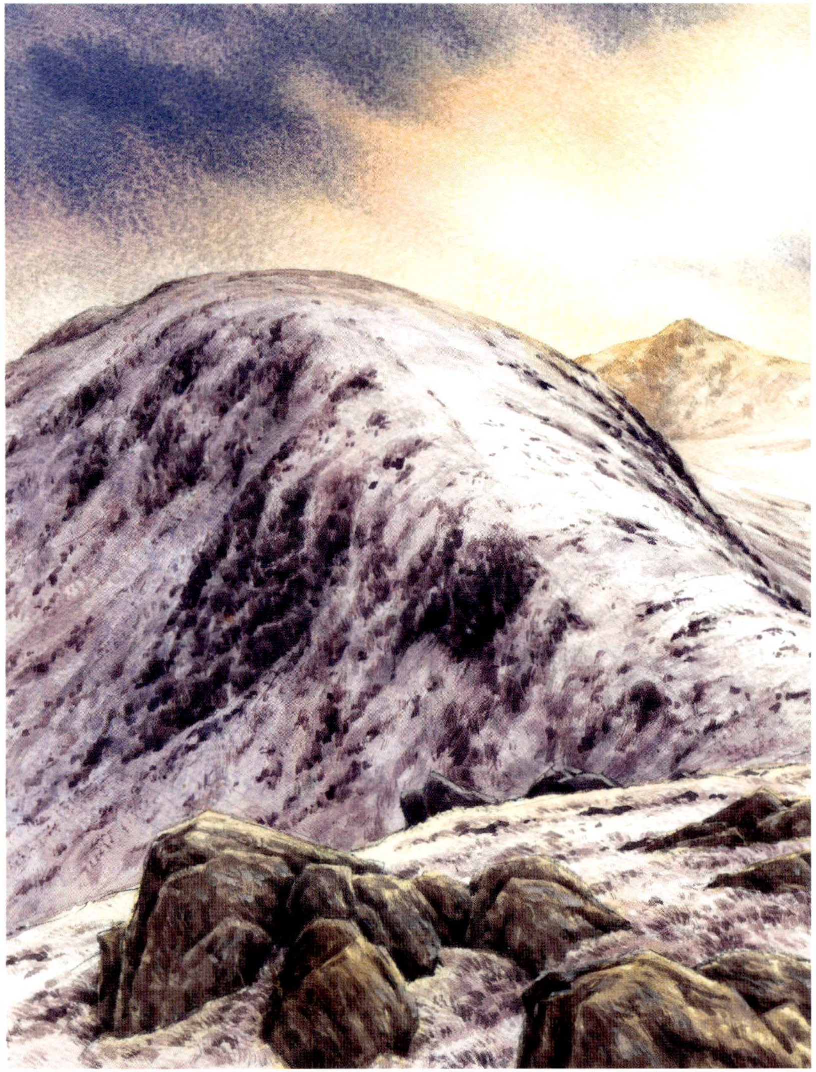

From Little How Crags 1/12/08
The breadth of the fell was narrowed by Wainwright which accentuated its drama. He also tweaked Coniston Old Man on the left and Dow Crag on the right to make them more obvious to the reader of the guide. This reference, along with others were obtained on a bitterly cold but beautiful day when the Coniston Fells were practically deserted.

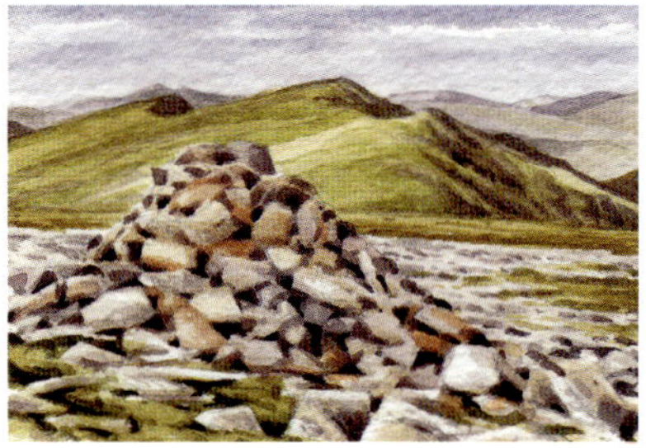

The north-east cairn 3/9/07
This pile of rocks stands a short distance from the main cairn and this is the view to the north.

Brim Fell

To free up space in Book Four AW could easily have omitted Brim Fell, he admits it is just a long ridge and his maps of Coniston Old Man and Swirl How almost meet so the ground could have been covered in those chapters. This is an example of AW taking the measured height of 2611' off the Bartholomew 1 inch map even though his 2½ inch O.S map indicated a height of 2597'. He visited the fell on 27th July 1958.

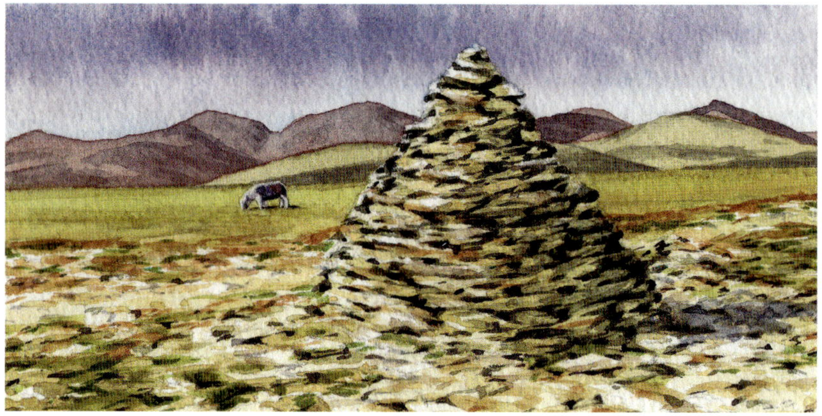

The summit 3/9/07
The cairn has been restored to this fine conical shape. Remarkably a Herdwick was grazing in the same place as AW had drawn a lone sheep.

Simon's Nick 1/12/08
The old mine level on the right is slowly being reclaimed by nature.

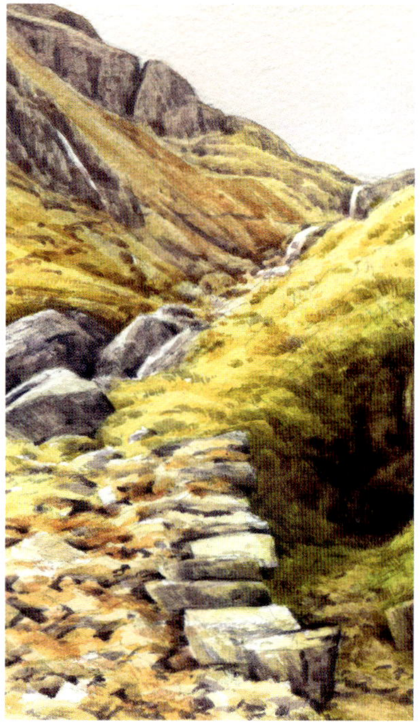

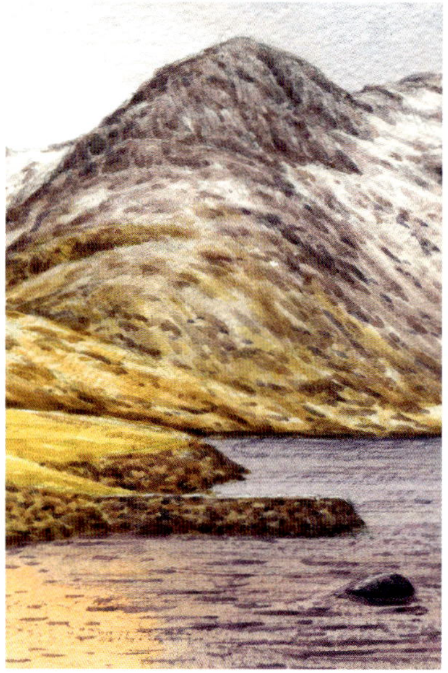

Raven Tor 1/12/08
The water level of Levers Water were much higher on my visit in comparison to the day of Wainwright's drawing.

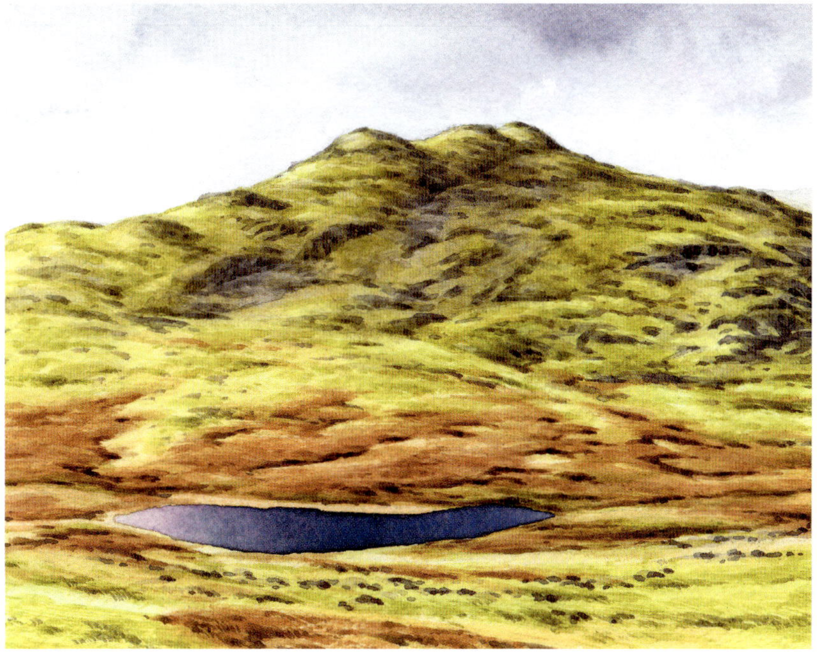

Cold Pike

Using the path that leads from Wrynose Pass summit to the top of Cold Pike is perhaps one of the easiest ways to gain a summit over 2000' in the district (Red Screes from Kirkstone Pass is shorter but steeper). For such little effort the rewards can be quite high, in the right weather conditions of course. There are fine views of some nearby southern fells as well as many of the eastern and far eastern hills at a distance. It is one of the quieter fells in the southern region.

From Pike o' Blisco 23/9/08
Red Tarn lies in the valley between the two fells. This view is from a location down from Pike o' Blisco's summit near Black Wars.

The summit 23/9/08
The size of the cairn is limited in size by the rock base on which it sits. From here on a clear day the multiple tops of Crinkle Crags and Bowfell are easy to appreciate.

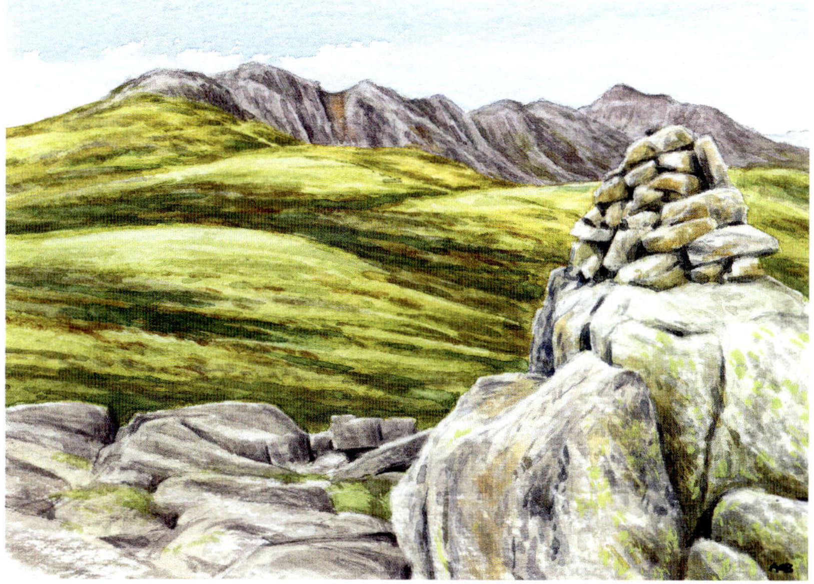

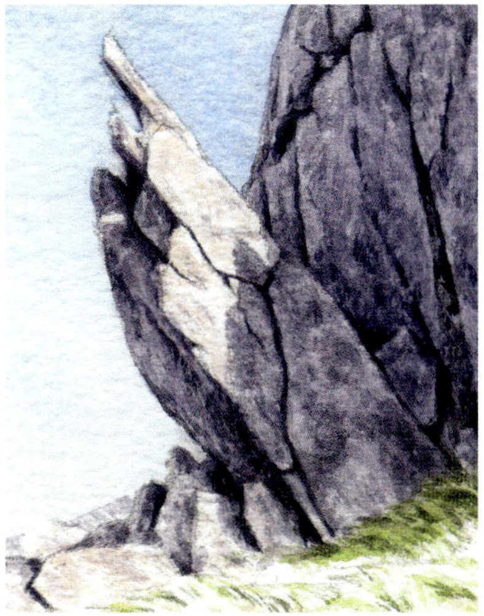

Cold Pike Tooth 23/9/08
Locating this large slab of rock that has come adrift from the crag isn't difficult especially as AW marks it in one of his drawings. It is worth finding though just to say you have been there and seen it for yourself.

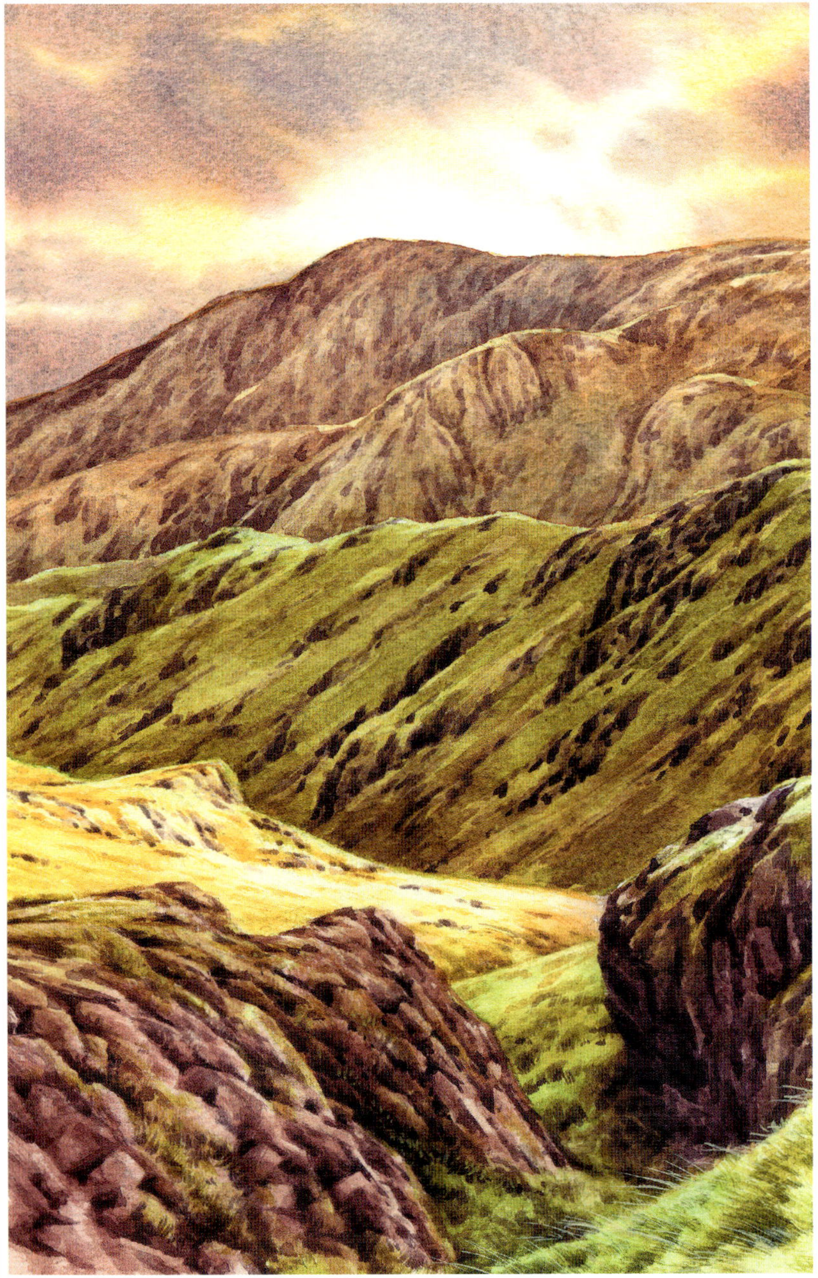

From Red Dell Head 3/9/07

Patches of late afternoon sun were illuminating the fell sides as we descended this indistinct path to the Coppermines Valley.

Coniston Old Man

Visitors to the quiet village of Coniston can't help but notice the large mountain that rises up above the streets and buildings. This is Coniston Old Man (also known as The Old Man of Coniston), a fell which has provided the local population with good income over the years either from tourism or from the industry of quarrying and mining which is now greatly reduced.

Waterfalls Church Beck 10/11/10

This series of falls is below the Miners Bridge adjacent to the road.

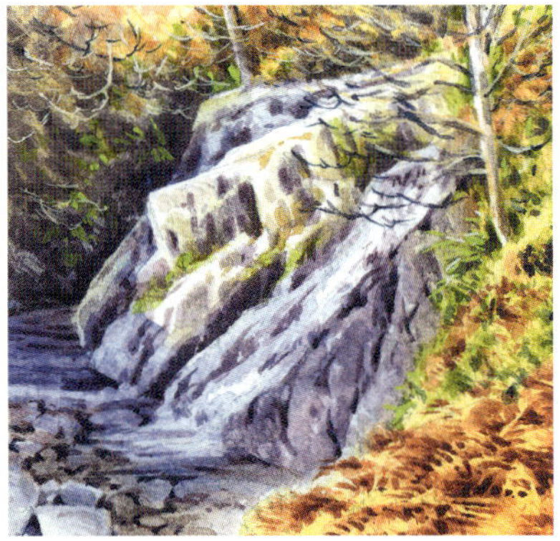

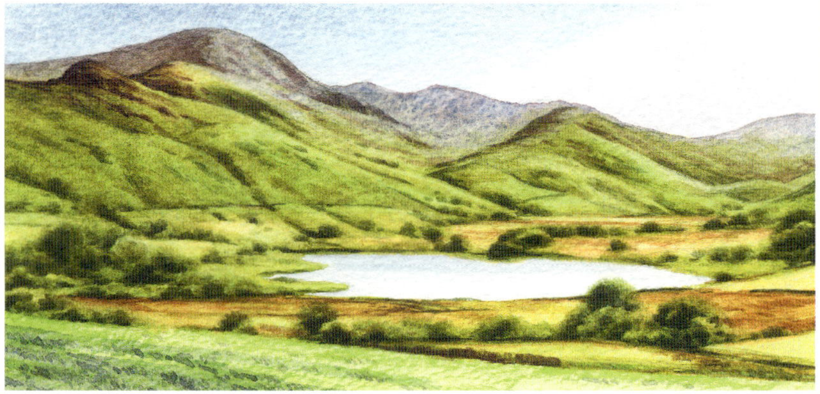

The northern Coniston Fells 2/8/09

As seen from near Little Langdale Tarn with Wetherlam on the left.

The Old Man from Low Water 10/11/10

An almost monochrome scene on this winter's day.

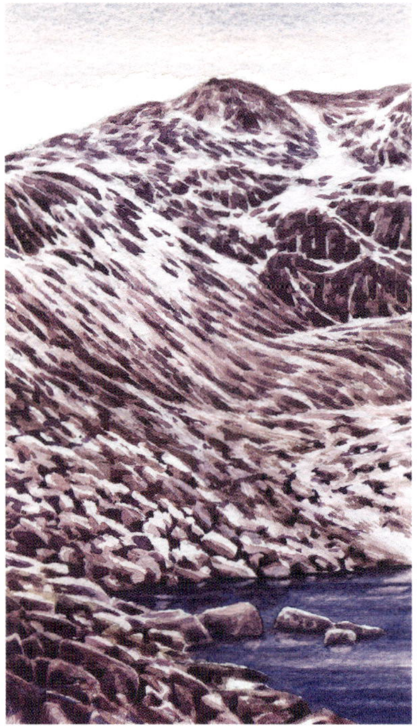

Charmer's Grave 30/1/09

This memorial stone is for a faithful hound who fell to her death off Dow Crag in late March 1911. Some of the engraved name and date can still be seen. It has suffered some damage over the years having been cast into the nearby stream at least once before being recovered and re-sited.

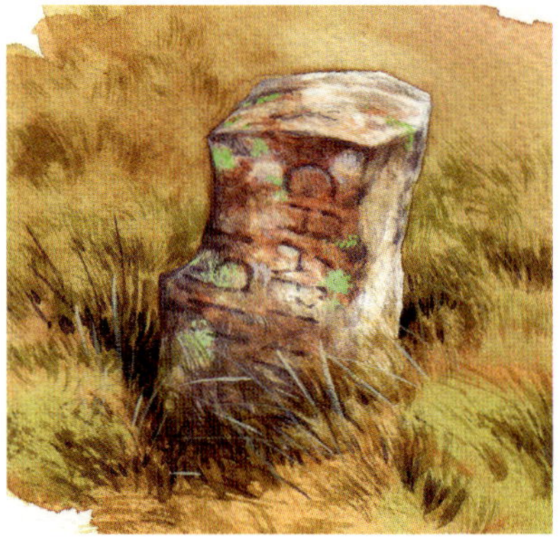

Boulder Valley 10/11/10

Aligning the large stones in this scene took a bit of detective work as this area has many such rocks, hence the name. Low Water Beck is in the foreground.

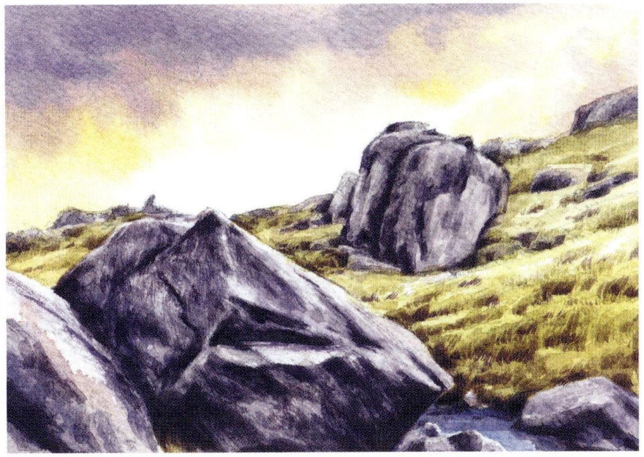

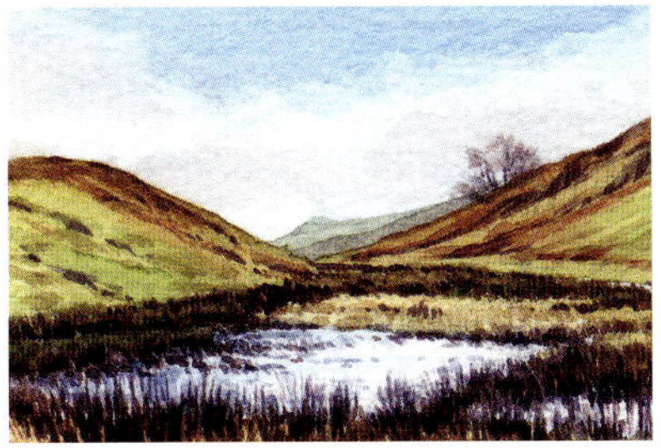

Boo Tarn 30/1/09

The tarn is still a pool of water but now very overgrown.

The Cave, Bursting Stone Quarry 30/1/09

The re-opening of the quarry for the extraction of slate has meant that the cave has been covered by the spoil heap. The small stream emitting from the pile was a clue to its possible location.

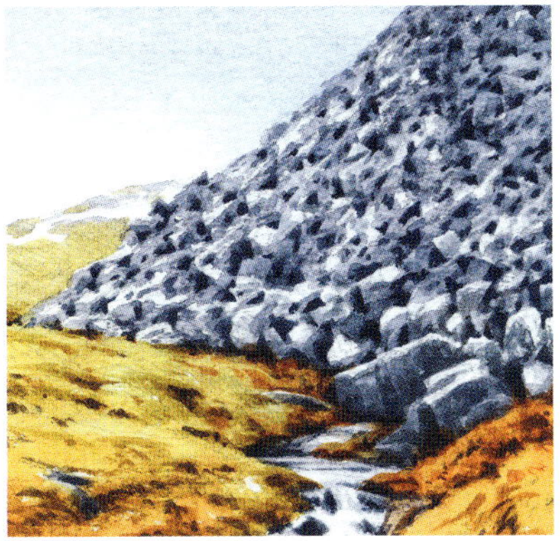

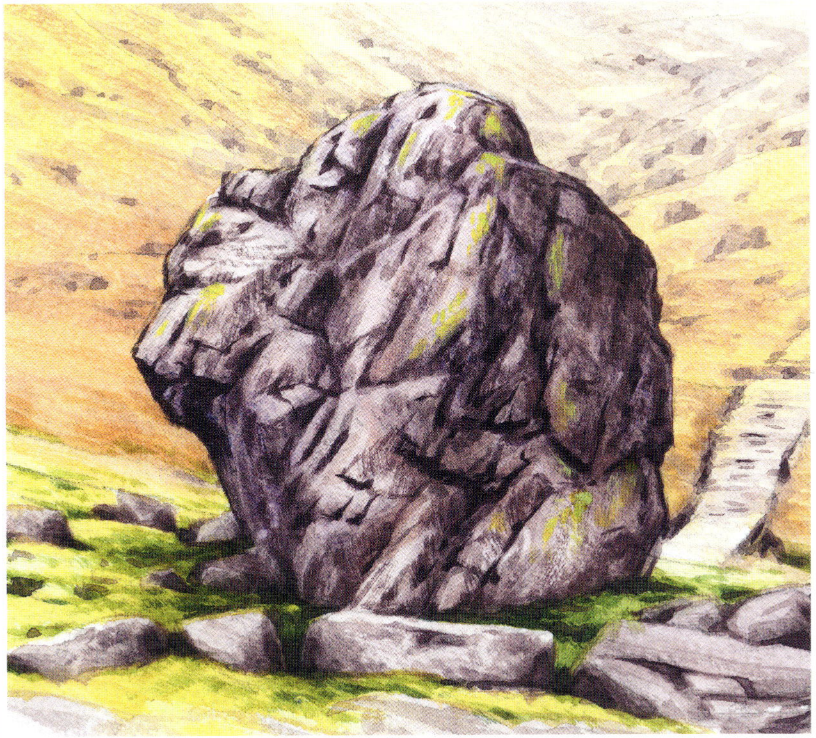

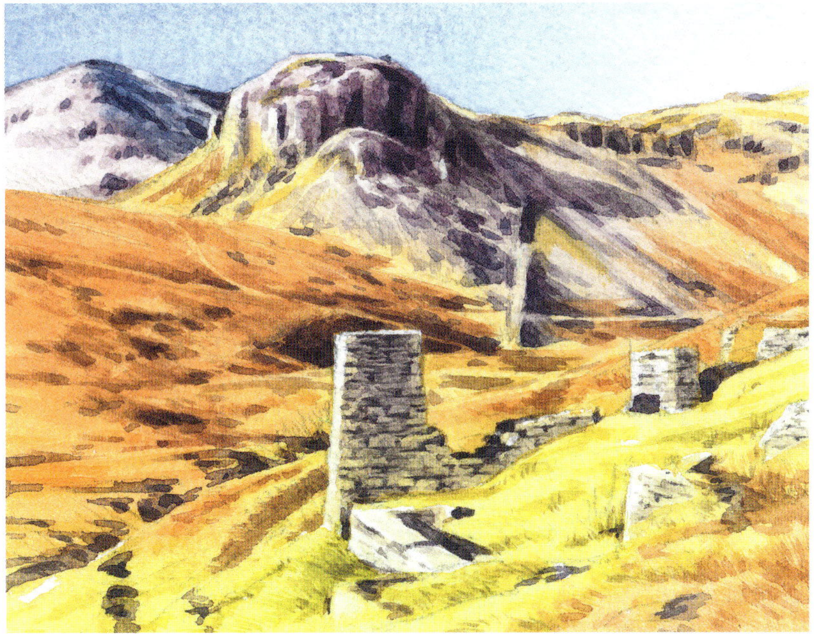

Coppermines Valley 10/11/10

The valley is covered with sites of old working such as this. Exploration of the remaining fragments of this industry is fascinating but take care, many of the shafts and workings are open and dangerous. Coniston Old Man summit is in the distance to the left of Kennel Crag.

The Pudding Stone 1/12/08

Finding this named stone in Boulder Valley was not too difficult, not only because AW marks it on the map but mainly due to its size. More of a challenge was to locate the other scene (above centre) as there was no sense of scale in that diagram. It took me more than one visit and several hours of comparing many rocks and angles before I found the right location. It was with some frustration that I realised that the solution was simple, the round boulder on the right was in fact The Pudding Stone but from the other side. Of course it's easy once you know the answer.

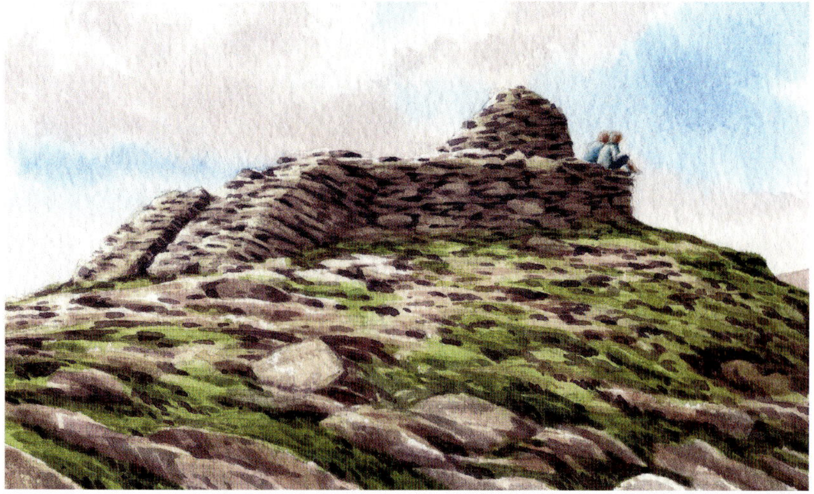

The summit 3/9/07

On this visit there was just me, the dogs and these two walkers who were sitting in the sun and looking to the hills to the north. As in Wainwright's day, this is a very popular top so don't expect it to be quiet for long. The cairn is now a broader structure and has been moved slightly to the left on the large stone built platform.

The summit from the north 1/12/08

The summit platform and the triangulation pillar seen from the path that passes close to the rim of the fell above Low Water.

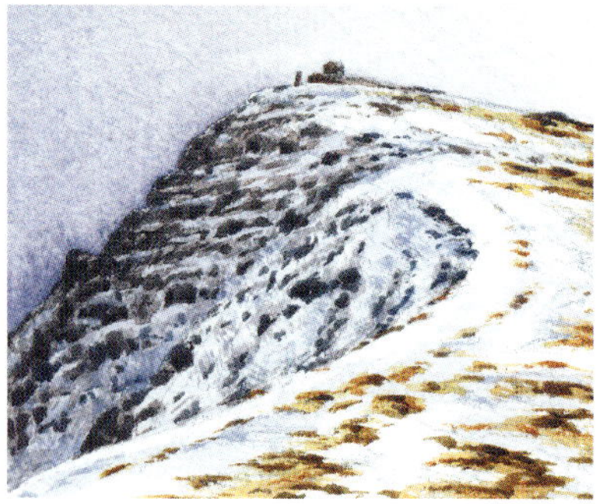

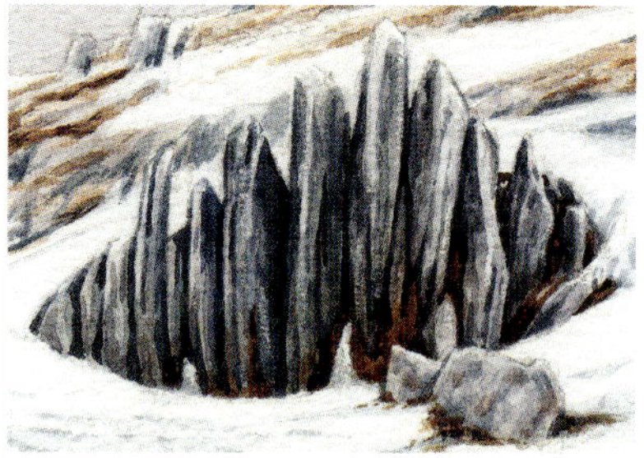

Typical rock formations 30/1/09

Examples of these plates of rock protruding from the turf are to be found near the summit. The driven snow didn't help my quest to find the exact ones but these were as close as I could find.

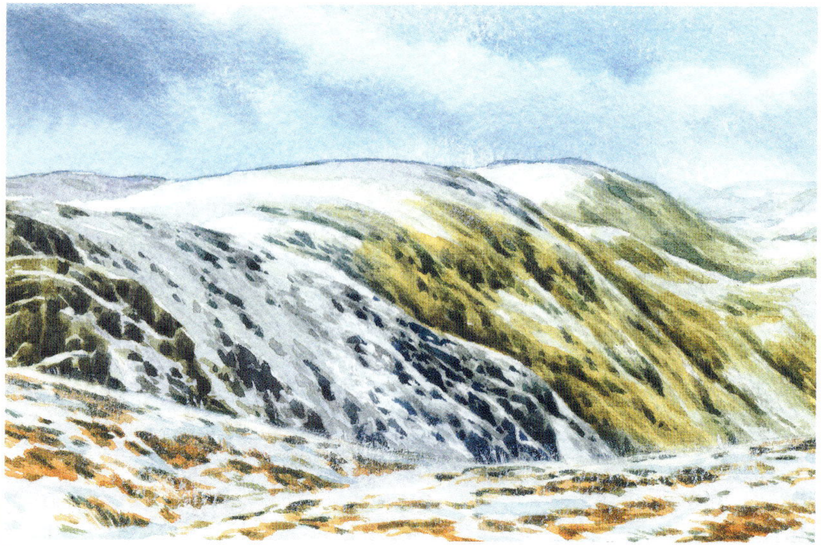

Looking north along the ridge 1/12/08

My route for this winter's day walk was planned with this scene in mind so that I could produce a similar seasonal version of AW's drawing in the guide book. A strong wind blew the fresh snow across the landscape.

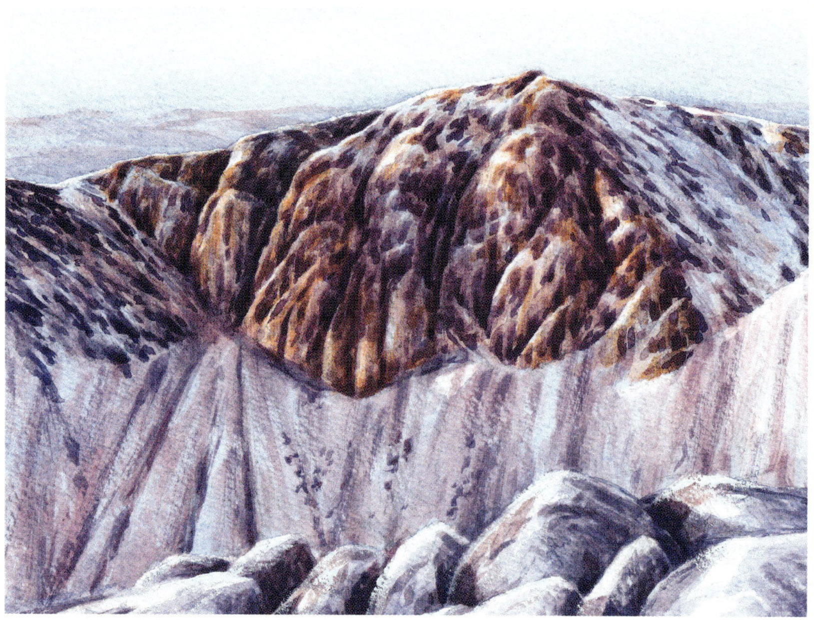

Dow Crag from the Old Man 1/12/08

With the dusting of snow and the low side light which accentuates the buttresses and gullies I opted to paint this winter version over a more plain late summer depiction.

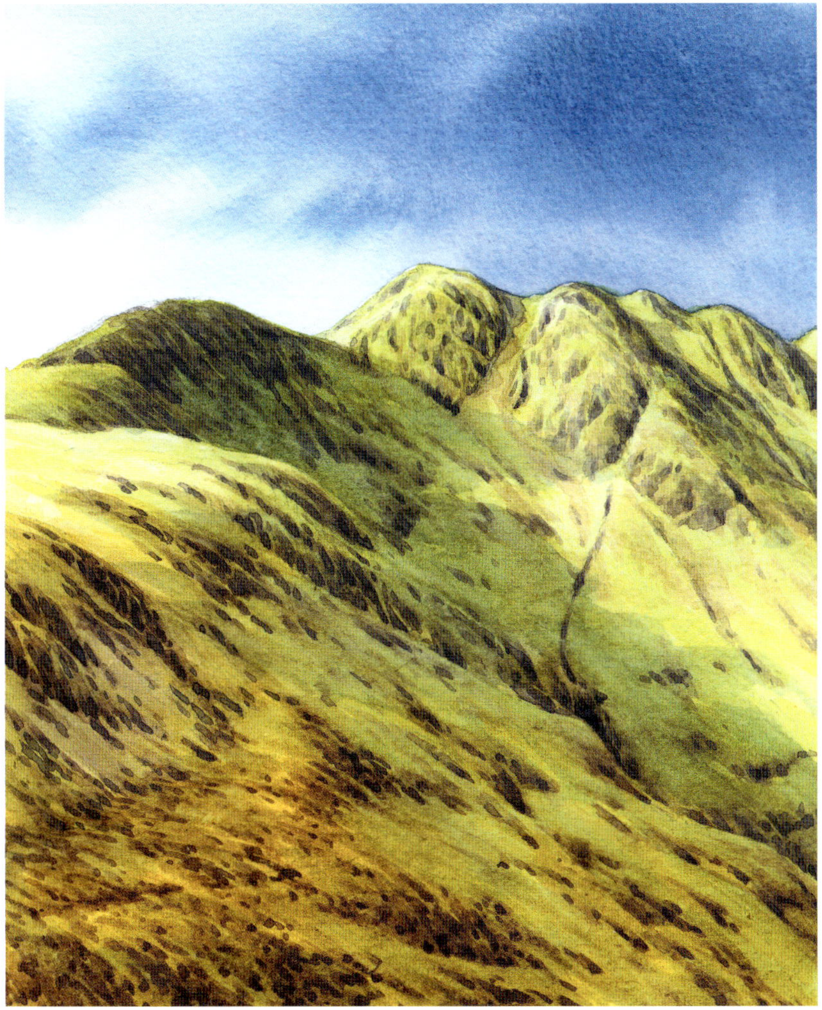

Crinkle Crags

There can hardly be any dispute that a traverse of the series of peaks and dips that form the ridge of this fell is one of the classic walks in the Lake District. In weather of poor visibility navigation can be an issue as sections of the route are rocky and paths can be difficult to follow. Enjoy it at its best in clear conditions.

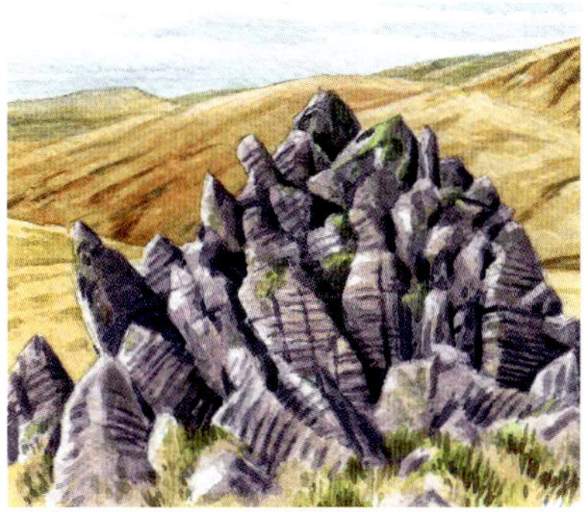

A strange outcrop 23/9/08

I had to descend from the main ridge down into Adam-a-Cove to locate this striated rock formation. Once found I then had to re-trace my steps back up several hundred feet to the ridge to continue my route. Just one of the unusual routes to find obscure subjects that I had to undertake during this project.

From Pike o' Blisco 24/10/08

This oblique view from Pike o' Blisco enabled AW to fit the long ridge of the five Crinkle Crags onto the page. Shelter Crags is just off the page to the right and the deep ravine of Crinkle Gill falls away to the bottom right.

The fourth and fifth Crinkles 23/9/08

Bowfell makes a rather impressive backdrop in this view. Even better for me were the patches of sunlight which added dimension to each top.

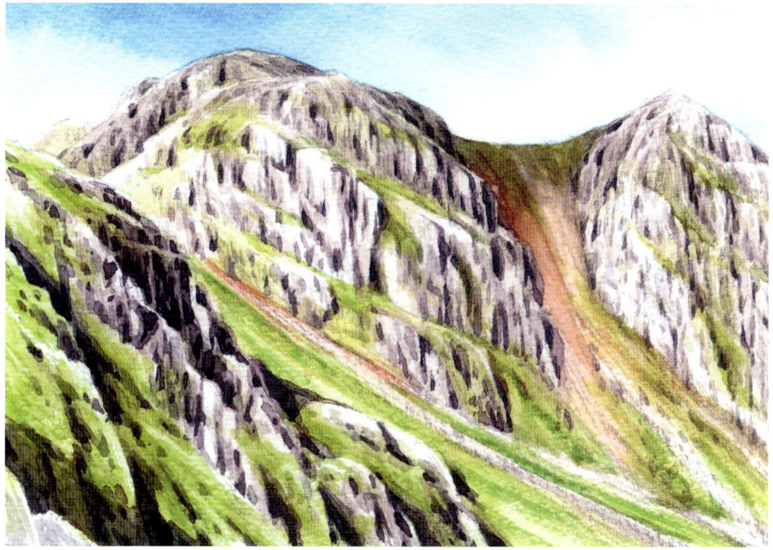

Looking north along the ridge 23/9/08

The highest Crinkle with the red scree gully of Mickle Door to its left.

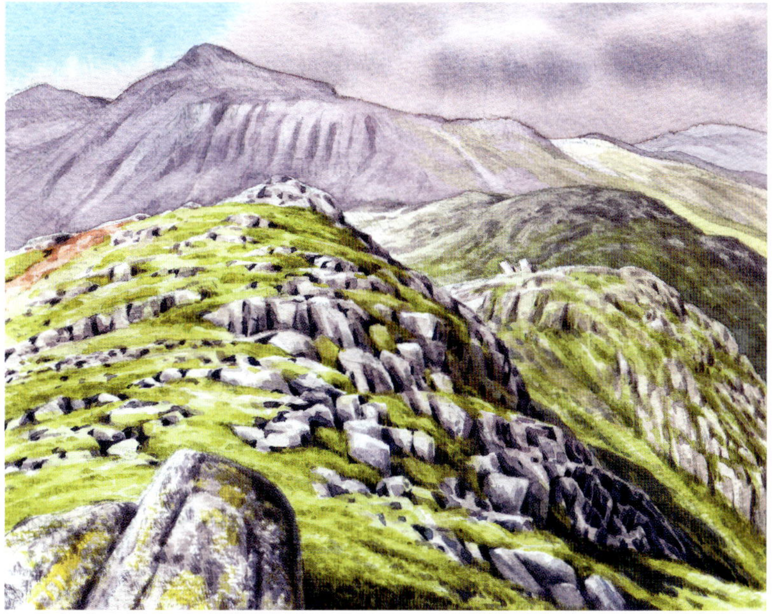

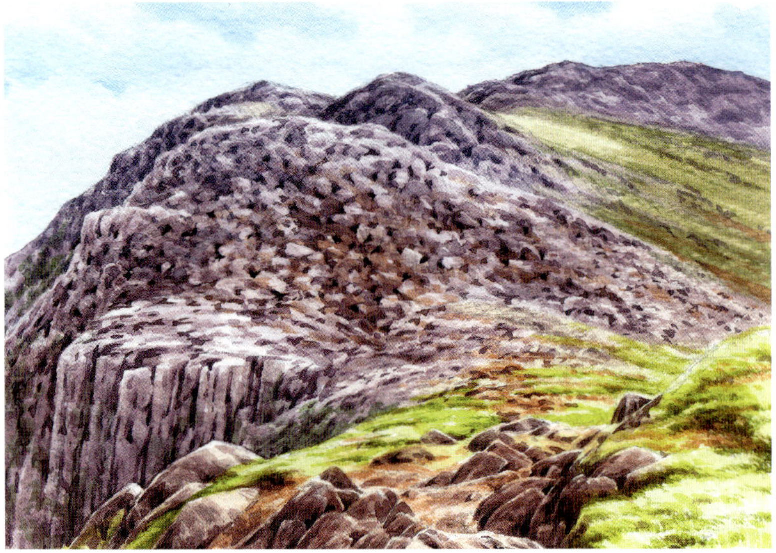

Looking south along the ridge 23/9/08

In this view from the path on Shelter Crags four of the five Crinkles can be seen. Long Top and the highest point is at the top right.

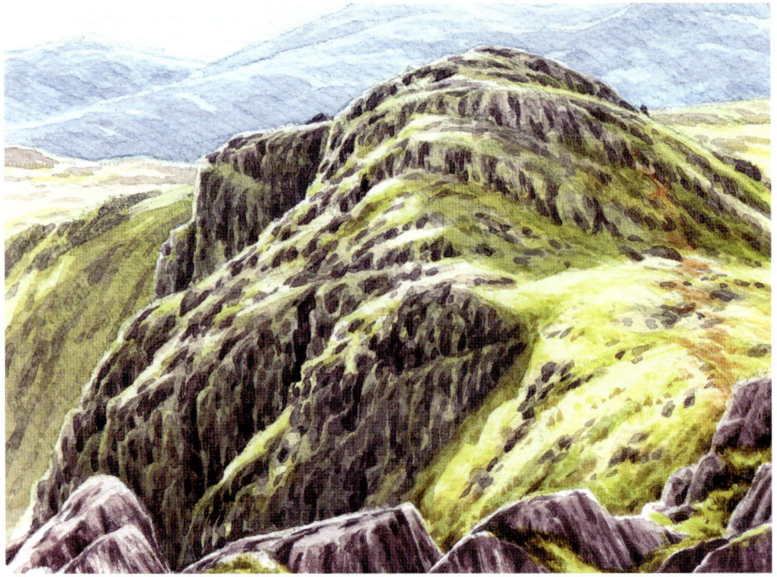

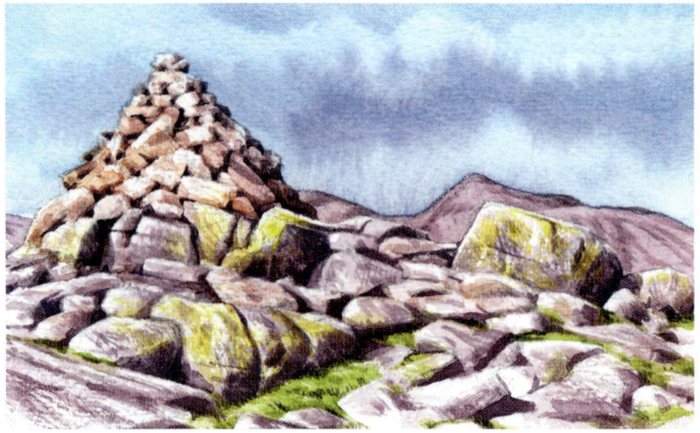

The summit 23/9/08

On this visit the cairn was a tidy pile. The rocks hereabouts were well covered in lichen.

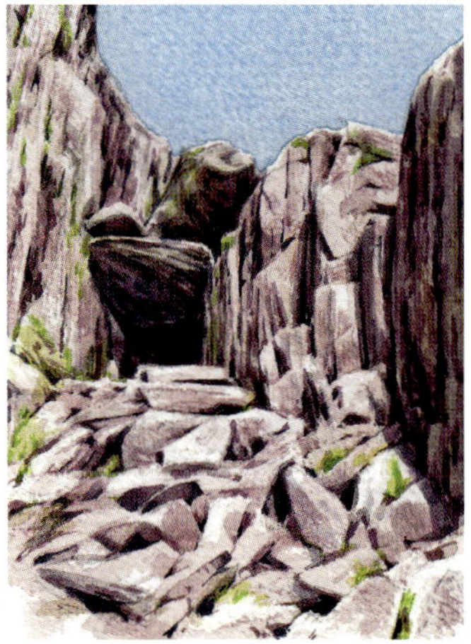

The Bad Step 23/9/08

A 10′ wall to the right of the chockstones is easier in ascent than descent. A couple of "hands on" moves and a bit of stretching will see the obstacle conquered. There is an easier alternative, a path around to the left which follows the base of the crag.

The fifth Crinkle 3/10/08

To reach the top of the fifth Crinkle from this point the route is either straight on to descend the Bad Step or re-trace your way back past the summit and take the easier path round to the west.

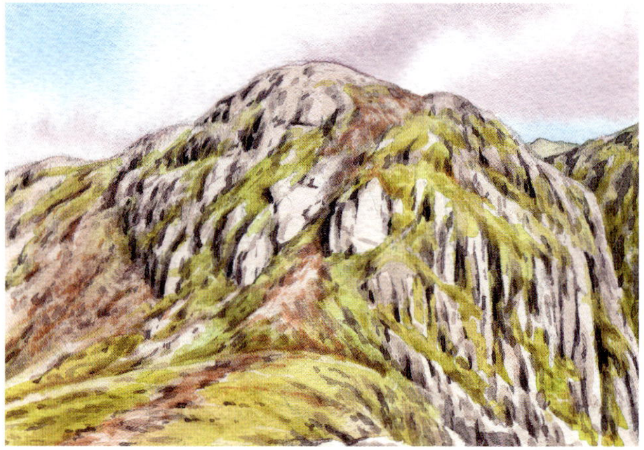

The Highest Crinkle from the south 3/10/08

The direct route to the top can be made via the red scree but you will encounter the Bad Step about half way up. The other route around to the left follows the base of the crag via a recently repaired path.

Bowfell 23/9/08

A great view of the gullies formerly known as the Churns of Bow Fell, but now as Bowfell Links, seen from Shelter Crags.

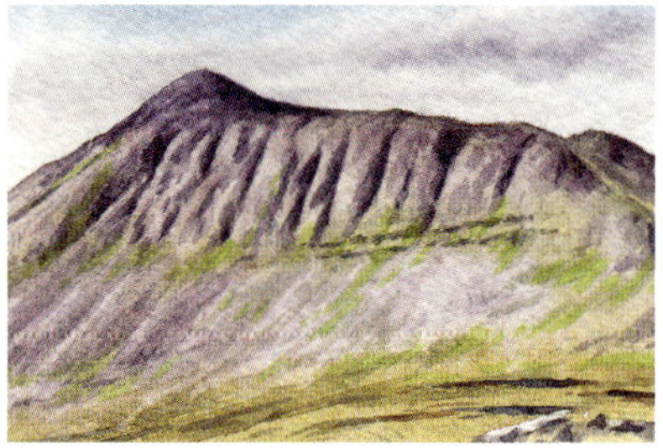

The Eastern Face 23/9/08

This aspect of the highest Crinkle had to be obtained from a point high above Gladstone Knott. The Eastern Terrace is clearly seen but the Crinkle itself is more squat than in Wainwright's illustration.

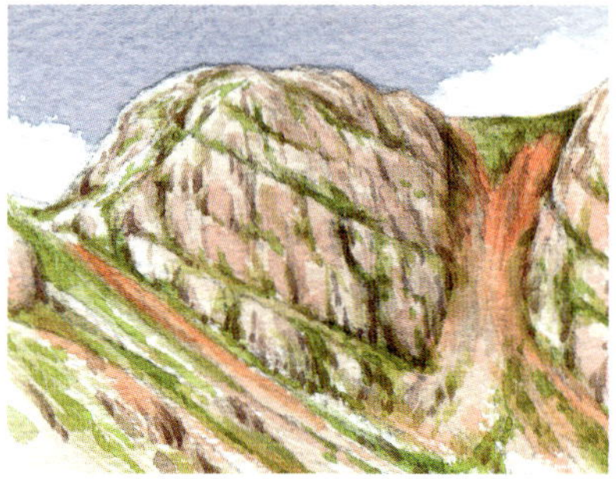

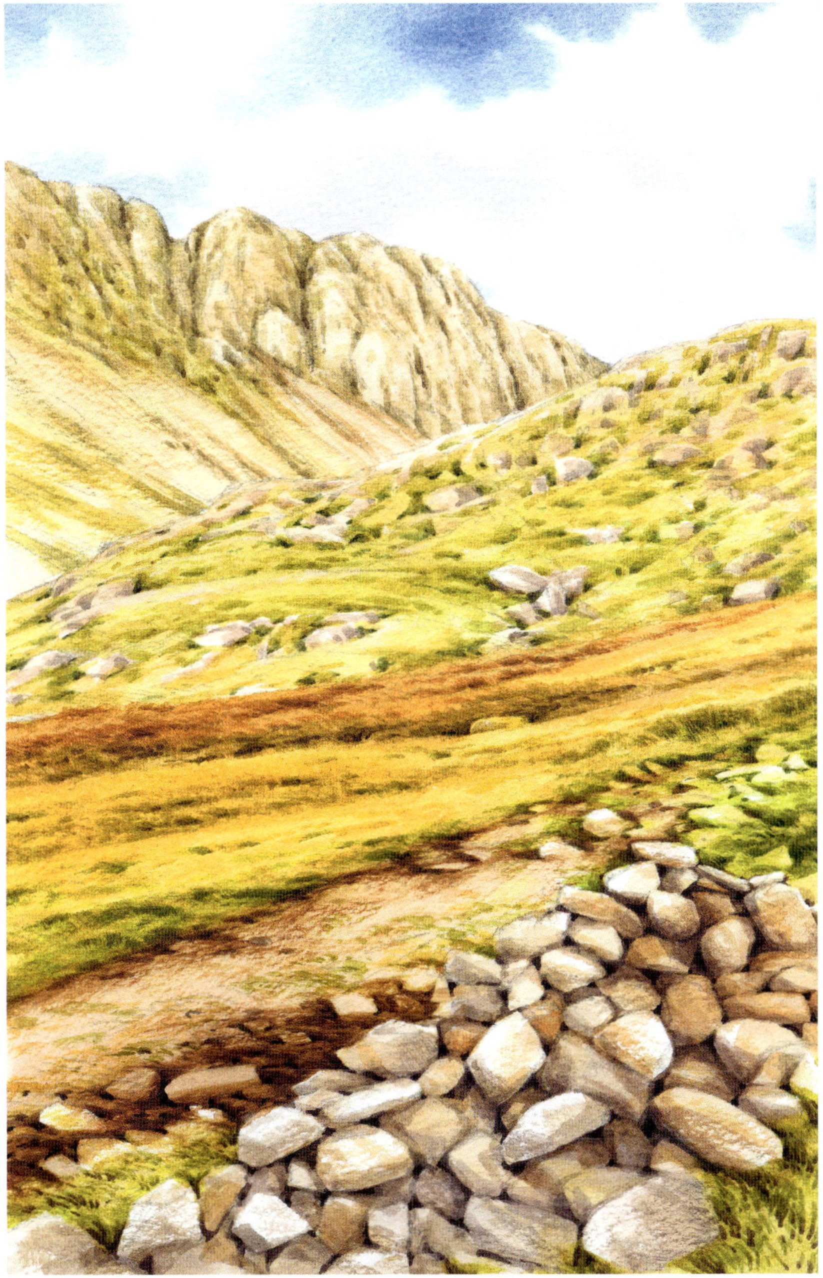

Dow Crag

The western slopes of Dow Crag from the summit to Seathwaite Tarn are fairly featureless and hardly get mentioned in the guide. The eastern face is a totally different story, near vertical rock buttresses loom above Goat's Water which are best viewed from high up on Coniston Old Man.

From The Cove 3/9/07

The path towards Goat's Water through The Cove passes by this large cairn which at one time was made mostly of quartz stones so AW marked it in his route maps as "white cairn". The addition of many more regular stones means the quartz and its white effect has been lost, as has the name of the cairn.

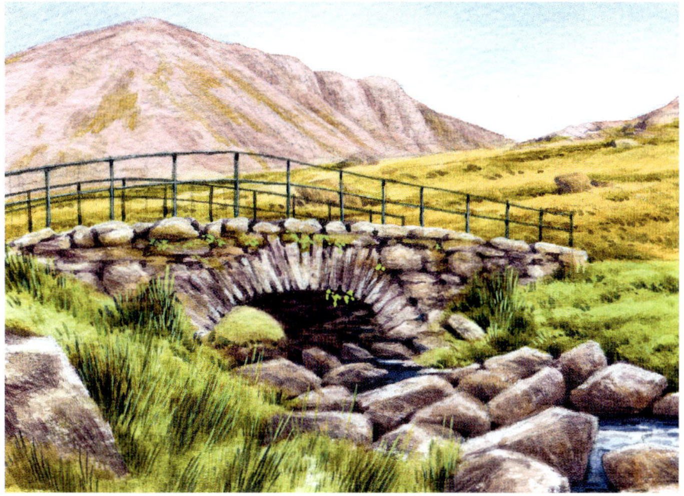

Cove Bridge 3/9/07

A bridge of some age with the unusual feature of handrails.

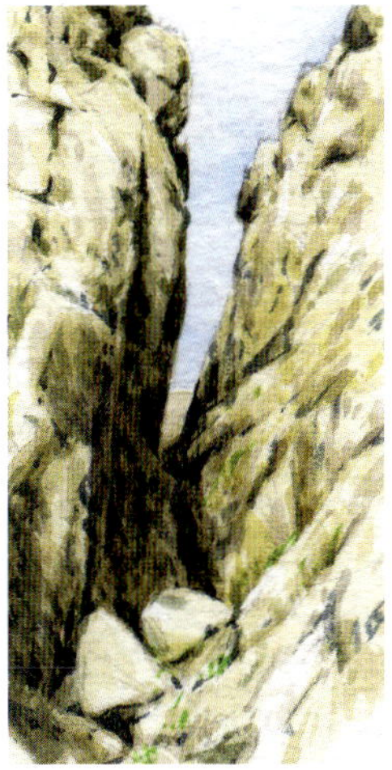

The entrance to Great Gully 3/9/07

A narrow cleft in the crag, passed by on the way to the South Rake.

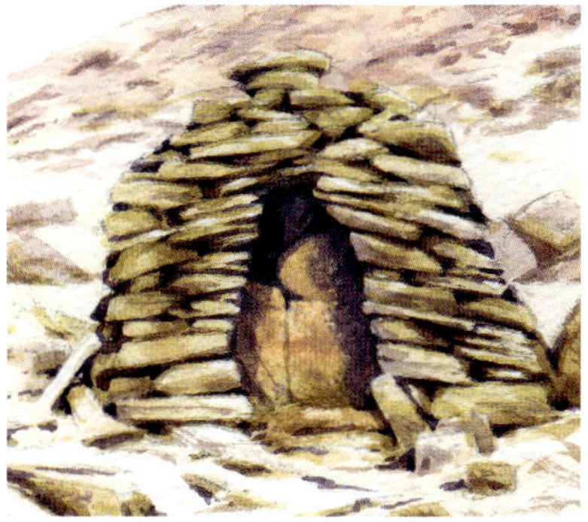

The shelter 1/12/08

To those old travellers on the Walna Scar road caught out in a storm this little shelter must have offered only basic protection.

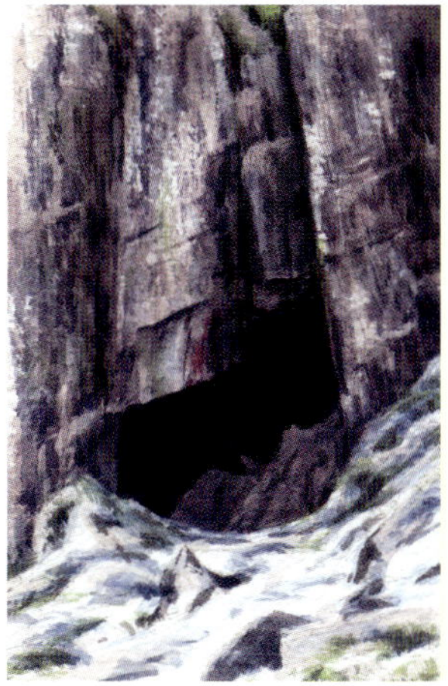

The big cave, Blind Tarn Quarry 1/12/08

These excavated workings extend for quite a way into the hillside with some wagon rails still in place.

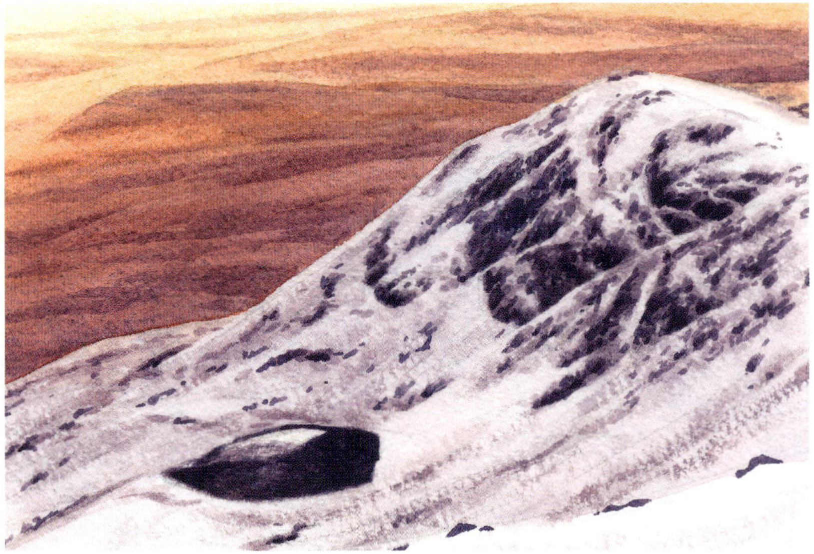

Brown Pike and Blind Tarn
1/12/08
Far in the distance Coniston Water was glowing in the winter light as I looked down from near Buck Pike.

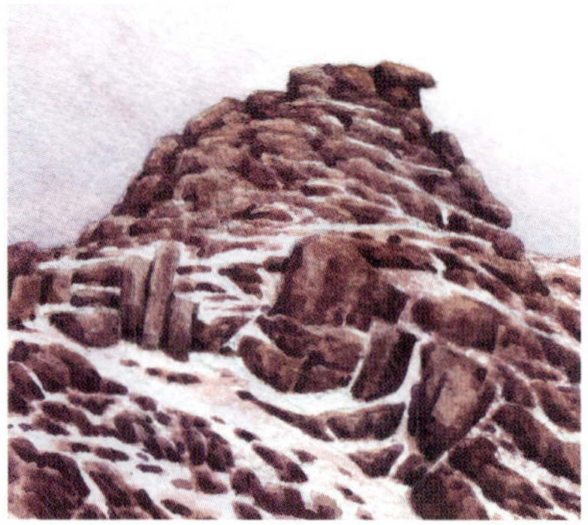

The Summit 1/12/08
A short scramble up to the left will see you on top of this lofty peak.

The summit ridge from the top of South Rake 1/12/08
The Rake drops steeply down over the snow covered edge.

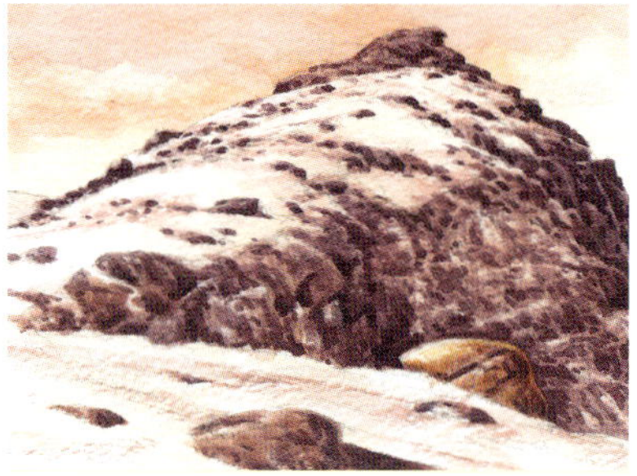

The head of Great Gully
1/12/09
One of three similar sketches on the approach to the summit.

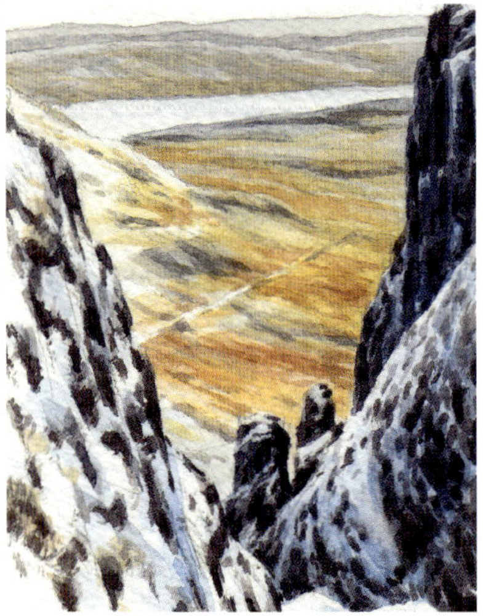

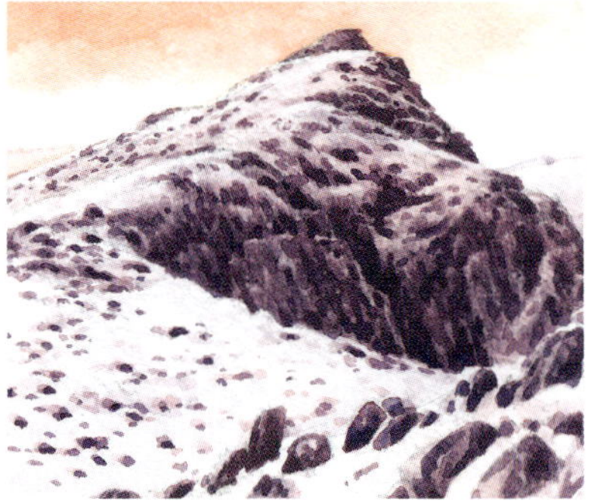

Looking down Easy Gully to the pinnacle 1/12/09
Coniston Water framed by crags.

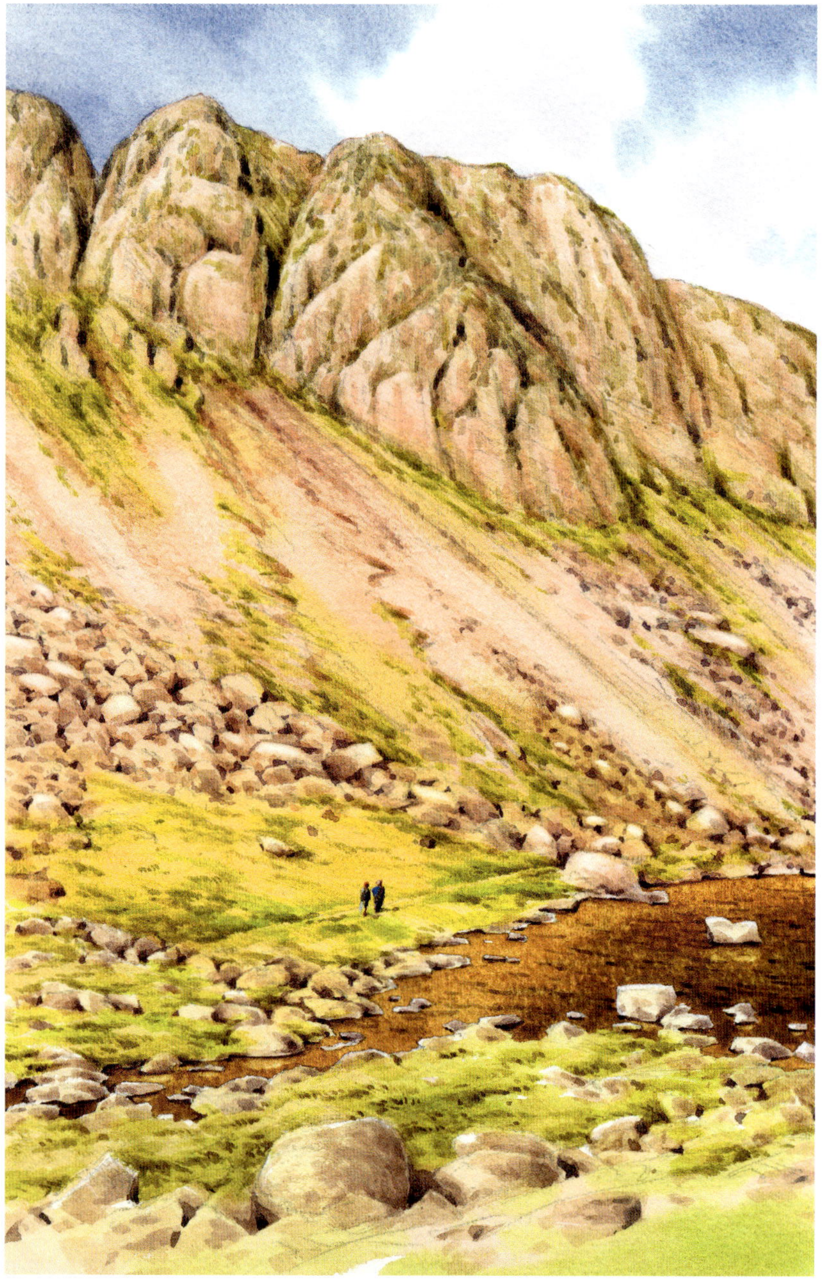

Dow Crag from Goat's Water
3/9/07
We had seen no other walkers up until this point but as we sat enjoying lunch two climbers appeared from The Cove and took the path to the crag, just as there are in AW's drawing. A real coincidence, the only thing missing was a covering of snow.

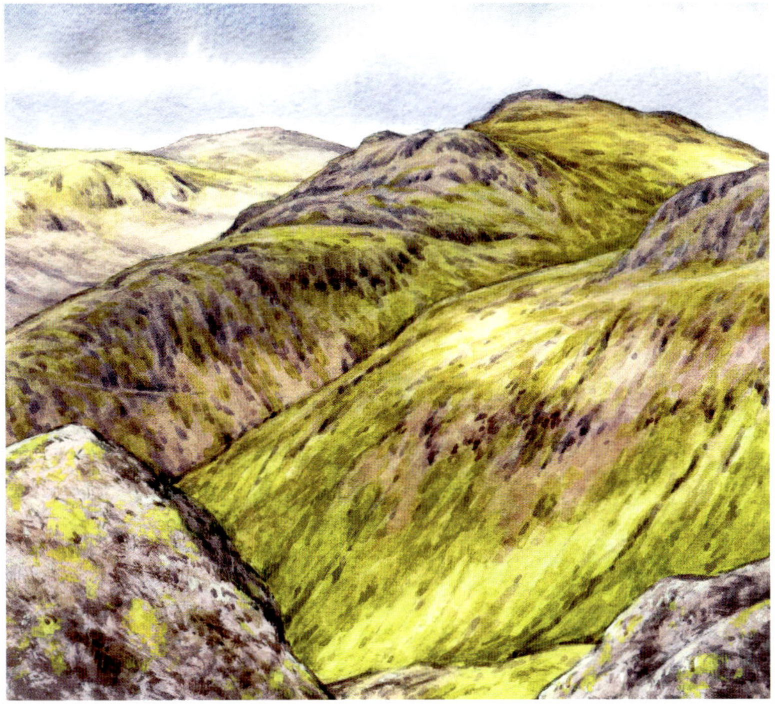

From Rest Gill, Crinkle Crags 23/9/08
The task of obtaining this reference required me to descend from the Crinkle Crags ridge alongside Rest Gill gully, seek out the exact location and take the photograph before climbing back up to the ridge via the 600′ steep and pathless slope. The rocks in the foreground are actually marked by AW in Crinkle Crags 8 as "bristly rocks", there is no other mention of them elsewhere in the guide. He omitted Great End in the distance from his illustration.

Esk Pike

Due to its positioning Esk Pike can be approached from four valleys, Eskdale, Langdale, Wasdale and Borrowdale. Each route has its own merits, with elements of interest and all have the rocky summit with its grand views as a goal. AW took the fell name Esk Pike from the 1 inch Bartholomew map of the day as it was unnamed on other maps.

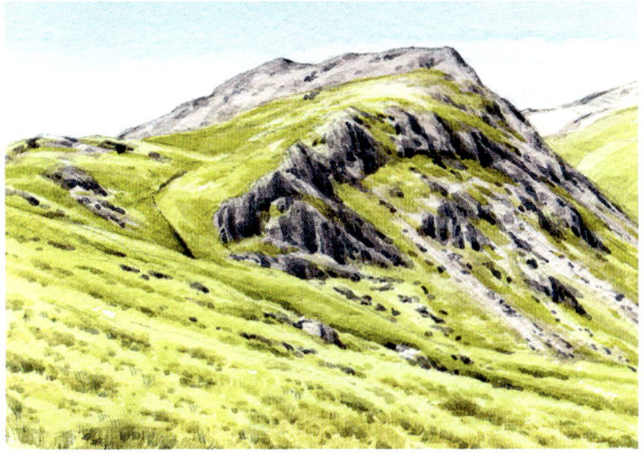

The approach to the summit 11/7/11
This south ridge remains mostly pathless but it's a location almost encircled by stunning fell scenery.

The summit from the top of the north buttress 3/10/08
The summit cairn is not visible from this point now. The shelter that Wainwright indicated is now not really worthy of such a definition.

Esk Pike from the wall shelter 3/10/08
The crumbling wall end of the shelter in AW's sketch has been repaired.

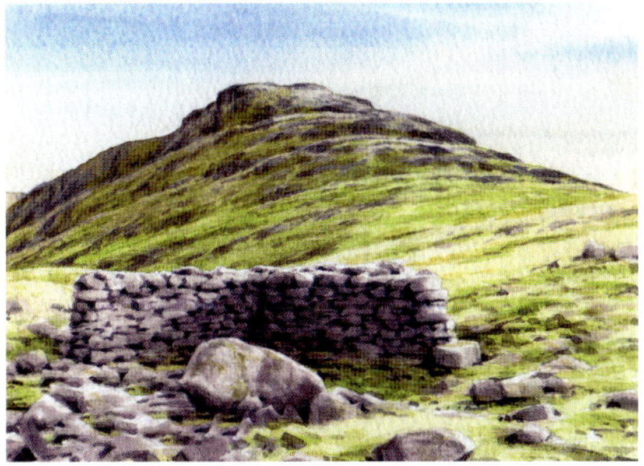

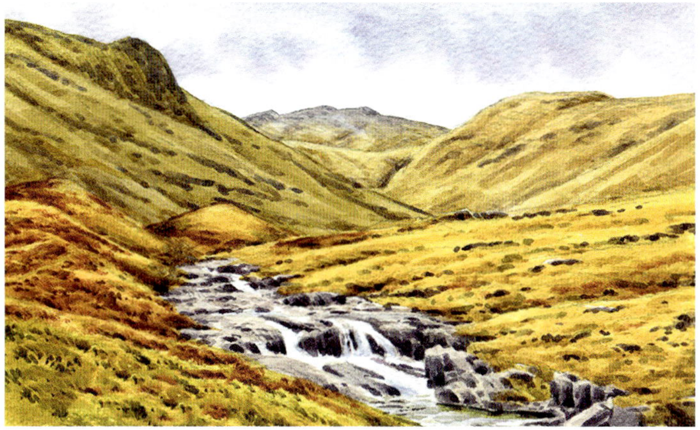

Esk Pike from Langstrath 4/10/11
This is a fine valley and is still unknown to many walkers. It is well worth exploring.

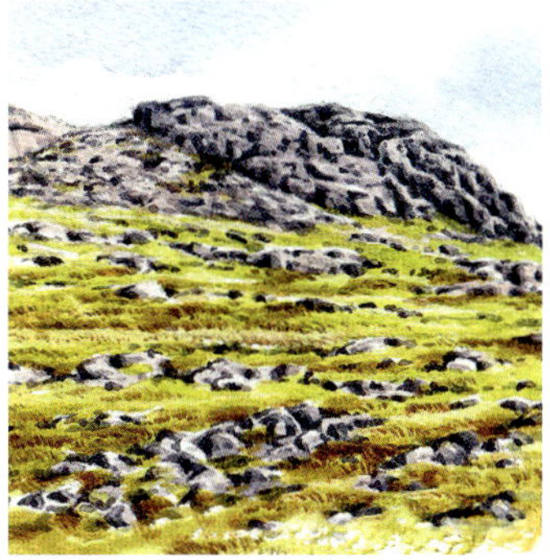

The summit 3/10/08
Many of the rocks on the Pike's summit have a strong orange colouration. Only a tiny cairn is in place here.

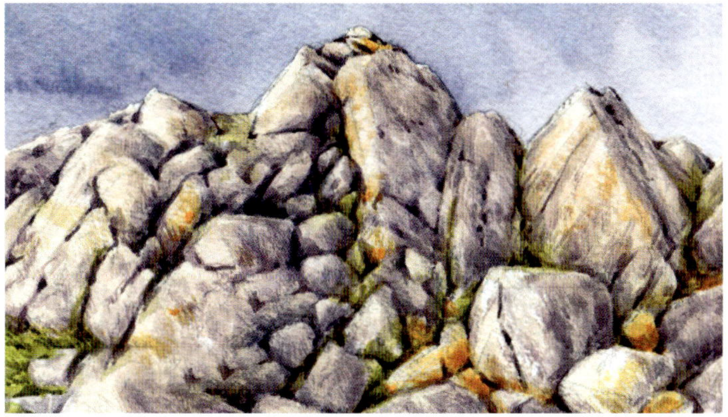

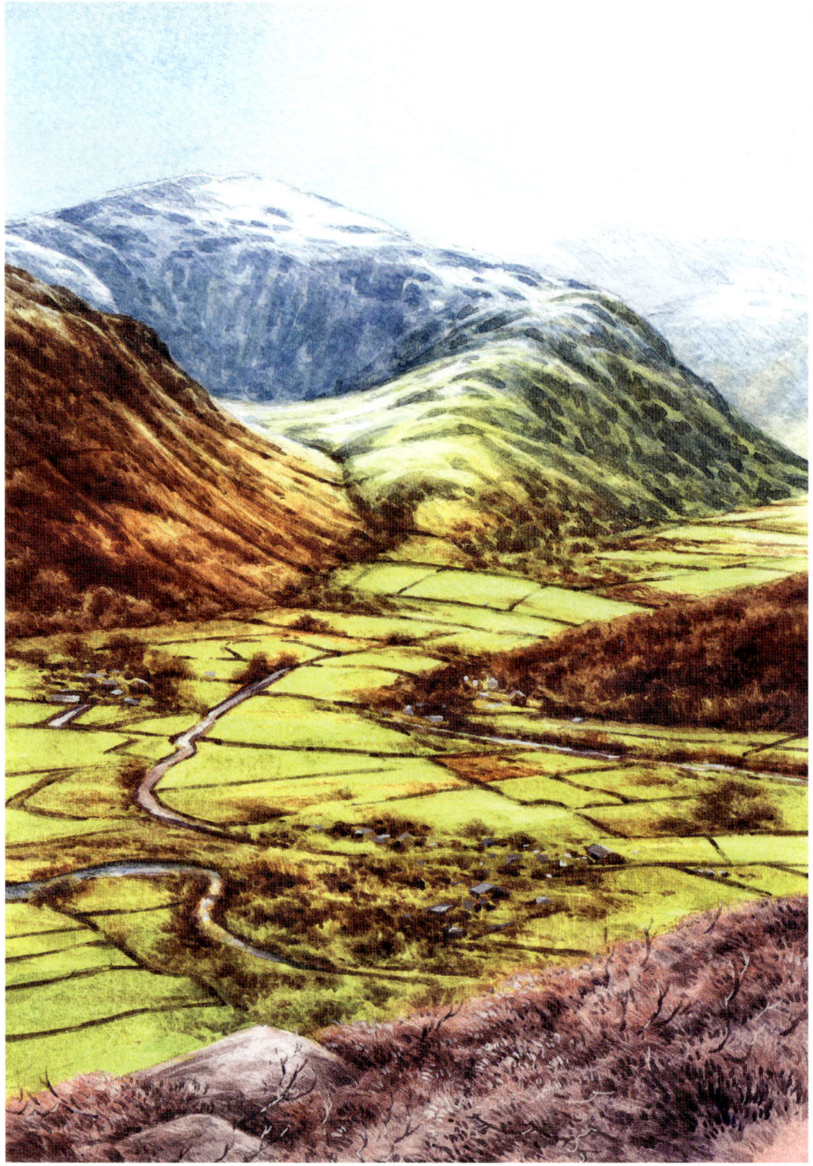

From Grange Fell 7/3/10
Early afternoon on a winter's day is not the best time to view this scene due to the sun's position. Rosthwaite is surrounded by snow capped fells.

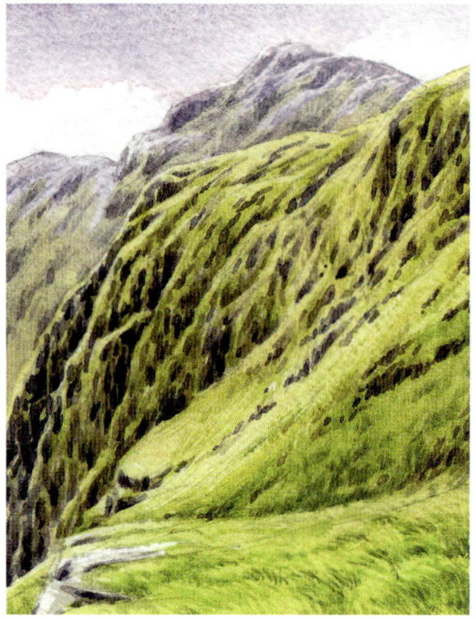

Comb Head and Raven Crag
12/6/09
The detour from the path is worth it for the view of Raven Crag. The name Comb in this area now ends with an "e" on the O.S. maps.

Glaramara

The ridge that runs south from Rosthwaite splits Borrowdale into two with Langstrath to the eastern side and the small valley of Grains Gill to the west. Along the ridge are three "Wainwright" tops, Rosthwaite Fell (Bessyboot), Glaramara and then Allen Crags. A variety of tarns and rocky outcrops fills this route with interest.

Tray Dub 4/10/11
This pool is far into the Langstrath valley but it is a delightful location and ideal for a summer picnic.

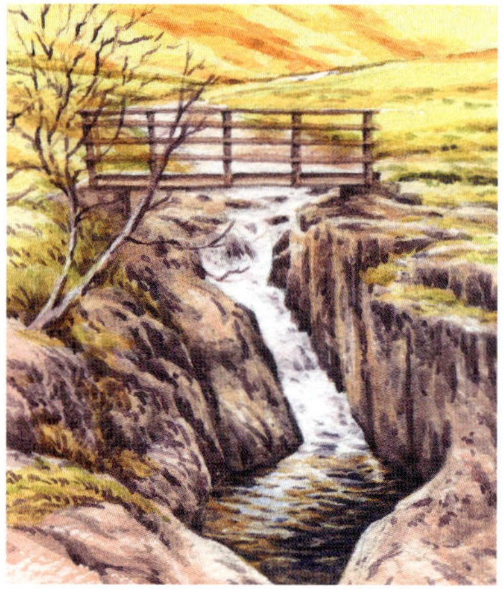

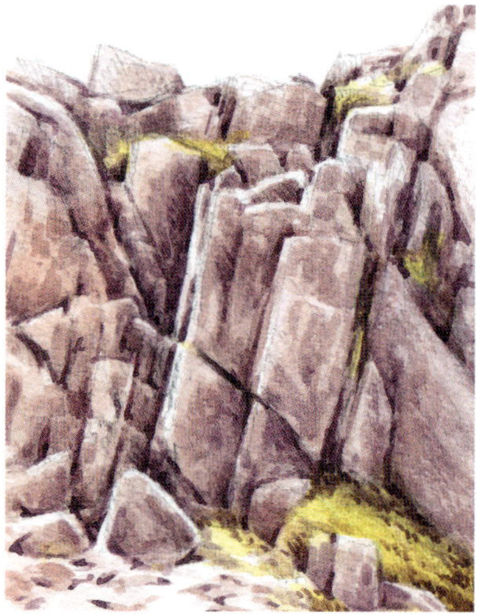

The 20' rock step 12/6/09
Most walkers will tackle this obstacle with ease. My problem was matching up the actual rock formation to his drawing.

The summit 12/6/09
There are two tops here and they are very alike. This is the north east one.

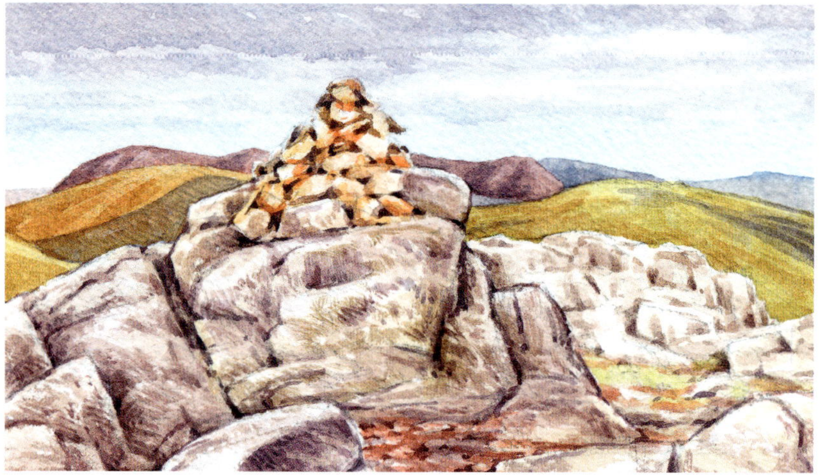

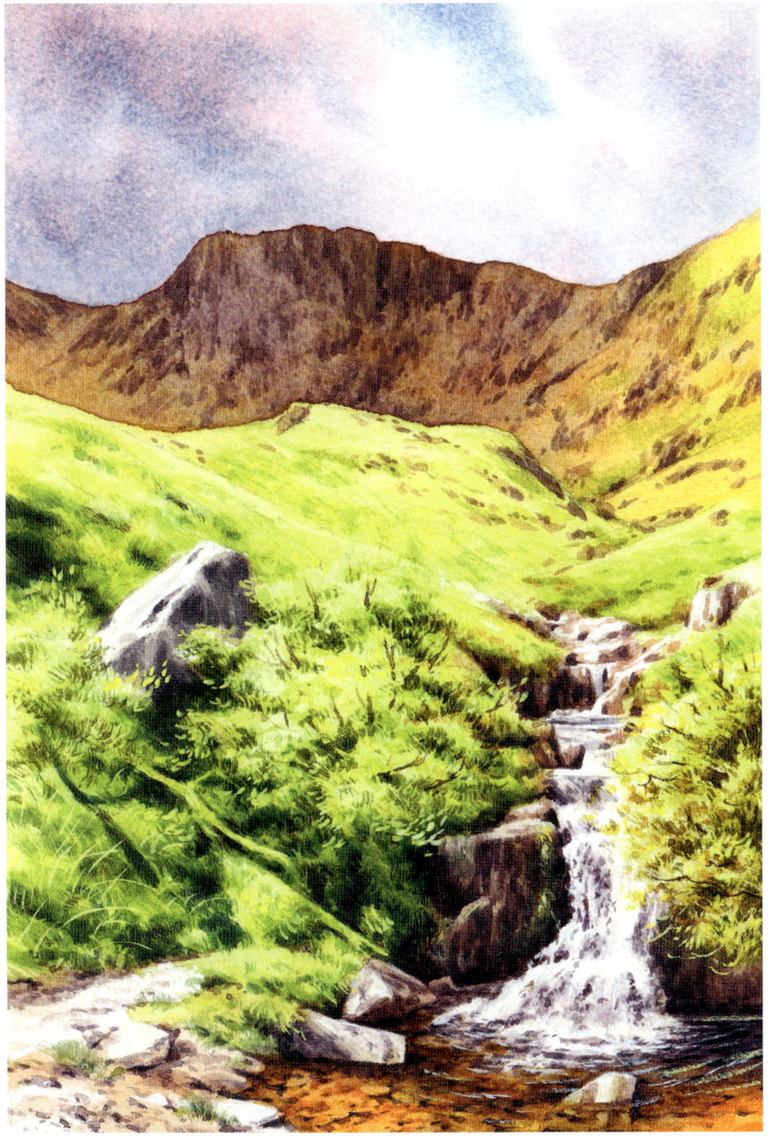

From Greenburn Beck 8/7/09
The footpath by the beck up into the valley is faint in places but it does lead up past these delightful falls and ascends Broad Slack to the summit ridge where some aeroplane wreckage can still be seen.

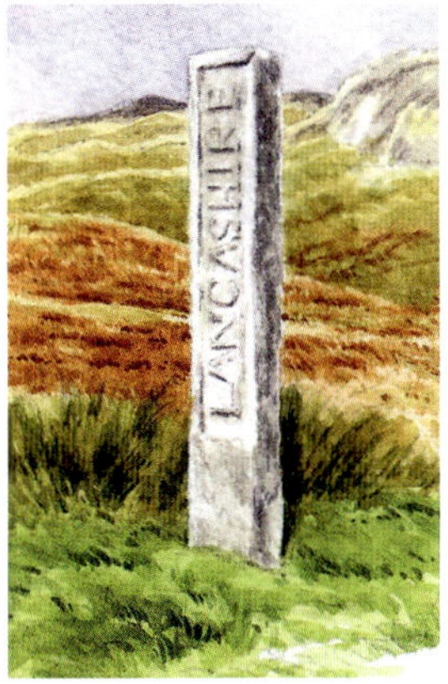

Hell Gill Pike 24/10/08
Deviate away from the path near Little Carrs to visit this fine viewpoint.

Three Shires Stone 24/10/08
Even though the Shires have since been formed into Cumbria the stone which dates back to 1816 still stands.

The summit 24/10/08 (below right)
A small cairn that holds a position close to the edge of the very top of the fell.

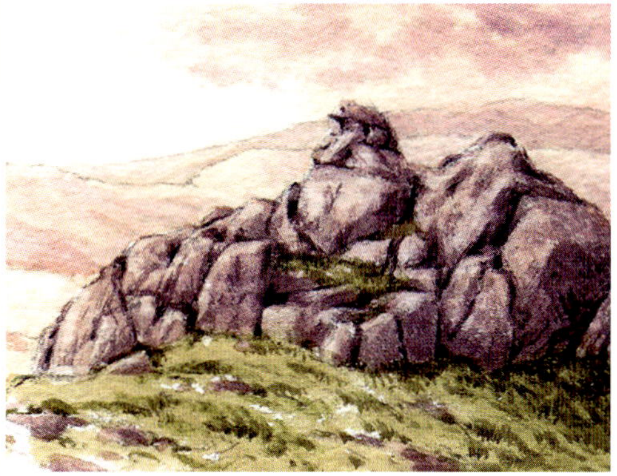

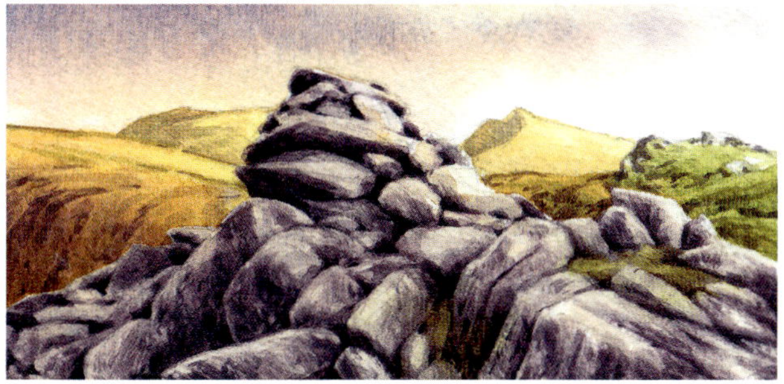

Great Carrs

Sited at the south western end of the Greenburn Valley, Great Carrs shows a formidable front to those who approach from this direction. Notably, not far from the summit is a memorial cairn to the eight man crew of a Halifax bomber who lost their lives here on the night of 22nd October 1944.

Great Carrs from Little Carrs 24/10/08
The rocky face of the summit drops steeply into the Greenburn Valley with Swirl How beyond.

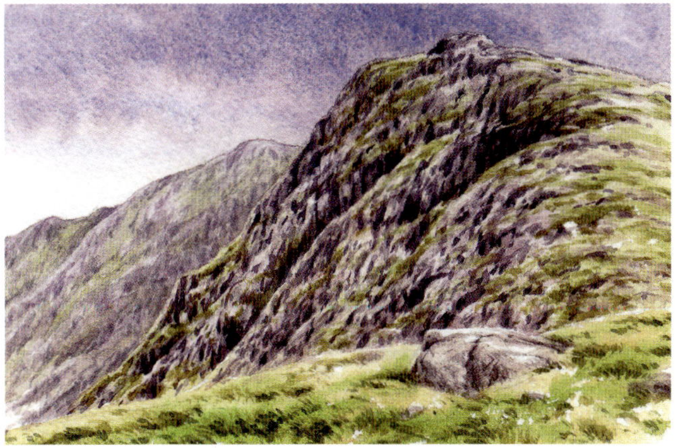

The summit ridge looking north 3/9/07
The furthest top is the actual highest point, the cairn can just about be seen.

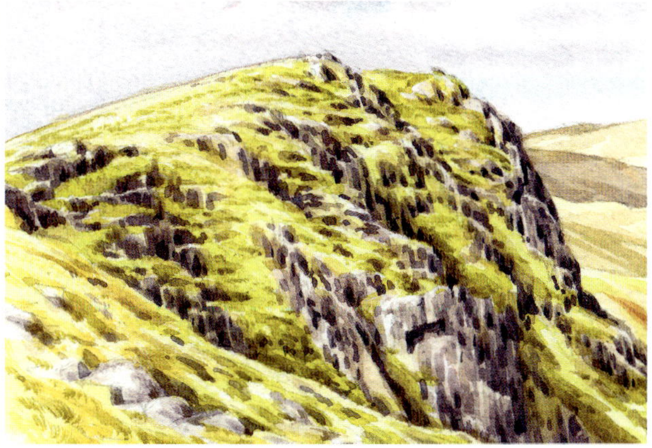

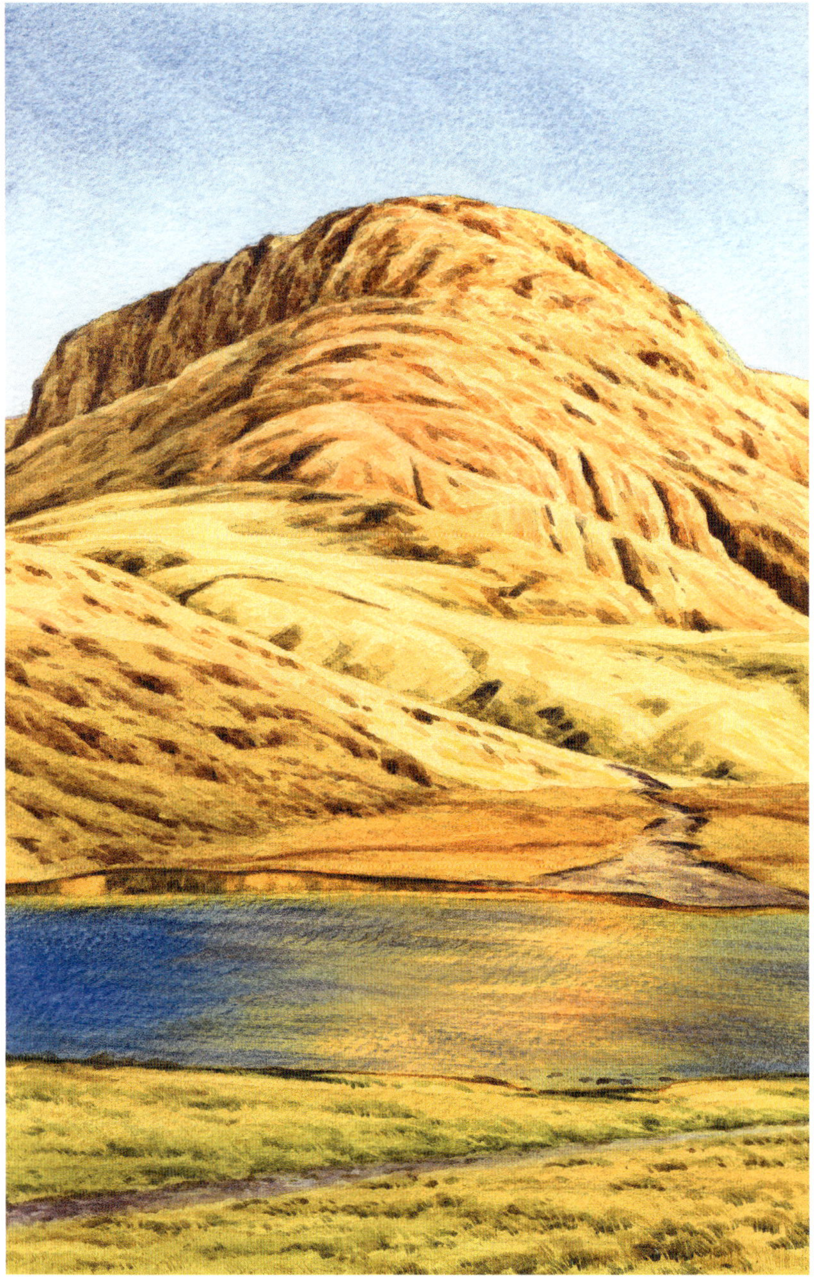

From Sty Head 10/4/11
As the evening sun was dropping in the west the fell was bathed in the warm light. Great End forms a superb backdrop above this tarn to those walkers using the path from Borrowdale.

Great End

Given its name there can be no surprise that this is one of the most popular fells which walkers choose to complete their round of the "Wainwrights". It is a grand fell with lots of character not least its gullied north-eastern face and its commanding view over Borrowdale and beyond.

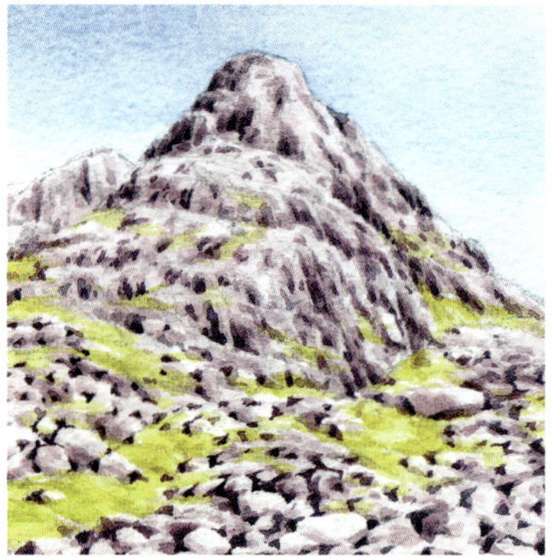

Cust's Gully

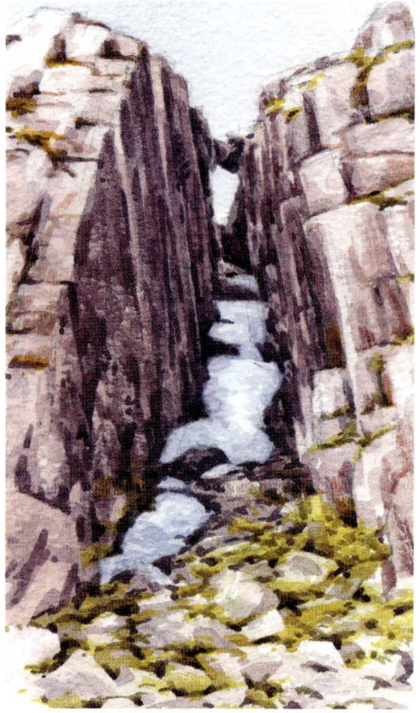

From below 10/4/11
Even in April the snow lay in the depths of the gully away from the warming sun. It covered the rough and rocky slope making progress difficult but I continued up into the ravine to get the next reference (top right).

Long Pike from near Lambfoot Dub 10/4/11
The tarn (Dub) is about 200′ feet above the popular Corridor Route and it remains a hidden gem.

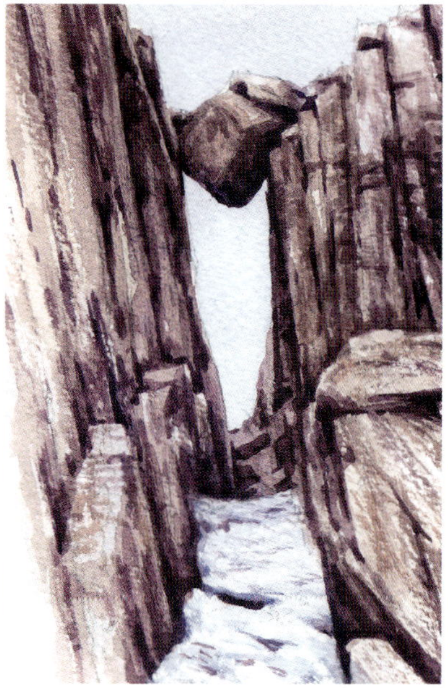

The pitch 10/4/11
Having obtained this reference I made a careful retreat back down over the patches of crusted snow.

From above 12/6/09
The chockstone wedged firmly in place supports a jumble of smaller rocks.

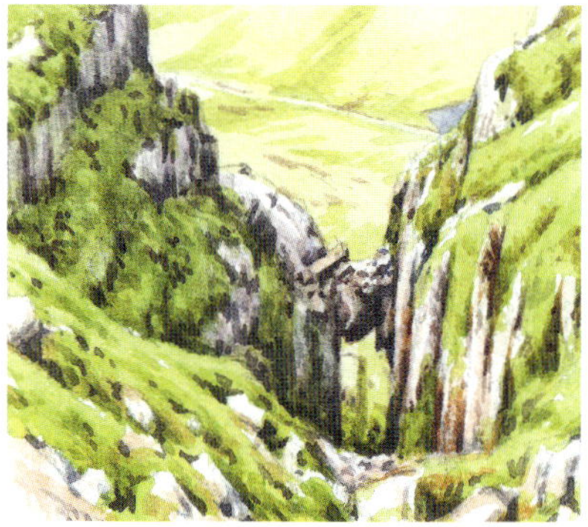

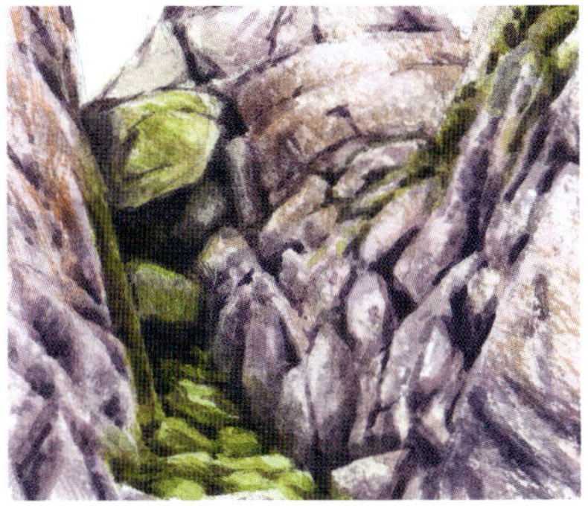

The branch gully 10/4/11

The sun seldom shines here so the rocks are covered with moss and are slippery. The avoiding route up to the right described by AW is also a place for care, requiring a bit of "hands on" work.

In Skew Gill 10/4/11

Working my way up the gill whilst trying to locate this view was a challenge as the safety of myself and the dogs was paramount. This was the closest likeness to his drawing that I could find.

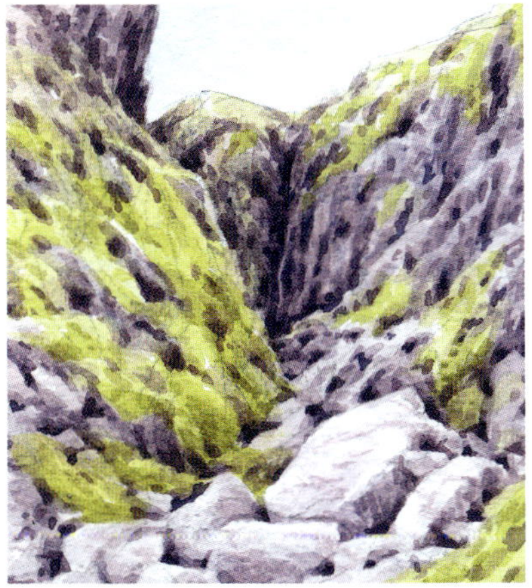

The summit 12/6/09

The cairn is small now but the building material lying around here is evidence of the decent column that stood here at some time in the past. Pillar shows itself above the north west cairn.

Skew Gill

The ascent up though the gill is not easy, it is rough and wet in places and requires an eye for spotting the potential hazards before you get to them. Sections that require scrambling especially near the top can be wet and slippery so enter the gill with caution. Retrospective views towards Great Gable from within its confines are exceptional.

The lower entrance, Skew Gill 10/4/11

The scree of the gill spills down onto the Corridor Route from where this reference was taken.

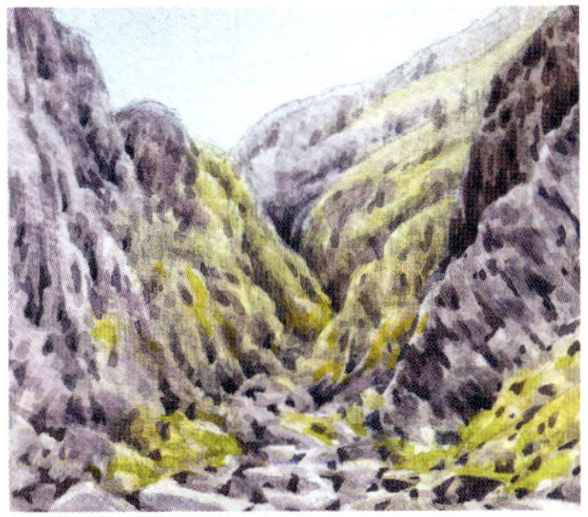

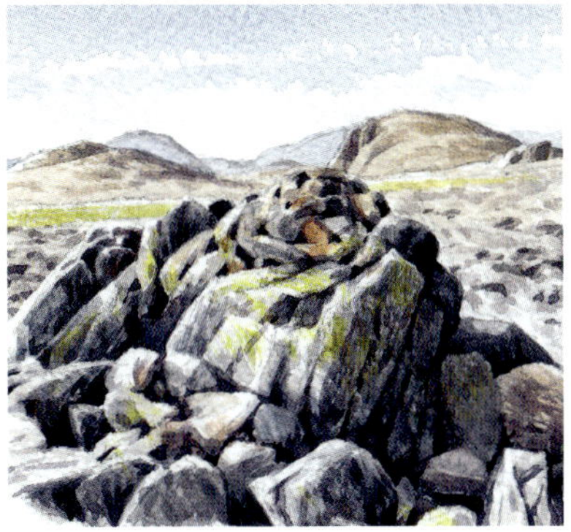

Borrowdale from the top of Central Gully 20/8/14

The title of Wainwright's sketch in the Pictorial Guide is a little misleading. A view from the top of the main Central Gully looks to the north east and Sprinkling Tarn cannot be seen. It took me three visits to ensure that I had the correct location for the sketch which is actually from the top of the side gully (C) in the guide, which leads off from Central Gully. To add to the confusion the wall on the right in his drawing is there but not the topmost section of the wall on the left. This was either a bit of artistic license or that area of rock has collapsed. In my research I have been unable to locate his original photograph which would have clarified the issue. It is still an excellent view, ideal for AW's full page portrait format.

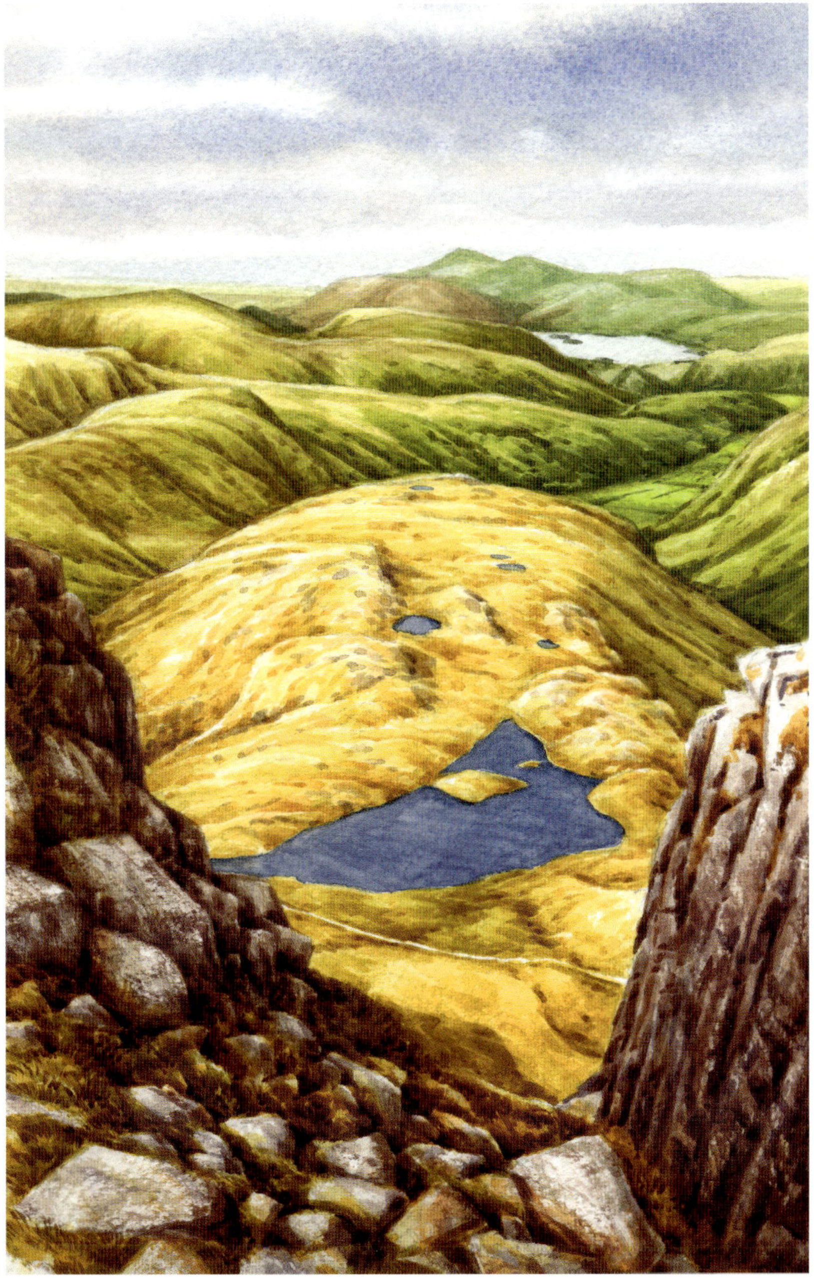

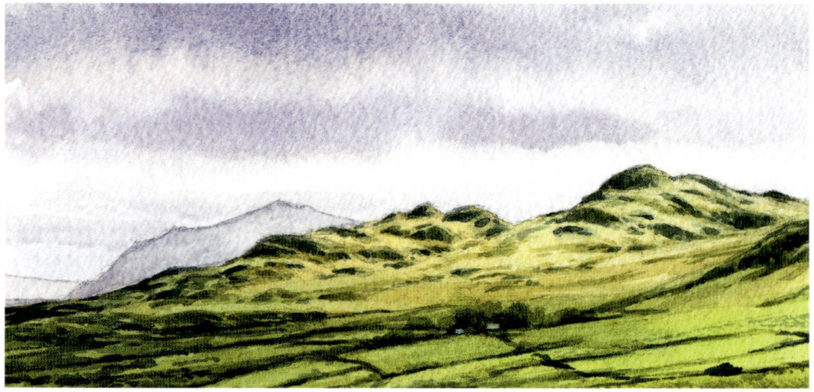

From Birker Fell 2/8/09
Green Crag is actually the high peak on the right with the lower rippled ridge on the left being named Crook Crag. Harter Fell is behind.

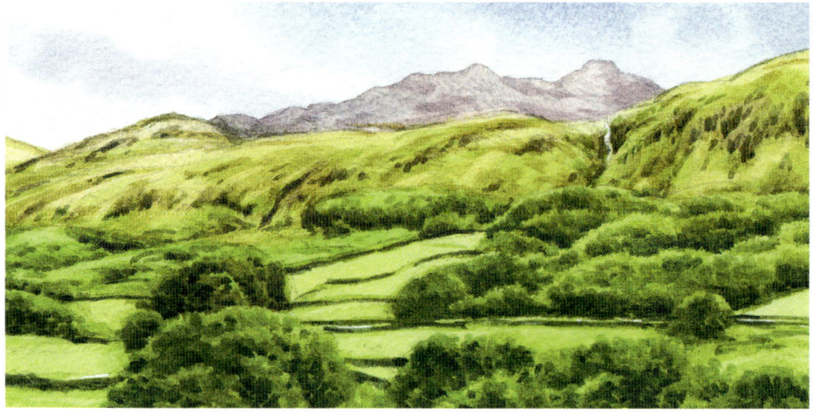

From Boot 2/8/09
Leaving the village of Boot on a footpath towards Boot Bank this view across the Eskdale valley presents itself, with the fell on the horizon. Birker Force waterfall can just be seen in front of the actual summit peak.

Green Crag

Four pages is the minimum allocation for fells in the Pictorial Guides and Green Crag fits into that category. Unusually, AW uses more than one illustration to depict the fell on the first page. The map of the fell cuts off abruptly just to the south west of the summit and perhaps this all reflects the shortage of book space for The Southern Fells.

The approach from Eskdale
24/8/09
As the footpath skirts round to the west of Kepple Crag this aspect of the fell comes into view with Crook Crag on the left.

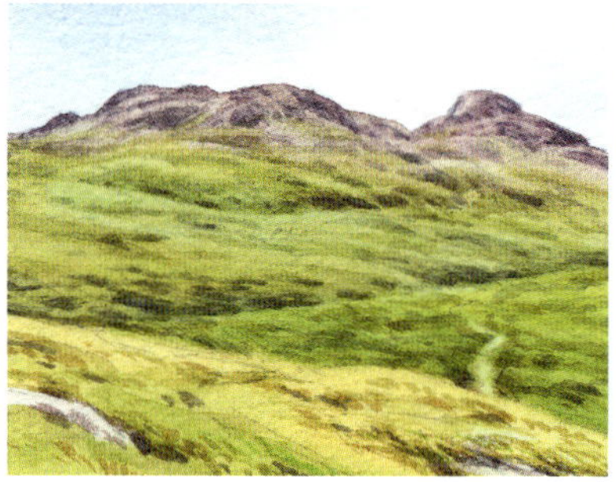

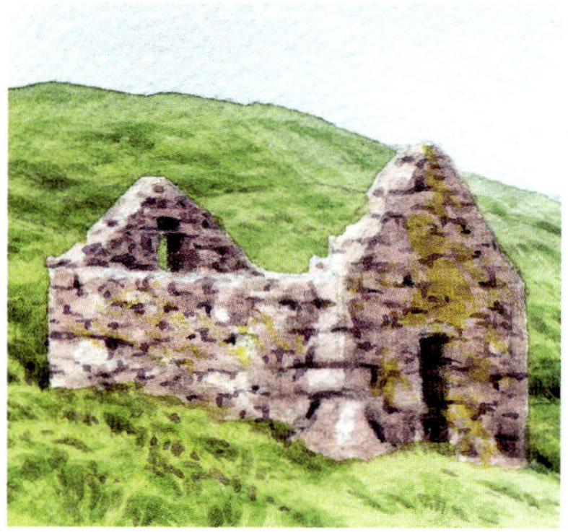

The Low Birker peat hut
24/8/09
The roof has collapsed in on this small single roomed storage hut. There is evidence of over 30 of these huts, known as Peat Scales in the Eskdale area. Peat was cut on the fell in May and left to dry outside until July after hay time when it was then brought into these buildings for storage for use over winter. Most farmsteads had their own hut. Once coal became more available to these remote areas the cutting and use of peat died out but there is evidence of the practice continuing until after the First World War.

The summit 24/8/09
No longer does the summit cairn look as if it has been there *"since the beginning of time"*, the rocks have been re-configured and added to. I have included Upper Eskdale as a backdrop.

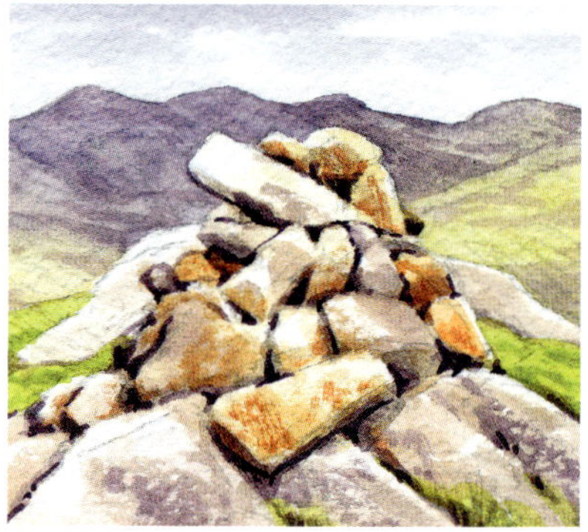

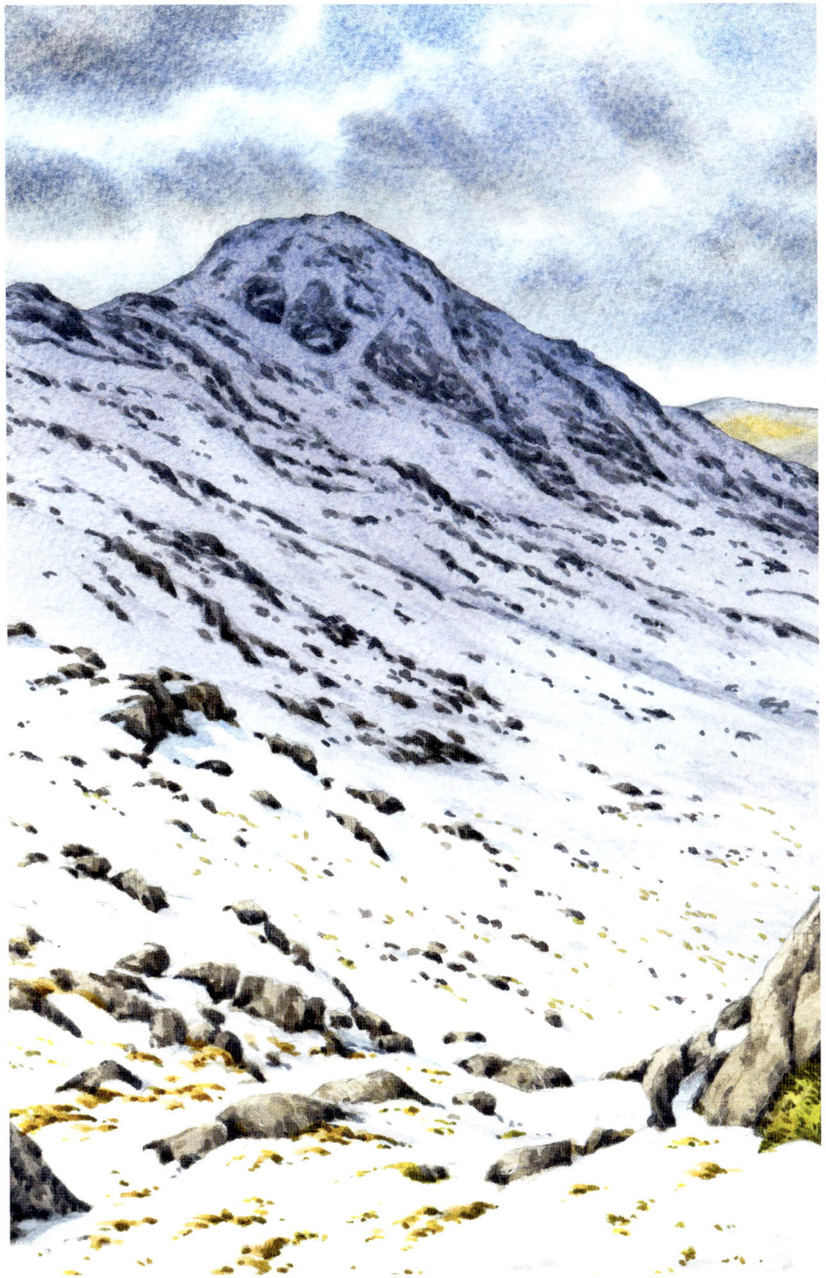

Grey Friar

Even though this fell sits out on a bit of a limb to the north west of the main Coniston Fell group it is easily visited in the completion of the classic round of these hills. I found that the ascent of Grey Friar from the south via Seathwaite Tarn and Calf Cove was an interesting and quiet route.

From Hell Gill Pike 23/3/14

I was keen to capture this scene in the same winter conditions as in AW's drawing so having seen the forecast I drove over to Wrynose Pass and walked up to this point. The patches of sun on the snow slopes were perfect for my needs. His drawing has raised a question for me though. How did Wainwright get here in winter with his limited transport? There is no evidence of similar conditions in drawings of nearby locations.

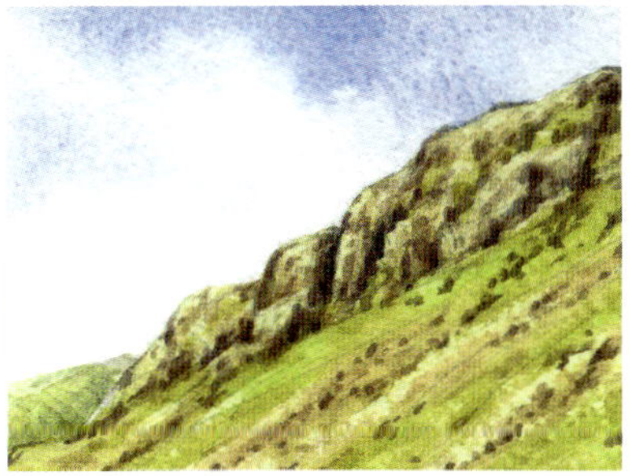

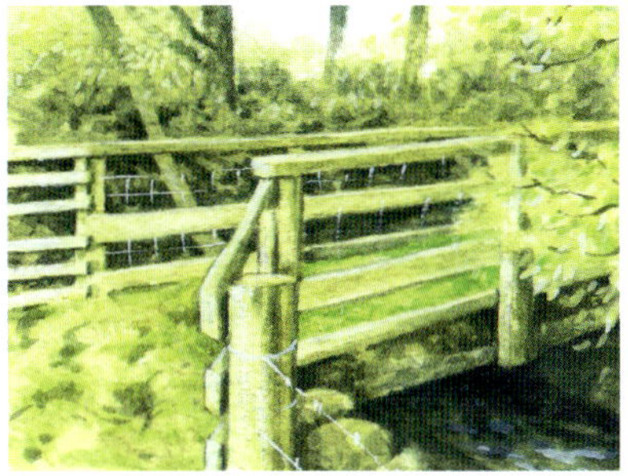

Footbridge over Long House Gill 2/8/09

After prolonged searching on more than one visit and asking locally, no evidence of the ancient footbridge could be found but this modern structure appears to be its replacement on the same site.

Big perched boulder, Calf Cove 24/7/14

There are several such boulders that sit proud of the ground here in Calf Cove. As he describes in the sketch title this one near the top of the cove is the biggest. It is about the size of a medium van.

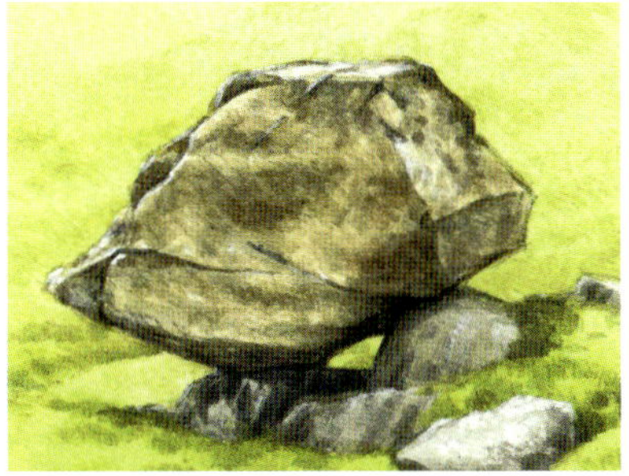

Tunnel entrance, Seathwaite Copper Mines 24/7/14

The level entrance has not gone as stated in the revised guide but merely collapsed in or been filled in for safety reasons.

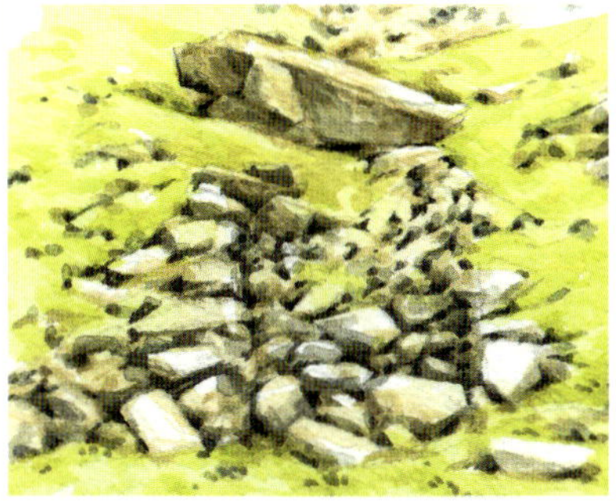

Grey Buttress, Great Blake Rigg 24/7/14

The crag as viewed from near the old tunnel entrance.

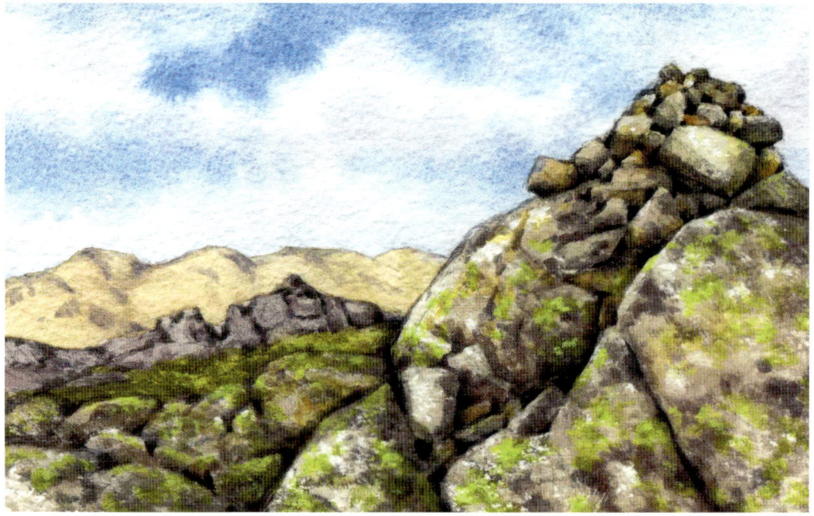

The summit 20/4/10
The north west summit, seen here in the middle distance may have the better views but this near point is the higher of the two tops.

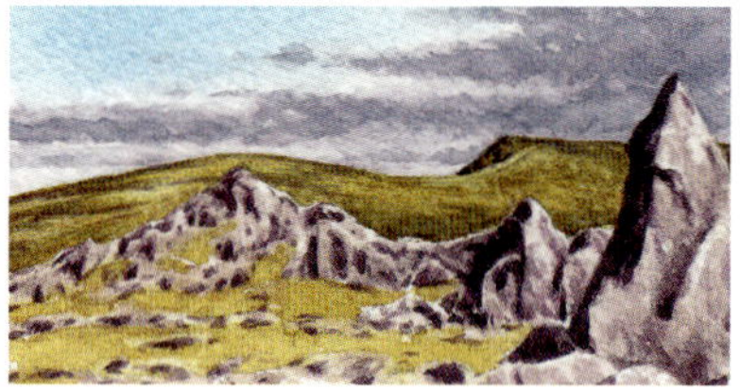

Swirl How from the pointed boulder 3/9/07
With its resemblance to the Swiss mountain this 6′ pinnacle has gained the name The Matterhorn Rock. It is located close to the path about 150 yards to the north east of the summit.

The Scafell Range 3/9/07
Moasdale on the far side of the Duddon Valley leads the eye to the distant Scafell massif from the north western cairn.

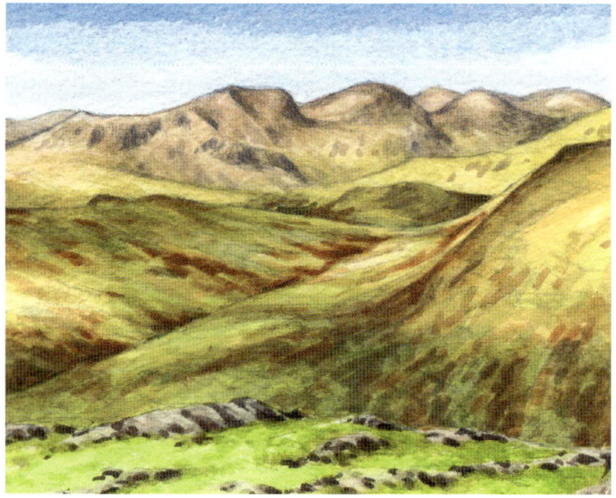

The Coniston Fells 3/9/07
This is the view to the south east from the highest point of the fell. Brim Fell, Coniston Old Man and Dow Crag with the col of Goat's Hause are featured.

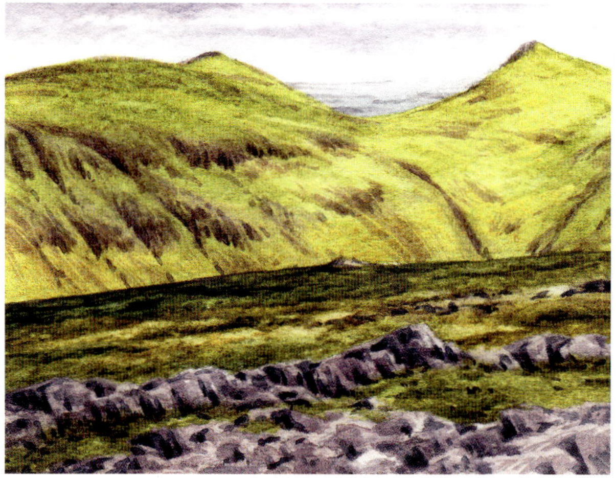

Nights on the fells.

Some people will be under the impression that Wainwright was one of those walkers who was solely a daytime visitor to the fells but this isn't quite true. It is well known of course that AW only took the bare essentials up onto the fells, a simple rucksack which apparently contained very basic rations, maybe a bit of fruit bought in a local shop, his camera, map and tobacco (a tin of Three Nuns for his pipe). As he couldn't use a compass he didn't take one. With him would also be his notebook and pencils, so it is logical that he also had a knife of some sort to sharpen his pencil and to clean out his pipe. In early forays to stay on the tops overnight AW took with him an army blanket for warmth but the extra weight didn't provide the added comfort that he needed so it was not taken on later trips. Even though there are no records of how often he did stay out on the tops there is an account where he spent the night on Harrison Stickle, watching a fox playing on a grassy shelf as the sun was going down. On these nights Wainwright did not sleep, instead he would pace about or sit in a sheltered spot, pondering his life and loves, waiting for the first hint of the new day to appear. Every half an hour he would allow himself a smoke, either from a cigarette or a pipe, this may also have helped to keep midges at bay. It must be assumed that most of these "bivouacs" as he called them were done during the short, warm nights of summer when his tweed suit would have at least kept off the night-time chill. He enjoyed these adventures as it allowed him to be on the fell tops at the start of the day, long before other walkers were about.

These days many of us also enjoy wildcamping out on the lake district fells but we normally allow ourselves the luxuries of a tent, stove, sleeping bag and decent food. During the course of this project I have experienced some superb nights out on the fells, watching the sun sinking into the sea beyond Ennerdale or the pink glow of predawn from Lingmell's summit, memories which will live with me for ever.

Wildcamping in the Lake District is tolerated as long as some basic rules are applied: Camp above the highest fell wall, leave no litter or any sign of the pitch, do not light fires, keep groups small to one or two tents, be unobtrusive, carry out everything that you carried in, perform toilet duties at least 100 feet from water and bury waste. At all times protect the environment and respect landowners and other users of the fells. On social media sites I regularly see photographs of campers not adhering to these simple rules, they are giving wildcampers a bad name, putting at risk this tolerance by the authorities which could so easily be withdrawn and the pleasure of wildcamping on the high fells overnight will be lost.

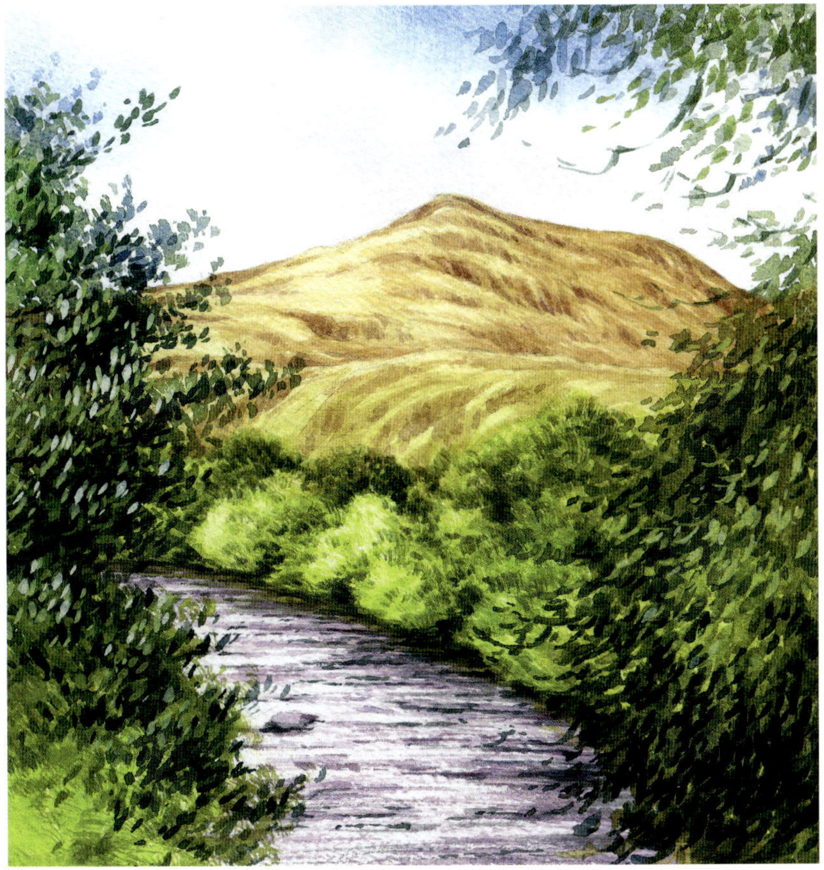

From Whahouse Bridge

15/7/09

This sketch is a good example as to why it would have been impractical to complete these sketches on location. The viewpoint is from the middle of the narrow bridge that crosses the River Esk, no place to set up an artist's easel.

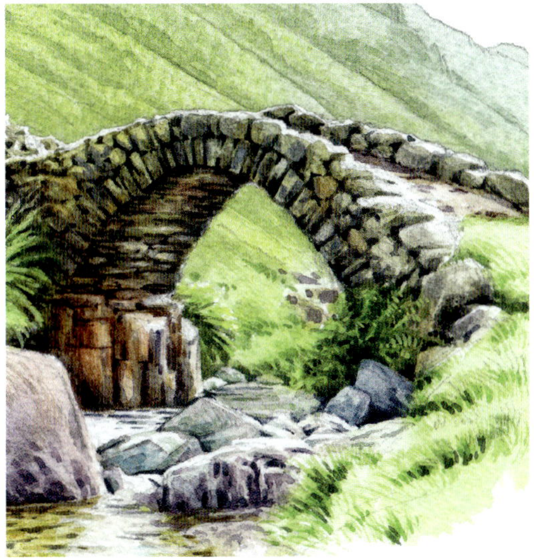

Lingcove Bridge 15/7/09

There are many old packhorse bridges in Cumbria but this one which spans Lingcove Beck near the junction with the River Esk is located in perhaps the most charming of all settings. Although it is two miles from the nearest road the walk to it is easy and worth the effort to enjoy the remote location for yourself.

Hardknott Pass 15/7/09

The cloud level was just a couple of hundred feet higher than the pass so I just managed to obtain my reference. The large cairn has gained a broader base at the expense of its height.

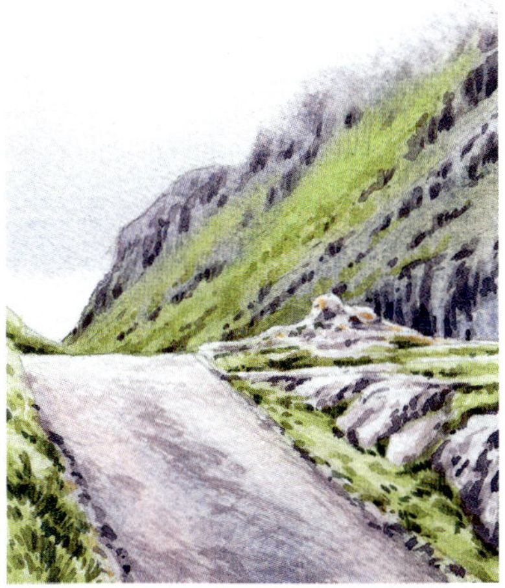

Hard Knott

The name is perhaps more associated with the Roman Fort or the high pass than the fell itself. There is limited parking space at the highest point of the Pass but from there the walk of less than a mile to the summit is not very taxing. The fell really sits on its own, not linked to others by ridges but a pleasant hour or two can be spent by visiting the fell top and admiring the Scafell Range and then exploring the area to find the Eskdale Needle and the lower top to the south west, Border End.

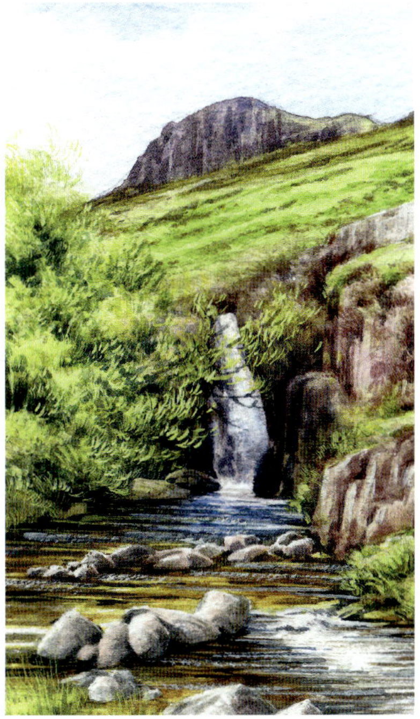

Lingcove Beck 15/7/09

From the same position where the view of the bridge above was obtained it is a simple matter of turning to the left and looking upstream to see this scene. The cascade is now partially hidden by trees but the comparison to AW's drawing can easily be made.

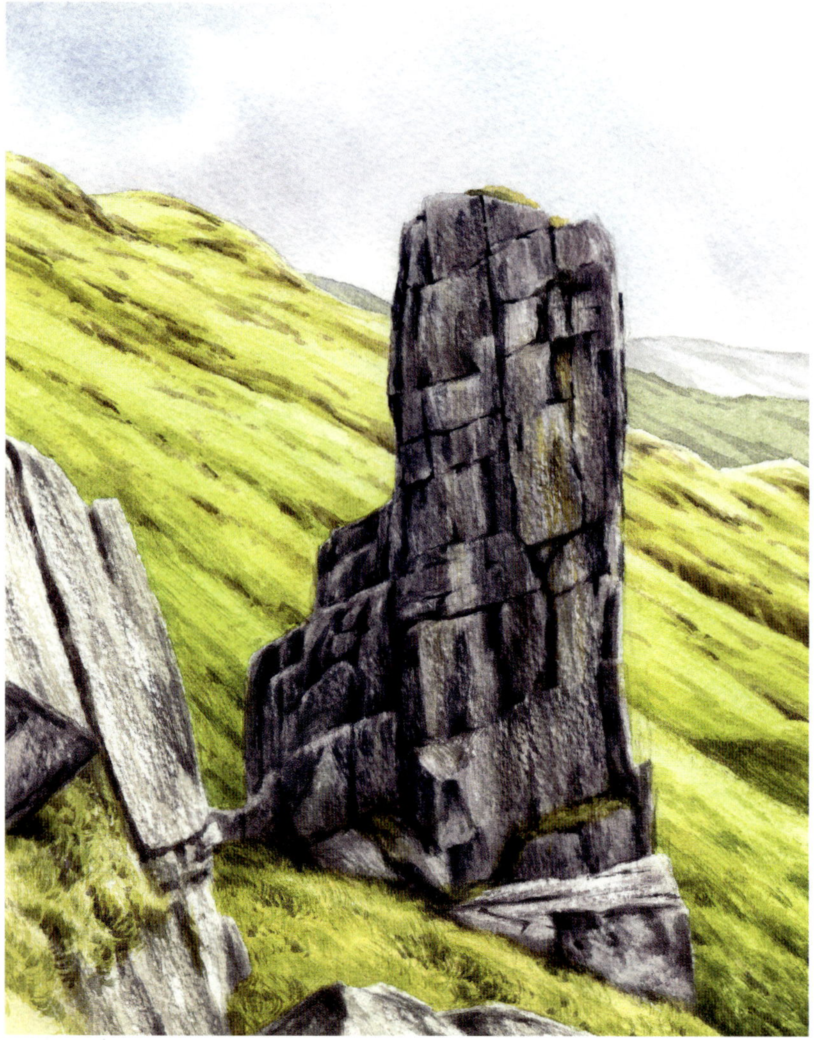

The Steeple 2/8/09

By studying his drawing and the black and white photograph which he used as a reference I was able to mark in my guide where the background horizon should be. This meant that once on location it was easier for me to confirm that I was standing in exactly the same place as where Wainwright had stood. He adjusted some of the rocks in the scene slightly but my sketch is as it was seen on the day of my visit.

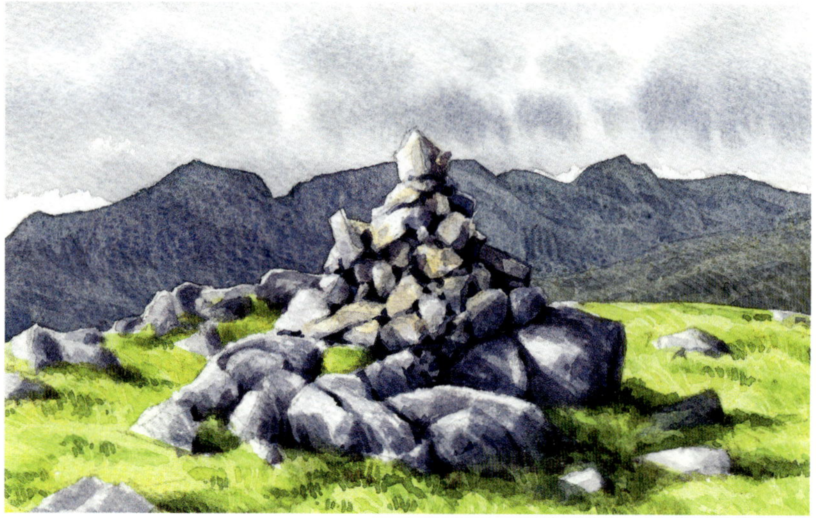

The summit 2/8/09

The cairn has been enlarged slightly and now spills over the rock on which it stands. Moving a short distance north from the summit provides a better view of the Scafells and Upper Eskdale.

The Steeple from the south 2/8/09

To visit The Steeple, also known as Eskdale Needle, which lies to the west of the summit, a descent of a couple of hundred feet down steep and pathless terrain must be made. If it is approached from a south westerly direction The Steeple itself and the distance Scafells make an excellent composition for either a photograph or painting.

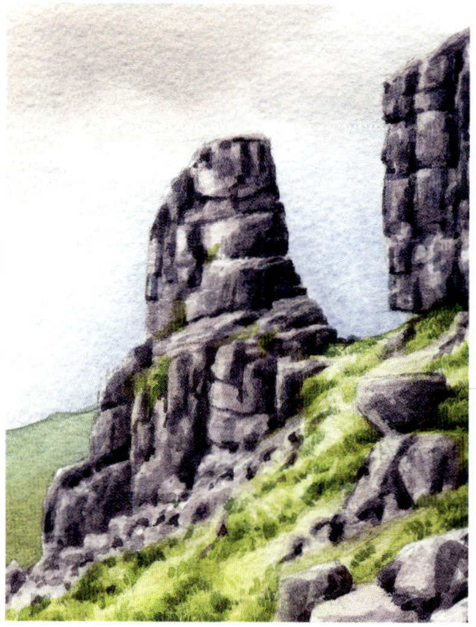

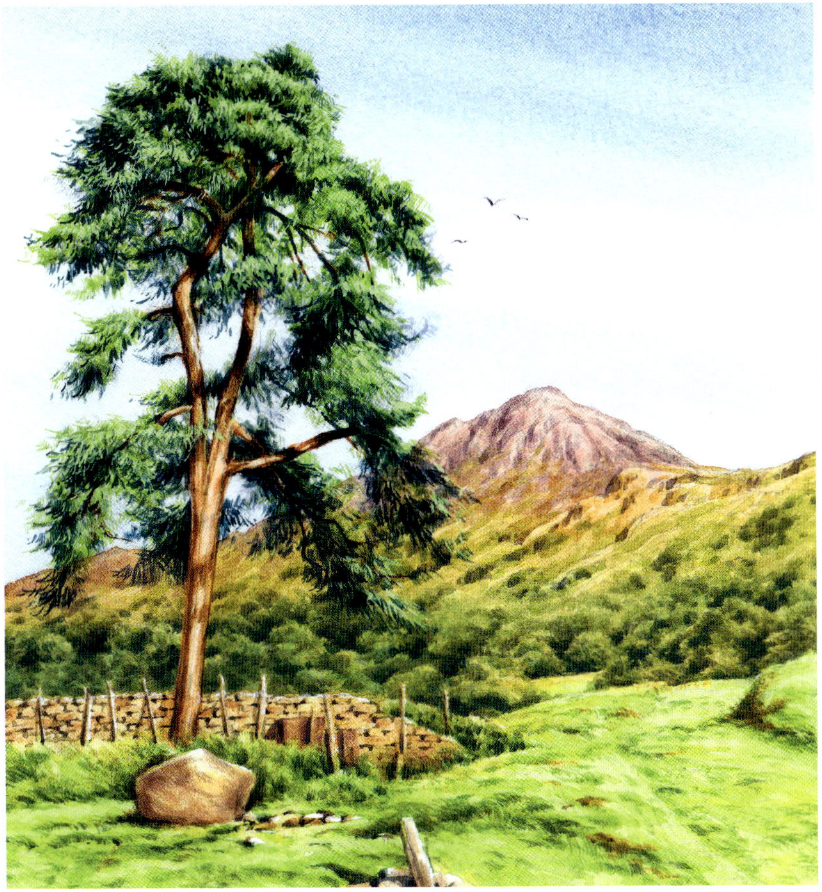

From Penny Hill 24/8/09
The walls have been altered under the lone pine.

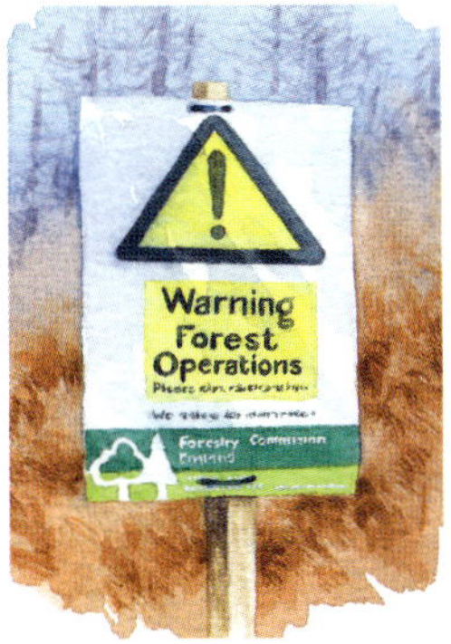

Forestry sign 23/2/10 The old signs have gone and this was the nearest modern equivalent that I could find.

Harter Fell

Much of the forest on the hill's eastern flanks have been felled. Heather blooms well in late summer on its higher slopes.

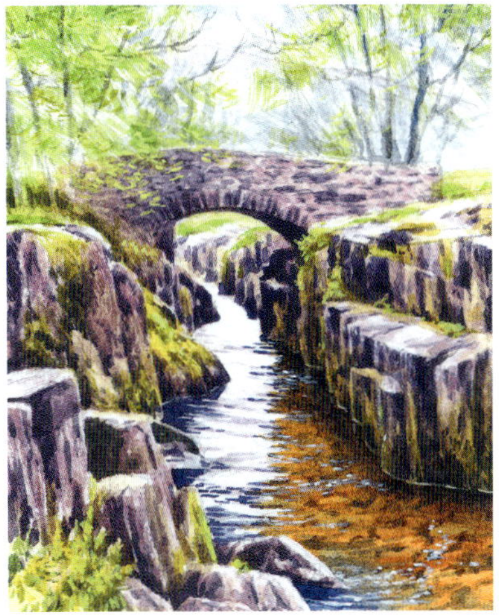

Birks Bridge 2/8/09
Clear waters of the River Duddon flow through this narrow gorge.

The official summit 24/8/09
The higher summit beyond has no flat space for a cairn or column.

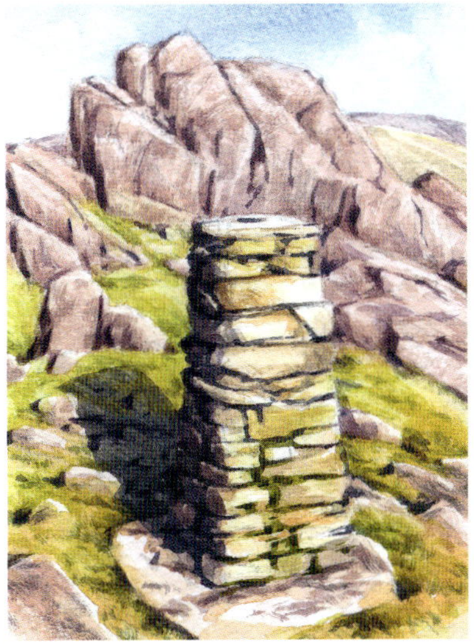

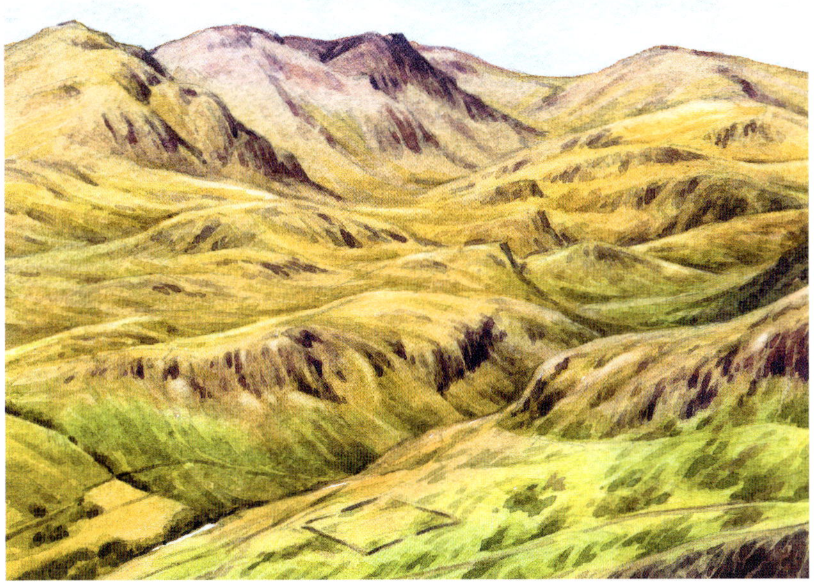

The head of Eskdale 24/8/09
A superb view with the Roman Fort included in the scene.

From the Walna Scar Path 2/8/09
The fell seen across the valley from just above Broad Haws.

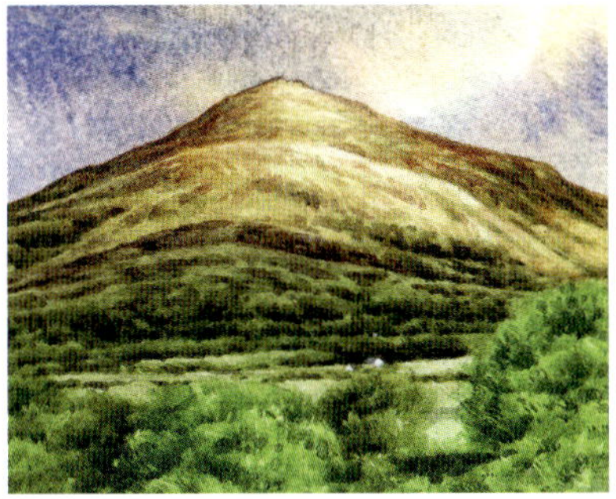

The summit 24/8/09
These rocks to the west of the pillar are not the actual true top.

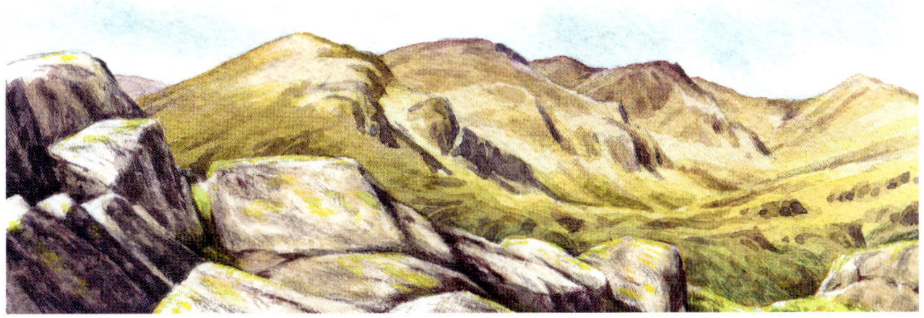

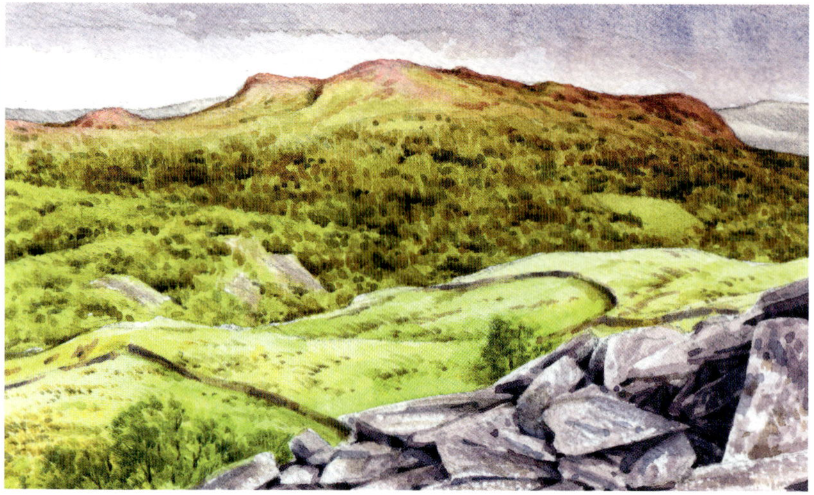

From Tunnel Quarry Low Fell 30/7/09
The wall shown in AW's illustration is all but gone with only a layer or two remaining, piles of untidy slate indicate its former construction.

From the north ridge 30/7/09
The north ridge of the fell has little in the way of paths so this viewpoint required some trekking through deep heather.

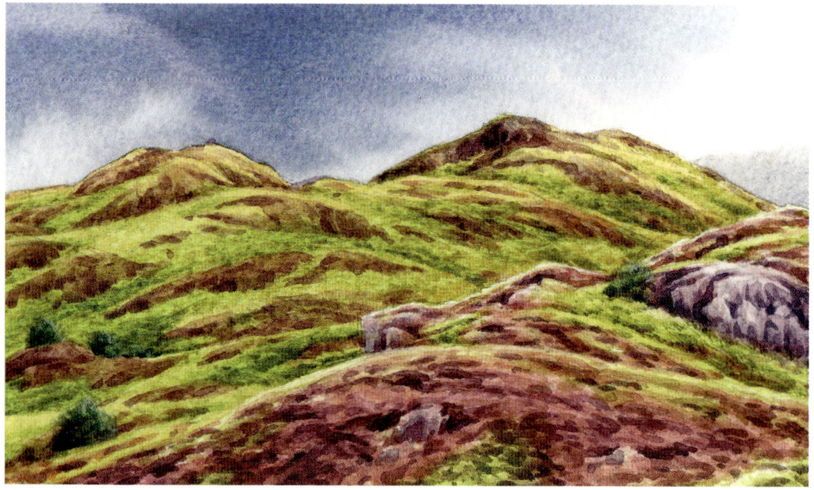

Holme Fell

Even though this fell only just rises above 1000' it is worthy of exploration. The lower slopes are cloaked with mixed native woodland which then higher up thins out to areas of heather and bare grey rocks that in late summer make a picturesque patchwork of natural colour. Man has left his mark here though and a look into to the nearby vast disused slate quarry of Hodge Close should also be on the itinerary of places to visit.

The big cairn of Ivy Crag
30/7/09
The only explanation as to why this cairn should be bigger than the one on the actual summit must be down to the availability of building materials. Grisedale Hause is the col to the right on the horizon.

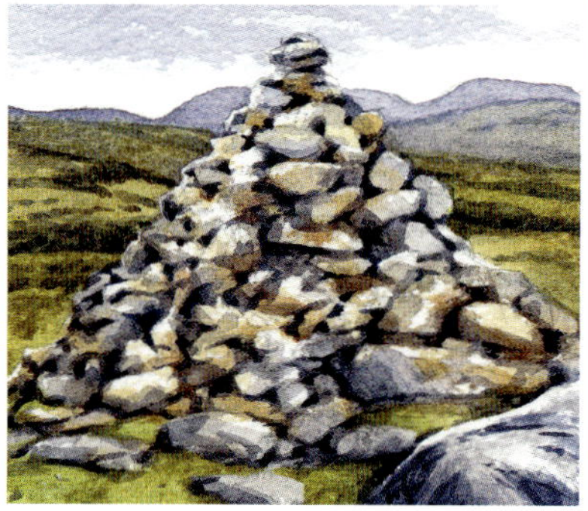

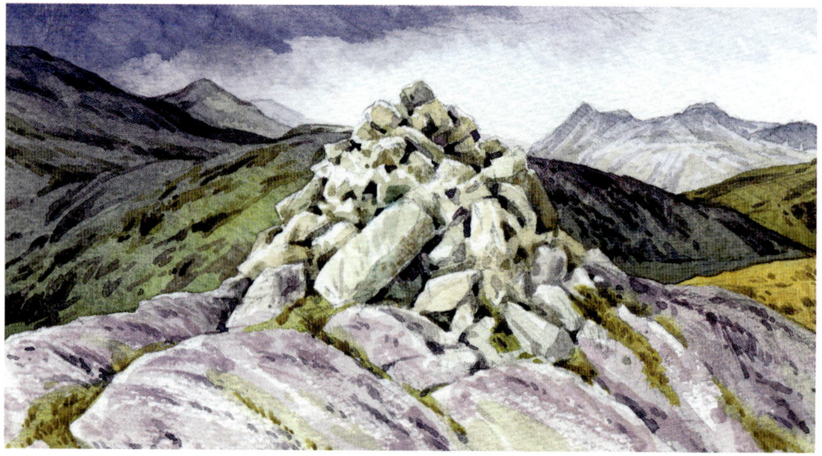

The summit 30/7/09
Now a cairn sits on the platform of rock that in AW's day was bare of any such adornment.

The admired Scot's Pine.

At the bottom of the Holme Fell 2 page, AW adds a note about a solitary Scot's Pine which he admired opposite the junction of the Hodge Close road, where there was a bus stop. Sadly the tree was blown down in a winter storm in the early 1980s and a younger pine is now sited at that location. There is however a fine mature specimen of such a tree about 100 yards along the road opposite the junction to Tilberthwaite which must have been there in AW's day but which didn't gain his admiration.

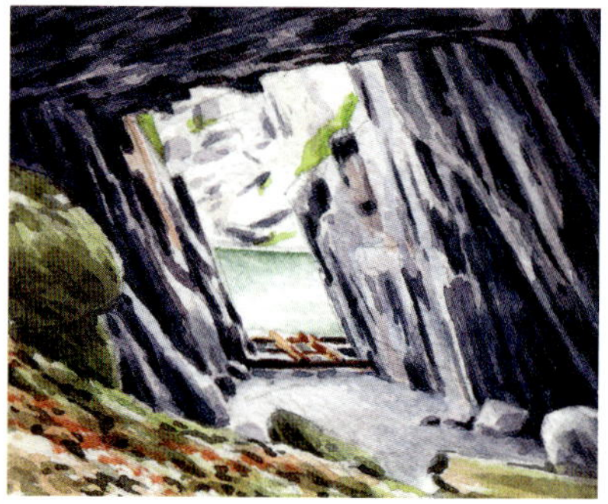

The arch 30/7/09
Perhaps due its small scale or more likely the quality of his reference photograph, Wainwright's sketch of this scene has some inaccuracies including the width of the hole and the appearance of the lake. It is an impressive site of the area's industrial past.

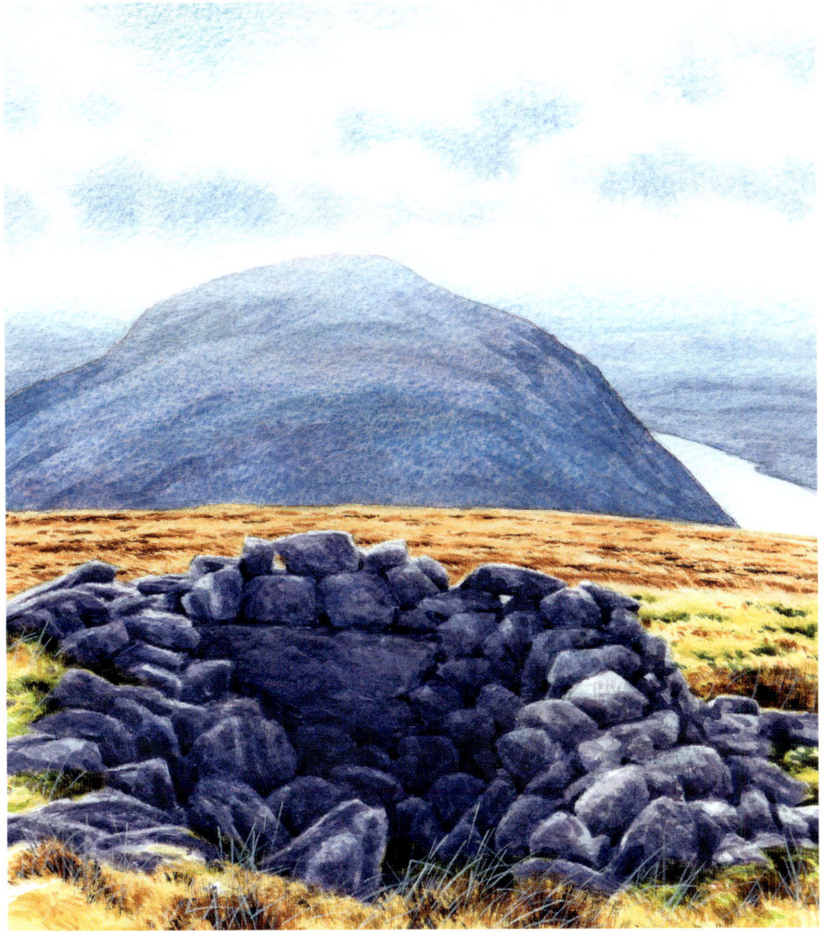

From Green How 31/3/09
This is a shelter of some age possibly built by shepherds. Away from regular walking paths it took some finding and remains relatively unchanged. The fell has a wider spread than depicted in the guidebook.

Illgill Head

The short cropped turf of the fell top makes for easy walking and is in total contrast to the steep cliffs of loose rock that fall to the very edge of Wastwater on the north western side of the fell.

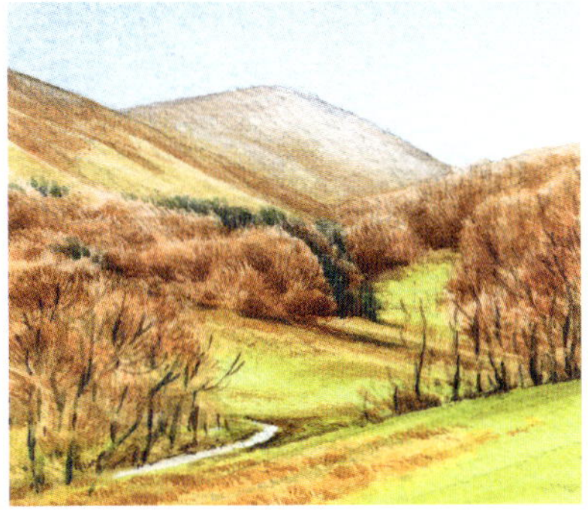

From Miterdale 31/3/09
The quiet valley of Miterdale, seen here from close to Bakerstead Farm which in AW's day was in ruins but is now an outdoor pursuits centre.

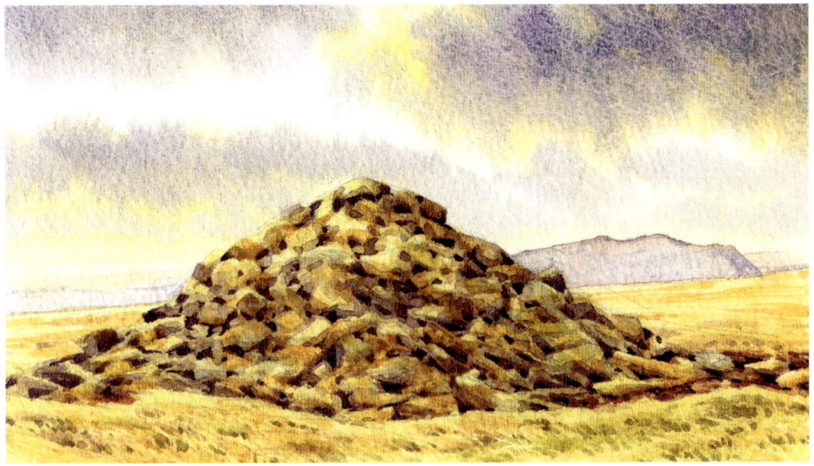

The summit 13/4/08
Using the shading in AW's drawing as a clue I concluded that the sketch should be from the north east so Whin Rigg is to the right of the cairn.

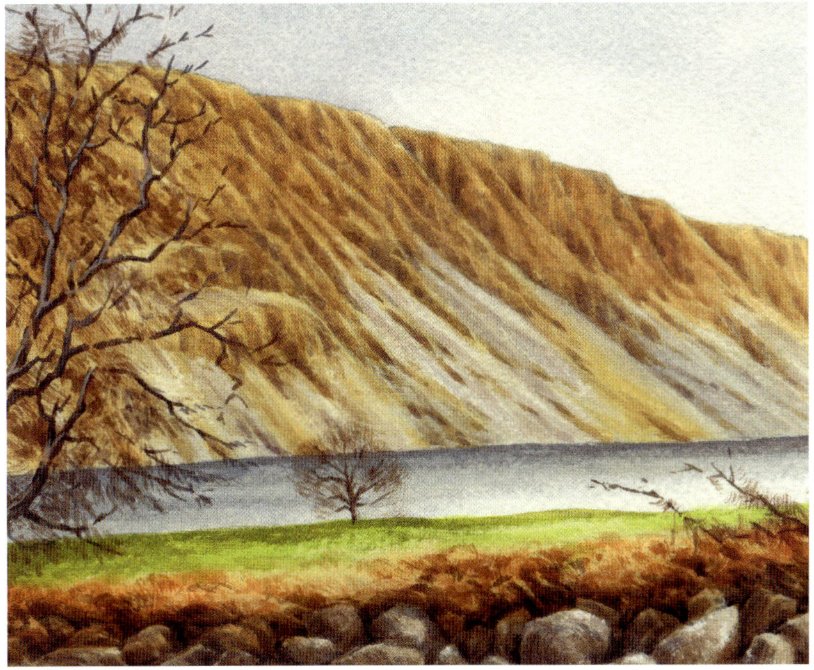

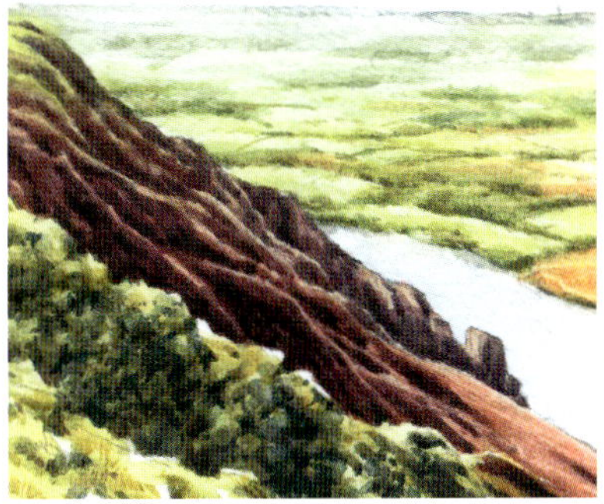

Wastwater from the summit 15/4/14
This spectacular view is from near the head of Great Gully.

Wastwater Screes 17/3/16
My original sketch of this view was incorrect so I had to revisit and then repaint the scene from this location near Overbeck Bridge.

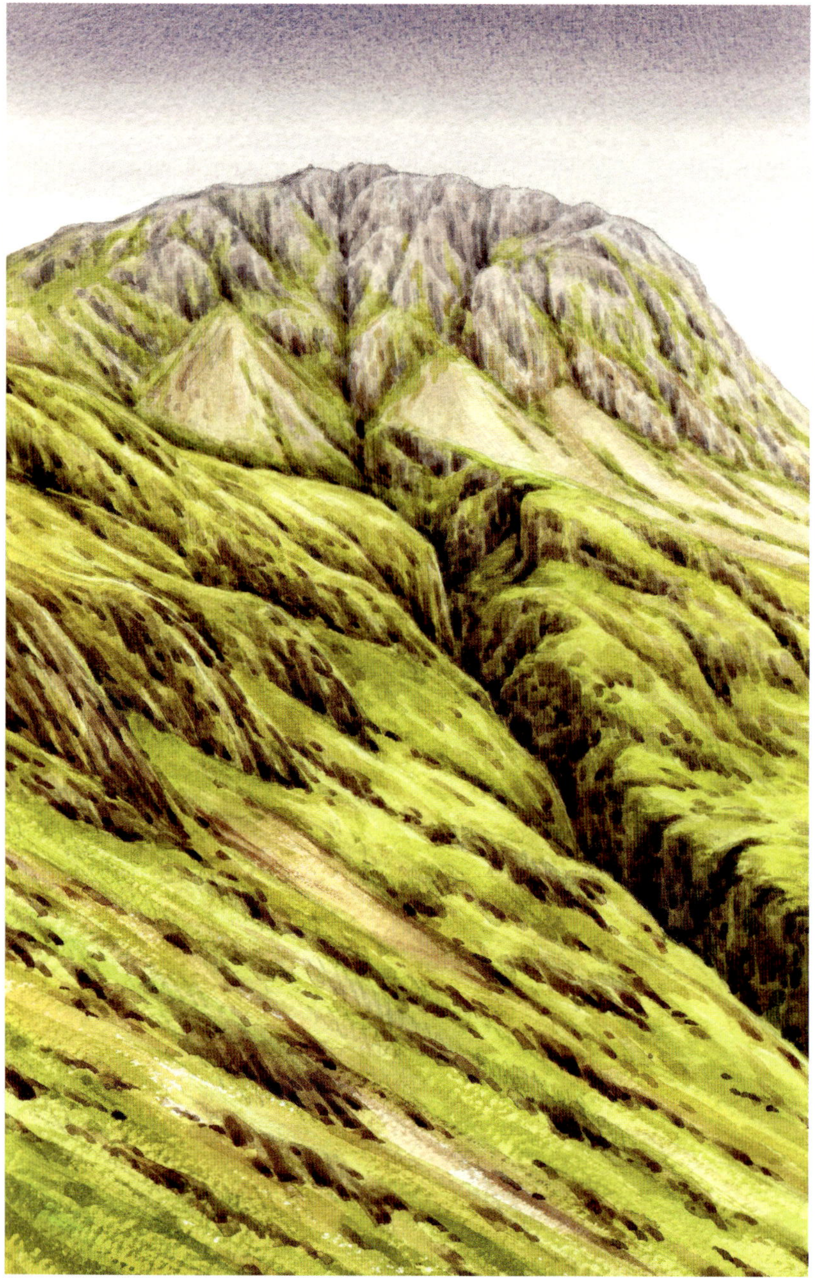

Lingmell

I have many fond memories of climbing Lingmell which includes a superb night's wild camping on its very summit, a star filled sky was followed by a glorious pink dawn. The views from the fell of Great Gable's steep southern flanks are second to none. The Pillar range, Mosedale and Wasdale Head are also well seen from this vantage point.

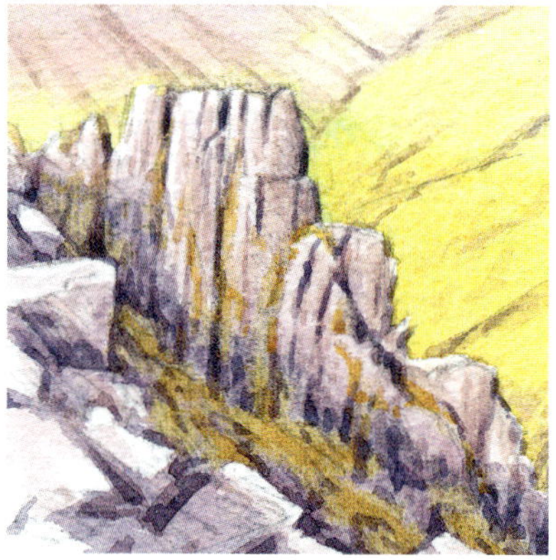

Summit arête 10/4/11
On looking down into Piers Gill from the summit this fin-like outcrop is just down to the left.

From the Corridor Route
23/8/13
There is a short rock step on the Corridor Route, this scene is taken from close to that point.

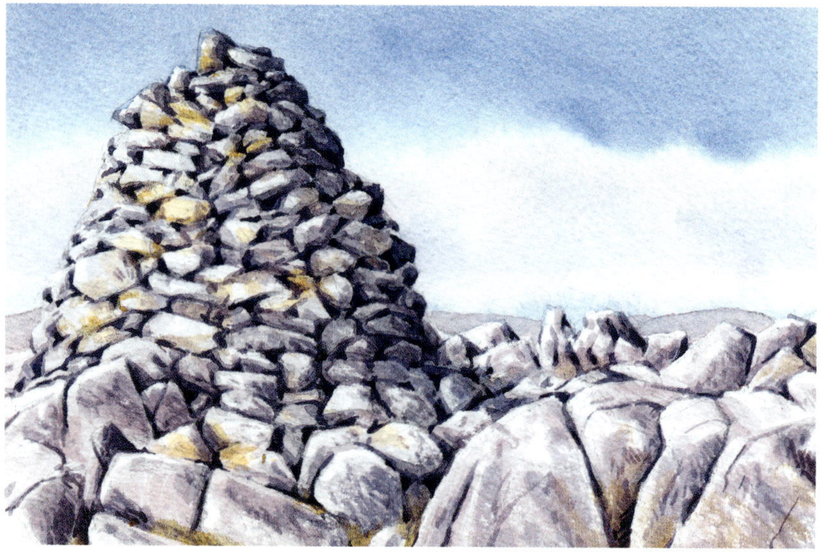

The summit 10/4/11
The tall slender column in his drawing didn't last long, it was already down by 1961. A short distance north of here is a more recent column, also tall and slender but with a commanding view of Great Gable.

Mickledore and Scafell Crag 10/4/11
Only by visiting the area of Goat Crags to the south east of Lingmell summit was I able to precisely line up the features in his illustration.

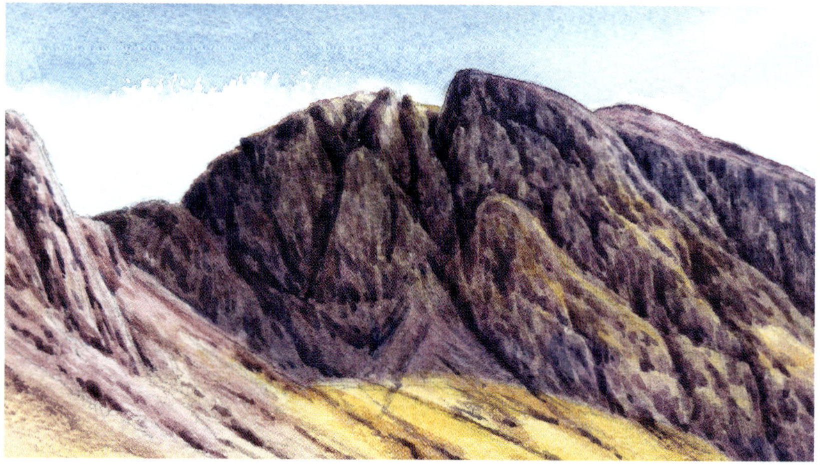

Piers Gill

A deep ravine with almost sheer sides in places. Take it from me, you don't want to venture into there by accident on a dark and damp night- but that was a long time ago.

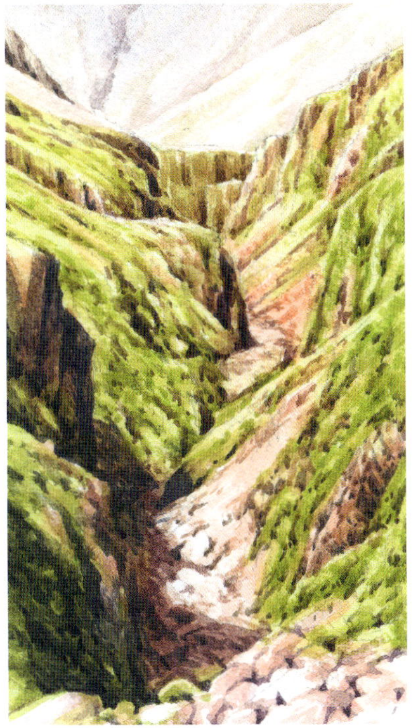

The upper section 4/7/06
The view that many people see of this ravine, looking down from the Corridor Route.

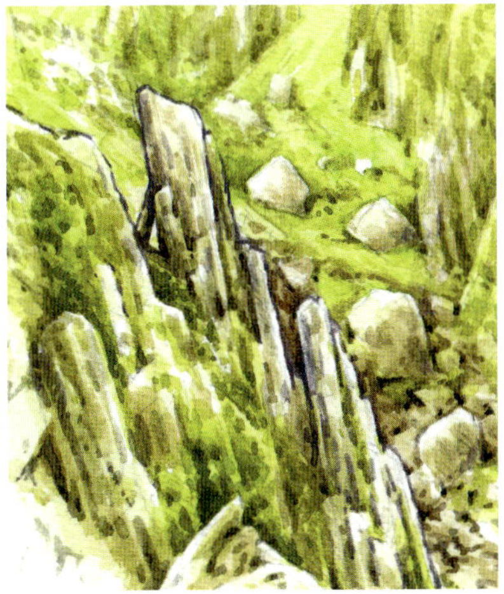

Pinnacles and spires 23/8/13
Locating these exact rock features took more than one visit to the gill.

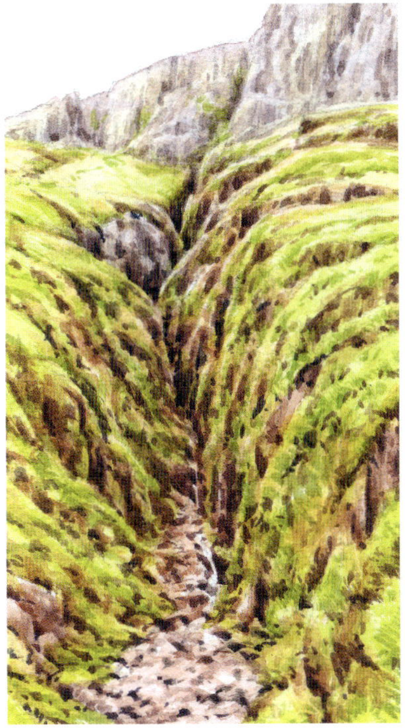

The lower section 4/7/06
Looking up the gorge, one of the earliest references obtained for the project.

Scafell Pike from Lingmell 10/4/11
The view from close to the fell's summit.

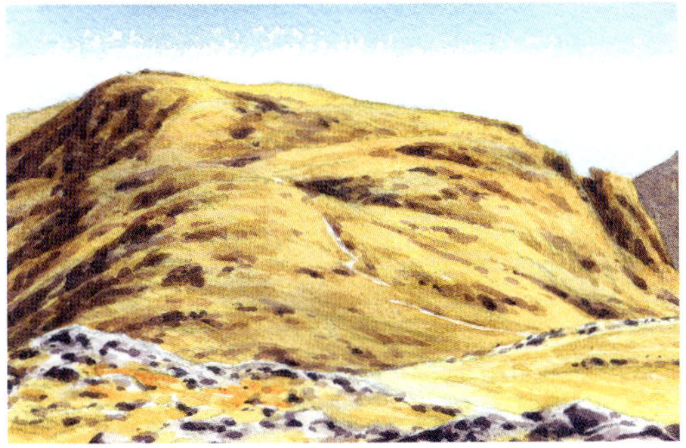

Great Gable from Lingmell 10/4/11
With one of Lakeland's giants neatly framed by the steep, rough walls of the ravine I would rate this as one of the best full page drawings in all of the Pictorial Guides. The wall on the right still has that rock that juts out which even though it is not as vertical as in Wainwright's illustration was still a good reference point for me when taking my photograph. I even managed to capture the shadow of Tophet Bastion in Great Hell Gill on Gable in a similar position which indicates that AW stood here at a comparable time of day.

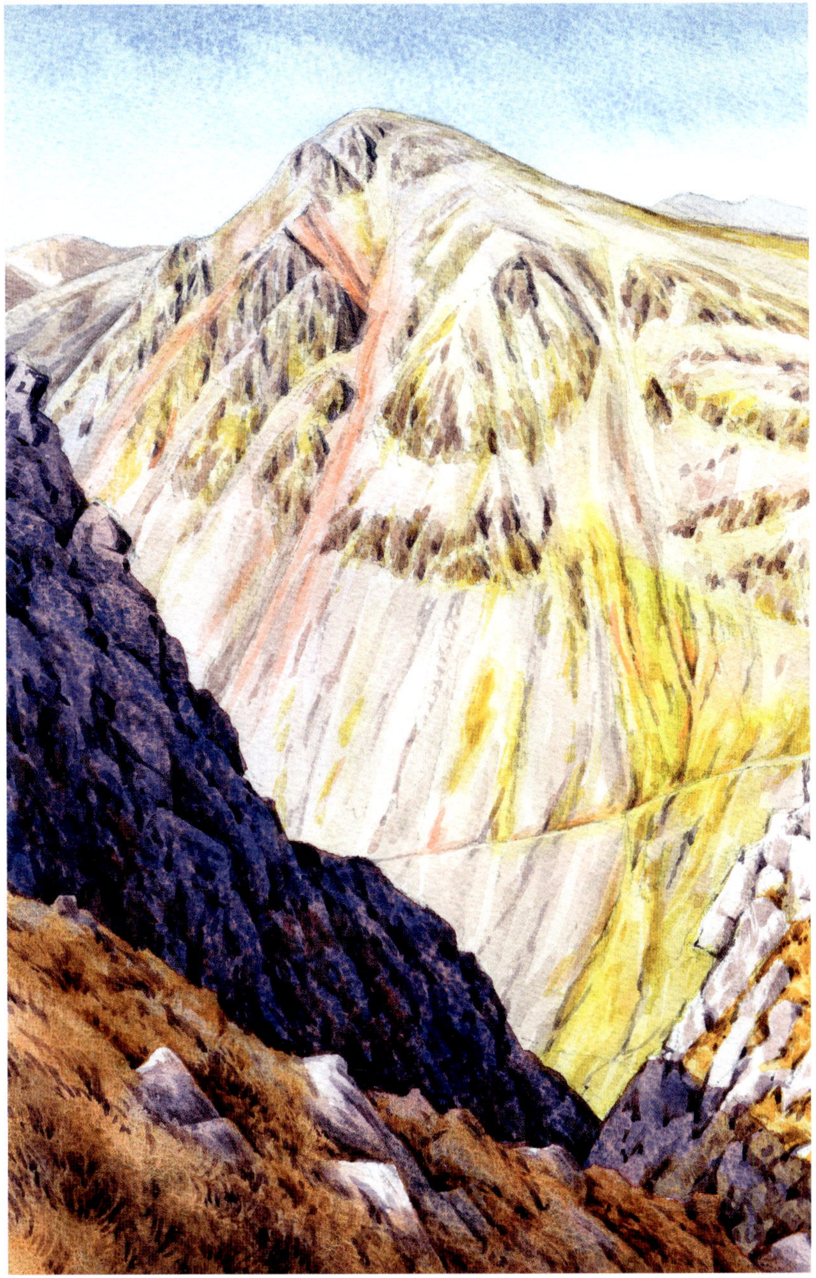

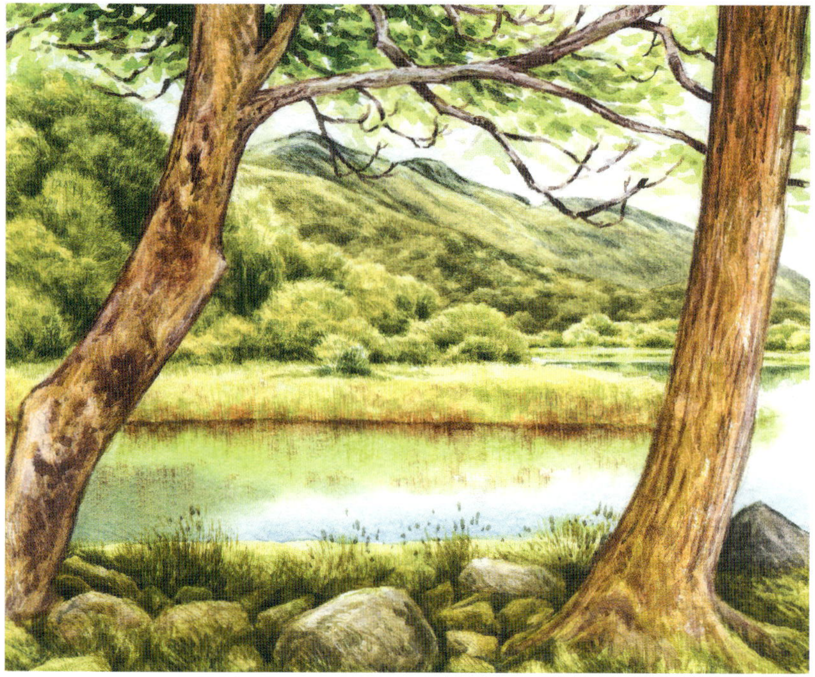

From Elterwater 10/6/11
I have used some artistic license to thin out the branches of the two trees that featured in AW's drawing so that the fell can be seen over the reflective waters of this serene lake.

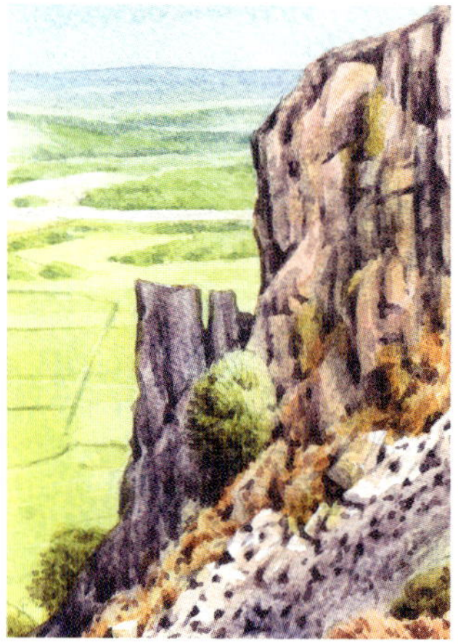

Oak How Needle 29/5/11
Elterwater Quarries as viewed from the Needle. No path exists to this location.

Lingmoor Fell
A visit to this fell's summit and along to Side Pike will give newcomers to Langdale a great insight to this area's dramatic and inspiring topography.

Bowfell 26/11/07
The ridge known as The Band leading up to the fell, from the west end of Side Pike.

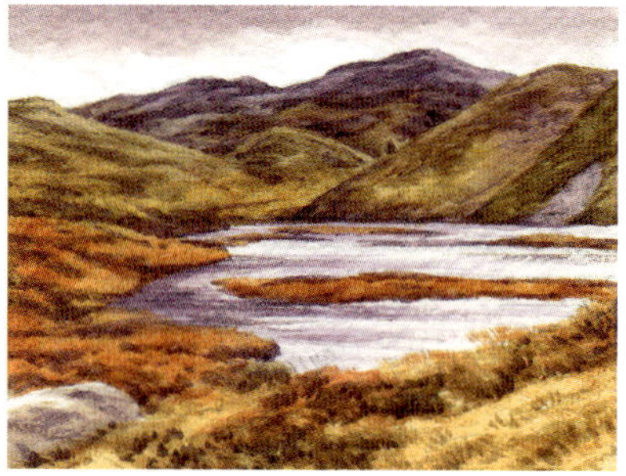

Lingmoor Tarn 25/11/07
The tarn outlet close to the ruined (dam?) wall which is not marked in the guide.

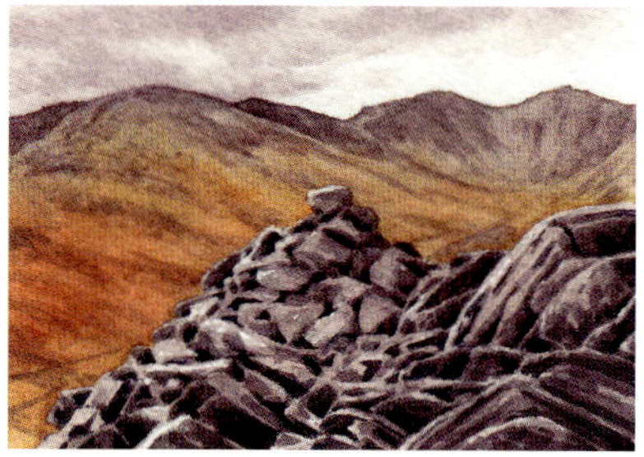

The summit 25/11/07
The most northern of the Coniston Fells beyond the small cairn.

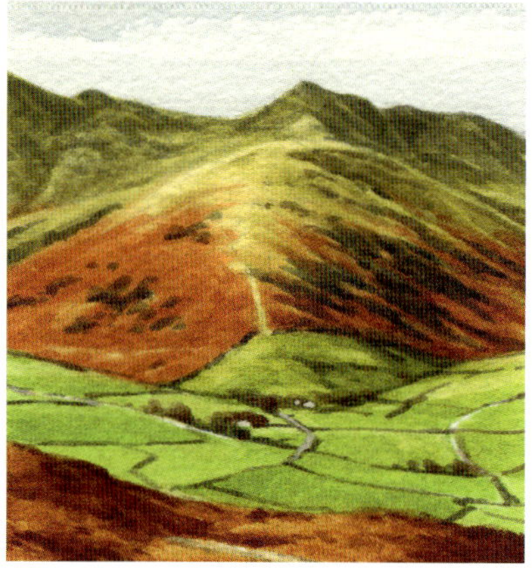

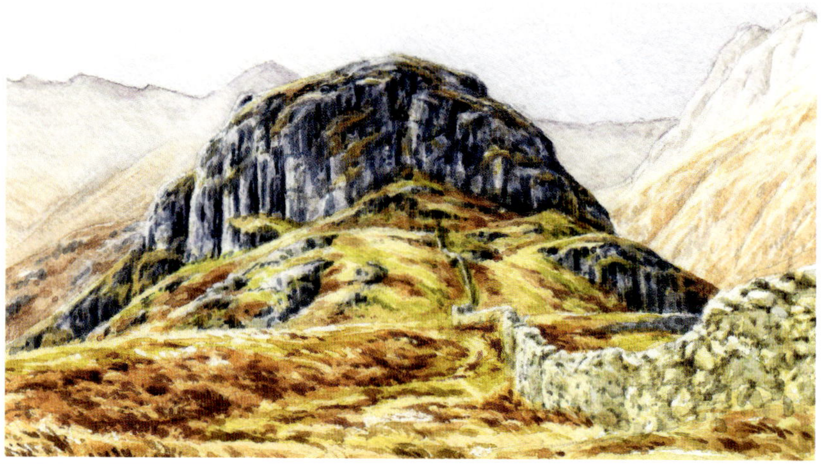

Side Pike 26/11/07
The top of the Pike is reached by a path round to the left at the base of the crag, this passes through a cleft in the rock called Fat Man's Agony. AW didn't mention this feature as his path took a lower and wider route and it appears that he may not have known of it at the time.

Langdale Pikes from Side Pike 26/11/07
Side Pike's small summit cairn has gone but the view is still breathtaking.

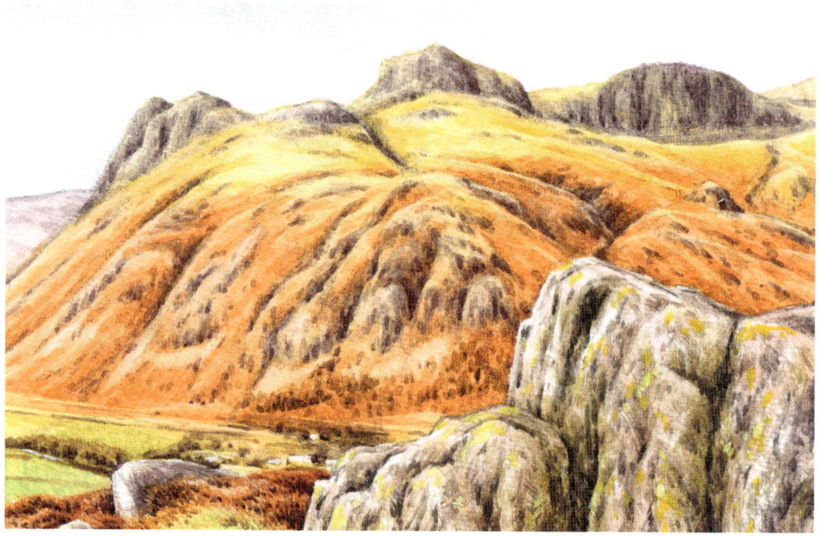

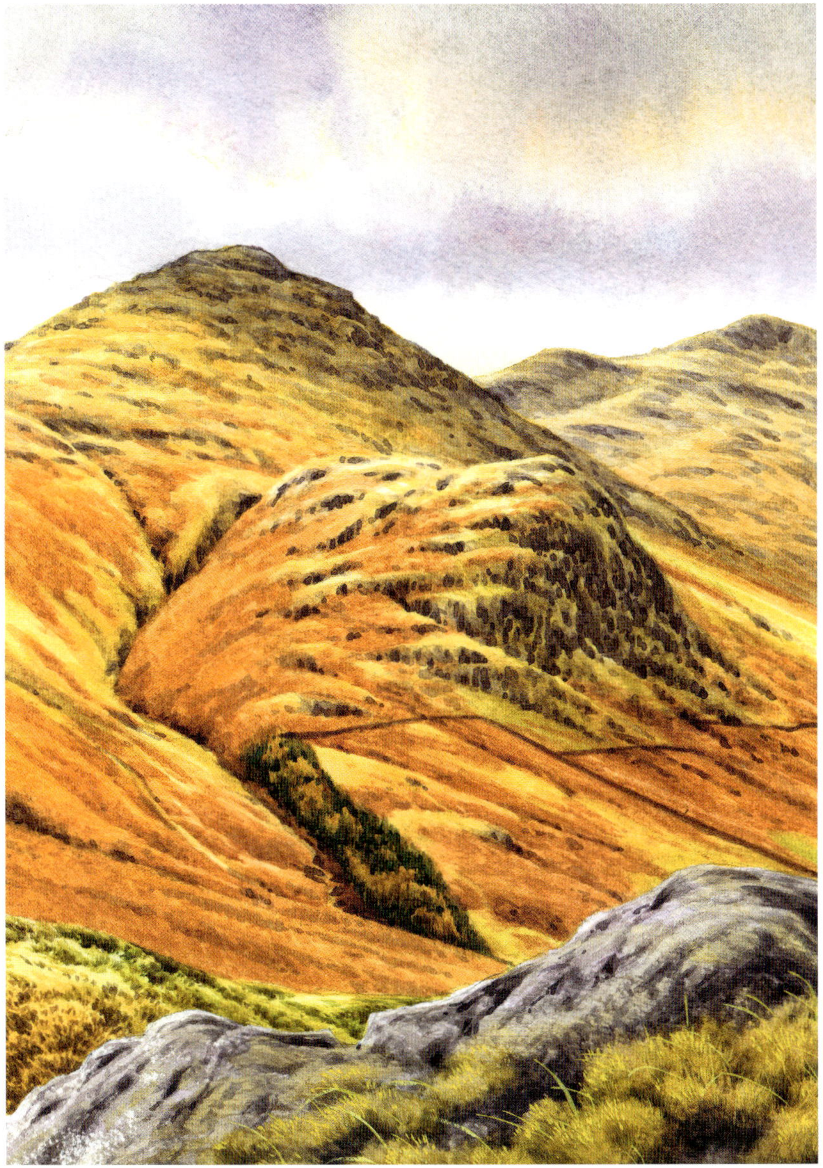

From Side Pike 26/11/07
The winter colours of the bracken covered fell side as seen from the western slopes of Side Pike. The summit cairn is no longer as obvious.

Pike o' Blisco

Even though this fell is not as popular as other Langdale giants, Pike o' Blisco still can easily hold its own in such notable company. Its conical peak shape draws attention from the valley floor which it overlooks. In my opinion it is best climbed from Great Langdale via Oxendale.

The Needle, Black Crag
24/10/08
There are records that this pinnacle was first climbed in 1955, a few years before AW's visit. Black Crag itself has over 100 climbing routes listed.

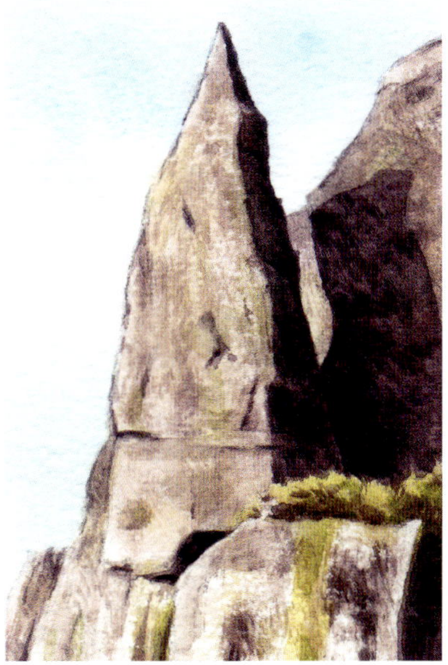

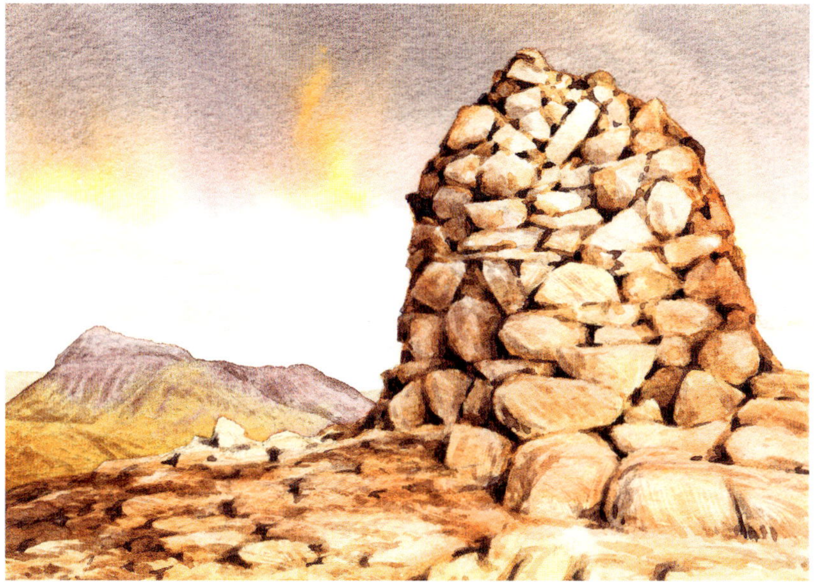

The summit 23/9/08
Before Book Four was completed in 1959 the tall cairn had been toppled but it had been rebuilt by 1961. The current version is more squat but some of its stones have been taken to make a fairly inadequate shelter nearby.

Bowfell from the summit
24/10/08
Looking across Oxendale from near the low wind shelter.

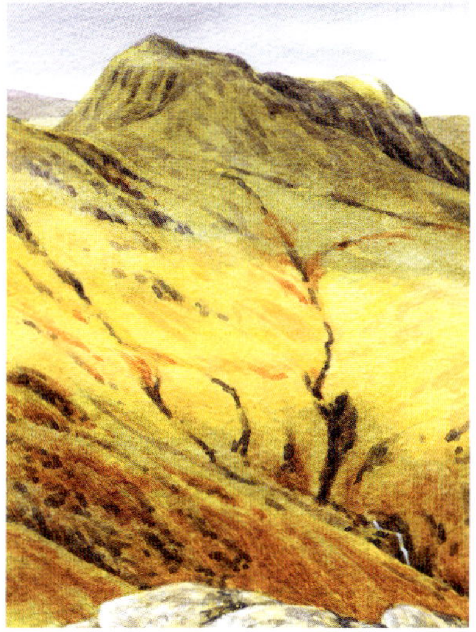

Kettle Crag 8/7/09
The Crag as viewed from the top of the road near Side Pike.

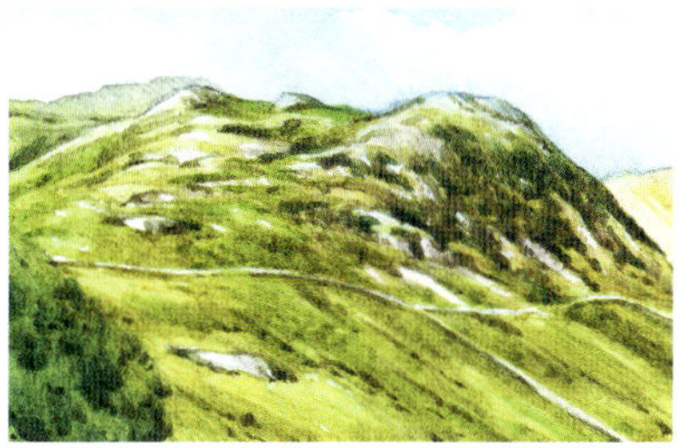

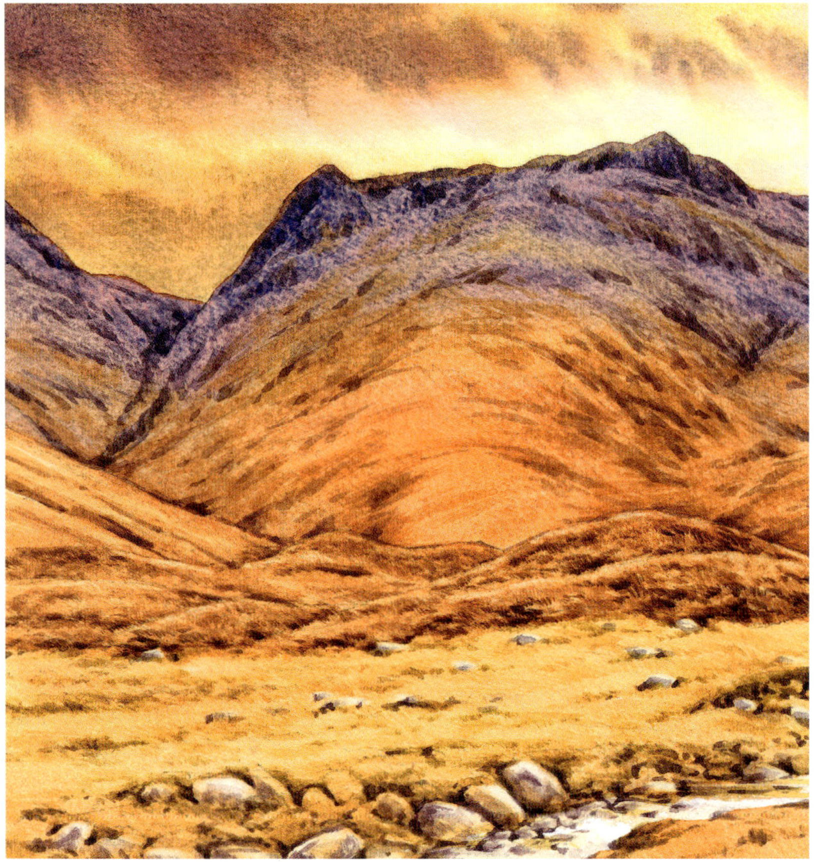

From Mickleden 8/7/09

I had to walk the one mile length of Mickleden surveying the changing scene before me until it matched up with the features of AW's drawing. It was late in the evening and the light was fading. The moraines in the valley bottom were the key, once their rounded shapes corresponded to the guide I knew I was standing in the right place. Due to the perspective it would appear that the top on the right (Buck Pike) is higher than the actual summit which it isn't of course, although Wainwright drew the peak on the left higher to accentuate the true top. The ravine of Rossett Gill is on the left.

Rossett Pike

The popular route to Scafell Pike from Langdale will see thousands of eager walkers pass along Mickleden every year. To them the target is England's highest mountain with little interest shown in lesser fells like Rossett Pike that they pass by, nor to the history of the trade route that they are following up and over Rossett Pass.

From the top of Rossett Pass 3/10/08

The crags drop down into the depths of Rossett Gill.

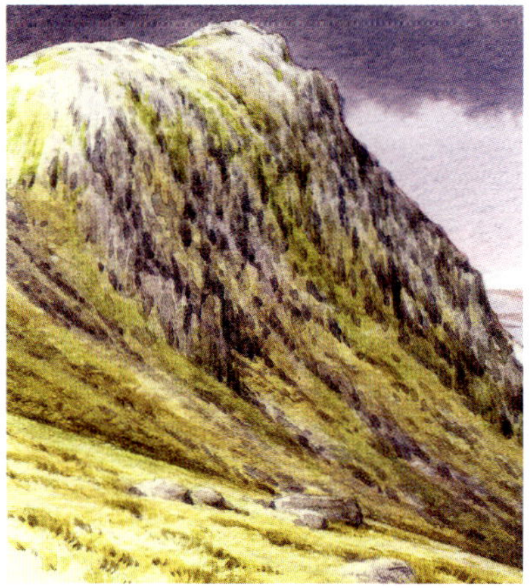

The summit 3/10/08

The loose arrangement of orange tinted rocks mark the recognised summit. The Mickleden cairn was easier to see from here in AW's day but it is now fallen. Its location is in between the two rocky outcrops in the mid distance.

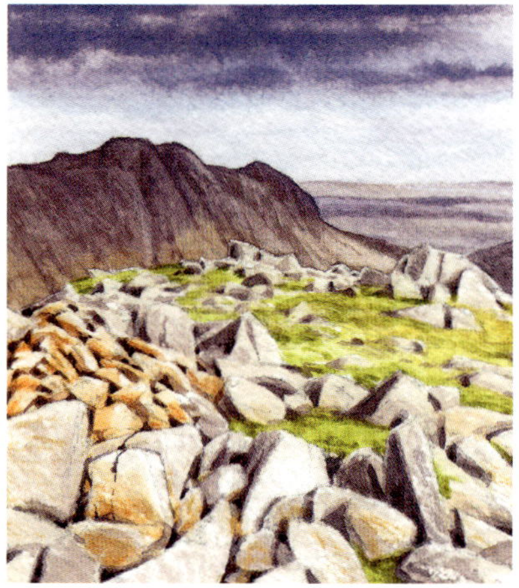

Mickleden 8/7/09

After a lengthy period of searching I just could not find the foreground rocks in his drawing, I now know that they were not in his reference photograph but artistic additions. Mickleden Beck takes a new route now.

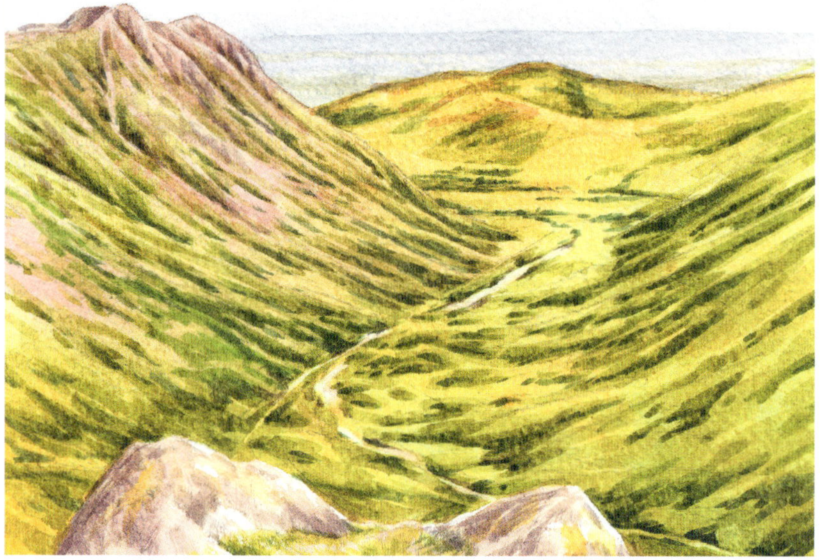

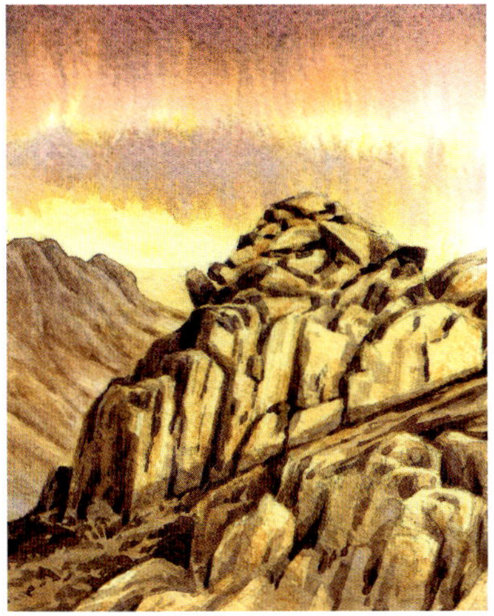

The Mickleden Cairn 3/10/08

The site of this cairn gives superb views along the length of the valley. Sadly the once tidy structure has seen better days.

The packwoman's grave 3/10/08

My sketch, like AW's drawing, does not give the exact location of this cross of stones which marks the site where this woman pedlar died, but modern research facilities easily identify the place. It was when travelling to Langdale from Wasdale in the late 18th century that she perished in a snowstorm. Her body was found some weeks later and buried at the site.

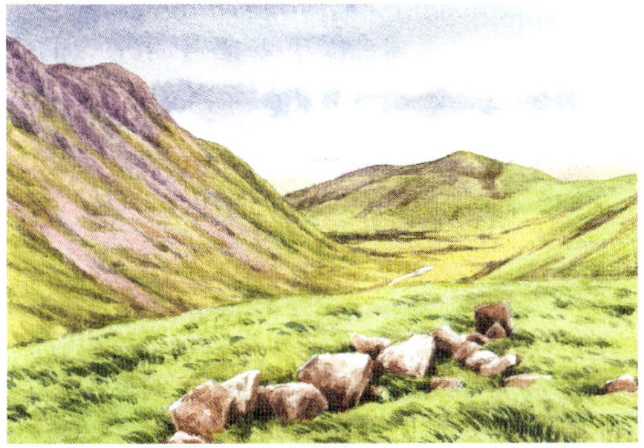

Rossett Pike and Rossett Gill

8/7/09

I recall in my early walking days in this area that the main route here was in the gill, a rough ankle twister of a place. Thankfully in recent years and after sections of the old pony route have been repaired, the old gill has been practically abandoned by walkers. This viewpoint is from part of the pony route on the grass ridge that is now totally unused and without paths. By comparing AW's drawing to my sketch it can be seen how the bad scarring to the left of the gill near the bottom has now almost fully recovered because of the footpath repair work.

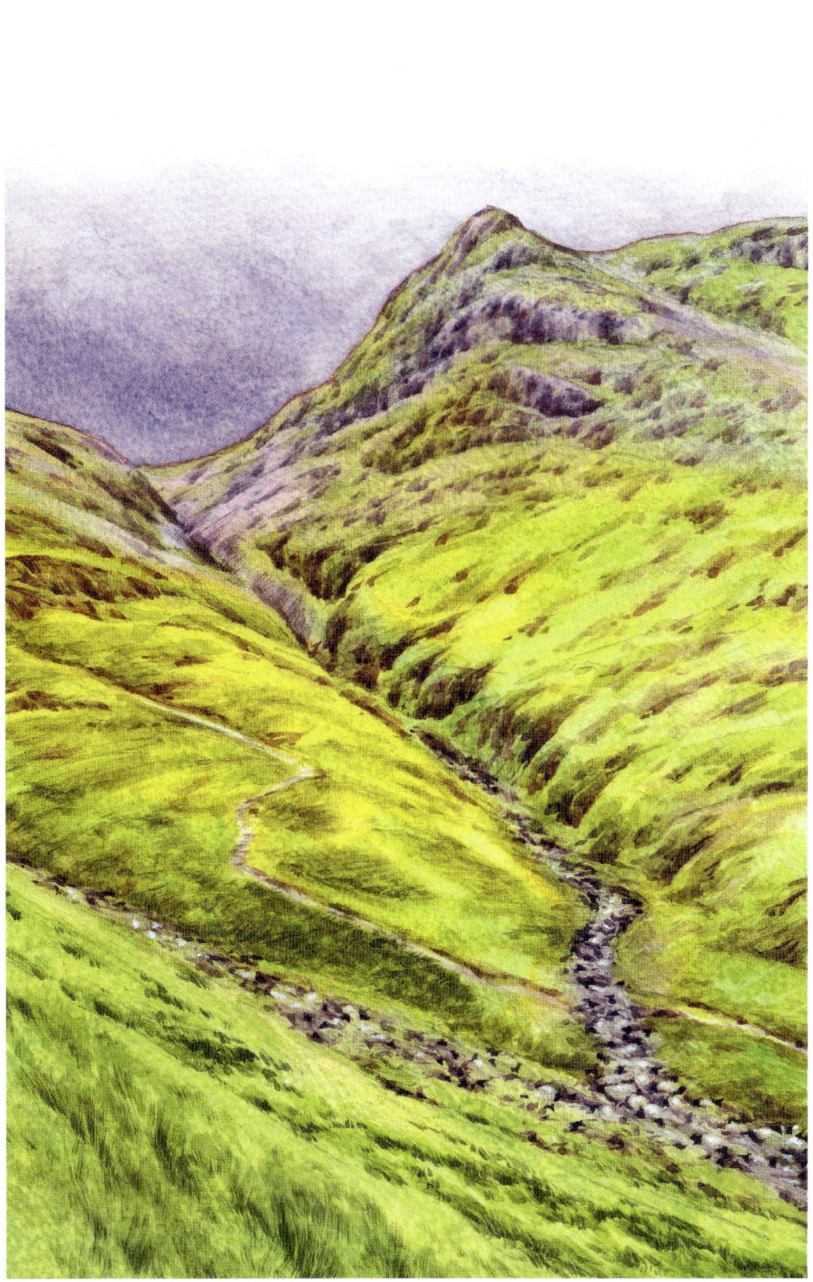

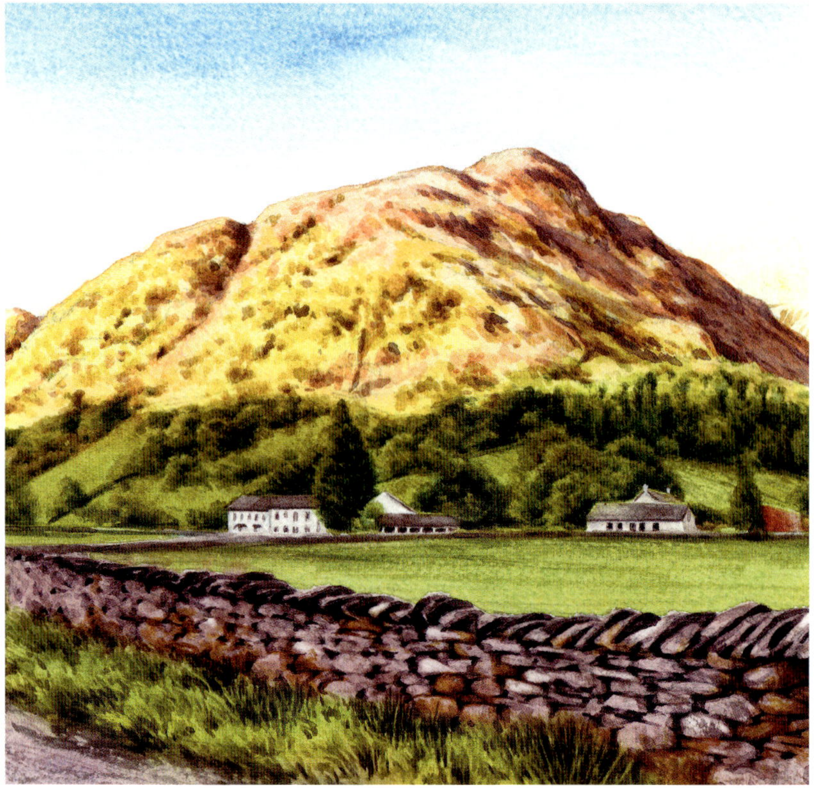

From Stonethwaite road end 12/6/09
The drama of the fell is reduced when seen in real life from this position, 100 yards from the junction with the Borrowdale road.

Rosthwaite Fell

The area of high ground that rises to the south of Stonethwaite village includes a number of tops and is generally covered by the name Rosthwaite Fell with recognised named features include Bessyboot, Rosthwaite Cam, Cam Crag and Dovenest Crag. It may seem odd that AW chose to class Bessyboot, the lowest of the tops as his summit for the book but this may be explained by the fact that Ordnance Survey maps of the time only marked one named spot height in this area, that of Bessyboot at 1807'.

South Chimney and Cave
12/6/09
Looking into the crack in the rock that is the entrance to the cave.

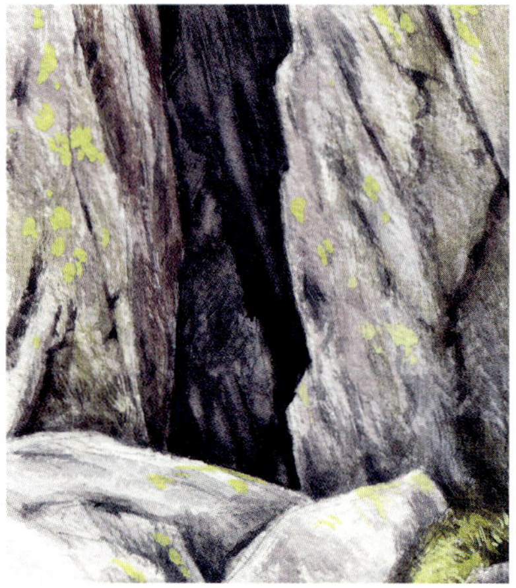

Doves Nest Caves

Doves Nest Crag 12/6/09
In truth the drawing which was a reference for this sketch (right) was more of an illustrative diagram by AW to show the routes on this climbers crag. If I omitted it though the sketch on the left would have been rather meaningless. The view of mine is from the scree path below the crag and that means the perspective is different to the sketch in the guide. It is certainly worth a visit if in the area of Combe Gill. Millican Dalton was a regular climber on this crag. AW was guided to the crag by A. Harry Griffin but refused to venture in.

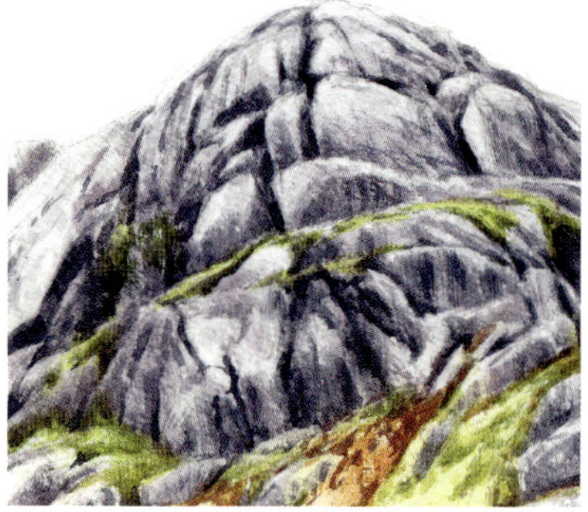

The summit 12/6/09
The cairn on Bessyboot shown here, now sits on top of the bedrock which is shaded in AW's drawing.

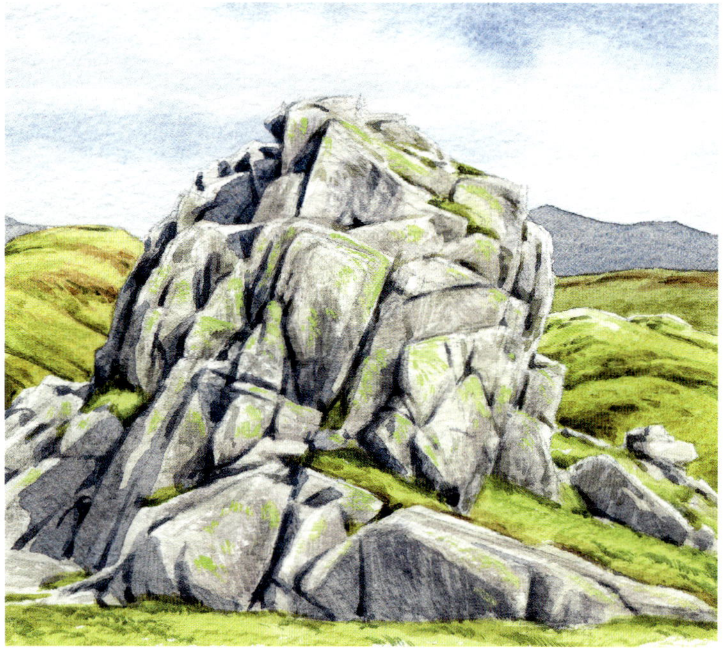

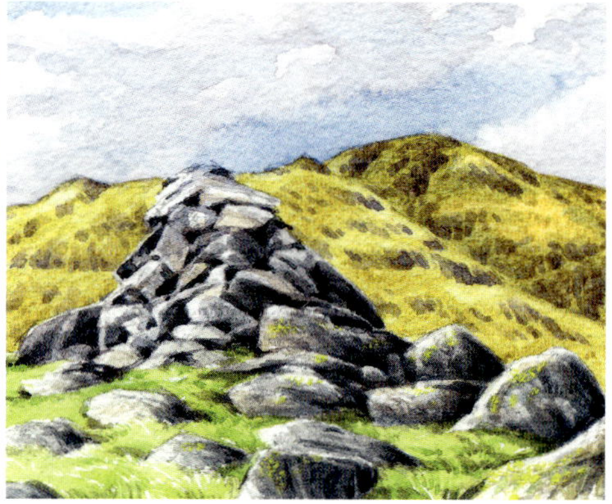

Rosthwaite Cam 12/6/09
This castle of rock is about 100' higher than the summit of Bessyboot. This craggy outcrop requires an easy scramble to access the very top. The small cairn in his drawing is now just one or two stones.

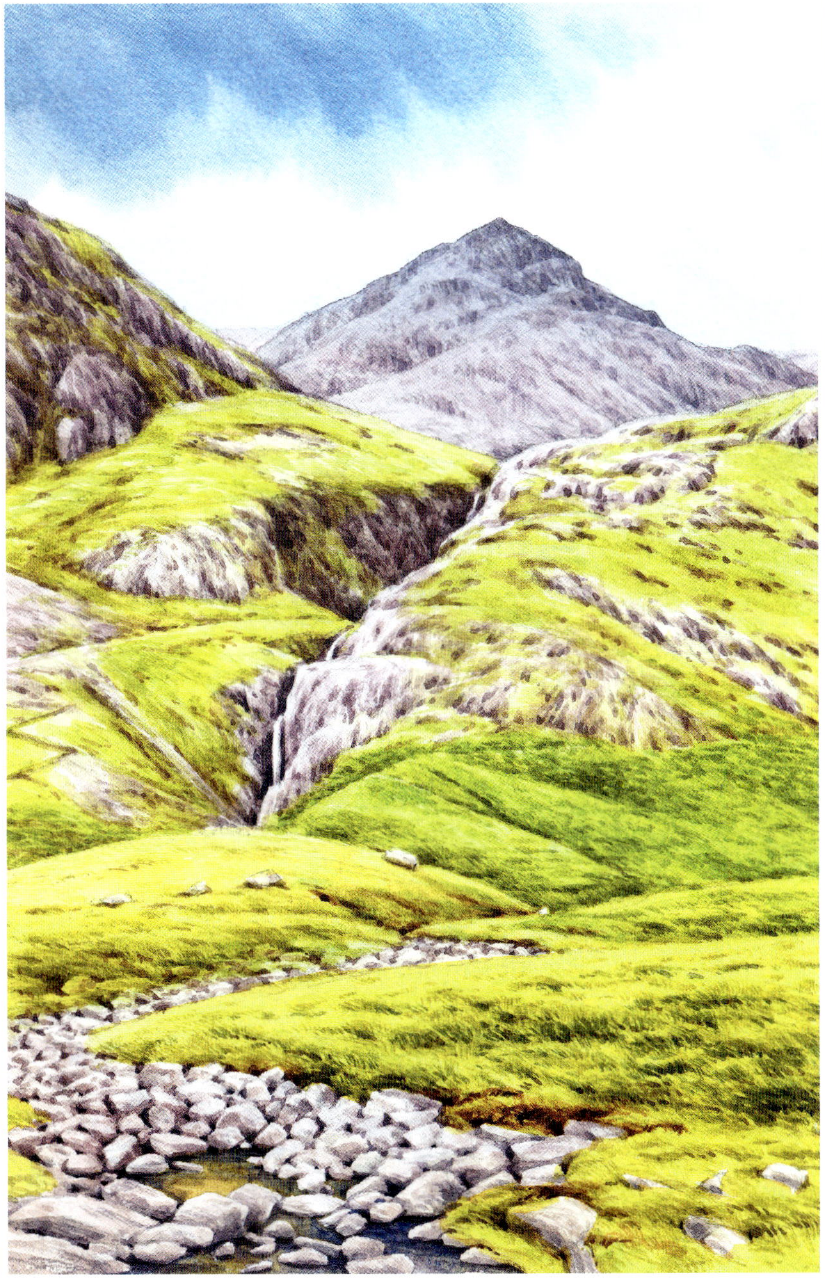

Scafell

From some directions, Scafell or Sca Fell according to the O.S. appears to be higher than its neighbour, Scafell Pike, but it loses out by about 50 feet. What is lacks in height it makes up for in character with a fearsome north face, Scafell Crag. Perhaps because of this crag and the barrier formed by Broad Stand the top, unlike its neighbour, is normally crowd free.

From Cam Spout 12/7/11

As impressive as it looks the peak in this sketch isn't actually the top of the fell but the high ground to the north of Greencove Wyke. The summit lies further back. To the right of the falls in AW's drawing can be seen random eroded paths scarring the turf, now the bare rock is exposed. An alternative route on the left hand side seems to be in regular use now.

The summit 20/4/10

Compared to the neighbouring summit of Scafell Pike, this top can be enjoyed in relative peace and quiet. AW's Deep Gill Buttress, to the right of the cairn is known as Symonds Knott. There is now a large cross of stones on the grassy saddle between the two points.

Broad Stand

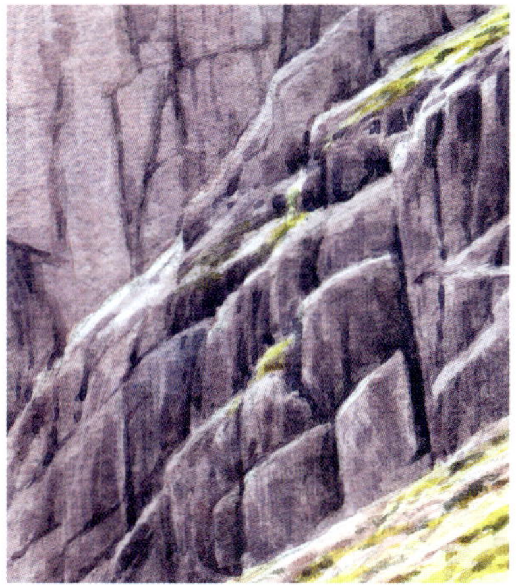

Not for walkers 10/4/11

A notorious accident black spot. The near vertical split is the entrance, known as Fat Man's Agony, from there the progress upwards is difficult to say the least.

Broad Stand and Mickledore

10/4/11

The almost impenetrable crags of Scafell which block the route between Scafell and Scafell Pike.

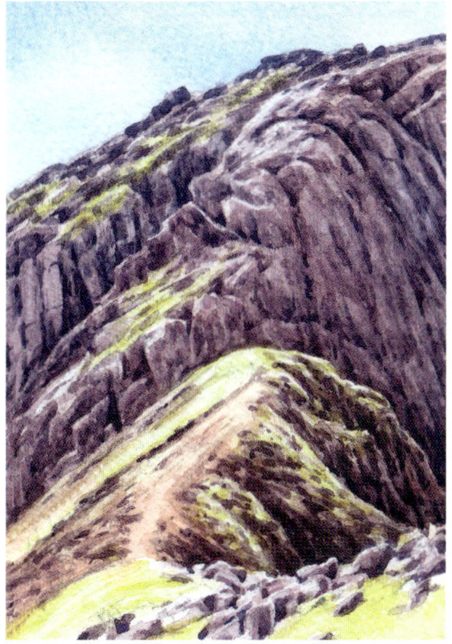

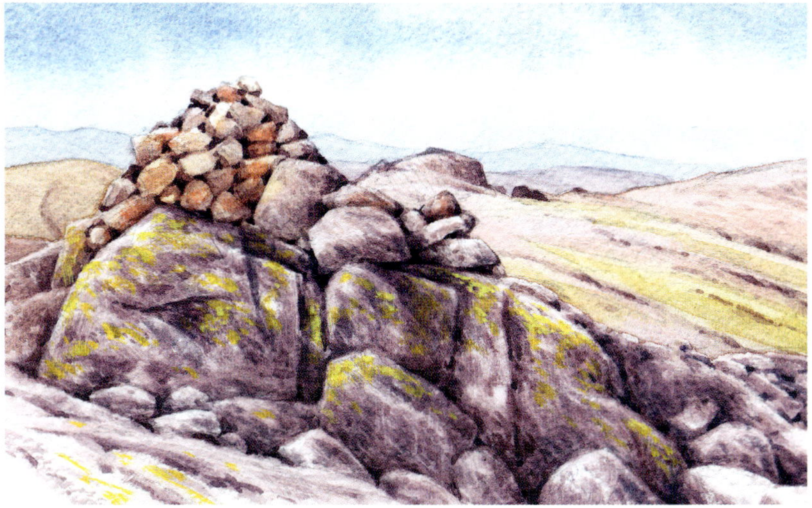

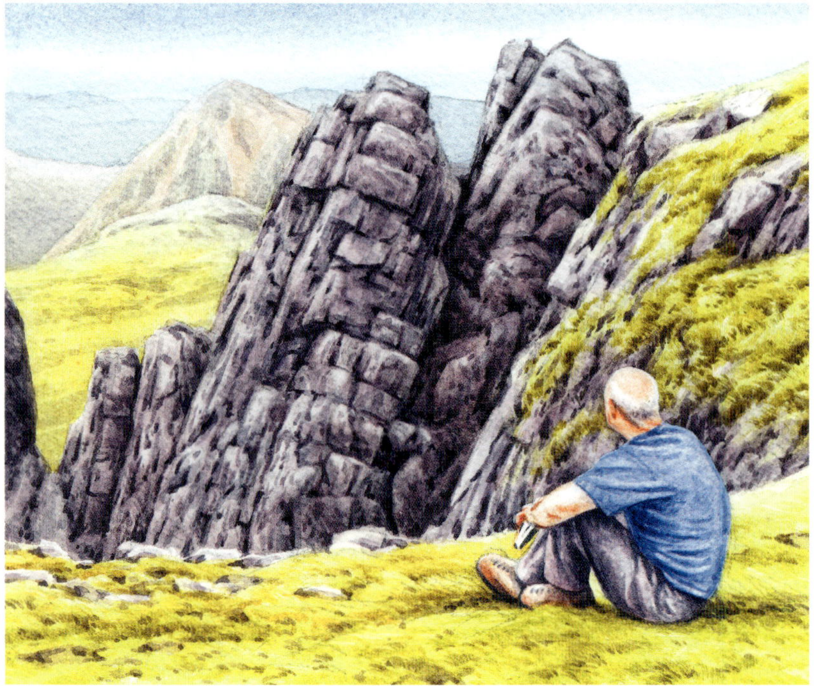

The head of Deep Gill 12/7/11

AW's self portrait drawing was a composite of two photographs (see right). The ground here drops away rather steeply into the gill. Note how some of the top of the left section of the cleft in the crag has fallen. At a distance is the distinctive shape of Great Gable.

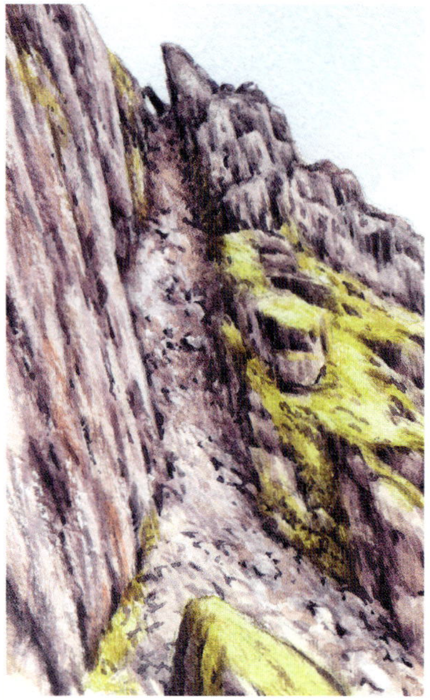

Lord's Rake- the first section

12/7/11

In the winter of 2001-2002 a major rockfall made the rake unstable, a large slab of rock fell into the gully and wedged itself between the walls. It can be seen here at the very top of the rake. It was precariously positioned and eventually fragmented and collapsed in late July 2016 luckily with no one underneath it at the time.

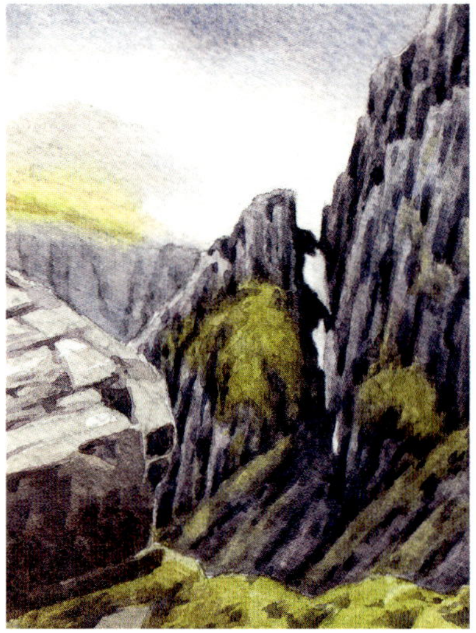

The start of Lord's Rake in descent 31/3/09

The last patches of snow cling on in this sun free gully with Scafell Pike in the mist to the left.

Wainwright's self portraits

Throughout the seven Pictorial Guides AW enhances a few of the sketches with figures to give a sense of scale to the landscape (e.g. see Pillar 5 and 6) or as comical space fillers (Kirk Fell 4). Some of these figures are so small they often go unnoticed by readers such as the two in the frontispiece of book 5 making their way towards Sharp Edge. However, he also felt the need to incorporate a self portrait of himself in one of the sketches in each of the books. I suspect that this was done more as a bit of mischief than vanity. In none of these poses is AW looking at the camera, he looks into the scene which not only leads the reader's eye into the picture but also cleverly avoids facial details of himself. It should be remembered that he was a shy man and these poses didn't give many clues about the relatively unknown author of these popular guides. Even his attire of tweed jacket, trousers and boots was the norm in that era so he just looked like a regular walker of the day.

As for the portrait compositions, it is clear from photographs that I have seen that some, if not all of the self portrait sketches were composite drawings of two photographs, one of the landscape itself and one of AW which he adjusted to fit his requirements, turning his head or adjusting the posture. It is possible that even though he had experimented with taking self-portraits with his cameras using the timer and string, propping up the camera with rocks, this system had limited success. It is evident that the photographs of himself which he used in these illustrations were more likely to have been taken by walking companions. The pose at the head of Deep Gill for instance (see left) is one taken from a photograph taken of AW sitting on Loft Crag looking towards Pike o' Stickle, he just married one with the other.

I on the other hand always carried a tripod so that I could set up the camera and use the self timer to adopt the required AW pose at the correct location and take a self portrait. It took several attempts each time but thanks to digital cameras I could check the images on site, something which would have been impossible for Wainwright to do. A couple of poses were more difficult than others to stage correctly but the results were more than satisfactory for my needs. Adopting these "Wainwright" poses has now become a popular challenge for other walkers too.

Apart from this one on the left the other self portrait sketches can be found in Clough Head (page 24), Harter Fell (page 81), Raven Crag (page 141), Binsey (page 206), Grasmoor (page 260) and to complete the set Yewbarrow (page 341) which was appropriately the final illustration of all of the 214 fells.

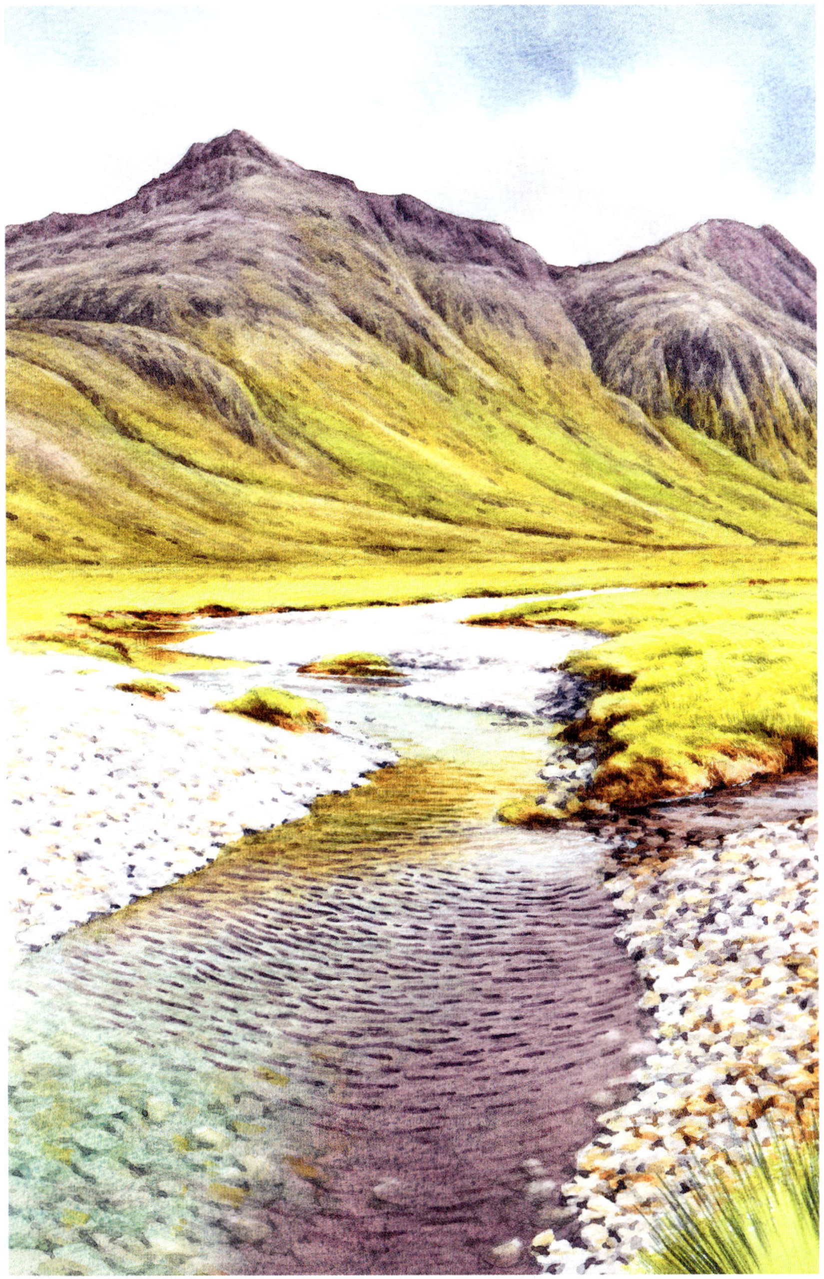

Scafell Pike

Many thousands of walkers every year set themselves the challenge to reach the highest point in England, Scafell Pike. Most tread the busy "tourist's" routes to get their "summit selfie". The majority have no idea that there is so much more to this iconic mountain.

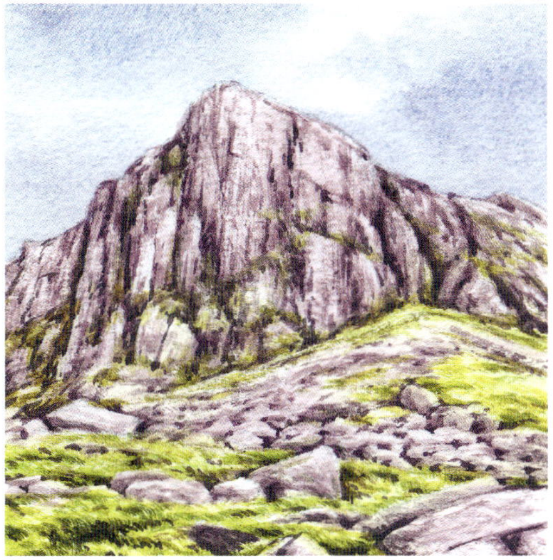

From Great Moss, Upper Eskdale 12/7/11

After an extensive search of the area I just could not find the cap of rock that he drew in the mid-distance. Once back in the studio I was able to compare my reference image to AW's photograph and it appears that the mound was actually made of peat and had since been eroded away, possibly taken by the river as it has grown in width and changed course slightly.

Dow Crag 12/7/11

On route to Little Narrowcove from Great Moss Dow Crag towers above the path. Only by diverting up from the route towards the crag's base was I able to locate the position required, complete with the angular blocks of rock which appear in the guide.

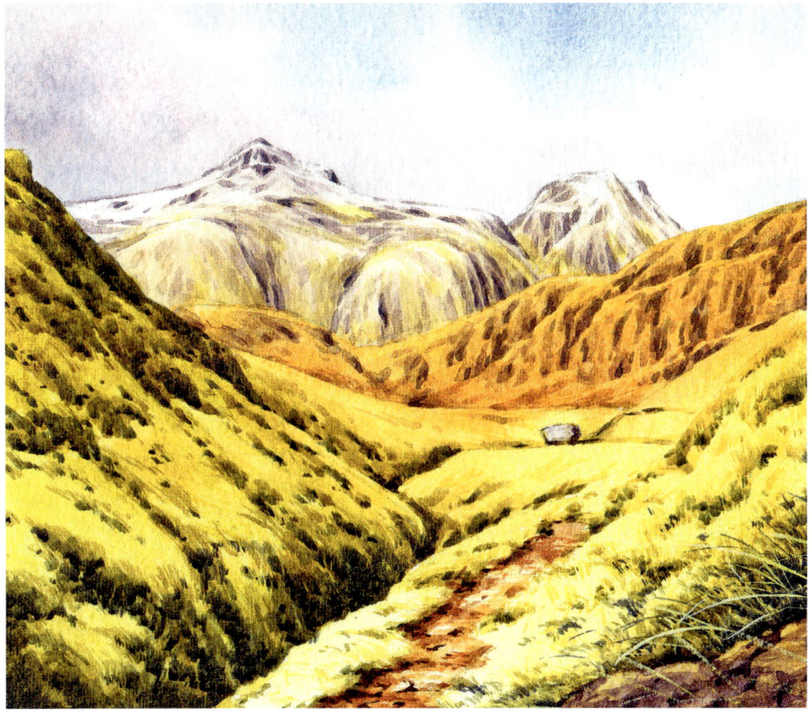

From the gorge of the Esk

5/3/07

Ascending from Lingcove Bridge towards Great Moss this imposing mountain scene comes into view. On my visit Scafell Pike and Ill Crag had a dusting of snow which only added to the spectacular vista. I produced another version of this scene for the front cover of the book.

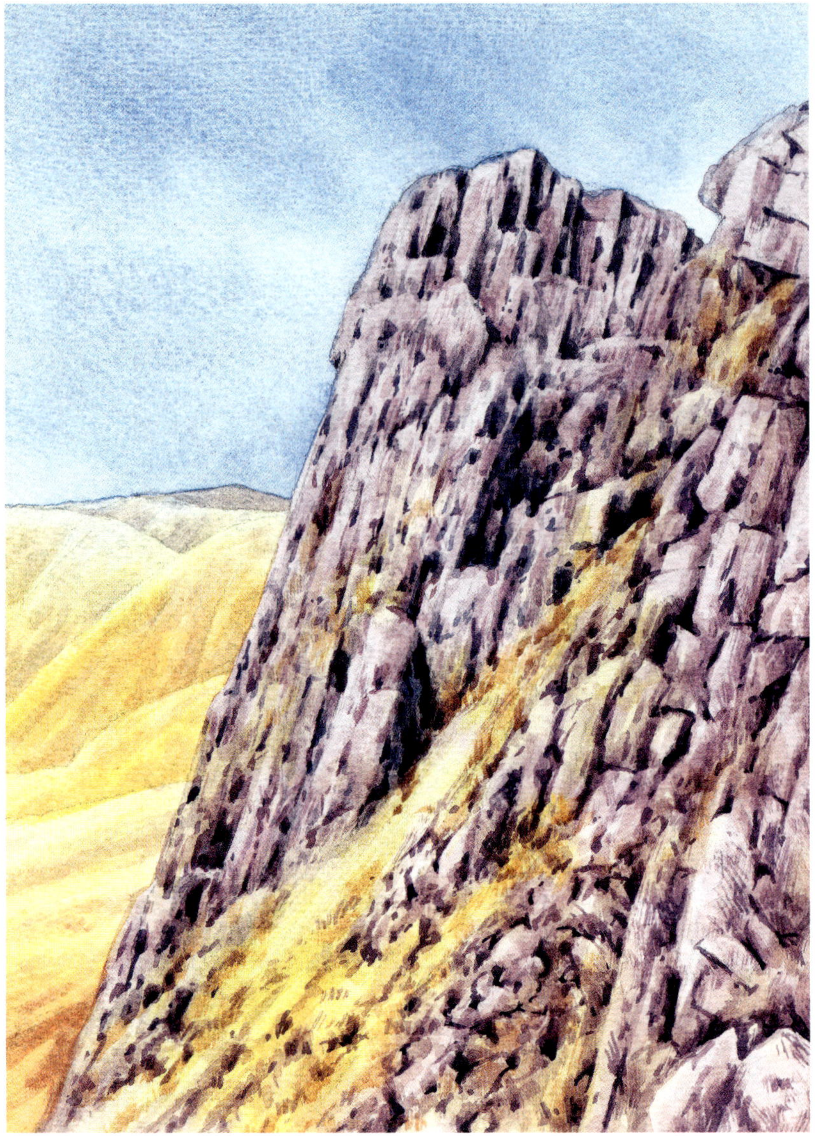

Pulpit Rock 10/4/11
The scale of this tall towering buttress of rock is best appreciated from Hollow Stones but this aspect, seen from the edge just above Mickledore gives a better close up view.

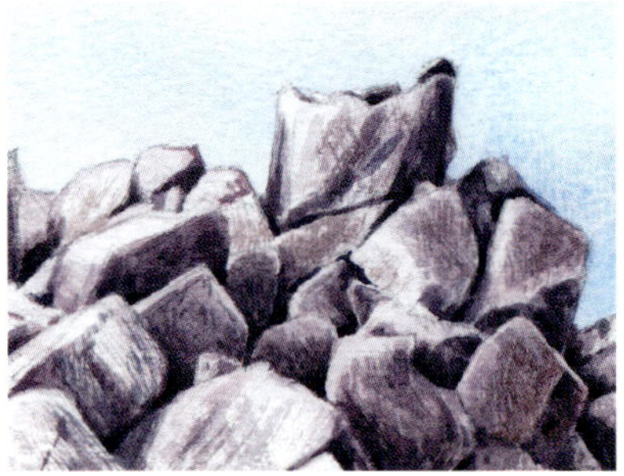

Broad Crag summit 12/6/09
The upper reaches of Broad Crag are mainly just a pathless rough boulder field and care is needed to gain the very top.

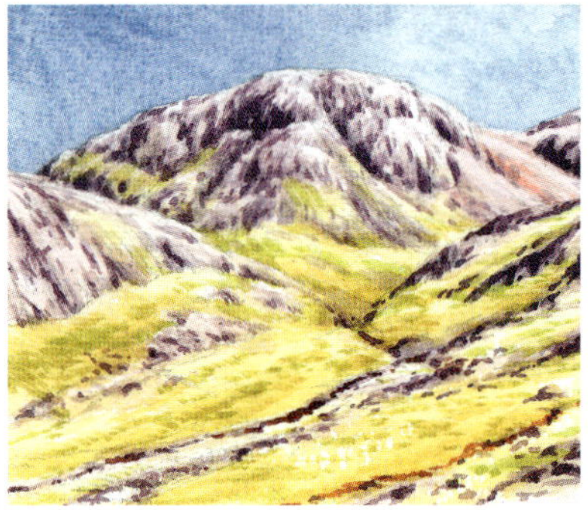

Broad Crag and Broad Crag col 10/4/11
From a point close to Lingmell col.

From Hollow Stones 3/6/11
Walkers ascending the fell from Brackenclose that have opted for the Mickledore route will be confronted by this dramatic scene with Pulpit Crag on the left and just out of view to the right is the sheer face of Scafell Crag.

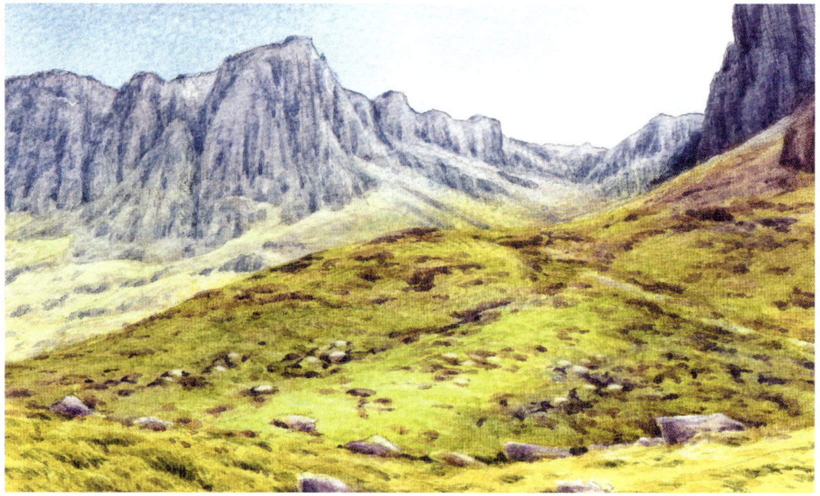

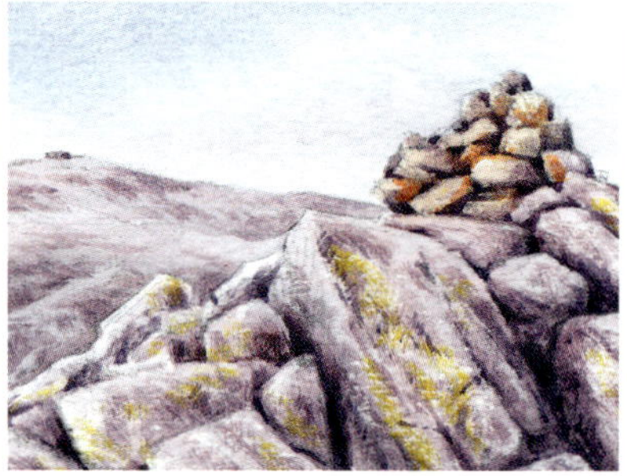

Ill Crag summit 212/6/09
The top of Scafell Pike is seen in the distance but the best view from here is down to the left, a superb aerial aspect of Upper Eskdale.

Broad Crag and Ill Crag

In his notebook AW lists both Broad Crag and Ill Crag as individual fells. They were two of the "Scafell Pikes" as this group was formerly known but they failed to make his final list. It is possible that he felt that they didn't have enough interesting features or potential routes of ascent for them to take up valuable space in Book 4 but they did each get a page to themselves.

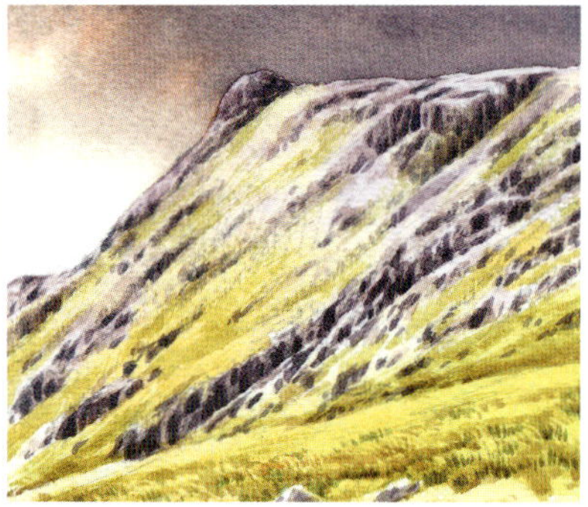

Ill Crag from the path above Esk Hause 12/6/09
The view to the left when heading up into Calf Cove on the wide path.

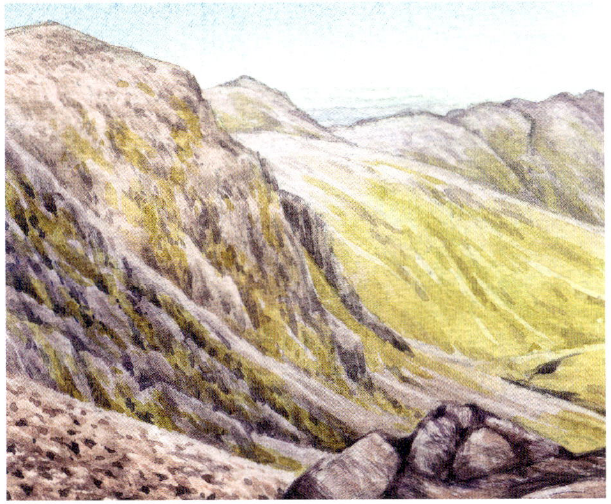

Looking down into Little Narrowcove 12/6/09
Heading from Broad Crag col to the summit this view is down to the left, looking into the cove shown below.

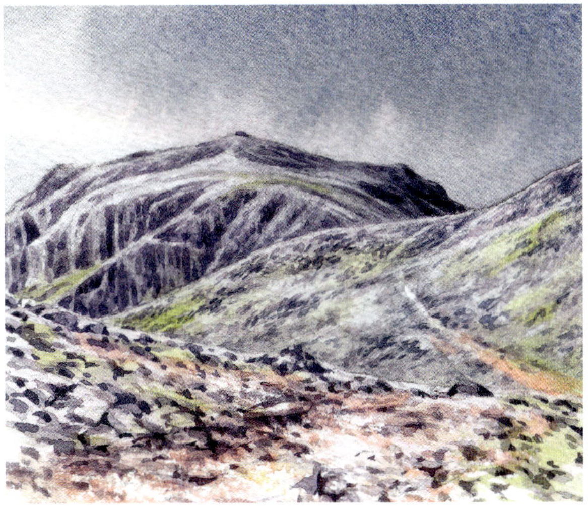

From the shoulder of Ill Crag 12/6/09
The summit of the fell is still some way off but the first view of the top is good incentive to press on.

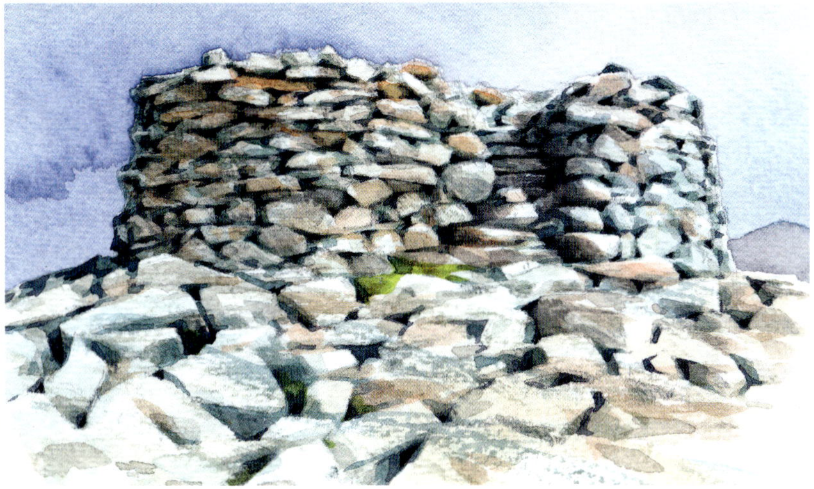

The summit 12/6/09
Even in AW's day this structure on the highest point of England was often busy with tourists, he would perhaps shudder at the numbers who stand here these days and the amount of rubbish and waste they leave behind.

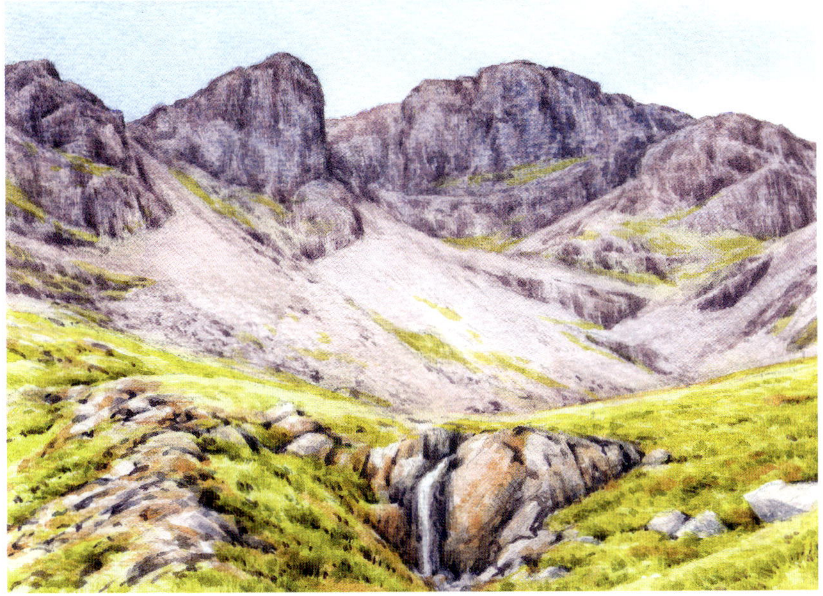

Little Narrowcove 12/7/11
Those walkers who have never ventured into this hidden valley will perhaps be surprised that the dramatic scenery in Wainwright's drawing is there in reality. Like the prow of a ship, Rough Crag juts out above steep scree slopes. The cove here is unknown to many but with its small beck and gentle falls the area is superb mountain terrain.

Taylorgill Force 10/4/11
This small sketch of the falls neatly fills a gap on Scafell Pike 15 although Taylorgill Force is some distance from the fell itself.

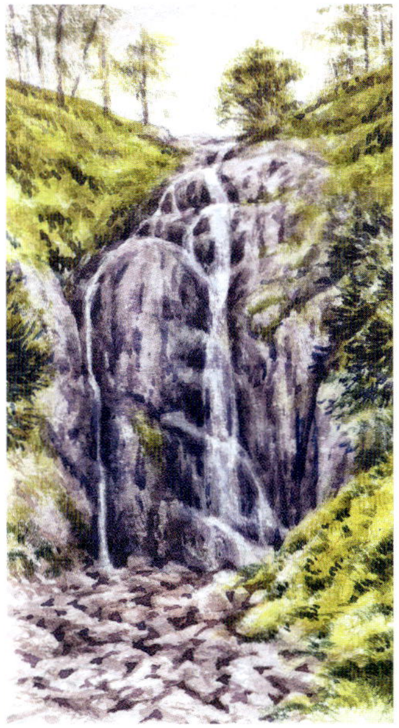

Lord's Rake 3/6/11
The view from Mickledore with Wastwater down to the right.

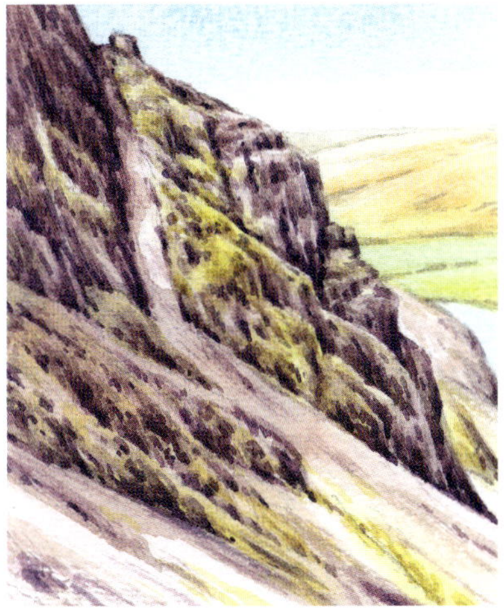

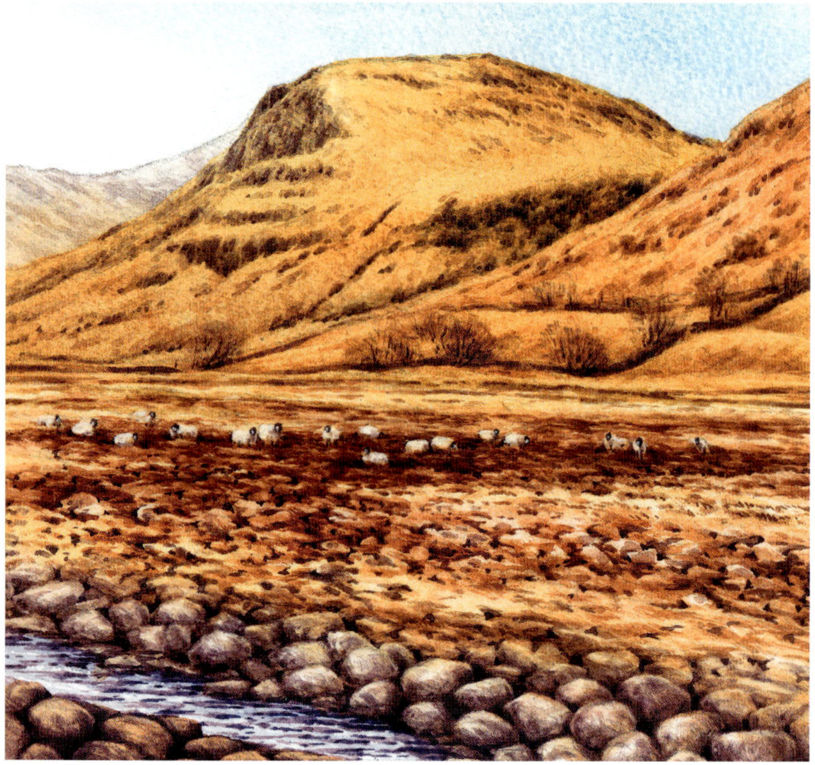

From Seathwaite 10/4/11
It was 5.30 in the morning when I took this reference at the start of a long day on the fells. There was a faint glow of dawn and just enough light to get my photograph. Sheep stood on the bare ground of late winter awaiting their food.

Seathwaite Fell

Positioned just to the south of the tiny hamlet of Seathwaite, this fell is bypassed by thousands of walkers every year, many of whom do not give this hill more than a second glance. The narrow lane to the hamlet is perhaps one of the most popular parking places for hikers heading off to fells such as Scafell Pike and Great Gable, it gets very busy.

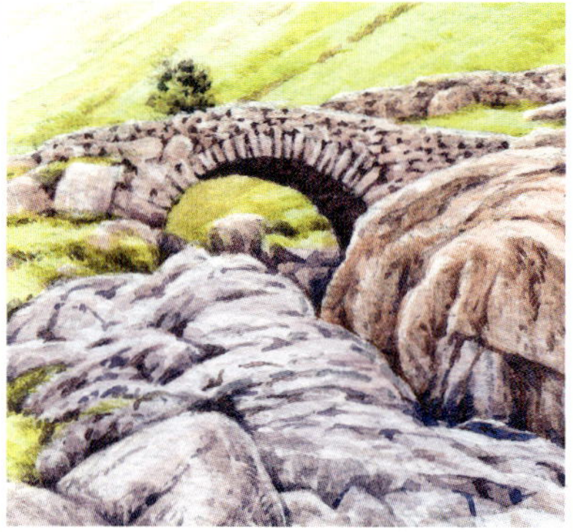

Stockley Bridge 10/4/11
One of the most popular old packhorse bridges in the district. Dating from the mid 18th century and part of the route from Borrowdale to Wasdale or Eskdale.

The summit 12/6/09
As AW states, this isn't the highest point of the fell, which is actually 100' higher, but it is where the only spot height, that of 1970', was marked on the map.

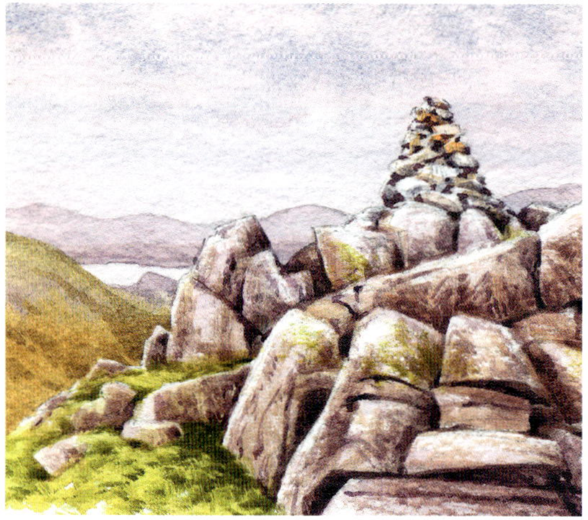

Tourism and AW

By the time Wainwright had published the complete set of the seven Pictorial Guides it was 1966 and the fells were more popular than ever, as were his guidebooks. Unsurprisingly some in the Lake District community blamed AW for this influx of visitors and even today there are people with the same opinion. In fact in later life even he admitted that the guides had played some part in bringing people to the fells, faint paths that he had described had in sections become distinct and eroded in places. Is this blame on Wainwright really justified?

The writing of guidebooks to the Lake District didn't begin with Wainwright in the 1950s, in fact the first were written as far back as 1773 when a solicitor from Barnard Castle, William Hutchinson, published *An Excursion to the Lakes of Westmorland and Cumberland* which is now considered to be the first popular travel guide to the region. Even Wordsworth wrote his own *Guide to the Lakes* which was published anonymously in 1810. Numerous publications followed and Wainwright himself used such guides in particular Baddeley's *Thorough Guide to the English Lake District,* first printed in 1880 which included Bartholomew maps but also another book, *Jenkinson's Practical Guide to the English Lake District* published in 1872, a guide that AW regarded to be the best written about the district. Nearly all these guidebook authors and others were blamed for bringing hordes of visitors to the region, spoiling the landscape but AW still gets the finger pointed at him, but why?

In some ways he unavoidably brought it upon himself. His guides were and still are the most popular with more than two million copies sold, pocket sized books that described the fells in such a detailed and unique way. More than that it was by coincidence that at the same time the area was becoming more accessible to the working man, families were starting to buy their first cars, the M6 motorway was in process of being built and with the Lake District becoming a National Park in 1951 it was more of a case of the masses coming to the area in rising numbers of their own accord. Once here, the Pictorial Guides were locally available for those who wished to explore the high fells. Wainwright's contemporary W.A.Poucher (of whom AW was a fan) published his book *The Lakeland Peaks* in 1960, at the time Wainwright produced Book 4 but Poucher's single volume was text heavy and only described 141 routes over 116 fells. AW's style, design, detail and humour made sales which left others in his wake but associated his name with the populariy of the Lake District. It's really only those seeking peace and quiet on the high fells who complain, many businesses still see Wainwright as a godsend.

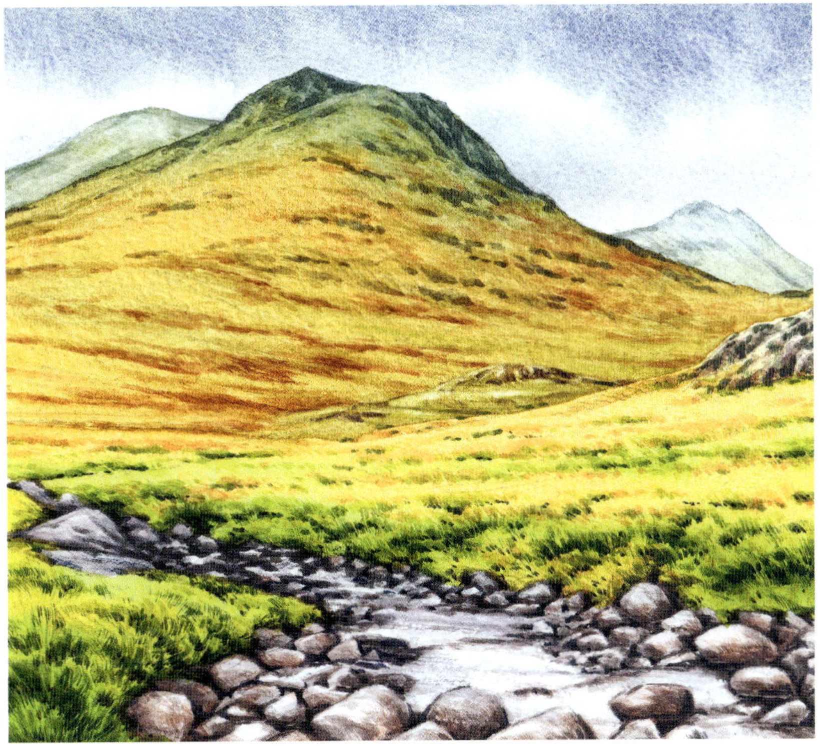

From Catcove Beck 12/7/11

The challenge of aligning the small water courses in these sketches often proved testing as they had often changed. Here, once I had the more solid features such as the rocky rise and outcrop on the right matched to the appropriate drawing, I did my best to correlate the stream as best I could but it is possible that AW used artistic license in his drawing. Scafell summit is to the left with Ill Crag on the right. Sadly I was unable to visit the area in the same wintery conditions as depicted in Wainwright's drawing.

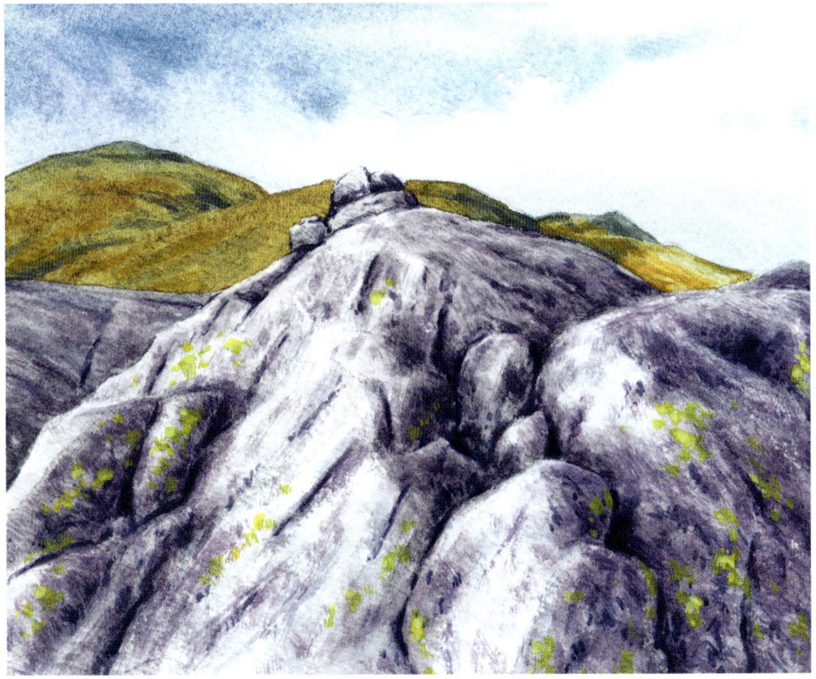

The summit 12/7/11

The first of my visits to this summit to obtain my reference was a fruitless trip as the low cloud restricted the view down to just a few yards. Needing to see the background fells I returned on a much clearer day. It is a lovely little rocky summit with just one or two stones to mark the highest point.

Slight Side

The inclusion of this fell on Wainwright's list may be questioned as it really is just part of Scafell's south ridge, but its qualification possibly stems from the fact that the top was a surveyed height on the 1 inch maps of the day and therefore drew his attention. The rocky nature of the summit requires a short scramble to gain the top from where there are fine views. It is normally visited in conjunction with a walk to Scafell, its parent fell. Steep crags lie to the east whereas the western slopes are uniform and featureless.

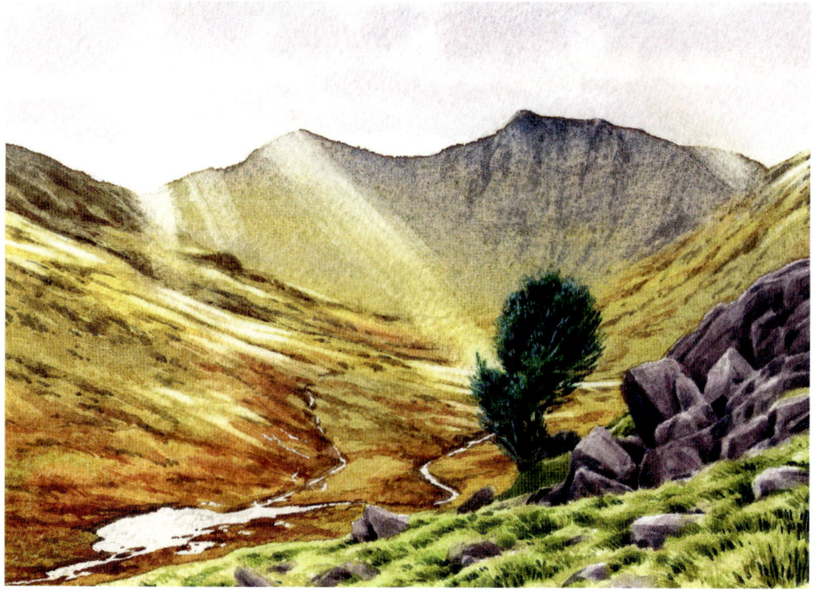

From Rough Crags 24/10/08

In my search for references it was always interesting as to whether the trees that featured in various AW's illustrations would still be there in some form. So imagine my surprise to find this holly tree, which is some distance from the path, not only still in place but almost unchanged in shape or size in the intervening 50 years. In the distance Swirl How is on the left and from this angle does look lower than Great Carrs on the right due to the perspective. AW however chose to give Swirl How dominance for the Pictorial Guide. Greenburn Tarn was once a reservoir but a storm in the winter of 1979/1980 burst the man made dam and lowered the water level.

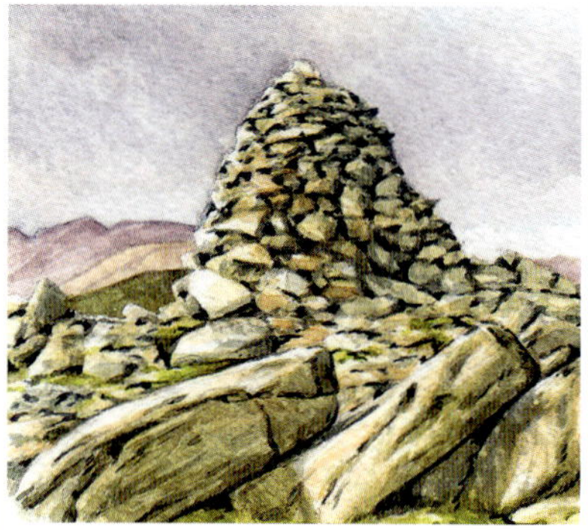

The summit 24/10/08

A neat conical cairn now marks the recognised top. The foreground slabs are like toppled dominos.

Swirl How

Today, with more accurate measuring devices available there is some question as to whether Swirl How could actually be just higher than Coniston Old Man, but there will only be a matter of a foot or two in it. Whatever the truth is, Coniston Old Man will always win the popularity contest though in this group of high fells.

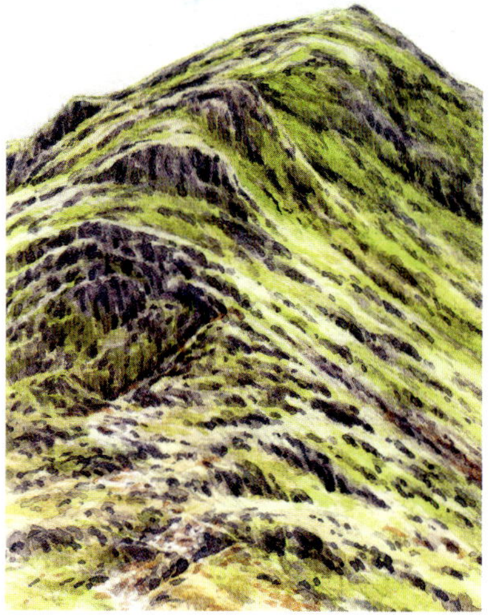

Prison Band 3/9/07

From just to the east of Swirl Hause on the path near Black Sails this is the prospect of the ridge to Swirl How's summit.

Lost crews on the fells

The brief but intense roar as a fast jet streaks through the valley will break the peace of a quiet day on the fells but before you have time to get the camera out it is gone. Whilst I appreciate that some will see this as an annoyance to their day, I, like many others will see this unexpected event as a bonus to being up on the fells, as on occasions you can actually be higher than the aircraft itself and watch as the skilful pilots twist their way along the valley and rise over the mountain passes.

The Lake District, like the other upland regions of the country, is classed as a low flying or tactical training area where fixed wing aircraft can fly as low as 250′ and rotary wing aircraft as low as 100′. This sort of training has been carried out in the area since before the second world war as it prepares the aircrew to fly in difficult terrain, something which cannot be achieved by flying over the sea. Sadly, such flying has resulted in accidents, more so in the days when navigation relied on fairly primitive equipment before technology removed some of the risks.

Most fellwalkers will be aware that the area has been the scene of many crash sites, some of which resulted in multiple fatalities including aircrew from countries other than the UK. Perhaps the most well known of these on the Wainwright fells is on Great Carrs where a memorial stands to the crew of the Halifax bomber which struck the fell in 1944 (page 171) which was mentioned by AW in the Pictorial Guide. The higher fells are littered with crash sites, both military and civilian, over sixty still show signs of the impact with either just fragments of the wrecks or more substantial sections of twisted airframe and engines. Whilst it may be interesting to go and locate such sites it must be remembered that the Protection of Military Remains Act 1986 means that removing of any souvenirs from such (military) sites, no matter how insignificant, is illegal whether there was a fatality involved or not.

One consequence of these military accidents is that as far back as 1938 there are records of RAF mountain rescues taking place, but in 1943 the Royal Air Force Mountain Rescue Service was officially formed as it was found that many aircrew who survived the crashes were dying of exposure prior to rescue. There are still four RAF MRS teams who, like their civilian counterparts, volunteer and take time off from their normal duties to attend call-outs, not just to recover aircrew but also to assist the civilian mountain rescue and emergency teams where needed. Until recently the familiar yellow Sea King helicopters were part of the RAF's Search and Rescue Force who were often to be seen flying throughout the fells coming to the aid of many a civilian casualty, lost on the fells.

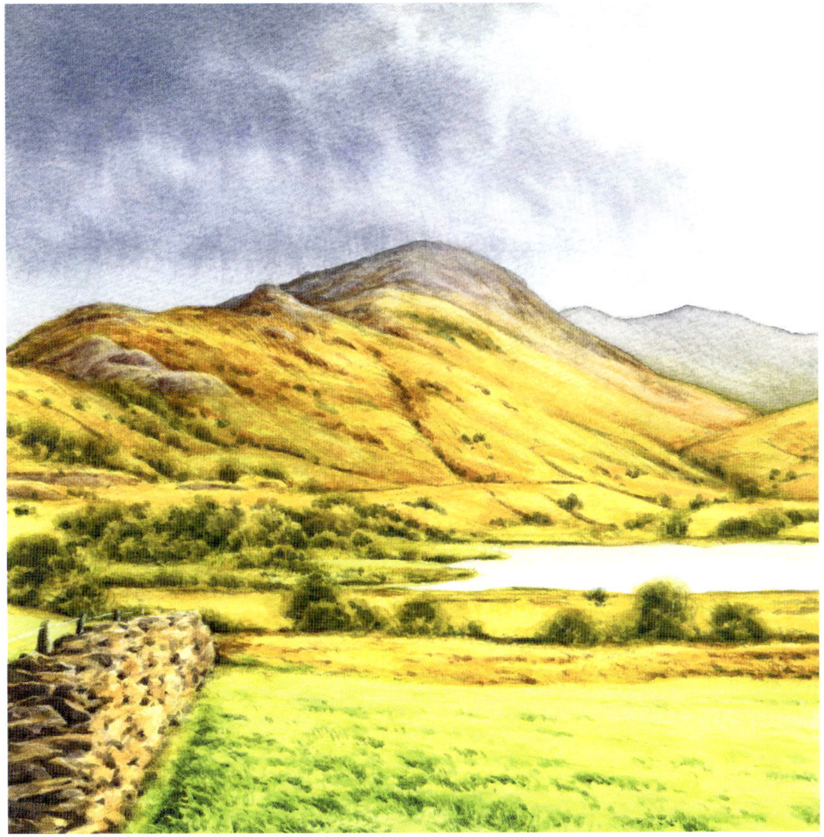

From Little Langdale 2/8/09

The valley of Little Langdale is still much quieter than the neighbouring Great Langdale but views such as this one mean it is popular with walkers, artists and photographers alike. This view is from the lane to High Birk Howe towards Slater's Bridge*.

*Slater's Bridge.

This ancient bridge which dates back at least to the 17th century crosses the River Brathay in three sections, one an arch of stone and the other two of solid slate slabs. It is marked on maps as Slater Bridge but AW and some historic signs in the area indicate Slater's Bridge (plural) which, as the bridge was used by quarrymen to get to and from work would seem to be grammatically correct. Surprisingly AW didn't include a drawing of this iconic bridge in the guide.

Wetherlam

The northernmost fell of the Coniston range, Wetherlam, like other fells in this area has seen industry working its flanks. Slate and copper has been quarried and mined here for centuries resulting in scars and holes in the landscape, many of which are being reclaimed by nature but as many are unfenced great care should be taken during their investigation. It is a fell of quality and visitors will enjoy exploring its history and terrain. One of the best routes of ascent is Steel Edge on its eastern side, a route not mentioned by Wainwright in the Pictorial Guide.

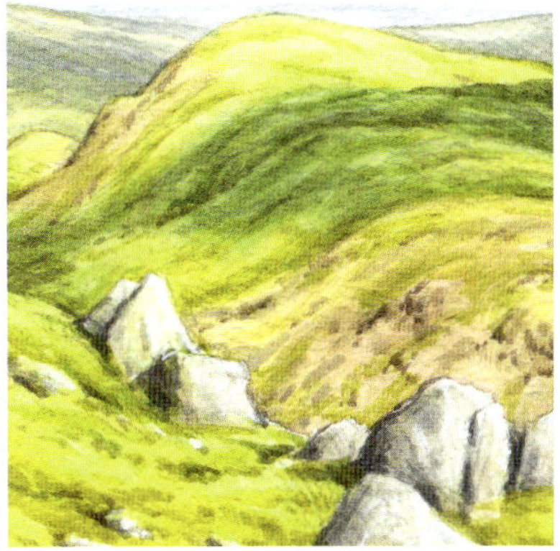

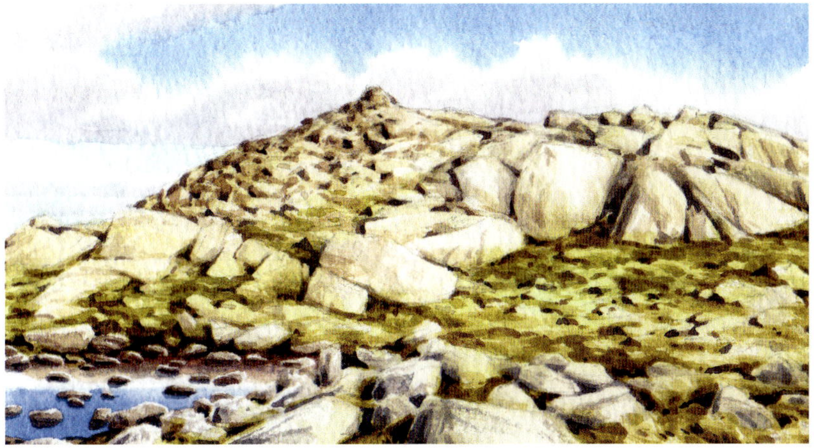

The summit 3/9/07

The small pool in the foreground can hardly be classed as a tarn, sometimes it is completely dried up and it now always seems to be smaller than depicted in AW's illustration.

Lanty Slee's Cave 30/7/09

Lanty Slee was a 19th century farmer and quarryman from the Little Langdale area, and this is just one of the locations where this notorious smuggler and illegal whiskey distiller apparently had one of his many stills and stashed his contraband. Exploring the landscape to find obscure locations of interest such as this can be an entertaining pastime when bad weather on higher ground disrupts fellwalking plans.

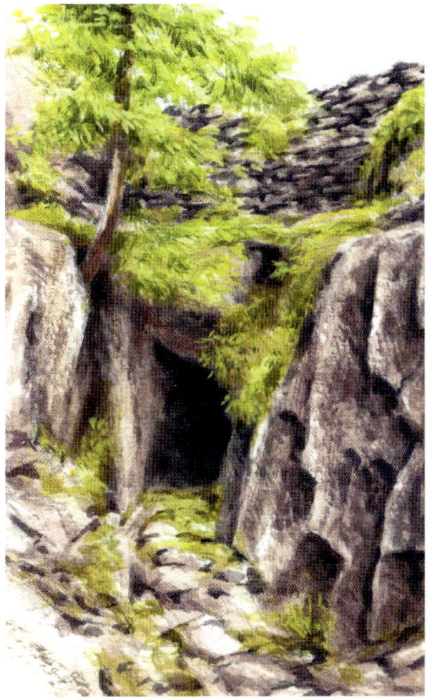

From Great Carrs 3/9/07

The view over the head of the Greenburn valley from close to Great Carrs summit.

Wetherlam's Hundred Holes - Typical copper-mine shafts

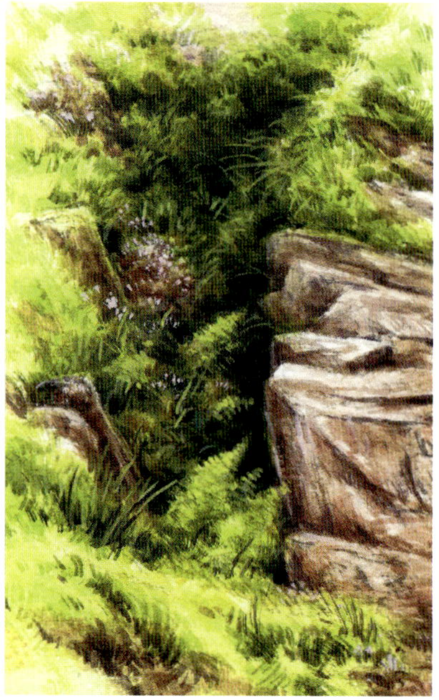

Shaft A 30/7/09
Ferns and foliage disguise this deep pit, the only one I found with the vertical wall on the right.

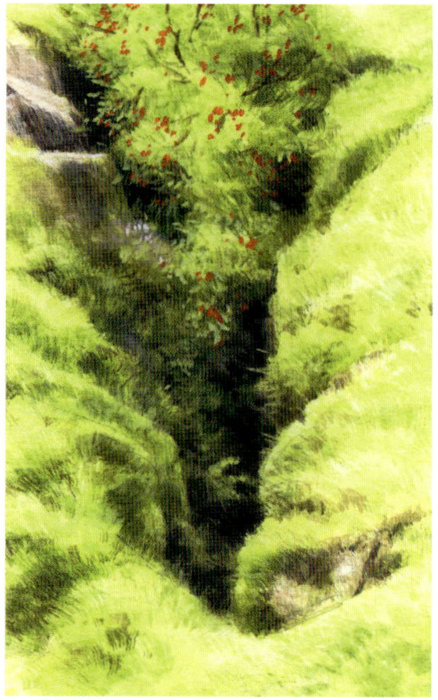

Shaft B 30/7/09
The rowan tree now fills the upper section of this cleft which resembles Wainwright's drawing.

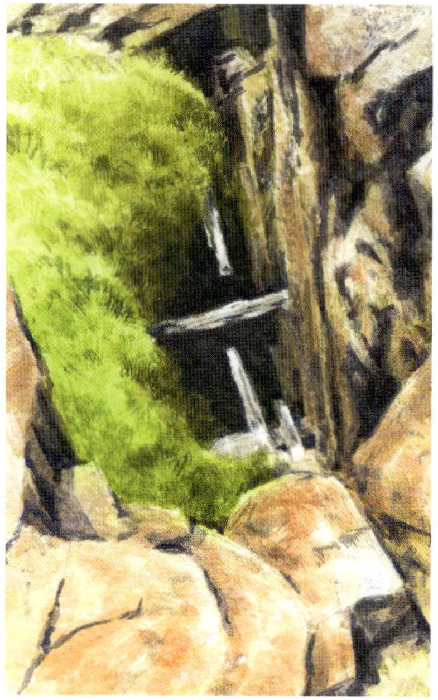

Shaft C 30/7/09
Even though they are in a state of decay the wooden spars in this fenced off shaft are still there.

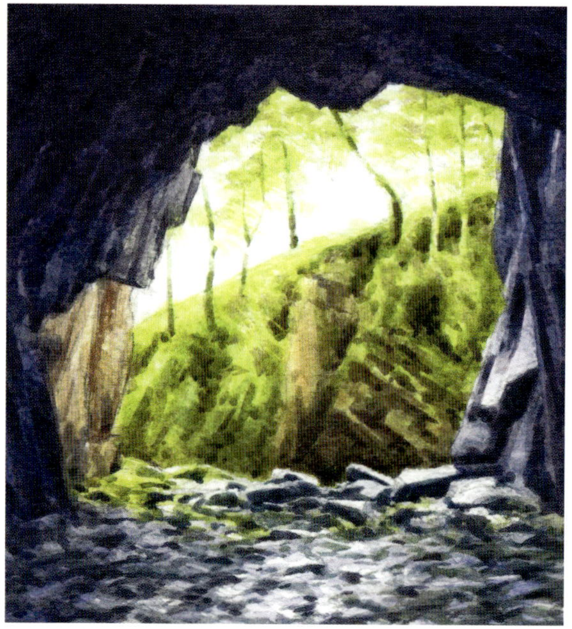

The Great Arch, Black Hole Quarry 30/7/09
The arch leads through to a large quarry chamber open to the sky. This view is looking out to the only way of entry. It is just in the woods to the south of Slater's Bridge, an old smithy building is close by.

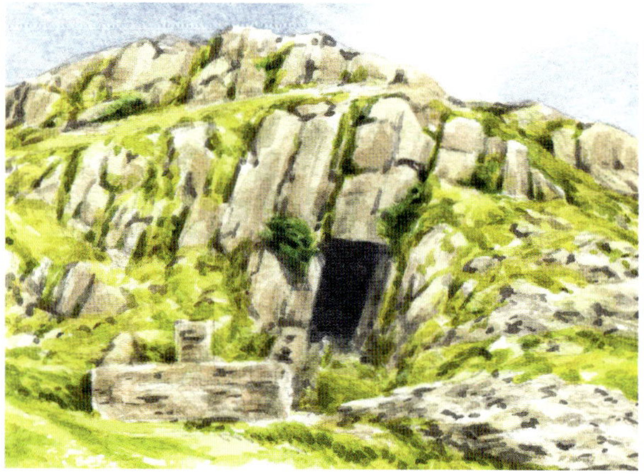

A quarry cave 30/7/09
This quarry entrance is quite some size, almost big enough to take a lorry. Due of its quiet location the walls of the small building in the foreground are virtually undisturbed.

A copper level 9/2/14
I had nearly given up on finding this level, assuming it had been filled in. However, it turns out to be located well away from the other shafts shown on this page. It is now gated.

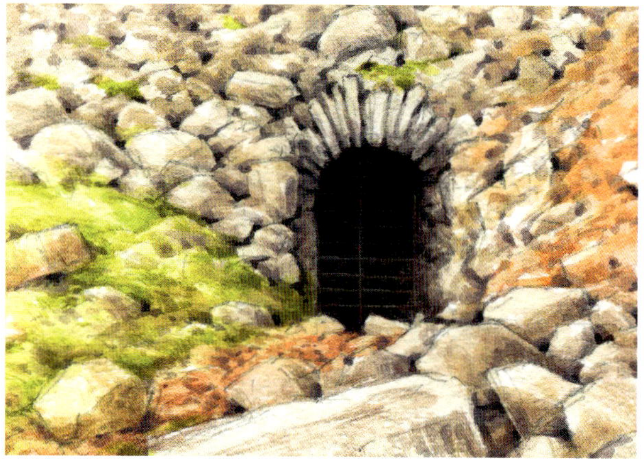

Cathedral Cave and Quarry.

Considering the detail that AW put into describing Wetherlam's quarrying activities it is a little odd that he makes no named mention of Cathedral Cave, a vast 40′ high quarried chamber in the fell side with a large central column which is now a popular visitor attraction. Either he didn't know of it or more likely it was out of bounds to the public as some quarries in this vicinity were still operating.

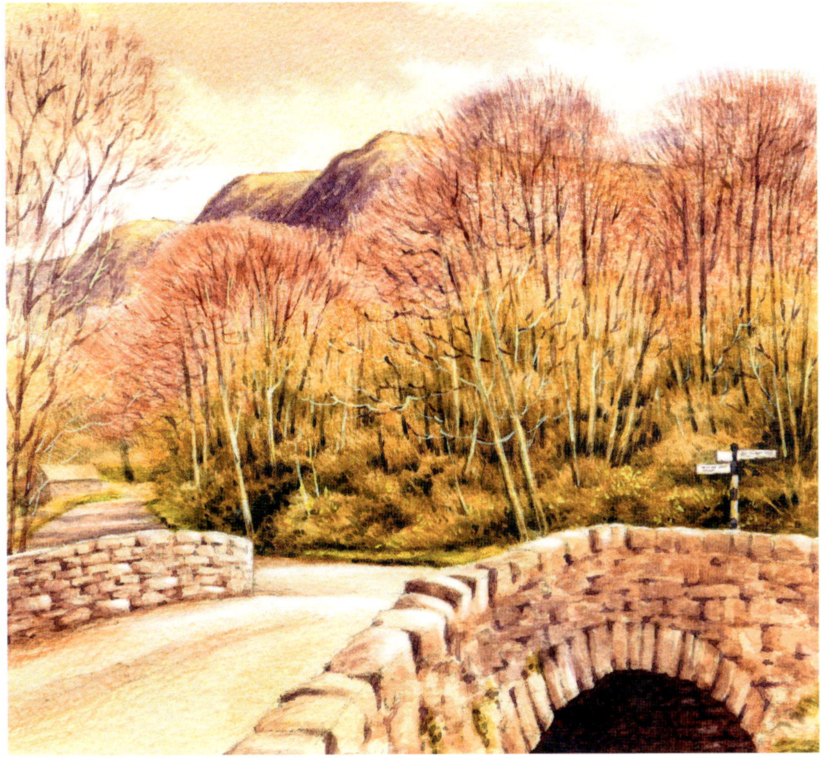

From Strands 13/4/08
The view was so nearly obscured by the trees, luckily I was here before they had come into leaf. This is Cinderdale Bridge just along the road from Nether Wasdale.

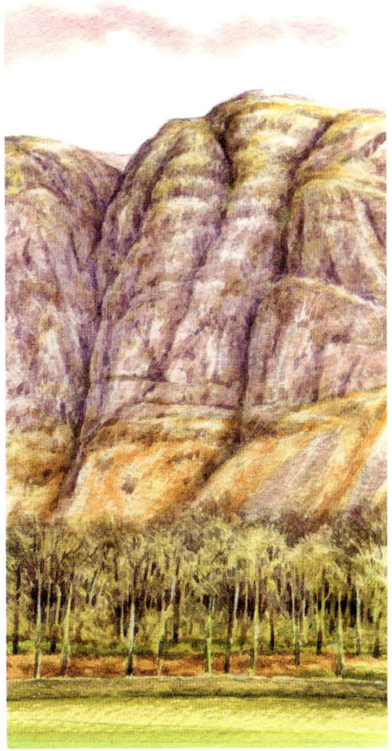

From near Woodhow 13/4/08
Unusually this drawing has no title in the guide but it is of the summit crags that drop down to Wastwater, here hidden behind Low Wood.

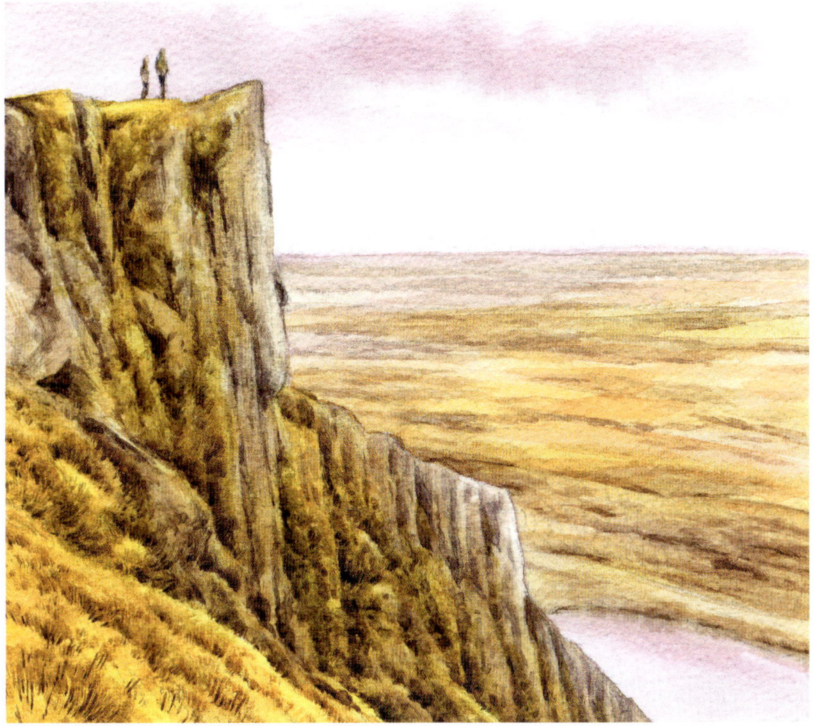

The two viewpoints 13/4/08
On a quiet day on the fell it was by pure chance that at the time I needed to take my reference photograph these two walkers appeared and then happened to stand in the right place, just like the figure in AW's illustration.

Whin Rigg

The tops of Whin Rigg and Illgill Head form the high ground above the impressive Wastwater Screes. The land between the two is pleasant walking with superb views of the lake and the giant mountains at the valley head.

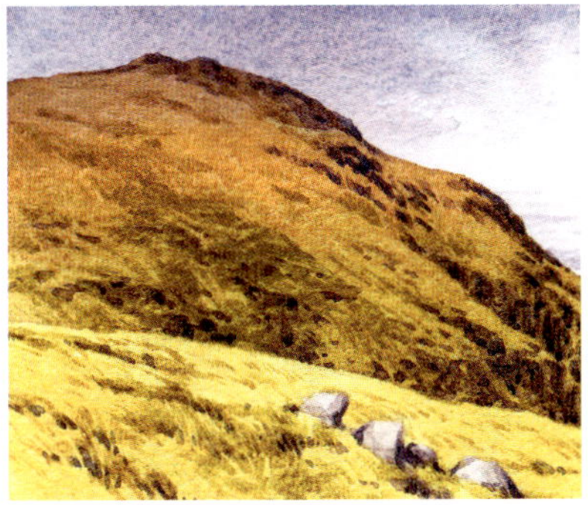

From the north east 13/4/08
Walking along the ridge from Illgill Head this view of the summit is taken from near the tarns.

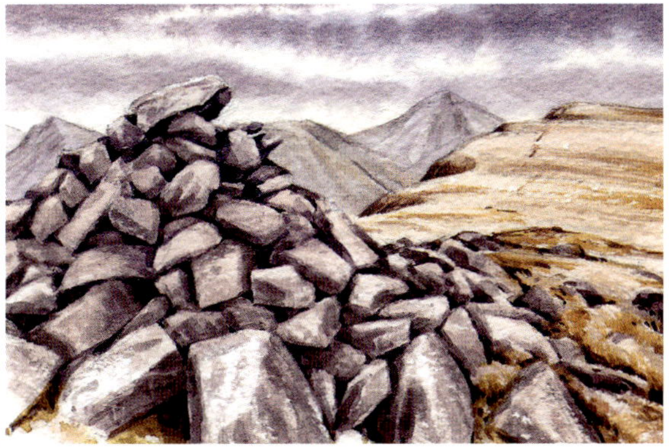

The summit 13/4/08
This cairn is the one close to the edge with Illgill Head and Great Gable in the distance. There is another high point 200 yards to the south east.

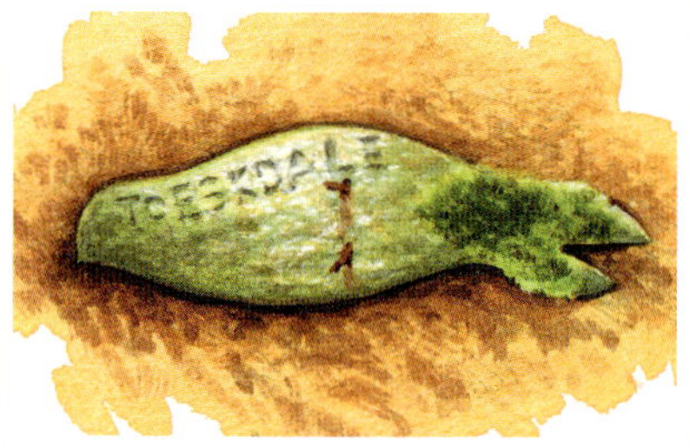

To Eskdale Sign 31/3/09

It was obvious to me that this wooden sign would probably have gone so, as an April Fool's day prank I made this exact replica complete with rusty nails and moss, carried it with me on the route and then photographed it on site. Needless to say, my efforts paid off, fooling many readers who read my walk report published on April 1st 2009.

Illgill Head from the ridge 13/4/08

The footpath that links the two fells is straightforward but detours to the edge above the screes can provide dramatic views towards Yewbarrow and Great Gable across Wast Water.

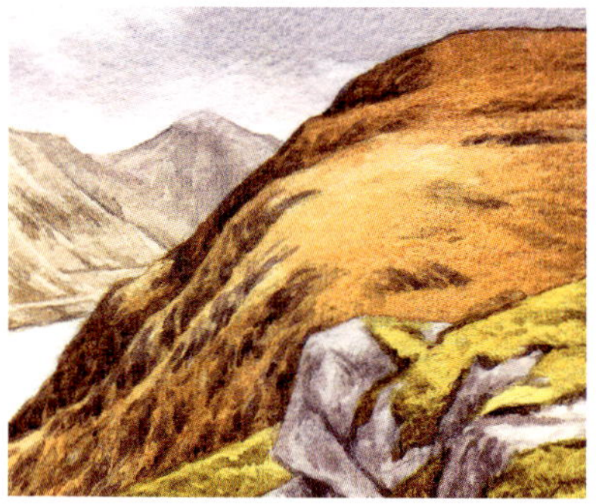

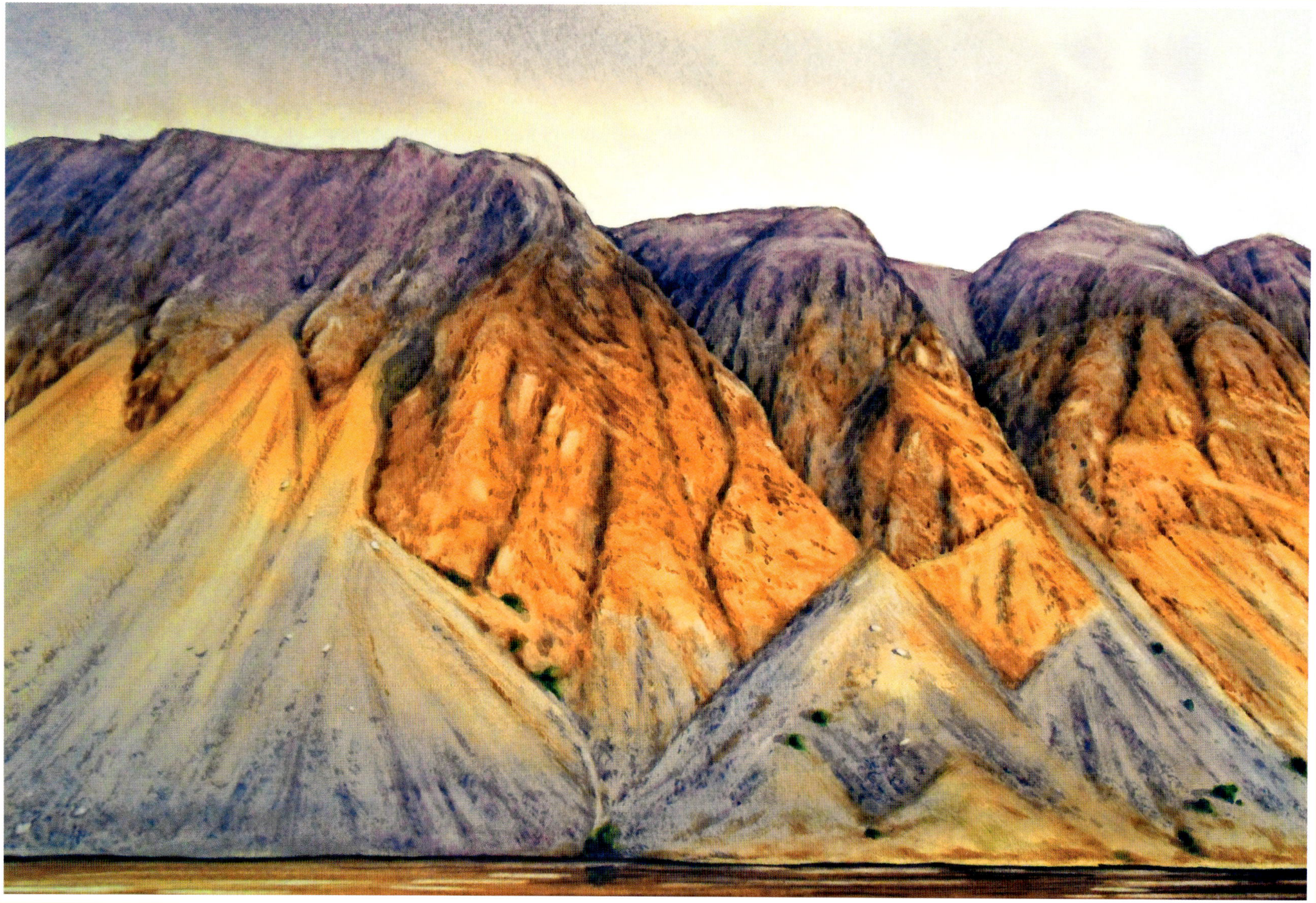

Wastwater Screes and Gullies 13/4/08

My route this day had taken me over Whin Rigg, Illgill Head and then a return via the Wastwater Screes path which basically runs along the base of the fans of crumbled rocks. It is an awkward route and best attempted when the rocks and boulders are dry. The bonus for me was that just as I returned to the car the setting sun appeared under the cloud cover and illuminated the screes with an orange glow, a truly majestic and memorable moment.

The Northern Fells

The area covered by Book 5 lies to the north of the A66 trunk road and the hills within this region can hardly be classed as the most exciting of fells in the Lake District, that is with the exception of one, Blencathra. This mountain may not quite top the 3000' mark but what it lacks in height it makes up for in quality. It isn't that the other fells should be dismissed out of hand, they are just more rolling and gentle than some of the hills that are featured in other Pictorial Guides, but then it is the variety which makes the fells on Wainwright's list so interesting. Eleven of the fells which featured in this guide did not appear on Wainwright's original series of fells whereas five others that were on those lists didn't make the final 214, such was the flexibility in AW's catalogue of hills (see notes in conclusion on page 342).

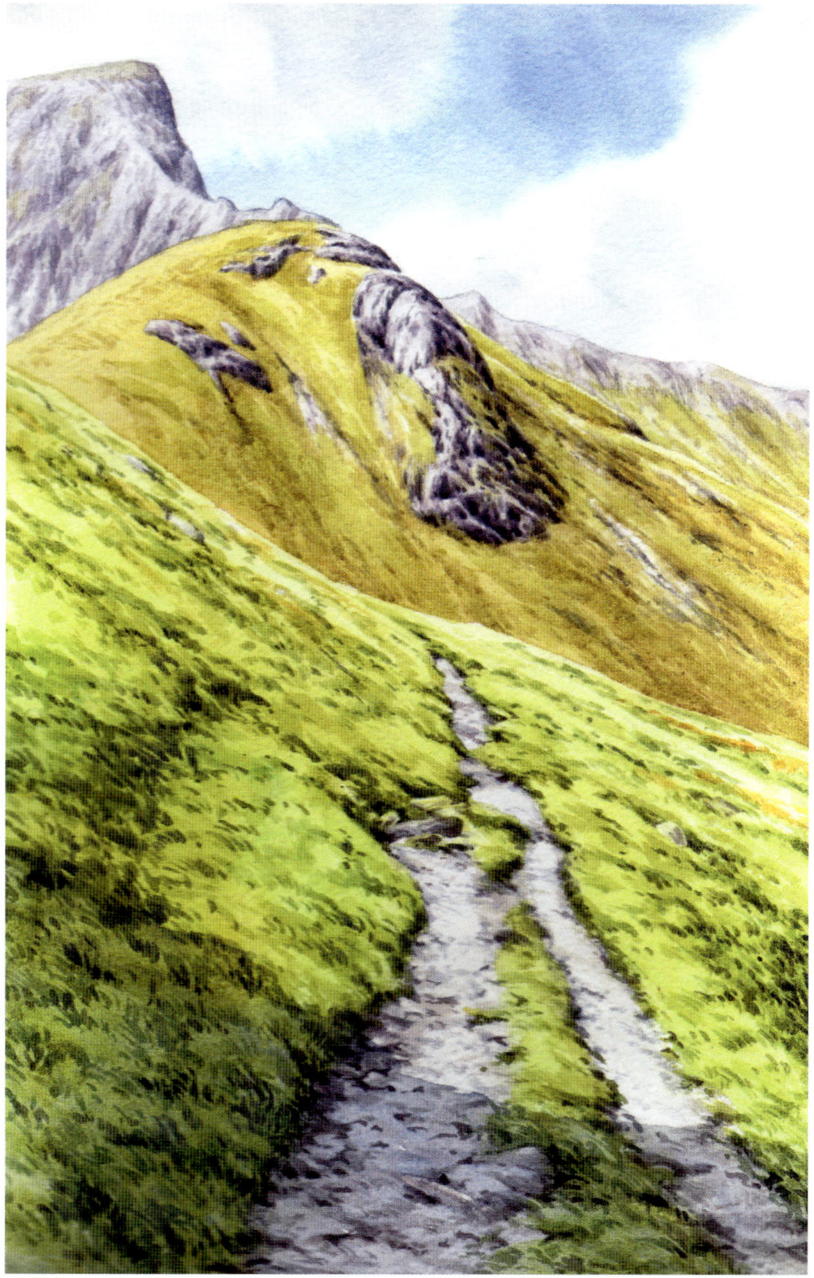

Frontispiece - Foule Crag and Brunt Knott 21/5/09

Fellwalkers who recognise this scene will have perhaps continued from this point up to the summit of Blencathra after crossing the knife edged ridge of Sharp Edge which can just be seen over the top of Brunt Knott. There are limited options in the northern fells region for a recognisable view of such drama for use as the frontispiece to the book. Unusually for this popular path, at the time of my visit there were no other walkers here, so my sketch is without the two tiny figures like those featured in AW's drawing, they are so small in fact that only the keenest eyes will have spotted them. My sketch is also free of the sheep which he depicted.

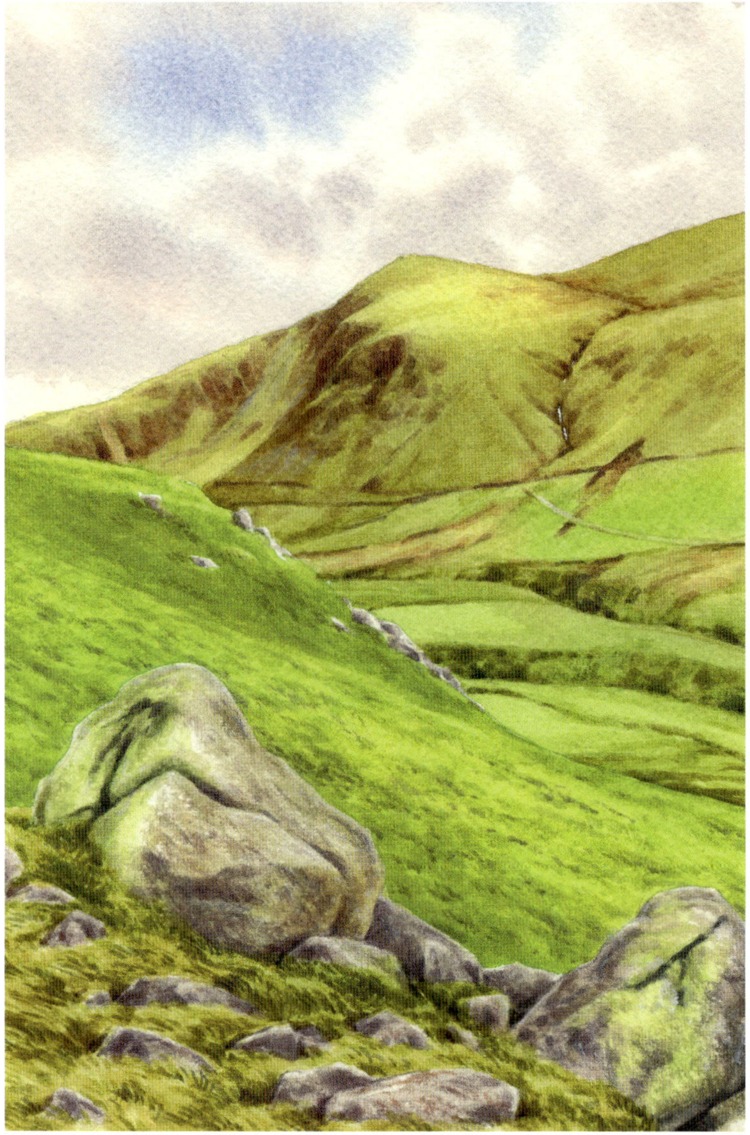

From Brockle Crag 20/5/09

This view to the fell is across the Dash Valley from the south-western slopes of Great Cockup. Brockle Crag is a scar of exposed quartz rocks. These oddly marked and shaped rocks were easily identifiable.

The approach along the Skiddaw House road 18/5/09

The road winds its way up past Dash Falls.

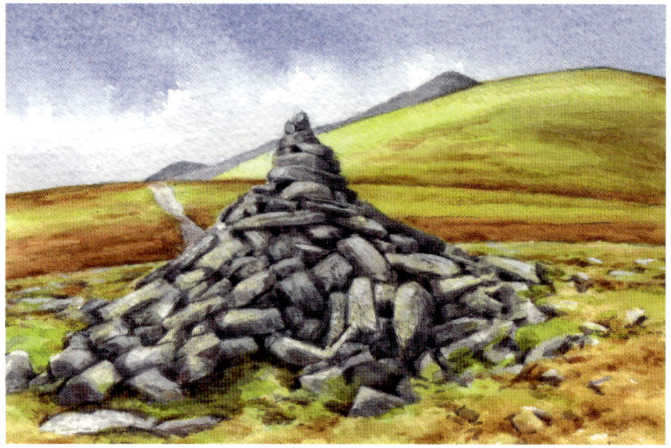

The summit 21/5/09

As AW stated, this cairn isn't at the highest point of the fell which can be seen to the left on the horizon at the corner of the fence. There now is a smaller cairn there.

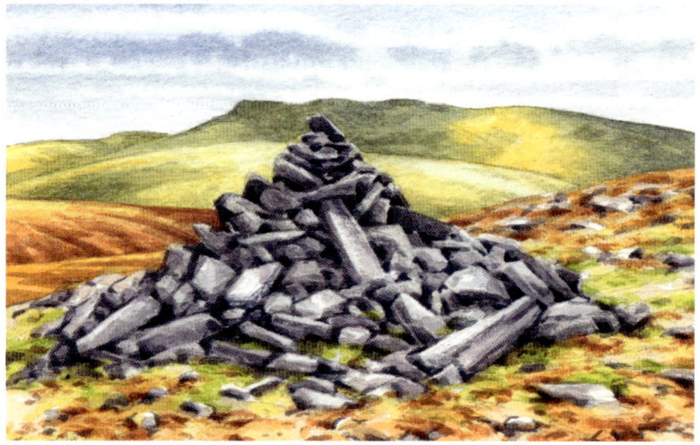

Blencathra from the summit of Bakestall 21/5/09

A different aspect of the cairn shown in the sketch above. Blencathra lacks an exciting profile from this angle.

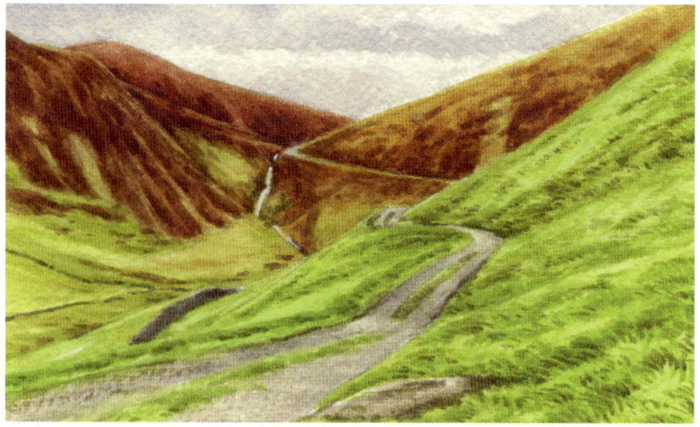

The head of the Dash valley

From the top of Dead Crags 21/5/09

Looking down on the Skiddaw House road.

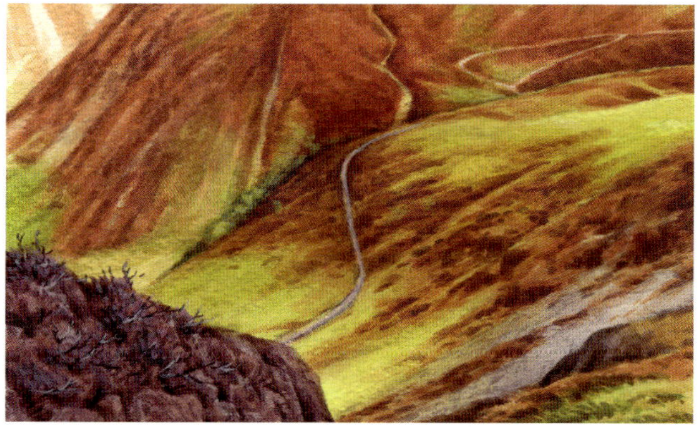

Bakestall

Without the two interesting features of Dead Crags and Dash Falls (Whitewater Dash) I doubt if Bakestall would have made it as a separate fell in the Pictorial Guide, even AW describes it as the name of a summit rather than a fell. A summit, unnamed on his 1 inch maps, which sits on the north-eastern spur of its parent fell, Skiddaw.

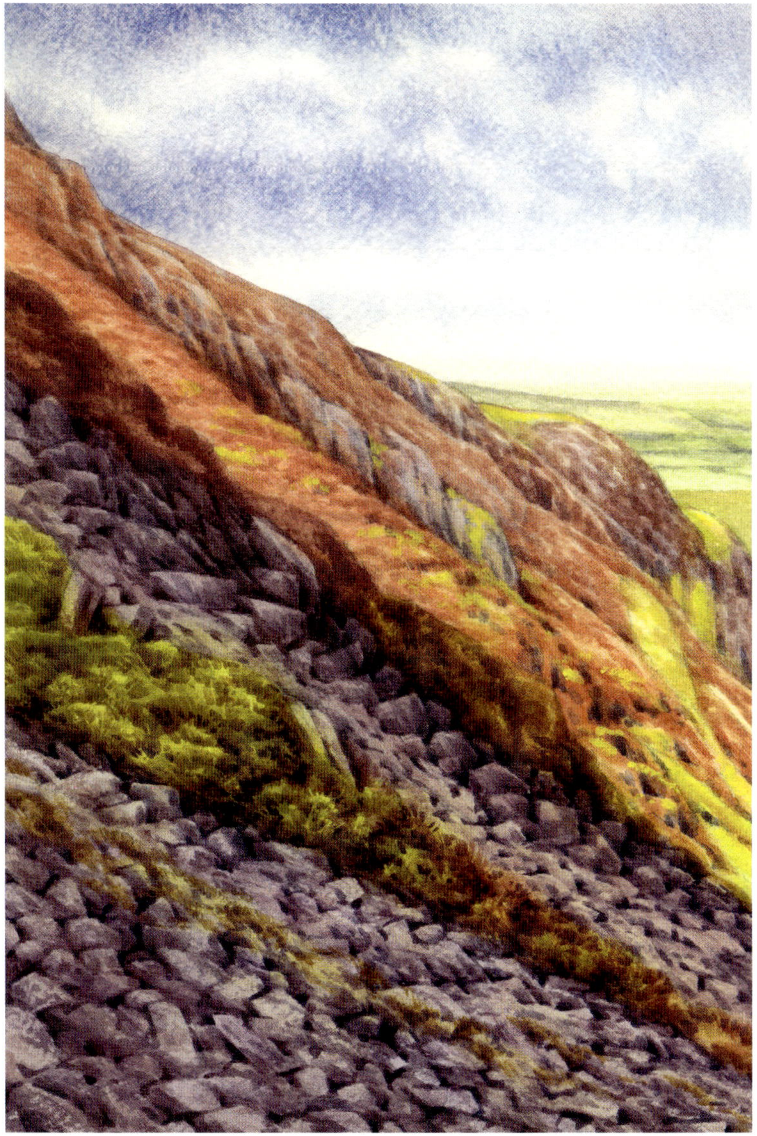

Dead Crags, from Birkett Edge 21/5/09
To match the illustration in the book with the actual terrain meant ascending the edge comparing his drawing to the land, a slow and challenging process but the only way to achieve the correct result.

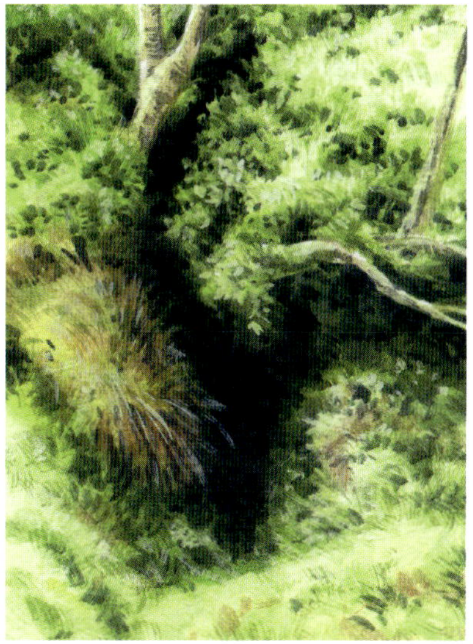

The old mine level, Dead Beck 21/5/09
Now almost hidden by vegetation.

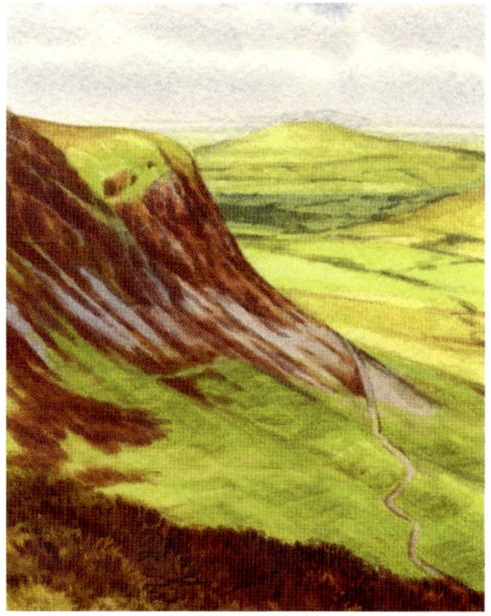

The Terminal Cliffs 21/5/09
Steep, unstable crags drop down to the floor of the Dash valley.

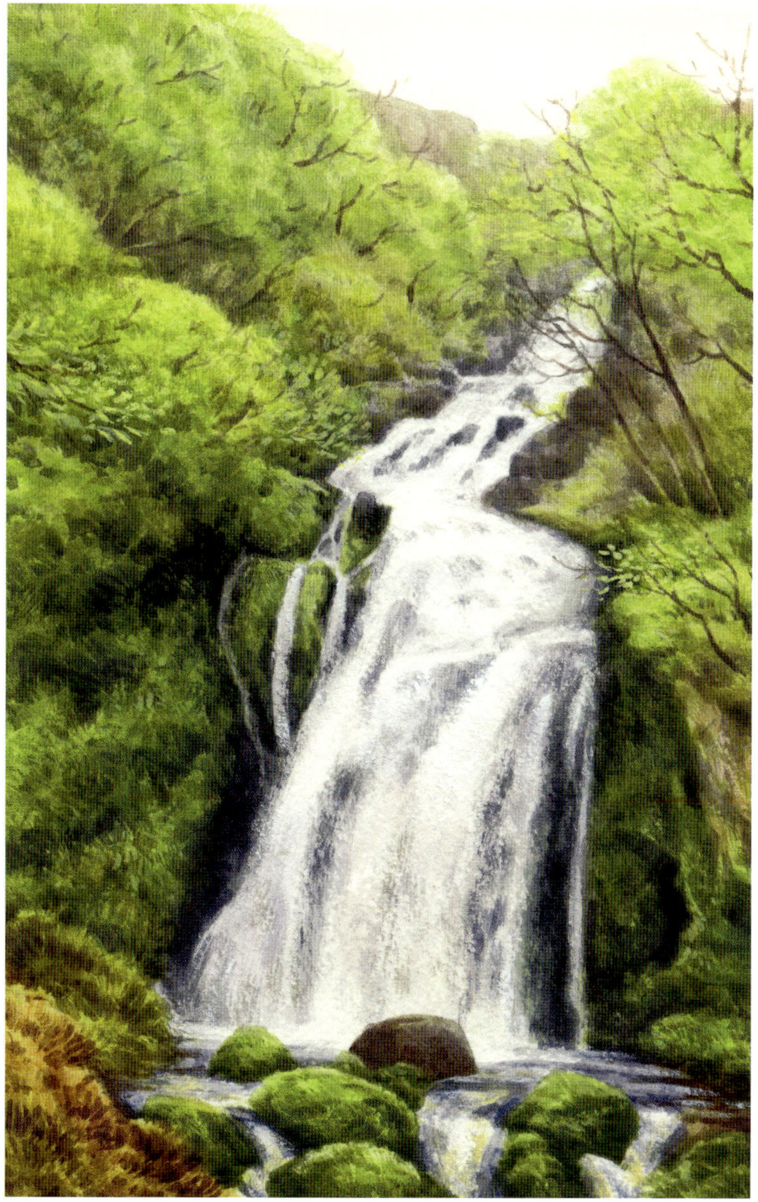

Dash Falls (Whitewater Dash) 18/5/09
A series of impressive cascades but access is difficult due to fencing.

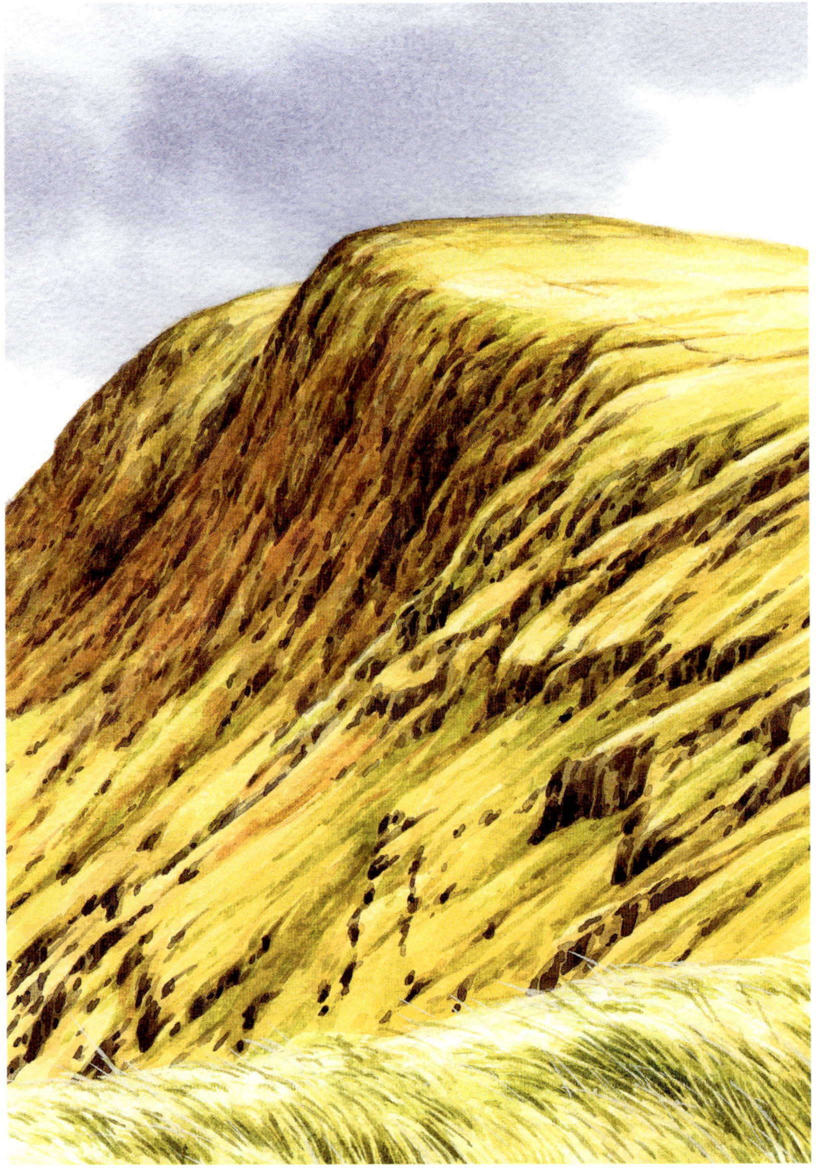

From the ridge leading to Bowscale Fell 28/8/08
The path here follows the edge that drops 600 feet into the valley of Bannerdale Beck. The route can just be seen heading up to the fell top.

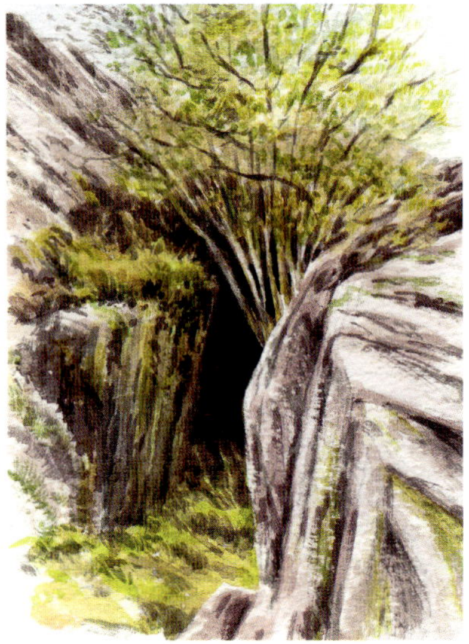

Upper level Bannerdale Mine 29/8/08
Some time was spent seeking out this secretive mine entrance.

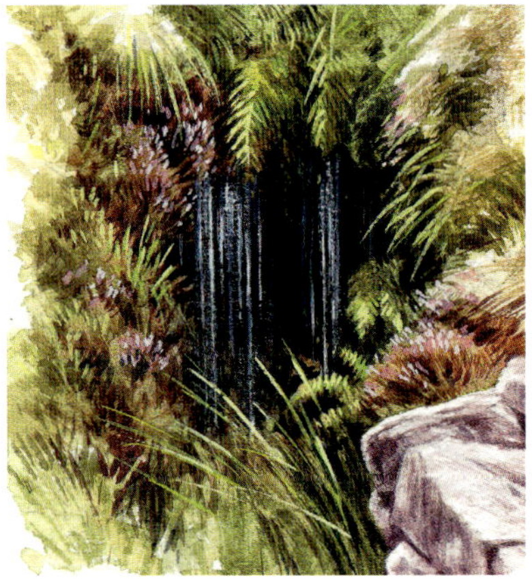

The lower mine level 29/8/08
The small overgrown opening has a curtain of water at its front.

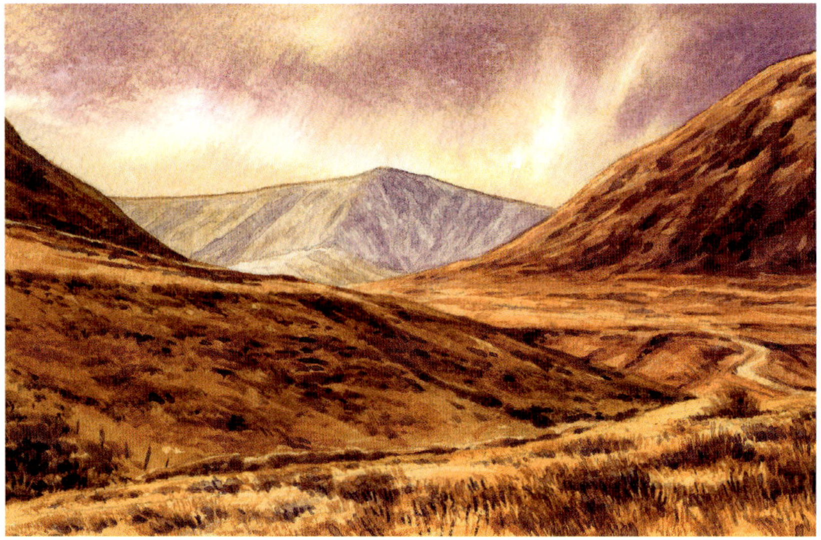

From Mungrisdale 29/8/08
The view that presents itself on the track west of the village alongside the River Glenderamackin.

Bannerdale Crags

Mungrisdale village is a good starting point for a walk up to this fell, with an easy route alongside the River Glenderamackin prior to heading up the steep and interesting east ridge. Once at the top, weather permitting the views can include the Coniston Fells, 20 miles to the south. A return to the start can incorporate a visit to nearby Bowscale Fell.

From the final tower of the east ridge 29/8/08
Close to the edge and away from the path it took time and care to locate the rocks from his drawing.

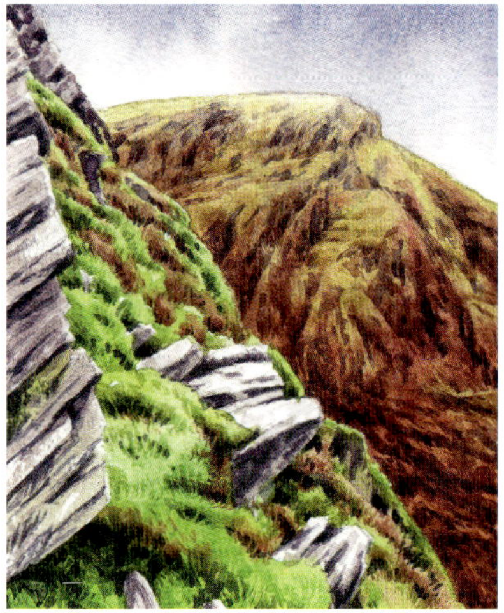

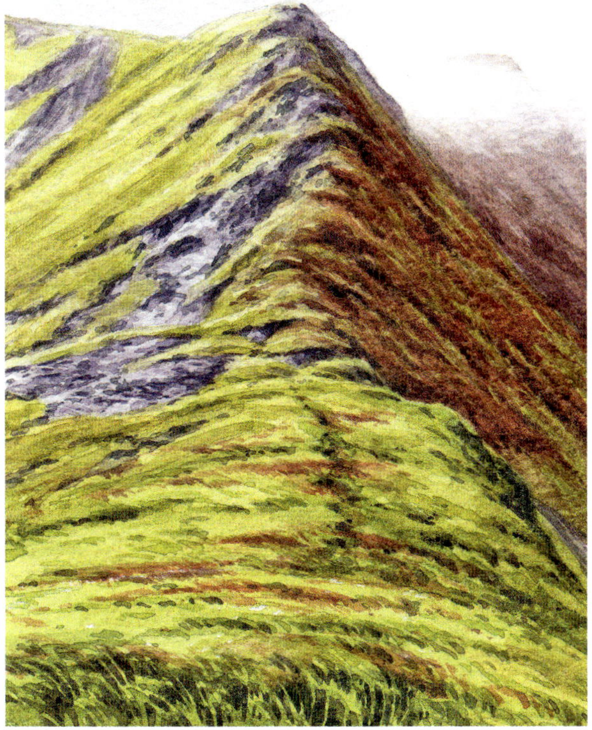

The east ridge with the summit to the right 29/8/08
The low cloud nearly put paid to my plans because if it obscured details of his illustrations I would have to return on another day. Before climbing the ridge I waited here for about an hour and gradually the weather improved so I continued on my way. This edge is the best route of ascent for Bannerdale Crags.

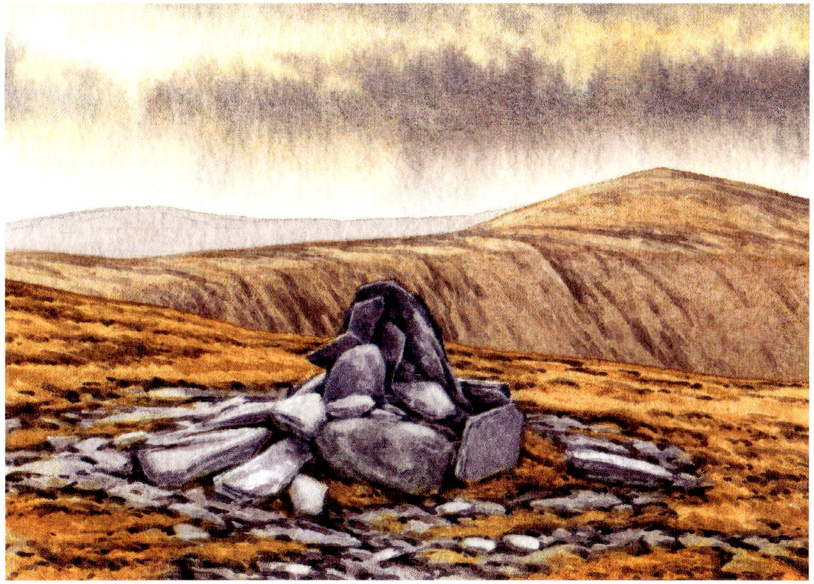

The summit 20/4/10
Another case of a fell summit where Wainwright acknowledges that there is higher ground nearby but this wasn't marked as such at the time. He opts to illustrate the summit area with the one of the two cairns that were located close to the edge of the crags. Bowscale Fell is to the right.

Bannerdale Mine, the ruined hut 29/8/08
The doorway has been walled up since AW's visit but the tree growing from the chimney breast within is now much larger. Nestled amongst the crags in the cove this old lead mine area is seldom visited by walkers.

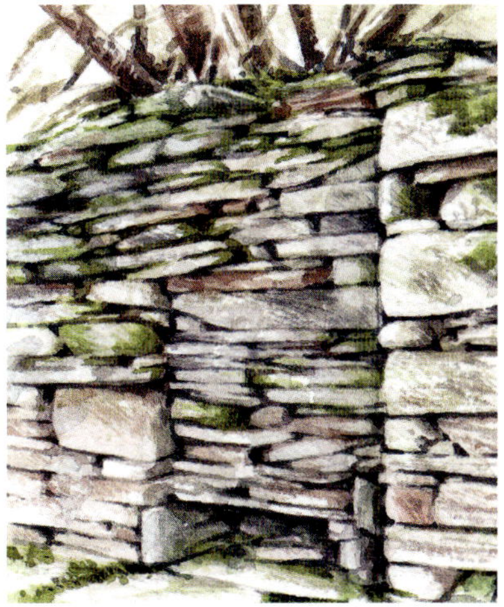

A natural cave 20/4/10
Open to the elements and with an uneven floor, only the sheep would use this as a shelter.

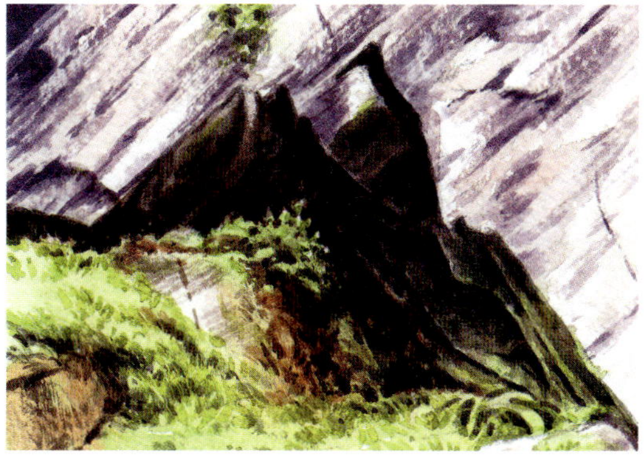

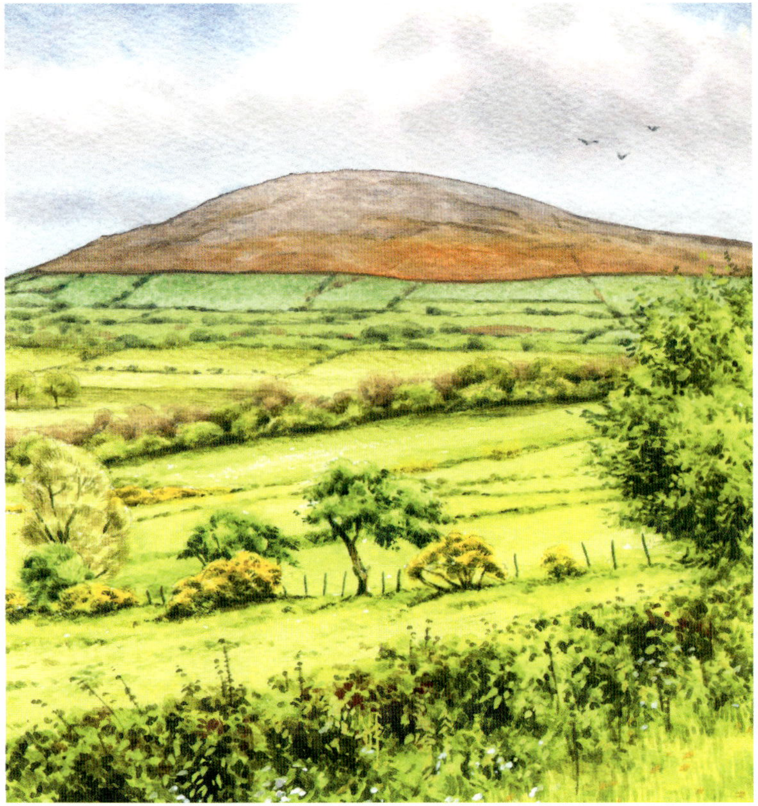

From Robin Hood, near Bassenthwaite 15/5/09
This view is from the road between Kilnhill and Uldale.

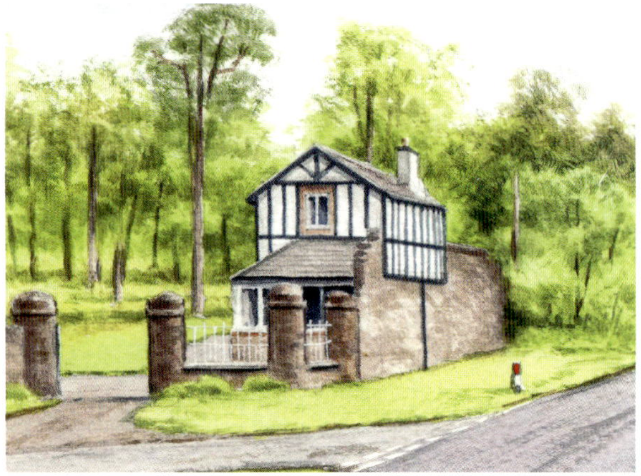

Binsey Lodge 15/5/09
Thinned out woodland and a roadside bollard are about the only changes to this scene in fifty years.

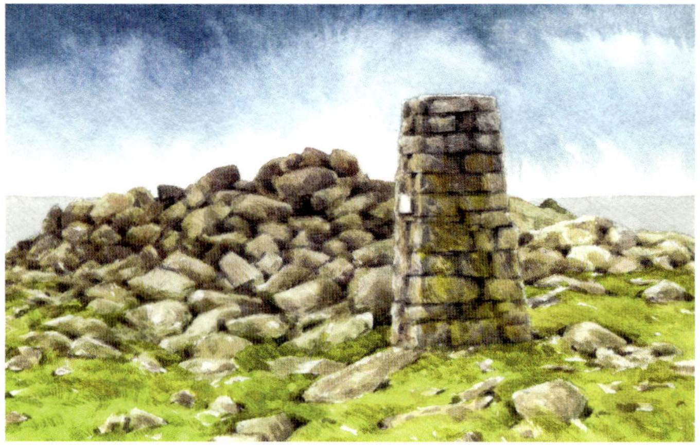

The summit 15/5/09
This cairn is more of a spread out affair now. There are another two cairns near the summit, one seen here just to the right of the pillar is the north-west cairn (shown below left). The other is just behind this point which has been constructed since AW's day.

Binsey

A fell for a gentle wander with merits of the views south to the Back o' Skiddaw and north to the Solway Firth. A small number of red grouse reside here in the heather.

On the top of Binsey 15/5/09
In his self portrait AW gives himself the tag of *"Ancient Briton"* and by coincidence both he and I would have been about the same age as we portrayed ourselves on this prehistoric tumulus. He had a full head of hair though.

The summit ridge
15/5/09
Now a slightly larger number of stones form the cairn.

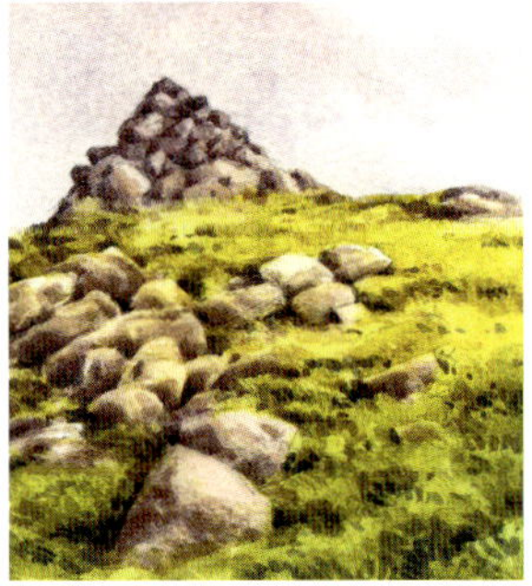

West Crag 15/5/09
The only sizeable area of exposed rock on the whole of the fell.

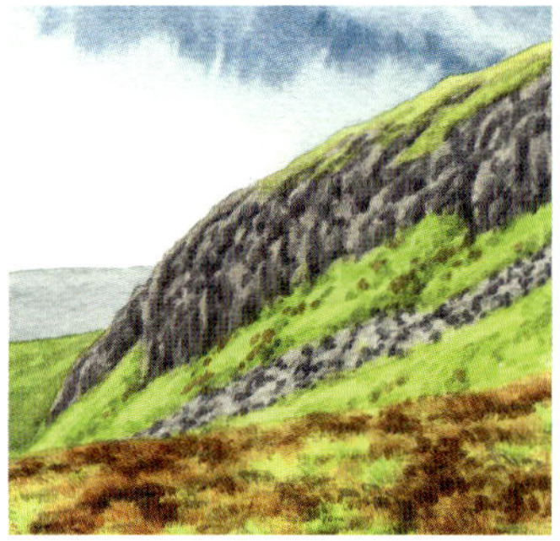

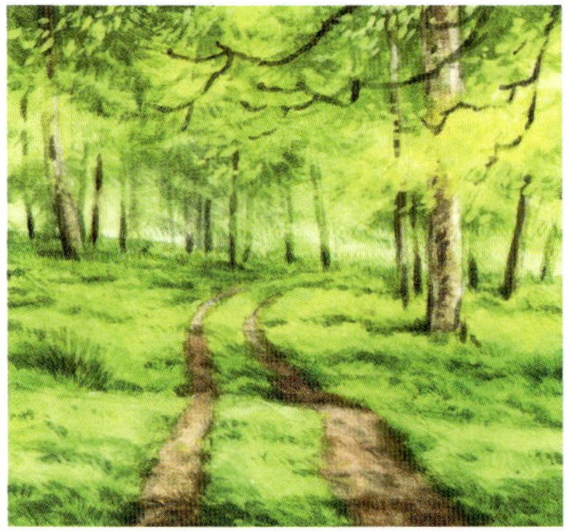

Private path in Binsey Plantation
15/5/09
The rhododendrons have been removed from this privately owned track near the lodge.

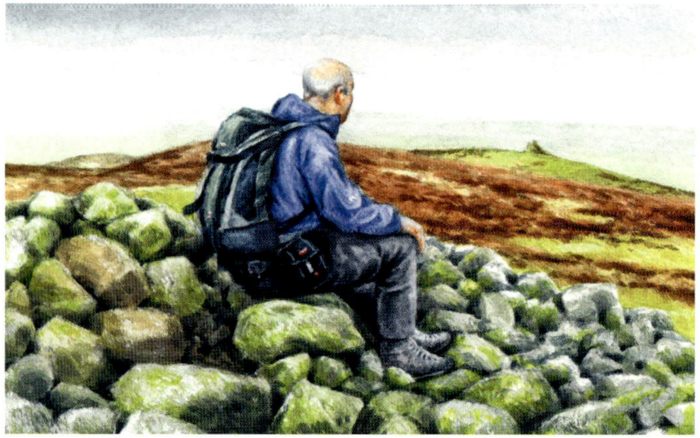

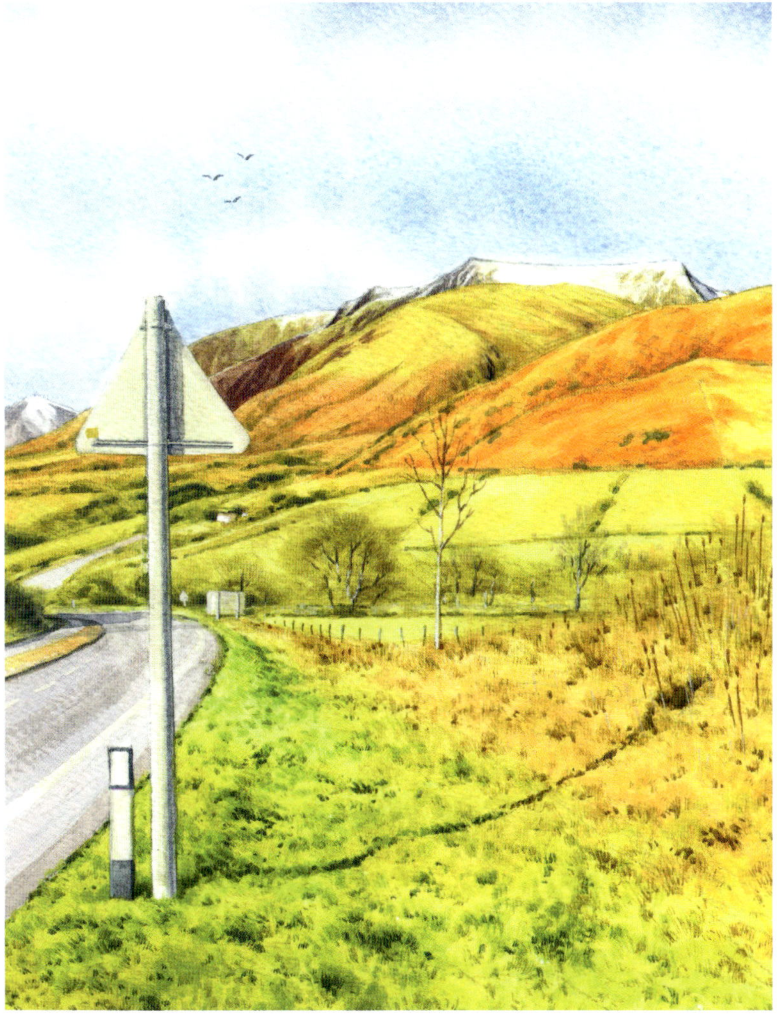

From Mungrisdale road End 5/3/07
The upgrading of the A66 widened the road and gone is the old sign. Both in AW's day and today this is how many people first see the fell as they approach from Penrith, so they can relate to this view. It also serves to illustrate the alternative name of Saddleback and features Blease Fell, Hall's Fell summit, Doddick Fell, Scales Fell, and Foule Crag, more than enough reason to use this view over any other as the opening page of the Blencathra chapter.

Blencathra

At 36 pages, Wainwright gave Blencathra more space than any other fell in the Pictorial Guides and called it "a *mountaineers' mountain*" and included it into his top six best fells. AW climbed Blencathra every Sunday in the winter of 1960/1961, a season of less snow than in previous years which obviously helped him in his task and in all of those visits he apparently met no other person. The south face of the fell is made up of a series of almost parallel ridges and gullies which he describes methodically in the chapter moving from west to east. No other fell is so complex with this number of possible routes of ascent, this is the main reason why he had to allocate it so many pages, not just because he liked it so much. Sharp Edge is the ridge which draws most attention but there is so much more to this fell and it takes more than one visit to discover its true character.

From Castlerigg Stone Circle 7/3/10
At 7.30 in the morning the rising sun cast a warming glow over these ancient rocks, a perfect foreground for the snow-capped fell.

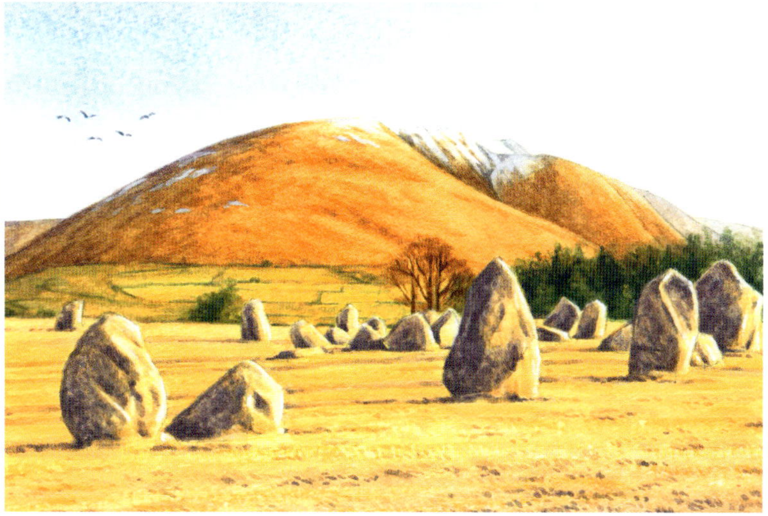

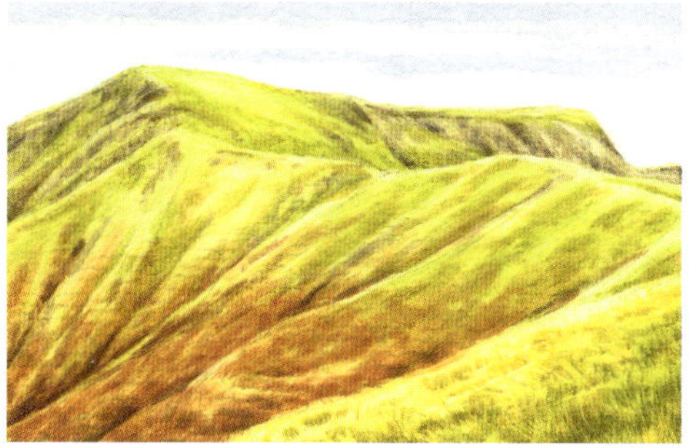

From Scales Fell to the summit 4/8/13
The rising ridge to the "Saddleback".

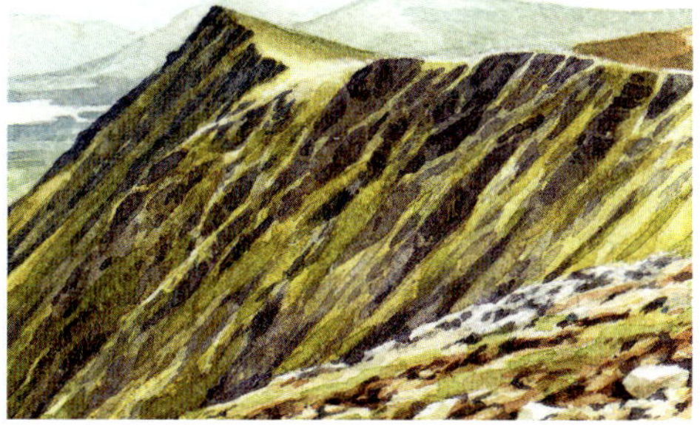

From the summit to Gategill Fell Top 13/3/09
The edge that drops down to Gate Gill.

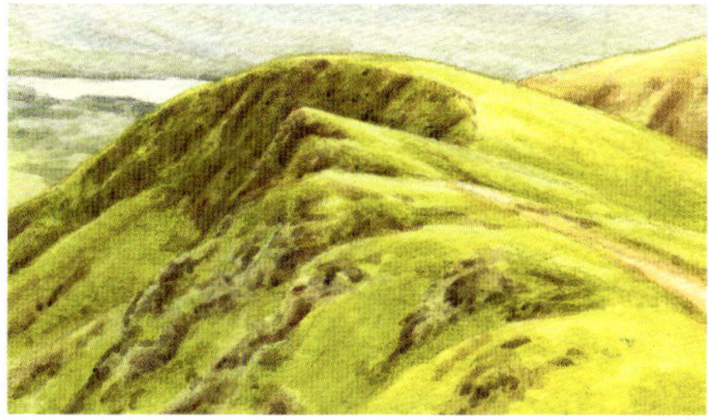

From Gategill Fell Top to Blease Fell 4/8/13
The view with a glimpse of Derwentwater.

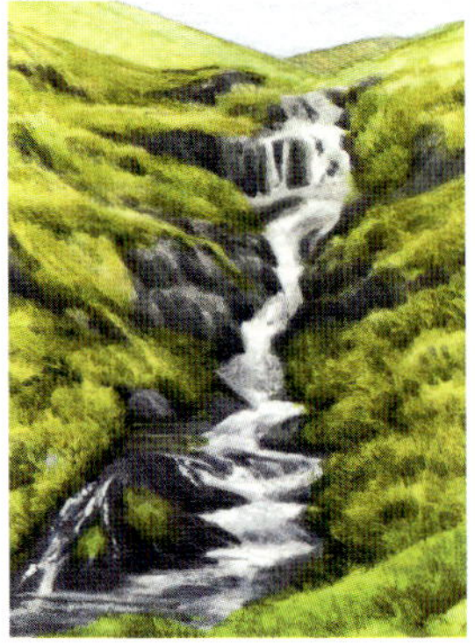

Roughten Gill
18/11/08

The lower of his two illustrated falls.

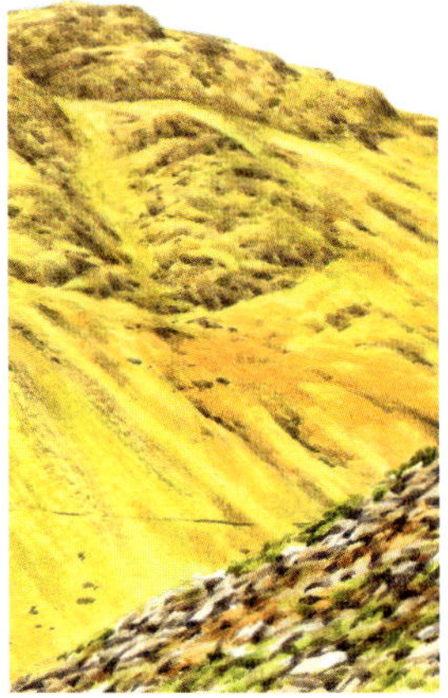

Knott Halloo 20/4/10
This rocky slate outcrop breaks through the heather covered slopes of Gategill Fell, seen here from the rough path 100 yards below the feature.

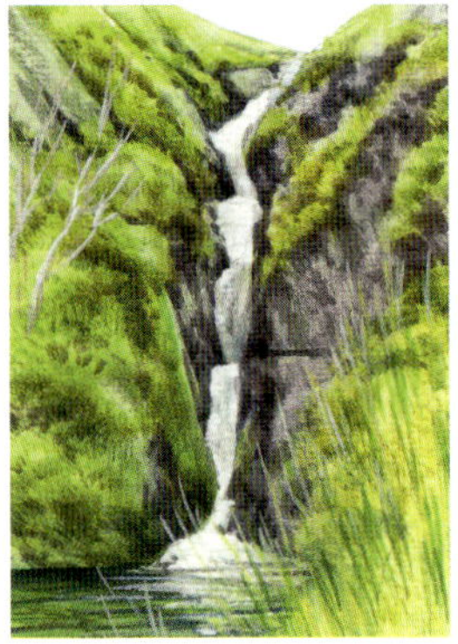

Roughten Gill
18/11/08

The upper falls. Trees have been planted in the ravine recently so in years to come this series of falls will be hidden from view.

Knowe Crags 4/8/13
Move to the west of the path above the two small rock shelters on Gategill Fell to obtain this view of the crags.

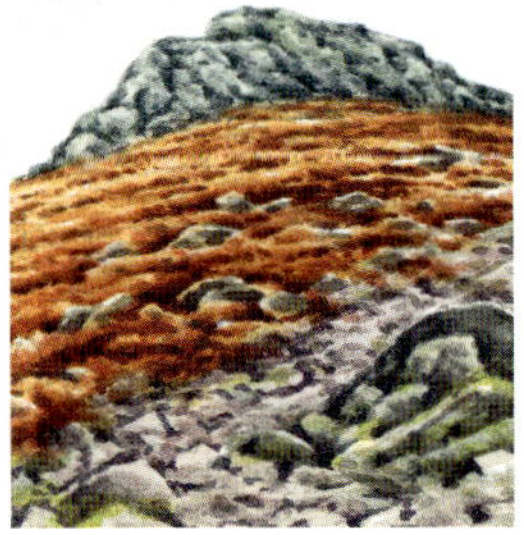

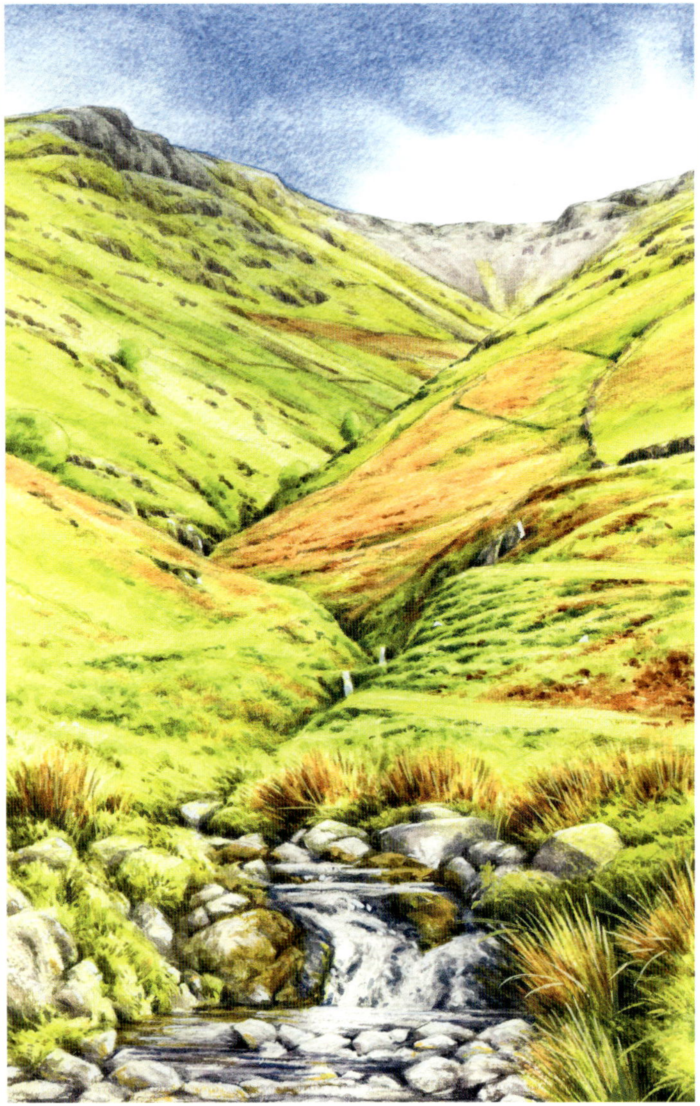

Blease Gill 16/5/09
Knowe Crags are up to the left and on the right are the slopes of Gategill Fell which can be ascended by a path near the wall. The near boulders in AW's drawing could not be found, most likely having been washed further downstream.

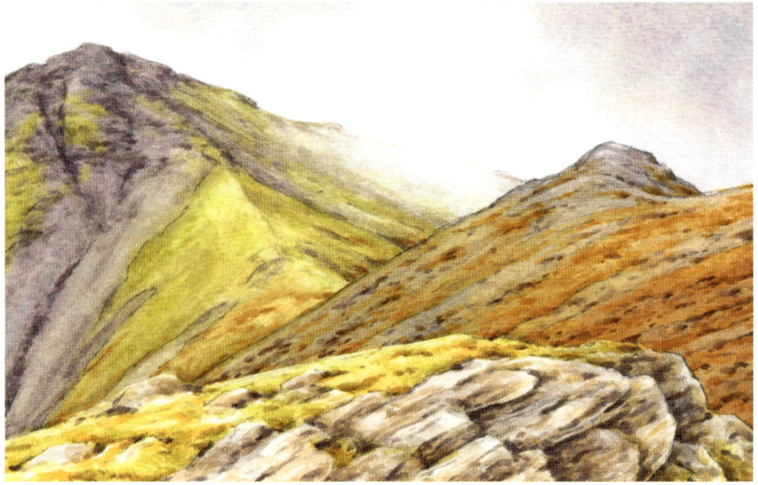

Looking to Gategill Fell Top 16/5/09
Cloud moved in after this, hiding the summit from view so another visit was required to get the references for the sketches below.

Gategill Fell

Looking up the ridge 4/8/13
Light on the undulating ridge.

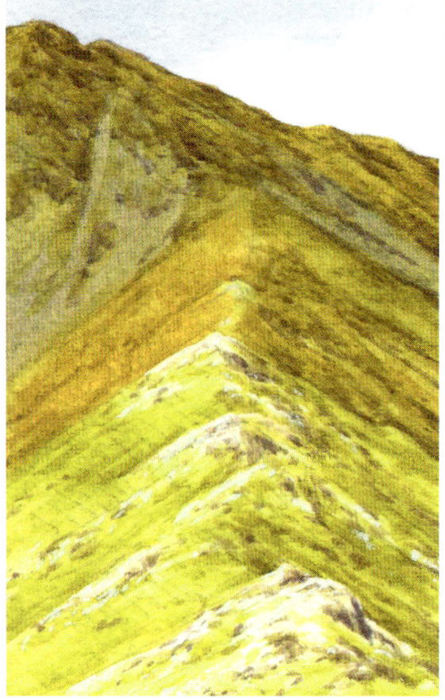

Looking down the ridge
4/8/13

Seen from the steep path just below Gategill Fell Top.

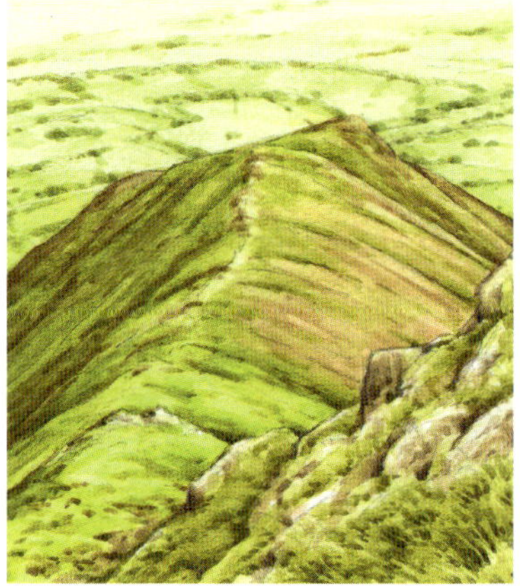

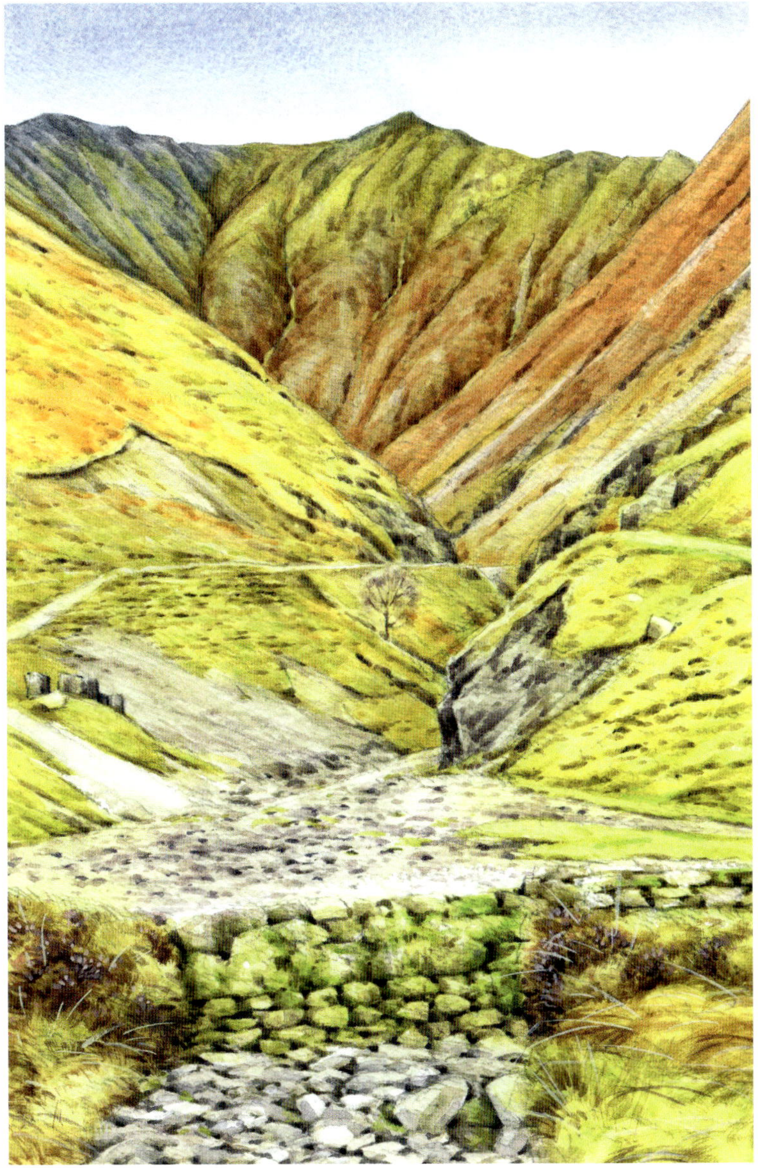

Gate Gill 27/4/10
Hall's Fell rises on the right and its ridge leads directly to the summit. The old mine hut is now in ruin but otherwise the scene is the same.

Looking down the ridge 13/3/09
This ridge was in AW's view the best route to ascend the fell and I fully agree with him.

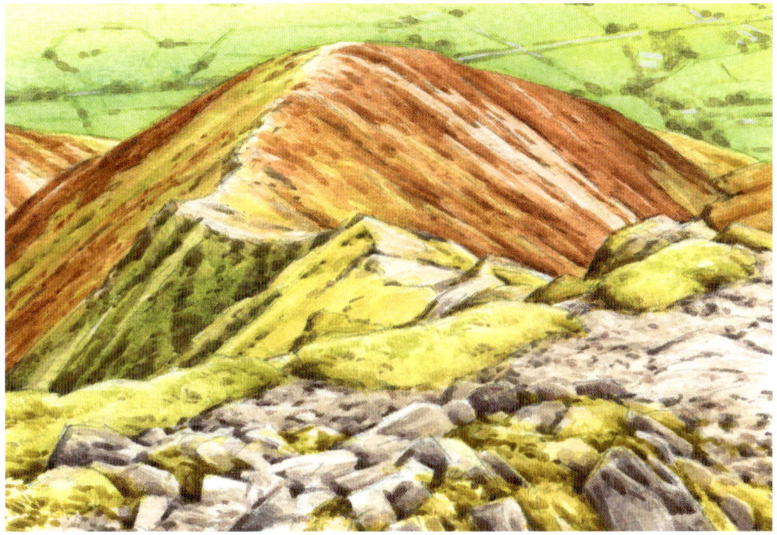

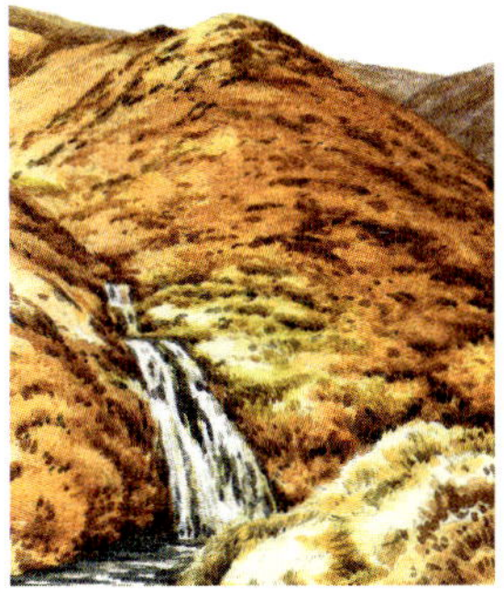

Foot of Middle Tongue 18/11/08
These cascades will be passed by those few who are using AW's Middle Tongue route to the summit.

Old levels Gategill Mine

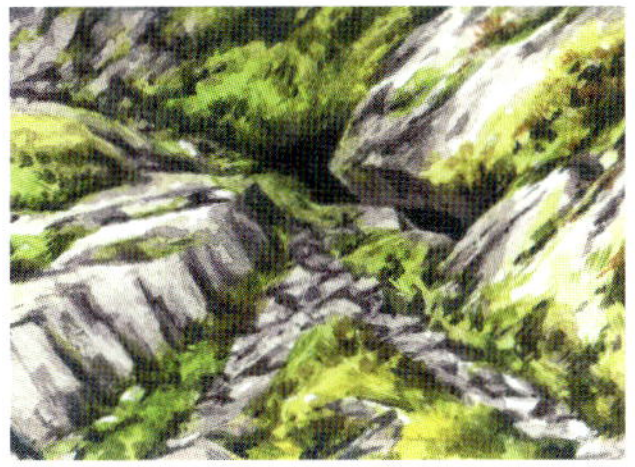

Old level 18/11/08
Debris from above has almost blocked the entry.

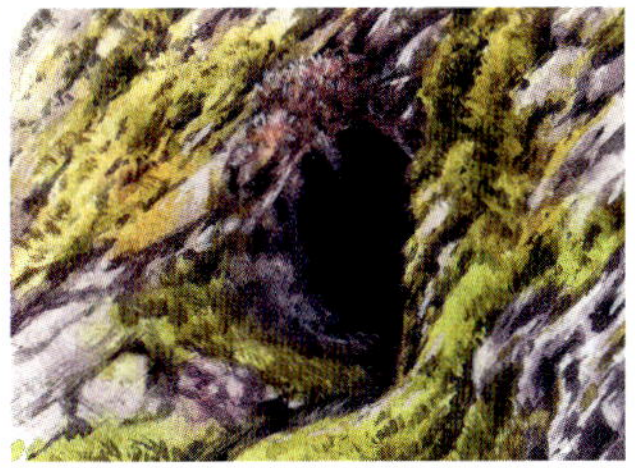

Old level 18/11/08
Dating back to about 1700 this was once one of the most productive lead mines in the whole of Cumbria.

The middle section 27/4/10
The Threlkeld valley is far below.

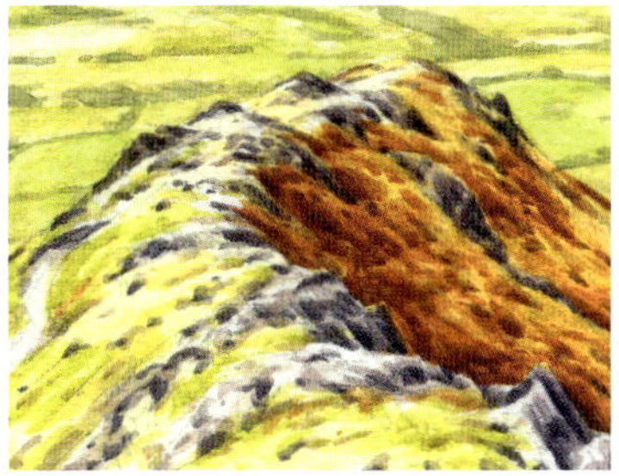

The curve in the ridge 27/4/10
Looking from the rocky section.

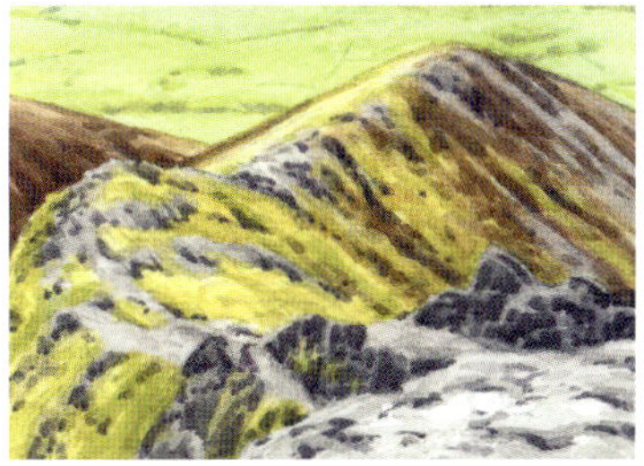

Hall's Fell

Looking up the ridge to the summit 27/4/10
The most exciting section of this fine ridge route to the top.

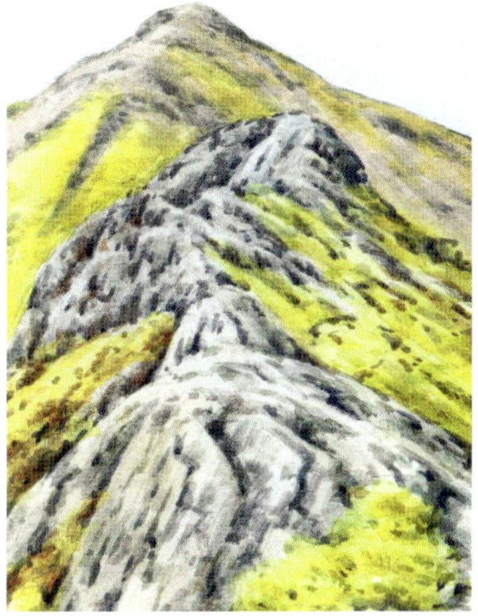

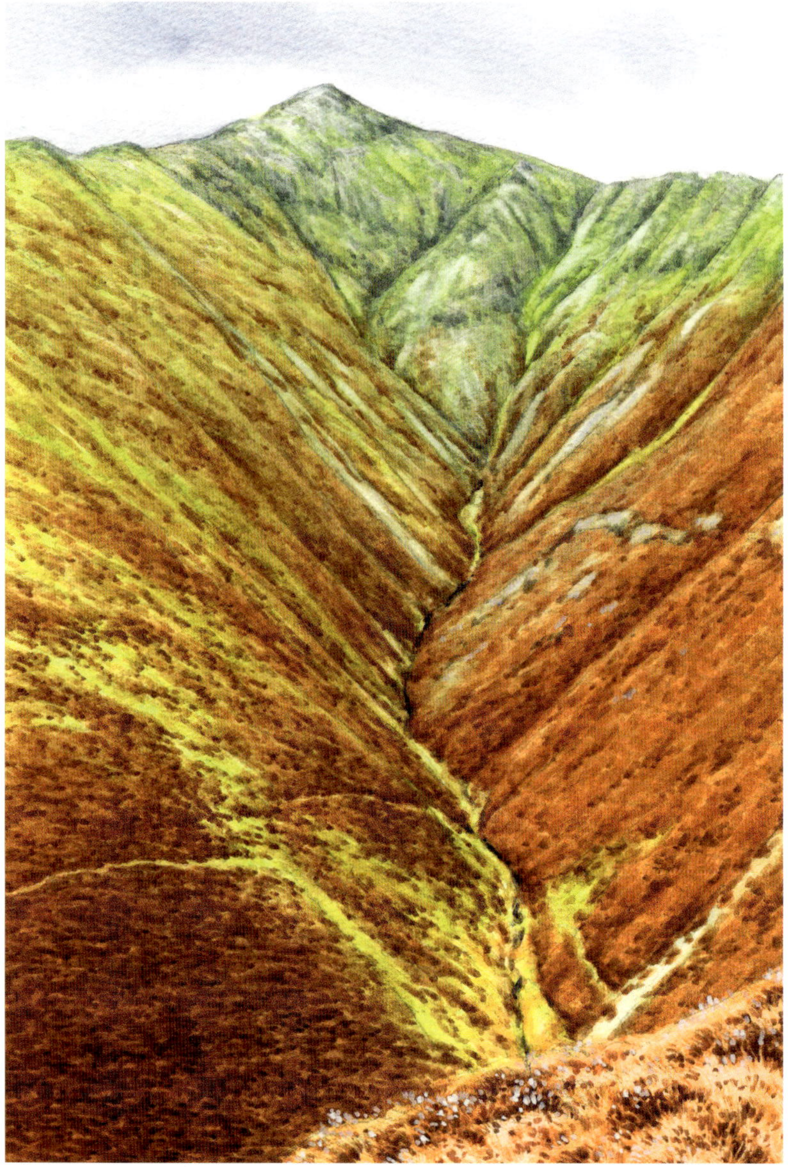

From 1350' on Doddick Fell 24/4/10
Unusually for AW he marks this viewpoint as a height and not a specific feature, by lining up the gill I was able to find the correct location.

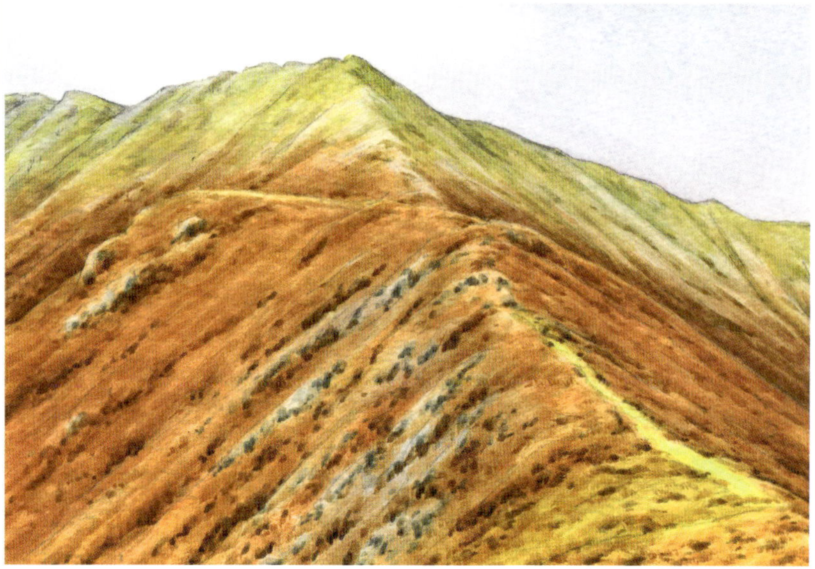

Looking up to Doddick Fell Top from 1450' 24/4/10
The grassy path through the heather follows the crest of this fine ridge.

Doddick Fell

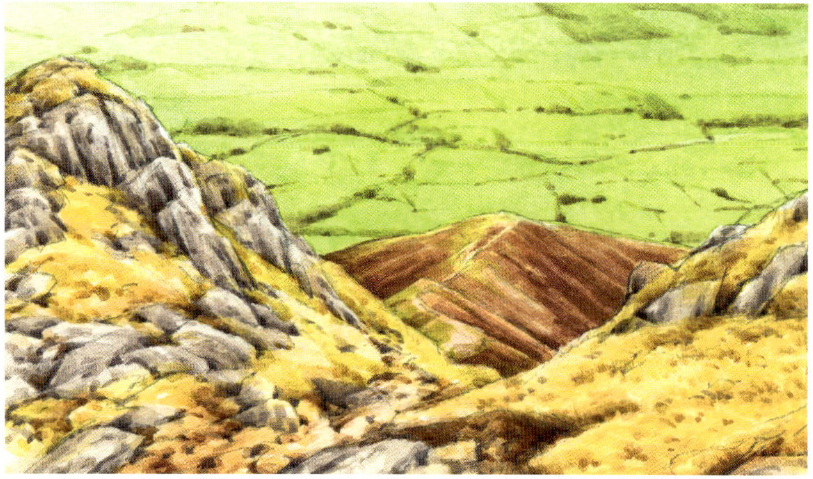

Looking down the ridge from Doddick Fell top 13/4/09
A gap in the summit ridge allows the path to come up to the fell top.

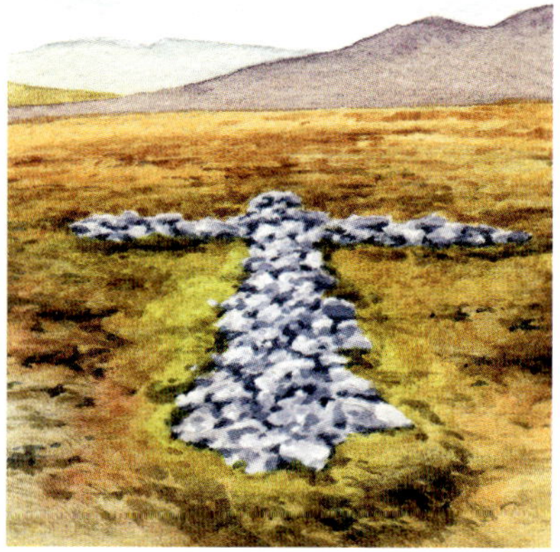

The White Cross 13/4/09
This memorial on the saddle remains relatively the same as in AW's drawing. There are actually three crosses in the area, this being the largest and most impressive. It is curious that the decent sized pool of water nearby is neither marked nor mentioned in the guide nor on maps as late as 1961. Its appearance gives the impression that it has been there for some time but obviously not.

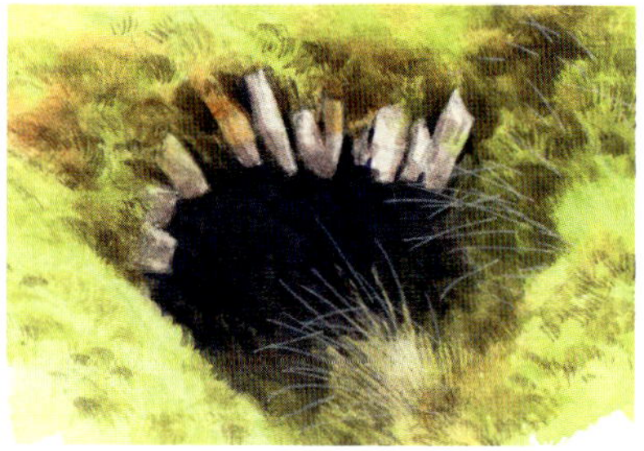

Old mine level 16/5/09
Several level entrances are hereabouts, this is the one in AW's drawing just south of Sinen Gill.

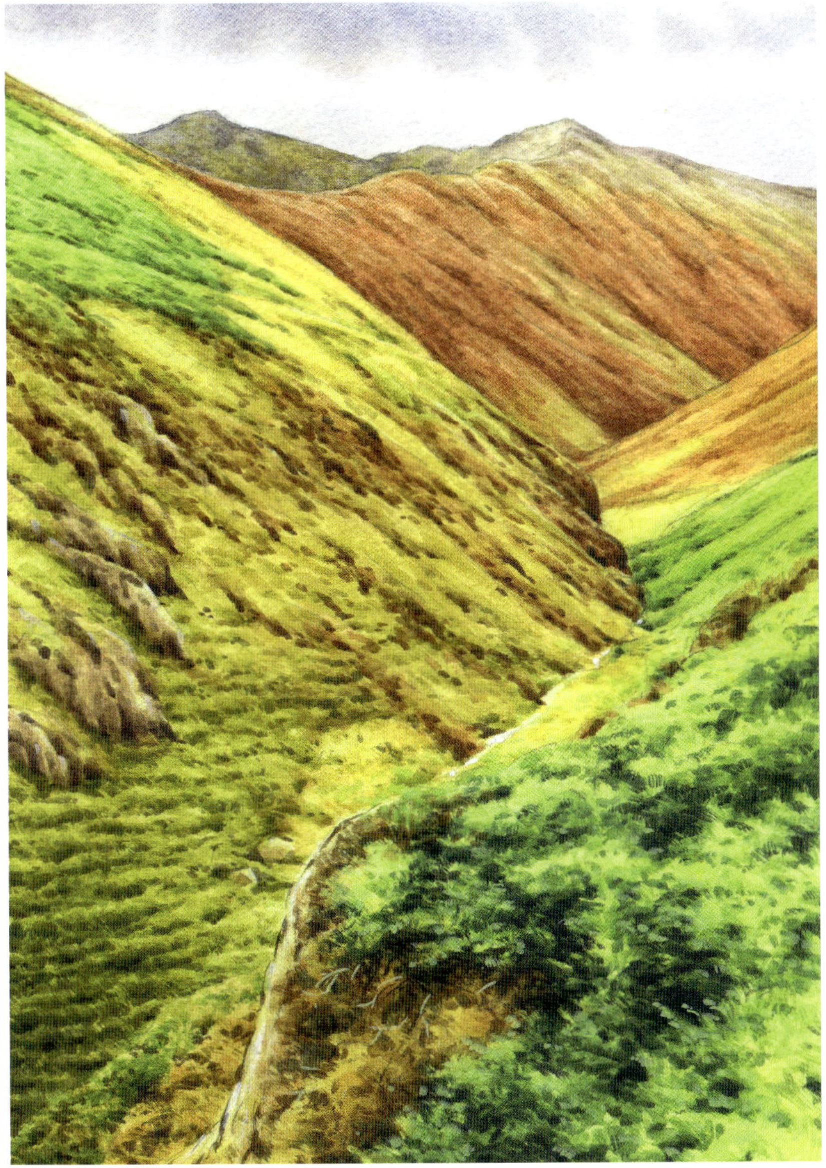

Scaley Beck 4/8/13
The footpath from which this view is seen is from a location under Goat Crags which is not as popular as the normal route over Scales Fell itself.

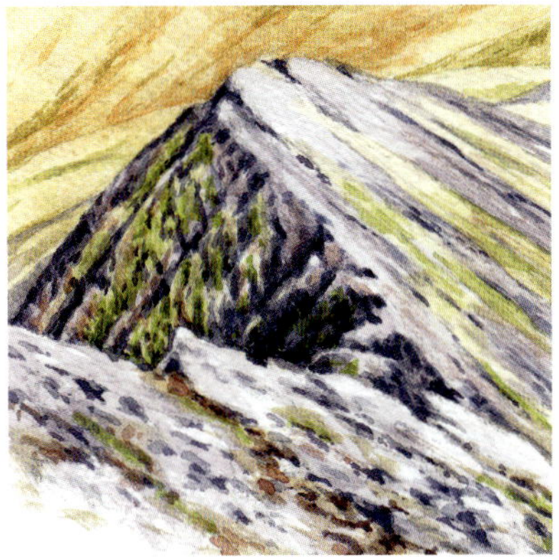

From Foule Crag 13/3/09
Sharp Edge from the rocks known formerly as Fool's Crags.

Sharp Edge

From Scales Tarn 21/5/09
The profile of the edge as seen from the outlet of the tarn.

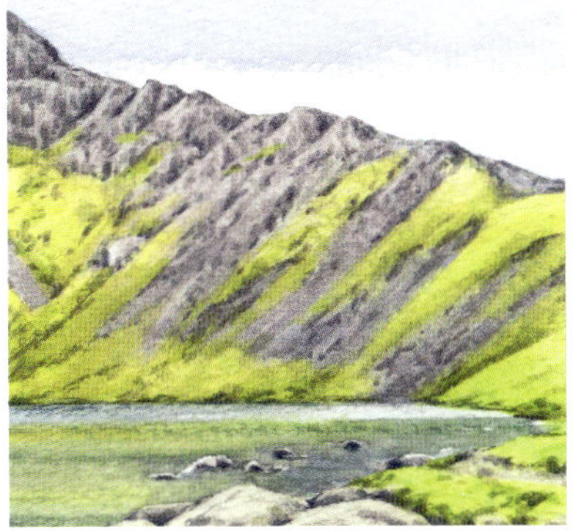

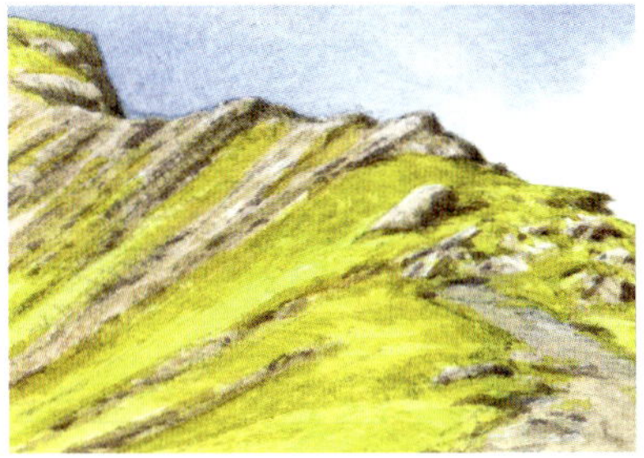

Approach from Scales tarn 15/4/12
A more obvious path now leads to this short but exciting ridge.

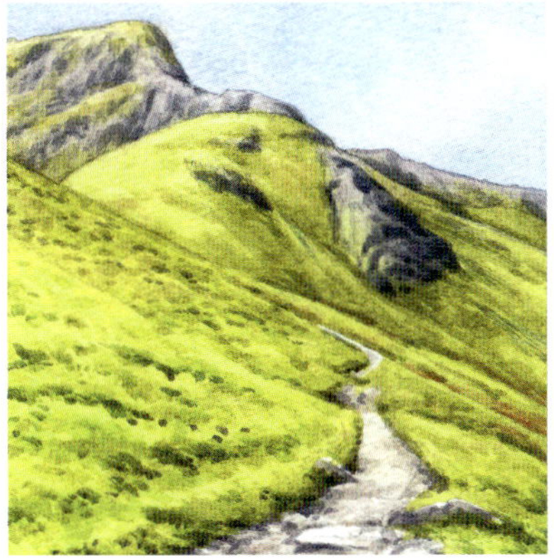

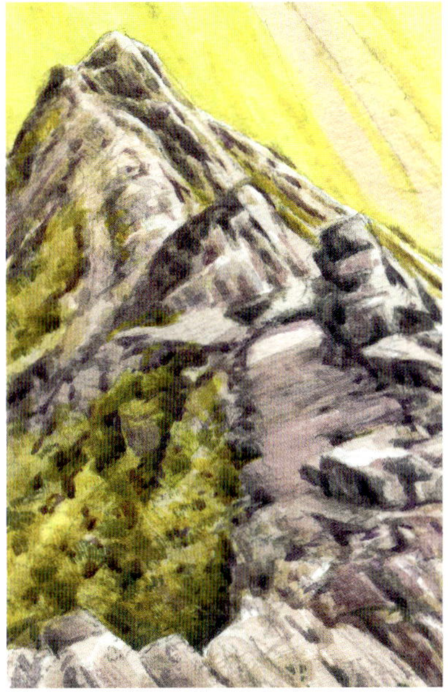

Looking east along the Edge 15/4/12
The length of the crest as viewed from the rise to Foule Crag.

The path from Scales 21/5/09
This is a smaller version of the view used as the frontispiece for Book 5.

The summit 13/3/09
The small cairn that was here in AW's day covered this triangulation station, in the form of a concrete ring, so he did not see it. The few modest stones at this summit sometimes get formed into a cairn close by.

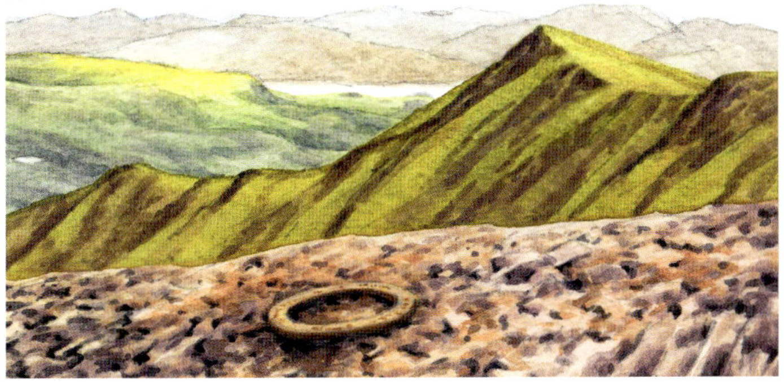

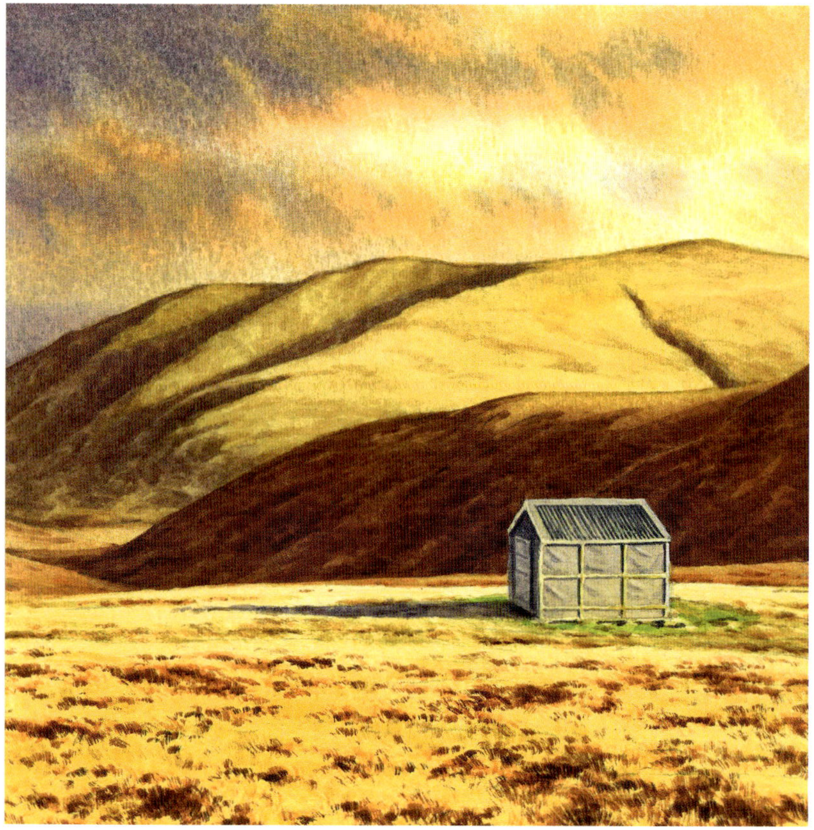

From the shooting box on Great Lingy Hill 6/8/09
The evening sun was low in the west as we passed by the hut which has had some modifications over the years, but remains a basic shelter open to all.

Bowscale Fell
Positioned approximately two miles directly west of Mungrisdale village Bowscale Fell is ideal for a short half day walking excursion from there. Try ascending the east ridge, visiting the summit and then descending via the heather covered tongue for a neat little circuit. Time it right and you can end your day in the village pub.

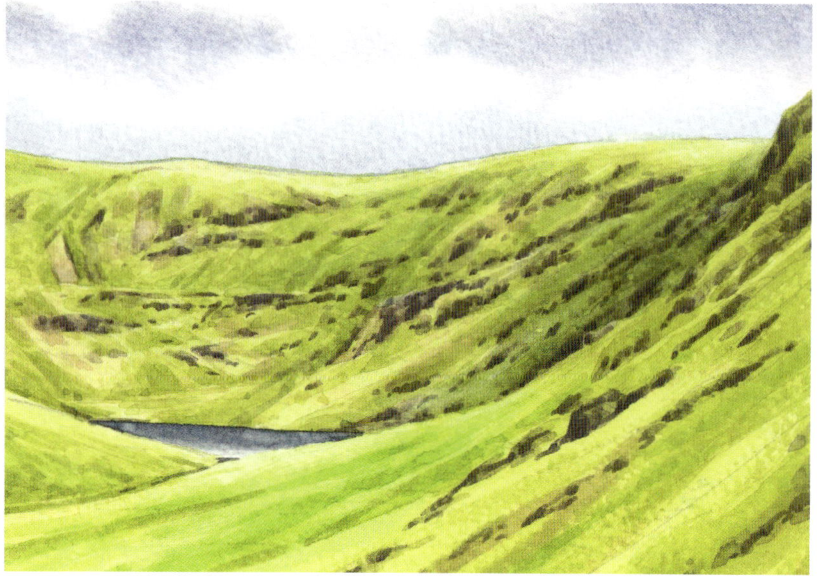

A glacial combe 15/4/12
With a steep back wall Bowscale Tarn is nestled in this natural bowl. This sketch is from the grassy rake which cuts down from Tarn Crags.

Point 1876' on the east ridge
29/8/08
There is no real virtue to this point, just the first of two undulations on the ascent of the east ridge.

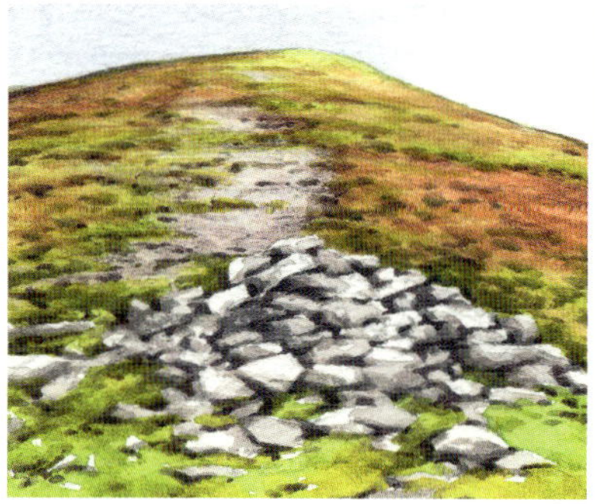

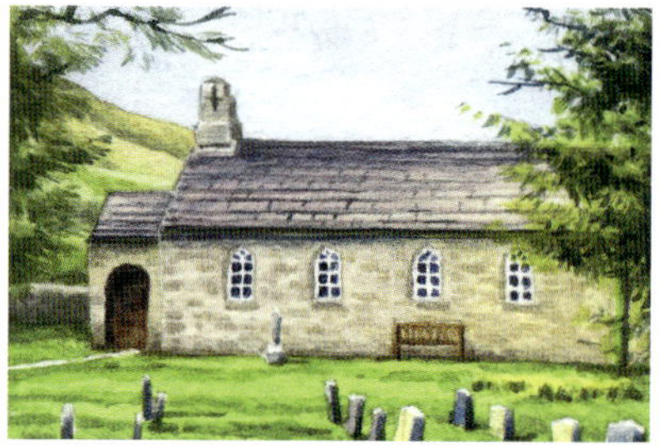

St Kentigern's, Mungrisdale
13/4/09
The once whitewashed walls of this small church which dates from 1756 are now back to bare stone.

Bowscale Tarn and moraine
29/8/08
A short distance to the north of the subsidiary summit the ground gently descends down towards the tarn. From here the glacial moraine that forms a lip of the tarn is easily identified.

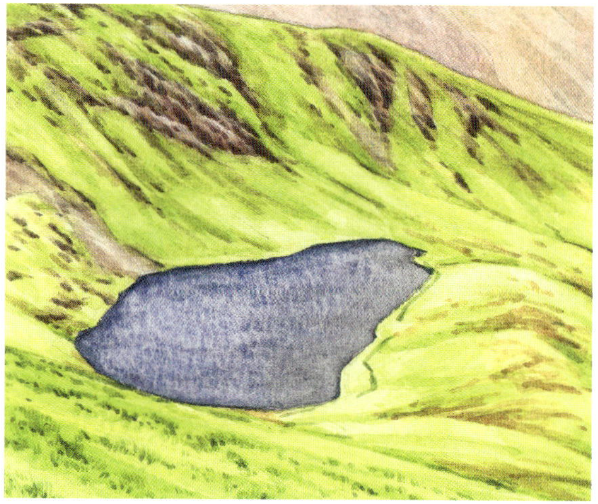

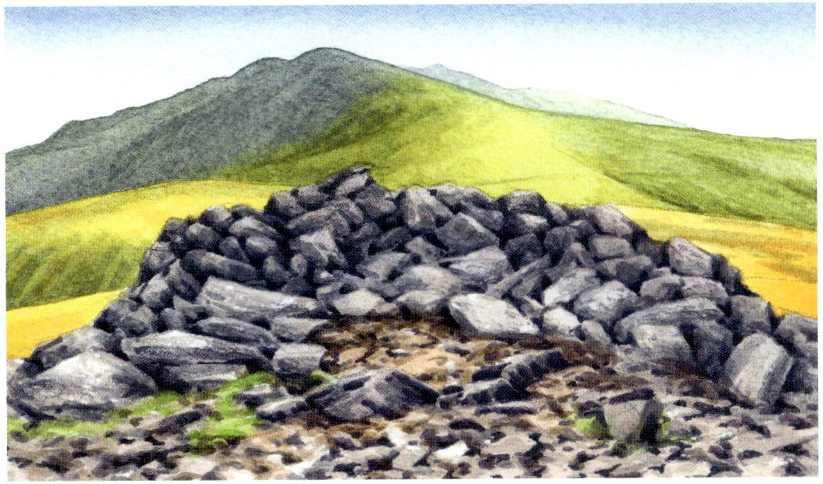

The summit 13/4/09

The wind shelter which occupies the highest ground has been extended but only really provides respite from winds coming in from the west. At this angle the north-eastern slopes of Blencathra dominate the scene.

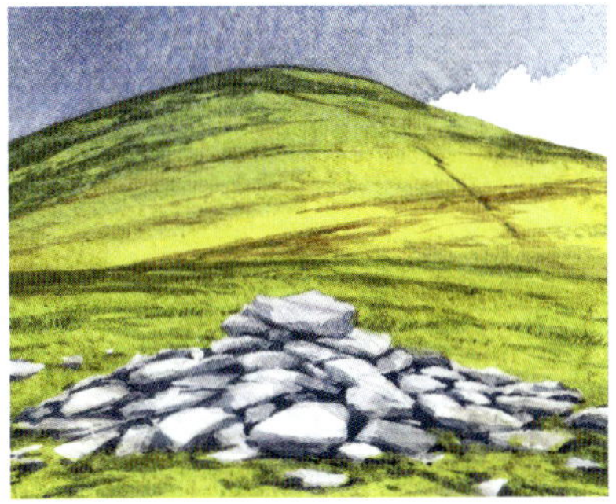

The subsidiary summit 29/8/08

A now larger flat cairn of slate marks this rise on the east ridge at just over 2200'. The path to the true summit cuts up the grassy slope ahead.

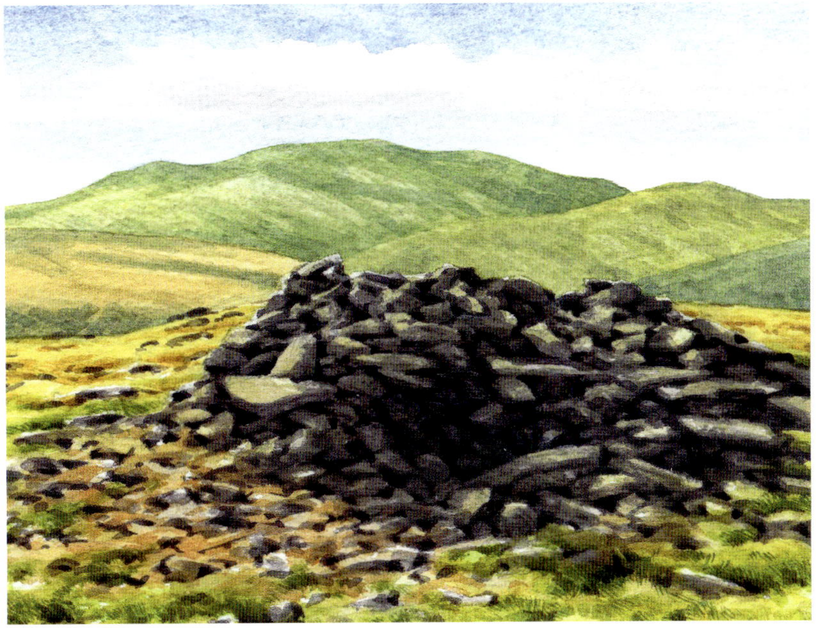

Looking west to Skiddaw 13/4/09

By moving slightly round to the left of the summit shelter the background is now formed by the Skiddaw group and Great Calva. Nearby is another cairn but it is lower in altitude to this mound.

Sheep on the fells.

There is estimated to be around 3 million sheep in Cumbria and Wainwright even dedicated Book Four *"to the hardiest of all fellwalkers - The Sheep of Lakeland"* so here is a short insight to the three main breeds found on the fells.

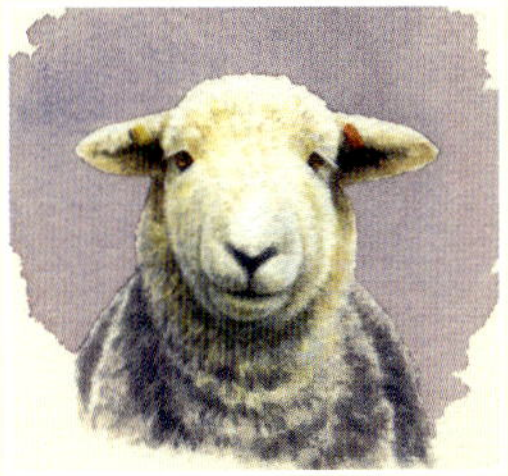

The Herdwick. This breed is almost synonymous with the area, the most hardy of all Britain's hill sheep found mostly in the central and western regions of this district. They can stay out in all weathers and are independent, needing little attention from humans. Over the centuries they have genetically evolved to become resistant to many diseases and parasites. Only the rams (known at Tups or Tips) have horns, lambs are born almost black and turn grey with age but all mature Herdwicks have white faces. Even though it appears that the sheep wander the fells at will they are "hefted or heafed" where they stay instinctively on one patch of ground, a trait passed down from ewe to lamb. Beatrix Potter was a respected breeder of this breed.

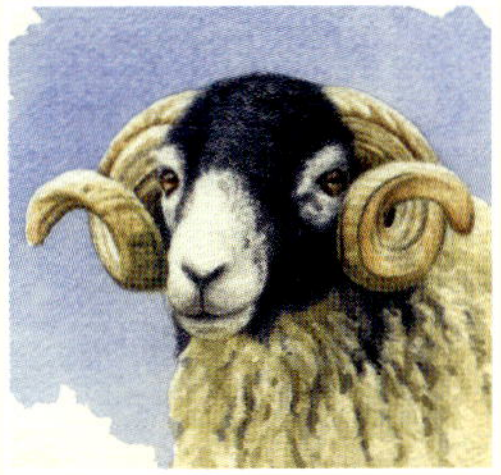

The Swaledale. Another hardy breed which originates from the valley of the same name in the Yorkshire Dales but which is adept at living on the high ground of the fells. Their fleeces are off white and they have black faces with white around the eyes and nose. Both tups and ewes have curled horns with the tup's being much larger and more curled as shown here. They are widespread throughout Cumbria.

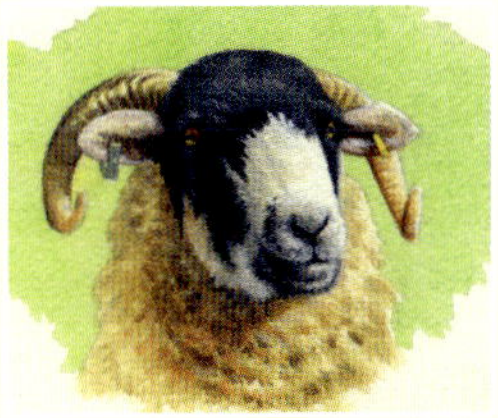

The Rough Fell. This breed is mostly found on the fells in the south and eastern area of Lakeland. They are not unlike Swaledales in looks but bigger in stature, the white on the black face is generally in one larger patch on the nose and not around the eyes. The Rough Fell fleece is more commercial than the tougher wool off the Swaledale.

All breeds produce good meat with a distinctive flavour but the fleeces are now very low in monetary value, almost costing more to actually shear than sell. The sheep will hopefully be on the fells for years to come, keeping the vegetation in short order.

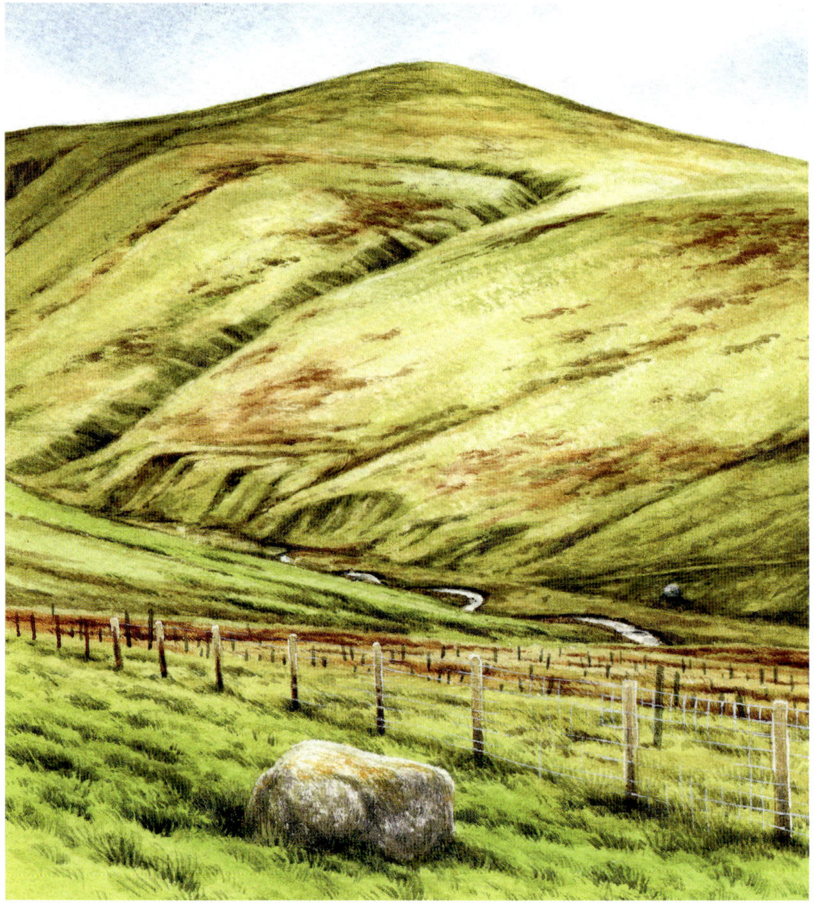

From Fell Side 20/5/09
The track from the hamlet of Fell Side towards Roughton Gill Mine provides this view. Land here has recently been planted with mixed trees.

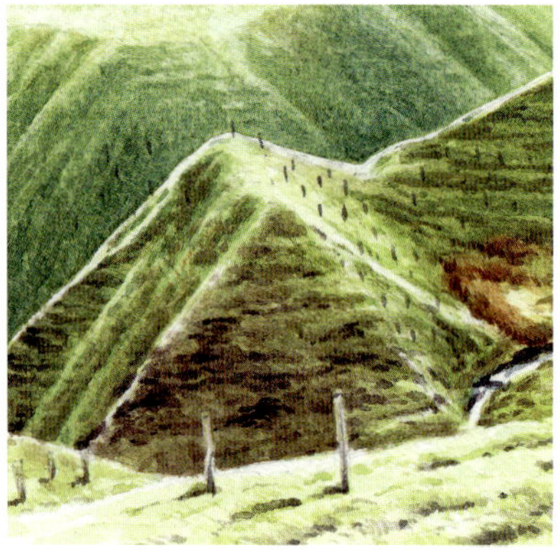

Saddleback, Charleton Gill
17/5/09
With the area now fenced off to protect the new planting, this feature is awkward to access.

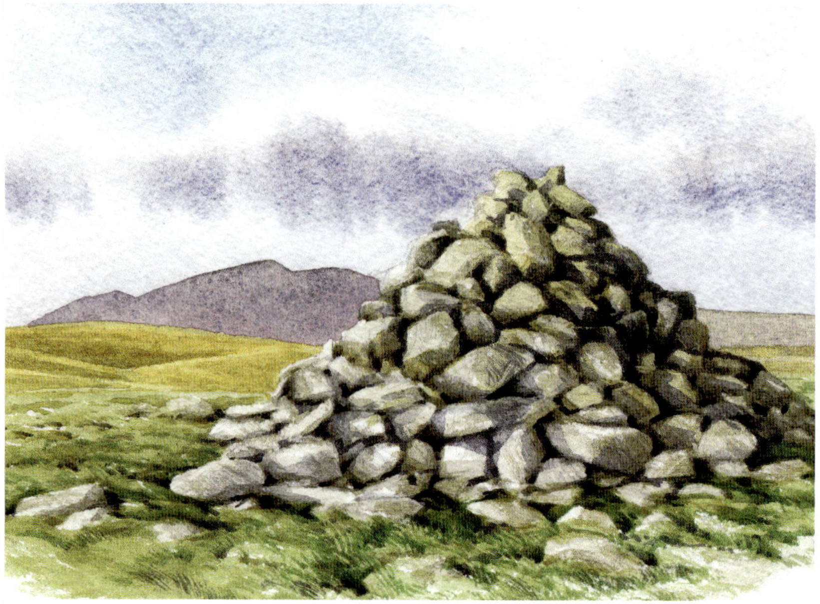

The summit 17/5/09
With no background detail at all in AW's drawing I opted to include the Skiddaw group as the far horizon. It is a substantial cairn in an area of short cropped turf.

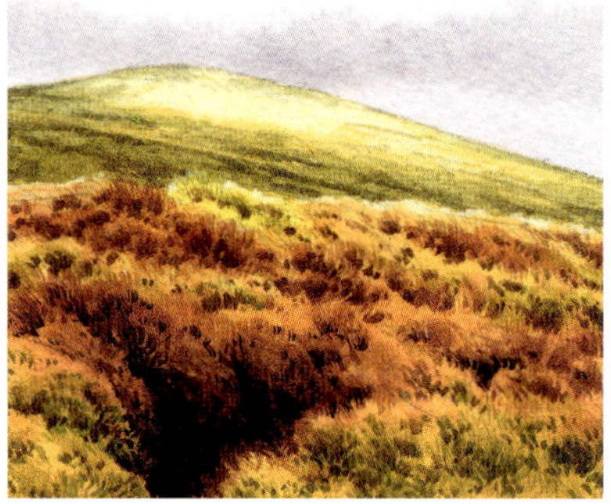

From Birk Moss 20/5/09
The Moss is basically a pathless bog and some time was spent trying to marry AW's view with a peat feature on the rough ground.

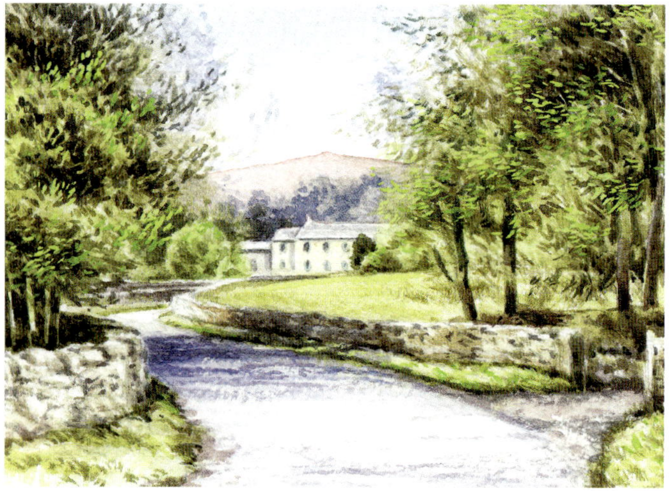

From the Caldbeck road near Fell Side
17/5/09
A copse of trees on the right now obscures some of the fell from view.

Brae Fell

In Wainwright's original lists Brae Fell did not get included, this was possibly because it is really just a slight rise on the northern ridge of Great Sca Fell and has little of interest to write about. However, its inclusion did add another fell to the contents of Book 6 and helped to fill up the volume.

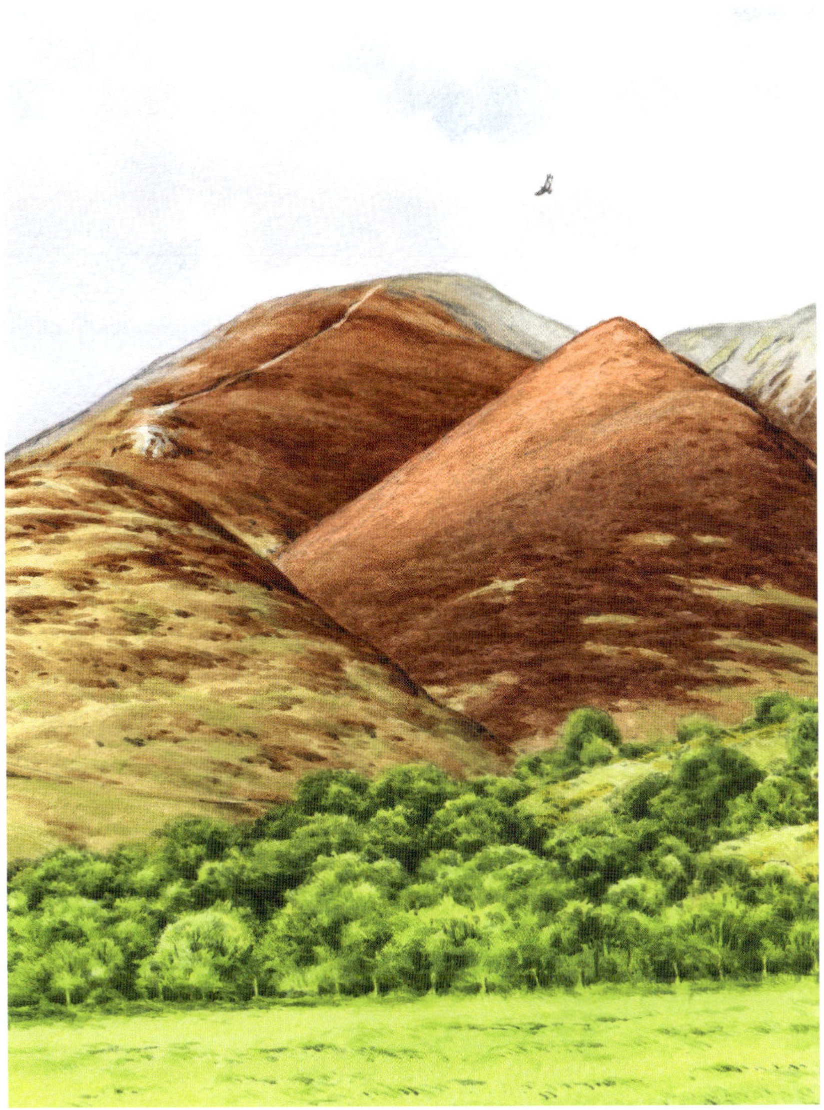

From the main road near Millbeck 17/5/09
In views such as this one which are taken from close to a main road I have always imagined AW perhaps biding his time waiting for a bus, or maybe in this instance walking his way back to Keswick for fish and chips after a good day on the fells.

The summit 22/5/09
Enough material to build a fine cairn but instead there is just a flat heap to go with the plateau of the highest point. A tarn lies in the dip between here and Skiddaw but it may be dry in summer.

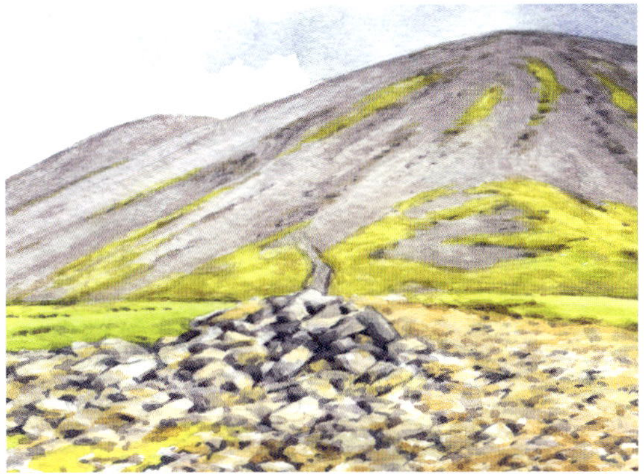

Carl Side

As part of the Skiddaw group Carl Side is a rounded topped fell which provides a welcome location for a break to those ascending Skiddaw from Millbeck before the onward climb.

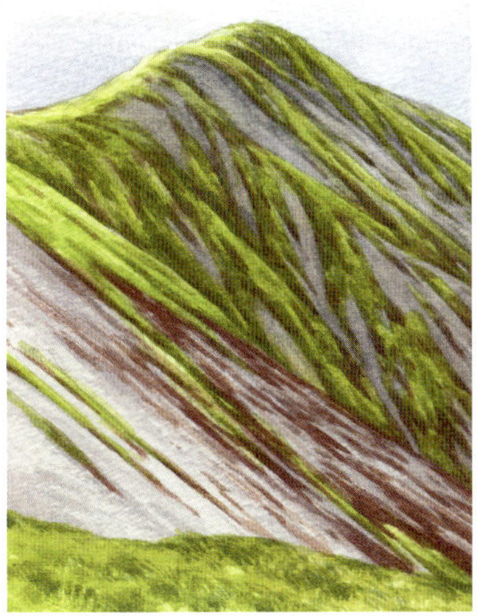

Skiddaw Little Man 22/5/09
The grey slate slopes of the fell as seen from Carl Side summit.

The summit of Carsledam 22/5/09
A little used path up the steep slope through dense heather.

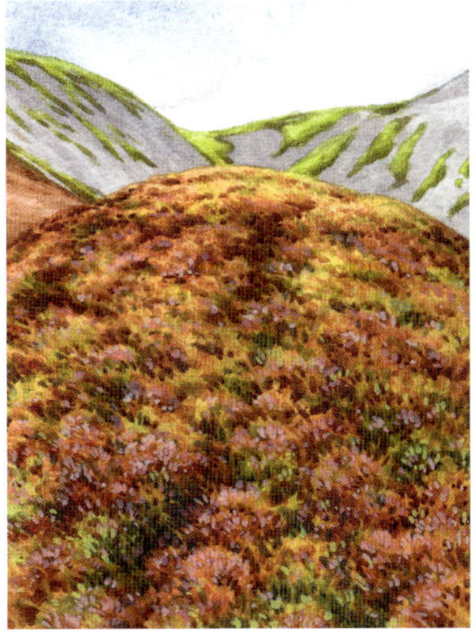

The cliffs of Doups 22/5/09
These crags are impressive when seen from the ravine at their base.

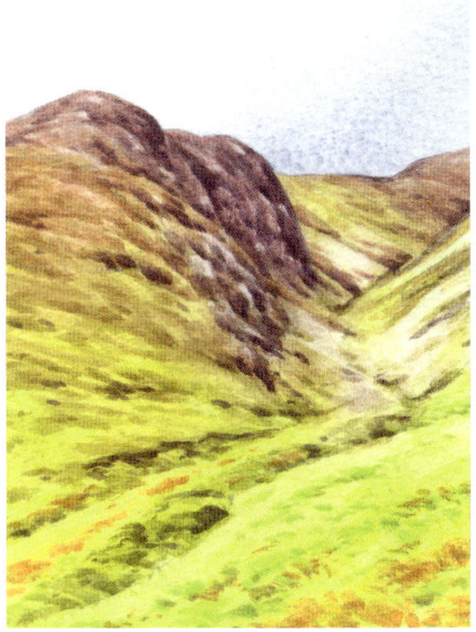

White Stones 22/5/09
An outbreak of bright quartz on the lower section of the south ridge which is actually marked on the map.

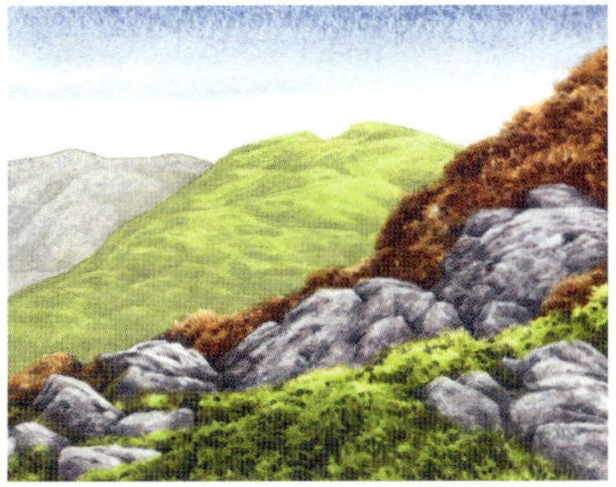

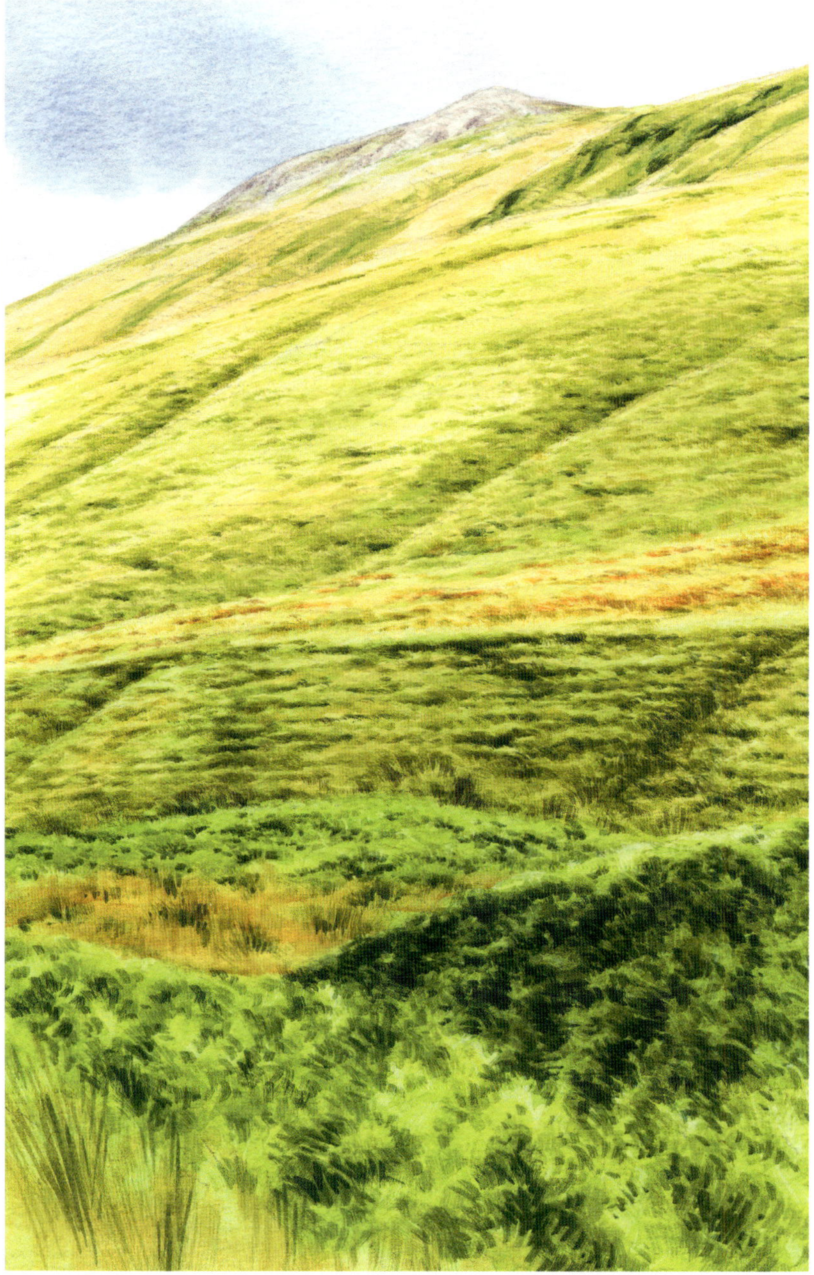

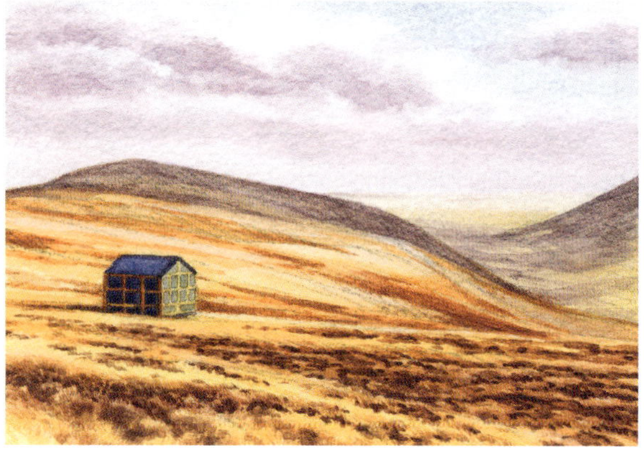

From the shooting box on Great Lingy Hill 25/12/08

A second time that the hut is featured in the Pictorial Guide, this time with the Mosedale valley down to the right and Carrock Fell beyond the hut.

Carrock Fell

It may not be the most aesthetically pleasing of fells but what it lacks in beauty it makes up for in interest. Man has left his mark on the fell throughout time, with the ancient ruins of a hill fort on the summit to the scars of mining activity on the lower slopes. In fact Carrock Fell also can claim to be the only fell in the district that Charles Dickens climbed back in 1857 aged 45 with his friend Wilkie Collins, who apparently sprained his ankle on the descent.

From the headwaters of Carrock Beck 6/8/09

This remote location close to Drygill Beck is not the best location for an interesting view of Carrock Fell, but it was the one chosen by AW, perhaps because the portrait format fitted his planned page layout.

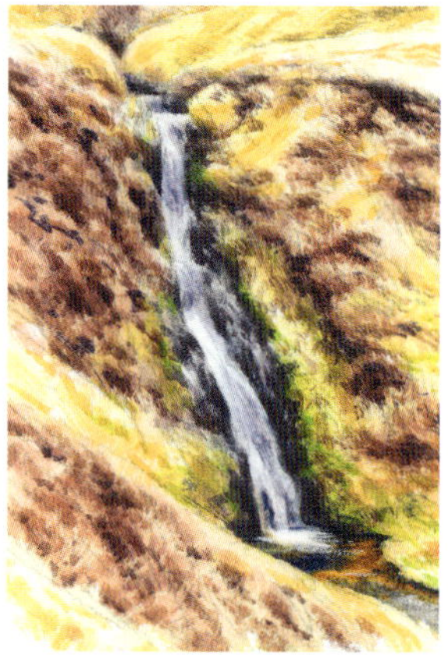

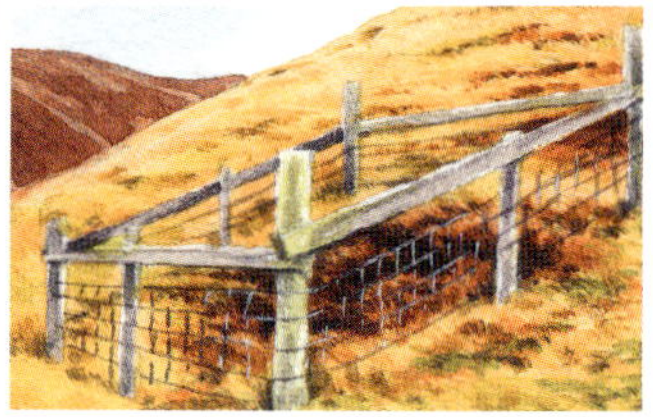

Open shaft, Carrock Mine 12/3/10

This deep hole on the fell side is now fenced off.

Waterfall, Brandy Gill 12/3/10

The tree at the top of the fall has gone. There is no path here and care should be taken near the ravine.

The crags of Carrock Fell 6/8/09

Only by taking the alternative route to the east peak which passes close to the cliff edge will this aspect of the crags be seen. Heather blooms well here in summer.

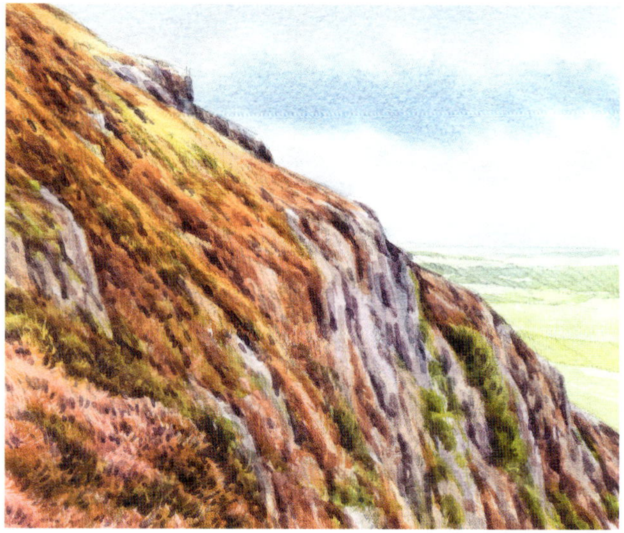

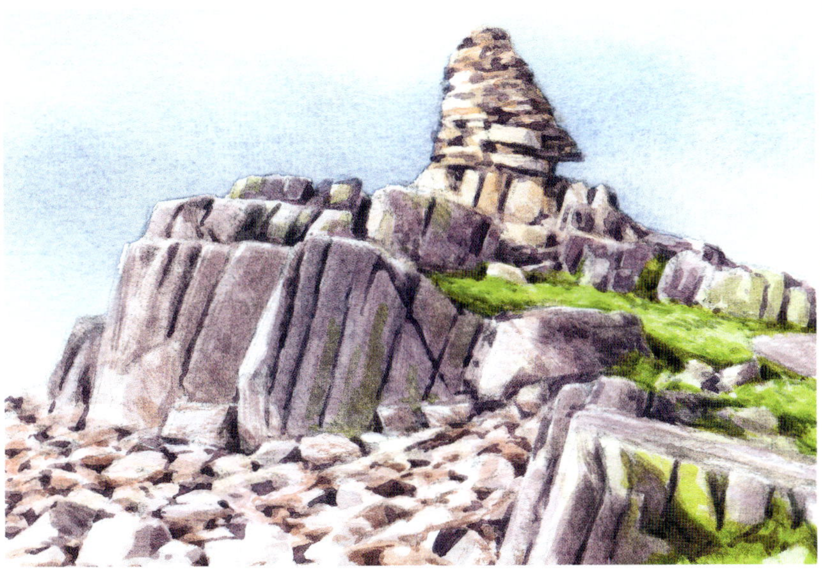

The summit 6/8/09
Currently the summit is topped with a decent cairn on a flat layer of bedrock. This is at the eastern end of the Iron Age Hill Fort which once occupied this fell top, evidence of which can still be seen (see below).

Carrock Fell from the Caldew Valley 6/8/09
The path that contours around the lower slopes of Knott near Wet Swine Gill provides this view of the heathery slopes of Carrock Fell.

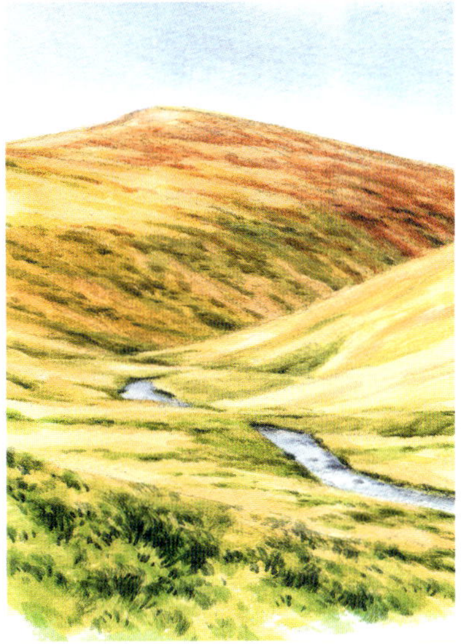

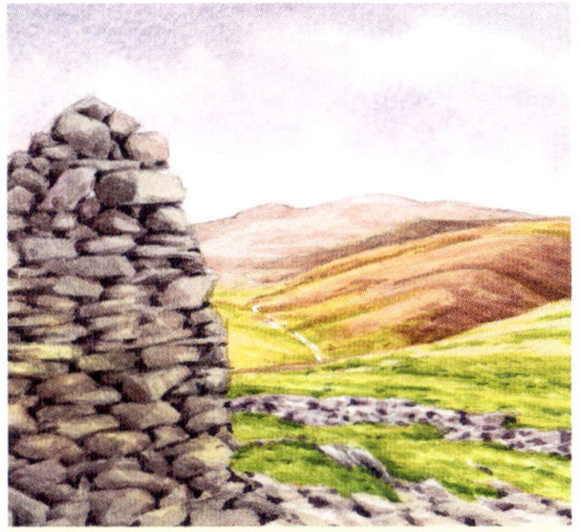

Skiddaw from the summit 6/8/09
The River Caldew leads the eye up to the distant Skiddaw range. The wall of the fort can be seen in the foreground.

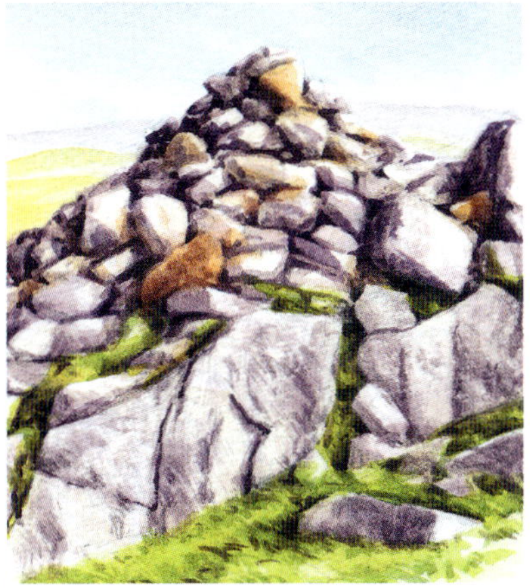

Cairn on east peak 6/8/09
The cairn here is worth a visit just for the view over to the Eden Valley alone. In the opposite direction a gently rising path leads through the rocky ramparts of the fort up to the summit.

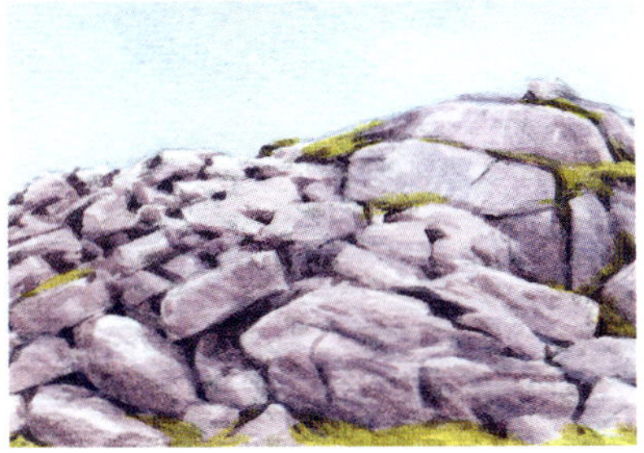

Original masonry 6/8/09
Sadly the best bit of the old wall has now fallen but due to AW's detailed diagram I was able to locate the section by the shape of the bedrock on the right.

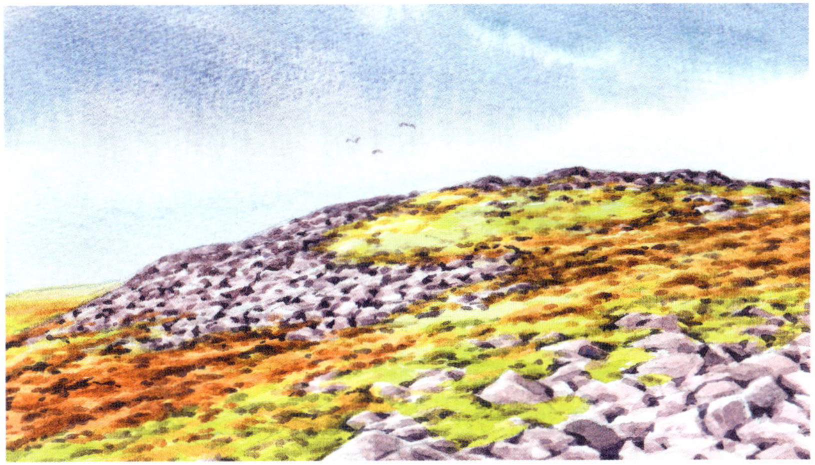

The collapsed walls of the fort 6/8/09
The approximate shape and size of the fort can be traced by the large ring of stones that once formed the walls. This view looks up to the fell summit across the gap which AW called the south gateway. If the amount of stone lying where the fort's walls once stood is anything to go by then this at one time must have been quite a substantial construction, dominating the local area.

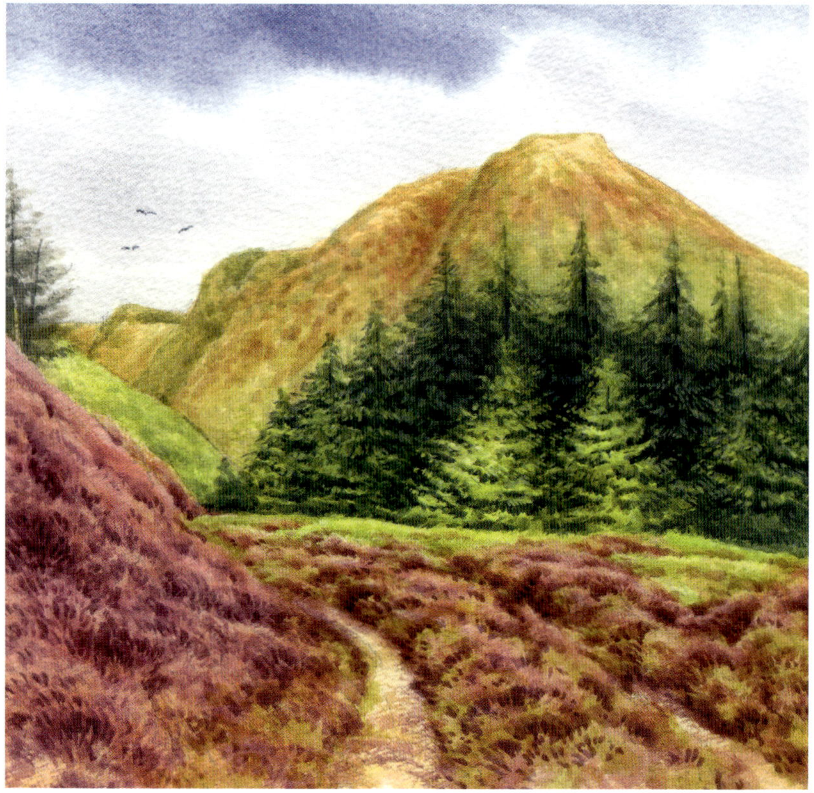

From Longside Wood 22/5/09
The timber stacks have been taken and the forest track here is now unused both by forestry wagons and walkers. It took some time to locate this exact spot.

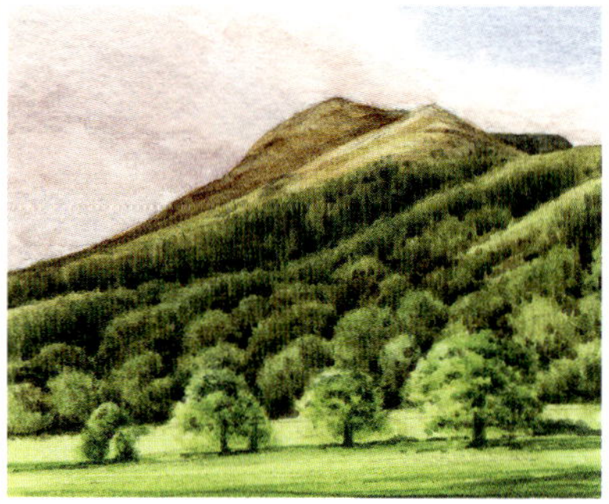

From Millbeck road end
16/5/09
The dense woodland now stops short of the summit.

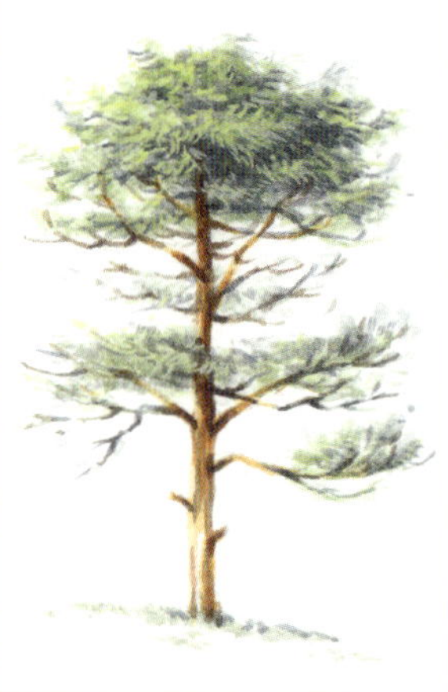

Scots pine

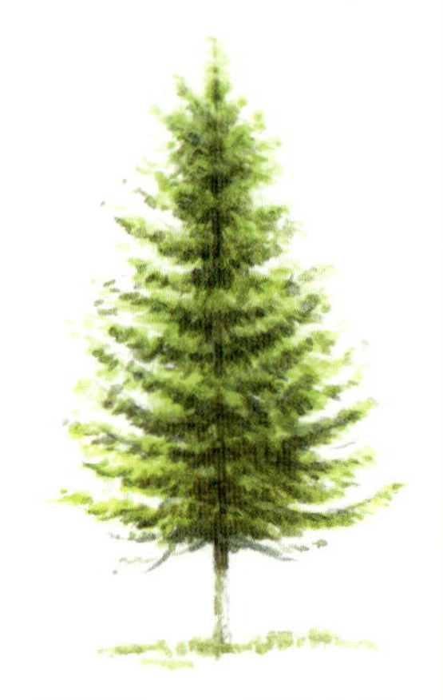

Larch

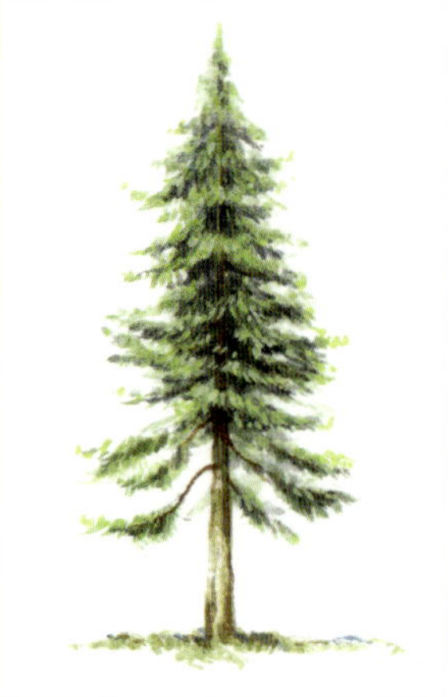

Douglas fir

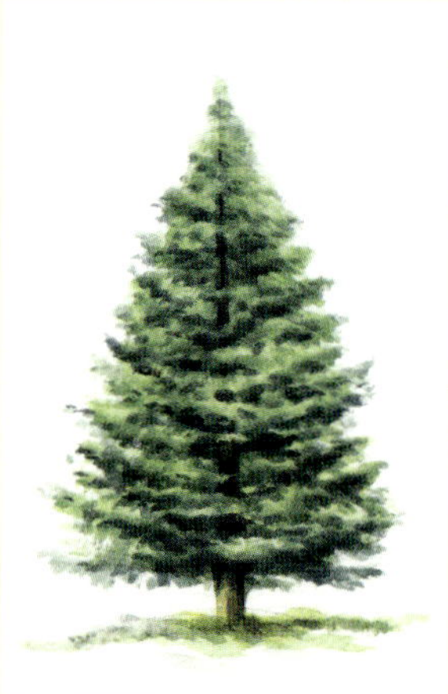

Sitka spruce

Dodd

This fell somehow made it onto Wainwright's final list despite the fact that at the time most of the slopes were covered with forestry practically to the very summit, and therefore views and routes were restricted. Twenty nine fells of the 214 like Dodd were not initially considered for inclusion, eleven of which are in the Northern Fells region, showing his need to fill what was a thin volume.

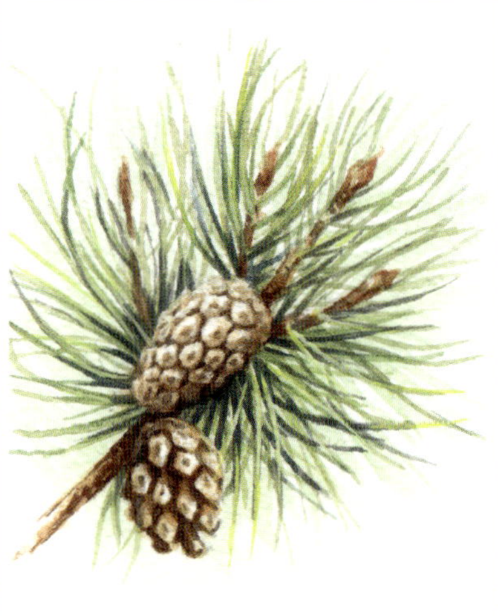

Scots Pine

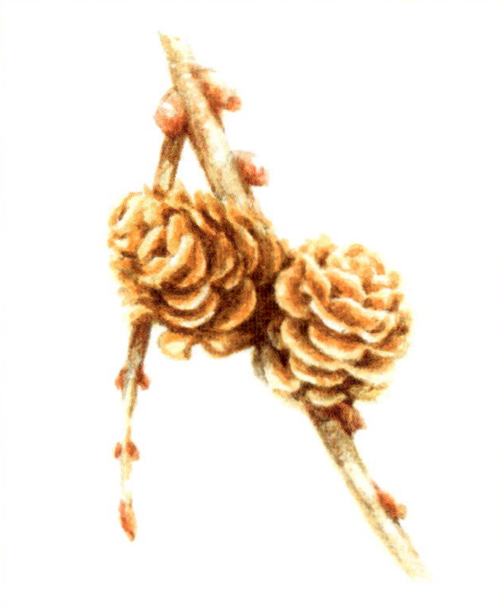

Japanese Larch-winter

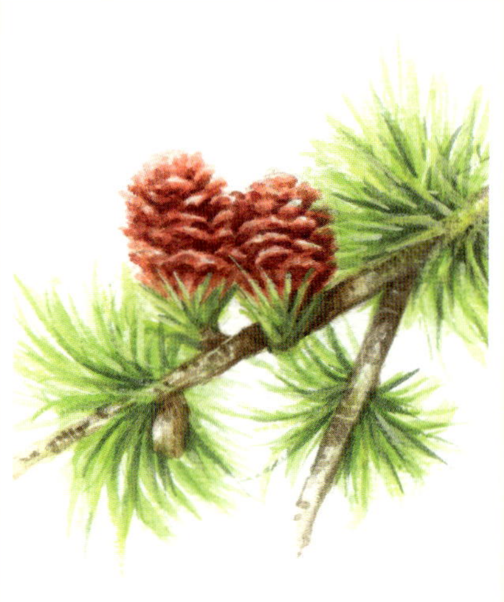

Japanese Larch-summer

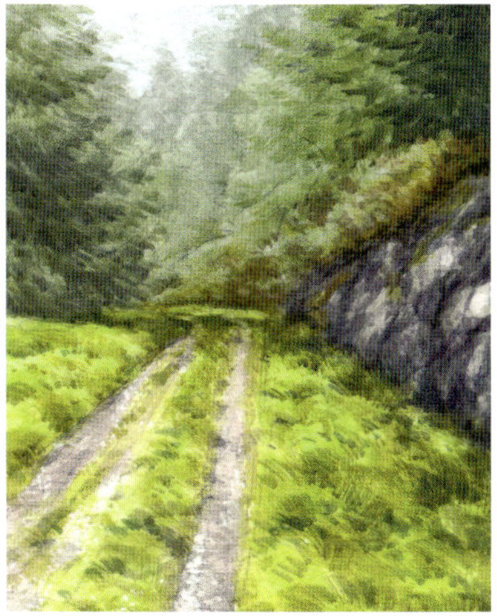

Forest road 14/3/12
There are miles of such tracks through the woods but this section was the nearest that I could find to AW's illustration.

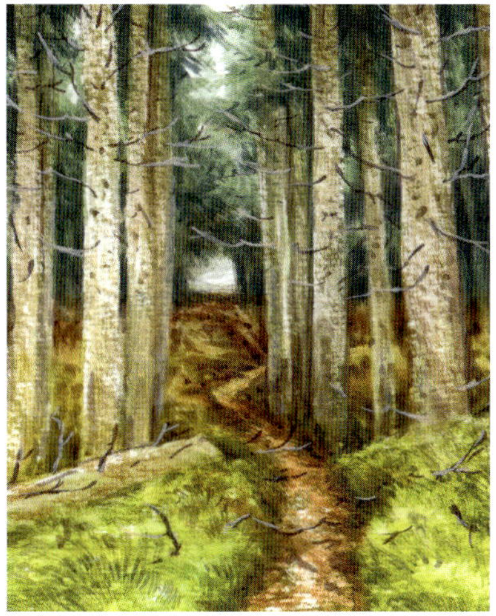

Forest path 14/3/12
By following the routes in the Dodd chapter shown by AW I guessed that I had my best chance of locating this place and I was right, here the path comes up from Dancing Gate.

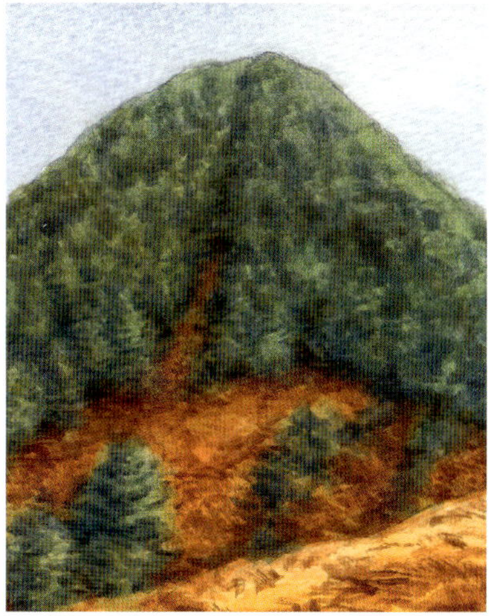

Fire-break 14/3/12
The fire-break is now indistinct on the north-west ridge as the trees have been felled and replanted since AW's visit.

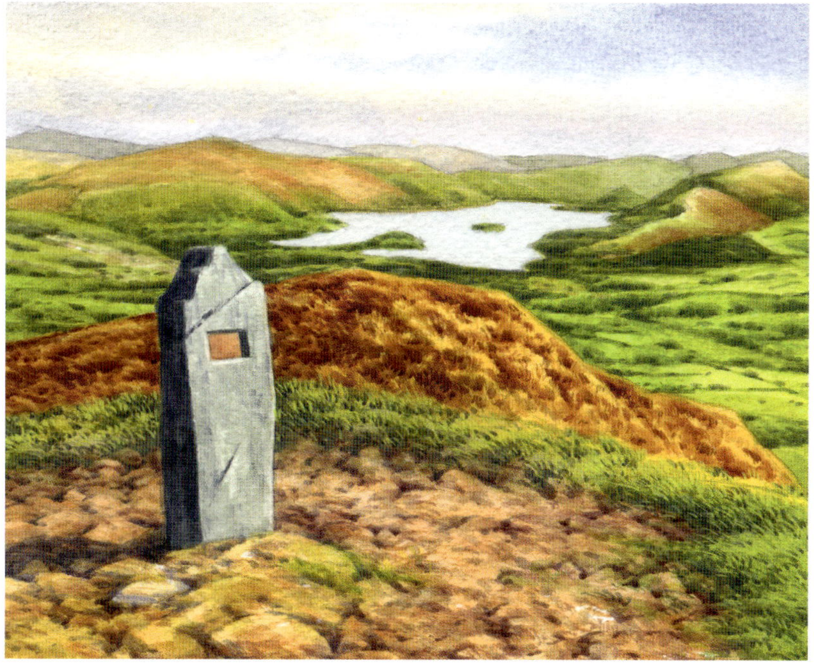

The summit 22/5/09
Now cleared of trees and with a slate memorial.

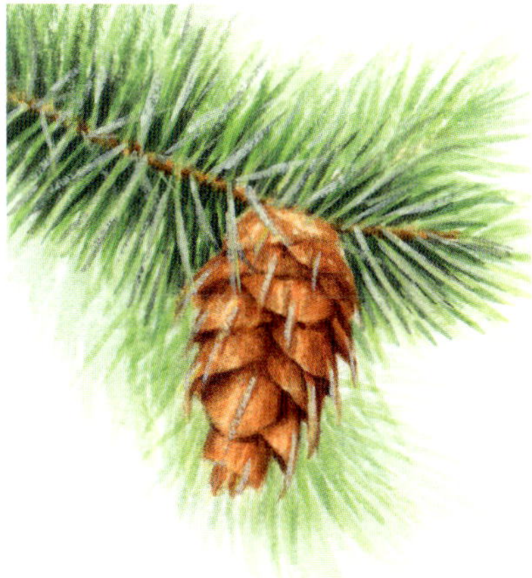

Douglas Fir

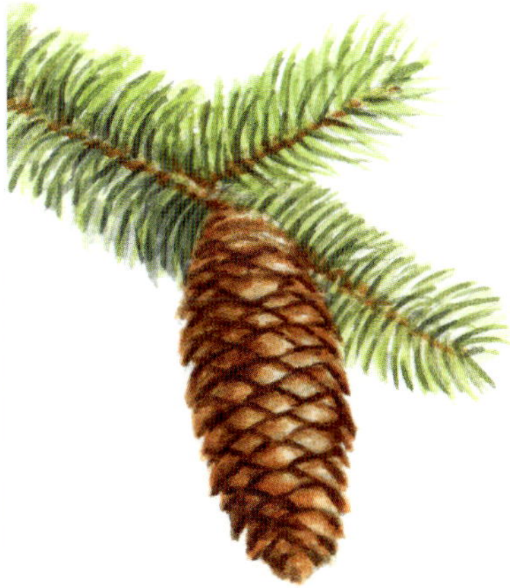

Norway Spruce

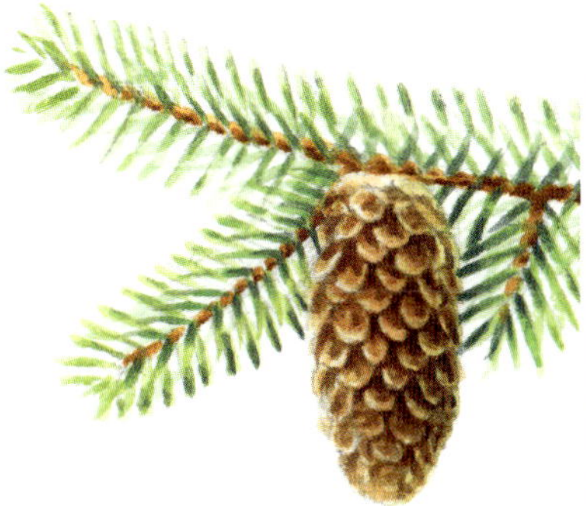

Sitka Spruce

The col 22/5/09
The crags of Long Doors.

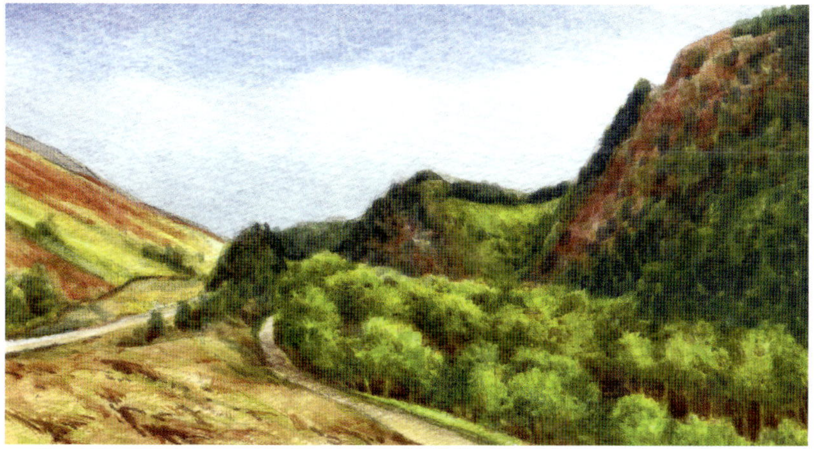

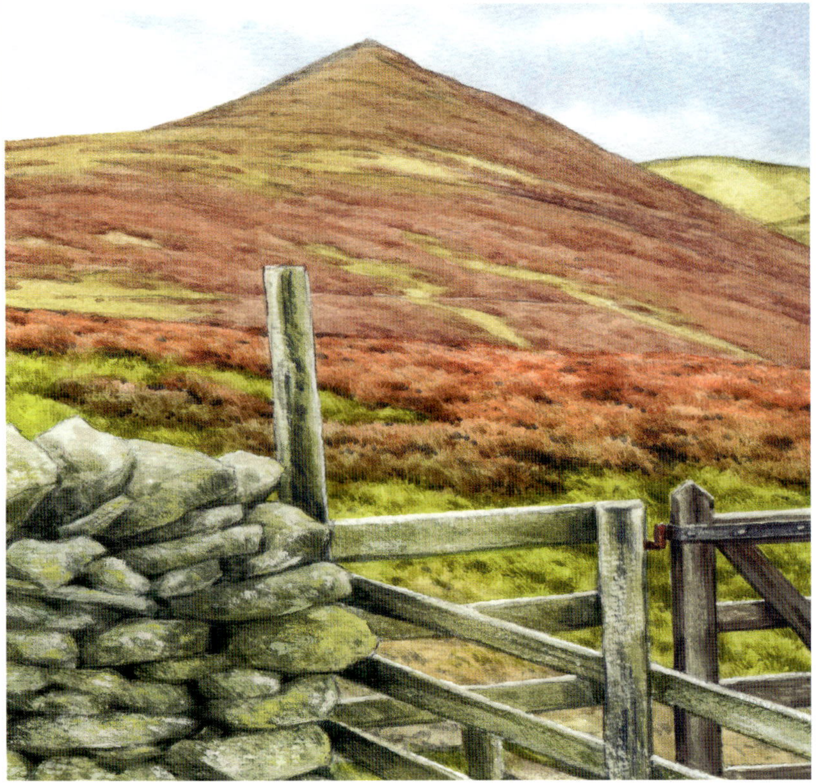

From the path to Skiddaw House 16/5/09

A more recent gate arrangement gives access to the path towards Skiddaw House. The hill has an almost total cover of heather on this side.

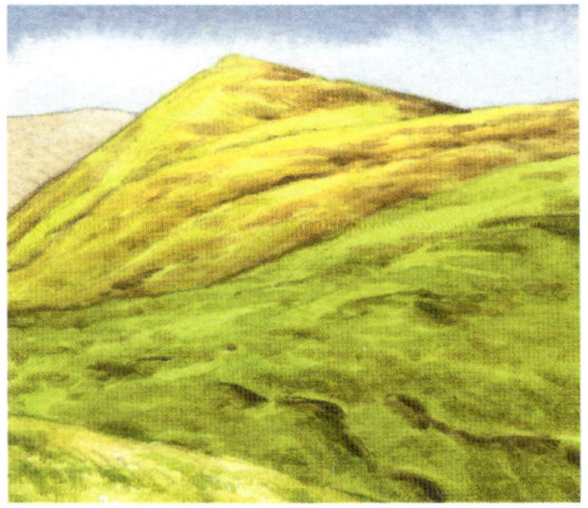

From Burn Tod 17/5/09

Burn Tod is a little visited west spur of Knott and a deviation from normal routes was required to enable me to obtain this reference.

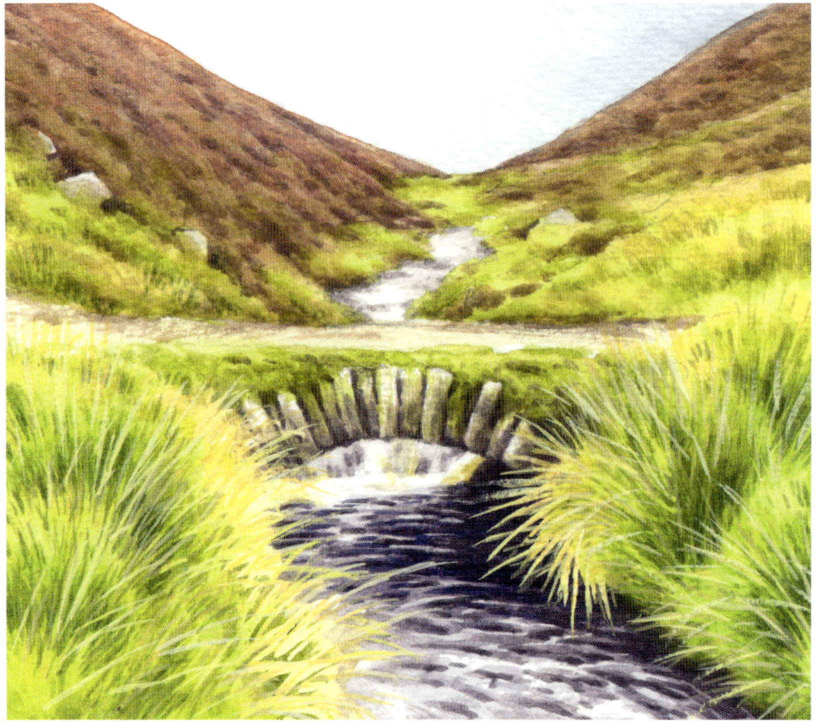

Bridge on the road to Skiddaw House 18/5/09

This neat little bridge spans Dash Beck before the stream tumbles down the drop of Whitewater dash. This rough track is really the only vehicular access to the house.

Great Calva

The fell is positioned at almost the centre of the northern fells region and consequently lies some distance from main roads. From the south Great Calva gives the impression that it is a conical heather clad peak, but north of the summit the crescent shaped contour of 2000' links the main top to the lower height of Little Calva to the west via an area of wet bog. Reaching the summit requires either a steep ascent through thick heather or a plod across damp peat. Dash Falls is the only real feature of note on this fell.

Circular sheepfold, Wiley Gill 18/5/09

Passing close to this fine example of dry stone walling is the footpath that follows the River Caldew down towards Mosedale. From here a direct but steep ascent to the fell top can be made by following the nearby fence which leads right to the south cairn.

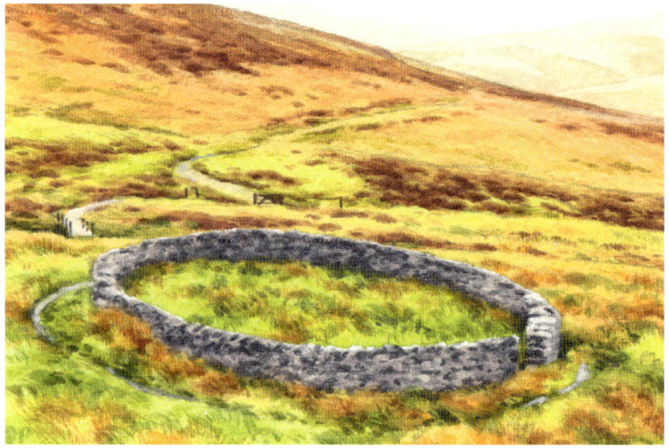

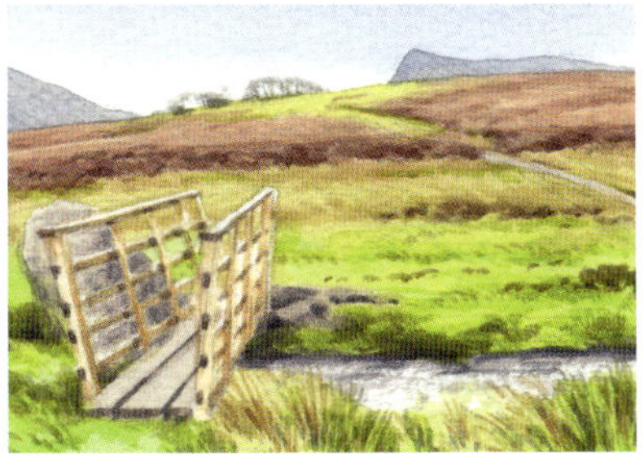

Footbridge A 18/5/09
This structure has replaced the one illustrated in the guide. Skiddaw House is in the copse of trees.

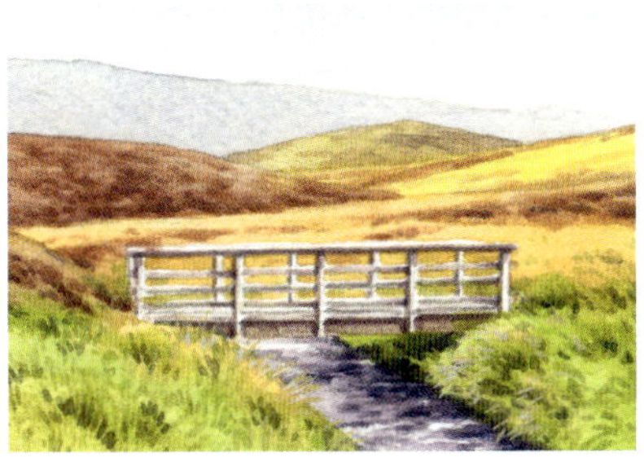

Footbridge B 18/5/15
Again, a new version of the simple bridge that was here in AW's day.

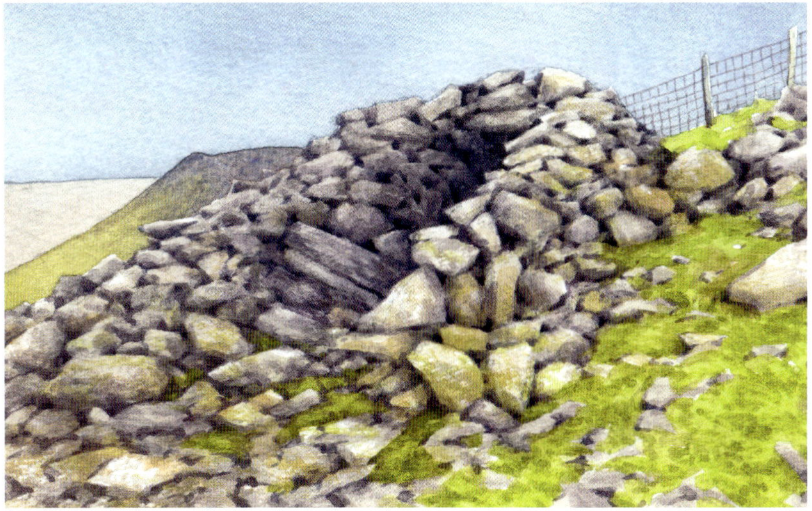

The summit shelter 18/5/09
To the east of the true summit a neatly formed shelter can be utilised in bad weather. Over the years it has been extended past the big boulder on the left of AW's drawing which is now in the middle of the far wall.

When is a forest not a forest?
The expanse of land to the south west of Great Calva is marked on maps as Skiddaw Forest but apart from a small copse around Skiddaw House the landscape is practically free from any trees. The reason is that the term Forest in this context refers to a large area of land which was a hunting ground for feudal landowners and not a woodland in the sense we use it now. Other "Forests" in the district include Grisedale Forest near Patterdale, the Deer Forest in Martindale and Copeland Forest near Wasdale as well as others.

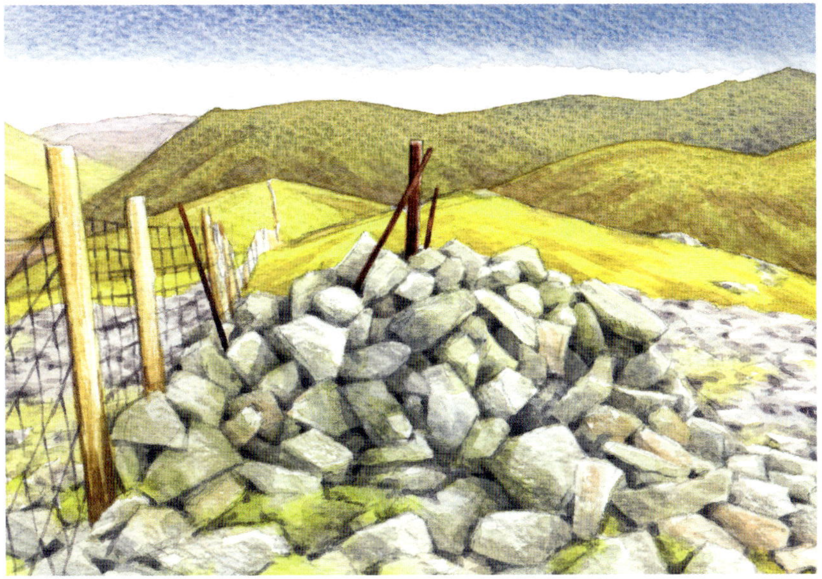

The summit 18/5/09
As has happened in other locations, the old iron fence has been replaced with a wooden post and wire version and the discarded rusty metal posts have been incorporated into this, the highest cairn as well as the lower southern one which sits on the far top along the fence line.

The south cairn 18/5/09
This lower top is the one seen when viewing the fell from the south. From here is an excellent vista along the Vale of St. John's and right through the gap of Dunmail Raise pass.

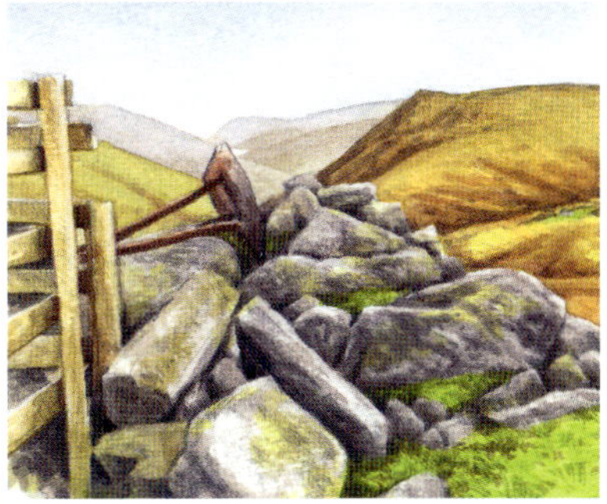

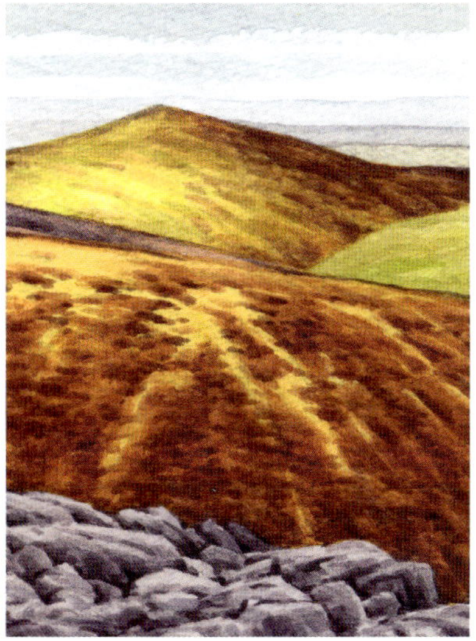

Carrock Fell from the top of Great Calva 18/5/09
In a north-east direction Carrock Fell is above the ridge of Snab.

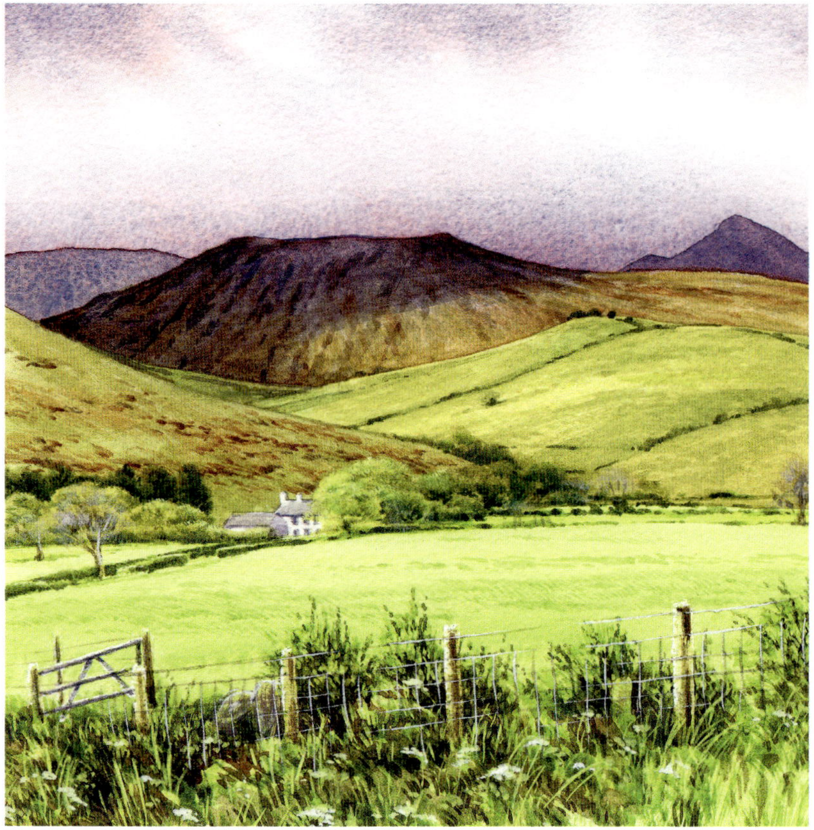

From Longlands 17/5/09
The embankment in the foreground has been modified and topped with a new fence but all else remains the same. I have included Skiddaw over to the right which Wainwright omitted.

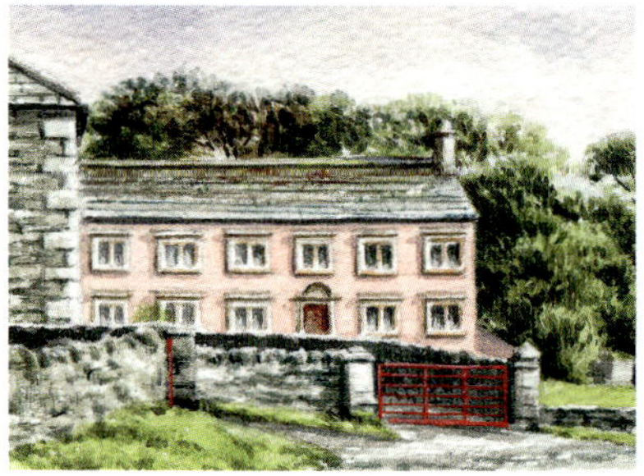

Orthwaite Hall 17/5/09
A fine house which dates back possibly to the early 17th century.

The Boulder 20/5/09
A large rounded boulder now of more interest to sheep with itchy backsides than curious walkers.

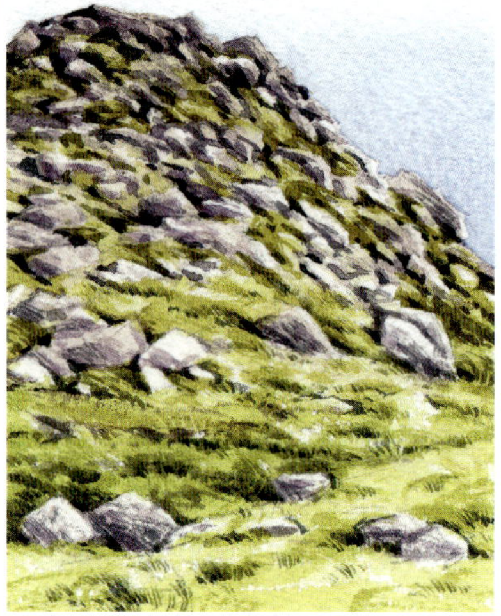

Brockle Crag 18/5/09
Numerous quartzite rocks lie amongst this jumble of boulders giving a speckled grey and white appearance from a distance.

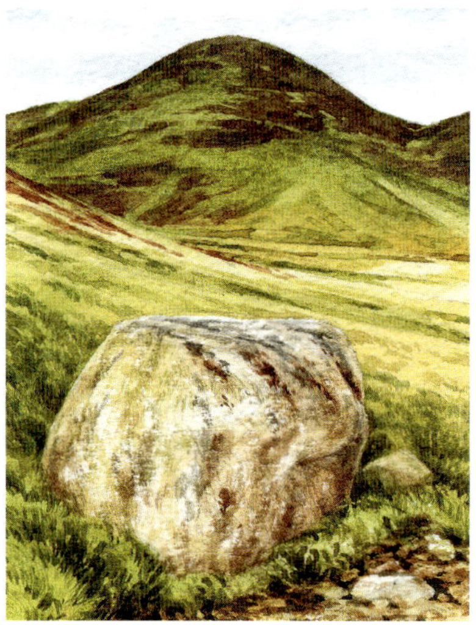

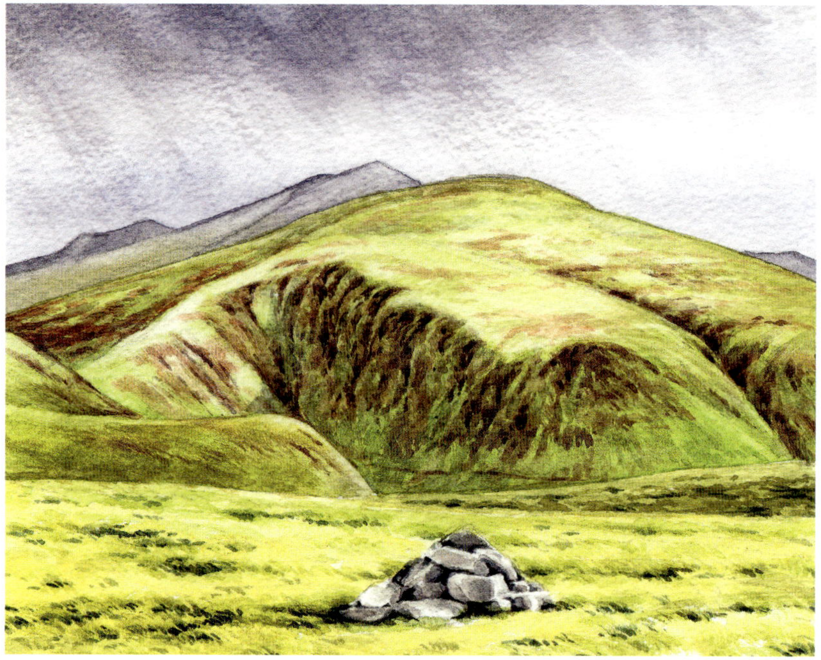

Great Cockup
A fell to while away an hour or two in simple exploration, perfect for a stroll on a warm summer's evening.

The summit 20/5/09
A small cairn now sits on this flat plateau to at least give some marker to the highest point. Grouse butts 300 yards to the east are now collapsed and out of use.

The Dash Valley 20/5/09
The valley comes into full view with Bakestall on the right when seen from the old track under Orthwaite Bank.

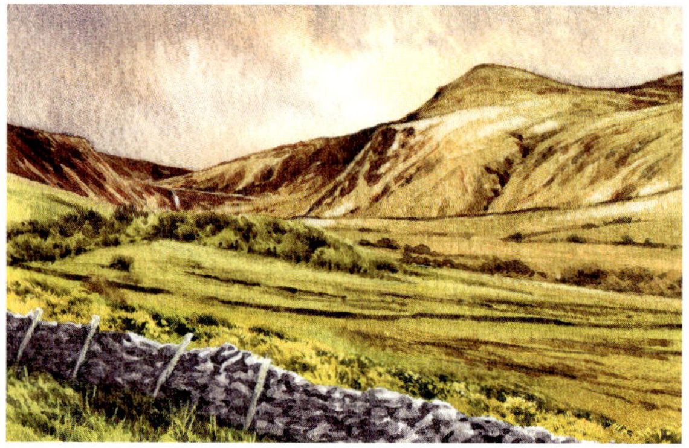

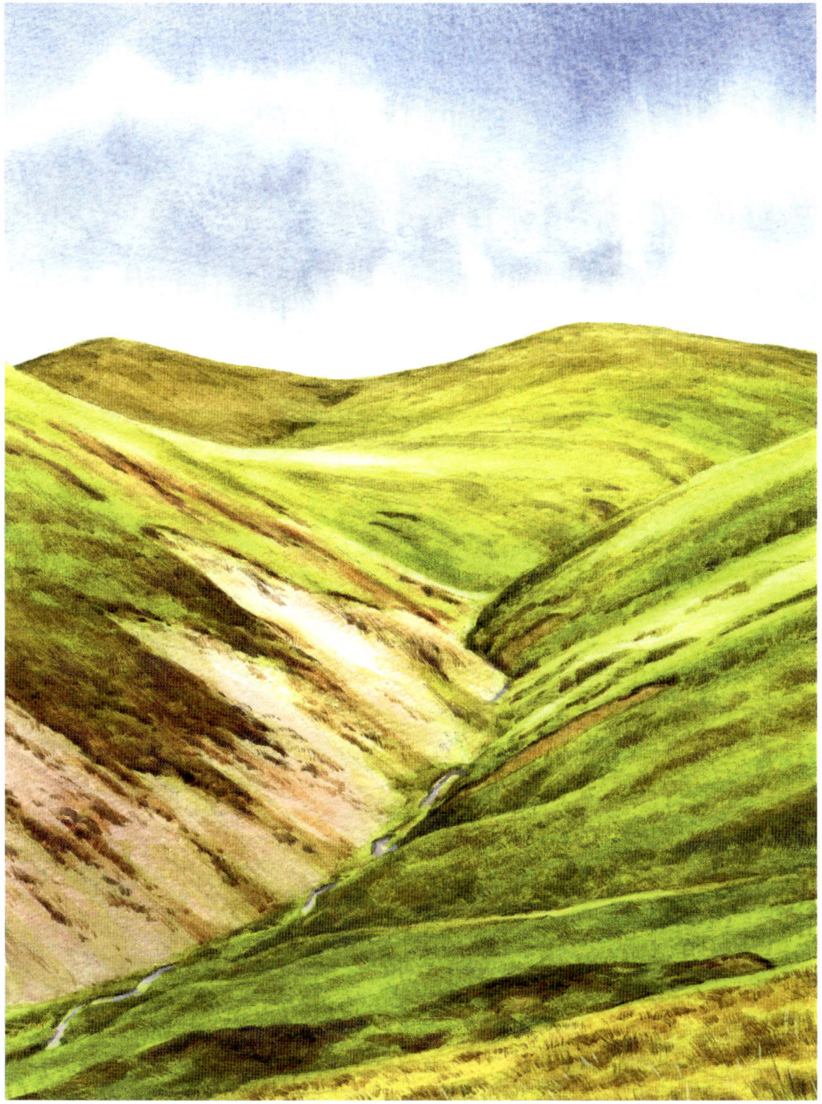

From Burn Tod 17/5/09
A visit to the area of Burn Tod, the western spur of Knott, does not feature on many walker's itinerary but AW obviously explored it as more than one of his drawings such as this one, which is from its northern slopes, appear in this guidebook.

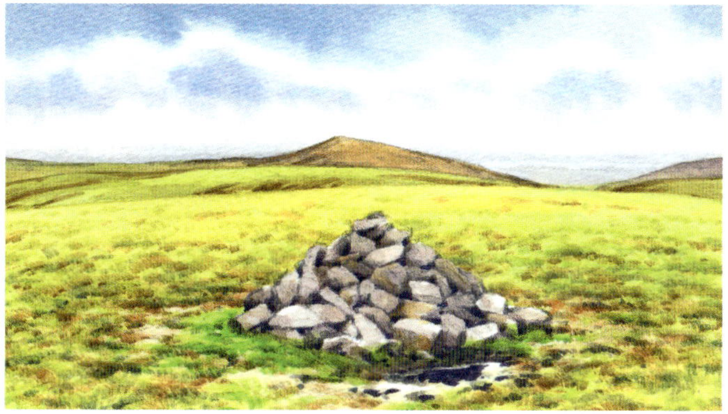

The summit 17/5/09
Over recent years visitors to this summit have made the effort to gather rocks from a distance to construct this cairn on the flat plateau.

Great Sca Fell

The use of the word "Great" in the name of the fell must only be there to differentiate between this and the neighbouring lower top of Little Sca Fell and not because of its mountain qualities. This fell can easily be incorporated into a route that includes a visit to several other tops in the vicinity.

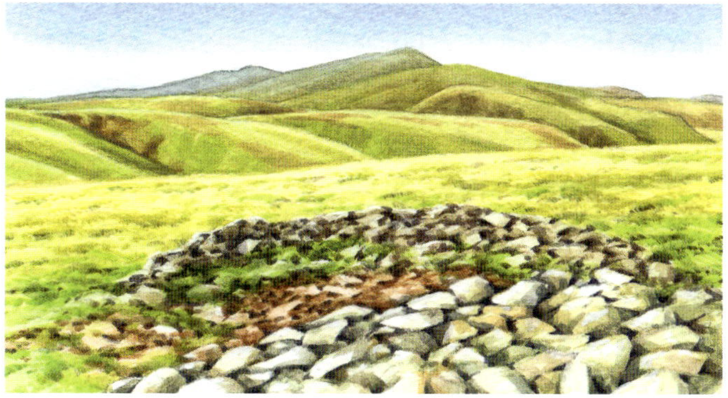

The summit of Little Sca Fell 17/5/09
The abundance of rocks have been used to build both a decent sized cairn and a low wind shelter around one half of a shallow dip in the ground.

From the Longlands valley 21/5/09
A basic farm track into this valley soon peters out and the path is indistinct. It is a route to the Sca Fells, both Great and Little which has not found much favour with walkers.

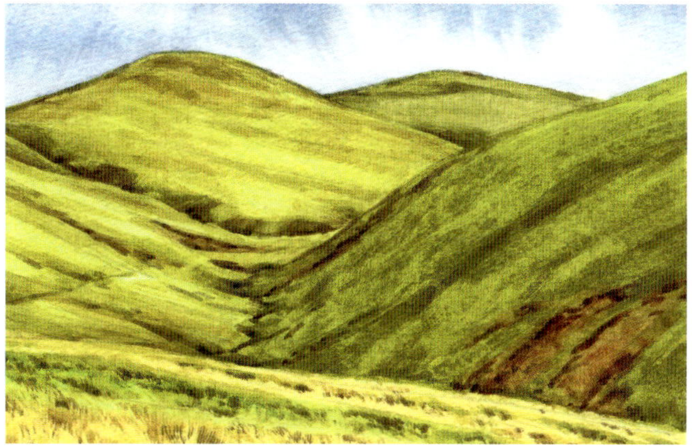

The top waterfall, Roughton Gill
20/5/09
A detour down off the thin path which passes through the gorge has to be made to see the fall from this angle. A remote place of peace and solitude.

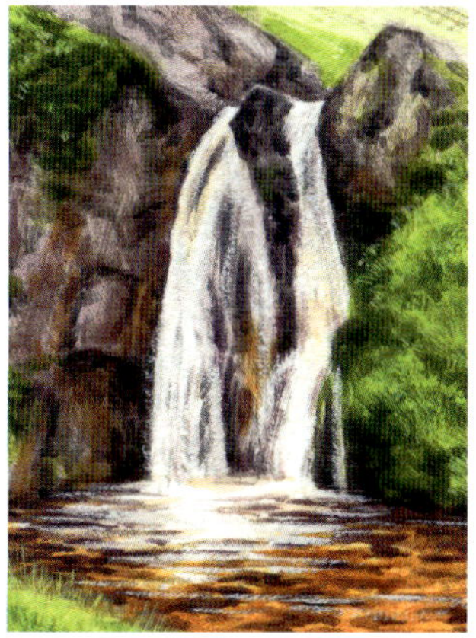

High Pike

Only by visiting the scarred northern side of the fell can an insight into High Pike's hidden treasures be gained. Mines dating back hundreds of years once provided wealth and employment here but those days are now long over. Time is trying to heal the wounds of industry. From the south the fell looks almost as nature intended.

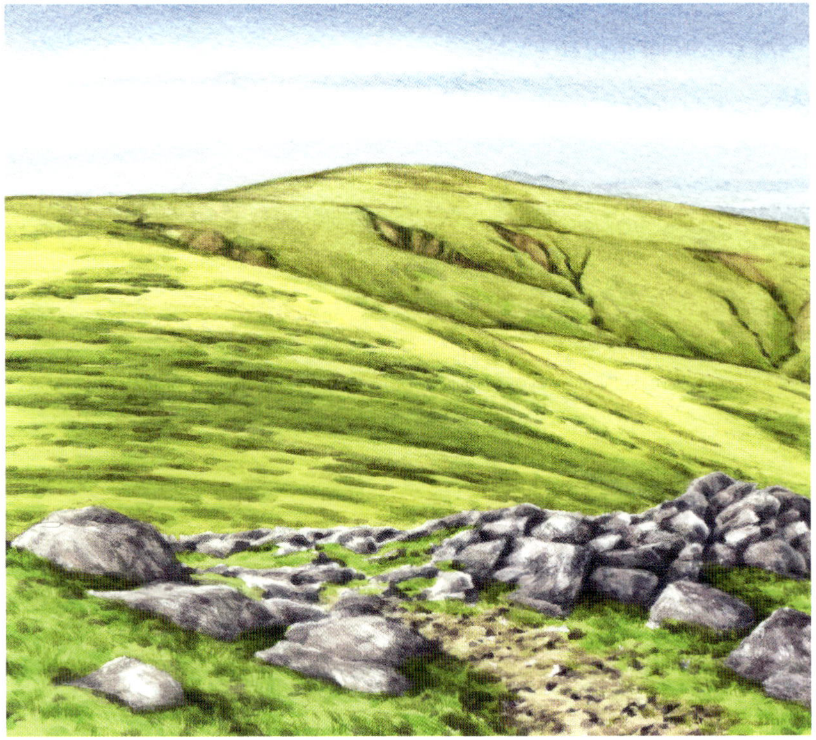

From the west gate, Carrock Hill Fort 6/8/09
The south eastern slopes of the fell are seen in this aspect as they drop down towards Driggith Mine and the valley of Carrock Beck.

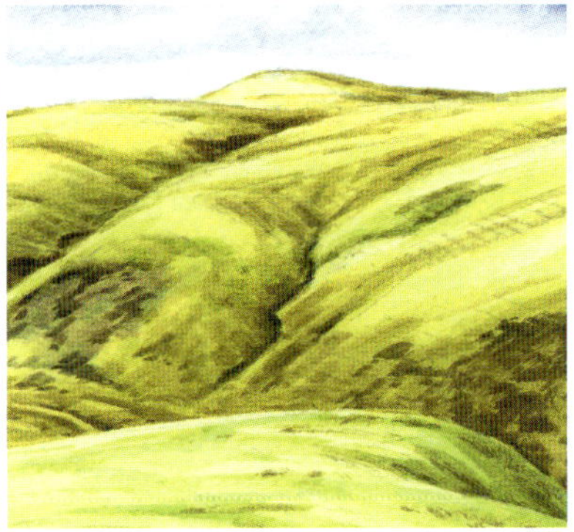

From Bowscale Fell 15/4/12
A view of High Pike from above Tarn Crags.

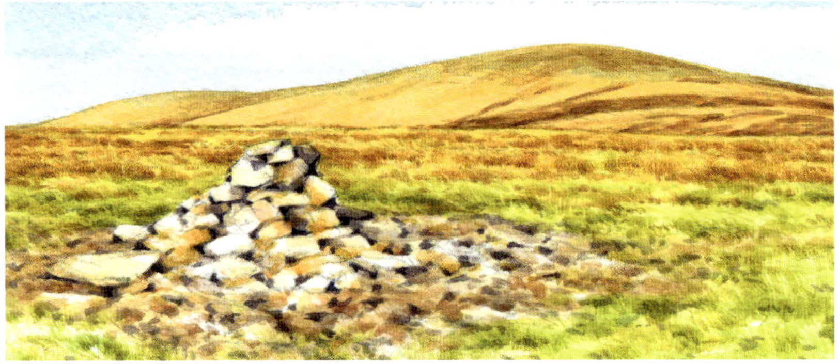

High Pike from Knott 12/10/10
Less of a pronounced top to High Pike than shown in AW's illustration.

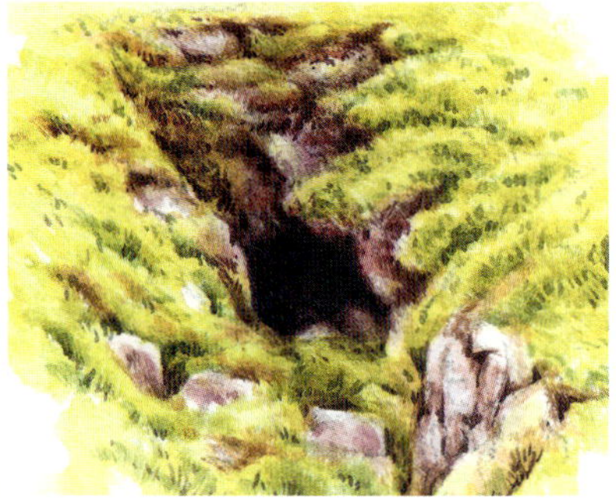

Old level, Hay Gill 17/5/09
Just east of the main valley track.

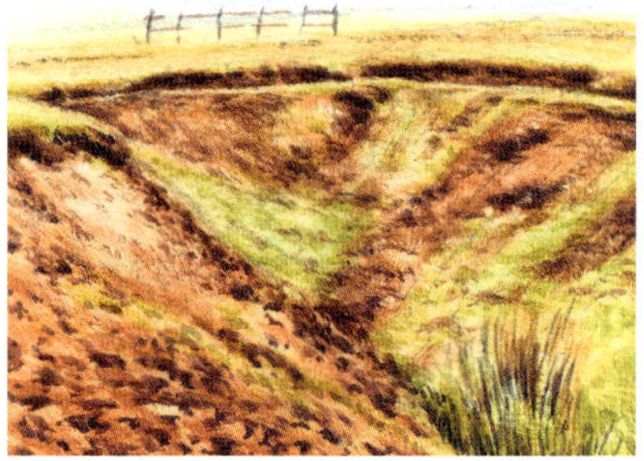

Old level, Potts Gill 15/5/09
The ground has now collapsed in.

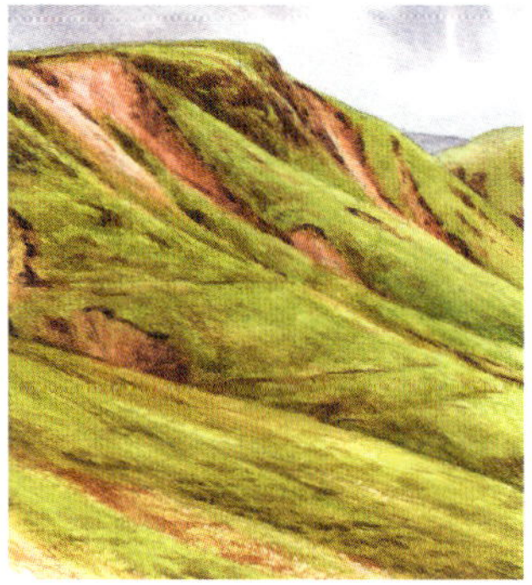

Iron Crag 20/5/09
The red scars of landslips.

Roughton Gill

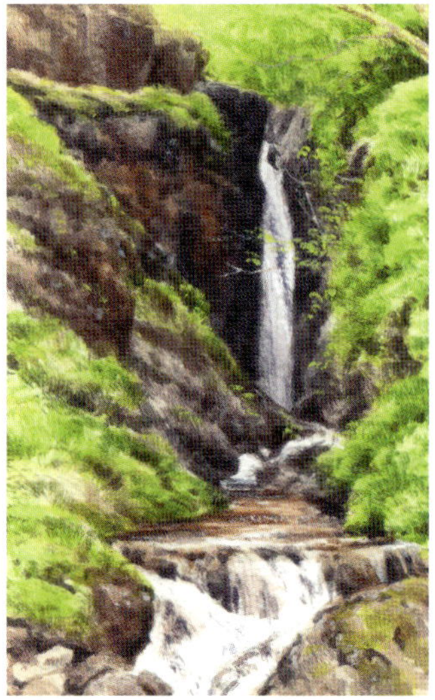

The lowest waterfall
20/5/09
The foreground rock wall on the right has now gone.

Old level, Dry Gill 6/8/09
Lush growth hides the scar.

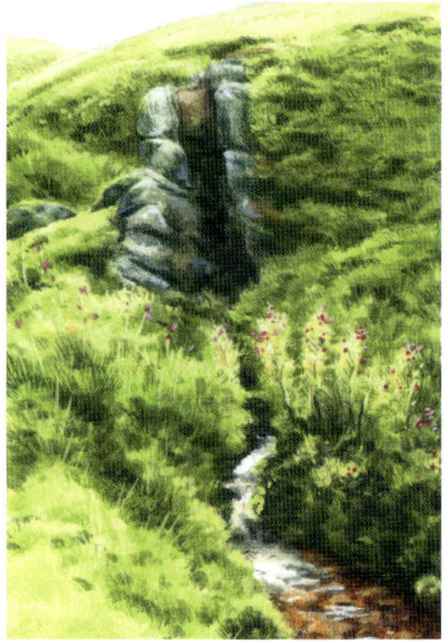

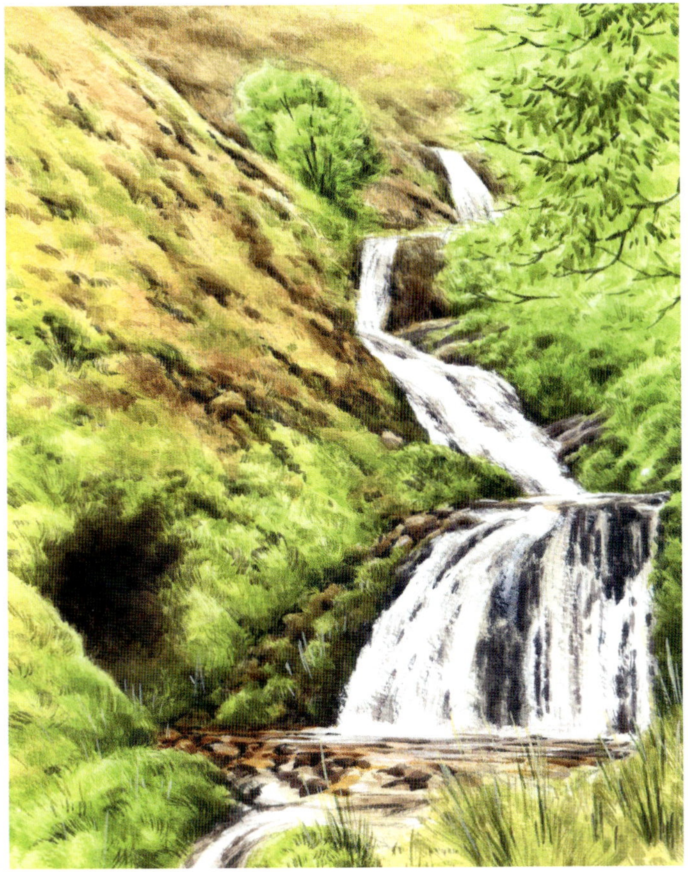

Death of an Industry 20/5/09

The old mine workings are slowly blending back into the landscape. The cascades of Roughton Gill spill down the ravine on the horizon.

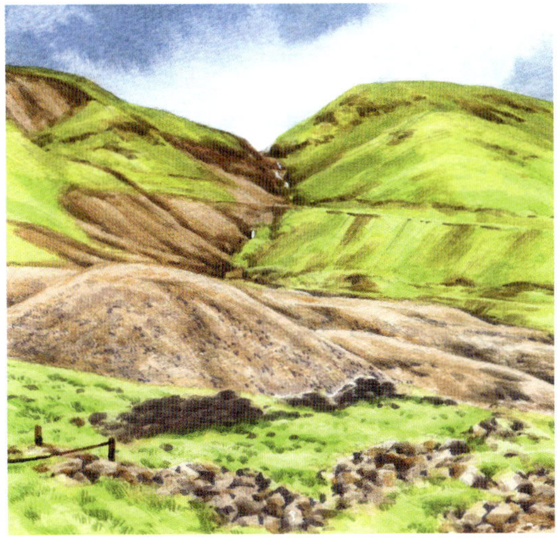

Old mine level and cascades 20/5/09

The gill has several impressive falls of which these are just a few. The level is open but overgrown with ferns and mosses.

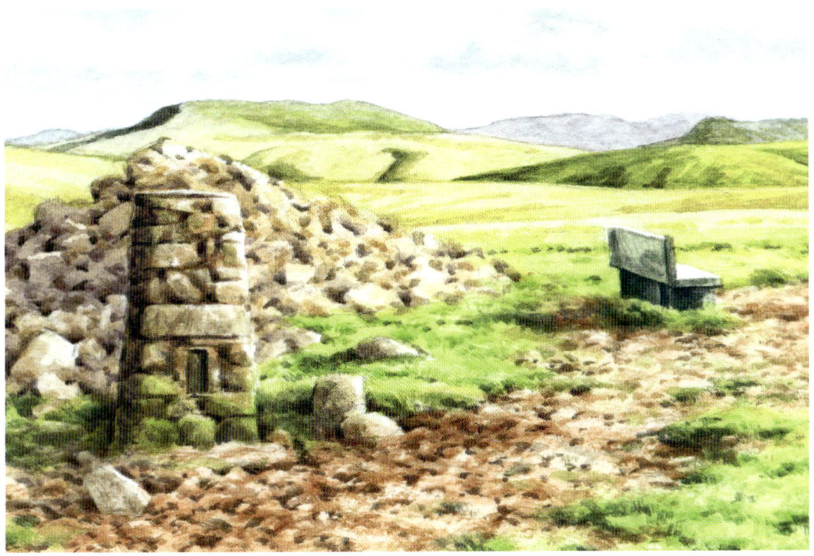

The summit looking south 6/8/09

The slate memorial seat that appeared in 1961 remains in place.

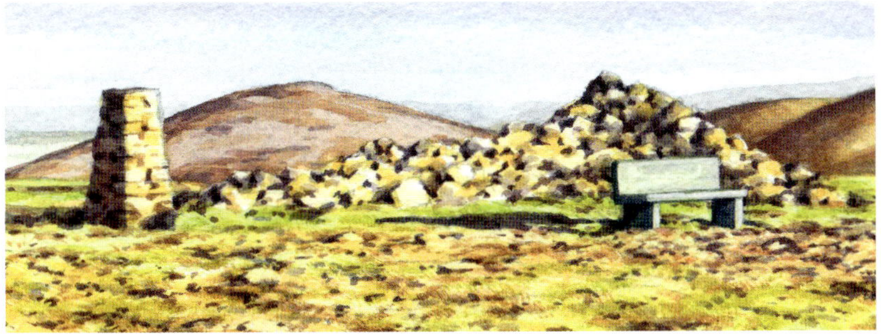

The summit looking south-east 12/10/10

AW depicted the two different seats in his drawings, I show the same seat twice.

The Dumpy Stone 15/5/09

This large boulder lies near the track to the disused Sandbed Mine.

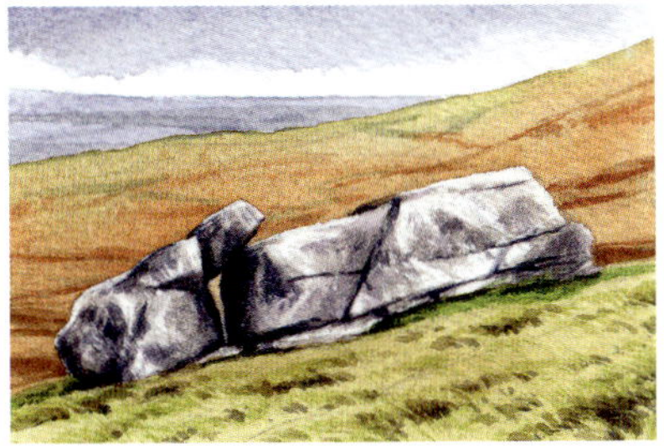

Howthwaite Stone 15/5/09

Located on the open fell just south of Calebrack Farm.

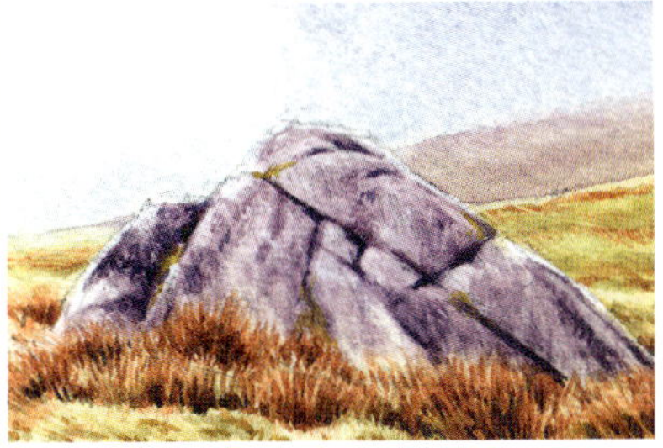

Nameless top above Iron Crag 25/12/08

A cairn sited on pathless terrain.

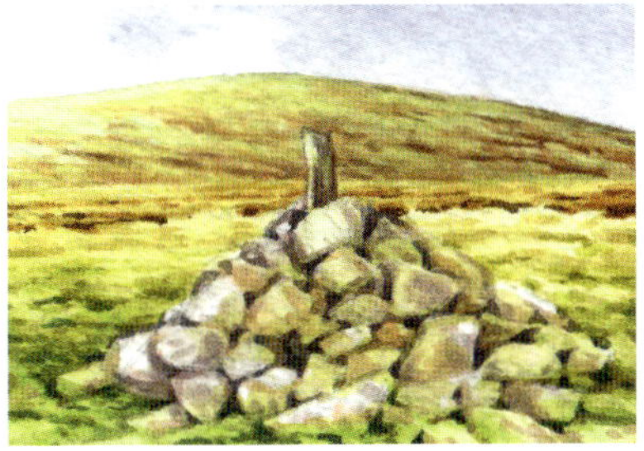

Great Lingy Hill 25/12/08

The small cairn lit with late afternoon sun on a Christmas day.

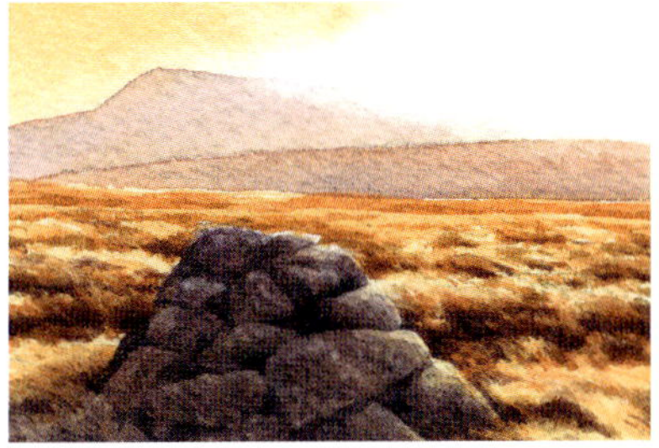

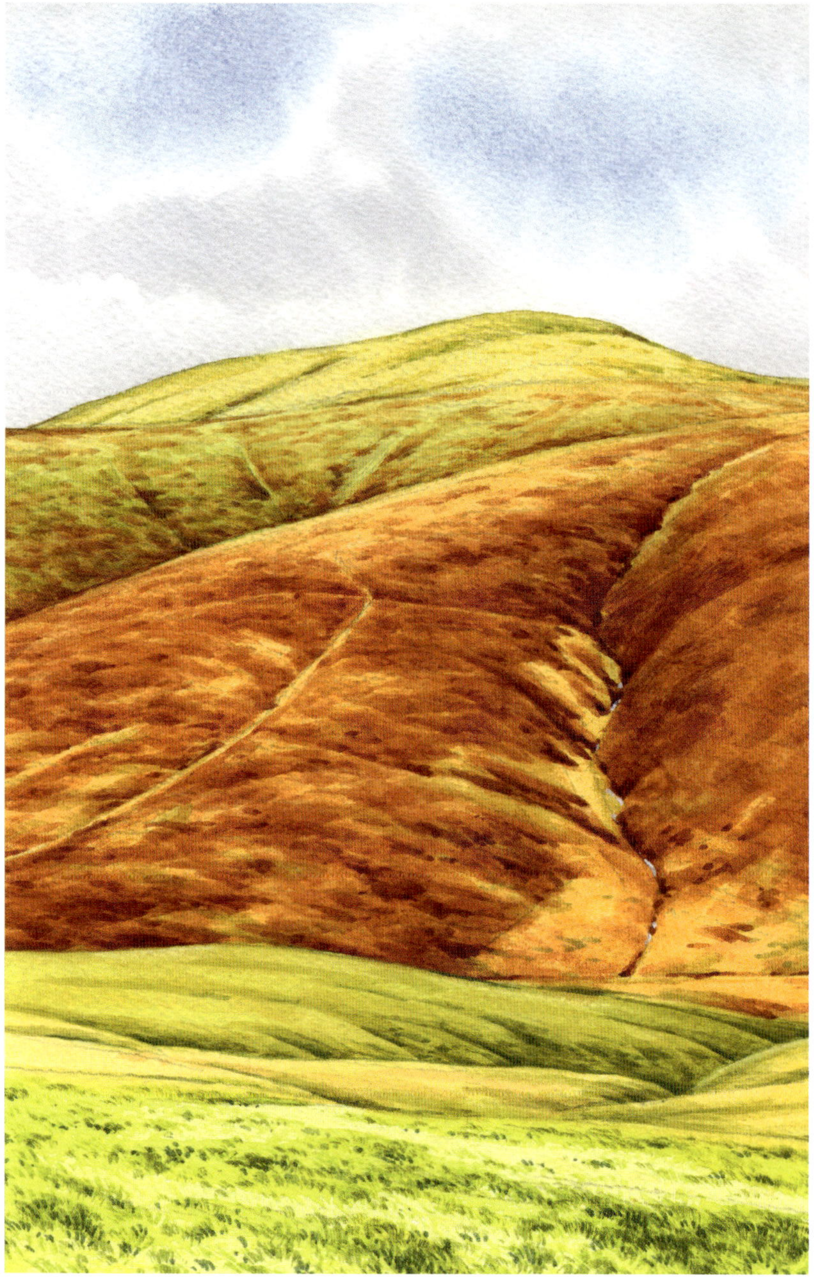

From Bowscale Fell 15/4/12

This view of the fell is taken from a point just to the north of Bowscale fell summit. The heather covered flanks of the fells are cut into by the valleys of Burdell Gill and Wet Swine Gill.

Cairn on Coomb Height 6/8/09

A number of stones have been added to give shape to this cairn which even now is on a route to the summit that only shows signs of infrequent use by walkers.

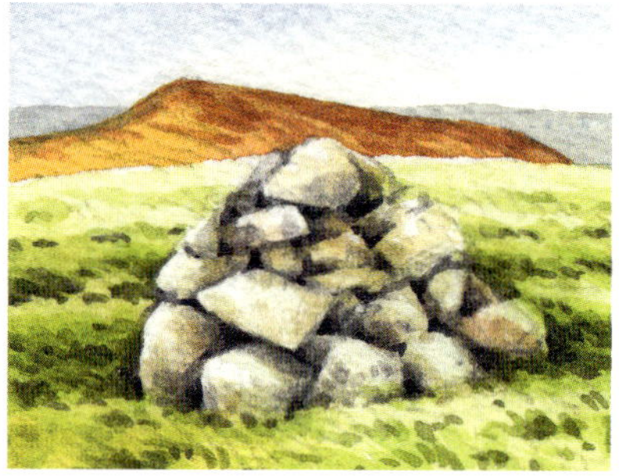

Knott

Once the 2000' contour has been reached on this fell the gradient eases and from then on up to the summit thc land consists of neatly cropped turf or heather, with just the occasional patches of wet or stony ground. Perhaps because of its situation geographically and the lack of interesting features Knott is one of the least visited fells in the area. Including it in a route that also takes in High Pike and Carrock Fell is a good option.

Path in the heather 6/8/09

In such an exposed location it is remarkable that this lone Scots pine tree is still standing, firmly fixed to the slopes of the fell near the River Caldew.

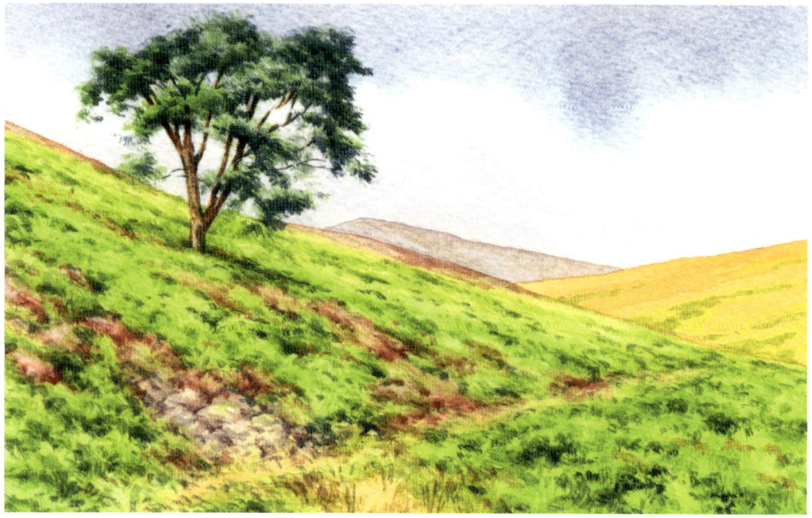

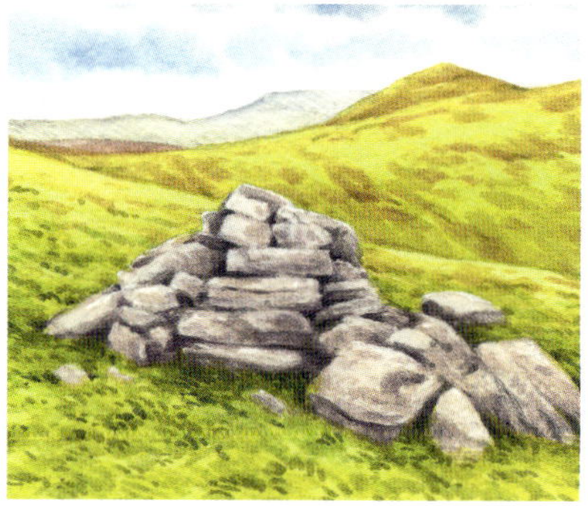

Cairn on Burn Tod 17/5/09

As indicated by AW, there is both a ruined (grouse) butt and a cairn on the top of Burn Tod. Due to the lack of popularity of this high ground the two structures show little sign of disturbance, as can be seen here the layers of stone in the cairn are unaltered. From this angle Great Calva and Blencathra are seen in the distance.

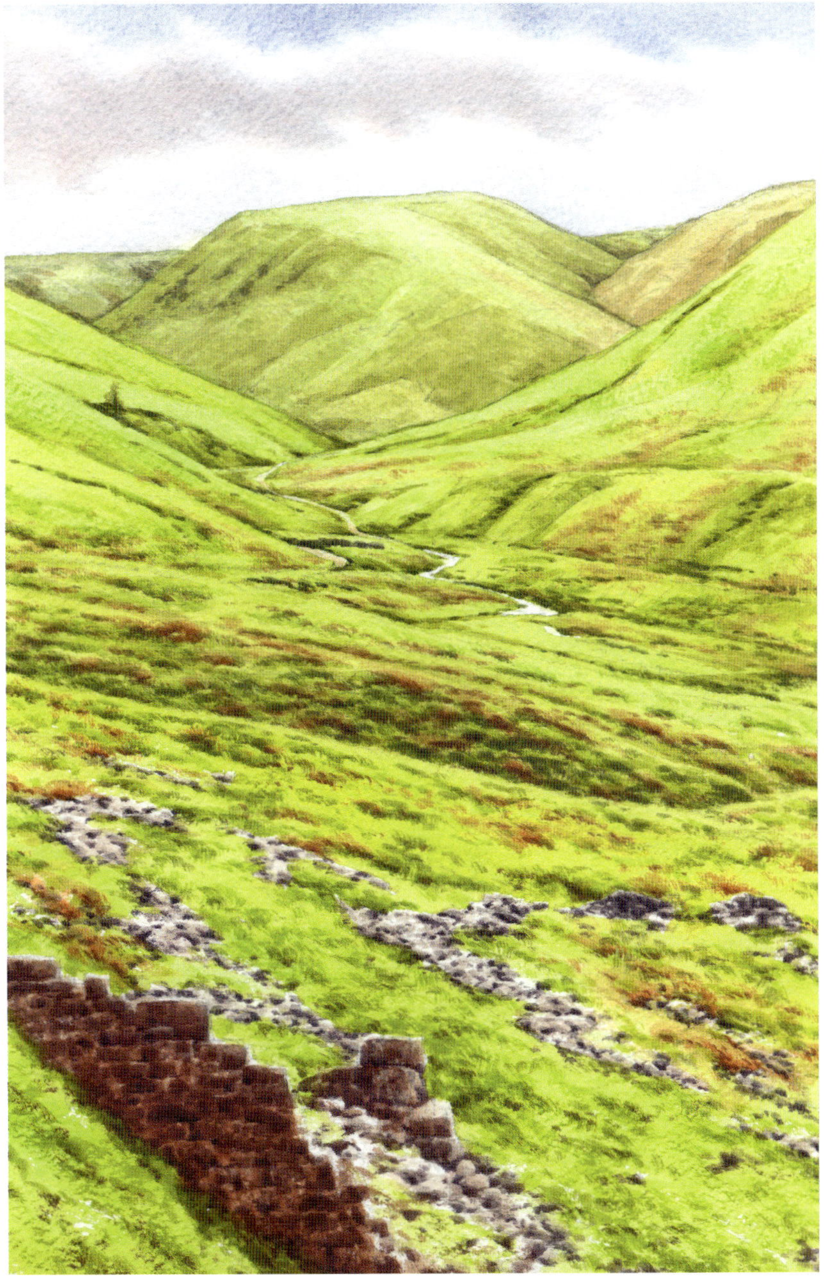

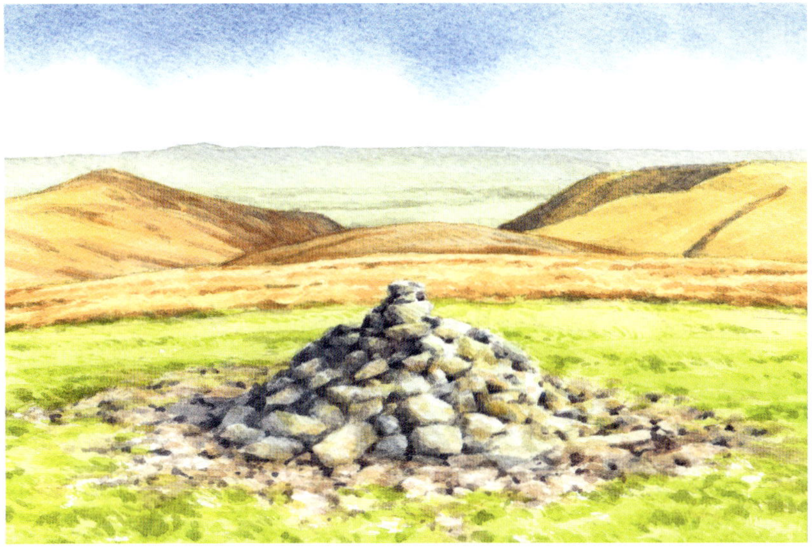

The summit 17/5/09

A more substantial cairn now adorns the flat top of the fell. AW's suggestion of having a cricket match up here may not as yet have been taken up but it is difficult to think of another fell with such a neatly cropped playing field.

Mosedale from the eastern shoulder 12/10/10

The ditch running north from here which AW mentions is actually the excavated Harding vein south of the Carrock Wolframite Mine. Wolframite is one of the main ores in tungsten.

The valley of Dale Beck 20/5/09

The few remaining standing sections of the walls of the old smelting mill are now crumbling. Yard Steel is the flat topped high ground at the head of the valley, which is shown as Ward Steel in the guidebook despite all references to it on maps showing it as Yard Steel. Most likely a spelling error by Wainwright.

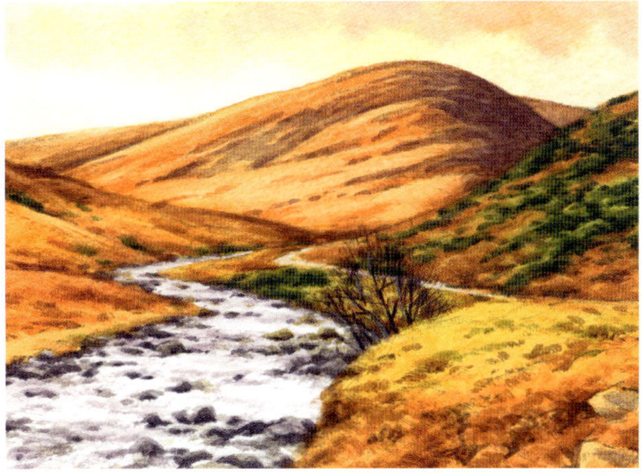

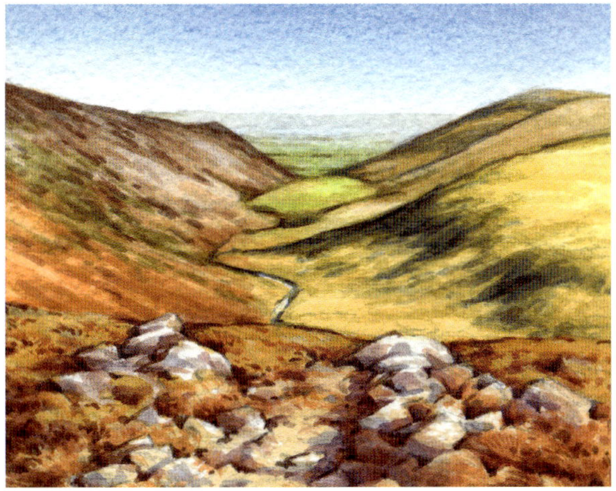

The eastern shoulder from Mosedale

25/12/08

Heading down through Mosedale at 2.30 pm on Christmas day and the low sun coloured the ridge a burnt orange.

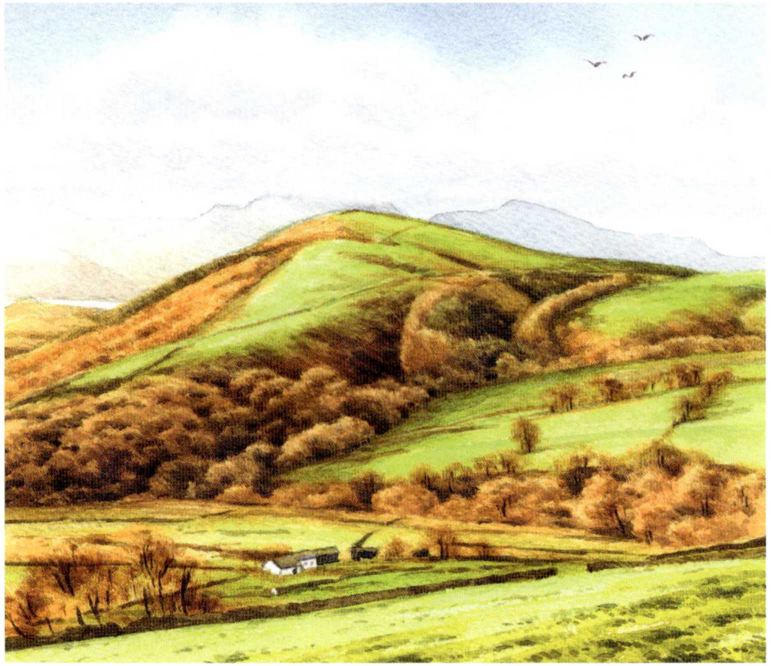

From Blencathra Sanatorium (now a field studies centre) 18/11/08

More precisely from the track heading into the Glenderaterra valley.

From the Orthwaite road 16/5/09

The wooded slopes of the fell as seen from opposite Thrushwood.

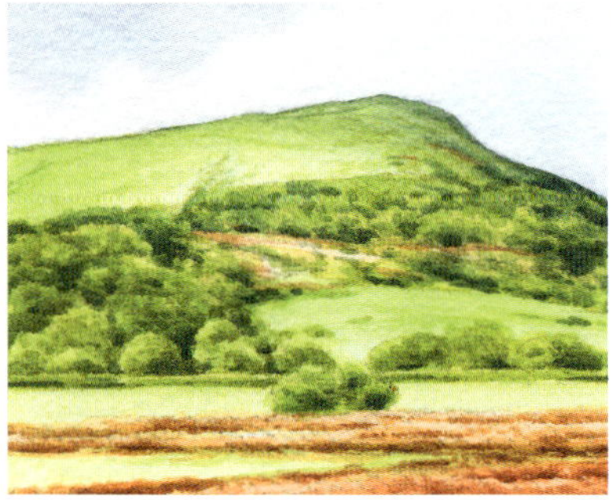

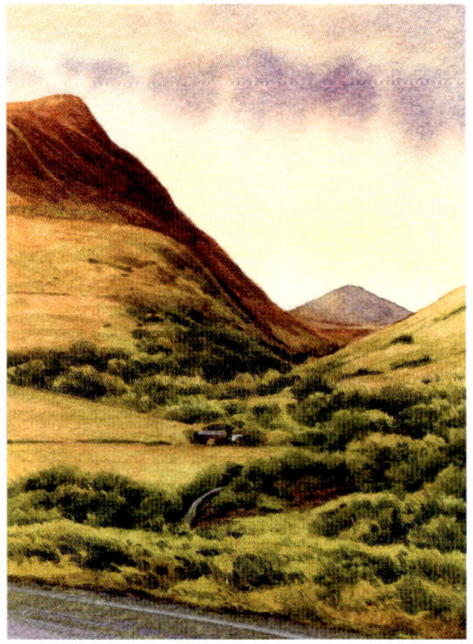

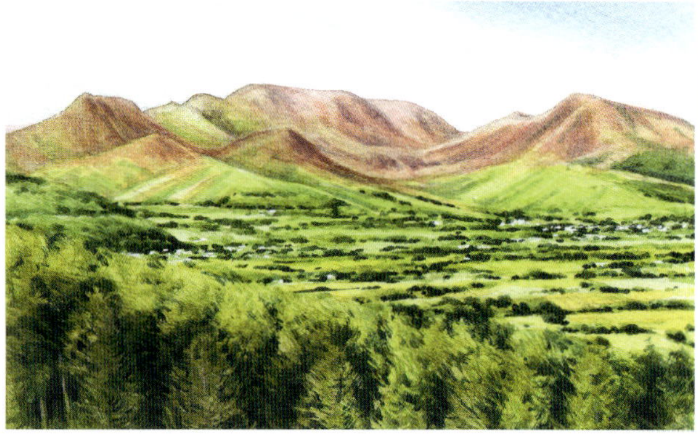

The Grasmoor group, from Gale road 31/7/12

A complex sketch of the valley and distant mountains.

Latrigg

This fell must claim the award for most return for so little effort, especially if accessed via the car park at Gale Road end. The view of mountain scenery to the south from the top is breathtaking. It is a perfect beginner's fell.

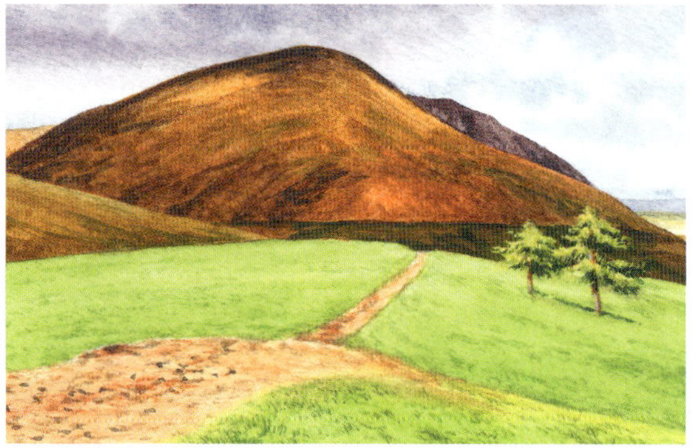

From the Penrith road 16/5/09

The modern A66 now cuts across the foreground.

The summit 16/5/09

Including Blease Fell as a backdrop adds interest to this rather plain fell top scene.

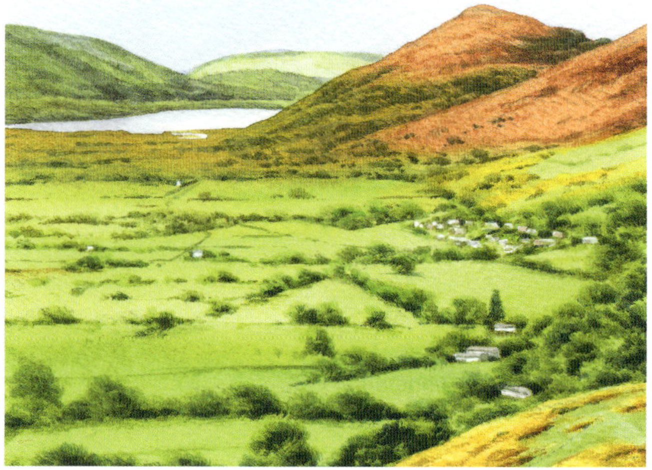

Underskiddaw, looking to Bassenthwaite Lake 16/5/09

Dodd's top is now de-forested but little else has changed.

Blease Fell, Blencathra, from the east ridge 31/7/12

All that remains of the tree is some partially buried roots.

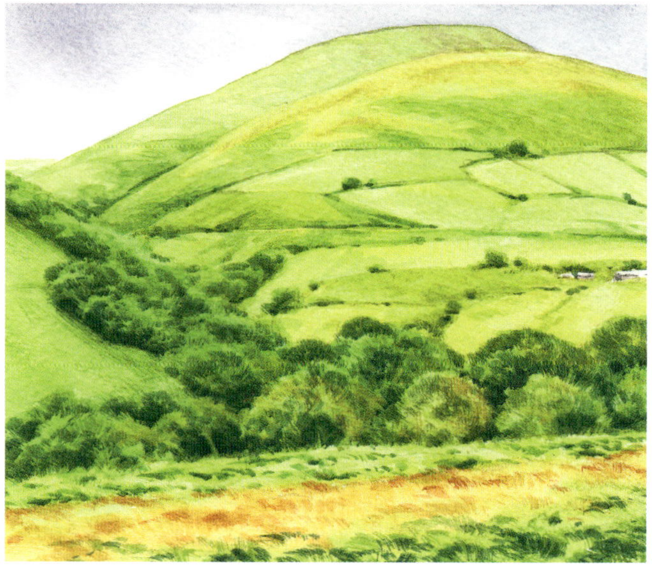

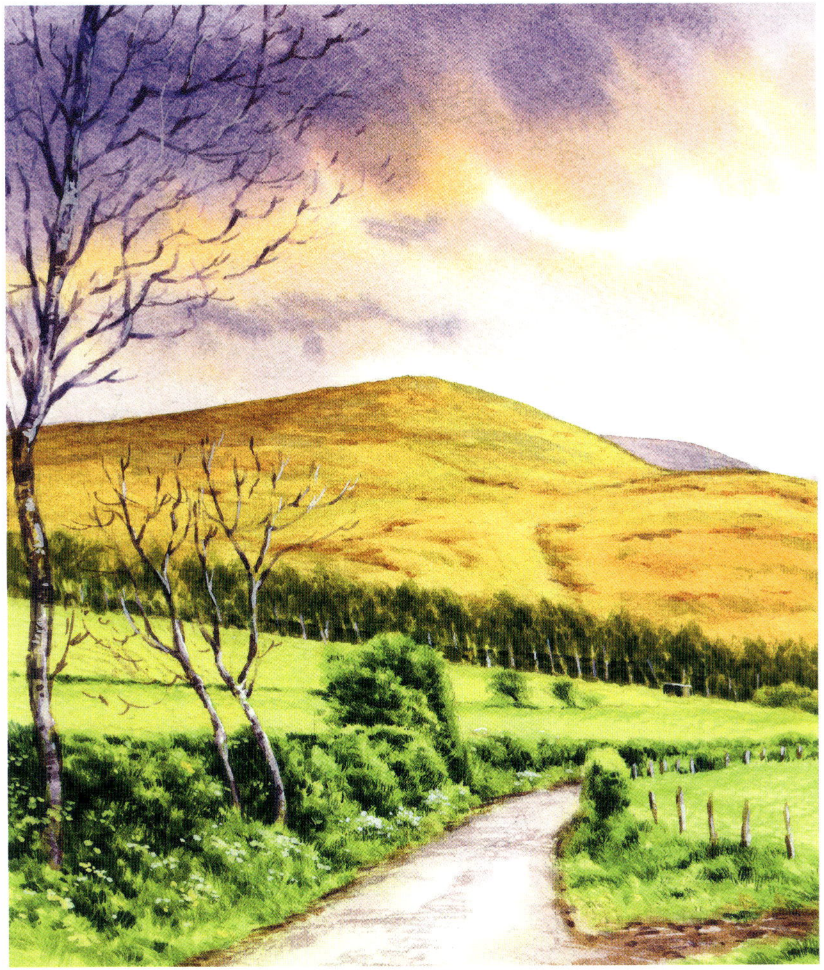

From the north-west 17/5/09
The same location was used for obtaining the view of Great Cockup but by just turning slightly to the left Longlands Fell presents this profile.

Longlands Fell

This is one of the Uldale Fells, gentle terrain which is hardly taxing for most walkers, except in mist. An area for getting away from crowds, especially over busy Bank Holiday weekends.

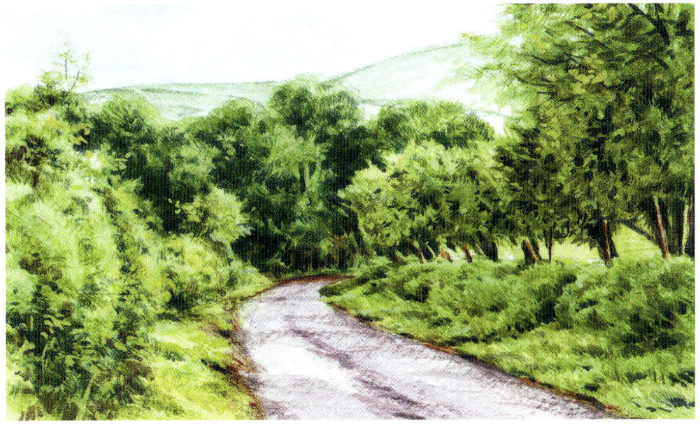

Longlands 17/5/09
Now these trees on the Orthwaite road obscure the hamlet.

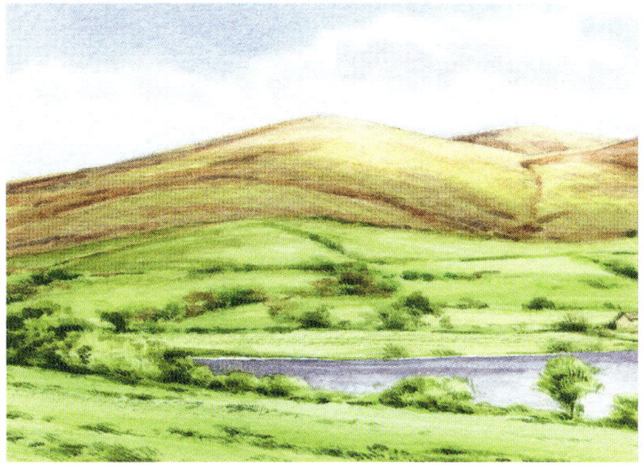

Longlands Fell, from Over Water 17/5/09
Over Water is the largest stretch of water in this area but this is the only time it is featured.

Skiddaw over Great Cockup 17/5/09
The view to the south-west from the summit.

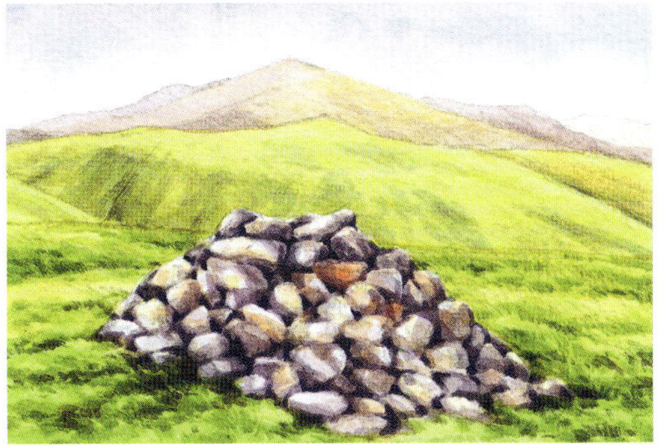

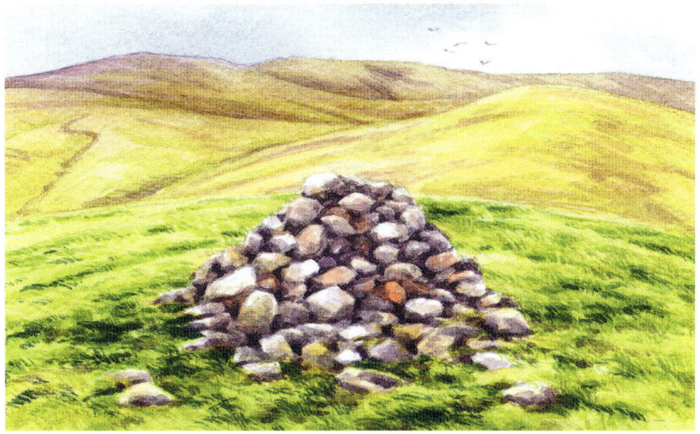

The summit 17/5/09
Some effort has been made to make the cairn into quite a pile of stones as none lie close by.

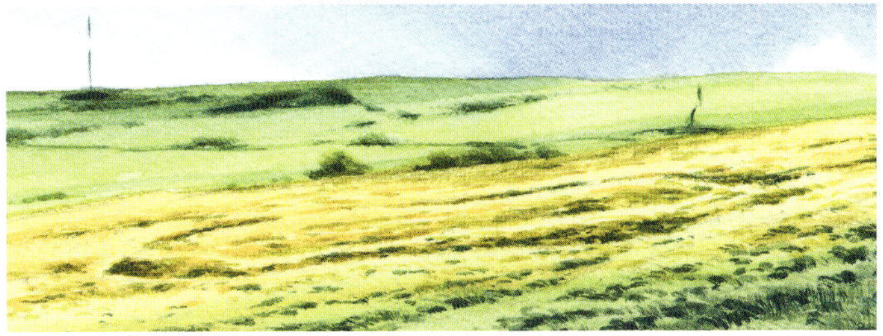

Aughertee Fell 21/5/09
The ancient enclosure is best seen when the sun is low and picks out the embankments. The Sandale transmitter mast is on the horizon away to the left.

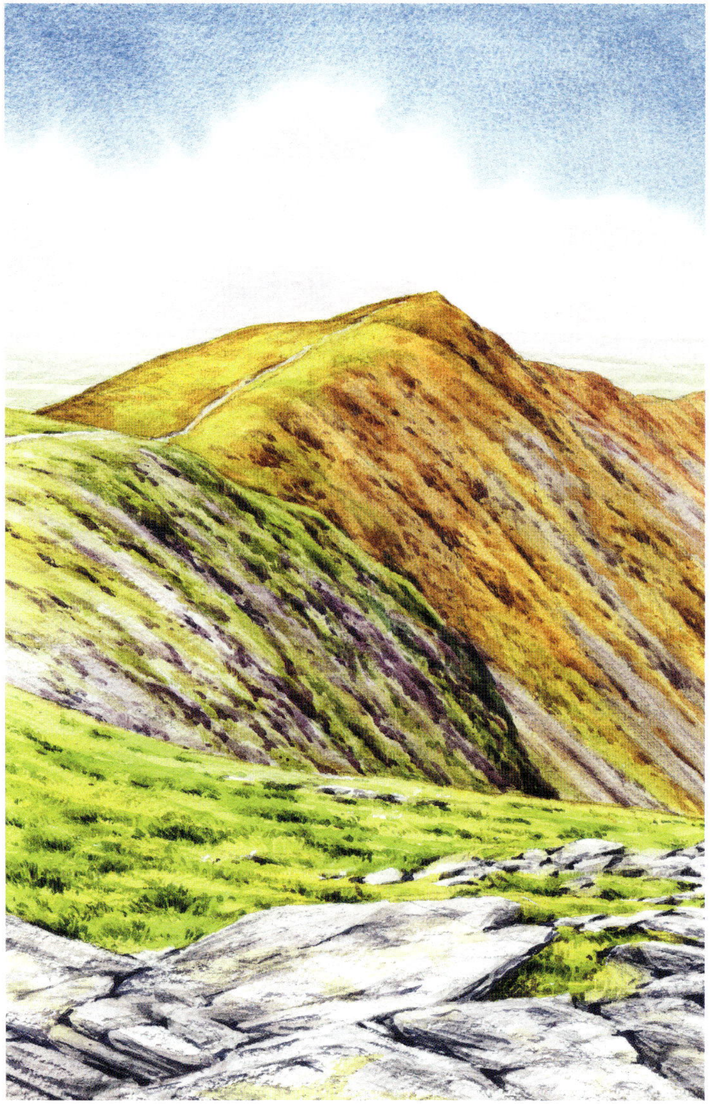

From Carlside col 22/5/09

The peak of Long Side does not in reality have the exaggerated profile that Wainwright gave it but even so, this angle does show the fell's most dramatic profile. The steep north-eastern slopes of loose scree and heather fall over 800′ into Southerndale.

The summit 22/5/09

A sprawling pile of slate marks the highest point of the fell with the undulating ridge descending to the north-west in the direction of the Solway Firth.

Long Side

There will be few who have visited the summit of Long Side without having first walked over the top of another hill. Its location means that this fell sits neatly between Ullock Pike and Carl Side on a fine heather clad ridge.

Longside Edge, looking from Ullock Pike 22/5/09

The highest point of this long ridge as seen from its neighbour.

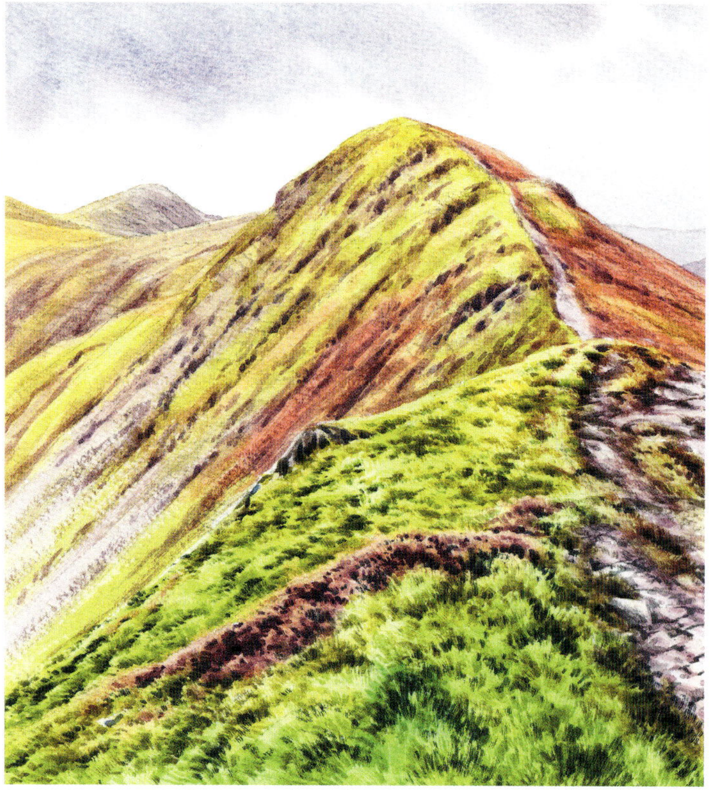

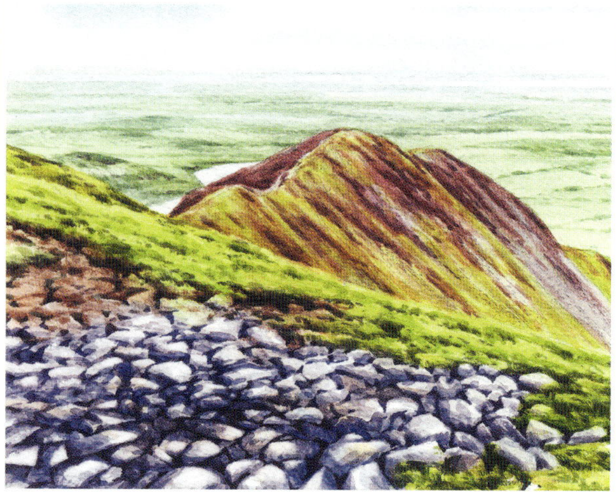

Dodd from Gable Gill 8/7/07

Mature trees have been felled and new saplings now replace them on Dodd's flank.

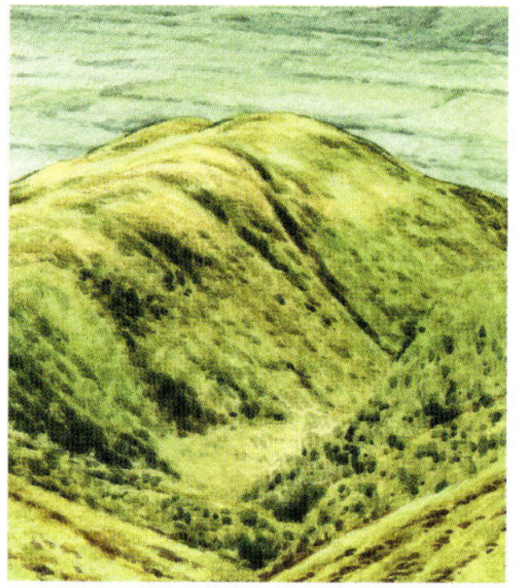

A cleft in the ridge 22/5/09

With Ullock Pike and a small section of Bassenthwaite Lake.

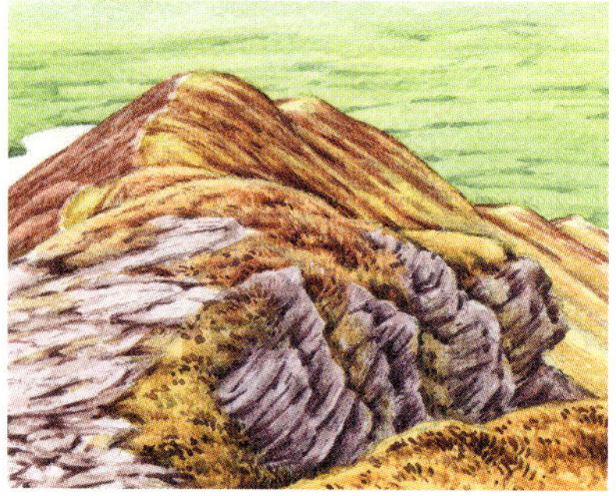

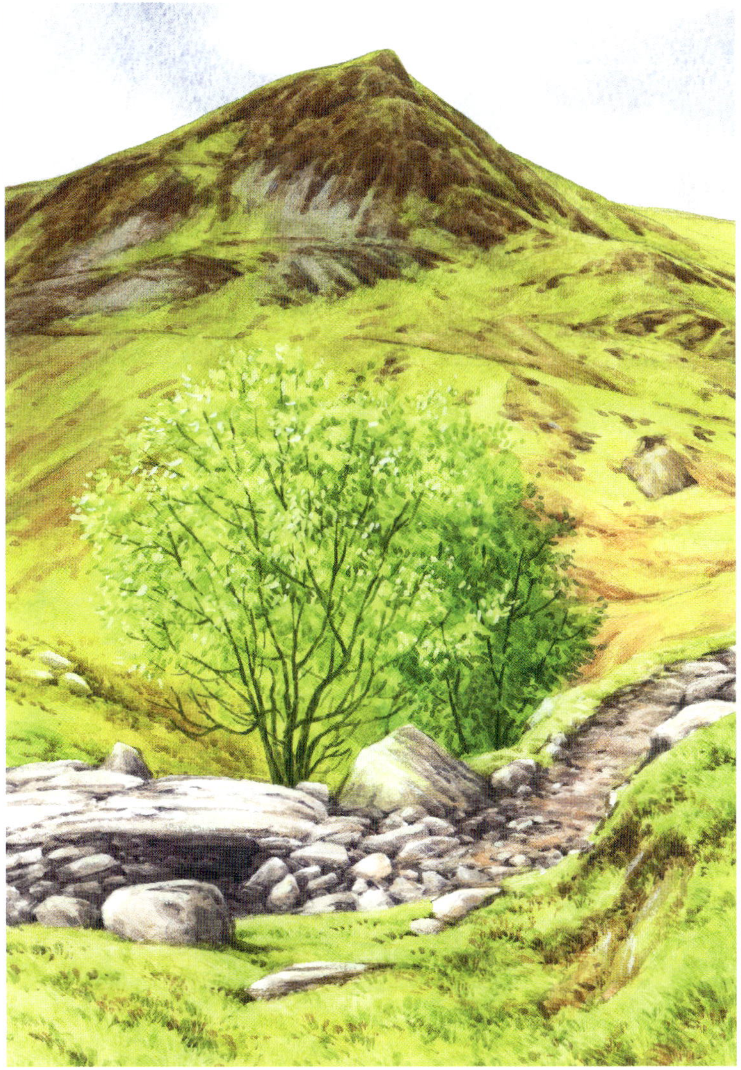

From Roughten Gill 16/5/09
It was always frustrating to get to a location such as this to find that trees had grown to obscure the view. Even more so here, as AW's composition was almost perfect, an old slate bridge adding foreground interest to a fine peak of a hill. I had to move back several paces to achieve the similar view, thanks to that new tree.

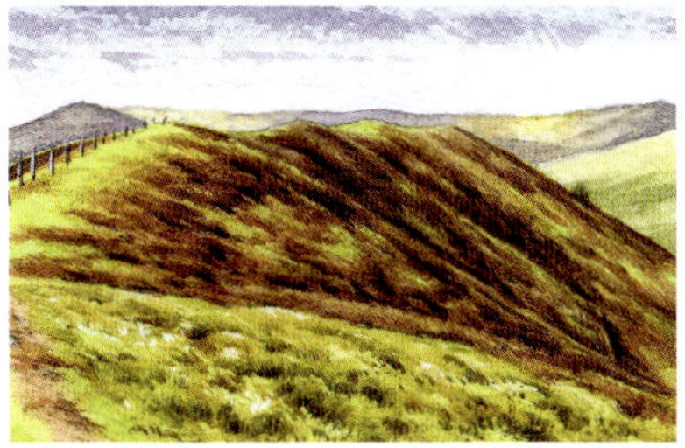

Burnt Horse ridge 19/5/09
A curious name that may mean the spur of land where burning has taken place.

Lonscale Fell

If it wasn't for the steep and craggy eastern face Lonscale Fell would be a rather mundane satellite of Skiddaw. A visit to the top of the east peak provides superb views especially to the south.

Lonscale Crags, from the path to Skiddaw House 19/5/09
The route can be seen continuing along the fell side. The rock ledge here now has another path alongside.

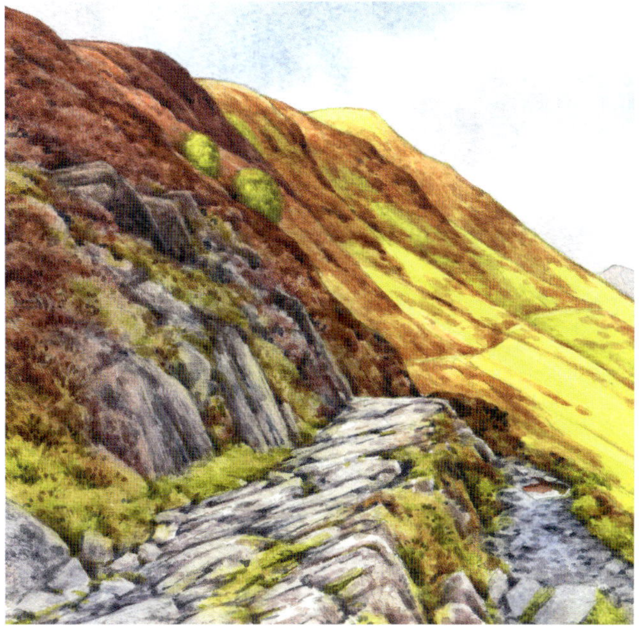

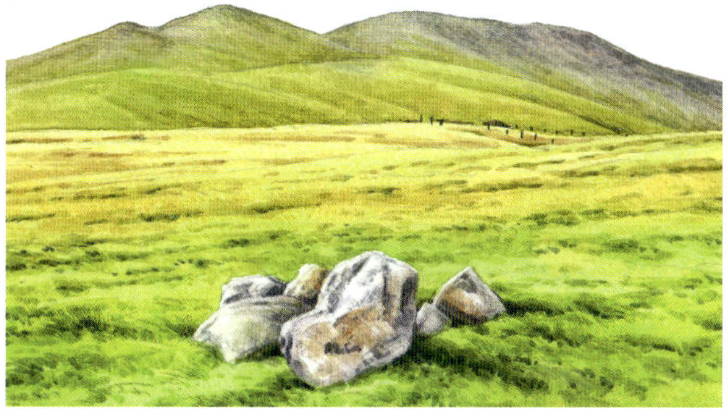

The summit 19/5/09
This is Wainwright's summit, marked with a few quartz rocks. A slate cairn nearby seems to be at the true top.

The summit tower, East Peak 19/5/09
The northern slopes of Blencathra form the backdrop in this view of the top section of AW's summit tower.

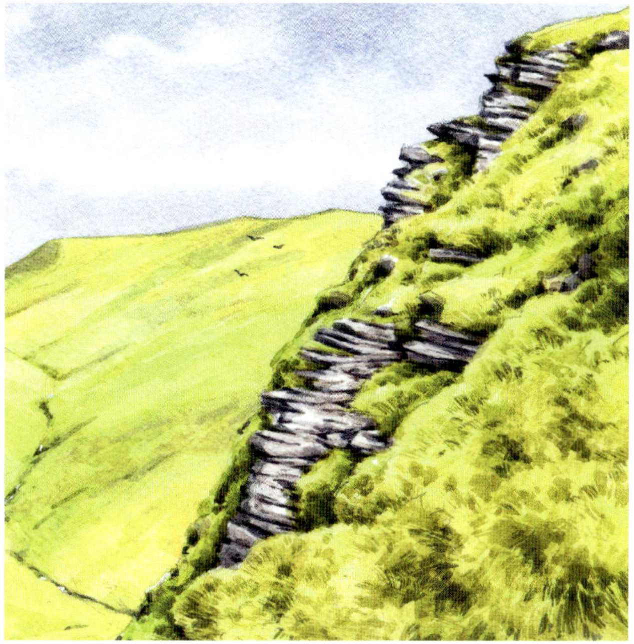

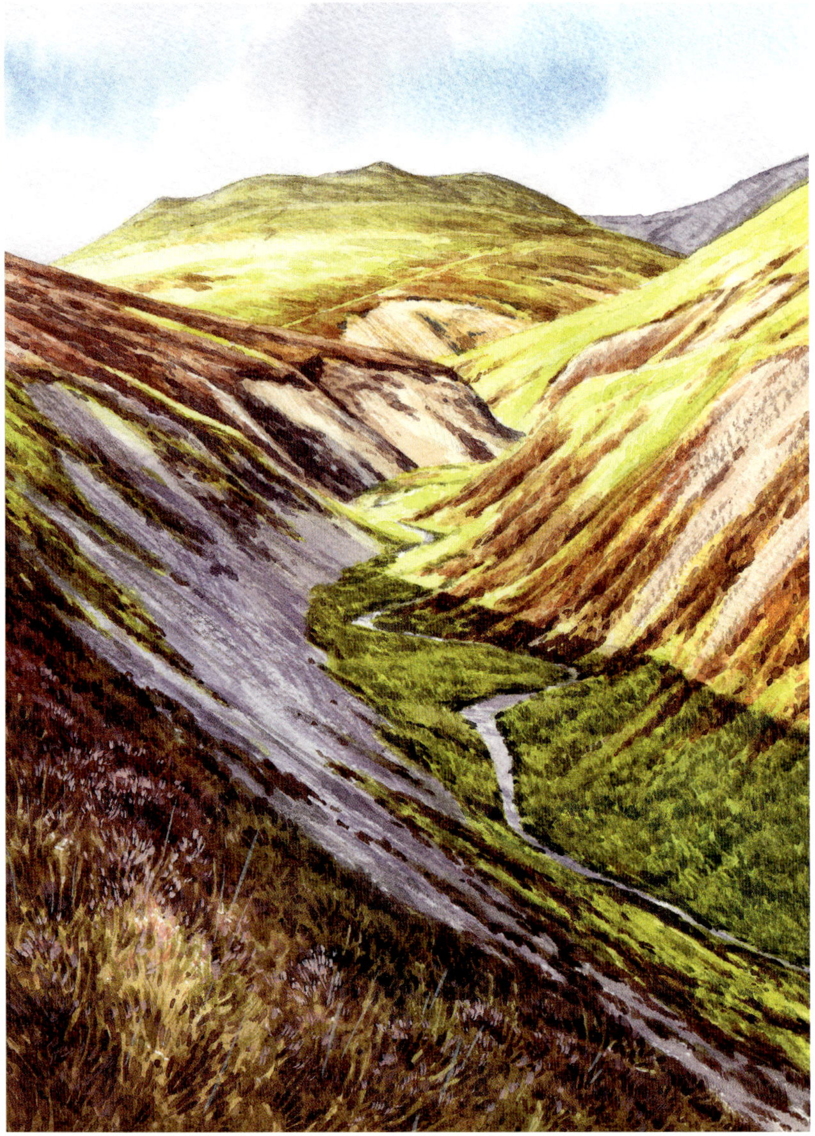

From Burntod Gill 20/5/09
South-west of Trusmadoor the footpath contours high above the beck, contouring the scarred valley walls. It is from here that this profile of the fell is seen, neatly framed by the ravine.

Meal Fell

This is one of the fells that was not on AW's original list, it may be due to the fact that on old one inch to the mile maps Meal Fell was not named. Features such as the stony summit, unusual in this area, and the curiosity of Trusmadoor may have helped to get it included on the final selection of the 214 fells in the Pictorial Guides.

Trusmadoor from Burntod Gill 17/5/09
In the Cumbric language *Trus* meant pass or gap, *-ma* is Brittonic for place with the English *door* added later. In this view, looking north-west, the distant shape of Criffel, 27 miles away across the Solway Firth can be seen.

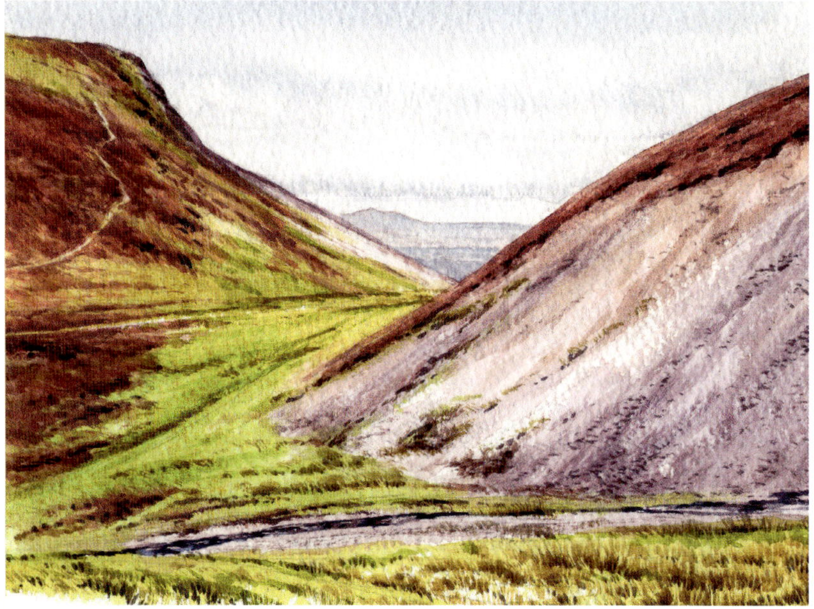

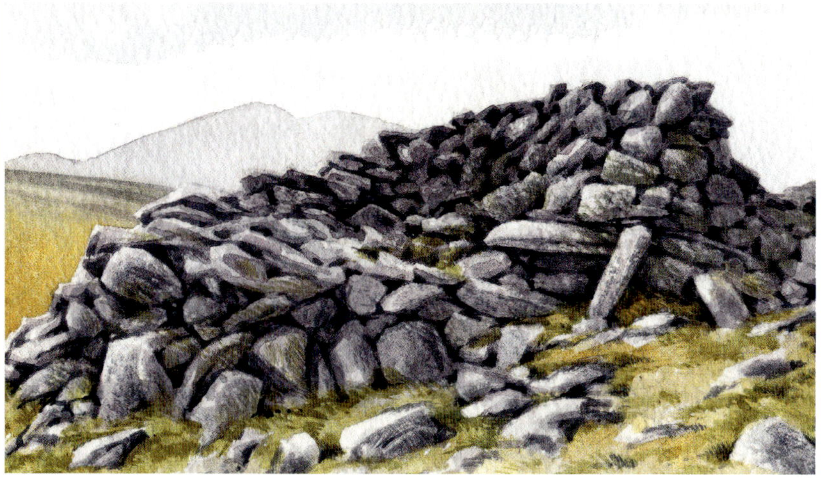

The summit 17/5/09
The large stone shelter is situated on the highest point and still serves its purpose in poor weather.

The summit from the west 17/5/09
What at first appears to be a large cairn turns out to be the shelter.

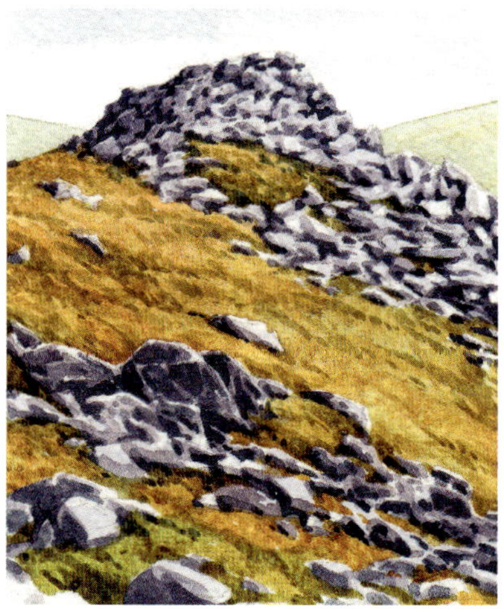

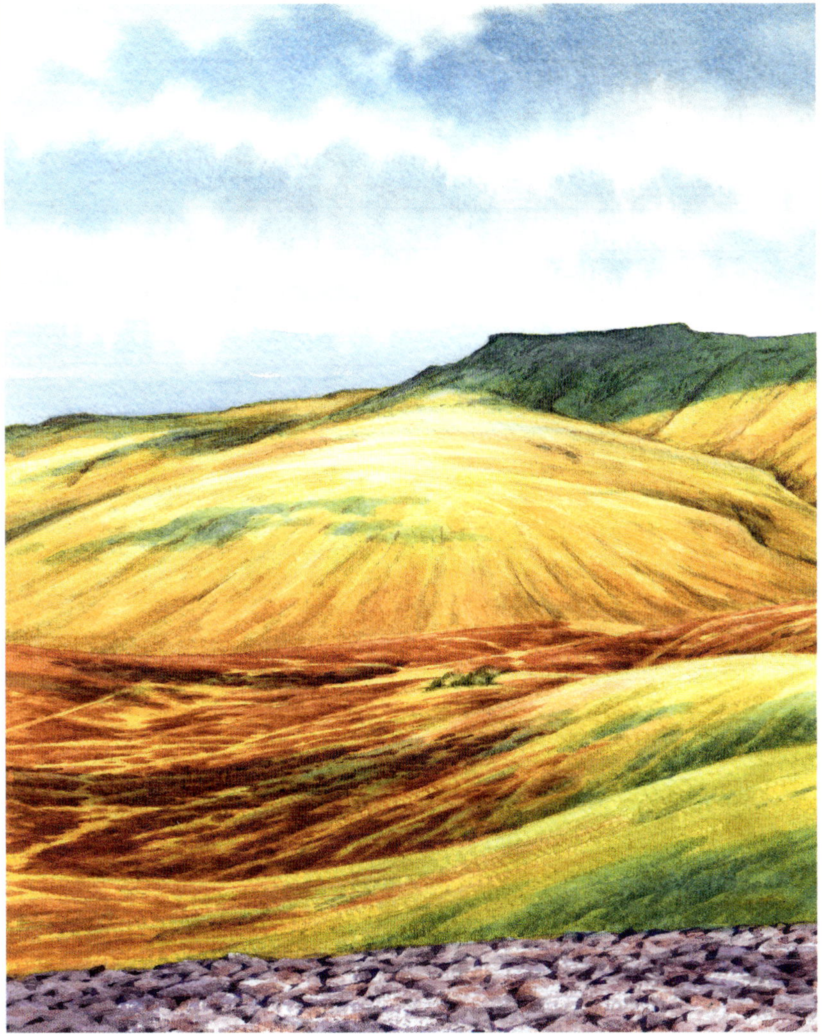

From Skiddaw 19/5/09

There are very few fells in the Pictorial Guides which are illustrated on the first chapter page by actually looking down on them, as in most cases the view looking up to a hill is normally more dramatic and inspiring. But then those two adjectives are not often connected with Mungrisdale Common, only by drawing this angle from near Skiddaw's summit where at least Blencathra acts as a foil does the hill look anywhere near interesting.

Mungrisedale Common

Walkers visit here out of curiosity or to put another tick on their list but despite its rather plain landscape AW did find several good subjects to draw that filled out the six page chapter. It takes a bit of walking and exploration to visit all these sketch locations.

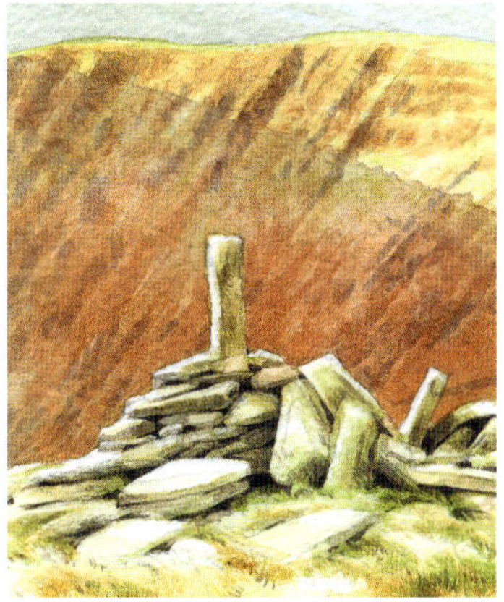

The first stone man 18/11/08

This structure sits between Sinen and Roughten Gills. Sadly the neat column has fallen since AW's visit.

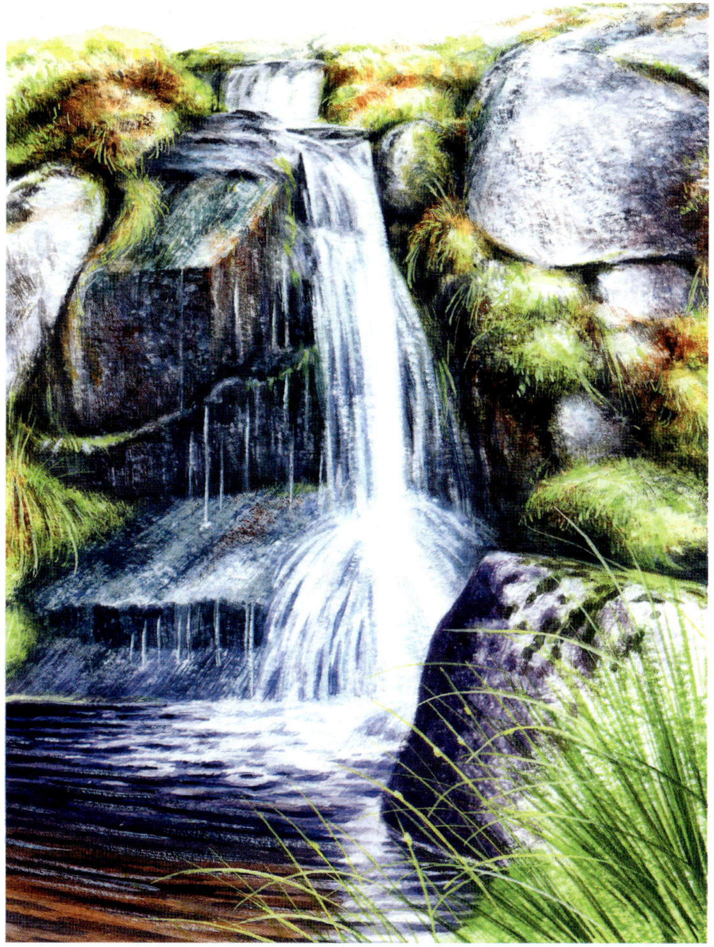

Waterfall, Sinen Gill 18/11/08

This waterfall is someway up the gill and not visible from the track through the Glenderaterra valley. The pink tinted Skiddaw granite is exposed here whilst the surrounding area is mostly of slate. The big boulder that sits in the pool is now more rounded.

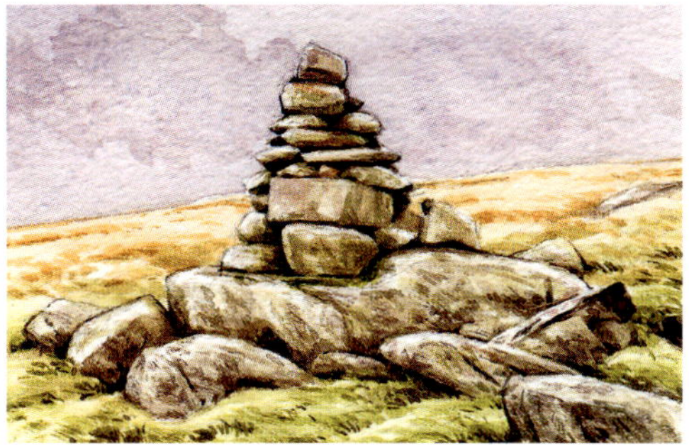

The second stone man 18/11/08

Located just to the west of the fell top this stone man is now more of a conical cairn, identified by its base of bedrock.

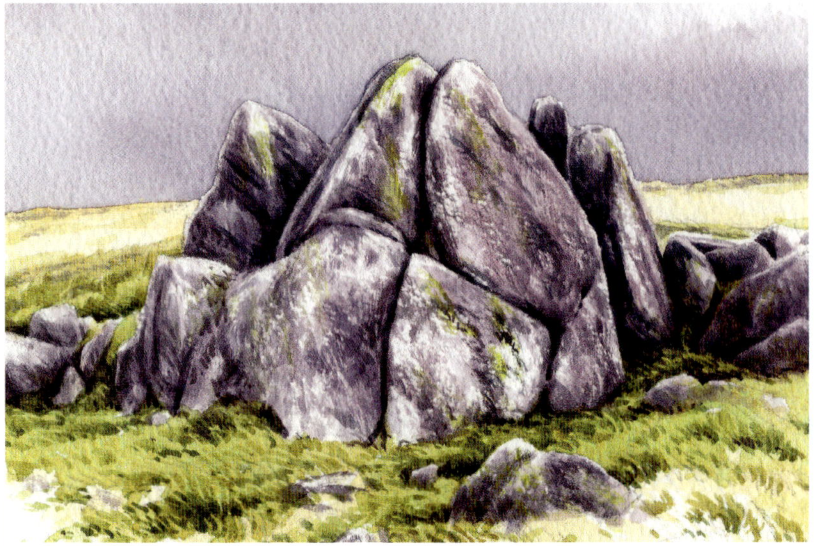

Cloven Stone 18/11/08

Walkers looking to find something of interest on their visit to Mungrisdale Common may more often than not seek out this split rock formation, which can be found along the path that runs south-west from the summit.

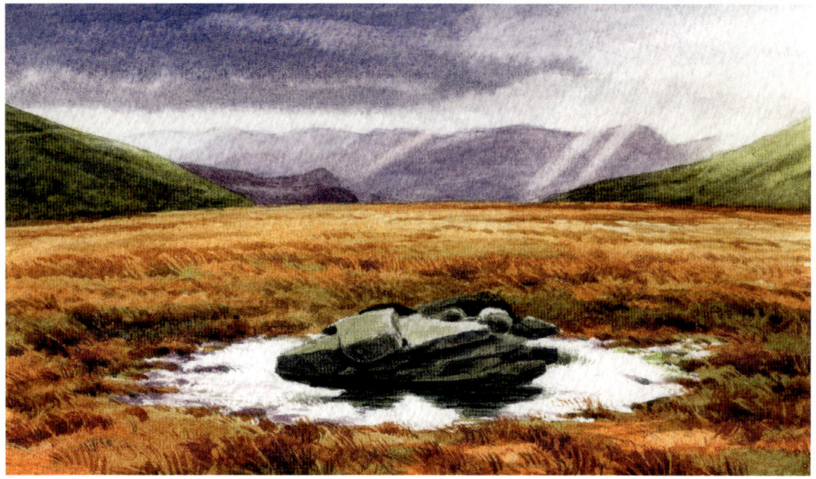

Looking south-west 18/11/08

In Wainwright's day there was nothing to mark the highest point of the fell so he didn't illustrate the summit, only the view to the south-west as I have done here. This cairn is a short distance from the actual location of AW's summit which is still devoid of a marker of any description.

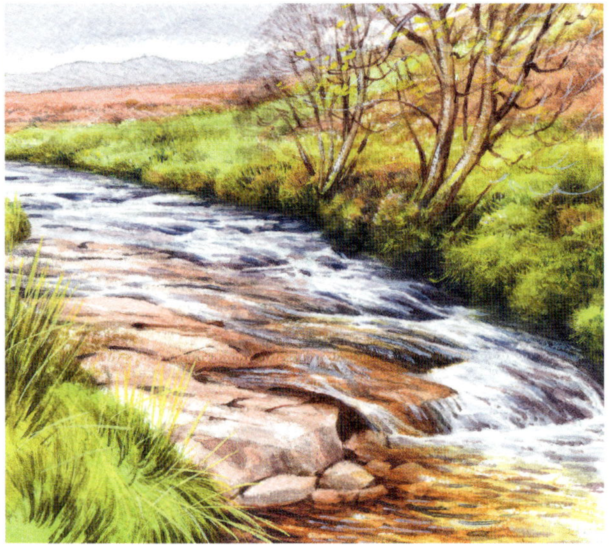

Granite slabs in the bed of the Caldew 6/8/09

Finding this reference required a long walk over difficult ground, closely following the banks of the river from near Skiddaw House downstream until the correct location was reached. Eventually the pink granite bedrock was exposed in the river bed and by fording the river I was able to match the location to AW's drawing, just north-east of where Blackhazel Beck joins the Caldew. I have yet to fathom out why AW was on this side of the river as there are no paths or routes.

The Stake 18/11/08

Unusually this boundary stone is engraved on all four faces, which indicated the estates whose boundaries met at this point. The ground here is very poorly drained so visiting The Stake usually means getting wet boots.

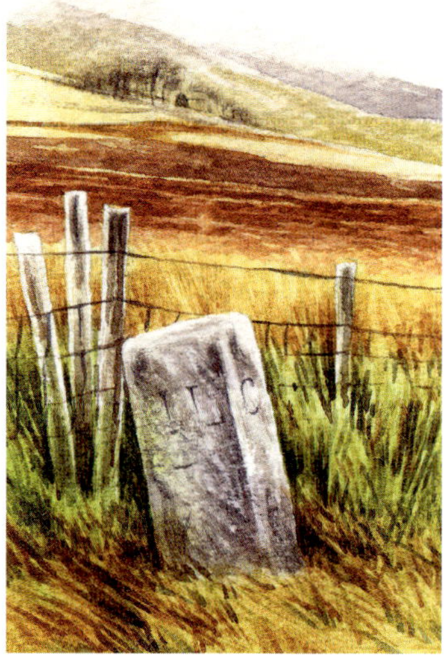

Why include this one?

Perhaps more than any other fell the question of why Wainwright included Mungrisdale Common in his final 214 often comes up in fell walker's conversations. Interestingly, this fell does not appear on either of AW's original lists but was added at a later date as he worked on the actual guides.

However, in my research for this project I have come up with my own theory regarding this matter. Firstly, the northern fell region covered by Book 5 is lacking in hills, only 24, so any opportunity for AW to increase the number of chapters and pages must have been taken. Despite Mungrisdale Common's reputation for being dreary he still manages to fill six pages with sketches, maps and details, more than the allocation to 37 other fells. Secondly, AW acknowledges that the Common is really a continuation of the northern slopes of Blencathra but by splitting the two he was able not only to write another fell chapter but also keep Blencathra to its 36 compelling pages. After all, Blencathra *"is a mountaineers' mountain"*, it would have been a shame to dilute its grandeur by including its dreary northern appendage. As the area of the Common still had to be mapped and featured, giving it a separate chapter was the obvious answer. Besides, it was his choice.

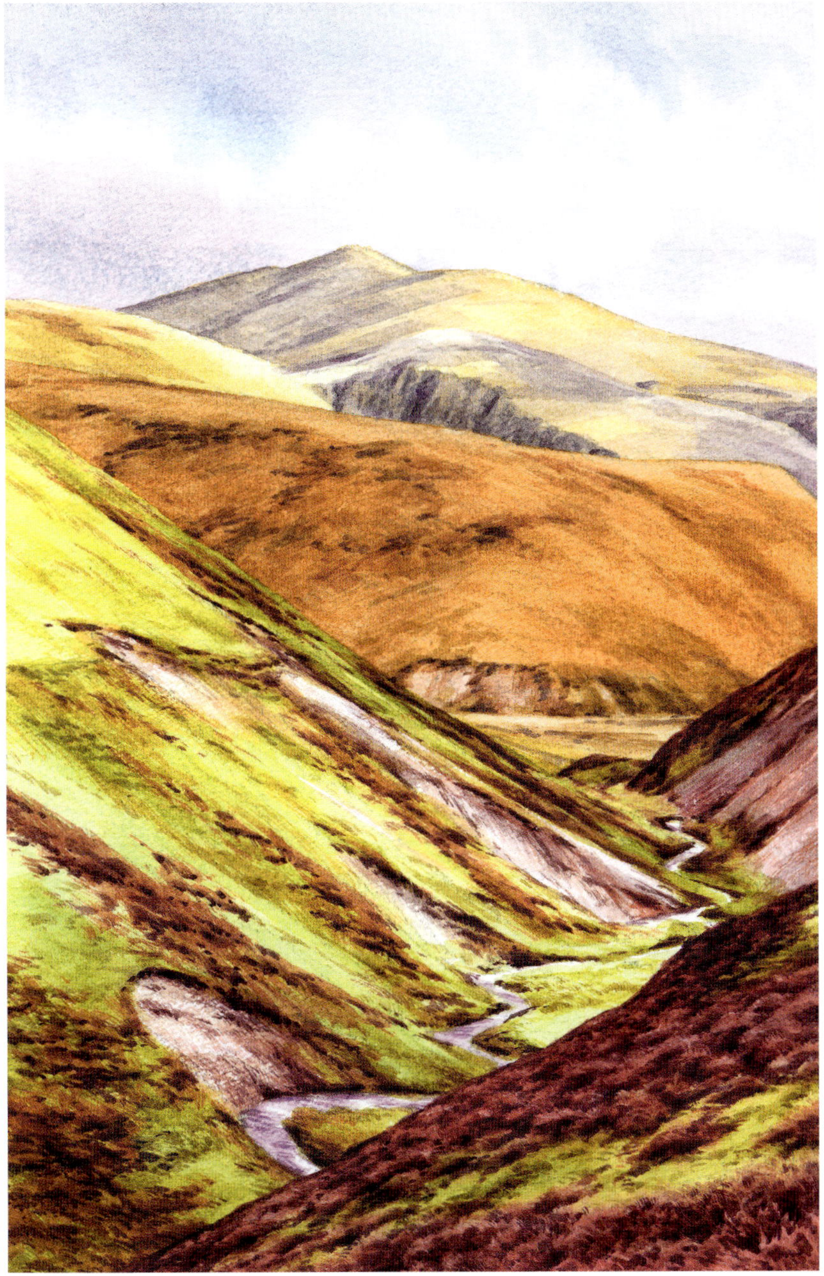

From Burntod Gill 20/5/09

Skiddaw only is the very top peak in this sketch, appearing over the ridges of Burn Tod, White Hause and then Bakestall. It is a pleasing view but it also illustrates the difficulty in capturing fells in the portrait format for the Pictorial Guides.

Skiddaw

Only four mountains on Wainwright's list reach over 3000' and Skiddaw is one of them. Consequently it is a popular fell for walkers especially to those who are based in the Keswick area. Despite its altitude, ascents can be made with relative ease on gradual slopes and without the hazards of steep drops or cliffs. Proper equipment should always be carried though, I have always found Skiddaw to be the windiest of hills.

Skiddaw House 18/5/09

One of the remotest buildings in England, this was once home to gamekeepers and shepherds. Pearson Dalton, the shepherd mentioned by AW eventually retired in 1969 after nearly 50 years of part time residence. The property is now a Youth Hostel Association bunkhouse.

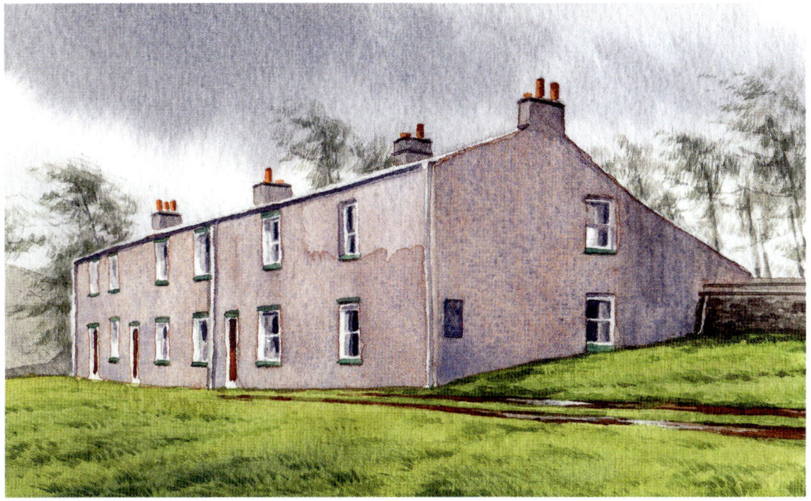

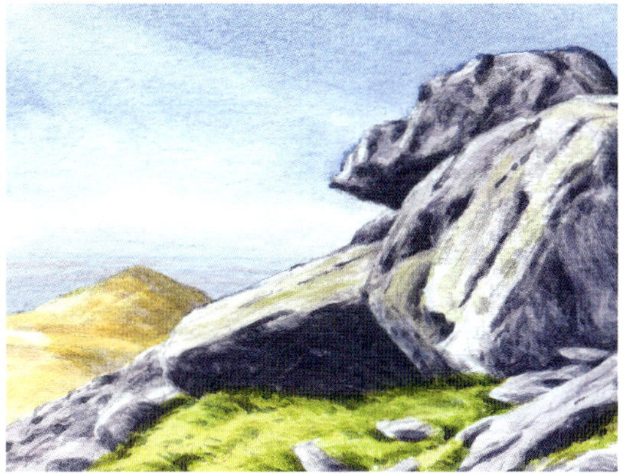

Fox Bield 19/5/09

Few cross the steep scree slopes to have a close look at this outcrop of rocks and boulders.

The Hawell Monument 16/5/09

An odd oblique angle from which to admire this tall memorial.

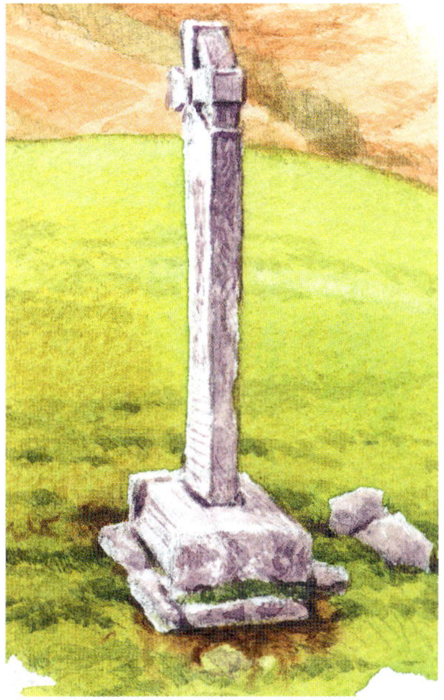

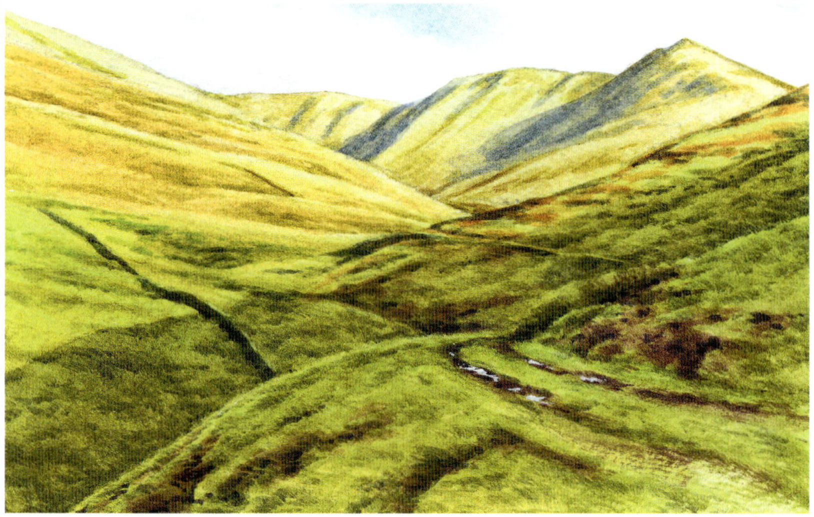

Southerndale 8/9/07
The view of the Ullock Pike ridge from the west, a great approach route.

Barkbethdale 8/7/07
Looking up this remote valley to the summit and screes of Skiddaw.

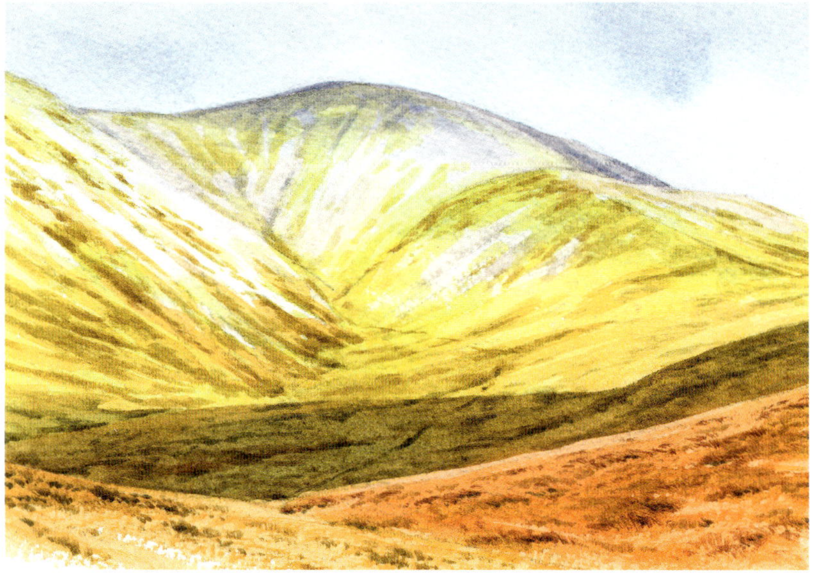

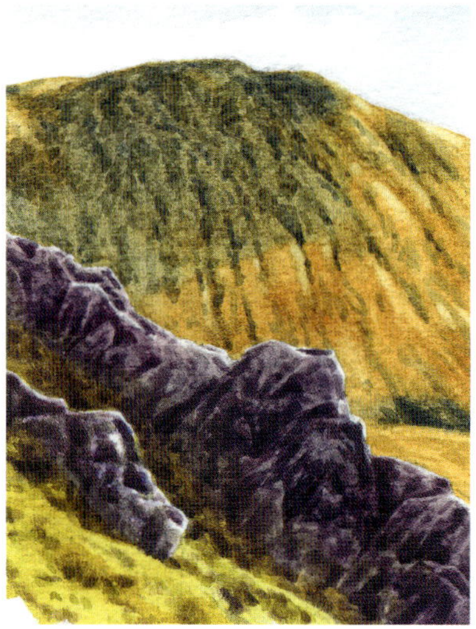

Ullock Pike, from Randel Crag 8/7/07
A slight diversion from the faint path enabled me to locate this outcrop.

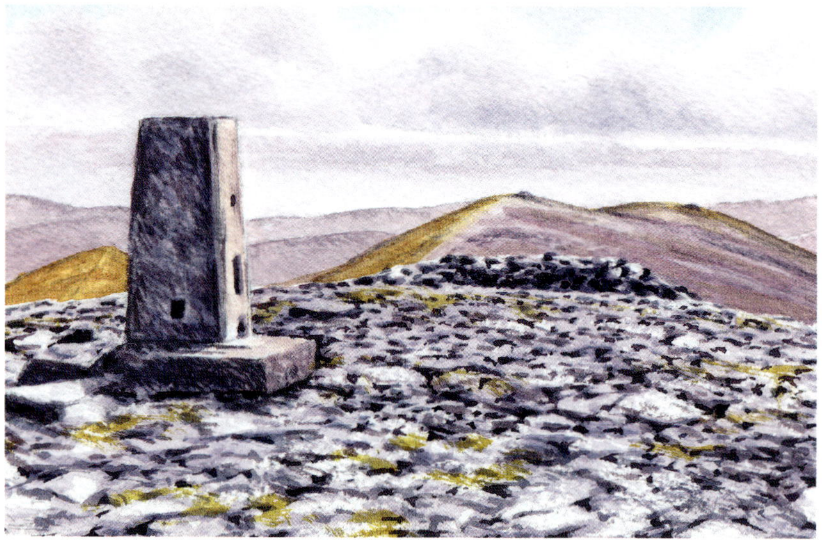

The summit, looking south 19/5/09
The cairn beyond the pillar has now been reformed into a shelter. The pillar itself appears to have had some restoration work including a new base. Just out of view to the right is a memorial cairn to commemorate the Queen's Silver Jubilee in 1977.

The summit, looking north from the south top 19/5/09
There are four separate tops over 3000′ here but they are merely rises on the high summit ridge with Skiddaw (High) Man being the true top, the others are unnamed on the O.S. map.

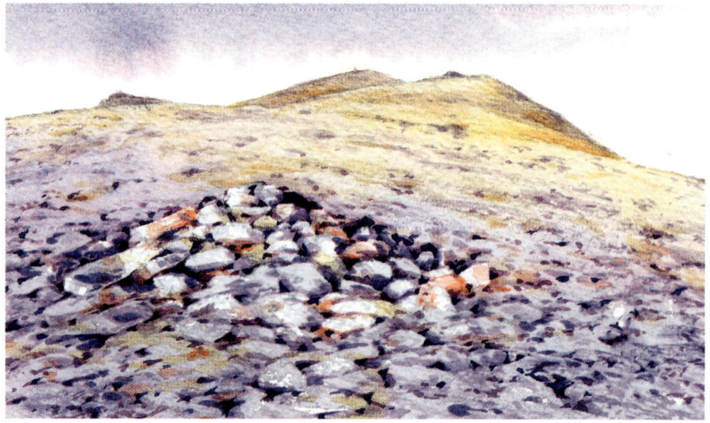

North top and Gibraltar Crag 19/5/09
This view is from near the north col on the indistinct path that comes up from Barkbethdale over Broad End.

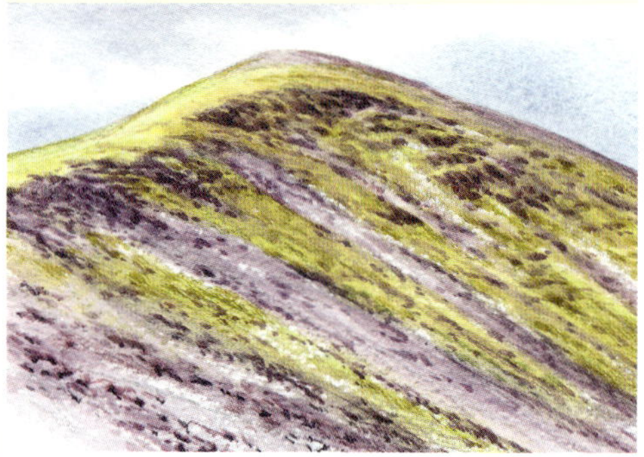

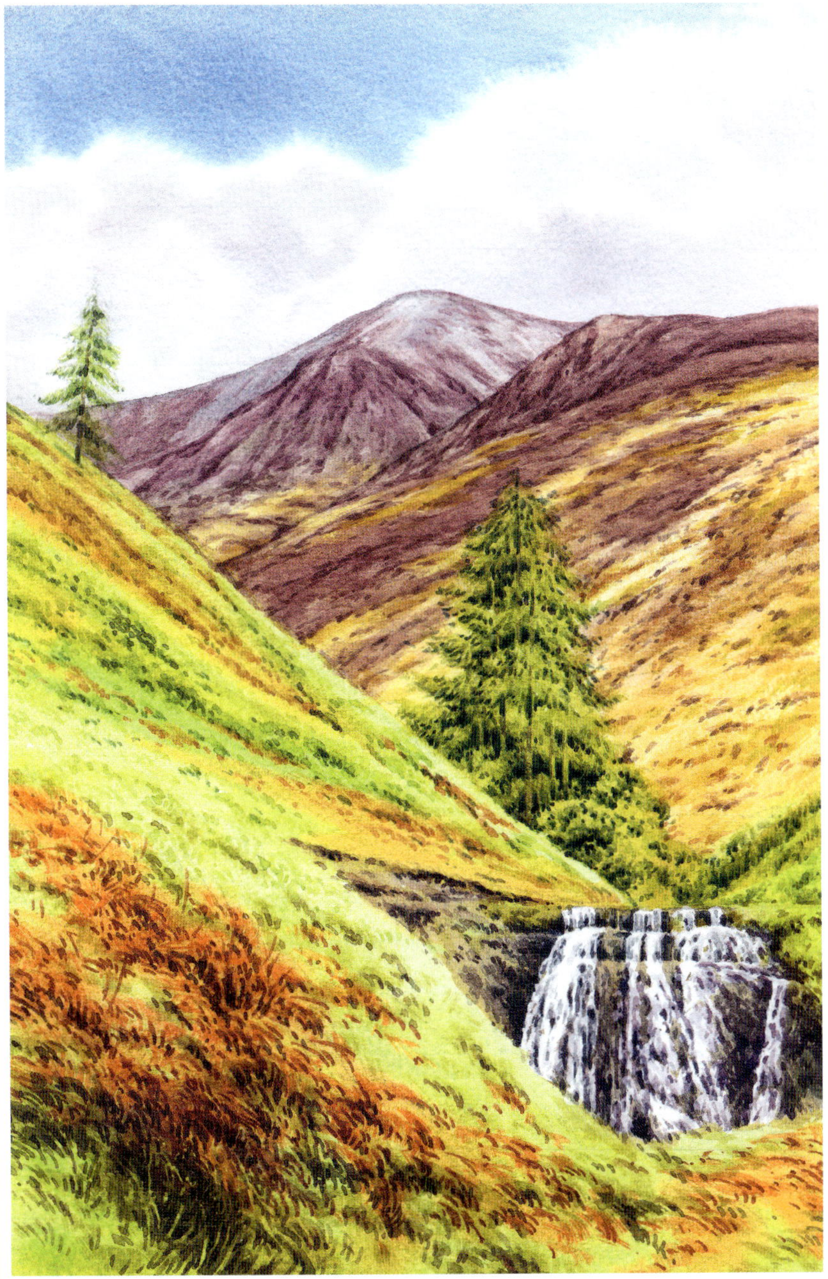

From the weir, Mill Beck
22/5/09
The weir has had alterations but all else is the same, even the trees are still in place.

Skiddaw Little Man

Just named as Little Man on various maps, this fell is rightly worthy of its own separate chapter in the guide. Wainwright waxes lyrical about the view from the summit, and justifiably so, to me it's a better panorama than that from the nearby and higher Skiddaw.

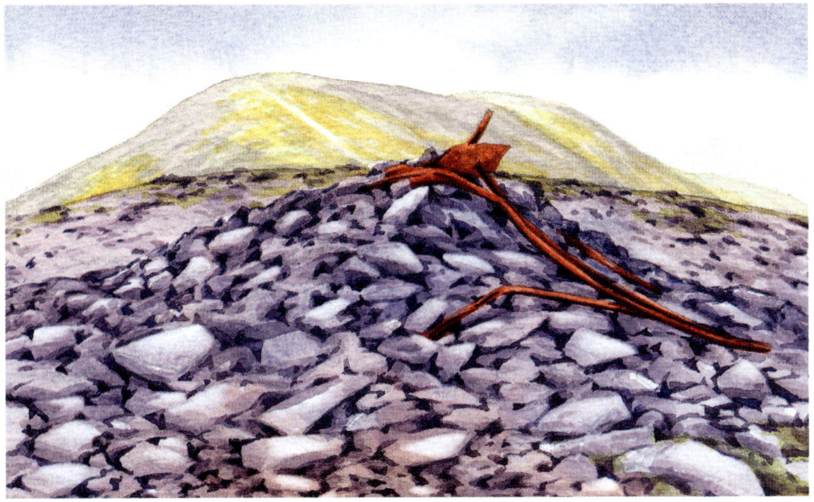

The summit cairn on Little Man 19/5/09
Rusting ironwork of the old fence lies on top of the pile of slate with the summit of Skiddaw behind.

The path to the hills, Applethwaite 22/5/09
A delightful woodland path that heads north out of the hamlet of Applethwaite.

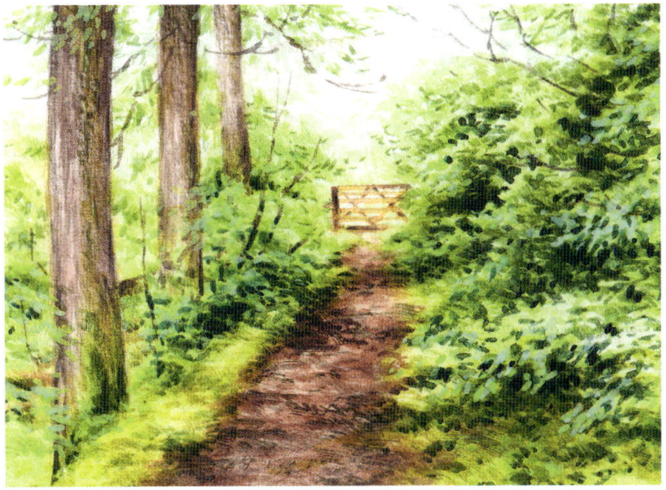

Waterfalls, Whit Beck
22/5/09
A series of hidden cascades which require effort to view.

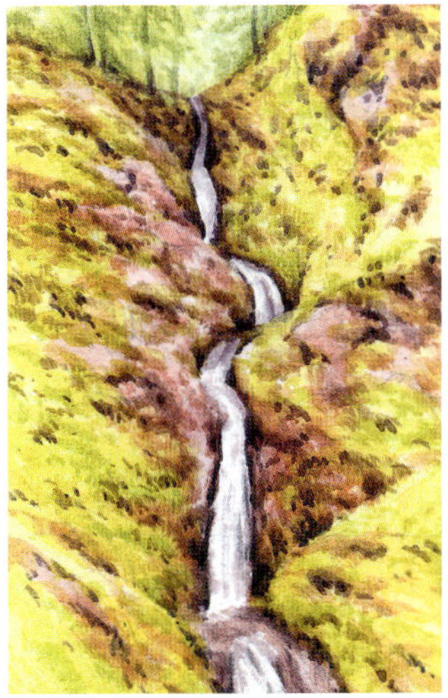

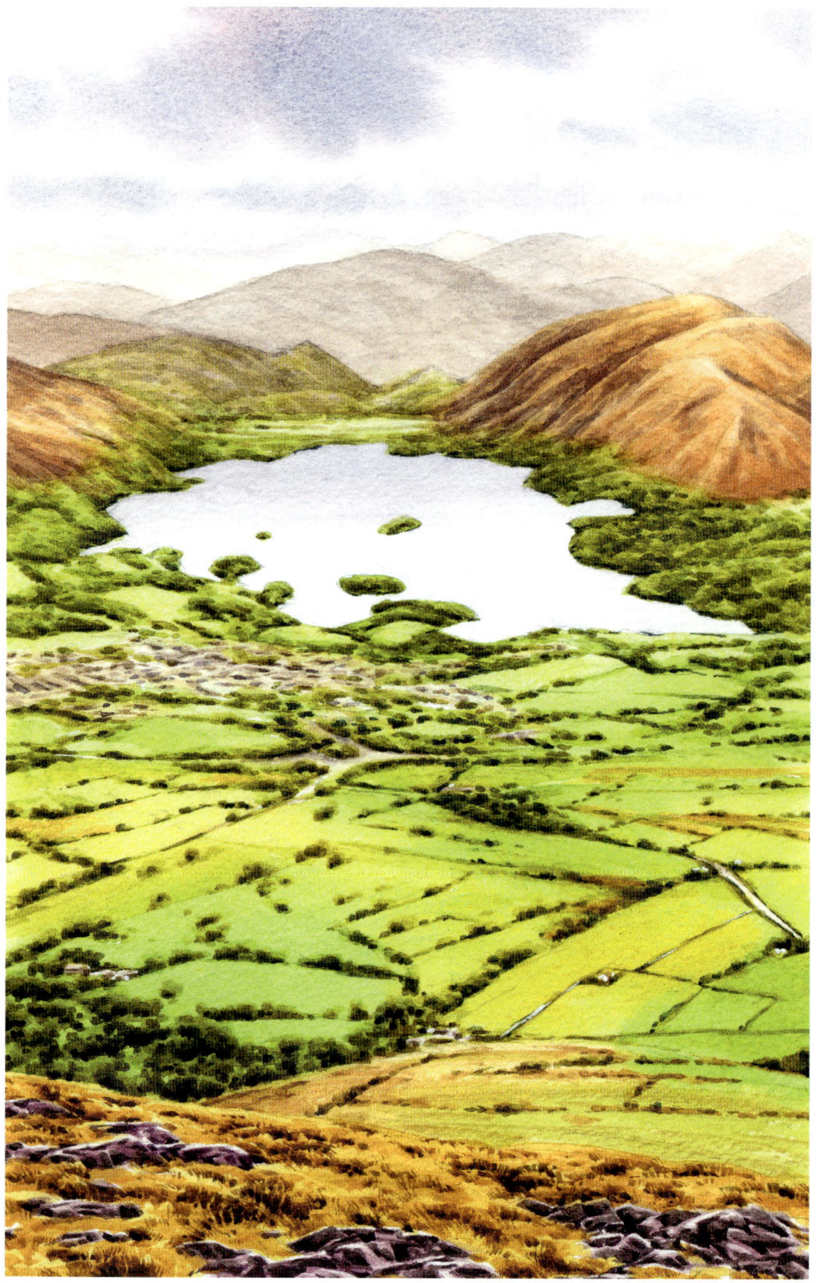

8' stake, Sale How 19/5/09
It would be remarkable if this was the same stake as in AW's drawing but it is certainly of an age.

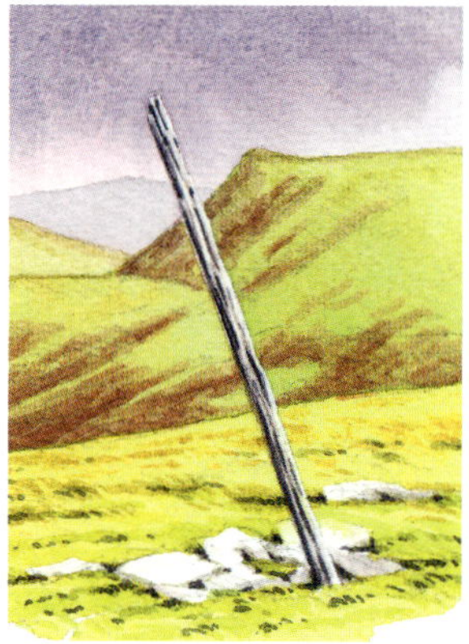

The cairn on Lesser Man 19/5/09
A larger cairn than that seen on the actual fell summit. Lesser Man was not named as such on either the 6 inch or 2½ inch O.S. maps of AW's day.

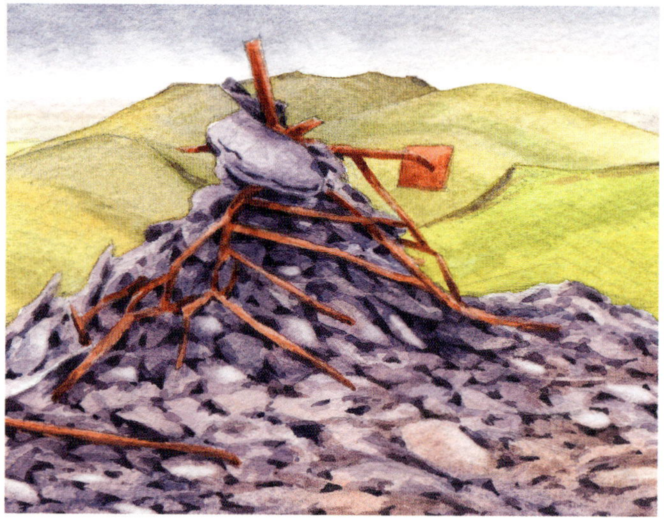

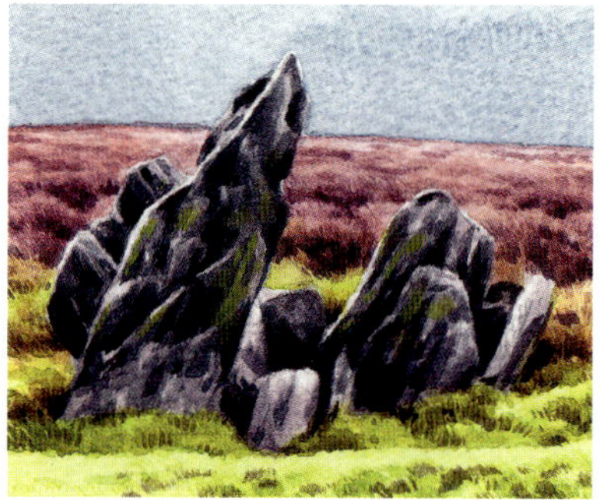

The two boulders 22/5/09
This is quite a deceptive sketch perspective wise as it is actually looking up a steep slope to the pointed rocks.

Looking south from the summit 19/5/09
The most annotated of all the full page drawings in the guides. In fact seen from a location100 yards south of the summit.

Looking down the south-west arête to Millbeck 19/5/09
I had to climb this narrow ridge twice to locate these pointed rocks but that wasn't a problem as this is the best ascent on all of the Skiddaw massif.

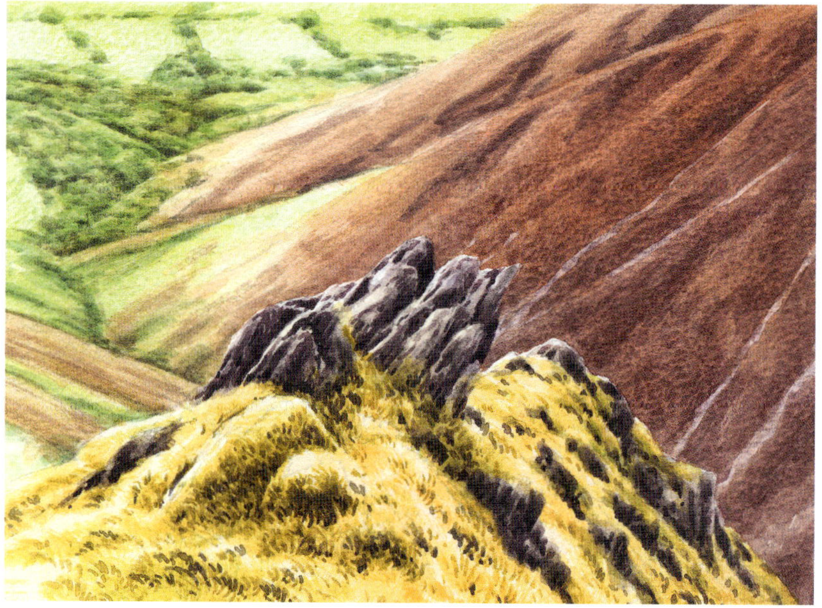

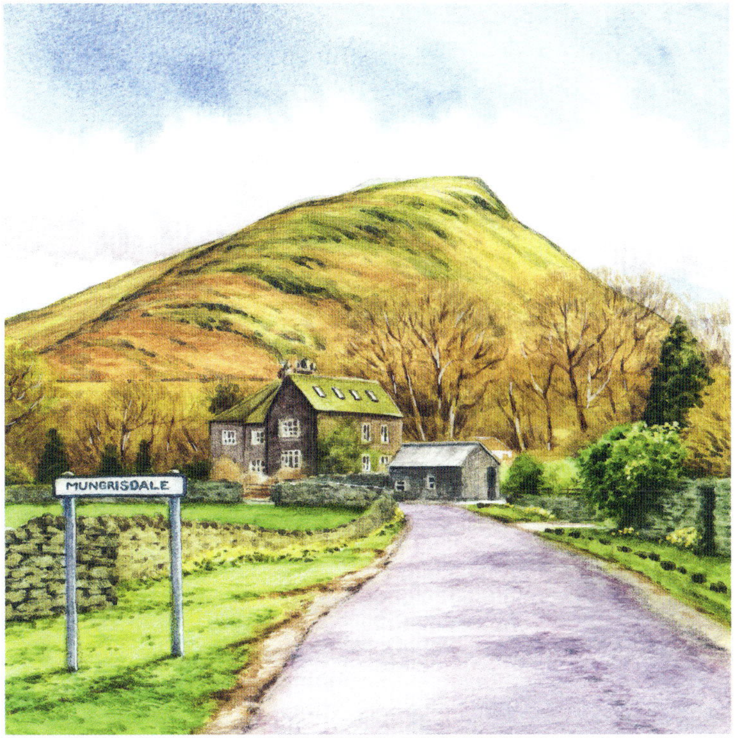

From Mungrisdale 13/4/09
The fell rises up behind the quiet hamlet of Mungrisdale which, apart from the new sign, has hardly changed since the late 1950s.

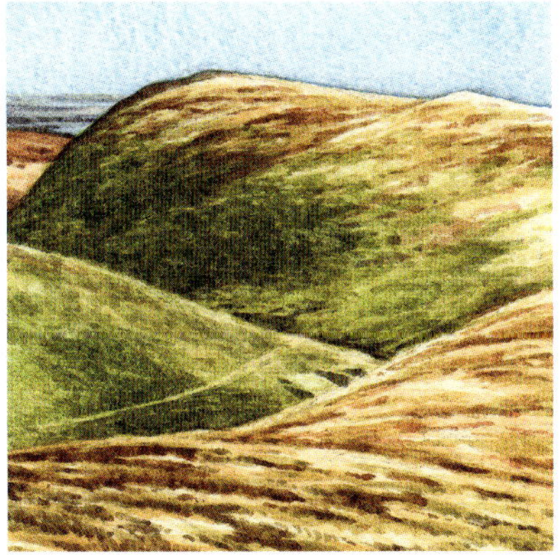

From Scales Fell
13/4/09
Looking down on the rounded slopes of Souther Fell and the valley of the river Glenderamackin.

Souther Fell

A whaleback shaped fell which is often ascended from the village of Mungrisdale. It is joined to Scales Fell by Mousthwaite Col so Blencathra can then be climbed without losing too much height.

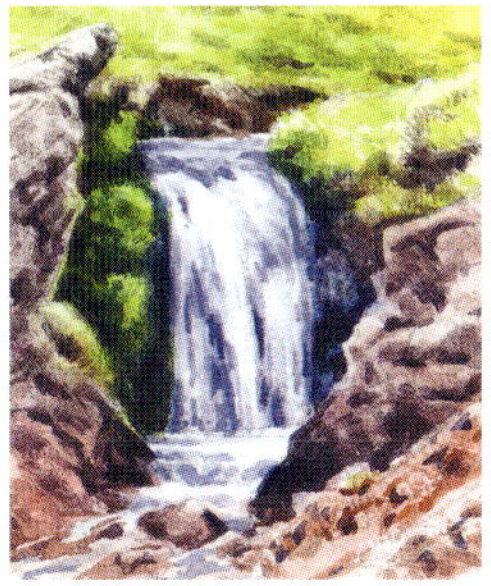

First waterfall
21/5/09
Not far from the old lead mine.

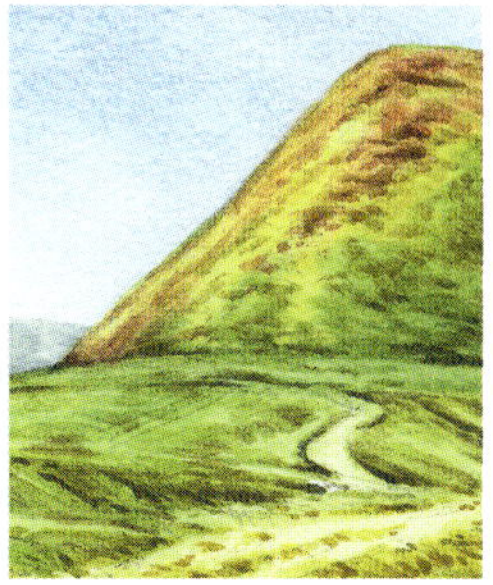

In Bannerdale
29/8/08 The Tongue rises up on the right.

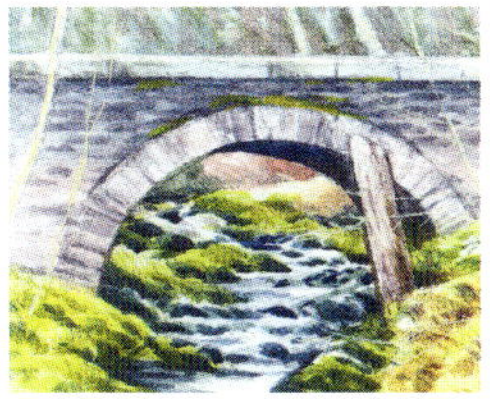

Second Bridge
18/12/07
This is in the village close to the inn.

First bridge 18/12/07
Now lost to flooding.

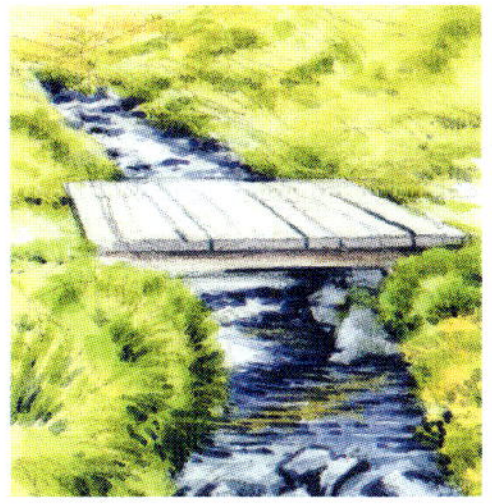

Mungrisdale
18/12/07 The village from the south side.

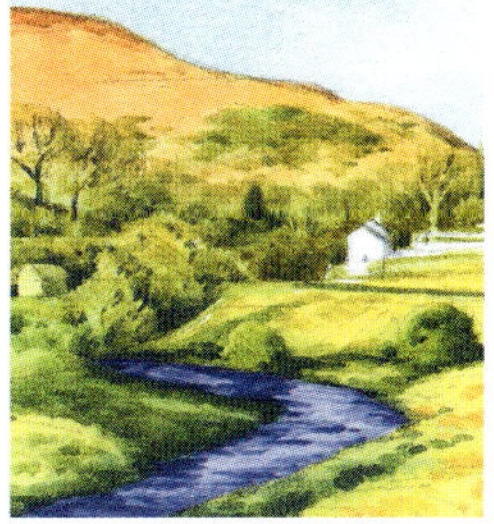

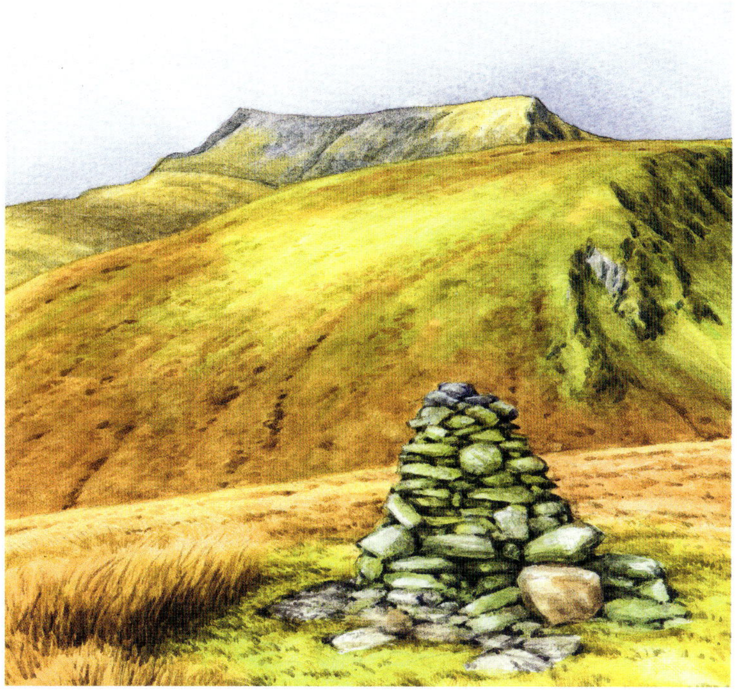

Blencathra, from a cairn on Souther Fell 13/4/09
This sizeable weathered cairn looks to be of some years but it is fairly recent, being just an enlargement of that depicted by AW.

The summit 13/4/09
One of the smallest summit drawings of any fell. No cairn to speak of and the posts have gone.

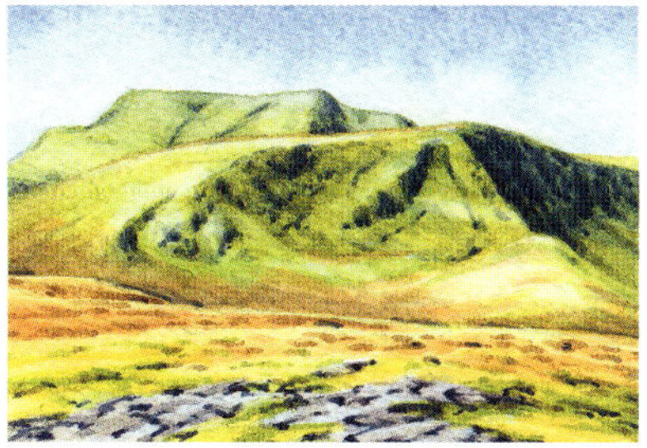

Blencathra from Mousthwaite col 13/4/09
A tiny sketch for such a fine view of Blencathra and Sharp Edge.

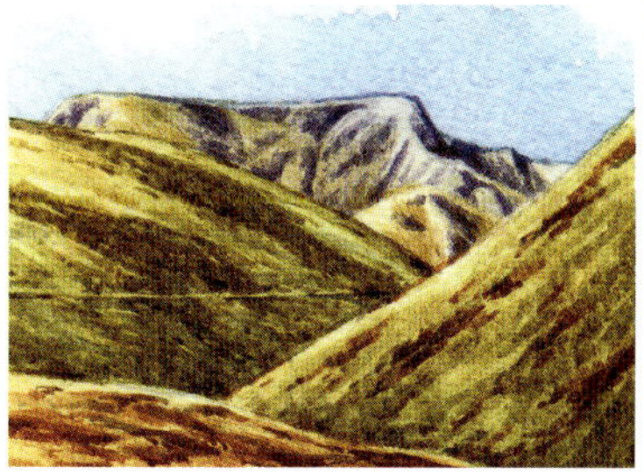

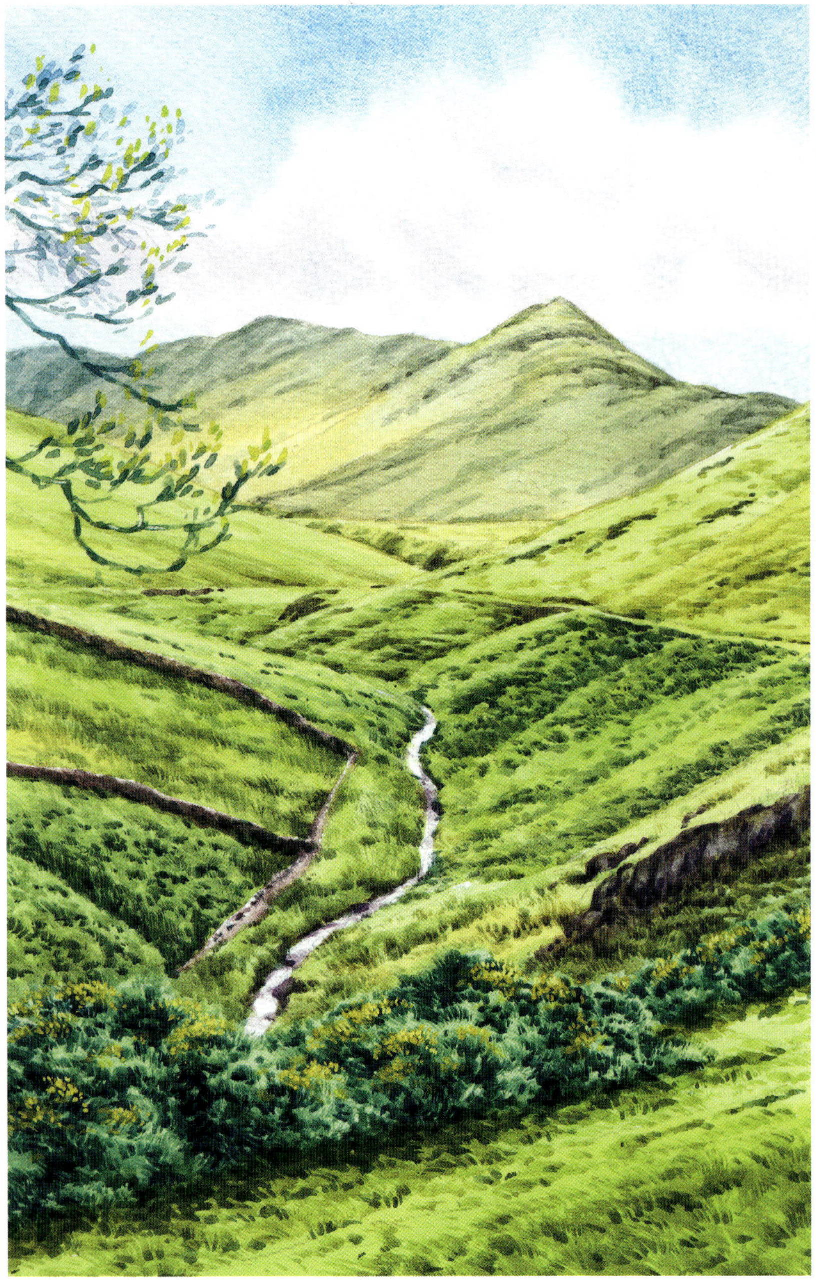

Ullock Pike

The high arm of land that reaches to the north-west from the Skiddaw massif is named as The Edge, the last high point on this ridge is Ullock Pike. The view from the summit to the north is uninterrupted to the hills of Dumfries and Galloway beyond the Solway Firth.

From Southerndale 8/7/07
In this view of the fell it does live up to its Pike (peak) name and gives walkers who are heading up to Skiddaw via this fine ridge an indication of what a great route lies ahead.

Ullock Pike from Chapel 17/5/09
On the main road to Keswick just out of the village of Chapel this view can be seen. The field patterns line up to match AW's illustration as does the ridge to the fells beyond. Skiddaw is just out of view in this depiction.

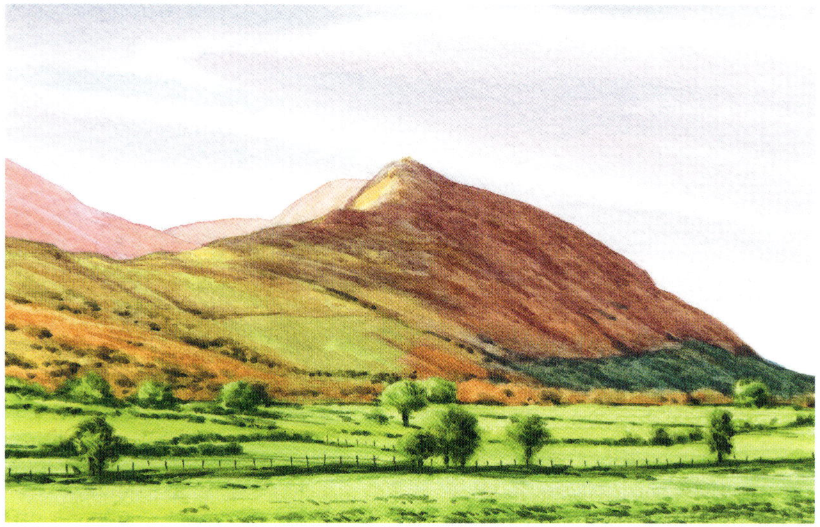

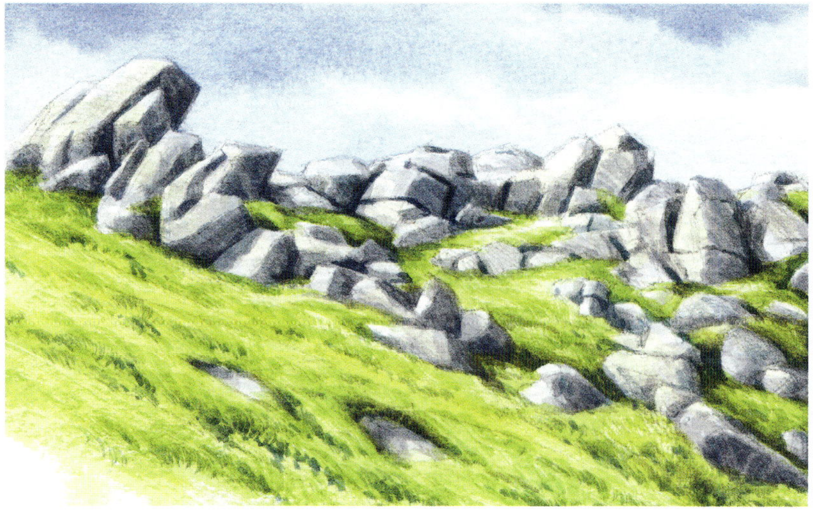

Watches 8/7/07
This natural outcrop of angular boulders on the lower section of Ullock Pike's northern ridge is an unusual feature on what is otherwise just an area of turf. The name is mostly likely to have come from this being a good look-out position at the times of border raiders coming down from the north.

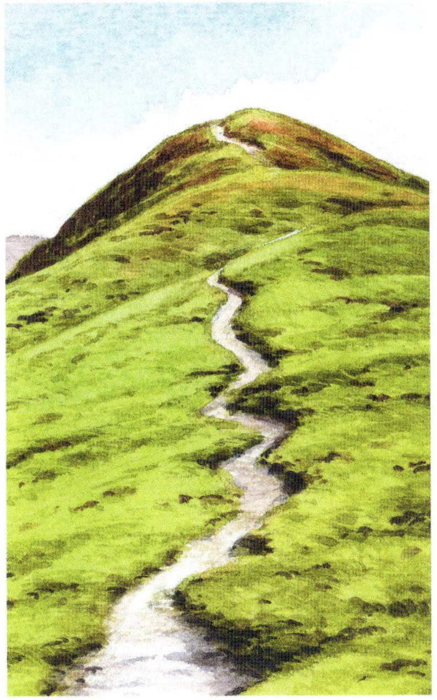

The last quarter mile 8/7/07
The approach to the summit along the north ridge known as The Edge. The clear path is easy to follow and the ridge provides excellent views.

Hanging Stone 9/8/11
It took me two attempts to obtain this reference which as a feature hardly warrants its naming on the map. It is well off the beaten track so getting to it requires tramping through dense heather which hides loose rocks. My bonus was being able to observe ring ouzels here at close quarters.

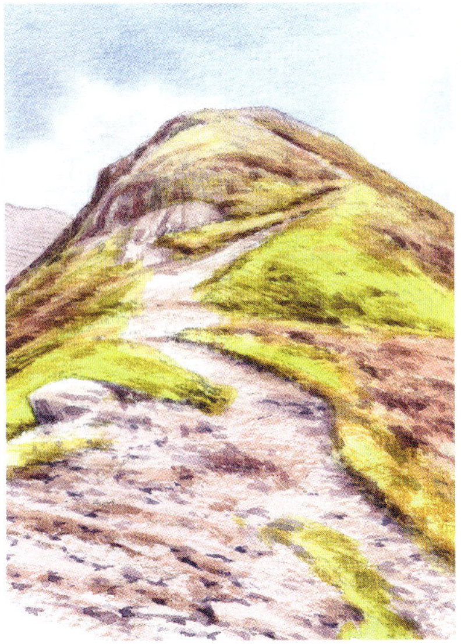

The true summit from the false one 22/5/09
If climbing the fell from the north there may be a little disappointment on reaching this summit to find that it isn't the true top, which in reality lies ahead.

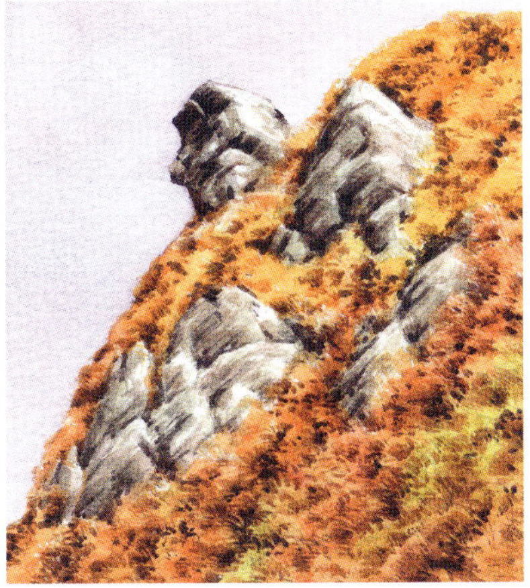

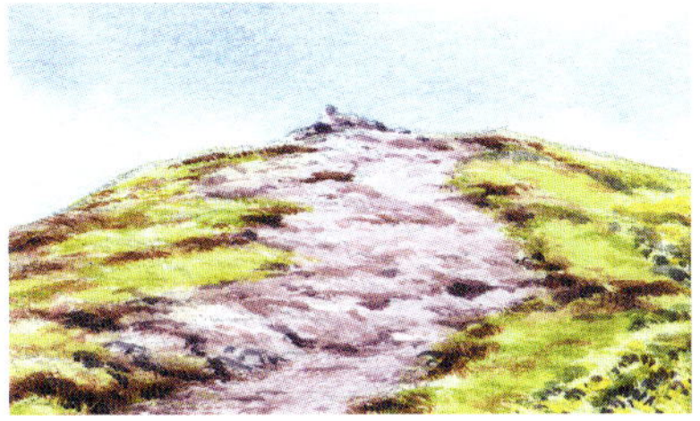

The summit 22/5/09
This was the smallest of all summit illustrations in the Pictorial Guides which didn't give me much clue as from which direction to obtain the reference. The passage of thousands of pairs of boots has eroded the thin topsoil to expose the bare rock but the path does pass just to the right of the top. So therefore I judged the angle of view to be from the south as shown here. It was a 50/50 option.

Bassenthwaite, from Ullock Pike 22/5/09
The aerial view of Bassenthwaite from just north of Ullock Pike's summit which doesn't quite fill the page fully, so AW had to include some skyscape, only the ninth time he added the detail of clouds in this volume. This neatly finished the pages of fell descriptions in Book 5 but uniquely in the seven guides this leads straight on to the personal notes in conclusion without a page break.

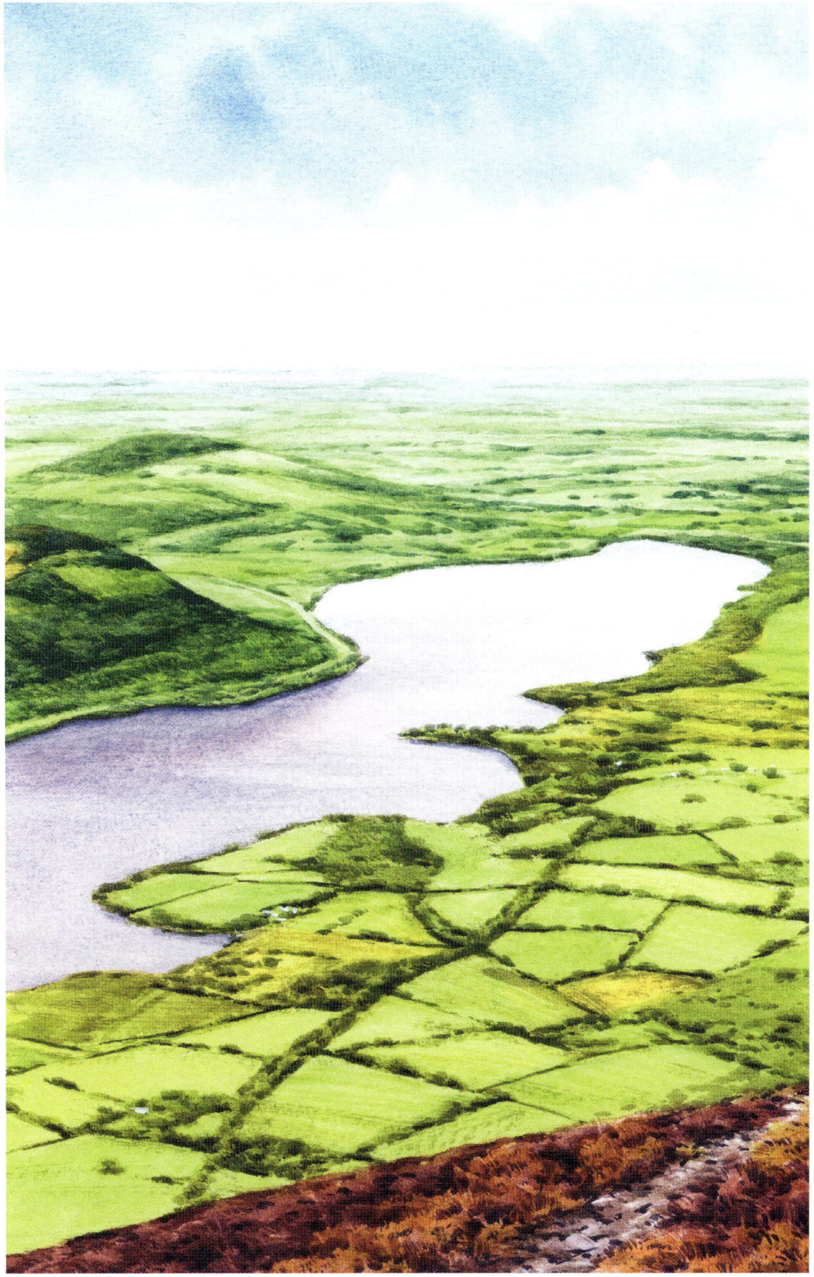

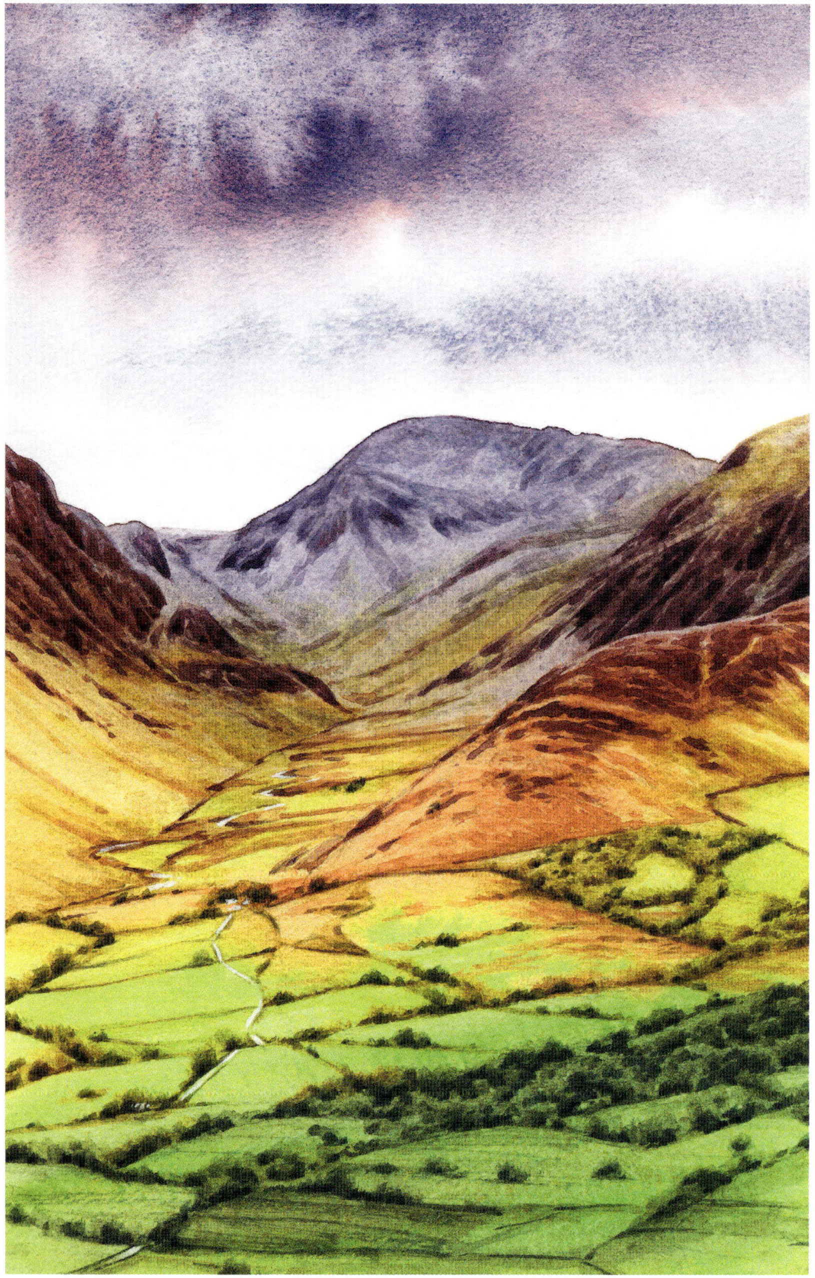

The North Western Fells

On current Ordnance Survey Explorer maps the 29 fells described by Wainwright in this, the sixth book in the series, are all included on a single sheet (OL4). The area is bounded by the River Derwent to the east and River Cocker on the west with their associated bodies of water. The fells contained herein may not be the highest in the Lake District but many are linked to their neighbours by fine ridges and provide some great days out walking.

Frontispiece - Newlands Valley and Dale Head 3/5/09

All but one of the seven frontispieces in the Pictorial Guides are untitled, AW leaving it to the reader to determine the location of the illustrated scene. This view is unique of all of those drawings in that it is of one fell in the guide, Dale Head as seen from another, Causey Pike, or more accurately Rowling End. A fine view it is too with the pastureland of the valley bottom surrounded by high fells on nearly all sides. In completing these sort of sketches which featured the agricultural landscape it was interesting to compare how the field boundaries had changed since Wainwright's day, thanks to the accuracy of his work.

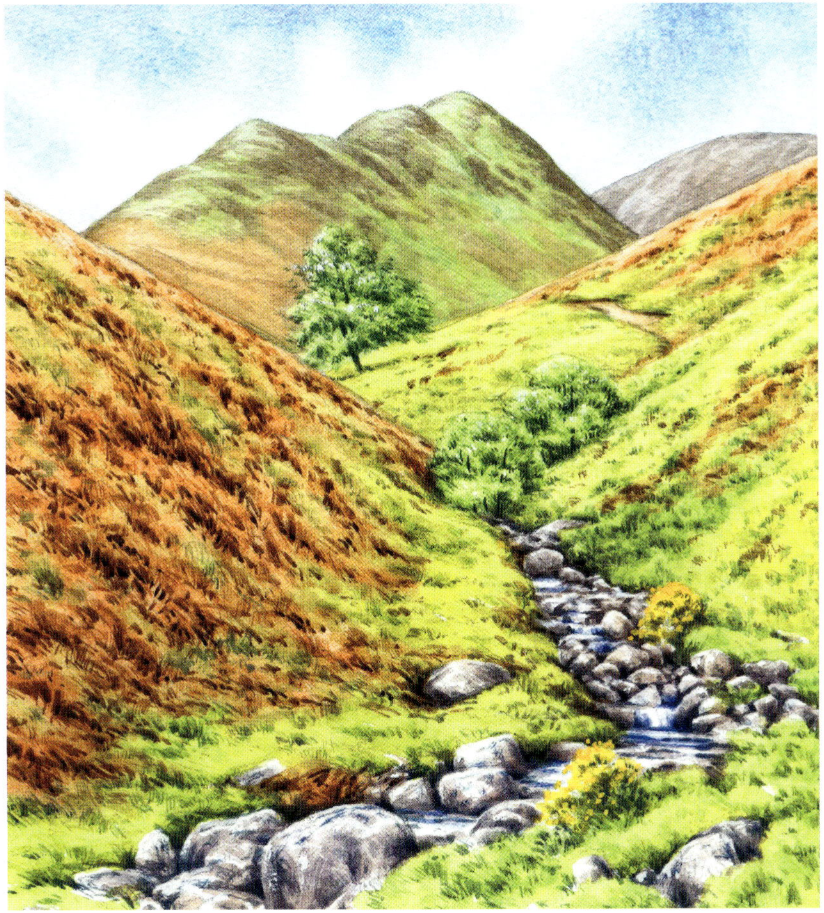

From Rigg Beck 16/5/08
A short distance along the footpath near where the Newlands road crosses Rigg Beck this view of the fell comes into view. It may not be as pronounced as in AW's illustration but it does present itself as a grand shapely fell. What was the small tree in the centre has now grown into a mature specimen of rowan and enabled me to line up the reference precisely.

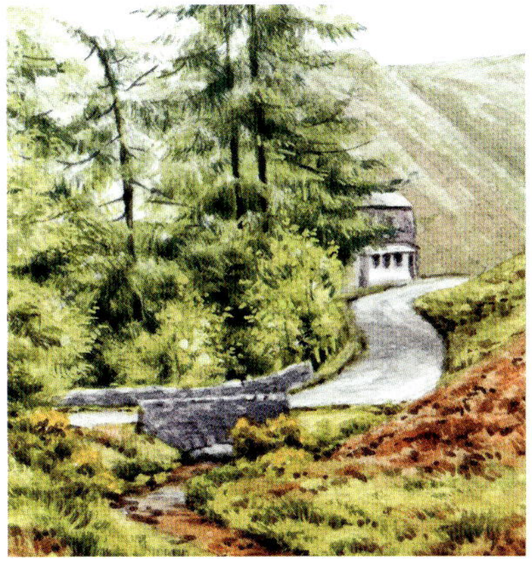

Rigg Beck 16/5/08
Just at the bend in the road stands the famous "Purple House" which was built in 1881 as a hotel. In the later half of the 20th century it provided cheap accommodation (2s 6d for a week) for actors and the like working in Keswick such as Bob Hoskins, Doug Scott, Ted Hughes and Victoria Wood. Fire regulations were then enforced bringing its closure and the place became derelict. A month after I took my reference photograph the wooden building was ironically destroyed by fire and now the site is occupied by a rather impressive private residence.

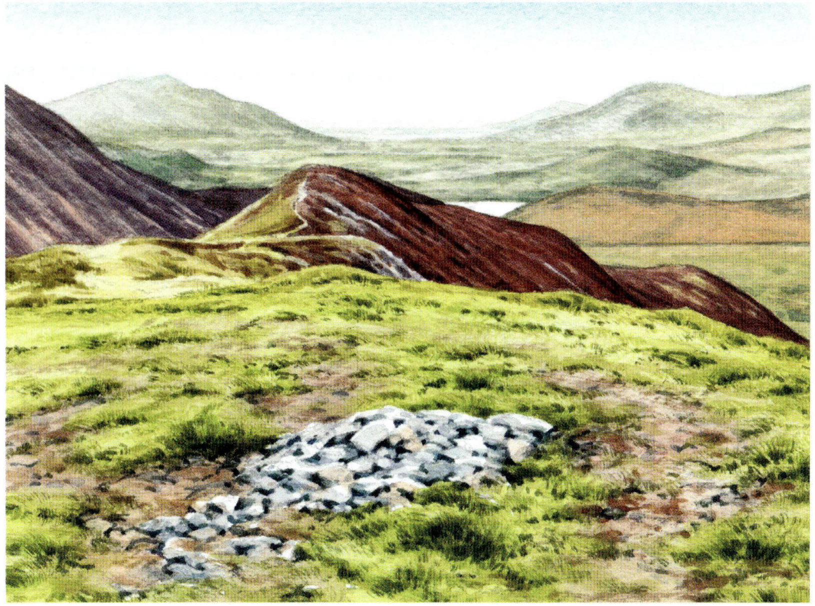

The summit 16/5/08
The view to the north-east beyond the small pile of stones that marks the highest point. Now rough grass has replaced the heather hereabouts.

The main summit from the east summit 16/5/08
Even this lower summit has a small cairn now. Whiteless Pike just peeks through on the right.

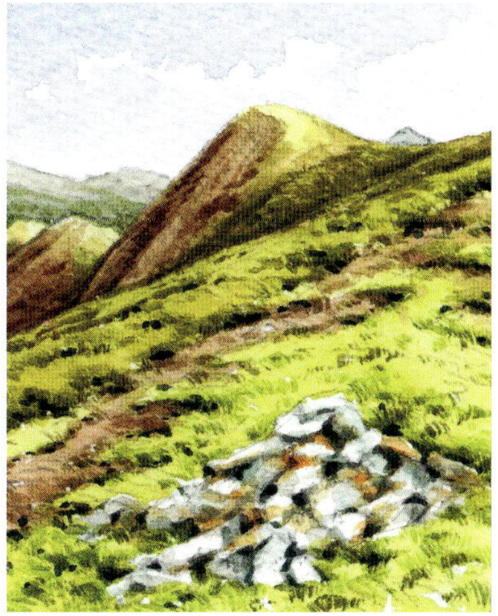

Ard Crags

Originally Wainwright had listed both this and Aikin Knott, at the eastern end of this ridge, as individual fells but only Ard Crags made the final cut. When combined with Knott Rigg this high ridge makes a delightful walk, especially in late summer when the heather is in full bloom.

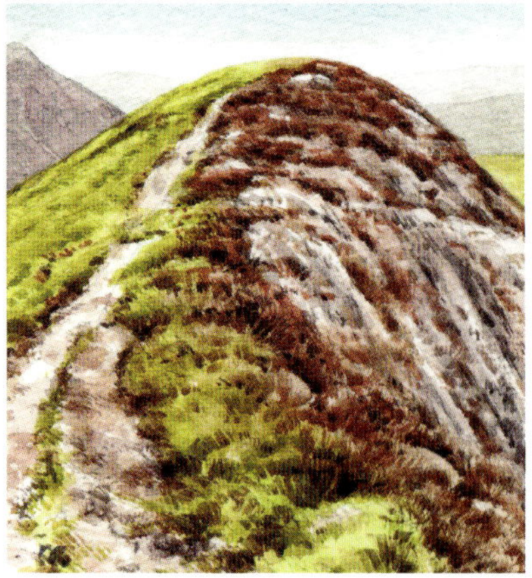

The summit crags 16/5/08
The path runs along the length of this fine ridge, the crags on the right fall away into Keskadale.

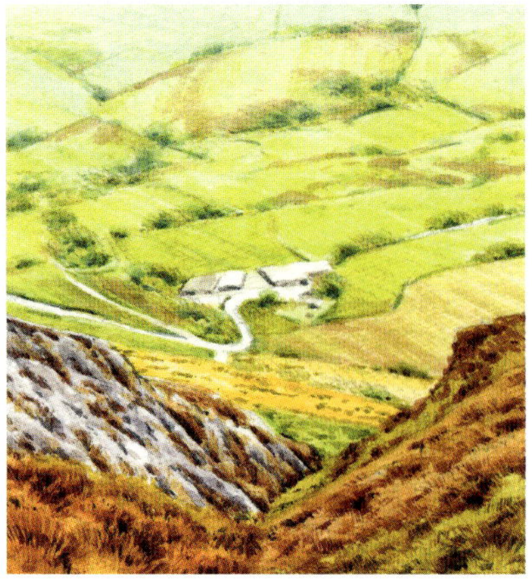

Looking down to Keskadale 16/5/08
Keskadale Farm at the sharp bend in the valley road, 1000' below.

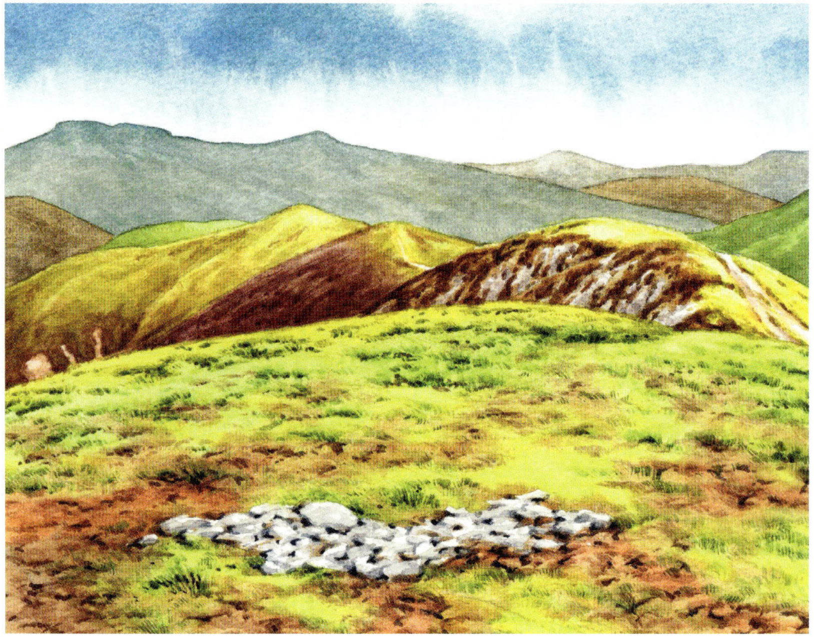

Looking southwest along the ridge to Knott Rigg 16/5/08
Walking between this summit and that of Knott Rigg along the ridge the eye is drawn to the mountains of the High Stile range beyond. The Buttermere valley separates the two groups.

Wainwright Society

On November 9th 2002 the inaugural meeting of The Wainwright Society took place at Ambleside Youth Hostel and over the following years the membership has grown to over 2000, with some notable figures in the field of fellwalking and mountaineering in the ranks and currently with the Chairman, Eric Robson, at the helm. The objectives of the Society are:

To keep alive the fellwalking traditions promoted by Alfred Wainwright through his guidebooks and other publications.

To keep faith with Wainwright's vision of introducing a wider audience to fellwalking and caring for the hills.

To encourage the benefits of association with people sharing those common interests.

To contribute to public debate on issues affecting landscape quality, and quality of life in upland areas of Britain and particularly the Lake District.

To foster and enhance Alfred Wainwright's standing in the field of long distance footpath walking.

Over the past 15 years the Society has become a major fund raiser with a different beneficiary each year. Over £100,000 (with matched funding) has been raised for groups and projects such as Mountain Rescue Teams, Lake District Mountain Rescue Search Dogs, The Calvert Trust, Animal Rescue Cumbria and Cumbria Wildlife Trust. Significant one off donations have also been made to other causes including flood appeals in Cumbria. The monies for these donations has been raised through various means including a successful calendar which has been produced since 2010.

Information boards at either end of the Coast to Coast long distance path as well as waymarking signs along the route have been funded by the Wainwright Society, as has the new iconic view indicator on Orrest Head in conjunction with Windermere Town Council.

Throughout the year the Society holds events such as a Memorial Lecture and group walks as well as producing a quarterly magazine, Footsteps. Being in the 21st century the Wainwright Society has an informative website and forum as well as a presence on social media. The Society has a comprehensive 214 Completers list and those who have achieved this goal can also obtain an official Completer's Certificate and badge.

To find out more about the organisation visit the website at www.wainwright.org.uk or by contacting the secretary at:
The Wainwright Society, The New House, Station Road, Bishops Lydeard, Taunton, Somerset TA4 3BU

aw The Wainwright Society

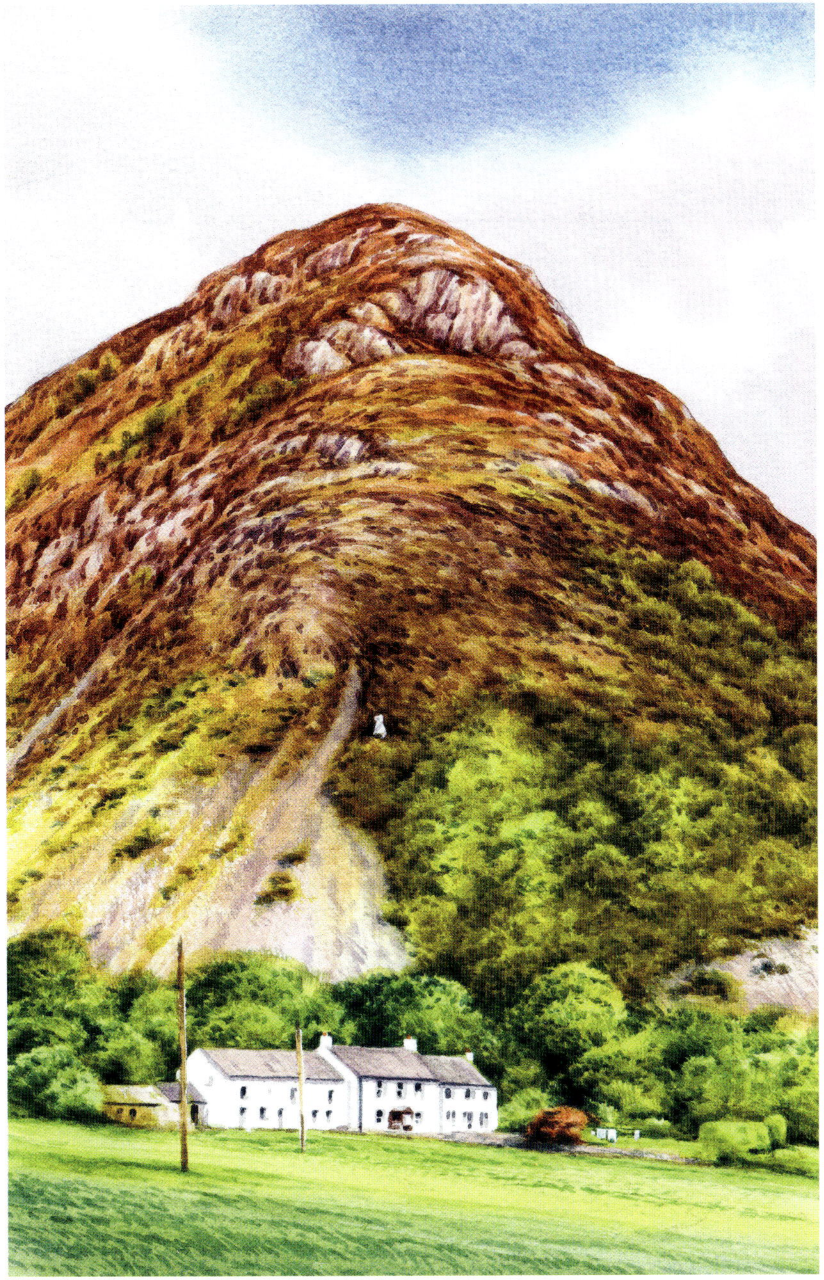

The Bishop of Barf 23/7/09
The steep path now passes to the left of the Bishop and not to the right as in the original guidebook. As a consequence this point below the Bishop is now overgrown with dense gorse making the obtaining of this reference rather difficult.

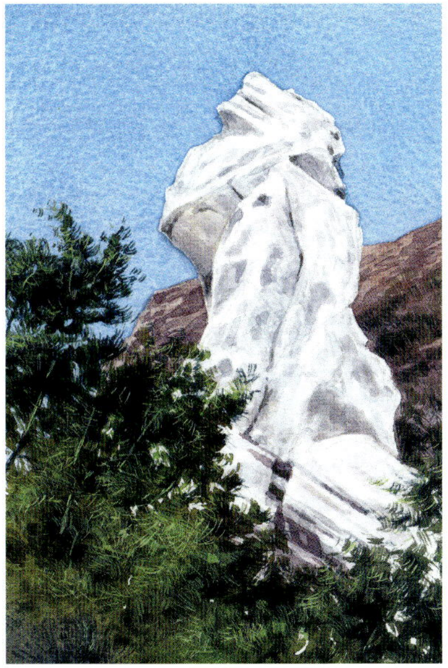

Barf

Whilst driving west along the A66 near Thornthwaite, Barf gives the appearance of a formidable fell with steep slopes made of scree, crags and heather. This is its bold front, from other approaches Barf is more of a gentle hill connected to Lord's Seat to the west by a pleasant rising ridge.

From the main road near Beckstones 23/7/09
The vegetation on the slopes of the fell changes from woodland and scrub on the lower sections to rich heather and exposed rock nearer the top. The Bishop is easily seen in this colour version.

The small rockface 23/7/09
Some of the forest in this area has been felled and the gap in the rocks where the path went is now more clearly seen. Due to the clearing of some trees an alternative path now bypasses this section, below and to the right.

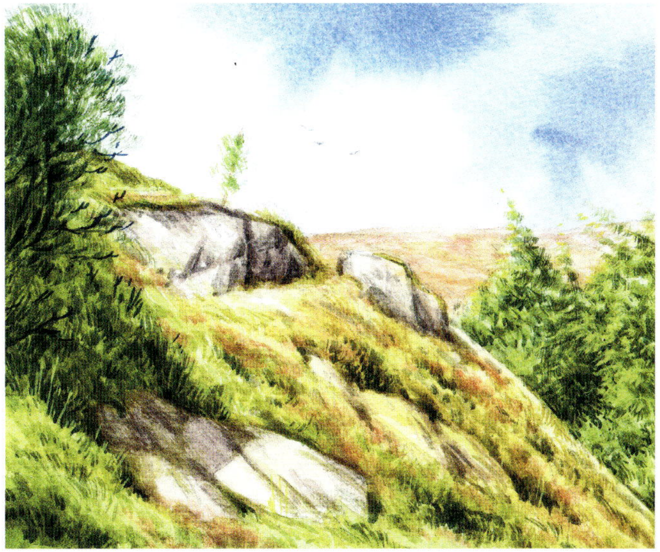

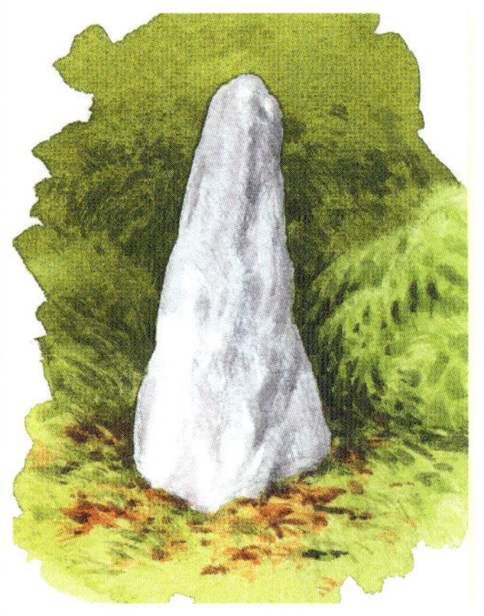

The Clerk 23/7/09

Sheltered in the woods the Clerk now also has a fresh coat of paint. He stands at about 3′ high and appears to be a natural if somewhat unusual column of rock.

The summit 23/7/09

The summit is devoid of a cairn of any substance. The turf is now worn away to reveal more of the underlying rock. This summit, or more precisely a point just to the north-east of it, provides excellent views of Bassenthwaite Lake and the Skiddaw massif, a great place to linger on a fine day.

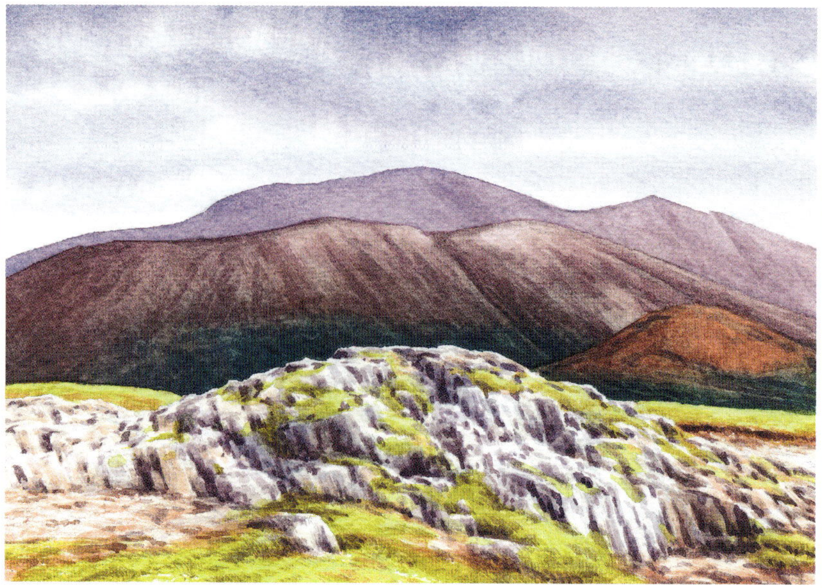

The Bishop - rear view 23/7/09

Standing on a steep scree slope of loose slate proved a challenge whilst lining up the elements in AW's illustration. Drawing or painting this scene on site would be almost impossible. The Bishop is now in a full white coat. At his feet the slate has been built up as a platform or pulpit.

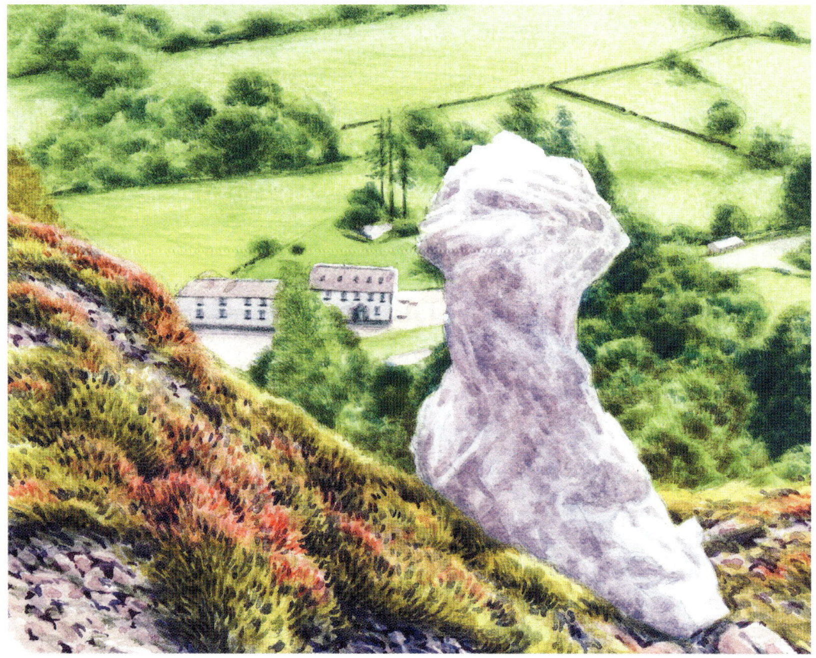

The Bishop of Barf

Local folklore has it that in 1783 the Bishop of Derry, as part of a drunken wager, tried to reach the summit of Barf on horseback. At a point near to the pinnacle of rock (left) the horse stumbled and both fell to their deaths, and were consequently buried at the foot of the slope near the smaller rock, The Clerk (top left). However, in reality at the time there were two Bishops of Derry, one Catholic and one Protestant, neither were involved in any such incident and both lived on to well past 1783. It is more likely that this was a myth perhaps fabricated by the Landlord of the Swan Inn to entice visitors to his establishment. The face of the pillar was painted white as far back as the 1880s which made it more visible from the hotel and gave it the appearance of a bishop in robes. Today it is repainted when needed, back and front, by Keswick Mountain Rescue Team. The Swan Inn is now private residences.

The top of Barf 23/7/09

Heather covers most of the upper reaches of the fell and now the path which links this top and that of Lord's Seat can clearly be seen working its way through the small hillocks.

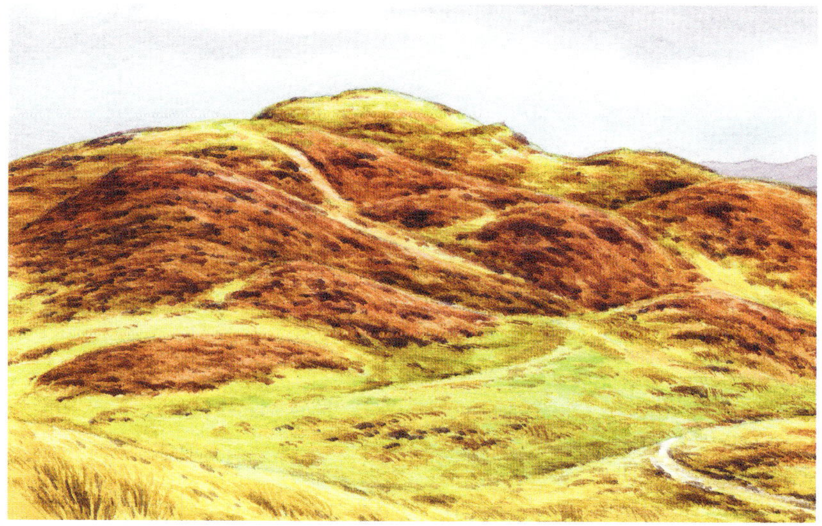

Barf, south side, from a forest road in Beckstones Plantation

23/7/09

It took some time to explore the forest roads that pass through the plantation to find this precise spot. Obviously the pile of logs were moved long ago so lining up the fell to the distant landscape was the only solution, made even more difficult in the fact that AW missed off some of the edge to Bassenthwaite Lake.

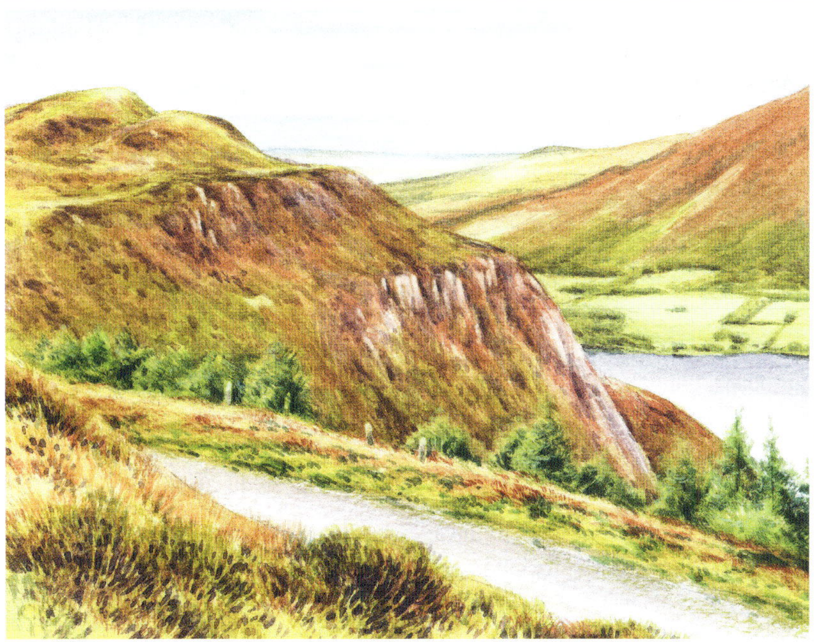

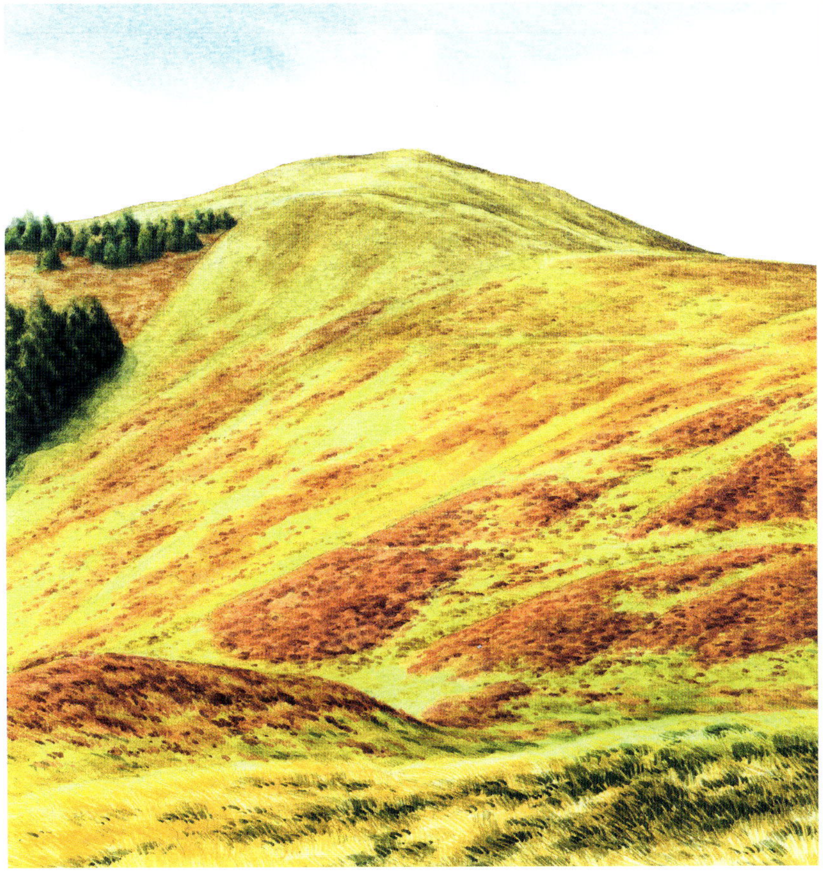

Lord's Seat from Barf 23/7/09

The slopes of fell are a mixture of grass and heather and in this view they fall down to Beckstones Gill on the left. The route to Lord's Seat from here sweeps round to the right and then up the easy rise to the summit.

Barf, north side, from a dead forest above Wythop Wood

3/5/11 (bottom right)

Of all the sketches required for this project this one is perhaps the one that provided the biggest surprise. The title in the Pictorial Guide is somewhat vague so I headed up though the forest from Woodend Brow with the intention of finding the location by lining up the top of Barf in the landscape. This area is totally pathless and nowhere near a route in the guide, this was obviously AW just exploring. Imagine my surprise after some time of wandering over the rough terrain when I came across this fallen tree, close comparison between the drawing in the book and the decaying timber confirmed that it was in fact the tree in his illustration, more decayed but still identifiable after fifty years. The upright trees in his drawing on the left and right have all but gone.

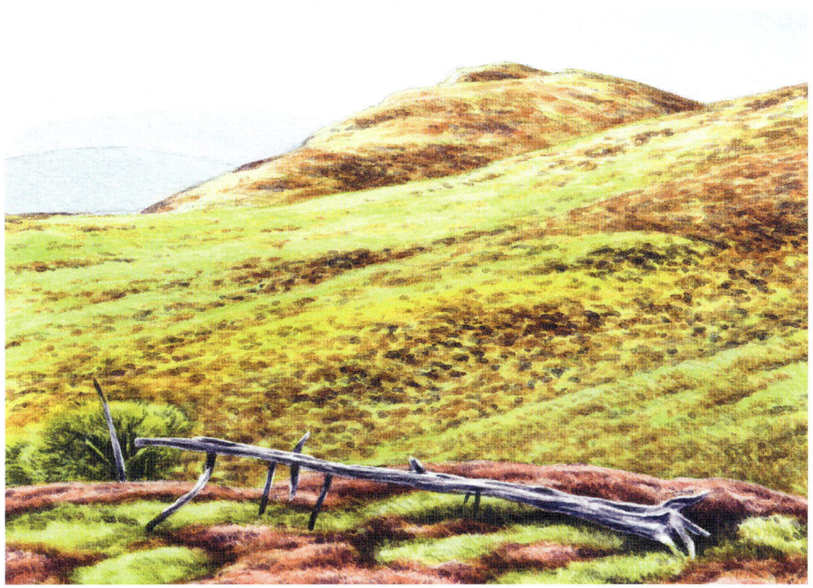

Barrow

Visitors to the village of Braithwaite with a couple of hours spare could use their time well by taking the easy north-east ridge of this fell to its summit. Then, by going on to Barrow Door before returning to the village a delightful circular route can be achieved.

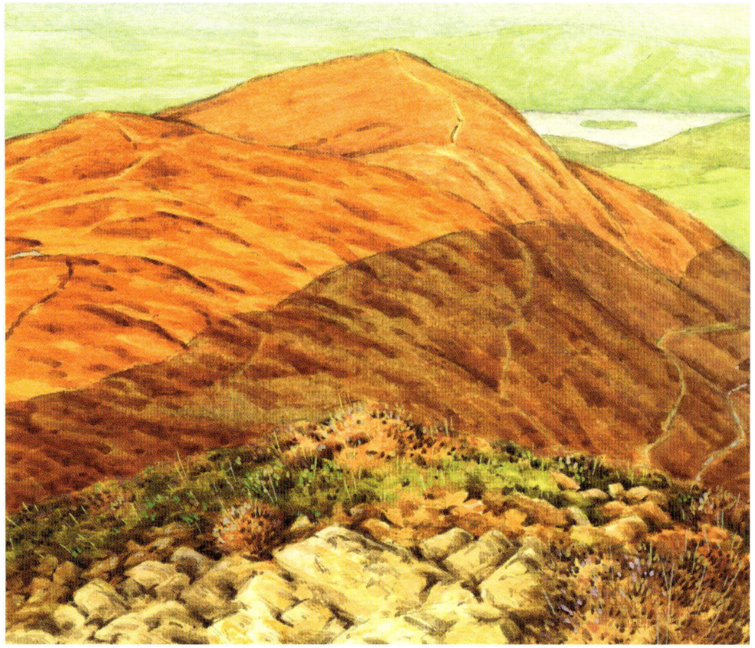

From Outerside 10/9/14
The last "official" reference required for the project at 5.30 in the evening, 49 years to the day after AW obtained his last informative details on Starling Dodd.

From Newlands Beck 14/5/08
The path near Little Braithwaite that runs alongside the beck.

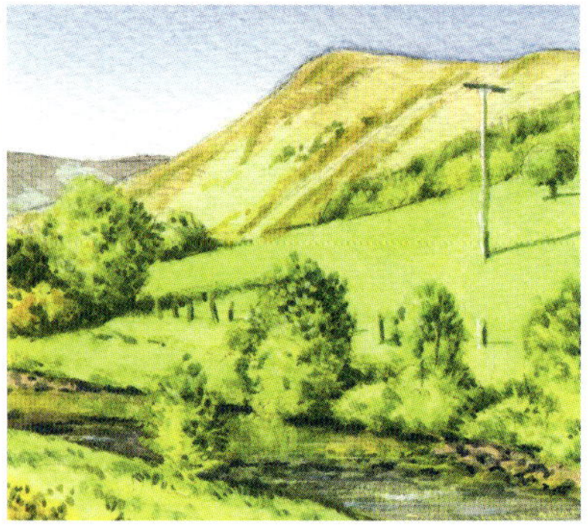

The old level 3/5/09
Found close to the path just above Stonycroft Bridge.

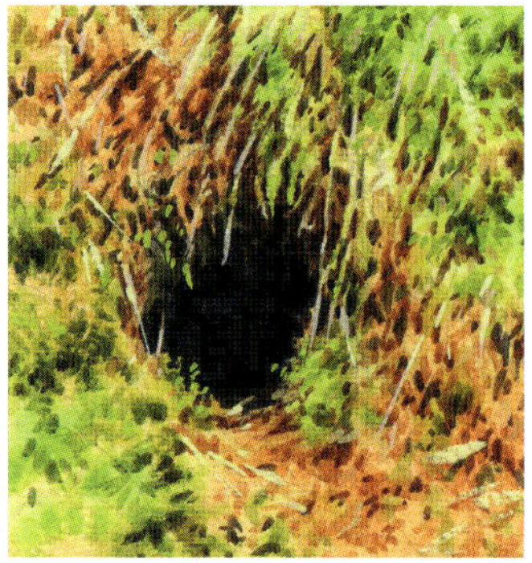

Barrow Gill

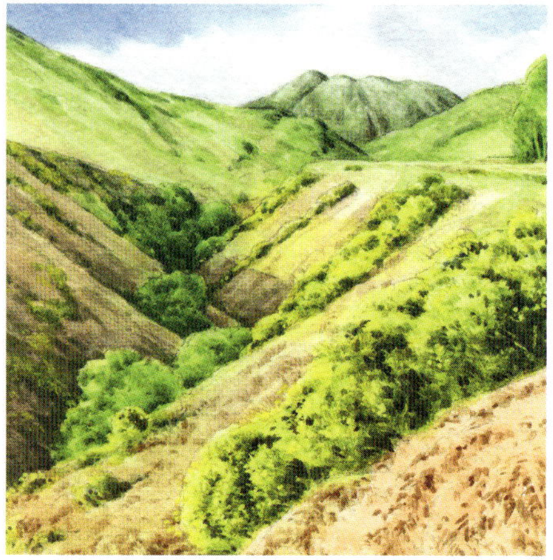

Looking up the gill 12/5/08
The ravine with Barrow Door and Causey Pike at the top. The gorse which thrives here was in full bloom on my visit.

Looking down the gill 12/5/08
This view into the deep gorge is seen from just off the path near Barrow Door.

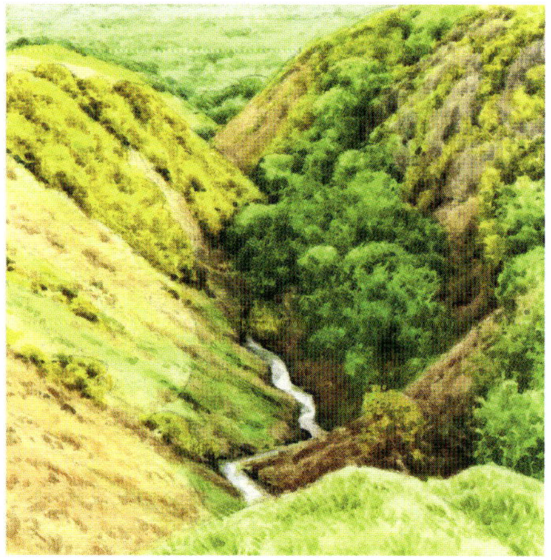

The summit 12/5/08
The turf has been now worn down to bare earth and rock with no permanent cairn to mark the highest point.

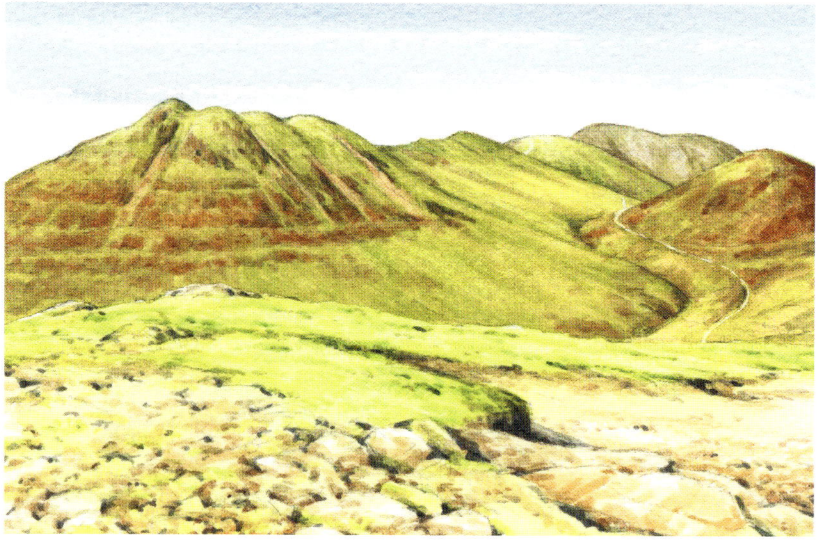

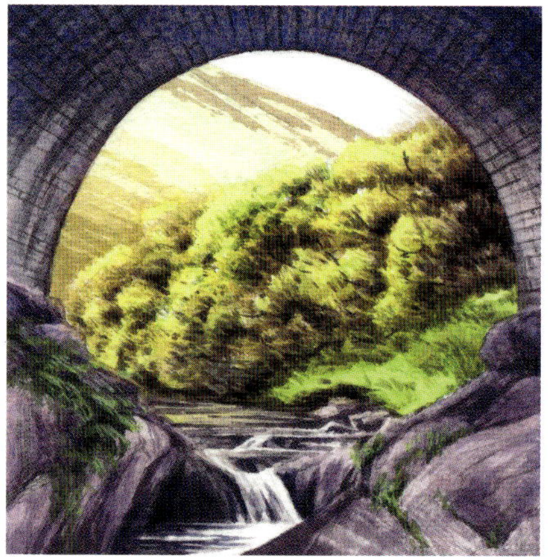

Under Stonycroft Bridge 16/5/08
Thick gorse has overgrown the dry watercut on the far bank through the arch. This bridge carries the main road from Braithwaite to Buttermere.

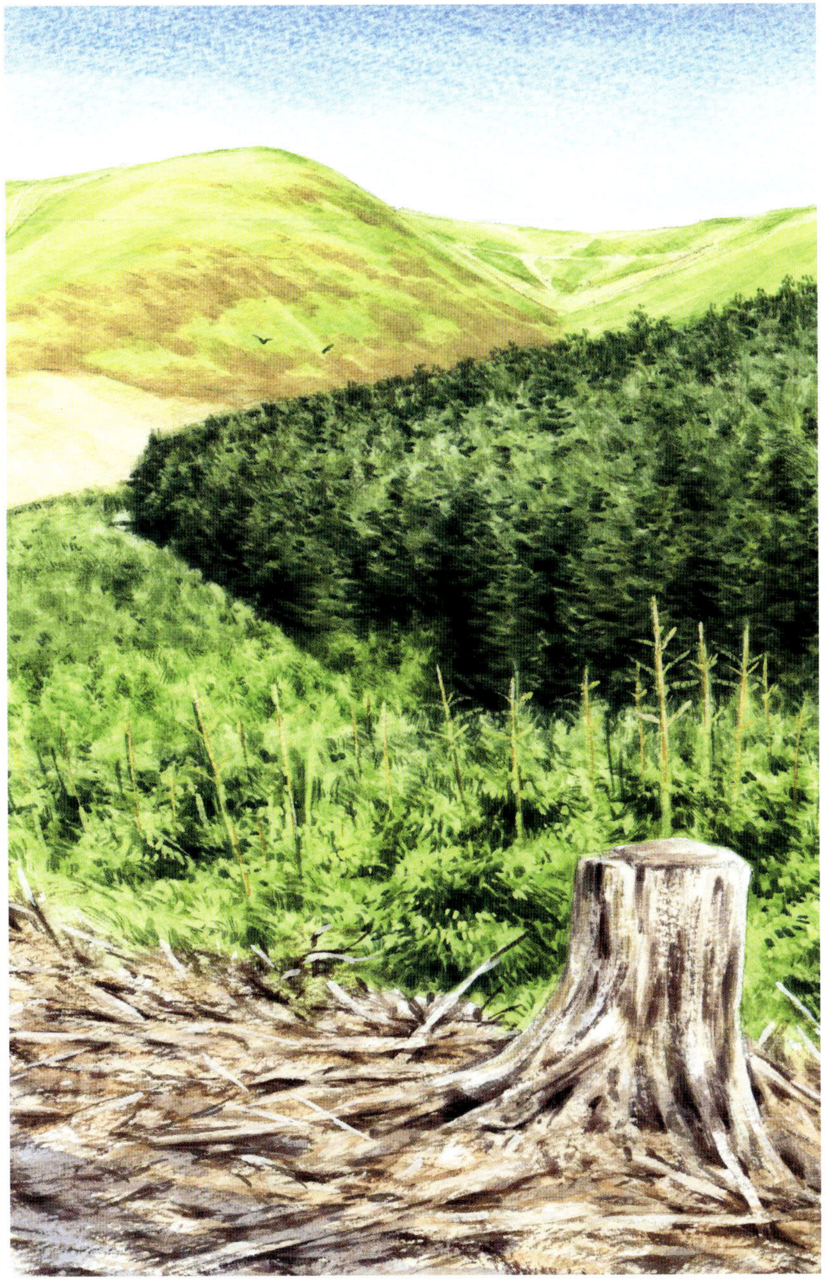

Broom Fell

I would guess that most visits to the summit of Broom Fell are accomplished as part of a route that has included nearby fells in the Whinlatter range. Direct ascents to the top of this fell can be made but they are unexciting and achieve little unless of course the walker is ticking off the fells in that manner. At least the fine summit column now provides this fell with a feature of quality.

From Aiken Plantation 13/5/08
The upright stone in AW's drawing could not be found but by referring to the pattern of the forestry blocks I was able to find the right location, and conveniently a stump of a felled tree provided a similar foreground feature.

The summit 11/5/08
The end of the old wall has not only been used as a ready supply of stones for the pillar but also as a basis for a low wind shelter. A new post and wire fence crosses the high ground in a north-south line.

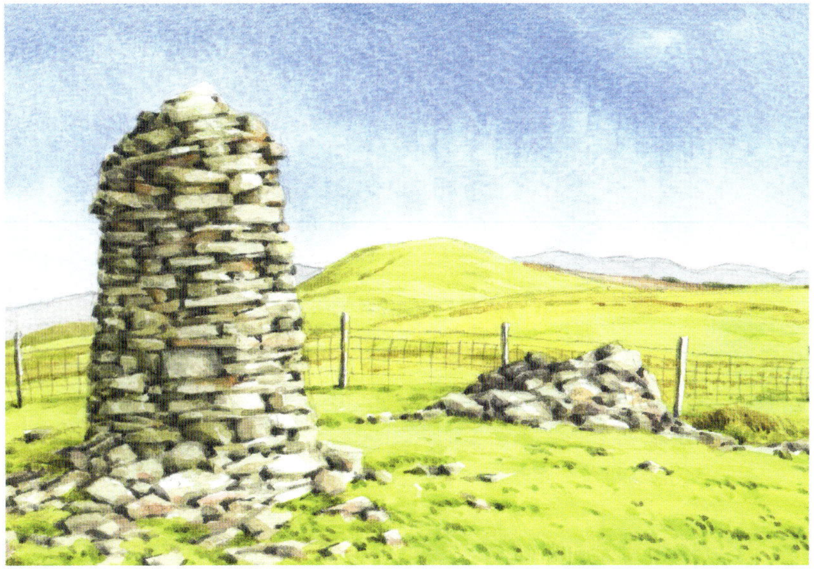

The summit 11/5/08
This tall pillar was built some time after AW's visit, it was constructed by John Lennox and the late Raymond Steel after they completed the Wainwright round in 1981. The materials came from the nearby derelict wall but in fact the highest point is 150 yards to the south-east of here.

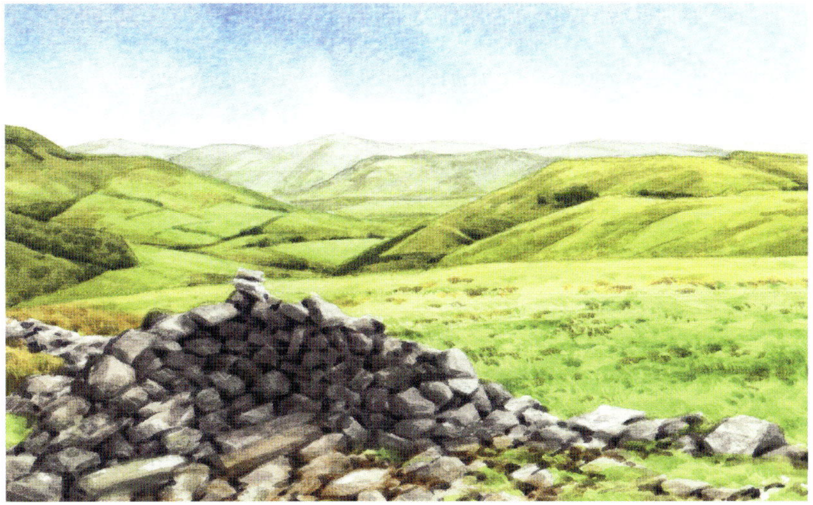

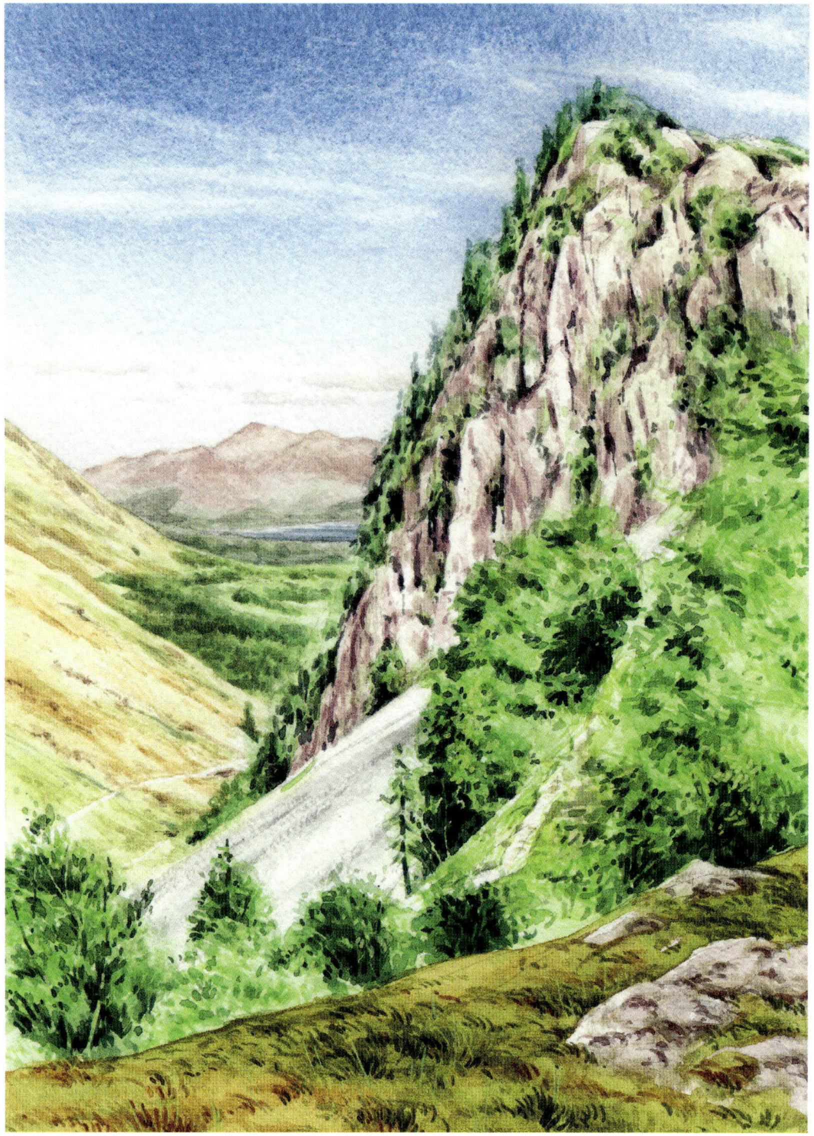

From the south 14/5/08
Wainwright's illustration captured not only the craggy face of the fell but also it featured the distant Derwentwater and the Skiddaw range. He took this view from the top enclosure on the route from Rosthwaite.

Quarries and caves of Castle Crag

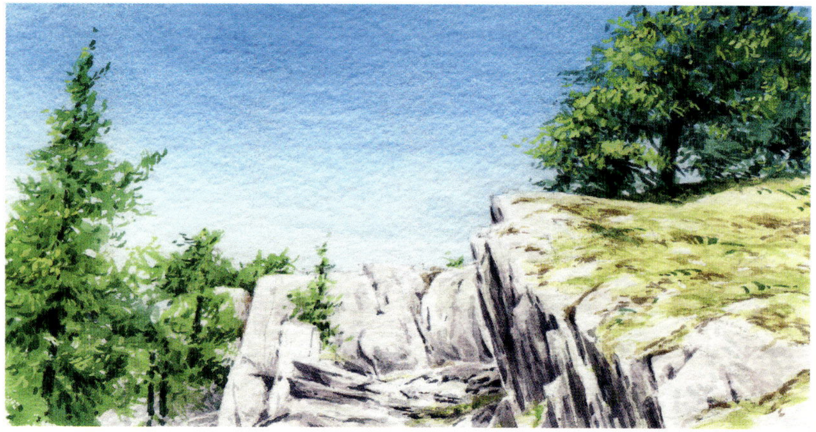

The summit quarry 14/5/08
In his illustration AW left out the lower details of the quarry including a neat dry stone wall. These days the quarry is filled with standing slabs of slate, erected by many walkers, just for fun.

Castle Crag

This is the only fell of the 214 with a height of less than 1000'. AW calculated it at 985' but it is now recognised as being only 951'. Castle Crag on the old 1 inch map did not have a trigonometrical point so that explains not only the reason why the height was only approximate in the Pictorial Guide, but also why the fell was not on his original list of fells. I would speculate that with the notoriety of Millican Dalton and his caves, other points of interest and the fact that AW classed this as "*the loveliest square mile in Lakeland*" Castle Crag easily earned its place in the guide.

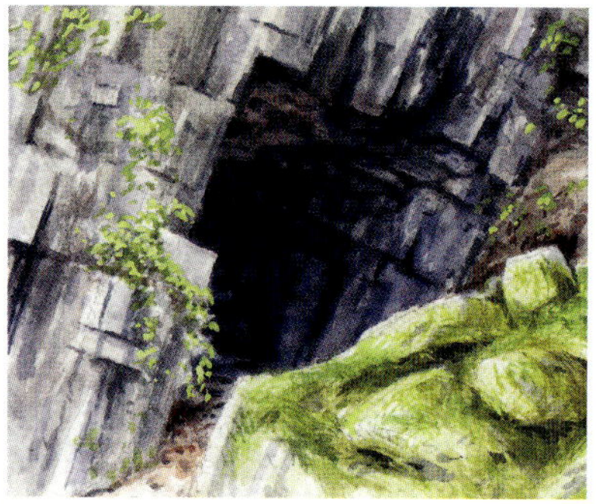

The attic 14/5/08
The opening to the higher cave where Millican Dalton slept whilst in residence (see page 251).

Millican's Cave 14/5/08
This is the larger cave entrance, just to the left of the Attic. Several of the trees featured in AW's drawing are now gone.

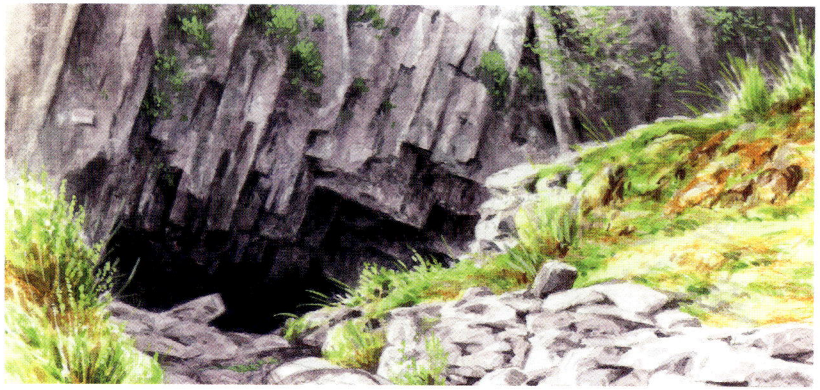

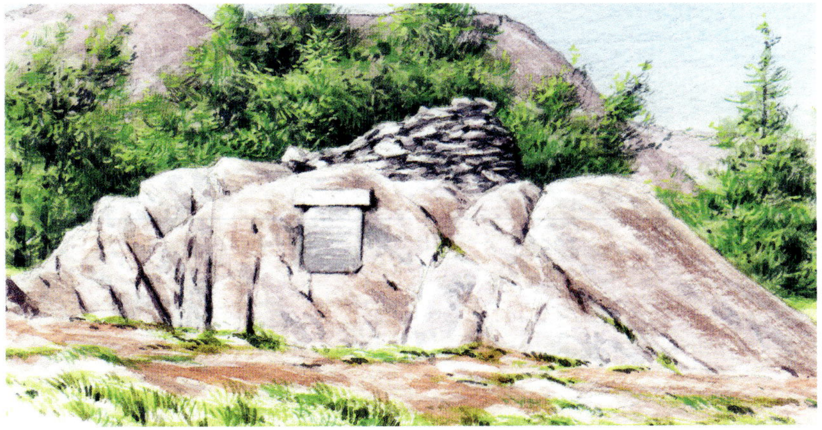

The summit 14/5/08

The round flat topped cairn that once sat on top of the summit platform of rock is now just a low wall not even making a full circle. A simple service is held here each Remembrance Sunday in front of the war memorial which is fixed to the rock.

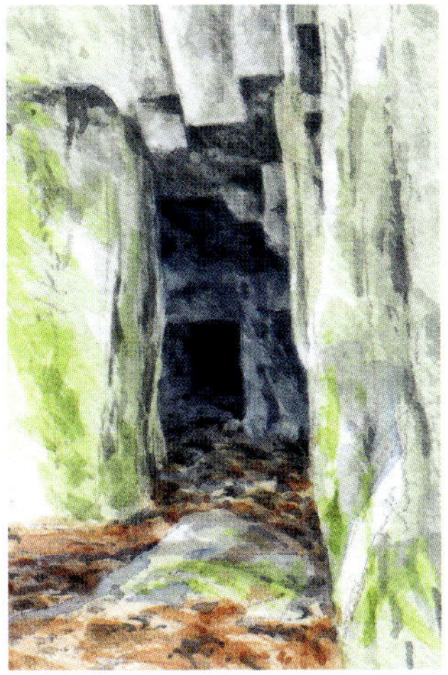

An old level 14/5/08

This level can be found a short distance from the stone shelter. Like all of these levels, care must be taken if venturing in to the old workings.

A typical stone store 14/5/08

This small building remains intact a few yards from the Rosthwaite route. It possibly served another purpose than a shelter as its proportions are diminutive.

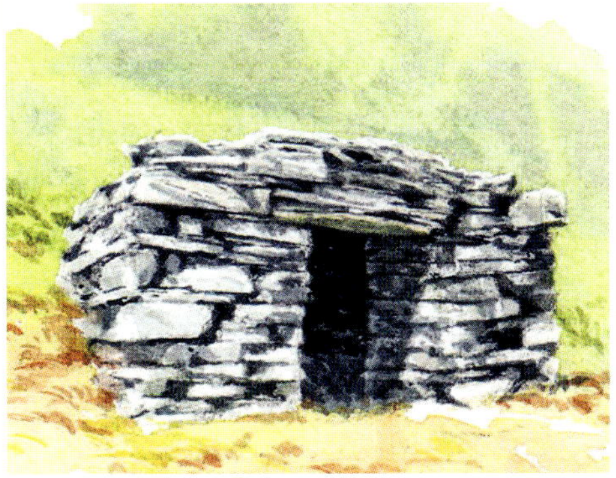

Millican Dalton and other men of the woods.

The caves on the eastern side of Castle Crag amongst the old slate quarries are a connection to one of the district's most famous historic characters, Millican Dalton. Born in 1867 at Nenthead near Alston into a Quaker family he was educated at Brookfield School, Wigton but after his father died the family moved down to Middlesex and then Essex. He and his brothers were adventurous types, spending time outdoors climbing trees and camping. Millican did have to gain employment which he did, as an insurance clerk in London. At the age of 36 though he turned his back on this boring life and went to Buckinghamshire where he built a rudimentary hut which he resided in during the winter. In the summer he headed to the Lake District and at first camped at High Lordore but later made his base in the caves on Castle Crag, returning to his hut when the weather turned colder. Furnishing his den with items picked up from the local rubbish tip at Grange and other locations he was a master of recycling. Millican lived frugally but did like his perks, Woodbine cigarettes, strong coffee and his own baked bread. It is a myth to think of him as a recluse though, he would often be seen out and about in Keswick and the local area. He took the title "The Professor of Adventure" and guided interested fee-paying parties on climbing, camping and rafting trips which often ended up around his camp fire at the caves for evenings of stimulating stories and conversation. He caused a stir by taking young ladies on these trips but he treated them as equals and with courtesy. His favourite local climbing ground was Dove's Nest Crags (see page 188) but he regularly climbed Napes Needle and on his fiftieth ascent he took with him the makings of a fire and brewed coffee on the very top of the pinnacle, he was also one of the early members of the Fell and Rock Climbing Club. His lifestyle was funded by his guiding services as well as sales of rucksacks, tents and other outdoor kit which he manufactured using basic equipment but to his own tried and tested designs. In total he spent 50 years guiding until he retired at the age of 75 even though he was still fit and nimble. He continued to spend the summers in Borrowdale and escaped to the warmer climes of Buckinghamshire for winter. Millican continued in this simple way of life until the winter of 1946 when accidently his hut burnt down and he resorted to living in a tent at the tender age of 79. The weather was too much for him though, being one of the coldest of the century and he fell ill, only to be admitted into Amersham Hospital where he died on 5th February 1947.

Dalton wasn't the only person to live rough in the district. In the 1860s George Smith, an artist by profession, had travelled down from Scotland and took up residence on the slopes of Dodd. His home was a simple affair, a structure made of branches and ferns build against a crag but he certainly wasn't as organised as Dalton. He became known as The Skiddaw Hermit and had meagre possessions. He was a competent portrait artist though and he would paint local farmers and landlords in exchange for liquor, he also did character assessments at local fairs by feeling the lumps on customer's heads. Smith's drinking got the better of him and he became a nuisance and left the area, eventually ending back up in Scotland where he died in an asylum in 1876.

More recently, but not of the same noteriety of Smith and Dalton was a Yorkshireman and former sailor called Fred Leake, he set up home for a time amongst the boulders in Great Wood under Walla Crag in the 1950s. He was a keen fellwalker and was well read, storing his books carefully to keep them dry. Later he moved to be nearer Falcon Crag where an overhanging rock gave him more protection from the elements and only in the worst of the weather would he take refuge in nearby Keswick.

No doubt characters like these would be frowned upon or moved on today but there must be some of us who would happily live out our lives in some quiet cave on a fellside, whether we would survive long without the trappings of modern day life is a different matter.

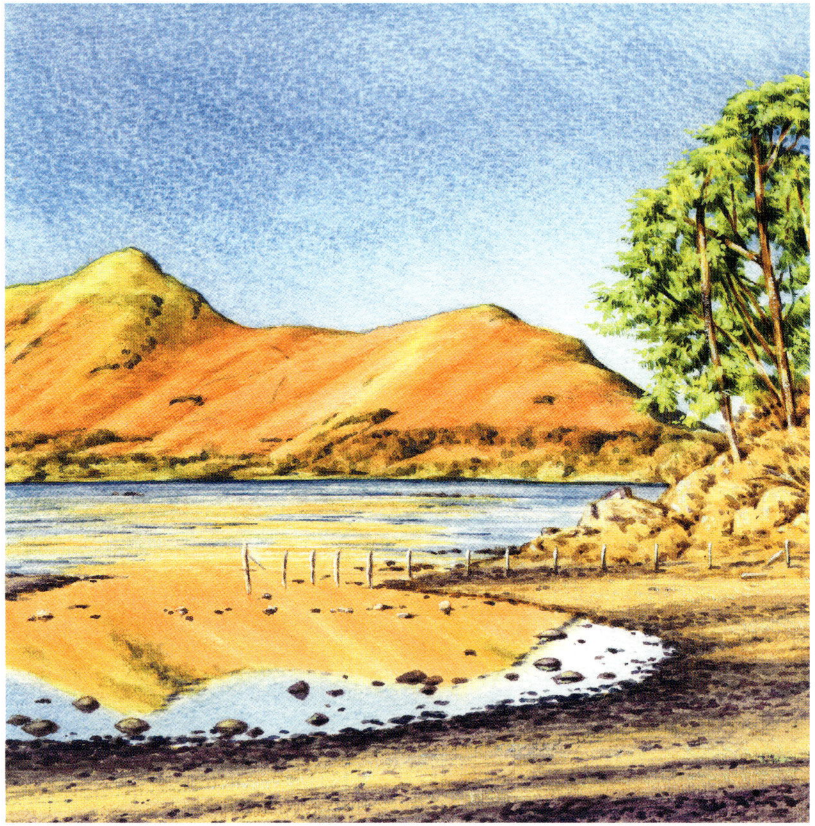

From Derwentwater 7/3/10
The water level of the lake was low on this visit of mine, early one morning in March, in comparison to AW's drawing. The Scots pines of Friar's Crag, the popular view point, are on the right.

Catbells

It is debatable as to which is the most popular fell of all in the Lake District, Helvellyn may just take the title but this one, Catbells, might be a contender. Its accessibility from Keswick and the ease of ascent up the north ridge means that it will be rare to have the fell all to yourself. It would seem that the name should properly be two words: Cat Bells.

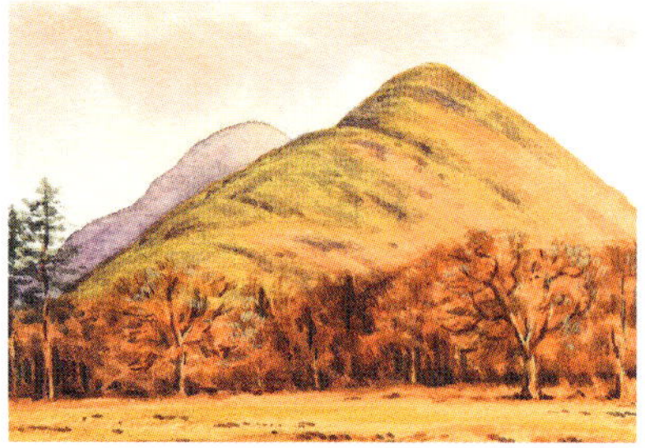

From the Portinscale path 14/3/12
AW simplified the shape of the twin peaks of the fell for his drawing giving them an almost perfect pyramidical shape. This is how they actually appear from the same location.

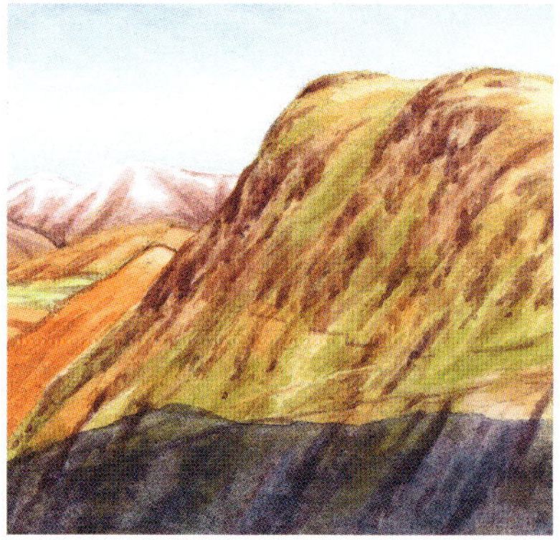

From Yewthwaite Combe 10/2/09
Aligning the view correctly in comparison to the illustration in the guide required some wandering on my part in the upper section of the combe. There is no path here, just steep ground.

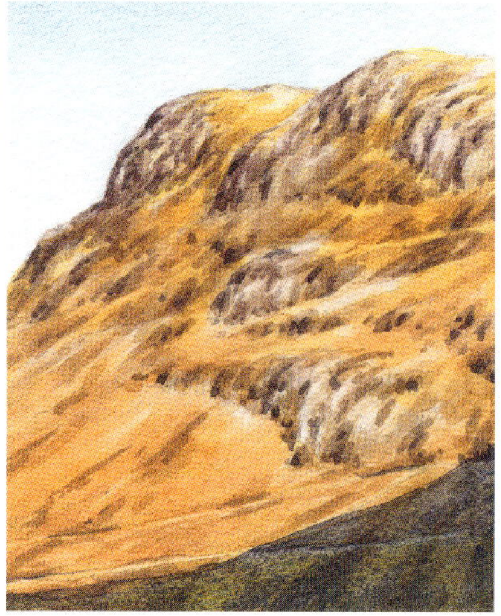

The crags of Mart Bield 10/2/09
Looking up to the crags from near Brunt Crag. Mart Bield is just south of the summit of the fell.

Workings at the Old Brandley Mine 10/2/09
The tree that hangs over the shaft with the two entrances is still there (below) and close by the mine level can be found with ease (right), both are near the path on the lower eastern slopes of the fell.

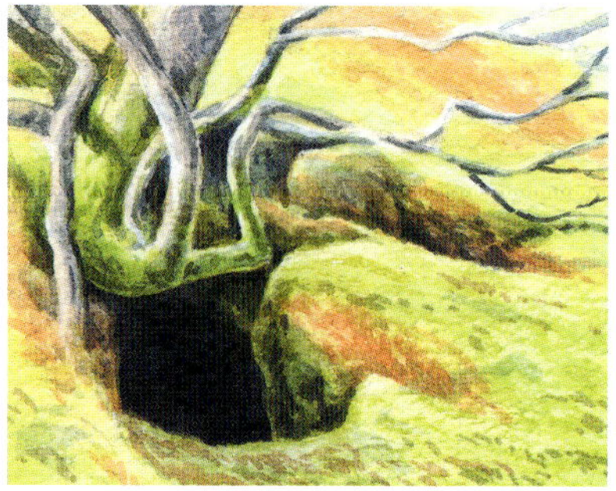

Caves and Caverns of Catbells

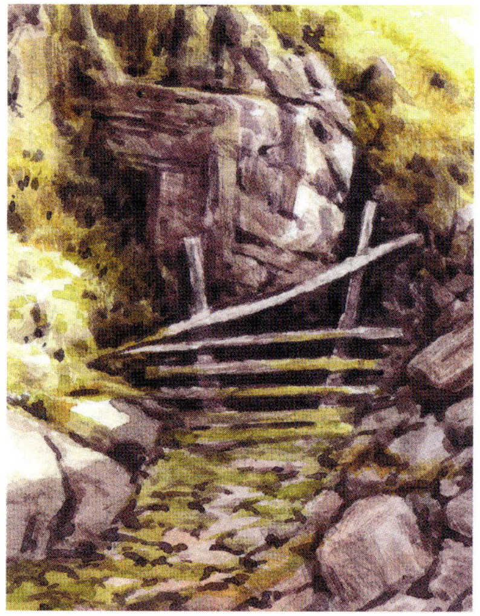

A dangerous hole at Yewthwaite Mine 10/2/09
This deep vertical shaft now has a rather flimsy wooden frame across the entrance. A stone that I dropped into the blackness fell a long way before coming to rest.

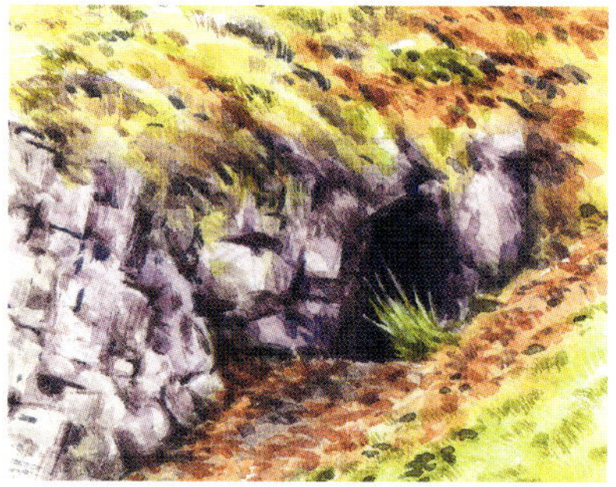

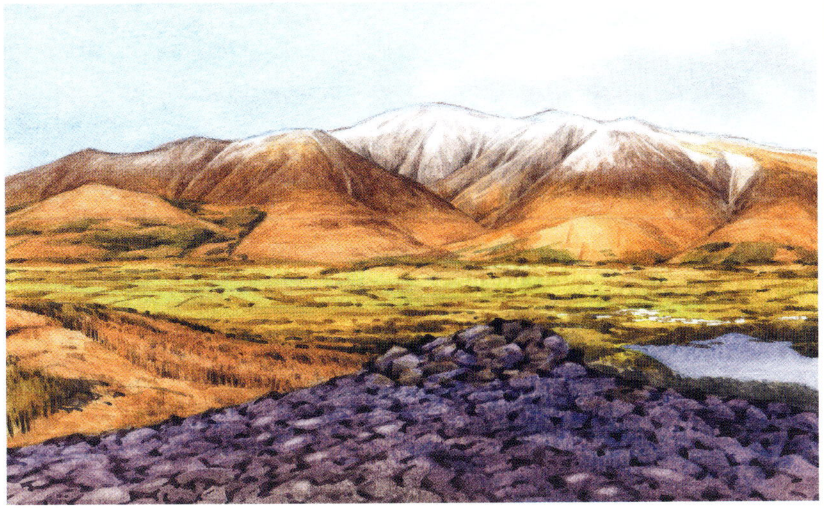

The summit 10/2/09

On this occasion a small cairn adorned the summit but more often than not there is just bare bedrock. It is a popular summit, one that families can achieve together.

Maiden Moor from Hause Gate 10/2/09

The sun bursts over Bull Crag on this winter's afternoon. The cairn here marks the crossing of the paths.

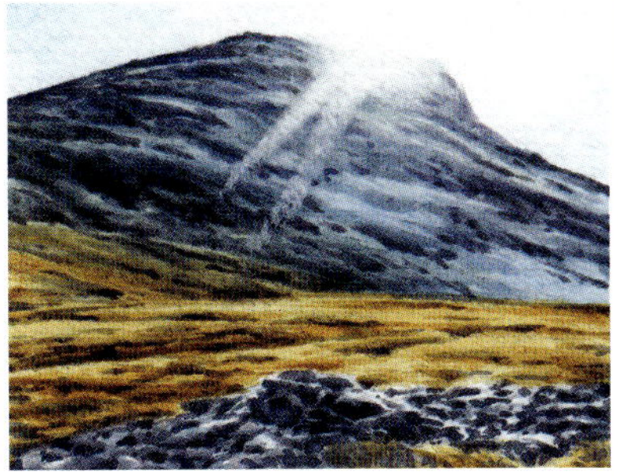

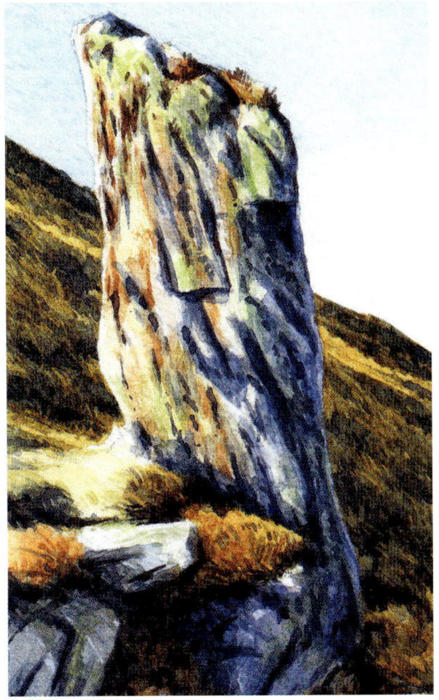

Catbells Pinnacle 10/2/09

This chest high tooth of rock can be visited by descending a hundred and fifty feet or so east from the summit down the steep pathless slope. It stands alone on the fell side.

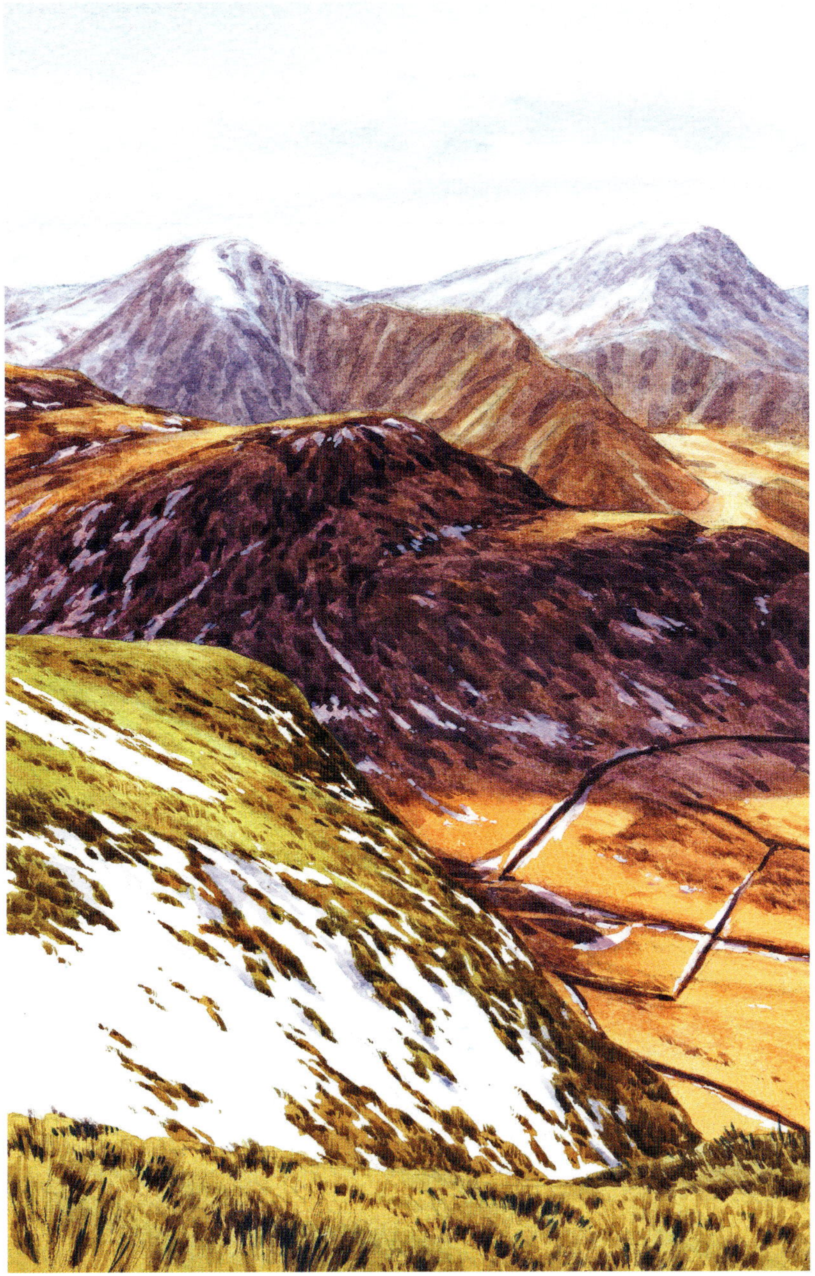

Hindscarth and Robinson from Catbells 10/2/09

My visit to Catbells on this day, during which I obtained most of the required references, was planned so that I could acquire this image in winter conditions not unlike that in Wainwright's illustration. The sun was not in the ideal position but at least the snow covering the high fells was adequate for my purpose. The exact location is just above the crags of Mart Bield, not far from the summit.

Causey Pike

The long undulating ridge of Causey Pike's summit looks similar to the knuckles of a clenched fist giving it a rather distinctive profile from most directions. The fell is one of those that make up the popular Coledale round and the views from its summit of other lakeland hills are extensive in all directions.

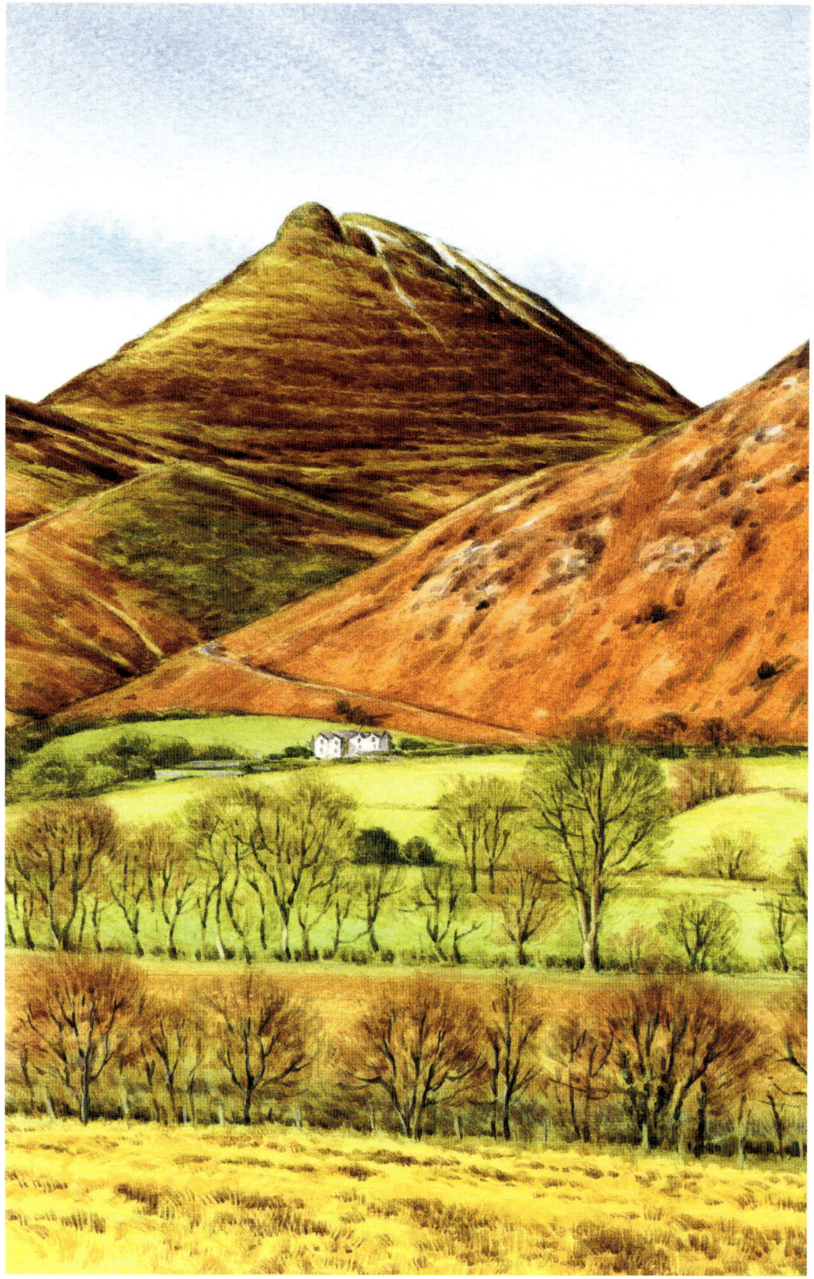

From Swinside 22/3/07
On the road that leads down from Swinside to Stair this scene comes into view. There was only the slight hint of snow on the top of the fell on this day.

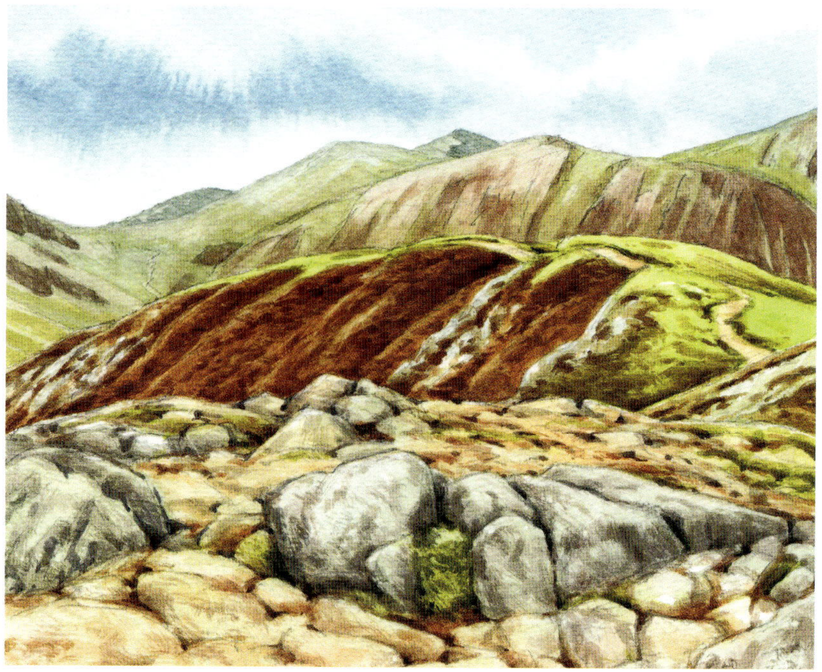

The summit 12/5/08
Many pairs of boots have crossed this popular summit and worn the grass out. Now it is almost bare rock with only a few available small stones to make a meagre cairn which is not always in place.

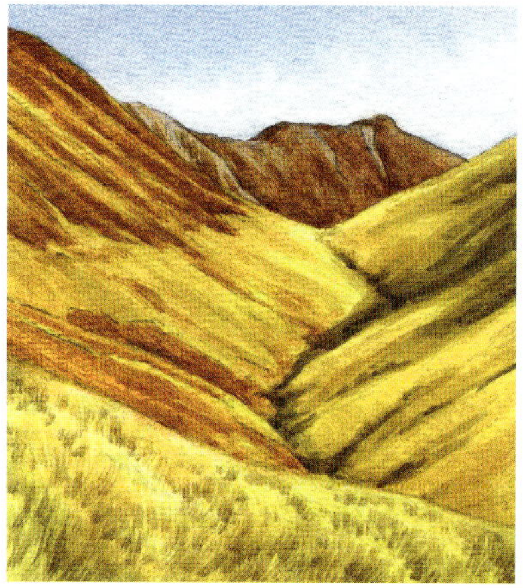

From Whiteless Breast 29/9/11
The valley leads the eye up to the ridge of Causey Pike and Scar Crags.

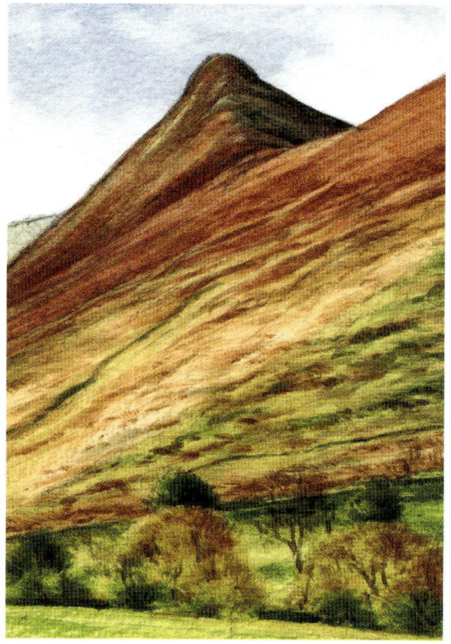

From Little Town 3/5/09
The distinctive peaked shape of the fell as seen from the road just north of the hamlet of Little Town.

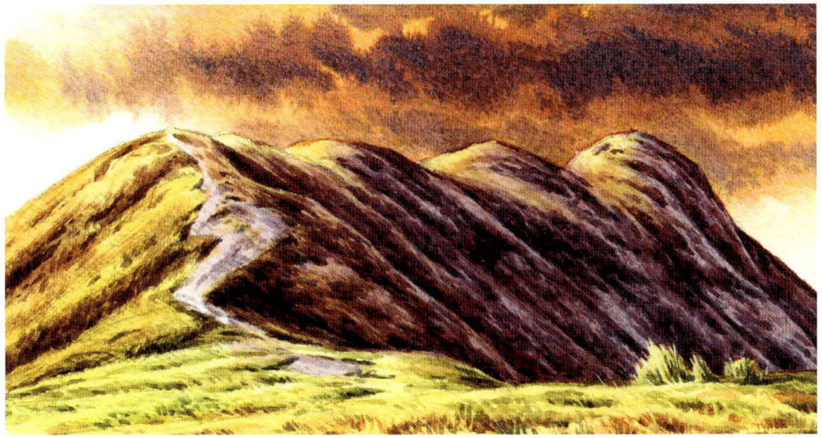

Looking back to Causey Pike from the depression 12/5/08
This aspect of the summit ridge shows the roller coaster like undulations that lead to the topmost peak at the far end.

The valley of Rigg Beck 5/9/12
A couple of paces south from the summit and this dramatic view of the valley comes fully into view. Unusually on the Causey Pike 10 page Wainwright even gives a key to the two drawings which neatly filled the last section of the fell chapter.

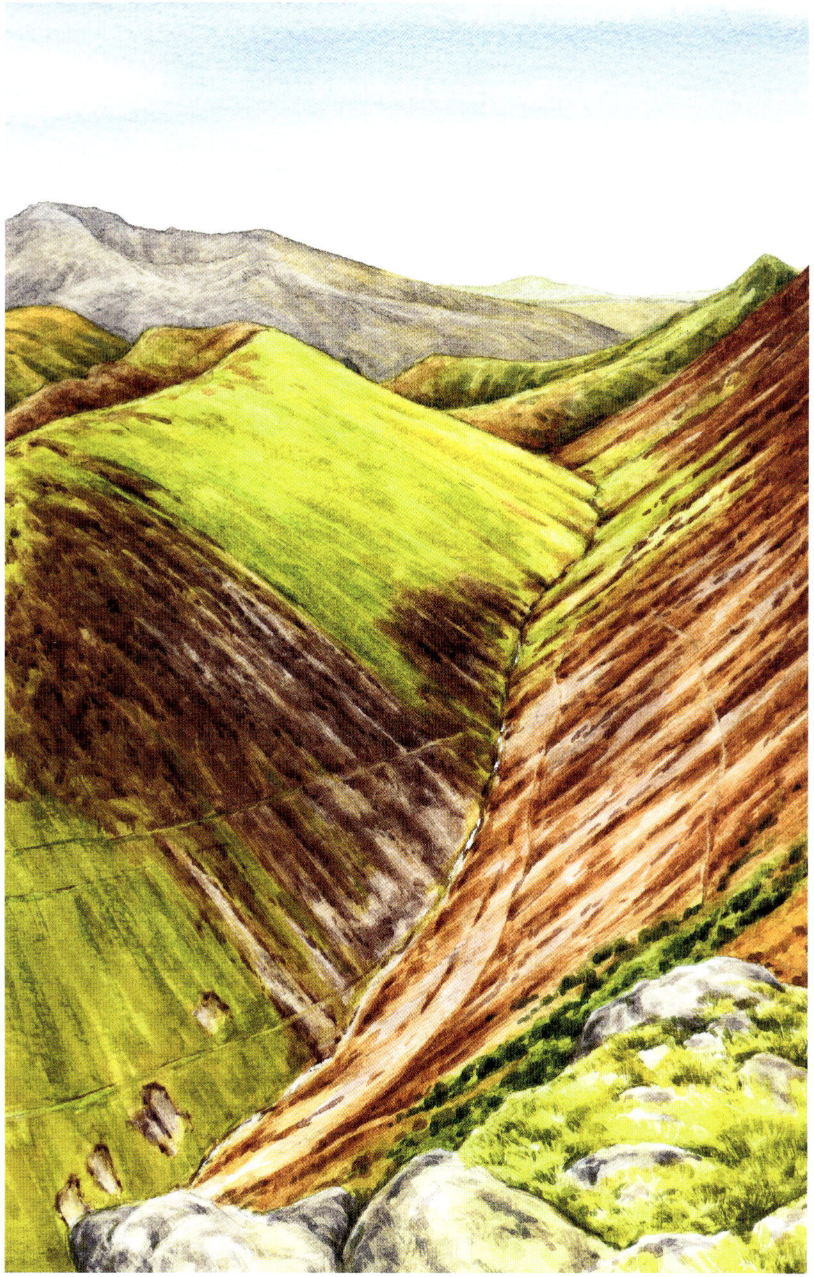

The ridge west from Causey Pike 5/9/12
By moving slightly to the north around the summit rocks AW was able to illustrate the ridge to Scar Crags and beyond. His drawing is slightly deceptive though as it would appear that the ridge continues to maintain height whereas in reality, as seen here, there is a deep col between Scar Crags and Sail.

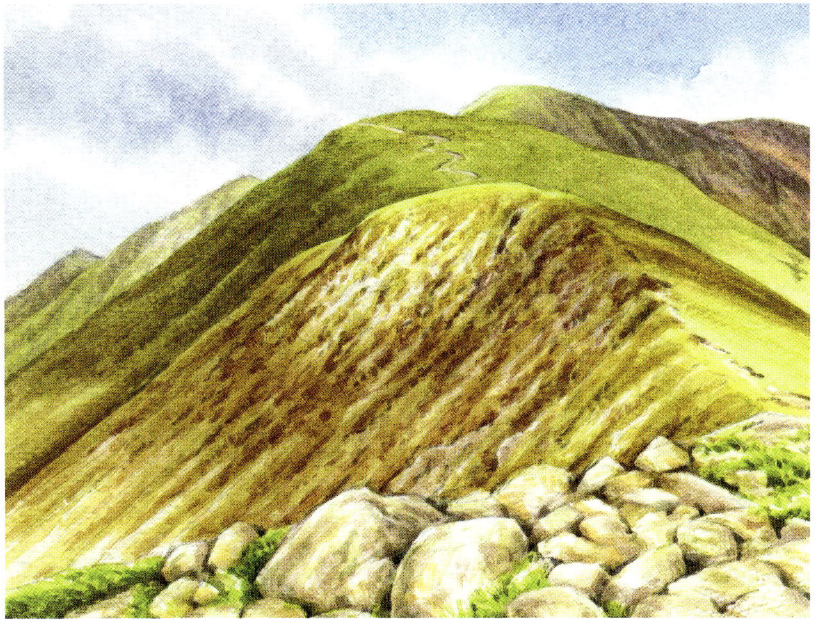

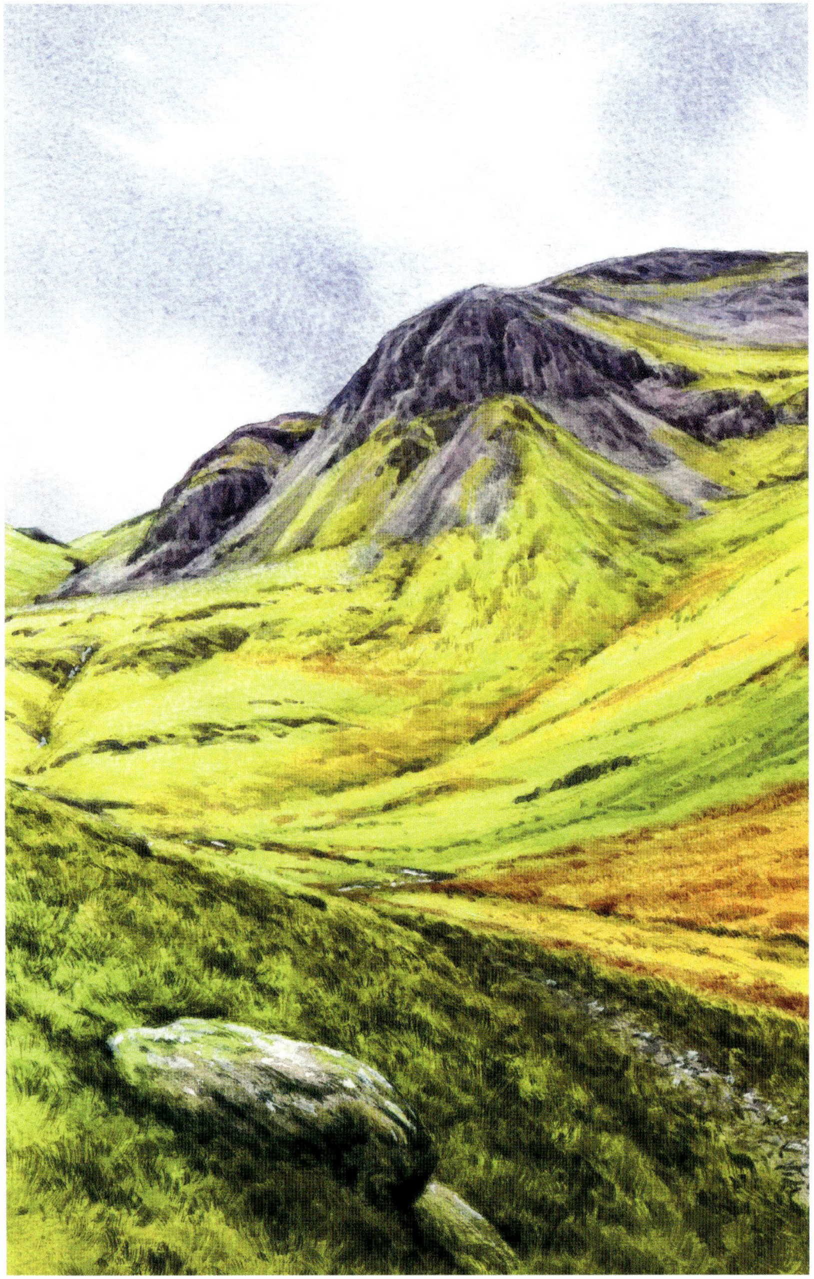

Dale Head

There are few fells with not only such a fine panoramic scene from the summit but also a grand view along the length of one of lakeland's finest dales, on this occasion, the Newlands valley.

Launchy Tarn 15/5/08

The backdrop is formed by High Spy in this view from near the fence just south of the tarn.

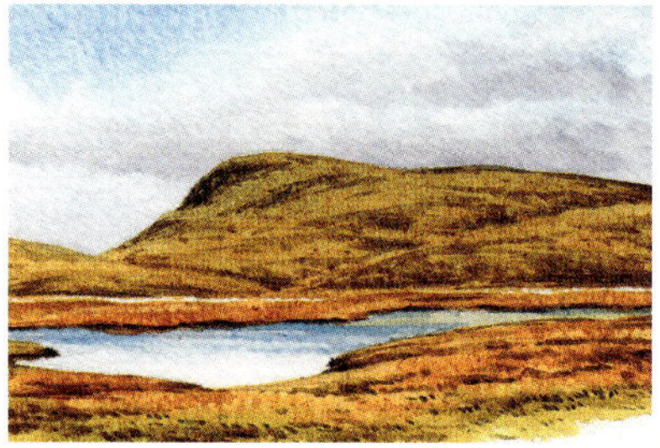

Dalehead Tarn from High Scawdel 15/5/08

It took me some time to pinpoint this location exactly, just north of Launchy Tarn, as AW's drawing of the rise of the ground on the right was slightly incorrect.

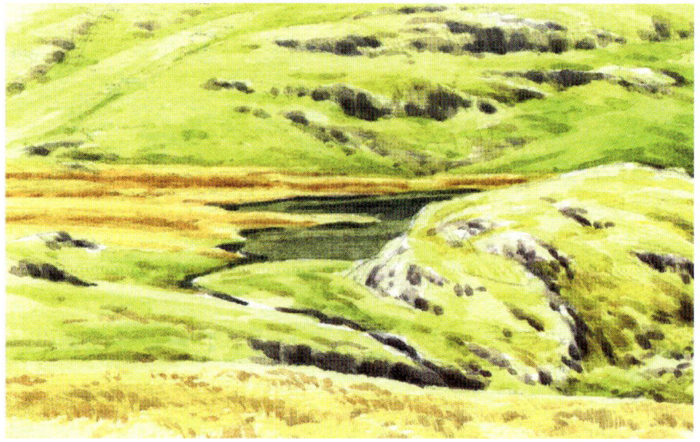

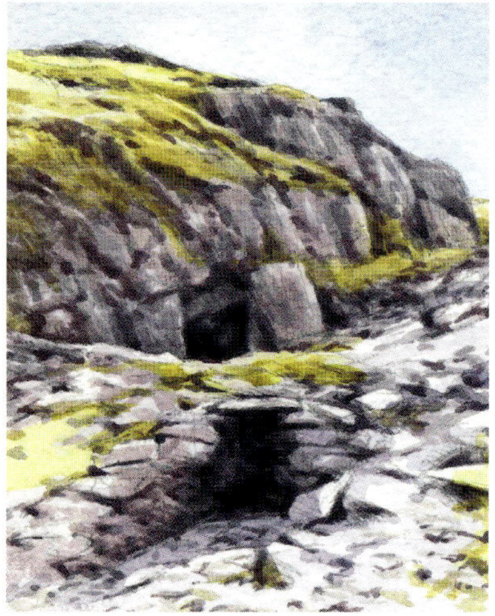

A level, Rigghead Quarry 3/5/11

There are several levels in the quarry and only by matching the skyline to AW's image was I able to find the correct entrance.

Mine cuttings near Far Tongue Gill 3/5/09

An unusual combination of mine cuttings, sheepfold and walls in this secluded spot away from main footpaths. Few walkers venture this way.

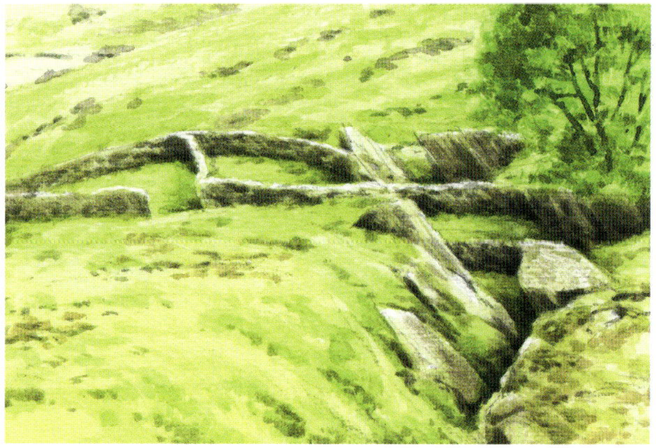

From Castle Nook 3/5/09

Walking south on the path that leads to the head of the Newlands Beck valley this view of Dale Head comes into view as the buttress of Castle Nook crag is passed. This is a remarkably quiet vicinity as most walkers circuit the valley on the high ground.

Copper Mines and Crags of Dale Head

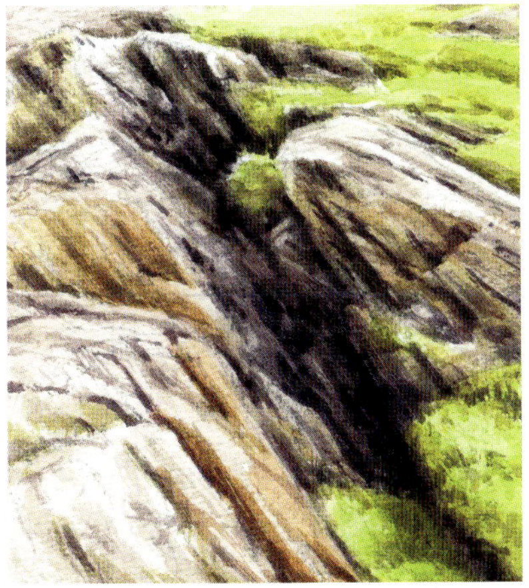

Two mine cuttings 3/5/09

The angled cutting on the left is actually a very deep open shaft.

The flooded cutting with the over hanging tree on the right forms an unusual deep pool.
Both are dangerous locations.

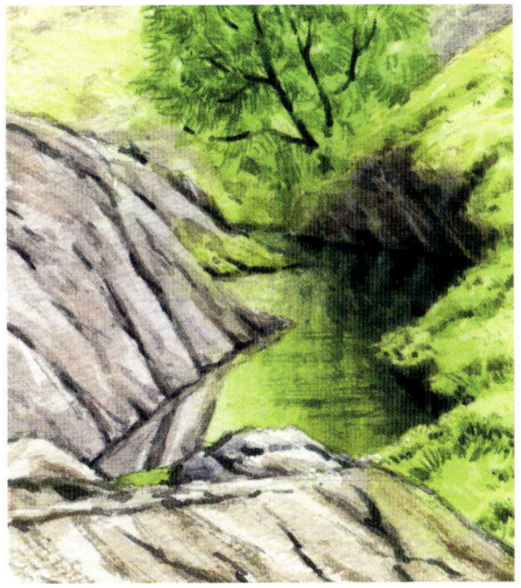

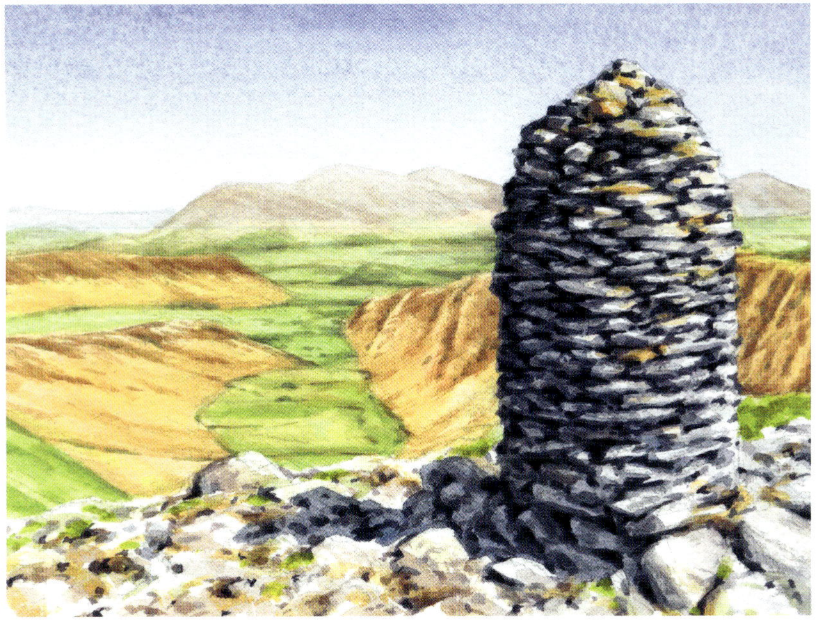

The summit 15/5/08

Shortly after AW's visit the cairn he illustrated had been wrecked, only to be re-built by 1963, but even this one isn't the replacement. The edifice that stands here has undergone several re-builds during its lifetime.

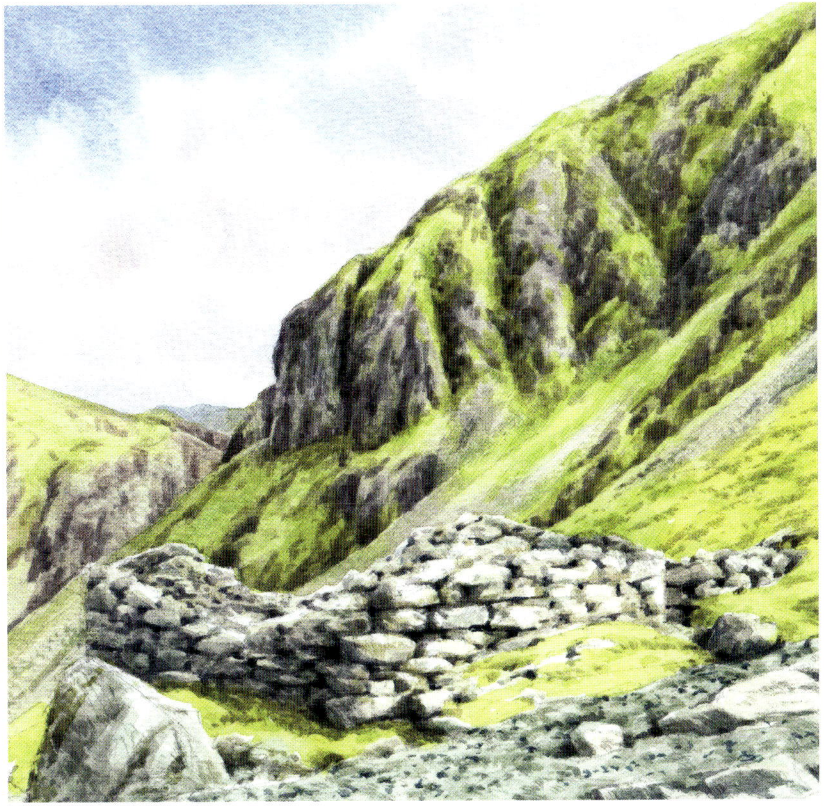

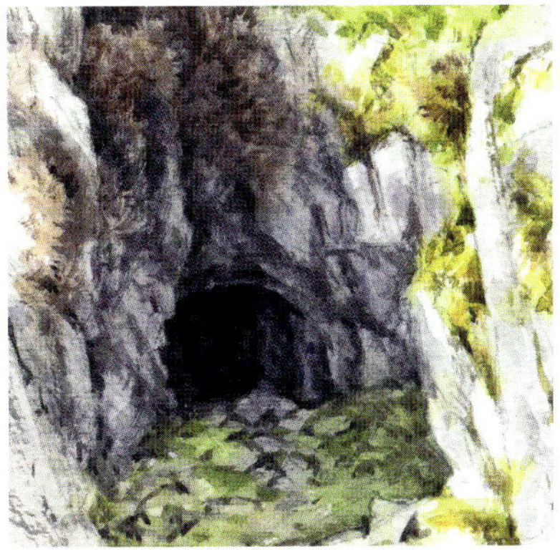

Old level 3/5/11

The old level, hut and quarries above Yew Crag are reminders of the area's industrial past, high above the Honister Pass.

The Hindscarth Ridge 15/5/08

The fence has gone and the well used path now splits to go both up and around the rocky rise.

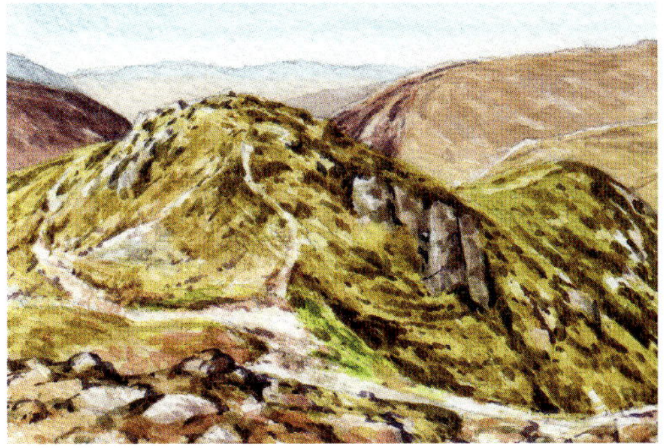

Dale Head Pillar and Gable Crag 3/5/09

The ruined mine buildings have remained almost untouched. Nearby it is easy to find samples of green malachite. What AW called Gable Crag is actually confusingly called Great Gable on various maps.

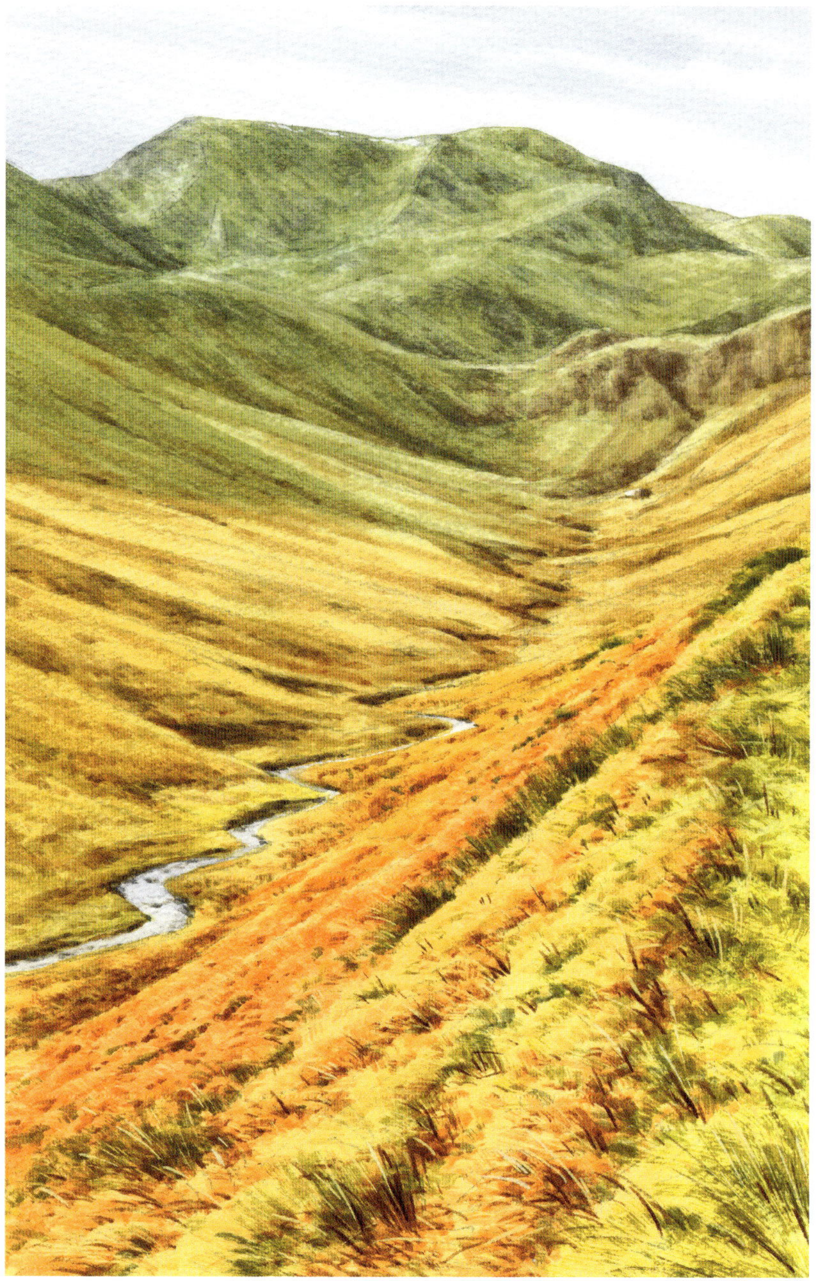

Eel Crag

As Wainwright explained in the Pictorial Guide, Eel Crag is really the north-east rough face of the fell and Crag Hill would seem to be the correct name. AW's title for the fell, which he took from the one inch Bartholomew map, only serves to prolong the confusion in the fell's name.

From Coledale 6/3/11

The peace of the valley with Eel Crag at the head can be deceptive. In both months of November 2009 and December 2015 heavy rains in this catchment area caused severe flooding in the village of Braithwaite at the foot of the valley.

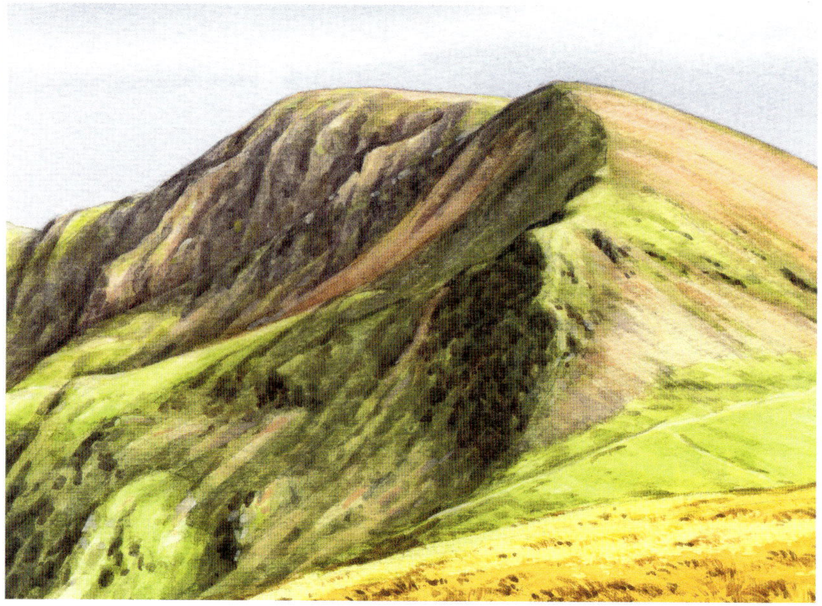

The north-east face, from the lower slopes of Sand Hill 13/5/08

The rocky buttresses of Eel Crag forming the north-east face of Crag Hill. This view is from near the fenced off shafts at the head of Pudding Beck.

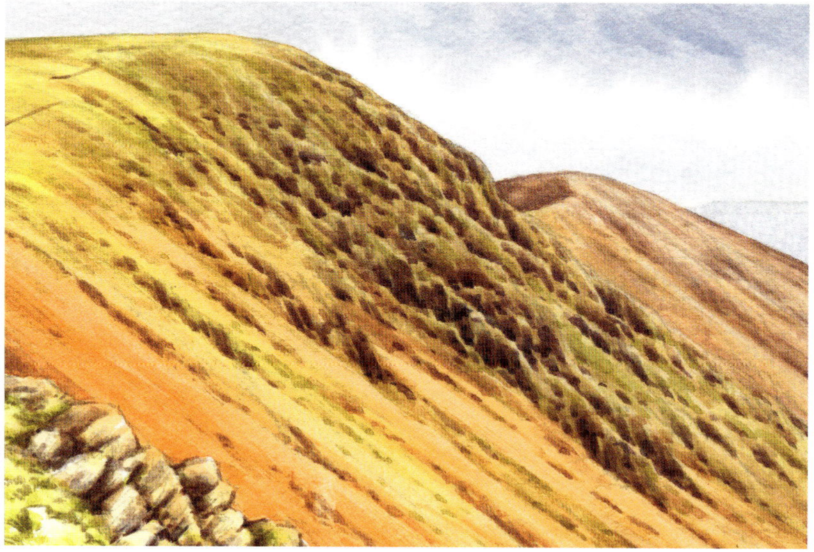

The south face, with Sail beyond, from Wandope 29/9/11

Near the very top of the ridge to Wandope summit from Addacomb Hole this view of the fell can be observed. The steep red scree slopes run down into the corrie.

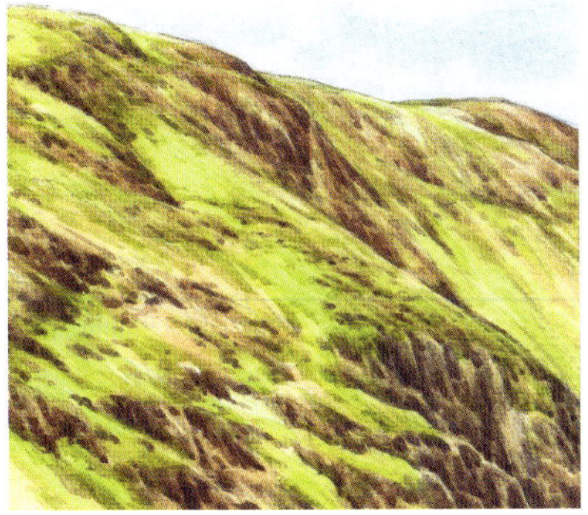

Eel Crag, from Sail 12/5/08

Scott Crag and Eel Crag seen from just north-west of Sail summit.

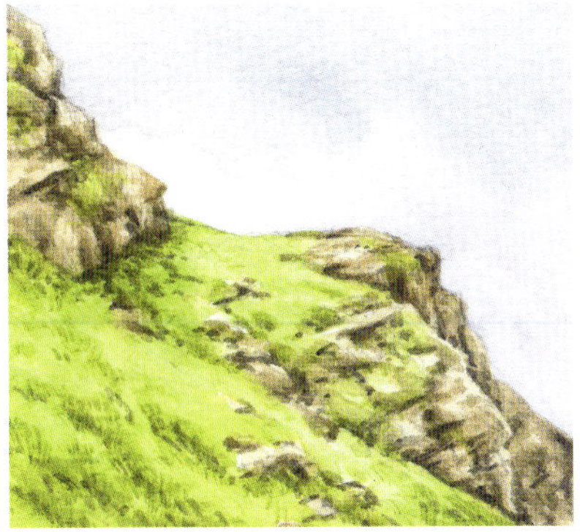

The end of the shelf 5/9/12

This route, the ascent from Braithwaite (Eel Crag 7), is still little used and the path is indistinct. These are the ways of the intrepid walkers who are looking to explore in detail already familiar fells.

Tower Ridge from the end of the shelf 5/9/12

By omitting from his drawing the background of the Sail ridge AW was able to give the profile of Tower Ridge a definite form without other distractions.

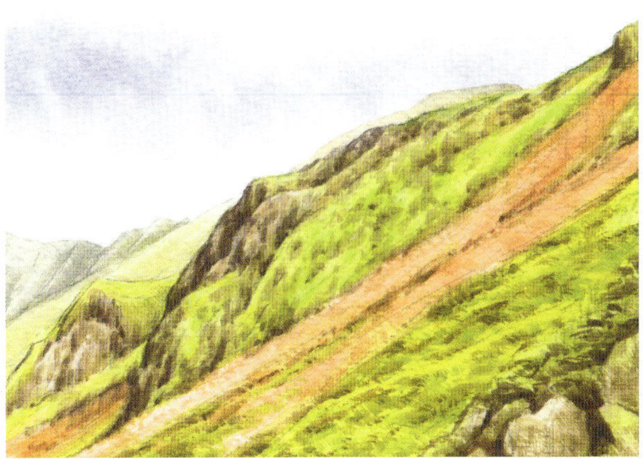

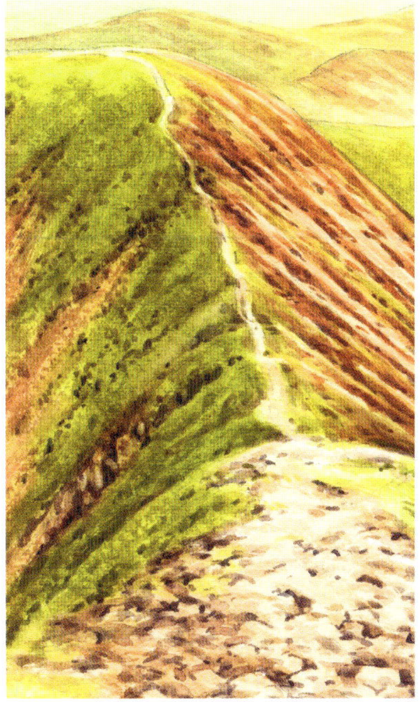

Looking to Sail from the east ridge 12/5/08

This ridge route is popular and the shallow topsoil is very prone to wear and erosion as shown here.

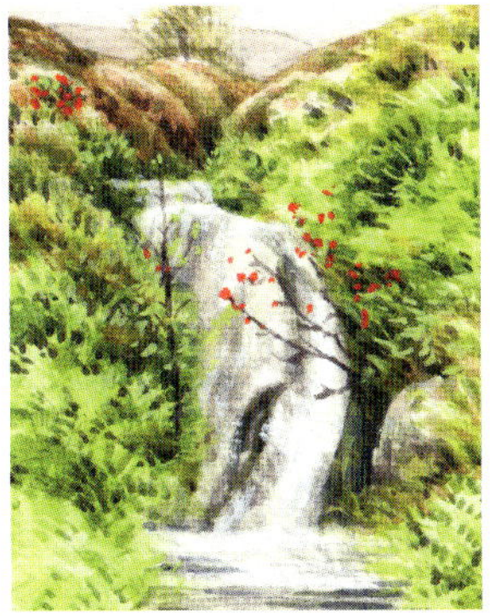

Waterfall, Rannerdale Beck 23/8/09

This is the waterfall drawn by AW just a short distance north of the sheepfold and the one he marks in the guide. There is a much more impressive fall about 300 yards further up the beck which is marked on the map and is incorrectly identified as this one in the revised guide.

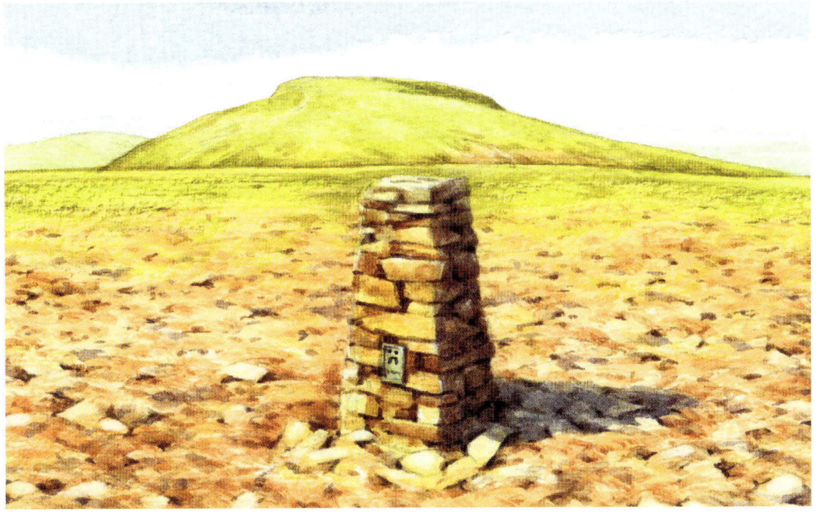

The summit 12/5/08

The stony summit plateau has at its top this triangulation column. On all of my visits it was showing damage near its base with stones missing. Consequently, since I obtained my reference photograph the pillar has toppled in one lump. On a recent visit it had been propped up into position but it needs a more permanent restoration if it is to survive. A mix of mortar and a bit of muscle power should put it right. Grasmoor is the fell behind and I was here just as the shadow from the column was almost the same as in AW's drawing.

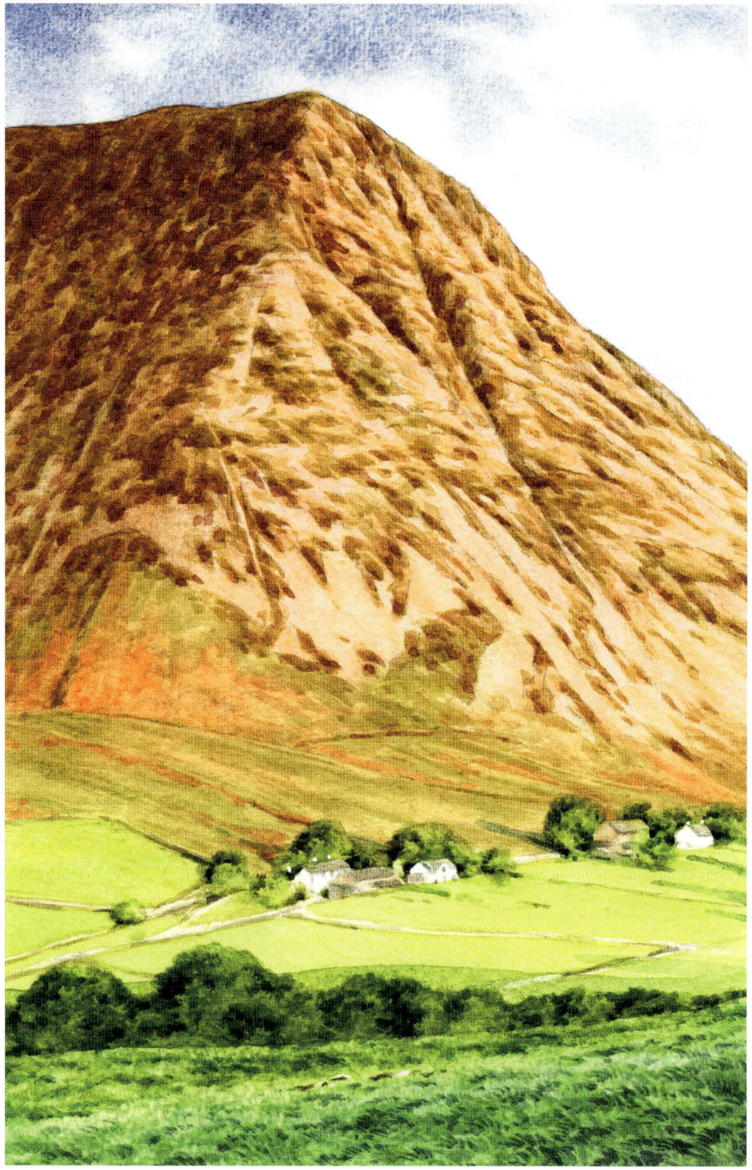

From Lanthwaite Hill 14/5/08
A search of this grassy slope revealed the remnants of the small tree in the foreground of AW's drawing, confirming this exact location.

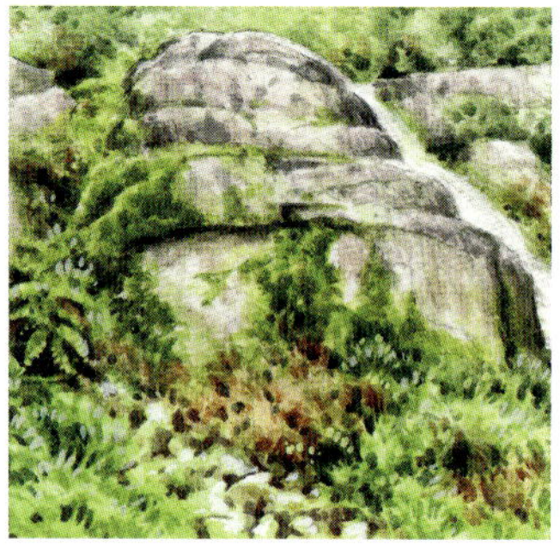

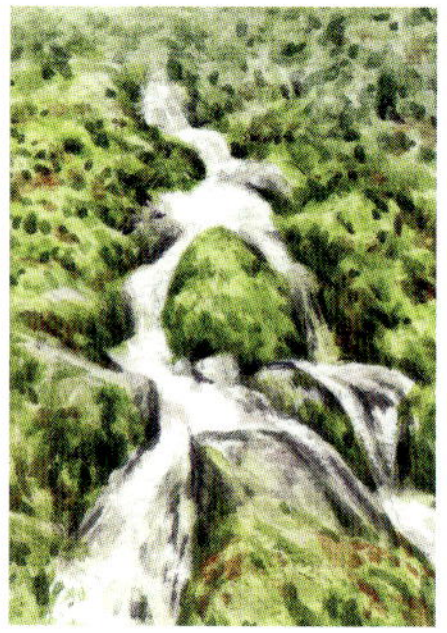

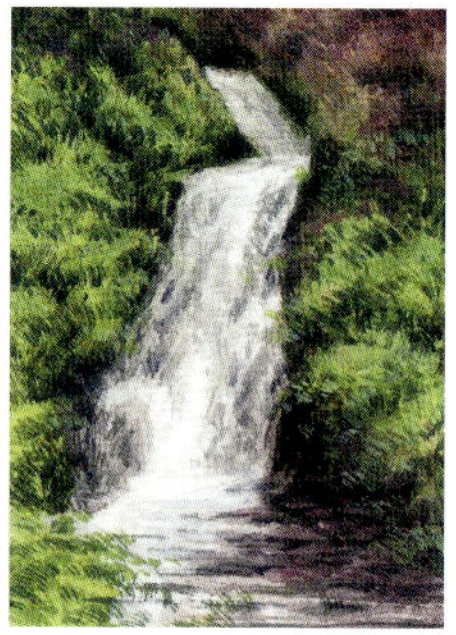

Cinderdale Beck 23/8/09
The course of the water in the stream has changed in places but I was able to find all the correct cascades.

Dove Crags (right) 11/8/13
A detailed search was rewarded in finding this precise location with the distinctive outline of crags.

The summit 28/9/11
On the highest point of the fell a large collection of rocks has been formed into a cross shaped low wind shelter.

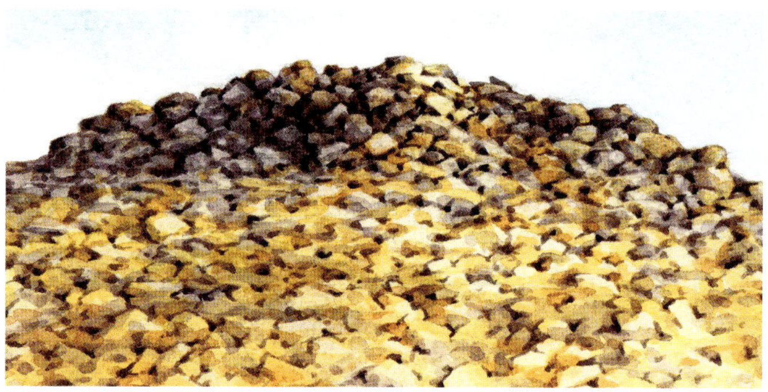

Grasmoor

Being the highest of the north-western fells, Grasmoor's rugged western face towers over Crummock Water. The summit can be attained easily from the east but in my opinion the best route of ascent is via the north-west ridge, an entertaining route that AW may have been the first to climb. He did so with a little difficulty, weighing 16 stone at the time and hence the reason he named a narrow gap on the ascent *"Fat Man's Agony"*.

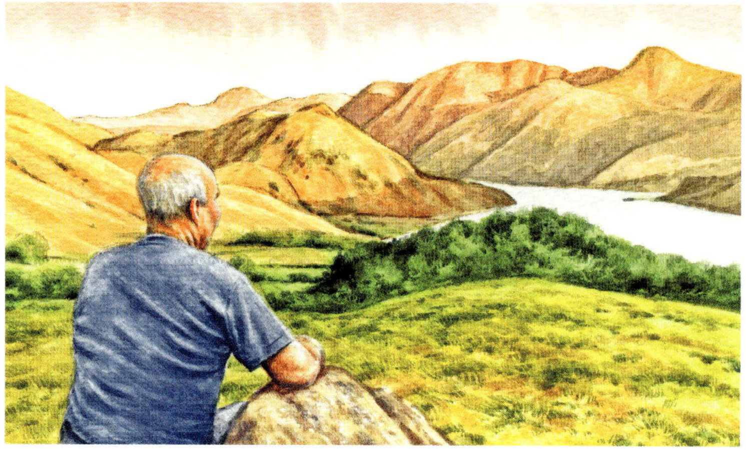

Grasmoor End, from Crummock Water (right) 23/2/10
The peak of the fell over Lanthwaite Wood from close to the weir.

Looking south-south-east from Lanthwaite Hill 14/5/08
In his self portrait AW combined a snap of himself leaning on a rock taken at another location with the scenic view of the High Stile Range. I did the same but without the Harris Tweed jacket and pipe.

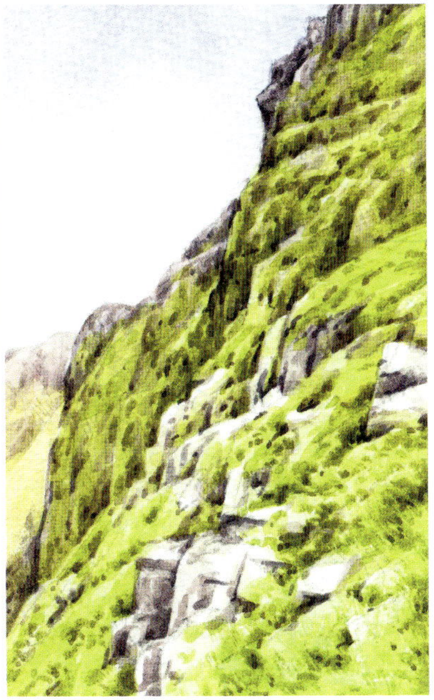

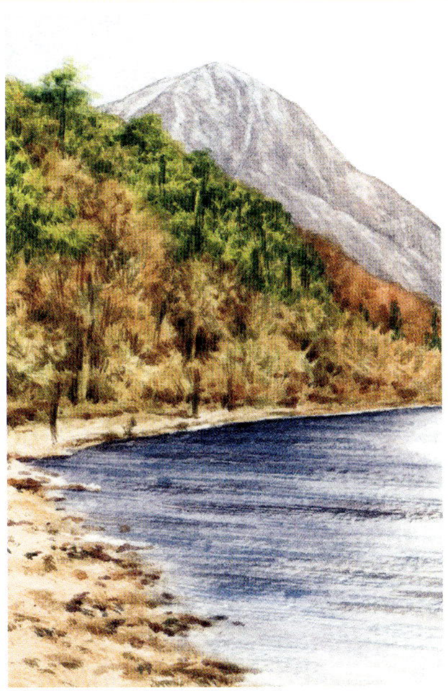

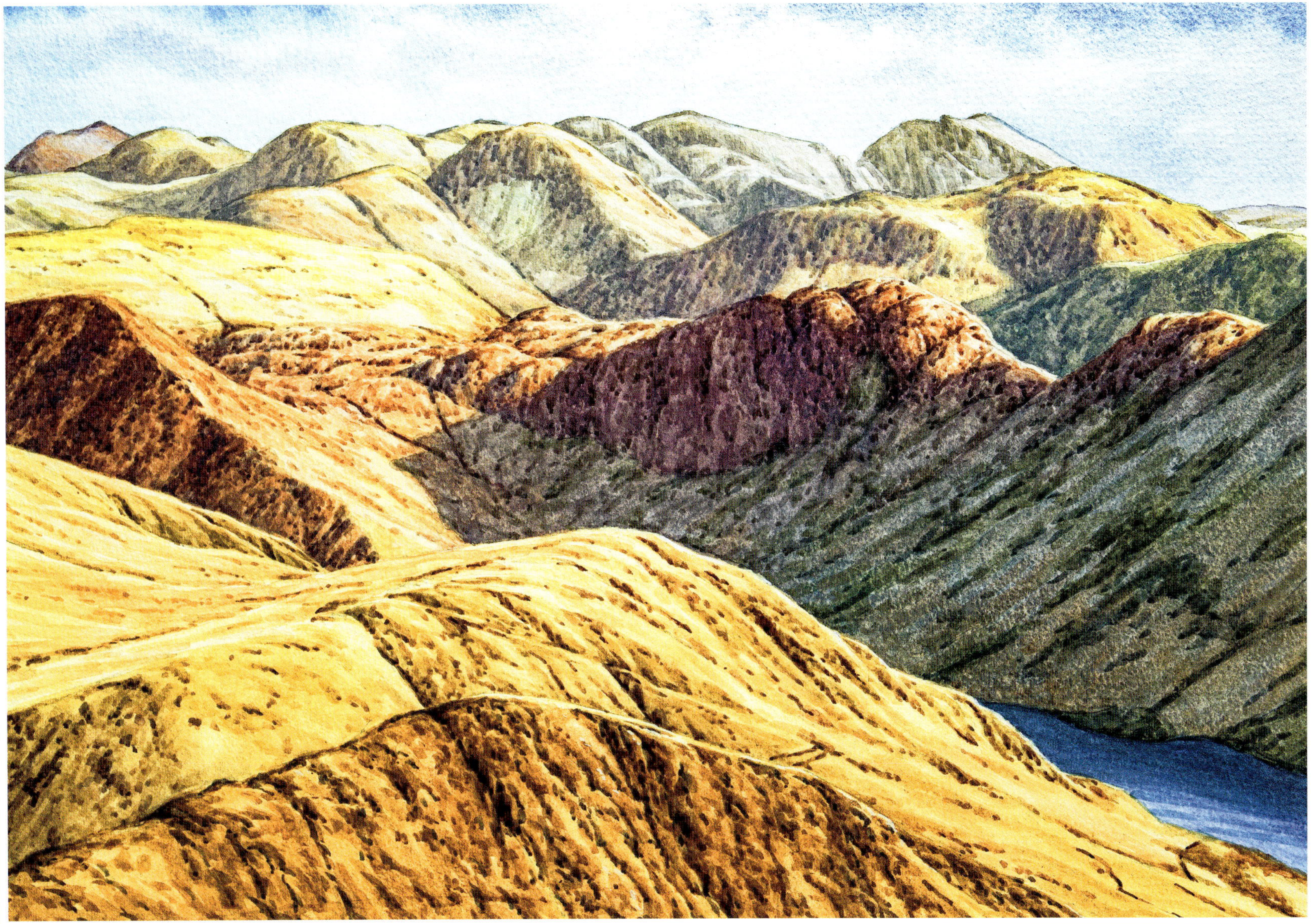

The Scafell group, from Grasmoor 28/9/11

The last of the three double page spreads in the Pictorial Guides was given over to this classic view which not only depicts the Scafell range but also fittingly Haystacks, positioned here centrally amongst its majestic neighbours, the fell where famously Wainwright's ashes were scattered in 1991.

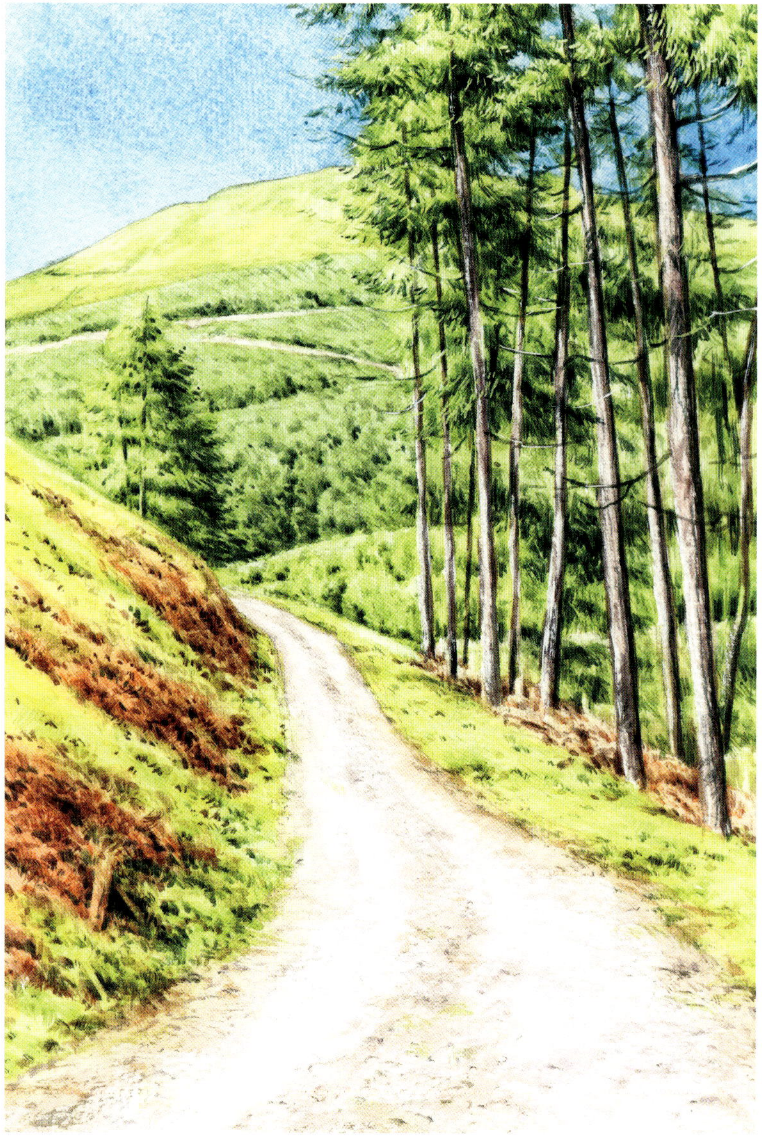

From Aiken Plantation 15/3/08
As the pines on the right have now matured they almost obscure the fell, but I decided to record the scene from the exact spot as a good comparison of how the forests have developed over the years.

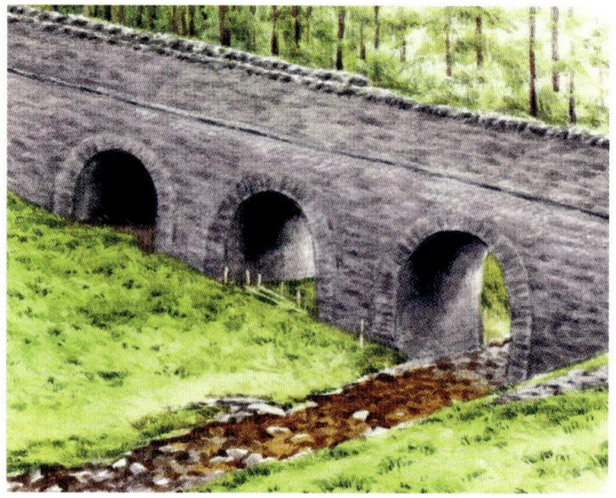

Scawgill Bridge on the Whinlatter road 11/5/08
The little footbridge across the river has gone but the footings can still be seen.

Graystones
On the O.S. maps of AW's day this area of high ground was properly called Kirk Fell but perhaps to avoid confusion with another hill of the same name Wainwright opted to use the title of the actual summit, Graystones, for the fell in the Pictorial Guides.

The biggest cairn on the fell 11/5/08
Located 300 yards west of the true top this cairn has the better view.

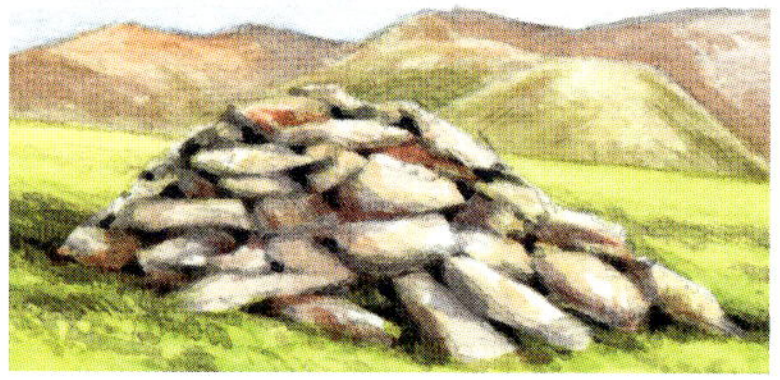

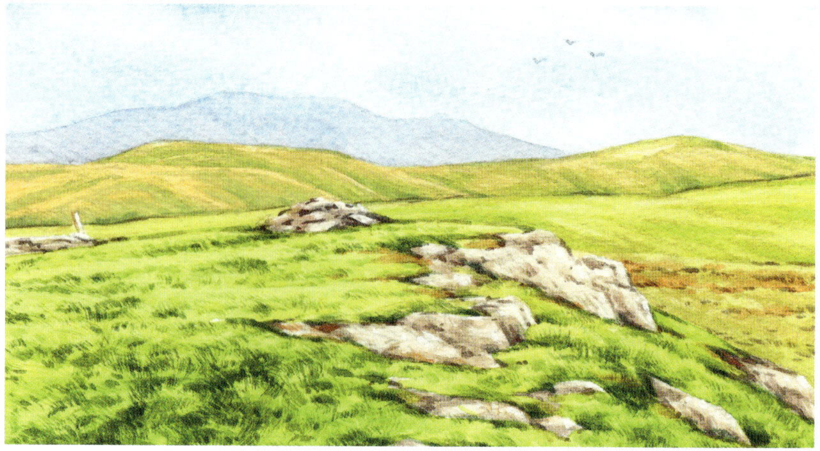

The summit 11/5/08
This point to the west of the wall now has a small cairn and in AW's day it was marked on the larger scale O.S. map with the trigonometrical point. A rise 150 yards south-east on the other side of the wall may just be higher.

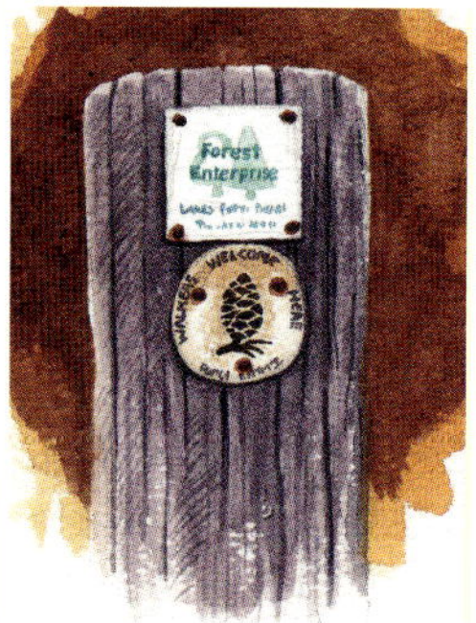

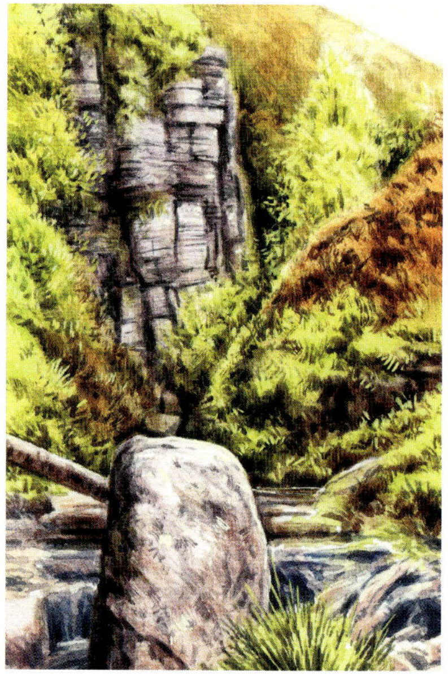

The gorge 11/5/08
The upright rock still stands, Spout Force being just round the corner out of view. Now a footpath up to the left gives access to a good view of the fall. The old "End of Public Footpath" sign has gone , but near the same location the one shown above can be found.

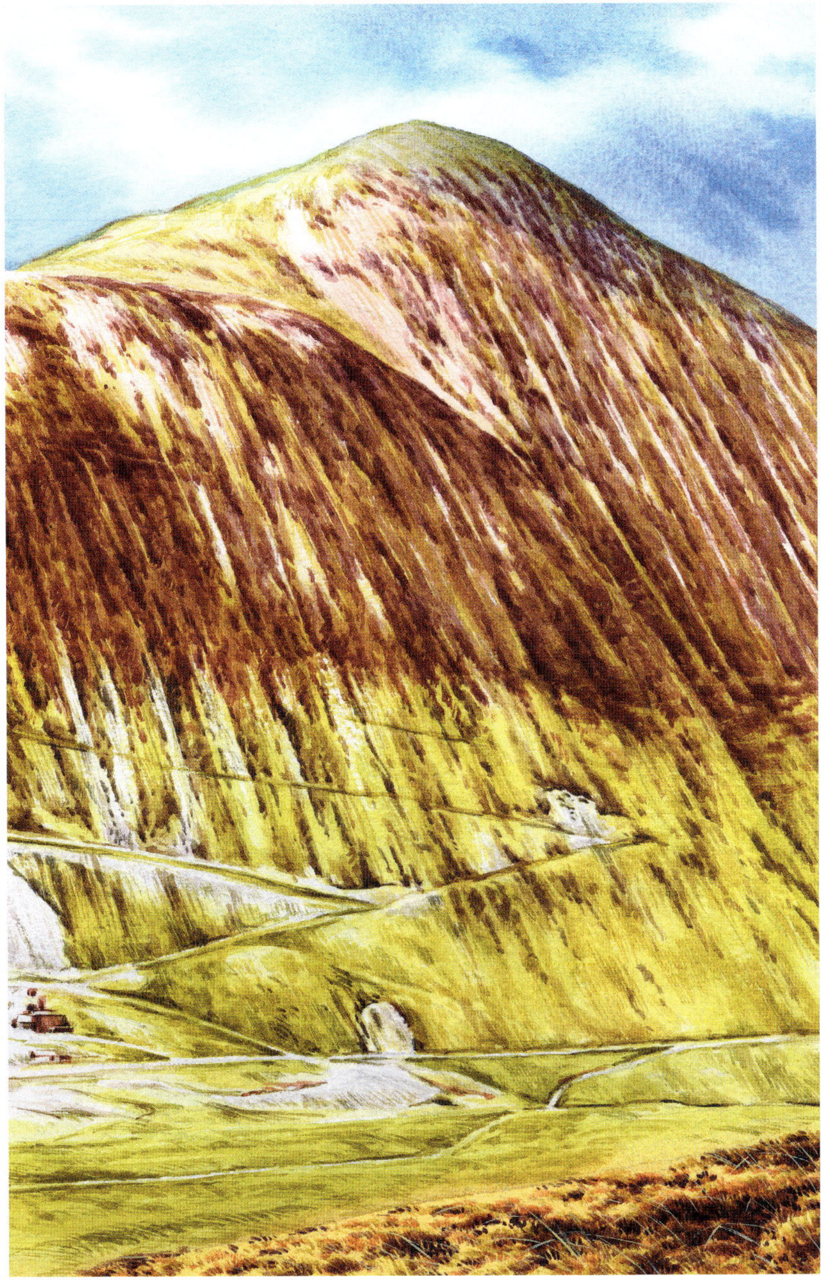

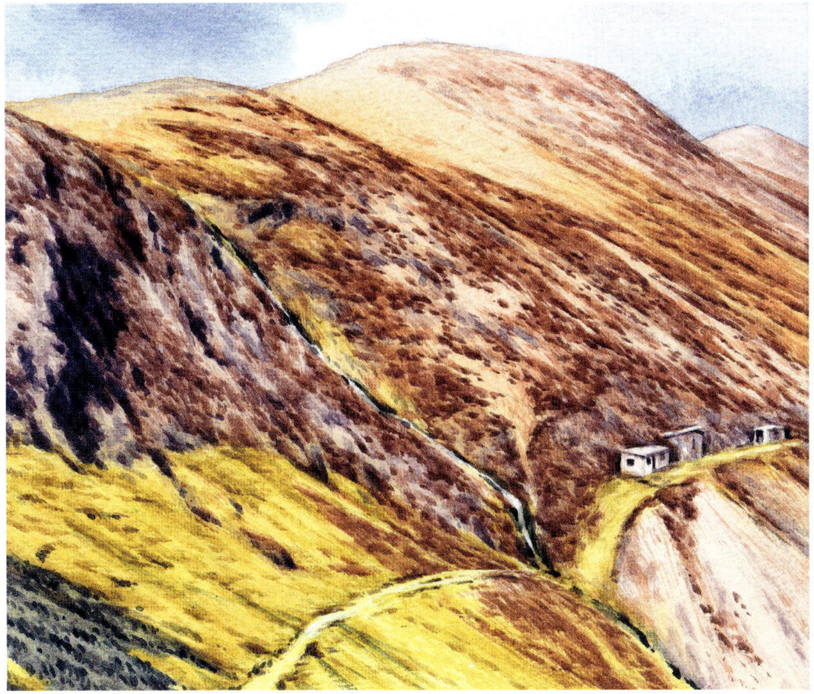

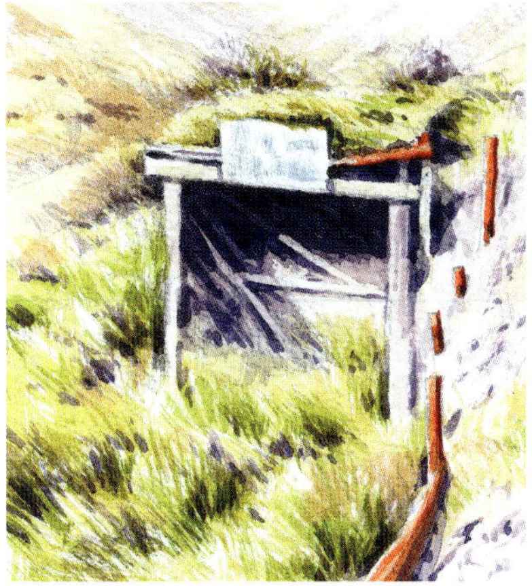

The main level 6/3/11
Only by consulting local mining expert Ian Tyler could I confirm that this was the correct level. The old railway tracks are now used as bank supports.

The summit 6/3/11
A cairn of slate pieces sits on the rocky top. Next to it will be seen an O.S. surface block, the alternative to a triangulation column.

High Force 6/3/11
The beck was all but dry on my visit, more of a trickle than a force.

Grisedale Pike

This is a fine peak shaped fell especially when viewed from the east, often visited as part of the excellent Coledale Horseshoe route.

From High Moss 12/5/08
I have slightly extended the scene to the left to include the buildings of the now disused Force Crag mine. Of interest are the mine tracks and route of the aerial ropeway which scar the fell side and were not in AW's illustration.

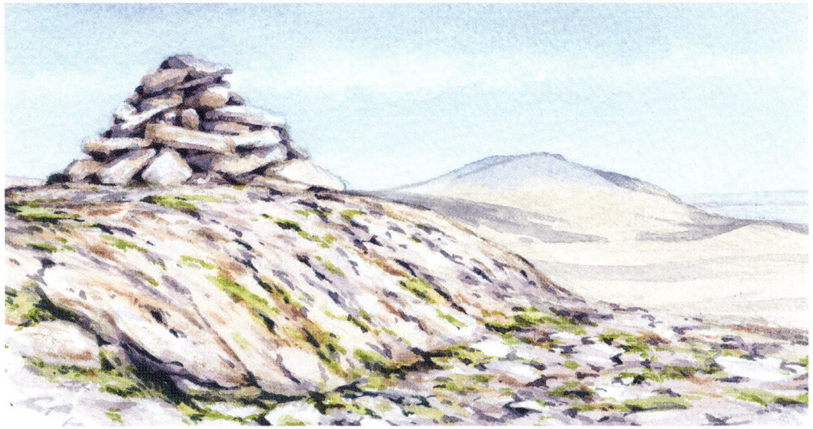

Force Crag Mine

In my efforts to locate the main level entrance of Force Crag Mine I had to spend some time searching the fell side scars of this now disused hive of industry. The mine was successfully but intermittently worked for lead, zinc and baryte from the 1860s and there is evidence that mining here may even have taken place as far back as the 1570s. At one time aerial ropeways brought ore down to the valley bottom to be processed. Force Crag Mine was the last working metal mine in the Lake District, closing in 1990. Parts of the processing mill were restored in 2004 and the National Trust have tours of the mine on certain days of the year. A new mine water treatment plant to extract polluting metals was opened near the mill in November 2015.

Low Force 6/3/11

The waters of the falls can just be seen on this sketch but the hut on the right in AW's drawing no longer exists.

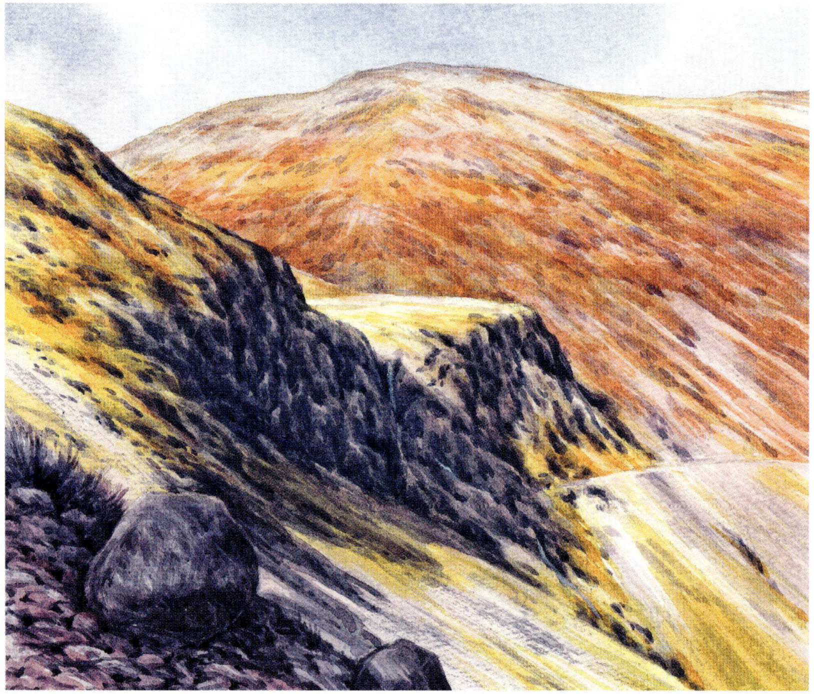

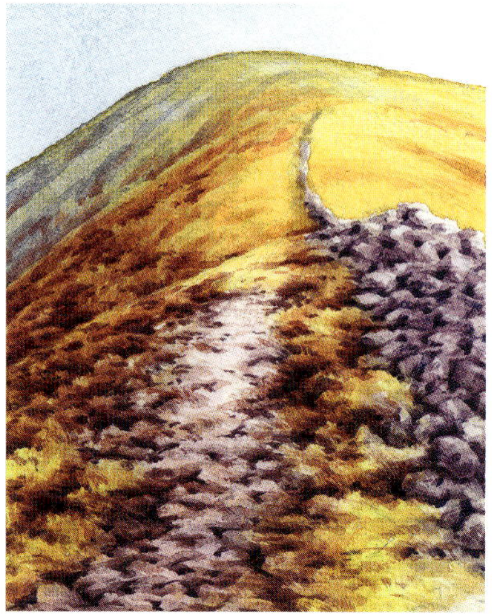

The north-east ridge 6/3/11

The length of the ridge had to be climbed to find this precise spot.

The north ridge 6/3/11

The cairn is now a little larger, sited to one side of the main ridge path.

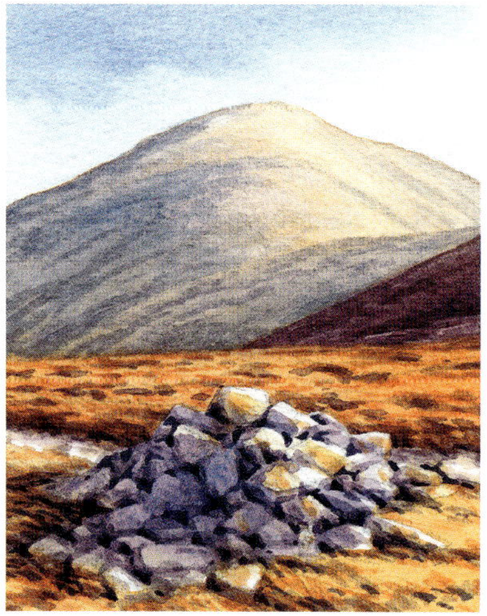

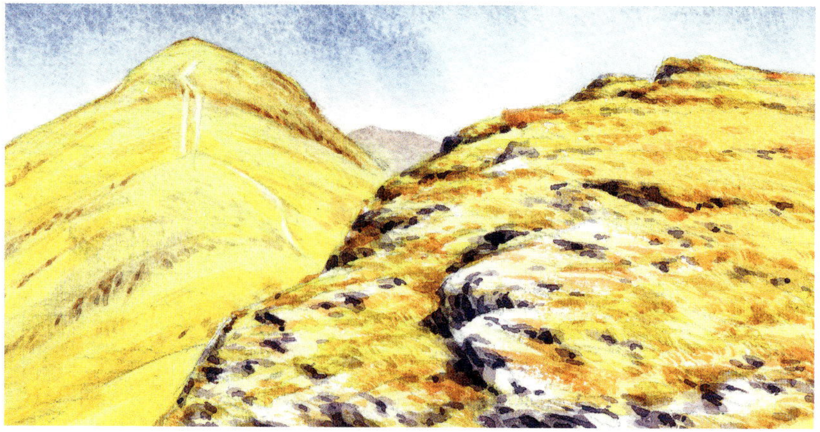

The main summit from the subsidiary summit 6/3/11

It is slightly odd that this distinctive subsidiary summit has no name.

The east ridge - the final section, from Sleet How 12/5/08

The steepest part of the ascent lies ahead but the path is easily followed.

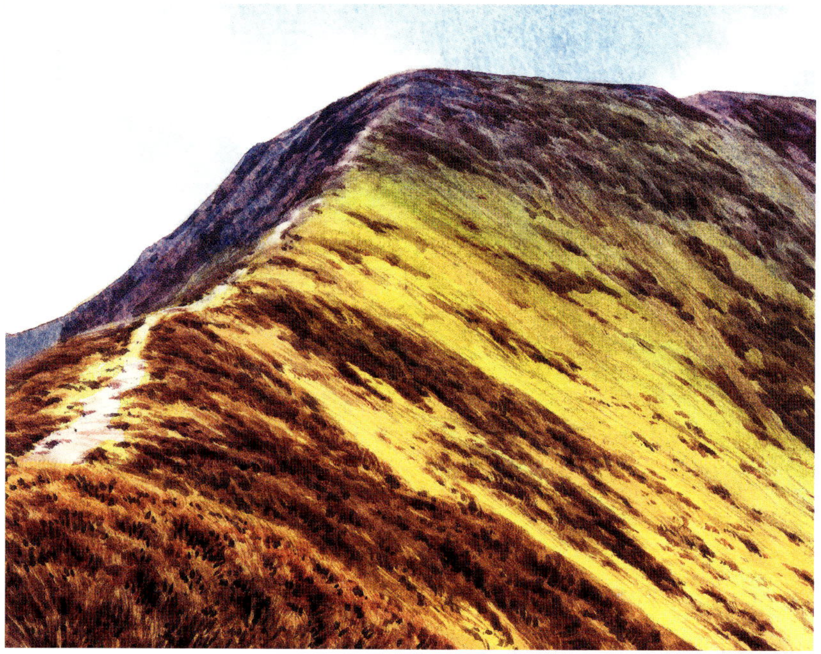

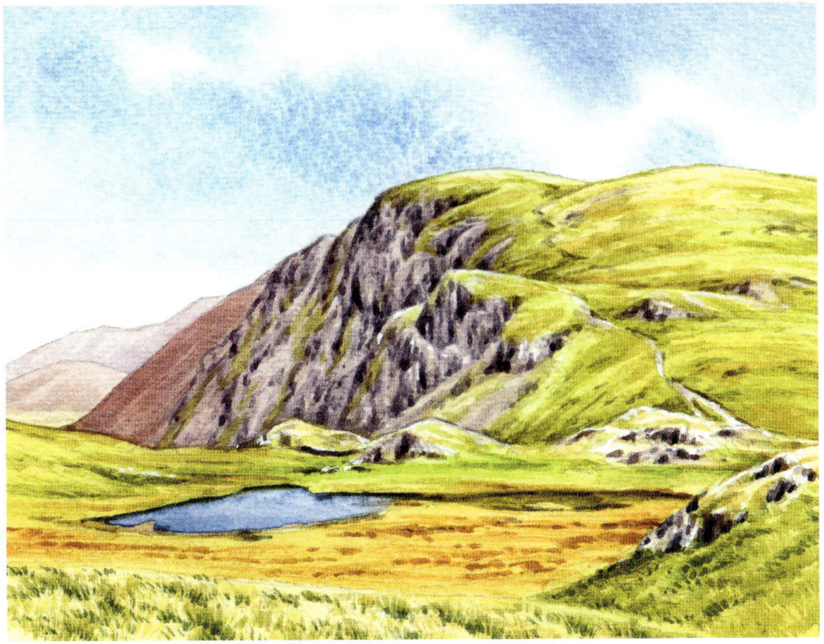

From Dalehead Tarn 15/5/09
The right hand section of the tarn is now quite reedy and a well defined path leads up towards the summit on the right. To the left of the crags in the distance is the Skiddaw range, omitted from Wainwright's drawing.

High Spy

In his Pictorial Guide AW gave various names for the fell but Eel Crags and Lobstone Band really only refer to features of the hill and the Scawdel Fell title is only shown on the Bartholomew maps of the day. High Spy is the name generally used today, it saves confusion.

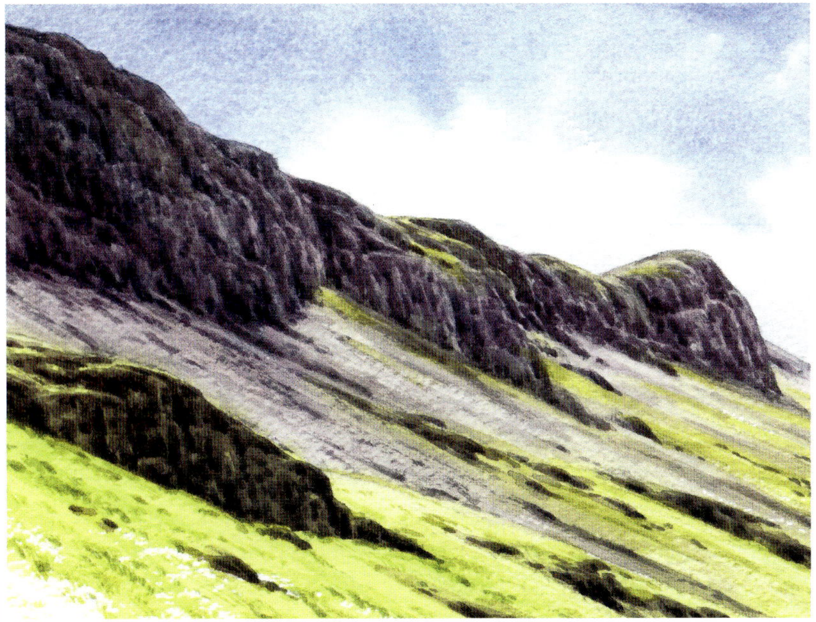

Looking south from Castlenook 3/5/09
The named crags shown here are a little more squat than as depicted in the Pictorial Guide.

Looking north from the foot of Miners Crag 3/5/09
The test for me for this sketch was to align the receding crags so that they matched the drawing in the guide, as I worked my way gingerly across the loose scree slopes.

Eel Crags

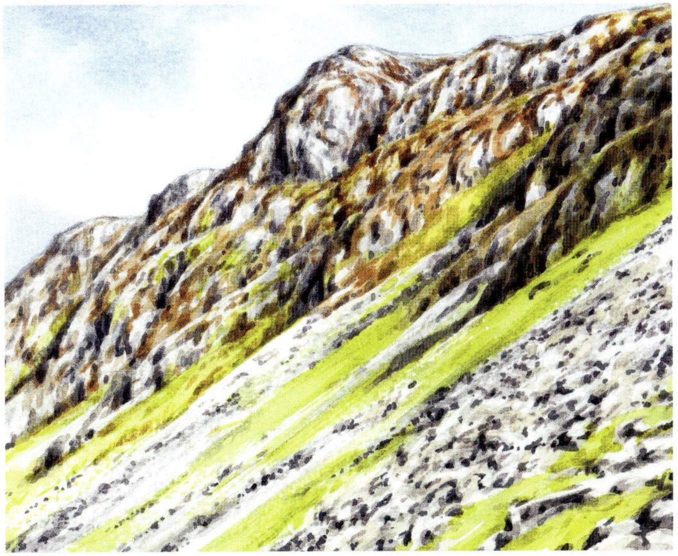

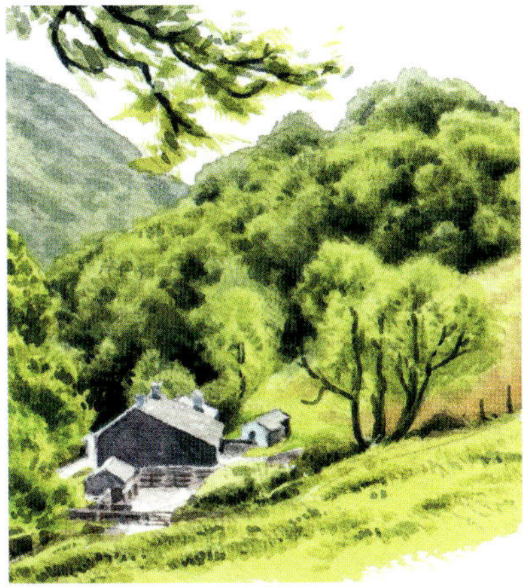

Hollows Farm 14/5/08
Nestled in the woods under Nitting Haws is this working farm. The viewpoint is unusual to walkers as it is away from any main path but on open access ground. AW must have just been having a wander when the scene caught his eye.

Joe Banks' Fold 20/4/10
Hidden away near Minum Crag is this derelict sheepfold, one of only a few in the area which is given their local name on the O.S. maps.

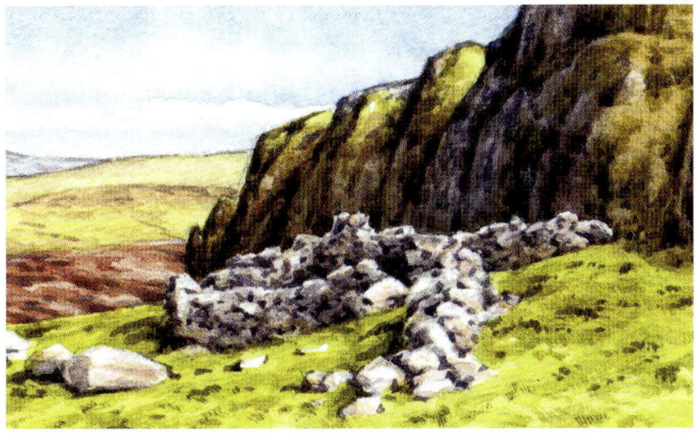

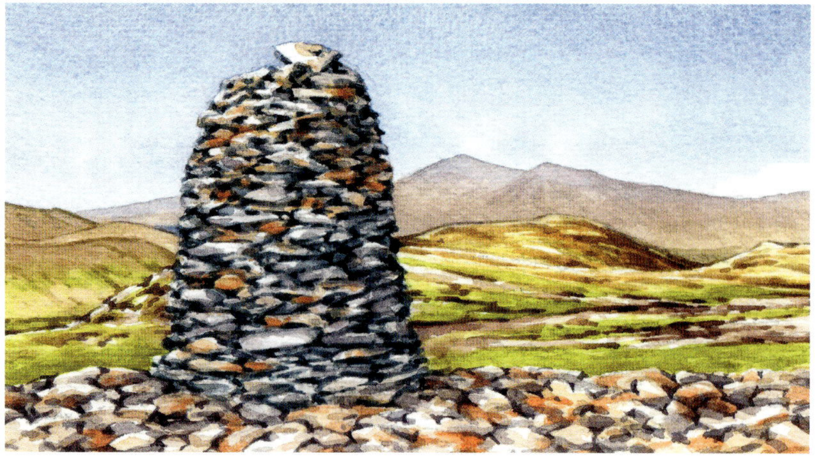

The summit 15/5/08

A substantial cairn which on this visit was in fairly good order but like others it is prone to damage.

Goat Crag, from Castle Crag

19/9/10

It was a dismal day when I stood here to get the reference, drizzle subdued the distant crag but the resulting sketch has a pleasing atmosphere. The two pines stand resolutely amongst the slate scree.

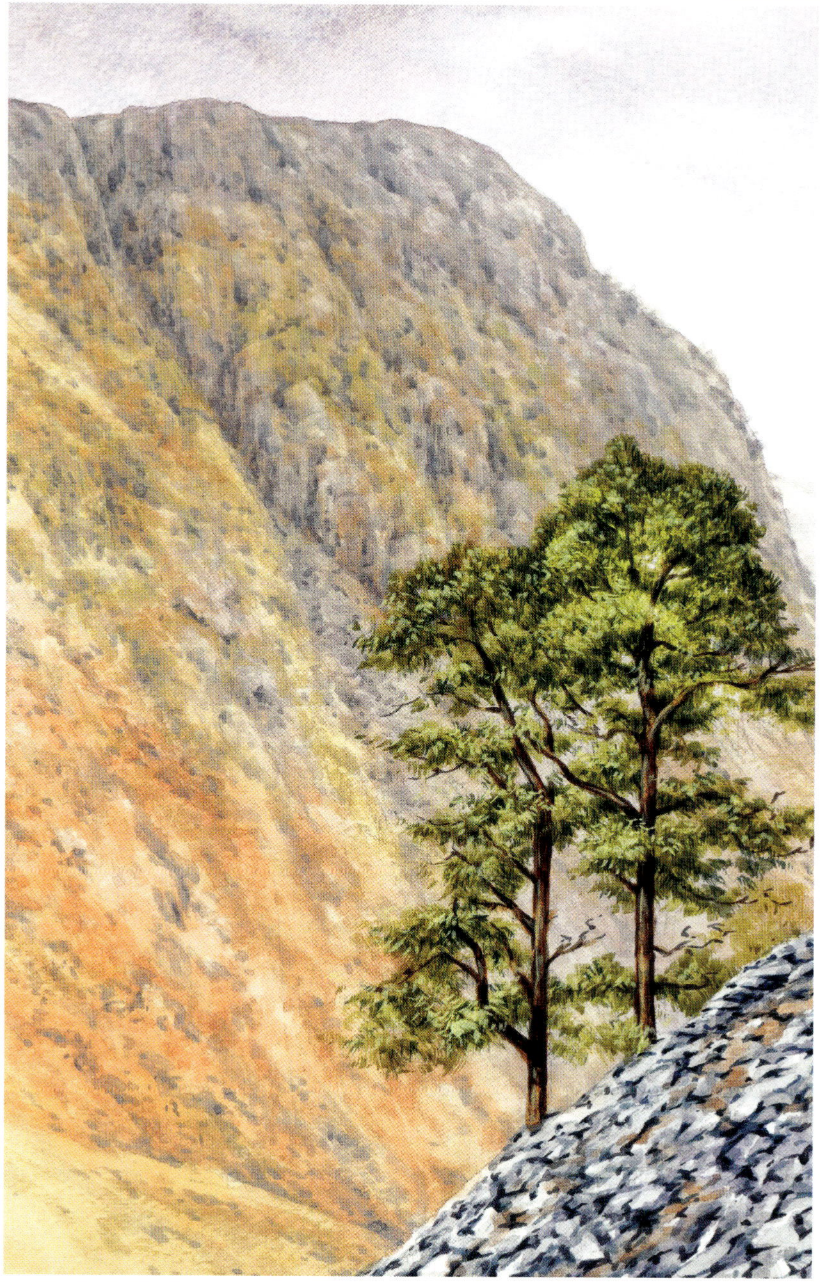

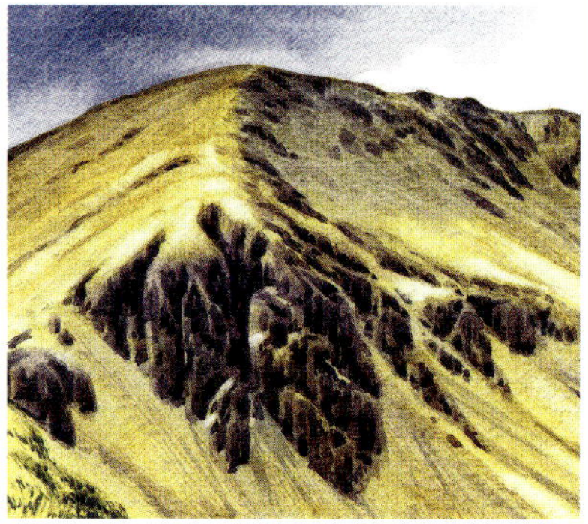

Dale Head from High Spy

15/5/08

The fell summit and Great Gable Crags from near High Spy summit.

The summit, looking south

15/5/08

A fine vista with High Spy summit on the left viewed from the edge of Eel Crags.

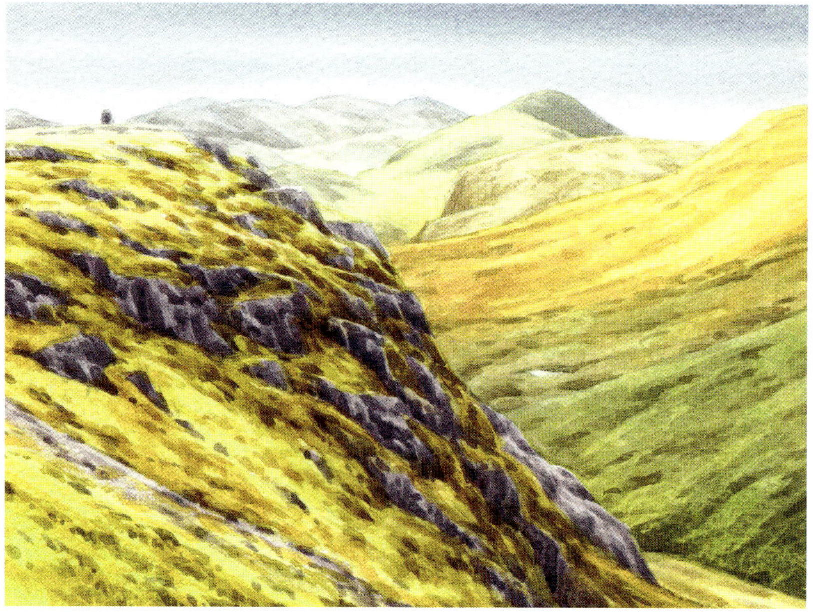

Staghorn moss 15/5/08

The only moss illustrated in the Pictorial Guides, not uncommon but interesting in shape and form.

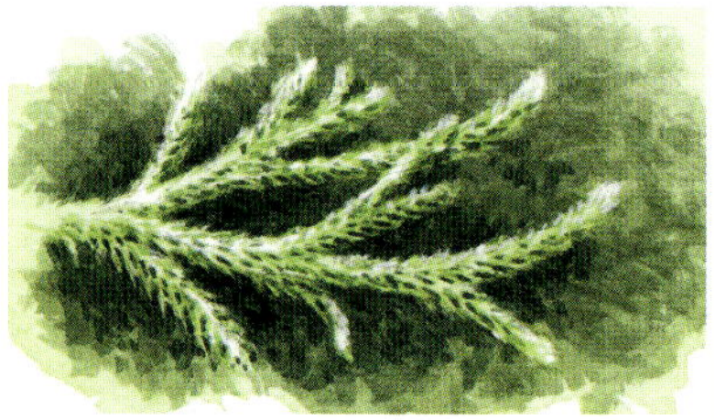

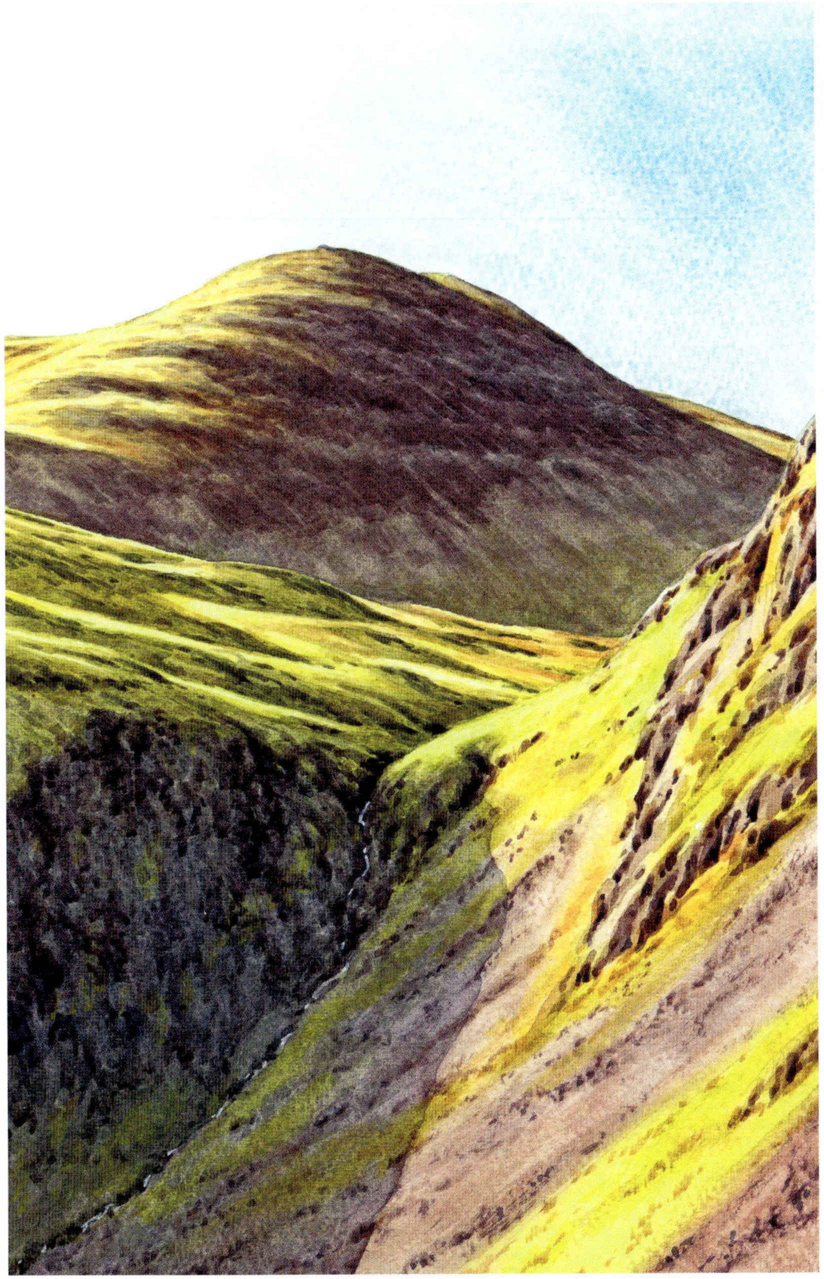

Hindscarth

From the ridge that links Dale Head to Robinson a high spur of land heads north into the Newlands valley. This forms the fell Hindscarth. It is basically a ridge which descends towards Little Town as Scope End. Many walkers will visit the summit as part of the classic Newlands round but the north ridge is well worth visiting especially when the heather is in bloom.

From High Snab Bank 15/5/09

On the ascent of Robinson via High Snab Bank a slight detour from the path near Blea Crags is needed to see this view as shown in the guide. Just out of view down to the bottom left is the small reservoir built to supply old mines in the valley.

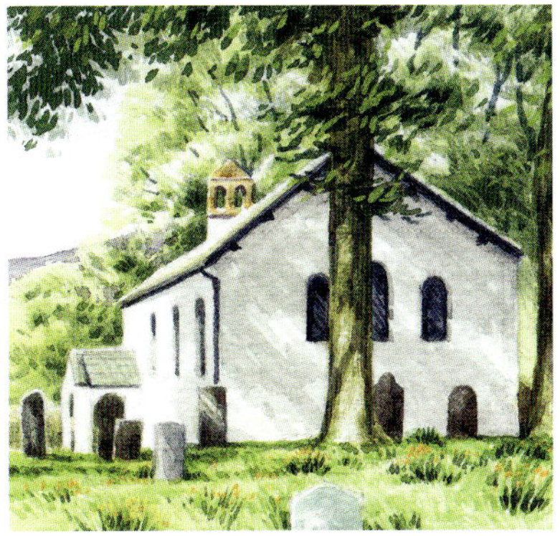

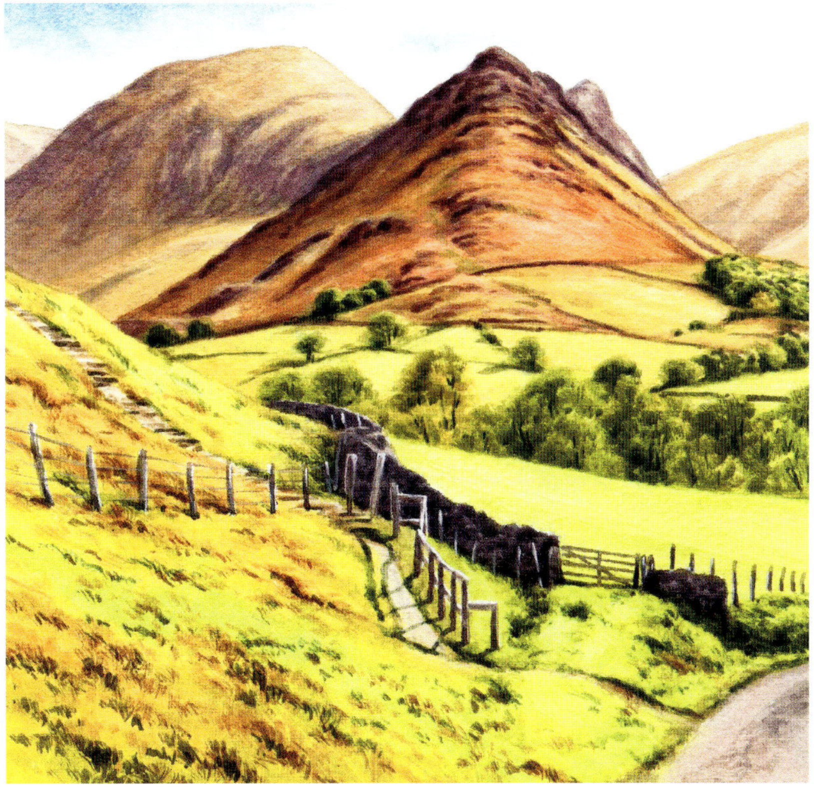

Scope End and Hindscarth from near Little Town 15/5/08

One of the few illustrations in the Pictorial Guides without a title. The hills in this classic lake district view may not be quite so angular as depicted in AW's drawing but it is still an inspiring scene for walkers and artists alike.

Newlands Church 15/5/08

This charming little church sits perfectly in the valley surrounded by high hills. More than one of the trees has gone and as to be expected the graveyard now has a few more residents. Not a bad place to be laid to rest.

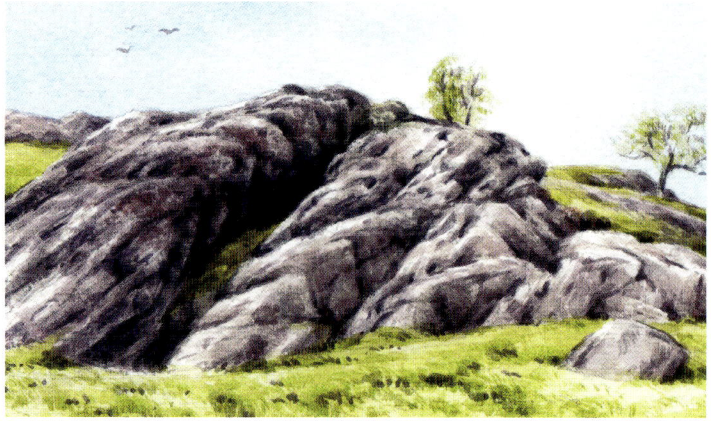

Upper Pan Holes 3/5/09

Just to the east of the ridge path on the lower slopes of Scope End this diagonal cut in the rock reveals the higher mine levels.

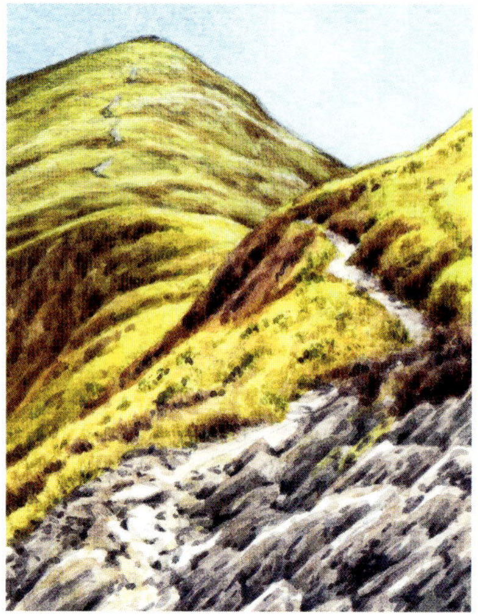

Looking south-west 3/5/09

The ridge path with the big cairn in sight on the peak ahead.

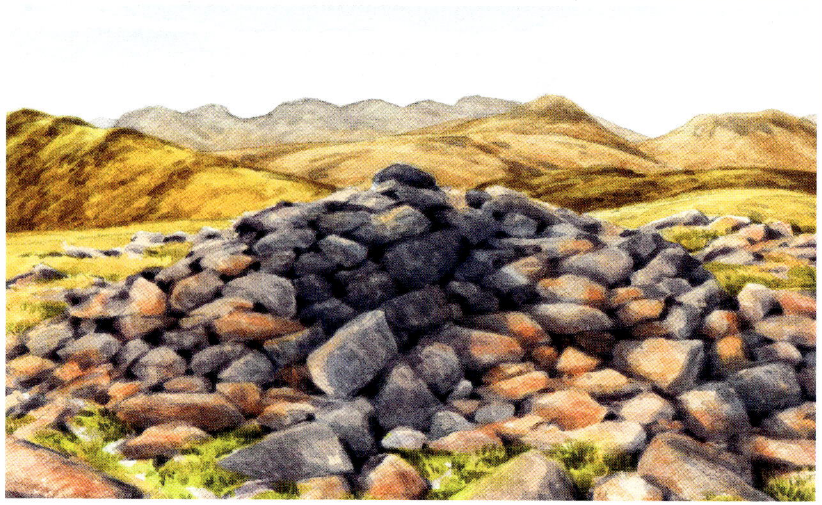

The summit 15/5/08

The cairn has been enlarged and formed into a low wind shelter with an impressive view of the mountains to the south.

Lower Pan Holes 3/5/09

Properly known as Grand Level this is the mine entrance just above the spoil heaps.

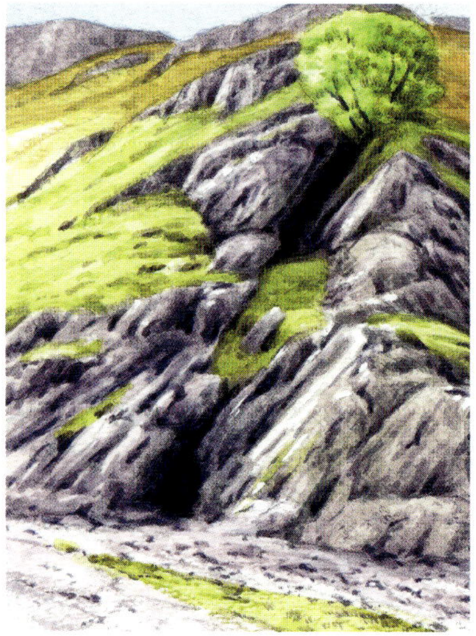

Goldscope Mine

Yet another mine in this area which tunnels deep into the mountain side in the quest of mineral extraction. The name is derived from the German "Gottesgab" meaning God's Gift. The mine was worked from as far back as the middle of the 16th century when expert German miners were brought in by the Company of Mines Royal to develop the potential of the mine. It was an excellent source of lead, copper and other metals which was worked up until the early 1900s.

A cairn of some antiquity 15/5/08

There is some question as to whether this cairn is as old as was once assumed. Maps of 1867 show it as a normal cairn but the revision of 1900 added the "antiquity" styling to the title. Current maps just show it as a cairn without any historic link.

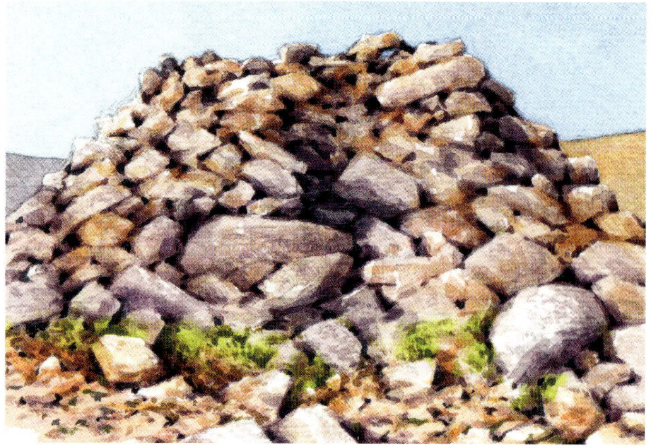

The ravine of Far Tongue Gill 3/5/09

AW's *"amazing ravine"* as seen from the ascent of Dale Head from Little Town.

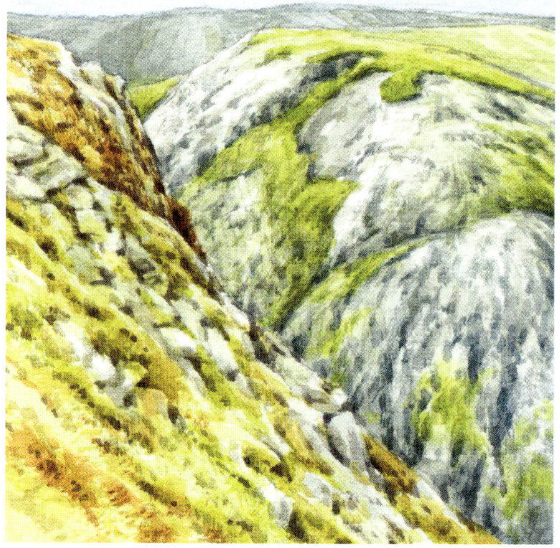

Hopegill Head

The Ordnance Survey always referred to this fell as Hopegill Head, only on the Bartholomew maps was the name Hobcarton Pike used that AW noted. The north-west face of the fell is formed by Hobcarton Crag, steep ground, with gullies and crags of loose rock where few venture, a place where I found myself on more than one occasion in search of the rare Alpine Catchfly, thankfully with successful results.

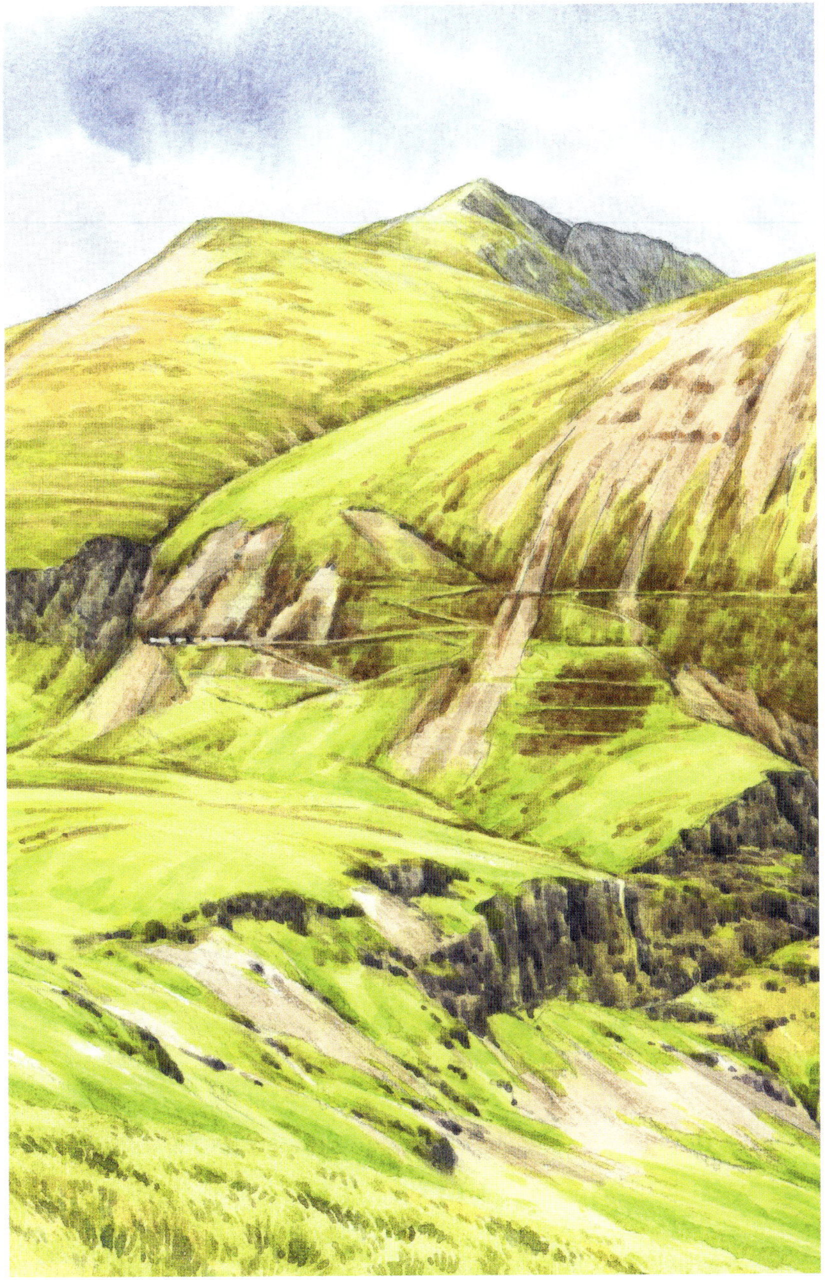

From Scar Crags 12/5/08

This is an unusual view of the fell as only the very top of Hobcarton Crag and the actual summit are in sight. The main section of the scene is taken up by Force Crag and the slopes of Grisedale Pike and Sand Hill. It was the best portrait view of the fell for AW's needs though.

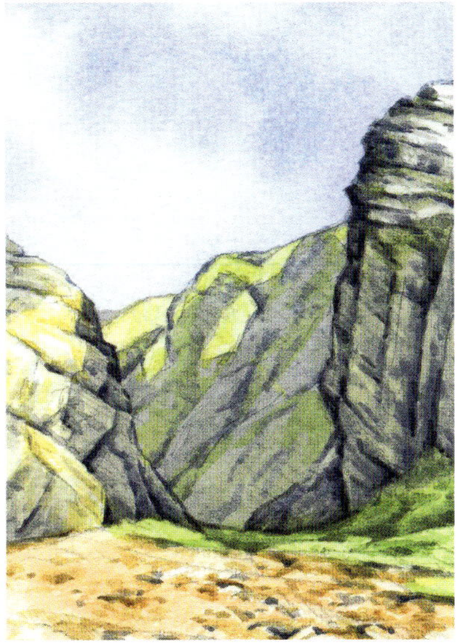

The Notch, Hobcarton Crag 13/5/08

I have stood on this spot on several occasions and even though I could match The Notch itself to AW's illustration, the background just does not configure to his drawing. I have shown the reality.

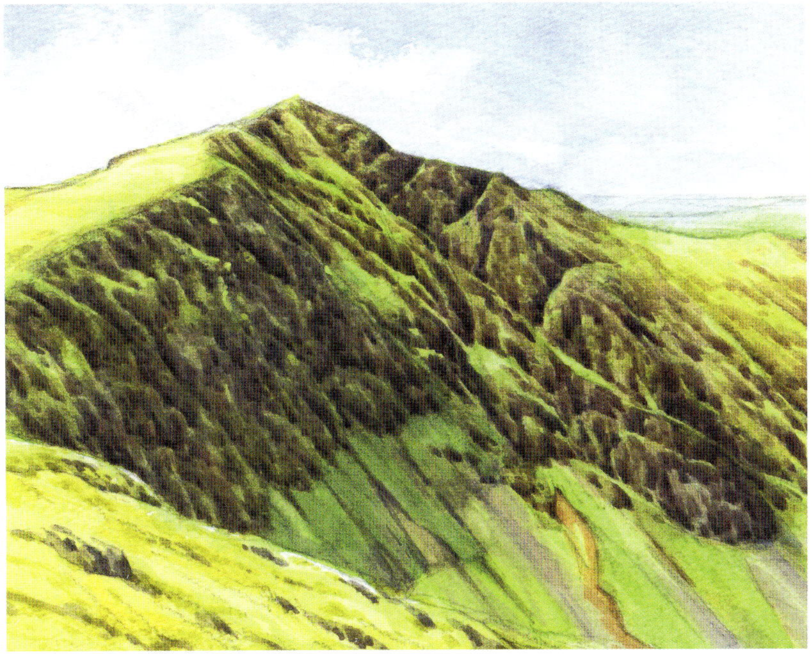

Hobcarton Crag 12/5/08

Seen from near the subsidiary summit of Grisedale Pike the face of the crag is seen in full. My quest to find the elusive flowering Catchfly meant that I ascended directly up one of the steep gullies shown in this sketch, not a route that I would recommend.

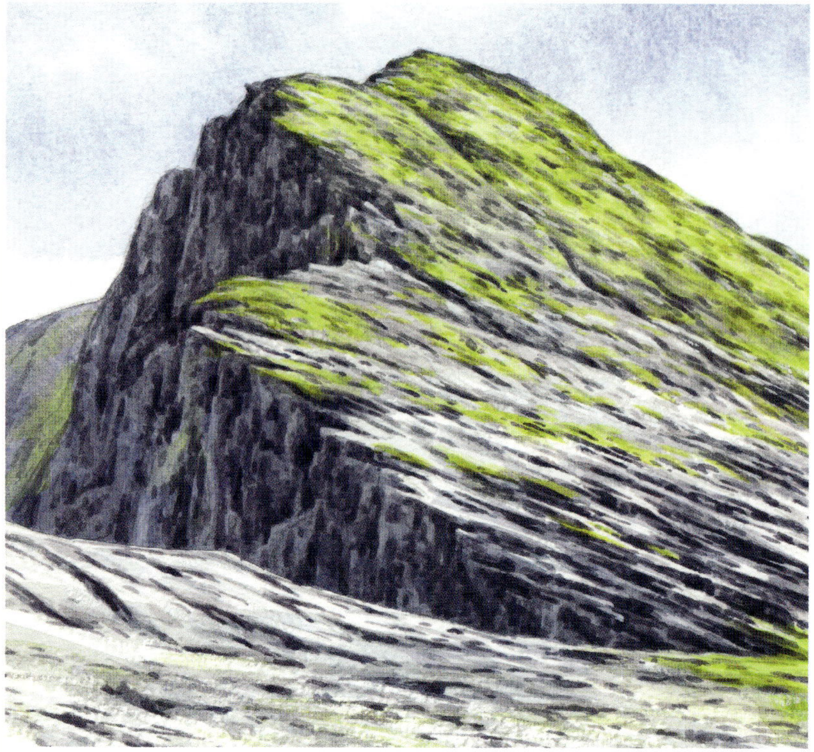

Hobcarton Crag 13/5/08
The upper section of the crag as seen on the north ridge approach.

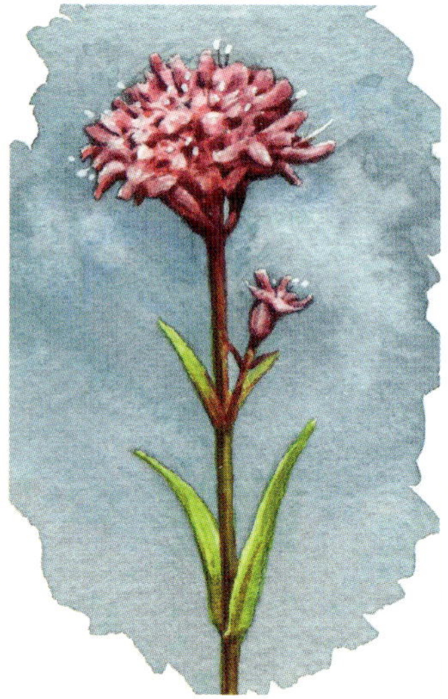

Viscaria Alpina 15/7/15
Only by scrambling up into the steep gullies of the crag was I able to see this rare beauty for myself, whether AW did the same is unclear but I have my doubts.

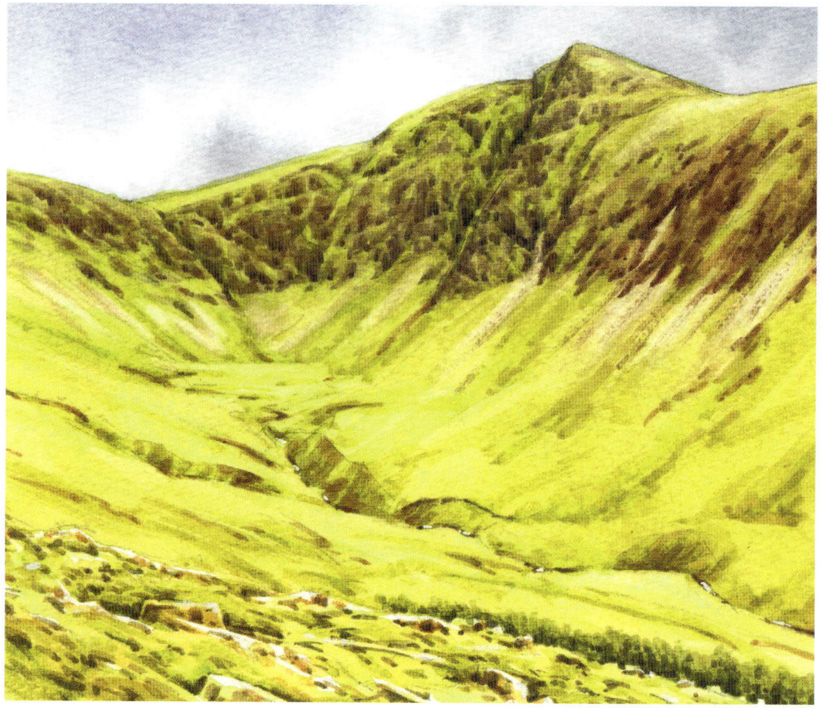

Hobcarton Valley and Crag 12/5/13
The forest has matured and been felled in this unfrequented location.

The summit of Hopegill Head, from the cairn on Sand Hill 6/3/11
A broad path now leads to the top.

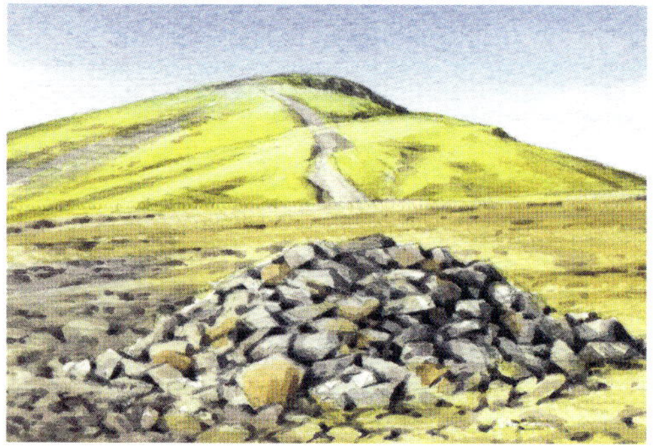

The summit 12/3/11
The bare rock of the highest point is only adorned with the smallest of cairns.

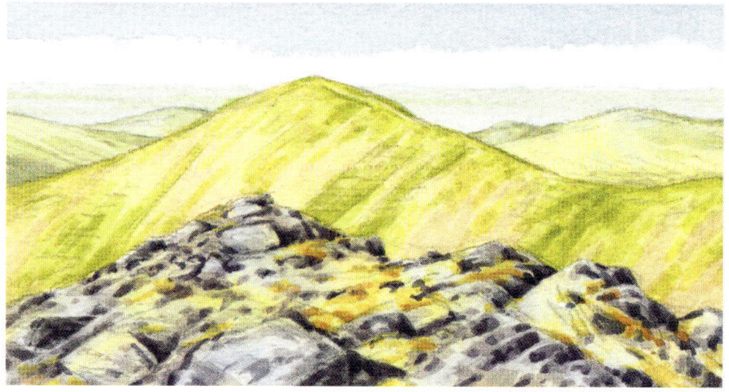

The ridge to Whiteside 6/3/11
One of my favourite ridge walks between two neighbouring fells.

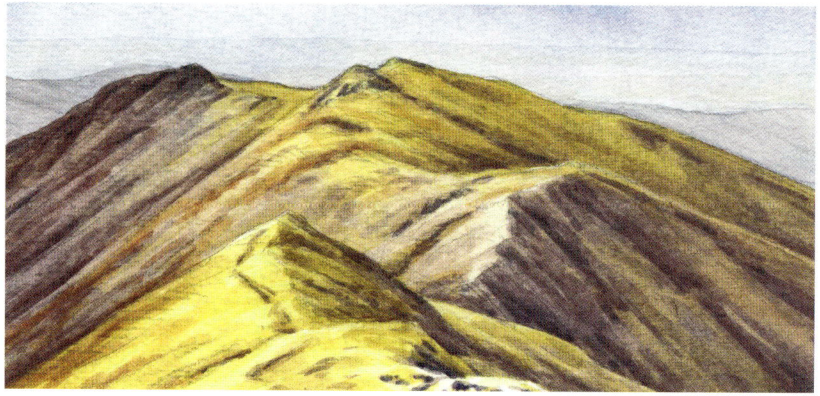

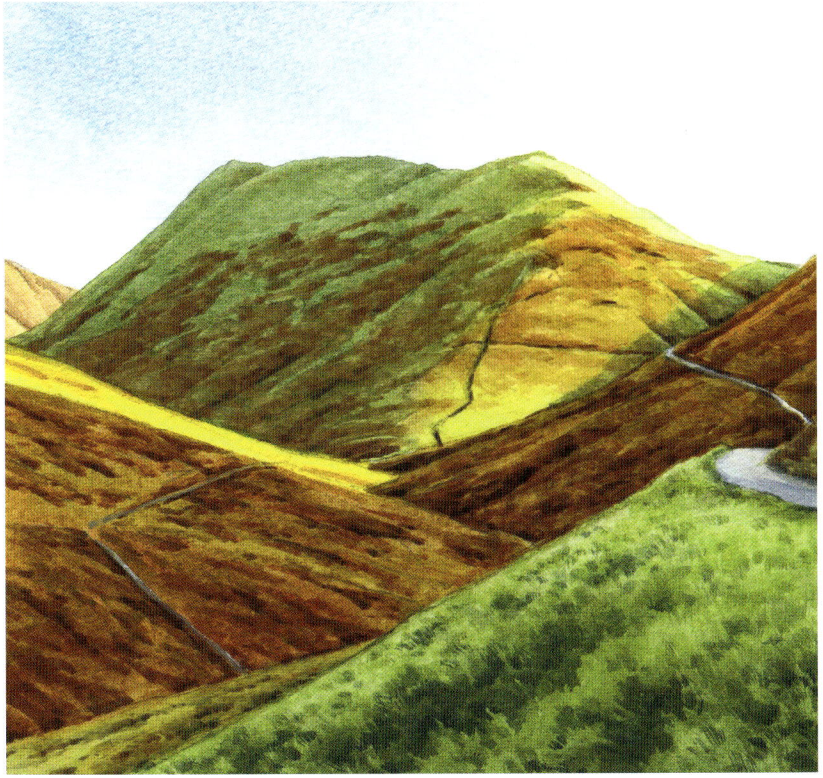

Knott Rigg

The steep walk from Newlands Hause to the summit may be one of the shorter fell ascents at just under a mile but the reward outweighs the effort. Many are tempted to continue along the ridge for another mile to the summit of Ard Crags. It is a there and back walk but pick the right day in late summer when the fells are cloaked in purple heather and it is a day you will not forget. Take a picnic and flask.

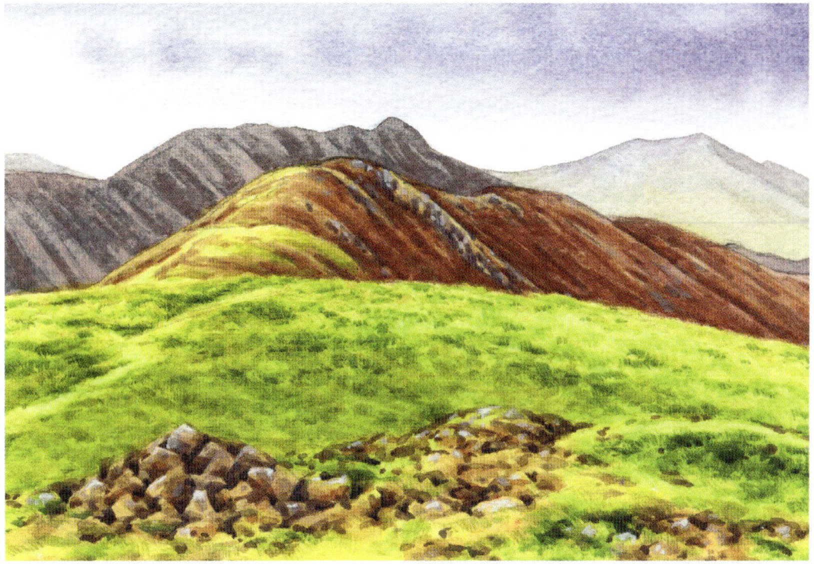

The summit 16/5/09

This minor cairn marks the highest point which was correctly identified by AW in the guide. Maps of the day pinpointed a lower height nearby.

From Buttermere 10/9/09

At just after 7.30 am on a bright September morning the early sun illuminates the slopes of the fell. The road up to Newlands Hause is on the right, a road popular with tourists which becomes tricky in winter conditions when ice forms.

Keskadale Edge and Ill Gill 10/9/09

I can just imagine Wainwright walking along this road and as he rounded the bend he was inspired to capture the view with its winding lane and peaked ridge for future use. The road is now more popular with motorists but it is still fairly quiet. Keskadale Farm is in the trees on the left.

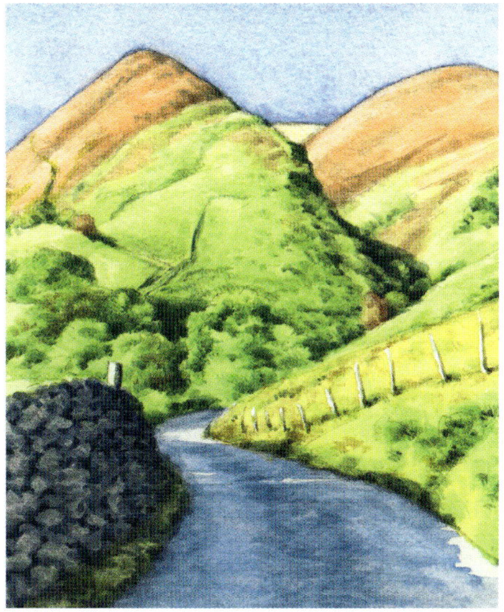

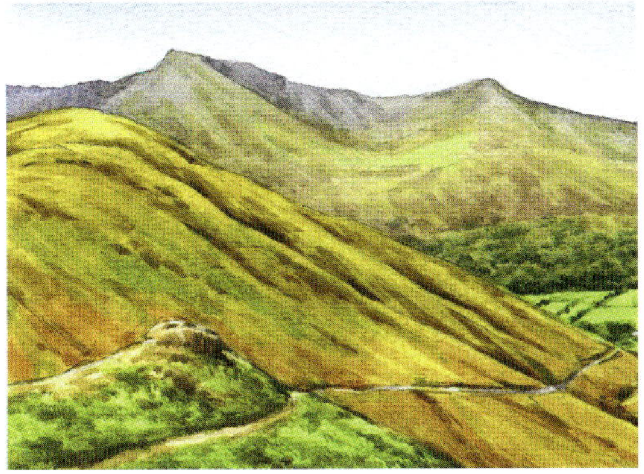

Looking down to the Buttermere valley 16/5/08

This view is a retrospective of the scene at the top left looking down to the road, with the valley and the High Stile range in the distance.

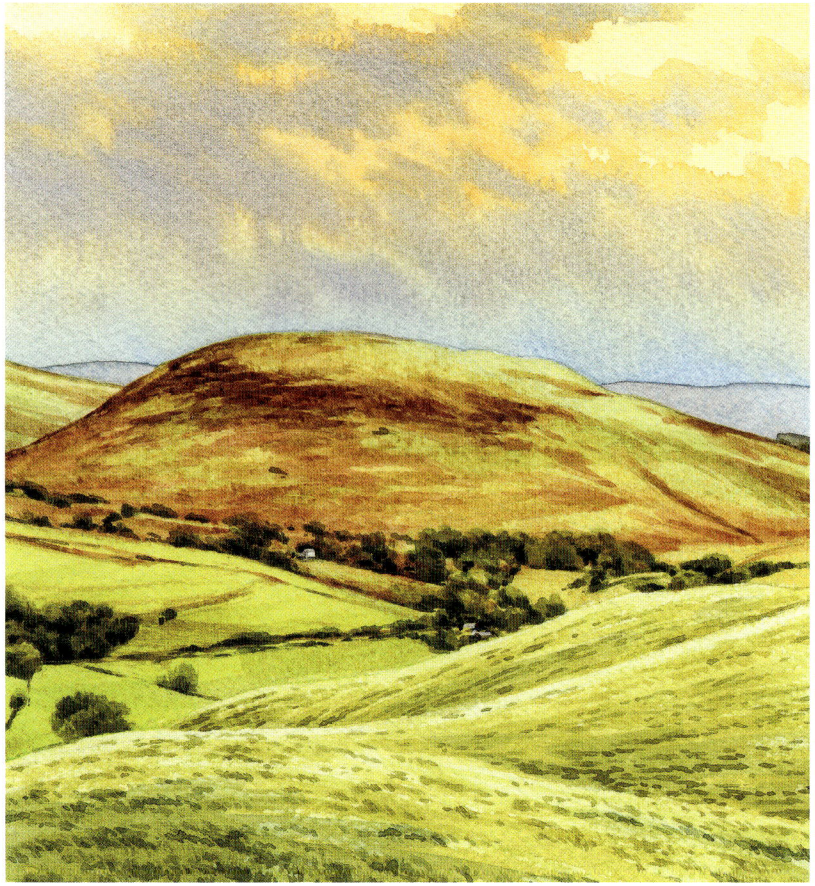

From Sale Fell 18/5/08
The rounded slopes of Ling Fell as viewed from the matching grazed flanks of Sale Fell, as seen from 100 yards east of the summit.

Ling Fell

The heather which once covered the fell and gave the hill its name is now patchy with bracken encroaching on the gentle slopes. Occasionally red grouse can be seen if you are lucky but the habitat now cannot support a decent population that there obviously once was, judging by the ruined shooting butts.

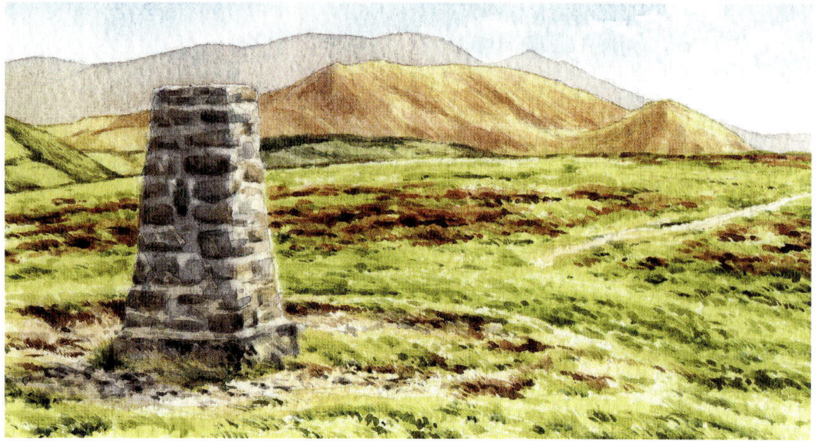

The summit 18/5/08
The view past the triangulation pillar towards the Skiddaw massif. Only one other column in the Pictorial Guides is drawn twice in the same fell chapter, that of High Pike in the Northern Fells.

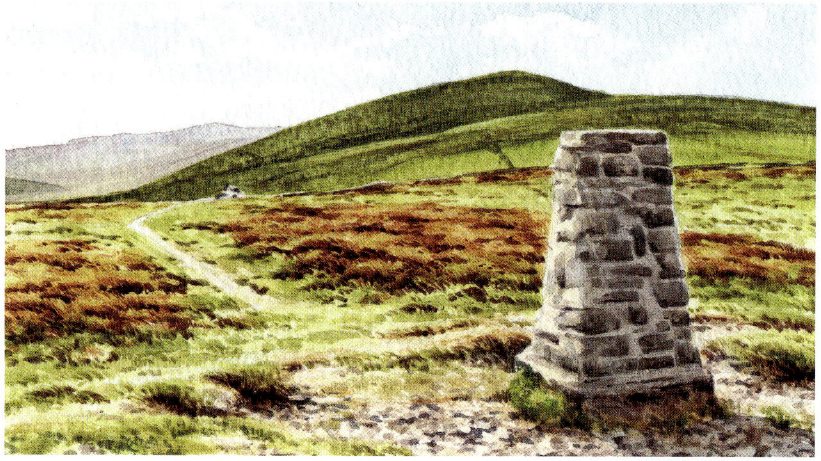

Looking south east 18/5/08
The stones that were shown at the foot of the pillar in AW's drawings have been moved and now form a small cairn a short distance from here, just visible in this sketch. That point may be just slightly higher than here but not by much, if at all.

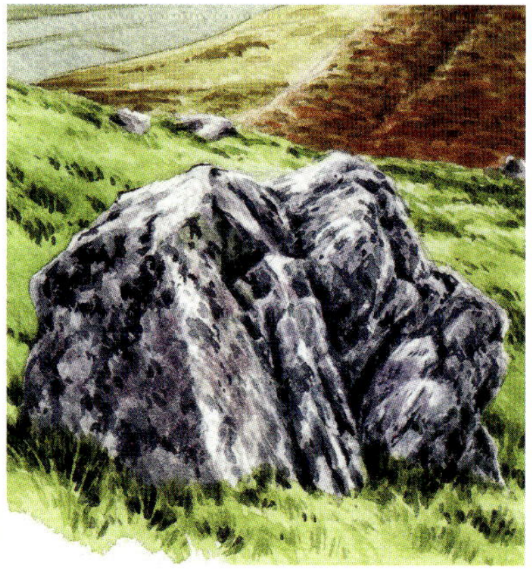

Speckled boulder, Tom Rudd Beck 18/5/08
There are several such boulders in this valley and some diligent searching was required to locate the correct one. It is about three feet high.

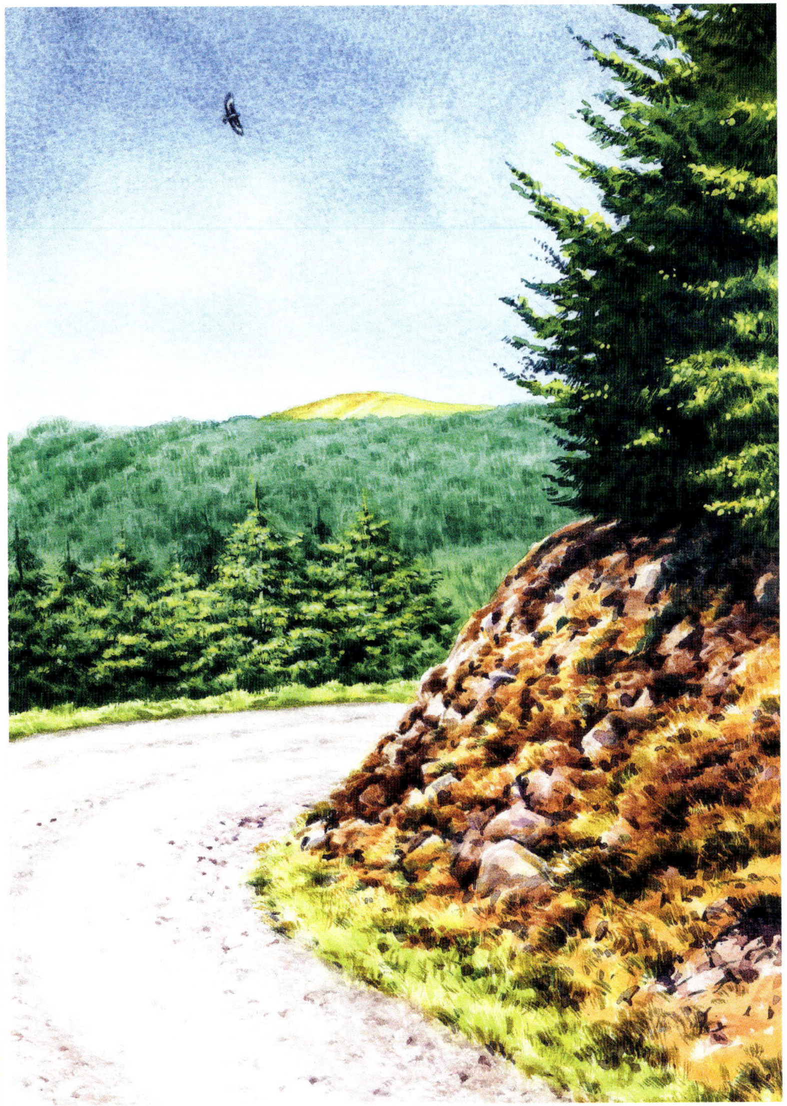

From a forest road in Comb Plantation 13/5/08
The numerous tracks through the forest were explored until I came across this, the exact location. Today the Forestry Commission plantation obscures all but the very top of the fell when viewed from here. A lone buzzard circles overhead.

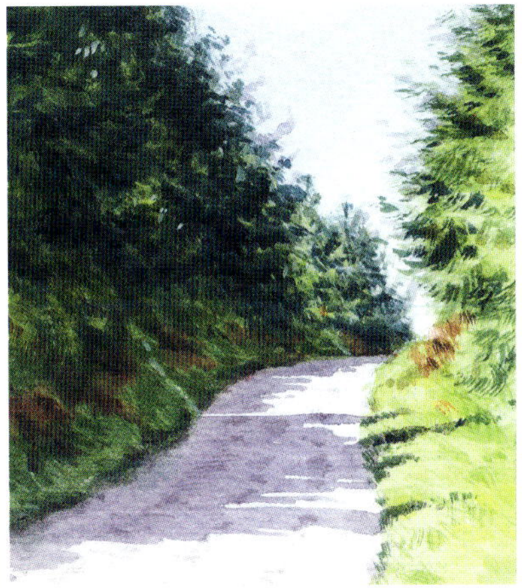

A forest road, Comb Plantation 13/5/08
The mature trees that featured in AW's illustration will most likely have been felled, this is the most similar scene that I could find to his view.

Lord's Seat

I have nearly always visited the summit of Lord's Seat whilst walking the "round" of the Lorton Fells. Its location means that the neighbouring hills of Broom Fell or Barf are easily visited. Its south-eastern slopes are still densely covered by forest.

Looking east to Barf 23/7/09
The forest fence has since been removed. The top section of Dodd now clear of trees.

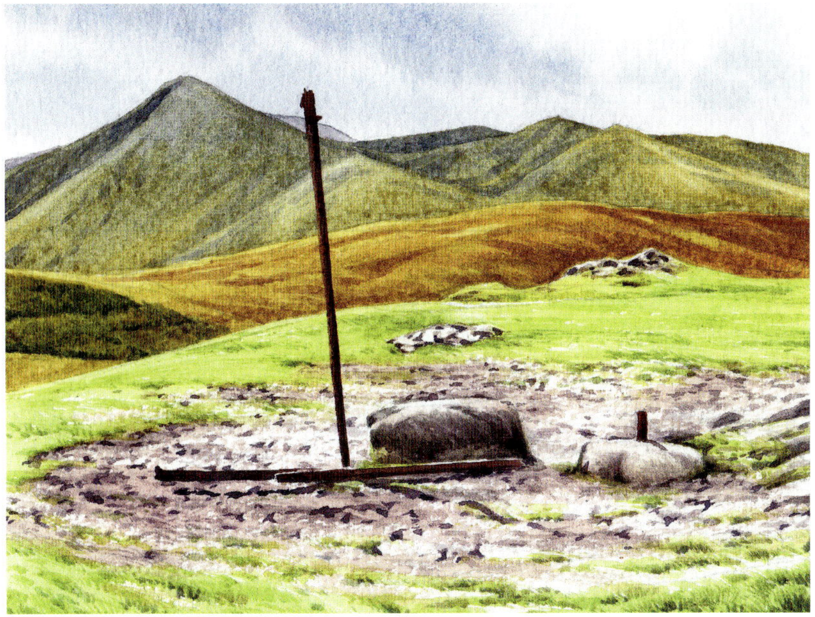

The summit 23/7/09
I was curious as to why the remains of the old iron fence seen here did not feature in AW's drawing, but my guess would be that he stood slightly forward of this point with the ironwork just behind him for a clearer view.

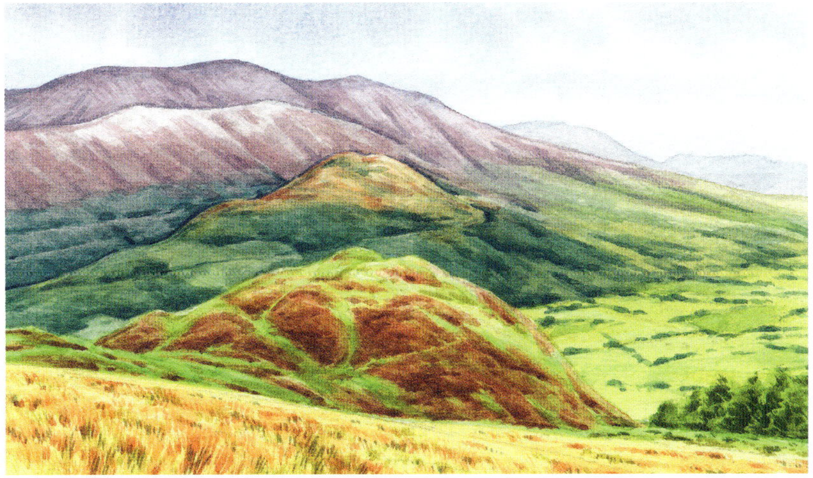

Maiden Moor

Before Wainwright, another well known author and artist, Beatrix Potter, had seen fit to make this fell famous. On the slopes above Little Town Mrs. Tiggy-Winkle lived in a house in the hillside by a big rock. The Newlands Valley can be easily identified in illustrations from that book.

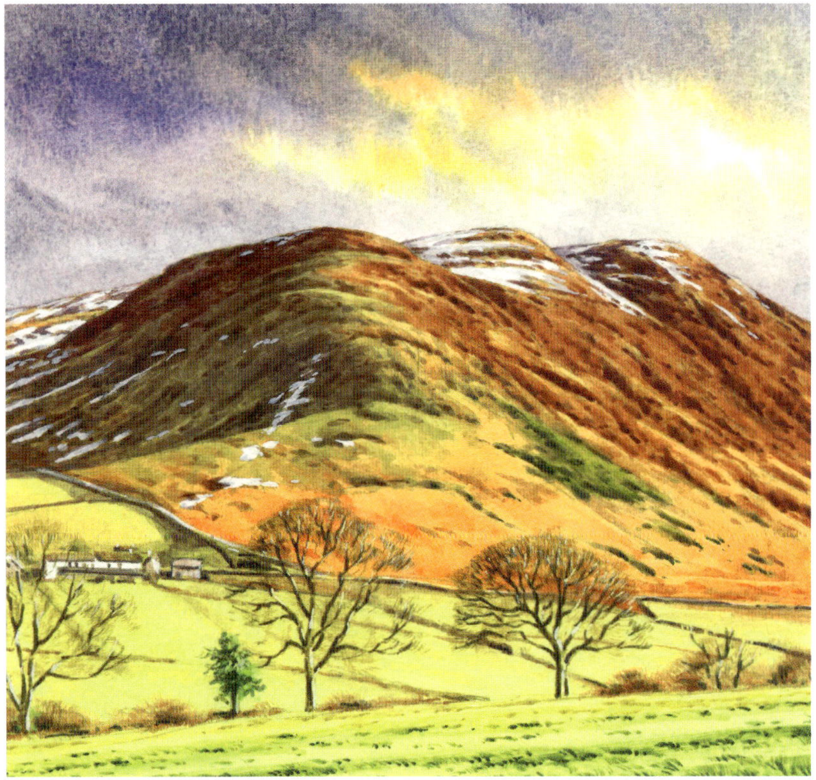

From Rigg Beck 22/3/07
The houses of Little Town give scale to the fell which rises up behind. This view is obtained on the narrow lane between Rigg Beck and Little Town.

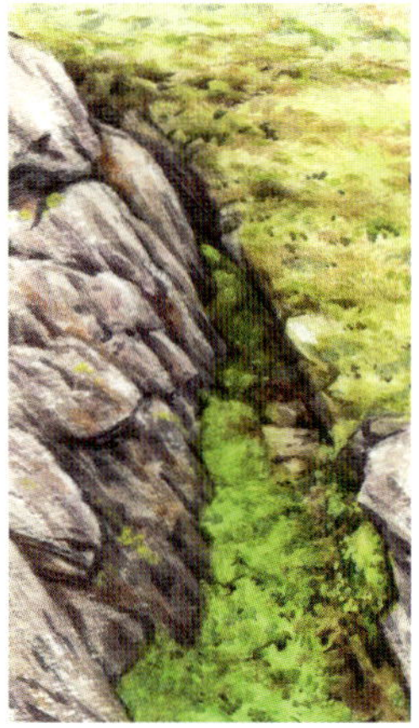

The entrance to Little Mine 3/5/09
This narrow cut is to be found on the steep ground above the valley track but away from regular paths.

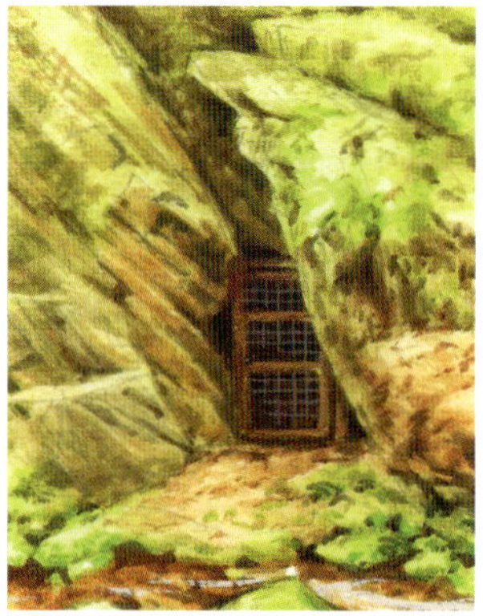

Lakeland's most exotic cave 23/5/14
The cave is now on private land (the reason it could not be found for the revised guide) and has lost some of its charm as the flowering shrubs have been cut back. A locked safety gate prevents exploration.

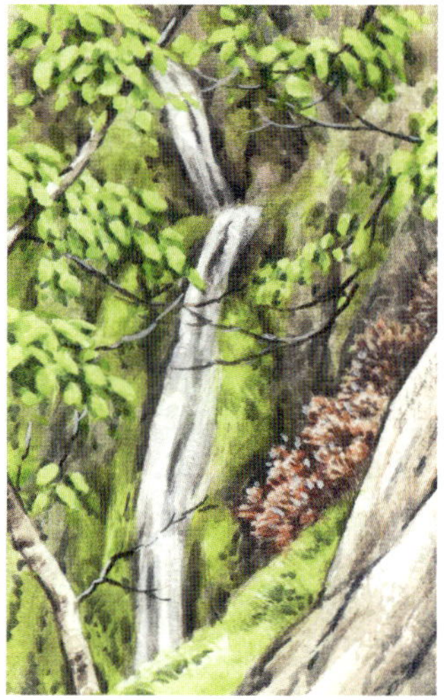

Waterfalls above Ellers Beck 3/5/11
The trees now almost hide these falls from full view.

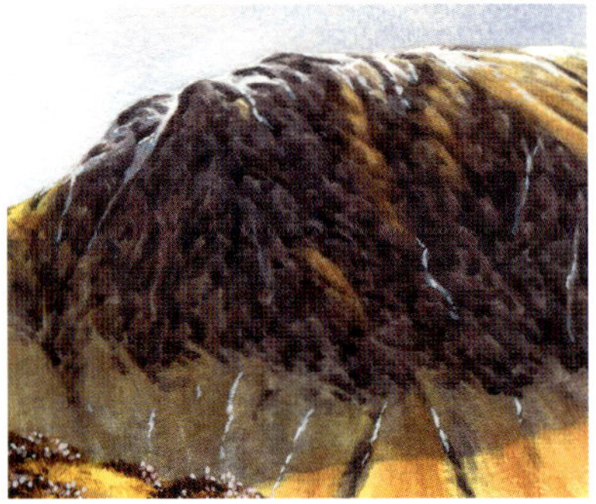

From Scope End 22/3/07
Snow lingers in the shaded gullies of Bull Crag on the western side of the fell.

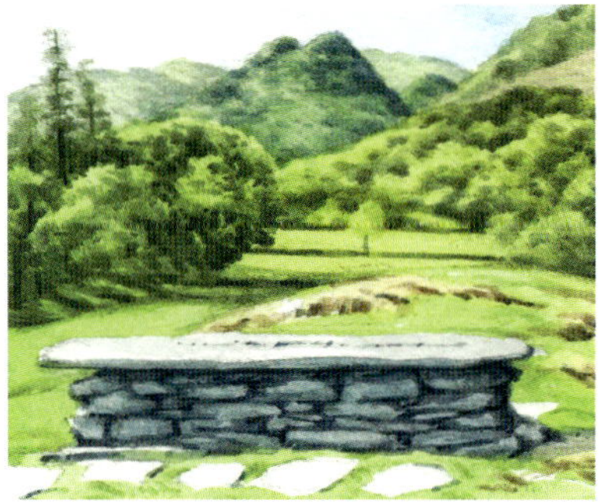

Peace How 14/5/08
This engraved slate seat records the donating of this property to The National Trust in 1917 by Canon Rawnsley, a founding member of the Trust itself.

The summit 15/5/08
This is AW's reckoned top, 100 yards from the small cairn which is the recognised top. Only from here can Bowfell be seen as in his summit view.

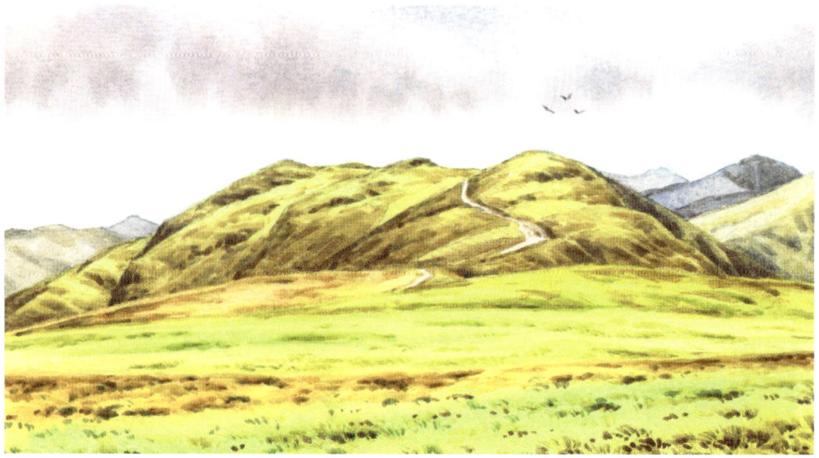

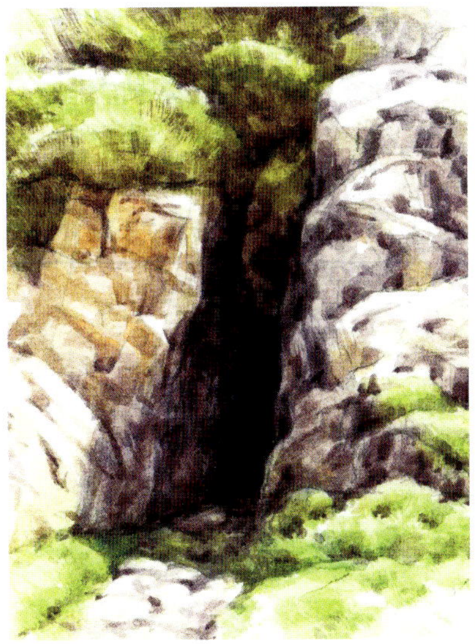

Entrance to the old level, Trap Knotts 15/5/08

Hidden in Yewthwaite Combe.

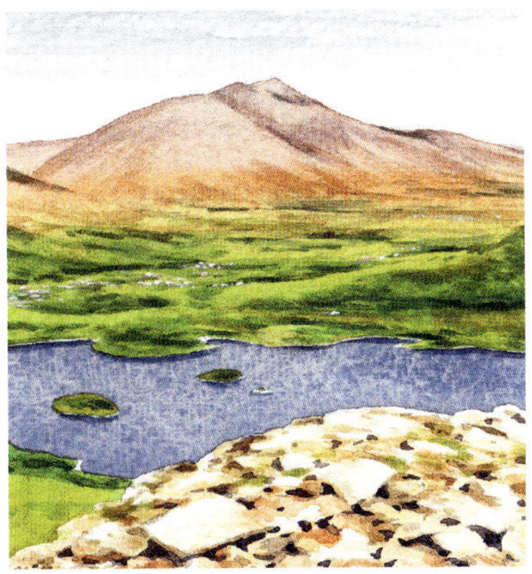

Blencathra from the north-east cairn 15/5/08

The cairn is now almost flattened but the view remains impressive.

The Newlands edge 15/5/08

The scene looking west from the north edge of the summit plateau of Maiden Moor.

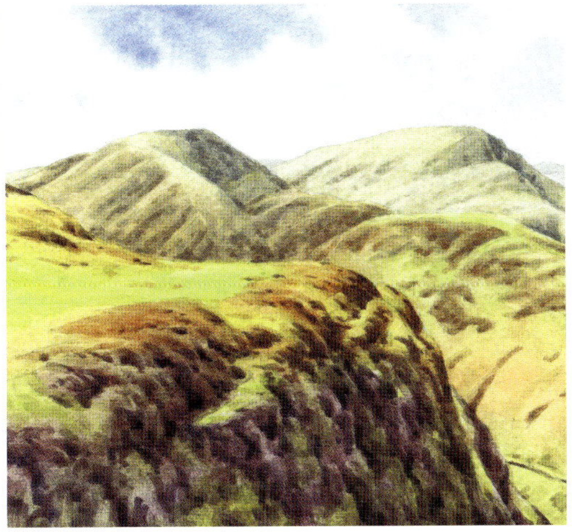

The cairn on Blea Crag 15/5/08

Today the once decent cairn is now a heap of rubble but the crag top is still well worth a visit.

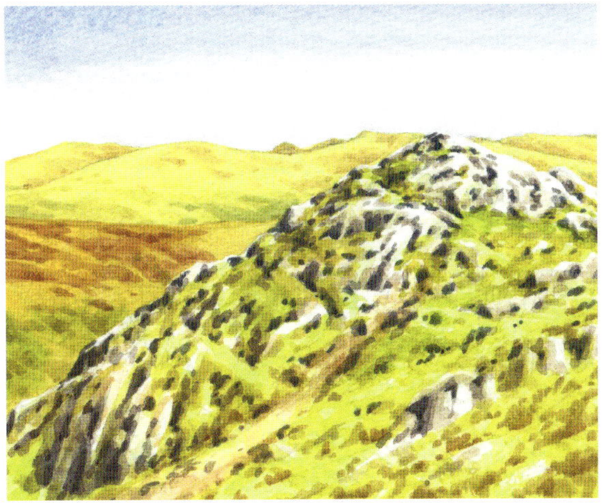

Mounds and pillars made by man.

For thousands of years, probably since he first occupied this landscape, man has seen fit to leave his mark by building mounds, cairns and pillars from the local available stone. The reasons for doing so are various, from the ancient ritual of marking a burial ground or important site to the more recent activity of indicating a summit of high ground or a fine viewpoint. The Lakeland Fells have numerous sites of antiquity which are clearly marked on current maps and are of major archaeological interest. Many books have been written on the subject and are worth reading.

On certain fell summits such as Seatallan, Binsey and Selside Pike will be seen substantial cairns which have been marked by the O.S. as historic. Often these cairns and other mounds denoted as tumuli have since been re-modelled into basic wind shelters by modern day walkers, many of whom I am sure are oblivious to the origins of such piles of stones. In more recent times cairns have become a feature of almost every fell top but even today a few defy having such adornment.

Elsewhere on the hills time has been taken to construct edifices of greater quality, stone towers and columns which even though they are hard to date may have been in place for many years but surprisingly others are more recent. Their reason for being built is often not obvious or recorded. In particular the Thornthwaite Crag "beacon" which once stood at about 14 feet high (page 110) but has now lost its top few feet. Wainwright mentions this obelisk on the day of his first venture onto the high fells in June 1930 but in researching this book I failed to find any mention of this pillar prior to 1912 on any old maps, so it is most likely to be a more recent construction, as is the column on Hallin Fell to the north. The term "beacon" is to be found on some recent maps and indeed also in the Pictorial Guides but this doesn't necessarily mean they were places where signalling fires were lit, many were previously marked as curricks, indicating they were most likely shepherd's cairns for finding their way in bad weather or for simply taking shelter.

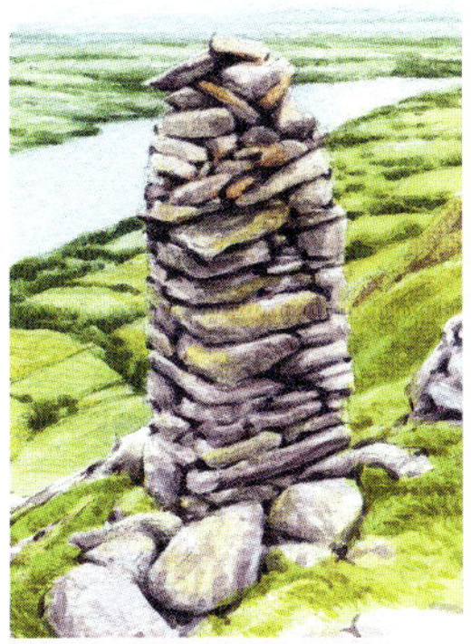

Even in recent years cairns and columns are still being built such as the one on the right, the more recent upper "tower" on Bonscale Pike which already looks as if it has been in place for years. It hasn't, but I doubt that it will outlive the mounds of ancient man.

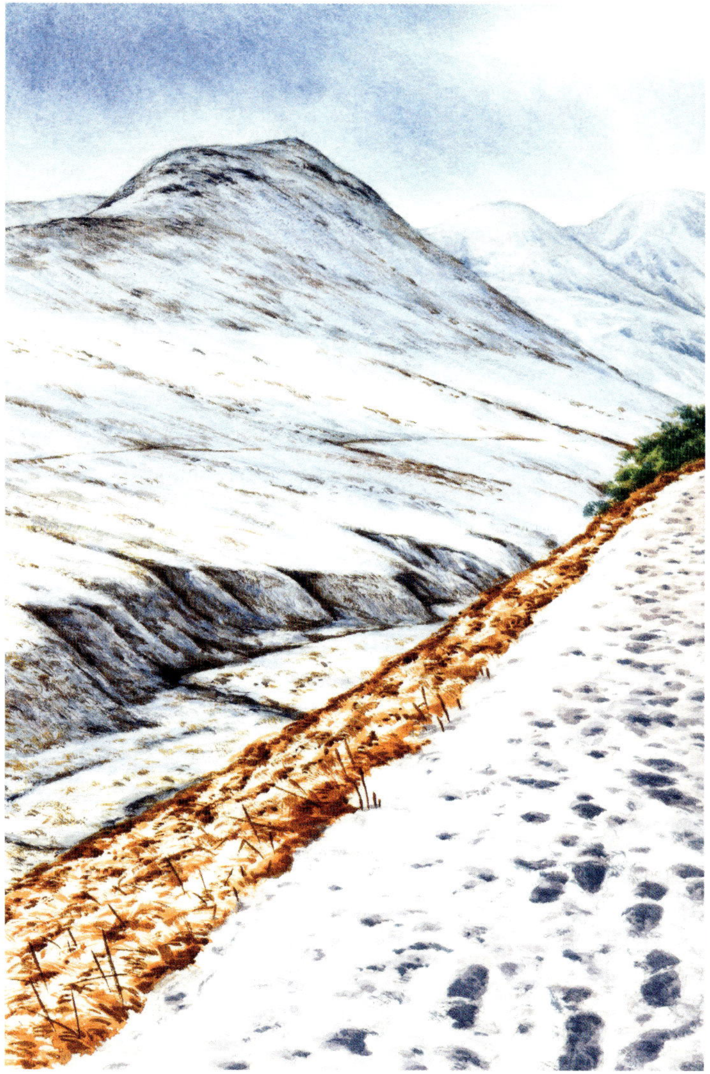

From Coledale 15/1/16

I had nearly given up on producing this sketch in the winter conditions as depicted by AW. However, late on in the proceedings a short period of snow enabled me to visit Coledale and obtain the reference with the valley in a covering of snow, showing evidence of more walkers than his lone footprints.

Outerside

Positioned in the heart of the Coledale valley Outerside is almost surrounded by higher hills on all sides, restricting views from the summit. I finished my second round of Wainwright fells for this project here on 10th Sept. 2014 obtaining my last official reference, exactly 49 years to the day after AW finished his field work on Starling Dodd. It was an emotional day.

The summit 12/5/09

By omitting the background, AW's illustration gave me free rein to produce this sketch with Eel Crag behind.

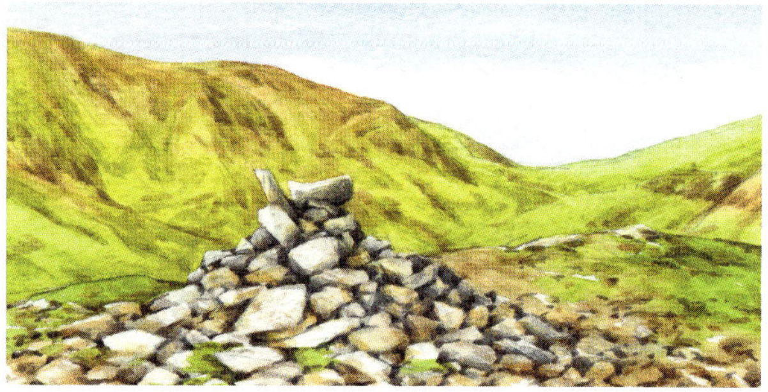

Stile End 12/5/08

The grassy path that heads up to Barrow Door is a pleasant way to gently ascend to the Coledale hills.

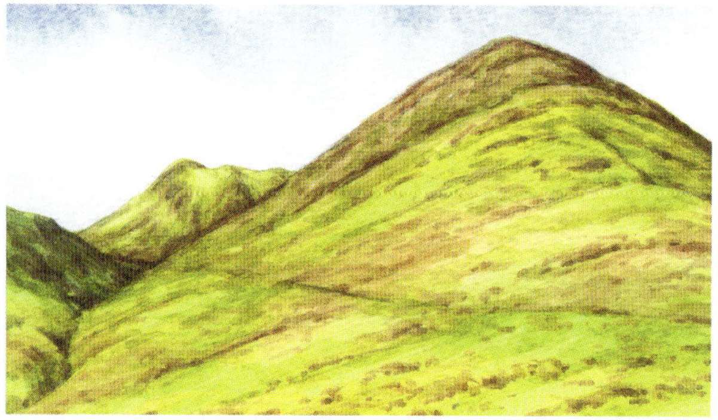

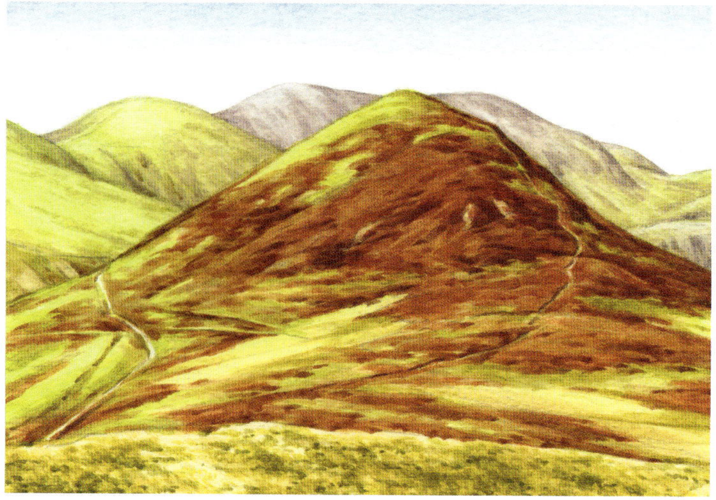

Outerside from Stile End 12/5/08

Stile End is a nice little top in its own right and a visit is recommended if walking in the area of Outerside and Barrow.

Sail Pass (left), Sail and Eel Crag from Outerside 12/5/09

AW's drawing showing only the top of the cairn appears that he ran out of space at the bottom of the page. I have included it in full.

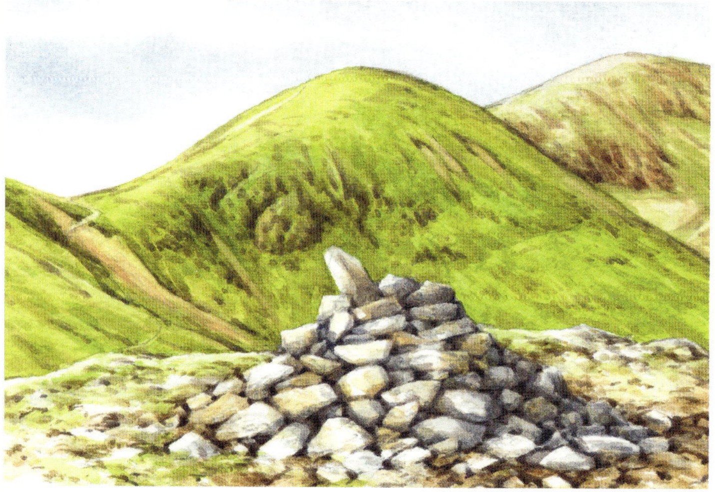

Dry stone walls - the dying art

Many visitors to the district will be impressed at the lines of dry stone walls that divide the pastures in the valley bottoms and then trace their way up over the fell sides like an endless grey snake. Even Wainwright was an admirer of this skill and called it *"a dying art"* alongside his detailed wall drawing (High Pike 4, Book One). The early inhabitants needed to use the fertile land in the valley bottoms for the growing of crops so any rubble was cleared and utilised in the construction of field boundaries, this not only defined properties but also could contain stock. The best example of this is perhaps seen at Wasdale Head where there was so much rock debris the walls ended up many feet wide in places. These fields in the valley near the farms were known as in-bye fields but as the farms extended up the fell sides the enclosed plots that were "taken" from the fell were known as in-take fields. Higher land beyond these walls was open fell. These walls were often constructed by the farmers and their families themselves. It is worth noting that the walls in some valleys are made of the rounded stones washed out of rivers which requires a different walling skill to those of the walls made from quarried stone.

The main period of walling took place in the 18th and 19th centuries during the Enclosure Movement which allowed wealthy landowners to delineate their land. However, there was a time restriction for the land to be enclosed so teams of professional wallers were employed to construct mile upon mile of wall. They could have been local labourers or out of work miners but many were from out of the area who moved from estate to estate. Normally the wallers would stay on site for six days a week and come down off the fell for one day to go to church or get supplies. An expert waller could build about five yards of wall a day depending on the construction and availability of material. Individual stones once selected were used, no energy was wasted in trying stones for size. At roughly one tonne per yard it was hard graft for little reward. Stone for the walls was either picked up from the fellside or where such material was limited, small quarries were dug to provide the needed stones. Space is restricted here to go into the design of the walls but they nearly all have a tapering profile, wider at the bottom than the top, the two faces are in filled with smaller stones and larger throughstones (throughs) placed horizontally across the width of the wall about halfway up which help to bind the two sides of the wall. Good walls can last for hundreds of years.

Across many fell tops can be seen the rusty remnants of metal fencing put in place around the 1870s when walling was impractical or too costly but the dry stone walls have outlived them by far.

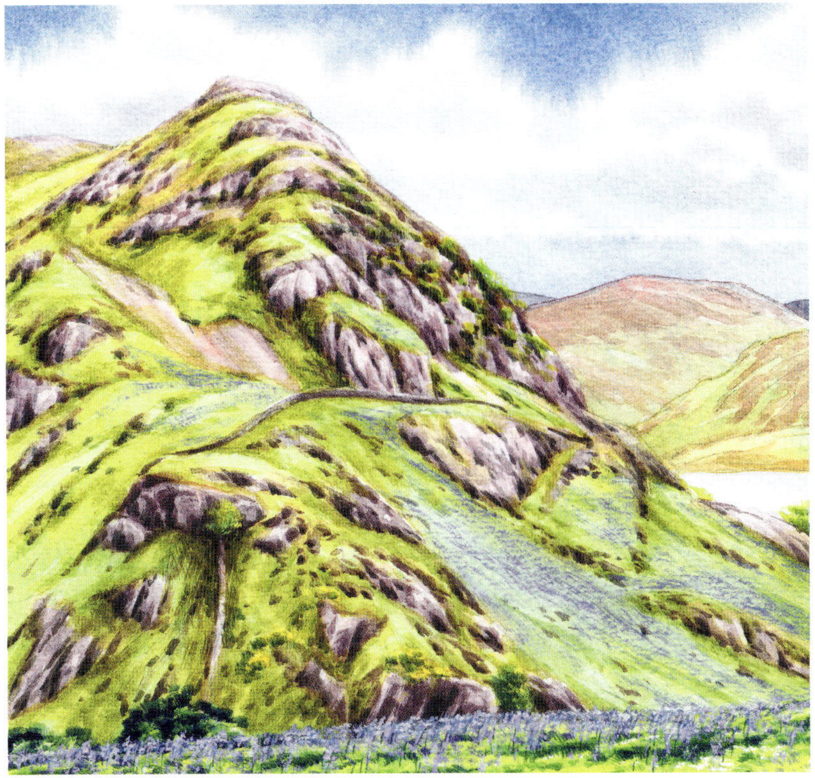

From High Rannerdale 17/5/08

The craggy north-western face of the fell is softened by the swathes of bluebells. The small tree in the bottom right of AW's illustration was in fact a rowan which has now died, I found its decaying boughs lying amongst the flowers.

Rannerdale Knotts

The lower slopes of the hill and the valley of Squat Beck are not only reputed to be the site of a battle in the 11th or 12th century, but these days are better known for the carpet of bluebells which bloom here in late spring each year, and have become a popular tourist attraction in their own right, usually in full bloom in late May. A fairly easy ascent of the fell can be achieved from Buttermere by the ridge along Low Bank, south-east of the summit.

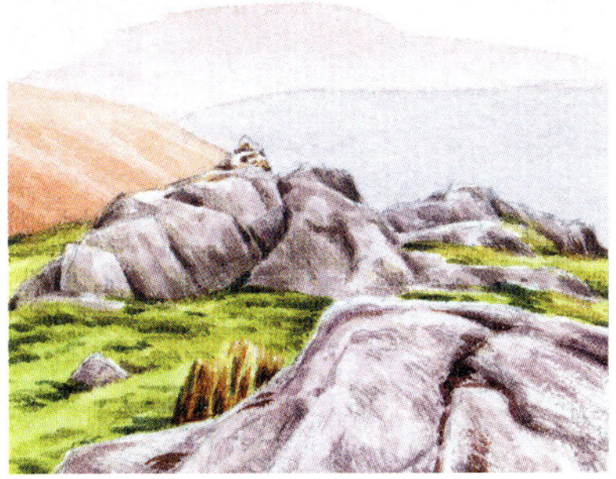

The main summit 17/5/08

A small cairn on a rock platform behind which and to the right can be seen the second summit. Robinson forms the far skyline.

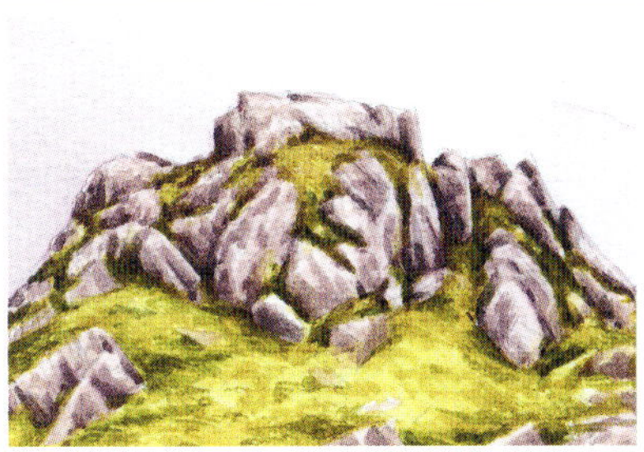

The second summit 17/5/08

A castle of bare rock devoid on this occasion of any form of cairn.

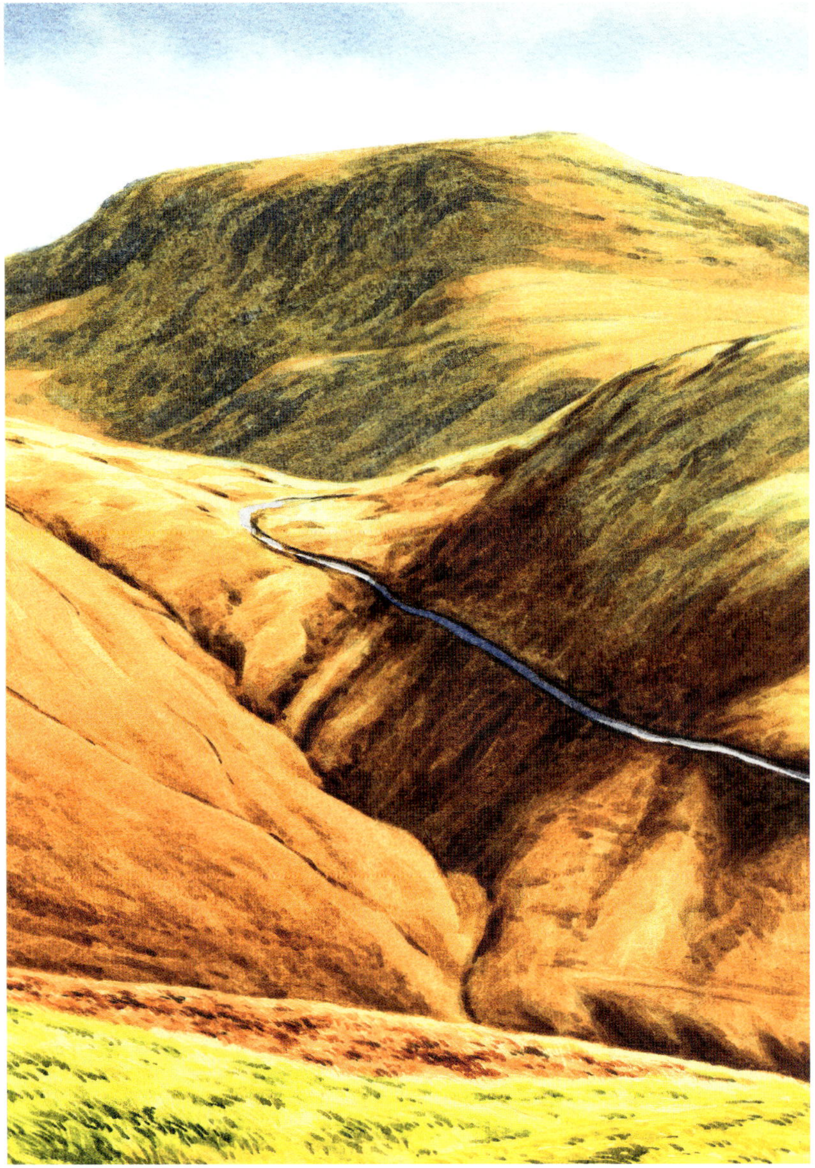

From Whiteless Breast 29/9/11
This location on the flank of Whiteless Pike provides a fine prospect of the west face of Robinson beyond Newlands Hause.

Robinson

From lower levels the best views of Robinson as a mountain are either from the Newlands Valley road or from across Buttermere. In my opinion the aspect of the fell from Whiteless Breast (left) does not do this fell justice but it meets the required format shape for the chapter page in the guidebook. Ascents made from either Newlands Church or Hassness will not disappoint.

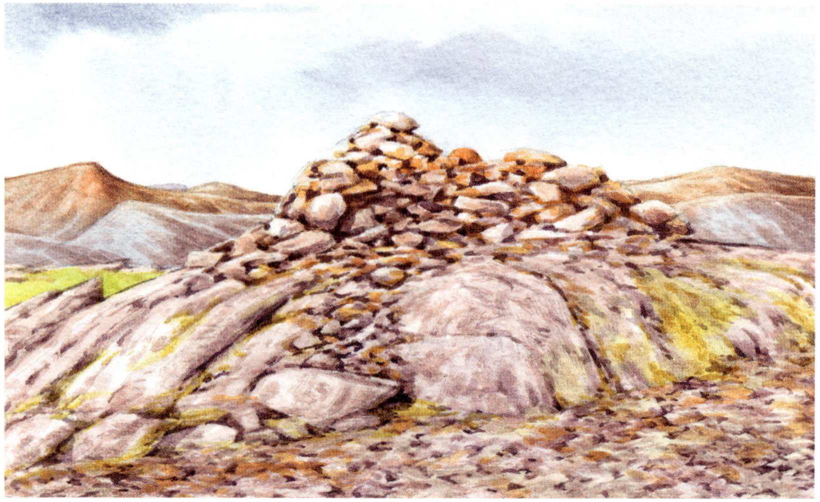

The summit 15/5/08
A rough cairn marks the summit on the more westerly of two rock ridges on the fell top. Away to the left is the distinctive coloured spur of Red Pike.

The lakeside tunnel 7/11/11
The sapling in the foreground of AW's drawing has matured, and now forms an obstacle on the path before the entrance to this low passageway through the rock.

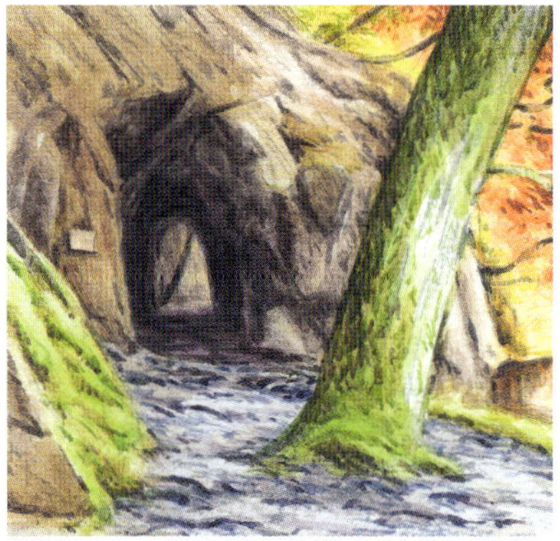

Cairn on High Snockrigg 7/11/11
At one time Wainwright included High Snockrigg on his potential list of fells, but it wasn't to be and it was demoted to get only a brief mention in the Robinson pages.

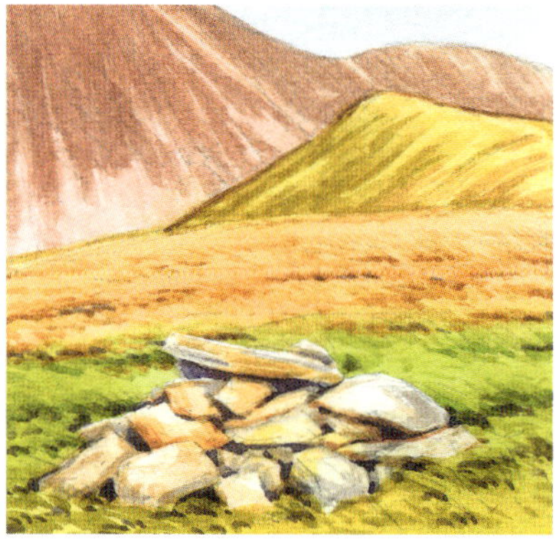

Hackney Holes 15/5/09
This natural feature on the hill is not unlike a disused quarry. The end of the wall highlighted by AW is still in place but serves no practical purpose.

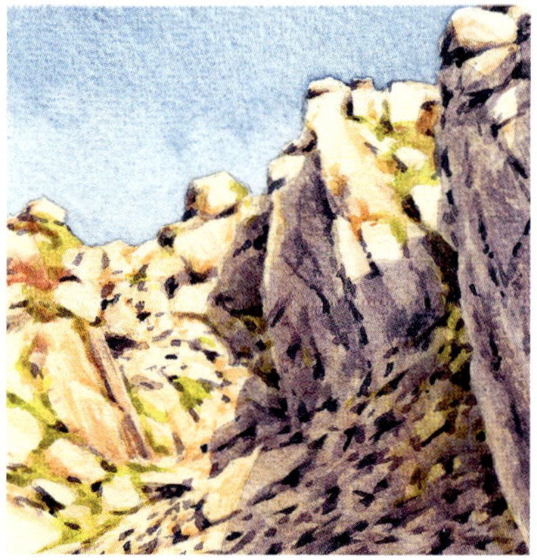

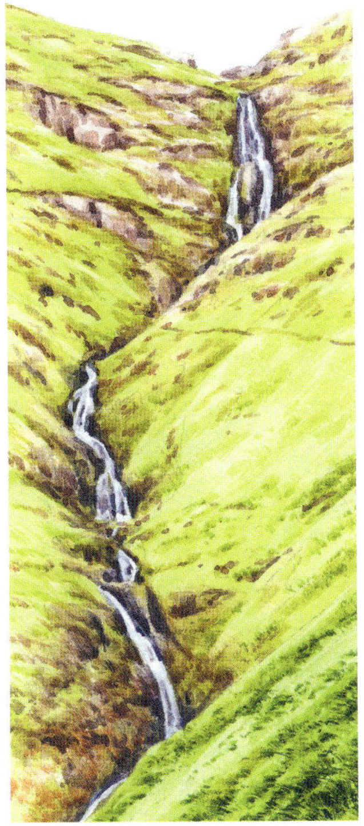

Moss Force, Newlands Hause 10/9/09

An impressive series of falls with an overall drop of over 300'. To fit it into a tight page space AW made it narrower than it is in reality.

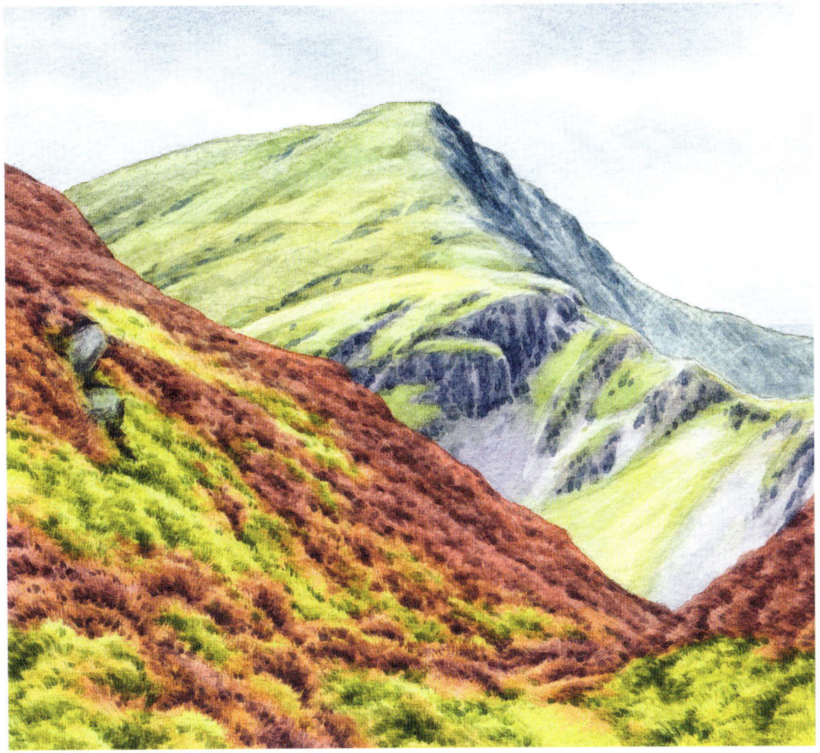

The north-east ridge of Robinson, from Scope End 3/5/09

This drawing by AW in the Pictorial Guide is one of my favourites. A great mountain vista that neatly finishes the fell chapter.

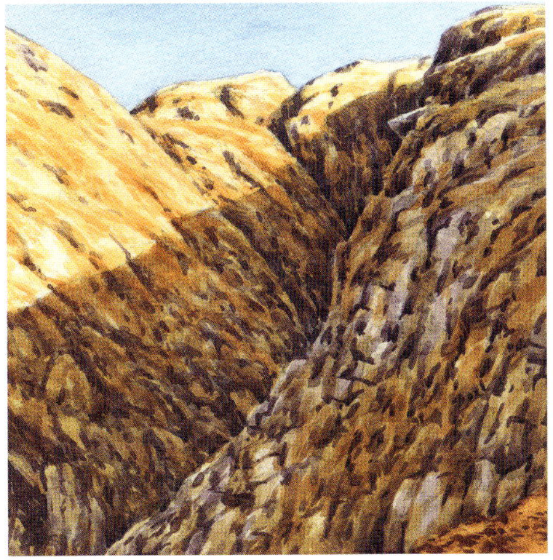

Goat Gills, Hassness 7/11/11

The ascent of Robinson from Hassness is steep but not without interest such as the views down into this ravine. On this route is the rowan tree which AW wondered if it would still be there in 1970, but it is alive even now.

Lake District Mountain Rescue

Hardly a week goes by without some form of news story where one of the Mountain Teams in the Lake District has come to someone's aid. The number of incidents and call-outs is steadily increasing year on year which can be attributed to several factors. There is no question that the fells are becoming more popular but sadly it appears that many folk who set off into the hills today are ill prepared, poorly equipped and lacking experience and often too reliant on mobile phones to direct them or get them out of trouble. Anyone who knows the fells will realise that even today getting a good signal is a hit and miss affair. Whilst it can be argued that even Wainwright didn't carry a compass or much kit he did know where he was in regard to a map and was prepared to take shelter or turn back when the weather was against him.

The ten rescue teams in the district can trace their histories back to the mid 1940s, before that time the system was more ad hoc with local farmers, police and climbers going to the aid of those missing or in trouble on the mountains. Over a period of time local Mountain Rescue Teams were officially formed, manned by unpaid volunteers from the local communities and currently the teams are: Cockermouth, Coniston, Duddon and Furness, Kendal, Keswick, Kirby Stephen, Langdale Ambleside, Patterdale, Penrith and finally Wasdale. In addition there is also the Lake District Mountain Rescue Search Dogs and the Cumbria Ore Mines Rescue Unit. It is a little known fact that in 1958 even AW was listed as a member of his local MRT in Kendal. Whether he actually went out on any call-outs is unclear. Today all these teams are under the umbrella body of The Lake District Search and Mountain Rescue Association and are autonomous but work and train together when needed. Not only do the teams attend incidents on the fells but they also support other services at times of flooding or other emergencies.

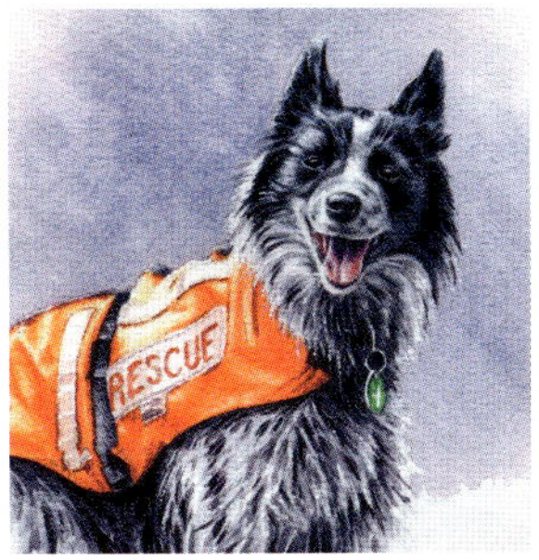

The team members are all unpaid volunteers, ready to attend an incident 365 days of the year and 24 hours a day, prepared to forgo family life or jobs to come to the assistance of others. Teams are solely funded by charitable donations. For more information visit: www.ldsamra.org.uk

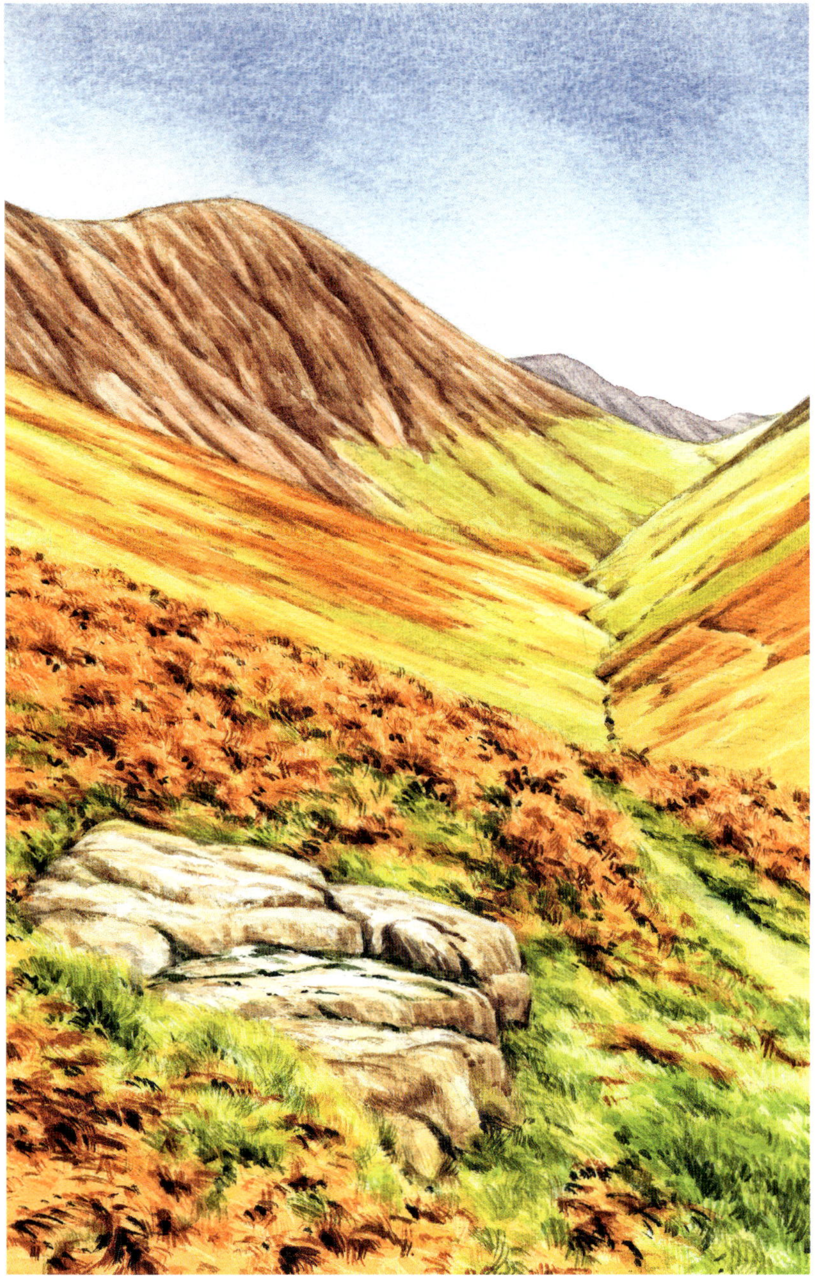

Sail

Due to its location on the east-west ridge that runs between Eel Crag and Causey Pike, Sail is often visited as part of the completion of this ridge. This is confirmed by the single path which crosses the summit. The limited routes here have resulted in the severe erosion of the fragile, thin soil layer, a topic that I cover on page 83.

From Sail Beck 29/9/11

This large, lone boulder sits adjacent to the path that contours the lower slopes of Wandope between Buttermere and Rigg Beck. Its exact location is just north of Third Gill and it makes perfect seat to take in this quiet valley. Sail Beck, which is about 300′ below this point, is one of the few becks in the district which is named after a nearby fell.

The summit 12/5/08

The area around this flat cairn has been worn down to the peat, it was dry on this visit but after a period of rain the pile of rocks becomes surrounded by its own shallow moat. The path that crosses the top is a few yards away.

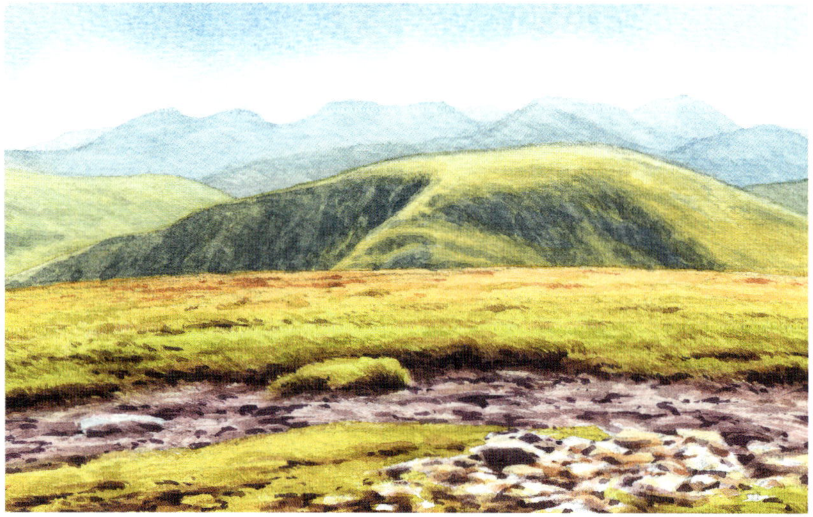

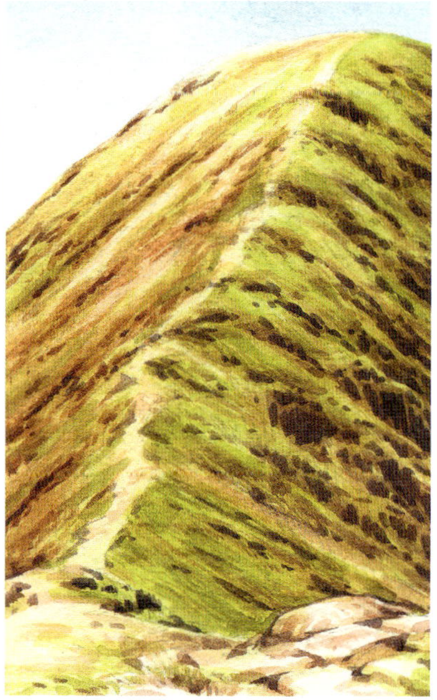

The ridge to Eel Crag 12/5/08

The path along the crest of the ridge was worn in AW's day but even more so now. This is a popular route as it forms part of the classic Coledale Round.

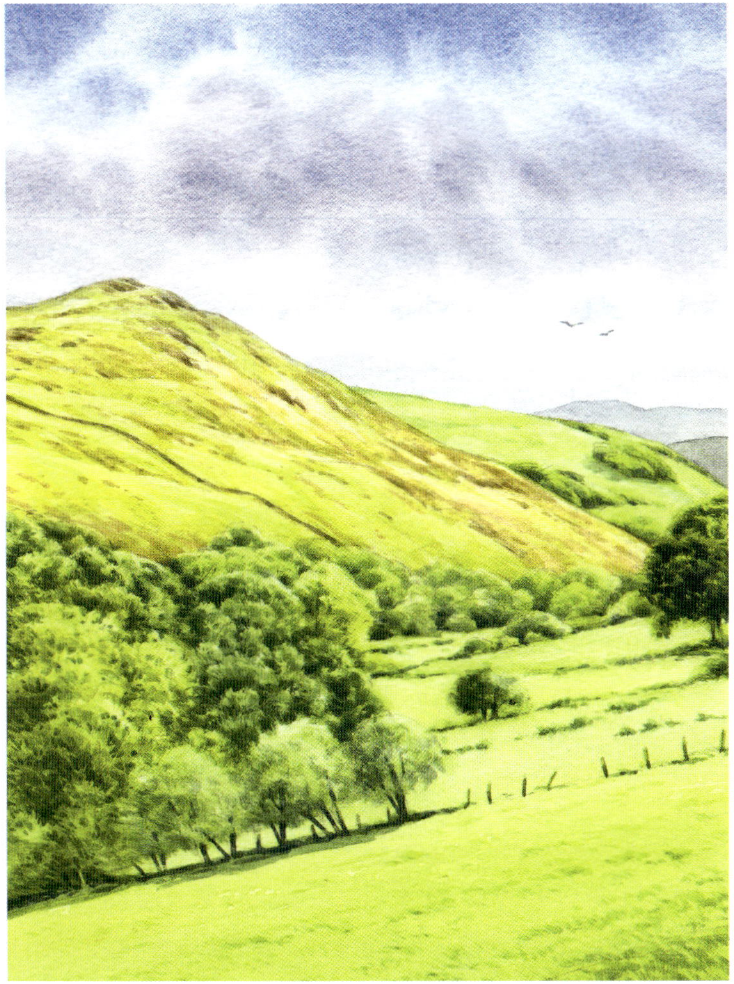

From the Wythop valley 18/5/08
The slopes of the fell are more gentle in gradient than shown in AW's illustration. This point of view is from the quiet country lane near Eskin.

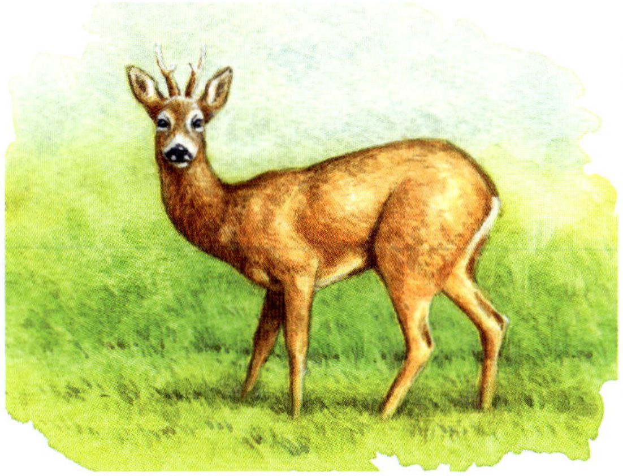

Roe Buck
By pure chance on my first visit to Wythop Mill a mature deer such as this, leapt across the road in front of the car as we drove up towards Kelswick.

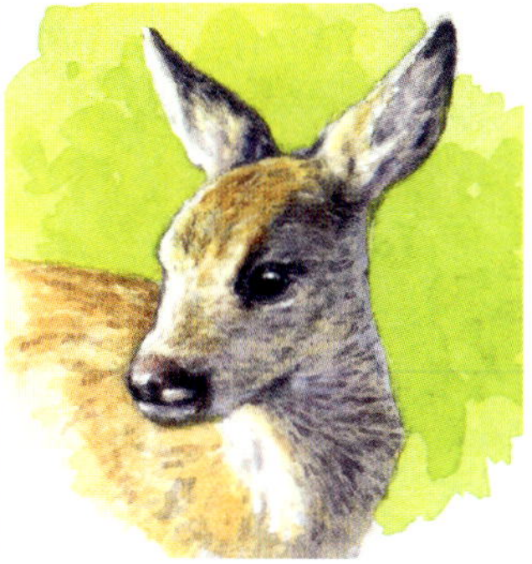

Baby roe deer
Plenty of woodland cover hereabouts for wildlife to take refuge.

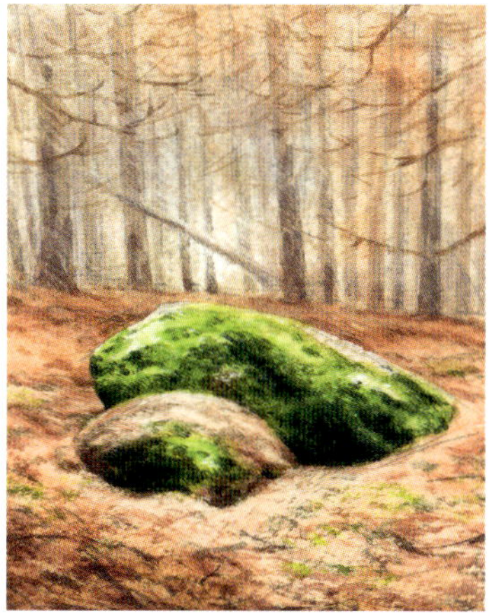

Ladies Table 10/2/09
This mossy boulder is hidden in the depths of the wood, years of fallen pine needles carpet the ground.

Sale Fell

This, the most northerly of the north-western fells, is not connected to any other hill but Sale Fell and its near neighbour Ling Fell can easily be completed on one walk.

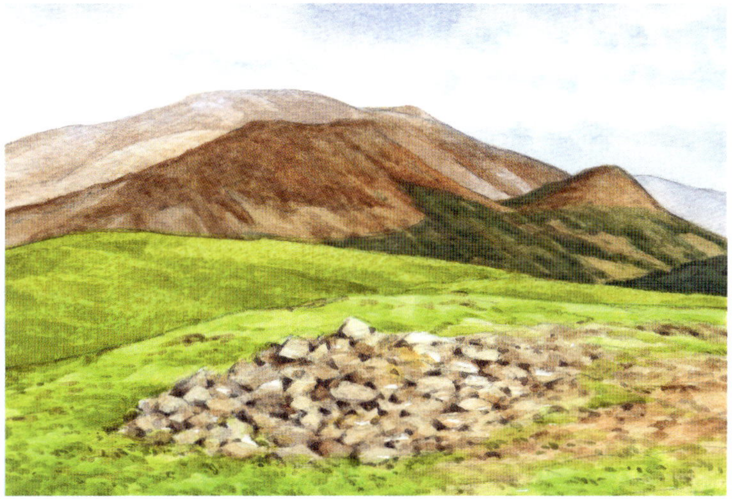

The summit 18/5/08
At the time of this visit the cairn was of a reasonable size, on subsequent occasions it had firstly almost doubled in size and then disappeared altogether. Cairns are not always permanent.

In Wythop Wood

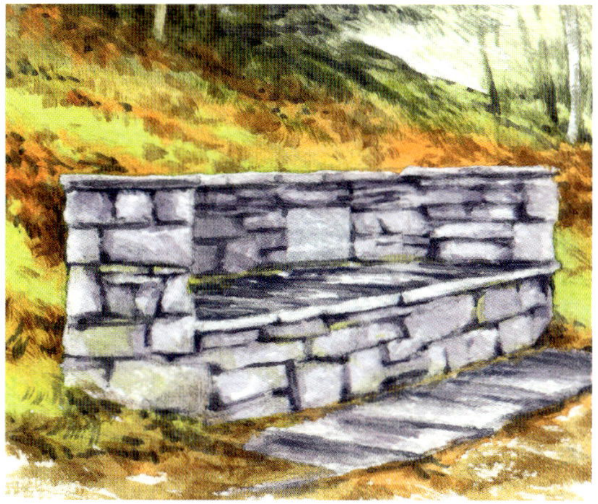

The Walton Memorial 10/2/09
Few fellwalkers will have sat on this stone seat as it is to be found in the woods, away from any paths to the high fells.

The Wythop Valley

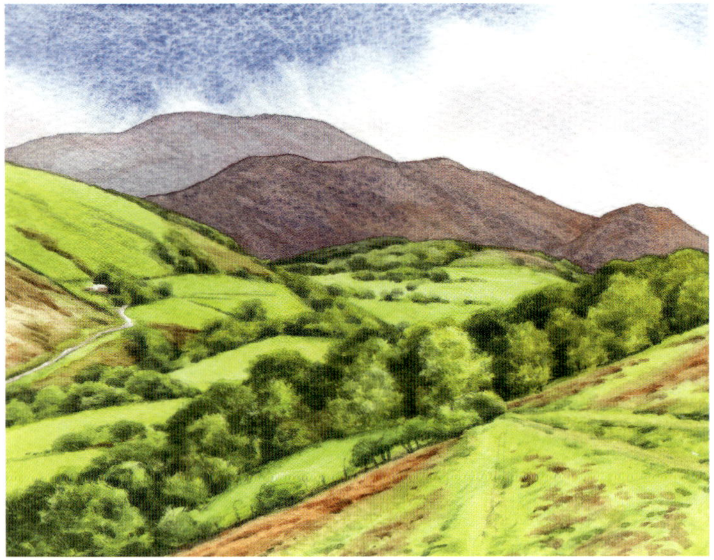

Looking up the Wythop Valley 18/5/08
The Skiddaw massif appears to be at the head of the valley.

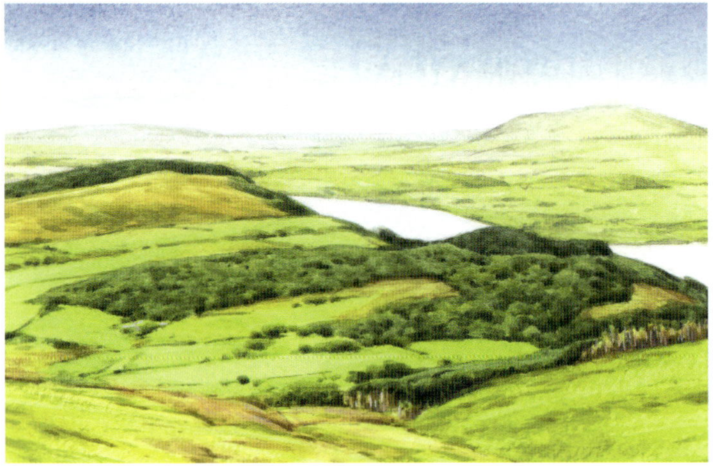

The view from Lord's Seat 11/5/08
The retrospective view of the scene looking to Lord's Seat (right)

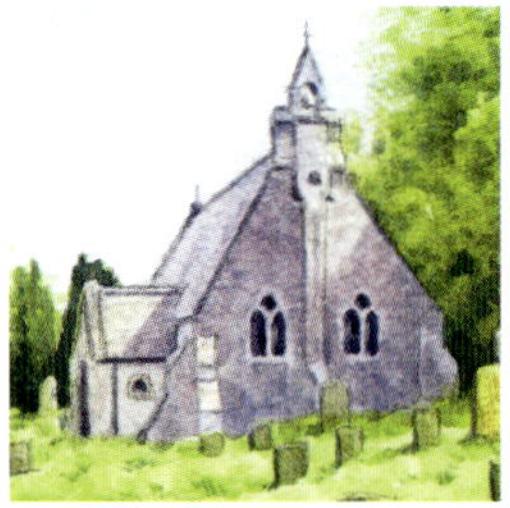

St Margaret's 18/5/08
Sited just by the road east of Wythop Mill this church replaced the old one (right).

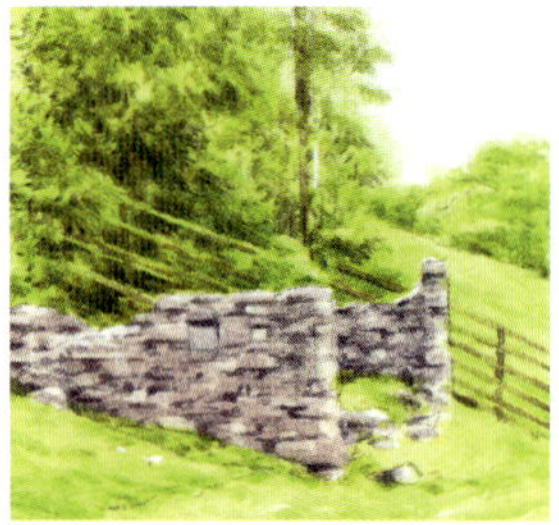

Site of Wythop Old Church 18/5/08
The ruins of the old church not far from Kelswick Farm.

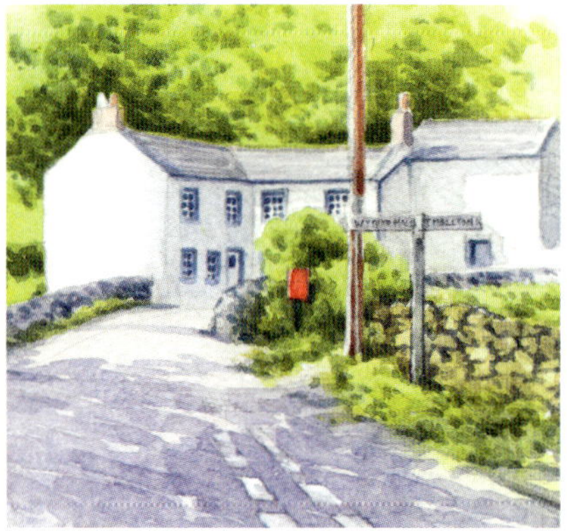

Cottages at Wythop Mill 18/5/08
Shrubs now screen the arch of the bridge.

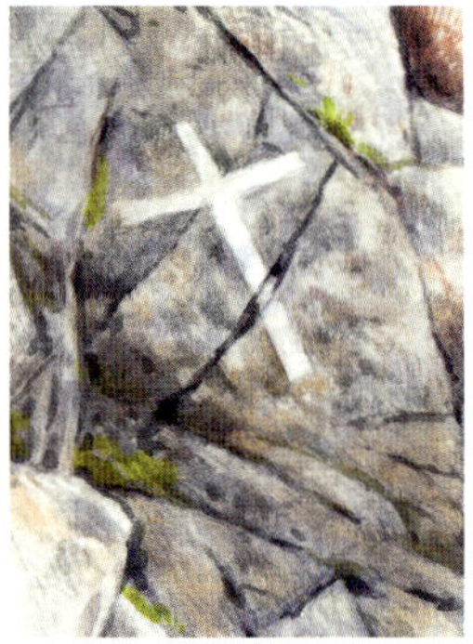

White Cross 18/5/08
Someone had given this cross a fresh coat of paint just prior to my visit. There are still no clues to its origin.

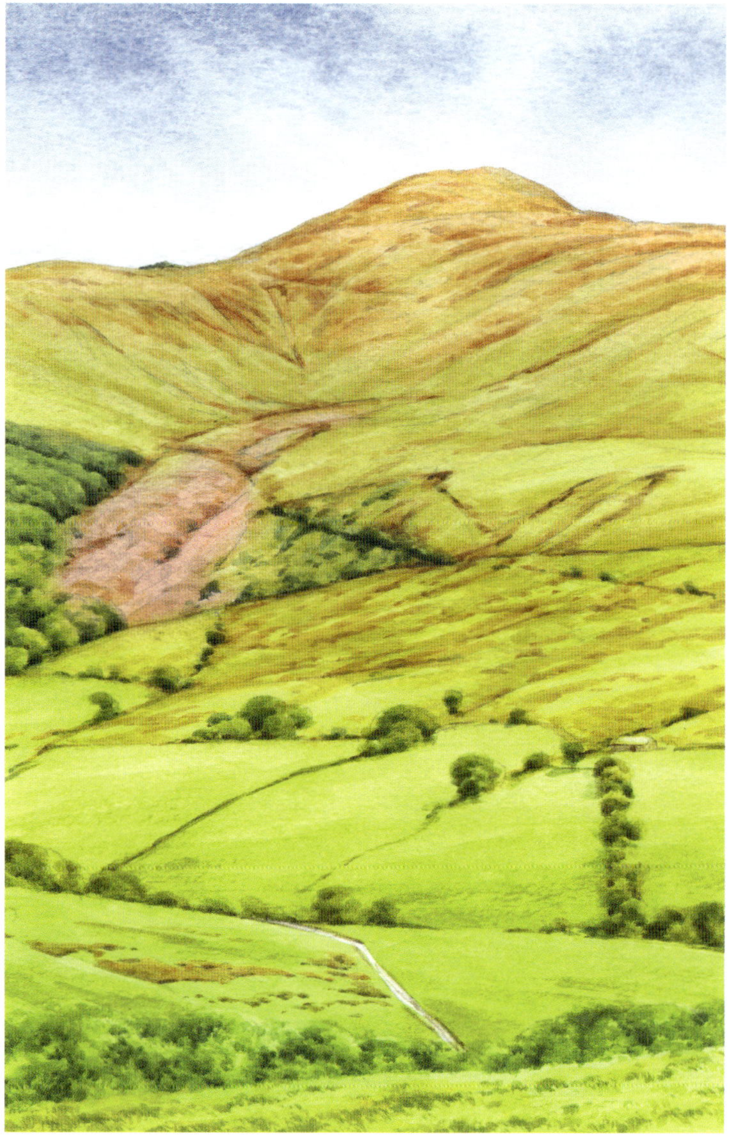

Looking across the Wythop Valley to Lord's Seat 18/5/08
This view from east of the old church is not the most inspiring of views, but it was useful to AW as it enabled him to fill a whole page and give the Sale Fell chapter an even number of pages.

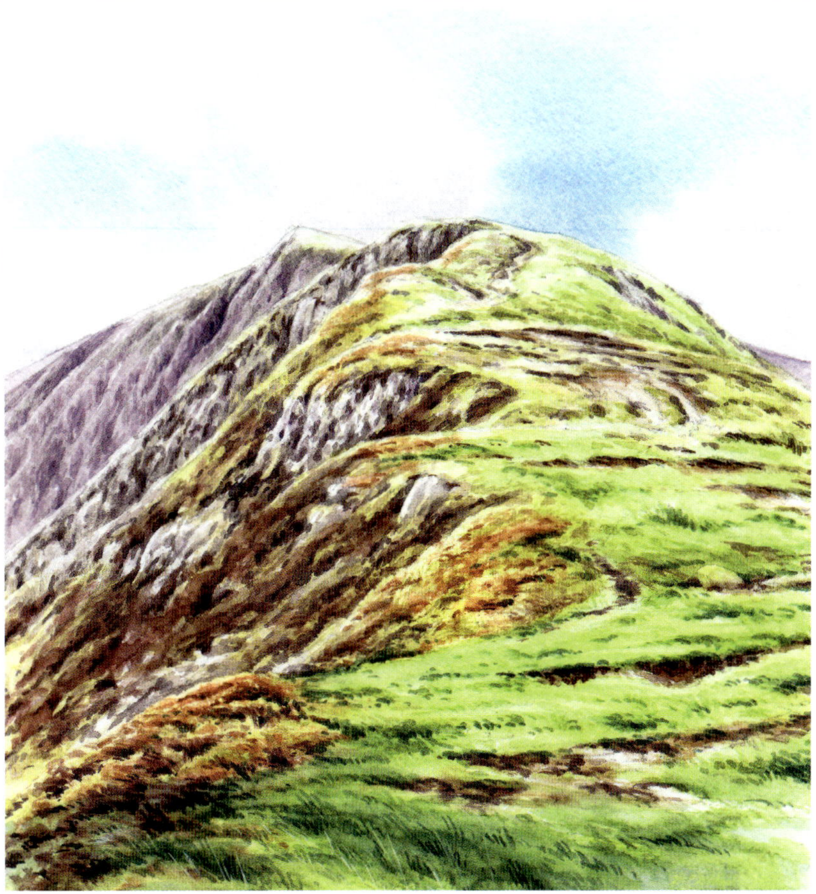

The eastern ridge 12/5/08
Unusually for the main fell illustration, Wainwright chose an aspect of Scar Crags from high up on the hill not far from the summit itself. Due to the fell really being just a rounded rise on the Causey Pike to Eel Crag ridge a good profile of the hill in isolation from a distance is hard to obtain.

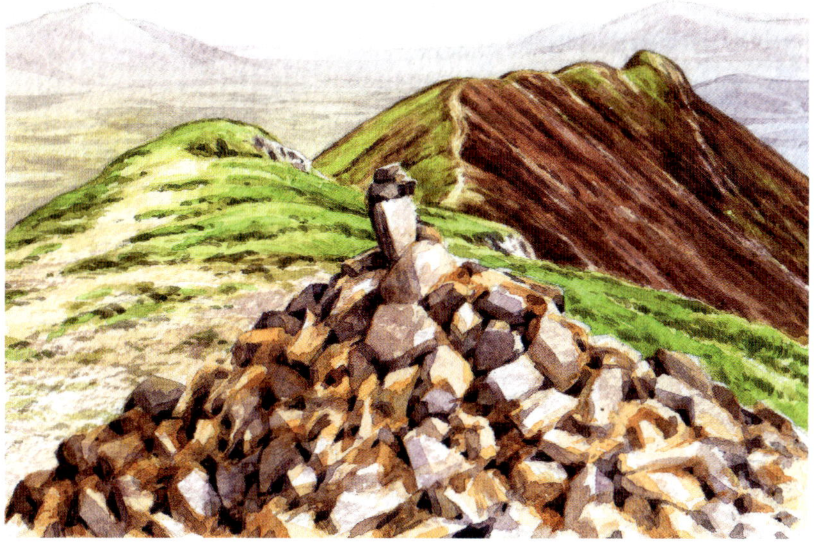

The summit 12/5/08
The cairn has grown to quite a size and spread over it can be seen the ridge to Causey Pike and in the distance Blencathra on the left and Clough Head on the right. The ridge path in this area is now much more worn.

Scar Crags

There is only one path that crosses the top of Scar Crags and access is normally only gained from the area of Sail Pass to the west or Causey Pike to the east. Otherwise the slopes of the fell in other aspects are abrupt, on the northern slopes are the scars of the old cobalt mine whereas on the steep scree southern slopes is the site of a crashed Hawker Hurricane, which hit the mountain in March 1941 sadly killing the young pilot. Some wreckage can still be seen but it is awkward to access for close inspection (see page 196).

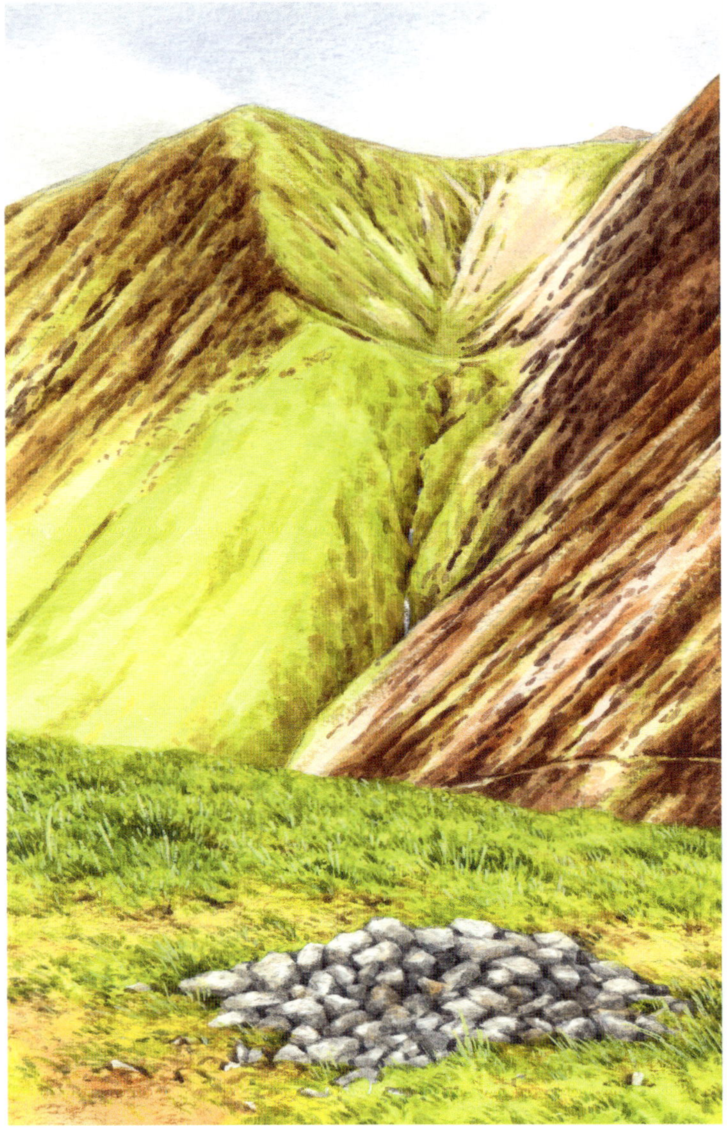

From Ard Crags 16/5/08
The fine hanging valley of Addacomb Hole is well seen in this aspect from the summit of Ard Crags with its now enlarged cairn. Omitted from AW's drawing, Grasmoor breaks the skyline.

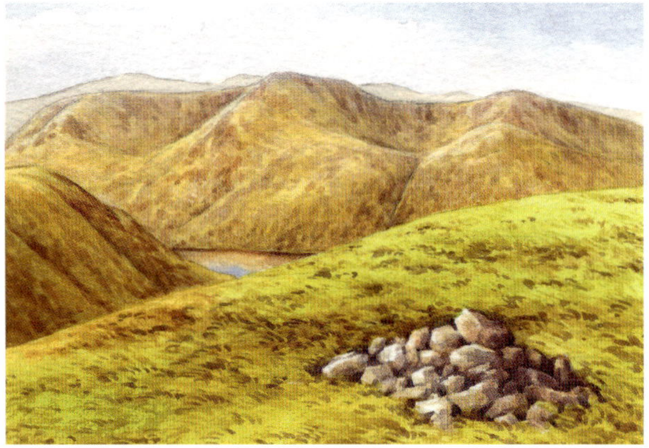

The summit 29/9/11
The slight increase in cairn size is perhaps a reflection of the lack of popularity of this top, some distance from the main Thirdgill Head Man to Coledale Hause footpath from which a detour is needed to visit it.

Wandope

Like many hill names, Wandope has had variations in the past but perhaps due to AW's comment and influence (see Wandope 2), Wanlope, a name used on earlier maps is now a name defunct. Few fells in the guides have all of their multiple routes of ascent starting at the one location, in this case Buttermere.

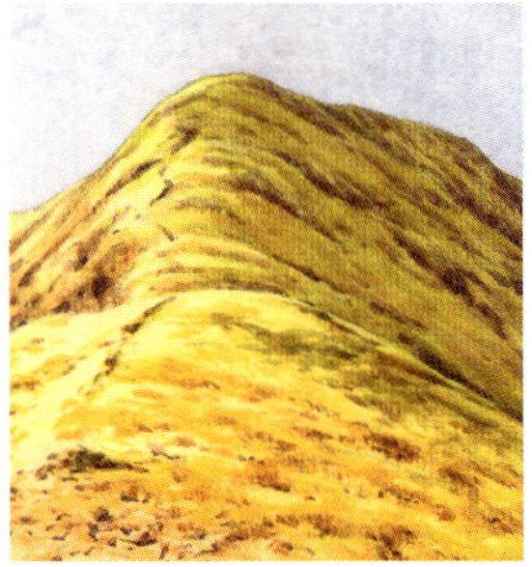

Looking down to Whiteless Pike from Thirdgill Head Man 29/9/11
This fine ridge provides great views of the High Stile range and the Buttermere valley.

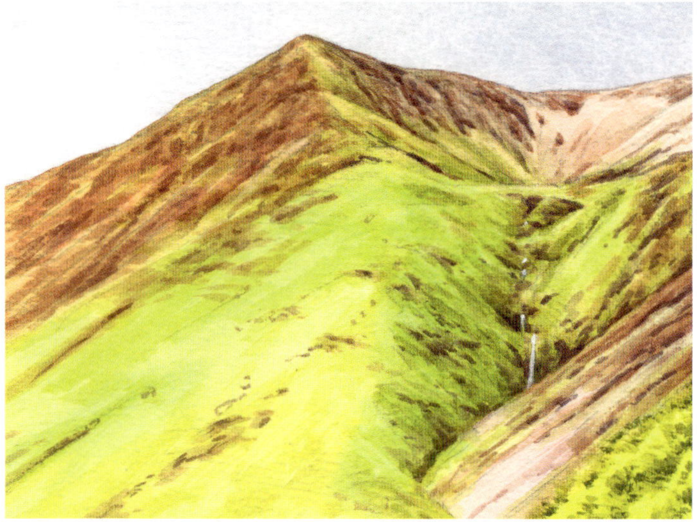

The Addacomb Ridge, from Sail Beck 16/5/08
Even though this is a similar sketch to the main fell illustration it is in fact taken from a point on the path near Sail Beck head.

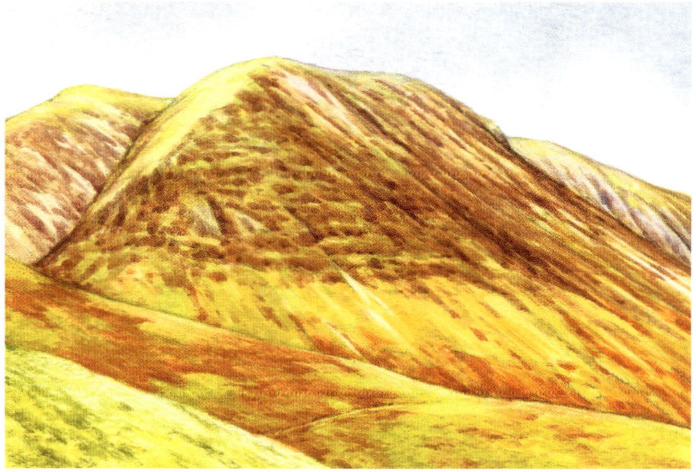

The Thirdgill Ridge, from Whiteless Breast 29/9/11
This area of Whiteless Pike remains pathless so I spent some time wandering on the hill side to pinpoint this exact location.

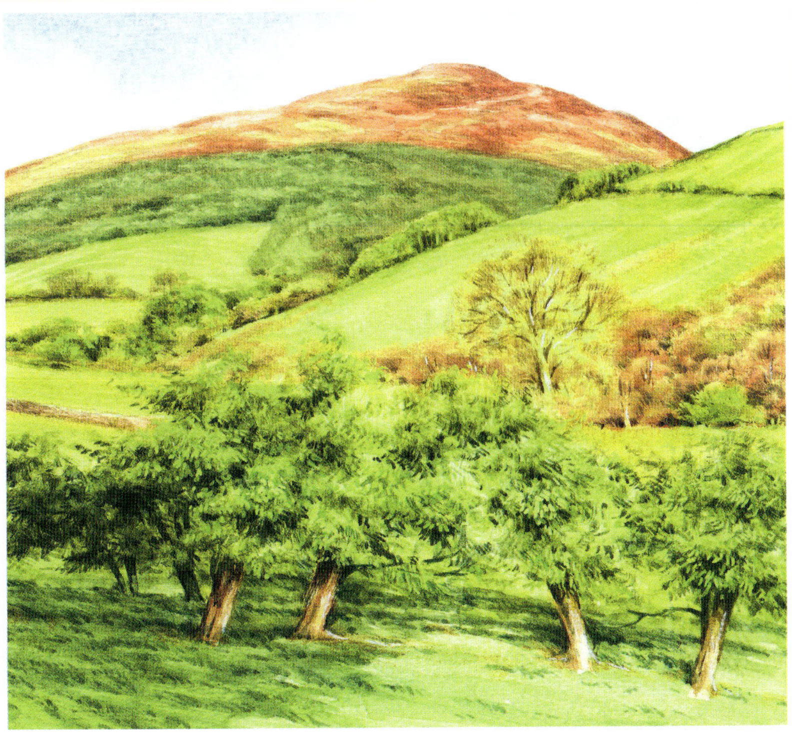

Whinlatter

Today the name Whinlatter is more associated with the Forest Visitor Centre than the fell which is featured here. A variety of outdoor activities are catered for throughout the forest as well as a live camera screening of the Bassenthwaite ospreys when they are nesting.

From High Lorton 3/5/09
This prospect is from the roadside just out of High Lorton on the Whinlatter Pass road. The fell side has been forested and the near wall in the hedgerow has gone.

The summit 20/4/10
This top, Brown How, has been calculated as not being the highest point of the fell which in fact is half a mile to the east.

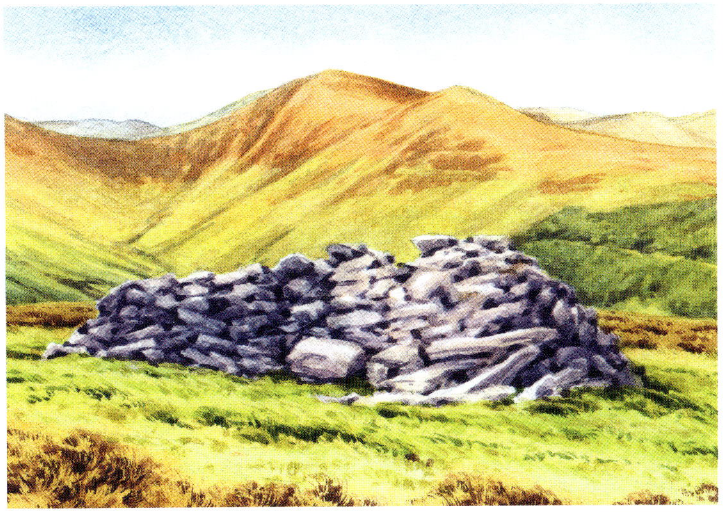

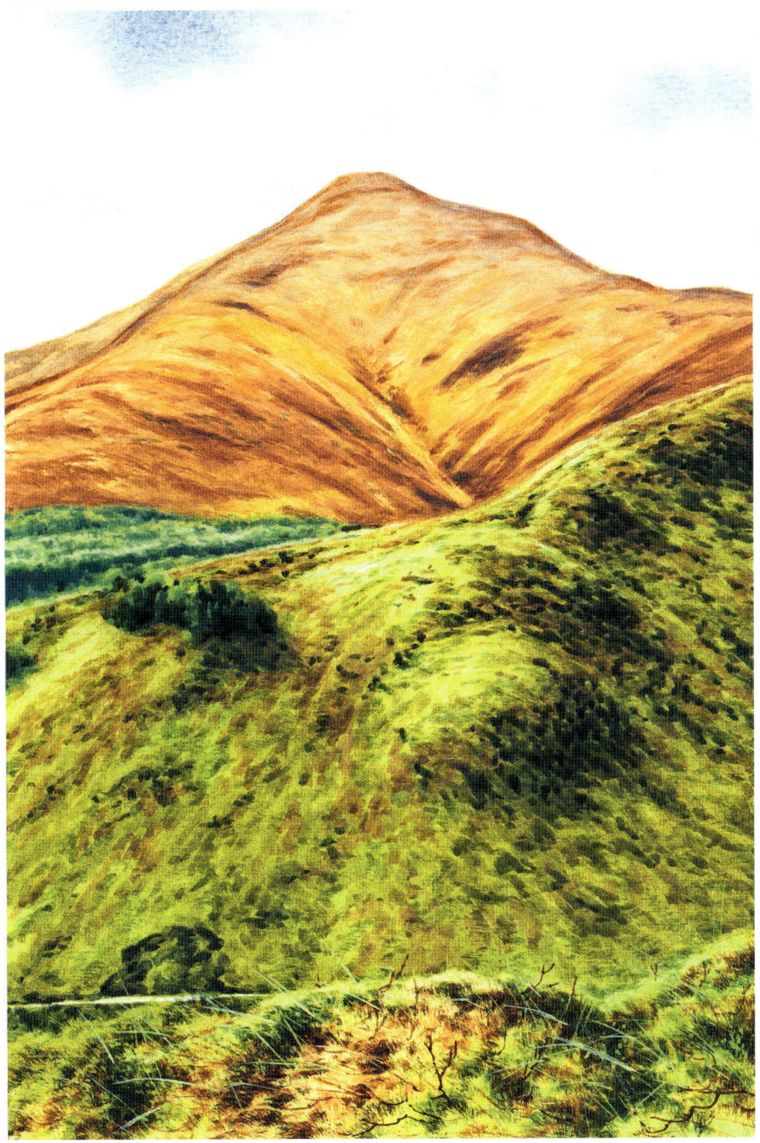

Grisedale Pike, from the east ridge of Whinlatter 13/5/08
Looking across the Whinlatter Pass, over Hobcarton End to the Pike. Two days earlier this view was partially obscured to me by smoke after a lightning strike had set fire to the eastern slope of the Pike.

Whinlatter Pass 3/5/09
Looking towards Black Crag.

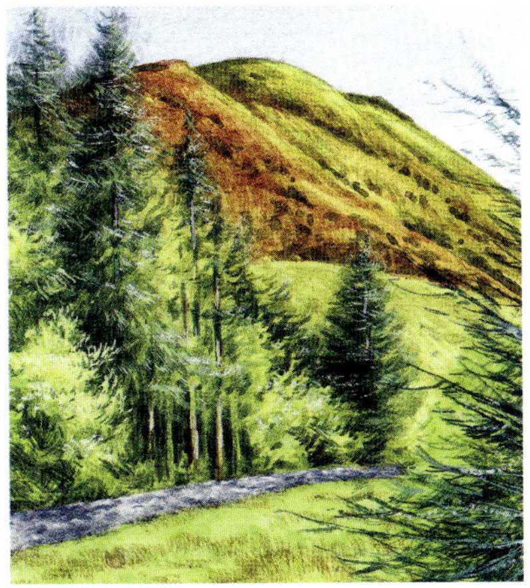

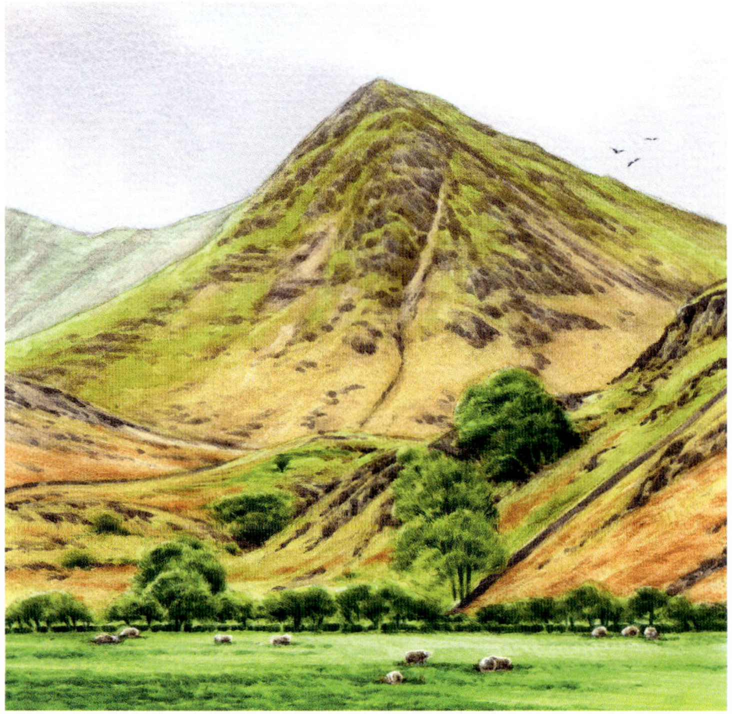

From Rannerdale Farm 17/5/08

On the road just south of the farm a gate on the left gives access to the field and it is from here that the view above is obtained. I was lucky in that sheep were grazing there just as they are shown in Wainwright's drawing.

Whiteless Pike

Wainwright calls Whiteless Pike *"the Weisshorn of Buttermere"* and indeed both mountains have a striking similarity of shape especially when the alpine peak is viewed from the east. The biggest difference of course is that the actual Weisshorn is approximately seven times the height at 14,783'. The ascent of Whiteless Pike from Buttermere is a pleasant and popular way to gain access to the heights of the Grasmoor group.

Whiteless Pike, from Thirdgill ridge of Wandope 29/9/11

Despite wandering around this area for some time I just could not match the foreground to Wainwright's illustration even though the ridge shape was correct. I can only guess that he invented the rocks to make a more pleasing composition, a ploy he used in a number of illustrations throughout the Pictorial Guides.

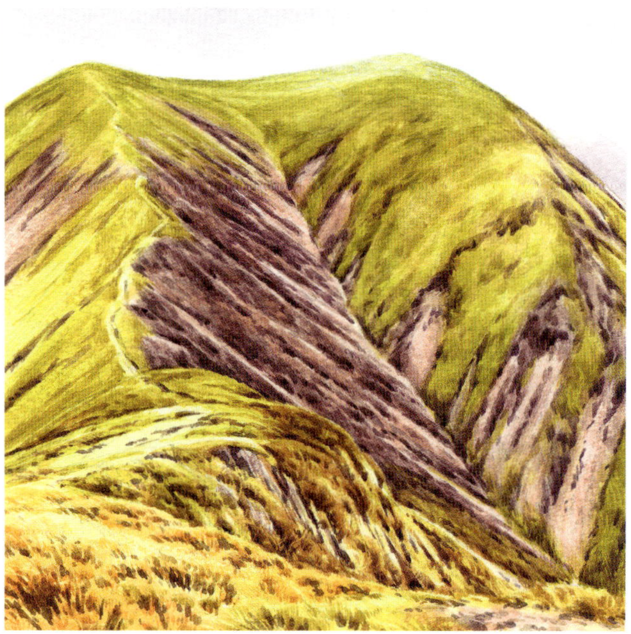

The ridge to Thirdgill Head Man 17/5/08

The neat V shaped ravine of Third Gill between the ridges that lead up to Wandope on the right and Thirdgill Head Man on the left. There are no named first or second gills.

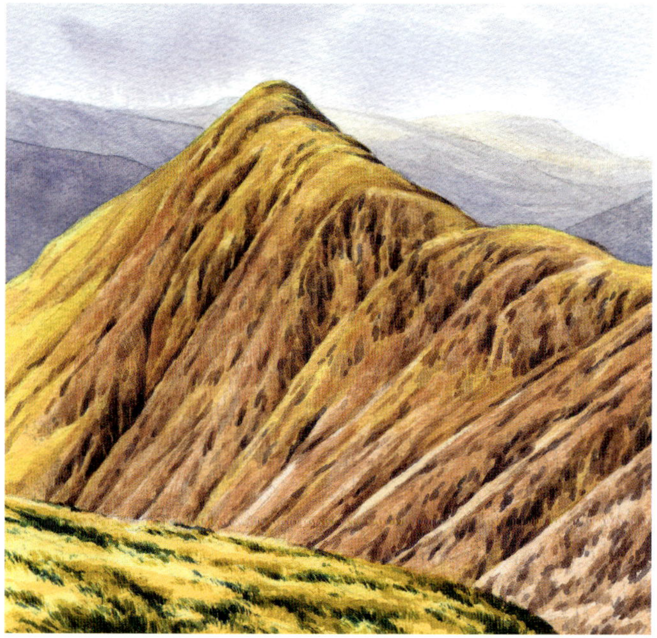

The Summit 29/9/11

More rock is now exposed at the summit but the cairn remains small. AW made an error in his drawing by misnaming Blencathra as Scar Crags which cannot be seen from this point as that fell is obscured behind Sail.

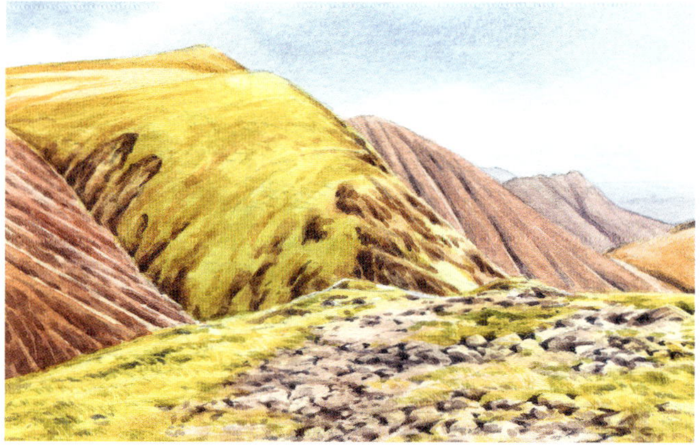

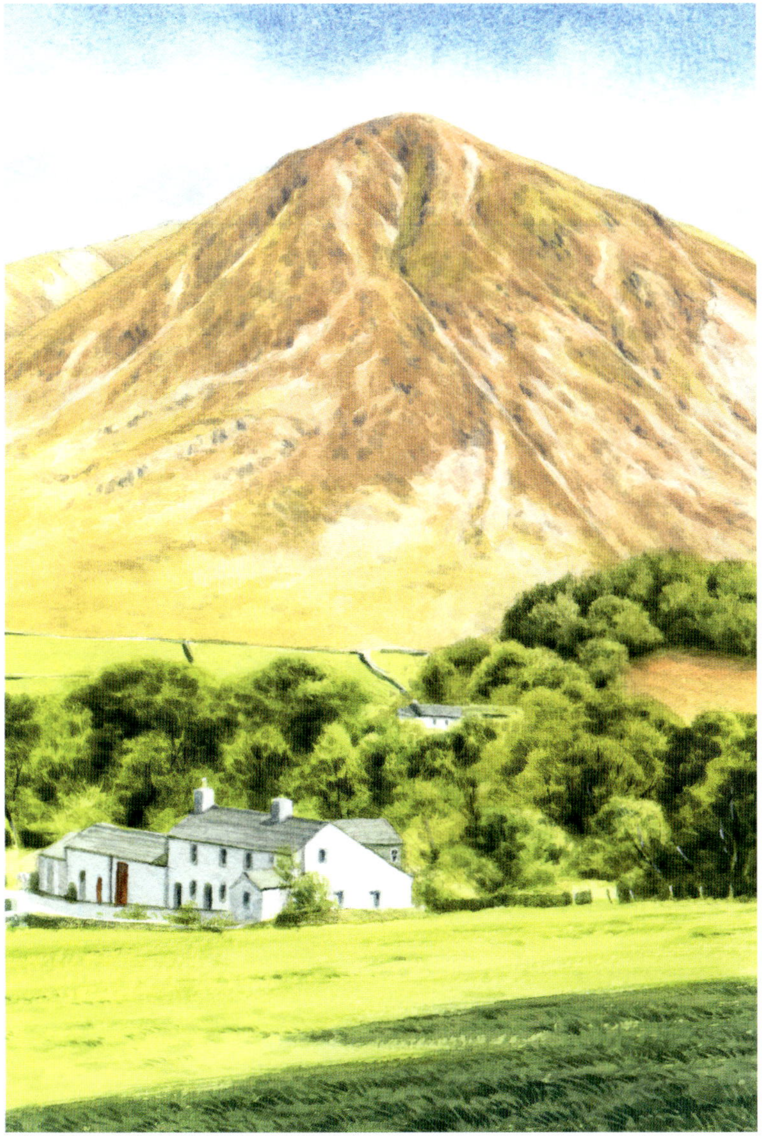

From the road to Scale Hill 13/5/08

The west end of the fell as seen from near Palacehow, Brackenthwaite. In a better artistic composition the house would be over to the right but AW filled that area with his location map on his page.

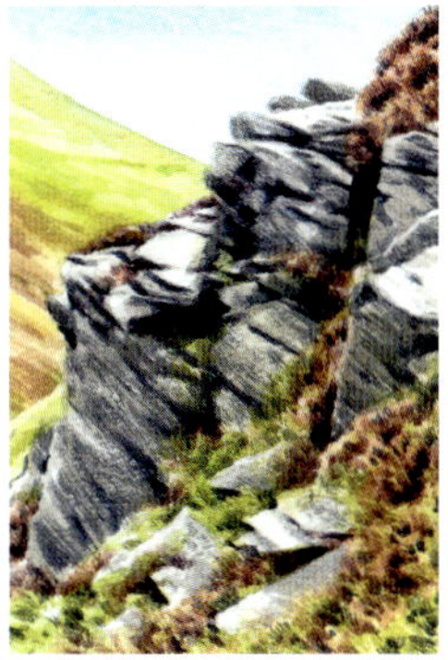

The rockstep 23/8/09

In the revised guide this feature could not be found but it is still in place on the higher path, but it is now avoided by a new route which passes just at the foot of the outcrop.

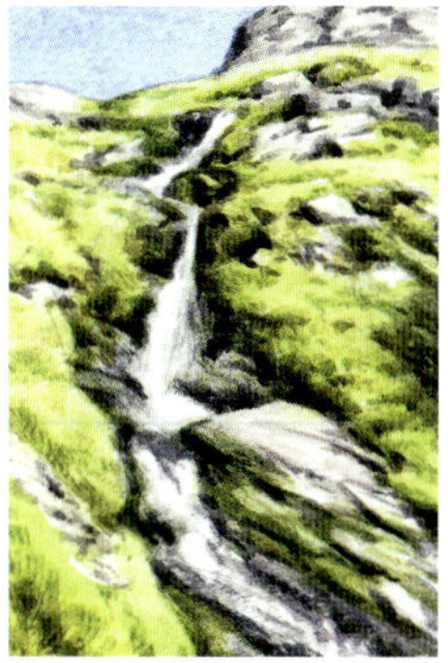

Waterfalls at the head of the gill 13/5/08

The falls on the left are just below Coledale Hause whereas those on the right are lower down the beck.

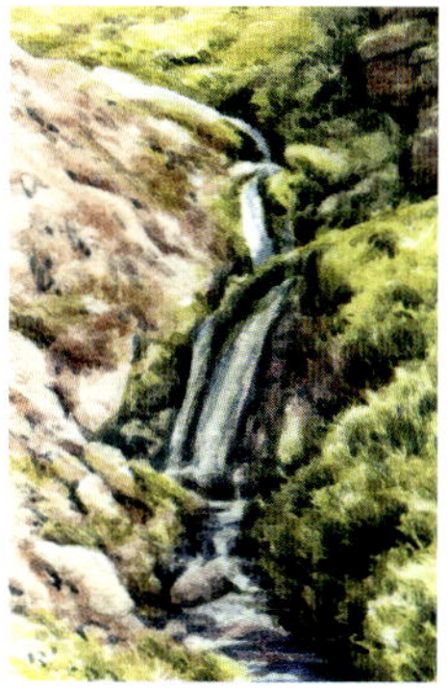

Whiteside

Unlike its namesake in the eastern fells this Whiteside is just one word. It is a fine mountain only let down by the restricted views from the summit. The feature of Gasgale Crags on the south facing side are best seen from near Dove Crags on Grasmoor, where the series of steep gullies and ridges can be fully appreciated. The ridge route between Whiteside and Hopegill Head is one of the best in the district.

Gasgale Gill

The lower section 13/5/08

From just under Whin Ben's end.

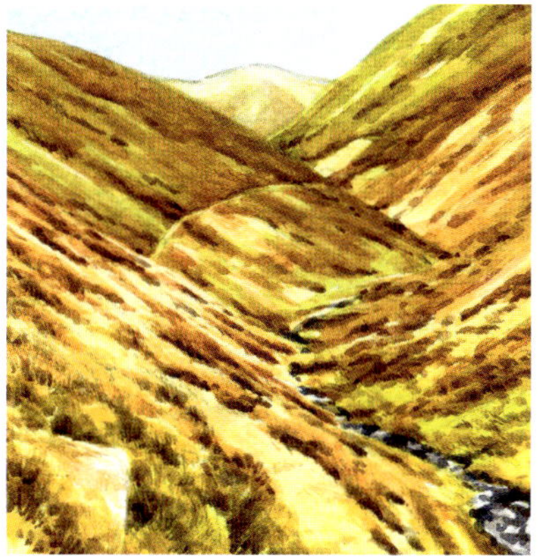

The middle section 13/5/08

Gasgale Crags are on the left here.

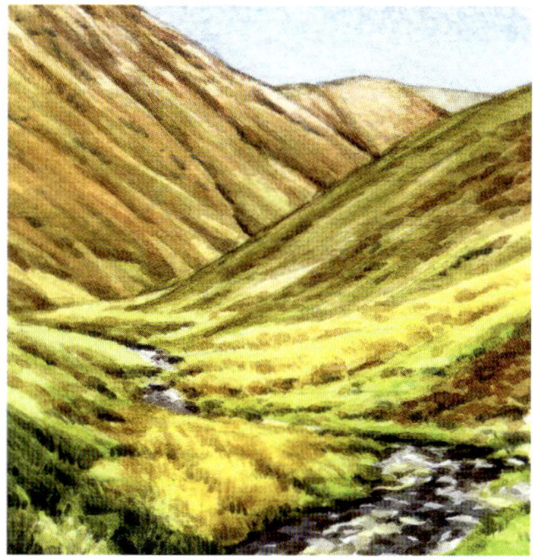

Looking east along the ridge 13/5/09

This view is from a point about five paces to the right of the summit view and gives only a slightly different perspective of the ridge which Wainwright rated highly, reflected in the fact that he drew the ridge three times in this guide.

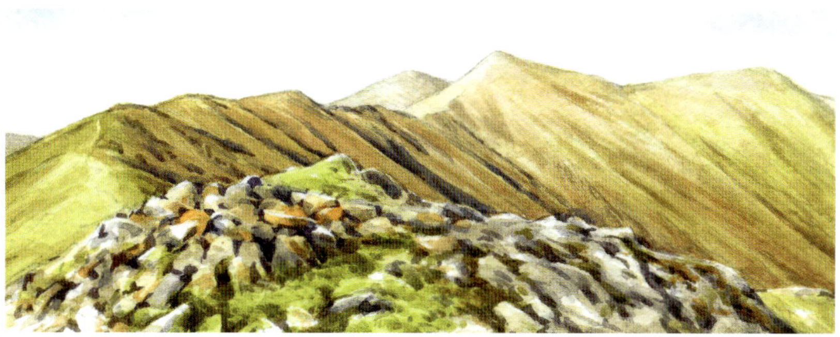

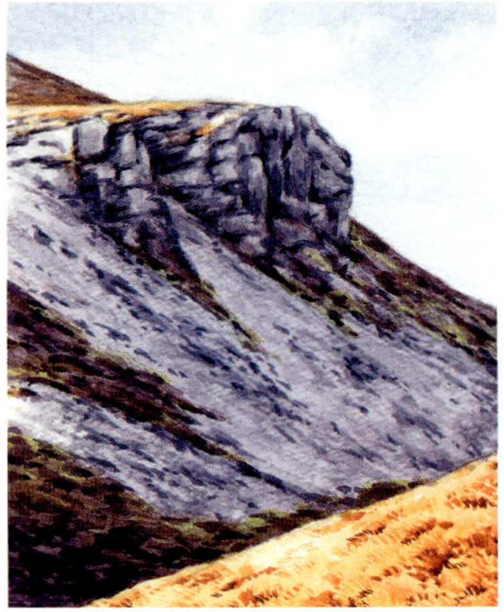

Dodd Pass 13/5/08
The crumbling cliff that stands guard over this dry gap near Dodd.

Cold Gill 13/5/08
The small bridge is no more but crossing the stream without your feet getting wet is not too difficult.

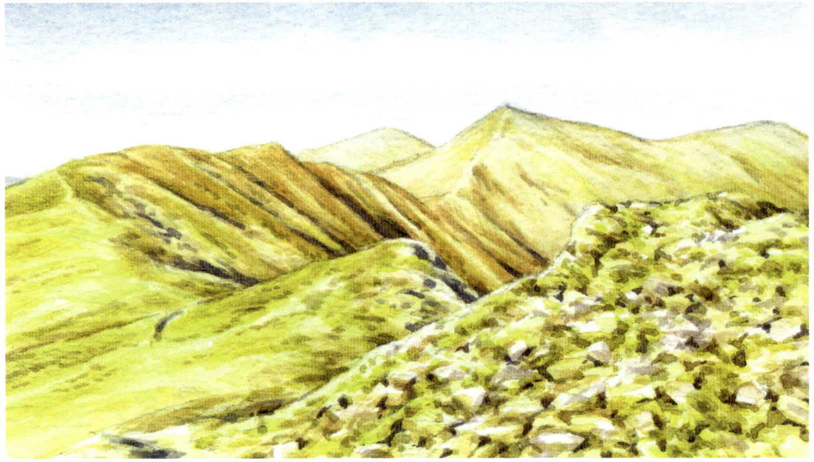

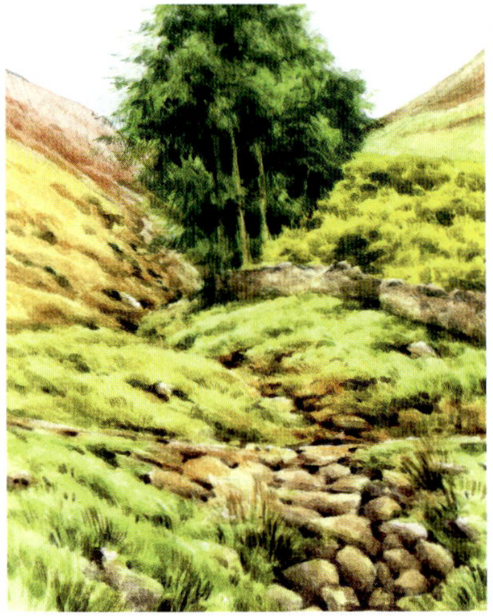

The summit 13/5/09
Yet again, AW recognises that this is not the true summit, that credit goes to the east top some 500 yards along the ridge which is at a height of 2359'. Once again it was a case of Wainwright using the official information provided on the one inch O.S. map of the time for use in the guidebook.

The summit rocks from the south 13/5/08
Seen from the edge of the crags.

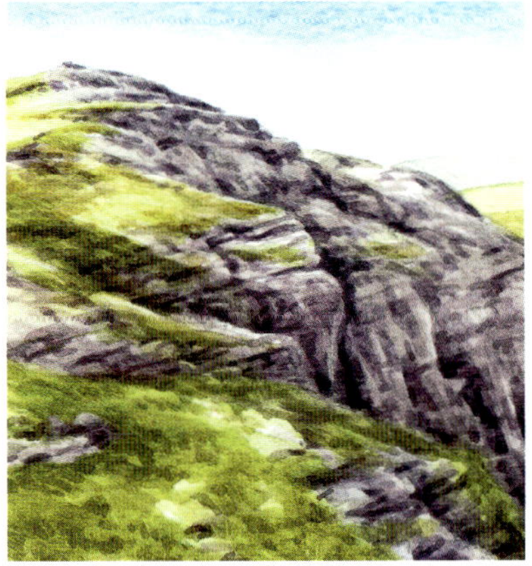

The summit rocks from the east 13/5/08
The top seen from along the ridge.

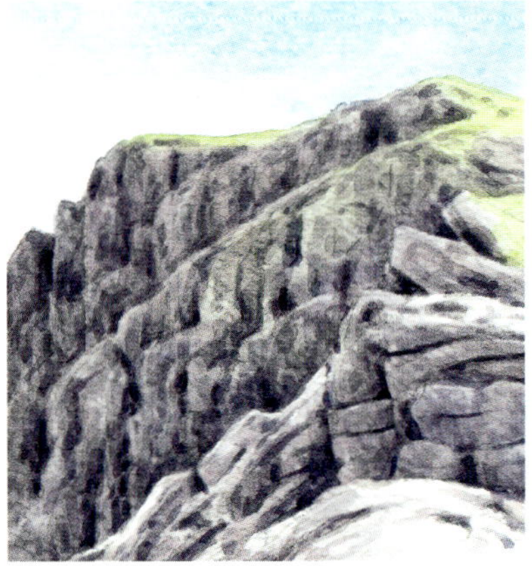

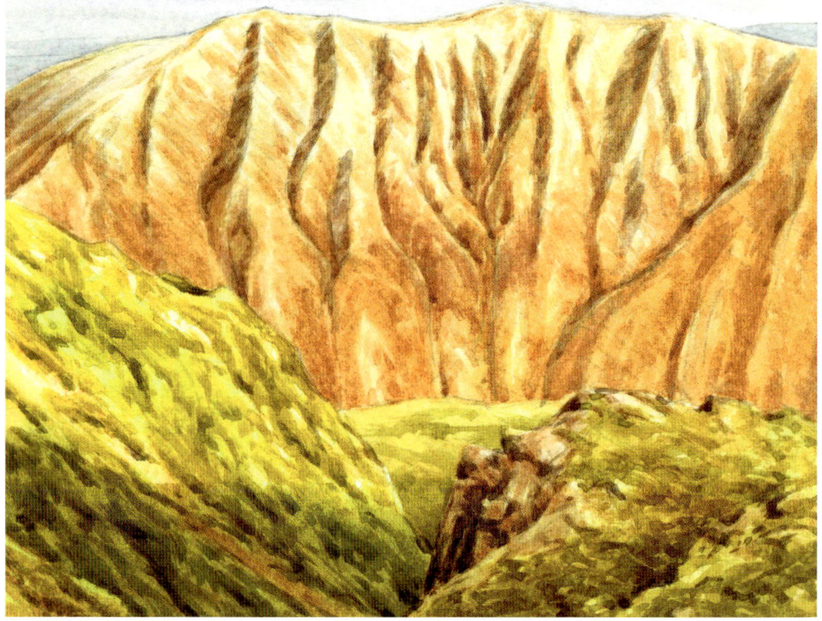

Whiteside and Whin Ben
14/5/08
Late evening sun on the fell side.

Gasgale Crags, Whiteside
29/9/11
The fine ridge fully seen in profile.

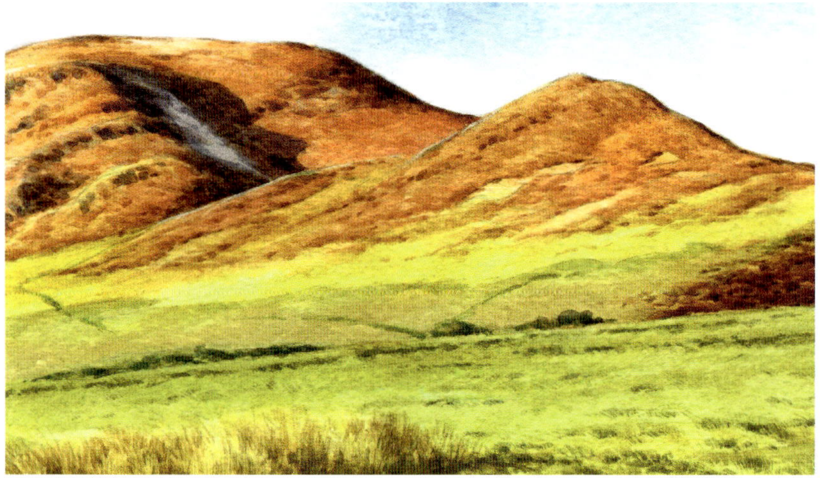

The Western Fells

In the personal notes in conclusion for Book Six, The North Western Fells, Wainwright mentions how he will go on to start his work on the last book, The Western Fells with mixed feelings. It would have undoubtedly been with some sorrow that he was nearing the completion of his major undertaking on his work for the Pictorial Guides, but also perhaps with some excitement that he was about to fully explore the fells that up until this time he had possibly only occasionally set foot on prior to the beginning of this work in 1952. The thirty three fells described in this last volume and illustrated with 262 sketches include not only majestic mountains such as Pillar and Great Gable but also the fell which was to become synonymous with the name of Alfred Wainwright, Haystacks.

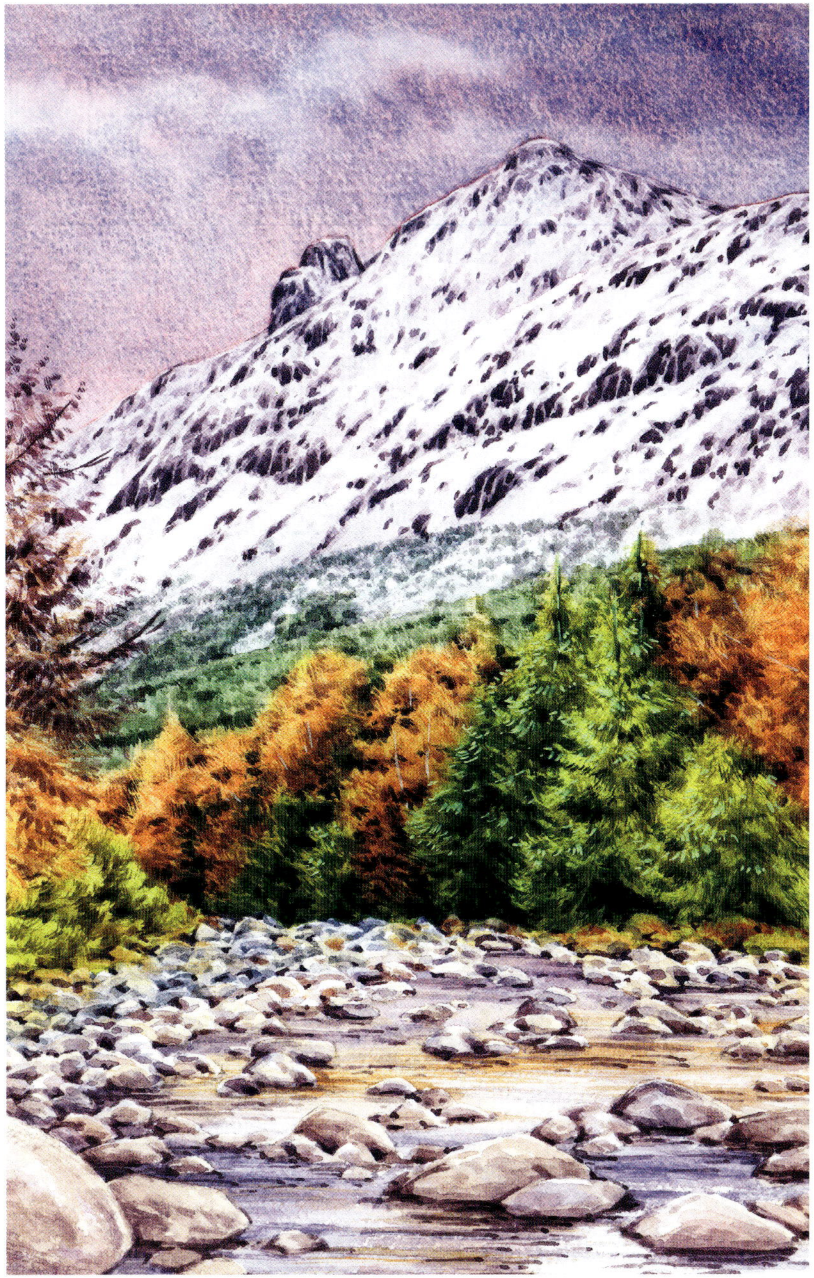

Frontispiece - Pillar and Pillar Rock from the River Liza 23/2/10

Although Wainwright did not title this frontispiece to the book the profile of Pillar and its rock of the same name from Ennerdale is unmistakable. I was determined to obtain this reference in similar winter conditions to his illustration so on a cold day in February I set off from home with the sole intention of completing this quest. Once in Ennerdale it was a case of walking into the valley from Bowness Knott, following the river upstream until the scene matched the drawing, checking continuously. Finally I reached the exact point some 300 yards down from the concrete bridge and about 50 yards off the forest road onto the riverbank. Photograph taken, it was a case of just returning home with a sense of achievement.

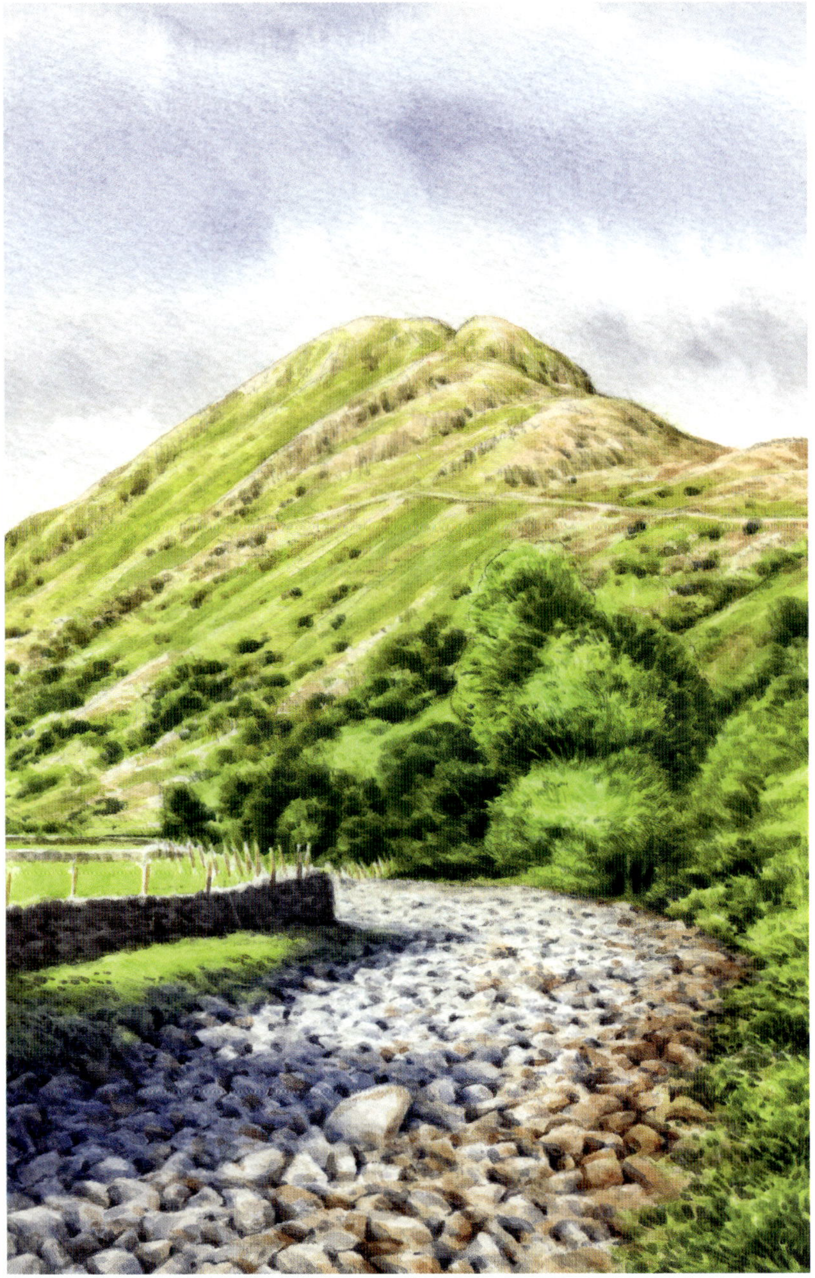

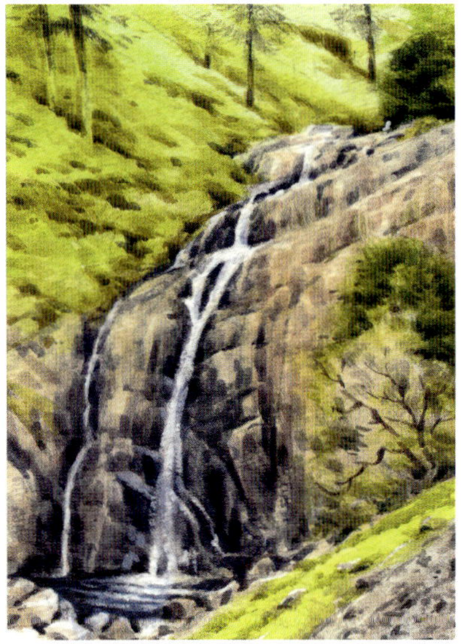

Base Brown

On approaching Seathwaite along Borrowdale, it appears that Base Brown stands separately from any other hills as it forms the right hand wall of the valley. It is in fact only linked by a ridge to one other fell, Green Gable, which is hidden from view.

From the Borrowdale Yews 12/6/09

The Borrowdale Yews were made famous in Wordsworth's poem of 1803 The Fraternal Four. Only three of the four yews survive and are the darker trees in this sketch. The beck was all but dry here on my visit.

Taylorgill Force 10/4/11

This is the second appearance of these falls (see Scafell Pike page 193) but this time from the path on the north side of the gorge.

Sour Milk Gill 17/4/09

This beck, one of three with this name in the district, has several cascades, all of which had to be investigated to determine which series featured in AW's drawing. The run of the falls remain mostly unchanged in this section which is seen here from near the less frequented path on the north side of the gill.

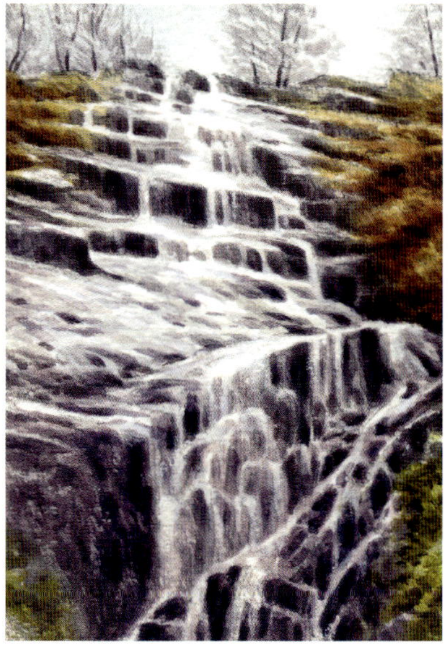

Fallen Stone 17/4/09

This huge boulder must have made a tremendous noise as it fell from the nearby crag but maybe man wasn't around to hear it. The path here is indistinct but the rock is easily visited on this ascent route of Base Brown.

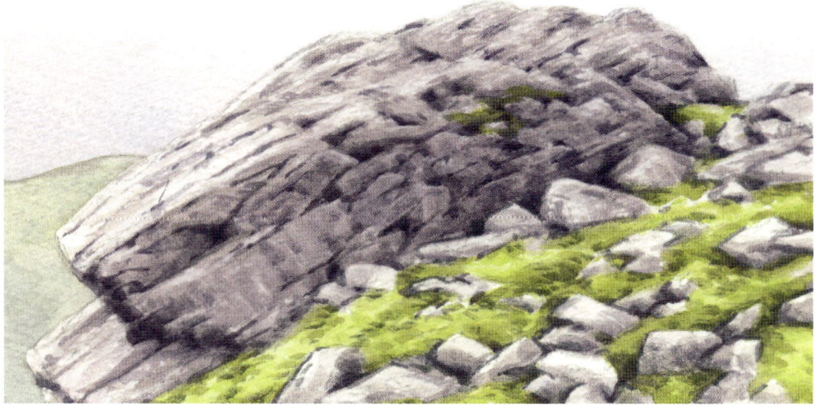

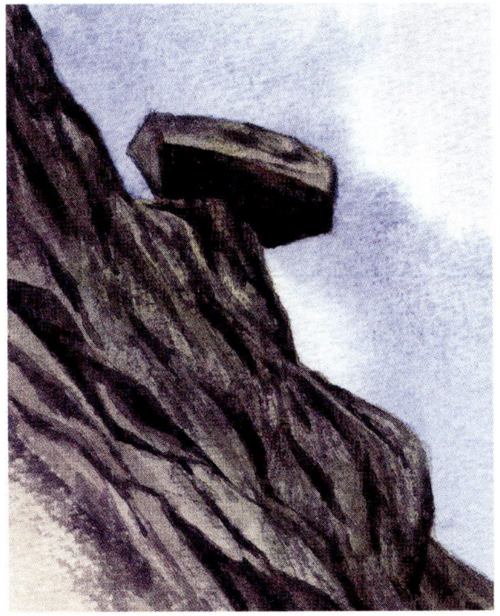

The Hanging Stone 17/4/09
Even though it looks delicately balanced from this viewpoint, the precarious rock has been in situ for many years and may be for some time to come.

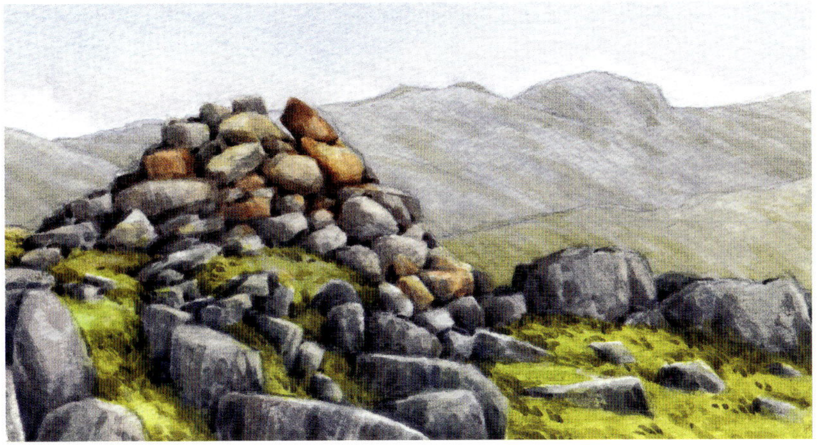

The summit 17/4/09
This view to the south over the small cairn shows Esk Pike as an almost symmetrically shaped top to the right of Allen Crags.

The top waterfall, Sour Milk Gill 17/4/09
A short detour off the main path is required to obtain this view.

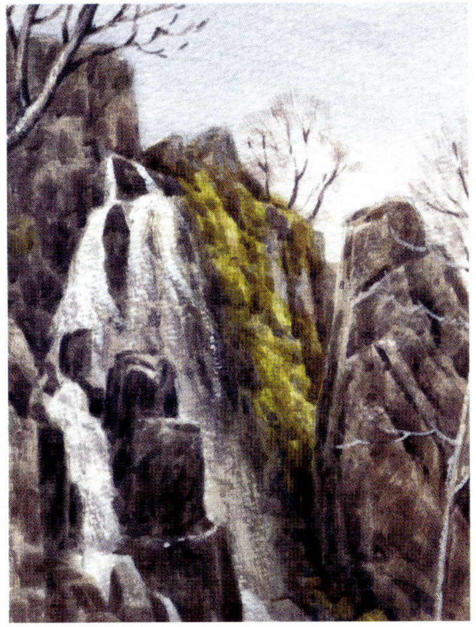

Seathwaite Slabs 17/4/09
The Slabs are easily visited from the path to the south of Sour Milk Gill.

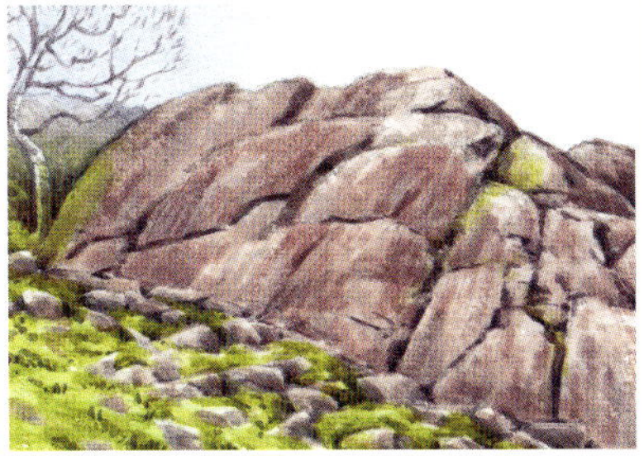

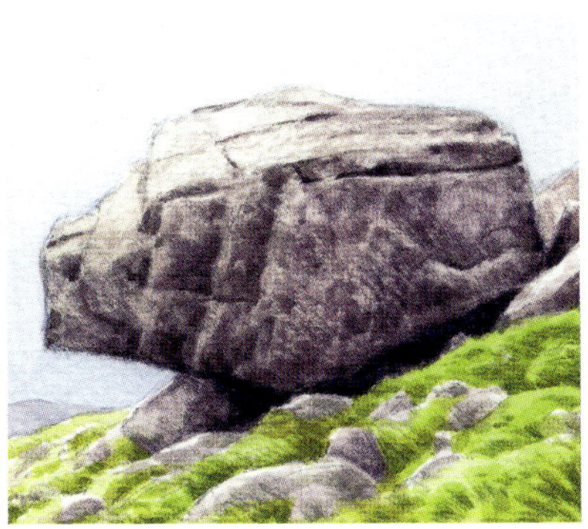

Perched boulder 17/4/09
This is not a different angle of the Hanging Stone but another rock altogether near the top of a gully.

The East Face above Taylor Gill 12/6/09
Many who descend from Sty Head to Seathwaite will see this feature on their left. The more adventurous will have taken the path on the north side of the gill.

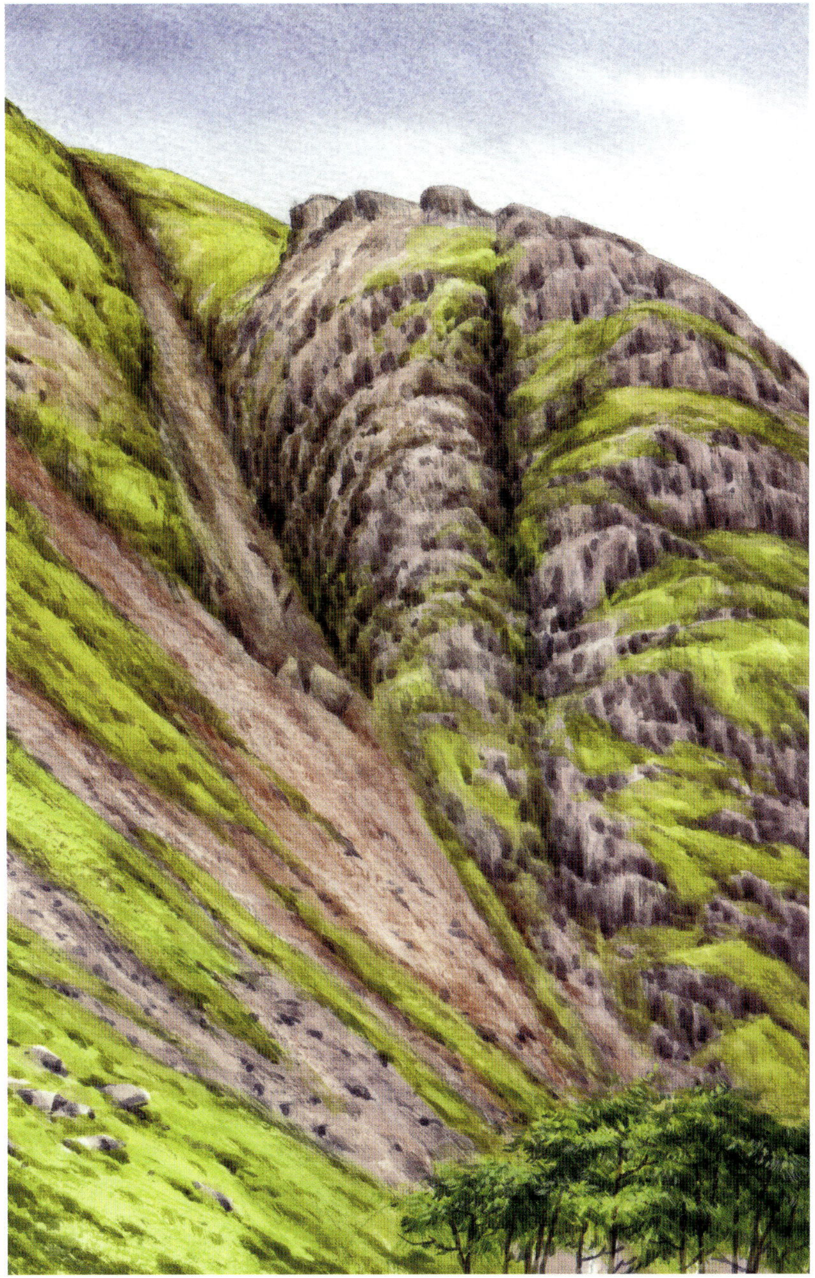

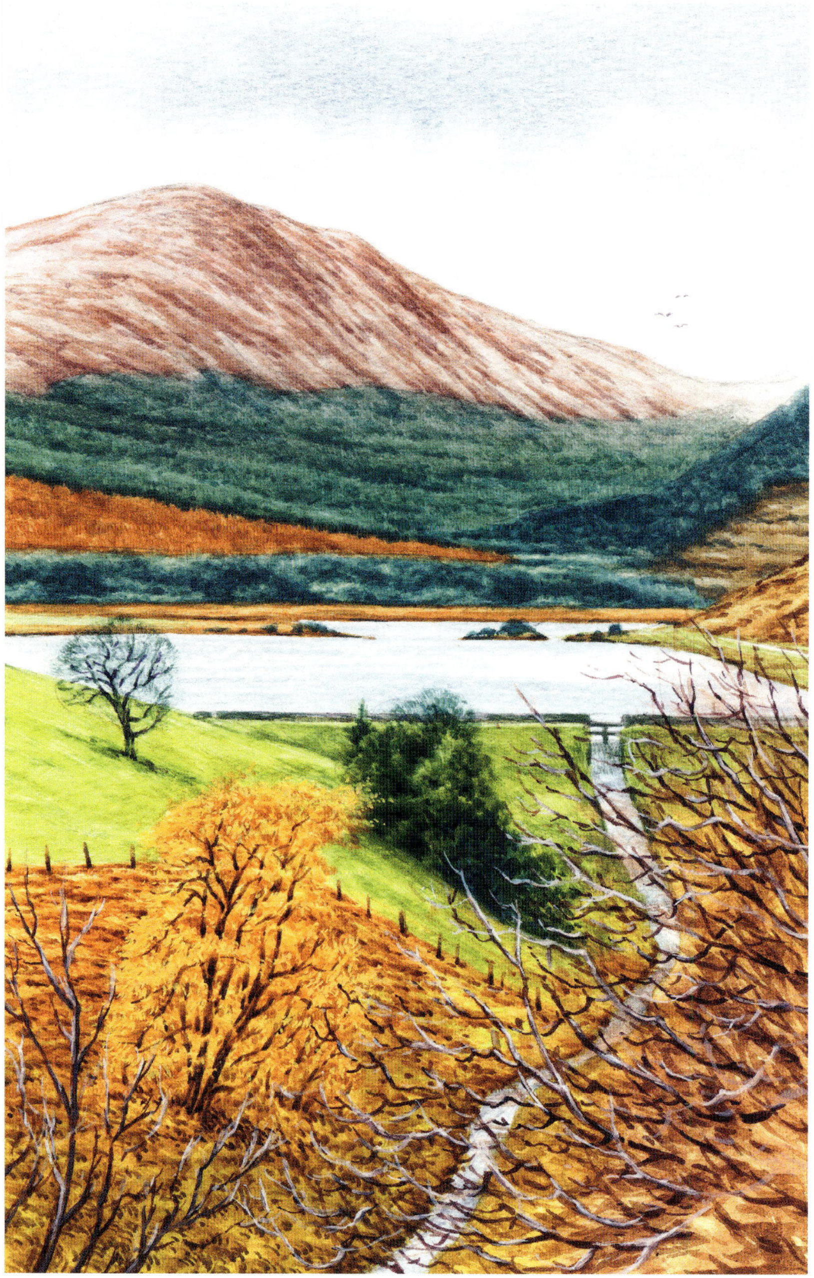

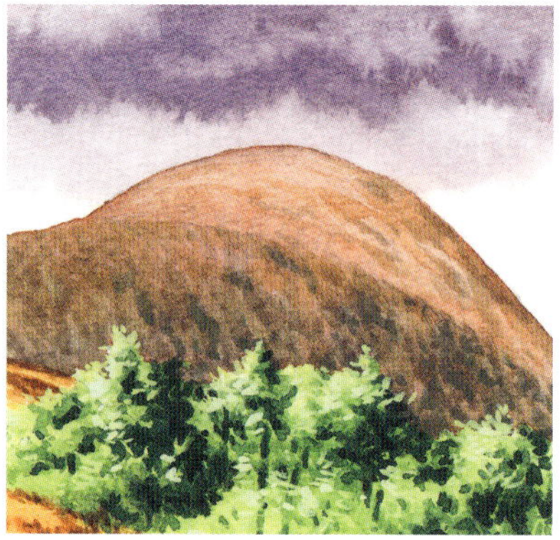

Knock Murton 6/11/08
No longer a *"forbidden peak"* this minor top is now on open access land and walkers are free to roam.

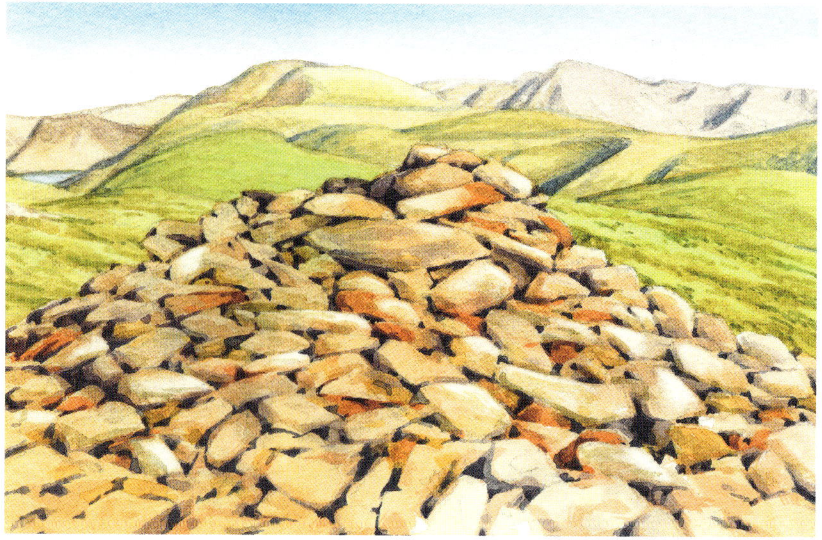

The summit 31/5/09
The enlarged cairn of coloured rocks that now sprawls over the highest point of the fell.

Blake Fell

The highest of the group known as the Loweswater Fells and with steep slopes on the west side, Blake Fell's summit not only has a lofty view of Cogra Moss but also is a fine place to watch a summer sunset.

From Cogra Moss 6/11/08
In 2015 there was a possibility that this reservoir, built about 1880 but not used as a water supply since 1975, was to be returned to its natural state by the relevant water authority. Following a strong campaign by the local community and interested groups this decision was rescinded. Consequently, this view of this water will remain the same for some time to come.

Ancient cairns, on Carling Knott 27/11/11
Carling Knott was on AW's original fell list but ended up as just a part of Blake Fell and hardly gets a mention.

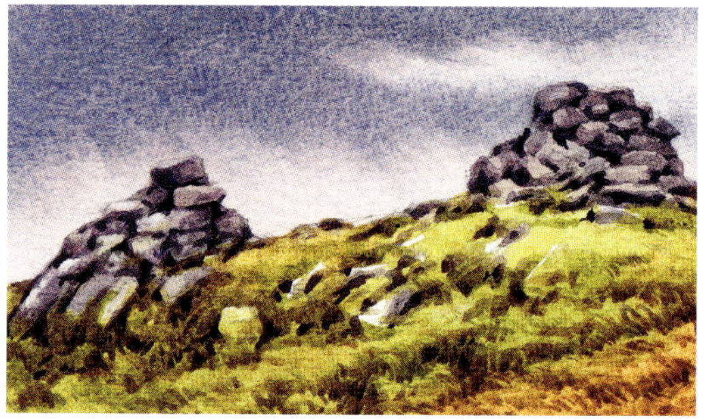

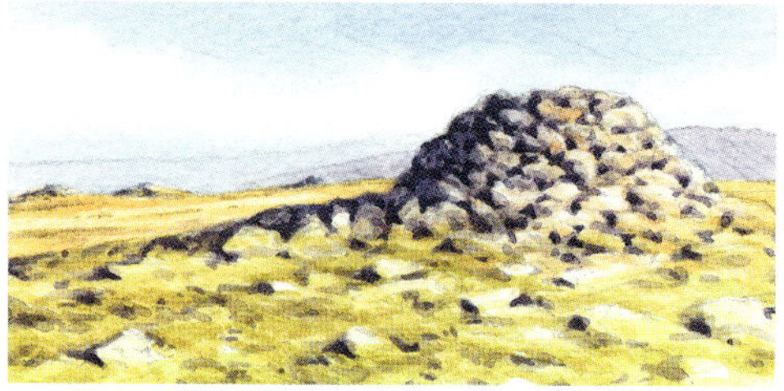

Knock Murton summit cairns 6/11/08
A wind shelter made of stones taken from these cairns has been constructed just behind this point of view.

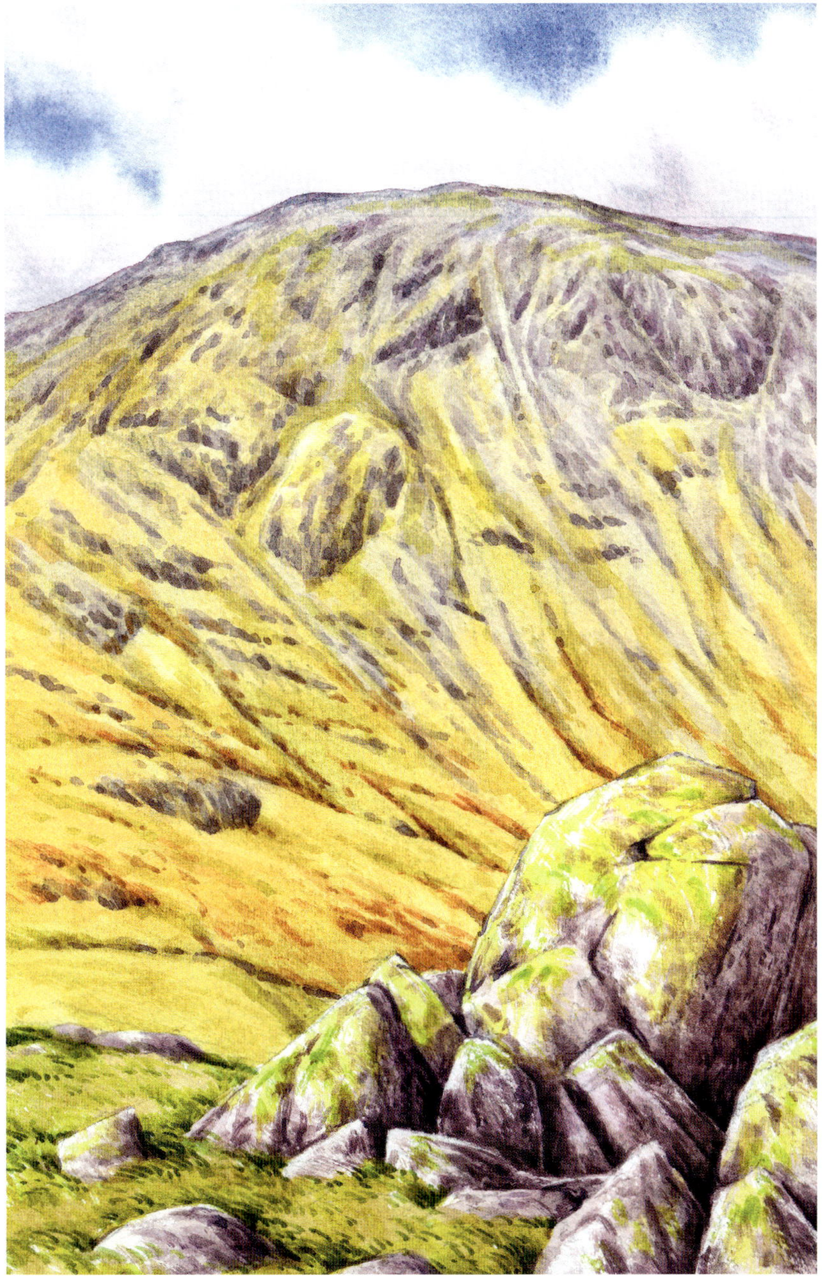

Brandreth

Due to its position on a high long ridge that connects Honister Pass to Great Gable, Brandreth is often visited on route between these two locations. The top is relatively flat and lacks real interest but the views from the slopes west of the summit of the Ennerdale and Buttermere valleys are truly outstanding.

From Base Brown 17/4/09
In a diligent search the nearest that I could find to the foreground rocks in Wainwright's drawing were these, a short distance west of Base Brown's summit. Brandreth lies across Gillercomb Head.

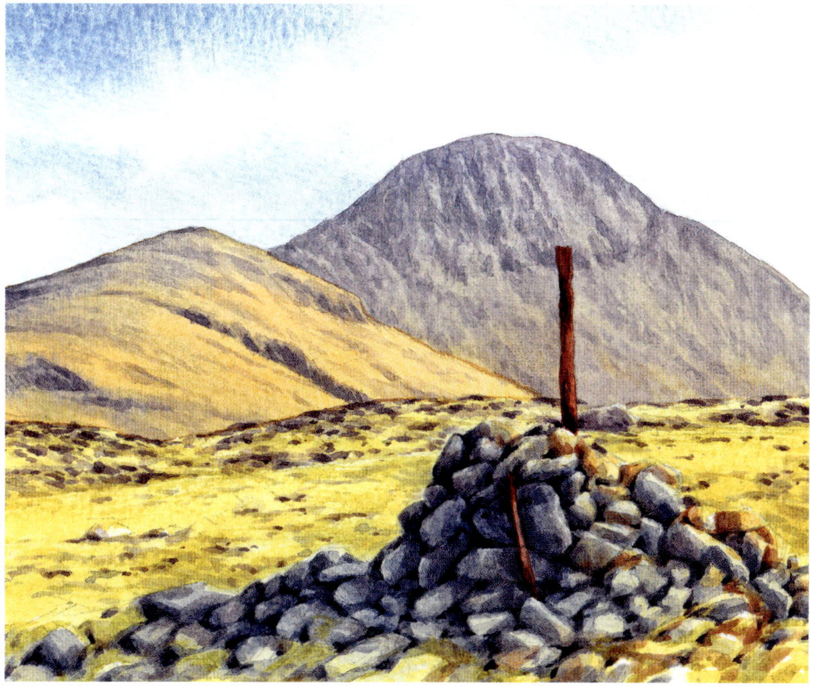

The summit 17/4/09
All that remains of the iron fence is one or two bars wedged into the cairn.

Great Round How 21/6/10
A reference obtained at 8.30 on the evening of the longest day as I headed towards Haystacks.

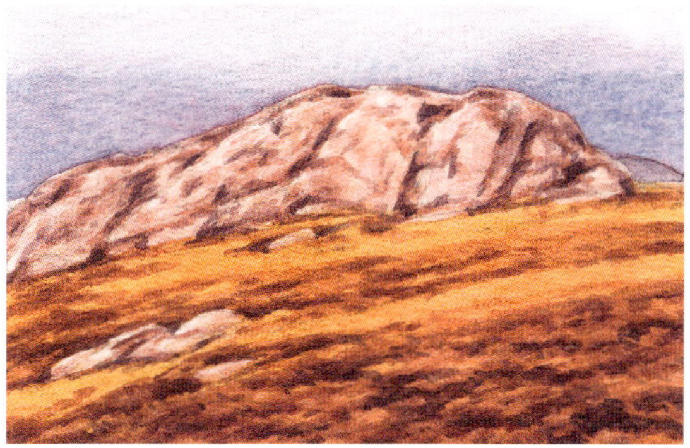

Gillercomb Head 17/4/09
The tarns are roughly the same in form today and I have included Kirk Fell in the distance.

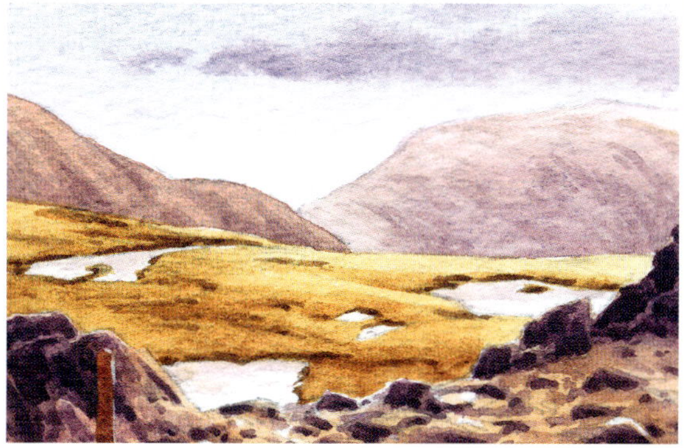

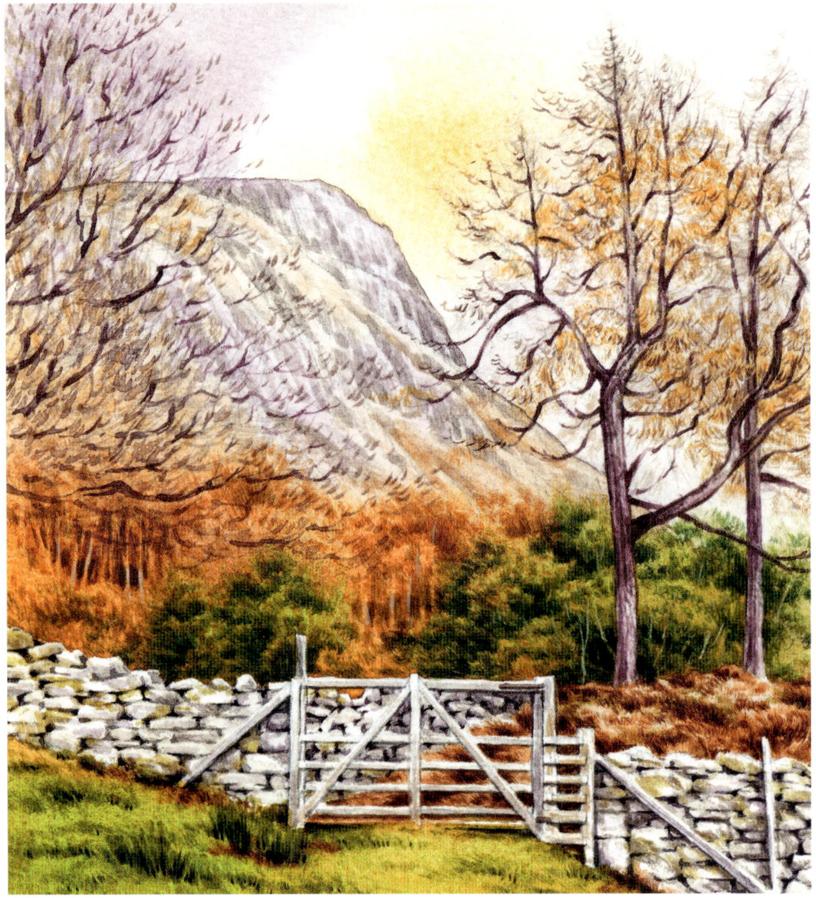

From Harrow Head 8/11/08
The big gate in the wall is a more recent addition and the fields now seem to be given over to woodland. The main tree still holds its original shape.

Buckbarrow

Neither Buckbarrow, Glade How nor Cat Bields were on AW's initial lists of fells despite the latter two being marked on the maps with measured heights. Perhaps the fact that it is the furthest from Seatallan and has views from the edge above the crags over Wasdale, Buckbarrow made the final 214 listing.

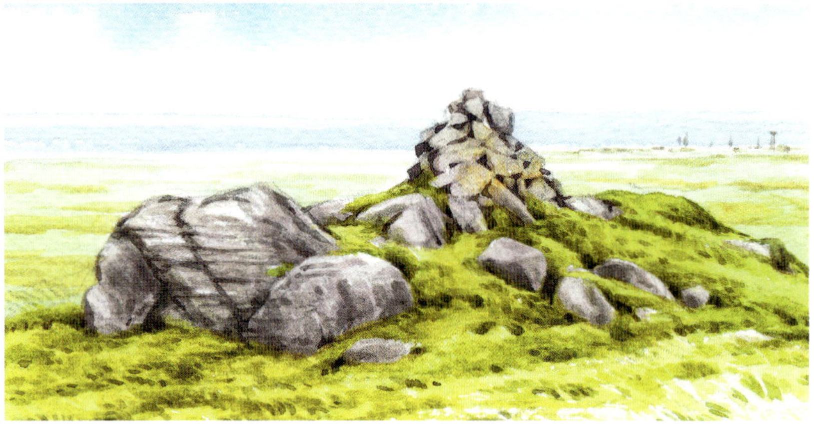

The summit 8/11/08
A cairn now sits on the rocky mound with Sellafield to the right.

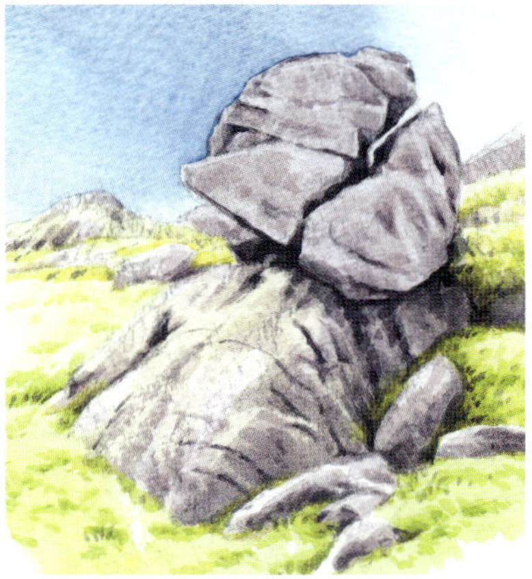

Perched and split boulder 8/11/08
This reference not only needed finding but required an accurate photograph that captures the light through the split as near as possible to AW's fine drawing. The background is included here.

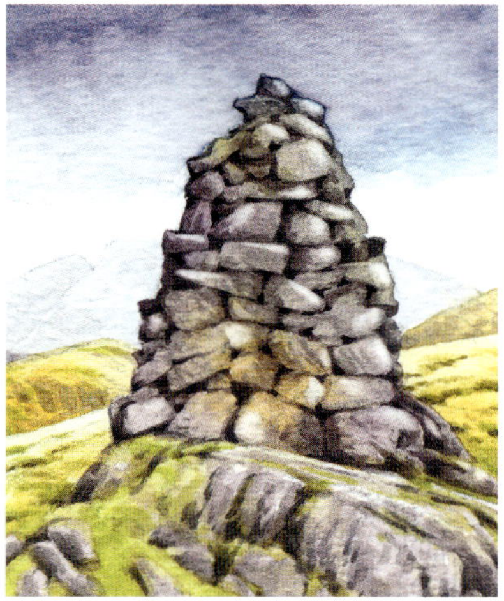

The cairn on Glade How 8/11/08
A fine old feature on a raised base.

Buckbarrow from Greendale 8/11/08
The southern, rough face of the fell with Pike Crag on the left.

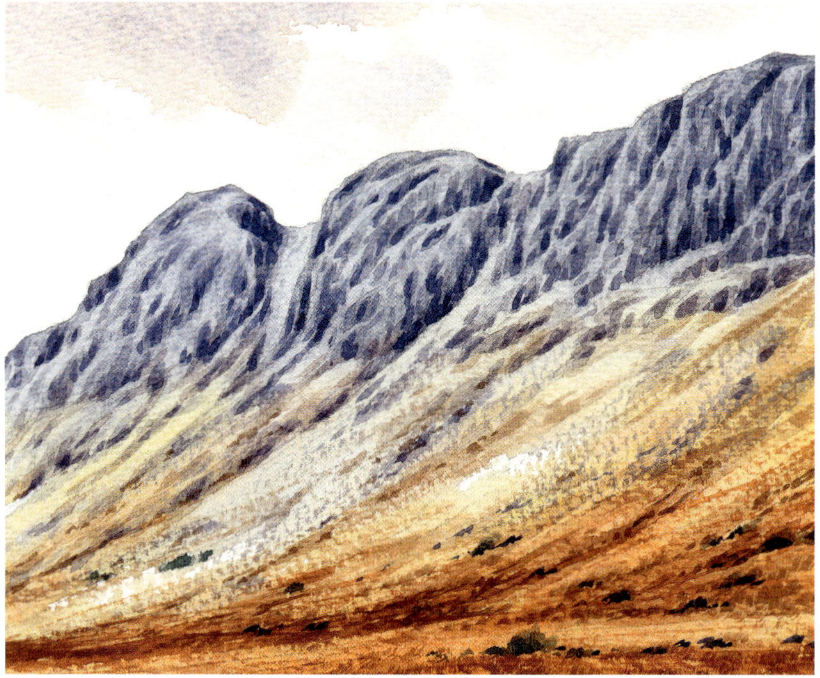

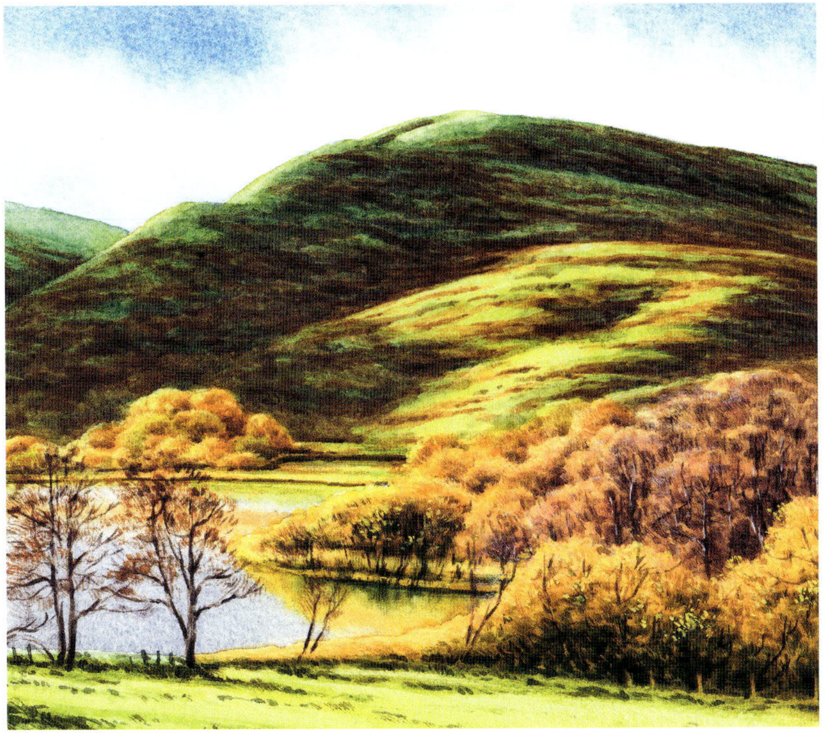

From Waterend 10/11/08
Another reference obtained from a roadside, this time from the road on the north side of Loweswater not far from the hall of the same name.

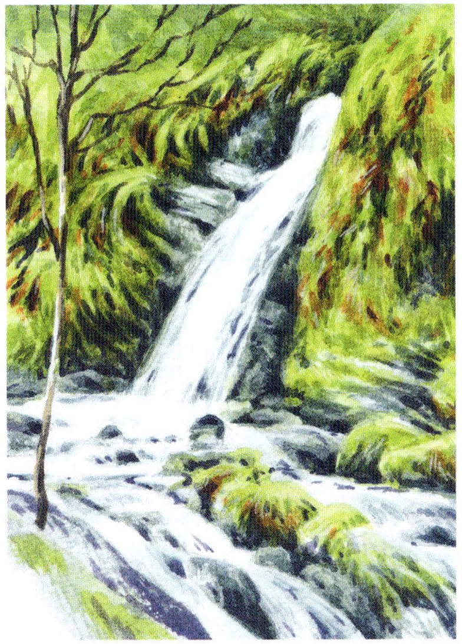

Holme Force 27/11/11
This charming fall is located in Holme Wood, a short walk from the car park at Maggie's Bridge. After heavy rain there can be two cascades, this is the one on the left.

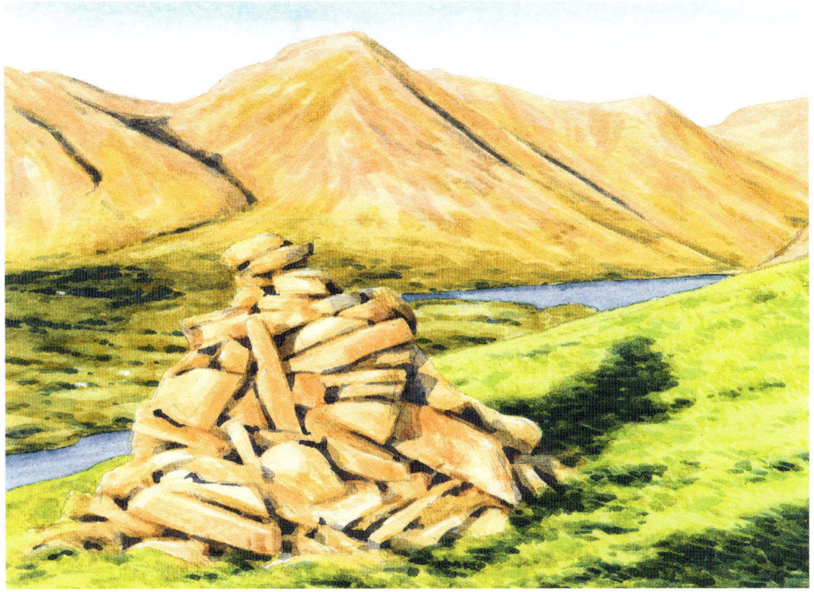

"...the only cairn on the fell." 31/5/09
This excellent view of the Grasmoor group seen over the now larger cairn at about 7.30 on a fine spring evening. Now that there is a small cairn at the summit this one loses its title of being the only one on Burnbank Fell.

Burnbank Fell

Anyone who only owns the revised versions of the Pictorial Guides will not recognise three of the sketches shown here. Due to the fact that AW's original route of ascent from Lamplugh had a short section across what is still private land, the original page "Burnbank Fell 4" was completely removed from the revised guide and consequently also eradicated were the drawings of the summit and *"the only cairn on the fell"*. In my opinion this revision could have been achieved with more sympathy for the original design and with some explanation of the amendment.

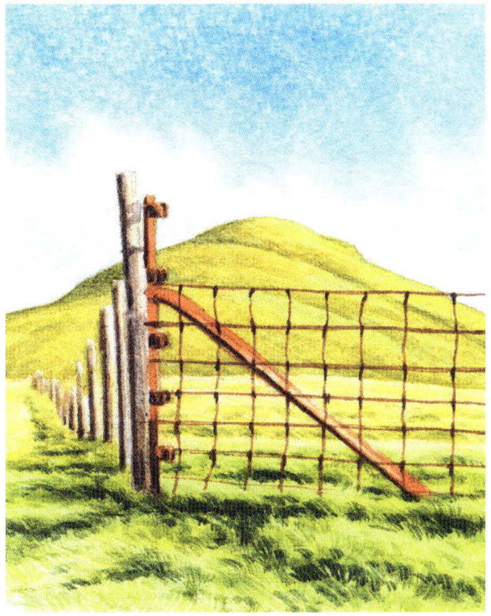

The summit 31/5/09
The top section of the iron post has gone and a more recent fence crosses the summit on the other side of which is a small cairn marking the highest point.

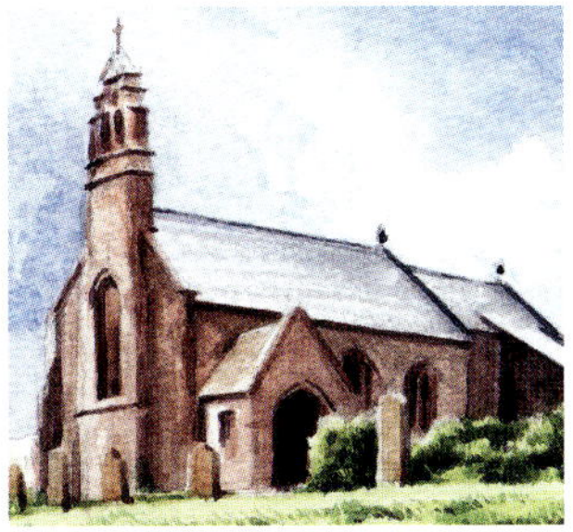

Lamplugh Church 7/11/08
Wainwright cleverly squeezes in this tiny detailed drawing, one of the smallest in all of the guides, into the bottom corner of the page (see note on the left).

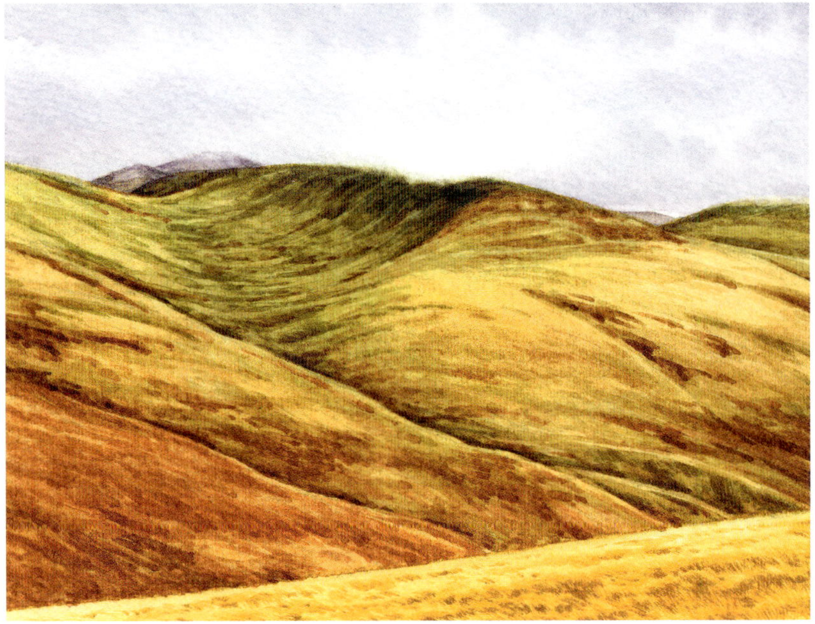

From Lank Rigg 14/9/11
Low cloud just lifted from the fell top at the right time to allow me to see the detail I needed. This view is from the western slopes of Lank Rigg.

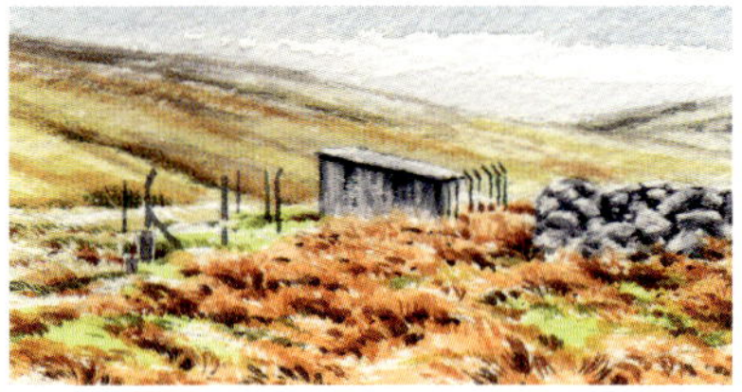

Water Intake Works 5/11/08
In the remote Worm Gill valley.

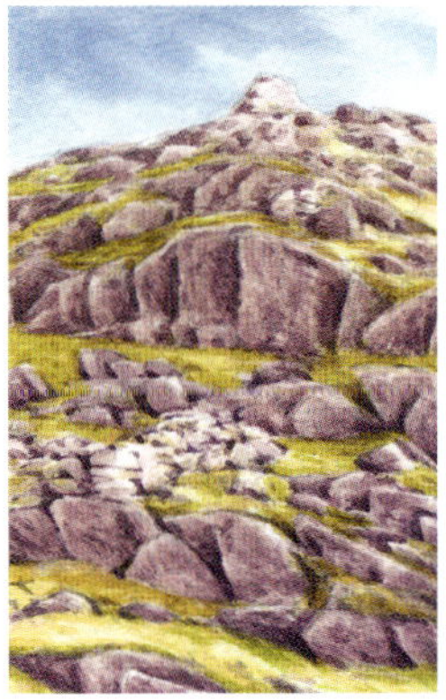

Little Gowder Crag 8/11/08
The wall needs some restoration.

The Antiquities of Stockdale Moor

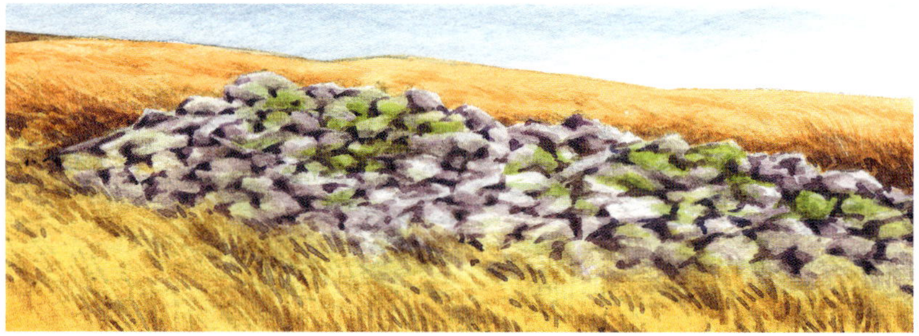

A tumulus 6/11/08
The largest rock pile on the moor.

An enclosure 6/11/08
The remains of an ancient bield.

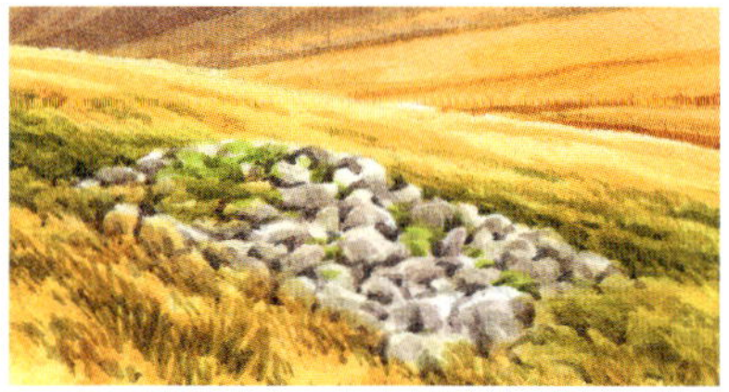

A cairn 6/11/08
Similar in look to AW's illustration.

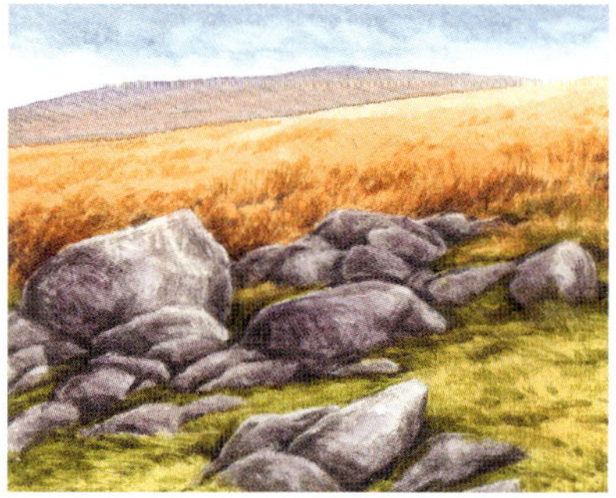

Caw Fell

On various maps the name of Caw Fell is usually placed one mile west of what AW denoted as this fell, he chose the spot height above Silver Cove as the summit. Caw Fell can be classed as the remotest of all Wainwright Fells.

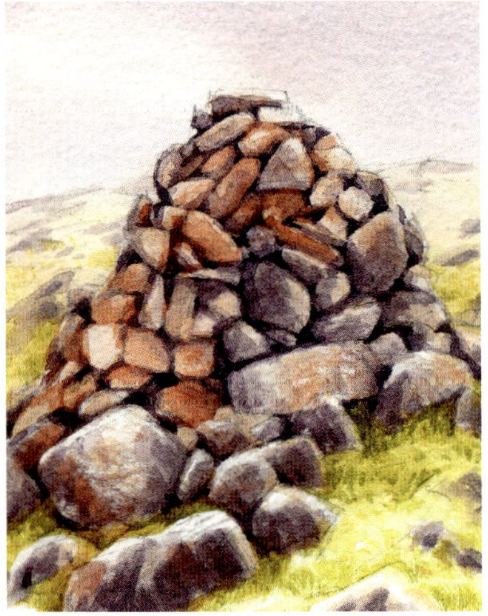

The summit 8/11/08
The pile of red coloured rocks that stands above Silver Cove.

From Ennerdale 23/2/10
The slopes of the fell seen from near the eastern end of Ennerdale Water.

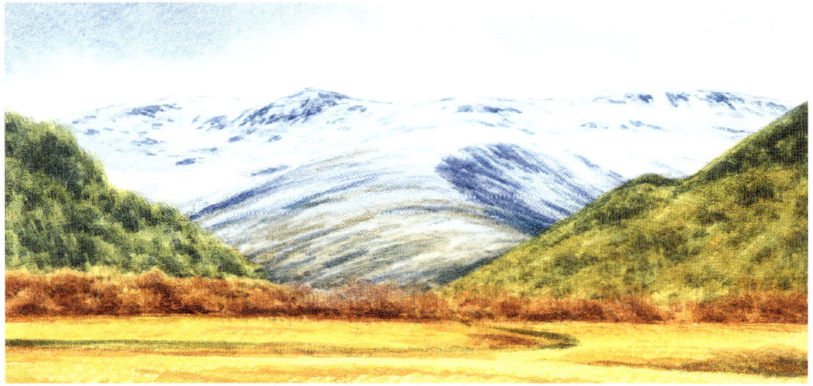

Sergeant Ford 6/11/08
The remaining stepping stones.

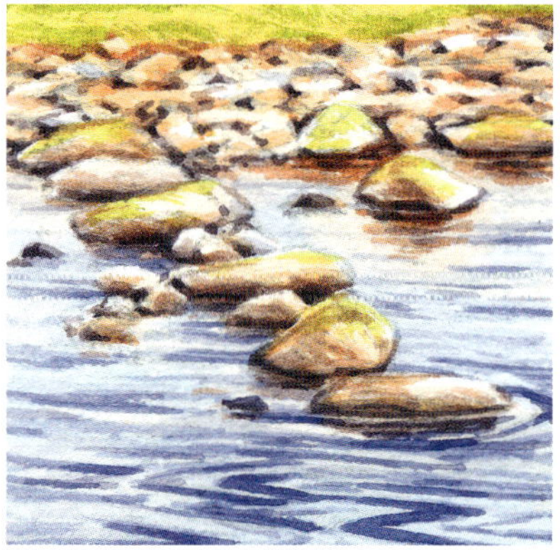

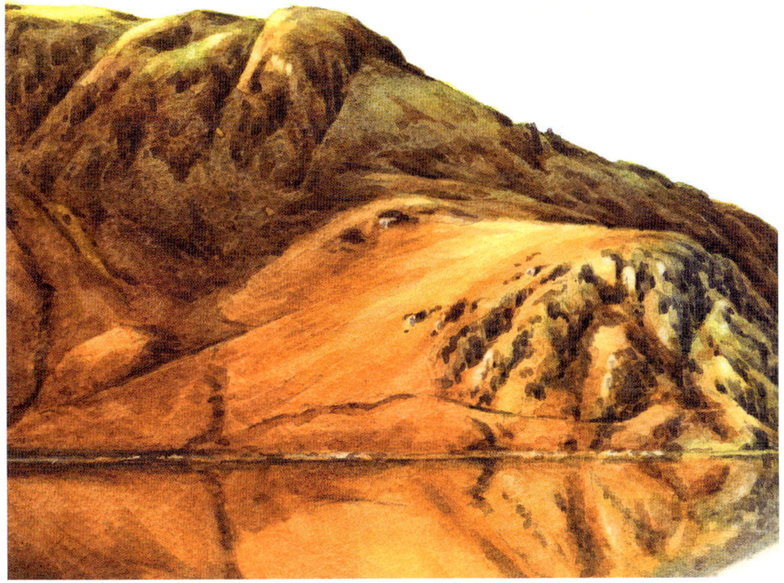

From Bowness Point 10/11/08
The first light of a November day illuminates the top of the fell and Angler's Crag across the flat calm Ennerdale Water.

Crag Fell

The best ascent of this hill is definitely the way up past the pinnacles on the north side. With impressive rock scenery and excellent views along Ennerdale I can highly recommend this route.

The summit 9/11/08
Bigger now than in AW's day this cairn gives some limited shelter.

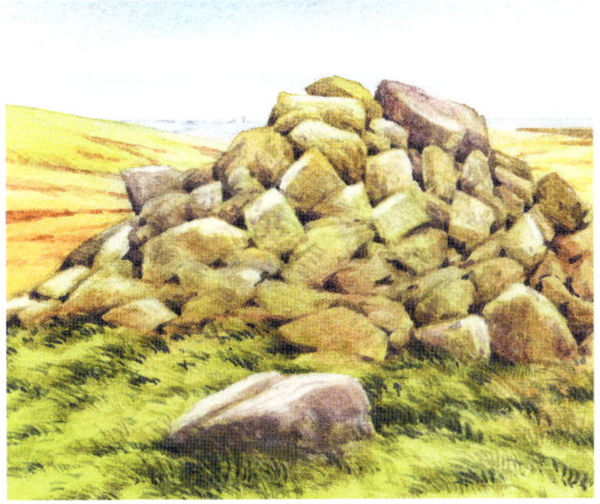

Crag Fell Pinnacles 9/11/08
The hint of the far shore of the lake in AW's drawing allowed me to pinpoint the angle of view exactly but the imposing columns are not quite so vertical as he depicted them.

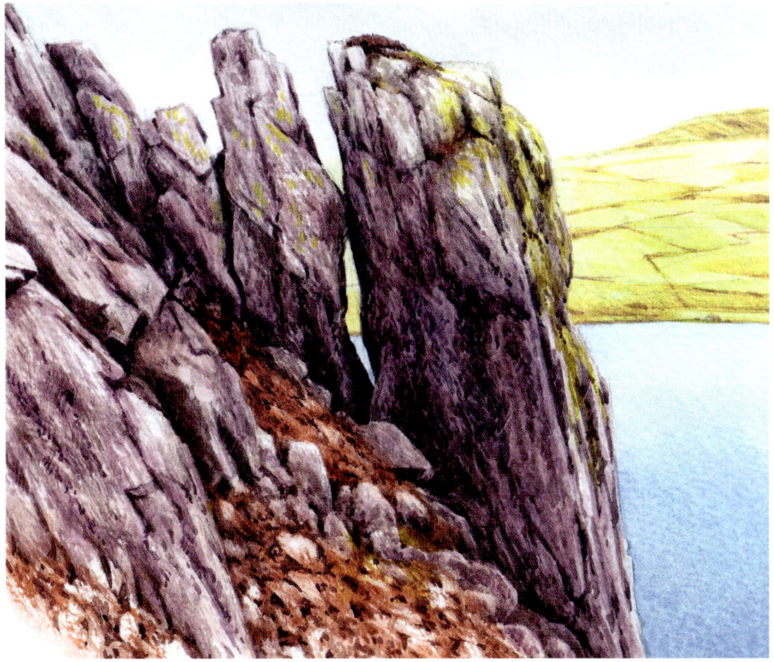

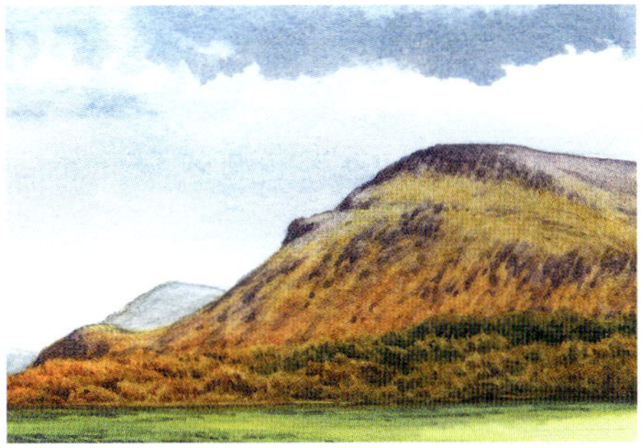

From Ennerdale Bridge 10/11/08
This more accurate profile is from the lane end to Low Moorend Farm.

Another of the Crag Fell Pinnacles 9/11/08
Great Borne is the backdrop.

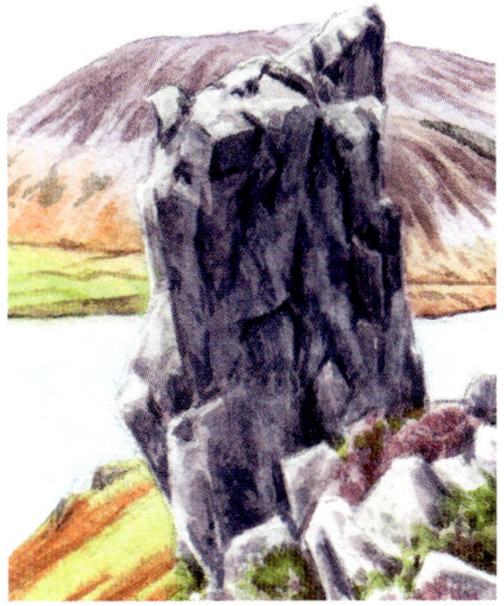

Angler's Crag 9/11/08
This footpath is now part of the popular Coast to Coast route.

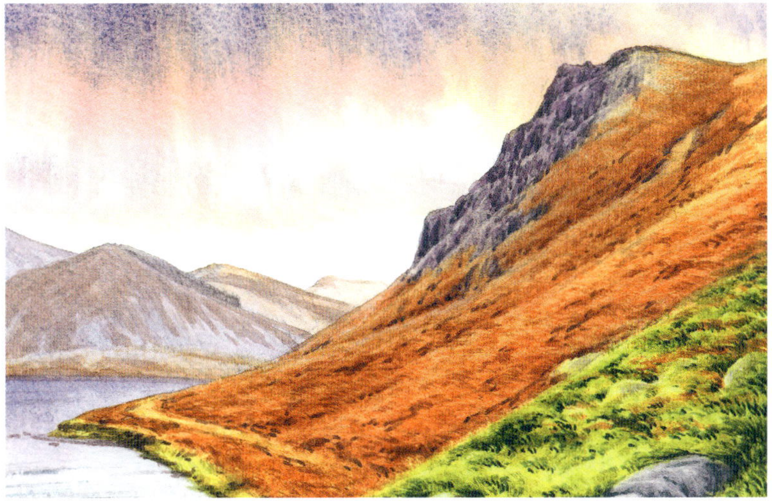

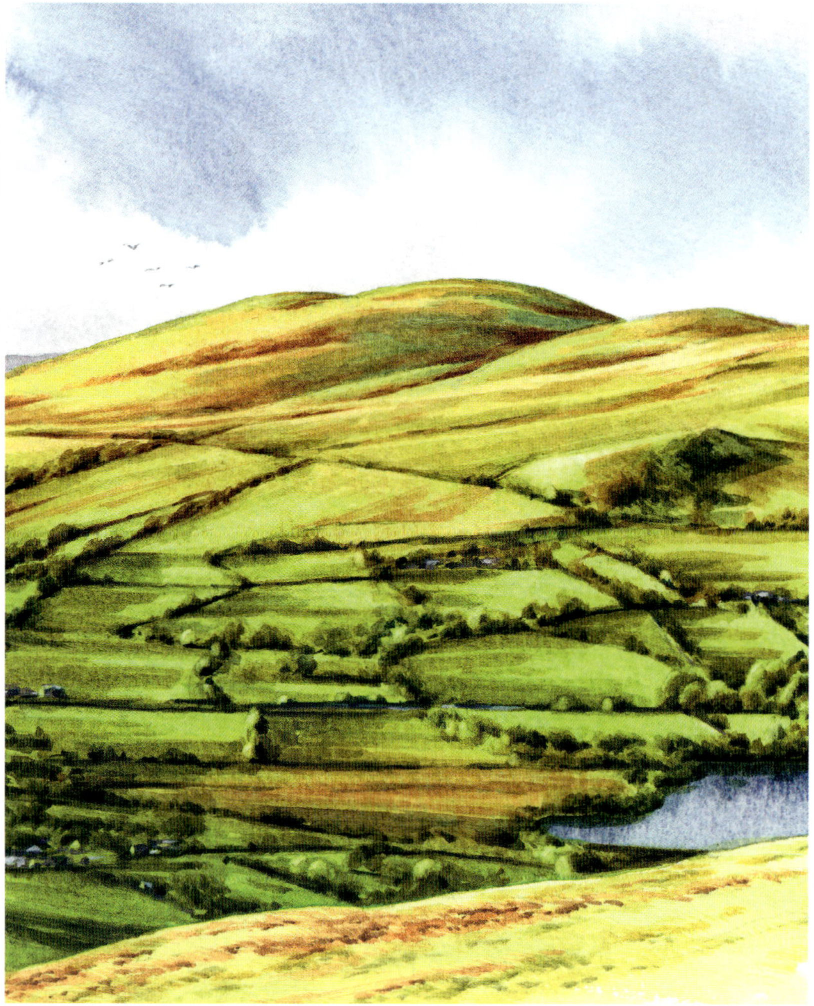

From the slopes of Burnbank Fell above Waterend 31/5/09

This is almost a retrospective view to that in the Burnbank Fell chapter "from Waterend". Here the prospect of Fellbarrow is taken from a point close to where Wainwright indicates an old level in Low Crag on the eastern slopes of Burnbank Fell. In his illustration AW employs the use of sky detail not only to fill up the space at the top of the page but the clouds with their solid ink outline help to define the rounded shape of Fellbarrow itself. He only depicts clouds on three occasions in book seven.

Fellbarrow

The two lowest hills of the Western Fells, Fellbarrow and Low Fell, are located at the north of this region and are joined together to form a neat area of high ground above Loweswater, and are ideal for exploring as a short day's outing.

Fellbarrow is another chapter in the new revised Pictorial Guides which has been chopped and changed. Whilst I respect the rights of private landowners over whose land AW may have shown a route, these pages could have been edited more sympathetically to maintain AW's original design. Even the ridge route to Low Fell with the detailed map has been cut. Now three of the sketches shown here, including the important summit view, are excluded from the new version of the guide, and Fellbarrow has become the only fell in all of the Pictorial Guides to have only one illustration within its description chapter, selling the reader short of sketches.

The summit 4/11/08

The rocks around the base of the triangulation pillar in AW's drawing have been moved five yards away to be formed into a low cairn. The summit is rather flat and uninteresting but the Grasmoor group does form an impressive scenic backdrop.

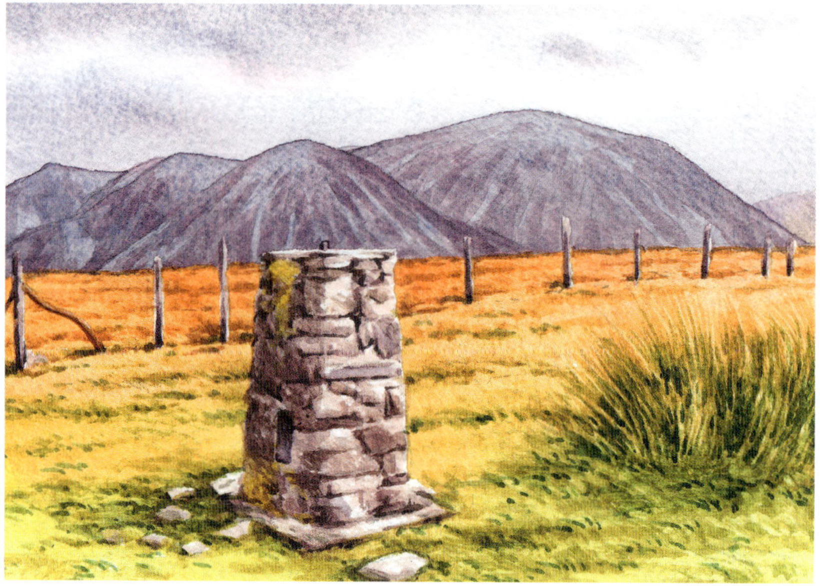

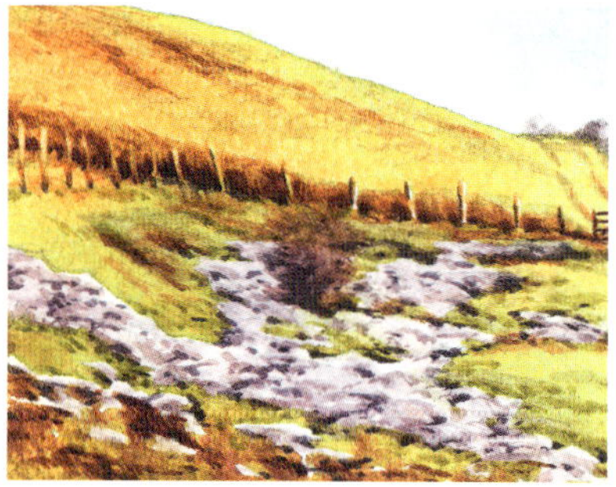

Ruins of Hatteringill 4/11/08

Hardly any wall is now over two feet high but the outline of the building can easily be defined.

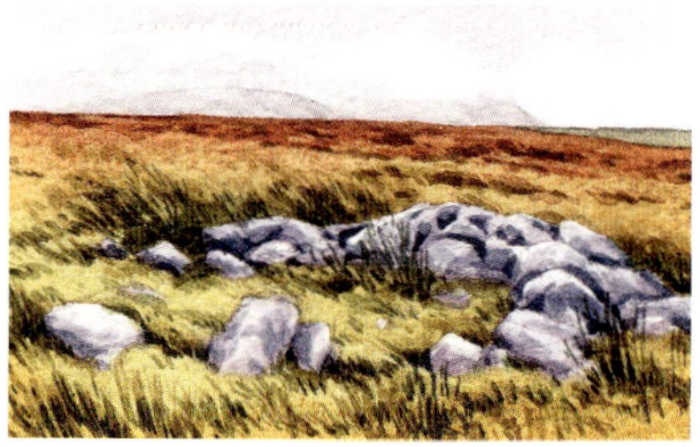

The stone ring 4/11/08

This circle of stones, some 60 yards west of the summit was marked on the 1900 6 inch O.S. map, most likely it was a former shooting butt.

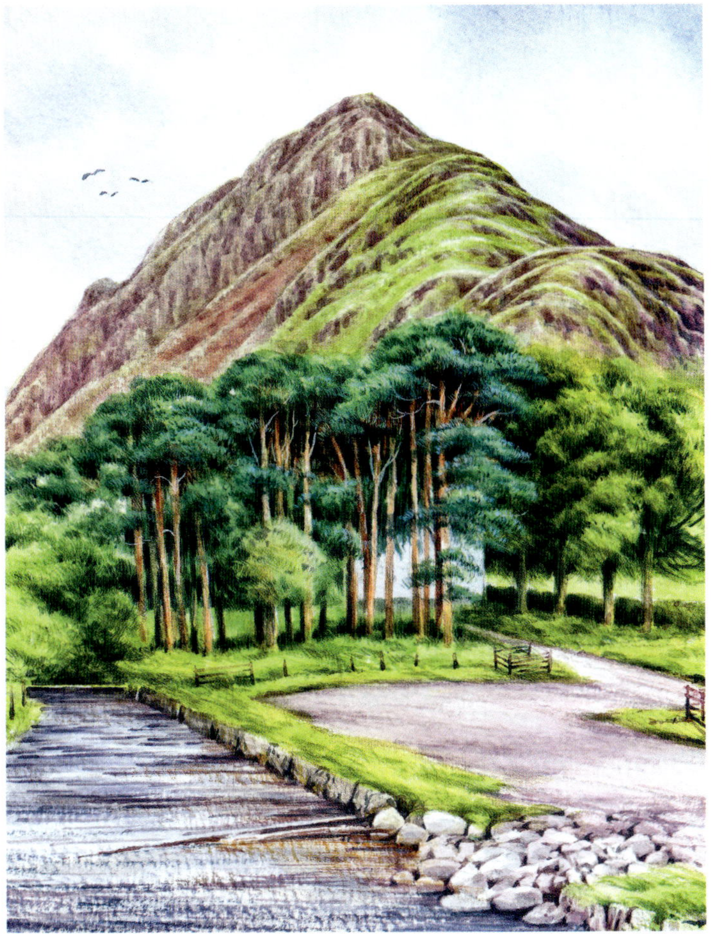

From Gatesgarth 10/9/09
A small surfaced area to the right of the river now provides a car park for visitors. Otherwise the scene is practically unchanged.

Fleetwith Pike

This imposing peak stands sentinel at the south-eastern end of Buttermere but it is a fell scarred by years of industry. For centuries man has tapped into the rich resource of slate deep within the mountain's heart.

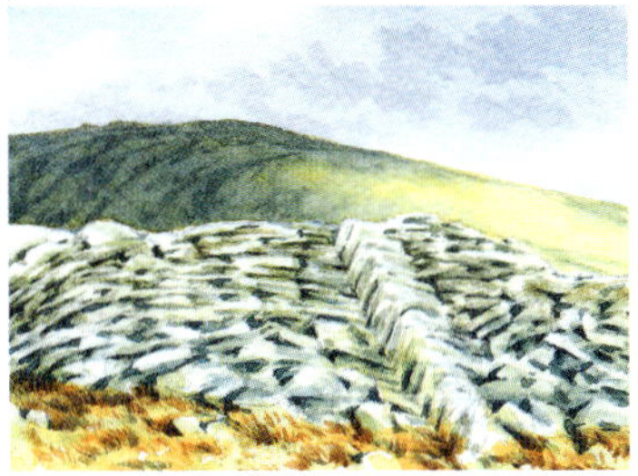

The Drum House 11/11/07
This aspect is from the south side with Dale Head behind.

Honister Crag 18/3/11
The high crags and steep scree runs above the Honister Pass road just in view, bottom right.

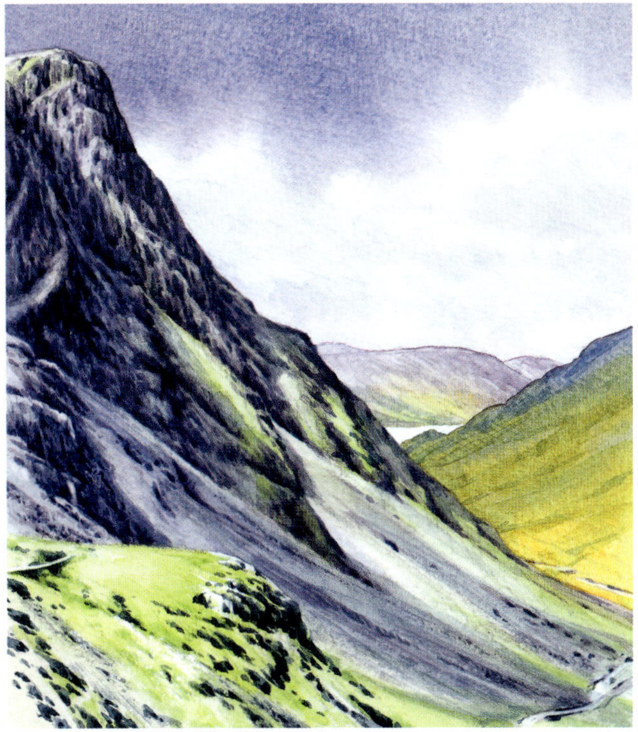

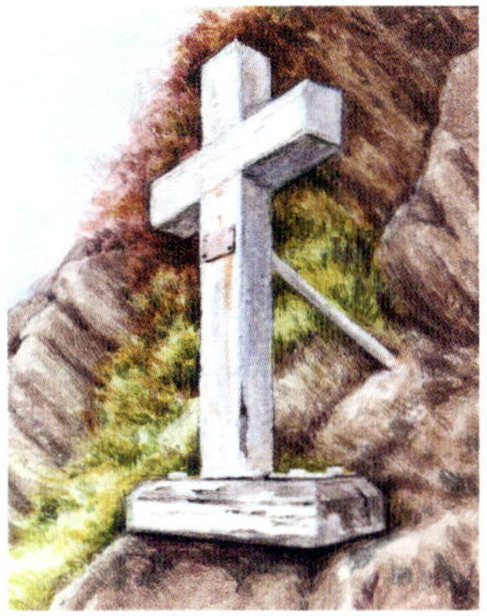

The White Cross 10/9/09
Since I obtained my reference for this sketch the 4′ high memorial to Fanny Mercer, who died here in 1887, has been fully refurbished.

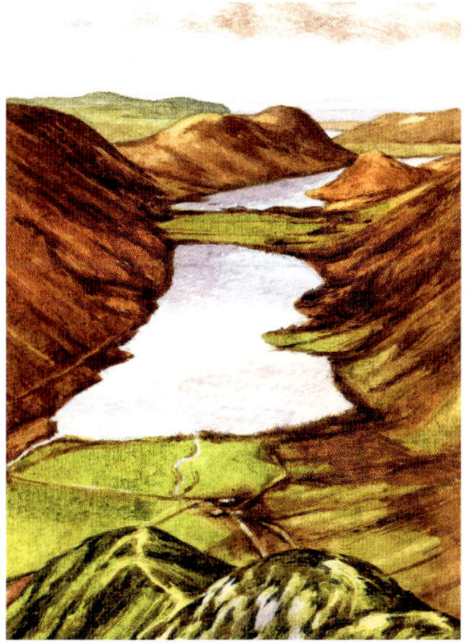

The Buttermere valley 12/11/07
The reward of a stunning view after climbing the ridge from Gatesgarth.

The summit 11/11/07
Although this cairn is now a little tumbledown, just 15 yards to the north-west is now a fine 5′ column with a grand view .

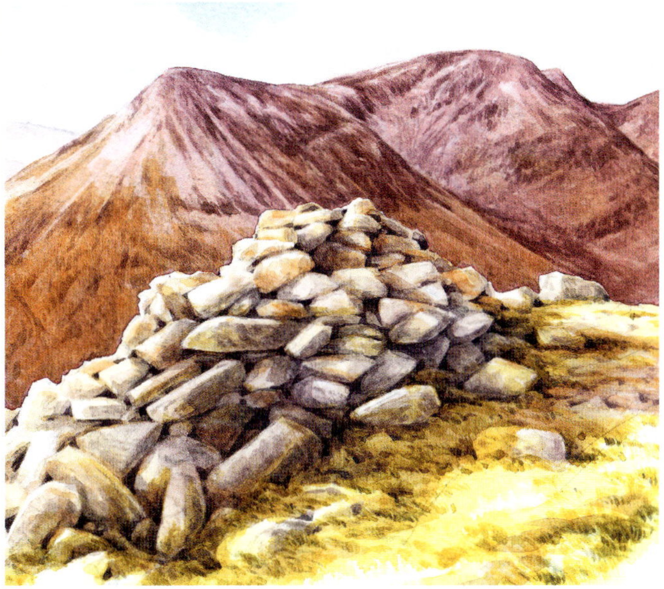

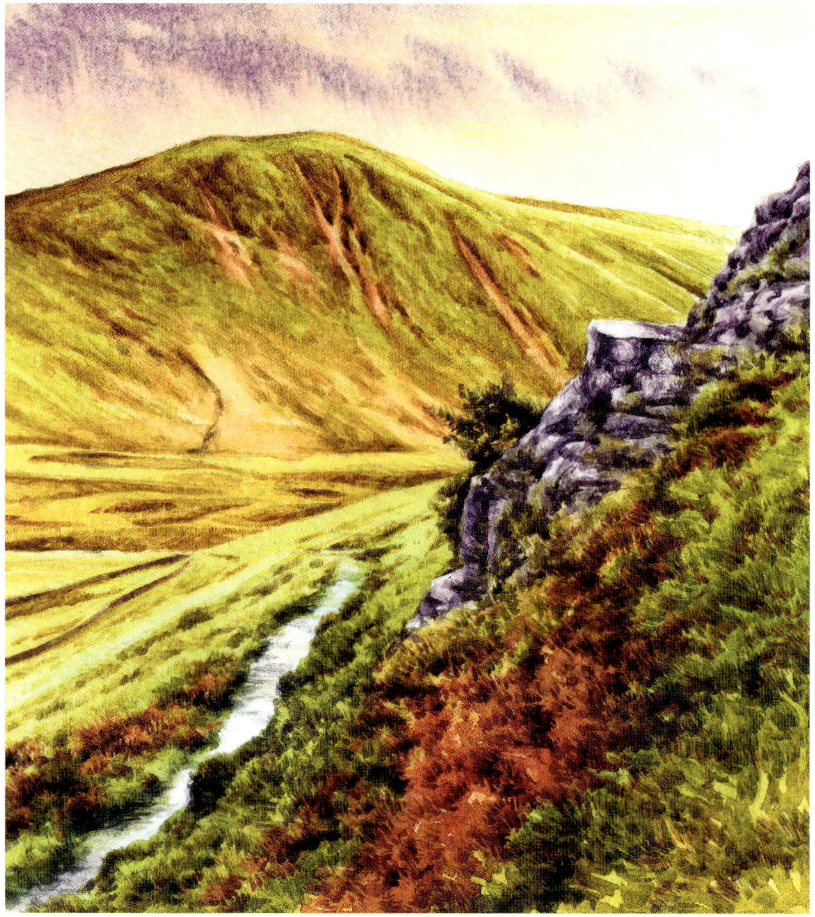

From the terrace path below Carling Knott 31/5/09
It was after 8pm but I was determined to seek out this outcrop of rock with the flat top to ensure accuracy in this sketch. My diligence paid off.

Gavel Fell
This is another of the hills in the group known as the Loweswater Fells and as such walkers usually visit Gavel Fell's simple top as part of a round of the hills in this area. Again, another fell which has lost pages and sketches in the revised version of the guide.

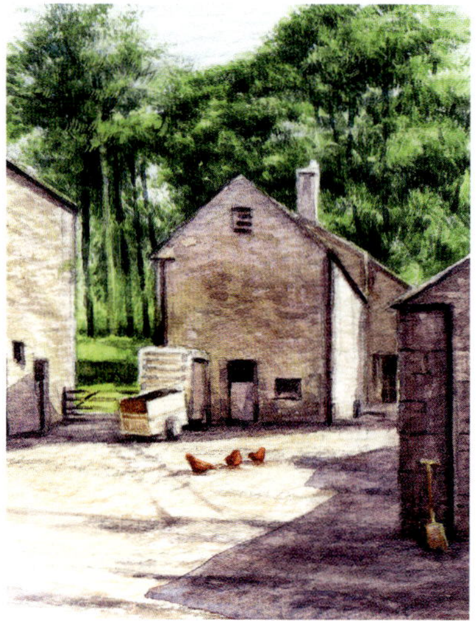

High Nook Farm 31/5/08
Only on close inspection of AW's drawing in the guide will the sow and her piglets be noticed in the yard. None were there on my visit so I took the liberty of adding hens in their place.

The subsidiary top 31/5/09
A quiet spot on a rise with splendid views over to the east. Another example of a sketch deleted from the revised Pictorial Guide.

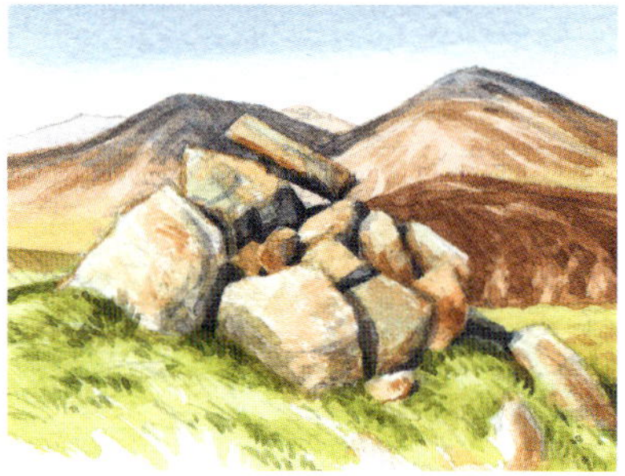

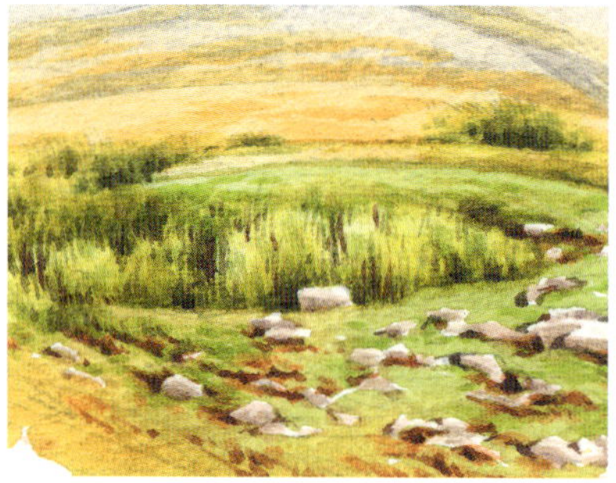

Pit Circle, Floutern Cop
10/11/08
Now hard to see amongst reeds.

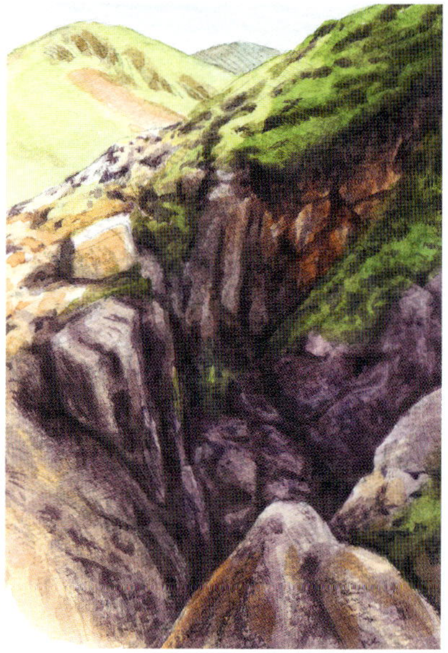

Old shaft, disused lead mines
31/5/09
The revised guide is wrong. This shaft is still there, unchanged, to be found if you look hard enough.

The summit 31/5/09
A summit with a fine view sadly not in the revised guide. On many tops the grass near the cairn gets worn thin, here it is almost pristine.

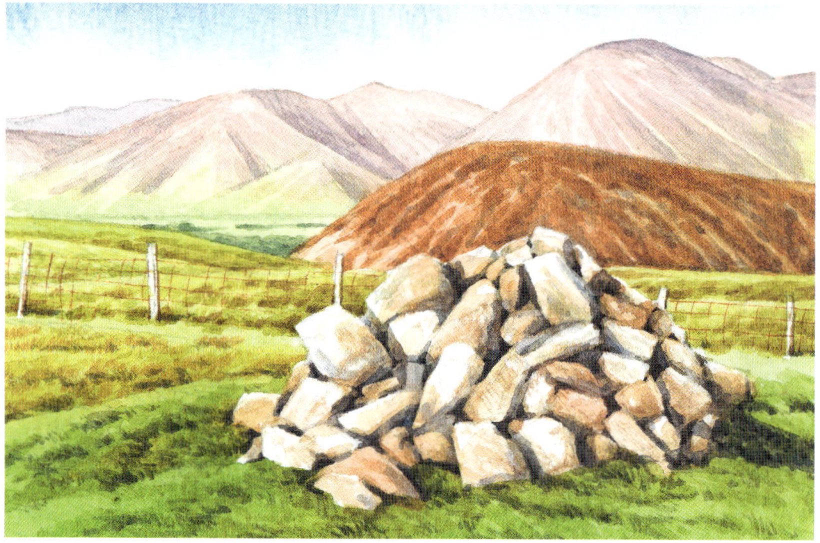

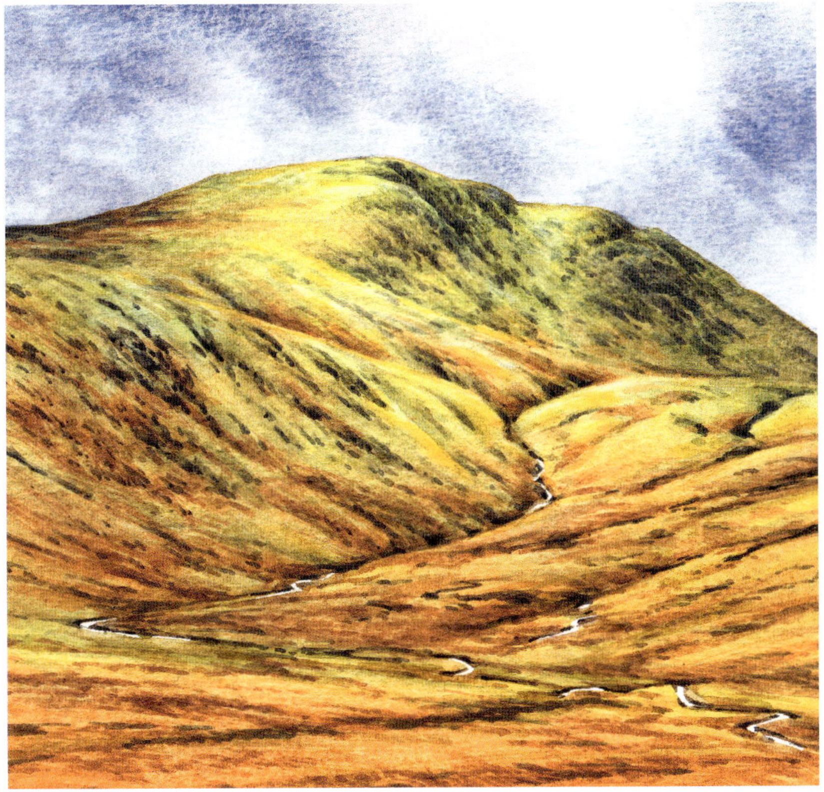

From Mosedale 10/11/08
The northern face of Great Borne seen across the head of Mosedale, an area of extensive marsh. This vista is from the path on the east side of the valley which takes a higher route above most of the morass.

Great Borne
Originally AW had listed Bowness Knott as a separate fell but perhaps due to the encroaching forest he decided to incorporate it into the Great Borne chapter. Wainwright's only direct route of ascent crossed land near Gill Beck which was and still is private. The best route of ascent now is via Rake Beck. Great Borne is more accurately the name of the summit whereas Herdus is the western portion of the fell with Scaw being the southern part.

The summit

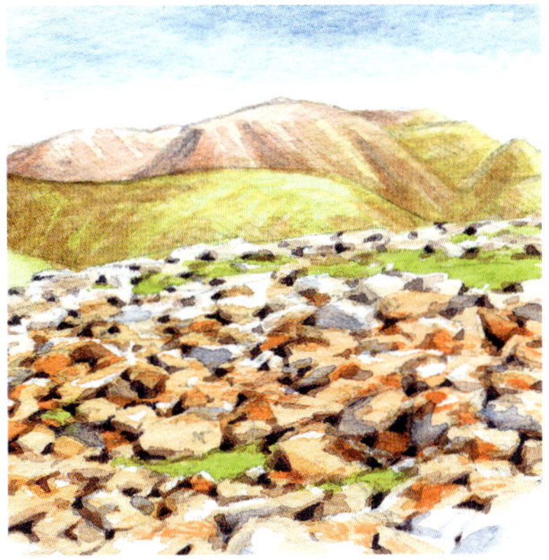

The big cairn on the north top 20/4/10
This substantial old cairn that was made mostly of pink granophyre rocks has been destroyed. Shame on those vandals for this act.

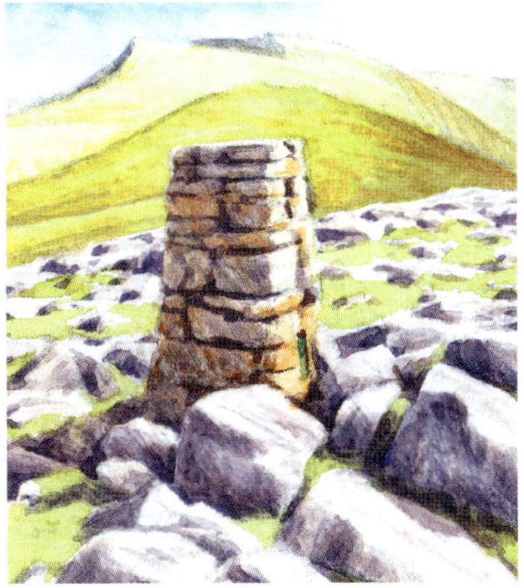

The column on the south top 10/9/09
There is a shelter close to here on the rocky summit plateau.

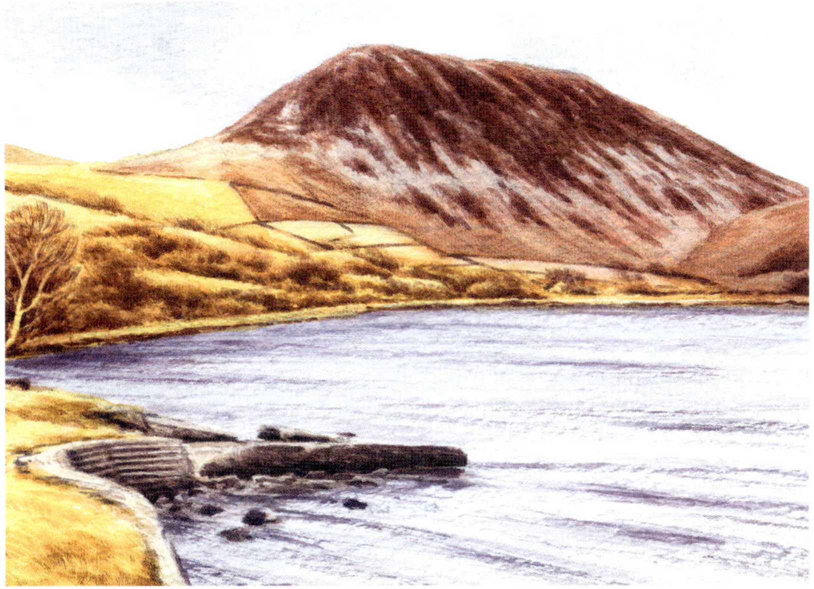

From Ennerdale 23/2/10
The crumbling jetty is all that remains of the Angler's Hotel which stood in this site until 1961 when it was demolished. What a view guests must have had, not only of Great Borne but of the whole length of Ennerdale.

Floutern Tarn 10/9/09
The tarn as seen from near the top of the pass. Red Pike is to the left.

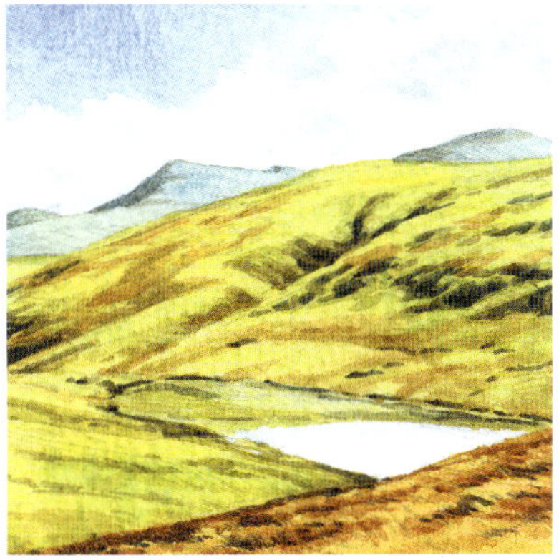

Bowness Knott 10/11/08
The forest was being cleared at the time of my visit, revealing the views.

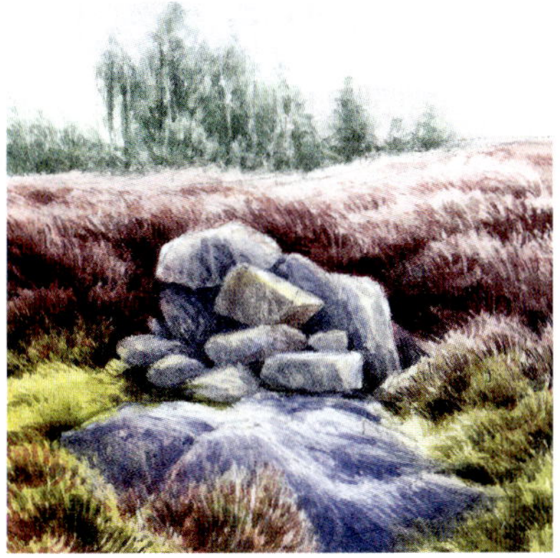

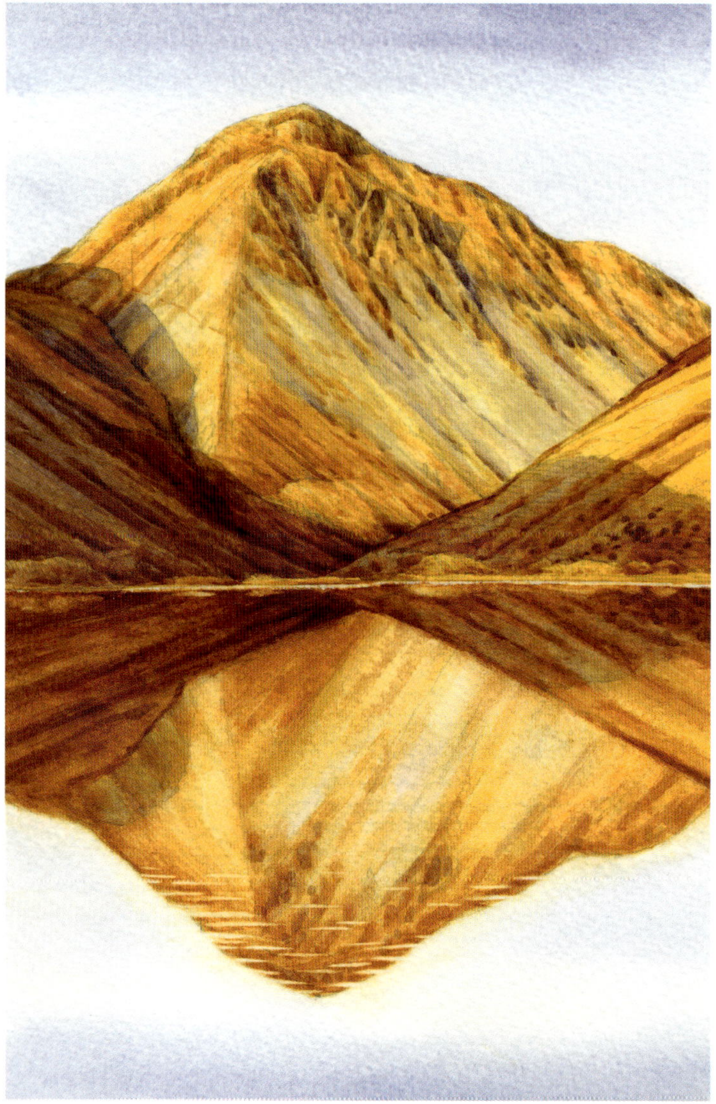

From Wastwater 14/4/14
The perfect mountain shape of Great Gable at the head of Wastwater could not have been better placed. This is only the centre focal point of what is a wide lakeland landscape which was voted "Britain's Favourite View" in 2007 in a television poll.

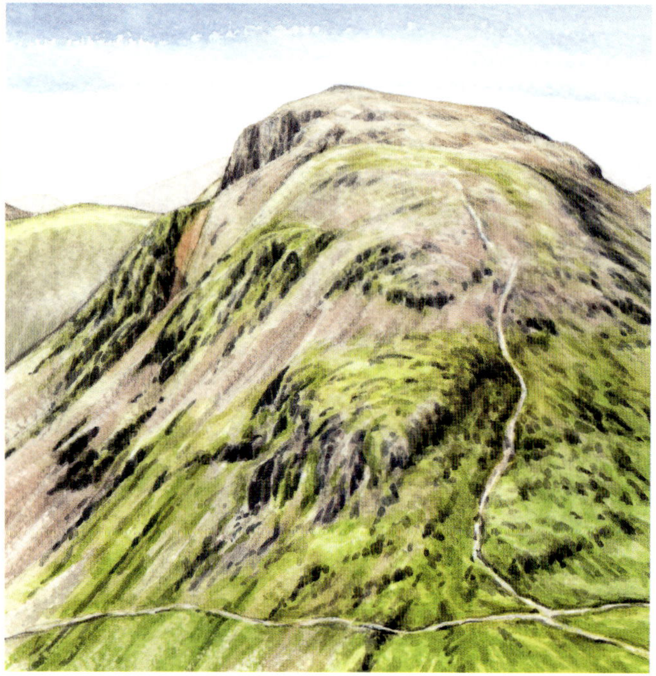

From Great End 12/6/09
The south west face of Great Gable from high up on The Band and an illustration which allowed AW to pinpoint features mentioned in the chapter.

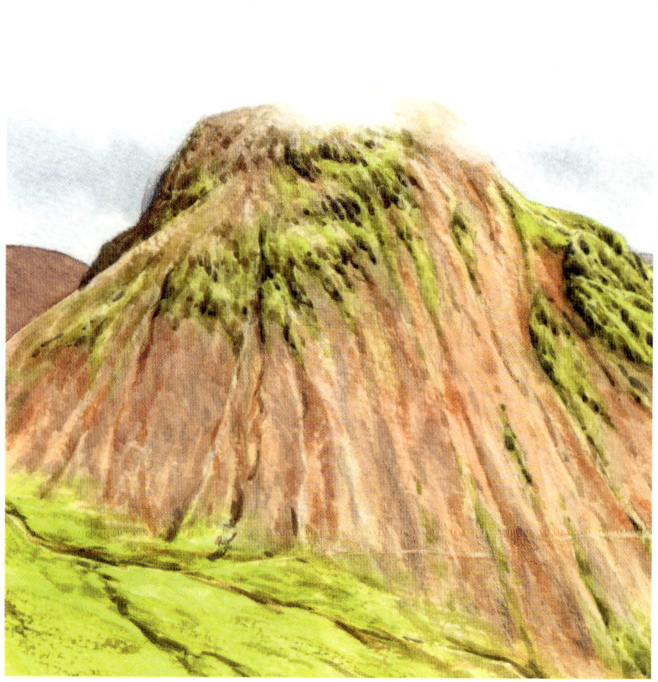

From the west 7/9/09
This aspect is from a point on Kirk Fell below the north-east summit.

Great Gable

In my opinion Great Gable is unrivalled in all of the Lake District Fells. During the course of this project I have visited its higher ground on five separate days and viewed it from a distance on numerous occasions, from all angles and in different seasons. Not once has it failed to inspire and excite me as it probably does for many other walkers, artists and photographers, as of course it did AW. He devoted 28 pages to the fell, just 8 less than for Blencathra.

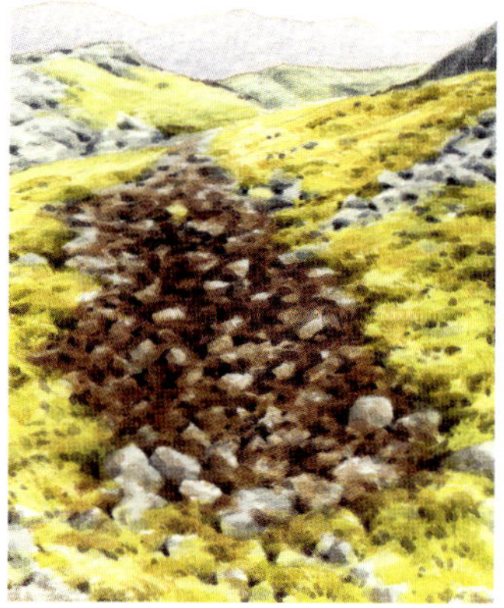

Dry Tarn 17/4/09
Named on the 6 inch O.S. map of 1900 with this title it is obvious that this dry pool, which is away from the regular path, has held little water for some time but the bed of the tarn curiously looks as if it was drained only yesterday.

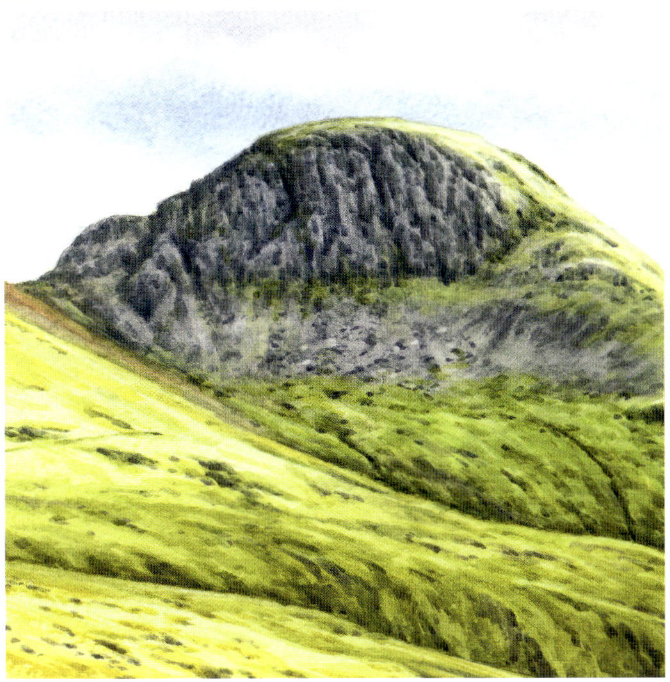

From the north 20/10/10
This is the prospect of Gable Crag as seen from Moses' Trod at a place directly between Brandreth and Brin Crag.

The Gable Girdle

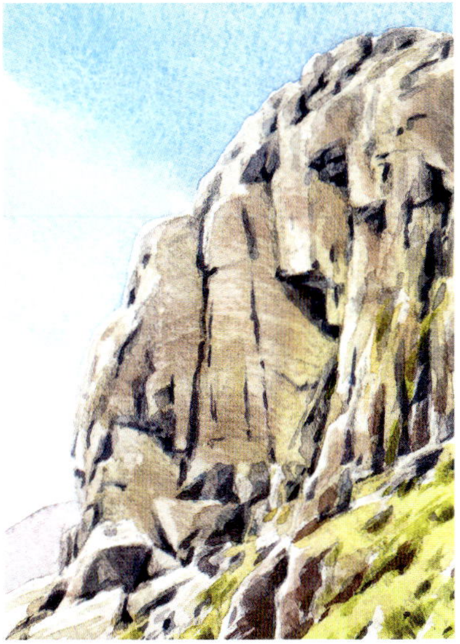

High Kern Knotts 17/4/09
This imposing crag has over 50 recognised climbing routes on it. The path passes close to the base.

Napes Needle 17/4/09
This iconic 70′ pinnacle can easily be missed when on the south traverse but a detour to the Dress Circle from where this view is obtained is well worth the effort. From other angles the topmost block which apparently rocks when stood on, looks to be defying gravity. The first ascent was in 1886 by W.P. Haskett-Smith.

The water-hole 17/4/09
A small cave from where clear water seems to constantly flow.

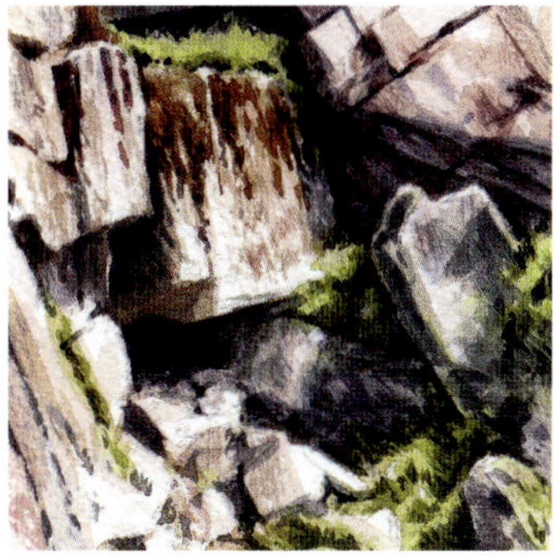

The Great Napes

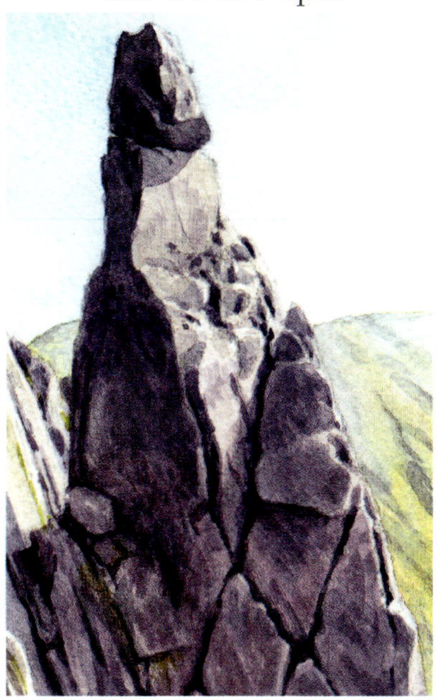

The Sphinx Rock 15/4/14
After a night's wild camp on Kirk Fell I was able to get to this position just as the early sun lit the face, great timing.

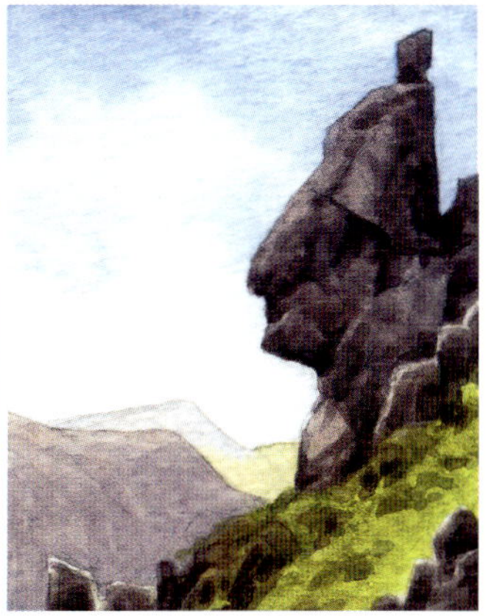

Moses' Trod

The hidden sheepfold 20/10/10
It took me two searches to find this structure which is away from the Trod.

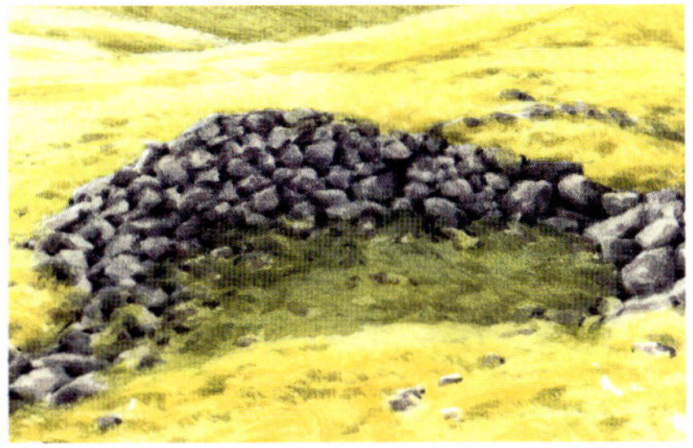

> **Moses Rigg**
> Mentioned by AW, this character worked at Honister Mine in the 1780s as well as doing a bit of smuggling on the side. It seems the Trod is the only route named after a person in Lakeland.

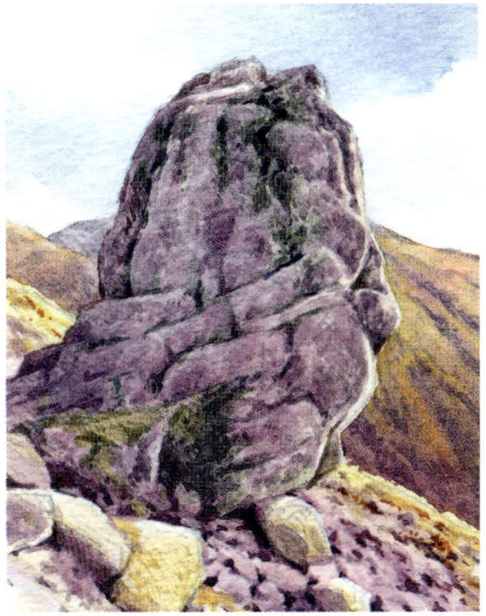

Moses' Finger 18/3/11
A natural pillar of rock in an area of loose scree on the Gavel Neese path overlooking Wasdale Head.

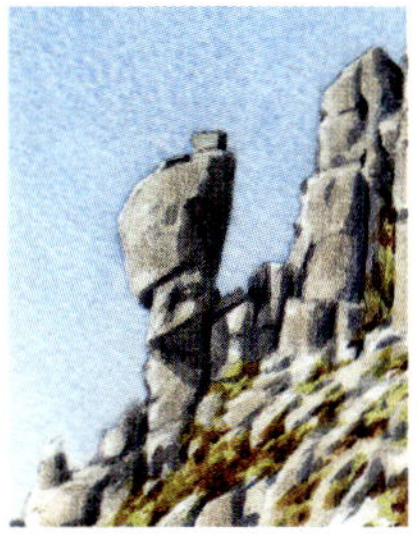

The Cat Rock 17/4/09
AW's tiny drawing seems to hint that Cat Rock actually has a tail, it hasn't, he just didn't draw in the rock under the "tail" shadow to give that idea. It is also known as Sphinx Rock.

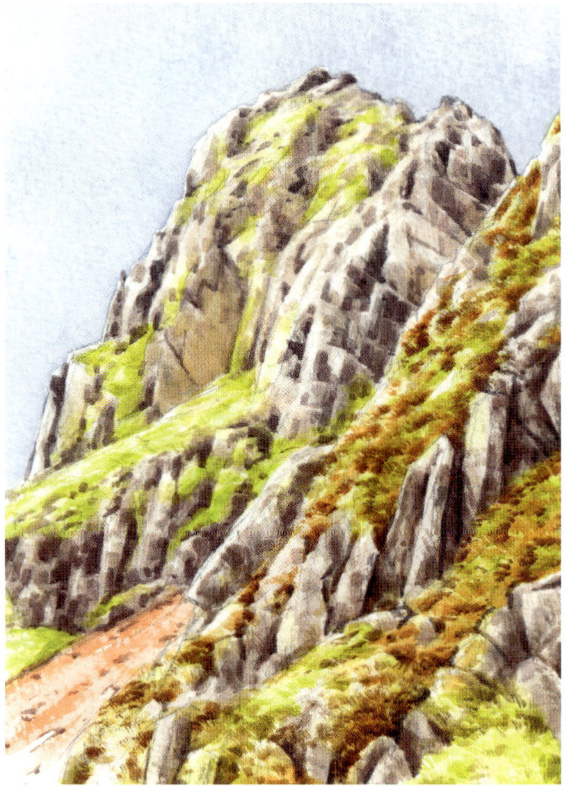

The Great Napes

Tophet Bastion 17/4/09

When completing the South Traverse in an east to west direction this huge tower of rock suddenly appears as you round a corner. It is wise to stop and take it all in and not let it cause distraction as you tread the narrow path. The name Tophet is a term for hell and Bastion is a fortification, combined to make a name fitting for this dramatic crag between the two "Hell Gates".

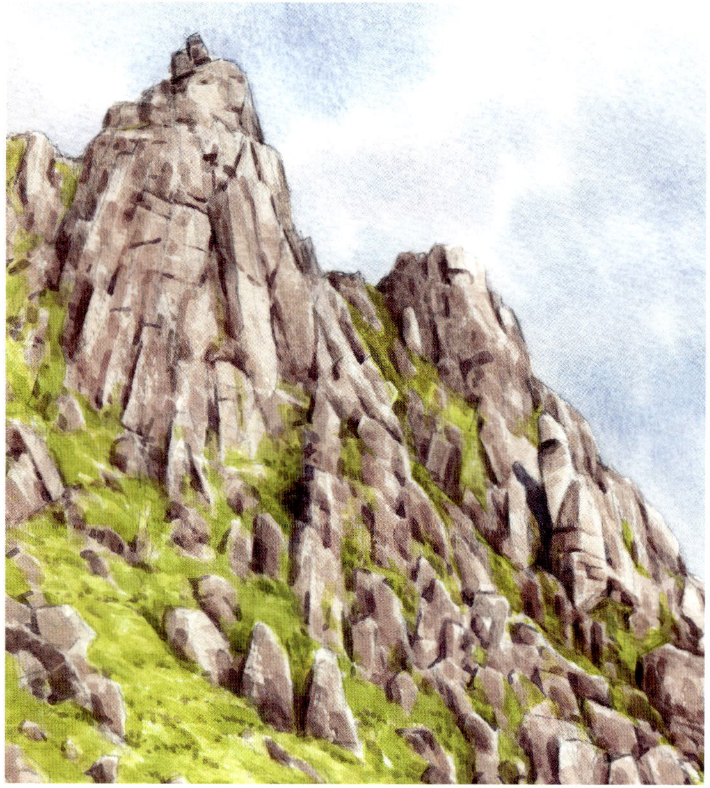

Looking upwards from just above the South Traverse 17/4/09

The rock scenery hereabouts is so impressive that Napes Needle is dwarfed by the nearby tall buttresses that make up The Great Napes.

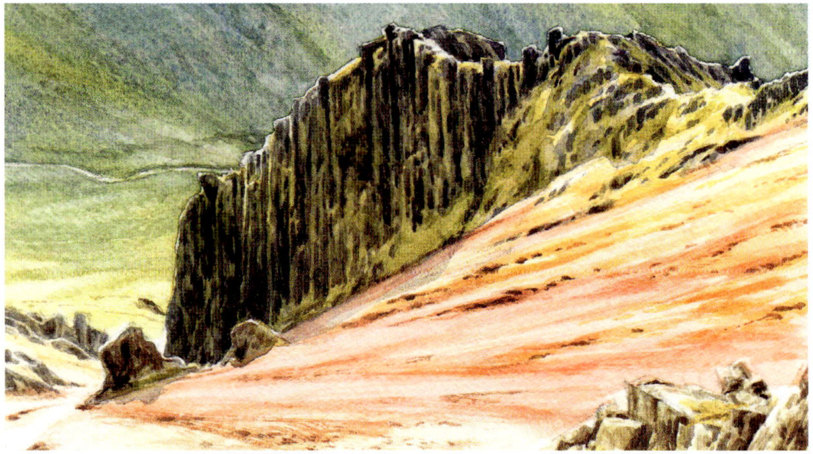

Looking steeply down on Tophet Bastion 11/11/07

The red scree run of Great Hell Gate and far below in the valley the ribbon of Lingmell Beck. The airy scene from the very edge of Westmorland Crags.

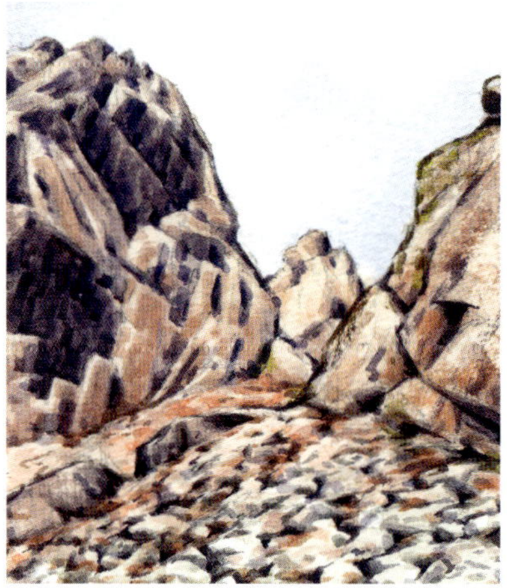

Little Hell Gate (left) 18/3/11

To get to this exact location where all the elements line up either an ascent or descent of this awkward scree run must be made. AW got himself into a position about half way up, near the right hand wall.

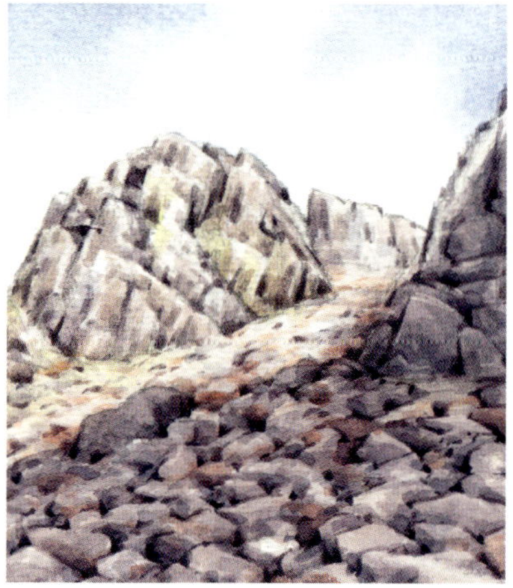

Great Hell Gate (right) 17/4/09

A view up this other long scree run from just above the South Traverse. Tophet Bastion forms the left wall.

The summit 17/4/09
In October 2013 this memorial plaque, dedicated to 20 members of the Fell and Rock Climbing Club who died in the First World War was replaced with a new, bright version, free from the previous spelling errors of the original. Each year on Remembrance Sunday, hundreds of walkers make a pilgrimage to this site to share two minutes silence at the 11th hour and pay tribute to those other lovers of these hills who have made the ultimate sacrifice for their country.

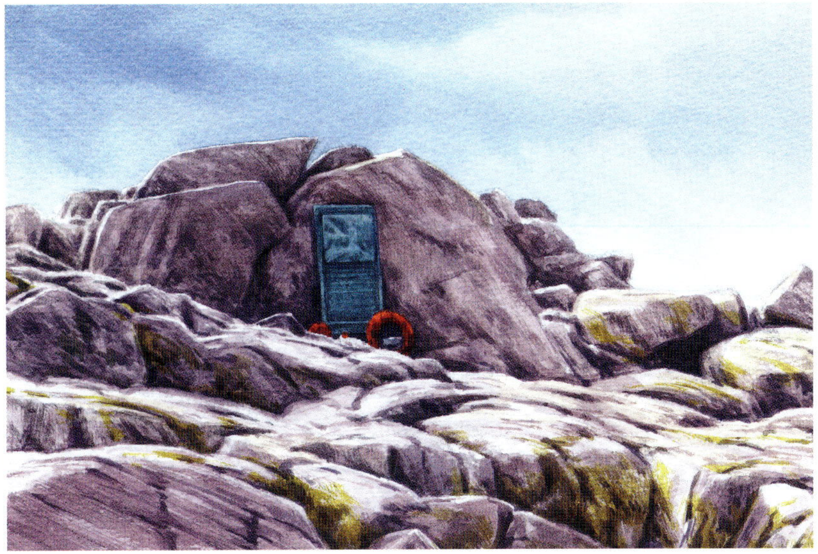

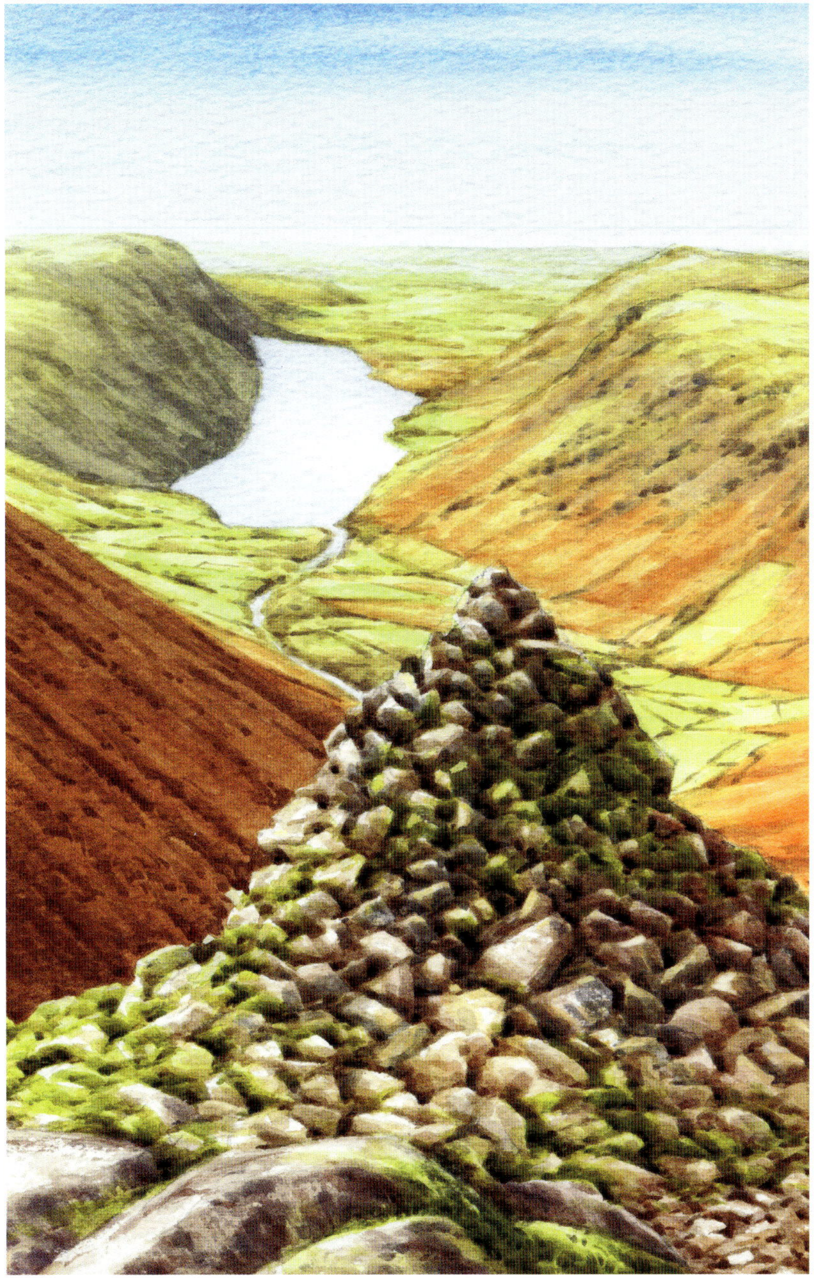

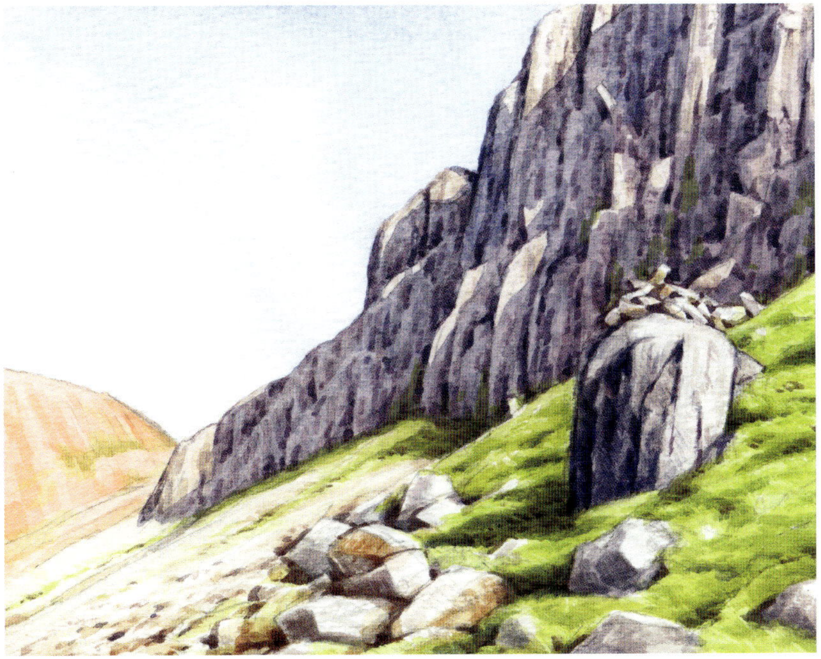

Westmorland Cairn 11/11/07
AW's drawing of this majestic view filled only three quarters of a page, thus allowing him space to detail the history of the cairn. I have taken the liberty of increasing the proportionate space in my sketch for this dramatic aerial view of Wasdale as I feel it deserves it. The cairn is a little larger but parts are now moss covered and relatively untouched since his day.

A place to remember... 17/4/09
The North Traverse, part of AW's Gable Girdle, starts here. Pass between the two cairns to continue on the path that hugs the base of Gable Crag towards Windy Gap.

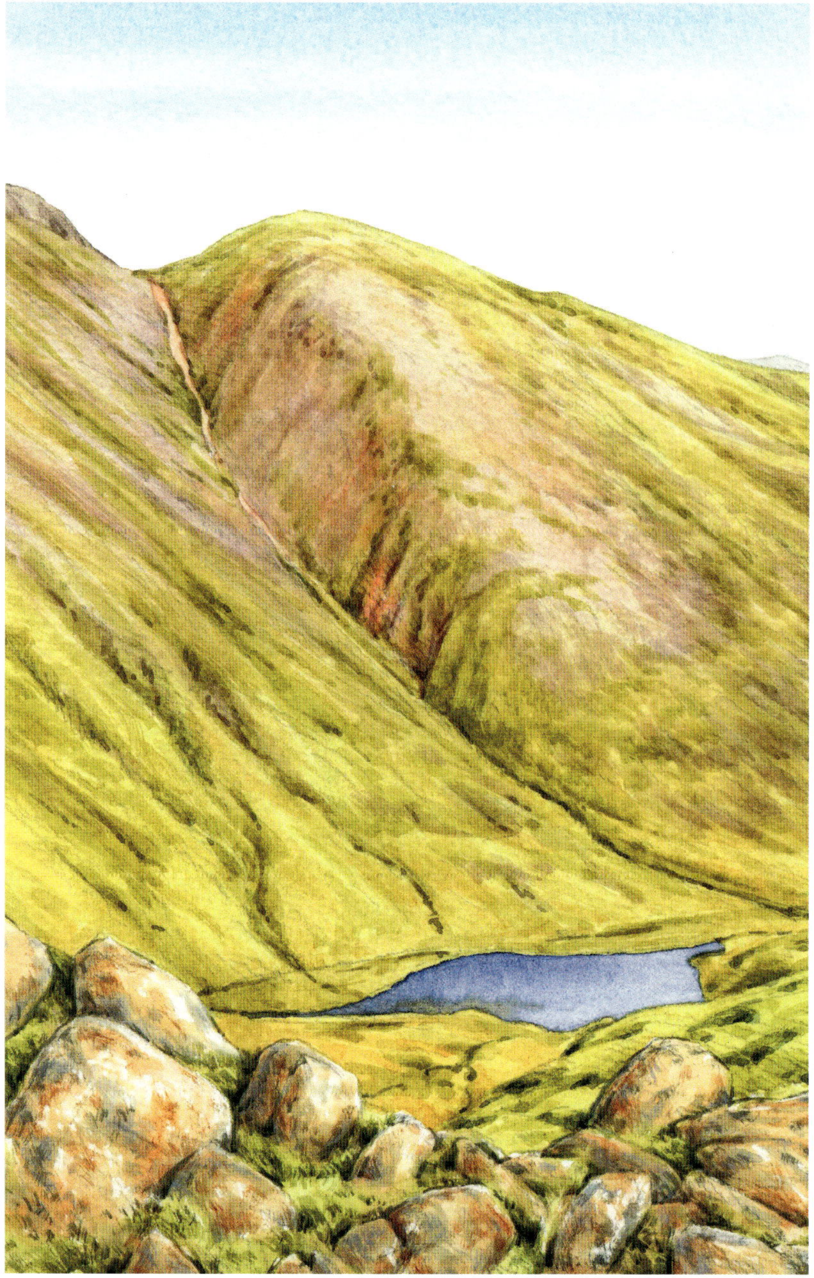

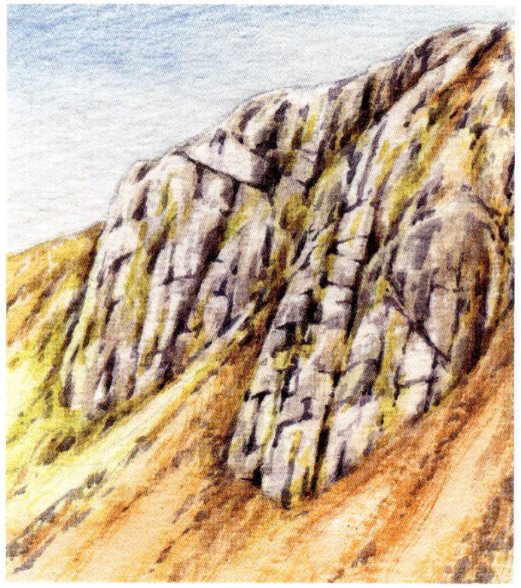

Greengable Crags 17/4/09
These 250′ crags west of the fell's summit have over 20 recognised climbing routes. Seen here from the path under Gable Crag.

Green Gable

This mountain is dominated by its near neighbour, Great Gable and because of this most walkers only spend a few moments on this fell's summit as they make their way either to or from the more notable adjoining fell.

From Great End 10/4/11
Sty Head and the tarn with the ravine of Arron Slack leading up to Windy Gap. Seen from a position on The Band of Great End.

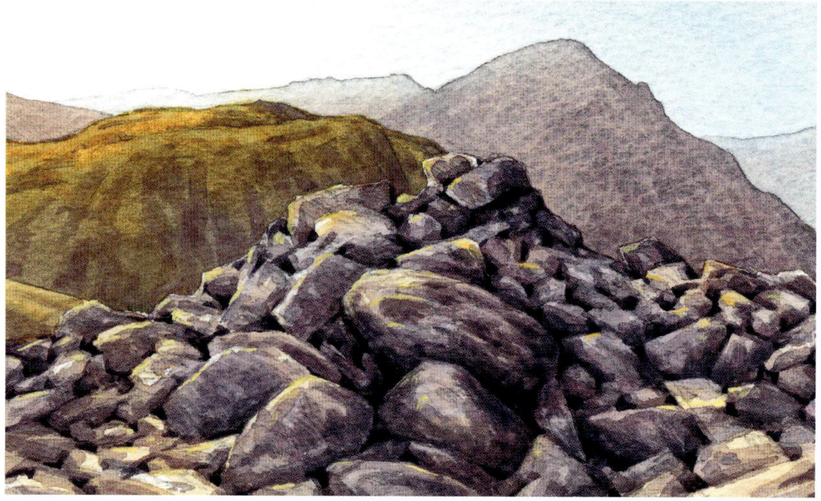

The summit 17/4/09
The iron fencing stake has gone and the cairn is now larger.

Windy Gap 17/4/09
The path across the gap is rich red in colour. The Scafells are seen in the far distance.

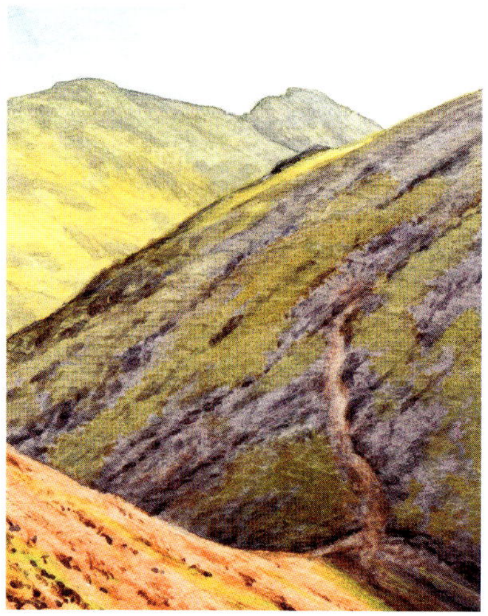

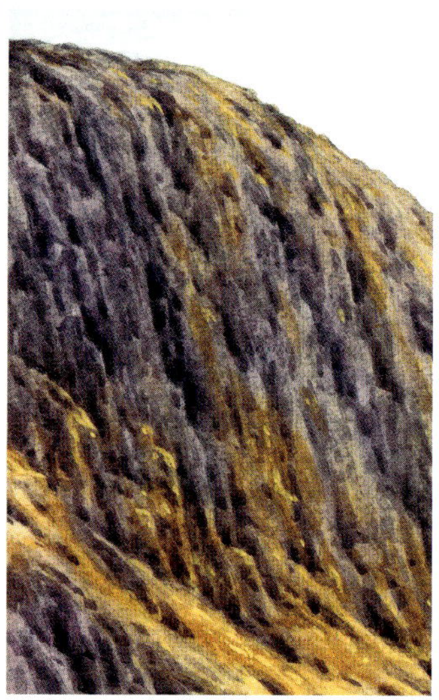

Gable Crag 17/4/09
A section of the impressive crag as viewed from the summit of Green Gable.

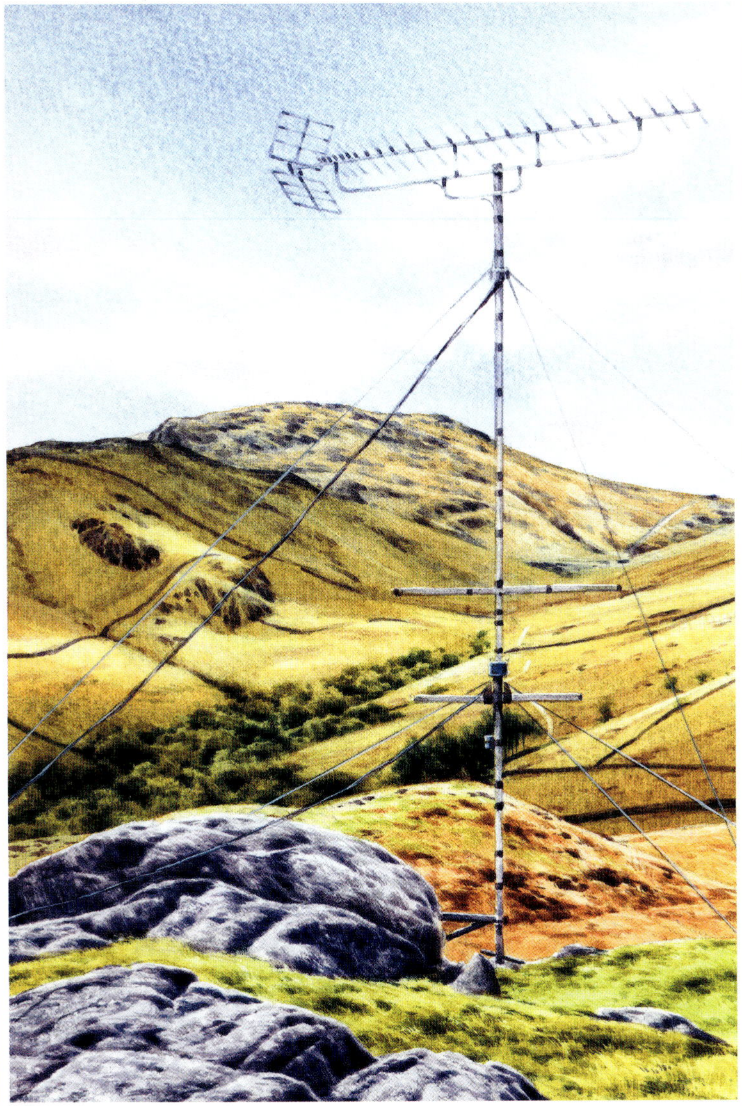

From the Seatoller Television Aerial on High Doat 3/5/11
Perhaps one of his most unusual illustrations, the aerial has been renewed and repositioned since AW's visit. High Doat is part of Dale Head in the North Western Fells region but provided Wainwright with what he considered the best view of Grey Knotts.

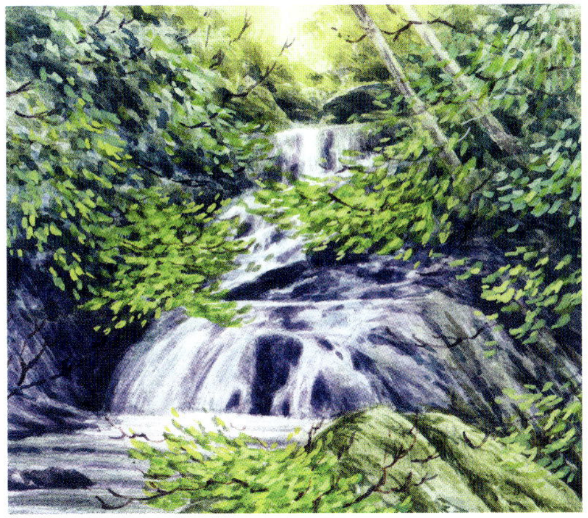

Hause Gill 10/9/09
This mountain stream runs down alongside the road from Seatoller as it heads up towards Honister Hause. The exact location for the sketch was only found after some time of comparing the book to the actual scene.

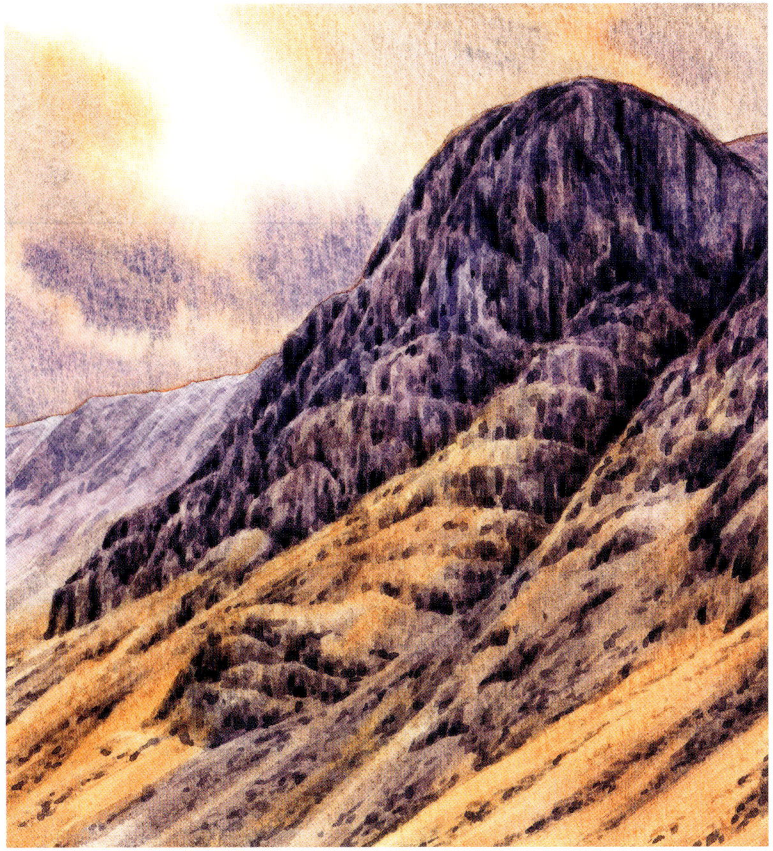

Raven Crag 17/4/09
This angle of view of the crag can be seen from the featureless area of moor above the Plumbago Mines, west of the summit.

Grey Knotts

Due to its location just to the south-west of Honister Hause, Grey Knotts is one of those fells whose summit is easily attained with little effort and is only one mile from the car park at Honister Mine. More often than not Grey Knotts features in routes to or from Great Gable which lies further to the south-west.

The John Bankes memorial stone 17/4/09
This slate slab, which has suffered some damage, is not in fact a memorial but just one of several markers for the various owners of the mining rights to the highly prized mineral, plumbago, also known as wad, black lead and graphite, which was mined here from as early as the mid 16th century. Pencil lead was only one of its many uses.

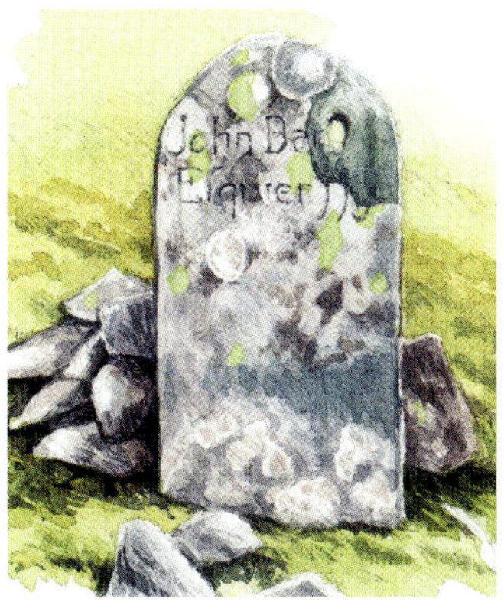

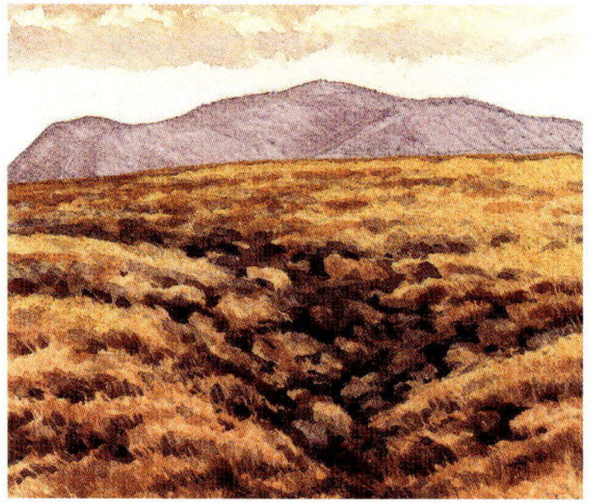

The uppermost level 17/4/09
Now overgrown and hard to find.

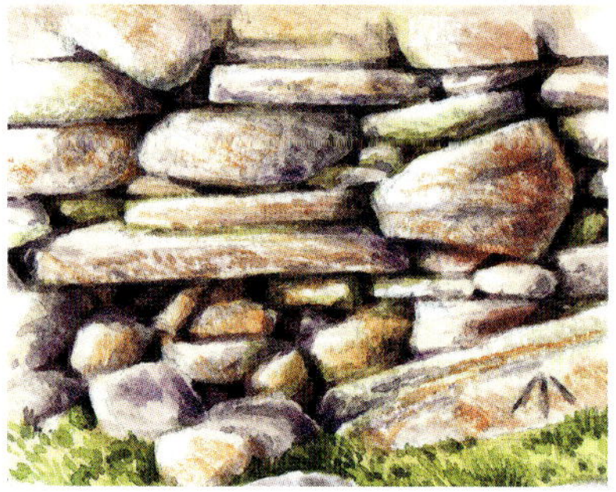

Benchmark 10/9/09
This is just one of thousands of benchmarks found across the land, used in the surveying and mapping of the country. The exact height of this one is 1169.8 feet.

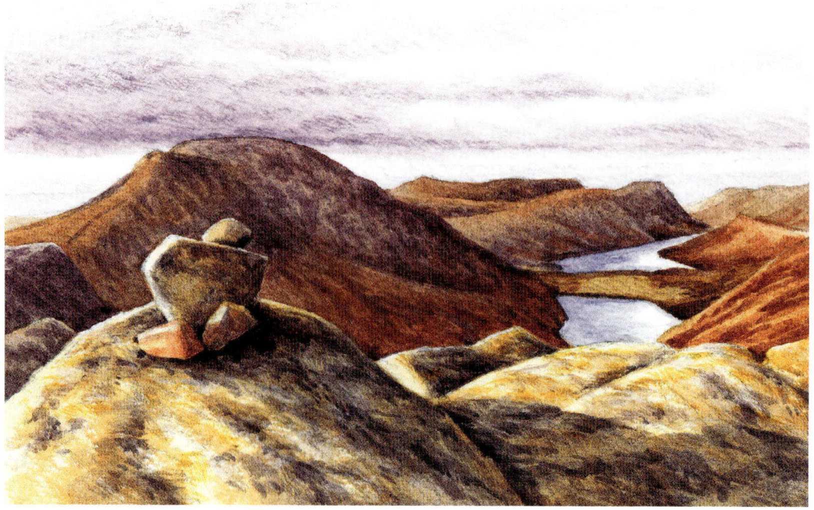

The summit 17/4/09
The two areas of high ground in the area of the summit are of a very similar height but this, the west one which is the slightly lower of the two, affords the best views over Buttermere and beyond.

The rock cutting 11/11/07
The old tramway route.

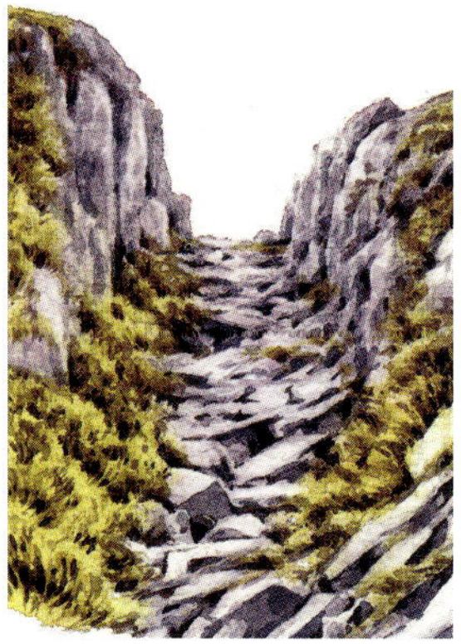

The skyline of Grey Knotts 11/11/07
Seen over the ruins of the Drum House, once part of the Honister Mine workings.

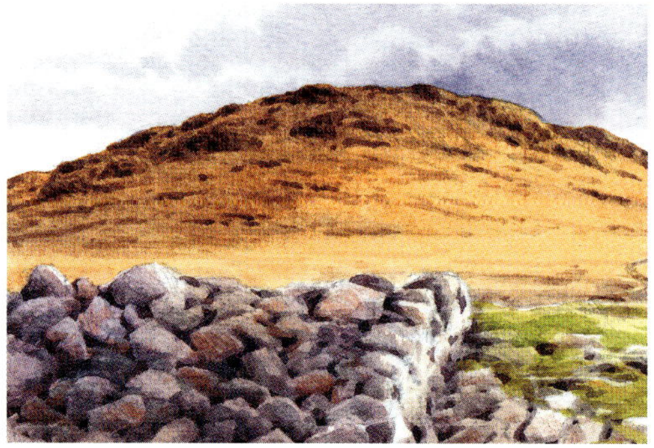

The west summit from the east summit 17/4/09
Looking towards Pillar.

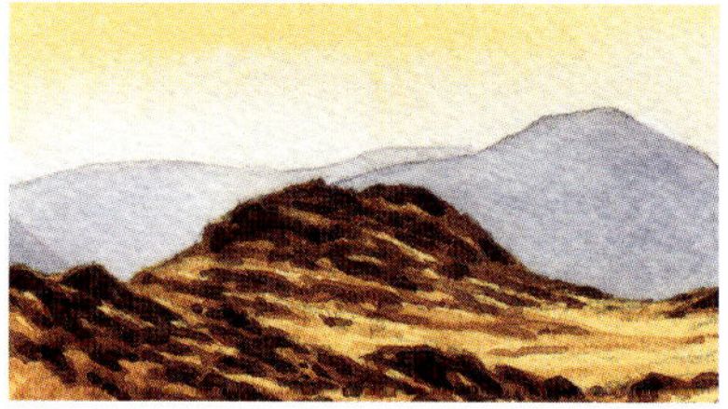

The east summit 17/4/09
This high point is marked with an O.S. triangulation bolt very close to the small cairn.

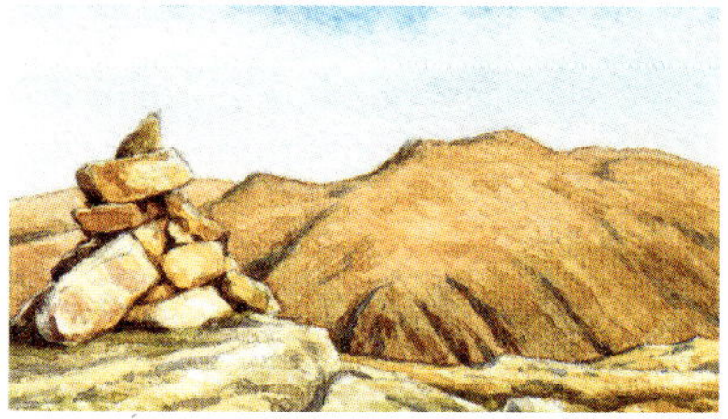

Gillercomb and Raven Crag 17/4/09
This view from the northern slopes of Base Brown shows the impressive front of Raven Crag, also known as Gillercombe Buttress, above the marshy valley floor. It is a popular location for climbing and bouldering

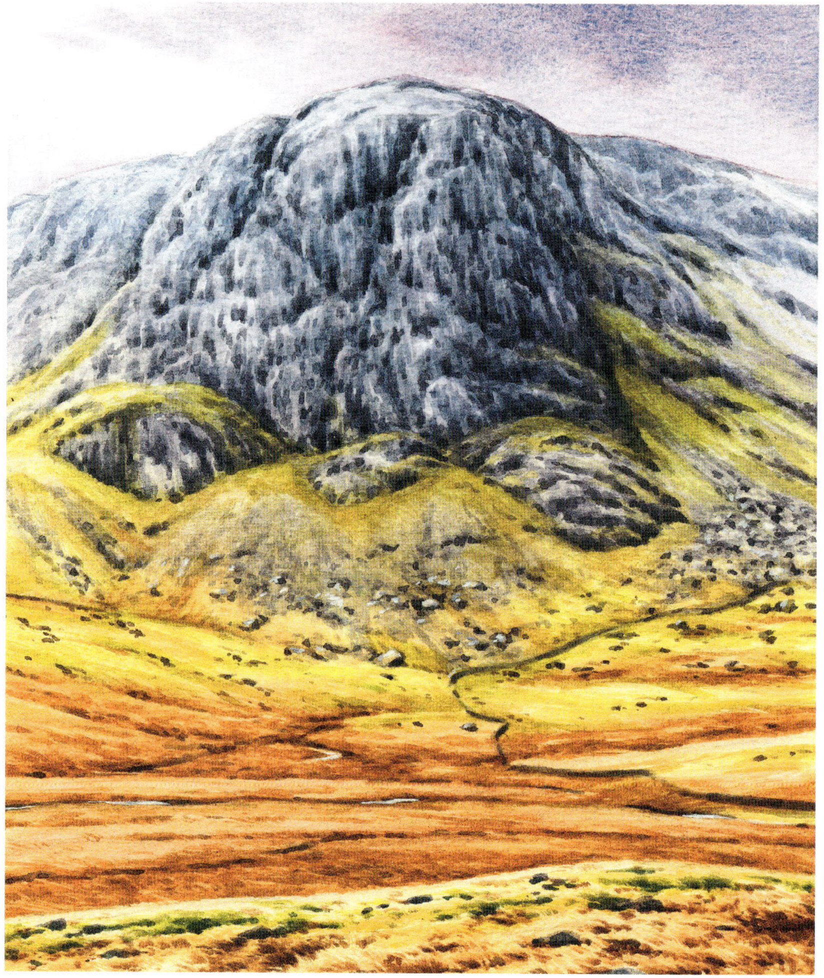

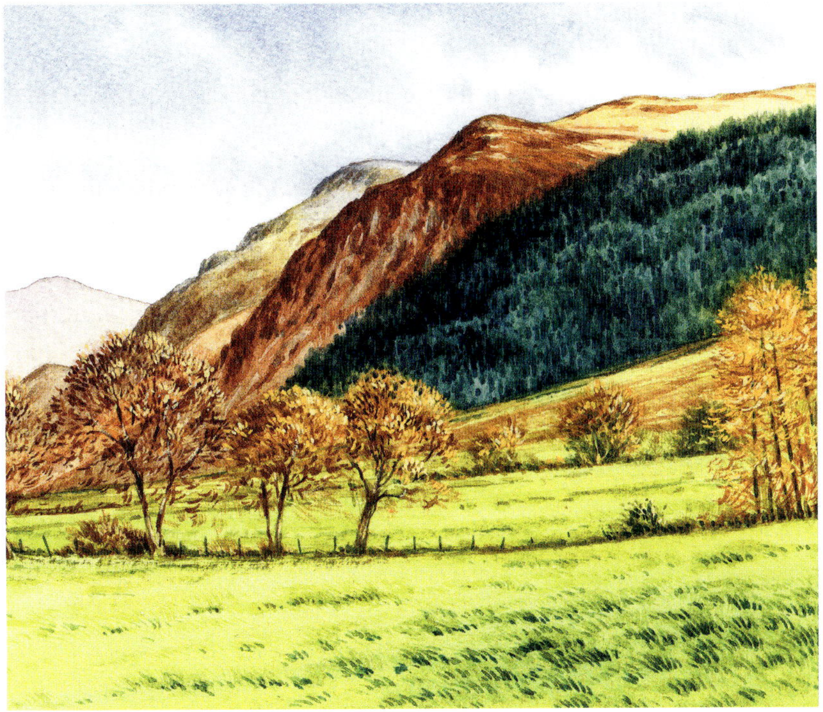

From Lanefoot 4/11/08
There were no cows in the field on my visit as in AW's drawing. Lanefoot is a farm just to the south-west of Ennerdale Bridge.

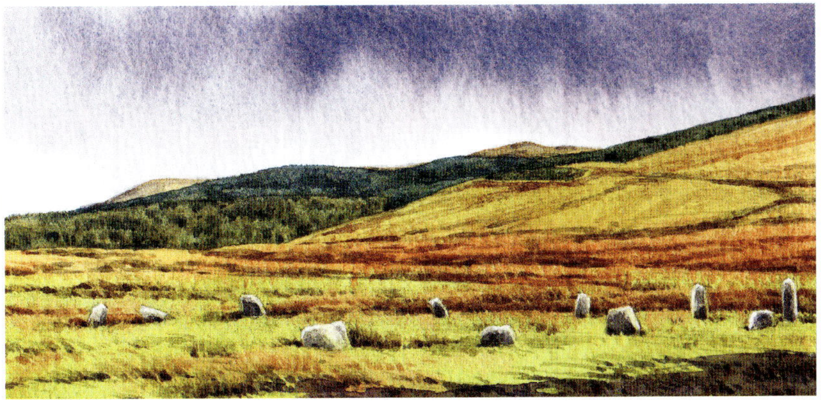

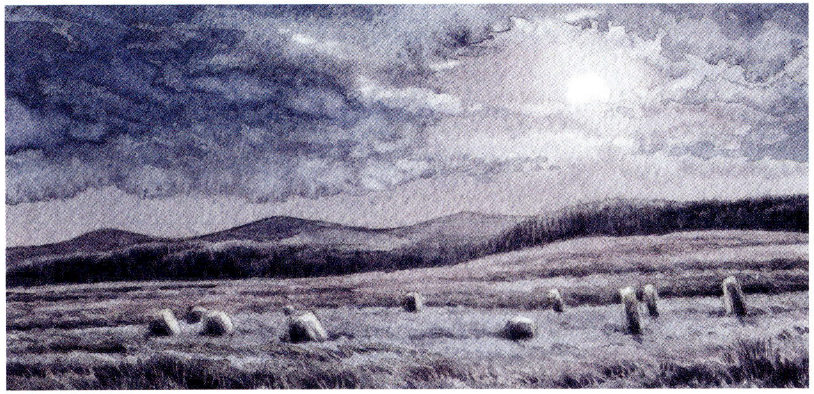

The Kinniside Stone Circle 4/11/08
Under a nearly full moon the circle takes on an ancient, mystical feel despite the fact that it owes its existence to a Dr Quine, who apparently re-set the stones here in concrete in 1925 after the original stones were supposedly purloined by a local farmer in the 18th century to use as gateposts. The real truth and myth seem to have become intertwined.

Grike

Wainwright wrote of Grike being transformed under a cloak of newly planted trees. Now those same trees have matured and been felled and once again the slopes of the hill are clear though not back to a natural state. Acres of tree stumps and brash still litter the landscape but at least it is better than dense forestry.

From Kinniside Stone Circle
20/4/10
Looking east towards Grike's summit, above the trees.

The Great Stone of Blakeley
4/11/08
This large natural boulder doesn't really live up to its name, being neither great in size or quality. It did however act as a boundary marker on old maps. The trees in the distance have been felled since my initial visit.

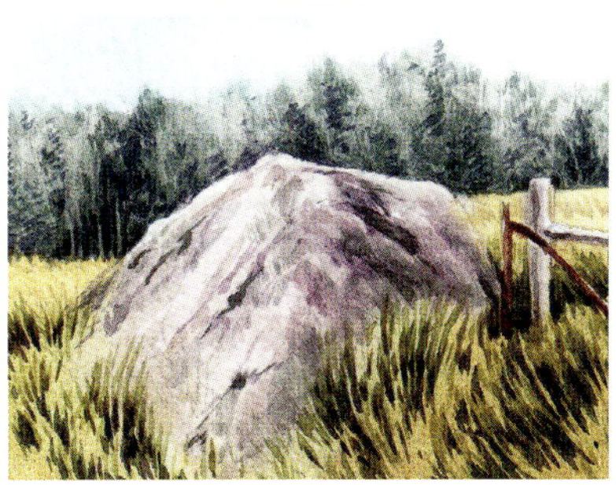

The summit 8/11/08
There are now three cairns on the summit plateau of Grike, two large ones and a smaller one which I expect will soon be incorporated into one of the greater cairns. The structures provide some shelter from the elements.

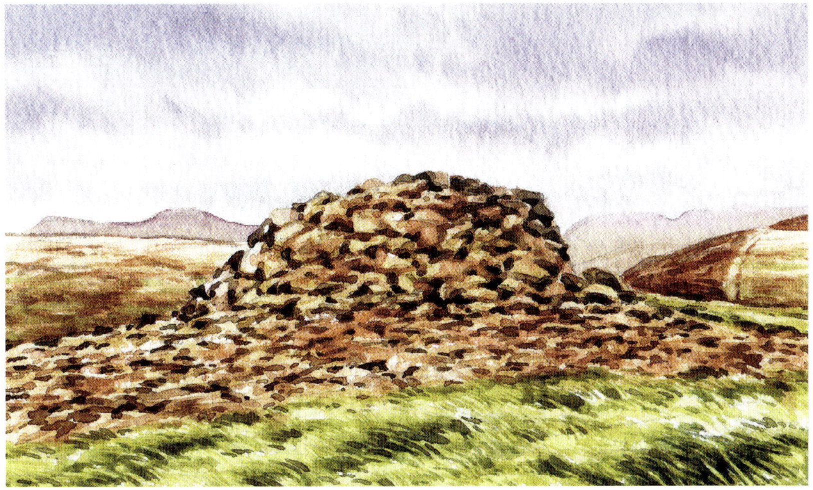

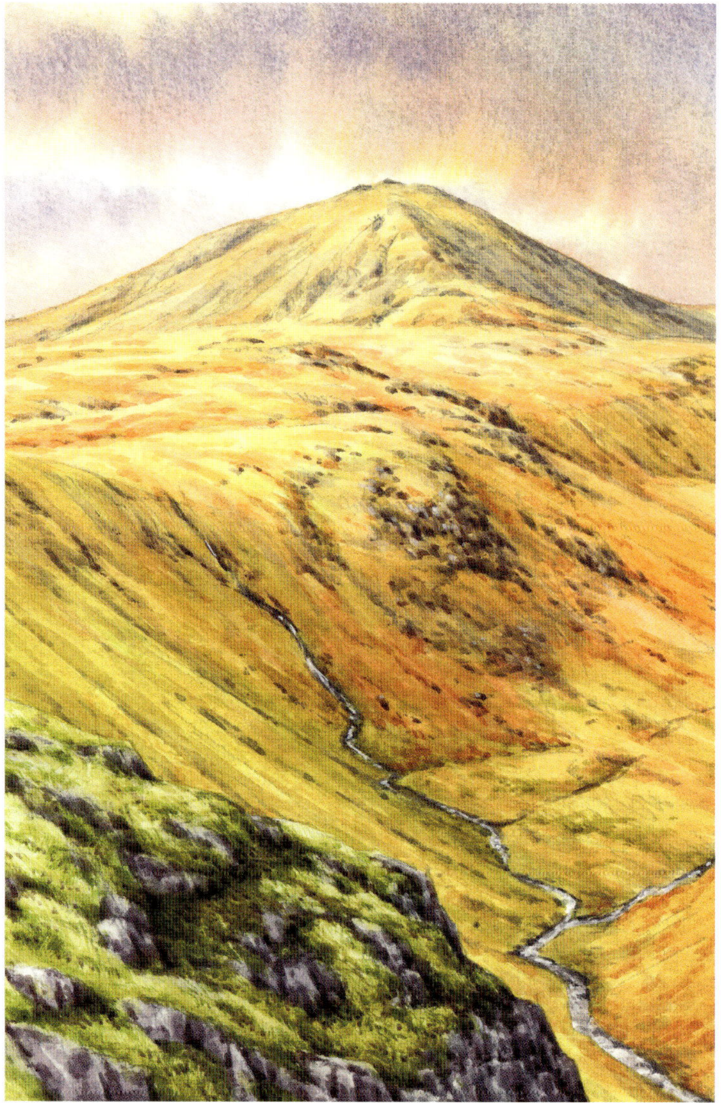

From Winscale Hows, Seatallan 8/3/14
The valley of Nether Beck leads the eye up to the uniformed slopes of Haycock. Paths in this area are faint so some time was taken over two visits to line up this exact viewpoint where very few walkers will have stood.

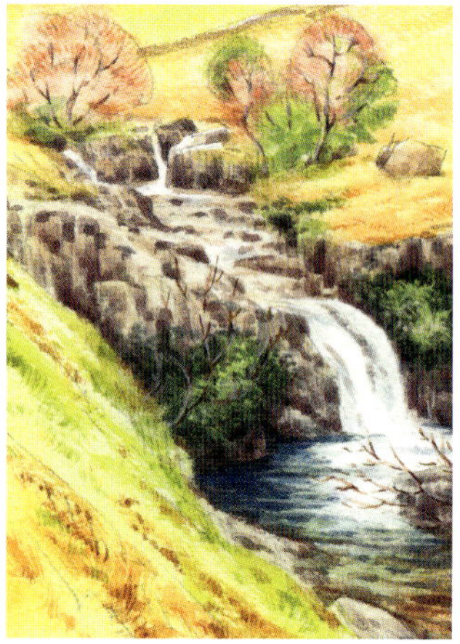

Waterfalls, Nether Beck 16/2/14
Cascades near Bowderdale.

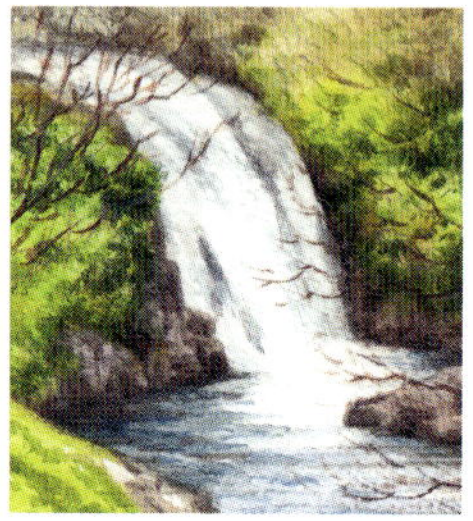

Waterfall, Nether Beck 16/2/14
A cropped version of the fall on the left.

The summit 9/11/08
The larger cairn on the north side of the wall, with Scoat Fell beyond.

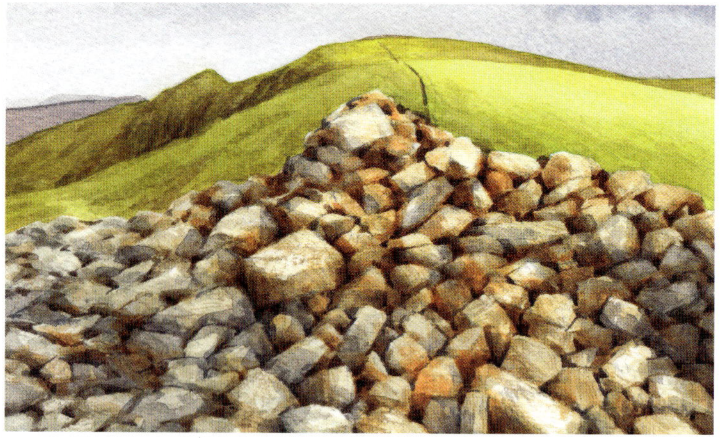

The summit 9/11/08
The second cairn on the summit, south of the wall and sited on a platform of rock.

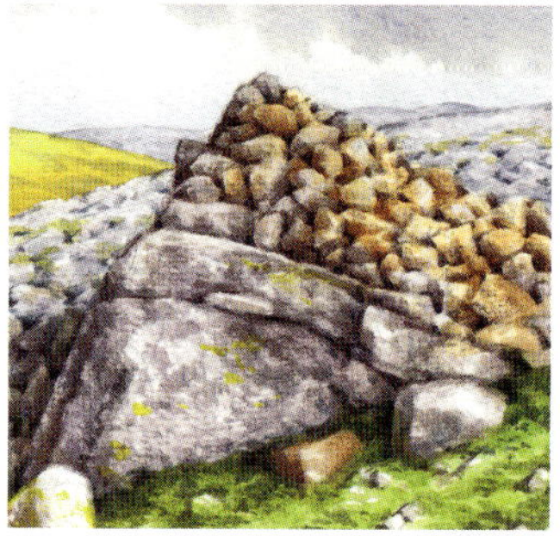

Haycock

With the Ennerdale valley to the north and Wasdale to the south, Haycock is a remote fell with no quick, short routes to its summit.

Little Gowder Crag 11/11/08
The Ennerdale boundary wall.

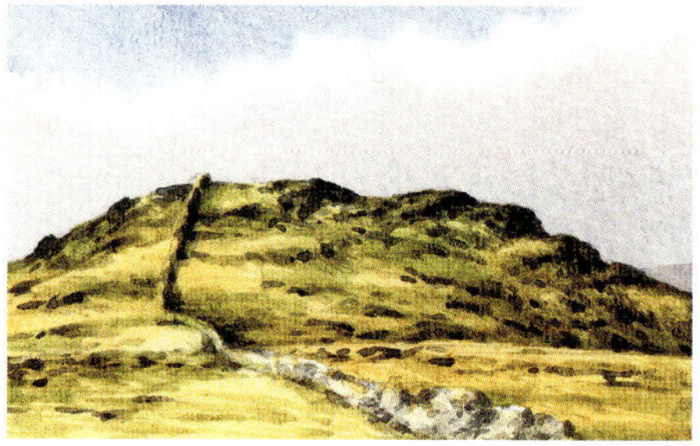

Haycock from Seatallan 8/11/08
More of a descriptive view than a sketch by AW but I thought justified inclusion.

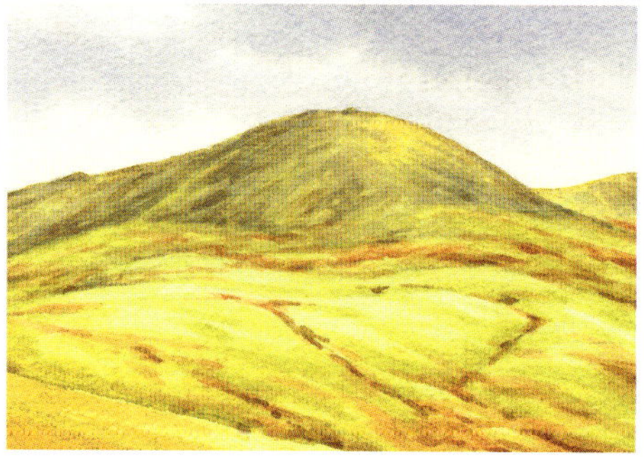

The footbridge 23/2/10
The old single plank bridge of AW's day over Silvercove Beck has been replaced with a more sturdy structure.

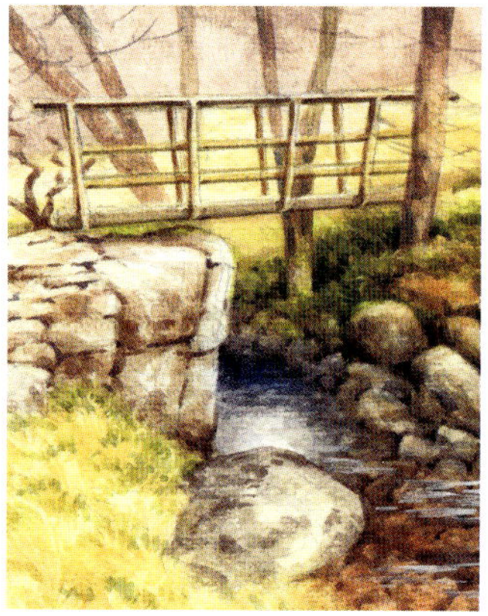

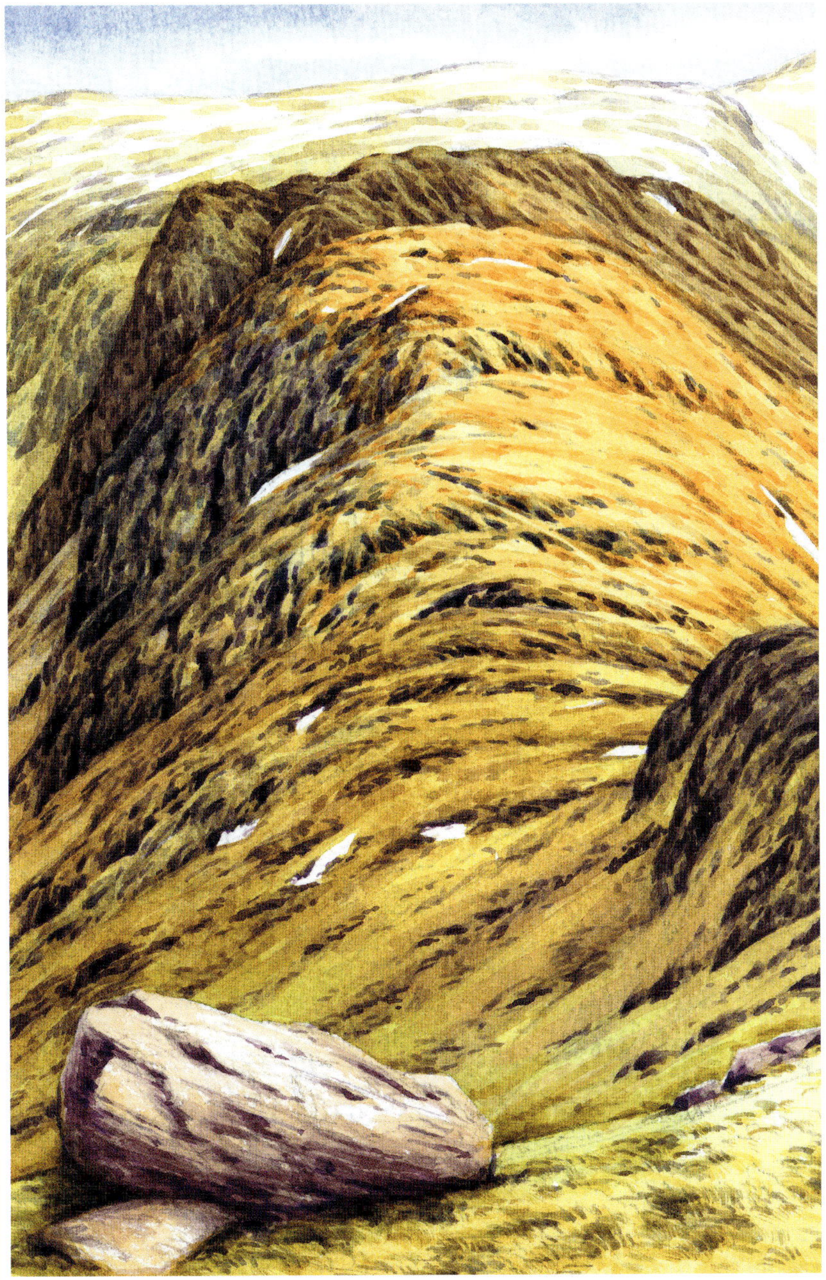

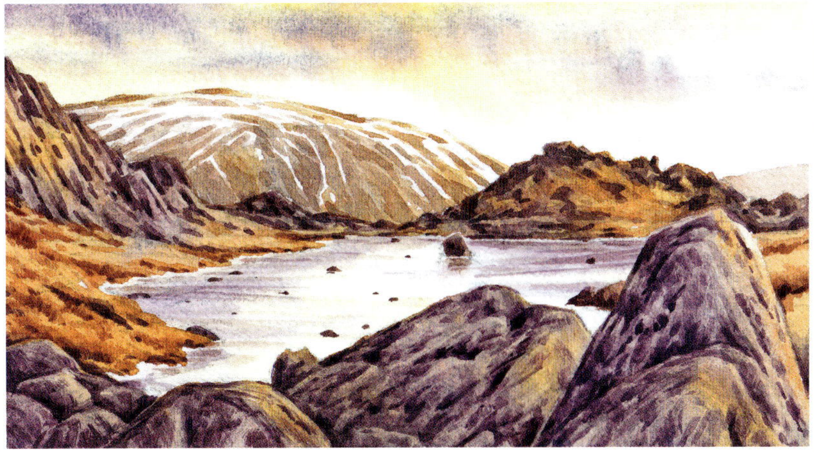

The summit tarn 10/2/10

This pool, close to the actual summit which is on the left, has no name. Looking to the south along its length Kirk Fell is seen in the distance. It is strange that AW chose to illustrate this and not the more picturesque Blackbeck or Innominate Tarns. Innominate (nameless) Tarn was in fact formerly known as Loaf Tarn but the name seems to have fallen out of use in the mid 19th century so confusingly there are two "innominate" tarns on the fell.

Haystacks

More than any other Lake District fell, Haystacks has become synonymous with the name of Alfred Wainwright, not least for the fact that he chose to have his ashes scattered here after his death in 1991. Haystacks is unique and individual, just as he was. Officially Hay Stacks on maps.

From Gamlin End, High Crag 22/3/11

On the large scale maps there is a "Marble Stone" marked on Gamlin End and AW obviously went and sought it out, even though he doesn't mention it. This is it. In his illustration he omitted the higher backdrop of Brandreth so that Haystacks wasn't overshadowed.

The north crags looking west from the slopes of Green Crag 10/2/10

The footpath wends its way up towards the summit of Haystacks, Blackbeck Tarn is just out of view to the left.

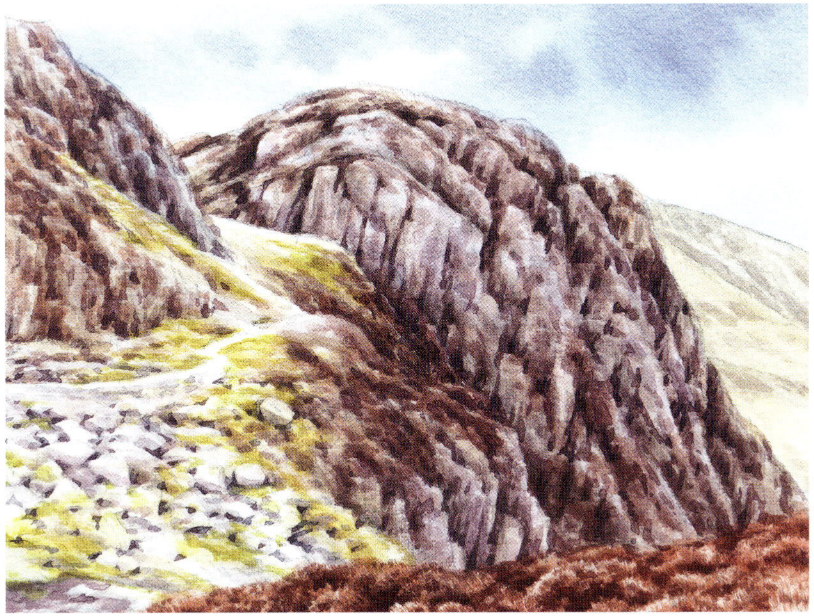

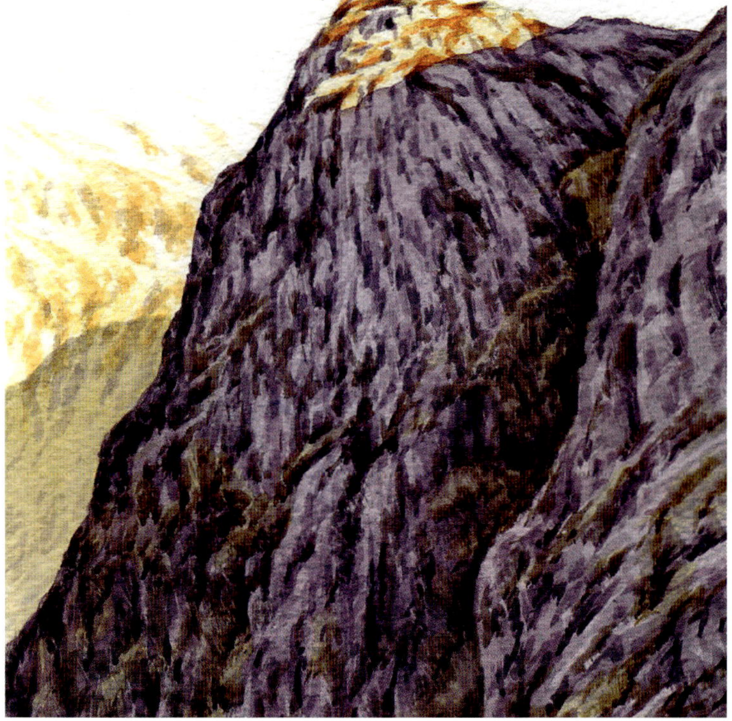

Big Stack 17/2/08
Sunshine and shadows on this rugged face of the fell.

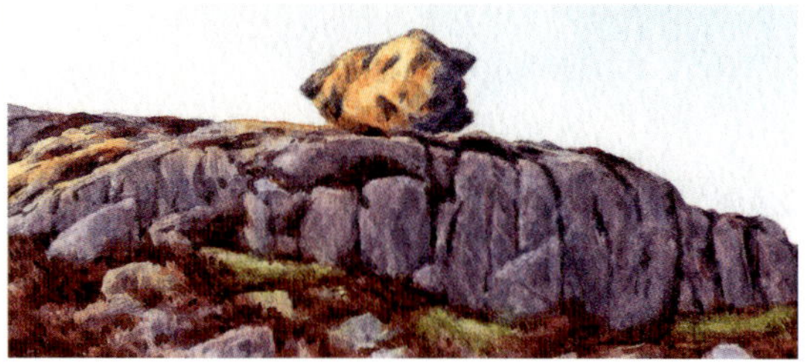

Perched boulder on a rock platform 17/2/08
The shape of the face on the right side of the boulder is accentuated in the afternoon light.

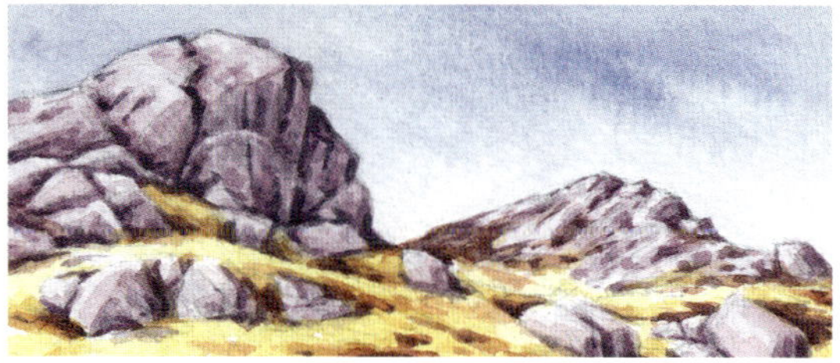

Typical summit tors 22/3/11
Of all the references for the project, this was the most frustrating to locate, taking six visits. The summit area is large and covered with rocky tors such as this and with no sense of scale to AW's drawing the only real clue was the dark shadow similar to that in the perched boulder sketch.

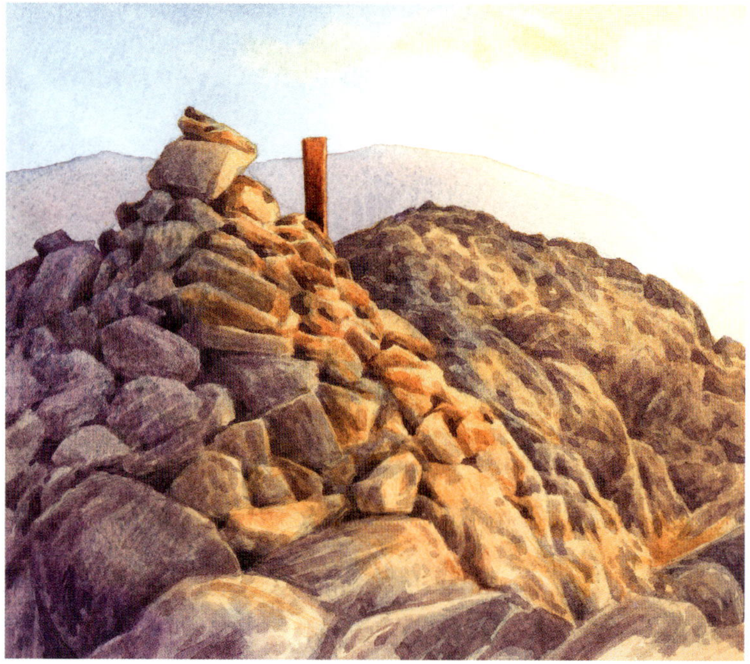

The summit 17/2/08
The iron post is still in place at the highest point although the top at the far (south) end of the ridge must be at a very similar altitude. It also has an iron post but it can't be seen from this angle now.

Looking south-east from Scarth Gap 17/2/08
Kirk Fell and Great Gable beyond.

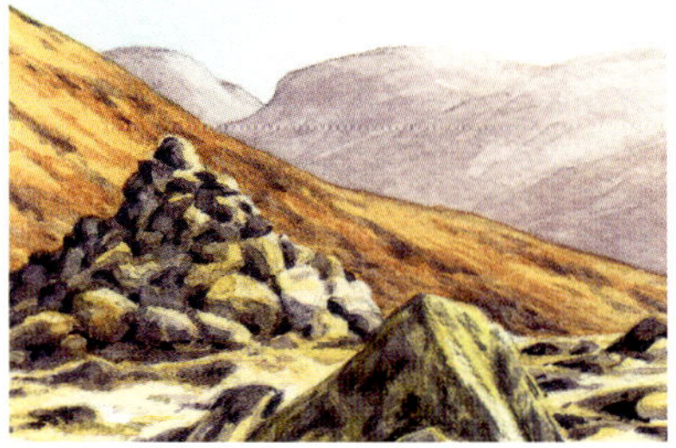

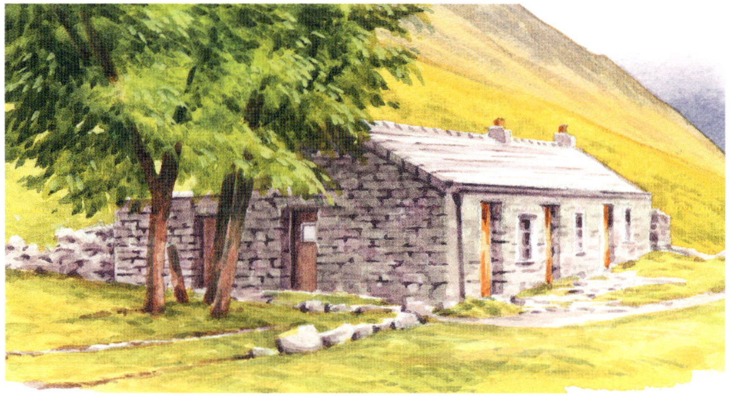

High Crag from Scarth Gap 17/2/08
The evening sun strikes the steep face of Gamlin End of High Crag.

Black Sail Youth Hostel 21/6/10
This remote bothy which opened in 1933 was once a shepherd's hut and is located at the eastern end of the secluded Ennerdale valley and is only accessible to the public by foot or bike. In 2013 the hostel underwent a major £325,000 refurbishment but it still maintains its unique and historic character.

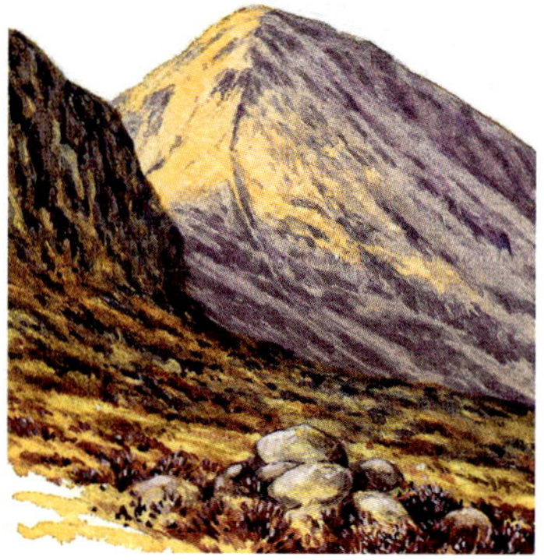

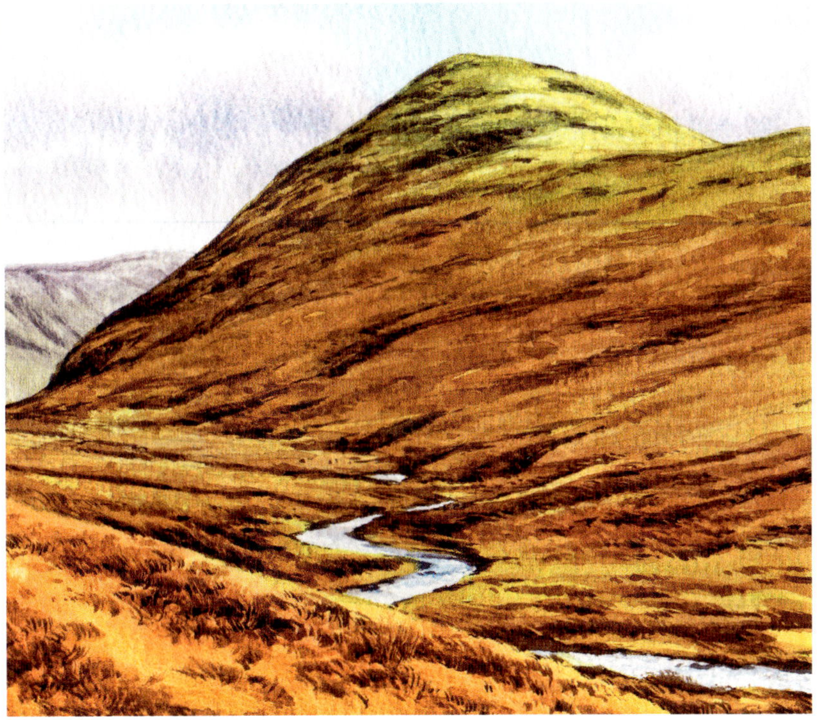

From Mosedale 7/11/08

This is the view of the fell as seen from the track that leads into the valley from Loweswater village. Mosedale itself is poorly drained and crossing from this side of the beck to the other to gain access to the fell usually involves getting boots and feet wet.

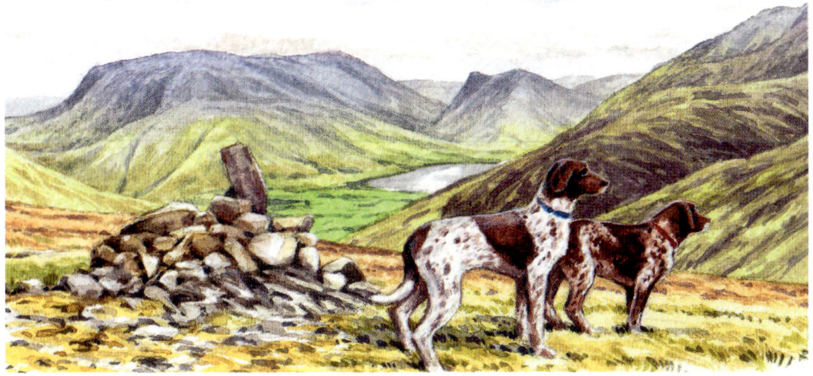

The summit 11/11/08

In Wainwright's illustration he included "Barmaid", a hound from the local kennels who followed him up onto the fell from the Kirkstile Inn. His drawing was actually a composite of two photographs with some artistic license, as in his reference photograph which he used to draw Barmaid and the cairn she was standing with Starling Dodd behind her so he changed the background to that of the view above. I of course was able to position both Zoe and Zeta in just the right place for my photograph.

Hen Combe

Situated as it is amongst the Loweswater Fells, Hen Comb is not the easiest fell to access. Including it in a route that takes in either Mellbreak or the other nearby fells to the north-west is a common practise. There is little inspiration for artists, photographers or explorers around the area of Hen Comb, this is reflected in the fact that AW only allotted the fell four pages.

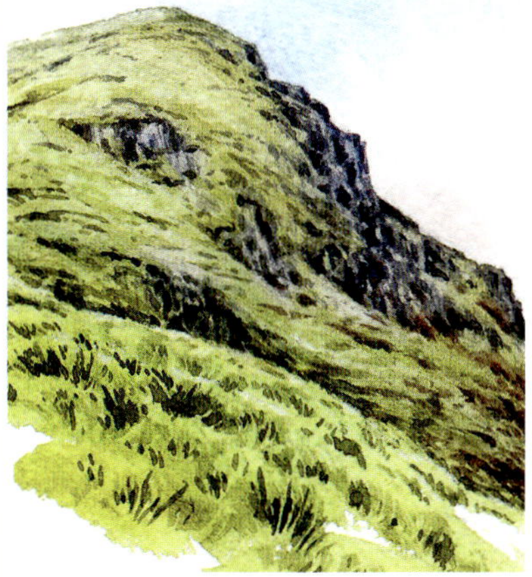

Little Dodd 11/11/08

The only real sections of exposed rock on this fell are here at Little Dodd and at Thrang Crags which are to the east of the summit.

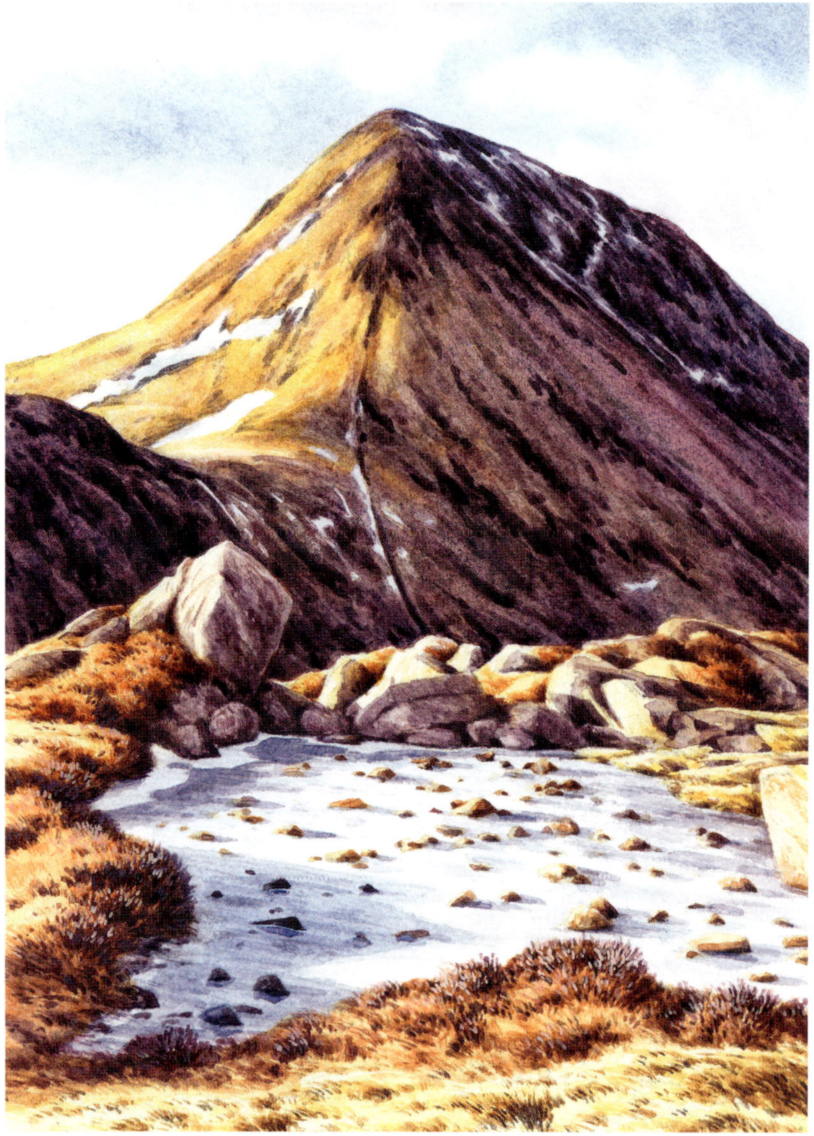

From Haystacks 10/2/10
This small pool, frozen on this visit, is passed by on the path to the summit from Scarth Gap. In error I have over exaggerated High Crag's shape just as AW did, something easily done to fit a fell to a limited sized page.

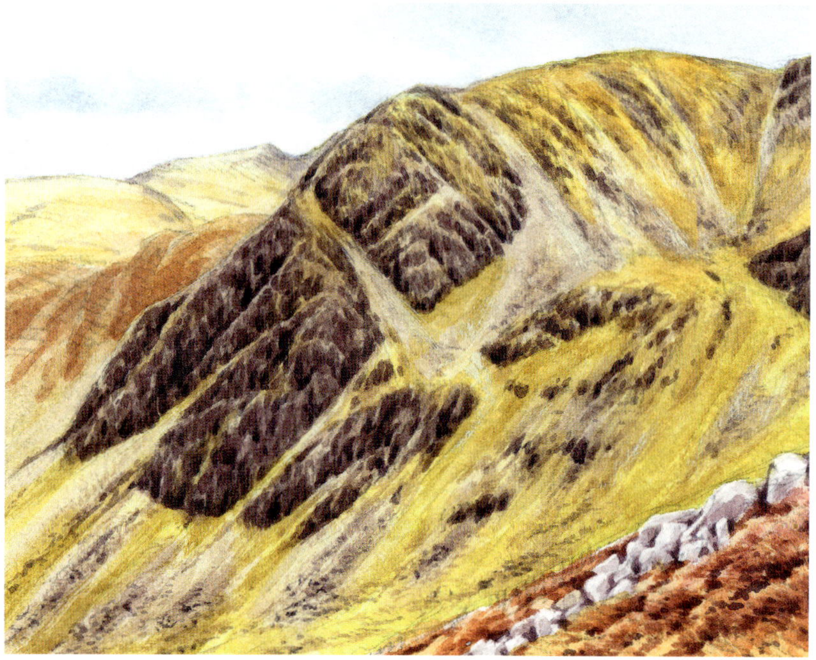

High Crag from the north-east ridge of High Stile 22/3/11
Sheepbone Rake on High Crag, seen slanting up to the left through the rock face is an exciting route of ascent for High Crag. Green Gable is in the far distance.

High Crag

The ridge that forms the high wall to the south-east of the Buttermere valley is rather fine fellwalking country, a lofty ridge of three fells which includes High Crag, providing superb views in all directions.

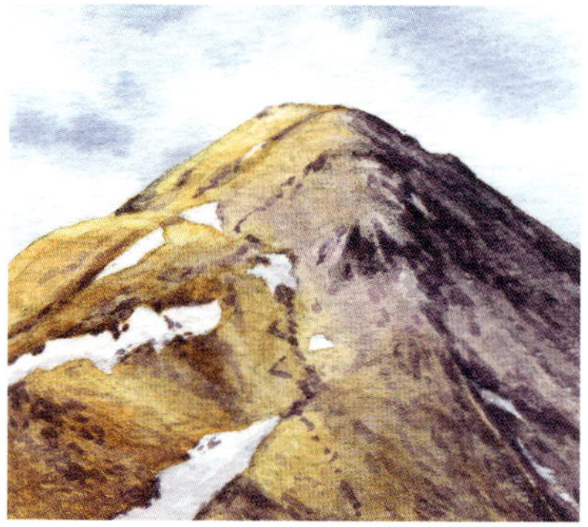

Gamlin End from Seat 10/2/10
The zigzag path on Gamlin End can just be seen. It has undergone some recent erosion repairs.

The summit 17/2/08
A few rods from the old iron fence still lie around the summit cairn. 10 miles away, beyond Dale Head, is the snow-capped Helvellyn range.

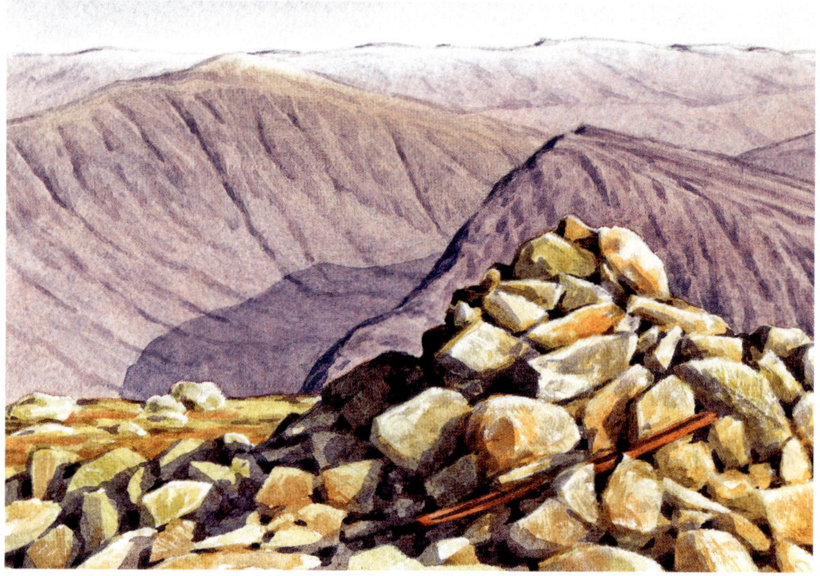

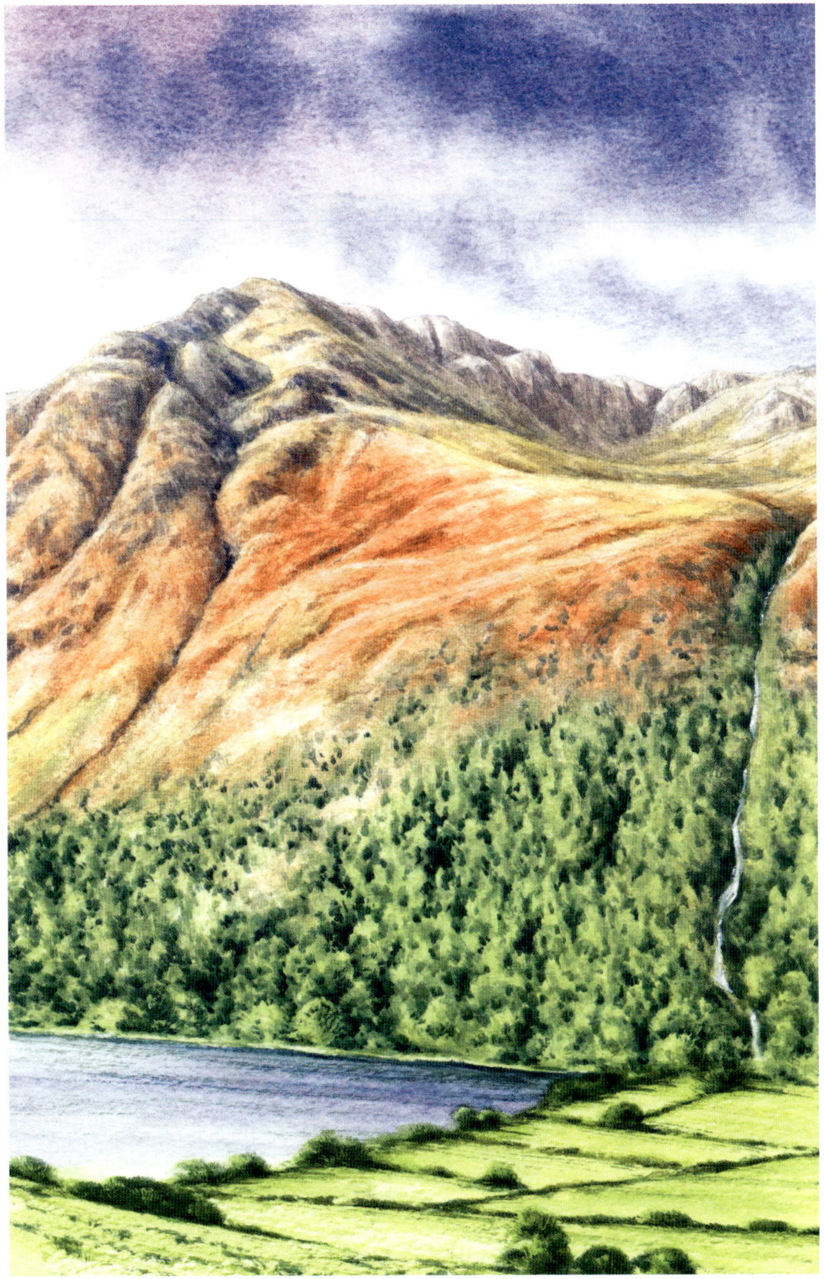

From Buttermere 29/9/11
More accurately, this view of the fell is from near the path junction at the eastern end of Low Bank.

High Stile

A fell which rises steeply from Buttermere's southern shore right up to the very summit at over 2600', an impressive sight even to those of us who have seen it often.

From Gatesgarth 20/10/10
The thin pines are young but the tree on the left with the bent trunk did feature in AW's drawing.

Dale Head and Fleetwith Pike 17/2/08
A dramatic aspect from the high spur above Grey Crag.

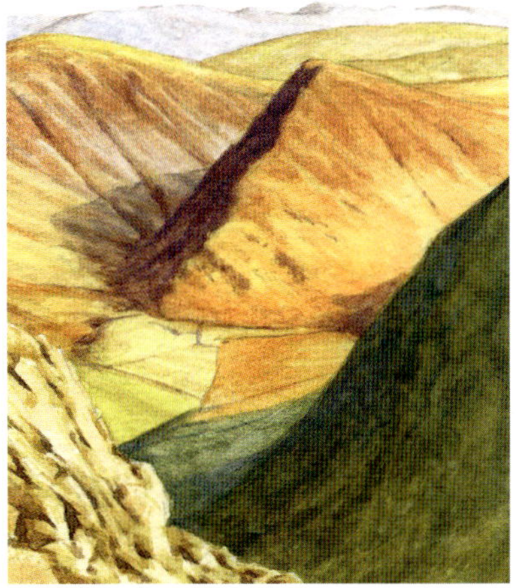

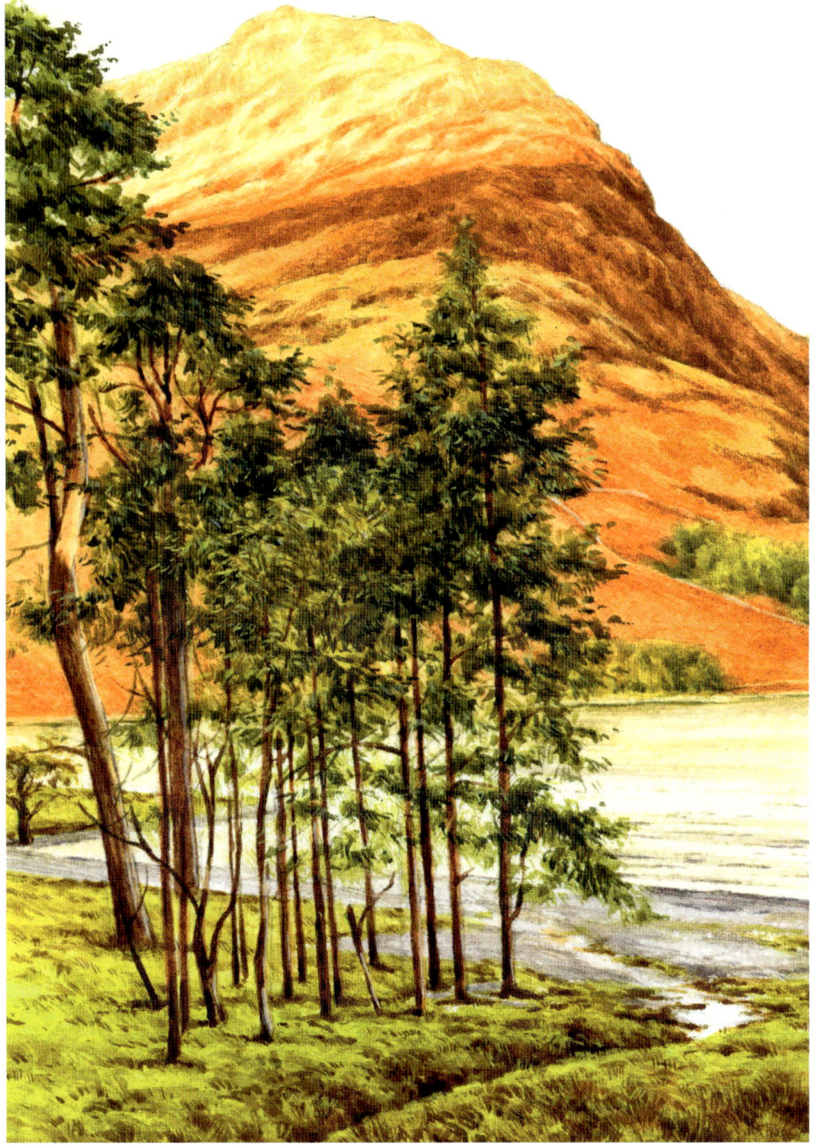

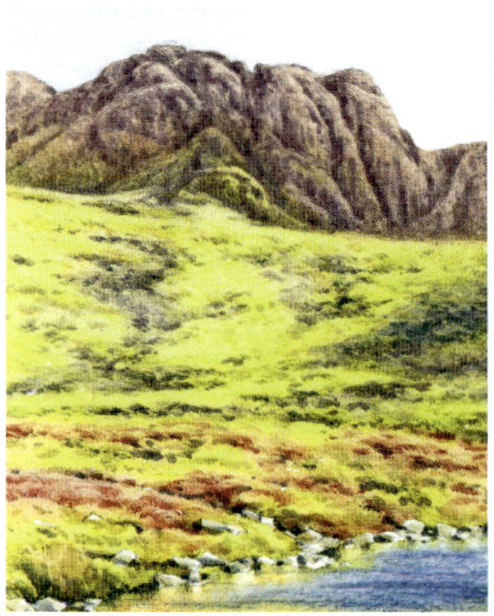

Chapel Crags from Bleaberry Tarn 10/9/09

This is a delightful location to spend some time, at a tarn nestled in a hollow surrounded by high mountain scenery.

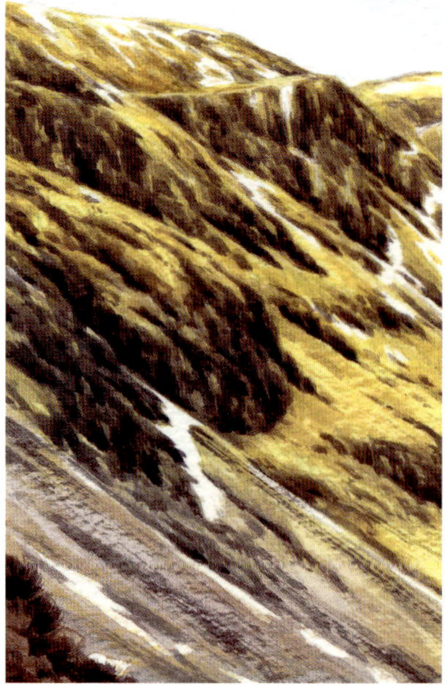

Eagle Crag from Sheepbone Rake 10/2/10

Sheepbone Rake features in a High Crag sketch (page 314)

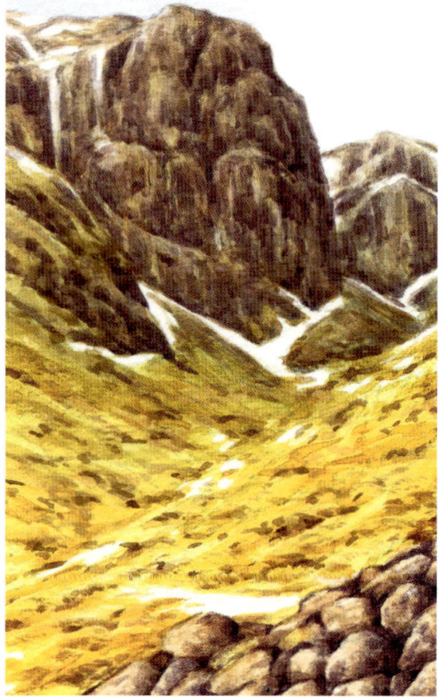

From the Comb to Eagle Crag 10/2/10

The crag is a popular climbing location with over 40 named routes of various grades.

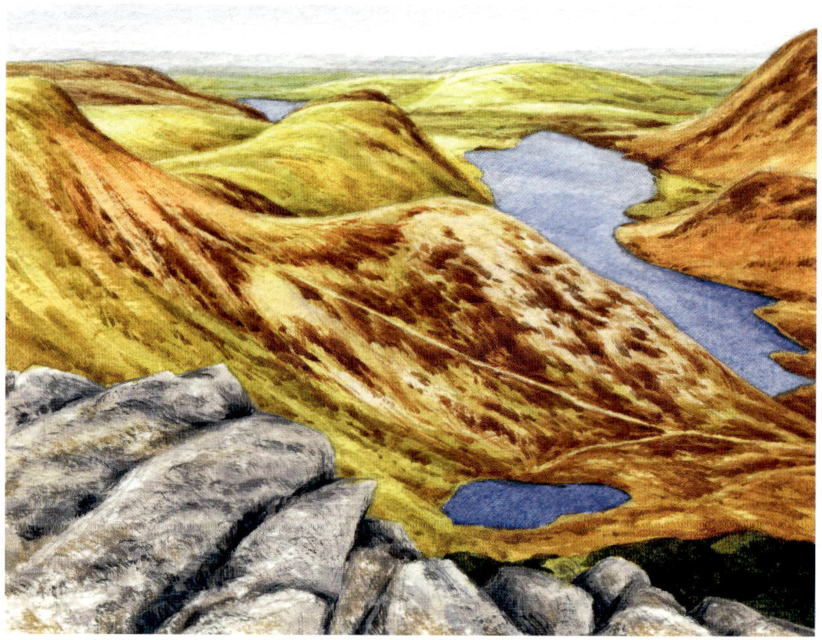

The view 22/3/11

And what a view it is. Sadly the tall pillar of stones which AW portrayed perched on the edge of the foreground rocks is no more but the rest of the superb aerial view of Bleaberry Tarn and Crummock Water is unaltered.

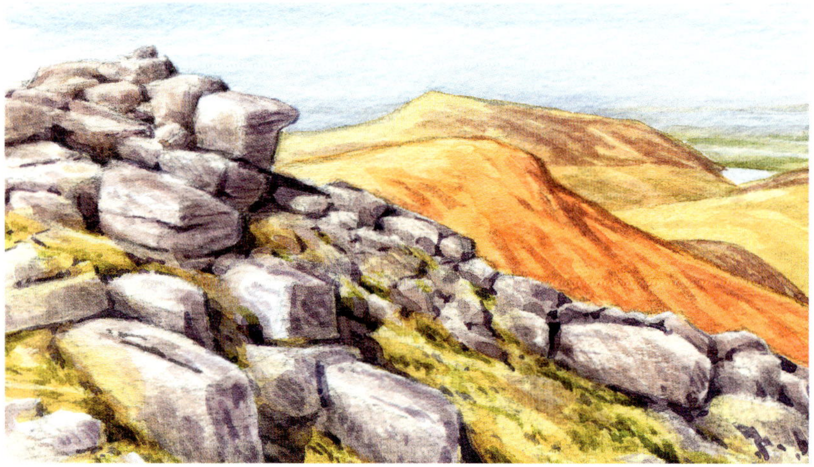

The summit 17/2/08

The tiny cairn in Wainwright's drawing has gone but the bedrock shapes could easily be identified. A section of Loweswater can just be seen in the distance.

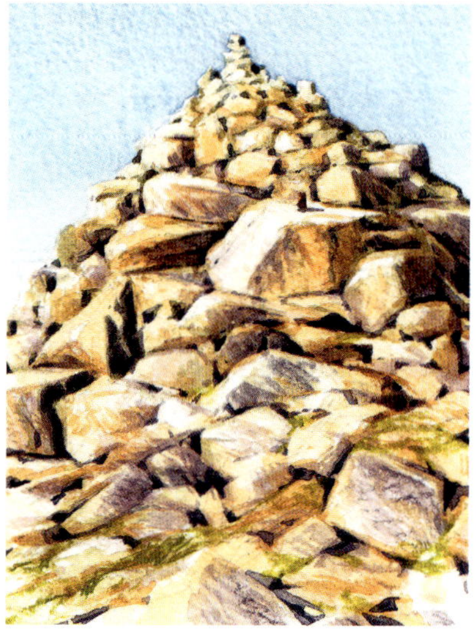

The summit cairn 17/2/08

This cairn is the one illustrated by AW that lay on the line of the old fence. The post has all but gone with just a short sharp spike protruding from the large block. The cairns 150 yards to the east, above Grey Crag are at a height of 2648', some four feet higher than the previous calculation.

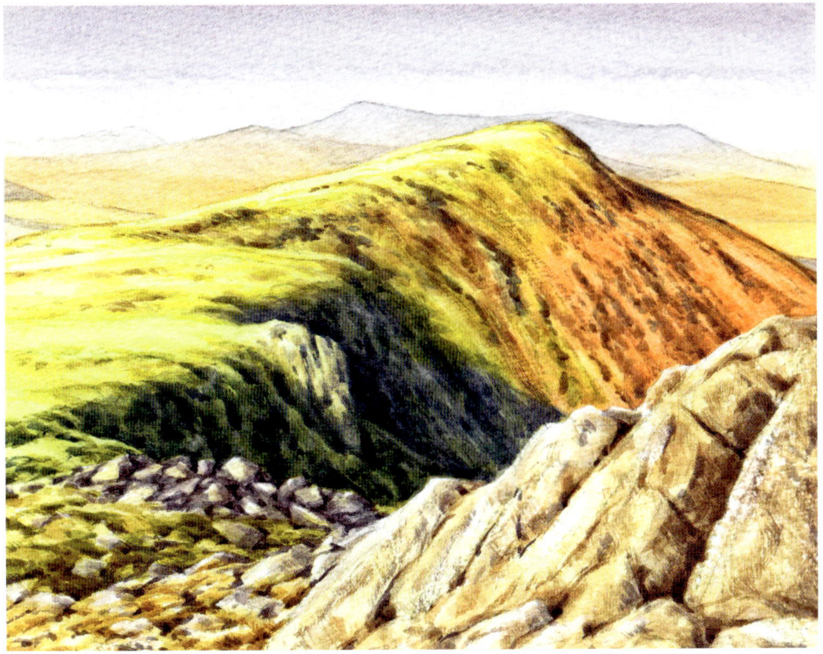

Red Pike from High Stile 17/2/08

The path from High Stile to Red Pike passes close to these rocks soon after leaving the summit. The distinctive colouration of Red Pike is clearly seen from this angle. The Loweswater Fells are on the far horizon.

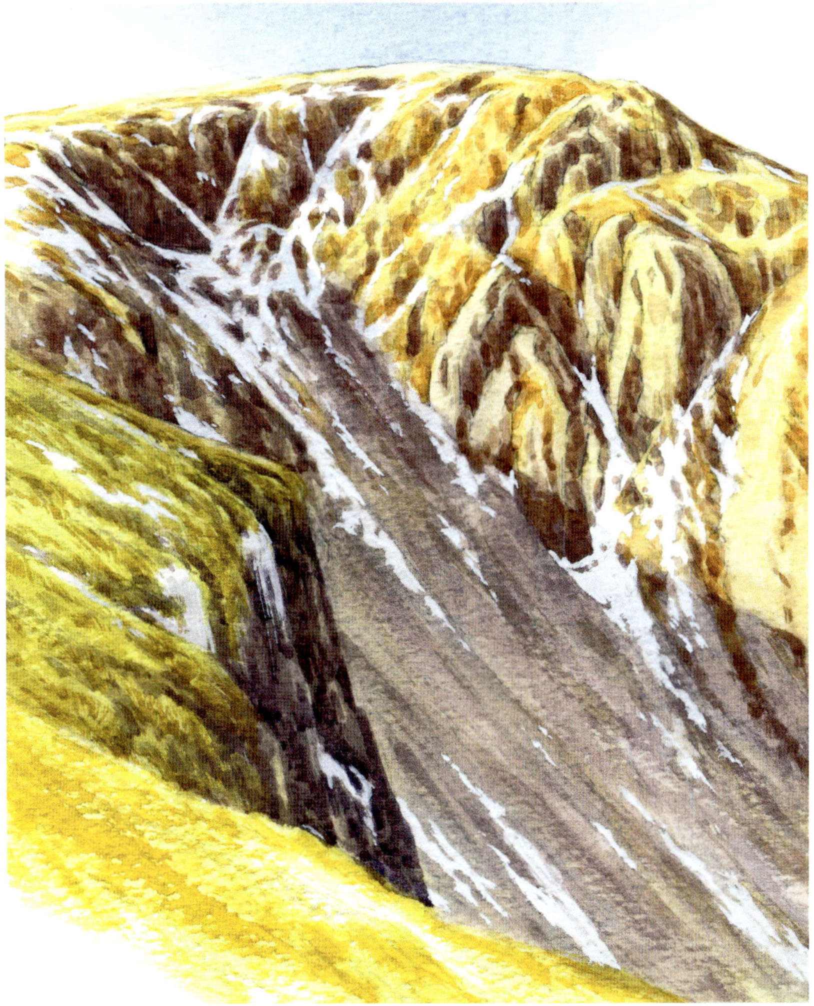

Looking back to High Stile 10/2/10

To see this exact view a deviation from the High Crag path towards the edge of the crags must be made. The grassy slopes abruptly drop over the cliff edge so care must be taken. Eagle Crag is seen near to hand and across the comb is Grey Crag (singular according to the current 1:25,000 O.S. map but plural in the guide) and above it is the highest point of High Stile. I was lucky with the weather, bright sunshine and some snow lying in the high gullies making this a great subject for a watercolour sketch.

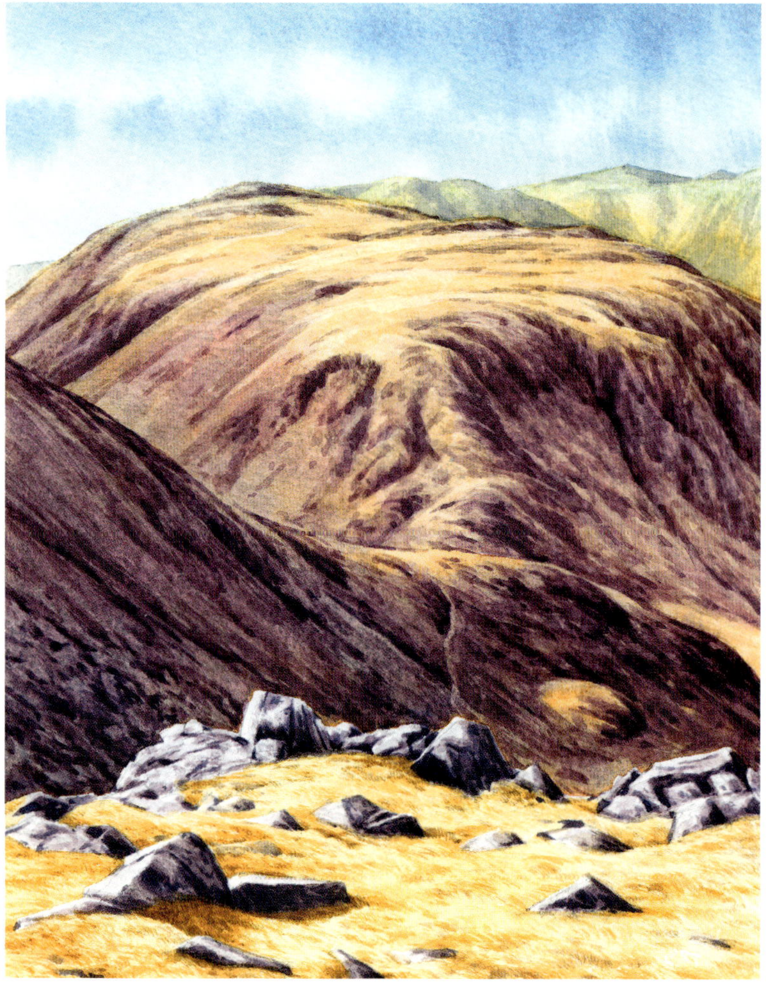

From Green Gable 18/3/11
Unfortunately the snow had all but gone on my visit with only small patches remaining in Windy Gap nearby. Kirk Fell is backed by Red Pike and Scoat Fell which AW chose to leave out of his illustration.

Kirk Fell

This mountain is often overlooked as it sits amongst giants at the head of Wasdale but it is well worthy of exploration.

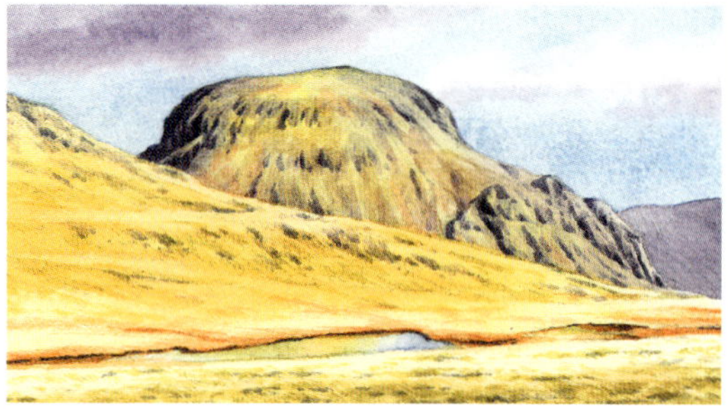

Great Gable from Kirkfell Tarn 20/10/10
The domed bulk of Gable rises above the south facing slopes of the fell.

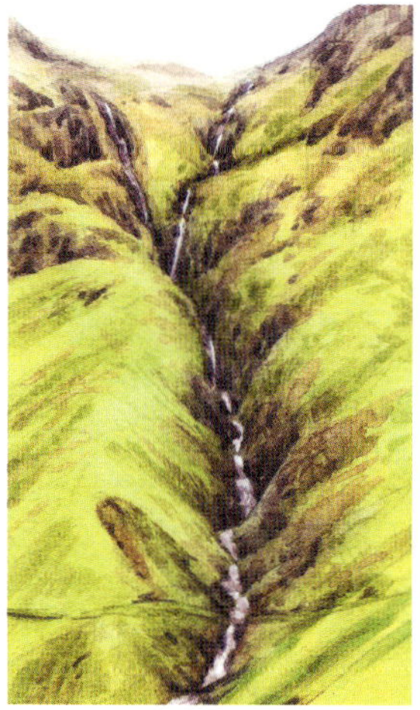

The ravine of Sail Beck 7/9/09
There is a faint path towards the summit via this ravine using the ground on the right. It offers an alternative to the usual routes but it isn't easy.

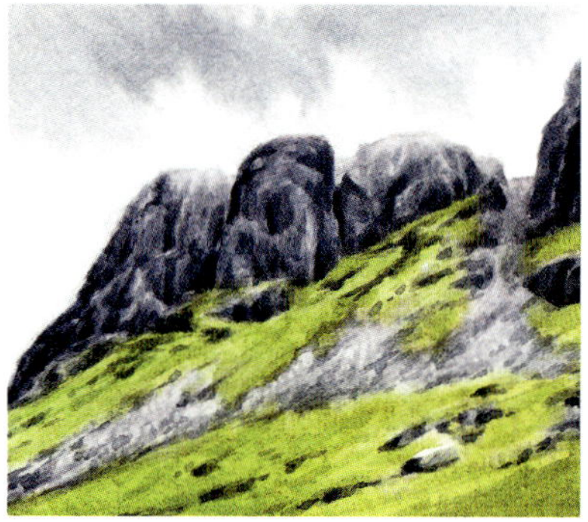

Boat How Crags 7/9/09
Clouds swirl around these imposing cliffs above the traverse path to Beck Head.

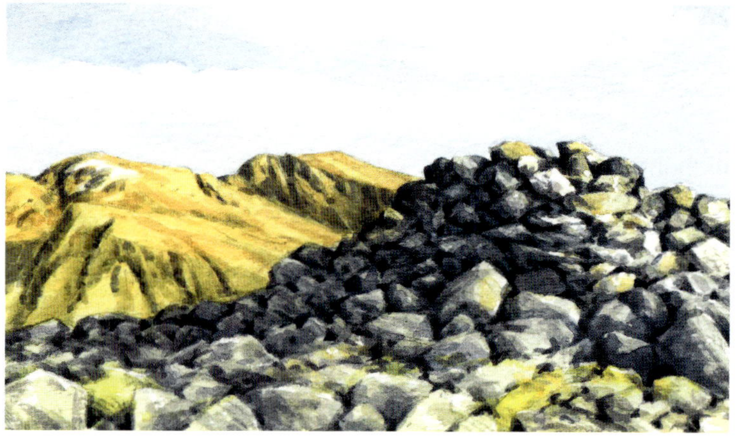

The summit 14/4/14
In error I missed obtaining this reference on previous visits so this time I combined the notorious direct ascent from Wasdale Head with a memorable wildcamp near here. One of my best days out.

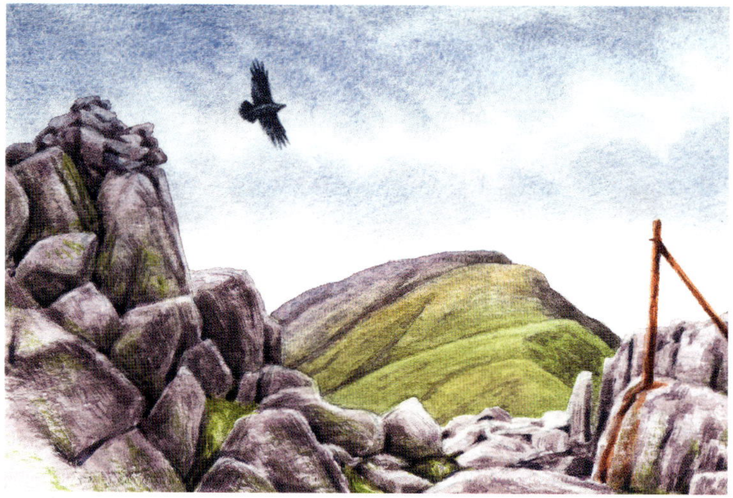

The north-east summit 7/9/09
One of the iron fence posts stands firm, above is a lone raven likely on the lookout for easy pickings.

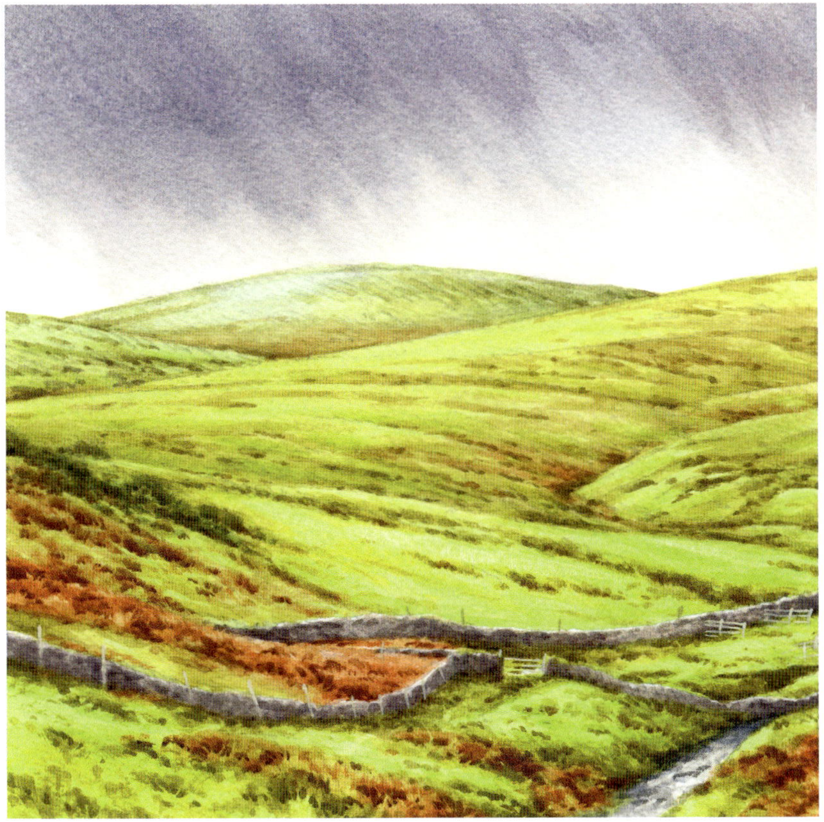

From Friar Moor near Coldfell Gate 5/11/08

The track follows Friar Gill before crossing over the River Calder and heading out to the open moor. A direct ascent of the fell may be accomplished across the moor but it is pathless and boggy in places.

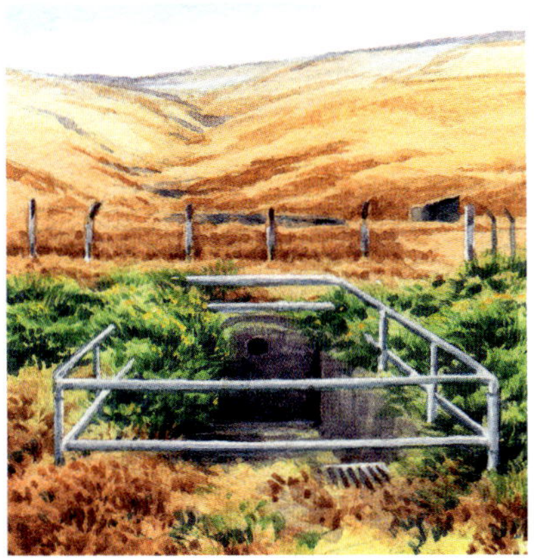

Water Intake Works, Worm Gill 5/11/08

Now derelict and overgrown. Also featured in Caw Fell (page 296).

Lank Rigg

This fell was possibly the most difficult for Wainwright to access, being so far from his Kendal home. It is certainly a remote fell and well away from the more popular walking routes even today.

Ancient enclosures and cairns on Tongue How, Town Bank 5/11/08

The references for the three sketches below were all obtained after some time searching across the fell side. By chance as I was wandering about across the moor I met Chris Jesty as he was researching information for the revised guide.

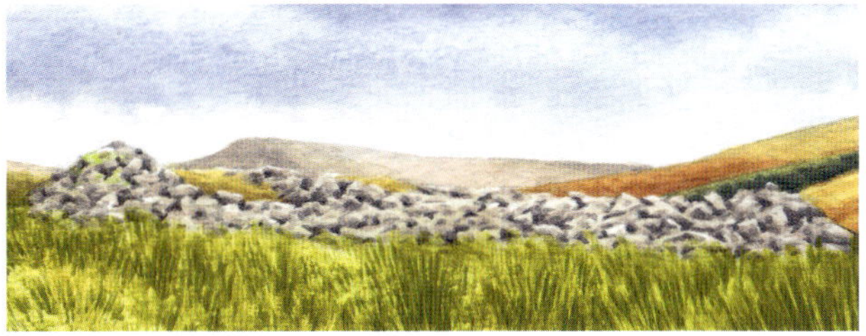

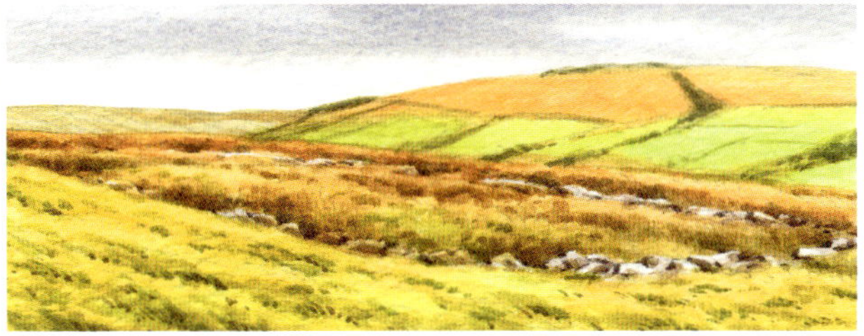

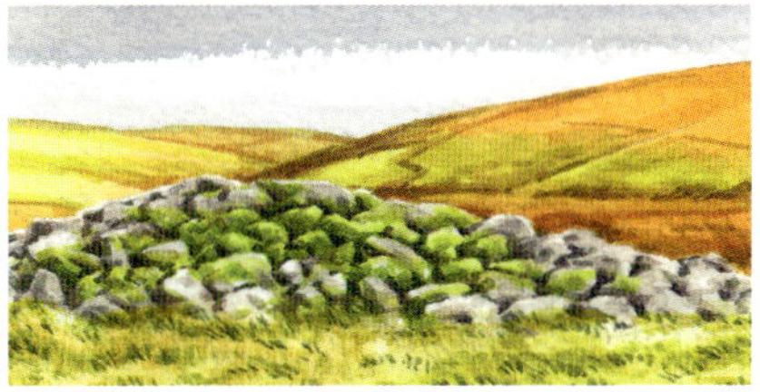

Matty Benn's Bridge 5/11/08

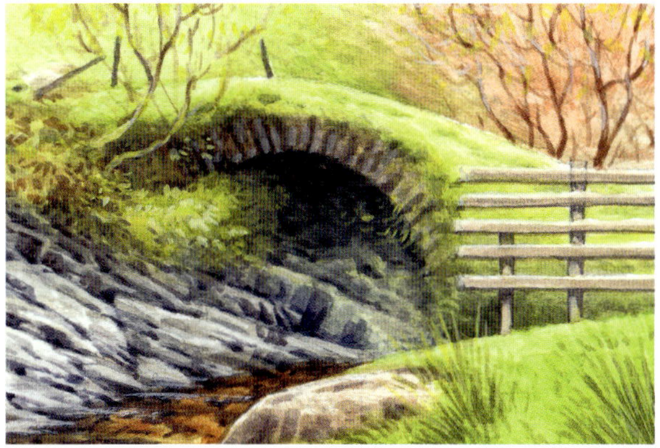

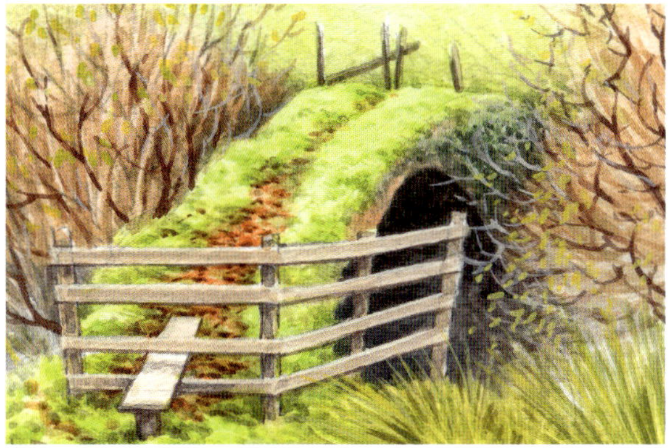

This ancient packhorse bridge is reputed to be the oldest in Cumbria as it dates back to the 17th Century. Monks from Calder Abbey used it so it goes by the name, Monks Bridge. Matty Benn's Bridge seems to be a more local name. Martha (Matty) Benn was a farmer's wife from nearby Brackenthwaite Farm in the second half of the 1800s. She regularly used the bridge as she travelled to Gosforth market on horseback. It seems that her return trip was usually done in a state of drunkenness and her name became connected to the bridge. Even though there is a stile at one end, the bridge is not on a public footpath.

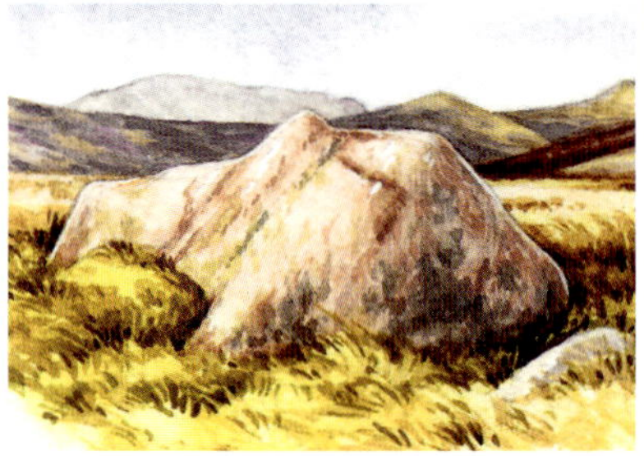

Whoap Summit 5/11/08

The lone pink boulder that marks the summit of this lesser top which birds obviously use as a handy perch. Grasmoor is the fell on the left in the far distance.

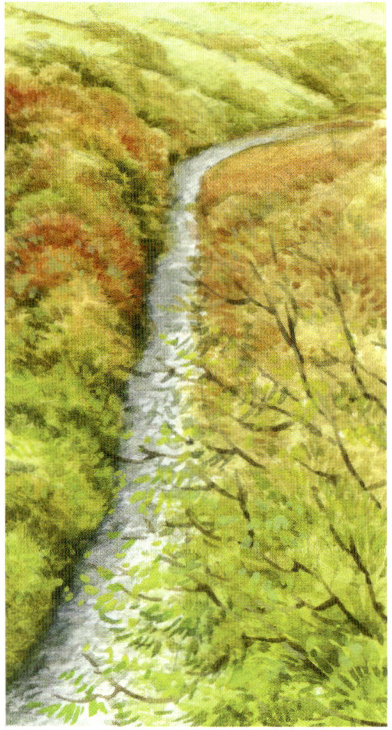

Lank Rigg's buried treasure

Wainwright's act of generosity in hiding a two shilling piece close to the summit in April 1965 didn't stay unclaimed for long. A day or two after the publication of Book 7, The Western Fells, in March 1966, a family from the Seaton area of Workington left home at dawn on Saturday the 12th and by 9.20 that morning had found the coin. Whether they spent it on a fish supper is unknown.

The tradition has been continued though, as a simple search around the summit area can reveal a small trove (last time I was there it amounted to £2.17), with walkers keeping up the spirit of Wainwright's "reckless act". This cache is under one or two of the stones of the small cairn which has since been formed close to the triangulation pillar, using the rocks which lay at random in AW's summit illustration.

The valley of the River Calder near Thornholme 6/8/11

Wainwright's map on Lank Rigg 5 shows Thornholme but not the location for this viewpoint, which after some investigating was found to be a short distance south of the farm. The steep bank is now thickly wooded and on private land so I obtained permission to access this position.

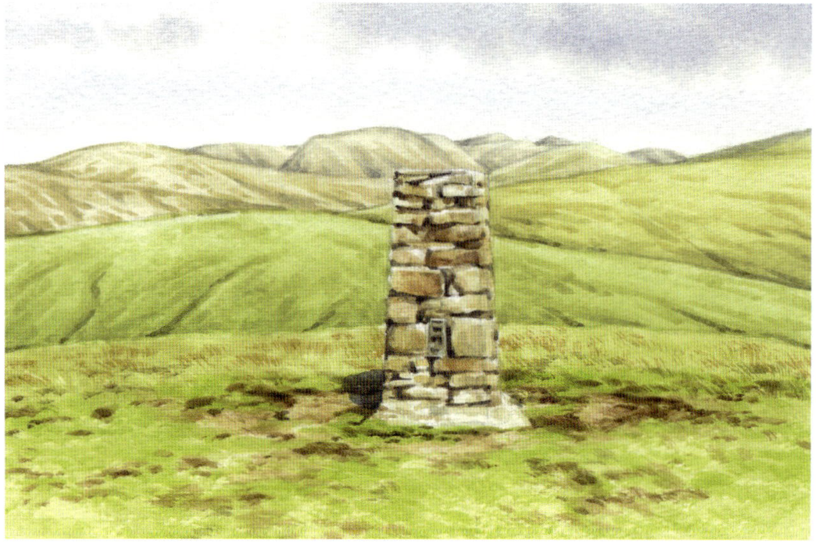

The summit 17/7/14

The triangulation pillar on the summit plateau. The scattering of stones in AW's drawing have since been formed into a small cairn nearby (see left).

Ancient and Modern 5/11/08

As with most historic tumuli on or near the summits of fells, this one has been re-shaped into a basic wind shelter. The four cooling towers of the Calder Hall nuclear power station shown in AW's drawing were demolished on Saturday 29th September 2007. What I have included is the Sellafield reprocessing plant which now occupies the same site.

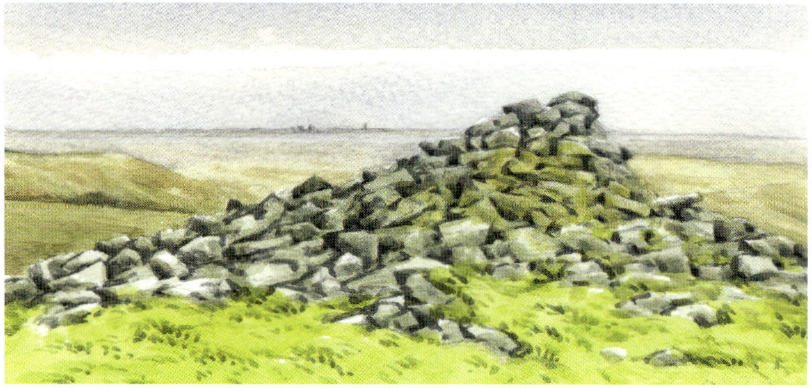

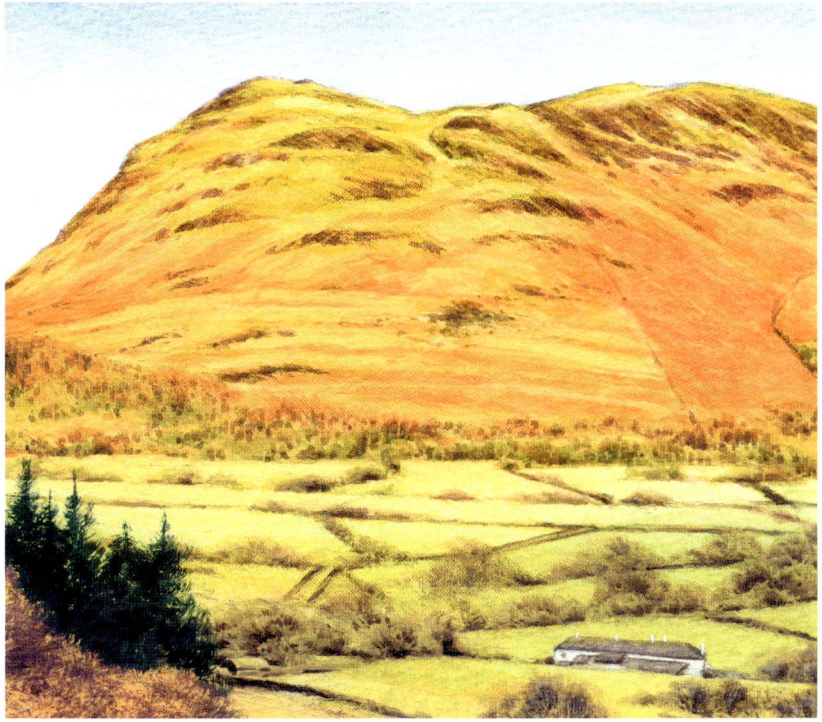

From Lanthwaite Hill 23/2/10

Looking across Lorton Vale to the south-eastern slopes of the fell. The former coaching Inn, Scale Hill, is the building in the sketch. AW used the area of Lanthwaite Hill (a name he likely took from the 1″ Bartholomew map) as a viewpoint for several sketches in the guides. The hill is marked as Brackenthwaite Hows on the O.S. maps but it has also been known as Scale Hill and Cinder Hill.

> **Low Fell**
>
> An excellent half day's walk can be had by visiting this hill and its near neighbour, Fellbarrow, preferably with Low Fell as the second top. The views south are more than ample reward for relatively little effort and afternoon or evening is the optimum time.

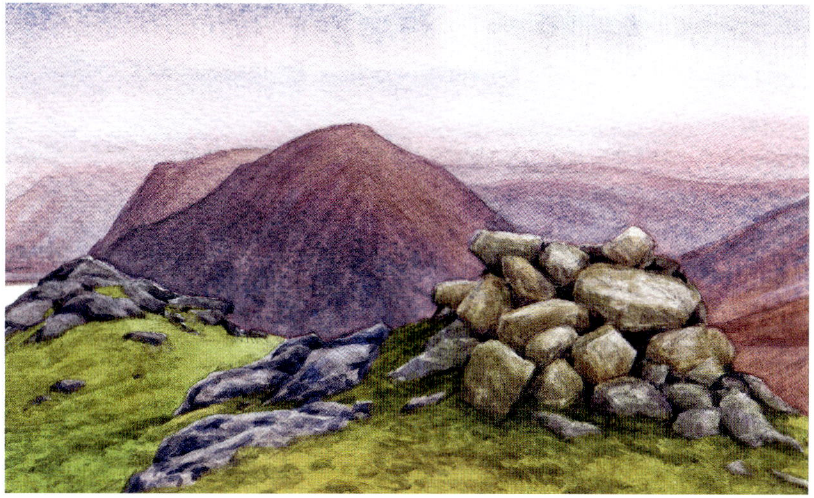

The summit 4/11/08

This is the cairn on the southern top of the fell which has outstanding views of the Crummock Water and Buttermere valley, this angle of view does not do the scene justice. Wainwright deliberated about the actual height of the fell which in his day had not been accurately surveyed and he estimated that the north top (below) was higher. It should not be assumed that because AW placed this sketch under the title "The summit" that it was the top of the fell but more likely it is there because it is a more picturesque scene.

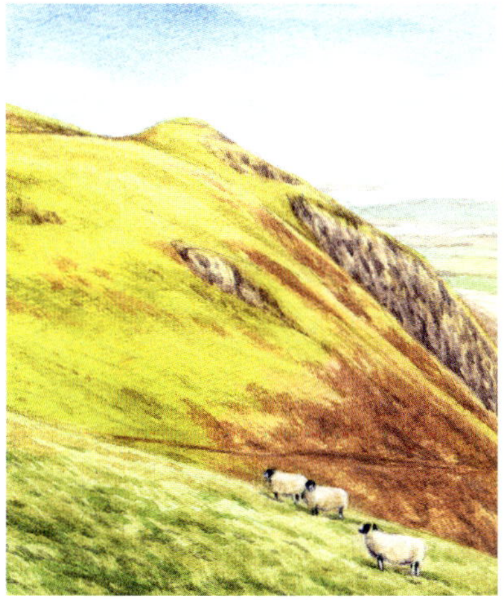

Watching Crag from the south 4/11/08

Remarkably there were sheep grazing on the near slope on my visit just as AW depicted in his drawing. He exaggerated the shape of the top skyline of the crag though.

Cairn on Darling Fell 4/11/08

Grasmoor behind Low Fell's south top was shrouded in cloud on this visit. The small, neat cairn has grown slightly since AW's day.

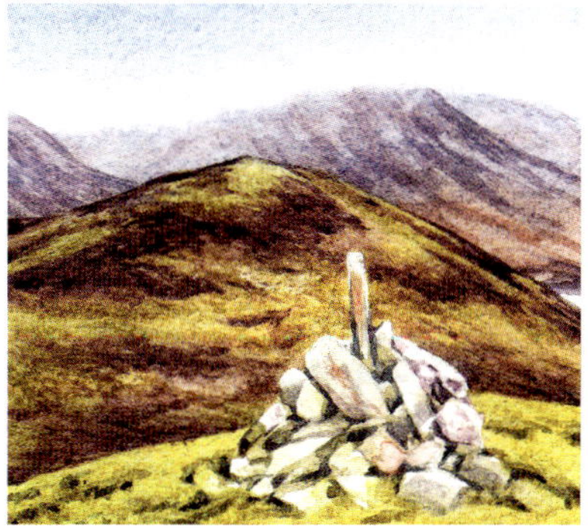

Cairn on the north top 4/11/08

AW was correct in his guess that this was the highest point of the fell, now measured at 1388′, some 28′ above his estimation for Low Fell (see above). It should be remembered that he worked out such heights by using the contour lines on his O.S. maps and by eye, no such gadgets as GPS.

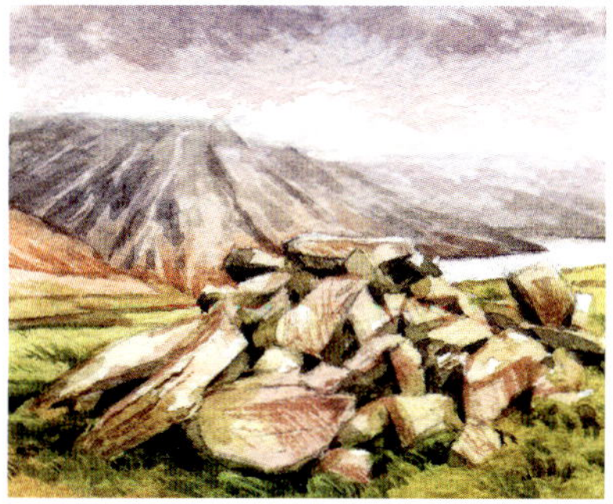

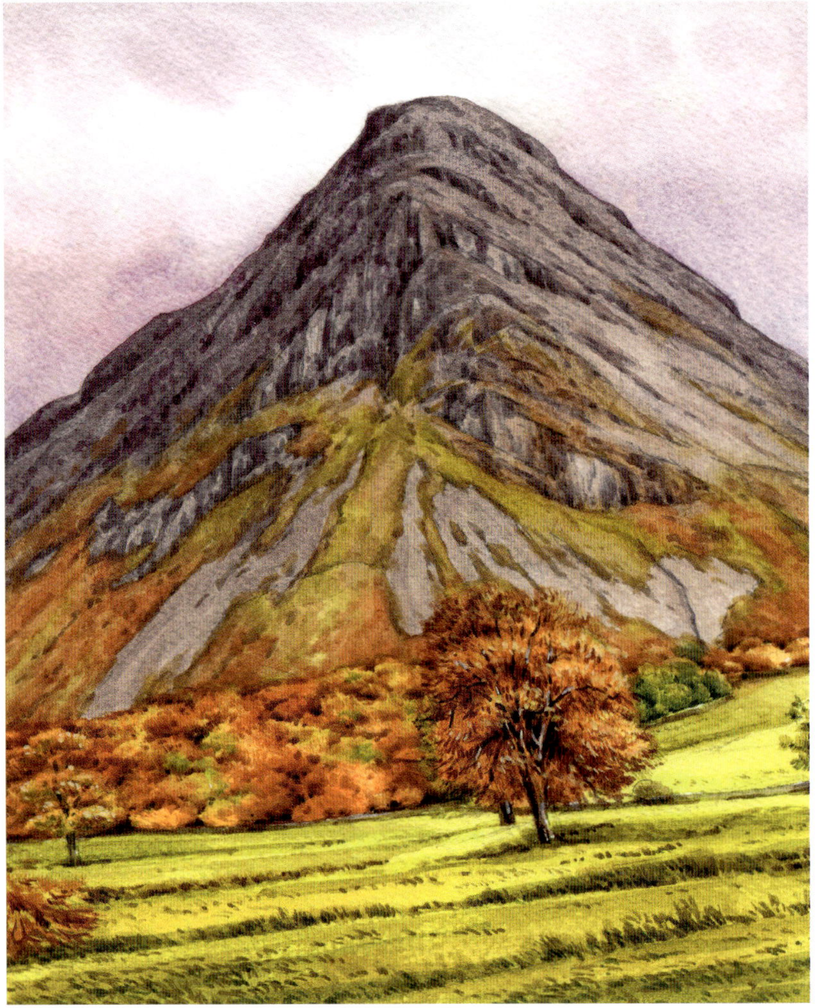

From Kirkhead 7/11/08

The pronounced shape of the fell as seen from the western end of Church bridge. Surprisingly perhaps, the mature trees in the pasture are still there, in fact the scene has changed little in fifty years.

Mellbreak

Individual in its character as well as position, Mellbreak hugs the western shores of Crummock Water and is not directly linked to another fell.

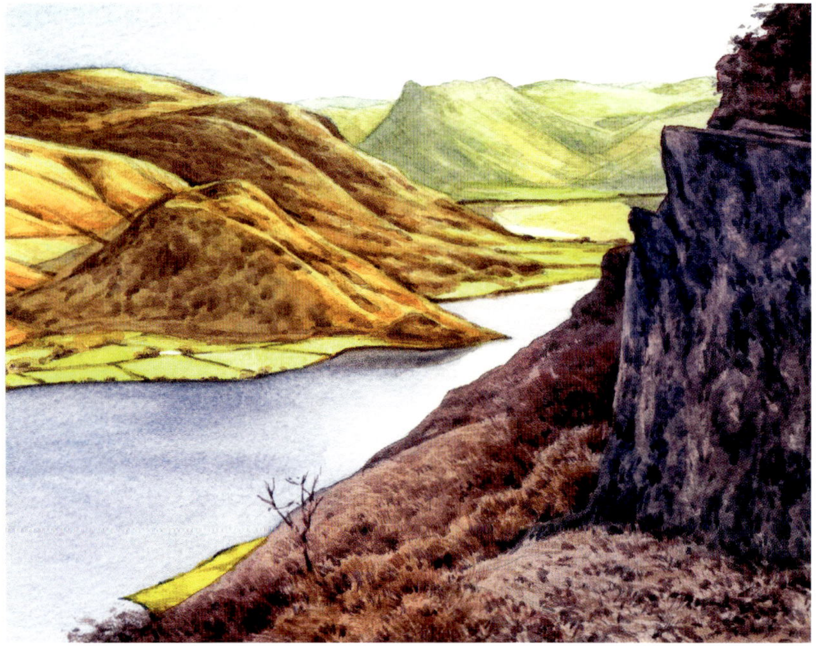

...a lovely peep... 10/11/08

A fine view indeed, and only a short diversion off the main route of ascent to the north top.

From Scalehill Bridge 24/8/09

This is a good place to access the layout of the fell, which is not unlike the long roof of a barn.

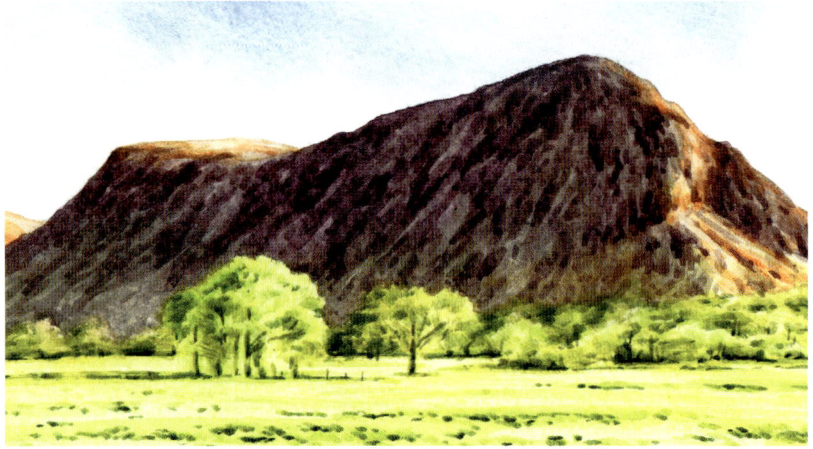

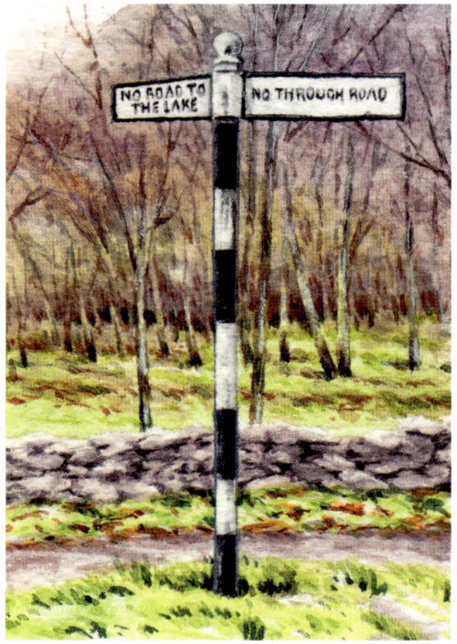

A negative signpost 7/11/08

The right hand sign has been replaced to clear up any confusion.

The Mosedale Tree 7/11/08

The lower branches of this old tree were used to identify from which angle I should sketch it. Very few trees in the district get noted on the O.S. maps. This holly, a larch on Fellbarrow and the Borrowdale Yews are in this small elite group.

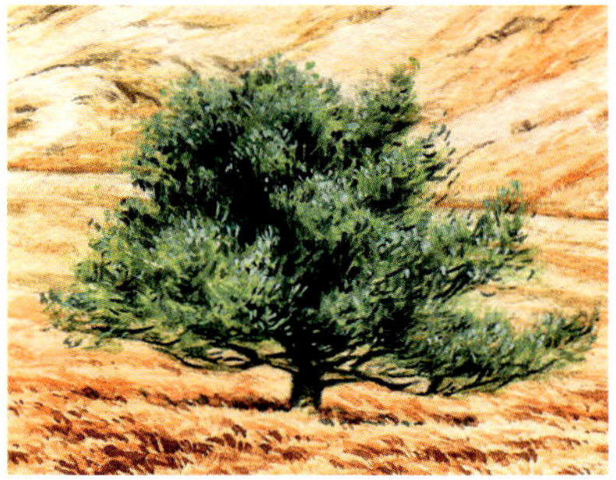

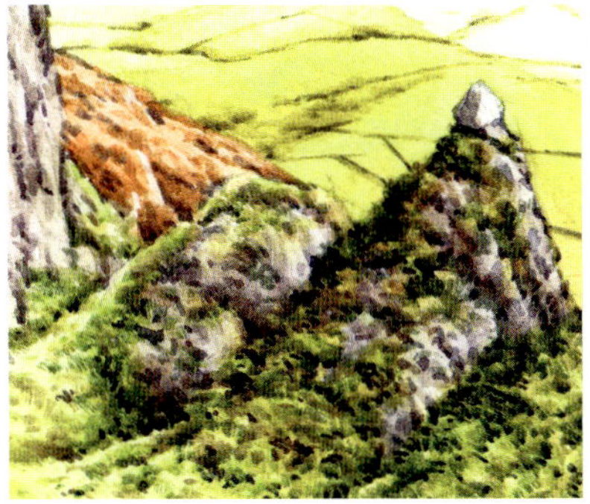

Pillar Rake, upper section
10/11/08
Looking down on the pillars.

The peninsula of Low Ling Crag 7/11/08
A small island linked to the shore by a crescent of shingle beach.

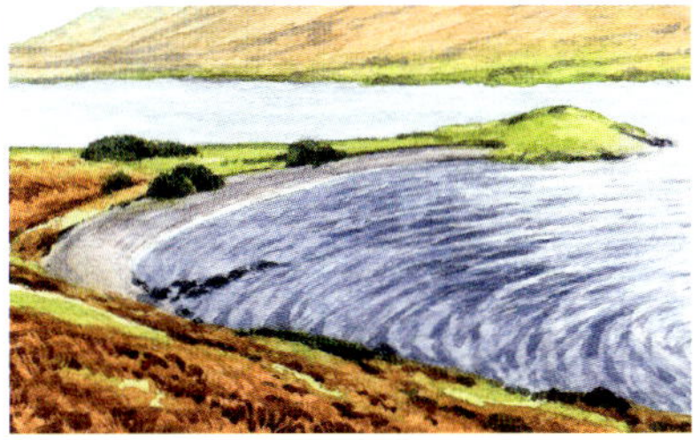

Iron Stone Crummock Water
7/11/08
The lone rock, just off shore.

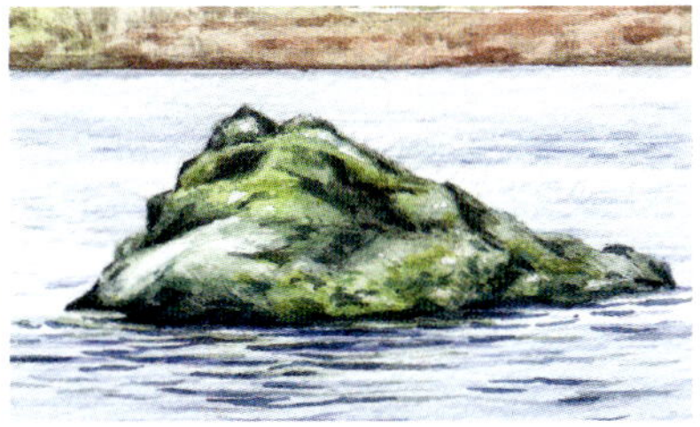

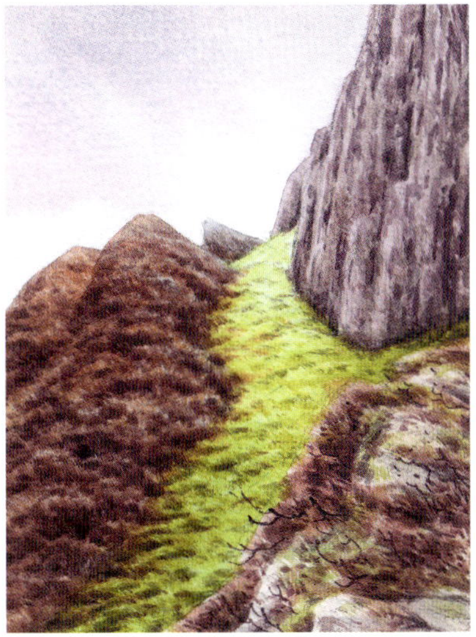

Pillar Rake, lower section
10/11/08
Looking up to the pillars from the grassy rake between the heather.

The summit 10/11/08
The cairn is now more of a wide sprawl of stones.

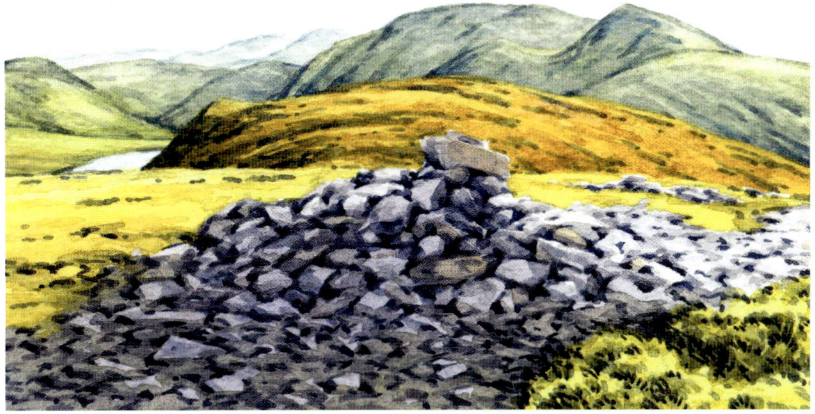

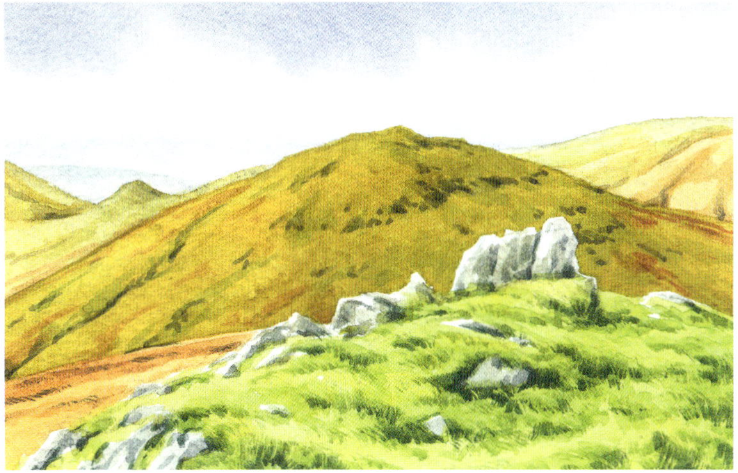

West from the south top
10/11/08
The cairn and fence posts are no longer here.

Grasmoor from the north top
20/4/10 A superb view of the fell.

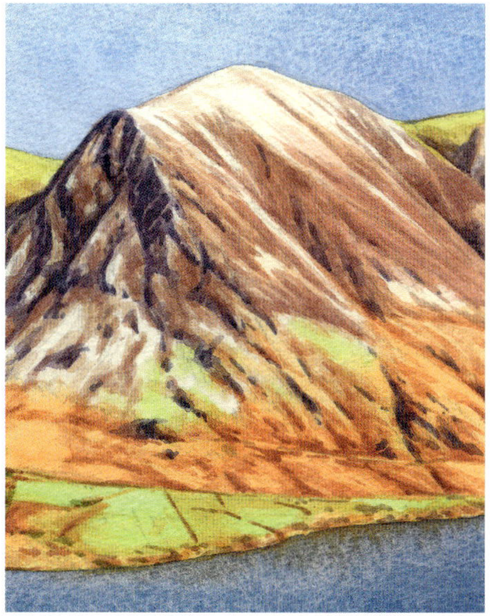

Rannerdale from the south top 10/11/08
An excellent aerial viewpoint over Crummock Water.

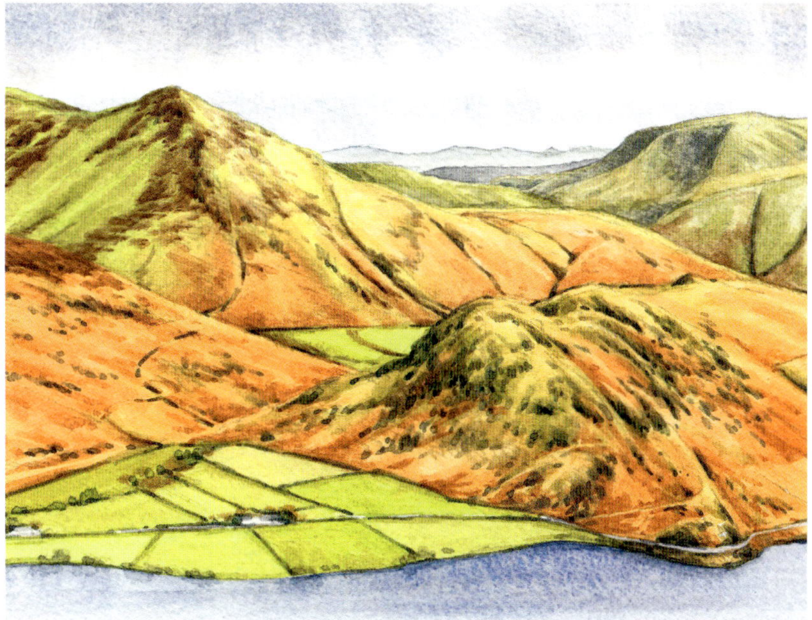

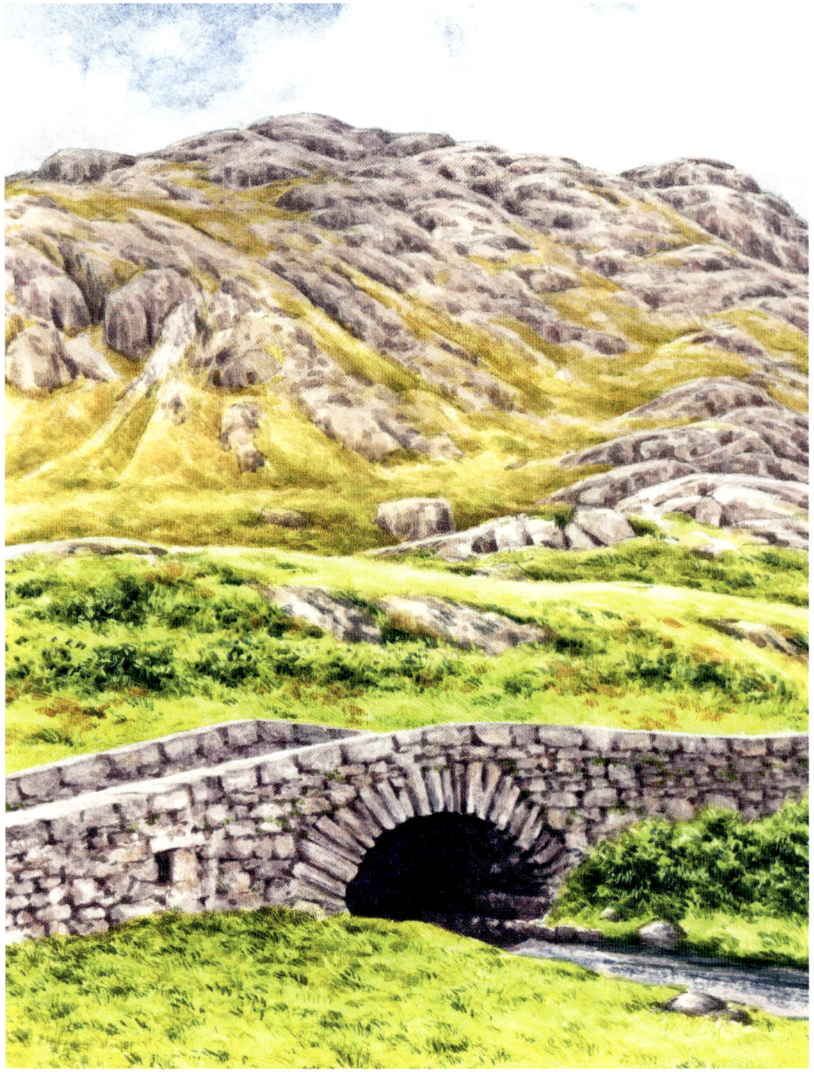

From Wastwater 17/9/09

This bridge is the one which spans Countess Beck and carries the road from Nether Wasdale up towards the valley head. The area here is a popular location for visitors to picnic and explore the shore of the lake in fine weather. The view to the right from near here is that of the length of Wasdale to Great Gable, a classic Lakeland scene.

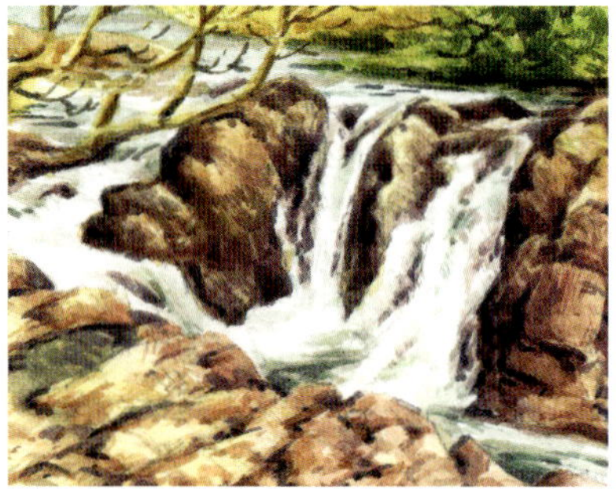

Waterfalls, Nether Beck 8/3/14

These charming falls also appear in the Haycock chapter.

Middle Fell

If any walker was to visit the Wasdale area for the first time I would strongly recommend that their initial route should be up to the summit of this fell. Positioned as it is, Middle Fell (in the right conditions) provides an excellent viewing point for many of the major mountains that surround the Wastwater valley.

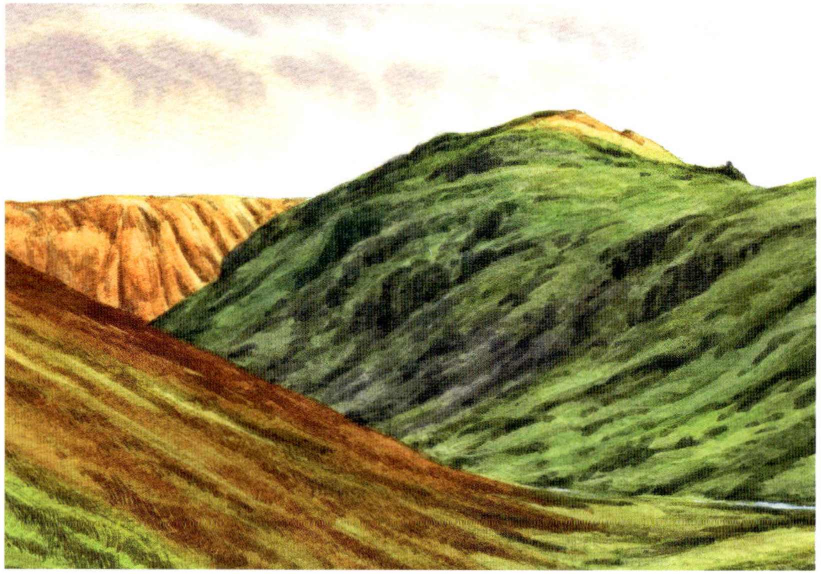

Middle Fell from the headwaters of Nether Beck 9/9/09

The time was 7.20 pm and the evening light was striking the Screes as I got to this reference location. It was dark by the time I returned to the car.

Greendale Tarn 9/11/08

The tarn outlet, perhaps not the best composition for a sketch but it neatly filled up the awkward space at the bottom of the Middle Fell 3 page.

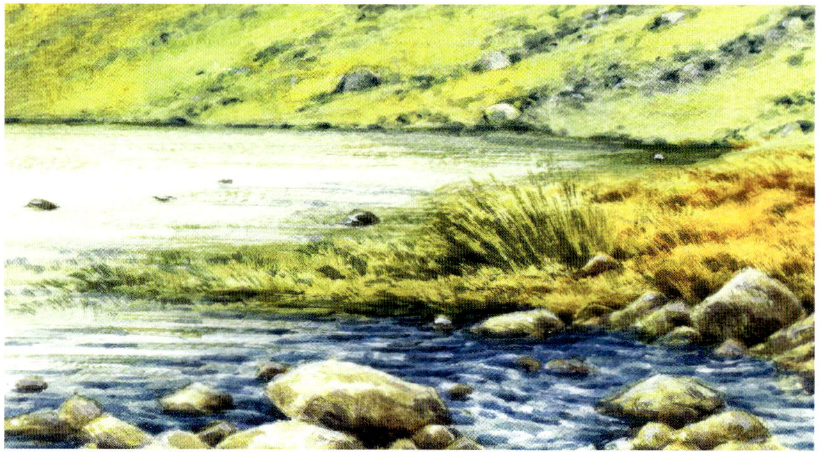

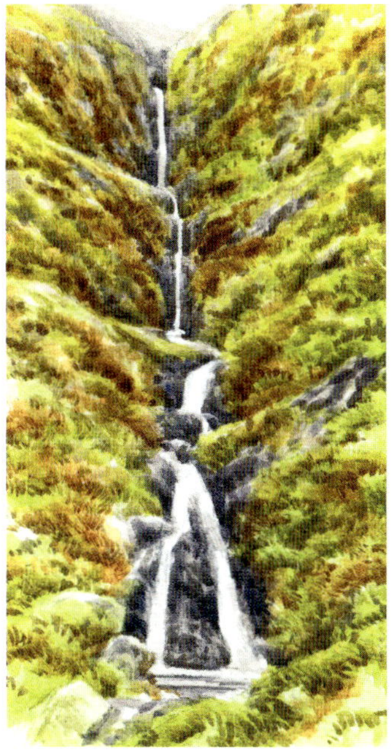

Cascades, Tongues Gills 11/11/08

These tall falls actually come down from the slopes of Seatallan. This ravine, which is just one of the Tongues Gills, is narrow and practically inaccessible.

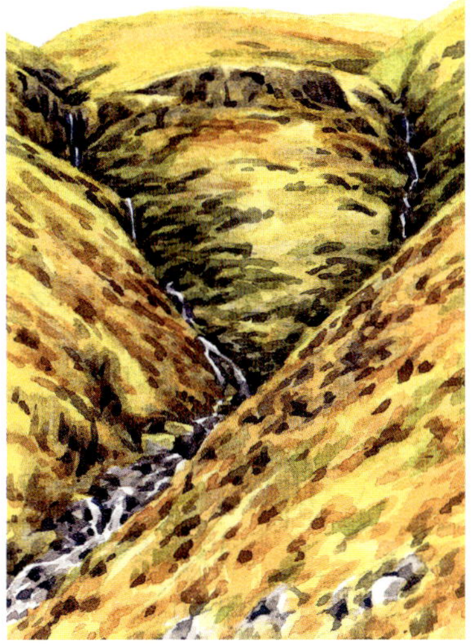

Tongues Gills 11/11/08

This scene, is from the narrow path to Greendale Tarn. The left hand ravine and cascades also feature in the sketch above left.

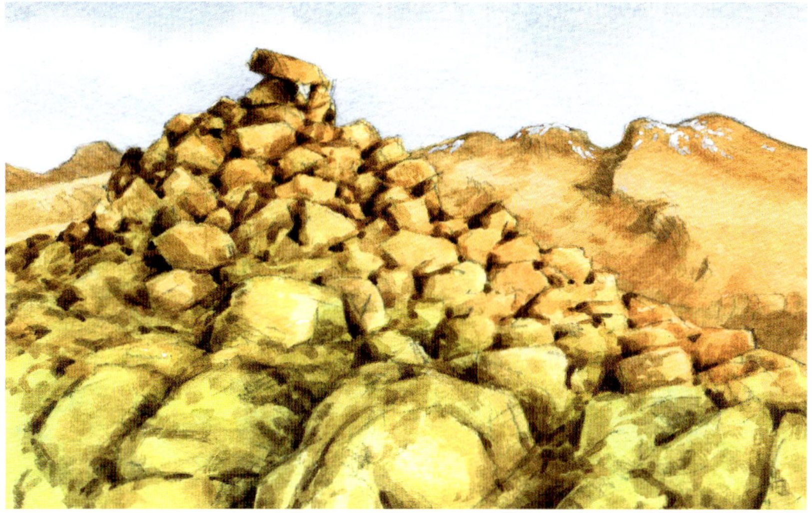

The summit 8/3/14

My first visit to this summit was when the cloud base was right down and I could see nothing of the view. How glad I was that on my second trip the air was clear and the full panorama revealed itself for it is one of the best, with the Scafell massif seen in its full glory. This exact viewpoint doesn't do it justice with the cairn obstructing some of the main subjects.

One word or two?

The name Wastwater is referred to by AW in the Pictorial Guides on several occasions. The O.S. split the name into two words - Wast Water but The National Trust, who own the lake as well as other local authorities such as the Wasdale mountain rescue team opt for the single word usage. Unusually, Wainwright is not consistent, using both versions. It appears that both variations are acceptable but the revised guides take the liberty of correcting AW by using Wast Water throughout when referring to the lake. For this book I use AW's version for the sketch titles.

Wastwater Screes from Middle Fell 8/3/14

The afternoon sunshine adds relief to these dramatic crags and scree falls. This vantage point is from Long Crag near Goat Gill, well away from any recognised path on the fell.

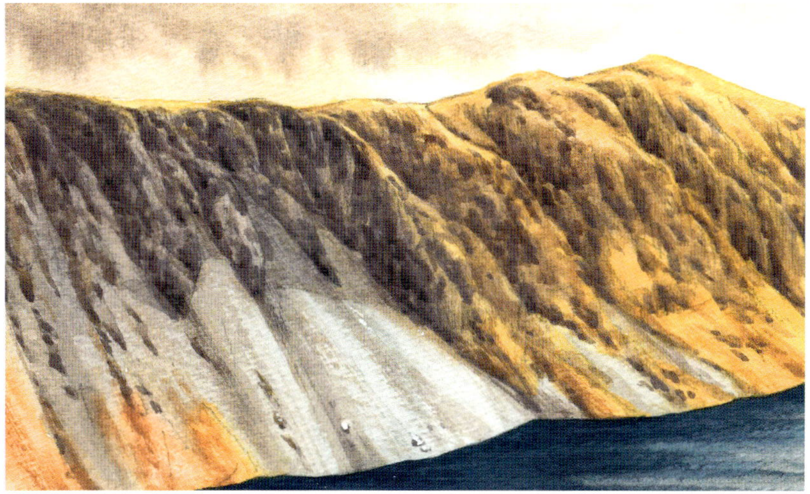

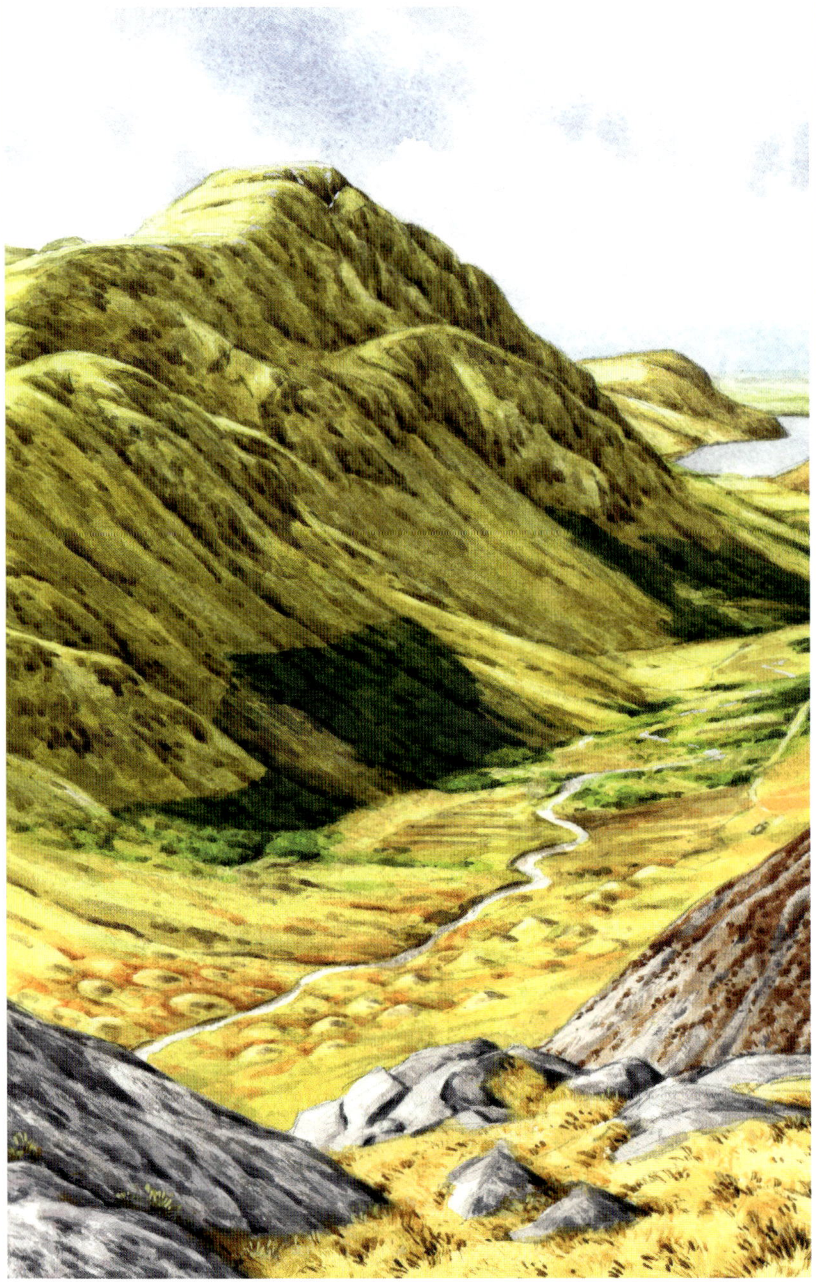

Pillar

It is a pretty sound bet that to many walkers who know the fells Pillar will be in their top ten, AW had it in his finest half dozen. A fell of character with a rugged northern front that reigns supreme over the wild and remote valley of Ennerdale and then with a more gentle side which holds a strong position over Mosedale and Wasdale Head. One visit will not reveal all of this mountain's secrets.

From Brin Crag, Brandreth

18/3/11

There is no doubt that Wainwright would approve of the current re-wilding of Ennerdale as it has resulted in the removal of acres of cultivated forestation in the valley. In this illustration AW invented the rocks at the bottom left to balance the composition, I found these to be a near likeness.

Pillar Rock from the east

7/9/09

It is difficult to give a sense of scale to this huge tower of rock in a sketch such as this. Only by standing here, near Robinson's Cairn, does the impact of the feature make its full impression.

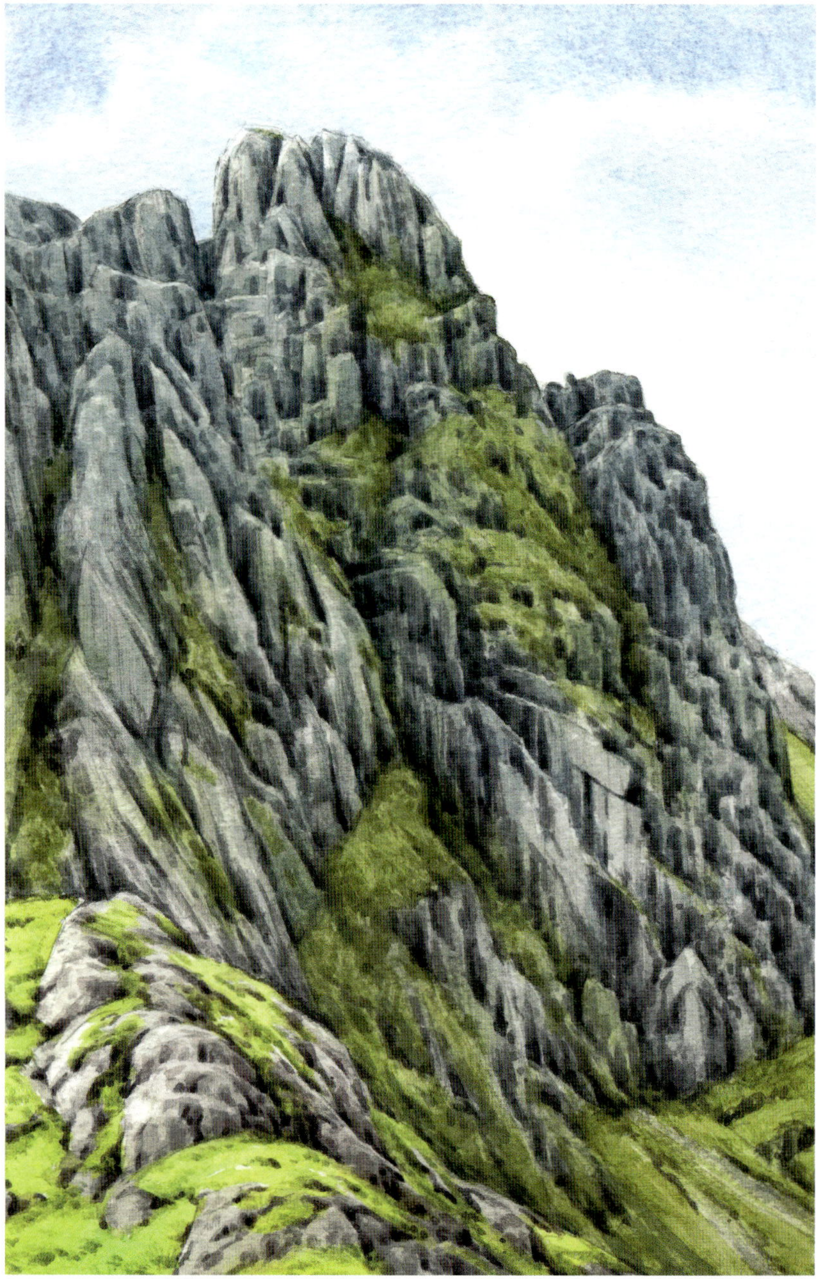

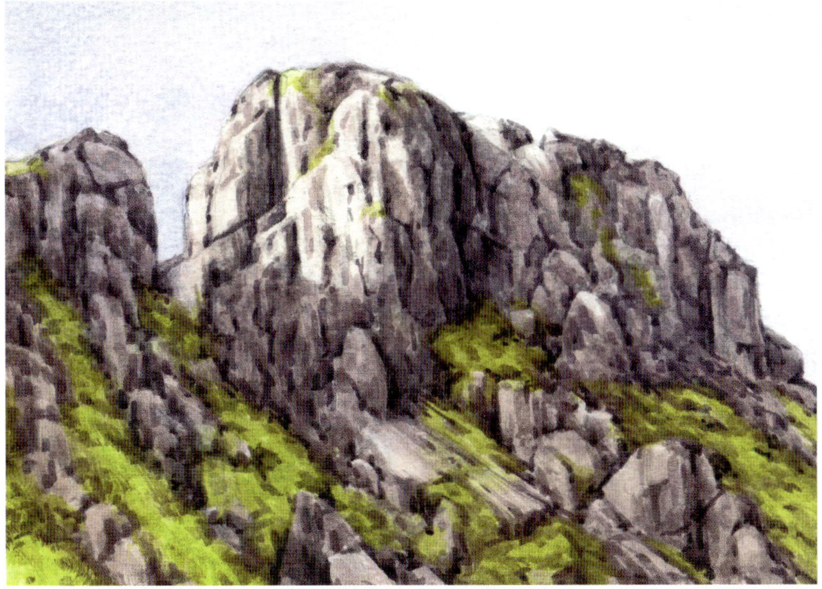

East face of High Man 9/9/09

The very top of Pillar Rock, known as High Man. This aspect can only be seen by those who dare to cross the Shamrock Traverse.

South Face of High Man 9/9/09

Pisgah, the near grassy mound is named after a mountain, Mount Nebo, in Jordan which was mentioned in the Bible, also the reason that the gully beyond is named Jordan Gap.

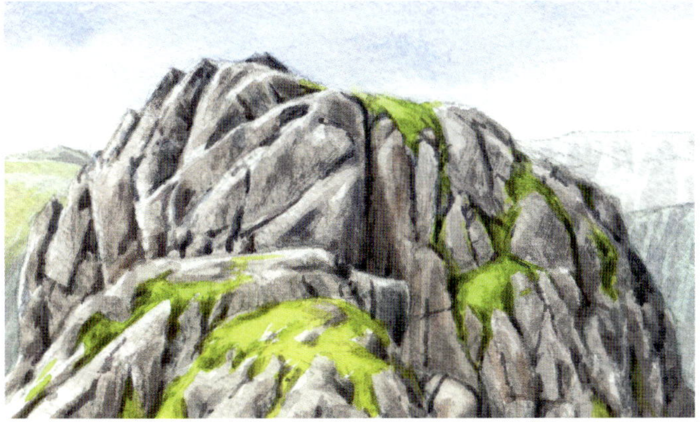

The concrete road-bridge

23/2/10

The bridge has had the addition of railings but more surprisingly the middle support column has been removed. The trees on the right have been felled.

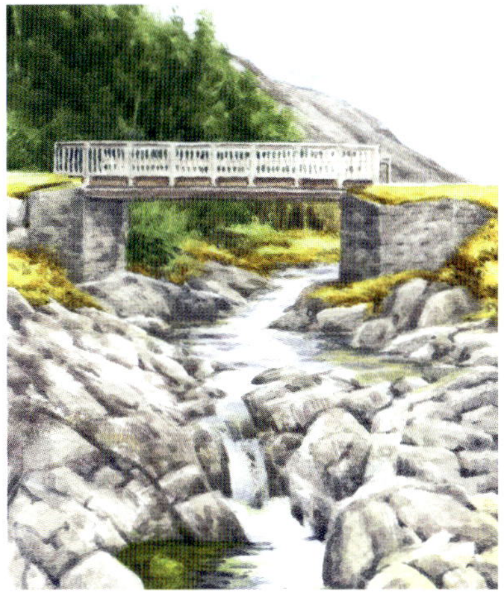

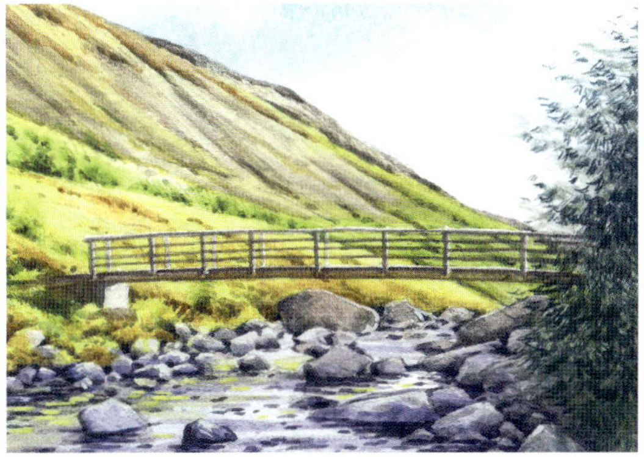

The memorial footbridge

20/1/10

This memorial bridge, built in 1959 is unchanged, as are the big boulders lying in the river bed but due to the fact that the trees are gone the whole scene has a much more open and pleasing feel.

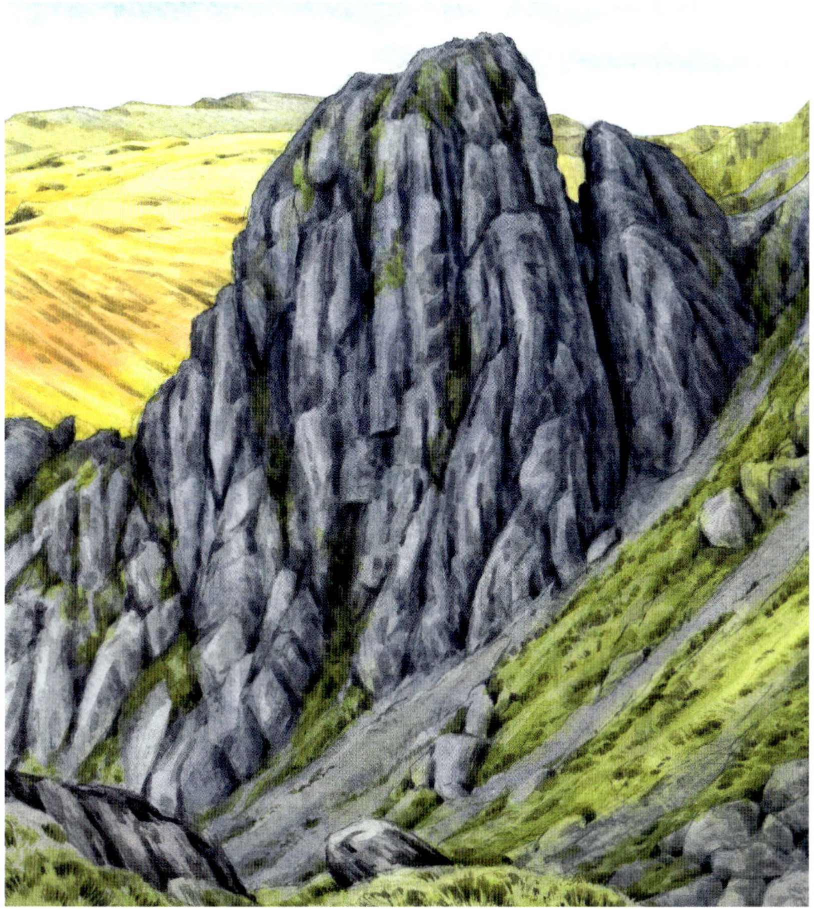

West Face of High Man

20/10/10

To reach this exact location, where very few walkers venture, required an amount of contouring across the high fellside above White Pike towards Pillar Rock. I can only assume that AW wanted to have a close inspection of the alternative, and darker side of the crag. West Jordan Gully is clearly seen here.

The High Level Route and Shamrock Traverse

This path which begins a short distance west of Looking Stead is an exhilarating way to ascend this fine fell and it also gives the humble walker a chance to get up close to the fabled Pillar Rock. The early section, known as The High Level Route, was apparently first used by John Robinson. It is narrow and contours the fell side to the cairn. From there the way to the summit is via Shamrock Traverse, a route which is rough up the initial zigzags and on the final pull up from Pisgah but with a middle section of an ascending shelf which tilts to the right. A short stretch of this slope has an area of seeping water which is mossy in summer and prone to icing in winter. This is where I would advise extra caution.

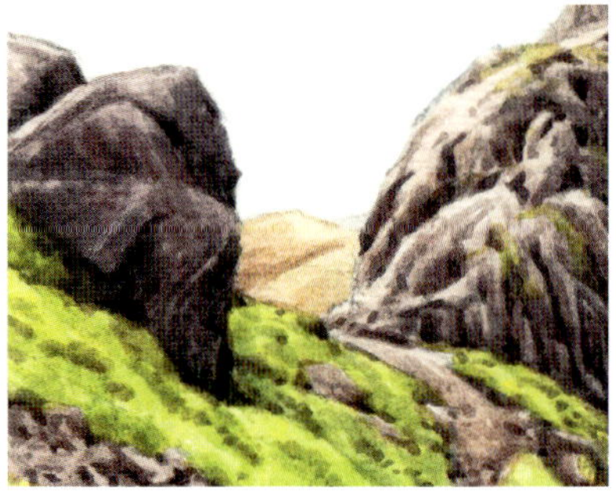

The start of the Traverse 9/9/09

The path proceeds up the grassy rake, the slightly testing place (see above) is along this section.

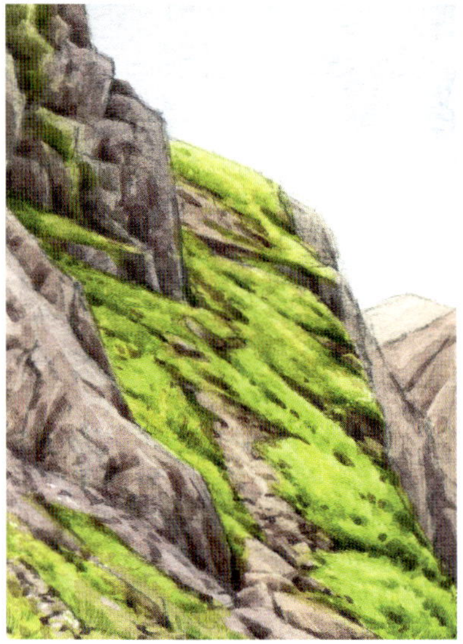

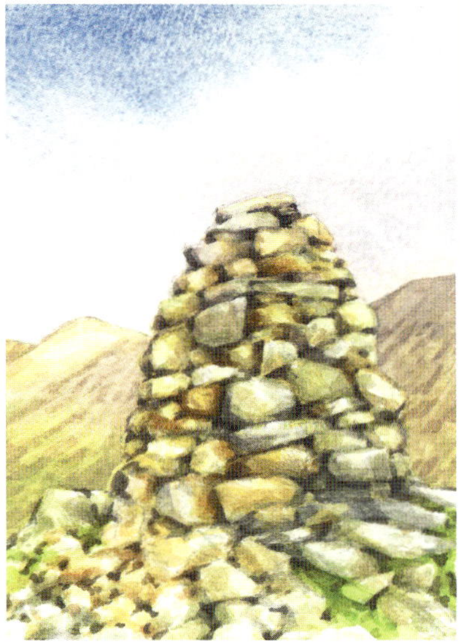

Pillar Rock from White Pike

20/10/10

Only the top of Pillar Rock can be seen from White Pike. To see the full west face of the crag (page 327) a direct approach across the boulder field must be made.

The end of the Traverse 9/9/09

The stretcher box in AW's drawing is no longer in place, backing against the rock on the left. In fact It had collapsed by November 1966, only a few months after this Pictorial Guide had been published.

Robinson's Cairn 9/9/09

This cairn was constructed on April 18th 1908 by members of the climbing fraternity in memory of a local climbing legend, John Wilson Robinson, who was president of the newly formed Fell and Rock Climbing Club until his death in 1907. Two months after the cairn was built a memorial plaque, which can be found close by, was put into place on June 13th. By pure coincidence this memorial cairn had undergone major restoration only two weeks prior to my visit. This was completed by current members of the club.

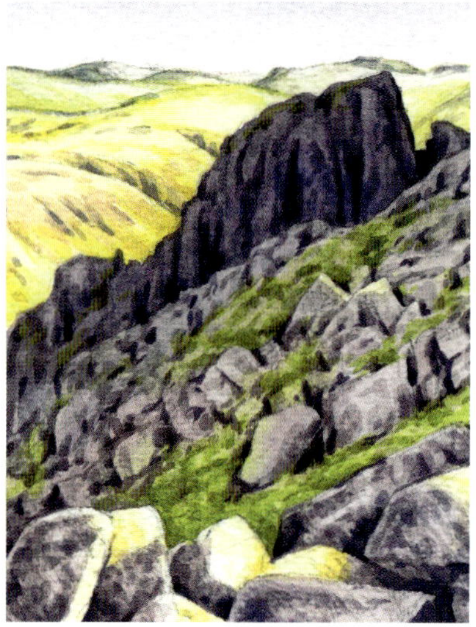

Pillar Rock from the north

20/10/10

No sketch can fully convey the breath-taking impression of this scene from within Pillar Cove.

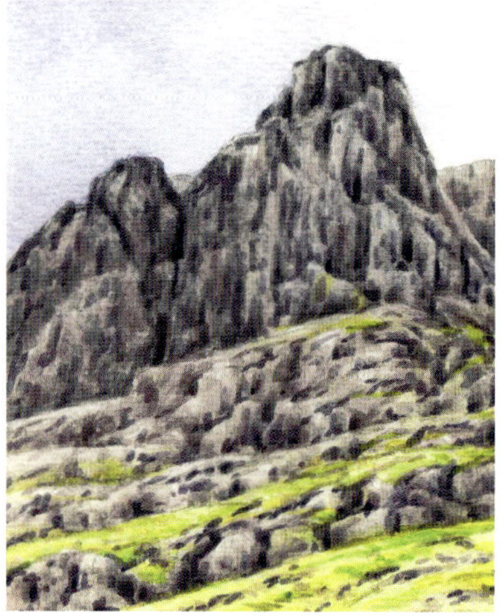

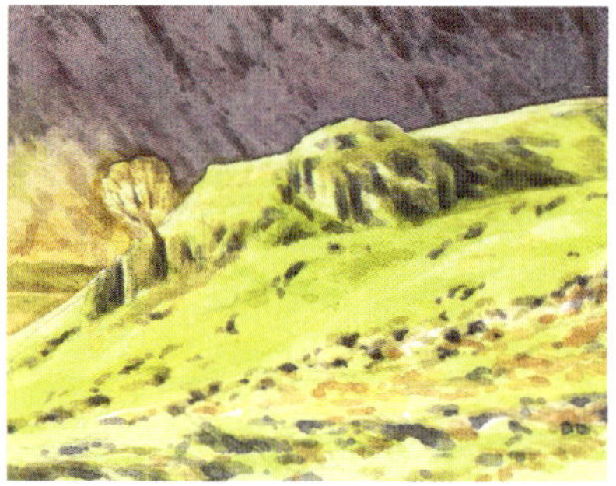

Path from Scarth Gap 20/10/10

Even though this illustration by AW was more of a route description than a filler sketch, I decided to include it as the features such as the tree and boulders were still in place and the light was rather inspiring.

The Pillar Ride 20/10/10

The forest having been cleared, this scene with Pillar Rock towering up out of the Cove looks more like a sketch from the high Andes.

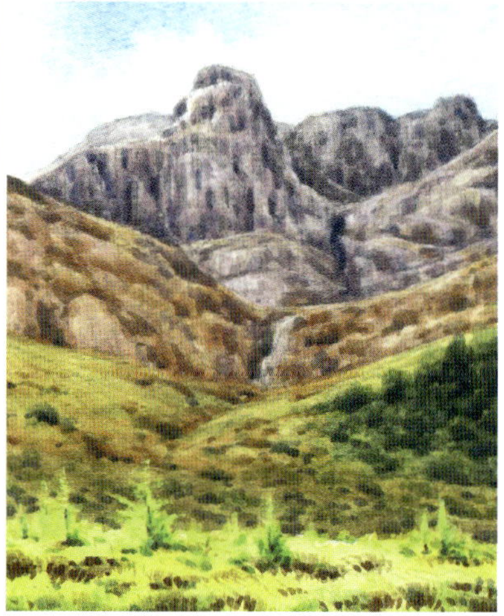

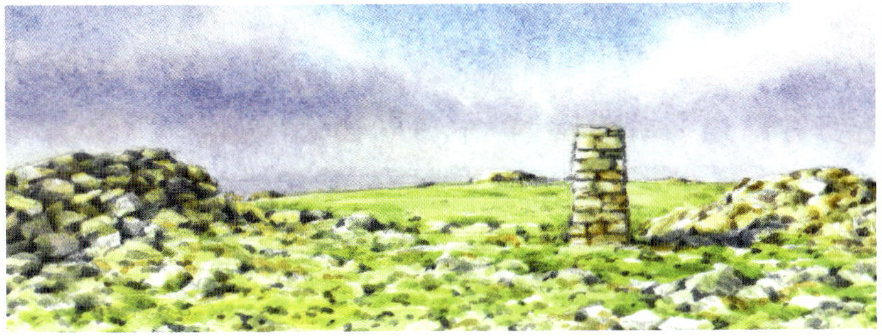

The summit 9/9/09

The plateau around the highest point is grassy and flat, an excellent location for a wild camp.

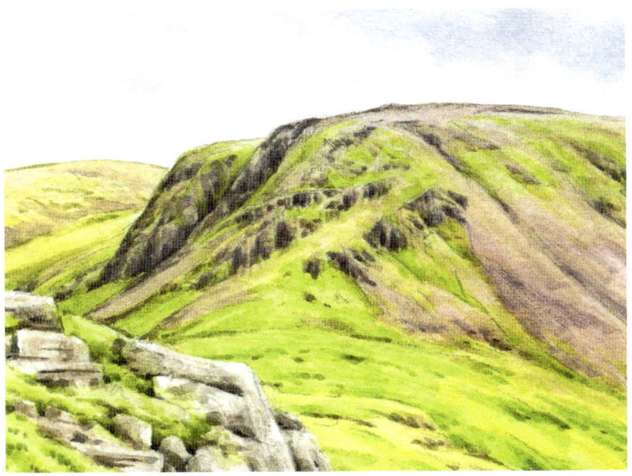

Kirk Fell from Looking Stead 7/9/09

The saddle here is Black Sail Pass and an ascent of Kirk Fell can be made using a rough path which winds up through the crags. Looking Stead was on AW's first list of fells.

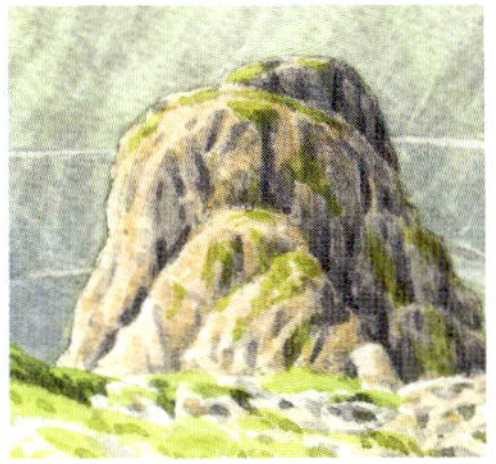

Pillar Rock as seen from the north shelter 9/9/09

A short walk from the shelter and this prospect of the Rock from above comes into view.

Animal Rescue Cumbria - The Wainwright Shelter

Wainwright's love of animals is well known, in fact it has been said that he preferred the company of animals to that of humans. His admiration for the wildlife that he encountered on the fells is well documented as was the distaste for the hunting of foxes and shooting of grouse. Whilst working on the Pictorial Guides it seems that dogs were the pets of choice but they were looked after by his then wife Ruth, when she walked out of the house for the last time the dog went too. In 1970 after AW and Betty were married she moved into the home and brought her cat, from then on cats were permanent residents, as many as 24 at a time but it seems about seven was the usual number, mostly those needing re-homing.

In the closing section of Book Seven AW indicated his plans to donate some of the proceeds of the sales of the Pictorial Guides to the local branch of the RSPCA so that a shelter could be built. The sum to be donated over a period of seven years beginning in January 1967 would have amounted to £120,000 in today's money. Sadly, the idea fell through much to AW's annoyance. In the meantime he and Betty made donations to an Animal Sanctuary near Ramsbottom which cared for old and sick donkeys. In the early 1970s they both became involved in the group Animal Rescue Cumbria whose aim was to find homes for pets who otherwise may have been put to sleep. AW was elected as Chairman and under his guidance the group was registered as a charity and became better organised. The plan was to build a permanent animal shelter near Kendal and with generous donations from AW and other fund raising activities they had accrued £30,000 by 1983, still well short of the required sum, but then AW sold the copyright to his books for £40,000 enabling the charity to then acquire a site near Grayrigg. By 1985 the centre, named Kapellan, was fully open. From the sale of original drawings, the royalties from coffee table books and films, AW was able to continue to help fund the charity even though it meant him forfeiting some of his valued privacy. It seems that he basically lived off his pension and donated most of the money that came in through his other work meaning that by 1990, the bank balance for Animal Rescue Cumbria was over £350,000, a substantial portion of which came from this man's generosity. Since AW's death though in 1991 the charity has had to rely on donations, fund raising and legacies, and with vet's bills alone at around £20,000 per year it is a costly business to keep what became known as The Wainwright Shelter running. For more information visit the website at: www.animalrescuecumbria.co.uk

ANIMAL RESCUE CUMBRIA
THE WAINWRIGHT SHELTER
Rescuing and rehoming since 1972

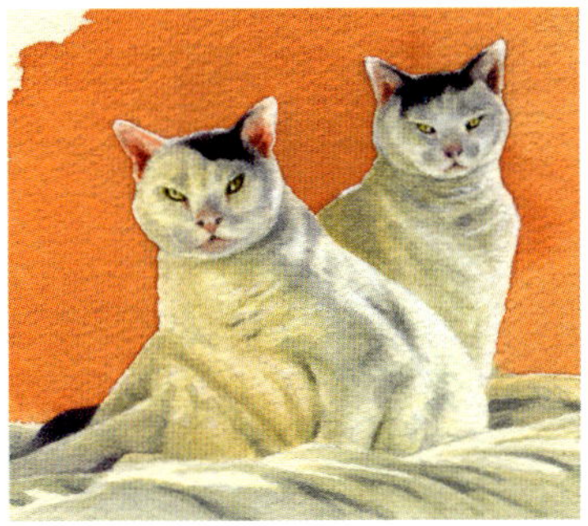

We are both dog and cat lovers so back in 2009 we decided that to bring cats back into our home we should look at adopting two from The Wainwright Shelter. I was tasked to go and have a look at a pair. On being shown potential cats the very first two that I saw were a four year old brother and sister and my heart melted. How appropriate that they were also black and white (in keeping with AW's work) so a couple of weeks later we were able to give them their forever home. They made our house a home and loved the freedom of living on a farm. I would like to think that AW would have approved of our choice even though we couldn't have the same number of cats as he had around his house.

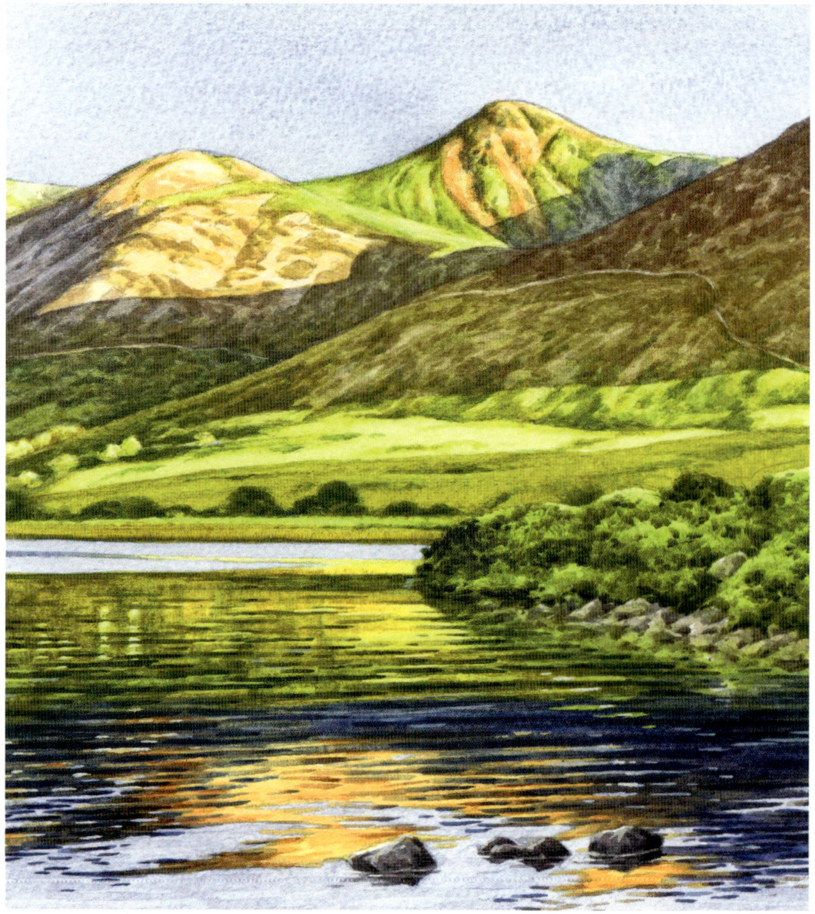

From Crummock Water 8/8/12
A perfect time for me to capture this scene as the late afternoon sun was highlighting the upper sections of Red Pike and Dodd.

Red Pike (Buttermere)
This fell, compared to its namesake in Wasdale, more distinctly shows the colouration from which both fells get their name. As one hill of the High Stile range, Red Pike forms part of an entertaining ridge route high above the Buttermere valley.

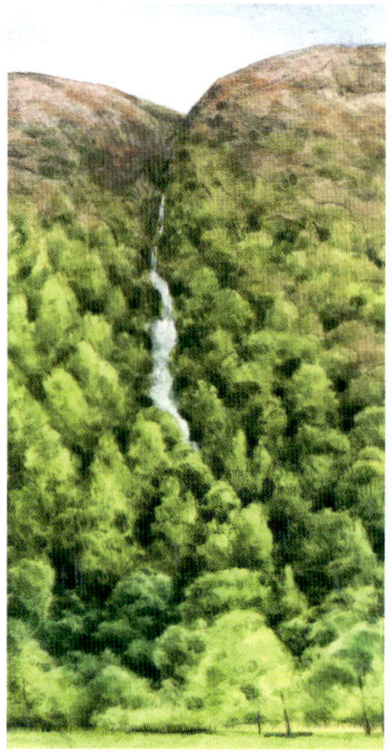

Sour Milk Gill
10/9/09
The mature wood now obscures the lower section of these fine cascades, here seen from the flat pastures at the western end of Buttermere lake.

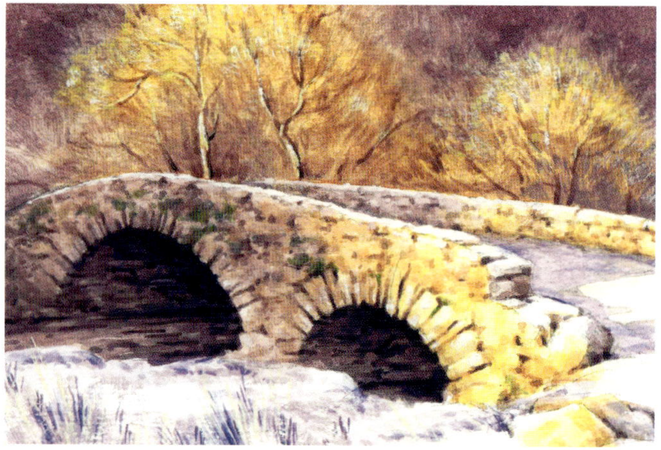

Scale Bridge 17/2/08
The winter sun brings warmth after a cold and frosty night. Scale Bridge is only a short walk from Buttermere village.

A simple cairn 10/9/09
A descent from The Saddle, below Red Pike, via the faint path into Ling Comb enabled me to locate this small cairn with its now fallen main stone. The drawing has been removed from the revised guide.

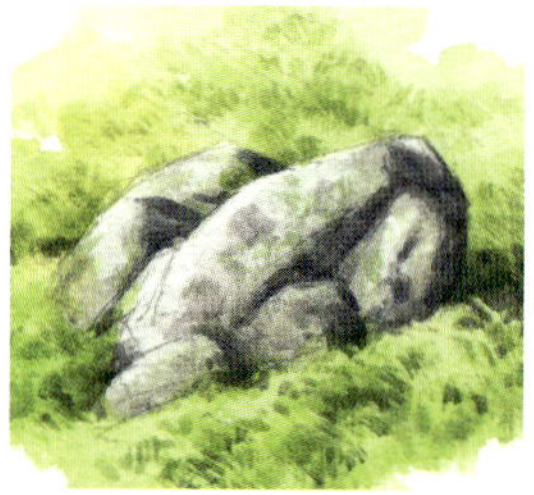

Lingcomb Edge, looking to Red Pike 17/2/08
There is now an obvious path on the lip of the fell above Ling Comb.

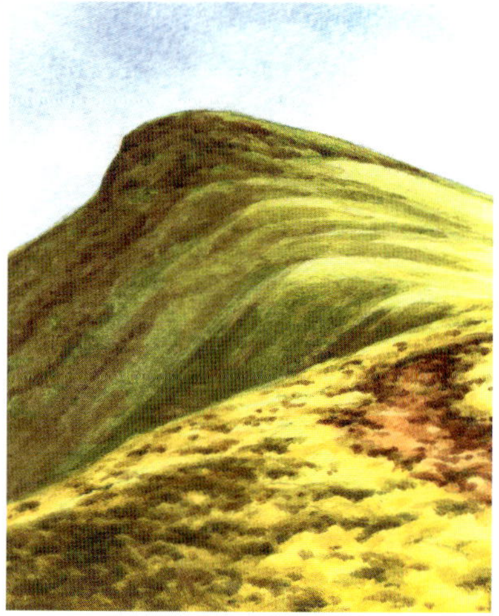

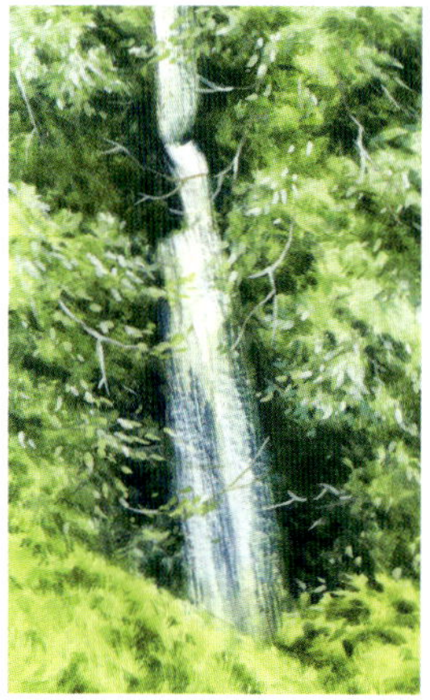

Waterfall, Far Ruddy Beck 8/8/12
This waterfall, with a drop of about 25 feet is now rarely visited, the path to it is overgrown and fallen trees make close access difficult. Obtaining a clear reference of it was almost impossible.

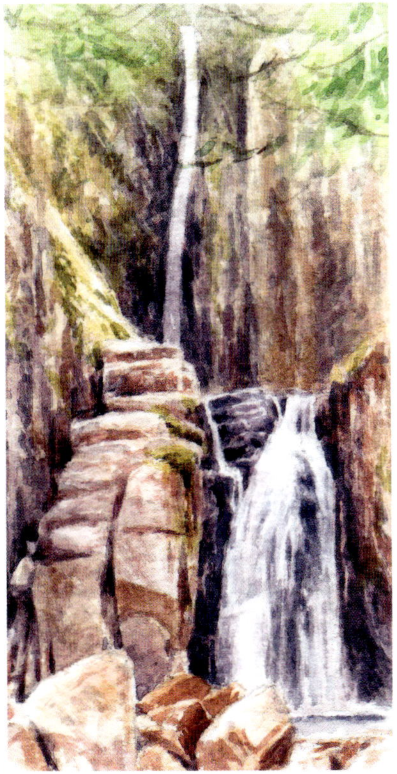

Scale Force 17/2/08

The rickety old ladder seen in AW's drawing is no longer there. To gain access to the upper section of the falls, the highest in the area, a bit of scrambling over wet and slippy rocks must be undertaken.

The summit, from Bleaberry Tarn 10/9/09

The outlet of this charming tarn provides foreground interest to this scene. Access to the summit from this direction is via a pitched path to the col from where the path is steep and rough on the rich red scree all the way to the very top.

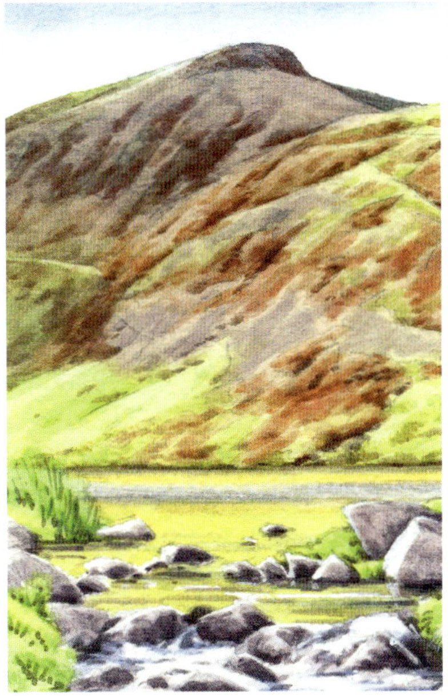

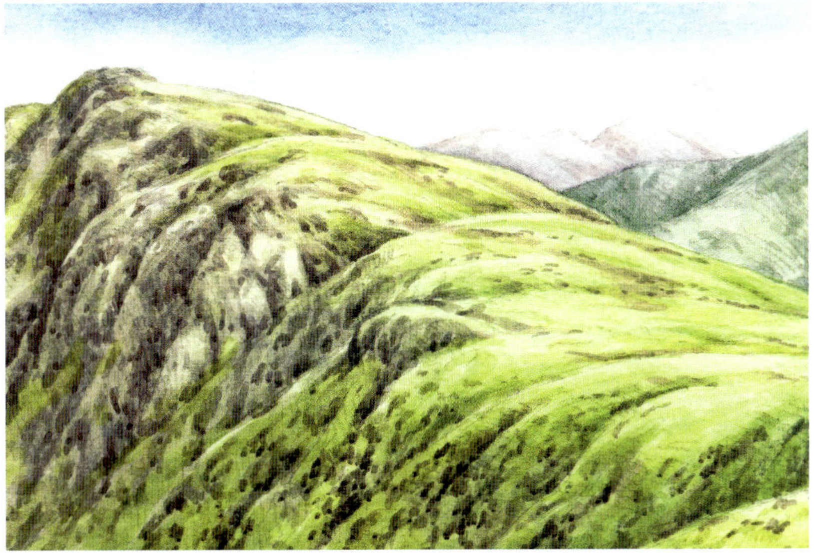

The ridge to High Stile 10/9/09

This scene illustrates the rising ridge to High Stile's summit, a route on which the high face of Chapel Crags can be observed. To the right can be seen the distant Scafells over the shoulder of Looking Stead.

Cairn on Lingcomb Edge 17/12/08

A neat pile of rocks that sits close to the drop into the comb.

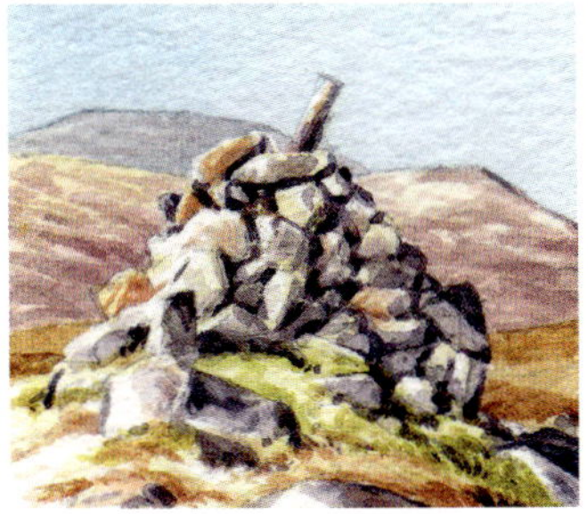

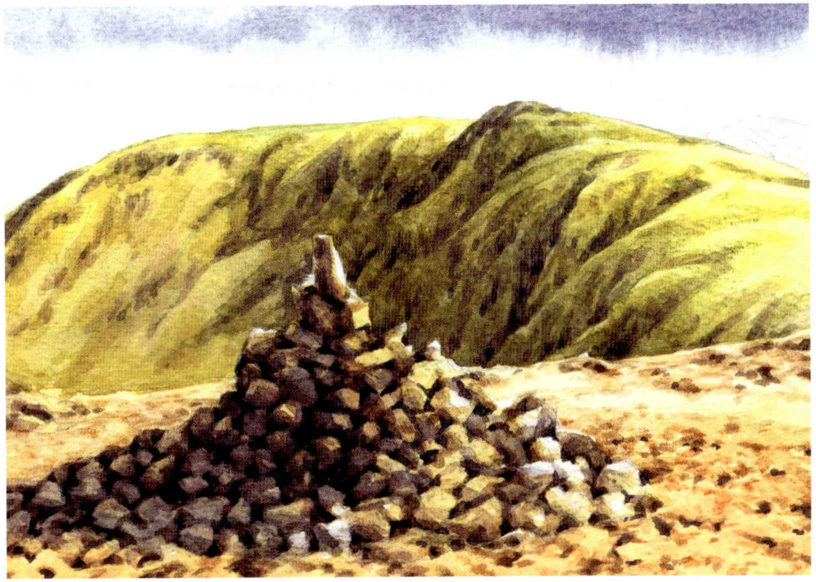

The summit 17/2/08

The huge single mound of stones of AW's day has been divided into two with one heap being shaped into a wind shelter. The summit is formed by a rounded butt of land which provides an excellent aerial view of Crummock Water and the Grasmoor group of fells.

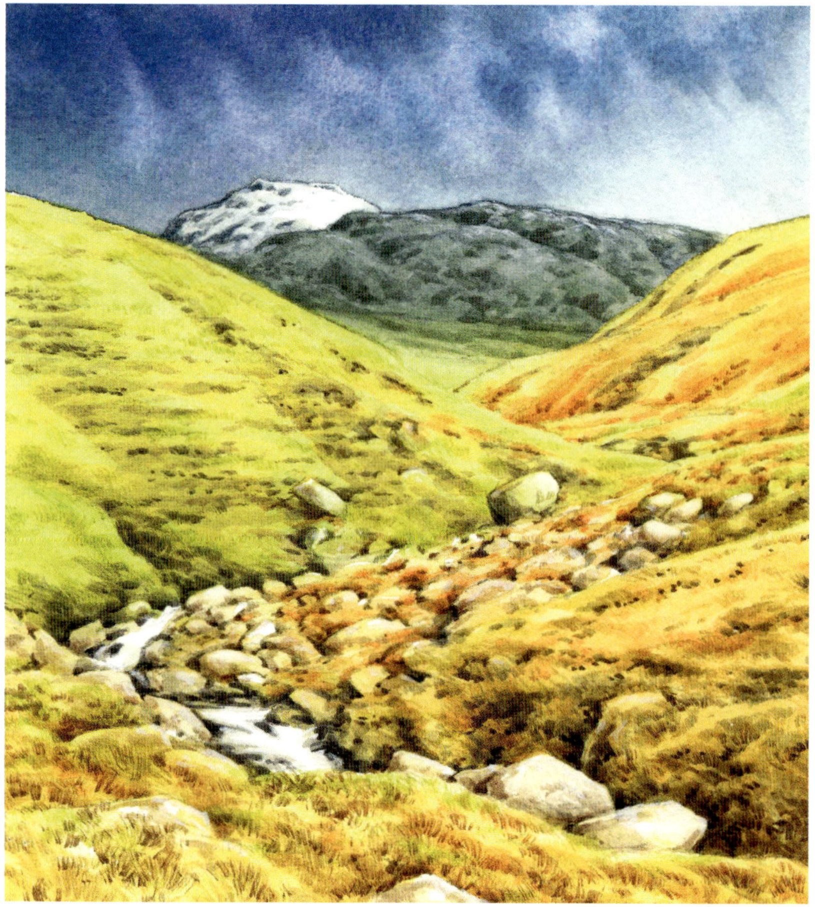

From Over Beck 6/2/14

Sometimes on my adventures I just got lucky with the weather. Here, with fresh snow of Red Pike's summit the sun broke through at just the right moment. Wainwright gave the fell some additional height in his drawing.

Red Pike (Wasdale)

Like many fells, Red Pike (Wasdale) has two sides, a formidable eastern face that steeply and ruggedly falls away into Mosedale and a western side that more gently slopes down to Scoat Tarn, Low Tarn and Over Beck. Red Pike was my initial inspiration.

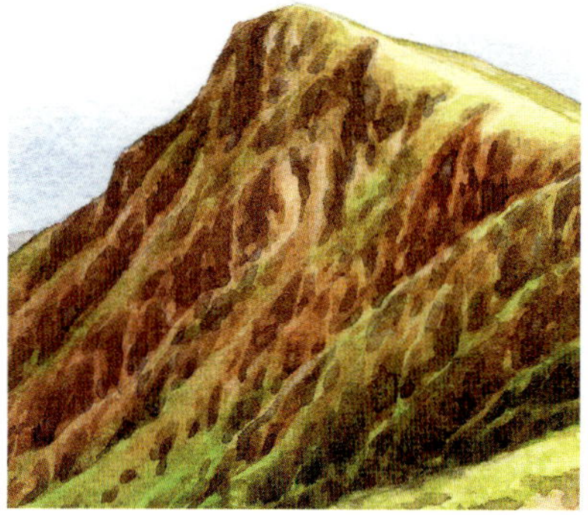

From Black Crag 2/7/06

This was the view that inspired the whole Wainwrights in Colour idea. Seen at 5.40 on a warm summer evening.

The cairn at 2629' 9/9/09

Note how the stones at the bottom right are still in place in this old cairn. Great Gable's distinctive dome forms the backdrop.

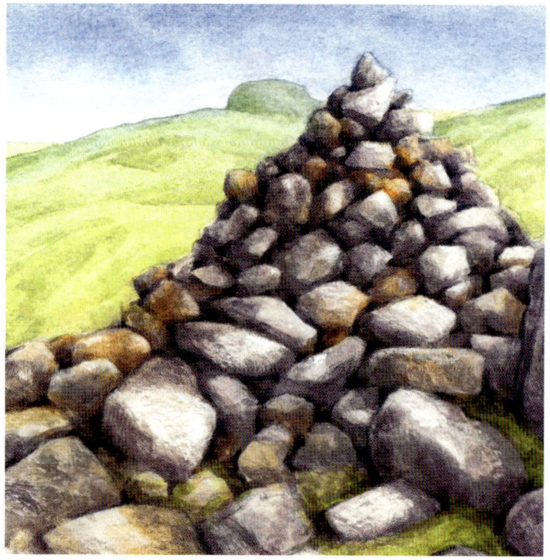

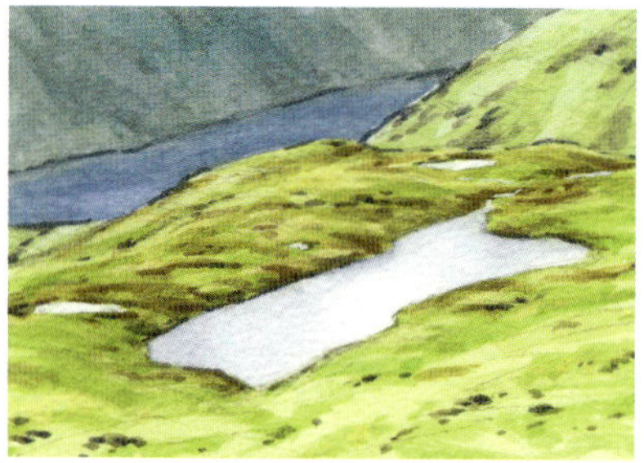

Low Tarn 9/9/09

This view of the tarn is obtained from the scree slope 150 yards west of the regular paths that cross the fell top. In my sketch I have included Wastwater and the base of The Screes.

Cairn near Low Tarn 16/2/14

The balanced column in the guide was unlikely to have survived, and it hasn't. Now just a jumble of rocks on a slight rise. Only AW's tiny cairn marker on Red Pike (W) 3 gave me any hint to its location. Seatallan lies beyond.

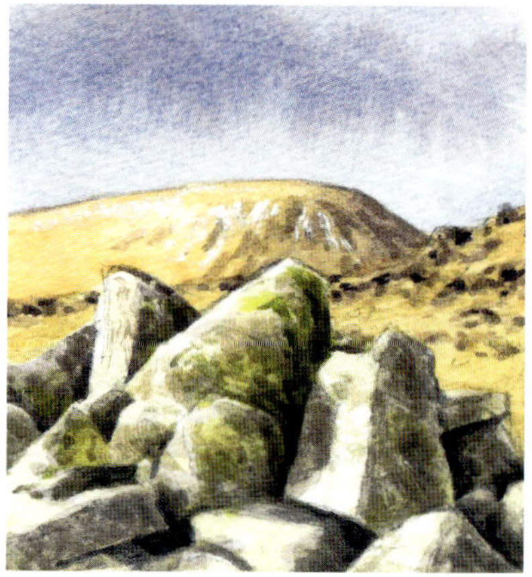

Bridge over Brimfull Beck 8/3/14

The footbridge has been replaced, making use of the buttresses that feature in Wainwright's guide.

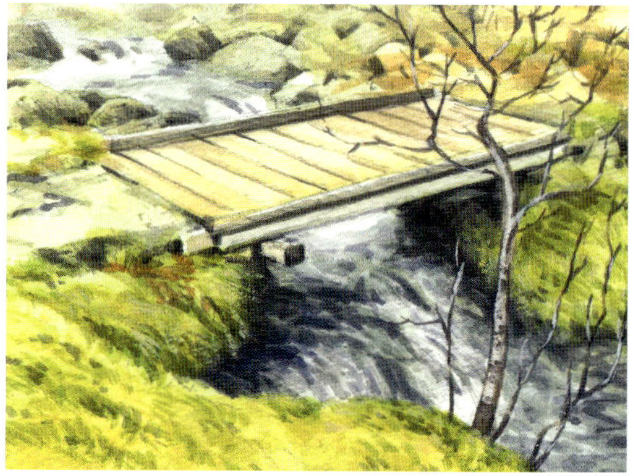

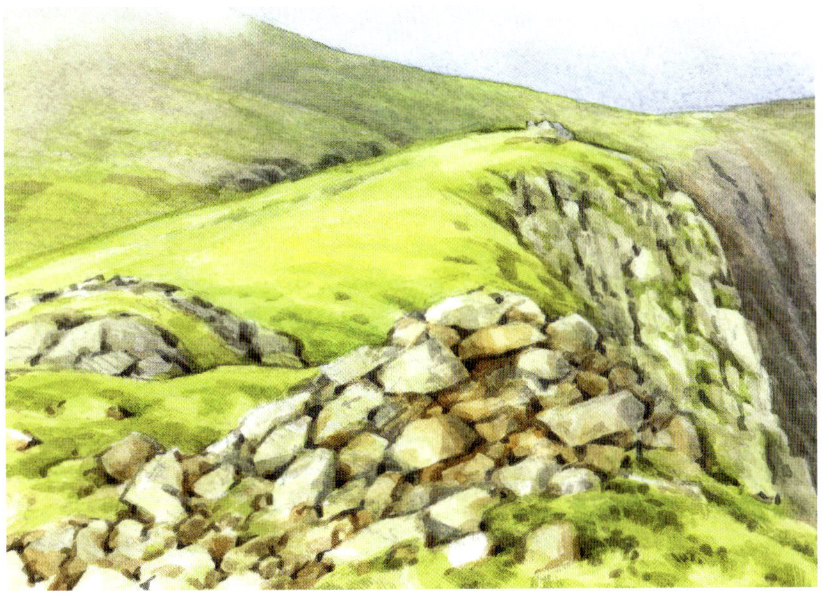

The summit 9/9/09

This cairn at the highest point sits right on the edge of a precipitous drop. The rise in the distance looks higher but it isn't, behind that is the col between Scoat Fell and Black Crag.

The summit cairn, looking east 9/9/09

Only on the 1 inch Bartholomew of AW's day was the summit height of 2707′ given, the O.S. maps of the time, both 1 and 2½ inch had only one measured height on the fell, that of the cairn at 2629′ (see page 332).

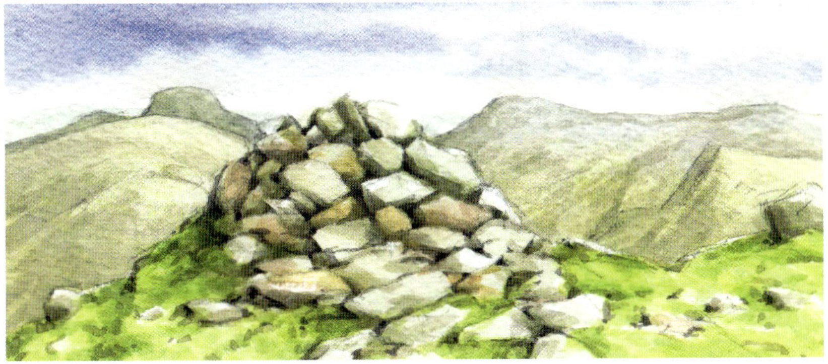

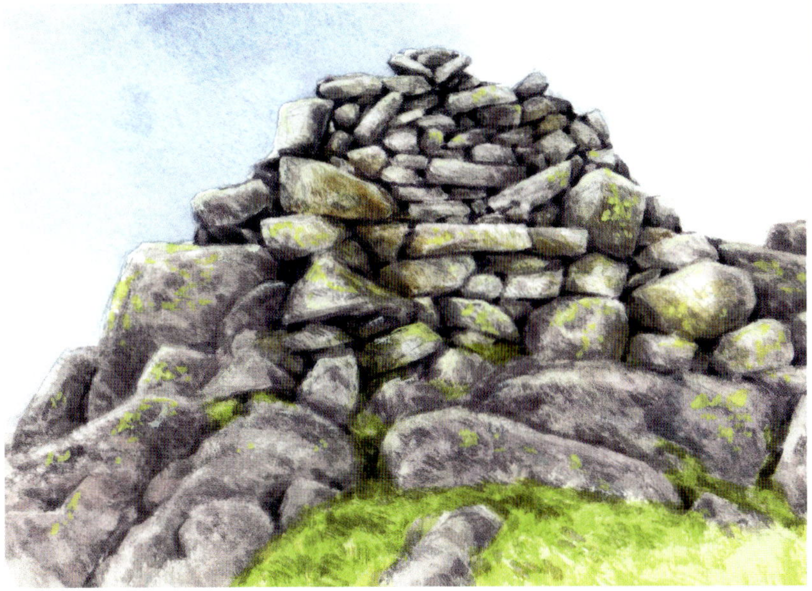

The Chair 9/9/09

Surprisingly perhaps, this substantial construction, a large stone armchair survives almost intact. It was such a feature of interest that it was even marked and named on the 6 inch O.S. map of 1900.

Stirrup Crag and Dore Head 9/9/09

This is the crag at the northern end of Yewbarrow. Far below to the left are the fields of Wasdale Head.

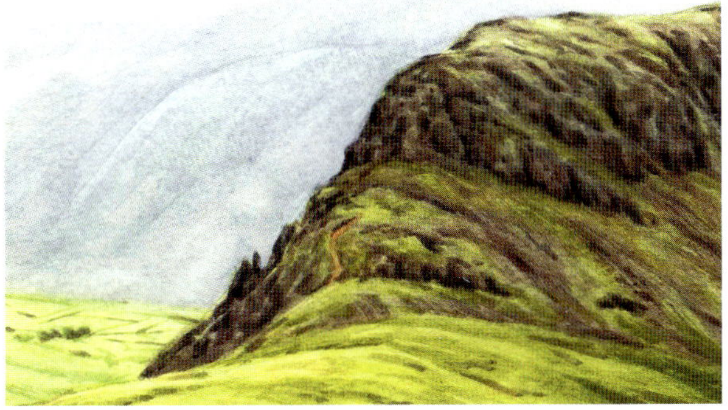

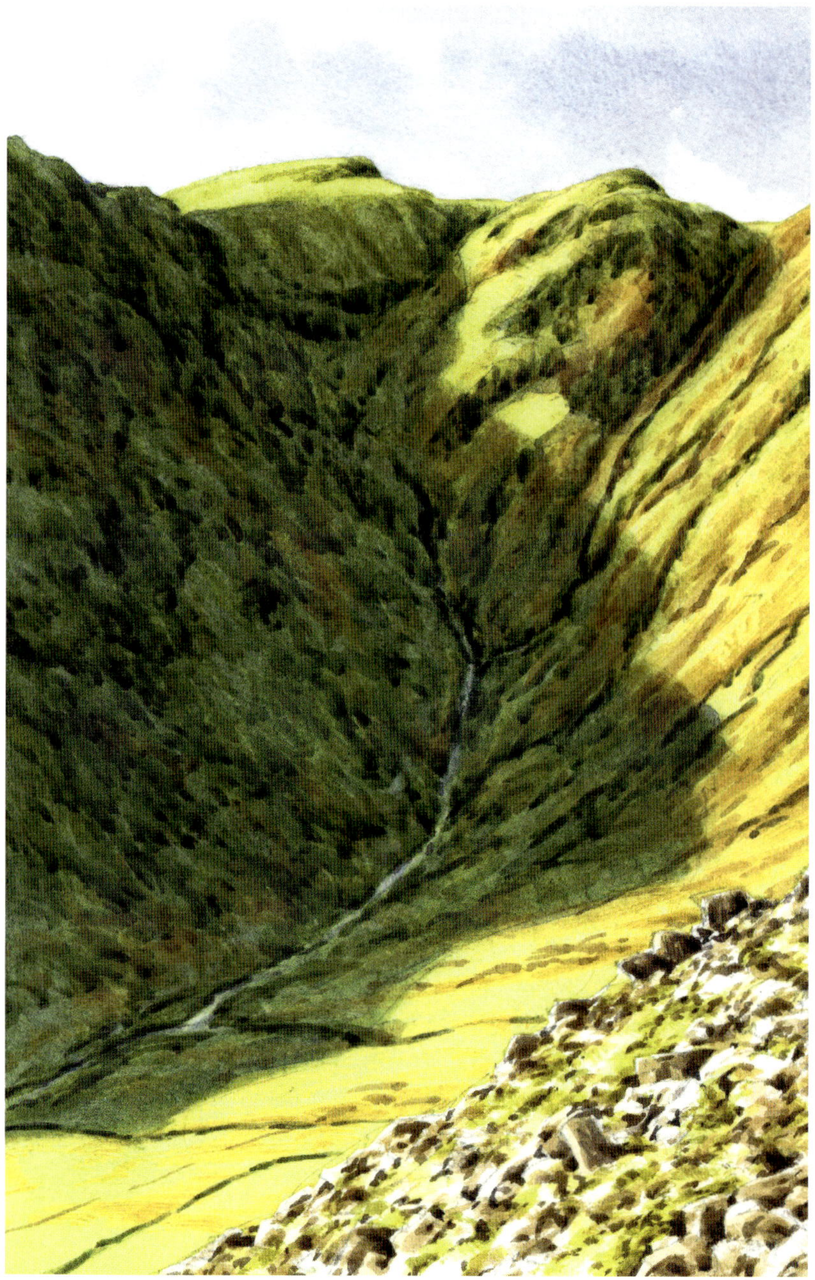

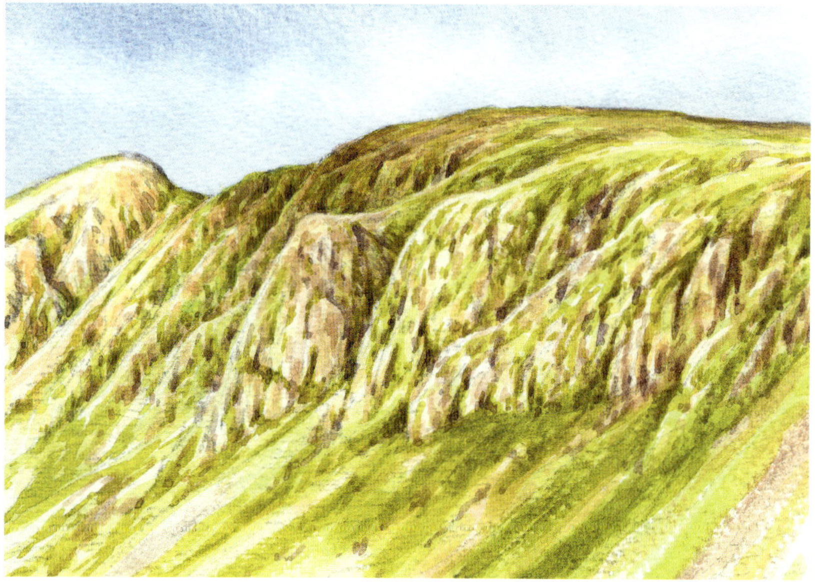

Steeple (left) and Scoat Fell, looking across Mirklin Cove 9/9/09

The upper reaches of Scoat's north-western ridge, above Tewit How provide this fine prospect of the crags above the Cove. The central one with the concave top is Haskett Buttress, one of the remotest climbing crags in the whole of the district.

From Kirk Fell 14/4/14

Anyone who has stood on this very spot to look down into the depths of Mosedale and across to Scoat Fell will perhaps have been taking a well earned rest, just as I did here. For this location is three quarters of the way up the steep, direct ascent of Kirk Fell from Wasdale Head and I was under the extra burden of my wildcamping kit. This is a route to take your time, unless of course you are a competitor in the Wasdale Show Fell Race which ascends this slope.

Scoat Fell

The name Scoat Fell actually covers the high ground which on O.S. maps is marked as Little Scoat Fell and Great Scoat Fell with Little Scoat Fell being the higher. In this case Great and Little likely refers to ground area and not height. It may not be high in the popularity stakes but I have some great memories of camping out on this summit.

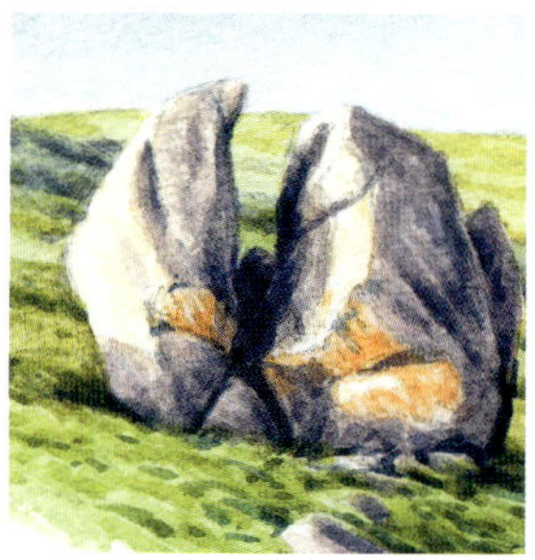

Split boulder, Scoat Tarn 9/9/09

This large boulder sits close to the path on the west side of the tarn.

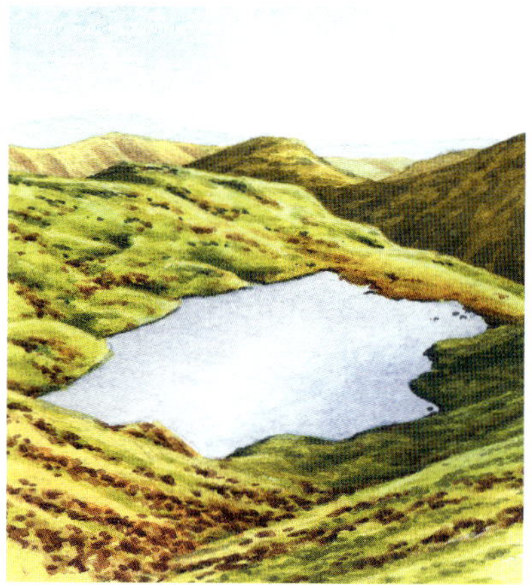

Looking back to Scoat Tarn from 2400' 9/9/09

Descending the path towards the tarn gave me the best opportunity to line up the elements in the scene to obtain my reference. The afternoon was near its end and I still had at least four other subjects to capture before getting back to my car at Netherbeck Bridge.

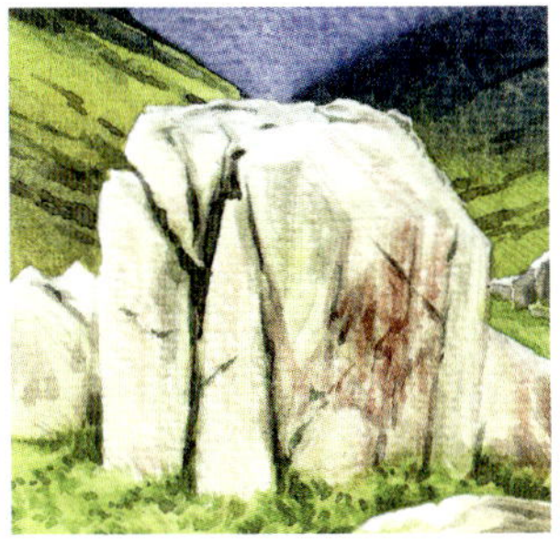

Split boulder 7/9/09

To the west of Mosedale Beck this 12′ high boulder stands alongside the path that continues up to the col between Red Pike and Scoat Fell. Due to the shape of the crack the boulder has gained the name Y Boulder on the O.S. maps, there can be no other natural feature with a shorter name.

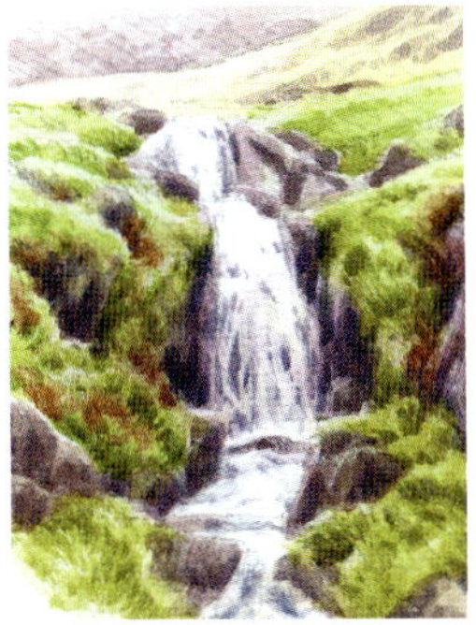

Falls in Mosedale Beck 7/9/09

By continuing on past the Y boulder, up alongside Mosedale Beck for another half a mile, this delightful small cascade will be seen down on your right.

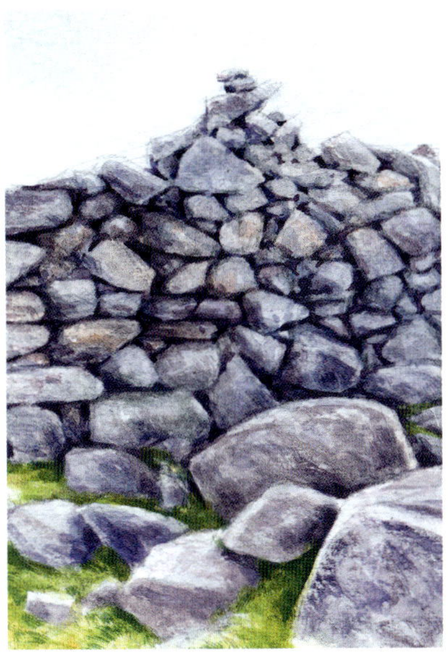

The summit 9/9/09

The Ennerdale boundary wall crosses the summit and occupies the highest point of the fell. On top of the wall is perched a small cairn.

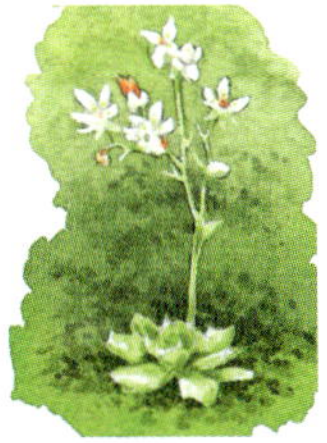

Starry saxifrage 12/7/11

The award for the smallest sketch by AW in all of the Pictorial Guides must go to his simple study of this delicate flower, an Arctic-alpine species of saxifrage not uncommon in the Lake District.

To Steeple 9/9/09

The Starling Dodd ridge behind Steeple gives the impression that I have angled this sketch but not so, this is how it looks in reality. This ridge route between Scoat Fell and Steeple is the shortest distance between any two Wainwright fells.

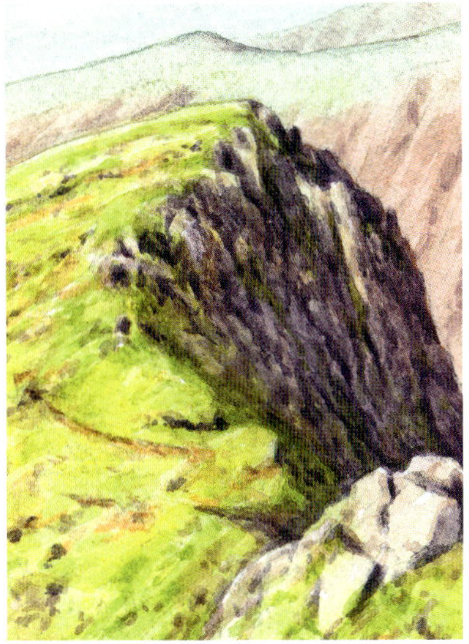

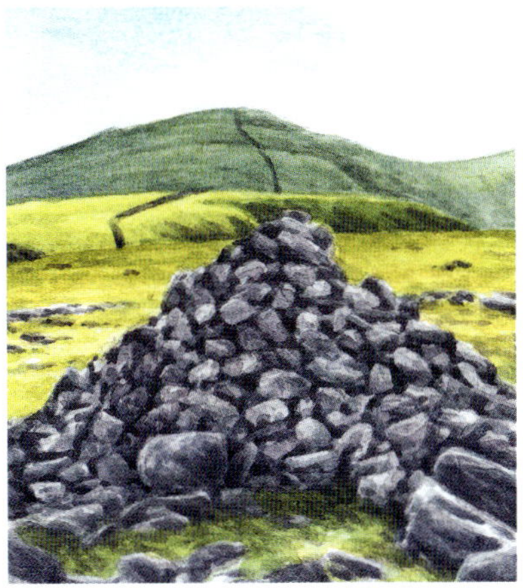

The summit cairn 9/9/09

This pile of stones, near the wall and on the flat ground is slightly lower than the actual summit. For those who feel the need to stand on summit cairns to "claim" the fell, this is the place to do so, not on top of the wall.

The re-wilding of Ennerdale

Around 1965 Wainwright wrote of *"a dark funereal shroud of foreign trees"* on the lower slopes of the Ennerdale valley but now things have changed dramatically and are continuing to do so. The dense blocks of Sitka Spruce which *"blocked out the light of day"* that were planted in the 1920s have now been harvested and since 2003 a programme to try to return the valley back to a more natural state has come into effect. Under the name Wild Ennerdale a partnership of landowners in the valley including United Utilities, the Forestry Commission, the National Trust and Natural England are working together to reinstate the landscape and ecology to a more natural state.

Some boundary fences have been removed, sheep numbers reduced and native Galloway cattle now graze the lower pastures. The River Liza, the only location in England for a population of migratory arctic char, now flows more freely. The marsh fritillary butterfly, previously extinct from Cumbria has had a successful re-introduction. There are hopes that even pine martens could soon return to join the other 100 species of wildlife found in the area. The Lynx UK Trust even put forward the idea to use Ennerdale as a trial site for the re-introduction of the animal but this was ruled out in the summer of 2016 as the site is too small.

Ennerdale is certainly going back to the wild, AW would be pleased.

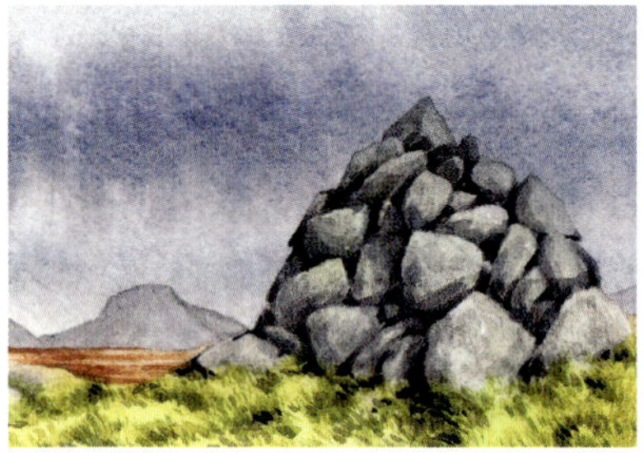

Cairn on Cat Bields 8/11/08
On my visit this cairn was a neat stack, slightly bigger than in AW's illustration. Worth looking out for is the 7′ tall column about half a mile east of this location built by the famous fell runner Joss Naylor.

Seatallan

A large expanse of ground that rises gradually up from Nether Wasdale Common to a height of 2266' is Seatallan, a fell which still remains fairly unknown to many hillwalkers. Much of the fell features terrain of tussocky grass over which there are few paths. Only the upper slopes on the north-western side show any real expanse of rocks.

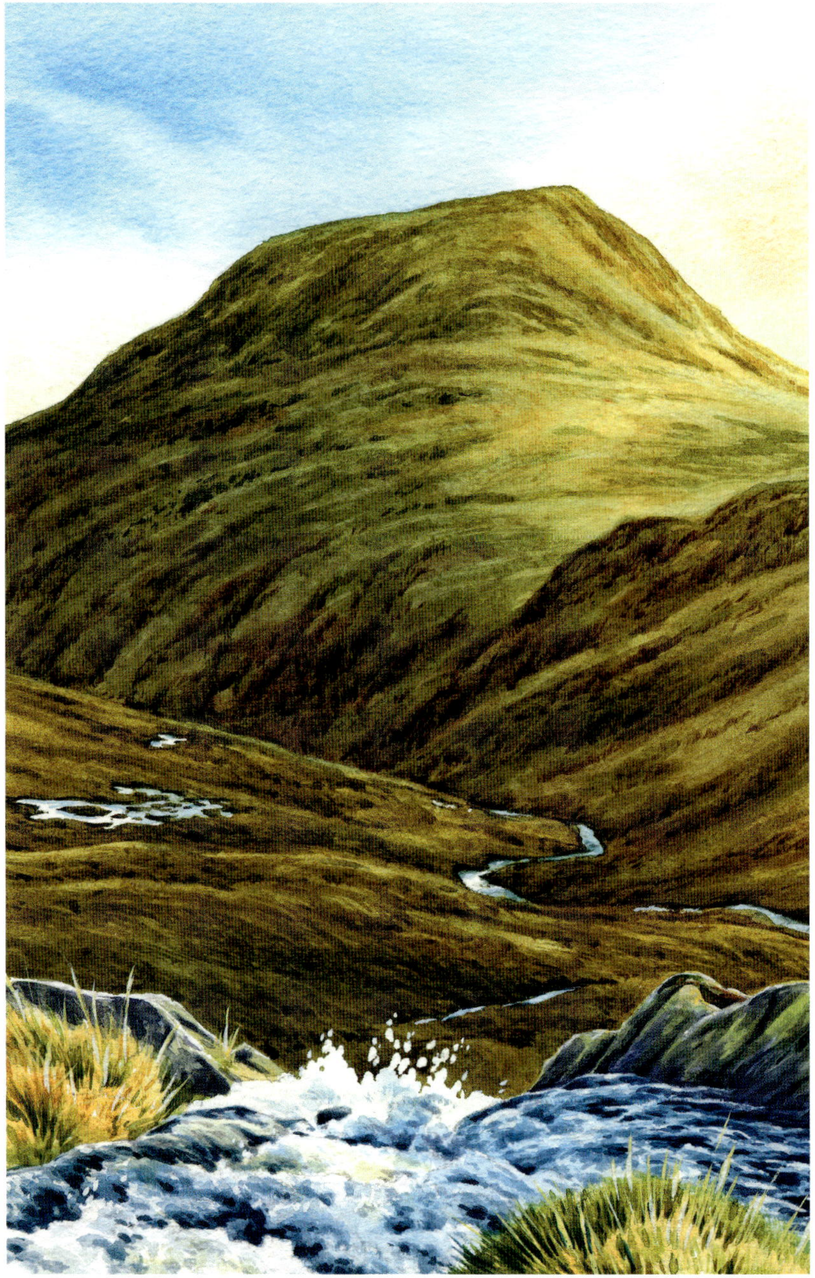

From below Scoat Tarn 9/9/09
The view across the Nether Beck valley as the evening light catches the slopes of Seatallan.

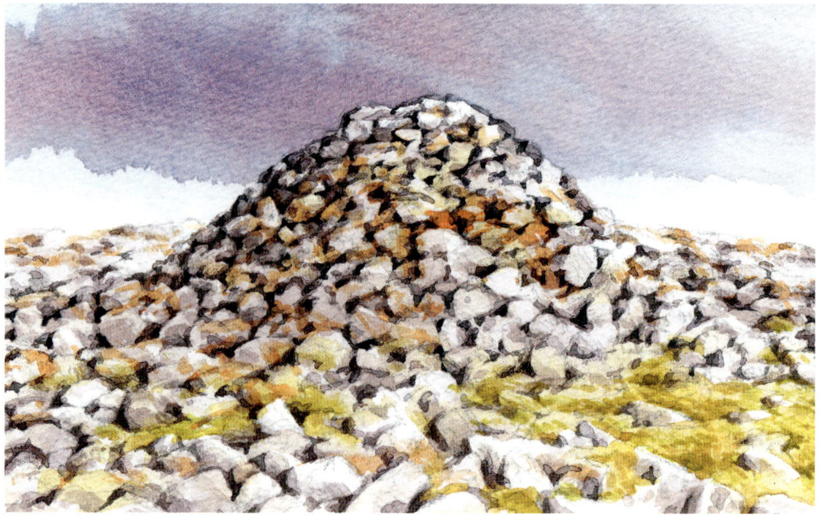

The summit 8/11/08
As with most of these ancient cairns and tumuli, modern visitors to the summit have spent some time re-working the stones into a form of shelter which is on the other side of this large heap.

The Scafell range from Seatallan 8/11/08
The triangulation pillar stands on an expanse of cropped grass, a short distance from the cairn. From here Scafell looks somewhat higher than Scafell Pike due to the perspective.

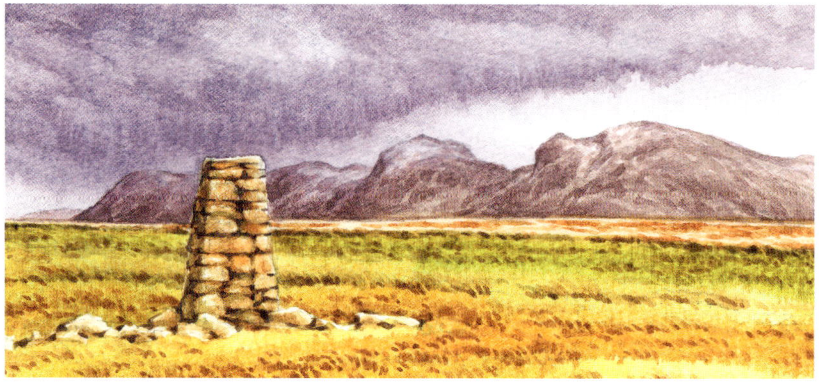

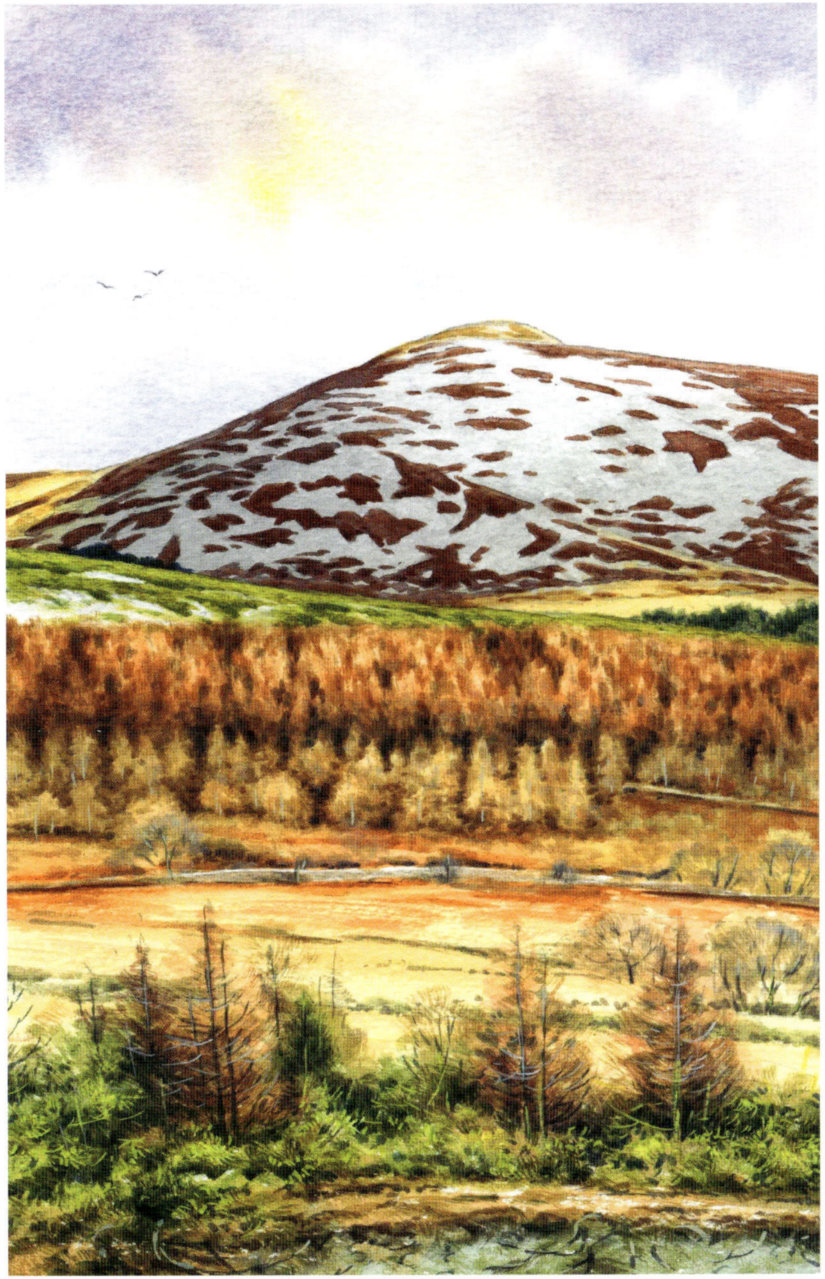

From Ennerdale 23/2/10
It took some detective work by me to locate this viewpoint which is actually from the track in Lingmell Plantations on the south side of the River Liza, which is hidden from view by the near trees. There has been a remarkable change to the fell since the days of AW's drawing in which he heightened the summit peak, the thin topsoil which bore the heather has been mostly eroded, exposing the grey stone scree underneath. Blocks of forestry have also been felled.

Starling Dodd

On Friday, 10th September 1965, AW's visit to Starling Dodd summit enabled him to complete the work for book 7, the final Pictorial Guide in the series. As will be noted, I chose to complete my first round of the fells for this project on this fell, 44 years to the day after his achievement.

The summit 10/9/09
At the time of AW's visit this cairn was a jumble of stones and ironwork from the old fence. Since 1997 someone has gone to the effort of separating the materials so that now, just off to the left of this cairn there is a matching cairn made of iron which resembles a Turner Prize exhibit.

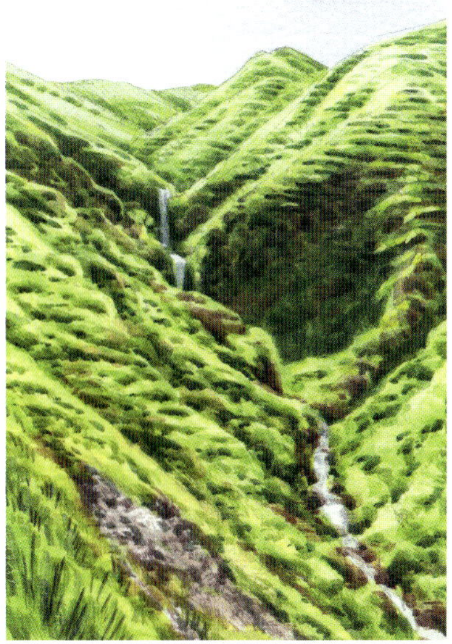

Red Gill, Mosedale 10/9/09
The unfrequented path here passes close to the edge providing a good view into the gill.

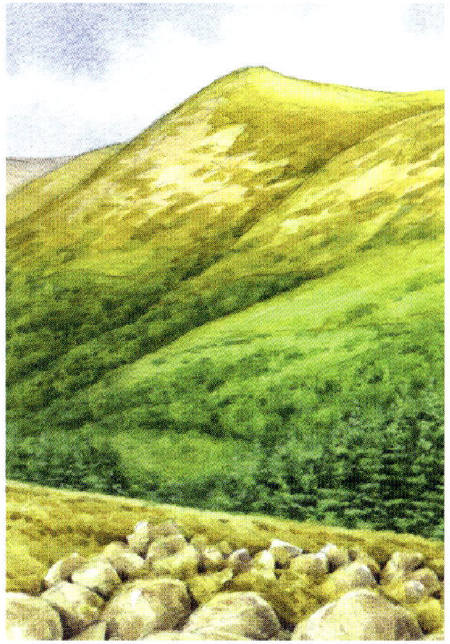

Starling Dodd from High Beck, Ennerdale 5/7/13
The path here, west of High Beck has fallen out of favour.

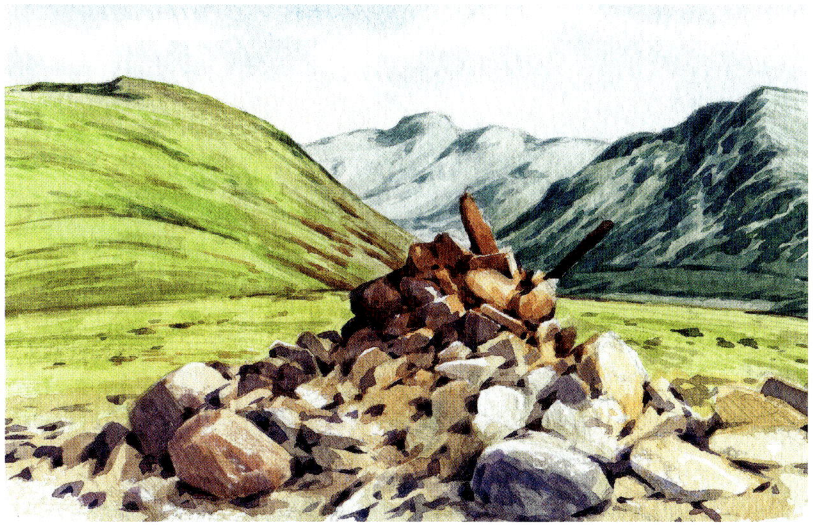

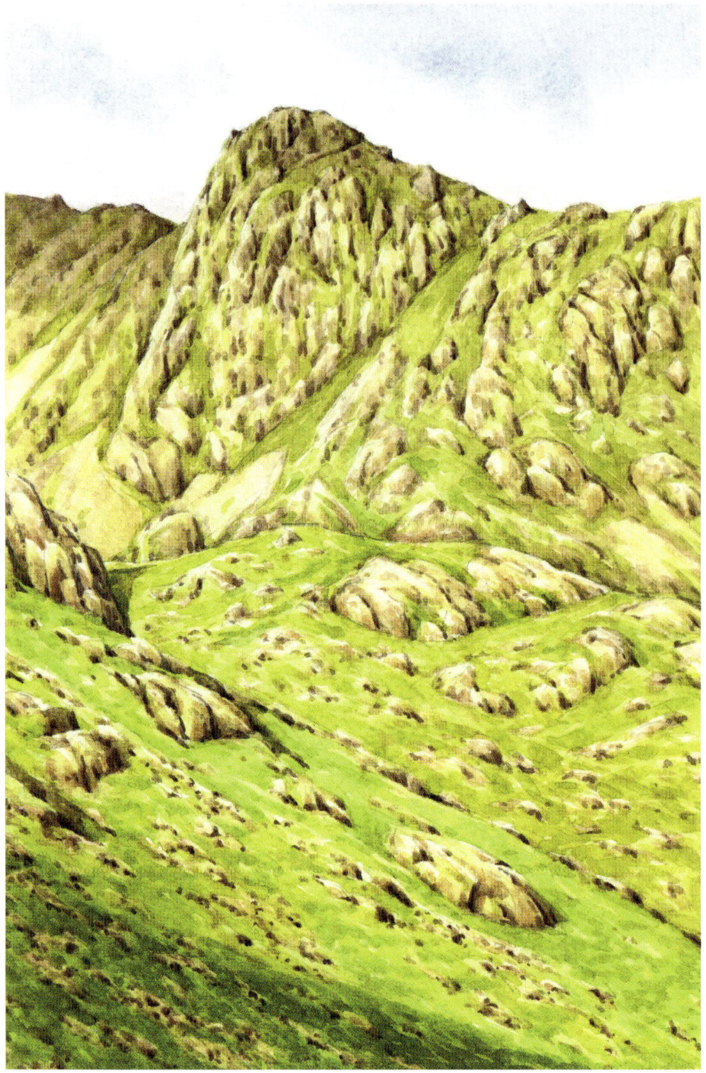

From Windgap Cove 18/7/14
After a night wildcamping on Scoat Fell I had planned my route of descent via the path that Wainwright indicated on the Pillar 12 page just to obtain this reference. Not only was this new ground for me but going by the indistinct track it is obviously unknown to many.

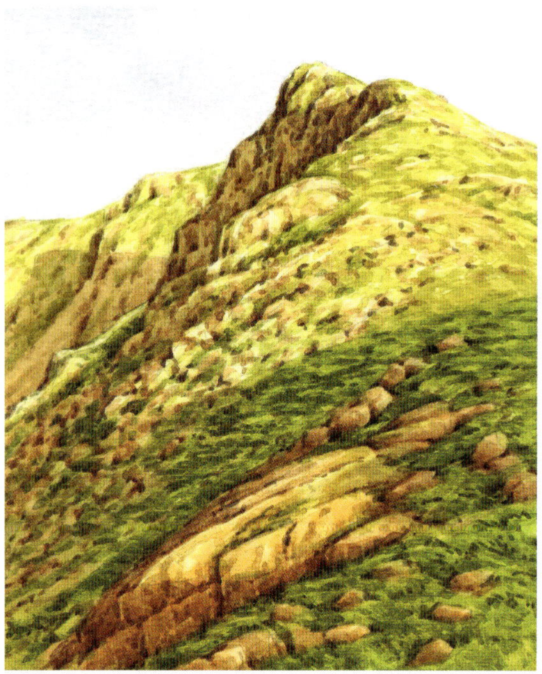

The north ridge 17/7/14
I had chosen a perfect evening to ascend this ridge, the summit is seen here from Long Crag.

The summit 9/9/09
Much of the grass on this small summit has been worn away and the cairn is now rather larger.

Steeple

Even though Wainwright admits that Steeple is just part of the neighbouring hill, Scoat Fell, he does class it as an individual fell for the purposes of his list. The fact that it was a measured height on the one inch maps of the time possibly influenced his decision. It is worthy of this inclusion.

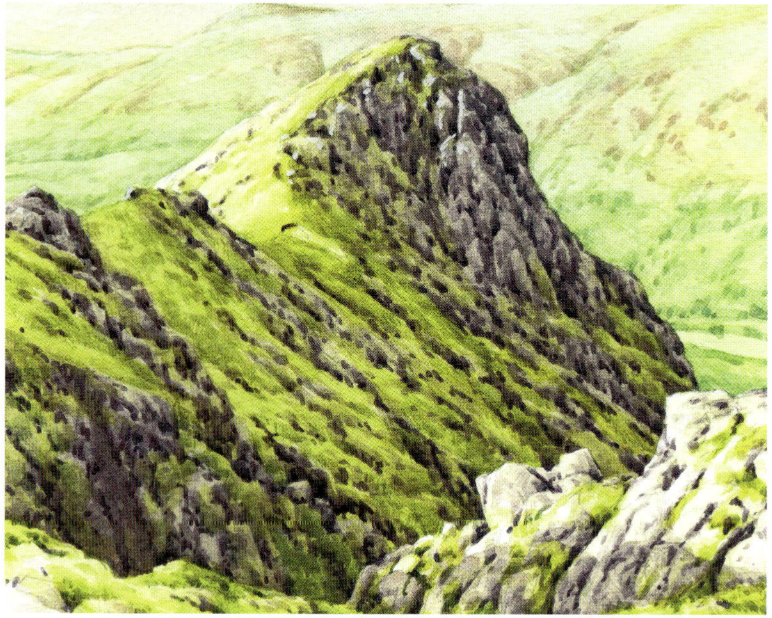

Steeple, as seen from Scoat Fell across Mirk Cove 9/9/09
Mirk Cove is in the upper reaches of Windgap Cove.

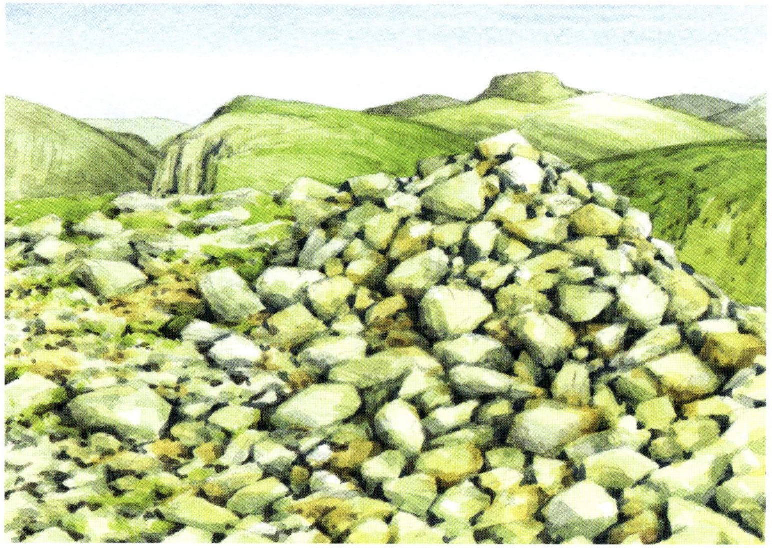

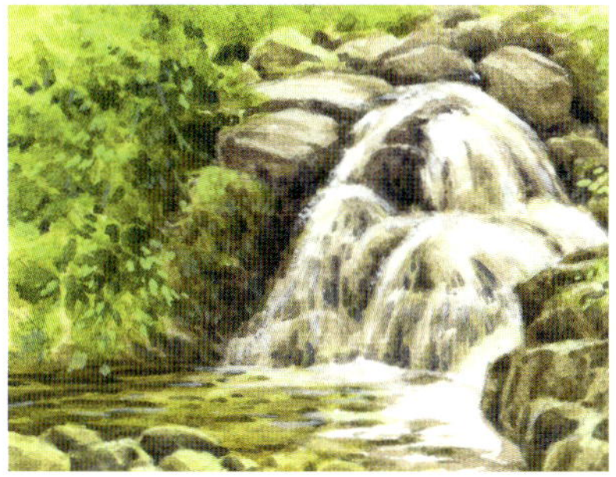

High Beck 5/7/13
This section of the beck is just below the forest track bridge.

Ridge Route 9/9/09
Ten minutes of good walking will get you to the summit of Scoat Fell.

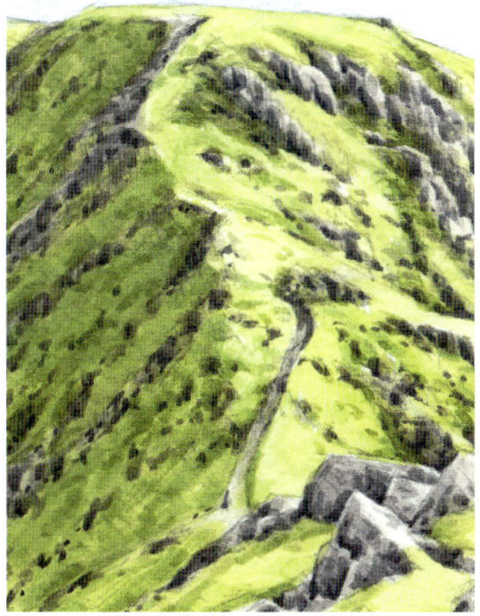

From Black Crag 18/7/14
Scoat Fell and Steeple as viewed from the rocky top of Black Crag.

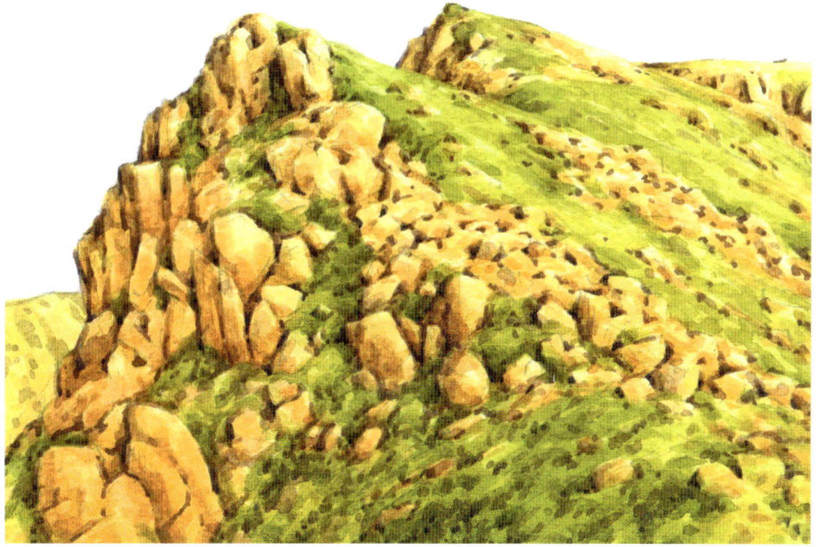

The upper part of the north ridge 17/7/14
The evening glow of the sun on the dramatic crags of the summit.

The east face from Black Crag 9/9/09
The near vertical buttress of Steeple drops down into Windgap Cove. Premium mountain scenery.

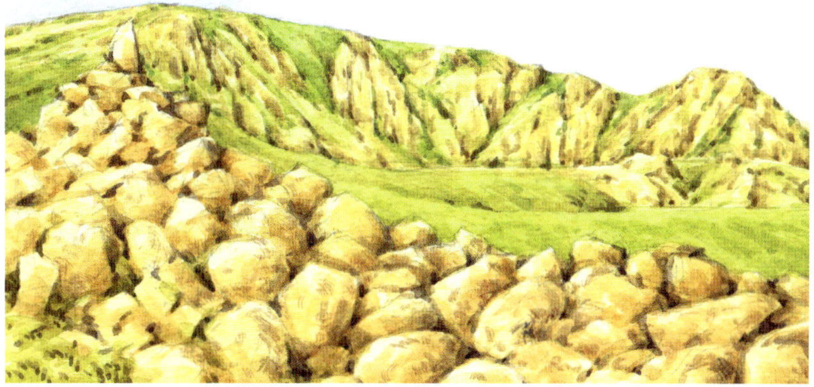

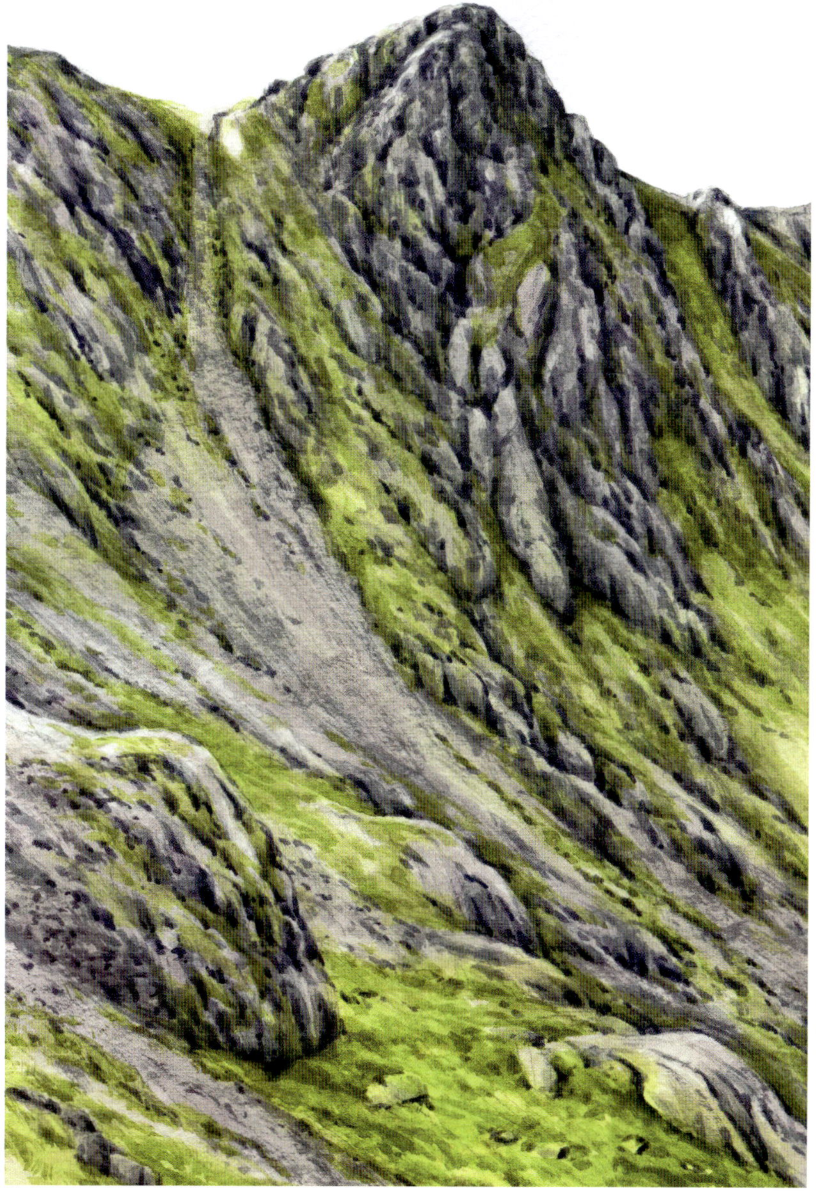

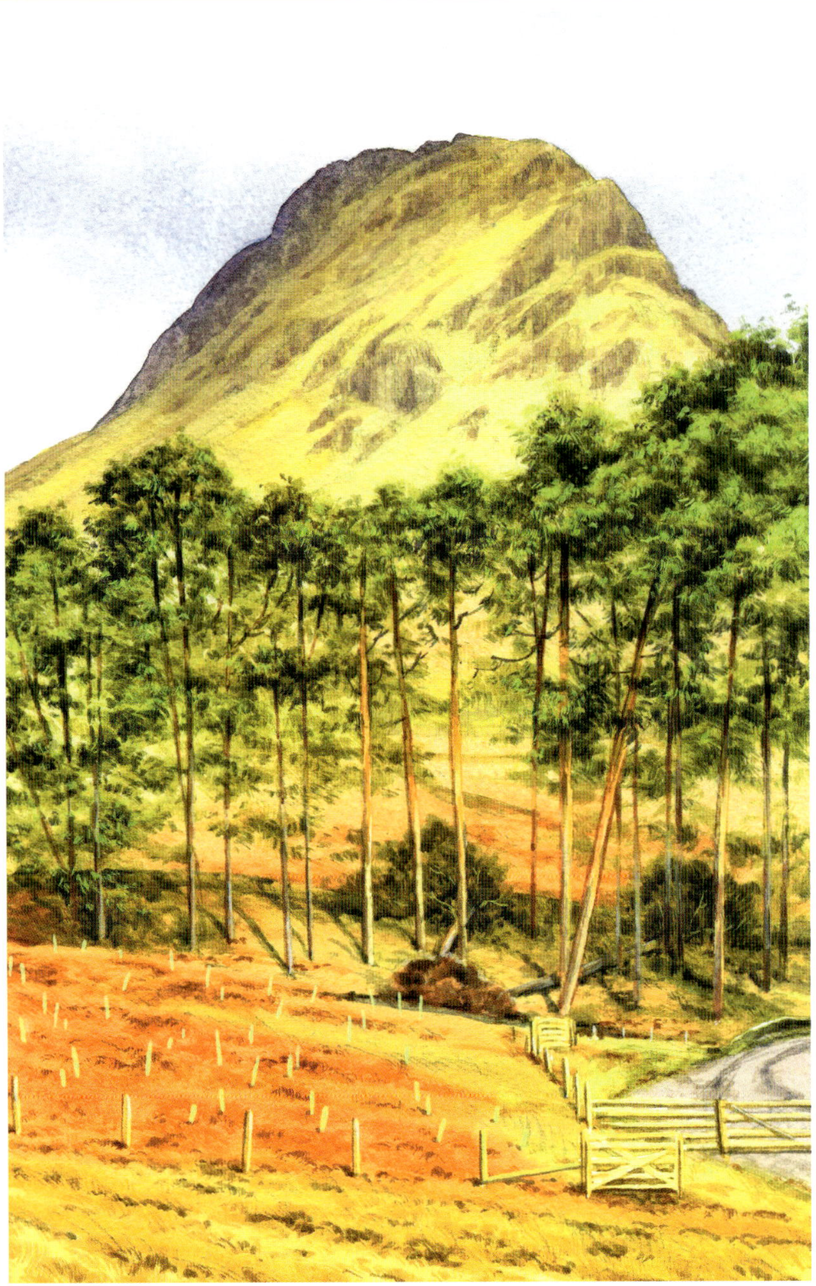

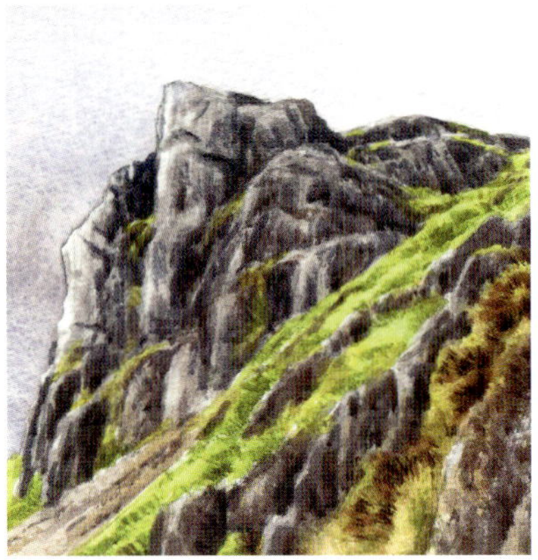

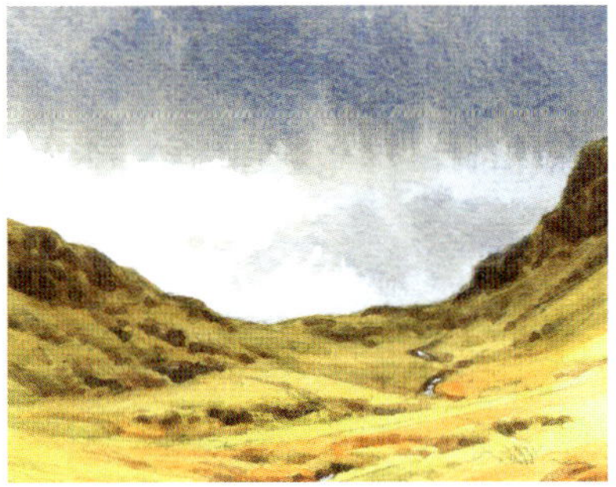

Yewbarrow

The head of Wasdale is home to several majestic mountains of which Yewbarrow is one. Attaining the top can be a bit of a challenge but the views are well worth all the effort.

From Netherbeck Bridge
7/9/09
A new fence protects the recently planted trees. The impressive view of the fell has not been diminished.

Dropping Crag 9/9/09
The route to the summit goes up a steep scree gully to the right of the crag.

The South Ridge
9/9/09
This large gap is often mistaken for the Great Door which lies further on. The regular path now cuts down to the right here, missing Great Door.

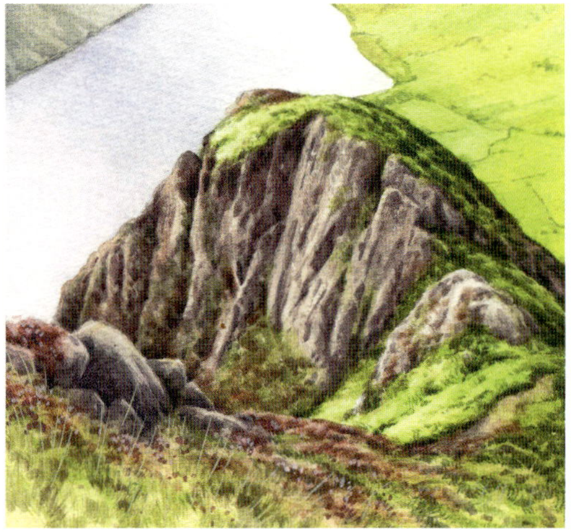

Dore Head 16/2/14
The col between Red Pike on the left and Yewbarrow on the right as seen from Great Knott.

Dropping Crag and Bell Rib
9/9/09
Bell Rib forms the sudden abrupt southern end of the fell.

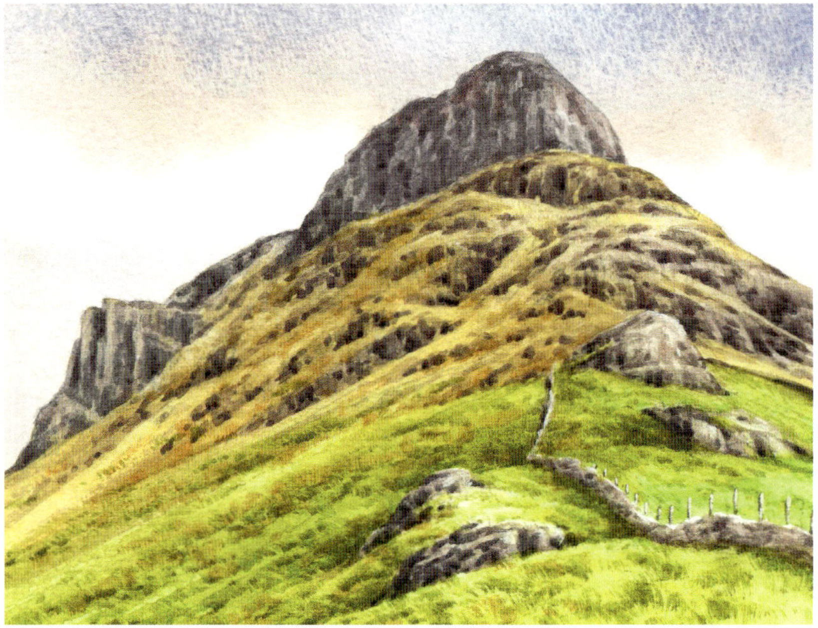

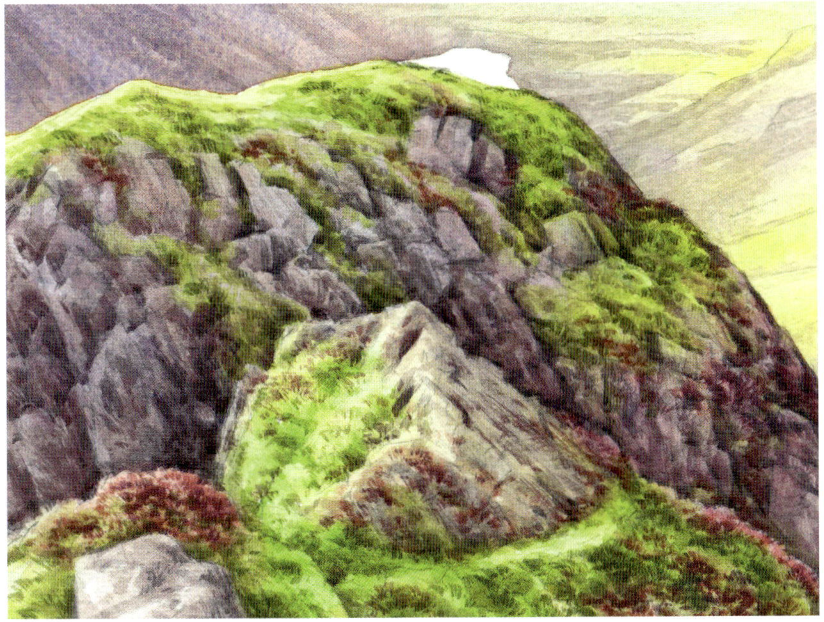

Great Door 9/9/09
The footpath here indicated by AW has now been bypassed but a visit to see this vertical narrow gash in the rock, just seen here on the left is worth the detour.

Ritson's Force 15/4/14
Enchanting falls in woodland not far from Wasdale Head.

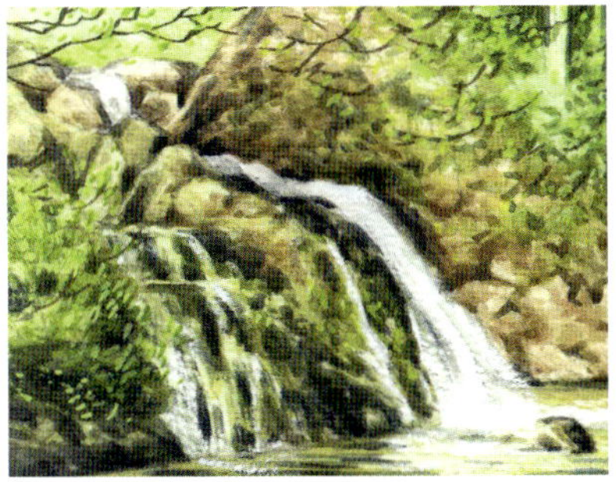

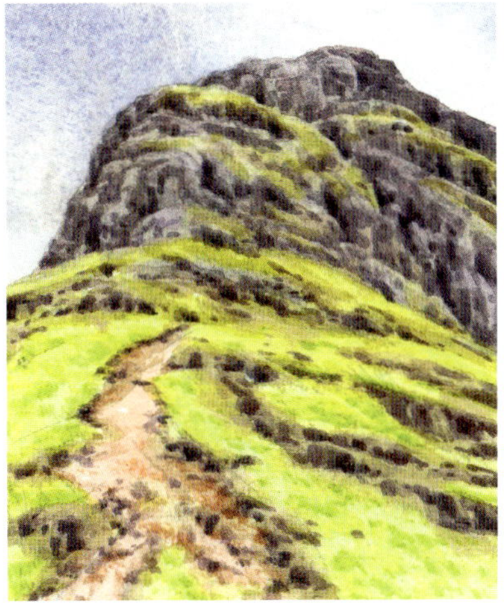

Stirrup Crag 9/9/09
This crag at the north end of the fell is perhaps easier to tackle in ascent rather than in descent.

The summit 16/2/14
For no explanation, the cairn has been moved slightly to the left off the angular block of bedrock on which it was in situated AW's drawing.

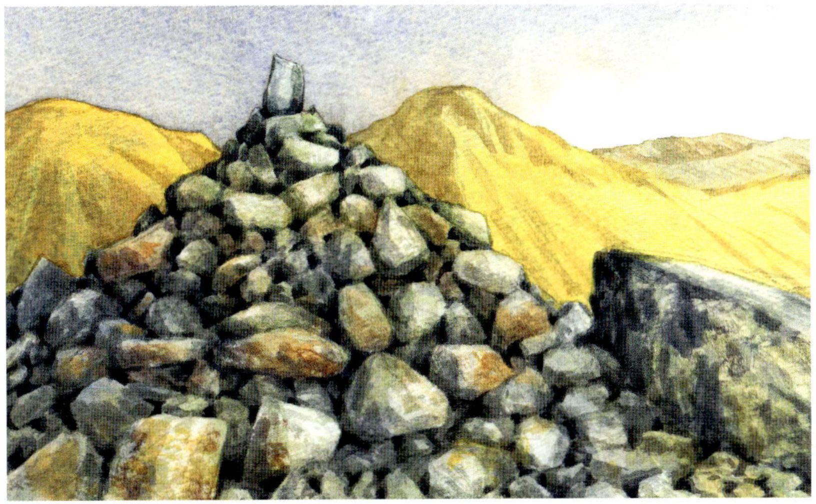

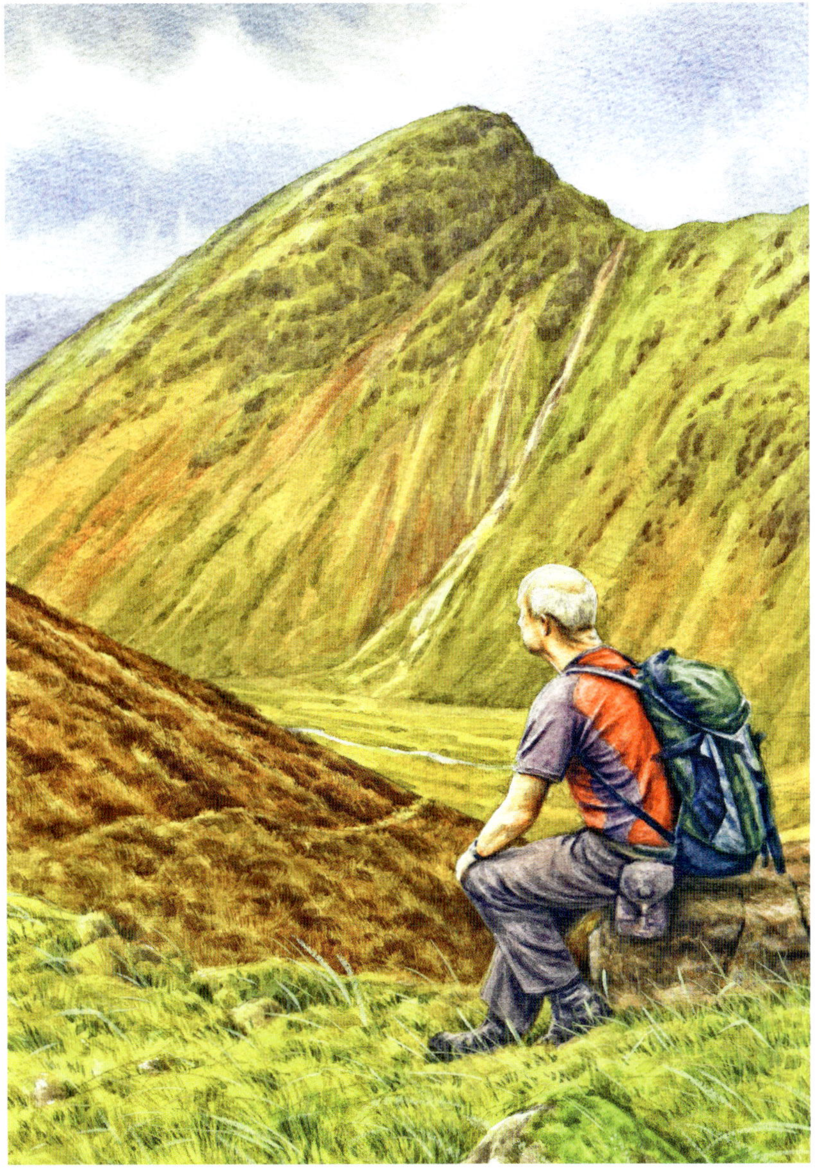

From Gatherstone Beck 7/9/09
Fittingly perhaps, Wainwright fills the very last page of the Pictorial Guide series with a self portrait in a reflective pose within an impressive setting.

Personal notes in conclusion

At the end of each Pictorial Guide Wainwright penned his thoughts on the book that he had just completed and what lay ahead. I can now fully understand why he did so and felt it only right to write something in a similar vein for The Wainwrights in Colour.

I now sit in my studio and reflect on the task that I have fully completed. The ten years plus since the original idea formed in my head on that hot summer's afternoon high on the Wasdale fells in some ways seems so long ago, but in other respects it seems like only yesterday. By looking back through the many pages of the book nearly every one of the 1500 sketches brings back strong memories for me, some with very emotional attachments. Great days of bright, clear weather or the less rewarding days where bad weather frustrated my efforts meaning that I had to plan a re-visit, but everyday was a joy to be out on the Lakeland Fells. On every single mile and foot of ascent I had at least one faithful hound by my side so I was never truly alone. The days where I had human company were few, mostly my wife Esther or other friends, all of whom put up with my wandering off at a tangent to seek out a lone rock or tree as a reference. I have come to understand something of why AW did the same, he may have been shy but he also was on a mission, work like this needs an element of concentration and perhaps selfishness. Walking in groups has no real appeal to me, I prefer to make my own way, taking time to stop and admire the landscape and scenery, and more so in the future when I will be back to sketching in the field, a pastime not for the impatient.

I now see AW's Pictorial Guides in a different light. I can't recall actually using them for guidance on routes but by seeking out the obscure locations for his sketches I was able to explore the Lakeland Fells comprehensively, not perhaps as fully as he did but more then the average fellwalker. I know that there are places that I have been to that even today are unfrequented by other fellwalkers, quite a claim in this popular area but the quiet places are still there, they just need seeking out.

The challenge of completing the "Wainwrights" is now a popular undertaking and almost every weekend of the year someone ticks off their final fell. This is no bad thing, it means that they have visited the hills in the four corners of Lakeland, just as AW intended them to do but this doesn't mean they "know" the fells, far from it. One simple visit to Blencathra's summit via Doddick Fell leaves many other routes to explore, the surface has only been scratched. My answer to those who complete and ask what next to do I would say go back and explore the fells properly, re-visit favourite fells, find the places of interest and do so in a different season. Even I plan to follow this same idea, there are places and fells which I know have much more to offer, secretive places which I have spotted and noted and are just begging for a re-visit.

Since I officially announced my idea of The Wainwrights in Colour I have been overwhelmed by the support from fellow lovers of the work of Wainwright and the Lakeland Fells. Not only from those who supported me by purchasing the original fells but also by the number of people who registered interest in obtaining a copy of this book. On the other side of the coin I realise that there are some folk who will see what I have been doing as using the Wainwright name to sell my work. I am never going to change there opinion but that was never the idea. This whole project has been a personal challenge and homage to AW and his unsurpassed work in producing the guidebooks. In doing so I have come to understand more about this man, his methods and not least the fells that he so loved. Hopefully through this book and the articles that accompany the sketches I have been able to pass on this information to give a better insight to all things "Wainwright".

The length of time taken to accomplish this task has been much longer than anticipated, but to be honest I strongly believe that the final icing on the cake in the form of this book is now a much better product than if I had taken only five or so years to complete. My paintings have definitely improved and my time taken to research AW's background have helped to make this book complete.

Out of curiosity I had photocopies of Wainwright's original handwritten notebooks analysed by an expert graphologist, a person who actually had very little knowledge of AW beforehand. The results were fascinating and I consider them worth sharing here. *"Emotional outlay: the slant of the writing shows a lack of outward emotional expressiveness, they will only show emotion to the closest confidants. The size of writing shows a great deal of concentration and attention to detail typically found in those doing precision work i.e. surgeons, accountants etc. they will not be the life and soul of the party.*

Traits: diplomacy, determination, quick thinking, fluidity of thought, socially selective. This writer is more than happy with their own company and can show levels of concentration which lapses into obsession on their given subject. The physical links between normally unlinked words (by an upward slanting line) shows a mind that is thinking way ahead of the pen (pencil) on the page. It is also a sign of generosity. This person will be able to follow a set course and display strong powers of the will. Willpower tends to intensify all other traits.

Summary: the writer is totally confident working in their own comfort zone, able to work out complex calculations with an analytical mind. They can hold their emotions in check indefinitely but can still display passion about their chosen subject."

When I first heard this analysis I got goose bumps, the expert had summed up AW perfectly (the accountant detail and the traits were not prompted by me). The explanation backs up the well documented shyness of the man and of course his determination which resulted in completing the work on the Pictorial Guides and other books. The graphologist was no medical expert but again without prompting he did hint that perhaps Wainwright was in the autistic spectrum which would help to explain his personality that over time has given him the tag of being grumpy and curmudgeonly. I never met the man so I feel that I have no right to judge. He was a man of his time and thankfully he was born when he was. No one today would even consider producing a range of guidebooks the way he did and I am pretty sure that many of the young generation today fail to appreciate that his series of Lakeland Guides were all designed, written and produced by one man with a dip pen and ink, not as a job but a heart felt passion. By co-incidence both AW and myself would have completed our tasks at roughly the same age (58) so that is how I have depicted him in my drawing on the right.

If my project, The Wainwrights in Colour helps in some way to keep the works of Alfred Wainwright in the public domain then I don't see that as being a bad thing. Do you?

Andy Beck January 2017

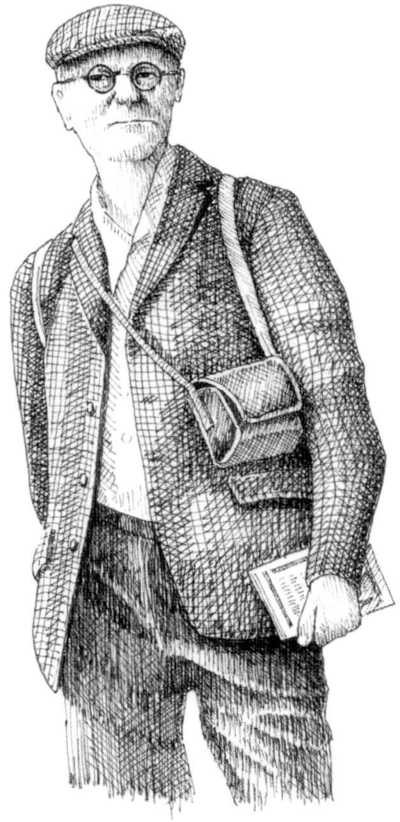

Thank you Mr. Wainwright

Credits & Bibliography

Credits

For simplicity of cross referencing between the Pictorial Guides and my sketches I have used Wainwright's titles throughout the book. I am grateful to Frances Lincoln Limited and the Wainwright Estate for this permission.

Picture titles from A Pictorial Guide to the Lakeland Fells:
Book One: The Eastern Fells
Book Two: The Far Eastern Fells
Book Three: The Central Fells
Book Four: The Southern Fells
Book Five: The Northern Fells
Book Six: The North Western Fells
Book Seven: The Western Fells

Bibliography

In addition to the Pictorial Guides listed above other published sources used for reference material in this book include:

Entwistle, M.D. *Millican Dalton a search for romance and freedom.* Blackburn. Mountainmere Research 2004
Davies, Hunter. *The Wainwright Letters.* London. Frances Lincoln Limited, 2011
Davies, Hunter. *Wainwright, The Biography.* London. Michael Joseph Limited. 1995
Wainwright, A. *Memoirs of a Fellwanderer.* London. Frances Lincoln Limited. 2003 edition
Wainwright, A. *Fellwanderer-the story behind the guidebooks.* Kendal. Westmorland Gazette. 1966
Whaley, Diana. *A Dictionary of Lake District Place-Names.* Nottingham. The English Place-Name Society, 2006

Index